English-Cantonese Dictionary

英 粵 字 典

Cantonese in Yale Romanization

Kwan Choi Wah 關彩華

Lo Chi Hung 羅智宏

Lo Tam Fee Yin 盧譚飛燕

Mak Tze Kuen 麥子權

Man Chiu Kwan 文肖群

Miu Wong Nga Ching 苗黃雅貞

Ng Shiu King, Pauline 吳少瓊

The Chinese University Press

New Asia – Yale-in-China Chinese Language

First published in 1991 by
New Asia–Yale-in-China Chinese Language Center
The Chinese University of Hong Kong

First copublished edition 2000

ISBN 962-201-970-6

Published by
The Chinese University Press
The Chinese University of Hong Kong
Sha Tin, N.T., Hong Kong
Fax: +852 2603 6692
+ 852 2603 7355
E-mail: cup@cuhk.edu.hk
Web-site: www.cuhk.edu.hk/cupress

and

New Asia–Yale-in-China Chinese Language Center
The Chinese University of Hong Kong
Sha Tin, N.T., Hong Kong

Printed in Hong Kong

Contents

Preface 1-2

Introduction 3-22

 1. Users' guide 3-4

 2. List of Symbols............... 4-5

 3. Brief Introduction to
   Cantonese Pronunciation 5-7

 4. Comparative
   Romanization Chart 8-11

 5. Grammatical Notes 12-21

 6. List of Abbreviation 22

The Dictionary 1

PREFACE

The impetus for compiling this Dictionary came from the interaction of teachers and students at the New Asia--Yale-in-China Chinese Language Center of The Chinese University of Hong Kong. Over the last several years these teachers and students have felt a growing need for having at their disposal a Dictionary which would emphasize the Cantonese spoken dialect and which would be portable, relatively cheap and thus available for ready reference. Since spoken Cantonese is somewhat different from written Chinese, it was decided that the Cantonese words and expressions would be given in spoken form and written in Yale Romanization. Therefore no Chinese character is provided. It was also decided that the words and expressions collected in this Dictionary would reflect those in common, everyday use.

To accomplish this, the Staff at the Center prepared the requisite materials while an Editorial Board co-ordinated the work.

The Staff consisted of:
Kwan Choi-wah
Lo Chi-hung
Lo Tam Fee-yin
Mak Tze-kuen
Man Chiu-kwan
Miu Wong Nga-ching
Ng Shiu-king, Pauline

The Editorial Board consisted of:
    Ng Lam Sim-yuk (Chairperson)
    Chik Hon-man
    Ho Cheuk-sang

Towards the end of this project Mrs. Miu Wong Nga Ching replaced Mrs. Ng to be the Chairperson of the Editorial Board. The final stages in the preparation of the dictionary for publication were carried out by her.

The Center would also like to express its gratitude to Brother Patrick Tierney of St. Joseph's College, Hong Kong, for checking the correspondence of meaning between each English and Cantonese word.

A 'Joint Venture' such as this, must of necessity contain flaws. Comments and suggestions for improvement will be gratefully received.

The compiler's sincerest hope is that the numerous students of Cantonese will find this Dictionary a real aid to everyday conversation and thus a treasure to possess.

LIU Ming
Director

INTRODUCTION

This Dictionary includes:

(i) a users' guide;

(ii) a brief introduction to Cantonese pronunciation in accordance with the Yale System of Romanization;

(iii) a comparative chart of four different systems of Romanization

(iv) grammatical notes; and

(v) an English-Cantonese dictionary containing some 15,000 separate entries.

Users' Guide

This dictionary is designed to help the user find the best word or phrase in Cantonese to express the meaning of an English word or expression. While, for the most part it follows standard conventions, users may find the notes below useful in familiarizing themselves with the format.

English words are listed in alphabetical order with each entry printed in a bold typeface. The part of speech is given, followed by the equivalent Cantonese word or phrase. Where the English word has more than one meaning, or demands a different Cantonese word or phrase in different contexts, these are separated by white numbers on a black background and an indication of the different meaning is given in brackets. Subsequently, the symbol ~ is used to represent the Cantonese word where simple examples are given of how it is used. Such examples are printed in italics. The sample entry below illustrates these conventions.

catch FV: ❶ (seize) jūk ❷ (intercept) làahnjiht ❸ (come upon sb. doing sth.) faatyihn; faatgok ❹ (get the meaning of) líhngwuih; mihngbaahk ❺ (become infected with) yíhm; yíhmdóu; yáuh ~ *behng* RV: ❶ (snatch) jáaujyuh; jūkjyuh ❷ (be in time for) góndóu ~ *fóchè* ❸ (capture) jūkjyuh; jūkdóu N: ❶ (cunning device) gwáigai (M: go) ❷ (of door) mùhnsēut (M: go) * **catch at** FV/RV: jūkjyuh * **catch it** PH: béi yàhn naauh

* **catch on** FV: ① lèihgáai; líuhgáai; líhngwuih ② (become popular) làuhhàhng héilàih * **catch up** FV: jèui; jèuiséuhng * **catch phrase** N: miuhgeui (M: geui) * **catch word** N: ① (of an article) biutàih (M: go) ② (slogan) biuyúh; làuhhàhngyúh (M: geui) * **catch a ball** VO: jipbō; jipjyuh go bō * **catch a cold** RV: láahngchàn FV: sèungfùng * **catch a disease** VO: yáuhbehng; yíhmbehng

The symbol ✳ marks the start of sub-entries. The nearest Cantonese equivalent is given for each. Where there is more than one meaning, the appropriate equivalents are listed, separated by numbers printed black on white. For convenience, symbols used in this dictionary are listed and defined below.

SYMBOLS

❶   main entry explanation
①   sub-entry explanation
~   represents immediately preceding Cantonese equivalent
·   marks the start of the example (except where ~ itself begins the example)
( )   enclosing English word before the definition
=   explanation
    enclosing English word after FV = the object of the FV
    enclosing Cantonese word = optional

/ = or

* marks the start of the sub-entry

A list of abbreviations used in this dictionary is given on page 22.

Brief Introduction to Cantonese Pronunciation

In pronouncing a syllable in Cantonese, three elements must be taken into account, namely, an <u>initial</u>, a <u>final</u> and a <u>tone</u>. The initial includes whatever is before the main vowel, the final includes the main vowel and whatever follows it and the tone is the voice pitch for the syllable. For the syllable, "ngáak", then, the initial is <u>ng</u>, the final is <u>aak</u> and the tone is high-rising.

Initials

An initial is the starting-off sound of a word.

Of the nineteen initials in Cantonese, ch, p, t, k and kw are aspirated while b, d, g, gw and j are unaspirated. The aspirated ch is articulated between the English ch and ts.

The remaining initials, f, h, l, m, n, ng, s, y and w have similar articulation to English.

1. Aspirated stops: i.e.
   P   T   K   CH   KW

2. Non-aspirated stops: i.e.
   B   D   G   J   GW

3. Nasals: i.e.
   M   N   NG

4. Fricative and Continuants: i.e.
   F   L   H   S

5. Semi-vowels: i.e.
   Y   W

Finals

A final is the concluding sound of a word and there are fifty one of these. The main vowel is the key part of the Cantonese final. The vowels may be either long or short and this affects the pronunciation.

1. Finals starting with "A"
   A
   AAI   <u>AI</u>
   AAU   <u>AU</u>
   AAM   <u>AM</u>
   AAN   <u>AN</u>
   AANG   <u>ANG</u>
   AAP   <u>AP</u>
   AAT   <u>AT</u>
   AAK   <u>AK</u>

2. Finals starting with "E"
   E   <u>EI</u>   ENG   EK
   EU   <u>EUI</u>   EUNG   <u>EUT</u>   <u>EUN</u>   EUK

3. Finals starting with "I"
   I   IU   IM   IN   <u>ING</u>
   IP   IT   IK

4. Finals starting with "O"
   O   OI   ON   <u>OU</u>   ONG   OT   OK

5. **Finals starting with "U"**
   U UI UN <u>UNG</u> UT <u>UK</u>

6. **Finals starting with "Y"**
   YU YUN YUT

The vowels in the underlined finals are shorter. The endings P T K are pronounced wihtout any burst of air.

Tones

The student of Cantonese will be well aware of the importance or tones in conveying meaning. Basically, there are seven tones which, in the Yale system, are represented by the use of diacritics and by the insertion of H for the three low tones.

The following chart will illustrate the seven tones:

1	2	3	4	5	6	7
High <u>Falling</u>	High <u>Rising</u>	Mid <u>Level</u>	High <u>Level</u>	Low <u>Falling</u>	Low <u>Rising</u>	Low <u>Level</u>
chàng	cháng	chang	chāng	chàhng	cháhng	chahng
bàai	báai	baai	bāai	bàaih	báaih	baaih

Below is a chart describing the relative differences between the seven tones:

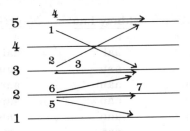

Comparative Chart of
Four Romanization Systems

Initials

Yale	IPA	Sidney Lau	Meyer-Wempe
p	p'	p	p'
b	p	b	p
t	t'	t	t'
d	t	d	t
k	k'	k	k'
g	k	g	k
ch	tʃ	ch	ch', ts'
j	tʃ	j	ch, ts
kw	k'w	kw	k'w
gw	kw	gw	kw
m	m	m	m
n	n	n	n
ng	ŋ	ng	ng
f	f	f	f
l	l	l	l
h	h	h	h
s	ʃ	s	s, sh
y	j	y	i, y
w	w	w	oo, w

Finals

Yale	IPA	Sidney Lau	Meyer-Wempe
a	a:	a	a
aai	a:i	aai	aai
aau	a:u	aau	aau
aam	a:m	aam	aam
aap	a:p	aap	aap
aan	a:n	aan	aan
aat	a:t	aat	aat

Comparative Chart of
Four Romanization Systems

Finals (Cont'd)

Yale	IPA	Sidney Lau	Meyer-Wempe
aang	a:ŋ	aang	aang
aak	a:k	aak	aak
ai	ai	ai	ai
au	au	au	au
am	am	am	am, om
ap	ap	ap	ap, op
an	an	an	an
at	at	at	at
ang	aŋ	ang	ang
ak	ak	ak	ak
e	ɛ:	e	e
eng	ɛ:ŋ	eng	eng
ek	ɛ:k	ek	ek
ei	ei	ei	ei
eu	œ:	euh	oeh
eung	œ:ŋ	eung	eung
euk	œ:k	euk	euk
eui	œi	ui	ui
eun	œn	un	un
eut	œt	ut	ut
i	i:	i	i
iu	i:u	iu	iu
im	i:m	im	im
ip	i:p	ip	ip
in	i:n	in	in
it	i:t	it	it
ing	iŋ	ing	ing
ik	ik	ik	ik

Comparative Chart of
Four Romanization Systems

Finals (Cont'd)

Yale	IPA	Sidney Lau	Meyer-Wempe
o	o	oh	oh
oi	o:i	oi	oi
on	o:n	on	on
ot	o:t	ot	ot
ong	o:ŋ	ong	ong
ok	o:k	ok	ok
ou	ou	o	o
u	u	oo	oo
ui	u:i	ooi	ooi
un	u:n	oon	oon
ut	u:t	oot	oot
ung	u:ŋ	ung	ung
uk	u:k	uk	uk
yu	y:	ue	ue
yun	y:n	uen	uen
yut	y:t	uet	uet

Tones

Yale		Sidney Lau		Meyer-Wempe	
high falling	à	high falling 1	a[1]	upper even	a
high rising	á	middle rising 2	a[2]	upper rising	á
middle level	a, at	middle level 3	a[3]	upper going	à
				middle entering	àt
high level	ā, āt	high level 1°	a[1]°	upper even	a
				upper entering	at
low falling	àh	low falling 4	a[4]	low even	ā
low rising	áh	low rising 5	a[5]	lower rising	ǎ
low level	ah, aht	low level 6	a[6]	lower going	ā
				lower entering	āt

Grammatical Notes

Parts of Speech
(Definitions, Uses, & Tests)

Adverbs (A)

An adverb modifies verbs or other adverbs.
There are three kinds of adverbs:

(1) It precedes the verb it modifies;
Kéuih <u>hóu</u> gòu. (He is very tall.)

(2) It precedes the subject;
<u>Daahhaih</u> ngóh móuh. (But I don't have.)
<u>Gám</u>, ngóh heui lā. (In that case I am going)

(3) It precedes the verb, but may be separated by the subjects;
Kéuih <u>sèuiyìhn</u> yáuh chín, . . .
(Although he is rich, . . .)
<u>Sèuiyìhn</u> kéuih yáuh chín, . . .
(Although he is rich, . . .)
In such cases, it is referred to as a movable adverb. (MA)

(4) It goes after the verb it modifies.
Kéuih gòu <u>gwotàuh</u>. (He is excessively tall.)
Ngóh heui <u>sìn</u>. (I go first.)

The test to determine whether certain verbal expressions are adverbs or other types of verb is:

A verbal expression is an adverb if 1. It may be used as a SV on other occasions: Kéuihdeih <u>gùnghòi</u> tóuleuhn nīgo mahntàih. (They discuss this problem openly.) Note: 'gùnghòi' is also a stative verb. 2. The verb which follows this expression cannot be dropped.

Q: Kéuih haih m̀haih <u>sìhsìh</u> làih a?
   (Does he often come?)
A: Kéuih <u>sìhsìh</u> làih.
   (Yes, he does.)

Compare this with auxiliary verb "háng"

Q: Kéuih háng heui ma? (Is he willing to do?)
A: Kéuih háng.   (Yes. or He is willing.)

Attributives (ATT.)

An attributive is a boundform serving as a noun-modifier. It may become a noun by adding the particle 'ge' at the end, i.e.

Kéuih haih nàahm hohksàang. (He is a male student.)
Kéuih haih nàahmge.   (He is a male.)

Auxiliary Verbs (AV)

An auxiliary verb normally takes other verbs or verb-object compounds as their objects, i.e.

Ngóh séung heui. (I want to go.) (I'm thinking of going.)
Ngóh jùngyi duhksyù. (I like to study.)

All auxiliary verbs have verbal functions and may be used as functive verbs.

Q: Néih jùngyi duhksyù ma? (Do you like to study?)
A: Ngóh jùngyi. (Yes, I do.)

In the "N AV FV" pattern, the negative particle "m̀" always goes before the AV. Ngóh m̀jùngyi heui. (I don't like to go.)

An auxiliary verb may be modified by the adverb 'hóu'.

Boundorms (BF)

A boundform is a syllable which cannot stand alone in normal speech. A combination of syllables including one or more boundforms is written together as a single word.

   . . . tùhng (together with)
e.g. tùhnghohk (schoolmate)
       tùhngsih   (colleague)

   . . . séuhng (go up on to something)
e.g. séuhng chè (get in a car)
       séuhng láu (go upstairs)

Co-Verbs (CV)

A co-verb plus its object forms a co-verb phrase modifying the main verb. The co-verb takes the place of the English preposition in expressing relationships.

> Kéuih hái Méihgwok làih ge.
> (He came from America.)

A co-verb and its object always precede the main verb and the main verb which is so modified may be either a functive verb or stative verb;

> Kéuih tùhng ngóh máaih syù.
> (He bought a book for me.)

A 'CV . . . FV' pattern may be modified by a negative particle or other adverbs, and the modifier goes before the co-verb; i.e.

> Kéuih m̀tùhng ngóh máaih syù.
> (He didn't buy a book for me.)

A co-verbial phrase may be stressed by the 'haih . . . ge' pattern, if the main verb of the sentence is a functive verb; i.e.

> Kéuih haih chóh syùhn làih ge.
> (It was by boat that he came.)

Equative Verbs (EV)

An equative verb states the equality of the two nouns between which it stands;

> Kéuih haih Jùnggwok yàhn.
> (He is a Chinese.)

> Kéuih sing Wòhng.
> (He is surnamed Wong.)

It is not customary to modify an object of an equational verb with a noun clause. Instead of saying: "Kéuih haih yātgo wúih góng Jùnggwokwá ge yàhn." (He is the man who can speak Chinese.), it is more idiomatic to say "Gógo yàhn wúih góng Jùnggwokwá." (That man can speak Chinese.)

Functive verbs (FV)

The term functive verb distinguishes a verb which predicates action or event from one which characterizes (SV). It may take an object.

Idiomatic Expressions (IE)

An idiomatic expression is a set phrase which carries a special meaning when used in a specific situation. It may not be a complete sentence. Yet it may stand alone without a subject or a verb;

Deuiṁjyuh.   (I'm sorry.)
Néih nē?   (How about you?)

Measures (M)

A measure is a boundform which can be preceded by a number (NU), a specifier (SP), or other indicator of quantity;

yātgo   (one)
nīgo   (this)
hóudò go (many)

Movable Adverbs (MA)

A movable adverb is one which can be used before or right after a subject.

Numbers (NU)

With the exception of a few, a number is essentially a counter. In simple counting or in reading off a list of numbers they are free forms. Otherwise are bound-forms and require measures (M) to complete them.

It may modify a noun;

yātbún syù   (a book)
yātgo yàhn   (a person)

It may be used as a noun;

Yātgo ṁgau.   (One is not enough.)
Ngóh yiu yātgo. (I want one.)

Nouns (N)

A noun may function as the subject or object of a verb or as modifier of another noun. It can be preceded by the combination SP-NU-M or by some portion of it.

Particles (P)

A particle is an indicator with a definite grammatical significance, though its exact English meaning is sometimes hard to translate;

Kéuih làihjó <u>la</u>.   (He has come.)
Kéuih sihk<u>gán</u> faahn.   (He is eating.)

Placewords (PW)

A placeword is a positional noun, which includes all proper names of places.

A noun followed by a positional suffix such as 'nīsyu', 'gósyu', 'seuhngbihn', etc. will have the same function o a placeword;

Chéng néih làih ngóh <u>nīsyu</u>.
(Please come to me.)

M̀gòi néih jàihái tói <u>seuhngbihn</u>.
(Please put it on the table.)

Certain common nouns such as 'ngūkkéi', 'hohkhaauh' 'poutáu' and 'jáugā' are treated as placewords. There ar other nouns, which should from the point of view of mean ing, be considered placewords, but which do not so func tion; i.e. hòh (river), hói (sea), sàan (mountain), sèhng (c ty), and gāai (street).

Only a placeword can be used as object of co-verb 'há and 'yàuh'.

A placeword can modify a noun either with or withou particle 'ge' in between, though the meaning may not t the same;

Jùnggwokyàhn   (Chinese people)
Jùnggwok ge yàhn   (people in China)

Post Verbs (PV)

A post verb may be suffixed to functive verbs to indicate certain relationships. The resulting compounds require an object just as co-verbs do;

Kéuih chóh <u>hái</u> gósyu. (He sits over there.)

Not all functive verbs can be followed by a post verb. It is correct to say "fanhái chòhngsyu" (sleep in bed), but it is wrong to say "sihkhái jáugā" (eat in a restaurant).

The "RV-PV" compound is different from "AV FV" pattern. The "FV-PV" is considered as one word, hence no other words can be inserted between them. The FV in the "AV FV" pattern however may be modified by other elements. For example, "Ngóh séung heui." (I'm thinking of going.) "séung" is an auxiliary verb; therefore, the main verb "heui" may be modified by adverbs like "tìngyaht", "sìhsìh", "m̀" etc.

Question Words (QW)

A question word is a noun or a place word used in asking a question; such as 'bīngo' (who), 'bīnsyu' (where).

A question word occupies in the sentence the same position as the word or words which replace it in the answer; i.e.

<u>Bīngo</u> haih hohksàang a? (Who is a student?)

The QW 'bīngo' is placed before the verb 'haih', because the answer to this question is 'Kéuih haih hohksàang.' (He is a student.) Hence 'bīngo' occupies the same position as 'kéuih'.

Gó go yàhn haih <u>bīngo</u> a? (Who is that man?)

The answer to this question could be 'Gógo yàhn haih Wòhng sìnsàang.' (That man is Mr. Wong.) Hence the QW 'bīngo' occupies the same place as 'Wòhng sìnsàang'.

A question word may be used in the following patterns

(1) indefinite patterns:
   Ngóh m̀heui bīnsyu.
   (I'm not going anywhere in particular.)

(2) inclusive or exclusive patterns:
   Ngóh bīngo dōu jùngyi. (I like everybody.)

Resultative Verbs (RV)

A resultative verb is a compound of two verbs, in which the first verb indicates the kind of action involved, while the second which is called the resultative verb ending (RVE) shows the result or extent of the action; 'heuidou' (reach), 'séyùhn' (finish writing)

Most of the resultative verbs have two forms:

(1) The actual form, in which the result has been actually attained;

   Ngóh táigin góga chè.
   (I saw that car.)

   Ngóh móuh táigin góga chè.
   (I don't see that car.)

(2) The potential form, in which the result of the action is conceived of as being possible or impossible of attainment;

   Ngóh wándākdóu néih gógo pàhngyáuh. (I could find your friend.)

   Ngóh m̀wándākdóu néih gógo pàhngyáuh. (I couldn't find your friend.)

Not all resultative verbs have actual form, for example 'sihkdākhéi' (can afford to eat) which has only the potential form.

Not all compound verbs are resultative, for example 'tènggóng' (hear it said that), 'mìhngbaahk'(understand) are not. The test for resultative is whether the compound can be converted into potential form.

Stative Verbs (SV)

A stative verb expresses quality or condition, hence describes rather than predicates action or event; 'hóu' (be well), 'mòhng' (be busy).

Use of stative verbs:

(1) They may be used as a verb of the subject; i.e.

Kéuih gòu. (He is tall.)

Note: unlike the adjective in English, a stative verb is not preceded by a verb to be.

(2) They may modify a noun; i.e.

hóu syù (good book)

Note: If it is a simple unqualified stative verb, the particle 'ge' is not necessary.

(3) They may be used in the following patterns:

A. . . . béi . . . . SV

Kéuih béi ngóh gòu. (He is taller than I.)

B. . . . tùhng . . . yātyeuhng SV

Kéuih tùhng ngóh yātyeuhng gòu.
(He and I are of the same height.)

C. . . . móuh . . . gam SV

Kéuih móuh ngóh gam gòu.
(He is not as tall as I.)

(4) They may describe a manner; i.e.

Kéuih hàahngdāk hóu faai. (He walks very fast.)

(5) Some stative verbs may be used as adverbs to modify other verbs; i.e.

Kéuih hóu fùnhéi gám wah . . .
(He happily said . . .)

(6) Some stative verbs may be used as a resultative verb ending; i.e.

táidāk chìngchó (can see clearly)

sáim̀gònjehng (cannot be washed clean)

Test for stative verbs:

(1) They can be modified by adverb 'hóu', and

(2) They do not take an object, but can modify a noun, and

(3) They can be used in one of the three patterns mentioned in 'Uses of stative verbs, section3'

Specifiers (SP)

A specifier points to a definite thing or things. It can stand before a noun, a NU-M compound, a NU-M-N compound, or another specifier; i.e.

gógo (that one)
gógo yàhn (that person)
lihngngoih gógo yàhn (the other person)

Uses of the SP-NU-M conpound are the same as NU-M compound.

Time Words (TW)

A time word indicates the time when a certain action or event has occurred or will occur. It may function as a noun or as an adverb; i.e.

Gàmyaht haih láihbaaiyāt. (Today is Monday.)
Ngóh gàmyaht làih (I'll come today.)

Verb-object Compounds (VO)

Some verbs in Chinese are commonly associated with generalized objects, which together form single concepts in the Western mind, and translate into single English intransitive verbs. Such are called VO compound;

sihkfaahn (eat)
séjih (write)

In English these generalized objects are more often implied, whereas in Chinese they are always expressed.

When a specific object is indicated, it replaces the generalized object. For instance, one says: 'Ngóh yiu sihk tóng.' (I want to eat candy.), never 'Ngóh yiu sihkfaahn tóng.'

The object of the VO compound, like other nouns may be modified by a stative verb, a SP-NU-M compound, or other elements.

Tests for VO compound:

(1) If it's English translation is a single intransitive verb,

(2) If the object is not a free form,
    'jóugok'   (to form a cabinet)
    'gónghohk' (give lectures)

(3) If the verb has a special meaning as in the expressions 'dálit' (to tie a knot), 'sauhyínghéung' (be affected)

An expression may look like a VO compound but actually be a FV;

gingwok (found a nation)

Abbreviations

A	: adverb	P	: particle
Adj. PH	: adjectival phrase	Patt	: pattern
Adv. PH	: adverbial phrase	PH	: phrase
ATT	: attributive	pl.	: plural
AV	: auxiliary verb	PN	: pronoun
BF	: bound form	PV	: post-verb
coll.	: colloquial expression	PW	: place word
CV	: co-verb	RV	: resultative verb
EV	: equative verb	RVE	: resultative verb ending
fig.	: figurative	sl.	: slang
FV	: functive verb	SP	: specifier
IE	: idiomatic expression	sth.	: something
lit.	: literary	SV	: stative verb
M	: measure	TW	: time word
MA	: movable adverb	U.S.A.	: Mainly American Usage
N	: noun	VO	: verb object
NuM	: number measure		

A

a   Nu: yāt

aback   A: heunghauhtan; dádoutan * **taken aback** PH: haakjó yāttiu

abacus   N: syunpùhn (M: go)

abalone   N: bàauyùh (M: jek)

abandon   FV: ❶ fonghei (things, duty) ❷ pàauhei (home, friends) * **abandon oneself to** A: jeuhnchìhng gám; bok-mehnggám * **abandon oneself to despair** PH: jih-bouh-jih-hei

abase   FV: bíndài

abash   Adj. PH: gokdāk chàahmkwáih; cháu; m̀ ngônlohk

abbey   N: jihyún; sàudouhyún (M: gàan)

abbreviate   FV/N: sūksé; gáansé (M: go)

abbreviation   FV/N: gáan-sé; sūksé (M: go)

abdicate   FV: ❶ fonghei (right) ❷ yeuhng; teui (throne) ~ *waih*

abdomen   N: tóuh (M: go); fūkbouh

abduct   FV: gwáaidaai

abductor   N: gwáaijílóu (M: go)

aberration   N: chosih (M: gihn); gwosāt (M: chi)

abeyance   FV: jùngjí; jaahm-sìh gokji

abide   FV: yánsauh; yùhngyán * **abide by** FV: ① jèunsáu

(regulations) ② gìnchìh (opinion)

ability   N: nàhnglihk; búnsih (M: júng)

abject   SV: ❶ hólìhn; cháam (situation) ❷ bèipéi (manner)

ablaze   RV: sìujeuhk * **ablaze with anger** SV: fógwán

able   AV: hóyíh; nàhnggau; wúih SV: búnsih; nàhnggon; lēk * **able-bodied man** N: jongdīng (M: go)

ablution   N: gònjehng ge séui * **perform ablution** VO: sáisàn IE: jàai-gaai-muhk-yuhk

abnegate   FV: ❶ hākjai (desire) ❷ fonghei (rights)

abnormal   SV: bintaai; kèiyìhng; m̀jingsèuhng

aboard   PH: hái (ship, plane . . .) syu/seuhngbihn ~ *sỳuhn* ~

abolish   FV: faichèuih

abominable   SV: hātyàhn-jàng; tóuyim

aboriginal   SV: búndeih

aborigines   N: tóuyàhn; búndeihyàhn (M: go) * **savage aborigines** N: sàangfàan (M: go)

abortion   N: ❶ (by accident) làuhcháan; síucháan ❷ (artificial) dohtòi; làuhcháan * **criminal abortion** N/VO: dohtòi; lohktòi; fèifaat dohtòi * **induced abortion** N: yàhngùng làuhcháan

abound   Adj. PH: yáuh hóudò; yáuh hóu fùngfu ge

about   CV: gwàanyù A: ❶ daaihyeuk; yeukmók; chàmdò

~ *luhk dímjùng* ❷ jóyáu; gamseuhnghá • *luhkdímjūng* ~ ✳ **about to** A: jèunggahn; jauhlàih; jauhlèih

above PW: (hái) . . . seuhngbihn ✳ **as above** PH: hóuchíh yíhseuhng ge ✳ **above all** A: sáusìn

abreast A: yàt paak ✳ **keep abreast** Adj. PH: jèuiséuhng sìhdoih

abridge FV: ❶ sūkdyún ❷ sàanseuk; sàanjit

abroad PW: hái ngoihgwok SV: hói ngoih

abrogate FV: faichèuih

abrupt SV: dahtyìhn ✳ **an abrupt turn** N: gāpwàan (M: go)

abscess N: chòng; nùhngchòng (M: go)

abscond FV: chìhmtòuh; tàujáu

absent FV: kyutjihk; móuhlàih; móuhdou ✳ **absent minded** Adj. PH: sàm-bāt-joihyìhn; sàm-sàhn-fóng-fāt; sàhn-bāt-sáu-se

absolute SV/A: jyuhtdeui

absolutely A: jyuhtdeui; yùhnchyùhn

absolution N: semíhn (M: go)

absolve FV: ❶ semíhn (sins) ❷ míhnchèuih (obligation)

absorb FV: ❶ sok; kāp (liquid) ❷ kāpsàu (experience, knowledge) ✳ **be absorbed in** Adv. PH: chyùhn-sàhn-gun-jyu, jyùnsàm; jaahpjùngjìngsàhn

abstain FV: gaai

abstemious SV: yáuhjitjai

abstract SV: chàu-jeuhng (opp. of geuihtái) N: jaahkyiu (of report) (M: dyuhn) ✳ **make an abstract of** FV: jaahkluhk; chyutsé

absurd SV: fòngmauh; m̀hahpléih; lèihpóu; sòh; múng; ngohng gèui (slang)

abundant SV: fùngfu; hóudò

abuse FV: ❶ (misuse) láahmyuhng ~ *kyuhnlihk* ❷ (treat badly) yeuhk doih ❸ (scold) naauh • *góng chòuháu ~ yàhn* N: baihbehng; waaih jaahpgwaan; ngokjaahp

abusive SV: ❶ naauhyàhnge ❷ béi yàhn láahmyuhng ge (privilege)

abyss N: sàmyùn; mòuhdái sàmtàahm (M: go)

academic(al) SV: hohkseuhtge ✳ **academic degree** N: hohkwái (M: go) ✳ **academic world** N: hohkseuhtgaai (M: go)

academician N: yúnsih (M: wái)

academy N: ❶ (school of higher learning) hohkyún (M: gàan) ❷ (society of distinguished men) hohkwúi (M: go)

accede FV: ❶ daapying (request) ❷ tùhng yi (terms)

accelerate FV: gàfaai VO: gàchūk; gàfaai chūkdouh

accelerator N: ❶ (of a car) yáu mùhn (M: go) ❷ gàchūkhei

accent N: ❶ (individual way of pronouncing) yàm; háu yàm (M: júng) ❷ (prominence to a syllable) chúhngyàm

accept FV: ❶ jip sauh (offer, gift, proposal) ❷ yìngsìhng; daapying (request) ❸ sàu (sth, offered) ~ m̀ ~ jìpiu a?

acceptable SV: hóyíh jipsauh ge • kéuih ge yigin haih ~

access FV: jipgahn

accident N: yi'ngoih; sātsih (M: chi) ✽ **by accident** SV/A: mòuhyijùng, ngáuhyìhn

accidentally A: ngáuhyìhn gám Adv. PH: yáuh gam ngāam dāk gam kíu

acclaim FV: hotchói; fùnfù

acclamation N: fùnfù; jaanséung

acclimatize VO: sīkying séuitóu

accommodate FV: ❶ (lodge) sàuyùhng; yùhng'naahp ❷ (supply) gùngying; gùngkāp ✽ **accommodate to** FV: sīkying; puihahp

accommodating SV: hóusàmdéi (háng bòng yàhn)

accompany FV: ❶ (go with) pùih ❷ (by music) buhnjau

accomplice N: tùhngdóng (M: go) bònghùng (M: go)

accomplish FV: ❶ daahtdou (purpose) ❷ yùhnsìhng (mission) ❸ sahtyìhn (plan) ✽ **accomplished in** A: sìhnchèuhng (yù); jìngtùng (yù); hóuwúih

accomplishment N: sìhngjauh (M: júng)

accomplishments N: geihnàhng; chòihnàhng (M: júng)

accord FV: ❶ (grant)béi; chibéi; sungbéi ❷ (consistent) fùhhahp ~ yiukàuh ✽ of one's own accord AV: jihyuhn Adv. PH: gàmsàm chìhngyuhn ✽ **in accord with** Patt: . . . tùhng . . . yātji • kéuihge yigin ~ ngóh (ge) ~

accordance FV: gàngeui; jiu ✽ **in accordance with** FV: gàngeui; yìjiu, jiu

according FV: (base on) jiu; gàngeui (see below) CV: (following) jiujyuh; jiu (see below) ✽ **according to** FV: jiu, gàngeui ~ ngóhdeih yìhgā ge chìhngyìhng làih tái, . . . CV: jiujyuh; jiu • néih yiu ~ ngóh sógóng ge heui jouh

accordion N: sáufùngkàhm (M: go)

accost FV: dàudaap

account N: ❶ (statement of money) jeung; sou (M: pùhn) ❷ (of bank) wuhháu (M: go) ❸ (report) boudouh; góngfaat (M: go) syutmìhng; jeuihseuht (M: dyuhn) ❹ (estimation) gúgai ❺ (reason) léihyàuh; yùhnyàn (M: go) FV: ❶ (consider) yìhngwàih ❷ (explain) gáaisīk ✽ **account for** FV: gáaisīk; syutmìhng; góngmìhng ✽ **give an account of** FV: gáaisīk; bougou; góngseuht ✽ **on account of** A: yànwaih; yànwaih . . . ge yùhngu ✽ **on no account** Adv. PH: chìnkèih m̀hóu; mòuhleuhn dím dōu m̀hóu ✽ **take account of / take into account** FV: háauleuih; jyuyi ✽ **turn to (full, good) account** FV: (chùngfahn, hóu hóu gám) leih yuhng ✳ **balance an account** VO: git yāt tiuh sou ✳ **make much (little) account of** FV: (m̀) juhngsih; (m̀) jyuyi

accountant N: wuihgaisī (M: go) wuihgaiyùhn (M: go)

accounting N: wuihgaihohk; wuihgai

accredit FV: ❶ (send) wáipaai ❷ (believe) sèungseun; seun yahm

accumulate FV: leuihjīk

accumulator N: dihnchìh (M: go)

accuracy N: jéunkoksing; jéunkokdouh (M: go)

accurate SV: jéunkok; jéun

accursed, accurst SV: tóuyimge; hātyàhnjàngge

accusation N: hunggou; hungsou

accuse FV: ❶ hínjaak; jí jaak (have done wrong) ❷ hunggou (have committed crime)

accused N: beihgou (M: go)

accustom FV: jaahpgwaan RVE: – gwaan

ace N: (on cards) yìnsí; yīn (on dice) yātdím SV: (first rate) daihyātlàuh; yātlàuh ✳ **within an ace of** A: gèifùh; jàangdī

acerbity N: (taste) sỳun; fú; gip SV: (language) hākbohk; jìmsyùn hākbohk

ache N: tung (M: júng)

achieve FV: ❶ yùhnsìhng (work) ❷ daahtdou (goal) ❸ dākdóu (success)

achievement N: sìhngjauh (M: júng)

achromatic SV: móuhsīkge

acid N/SV: syùn

acidify FV: sỳunfa; binsỳun

acidity N: syùnsing; syùndouh

acknowledge FV: sìhng-yìhng (truth) PH: tùhngjì sàudóu (news)

acknowledgement VO: jíjeh; mìhngjeh N: jehchìh (M: pìn)

acolyte N: johsáu (M: go)

acoustic SV: tìnggokge

acoustician N: sìnghohkgà (M: wái)

acquaint FV: yihngsīk; suhksīk; sīk ✳ **be acquainted with** FV: yìhngsīk; suhksīk; sīk Patt: PN₁ tùhng PN₂ sèungsīk ✳ **make acquaintance of** FV: gitsīk (PN); gitgàau ✳ **have acquaintance with** Patt: deui (subject) yáuh yihngsīk

acquaintance N: suhkyàhn (M: go)

acquiesce FV: mahkyìhng; mahkhéui

acquire FV: hohkdóu (knowledge, skill)

acquit FV: sīkfong

acquittal N: (set free) sīkfong PH: (not guilty) mòuhjeuih sīkfong; sỳunpun móuhjeuih

acre M: yìngmáuh

acrid SV: ❶ (smell) gùng-beihge; laahtge ❷ (temper, manner) jìmhāk

acrimonious SV: ❶ (words) hākbohk; jìmhāk ❷ (quarrel) kehkliht; sàileih

acrobat N: jaahpgeihyùhn; jaahpgeih yínyùhn (M: go)

acrobatics N: dahkgeih (M: júng); jaahpgeih (M: júng)

across BF: -gwo · hàahng-gwo; gìnggwo; wàahnggwo PW: hái . . . deui mihn

act N: (law) faatngon (M: tiùh) M: (of a play) mohk FV: jouh ~ hei ✳ **act as** FV: jouh; dàamyahm ~ faatleuht gumahn ✳ **act for** FV: doihléih; doih ✳ **act like** FV: hóuchíh ~ hóuchíh ✳ **act when you see a chance** PH(V): gin-gèi-hàhng-sih ✳ **act without noise or ostentation** Adv. PH: bāt-duhng-sìng-sīk; jihngjíngdéi

acting ATT: doih · ~ jújyahm, ~ haauhjéung FV: (pretending) jadai · kéuih ~ jē

action N: hàhngduhng; géuiduhng (M: júng) · kèihgwaai ge ~ ✳ **take action** VO: chóichéui hàhng-duhng ✳ **take action against** FV: hunggou/gou .PN. ✳ **put into action** FV: saht hàhng ✳ **in action** FV: jeunhàhng gán; jouhgán

active SV: ❶ (energetic) wuht put ~ ge saimànjái ❷ (engage in social life) wuhtyeuk · hái sèunggaai hóu ~ ✳ **on active service** SV: yihnyihk ~ gwànyàhn

activist N: jīkgihk fahnjí (M: go)

activity N: wuhtduhng (M: júng) ✳ **extracurricular activities** N: fo'ngoih wuhtduhng ✳ **outdoor activities** N: wuh'ngoih wuhtduhng ✳ **social activities** N: séhgàau wuhtduhng

actor N: yínyùhn (M: go)

actress N: néuihyínyùhn (M: go)

actual SV: ❶ sahtjoihge; sahtjaige ❷ koksahtge

actually A: ❶ kèihsaht ~ kéuih m̀jùngyi ❷ sahtjaiseuhng ~ kéuih sìnji haih lóuhbáan

acupuncture N: jàmgau ✳ **acupuncture anaesthesia** N: jàmchi màhjeui

acute SV: ❶ (sharp) jìmge; jìmyeuihge ~ gok ❷ (keen) (of senses) máhnyeuih; lìhngmáhn ~ ge chaugok ❸ (of pain) gányiu, gàaugwàan · tung dāk ~ ❹ (of diseases) gāpsing (ge)

A.D. TW: gùngyùhn (hauh)

adage N: gaakyìhn; yihmyúh; jàmyìhn (M: geui)

Adam N: A-Dòng ✳ **Adam's apple** N: hàuhwát (M: nāp, go)

adapt FV: ❶ sīkying (environment) ❷ góipìn; góisé (writings) · jèung síusyut ~ sèhng heikehk ❸ góijòng (design)

adaptability N: sīkying-lihk; sīkying nàhnglihk (M: júng)

adaptor N: (electric) maahn-nàhng (chaap) sōu (M: go)

add FV: gà ✳ **add up** (together) RV: gàmàaih (yāt chái) ✳ **add up (to)** PH:

gàmàaih yātguhng yáuh . . . *
add to FV: jànggà ~ fuh dàam

addendum N: bóuwàih;
bóupīn (M: dyuhn)

adder N: fūksèh (M; tìuh)

addict N: (a drug addict)
douhyáuh; yáhn gwànjí (M:go)
* **addicted to** VO: ①
séuhngyáhn • yámjáu wúih ~
② séuhngjó . . . yáhn; yáuh . .
. yáhn ~duhk ~

addiction N: yáhn; pīkhou
(M: júng)

adding machine N: gaisyungèi; gaisougèi (M: ga)

addition N: gà (faat) * in
addition MA: chèuihchí
jí'ngoih ~ néih juhngyáuh
mātyéh tìm a? * in addition
to Patt: chèuihjó . . . jí'ngoih ~
néih ~ juhngyáuh bīngo a?

additional SV: lihngngoih
ge; fuhgà ge

addle SV: wùhtòuh * addle-
head N: wùhtòuhchùhng (M:
go)

address N: ❶ (place of
residence or business) deihjí (M:
go) ❷ (mailing address) tùng-
seunchyu; tùngseun deihjí (M:
go) ❸ (speech or talk) yínsyut
(M: pìn) * give an address
VO: faatbíu yínsyut • heung .
. . ~ * address to FV: sébéi
• nīfùng seun ~ bīngo sàu a?
* address as FV: chìngfù ~
kéuih jouh . . .; Dímyéung ~
kéuih a?

addressee N: sàuseunyàhn
(M: go)

adduce FV: géuichēut

adept Patt: deui . . . hóu-

joihhòhng ~ yíngséung ~

adequate SV: jūkgau; gau

adhere RV: chìjyuh

adhesive SV: yáuhnìm-
sing(ge) * adhesive tape N:
gàaubou (M: faai)

adhoc BF: dahkbiht(ge);
jyùnjaak(ge) ~ wáiyùhnwúi;
~ síujóu

adieu N: joigin * bid adieu
VO: goubiht; góng joigin

adjacent PW: gaaklèih;
fuhgahn; jógán

adjective N: yìhngyùhng-
chìh (M: go)

adjoin FV: ❶ sèunglihn;
lìhnmàaih • N₁ tùhng N₂ ~ ❷
gahnjyuh • N₁ ~ N₂

adjourn VO: yàuwúi

adjudicate FV: syùnpun

adjudication N: punkyut
(M: go)

adjudicator N: sámpungùn
(M: wái)

adjust RV: gaaungāam;
gaaujéun ~ go mohngngyúhn-
geng FV: gaau; tiuhjíng

administer FV: gúnléih

administration N: ❶ (of
affairs) gúnléih •gùngsèung ~
❷ (of a government) hàhngjing
bouhmùhn

administrative SV:
hàhngjing(ge)

admirable PH: lihngyàhn
puifuhk ge

admiral N: hóigwàn seuhngjeung (M: go)

admire FV: puifuhk; yàmpui

admission N: (price of entrance) piuga; yahpchèuhngfai

admit FV: ❶ sihngyìhng (mistake) ❷ sàu (students) Patt: béi/jéun .PN. yahplàih

admonish FV: gínggou; hyungaai

adolescence N: chìngchèunkèih (M: go)

adolescent N: chìngsiunìhn (M: go); chìngnìhn nàahmnéuih; nìhnchìngyàhn

adopt FV: ❶ chóiyuhng; yuhng (idea, custom, etc.) ❷ sàuyéuhng (child)

adore FV: ❶ sùhngbaai (God) ❷ gìngpui

adorn FV: jòngsīk

adornment N: jòngsīkbán (M: gihn)

adrift FV: piubok; piulàuh

adroit SV: suhklihn(ge)

adulate VO: paakmáhpei

adult N: daaihyàhn; sìhngyàhn (M: go) * **adult education** N: sìhngyàhn gaauyuhk

adulterate BF: (make impure) kàujó- ~ *séui ge ngàuhnáaih*

adulterer N: gàanfù (M: go)

adulteress N: yàhmfúh (M: go)

adultery FV: tùnggàan • . . . *tùhng . . .* ~ N: tùnggàanjeuih

adumbrate FV: ngàuwaahk ~ *chēut daaihkoi ge chìhngyìhng*

advance FV: ❶ (go forward) chìhnjeun ❷ (progress) jeunbouh ❸ (rise) tàihgòu; seuhngjeung • *mahtga ~ jó yátsìhng* ❹ (move forward as a date) tàihchìhn * **in advance** A: yuhsìn; sìhchìhn * **to advance money** FV: yuhjí

advanced SV: ❶ (of courses) gòukāp(ge) ❷ (of studies) gòusàamge ❸ (of technology) sìnjeun ge ❹ (old) nìhngéi daaih ge; séuhngjó nìhngéi ge

advantage N: yàudím; hóuchyu (M: go) Patt: deui .N. . yáuhleih * **take advantage of sb.** FV: ngāak .PN. VO: wán .PN. bahn

advantageous SV: yáuhleih; yáuhjeuhksou • *deui .PN.* ~

adventure VO: mouhhím

adventurer N: mouhhímgà; taamhímgà (M: go)

adventurous SV: gau chigīk

adverb N: fuchìh (M: go)

adversary N: deuisáu; dihksáu (M:go)

adverse SV: ❶ (unfavourable) bātleihge; m̀hóuge ❷ (contrary or hostile to) dihkdeui; fáandeui * **adverse winds** SV/N: ngaahkfùng, yihkfùng * **adverse fortune** N: sèuiwahn • *hàahng ~*

adversity N: waahn naahn; yihkgíng; ngàakwahn

advertise VO: dànggwónggou; maaihgwónggou; maaih goubaahk

advertisement N: gwónggou; goubaahk (M: dyuhn)

advice N: jùnggūk; yigin (M: go) ∗ **letter of advice** N: jingsīk tùngjì

advisable SV: mìhngji ge; sīkdongge

advise FV: hyun Patt: wah . . . yìnggòi • yìsàng ~ kéuih ~ yàusīk

adviser/advisor N: gu-mahn (M: wái)

advocate FV: jyújèung; tàihcheung N: (Barrister) bìhnwuh leuhtsī (M: wái; go)

A-energy N: yùhnjí nàhng

aeon N: wìhngsai

aerial SV: ❶ (exist in the air) hùngjùng ❷ (immaterial) hèuiwaahn N: tìnsin (M: tiuh)

aerobatics N: dahkgeih fèihàhng bíuyín (M: júng)

aerobus N: hùngjùng bàsí (M: ga)

aerodrome N: fèigèi-chèuhng (M: go)

aerodynamics N: heitái duhnglihk hohk

aerogram N: yàuhgáan (M: fùng)

aerolite N: wàhnsehk (M: gauh)

aeromap N: hòhnghùng deihtòuh (M: fùk)

aeronautics N: hòhng-hùnghohk

aeroplane N: fèigèi (M: ga, jek)

aerosol N: yìn; mouh ∗ **aerosol bomb** N: panmouhhei (M: go)

aesthetic SV: méihhohk ge; sámméihge

aesthetics N: méihhohk; sámméihhohk

afar SV: yúhn ∗ **from afar** A: lèihyúhn

affable SV: hóusèungyúh; hóuyàhnsí

affair N: sih; sihgon; sihchìhng (M: gihn)

affect FV: ❶ (have effect on) yínghéung ❷ (move the feelings) gámduhng • sauh ~ ❸ (of diseases) chyùhnyíhm; gám-yíhm • sauh ~

affected SV: jìjíng; jouhjok; hèuingaih

affecting SV: gámyàhnge; duhngyàhn ge

affection N: (love) ngoi; gámchìhng

affectionate SV: chànngoi ge

affidavit N: syùnsaihsyù (M: fahn); syùnsaihjí (M: jèung)

affiliate FV: gàyahp (a socie-ty) ∗ **affiliated member** N: jaanjoh wúiyùhn

affinity N: (having an attra-tion for) yùhnfahn; yùhn (M: júng) • ngóh tùhng néih yáuh ~

affirm FV: hángdihng

affirmative SV: hángdihng ge

affix FV: fuhgà; nìhm; tip N: fuhgín ∗ **affix a postage stamp** VO: nìhm yàuhpiu; tip sihdàam ∗ **affix a seal** VO: dámyan ∗ **affix a signature** VO: chìmméng; chìmjí; gàchìm

afflict FV: jitmòh; jòujāt

affliction N: fúnaahn; tungfú (M: júng)

affluent SV: fùngfu; fuyuh

afford RV: fuhdàam dāk héi; máaihdākhéi, béidākhéi; . FV. dāk héi . O .; (negative) V-m̀héi • jeuk ~ gam gwai ge sàam

afforest FV: luhkfa

affray N: jàngjāp VO: dágàau

affront FV: móuhyuhk PH: dòngjung móuhyuhk VO: lohkmín • lohk PN mín

Afghan N: ❶ A-fu-hohn yàhn (M: go) ❷ A-fu-hohn wá (M: júng)

afloat FV: ❶ fàuh (on air or water) ❷ làuhchyùhn (rumour)

afore A: chìhnbihn; seuhngbihn * **aforesaid** Adj. PH: chìhnbihn só góng ge; seuhng seuht ge * **aforethought** Adj. PH: yáuh yuhmàuh ge

afraid FV: pa

afresh A: joi; chùhngsàn

African N: Fèijàuyàhn (M: go)

after Adv. PH: hái . . . jìhauh; yíhhauh * **the day after** TW: daihyihyaht * **after-care** PH: behnghauh tiuhyéuhng * **aftermath** N: yùhbō; gitgwó * **after all** A: gauging; doudái * **after-thought** RV: séungfàanhéi FV: fáansíng * **after death** SV: sànhauh; séihauh

afternoon TW: hahjau

afterwards TW: hauhlòih; yíhhauh; sāuméi

again A: yauh; joi * **again and again** A: léuihchi * **once again** A: joichi

against FV: ❶ fáandeui; fáan (a person, policy, proposal, etc.) ❷ ngàaijyuh, bahngjyuh (wall, tree, etc.) * **against law** SV: faahnfaat * **against current** SV: yihkséui; ngaahkséui * **against wind** SV: yihkfùng; ngaahkfùng * **against one's will** FV: míhnkéuhng * **against one's conscience** Adj. PH: wàihbui lèuhngsàm

agape PH: maakdaaih go háu

agate N: máhnóuh (M: nāp)

age N: ❶ seui • Néih géidò ~ a? ❷ nihngéi (M: go) • Néih yáuh géidaaih ~ a? ❸ nihnlìhng (M: go) • Néih ge ~ haih géidò a? ❹ sìhdoih (M: go) • nígo haih dihnnóuh ge ~ * **over age** SV: chìulìhng * **for an age** TW: hóunoih; hóu chèuhng ge sìhgaan * **the aged** N: lóuhyàhn; lóuhyàhngà; (male) baakyēgūng; (female) baakyēpó * **in all ages** TW: lihkdoih

agency N: doihléih (M: go)

agenda N: yíhchìhng (M: go, hohng)

agent N: ❶ doihléihyàhn; doihléihsèung; doihléih (M: go) ❷ (of house etc.) gìnggéi (M: go)

aggravate FV: ❶ (make angry) liuh; gīknàu ❷ (make worse) gàchúhng ~ kéuihge jeuih

aggregate FV: jeuihjaahp

aggression N: chàmleuhk (M: chi)

aggressive SV: ❶ (disposed

to attack) ngahjah, badouh • *nīgo yàhn hóu* ~ ❷ (offensive) gùnggīksing ~ *móuhhei*

aggressor N: chàmleuhkjé (M: go)

aggrieved VO: sauhwáiwāt

aghast RV: haakdou sòhjó; haaksòhjó

agile SV: lihngmáhn; máhnjiht

agitate SV: (cause anxiety to a person's feelings) gīkduhng • *kéuih tènggin waaih sìusīk, hóu* ~ FV: (shake, stir up) yiuh; gáau * **agitate for** FV: faatduhng; sinduhng

ago A: chìhn, jíchìhn • *nīdī haih léuhngnìhn* ~ *ge sih * **long ago** TW: hóu noih jíchìhn * **a while ago** TW: móuhgéinoih jíchìhn

agog AV: hotmohng • *dī saimānjái* ~ *gin kéuihdeih ge fuhmóuh*

agony N: tungfú PH: gihkdaaih ge tungfú (M: júng)

agrarian SV: tóudeih ge; nùhngyihp ge

agree FV: ❶ (consent) tùhngyi; yìngsìhng ❷ (accept as correct) fùhhahp ~ *yiukàuh* SV: ❶ (in harmony) yātji ~ *ge yigin* ❷ (get on well) tàuhkai • *kéuihdeih léuhng go yàhn hóu* ~ * **agree to** FV: tùhngyi * **agree with** (a person) FV: jaansìhng * **agree with** (certain kind of food, etc.) FV: sauhdāk

agreement N: hipdihng; hipyíh (M: go) * **by agreement** Adj. PH: daaihgā tùhngyi ge; yeukdihngge * **enter into an agreement** VO: chìmmahp-

tùhng; dájó hahptùhng

agriculture N: nùhngyihp

agriculturist N: nùhnghohkgā (M: wái, go)

agrobiology N: nùhngyihp sàngmahthohk

aground FV: gokchín

ague N: yeuhkjaht; faatláahng VO: dáláahngjan; faat láahng

ahead A: hái chìhnbihn * **go ahead** PH: ① gaijuhk heungchìhn .FV .; ② *gaijuhk V lohkheui* * **ahead of** Adv. PH: hái . ˙. chìhnbihn * **look ahead** PH: waih jèunglòih dásyun IE: meihyúh chàuhmàuh

aid FV/N: bòngjoh; wùhnjoh; gaujai * **with the aid of** FV: jejoh yù . . . * **first aid** N: gāpgau * **deaf aid** N: johtinghei (M: go) * **visual aids** N: sihgok gaaugeuih

aide N: johsáu; fugùn (M: go)

AIDS N; oijī behng

ailment N: behngtung; behng (M: júng)

aim FV: ❶ mìuhjéun (a target) ❷ jijoih (have a plan or intention) N: (goal) muhkdīk; muhkbīu

aimless SV: móuh muhkdīk ge

air N: hùnghei VO: tùnghei; tùngháhhei * **put on high airs** SV: láansíng; láanlēk; sàchàhn * **on the air** FV: gwóngbo * **travel by air** VO: chóh fèigèi * **in the air** N: yìuhchyùhn * **open air** SV: louhtìn

airbus N: hùngjùng bàsí (M: ga)

aircast N: mòuhsindihn gwóngbo

air-conditioned SV: yáuh-láahngheige; yáuh hùngtiùh ge

air-conditoner N: láahng-heigèi (M: ga, bouh)

aircraft N: fèigèi (M: ga, jek)

aircraft carrier N: hòhng-hùng móuh laahm (M: jek)

aircrew N: gèiyùhn; hùng-kàhnyàhnyùhn (M: go)

air current N: heilàuh (M: douh, gú)

air cushion N: heidín (M: go)

airdrop FV: hùngtàuh

airfield (see airport)

air force N: hùnggwàn (M: deuih)

air-gun N: heichèung (M: jì)

air-hostess N: hùngjùng síujé (M: wái)

airless PH: hùnghei m̀làuh-tùng SV: guhk

air letter N: hòhnghùng yàuhgáan (M: fùng) hòhnghùng seun (M: fùng)

airlift VO: hùngwahn bóukāp FV: hùngwahn

airline N: hòhnghùng gùngsī (M: gàan)

airliner N: bàangèi

airmail N: hòhnghùng yàuhgín; hùngyàuh (M: gihn)

airport N: fèigèichèuhng gèichùhng (M: go)

air raid N/FV: hùngjaahp (M: chi)

air raid alarm N: fòhng-hùng gíngbou (M: chi)

air raid shelter N: fòhng-hùng duhng; fòhnghùngdúng (M: go)

airtight SV: m̀lauhhei

airway N: hòhngsin (M: tiùh)

airy SV: ❶ (full of fresh air) hùnghei làuhtùng ❷ (immaterial) hùnghèui ❸ (not sincere) hèuingaih

aisle N: tùngdouh; jáulóng (M: tiùh)

ajar SV: bunyím; bunhòi

akimbo Adj. PH: léuhng jek sáu chàjyuh (tiùh) yìu

akin Adj. PH: yáuh hyuttúng gwàanhaih

a la mode SV: sìhhìng

alacrity SV: sóngfaai

alarm FV: gèng N: gíngbou * **alarm clock** N: naauhjùng (M: go) * **fire alarm** N: fógíng * **burglar alarm** N: fòhng douh gíng jùng (M: go)

alarming SV: dākyàhngèng

alas P: ai-ya; àihyàh; ài-ya

Alaskan N: A-làai-sì-gà yàhn (M: go)

Albanian N: A-yíh-bà-nèih-a yàhn (M: go)

albatross N: seuntìnyúng (M: jek)

album N: géinihmbóu; géinihmchaak (M: bún) ✻ **photo album** N: séungbóu (M: bún) ✻ **stamp album** N: jaahpyàuhbóu (M: bún)

albumen N: ❶ (white of egg) dáanbáak ❷ (substance as in white of egg) dáanbaahkjāt

alchemy N: lihngàmseuht; dímgàmseuht (M: júng)

alcohol N: ❶ (liquor) jáujìng ❷ (medicinal) fójáu

alcoholic N: jáugwái (M: go)

alert SV: gèigíng; síngséui; làuhsàm FV: tàihfòhng N: gíngbou ✻ **on the alert** VO: tàihgòu gínggok FV: làuhsàm; gujyuh

alfresco SV: louhtìn ge; wuh'ngoih ge

alga N: hóichóu

algebra N: doihsou

Algerian N: A-yíh-kahp-leih-a yàhn (M: go)

alias N: bihtméng (M: go)

alibi PH: m̀joihchèuhng ge jinggeui; m̀joihchèuhng ge jingmìhng (M: go)

alien N: ngoihgwok yàhn (M: go) ATT: ngoihgwok

alienate FV: ❶ (turn away friendship, etc.) sòyúhn • *tùhng PN ~ / ~ PN* ❷ (cause sb. to lose his friends) lèihgaan; tiubuht lèihgaan • *kéuihdeih ge gámchìhng* ❸ (transfer ownership) jyúnyeuhng

alienist N: jìngsàhnbehng yìsàng; jìngsàhn fō yìsàng (M: wái)

alight FV: ❶ lohk (chè, máh) ❷ gonglohk SV: ❶ (on fire) dímjeuhkge ❷ (bright) faatgwòng ge

align PH: ❶ (put in a line) pàaihsìhng yāt hòhng ❷ (form a line) jouhsìhng yāt tìuh jihksin VO: (come into agreement) gitmàhng • *nīgo gwokgà tùhng gógo gwokgà ~*

alike SV: ❶ (quality) sèungtùhng; yātyeuhng ❷ (appearance) chíhyéung; sèungchíh Adv. PH: deui . . . (dōuhaih) yātyeuhng • *kéuih màhmā ~ kéuihdeih géi hìngdaih ~*

alimentary SV: yáuh yìhngyéuhng ge; jìbóu ge

alimony N: sìhmyéuhngfai (M: bāt)

aliquant SV: chèuihm̀jeuhn ge

aliquot Adj. PH: chèuihdākjeuhnge

alive SV: sàang; sàangmáahng

alkaline SV: gáansing

all MM: gogo; jìjì etc. ~ *dōu hóu* Adj. PH: sóyáuhge ~ *hohksàang dōu làihchàih laak* RVE: saai • *kéuih sái ~ kéuih ge chín* SP: sèhng •*kéuih ~ máahn dōu móuh fan* ✻ **all kinds of** SV: goksìk gokyeuhng; gokjúng ✻ **all the way** A: yātlouhgám ✻ **not at all** Adv; PH: yātdī dōu m̀; yātdī dōu móuh; yātdī dōu móuh; yùhnchyùhn m̀ ✻ **all around** PW/A: seiwàih ~ *dōu yáuh yàhn •* ~ *gám mohng* ✻ **all in all** Adj. PH: jeui gányiu ge Adv. PH: júngkwut làih góng ✻ **all at once** A: dahtyìhn; fātyìhn-

gàan * **all but** Patt: chèuihjó
. . . ji'ngoih, kèihtà ge dōu . .
. ~ *kéuihdeih sàamgo* ~, ~
móuhlàih * **all gone** PH:
móuhsaai laak; yātdī dōu móuh
laak * **all over** PH: yùhnsaai
* **all right** PH: dāk;
móuhmahntàih * **all the
same** PH: yùhnchyùhn yātyeuhng; dōuhaih yātyeuhng *
all the time PH: sèhngyaht-
dōu; yātjihkdōu * **all
together** A: yātchái; yātchàih
* **that's all** PH: haih gamdō
la; móuh la * **all round** Adv.
PH: dò chòih dò ngaih ~ *ge
yàhn*

allay RV: gáamhèng, gáamsíu

allege FV: jadai wah · *kéuih
~ yáuhbehng*

alleged SV: yáuh yìhmyìh ge;
yìhmyìh * **the alleged** N: yìh-
fáan (M: go)

allegedly A: sityìhm · *kéuih
~ faahn tàusit jeuih*

allegiance N: jùngsìhng (M:
júng)· *deui . . . bíusih* ~ VO: ❶
haauhjùng; jeuhnjùng · *deui
gwokgà* ~ ❷ hinsàn ·
gwànyàhn ~ *béi gwokgà*

allegoric SV: yáuh yuhyi ge
* **allegoric tale** N: yuhyìhn
(M: go)

allegory N: yuhyi; yuhyìhn
(M: go)

allegro SV: hìngfaai; wuhtput

allergic SV: máhngám *
allergic to PH: deui . . .
máhngám

allergy N: máhngám; máhn-
gámjing; gwomáhnjing (M:
júng)

alleviate FV: gáamhèng

alleviative N: jítungyeuhk
(M: júng)

alley N: hohngjái; hóng (M:
tiuh) * **blind alley** N: gwahttàuh hóng (M: tiuh)

alliance N: lyùhnmàhng;
tùhngmàhng; màhnggwok;
màhngyáuh (M: go)

allied troops N: màhng-
gwàn (M: jì)

allocate FV: ❶ buht (fund,
land, people) ❷ fànpui (duties,
money, things, people) ~ *N béi
PN/N*

allot FV: fànpui

allotment M: fahn

allow FV: (informal) béi;
(formal) jéun

allowance N: (sum of
money) jèuntip (M: bāt) *
make allowance for Patt:
nihmjoih; háauleuihdou ·
*néih chòchi faahncho, sóyíh m̀
faht néih* * **housing
allowance** N: fòhngngūk jèuntip (M: bāt)

alloy N: hahpgàm (M: júng)

allude FV: ❶ (refer to indirectly) ngamsih · *kéuih ~
ngóh m̀hóu gám jouh* ❷ (speak
of) tàihhéi

allure FV: ❶ (tempt) yáhnyáuh ❷ (attract) kāpyáhn

allurement N: kāpyáhnlihk; yáuhwaahklihk (M: júng)

alluvial N: chùngjīk tóu

alluvium N: sàjàu (M: go)

ally N: (tùhng) màhnggwok
(M: go)

alma mater N: ❶ (mother school) móuhhaauh (M: gàan) ❷ (school song or anthem) haauhgō (M: sáu)

almanac N: tùngsing; tùngsyù (M: bún)

almighty SV: maahnnàhng; chyúhnnàhng

almond N: hahng; hahng-yàhn (M: pò) ✳ **almond nuts** N: hahngyàhn (M: nāp)

almost A: ❶ (with negative V.) gèifùh; chàmdò ~ m̀geidāk kéuih sing māt ❷ (nearly) jàangdī ~ ditdài ❸ (refer to time) jauhlàih ~ gaujùng la

alms N: ❶ (money) gaujaigàm (M: bāt) ❷ (things) gaujaibán (M: gihn)

aloft SV: gòu A: hái seuhngbihn ✳ **to go aloft** PH: (go up the masthead of a ship) pàh séuhng wàlhgòn (déng) VO: (colloq.) gwàisài; séuhngsàitin PH: heuiséi

alone A: (by oneself) jihgéi; jihgēi; yātgo yàn SV: (lonely) gùduhk ✳ **let alone** Patt: ... lìhn .N. dōu .:V., m̀sáigóng .VO laak · kéuih lìhn faahn dōu móuh dāk sihk, m̀sái góng heui hohkhaauh duhksyu laak ✳ **let (leave) sb. alone** PH: máih léih kéuih; m̀hóu chói kéuih ✳ **let (leave) sth. alone** PH: ting kèih jihyìhn

along FV: seuhnjyuh; yùhnjyuh ~ nītiuh louh hàahng ✳ **come along** PH: làih lā! ✳ **along shore** Adj. PH: yùhnngohn; yùhnhói ✳ **get along with** FV: sèungchyúh ✳ **carry along with** RV: daaimàaih ✳ **along side** A: paakjyuh; paakmàaih

aloof RV: lèihhòidī; beihhòidī; hàahngyúhndī

aloud SV: daaihsèng

alp N: gòusàan; gòufùng (M: go)

Alps N: A-yíh-bèi-sì sàan (M: go)

alphabet N: jihmóuh (M: go)

alphabetic Adv. PH: jiujihmóuh seuhnjeuih

alpinist N: pàhsàangà (M: go)

already A: yíhgìng

also A: dōu; yihkdōu; yihk ✳ **not only..., but also...** Patt: m̀jí ..., juhng ... (tìm)

altar N: ❶ (church, temple, public) jaitàahn (M: go) ❷ (in a household) sàhntói; sàhntòih (M: go)

alter FV: góibin; gói; gànggói

alteration N: bingàng; binduhng (M: júng)

alternate A: lèuhnláu ✳ **alternate days** A: gaakyaht ✳ **alternate current** N: gàaulàuh dihn

alternative N: syúnjaahk (M: go, júng); hónàhngsing; syúnjaahksing

although MA: sèuiyìhn; jauhsyun

altimeter N: gòudouhgai (M: go)

altitude N: gòudouh (M: go)

alto N: ❶ nàahm gòu yàm ❷ néuih dài yàm

altogether A: hahmbah-laahng; yātguhng; júngguhng

altruism N: leihtàjýuyih

altruist N: leihtàjýuyihjé (M: go)

alum N: baahkfàahn; mihng-fàahn

aluminium N: léuih; tài

alumna N: néuih haauhyáuh (M: go)

alumnus N: nàahm haauh-yáuh (M: go)

always A: sìhsìhdōu * not always A: meihbīt; m̀haih yātdihng

am EV: haih

a.m. TW: seuhngjau

amah N: ❶ (maid servant) (néuih) gùngyàhn (M: go) ❷ (nursemaid) bóumóuh; náaihmā (M: go)

amalgamate FV: hahpbing

amass FV: jīkjeuih (riches)

amateur SV: yihpyùh

amatory SV: ❶ (of lovers) chìhng ~ gō, ~ sī ❷ (pornographic) wòhngsīk, sīkchìhng * amatory potions N: chèunyeuhk (M: júng)

amaze PH: lihng .PN. gìngkèih; haakjó PN yàttiu • nīgo siusīk ~ ngóh ~

amazing SV: gìngkèih

ambassador N: daaihsi (M: wái, go)

amber N: ❶ fúpaak ❷ fúpaaksīk

ambiguous SV: hàhmwùh; m̀chìngchó PH: mòuh-lìhng-léuhng-hó

ambition N: ❶ (in good sense) póuhfuh; hùhngsàm; jìhei (M: júng) ❷ (pejorative) yéhsàm (M: júng)

ambitious SV: ❶ yáuhjìhei ❷ yáuhyéhsàm • deui . . . ~

ambulance N: gausèung-chè; sahpjihchè; gauwuhchè (M: ga)

ambuscade, ambush FV: màaihfuhk; fuhkgīk N: fuhkbìng

ameba, amoeba N: bin-yihngchùhng; a-máihbā (M: tiuh)

ameliorate RV: binhóu; góisihn FV: góijeun

amen P: ❶ (Christian) a-mùhn ❷ (Catholic) a-maahng

amenable SV: ❶ (responsible) yáuhjaakyahm; yáuhyih-mouh ❷ (responsive) tèng-gaau; tèngwah

amend FV/RV: góijing; sàujing; sàugói

amendment N: sàujing-ngon (M: go)

amenity SV: sỳusīk; yùh-faai; séyi

America N: Méihjàu * North America N: Bāk Méih-jàu * South America N: Nàahm Méihjàu

American SV: Méihgwok ge N: Méihgwokyàhn (M: go) * American currency N: Méihgàm

amiable SV: hóupèihhei; wòh'ói; yáuhsihn; hóusèungyúh

amid(st) PW: hái . . . jùnggàan

amino acid N: ngòngèisyùn

amiss SV: m̀seuhnngáahn; m̀yùhyi ＊ please don't take it **amiss** PH: chéng néih m̀hóu gin'gwaai

amity N: yáuhhóu ge gwàanhaih SV: wòhmuhk; yáuhhóu

ammonia N: a-mùng-nèih-a, ngòn

ammunition N: dáanyeuhk; gwànfó (M: pài)

amnesty FV/N: daaihse; dahkse (M: chi)

among Patt: hái . . . léuihbihn ~ góbàanyàhn ~ A: kèihjùng ・ gósyu nǵhgoyàhn, ~ yáuh léuhnggo haih saimānjái

amorous SV: dòchìhng ＊ **amorous looks** Adj. PH: hàhmchìhng mahkmahk ＊ **amorous songs** N: chìhnggō (M: sáu)

amorphous SV: móuhdihng yìhng(ge); m̀dihng-yìhng(ge)

amount N: ❶ (quantity) souleuhng ❷ (total) júngsou ❸ (value) gajihk

ampere M: ngòn; ngònpùih

ampere meter N: dihnbìu (M: go)

amphibian N: léuhngchài duhngmaht (M: jek) SV: léuhngchài

ample SV: chùngjūk

amplifier N: ❶ fongdaaihhei (M: go) ❷ (for sound) kwongyàmhei (M: go)

amplify FV: kwongdaaih; fongdaaih

amplitude N: (physics) janfūk

amputate FV: ❶ geujó (arm, leg) ❷ chitchèuih

Amsterdam PW: A-móuh-sī-dahk-dāan

amulet N: fùh; wuhsànfùh (M: douh)

amuse FV: yùhlohk; lihng PN hòisàm

amusement N: yùhlohk; sìuhín (M: júng) ＊ **amusement park** N/PW: yàuhlohkchèuhng (M: go)

amusing SV: hóusiu, yáuhcheui

anaemia N: pàhnhyutjing; pàhnhyut

anaesthesia N: màhjeui

anaesthetic N: màhjeui-yeuhk; màhjeuijài (M: júng)

anaesthetist N: màhjeuisī (M: wái, go)

analogic(al) SV: leuihchíh

analogue PH: sèungchíh ge yéh; leuihchíh ge yéh (M: júng)

analogy N: (process of reasoning between parallel cases) leuihtèuifaat; tèuiléihfaat (M: júng) ＊ **by analogy** PH: yùhchíleuihtèui

analyse FV: ❶ fànsīk ❷ (in chemistry) fayìhm

analysis N: fànsīk

anarchism N: mòuhjìngfú jýuyìh (M: júng)

anarchy N: mòuh jìngfú johngtaai

anatomic(al) SV: gáaifáuhohk seuhng(ge)

anatomy N: gáaifáuhohk

ancestor N: jóusìn; jóujùng

ancestral SV: ❶ (belong to ancestors) jóusìn ge ❷ (having come from ancestors) jóuchyùhn ge ✻ **ancestral home** N: jóungūk (M: gàan) ✻ **ancestral temple (hall)** N: chìhtóng (M: gàan) ✻ **ancestral tablet** N: sàhnjýupáai (M: go)

anchor N: nàauh (M: go) VO: pàaunàauh

ancient SV: ❶ (old day) gúdoih(ge) ❷ (things) gúlóuh(ge); gauhsīk(ge) BF: gú - • ~ yàhn

ancillary SV: fuhjoh

and CV: (between Ns) tùhng; tùhngmàaih • nīdī ~ gódī A: ❶ (between Vs) V yùhn yauh V ❷ (between SVs) yauh SV1 yauh SV2 ✻ **(M) and (M)** Patt: hóudò hóudò (M) N • tái jó ~ ~ (bún) syu ✻ **better and better/getting more and more** SV/ Patt: yuht làih yuht SV ✻ **and so on (forth)** PH: dángdáng ✻ **and then** A: yìhnhauh; yìhnjìhauh ✻ **and yet** A: daahnhaih; bātgwo

anecdote N: cheuisìh; yahtsìh (M: gihn)

anemometer N: fùngchūkgai (M: go)

anew A: chùhngsàn

angel N: tìnsi (M: go)

anger FV: nàu; faatnàu

angina N: sàmgáautung (jìng)

angle N: ❶ gok, gokdouh (M: go) ❷ (point of view) gùndím; táifaat (M: go) ✻ **right angle** N: jihkgok (M: go) ✻ **at right angles to (with)** N: . . . tùhng . . . sìhng jihkgok

angry SV: nàu; fáhnnouh

anguished SV: baingai

angular SV: ❶ (have angles) yáuhgokge ❷ (of persons) sau máang máang

anil N: làahmdihn

animal N: duhngmaht (M: jek, júng)

animate SV: (living) yáuhsàngmihng ge FV: (make lively) lìhng dou . . . yáuh sàang hei

animated Adj. PH: héuihéuiyùhsàng SV: sàangd;uhng

animosity N: sàuhhahn; dihkyi (M: júng)

ankle N: geukjàang (M: go)

annals N: ❶ (history) pìnnìhnsí (M: bún) ❷ (record of work) nìhnbou (M: bún)

annex FV: ❶ (take possession of) bihngtàn • daaihgwok ~saigwok ❷ (add as subordinate part) fuhgà

annihilate FV: sìumiht; chìmmiht (army)

anniversary N: jàunìhngéinihmyaht; jàunìhn géinihm

Anno Domini (A.D.) TW: gùngyùhn

annotate FV: jyugáai; jyusīk

annotation N: jyugáai; jyusīk (M: go)

announce FV: syùnbou

announcement N: tùnggou; káisih (M: dyuhn)

announcer N: boyàmyùhn (M: go)

annoyance N: sòuyíu · *deui . . . jouhsèhng ~*

annoying SV: mángjáng; fàahn

annual SV: ❶ yātnìhn ge ❷ yātnìhn yātchi ge

annuity N: yéuhnglóuhgàm (M: bāt)

annul FV: chéuisìu; faichèuih

annum NuM/TW: yāt nìhn

anodyne N: jítungyeuhk (M: júng)

anoint VO: chàhyàuh

anomalous SV: m̀kwàijākge; yihsèuhng ge

anonymity N: mòuhmìhngsih (M: go)

anonymous SV: nīkmìhng (ge)

anorak N: ❶ (general) taaihùnglāu (M: gihn) ❷ (for snow) syutlāu (M: gihn) ❸ (for wind) fùnglāu (M: gihn)

another SP: (different) lihngngoih ~yāt go Nu: (different) daihyih ~yaht joi làih A: (additional) joi; yauh; juhng ~ yiu yāt bùi chàh tìm ✳ **another day or two** PH:

joigwo yātléuhng yaht ✳ one **after another** Adv. PH: yāt go gànjyuh yāt go ✳ one **another** A: béichí; wuhsèung ✳ one **way or another** A: júngjì

answer FV: ❶ daap; wùihdaap (question) ❷ wùihfūk (letter) ❸ ying (a call) · *ngóh giu kéuih, kéuih móuh ~* N: ❶ (of exercises) daap ngon (M: go) ❷ (of question) daapfūk (M: go) · *ngóh deui kéuih ge ~ m̀ múhnyi* ✳ **answer for** FV: deui . . . fuhjaak/bóujing . . . ✳ **answer to** FV: . . . tùhng . . . sèungfùh

ant N: ngáih (M: jek)

antagonist N: deuisáu; dihksáu (M: go)

antagonistic(al) SV: deuilahp; dihkdeui

Antarctic N: Nàahmgihk ✳ **Antarctic ocean** N: Nàahmbìngyèuhng

antecedence N: sìnlaih (M: go) yíhchìhn ge sih (M: gihn)

antechamber N: jipdoihsāt (M: gàan)

antediluvian SV: gúlóuh; sáugauh

antelope N: lìhngyèuhng (M: jek)

ante meridiem (A.M.) TW: seuhngjau

antenna N: ❶ (of insects) jūksòu; jūkgok (M: tìuh) ❷ (of wireless aerial) tìnsin (M: jì)

anthem N: ❶ (sung in church) jaanméih sī (M: sáu) ❷ (of school) haauhgō (M: sáu) ✳ **national anthem** N: gwokgō (M: sáu)

anthology N: ❶ (of prose) màhn syún; màhn jaahp (,M: bún) ❷ (of verse) sī syún; sī jaahp (M: bún) ❸ (both prose and verse) sī màhn syún; sì màhn jaahp (M: bún)

anthracite N: mòuhyìnmùih

anthropology N: yàhnleuihhohk

anti- BF: fáan- * **anticommunist** SV: fáanguhng **anti-war** SV: fáanjin * **anti-imperialism** N: fáan daigwok jyúyih * **anti-missile** SV: fáan douhdáan

anti-aircraft SV: ́fòhnghùng ge * **anti-aircraft guns** N: gòusehpaau (M: hám, jì)

antibiotic N: kongsàngsou (M: júng)

antibody N: kongtái (M: júng)

antic SV: fùihàaih; waahtkài

anticancer SV: kongngàahmge

anticipate FV: (expect) yuhliuh A: (do before) yuhsìn

anticlockwise PH: fáan sìhjàm fòngheung; yihk sìhjàm fòngheung

antidote N: gáaiduhkyeuhk; gáaiduhkjài (M:júng)

antifertility N/VO: beihyahn

antimony N: tài

antipathy N: fáangám (M: júng)

antiquated SV: gúlóuhge

antique SV: gúdoihge N: ❶ (works of art) gúdúng; gúmaht (M: gihn) ❷ (ancient remains) gújīk

antirheumatic N: kongfùngsāp yeuhk (M: júng)

anti-semite N: fáanyàuhtaaijyúyihjé

antiseptic N: fòhngfuhjài (M: júng)

antisocial SV: fáan séhwúi ge

antitank SV: fáantáanhāk

antithesis N: deuingáuh; ngáuhgeui

antitoxin N: kongduhksou

antler N: luhkgok (M: jì, jek)

antonym N: sèungfáanchìh (M: go)

anus N: gòngmùhn (M: go)

anxiety N: yàuleuih (M: júng)

anxious SV: yàuleuih; dàamsàm * **be anxious to** A: hotmohng; hóuséung

any BF/N/Patt: ❶ yahmhòh-; bīngo; mātyéh; mòuhleuhn QW dōu; QW . . . dōu • kéuih móuh mahngwo yahm hòh yàhn • kéuih bīngo dōu móuh mahngwo • kéuih mātyéh dōu m̀jì • géisí làih dōu dāk ❷ (for question) yáuhmóuh QW * **in any case** Adv. PH: mòuhleuhn yùhhòh * **at any cost** Adv. PH: bātsīk yahmhòh doihga * **not any longer (more)** A: m̀joi; móuhjoi * **if any** PH: yùhgwó yáuh ge wá

anybody PN: yahmhòhyàhn; mòuhleuhn bīngo

anyhow A: ❶ wàahngdihm ~ *móuhsihjouh, bātyùh heui táihei* ❷ mòuhleuhn yùhhòh, mòuhleuhn dím ~ *dōu m̀jéun yahpheui*

anything N: mòuhleuhn mātyéh dōu, mātyéhdōu · *kéuih ~ sihk* ✻ anything else N: daihyihdī yéh ✻ anything but A/Patt: ① bihng m̀ . . . · *kéuih ~ leng* ② chèuihjó . . . ji'ngoih, mātyéhdōu . . .

anyway A: wàahngdihm

anywhere PW: mòuhleuhn bīnsyu; bīnsyu dōu

aorta N; daaihduhngmahk (M: tìuh)

apart FV: sèunggaak · *gó léuhnggàan ngūk ~ yāt léih* ✻ take someone apart RV/PH: jèung PN làaimàaih yāt bihn ✻ take something apart RV/PH: jèung . . . chaakhòi ✻ set/put something apart RV: fànhòi; jàihòi; jàimàaih yāt bihn ✻ tell two things/persons apart RV: táidākchēut; fàndākchēut ✻ apart from Patt: chèuihjó . . . ji'ngoih

apartment N: toufóng (M: gàan) ✻ apartment house N: gùngyuh daaihhah (M: joh, gàan)

apathetic SV: láahng-daahm, mohk-bāt-gwàansàm

ape N: máhlàu, sìngsìng (M: jek) FV: mòuhfóng

aperture N: ❶ lūng (M: go); la (M: tìuh) ❷ (of camera lens) gwònghyun (M: douh)

apex N: díngdím; jeuigòudím (M: go)

aphorism N: gaakyìhn (M: geui)

apiece A: múihgo; múih-gihn; múih yàhn

Apollo N: A-Bō-lòh

apologize FV: douhhip ✻ apologize to PN FV: heung PN ~ ✻ apologize for . . . FV: waih . . . ~

apoplexy VO/N: jungfùng

apostasy VO: binjit; buhn-gaau

apostle N: sitòuh (M: go)

apothecary N: yeuhkjàisī, maaihyeuhk ge yàhn (M: go)

appalling SV: dākyàhn-gèng; haakséiyàhn

apparatus N: yìhhei (M: fu, gihn, ga)

apparent SV: mìhnghín

apparition N: gwáiwàhn; yàulìhng; yíu-mō-gwái-gwaai (M: go, jek)

appeal FV: ❶ (earnest request) hánkàuh; chíngkàuh ❷ (in law) seuhng sou ❸ (attract) kāpyáhn   PH: yáhnhéi hingcheui

appear FV: ❶ (come into view) chēutyihn ❷ (arrive) dou VO: ❶ (of actor etc.) chēut-chèuhng ❷ (legal) chēuttìhng ✻ appear to be Adv. PH: táihéilàih hóuchíh ✻ it appears that A: chíhfùh

appearance N: ngoihbíu; ngoihmaauh ✻ in appearance A: ngoihbíuseuhng; táihéi-séuhnglàih ✻ keep up appearances SV: gu mihnjí

appease FV: ❶ pìhngsīk

(anger) ❷ múhnjūk (desire)

appellant N: seuhngsou-yàhn (M: go)

append FV: fuhgà

appendage N: fuhsuhk ge yéh; fuhsuhkbán; fuhgà ge bouhfahn

appendicitis N: màahng-chéung yìhm

appendix N: ❶ (of books) fuhluhk (M: go) ❷ (of body) màahngchéung; wàahng-ngà chéung (M: tiùh)

appertain A: suhkyù; gwàanyù

appetite N: waihháu • *hóu ~ ; móuh ~*

applaud VO: ❶ (clap hands) paakjéung; paaksáu; paak sáu-jéung ❷ (call aloud) hotchói

apple N: pìhnggwó (M: go) * **apple pie** N: pìhnggwó päi (M: gihn) * **apple sauce** N: pìhng-gwó jeung * **the apple of one's eye** N: jeui sàmngoi ge yéh/yàhn

appliance N: yuhnggeuih; heigeuih (M: gihn)

applicable SV: hahpsīk; ngāamyuhng

applicant N: sànchíngyàhn (M: go)

application N: sànchíng * **application form** N: sàn-chíngbíu (M: fahn)

applied SV: yingyuhng; sahtyuhng * **applied mathematics** N: yingyuhng souhohk

apply FV: ❶ chàh (ointment etc.) ❷ tip (plaster) * **apply for** FV: sànching * **apply to** FV: yingyuhng Patt: deui . . . hahpyuhng

appoint FV: ❶ (choose and name) wáiyahm; yahmmihng; jípaai ❷ yeukdihng (sìhgaan)

appointment N: ❶ (ar-rangement to meet) yeuk; yeukwuih (M: go) ❷ (position) jīkwaih (M: go) * **make an ap-pointment with** PH: tùhng . . . yeukhóu

apportion FV: fànpui

appraise FV: ❶ (set a value on) gúga; gúgai ❷ (give definitive judgement) pìhngga; gaamdihng

appreciable SV: gámgok-dóuge; gindóuge

appreciate FV: ❶ yàn-séung; gaamséung (art, scenery, etc.) ❷ gámgïk (favour or kindness) ❸ séungsīk (talent or ability) VO: (rise in value) jàngjihk

apprehend FV: ❶ (under-stand) líuhgáai ❷ (fear) yàuleuih ❸ (arrest) jūk; làai; kèuibouh

apprehensible SV: hóyíh léihgáai ge

apprentice N: hohksìjái; hohksī (M: go)

approach FV: làihgán; jèunggahndou • *dùngtin ~ la, tìnhei yuht làih yuht láahng* N: fòngfaat (M: go) * **at the ap-proach of** Patt: jèunggahn dou . . . gó jahnsí

approachable SV: hóyíh chàngahn ge

appropriate SV: sīkdong;

ngàam FV: (put on one side for special purpose) buht, buhtchēut

approval N: pàijéun; jaansìhng

approve FV: ❶ (formally agree and support) pàijéun ❷ (to vote into effect) tùnggwo

approximate FV: jipgahn · *kéuih sógóng ge ~ sihsaht* SV: daaihyeuhk; chàmdō; yeuhkmók · *~ NuM* gamseuhnghá · *NuM ~*

apricot· N: hahng

April N/TW: seiyuht ✳ **April Fools' Day** N/TW: yùhyàhnjit

apron N: wàihkwán (M: tìuh)

apt SV: ❶ chùngmìhng ❷ (well-suited) hāpdong; sīkdong ✳ **apt at** A; hóusīk ✳ **apt to** Adv. PH: hóuyùhngyih(wúih) · *~ laahn*

aptitude N: chòihnàhng; nàhnglihk; jìjāt

aquaplane N: waahtséuibáan (M: faai)

aquarium N: ❶ (building) séuijuhkgún (M: gàan) ❷ (pond) gàmyùhchìh (M: go) ❸(glass bowl) gàmyùhgòng (M: go)

Aquarius N: Séuipìhngjoh (M: go)

aquatic SV: séuiseuhng(ge)

aqueduct N: sȳuséuigún (M: tìuh)

Arab N: A-lāai-baak

arable SV: sīkhahp gàangjung ge

arbiter N: gùngjing yàhn; chòihpun (M: go)

arbitament N: chòihkyut (M: go)

arbitrary SV: ❶ yahmyi ❷ (dictatorial) duhkchòih; jyùnwàahng

arbitrate FV: tiuhtìhng; juhngchòih

arbour N: pàahnggá; lèuhngtíng (M: go)

arc N: wùh; wùhyìhng (M: go)

arcade N: gúnglòhng (M: tìuh)

arch N: gúng (M: go) SV: tiupèih FV: gúnghéi

arch- SV: jyúyiu; daaih ✳ **arch enemy** N: daaihdihk; jyúyiu dihkyàhn

archaeologist N: háaugúhohkgà (M: go)

archaeology N: háaugúhohk

archaic SV: gú; gúgauh

archbishop N: daaihjýugaau (M: go)

archer N: gùngjinsáu (M: go)

archery N: jinseuht

archipelago N: kwàhndóu

architect N: ginjūksī; waahkjīksī (M: go)

archives N: dóngngon

archway N: pàaihlàuh; gúngmùhn (M: douh, go)

Arctic SV: bākgihk N: Bākgihkkhyùn ✳ **Arctic Ocean** N: Bākbìngyèuhng

ardent SV: yihtliht; yihtsâm

ardour SV: yihtchihng

arduous SV: ❶ (difficult) gàangeuih ~ ge gùngjok ❷ (slope) che, hímjeun

are EV: haih

area N: ❶ mihnjīk (M: go) ❷ (district) kèui (M: go)

arena N: móuhtòih; lèuihtòih (M: go)

Argentine N: A-gàn-tihng yàhn (M: go)

argentine SV: ngàhnsīkge

arguable SV: yáuh jàng-leuhnsìng ge

argue VO: ngaaugēng; ngaai-gàau • *Kéuihdeih ngaai mātyéh gàau a?* FV: ngaau, ngaai, jàngbihn • *tùhng kéuih ~* ✳ **argue with somebody about something** Patt: PN1 tùhng PN2 ngaau . . . ge sih

argument N: léihyàuh, leuhngeui (M: go)

arid SV: ❶ gònchou ❷ (of field) sau

aright SV: móuhcho; ngāam

arise FV: ❶ (come into existence) chēutyihn; faatsàng ❷ (get up) héisàn ✳ **arise from** Patt: yàuh . . . yìh yáhnhéi

aristocracy N: gwaijuhk

arithmetic N: syunseuht ✳ **arithmetical progression** N: syunseuht kāpsou

ark N: ❶ (in the Bible) fòngjàu (M: jek) ❷ (fig.) beihnaahnsó (M: daat)

arm N: ❶ (upper limbs) sáubei (M: jek, deui) ❷ (of a chair) fùhsáu (M: go, jek) ❸ (weapons) móuhhei; bìnghei (M: júng) ✳ **arm in arm** Adv. PH: sáu-làaisáu; sáutòsáu ✳ **(welcome) with open arms** Adv. PH: yihtliht gám (fùnyìhng) ✳ **in arms** SV: móuhjòng ge; daaimóuhhei ge ✳ **armed with** Patt: yuhng . . . jouh móuhhei; daaijyuh . . . ge jòngbeih

armament N: bìnghei (M: gihn); móuhjòng; gwànbeih

armature N: kwàigaap (M: gihn)

armchair N: ngònlohkyí (M: jèung)

armistice VO: yàujìn; tìhng-jìn

armlet N: beijèung (M: go)

armo(u)r N: ❶ (for body) kwàigaap (M: gihn) ❷ (for tanks, warships) titgaap (M: fu) ❸ (collective) jònggaap bouhdéui (M: deuih)

armpit N: gaaklàakdái (M: go)

army N: ❶ (military forces on land) luhkgwàn; gwàndéui (M: deuih) ❷ tyùhntái (M: go) ✳ **be in the army** VO: dòngbìng

aroma N: ❶ hèunghei; hèungmeih (M: jahn) ❷ (fig.) wáhnmeih • *nī sáu sī hóu yáuh ~*

around PW: hái jàuwàih; hái . . . jàuwàih A: ❶ daaihyeuk • ~ *NuM* ❷ wàihjyuh ~ *wùhbīn hàahng* ✳ **all around** PW: seiwàih

arouse FV: ❶ (awaken) giu-séng; jíngséng ❷ (stir up) gīkhéi; yáhnhéi

arraign FV: ❶ chýuhnseun; tàihseun (on criminal charge) ❷ jíjaak (on fault)

arrange FV: ❶ (put in order) báai; jíngléih ❷ (make plans) chàuhbeih; gaiwaahk ❸ (take care of) baahn léih; baahn tóh ✻ **arrange with somebody** Patt: tùhng PN sèunglèuhng hóu; tùhng PN yeukhóu

arrant A: gihkjì; jyuhtdíng

arrears N: ❶ (money) jaai, jàang lohk yàhn ge chín (M: bāt) ❷ (work) sáuméih

arrest FV: ❶ làai, kèuibouh (a wrongdoer, etc.) ❷ kāpyáhn (attention) ❸ fòhngngoih (movement)

arrive FV: dou

arrogant SV: sàchàhn; jihdaaih; giungouh

arrogate FV: mouhyihng • ~ haih chàaiyàhn

arrow N: ❶ jin (M: jì) ❷ (mark) jin jéui (M: go) • jiujyuh ~ só jí ge fòngheung hàahng

arsenal N: gwànfófu (M: go)

arson VO: fongfó

art N: ngaihseuht; méihseuht ✻ **bachelor of arts** N: màhnhohksih ✻ **art gallery** N: ngaihseuhtgún; méih-seuhtgún (M: gàan)

artery N: duhngmahk ✻ **arteries of traffic** N: gàautùng gonsin (M: tìuh)

artful SV: gáauwaaht

arthritis N: gwàanjityìhm

article N: ❶ (thing) yéh; mahtgín (M: gihn) ❷ (written composition) màhnjèung (M: pìn) N/M: (clause in document) tiuh; hohng

articulate VO: faatyàm

articulation VO/N: faat-yàm (M: go)

artifice N: geihháau; sáu-dyuhn

artificer N: geihgùng (M: go)

artillery N: ❶ daaihpaau (M: hám, jì) ❷ (army) paaubìng (M: deuih)

artist N: ngaihseuhtgà (M: go)

artless SV: jihyìhn; tìnjàn

as FV: hóuchíh • kéuih ~ ngóh gam fèih ✻ **as a matter of fact** A: kèihsaht ✻ **as above** A: yùhseuhng ✻ **as far as** A: jeuhn ~ ngóh só ngàhng-gau jouh ge ✻ **as follows** A: yùhhah ✻ **as for** A: jiyù ✻ **as (so) long as** A: jíyíu ✻ **as soon as** Patt: yāt . . . jauh . . . ~ sihkyùhn faahn — chēutgàai ✻ **as usual** A: jiuseùhng ✻ **as you please** Adv. PH: chèuih néih jùngyi; chèuihbín néih

asbestos N: sehkmìhn

ascend FV: sìng; seuhngsìng

ascent N: chèhbō (M: go, douh)

ascertain FV: kokdihng

ascetic N: fúhàhngjé (M: go)

ascribe FV: laaih • kéuih ~ kéuihge sàntái mhóu, lìhng kéuih sātbaaih

ash N: fûi * **ash tray** N: yìn-
fûijùng; yìnfûidíp (M: jek, go)
* **ash bin** N: laahpsaapsèung
(M: go)

ashamed SV: cháu, sàuchí;
chàahm kwáih; m̀hóu yisi

ashore PW: ngohnseuhng;
luhkseuhng

ashy SV: chòngbaahk; fûi-
baahk

Asia PW: A-jàu

Asian N: A-jàu yàhn (M: go)

aside PW: pòhngbīn * **put
aside** PH: jài màaih yāt bihn

ask FV: ❶ mahn (question) ❷
giu; chéng (request) * **ask
about** FV: mahn; sèunmahn;
dáting * **ask after** FV:
mahnhauh * **ask for** FV: yiu;
yiukàuh * **ask for someone**
FV: wán; taam * **ask leave of
absence** VO: chéngga * **ask
sick leave** VO: chéngbehng ga
* **ask the way** VO: mahnlouh

askance A: ngáahnlaihlaih
~ *gám tái*

askew SV: mé; che

aslant A: chèhchèhdéi;
chechédéi

asleep RV: fanjeuhk SV: bei
• *ngóh ge geuk ~, m̀kéidāk
héisàn*

asparagus N: lòuhséun;
louhséun (M: jì)

aspect N: ❶ (appearance)
ngoihmaauh (M: go) ❷ (of affairs) fòngmihn (M: go) FV:
(face) heung

aspen N: baahkyèuhng
(syuh) (M: pò)

asphalt N: laahpchèng

asphyxiate FV: jahtsīk

aspirant PH: yáuh seuhng-
jeunsâm ge yàhn; yáuh
yéhsàmge yàhn (M: go)

aspirate N: sungheiyàm (M:
go)

aspiration N: ❶ (breath)
fūkāp ❷ (desire) yuhnmohng;
sàmyuhn (M: go)

aspirator N: kāpheigèi (M:
ga)

aspire FV: hotmohng

aspirin N: asīpātlìhng (M:
nāp)

aspiring SV: yáuhjìhei

ass N: ❶ (animal) lèuihjái (M:
jek) ❷ (person) bahndáan;
chéunchòih; sòhgwà (M: go)

assail FV: dá; gùnggīk

assassin N: chīkhaak;
chi'haak (M: go)

assassinate FV: hàhng
chīk; hàhngchi; ngamsaat

assault FV: jaahpgīk; ngáu-
dá

assay FV: fayihm; fànsīk

assemblage N: jòngji

assemble FV: ❶ (gather
together) jaahphahp; jeuihjaahp ❷ (fit together) jòngpui

assembly N: jaahpwúi;
wuihyíh (M: go)

assent V: ❶ tùhngyi; jaansìhng ❷ (official) pàijéun

assert FV: ❶ wàihwuh

(rights, etc.) ❷ (declare) syùn-chìng ❸ (affirm) dyundihng

assertive SV: hángdihng

assess FV: gúga; pìhnggú

assets N: jìcháan; chòicháan

assiduous SV: ❶ (constant attention) jyùnsàm ❷ (persevering) yáuh hàhngsàm; yáuh ngaihlihk

assign FV: ❶ (allot) fànpui ~ gùngjok ❷ (appoint) jídihng ~ sìhgaan, deihdím ❸ (appoint) jípaai; wáipaai (sb. for a task)

assignment N: jídihng ge gùngjok (M: gihn) wáipaai ge yahmmouh (M: go)

assimilate FV: ❶ sìufa; kāpsàu (food, etc.) ❷ tùhngfa (social group)

assist FV: bòngjoh; bòng-mòhng

assistant N: johsáu (M: go) ATT: fu ~ gìngléih

associate FV: ❶ gitgàau (friend) ❷ lyúhnséung (one thing with another) ~ héi/dou daihyih gihn sih ✻ associate with someone Patt: tùhng .P.N. jouhpàhngyáuh; tùhng .P.N. gitgàau

association N: wúi; gùng-wúi; hipwúi (M: go)

assorted BF: jaahpgám; jaahp

assume FV: ❶ (suppose) gáchit; gádihng; dong ❷ (undertake) dàamyahm ✻ assume office VO: jauhjīk; séuhngyahm

assumption N: gáchit (M: go)

assurance N: ❶ (promise) bóujing ❷ (self-confidence) jih-seun ❸ (insurance) bóuhím ❹ (impudence) jihdaaih

assure FV: wah ... yātdihng; heung ... bóujing; dàambóu

asterisk N: sìnghouh (M: go)

astern PH: hái syùhnméih

asthma N: hàauchyúnbehng

astigmatism N: sáan gwòng

astonishing SV: gìngkèih

astound Adj. PH: lìhng yàhn jangīng

astray VO: dohngsātlouh IE: (fig.) ngh-yahp-kèihtòuh • gógo hauhsàang jái ~

astride A: maakhòi deui geuk

astrologer N: sìngseunggà; fùngséui sìnsàang (M: go)

astrology N: sìngseung-hohk

astronaut N: taaihùngyàhn (M: wái)

astronomy N: tìnmàhn-hohk

astrophysics N: tìntái mahtléihhohk

astute SV: jìngmìhng

asunder FV: fànsaan

asylum N: sàuyùhngsó; beiwuhsó (M: gàan) ✻ mental asylum N: jìngsàhn behng yún; sàhngìng behngyún (M: gàan)

at CV: hái ✻ at all A:

yùhnchỳuhn ∗ **at first** TW: jeuichò; héisáu gójahnsí ∗ **at last** TW: jeuihauh; jùngyù ∗ **at least** A: jeuisíu; jeuidài haahndouh ∗ **at most** A: jeuidò ∗ **at once** TW: jīkhāak ∗ **at random** A: chèuihyi ∗ **at all cost** IE: bātsīk doihga ∗ **at table** TW: sihkgán faahn gójahnsí Adv. PH: hái jihk seuhng

atavism N: gaakdoih wàihchỳuhn

atheism N: mòuhsàhnleuhn

Athenian N: Ngáhdínyàhn (M: go)

athlete N: wahnduhngyùhn (M: go)

athletics N: wahnduhng (M: júng)

Atlantic N: Daaihsàiyèuhng

atlas N: deihtòuh (M: bún)

atmosphere N: ❶ (gases surrounding the earth) daaihhei ❷ (air) hùnghei ❸ (mood) heifàn (M: júng) · *sànnihn ge* ~

atom N: yùhnjí (M: nāp) ∗ **atomic bomb** N: yùhnjí dáan (M: go) ∗ **atomic energy** N: yùhnyínàhng

atomizer N: panmouhhei (M: go)

atone FV: ❶ suhk ~*jeuih* ❷ bóuséuhng ~ *syúnsāt*

atrocious SV: hùngchàahn; chàahnbouh

attach FV: ❶ (adhere) nìhm; tip; chì ❷ (fasten or join) fuhgà; fuhséuhng ~ *syutmìhngsỳu* ∗ **attach oneself to** FV: gàyahp

attaché N: líhngsihgún yàhnyùhn (M: go) ∗ **military**

attaché N: móuhgùn (M: go)

attachment N: fuhgín, fuhsuhkbán (M: gihn)

attack FV: ❶ dá ❷ (military) gùngdá; jeungùng ❸ (of disease) faatjok; dahtfaat · *sàmjohngbehng* ~

attain FV: ❶ (reach) daahtdou ~ *muhkbiu* ❷ (achieve) dākdóu

attainment N: sihngjauh (M: júng)

attempt FV: sèuhngsi; kéihtòuh ∗ **make an attempt to do** PH: siháh jouh

attend FV: ❶ (be present) chēutjihk; dou ❷ (look after) dáléih; jiugu ❸ (serve) fuhksih ~ *lóuhyàhn tùhngmàaih behng yàhn* ∗ **attend to** A: yuhngsàm; jyùnsàm

attendant N: fuhkmouhyùhn; chèuihhàhng ge yàhn (M: go)

attention N: jyuyi ∗ **attract (draw) sb's attention to** PH: yáhnhéi PN ge jyuyi ∗ **pay attention to** FV: jyuyi; làuhsàm; léih

attentive SV: jyùnsàm

attenuate FV: binsai; binbohk

attest FV: ❶ (give proof) jingmìhng ❷ (declare on oath) syùnsaih

attestation N: jingmìhngsyù; syùnsaihjí (M: jèung)

attire N: fuhkjòng (M: tou)

attitude N: taaidouh (M: júng) ∗ **strike an attitude** IE: jòng mòuh jok yeuhng

attorney N: leuhtsī (M: wái)
✻ **attorney general** N: leuht-
jingsī; gímchaatjúng jéung

attract FV: ❶ kāpyáhn ❷ (as
a magnet) sip • *yuhng siptit ~
héi dī dēng*

attraction N: ❶ kāpyáhnlihk; kāplihk ❷ (physics)
yáhnlihk

attractive SV: leng (lady
etc.)

attribute N: ❶ (symbol) biuji (M: go); jeuhngjīng (M: júng)
❷ (characteristic) bánsing (M:
júng)

attributive N: sàusīkyúh
(M: go)

attrition FV: sìuhou

auburn N/SV: chàhsīk;
jésīk

auction N/FV: paakmaaih
(M: chi)

audacious SV: daaihdáam;
lóuhmóhng

audible SV: tèngdākginge

audience N: tèngjung
(listen); gùnjung (watch)

audio SV: tènggokge; ting-
gok ge ✻ **audio-visual aids** N:
sihting gaaugeuih; sihting
gaauchòih

audiphone N: johtinghei
(M: fu)

audit VO: hahtsou; chàh-
jeung

auditor N: ❶ (listener)
pòhngtingsàng (M: go) ❷ (of accounts) hahtsouyùhn (M: go)

auditorium N: daaihláih-

tòhng; yíngóngtèng (M: gàan,
go)

augment FV: jànggà; jàng-
daaih

August TW/N: baatyuht

august SV: yáuhwàiyìhm ge

aunt N: ❶ (paternal older
brother's wife) baaknèuhng ❷
(paternal younger brother's wife)
a-sám ❸ (paternal older sister)
gùmā ❹ (paternal younger
sister) gù jē ❺ (maternal older
sister) yìhmā; daaihyìh ❻
(maternal younger sister) a-yī ❼
(maternal brother's wife) káhm-
móuh; a-káhm ❽ (paternal
sisters in general) a-gū ❾ (maternal sisters in general) a-yī

aural SV: tènggokge; yíhge
✻ **aural surgeon** N: yíh fō
yìsàng (M: wái)

aureola N: gwònglèuhn;
gwòngwàahn; gwòngwàhn (M:
go)

aurora N: chýuhgwòng

auspice N: (prophetic token)
yuhsiuh (M: júng) FV: (help and
favour) jaanjoh

auspicious SV: gātleihge;
hóuyitàuh ge ✻ **auspicious
day** N: hóuyahtjí (M: go)

austere SV: ❶ (strict)
yìhmsūk ❷ (simple) poksou

austerity N: fúsàu; fúhàhng

Australia N/PW: Oujàu

Australian N: Oujàuyàhn

Austria N: Oudeihleih

authentic SV: jànge; seundākgwo ge

author N: jokjé; jokgà (M: wái)

authoritative SV: yáuh-kyùhnwàige; gùn fòngge

authority N: ❶ (power) kyùhnlihk; kyùhnwài (M: júng) ❷ (person with special knowledge) jyùngà (M: go) ❸ (govt.) jingfú dòngguhk

authorize VO: sauhkyùhn

auto N: heichè (M: ga)

autobiography N: jihjýun (M: pìn, bún)

autocracy N: duhkchòih jingjih; duhkchòih jingfú (M: go)

autograph N: chànbāt chìmméng ✳ **autograph album** N: géi nihm chaak (M: bún)

automatic SV: jihduhng

automobile N: heichè (M: ga)

autonomous SV: jihjih ge

autopsy VO: yihmsī

autotype N: fūkyanbán (M: gihn)

autumn N: chàutìn; chàugwai

auxiliary SV: fuhjoh(ge)

avail SV: yáuhyuhng; yáuhyīk ✳ **avail oneself of an opportunity** VO: chan gèiwuih; leihyuhng gèiwuih ✳ **of no avail** SV: móuhyuhng; móuh haauh

available SV: yáuhhaauh Adj. PH: hóyíh yuhng; hóyíh wándāk dóu

avalanche N: syutbàng

avant-garde N: sìnfùng (M: go)

avaricious SV: tàamsàm

avenge PH: waih / tùhng .P.N. bousàuh

avenue N: louh; gāai (M: tìuh)

average SV: pìhnggwàn ~fànsou

averse AV/FV: jàng; m̀jùng-yi

avert FV: ❶ (turn away) beihhòi ~kéuihge sihsin ❷ (prevent) beihmíhn; fòhngjí ~yi'ngoih

aviation ATT: hòhnghùng

aviator N: fèihàhng yùhn (M: go)

avid FV: hotmohng dākdóu

avocation N: fuyihp (M: júng) PH: yihpyùh ge sihou

avoid FV: ❶ beihmíhn (thing) ❷ beihhòi (person)

avouch FV: bóujing

avow PH: gùnghòi sìhng-yihng

await FV: dáng

awake FV/SV: séng RV: ❶ (naturally) fanséng ❷ (by someone) giuséng ❸ (by noise) chòuhséng

awaken FV: (fig.) gokngh

award FV: ❶ (grant by official decision) bàanfaat; bàansauh ❷jéung; séung N: jéungbán (M: gihn); jéung (M: go)

aware FV: jì; jyuyi; gokdāk

away FV: ❶ lèihhòi ~ *nīsyu sàamgo yuht* ❷ heui ~ *jó léuihhàhng* ❸ jáu • *ngàam-ngàam* ~ *jó* RV: ❶ -jáu • *daai* ~; *nīk* ~; *ló* ~ ❷ -hòi • *nīk* ~; *hàahng* ~ ❸ -saai • *móuh* ~; *m̀gin* ~ Patt: (distance) lèih . . . yáuh NuM (yúhn) • *hohkhaauh* ~ *nīsyu* ~ *léuhng léih* ✻ keep . . . away from Patt: m̀hóu béi . . . jipgahn . . . ✻ do away with FV: m̀yiu; faichèuih ✻ right away TW: jīkhāak ✻ pass away VO: gwosàn

awe FV: haak; gingwai

awful SV: ❶ (dreadful) dākyàhngèng ❷ (not handsome) nàahntái A: gihkjì; fèisèuhng; hóu

awhile Adv. PH: gwojó yātjahngàan

awkward SV: leuhnjeuhn

awl N: yēui (M: jì)

awning N: yàhmpùhng (M: go); boujeung (M: faai)

awry SV: kūk; mé; che PH: (wrong) chēutjócho

axe N: fútáu (M: bá)

axiom N: gùngléih; dihngléih (M: tiuh)

axis N: juhk; juhksàm (M: tiuh)

axle N: juhk; chèjuhk (M: tiuh)

ay, aye P: haih-a; hóu-aak N: jaan sìhng piu

azalea N: douhgyùnfā (M: dó, déu, pò)

azure N/SV: tìnlàahm (sīk); waihlàahm (sīk)

B

B.A. N: màhnhohksih

babble SV/FV: ❶ (repeat foolishly) lōsō ❷ (reveal a secret by talking too freely) dōjéui

baby N: bìhbījái; bìhbī; sōuhājái (M: go)

bachelor N: ❶ (man) dàansàn ge yàhn; dàansàn gwálóu (M: go) ❷ (degree) hohksih (M: go)

bachelorhood Adj. PH: duhksàn

back N: ❶ (of the body) buijek (M: go) ❷ (of a chair) pèng (M: go) ❸ (reverse side) hauhbihn PW: hauhbihn RVE: -fàan • *béi* ~ FV: tanhauh; heung hauh tan ✻ at one's back PH: hái buihauh jìchìh ✻ back and forth PH: V làih V heui ✻ (do, say sth.) behind sb's back Adv. PH: ngamjùng; hái buihauh . . . ✻ back down FV: yeuhngbouh ✻ back to back A: bui deui bui; bui heung bui ✻ back up FV: ① jìchìh ② tanhauh (vehicle) ✻ back pay N: bóusàn; bóuséui (M: bāt) ✻ back out FV: tantáaih

backache N: buitung

backbite PH: hái buihauh jungsèung

backbone N: jekgwāt; yìugwāt (M: tiuh)

backdoor N: hauhmún (M: douh)

background N: buigíng (M: go)

backhanded SV: fáansáu ~ *dá nī go bō*

backless SV: móuhpèng(ge) ~ *yí*

back number SV: gwokèihge; gwosìhge ~ *jaahpji*

backseat N: hauhjoh

backside N: peigú (M: go)

backslide FV: dohlohk

backstage N: hauhtòih (M: go)

backstairs N: hauh làuhtài (M: douh, tòhng)

backstroke N: (swim) buiwihng; yéuhngwihng

backtalk VO: bokjéui

backward A: heung hauh

bacon N: yìnyuhk (M: faai, gauh)

bacteria N: saikwán

bad SV: waaih, m̀hóu ✱ **bad word** N: chòuháu (M: geui) ✱ **bad debt** N: laahnjeung (M: bāt) ✱ **bad temper** SV: m̀hóu pèihhei ✱ **bad weather** PH: tìnhei m̀hóu ✱ **not bad** IE: m̀cho ✱ **go bad** RV: binwaaihjó ✱ **too bad** PH: jànhaih baih laak! ✱ **go from bad to worse** Adj. PH: yuht làih yuht waaih IE: múih hah yuh fong

badge N: fàijèung, kàmjèung (M: go) BF: fài · *haauh ~* · *wúi ~*

badger FV: fàahn · *kéuih ~ dou ngóh séung m̀ yìngsìhng kéuih dōu m̀dāk*

badminton N: yúhmòuhkàuh (M: go)

baffle RV: nàahndóu · *béi gógo mahntàih ~ ngóh*

bag N: doih, dói (M: go) · *bou ~* · *sáu ~* FV: ❶ (put into a bag) doih ~ *lohk go dói syu* ❷ (catch) jūk ❸ (colloq.) sàauh · *kéuih ~ jó ngóh jì bāt* ✱ **handbag** N: sáudói (M: go) ✱ **travelling bag** N: léuihhàhngdói (M: go) ✱ **let the cat out of the bag** IE: sitlauh fùngsìng

baggage N: hàhngléih (M: gihn) ✱ **baggage-office** N: hàhngléihfóng (M: gàan)

bagpipe N: fùngdehk (M: jì)

bail N: bóusīkgàm (M: bāt) FV: bóu; dàambóu (sb. out)

bait N: neih; leih

bake FV: guhk

baker N: mihnbāau sìfú (M: go)

bakery N: mihnbàaupóu (M: gàan)

balance N: ❶ (steelyard) chìng (M: bá) ❷ (beam balance) tìnpìhng (M: go) ❸ (difference, of accounts) chà'ngáak (M: go) · *léuhng tiùh sou ge ~* ❹ (deposit) chyùhnfún · *ngàhnhòhng ge wuhháu yáuh géidō ~ a?* ❺ (amount owed) méihsou (M: tiùh) SV: (steady) pìhnghàhng; wán · *yànwaih taai daaihfùng, jek téhng m̀ ~* ✱ **be (hang) in the balance** IE: yùhn-yìh-meih-kyut; meih yáuh kyut dihng ✱ **balance of**

power IE: sai-gwàn-lihk-dihk ✻ **balance-sheet** N: jìcháan fuhjaai bíu (M: jèung)

balcony N: louhtòih (M: go)

bald SV: gwòngtàuh ✻ **bald-head** N: gwòngtàuhlóu (M: go)

balderdash N: faiwá (M: dèui)

bale M: bàau; jaat

balk, baulk N: ❶ (wood) muhkfòng (M: tìuh) ❷ (hindrance) jó'ngoih FV: jó'ngoih

ball N: ❶ bō (M: go) ❷ (dancing) móuhwúi (M: go) BF: ❶ -kàuh • *jūk* ~ • *hà* ~ ❷ (of minced meat)-yún • *yuhk* ~ ✻ **ball-pen** N: yùhnjíbāt (M: jì) ✻ **ball-room** N: móuhtèng (M: gàan)

ballad N: màhngō (M: sáu)

ballet N: bālèuihmóuh (M: jek)

ballistic SV: daahndouh(ge) ✻ **intercontinental ballistic missiles** N: jàujai daahndouh fèidáan (M: go)

balloon N: heikàuh (M: go) ✻ **balloon-fish** N: gàipóuhyú; hòhtyùhn (M: tìuh)

ballot N: syúnpiu (M: jèung) VO: ❶ tàuhpiu ❷ (draw lots) chàuchìm ✻ **ballot-box** N: tàuhpiu sēung (M: go)

balm N: hèungyàuh; yàuh SV: hèung ✻ **balm cricket** N: sìhm (M: jek)

balsam N: (flowering plant) fuhngsìnfā (M: pò, déu)

bamboo N: jūk (M: jì, pò) ✻ **bamboo shoot** N: jūkséun (M: go)

ban FV: gamjí

banana N: jìu; hèungjìu (M: jek; sò for bunch)

band N: ❶ (strip of material) dáai (M: tìuh) • *bou* ~ ❷ (hoop) kwù (M: go, tìuh) • *jeuhnggàn* ~ • *tit* ~ ❸ (a group of musicians) ngohkdéui (M: deuih) ✻ **band together** PH: hahpmàaih yātchái ✻ **band master** N: ngohkdéui jífài (M: go)

bandage N: bàngdáai (M: tìuh) FV: jaat; bóng

bandit N: chaahk; féitòuh (M: go)

bang FV: ❶ (hit violently) johng ❷ (close violently) bàahng • *daaihlihk* ~ *màaih douh mùhn* SV: bàahngbáang sèng N: (hair) làuhhói (M: jàp)

bangle N: ngáak (M: jek)

banian, banyan N: yùhng-syuh (M: pò)

banish PH: kèuijuhk chēut-gíng FV: sìuchèuih

bank N: ❶ (coast) ngohn (M: go); tàih (M: tìuh) ❷ (for money) ngàhnhòhng (M: gàan) N/M: (heap or pile) dèui (M: go)

banker N: ngàhnhòhng gà (M: go)

banking N: ngàhnhòhng-yihp; ngàhnhòhnghohk

banknote N: ngàhnjí (M: jèung)

bankrupt VO: pocháan

banner N: ❶ kèih (M: jì) ❷ (announcement for slogans etc.) biuyúh, wàahngngáak (M: jèung, fūk) ❸ (headline in newspaper) tàuhtìuh (sànmán)

banquet N: yinwuih (M: go)

bantam N: ❶ ngáigeukgài (M: jek) ❷ (boxer) yúhleuhng kāp kyùhnsī (M: go)

banter FV: siu

baptism N: sáiláih

baptist mission N: jamseunwúi

baptize VO: ❶ (baptized) sauhsái; líhngsái ❷ (give baptism) sìsái

bar N: ❶ (wood or metal) gwan (M: tìuh) ❷ (railing) làahn'gòn (M: tìuh) ❸ (where drinks are served) jáubā (M: go, gàan) FV: jó; dóng ✳ **bar the way** PH: jójyuh tìuh louh

barb N: douchi ✳ **barbed wire** N: titsìmóhng (M: go)

barbarian N: yéhmàahnyàhn (M: go)

barbaric SV: yéhmàahn

barber N: fèifaatlóu (M: go) ✳ **barber shop** N: fèifaatpóu (M: gàan)

bare SV: dácheklaak; dá—daaih cheklaak ✳ **bare faced** SV: mòuhchí; bèipéi ✳ **bare footed** SV: dáchekgeuk

barely A: (just) gángán · háausíh ~ kahpgaak

bargain N: ❶ (agreement to buy or sell) gàauyihk ❷ (sth. cheap) pèhngyéh; dáimáaih ge yéh VO: góngga

barge N: (for goods) boktéhng; dánsyùhn (M: jek)

baritone, barytone N: nàahmjùngyàm

bark N: ❶ (of tree) syuhpèih (M: faai) ❷ (of dogs) gáufaih sèng FV: (of dogs) faih

barley N: daaihmahk (M: pò) ✳ **pearl barley** N: yìmáih (M: nāp)

barmaid N: bànéui (M: go)

barn N: ❶ gūkchòng (M: go) ❷ (livestock) ngàuh/máhfòhng (M: go)

barometer N: heingaatbíu; fùngyúhbíu (M: go)

baron N: ❶ nàahmjeuk (M: wái) ❷ (rich man) yáuhchínlóu (M: go) BF: (great industrial leader) — daaihwòhng (M: go) · sehkyàuh ~

barracks N: bìngfòhng; gwànyìhng (M: go)

barrel N: túng (M: go)

barren SV: (of land) sau PH: (of women) m̀nàhnggau sàangyuhkge; móuh sàangyuhk ge

barricade N: louhjeung (M: go) VO: chitji louhjeung

barrier N: jeungngoih

barrister N: daaihleuhtsī (M: wái)

barrow N: ❶ chèjái; sáutèuichè (M: ga) ❷ (tumulus) gúmouh (M: go)

barter FV: gàauwuhn

base N: ❶ (foundation) gèichó; gàngèi (M: go) ❷ (of armed forces, etc.) gèideih (M: go) SV: bèipéi; hahjihn ✳ **base of operations** N: gàngeuideih (M: go) ✳ **based on** FV: gàngeui ✳ **base-line** N: gèisin

(M: tìuh)

baseball N: páahngkàuh; lèuihkàuh (M: go)

basement N: deihlòuh (M: go)

bash FV: bōk · *daaihlihk ~ laahn dī yéh*

bashful SV: pacháu

basic SV: ❶ gèibún ❷ (chem.) gáansing

basilica N: daaihgaautòhng (M: gàan) ✻ **the basilica of St. Peter's in Rome** N: Lòhmáh Sing Béidāk Daaih gaautòhng

basin N: ❶ pùhn (M: go) · *mihn ~* · *sáisáu ~* ❷ (geog.) pùhndeih (M: go)

basis N: gèichó (M: go) ✻ **on the basis of** FV: gàngeui

bask VO: ❶ (under the sun) saaitaaiyèuhng ❷ (have warmth) bouhnýuhn

basket N: láam; lō; lēi (M: go)

basketball N: làahmkàuh (M: go)

bass N: ❶ (singer) nàahmdàiyām (M: go) ❷ (music) dàiyām ❸ (fish) lòuhyú (M: tìuh)

bassinet N: ❶ yìuhlàahm (M: go) ❷ bìhbīchè; yìngyìhchè (M: ga)

bassoon N: bàchùhnggún (M: jì)

bastard N: (child) sìsàngjí (M: go) SV: (things) gá

baste FV: ❶ tiu, lỳuhn (clothes) ❷ (beat) (coll.) chai

bastion N: (gwànsih) geui-

dím (M: go)

bat N: ❶ (animal) pìnfūk; fūksyú (M: jek) ❷ (in games) kàuhpáak (M: faai, go, jì)

batch N/M: pài

bathe VO: chùnglèuhng; sáisàn FV: sái; jam

bath-house N: yuhksāt (M: gàan)

bathing VO: yàuhséui ✻ **bathing-cap** N: wìhngmóuh (M: déng) ✻ **bathing-costume** N: wìhng yī (M: gihn)

bathrobe N: yuhkpòuh (M: gihn)

bathroom N: chùnglèuhngfóng; yuhksāt (M: go, gàan)

bathtub N: chùnglèuhng gòng; yuhkgòng (M: go)

baton N: ❶ (policeman's) gínggwan (M: jì) ❷ (for conductor) jífàipáahng (M: jì)

battalion M: yìhng

batter FV: johng · *~ laahn*

battery N: ❶ (single voltaic cell) dihnsām; dihnchìh (M: gauh) ❷ (group of connected electric cells) dihnchìh (M: go) ❸ (army unit) paaubìng (M: lìhn) ❹ (emplacement) paautòih (M: go)

battle N: jeung; jinsih (M: chèuhng) N/FV: (combat between persons) bokdau (M: chèuhng) ✻ **battle cruiser** N: chèuhnyèuhng laahm (M: jek) ✻ **battle-plane** N: jindaugēi (M: ga, jek) ✻ **battle-ship** N: jinlaahm; jýulihklaahm (M: jek) ✻ **battle field** N: jinchèuhng (M: go)

batty SV: chìsin

bawdy SV: hàahmsāp; hah-làuh; dàikáp cheuimeihge

bawl FV: ngaai; daaihsèng-ngaai

bay N: ❶ (of sea) hóiwāan (M: go) ❷ (tree) yuhtgwaisyuh (M: pò) ✴ **bay-line** N: (titlouh) jisin (M: tìuh)

bayonet N: chìdōu (M: bá)

bazaar N: maaihmahtwúi (M: go)

B.C. TW: gùngyùhnchìhn; géiyùhnchìhn

be EV: haih · kéuih ~ Chàhn sàang FV: jouh · kéuih séung jèunglòih ~ yīsāng CV: (followed by PW) hái · ngóh ~ nīsyu A: (suggestion or command) mhóu (with SV of opp. meaning) ~ chòuh A: yiu (optional) · tìngyaht ~ jóudī làih ✴ **be . . . ing** Patt: ① (continuous tense) FV gán · sihk ~ faahn ② (future tense) wúih FV/FV · néih tìngyaht wúih m̀ wúih heui a? néih heui m̀ heui a? ✴ **be . . . by . . .** Patt: (wúih) béi . . · ~ yàhn naauh

beach N: hóitāan (M: go)

beacon N: ❶ (lighthouse) dàngtaap (M: go) ❷ (signal) seunhoùhdàng (M: jáan)

bead N: jyùjái (M: nāp, chyun for string)

beak N: ❶ (of birds) jéui (M: go) ❷ (nose) ngàubeih (M: go)

beam N: ❶ (timber) wàahng-lèuhng (M: tìuh) ❷ (ray) gwòngsin FV: ❶ faatchēut (light, warmth) ❷ faatseh (wireless telegraphy) ✴ **beam** weapon N: séigwòng móuhhei

beaming FV: ❶ (fig.) mèihsiu PH: símsímfaatgwòng

bean N: dáu, dauh (M: nāp) ✴ **bean curd** N: dauhfuh (M: gauh, gihn) ✴ **bean sprouts** N: ngàhchoi

bear N: ❶ (animal) hùhng; hùhngyán (M: jek) ❷ (person) chòuyàhn (M: go) FV: ❶ (give birth to) sàang ~ saimānjái ❷ (support) jichìh · nītiuh muhk taai yau, m̀ nàhnggaū ~ gám ge chúhng leuhng ❸ (support) fuhdàam, fuh (responsibility, expense) · Bīngo ~ nīgo jaakyahm a? ❹ (endure) dái, yán · ngóh m̀ ~ dāk kéuih gam láahn · kéuih hóu ~ dāk tung ❺ (carry) joi · nīga chè hóyíh ~ géi chúhng a? ❻ (have) yáuh · kéuih ~ chēung ❼ (produce) jichìh ❽ (yield) cháan-sàng ❾ (push) ngúng ❿ (on a pole) dàam ⓫ ❷ (on the palm or shoulder) tok ⓫ ❷ (between two people) tòih ✴ **bear sb. out** Patt: tùhng . . . jouh jing yàhn ✴ **bear out** VO: jokjing ✴ **bear in mind** RV: geijyuh ✴ **bear on/against** RV: gahmjyuh ✴ **bear with** FV: yùhngyán; yánsauh

bearable PH: hóyíh yánsauh ge; hóyíh yùhngyán ge

beard N: wùhsōu; sōu (M: jāp, bāt)

bearer N: (of a cheque) chìhpiuyàhn (M: go)

bearing N: (of a machine) bēlíng; juhksìhng ✴ **lose one's bearings** PH: màihsātjó fòngheung

beast N: ❶ yéhsau; máahng-sau (M: jek) ❷ (person)

ngokyâhn; yìgùn kàhmsau (IE) (M: go)

beat FV: ❶ (hit or strike) dá ❷ (defeat) yèhngjó ❸ (move up and down regularly) paak ❹ (of the heart) tiu N: (mark of rhythm in music) paakjí (M: háh) * **beat up** FV: duhkdá

beautiful SV: ❶ leng ❷ (of weather) hóu

beautify FV: méihfa

beauty N: méihlaih * **beauty parlour** N: méihyùhngyún; faatyìhngngūk (M: gàan) * **beauty spot** N: ❶ (of person) ji (M: nāp) ❷ (place) mìhngsing

beaver N: hóilèih (M: jek)

because A: yànwaih

become FV: ❶ binsèhng • *yàuh waaihyàhn ~ hóuyàhn* ❷ sihngwaih ~ *yātgo hóu chēutméng ge hohkjé*

bed N: ❶ chòhng (M: jèung) ❷ (of the sea, etc.) hòhchòhng (M: go) * **go to bed** PH: heui fangaau * **make the bed** VO: jāpchòhng; pòuchòhng * **take to (keep) one's bed** RV: behngdāijó * **bed-bug** N: muhksāt (M: jek) * **get up on the wrong side of the bed** Adj. PH: sàmchìhng m̀hóu * **bed-clothes** N: péihpōu * **bed-pan** N: bihnpùhn (M: go) * **bed-side** PW: chòhngbīn * **bed-spread** N: chòhngkám (M: go) * **bed-sheet** N: chòhngdāan (M: jèung) * **bed-room** N: seuihfóng (M: gàan, go) * **bed-wetting** VO: laaihniuh

bedding N: chòhngpòu

bee N: mahtfùng (M: jek) * **bee-garden** N: yéuhngfùngchèuhng (M: go) * **bee-hive** N:

mahtfùngdau (M: go) * **bee-line** N: jihtging; jihksin (M: tiuh) * **beeswax** N: mahtlaahp (M: gauh)

beef N: ❶ ngàuhyuhk (M: gauh) ❷ (muscle of men) gèiyuhk (M: gauh) * **beef-steak** N: ngàuhpá (M: gihn)

beep N: bībīsèng; dyūtdyūtsèng

beer N: bējáu (M: jì, bùi)

beestings N: chòyúh

beet-root N: tìhmchoitàuh (M: go)

beetle N: ❶ (insect) gaapchùhng (M: jek) ❷ (tool) daaihchèuih (M: go)

befall FV: faatsàng RV: yuhdóu

befit A: yìnggòi

before TW: ❶ jíchìhn • *sihkfaahn ~ sáisáu* ❷ yíhchìhn ~ *kéuih haih hohksàang, yìhgà haih sìnsàang* PW: ❶ (face to face) hái PN mihnchìhn ❷ (location) hái (thing) chìhnbihn • *kéih ~ hāakbáan ~* ❸ (arrangement) N1 hái N2 jichìhn/chìhnbihn • *néihge méng ~ ngóhge ~* * **as before** Adv. PH: tùhng/ hóuchíh yíhchìhn yātyeuhng * **before all** A: sáusìn * **before long** A: m̀sái géi nói; jauhlàih * **not long before** TW: móuh géi noih jì chìhn

beforehand A: sihsìn

beg FV: ❶ (as a beggar) hāt ❷ (ask) kàuh * **beg sb. off** PH: tùhng PN kàuhchìhng * **beg your pardon** PH: chéng néih joi góng yātchi

beget FV: sàang RV: jouh-sèhng; lihngdou yáuh

beggar N: hātyī (M: go)

begin A: héisáu, hòichí * **begin at** Patt: yàuh . . . héi, yàuh . . . hòichí * **from beginning to end** PH: yàuh tàuh ji (dou) méih

beginner PH: chòhohk ge yàhn N: sàndìng (M: go)

beginning N: hòichí

begrudge FV: douhgeih PH: deui . . . bātmúhn

behalf FV: doihbíu * **on behalf of** FV: doihbíu . . .

behaviour N: hàhngwàih; géuiduhng

behead VO: jáamtáu

behind PW: hái . . . hauh-bihn * **behind one's back** Adv. PH: hái .PN. buihauh * **behind time** SV: gwokeìh; gwosìh * **lag (fall) behind** FV: lohkhauh * **leave behind** RV: làuhdài * **left behind** RV: lauhjó; lauhdàijó; laaihdàijó

behind hand FV: tò SV: lohkhauh

being PH: chyùhnjoih ge yéh * **come into being** FV: yìhngsìhng; faatsàng * **for the time being** TW: jaahmsìh

belabour FV: daaihlihkdá

belated SV: yìhnnghjó ge; jóchìhjó ge

belch VO: dá sīyīk FV: pan-chēut • fósàan ~ fóyihm

beleaguer FV: bàauwàih; wàihkwan; wàihgùng

belfry N: jùnglàuh (M: go, joh)

Belgian N: Béileihsìhyàhn (M: go)

belief N: seunsàm; seun-nihm (M: go)

believable SV: seundākgwo ge

believe FV: seun; sèungseun * **believe in** FV: ❶ sèungseun ❷ seunfuhng (religion) * **make believe** A: jadai

believer N: seuntòuh (M: go)

bell N: jùng (M: go) * **ring the bell** VO: dájūng; hàaujùng * **bell-boy** N: sihjái; fuhkmouhyùhn (M: go) * **bell-wether** N: sáulíhng (M: go)

bellow FV: giu N: giusèng

belly N: tóuh (M: go) * **belly-ache** N: tóuh tung * **belly-band** N: tóuh kù; tóuhdàu (M: go)

belong FV: suhkyù

belongings N: mahtgín; chòihcháan

beloved SV: chàn'oige PH: só oi ge yàhn

below PW: hái . . . hahbihn SV: ❶ dàigwo, • gàmyaht ge heiwàn ~ sahpdouh ❷ hahbihn, hauhbihn • syù ~ ge gáaisīk Patt: hái .NuM. yíhhah

belt N: ❶ dáai (M: tìuh) ❷ (zone) deihdaai (M: go) BF: -daai • yiht ~ * **tighten one's belt** VO: jaatjyuh futàuh; (coll.) jaatpaau

bemoan FV: yun

bench N: chèuhngdang (M:

jèung)

bend FV: ❶ wāt, wātkūk ❷ (submit) wātfuhk • . . . *heung* . . . ~ ✳ be bent on Adv. PH: yātsàm yātyi; jyùnsàm ✳ the bends N: chàhmsèung behng ✳ bend down FV: wùdài (sàn, tiuhyīu)

beneath PW: hái . . . hahbihn A: m̀jihkdāk

benediction N: jūkfūk; jūktóu

benefactor N: ❶ (to an individual) yànyàhn (M: go) ❷ (to an institution) jaanjohyàhn (M: go)

beneficial SV: yáuhyīk PH: deui . . . yáuhyīk

beneficiary N: sauhyīkyàhn (M: go)

benefit N: leihyīk; hóuchyu PH: deui . . . yáuh hóuchyu; deui . . . yáuh leih

benevolence N: yàhnchìh; sihnsàm

benevolent SV: yàhnchìh; chìhbēi

benign SV: ❶ (person) wòh'ói hóuchàm; chìhchèuhng ❷ (climate, etc.) wànwòh ❸ (tumour) lèuhngsing

benignant SV: yàhnchìh

bent N: ngoihou; oihou

bequeath FV: sung

bequest N: wàihcháan (M: bāt)

bereave FV: lójó, mōkdyuht

bereaved Adj. PH: séijó chànyàhn ge

beriberi N: geukheibehng

Berlin PW/N: Paaklàhm

berry N: chóumùih (M: go)

berth N: ❶ (in a train, etc.) ngohpōu (M: jèung) ❷ (at a wharf) tìhngbok ge deihfòng (M: go, daat)

beseech FV: hánkàuh; chíngkàuh

beset FV: ❶ (close in) bàauwàih; wàihkwan ❷ (ornament) sèung ~ jó jyunsehk ge gaaijí

beside PW: hái . . . pòhngbīn FV: tùhng . . . béigaau ✳ beside the mark SV: lèihtàih ✳ beside oneself VO: faatkwòhng; mòhngyìhng

besides Patt: (in addition to) chèuihjó . . . jì ngoih, (juhng yáuh) . . . ~ *ngóhdeih* ~ , *juhng yáuh léuhng go yàhn làih* A: (moreover) yìhché • *gàmyaht ngóh m̀dākhàahn, ~ lohkyúh, ngóh m̀heui la*

besiege FV: bàauwàih; wàihgùng

best SV: jeuihóu ✳ at the very best PH: jeuidò jauh haih . . . ✳ do one's best IE: jeuhnlihk yìhwàih; jeuhnlihk jouh ✳ to the best of one's knowledge PH: jiu PN sójì ✳ best man N: buhnlóng (M: go)

bestial SV: sausing ge

bestiality N: sausing; sauyuhk

bestow FV: sungbéi; chibéi

bet FV: dóu; syùdóu; dádóu

betake FV: heui ✳ betake oneself to arms VO: yuhng móuhlihk ✳ betake oneself

to one's heels IE: líu jì
daaihgāt; gaaugeuk (coll.)

betel nut N: bànlòhng (M:
go)

betray FV: buibuhn; chēut-
maaih

betroth VO: dihngfàn

betrothal N: dihngfànláih
(M: go)

better SV: hóudī ge ✳ **better
than** Patt: N1 hóugwo N2; N1
hóudī ✳ **getting better** SV:
hóudī; hóujódī ✳ **had better**
A: jeui hóu . . . ~ m̀hóu gám-
jouh ✳ **be the better for** Patt:
deui . . . fáanyìh hóudī ✳ **better than nothing** PH: hóugwo
móuh

betterment FV/N: gói-
lèuhng; góijing

between PW: hái . . . tùhng
. . . jìgàan ✳ **between two
fires** IE: jeun teui léuhng
nàahn; jeunteui wàihgūk

bevel N: chegok; chèhmín
SV: che

beverage N: yámbán; yám-
liuh

bevy M: bàan

bewail FV: òidouh

beware FV: tàihfòhng; síusàm

bewilder FV: màihwaahk

bewitch FV: màihwaahk

beyond PW: **❶** (on the far
side of) hái . . . góbihn ~
tiuhkiùh ~ **❷** (farther away)
(hái) . . . jìngoih • m̀hóu hàahng
chēut gó tiuh wòhng sin ~FV:
chìugwo, gwojó • m̀hóu ~

gótiuh wòhngsin A: **❶** (of time)
chìhgwo, chìugwo • m̀hóu ~
sahpdím fàanlàih **❷** (out of
reach) . . . yíhngoih • nīdī haih
ngóhdeih nàhnglihk ~ ge sìh ✳
beyond control RV: gúnm̀-
dihm ✳ **beyond doubt** IE:
hòuh mòuh yìh mahn

biannual Adj. PH: léuhngnìhn yātchi ge

bias N: **❶** (prejudice) pìngin
(M: go) **❷** (predisposition)
pīkhou **❸** (of cloth) chèhsin SV:
che

bib N: háuséuigīn (M: go)

bible N: singgìng (M: bún)

bibliography N: **❶** (list of
books) syùmuhk (M: go) **❷**
(study of authorship, editions,
etc.) muhkluhkhohk

bicarbonate N: sōdá

bicentenary PH: yihbaak
jàunìhn géinihm

bicker VO: ngaaigàau N/FV:
háugok

bicycle N: dāanchē (M: ga) •
cháai ~

bid FV: **❶** chēut (price) **❷**
(command) fànfu VO: (cards,
bridge) giupáai ✳ **bid fair to**
Adv. PH: hóu yáuh/daaih
hónàhng ✳ **enter a bid** VO:
tàuhbīu

bier N: gùnchòih gá (M: go)
sìtáigá (M: go)

big SV: daaih ✳ **big wig** N:
daaihhāng (M: go)

bigamy N: chùhngfàn

bigot N: wàahngu fahnjí (M:
go)

bilateral SV: sèungbīn(ge) ~ *hipdihng*

bile N: ❶ dáamjáp ❷ (fig.) chau pèihhei ✻ **bile-stone** N: dáamsehk (M: nāp)

bill N: ❶ (statement of charges) jeungdāan (M: jèung) ❷ (poster, etc.) hóibou; gàaijiu (M: jèung) ❸ (proposed law) yíh'ngon (M: go) ❹ (bank note) ngàhnjí (M: jèung) ❺ (of bird) jéui; jeukjéui (M: go) ✻ **bill of exchange** N: wuihpiu (M: jèung) ✻ **bill collector** PH: sàusou ge yàhn (M: go)

billet N: yìhng; sūkyìhng (M: go)

billiards N: tóibō

billion Nu: sahpyīk

billow N: daaihlohng (M: go)

bimonthly N: (periodical) sèungyuhthōn (M: bún)

bin N: sèung; túng (M: go) ✻ **dust bin** N: laahpsaapsèung; laahpsaaptúng (M: go)

bind FV: ❶ bóng; jaat (sth. or sb. with rope etc.) ❷ dèng; dèngjòng (books, etc.) ❸ yeukchūk (by legal agreement, etc.)

binocular N: sèungtúng mohngyúhngeng (M: go)

biochemistry N: sàngmaht fahohk

biography N: jyuhngei (M: bún, pìn)

biology N: sàngmaht hohk

biophysics N: sàngmaht mahtléihhohk

biotic SV: sàngmihngge; sàngmahtge

bipartisan SV: léuhnggo-dóngge

birch N: baahkwàhsyuh (M: pò)

bird N: jéuk, jeukjái (M: jek) ✻ **a bird in the hand** PH: geidāk leihyīk; sahpnàh gáuwán ge yéh ✻ **birds of same feather** IE/N: yātyàu jihohk (Neg.); tùhng sèng tùhng hei ge ✻ **kill two birds with one stone** IE: yāt géui léuhngdāk; yāt chí (jin) sèung dīu ✻ **bird's eye view** N: níuhhaahm tòuh (M: fūk) ✻ **bird-man** N: fèihàhnggā (M: go)

bird's-nest N: jeukjáidau; jeukchàauh; yinwō (M: go)

birth FV: sàang VO: chēutsai ✻ **give birth to** FV: ❶ sàang ~ *saimānjái* ❷ cháansàng, yáhnhéi ~ *waaih ge yínghéung* ✻ **birth certificate** N: chēut-saijí (M: jèung) ✻ **birth control** FV/N: jityuhk

birthday FV/N: sàangyaht • *néih géisí ~ a?*

birth-mark N: ji; mák; mahksí (M: nāp)

birth-right PH: daaihjái ge gaisìhngkyùhn

biscuit N: bénggòn (M: faai)

bisect PH: fànhòi léuhng fahn

bisexual SV: léuhngsing ge; chìhùhngtùhng tái ge

bishop N: jyúgaau (M: go)

bit Nu: yātdī ✻ **a bit of** Nu: dītgamdēu ✻ **a bit at a time** Adv. PH: maahnmáan gám; yāt bouh yāt bouh gám ✻ **bit by bit** A: juhkdī ✻ **do one's bit** VO: jeuhn (jihgéi ge) búnfahn ✻ **not a bit** N/Adv. PH: yātdī dōu móuh

bitch N: ❶ (animal) gáuná (M: jek) ❷ (woman) dohngfúh; yàhmfúh (M: go)

bite FV: ngáauh M/N: daahm · béi sèh ngáauh jó yāt ~ N: (of insect) naan (M: nâp) · yāt nāp mān ~ ✻ **bite in** FV: lá; fuhsihk

bitter SV: ❶ (taste) fú ❷ (severe) leihhoih; gàaugwàan

bivouac FV/VO: louhyìhng

biweekly N: (periodical) bunyuht hōn; sèungjàuhōn (M: bún)

bizarre SV: gúgwaai

black SV: hāk, hāak N: ❶ (colour) hāk; hāksīk ❷ (race) hākyàhn ✻ **black out** FV: cháh; cháhjó · ~ nī go jih ✻ **in black and white** Adj. PH: baahkjí hākjih ✻ **black-spot** N: hākdím (M: go) ✻ **black market** SV/N: hāksíh ✻ **black-browned** Adj. PH: sàuh mèih fú mihn

black-beetle N: gaahtjáat (M: jek)

black-board N: hākbáan (M: faai)

blacken FV: féipóhng VO: góng waaihwá

black Friday N: hāksīk sìngkèihngh

black-guard N: ngokyē (M: go)

black hand N: hāksáudóng

black-hearted SV: hāksām

black-letter N: hāktáijih

black-list N: hākmìhngdāan (M: jèung) · yahpjó ~

black mail FV: dádāan; laahksok

black-out VO: sīkdāng PH: dàngfó gúnjai

black-smith N: dátitlóu (M: go)

bladder N: ❶ (organ of body) pòhng gwòng (M: go) ❷ (of ball) dáam (M: go) · bō ~ ❸ (of fish) pōk (M: go) · yùh ~ ❹ (general) pōk (M: go) · séui ~

blade N: ❶ (of a knife) dōuháu; dōufùng (M: go) ❷ (razor) dōupín (M: jèung) ❸ (small knife) dōujái (M: bá, jèung) BF: -yíp (M: faai) · fùngsin ~ ✻ **blade-bone** N: gìngaap gwāt (M: faai)

blame FV: gwaai; yun

blanch PH: bindāk chòng baahk

bland SV: ❶ (manner) wànwòh ❷ (of food, etc.) móuhmeih ge; táahm

blank SV: ❶ (of paper) hùngbaahk ❷ (expression) móuhbíuchìhng N: ❶ (space) hùngwái (M: go) ❷ (of a form) hùngwái; hùngggáak (M: go)

blanket N: jīn (M: jèung) FV: kám · wán jèung jīn làih ~ sīk dīfó RV: kámjyuh

blare FV/SV: chòuhhèui bàbai · gódī yàhn háisyu ~

blaspheme FV: sitduhk; naauh · m̀hóu ~ seuhngdai

blasphemous SV: sitduhk sàhnlìhng ge

blasphemy N: bātging; PH: m̀jyùnging ge taaidouh; deui . . . m̀jyùnging

blast M: jahm; jahn • *yāt ~ fùng* N: baauja FV: ja; jalaahn ✻ **blast furnace** N: yùhnglòuh (M: go)

blatant Adj. PH: daaih cháau daaih naauh FV: gwà gwà giu; chòuh chòuh bai

blaze N: ❶ (flame) fóyìhm ❷ (fire) fó (M: chèuhng) • *gau sīk gó chèuhng ~* ✻ **blaze up** RV: siu héi (séuhng) làih

bleach FV: piubaahk

bleaching BF: piubaahk - • *~ séui* ✻ **bleaching out** SV: làtsīk

bleak SV: ❶ (of weather) yàmngam ❷ (bare) fònglèuhng ❸ (fig., dreary) chàilèuhng ❹ (of prospects) ngamdaahm

bleat N; yèuhngmēsēng (M: bá) FV: yèuhngmēgiu

bleed VO: ❶ làuhhyut; chēuthyut ❷ (draw blood) chàuhyut • *yīsāng tùhng behngyàhn ~*

blemish N: hàhchì (M: dím); kyutdím (M: go) FV: syúnhoih

blend FV: kàumàaih, gáau-wàhn

bless FV: bóuyauh; jūkfūk

blessed SV: sàhnsingge, hahngfūkge

blessing FV/N: jūkfūk

blind SV: màahng N: lím; chèunglím (M: tòhng) ✻ **blind**

man/girl N: màahnglóu; màahnggùng/mūi (M: go) ✻ **venetian blind** N: baakyihplím (M: tòhng)

blindly A: màahngmuhk gám; màahngjùngjùng gám

blink VO: jáamngáahn FV: (twinkle) sím

bliss N: ❶ fūk; fūkhei ❷ (heaven) tìntòhng • *séuhng ~*

blister N: séuipōk (M: go)

blitz símdihnjin (M: chèuhng)

blizzard N: bouhfùngsyut (M: chèuhng)

bloat SV: yúngjúng

blob M: ❶ (drop) dihk❷ (spot) daat • *yāt ~ laahttaat yéh*

bloc N: jaahptyùhn (M: go)

block M: (solid piece of) gauh *yāt ~ muhk* N: ❶ (cutting board) jàmbáan (M: faai) ❷ (pulley) waahtlèuhn (M: go) FV: jósāk, sākjyuh • *tiuh louh béi dī fomaht ~* ✻ **block in** VO: waahk chóutòuh ✻ **block letter** N: daaihkáai; daaihgàai

blockade FV: fùngsó, dóusāk

blonde SV: táahmwòhngsīk; chínwòhngsīk

blood N: hyut (M: dihk) ✻ **blood-corpuscle** N: hyutkàuh ✻ **blood-letting** VO: chàuhyut ✻ **blood plasma** N: hyutjèung ✻ **blood poisoning** PH: hyut jungduhk ✻ **blood pressure** N: hyutngaat • *~gòu/dài* ✻ **blood relation** PH: yáuhhyutyùhn gwàanhaih ge chànsuhk ✻ **blood serum** N: hyutchìng ✻ **blood-shed** VO: làuhhyut N: làuhhyut sihgín ✻

blood stain N: hyutjīk (M: daat) * **blood stained** SV: hyutsèngge * **blood test** VO: yìhmhyut * **blood transfusion** VO: syùhyut * **blood vessel** N: hyutgún (M: tìuh) * **blood worm** N: sàchúng (M: tìuh)

bloody SV: hyutsèngge; làuhhyutge

bloom N: ❶ fā (M: déu) ❷ (time of greatest beauty) chìngchēun VO: hòifā

blooming SV: mauhsihng

blossom N: fā (M: déu) VO: hòifā * **in blossom** Adj. PH: fā jingjoih sihnghòi

blot N: wùjīk; mahkjīk (M: daat, dím)

blotch N: bàandím (on the skin) (N: daat)

blotter N: yanséuijí (M: jèung)

blouse N: néuihjòng sēutsàam (M: gihn)

blow FV: chèui VO: (breathe hard and quickly) chýunhei N: (hard stroke) dágīk (M: háh) * **blow the nose** VO: sangbeih; sangbeihtai * **blow off** RV: chèuisaan · *dī mouh béi fùng ~* * **blow over** FV: gwoheui · *bouhfùngyúh hóufaai jauh wúih ~* * **blow out** RV: chèuisīk (jáandàng) FV: baau (tàai) · *ga chè ~ jó tàai* VO: lauhhei * **blow fish** N: hòhtyùhn (M: tìuh) * **blow fly** N: daaih wūyīng (M: jek) * **blow up** VO: dáhei

blubber N: kìhngyùh yàuh FV: daaihsèng haam VO: soufú · *kéuih deui ngóh ~*

bludgeon N: gínggwan (M: jì)

blue N: làahmsīk SV: làahm * **blue bell** N: yéh fùngseunjí; làahmjùngfā (M: pò, déu) * **blue collar** N: làahmléhng; gùngyàhn (M: go) * **blue jacket** N: séuibīng (M: go) * **blue movie** N: sīkchìhng dihnyíng; síu dihnyíng; wòhngsīk dihnyíng; (coll.) hàahmpín (M: chēut) * **blue print** N: làahmtòuh (M: go, fūk)

bluff SV: ❶ che, dáuche ❷ (of a person) sēutjihk N: yùhnngàaih (M: douh, go) FV: húnghaak VO: pàaulohngtàuh · *kéuih pàau ngóh lohngtàuh*

blunder VO: faahn daaihcho

blunt SV: deuhn

blurred SV: mùhng; mòuhwùh; (coll.) mùhngchàhchàh

blurt PH: háufaaifaai ngāp jó chēut làih

blush PH: mihnhùhng · *kéuih faai mihn hùhng saai, gokdāk m̀hóu yisi* FV/SV: pacháu

boa N: móhngsèh (M: tìuh)

boar N: jyùgùng (M: jek)

board N: ❶ (wood) báan (M: faai) · *hāk ~ · bougou ~* ❷ (committee) wúi (M: go) ❸ (food) fósihk (M: chàan) ❹ (deck) gaapbáan (M: faai) * **above board** SV: gùnghòi ge; gwòngmìhng jingdaaihge * **on board** PH: hái (syùhn, fèigèi, chè) seuhngbihn * **to board** VO: bàau fósihk

boarding N: deihbáan (M: faai) VO: daapsihk · *hái*

hohkhaau ~ * **boarding school** N: geisūk hohkhaauh (M: gàan)

boast FV: jih'kwà FV/VO: chèuingàuh; chèdaaihpaau

boaster N: daaih paau yáu (M: go)

boat N: ❶ syùhn (M: jek) ❷ (small) téhng; téhngjái (M: jek) * **go boating** PH: heui pàhtéhng * **burn one's boats** IE: po fú chàhm jàu * **boat people** N: téhnggà

bobbin N: juhksàm (M: tiùh)

body N: ❶ sàntái (M: go) ❷ (corpse) sìtái ❸ (piece of matter) mahttái (M: gihn) BF: (main part of a structure) — sàn • chè ~ M: kwàhn; bàan • *yāt* ~ *yàhn* * **body guard** N: bóubīu (M: go)

bog N: jíujaahk (M: go)

bogey, bogie, bogy N: ❶ (evil spirit) yíumō; yíugwaai; yíu mō gwái gwaai (M: jek) ❷ (unknown object) bātmìhng fèihàhng mahttái (M: gihn)

bogus SV: gá; ngaihjouhge

boil FV: bòu N: chōng (M: go) * **keep the pot boiling** VO: wàihchìh sàngwuht * **boil down** RV: bòugihtdī * **boil up** RV: bòugwán

boiler N: wòlòuh (M: go)

boiling SV: gwán * **boiling point** N: faidím

bold SV: daaihdáam; dáamchòu * **bold-faced** SV: mìhnpèihháuh

Bolshevik N: Bou-yíh-sahp-wàih-hāk

bolt N: ❶ (for the door) sēut (M: go) • *mùhn* ~ ❷ (screw) lòhsìdēng (M: nāp) FV: (run away) tòuhpáau; jáu IE: (swallow) lòhngtànfúyit

bomb N: jadáan (M: go) * **bomb-proof** SV: fòhngdáan

bombard FV: gwàngja

bombast N: daaihwah

bombastic SV: daaihháuhei

bomber N: gwàngjagēi (M: ga)

bona fide SV: yáuh sìhngyi ge; sìhngsaht

bond N: ❶ (agreement) hahptùhng; kaiyeuk (M: fahn) ❷ (printed paper acknowledging money has been lent) jaai gyun (M: jèung); gùngjaai ❸ (sth. that joins) yeukchūk

bondage N: chūkbok

bone N: gwāt (M: gauh, tiùh) * **bone of contention** PH: yáuh ngaaugiuh ge mahntàih (M: go) * **bone up on** FV: jyunyìhn * **make no bones about doing** Adv. PH: hòuhmòuhgugeih; hòuhbātyàuhyìh * **feel in one's bones** IE: jìkèihyìhn, bātjì kèih sóyíhyìhn * **to the bones** Adj. PH: sv dou yahpgwāt * **bone head** N: bahndáan (M: go)

bonfire N: yìhngfó

bonnet N: (néuihjòng) móu (M: déng)

bonny, bonnie SV: gihnméihge

bonus N: fāhùhng; jéunggàm (M: bāt)

book N: ❶ syù (M: bún) ❷

(blank) bóu (M: bún) FV: ❶ (write down) dànggei ❷ (order for seats etc.) dehng ✳ off the books VO: chèuihméng ✳ on the books PH: yíhgìng jyujóchaak ✳ without books SV: móuhgàngeui

book-case N: syùgwaih (M: go)

booking N: dànggei; yuhyeuk ✳ booking office N: sauhpiuchyu

bookish Adj. PH: duhkséisyù

book-keeper N: bouhgeiyùhn (M: go)

book-keeping N: bouhgei

booklet N: syùjái (M: bún)

book-mark N: syùchìm (M: jèung)

book-seller N: syùsèung (M: go)

book-shelf N: syùgá (M: go)

book-stall N: syùtàan (M: dong, go)

book-store N: syùdim; syùguhk; syùgúk (M: gàan)

book-worm N: syùchùhng (M: tiuh)

boom N: ❶ (of derrick) diubei (M: jì) ❷ (logs) làahnsàan (M: douh) ❸ (of trade) fàahnwìhng ge gíngjeuhng; gínghei ❹ (a sound) gwàhng gwáng sèng; lùhnglúng sèng

boost FV: jìchìh; tèuigéui; búng

boot N: hēu (M: pair-deui, jek) FV: tek ✳ to boot A: yìhché

booth N: ❶ tàanwái (M: go) ❷ (for telephone) dihnwátíng (M: go)

booty N: ❶ jòngmaht; chaahkjòng (M; gihn) ❷ (from enemy in war) jinleihbán (M: gihn)

booze FV: kòhngyám; bouhyám

borax N: pàahngsà

border N: ❶ (of anything) bīn (M: tiuh) ❷ (land) bìngaai (M: tiuh) ✳ border on FV: tùhng . . . sèunglìhn/chìjyuh . . . ✳ on the border of TW/A: ngàamngàamséung ✳ border-line N: gaaisin (M: tiuh)

bore VO: jyunlūng SV/FV: fàahn • kéuih haih yātgo hóu ~ ge yàhn, sihsih dōu làih ~ ngóh PH: lihng yàhn tóuyim ge yàhn (M: go)

boring SV: muhn

born VO: chēutsai • néih géisí ~ ga ?

borough N: jihjihkèui (M: go)

borrow FV: je

bosom N: ❶ (breast) hùng (M: go) ❷ (inmost part) noihsàm (M: go) ✳ bosom friend N: jìgéi pàhngyáuh (M: go)

boss N: lóuhbáan; bōsí; sihtáu (M: go) FV: jí; jí fài

botanist N: jihkmahthohkgà (M: go)

botany N: jihkmahthohk

botch Adj. PH: chòu ge sáugùng

both Nu: léuhng Patt: yauh

SV1 yauh SV2; m̀jí V1 juhng
V2; N1 tùhngmàaih N2 dōu

bother FV: sòuyíu; gwán-
gáau ~ saainéih, m̀hóuyisi! *
bother about PH: waih . . .
dàamsàm

bottle N: jēun (M: go) * bottle green N: sàmluhksīk *
bottle neck N: jēungéng
deihdaai (M: go) * bottle up
FV: ngaatyīk; yánchòhng ~
fáhnnouh

bottom N: dái * bottoms
up IE: yám sing * from the
bottom of one's heart SV:
yàuhchùngge; chùngsàm ge *
bottom up FV: dìndóu;
doujyun

bottomless SV: móuhdáige
* bottomless pit N: mòuhdái
sàmyùn (M: go)

bough N: syuhjì (M: jì)

bouillon N: yuhktòng

boulder N: daaihsehktàuh;
yùhnwaaht ge sehk (M: gauh)

boulevard N: làhmyam
daaihdouh (M: tiuh)

bounce FV: fáandaahn;
daahn PH: (rush angrily) lyuhn
chùng lyuhn johng

bound N: ❶ (limit) faahnwàih; gaaihaahn (M: go) FV: ❶
(set bounds) haahnjai ❷ (jump)
tiuhéi; daahn * bound to A:
yātdihng; bītdihng * bound
for FV: heui * bound up in
SV/A: jyùnsàm; màaih-tàuh-
màaih-nóuh * bound up with
PH: tùhng . . . yáuh mahtchit
gwàanhaih * by leaps and
bounds Adj. PH: daht fèi
máahng jeun * know no
bounds A: móuh haahnjai gám

boundary N: gaaisin;
gèunggaai (M: tiuh)

boundless SV: mòuhhaahn

bountiful SV: ❶ (generous)
hóngkoi ❷ (abundant) fùngfu

bouquet NuMN: yātjaatfā

bourgeoisie N: jìcháan
gàaikāp (M: go)

bout NuM: yātchi N: wùihhahp (M: go)

boutique N: sìhjòngpóu;
sìhjòngdim (M: gàan)

bow N: ❶ (for shooting ar-
rows) gùng (M: bá) ❷ (of a ship)
syùhntàuh (M: go) ❸ (curve)
gùngyìhng; wùhyìhng (M: go) ❹
(neck wear) léhng fā; bōutāai
(M: go) FV: gūkgùng • heung .
. . ~

bowel N: ❶ chéung (M: tiuh)
❷ (innermost part) noihbouh *
bowel movement N: daaih-
bihn

bowl N: ❶ wún (M: jek) ❷
(game) muhkkàuh

box N: ❶ (small) háap (M: go)
❷ (large) sèung (M: go) * box-
office N: sauhpiuchyu (M: go)
* box up VO: jòngsèung;
yahpsèung

boxer N: kyùhngīkgà; kyùhnsáu (M: go)

boxing N: kyùhngīk; sài-
yèuhng kyùhn

boy N: ❶ nàahmjái (M: go) ❷
(son) jái (M: go) ❸ (servant, in
hotel, etc.) sihjái; fógei (M: go)
* boy friend N: nàahmpàhng-
yáuh (M: go) * boy scout N:
tùhnggwàn (M: go, deuih)

boycott FV: dáijai; bùigoi

boyhood N: siunìhn sìhdoih

bra N: hùngwàih; (coll.) yúhjaau (M: go)

brace N: jìgá (M: go) RV: bónggán * **brace oneself up** FV: janjok; tàihhéi jìngsàhn

bracelet N: sáungáak; ngáak (M: jek)

bracket N: (sign) kwutwùh (M: go)

brag VO: chèuingàuh; chèdaaihpaau

braggart N: daaihpaau yáu (M: go) chèuingàuh daaihwòhng (M: go)

braid N: (hair) bīn (M: tìuh)

brain N: nóuh (M: go) * **beat one's brains** Adj. PH: gáau jeuhn nóuhjáp * **brain fever** N: nóuh(mók) yìhm * **brain wave** N: nóuh dihnbō * **brain-worker** PH: nóuhlihk lòuhduhng ge yàhn (M: go) * **brain washing** N/VO: sáinóuh * **brain drain** PH: yàhnchòih ngoih làuh

brainless SV: chéun; móuhnóuh

brainy SV: chùngmìhng

braise FV: màn

brake N: (of cars) jai (M: go) · sáu ~ · geuk ~ VO: saatchè; saatjai PH: saattìhng ga chè

bran N: hòng; mahkhòng

branch N: (of tree) syuhjì (M: jì) ATT: ❶ jì (of railway, river, road) ~ sin ❷ fàn (of school, office, firm, store) ~ gúk * **branch out** FV; faatjín * **root and branch** SV: chitdái

brand N: (trademark) māktàuh; sèungbīu (M: go) VO: dáyan FV: móuhyuhk (sb. with infamy)

brandish FV: móuh, móu ~ gim

brandy N: bahtlāandéi (jáu) (M: jì)

brand-new SV: chyùhnsàn ge

brass N: wòhngtùhng; tùhng * **brass band** N: tùhng gún ngohkdéui (M: deuih)

brassy SV: mihnpèihháuh

brat N: (coll.) lèngjái (M: go)

brave SV: yúhnggám FV: mouh (danger) * **brave it out** PH: díngngaahngséuhng; séidíng

bravo PH: hóuyéh!

brawl VO: ngaaigàau

brawn N: ❶ (meat) jyūyuhkgōn (M: faai) ❷ (muscle) gèiyuhk (M: gauh)

brawny SV: daaihjek

Brazilian N: Bàsàiyàhn (M: go)

breach FV: wàihfaahn; powaaih (law, contract, etc.)

bread N: mihnbāau (M: go, faai) * **bread-crumb** N: mihnbàauhòng

breadth N: futdouh * **by(to) a hair's breadth** IE: (dangerous) chìn-gwàn-yāt-faat

break FV: ❶ jínglaahn ❷ (smash) dá laahn ❸ (by dropping) ditlaahn ❹ (with fingers) mītlaahn ❺ (tearing) sìlaahn *

break away PH: dahtyìhn lèihhòi FV: gaai, gaaichèuih (habit) ✳ **break appointment** VO: sātyeuk ✳ **break contract** VO: wái yeuk; wàihfáan hipdihng ✳ **break down** FV: ① (of machine) waaih ② (by force) tèuifàan; fánseui ③ (collapse) ngàhgáai ✳ **break forth** FV: baaufaat ✳ **break in** FV: ① (train) fanlihn ② (interrupt) dátyúhn PH: (enter a building by force) po-mùhn-yahp-ngūk ✳ **break a law** VO: faahnfaat ✳ **break off** FV: týuhnjyuht ✳ **break out** RV: (escape) jáulàt ✳ **break record** VO: dápo géiluhk; po géiluhk

breakable Adj. PH: dádāk laahn ge; yih laahn ge

breakage N: ❶ (broken place) lihthàuh (M: go) ❷ (broken articles) syún hou; laahn jó ge yéh

breakdown N: bàngkúi · *jìngsàhn* ~ ✳ **nervous breakdown** N: sàhngìng sèuiyeuhk

breaker N: (of wave) seuilohng; lohngfā

breakfast N: jóuchāan (M: chāan)

breast N: ❶ hùnghàuh; sàmháu (M: go) ❷ (of woman) yúhfòhng; náaih (M: go) ✳ **breast pump** N: kāpnáaihhei (M: go) ✳ **breast stroke** N: wāsīk · *yàuhséui yàuh* ~

breath N: hei; fùkāp (M: daahm) ✳ **in a breath** A: jīkhāk ✳ **out of breath** VO: chýunhei A/IE: seuhnghei m̀jip hah hei ✳ **spend (waste) one's breath** A: sàaihei ✳ **take breath** VO: táuhei; hitháhhei

breathe FV: fùkāp VO: táuhei ✳ **breathe freely again** PH: sùng yāt háu hei; sùng yāt daahm hei

breathlessly A: heichyúnchyúngám

breathtaking SV: dākyàhngèng

breed FV: ❶ (keep animals) yéuhng ❷ (reproduce) sàang; fàahnjihk N: (kind) júng · *lèuhng ~ge máh* ✳ **breed up** FV: yéuhngdaaih; yéuhngyuhk; gaauyéuhng

breeding N: fùfa; fàahnjihk

breeze N: (wind) mèihfùng (M: jahm, jahn)

brew FV: yeuhng

brewery N: yeuhngjáuchóng (M: gàan)

bribe FV: sàumáaih; kúilouh N: kúilouh VO: sáihākchín ✳ **take a bribe** VO: sàu hākchín; sauh kúi

bribery N: kúilouh

brick N: jyùn (M: gauh) ✳ **like a brick** IE: yúhng wóhng jihk chìhn ✳ **brick field** N: jyùnchóng (M: gàan) ✳ **brick kiln** N: jyùnyiùh (M: go) ✳ **brick-layer** N: nàih séui sìfú; nàihséui lóu (M: go)

bridal N: fānláih (M: go)

bride N: sànnèuhng; sànnéung (M:go) ✳ **bride cake** N: ganéuibéng (M:go)

bridegroom N: sànlóng; sànlòhnggō (M: go)

bridesmaid N: buhnnéung (M: go)

bridge N: ❶ (structure of wood, steel etc.) kìuh (M: tìuh, douh) ❷ (card game) kìuhpáai (M: pòu)

bridle N: màhgèung (M: tìuh) FV: yeukchūk

brief SV: gáandyún ✻ **brief bag** N: sáutàihbàau; sáutàihdói (M: go) ✻ **brief case** N: gùngsìhbàau; gùngsìhgīp (M: go)

brier N: ❶ gìnggīk (M: pò) ❷ (wild rose) yéh chèuhngmèih (M: pò)

brigade M: ❶ (army unit) léuih ❷ (organized body of persons) deuih

bright SV: ❶ (of light) gwòng ❷ (with hope) yáuh hèimohng ❸ (clever) chùngmìhng ✻ **bright and early** TW/N: chìngjóu

brightness N: gwòngleuhng

brilliance N: gwòngfài (M: douh)

brilliant SV: ❶ gwòng-mìhng ❷ (of person) chùng-mìhng; yìngmìhng

brim N: bīn (M: tìuh)

brindle N: bàanmàhn (M: tìuh)

bring FV: nìnglàih; nīklàih; daailàih; nìng N làih, daai N làih; nīk N làih ✻ **bring about** RV: yáhnhéi; jouhsèhng ✻ **bring back** RV: nīkfàanlàih ✻ **bring forward** FV: tàihchēut ✻ **bring in** FV: yáhnjeun • ~fògeih ✻ **bring over** FV: lìhng ... góibin ✻ **bring round** RV: gauséng ✻ **bring up** RV: yéuhngdaaih ✻ **bring to light**

FV: faatyìhn; gùngbou

brink N: bìn; gaai (M: tìuh) ✻ **on the brink of** Adj. PH: hái ... ge bīnyùhn • ~ séimòhng ~

brisk SV: wuhtput; hìngfaai

bristle N: jyùjùng; jyù-jùngmòuh (M: tìuh)

Britannic SV: Yìnggwokge; Bātlihtdīng

British SV: Yìnggwokge ✻ **British pound** M/N: Yìngbóng (M: bohng)

brittle SV: cheui; yìh-seuige; yìhlaahnge

broad SV: fut ✻ **broad minded** SV: daaih leuhng; fùnwàhng daaihleuhng

broadbean N: chàahmdáu (M: nāp)

broadcast N/FV: gwóngbo

broaden FV: gàfut; fongfut

Broadway N: Baaklóuh-wuih

brochure N: gáangaai (M: bún)

broil FV: sìu

broken SV: laahnjó; lihtjó ✻ **broken-hearted** SV: sèung-sàm

broker N: gìnggéi (M:go)

brokerage N: yúnggàm; gìnggéiyúng (M: bāt)

bronchitis N: jìheigúnyìhm

bronze N: chèngtùhng; gútùhng ✻ **bronze colour** N: gútùhng sīk ✻ **bronze age** N: tùhnghei sìhdoih; chèngtǔhnghei sìhdoih (M: go)

brooch N: sàmháujàm (M: go)

brood FV: bouh; fù

brook N: kài (M: tìuh) FV: yùhngyán; yánsauh

broom N: soubá (M: bá)

broomcorn N: gòulèuhng (M: pò)

broth N: tòng (M: wún)

brothel N: gabouh; gàidau; geihjaaih; geihjáai (M: go)

brother * **brothers** N: hìngdaih (M: go) * **older brother** N: gòhgō; a-gō (M: go) * **younger brother** N: dàihdái; sailóu (M: go) brother-in-law N: ① (elder sister's husband) jéfù (M: go) ② (younger sister's husband) muihfù (M: go) ③ (husband's elder brother) daaihbaak (M: go) ④ (husband's younger brother) sūkjái (M: go) ⑤ (wife's elder brother) daaihkáuh (M: go) ⑥ (wife's younger brother) káuhjái (M: go) ⑦ (wife's elder sister's husband) kàmhìng (M: go) ⑧ (wife's younger sister's husband) kàmdái (M: go) * **brother's son** N: jahtjái; jái (M: go) * **brother's daughter** N: jahtnéui (M: go)

brotherhood N: hìngdaih gwàanhaih; sáujūk jì chìhng

brotherly SV: yáuhngoi

brow N: ❶ (hair above the eye) mèih; ngáahnmèih (M: tìuh) ❷ (forehead) ngaahk; ngaahktàuh (M: go) ❸ (of slope) yùhnngàaih (M: go, douh)

browbeat FV: húnghaak

brown N: gafēsīk; jyùgònsīk

* **brown sugar** N: wòhngtòhng

browse VO: sihkchóu FV: làuhláahm (dísyù)

bruise N: yú; yúhāk (M: daat) RV: johngyú; hámyú

brunt N: chùnggīk * **bear the brunt** IE: sáu-dòngkèih-chùng

brush N: ❶ cháat (M: go) ❷ (used by painters etc.) mòuhbāt (M: jì) ❸ (bushes) gunmuhkchùhng (M: go) FV: chaat * **brush aside** FV: m̀léih * **brush off** RV: chaatlāt * **brush up** FV: wànjaahp

brusque SV: chòulóuh; lóuhmóhng

brutal SV: chàahnyán; móuhyàhnsing; yéhmàahn

brutality N: bouhhahng (M: júng)

bubble N: póuh VO: hēipóuh * **blow bubbles** FV: waahnséung * **bubble car** N: fòhngdáan chè (M: ga)

buck N: ❶ (of deer) hùhnglúk (M: jek) ❷ (of rabbit) hùhng tou (M: jek) * **buck up** A: tàihhéi jīngsàhn; faaidī! * **buck horn** N: luhkgok (M: jek, jì)

bucket N: túng (M: go) * **kick the bucket** FV: (coll.) dèngjó; gwàjó; hèungjó

Buckingham Palace N: Baahkgàmhon gùng (M: joh)

buckle FV/N: kau (M: go)

bud N: ❶ (general) ngàh (M: jì) ❷ (of flower) lām (M: go) VO: chēutngàh; chēutlām

buddha N: faht; pòuhsaat; fahtjóu (M: joh, go)

buddhism N: fahtgaau

buddhist N: fahtgaautòuh (M: go) ✻ **buddhist scripture** N: fahtging (M: bún) ✻ **buddhist nun** N: sìgū (M: go) ✻ **buddhist monk** N: wòhséung (M: go)

budge FV: yūk ✻ **don't budge** PH: máih yūk

budget FV/N: yuhsyun (M: go) N: yuhsyunbíu (M: jèung, go)

buff BF: – màih · jūkkàuh ~ · máh ~

buffalo N: séuingàuh (M: jek)

buffer N: ❶ (apparatus) wùhnchùnghei (M: ga) ❷ (person) (coll.) chéunchòih (M: go)

buffet FV: dá N: yámsihk gwaihtói; síumaaihbouh (M: go) ✻ **buffet car** N: chàanchē (M: ga) ✻ **buffet dinner (or lunch)** N: jihjohchāan (M: chàan, go)

bug N: sāt; muhksāt (M: jek)

bugle N: labā; houhgok (M: go) VO: chèui labā; chèui houhgok

build FV: héi (building) built-in (furniture) ATT.: yahp-chèuhng – ✻ **build up** RV: ① (make) jouhsèhng; héisèhng ② (fill) sākjyuh

builder N: deihpùhn gùng-yàhn; ginjūk gùngyàhn (M: go)

building N: láu; daaihhah; ginjūkmaht (M: joh, gàan)

bulb N: ❶ (electrical) dàngdáam; dihndàngdáam (M: go) ❷ (plant) kàuhhàng (M: go)

Bulgarian N: Bóu-gà-leih-nga yàhn (M: go)

bulge M: gauh · gúnghéi / jeunghéi yāt ~ RV: gúnghéi; jeunghéi; dahthéi; baauhhéi

bulk ✻ **in bulk** SV: daaih-leuhng; daaihpài ✻ **the bulk of** N: daaihbouhfahn

bulky SV: daaihgauh; lauh-bauh

bull N: ❶ (male cow) ngàuhgùng (M: jek) ❷ (official order) fanlihng (M: go, douh) ✻ **bull dog** N: hàbàgáu (M: jek) ✻ **bull doze** FV: húnghaak ✻ **bull dozer** N: cháannàihchè (M: ga) ✻ **bull-ring** N: daungàuhchèuhng (M: go)

bullet N: jídáan (M: nāp) ✻ **bullet-proof** ATT: fòhngdáan; beihdáan ✻ **bullet train** N: jídáan fóchè (M: ga)

bulletin N: gùngbou (M: fahn) ✻ **bulletin board** N: bougoubáan (M: faai)

bullion N: ❶ (gold) gàmtíu (M: tìuh) ❷ (silver) ngàhntíu (M: tìuh)

bullock N: yìmjó ge ngàuh (M: jek)

bully FV: hà N: ngokba (M: go)

bulwark N: bóuléuih (M: joh, go)

bumble-bee N: daaih wòhngfùng (M: jek)

bump FV: ❶ (strike against) johng ❷ (jerky motion) dan N: (swelling on the body) láu; làuh (M: go)

bumper N: (of car) bàmbá (M: tiùh); gáamjanhei; beihjanhei (M: go)

bumpkin N: hèunghálóu (M: go)

bumpy SV: dan • *ga chè/tiùh louh hóu* ~

bun N: mihnbàau (M: go)

bunch M: ❶ chàu (of keys, grapes) ❷ jaat (of flowers, vegetables) ❸ bàan; jah; dèui (of people)

bundle M: ❶ jaat; bàau ❷ (heap) dèui

bungalow N: pìhngfòhng (M: gàan)

bungle PH: jouh dāk hóu léhféh; jouh dou wùlèidāan dōu/wùlèi máhcháh

bunk N: (of train) ngohpòu (M: jèung) ✻ **bunk bed** N: lūkgáchòhng (M: jèung)

bunker N: syùhn ge yihnlíuchòng

bunting N: chóikèih (M: jì)

buoy N: séuipóuh; fàuhbīu (M: go) ✻ **life buoy** N: gausàanghyūn (M: go)

buoyance N: fàuhlihk (M: douh)

burden N: ❶ fuhdàam (M: júng, go) ❷ (tonnage) dēunwái ✻ **be a burden to** PH: deui . . . haih yāt júng fuhdāam

burdensome SV: màhfàahn; leuihjeuih

bureau N: ❶ (desk) séjihtói (M: jèung) ❷ (office) guhk; só; chyúh; gúk • *léuihyàuhguhk • sànmàhnchyúh* ❸ (chest of drawers for clothes, etc.) yī gwaih (M: go)

bureaucracy N: gùnlìuh jyúyih

bureaucrat N: gùnlìuh (M: go)

burglar N: cháak; chaahk; syúmō (M: go)

burial N: jongláih (M: go) ✻ **burial case** N: gùnchòih; gùnmuhk (M: fu) ✻ **burial ground** N: sàanfàhn (M: go)

burlesque FV: (make fun of) fungchi; jàaufung N: bíuyín (M: chèuhng)

Burmese N: Míhndihnyàhn (M: go) Míhndihnwá

burn FV: sìu ✻ **burned** SV: nùngjó ✻ **burn down** (building etc.) PH: béi fó sìu jó ✻ **burn in** FV: fuhsihk; lá

burner N: ❶ (of lamp) dàngtàuh (M: go) ❷ (of stove) lòuhtàuh (M: go)

burrow N: lūng (M: go) VO: gwahtlūng

bursar N: wuihgai jyúyahm (M: go)

burst FV: baau; liht ✻ **burst forth** FV: baaufaat; panchēut ✻ **burst into** Patt: fātyìhn/dahtyìhn . ᵛ. héiséuhnglàih ✻ **burst on (upon)** FV: dahtyìhn chēutyìhn ✻ **burst up** FV: ① baauja ② (fail) sātbaaih; dóutòih

bury FV: màaihjong; jong

bus N: bàsí (M: ga, bouh) ✻ **bus stop** N: bāsíjaahm (M: go) ✻ **miss the bus** VO: sātjó gèiwuih; chogwo gèiwuih

bush N: ngáisyuh (M: pò)

bushel M: pòuhsīkyíh

busily A: chùngmòhng

business N: ❶ (trade) sàangyi (M: dàan) ❷ (task) gùngjok (M: gihn) ❸ (duty) jaakyahm (M: go) ❹ (matter) sih (M: gihn) ❺ (right) kyùhnleih (M: júng) ✳ **businessman** N: sàangyilóu; jouh sàangyi ge yàhn (M: go) ✳ **business hours** N: yìhngyihp sìhgaan ✳ **have no business to do** PH: móuhkyùhn jouh ✳ **mean business** PH: haih jànge

bust FV: ❶ baauliht ❷ sātbaaih; pocháan • *sàangyi* ~ N: ❶ (stone cutting or bronze etc.) bunsànjeuhng; bunsàndiusoujeuhng (M: go) ❷ (of woman's body) hùngbouh (M: go)

bustling SV: yihtnaauh

busy SV: ❶ (of a person) mòhng; m̀dākhàahn ❷ (of a place) yihtnaauh ❸ (of a telephone line) yáuhyàhngónggán; m̀tùng ✳ **busy body** PH: jyúsih ge yàhn; hou gún hàahnsih ge yàhn (M: go) ✳ **get busy** PH: héisáu jouh ✳ **not busy** SV: dākhàahn

but A: daahnhaih, bātgwo Patt: chèuihjó . . . ji'ngoih • ~ *kéuih* ~ , *gogo dōu heui* ✳ **all but** A: gèifùh; jàangdī ✳ **but for** A: yùhgwó m̀haih ✳ **but rather** A: yìhnìhngyún ✳ **but what** A: yìhm̀ ✳ **but yet** A: daahnhaihjuhng

butcher N: ❶ (of pigs) tòngjyùlóu (M: go) ❷ (of cows) tòngngàuhlóu (M: go) FV: tòng ✳ **butcher bird** N: baaklòuhjéuk (M: jek)

butler N: nàahmgúngà (M: go)

butt N: ❶ (cask for wine) jáutúng (M: go) ❷ (target) bá (M: go) ❸ (thicker end of fishing-rod, etc.) beng (M: go, tiùh) ❹ (person) jàausiu ge deuijeuhng (M: go) FV: johng

butter N: ngàuhyàuh (M: gauh, pound—bohng) ✳ **butterscotch** N: náaihyàuhtóng (M: nàp)

butterfly N: wùhdíp; wùhdihp (M: jek)

buttocks N: ❶ (refined) tyùhnbouh (M: go) ❷ (coll.) peigú (M: go) ❸ (very coll.) sífāt (M: go)

button N: ❶ (of clothing) náu (M: nàp) ❷ (electrical switch) jai (M: go) ✳ **button hole** N: náumùhn (M: go) ✳ **button up** VO: kaunáu ✳ **not worth a button** Adj. PH: yātgosīn dōu m̀jihk

buxom SV: táitaai fùngmúhn; gihnméih

buy FV: máaih ✳ **buy in** FV: (daaihpāi) máaihyahp ✳ **buy out** FV: máaihtùng ✳ **buy over** FV: sàumáaih ✳ **buy up** RV: máaihsaai ✳ **buy things** VO: máaihyéh ✳ **a good buy** PH: máaihdāk hóu dái

buzz N: wàngwàngsèng; wàhngwáng sèng A: wàngwàngsèng gám

buzzard N: yìng (M: jek)

by CV: ❶ (location) hái . . . pòhngbīn • *kéuih chóh* ~ *ngóh* ~ ❷ (by someone or something who causes an event) béi • *Ngóh búnsyù* ~ *kéuih jínglaahnjó* ❸ (not later than) (hái) TW jìchìhn · tìngjìu ~ jouhhéi béi ngóh ❹ (when the time indicated comes) gójahnsí · kéuih làihdou ~ yíhgìng tìnhāk laak ❺ (by a quantity) dyun (M) · maaih nīdī choi, ~ gàn dihng ~ bohng a? ❻ (by a period of time) ngon TW · jòugàm haih ~ yuht gai ❼ (by way of) yàuh ~ séuilouh yīkwaahk luhklouh heui a? ~ nītiuh louhheui ❽ (through the agency, means or instrumentality) yuhng N (làih) . . . · jèung tói haih ~ muhk jouh ge ❾ (by means of) kaau (FV/VO) . . . · kéuih ~ maaih boují wàihchìh sàngwuht ❿ (during) ge sìhhauh, gójahnsí · yehmáahn ~ FV: ❶ (by means of transportation) chóh, daap · ngóh ~ fóchè làih ❷ (send) gei ~ hùngyàuh ❸ (stand by sb.) jìchìh ❹ (go by) gìnggwo · múihyaht dōu ~ yàuhgúk ❺ (according to) jiu, gàngeui ~ ngóh ge bíu, yìhgā haih léuhngdím ✳ by and by A: yāt-jahnggàan, yātján ✳ by and large Adv. PH: yātbùn làihgóng ✳ by the way PH: góng hòi yauh góng, . . . ✳ by all means A: yātdihng yiu ✳ by all means not A: chìnkèih mhhóu ✳ by mistake Adv. PH: mgokyi .FV chojó ✳ by order of VO: fuhng . . . (ge) mihng; jèunjiu . . . ge yijí ✳ by oneself N: jihgéi; PN: jihgéi, jihgēi ✳ by oneself (alone) A: jihgéi/jihgēi yātgoyàhn ✳ by turns AV: lèuhnláu ✳ day by day Patt: yātyaht SV gwo yātyaht ✳ near by PW: fuhgahn

bye-bye PH: bāaibaai; joigin

bygone SV: yíhwóhng ge; gwoheui ge

C

cab N: dīksí (M: ga)

cabaret N: gòtèng; móuhtèng (M: gàan) ✳ **cabaret girl** N: móuhnéui; gònéui (M: go)

cabbage N: yèhchoi (M: pò) ✳ **Chinese white cabbage** N: baahkchoi (M: pò)

cabin N: ❶ (of ship) syùhnchòng (M: go) ❷ (of aircraft) gèichòng (M: go) ❸ (house) ngūkjái (M: gàan) ❹ (of railway) seunhouhsāt (M; go)

cabinet N: ❶ (furniture) gwaih (M: go)˙ ❷ (council) noihgok (M: go) ✳ **cabinet meeting** N: noihgok wuihyíh (M: go)

cable N: ❶ (of an anchor) nàauhlín (M: tìuh) ❷ (rope) laahm (M: tìuh) ❸ (on the ocean floor) hóidái dihnlaahm (M: tìuh) ❹ (message) dihnbou (M: fùng) ✳ **cable car** N: laahmchè; diuchè (M: ga)

caboose PH: gaapbáan seuhngbihn ge chyùhfóng (M: go)

cactus N; sìnyàhnjéung (M: pò)

caddy N: chàhyihpgun (M: go)

cadence N: wàhnleuht; jitjau; paakjí (M: go)

cadet N: ❶ (student at a naval college, etc.) gwànhaauh hohksàang (M: go) ❷ (young people under training) lihnjaahpsàng (M: go) ❸ (younger son) saijái (M: go)

cadre N: gonbouh (M: go)

Caesar N: Hóisaat daaihdai ✳ **caesar birth** PH: fáufūk sàngcháan

café N: gafēsāt (M: gàan)

cafeteria N: sihktòhng; faahntòhng (M: gàan)

caffeine N: gafēyān

cage N: lùhng (M: go)

cajole FV: tam

cake N: ❶ (ordinary) béng (M: go, gihn) ❷ (sponge) daahngōu (M: go, gihn) M: gauh • yāt ~ fàangáan

calamity N: jòinaahn (M: chèuhng)

calcium N: koi

calculate FV: ❶ gai, gaisyun ❷ (rely) jímohng ❸ (suppose) gokdāk; yìhngwàih

calculation N: gúgai

calculator N: (machine) gaisougèi (M: ga)

calculus N: ❶ mèihjīkfàn ❷ (med.) gitsehk (M: nāp)

caldron, cauldron N: daaihbōu (M: go)

calendar N: ❶ (almanac) yahtlihk (M: go) ❷ (monthly) yuhtlihk (M: go) ❸ (system) lihkfaat (M: go) ✳ **school calendar** N: haauhlihk (M: go) ✳ **solar calendar** N: sànlihk; yèuhnglihk ✳ **lunar calendar** N: gauhlihk; yàmlihk

calf N: ❶ (young cow) ngàuhjái (M: jek) ❷ (of the leg) síutéui (M: go)

calibrate FV/RV: gaaujéun

calibre N: háuging; jihkging

calico N: ❶ (white) baahkbou (M: faai) ❷ (printed) fàbou (M: faai)

call FV: ❶ (shout) giu ❷ (visit) taam; wán PN chóh ❸ (name) giu N jouh; giujouh • ngóh ~ kéuih ~ ngàuhjái • kéuih ~ ngàuhjái ❹ (summon) giu ~ yìsāng ✳ **call back** RV: giu . . . fàanlàih FV: chéuisìu ✳ **call back (sb. on telephone)** VO: fūkdihnwá béi PN ✳ **call down** FV: yiukàuh ✳ **call for help** PH: yiuyàhn bòngsáu ✳ **call on** FV: (visit) fóngmahn ✳ **call off sth.** FV: chéuisìujó; tìhngjíjó ✳ **call over** VO: dímmēng ✳ **call (sb.) up** Patt: dádihnwá béi PN ✳ **call upon** FV: chíngkàuh ✳ **on call** PH: chèuih chyùhn chèuih dou ✳ **so called** PH: sówaih ✳ **call bell** N: dihnjùng (M: go) ✳ **call box** N: gùngjung dihnwátihng (M: go) ✳ **call girl** N: yingjiuh néuihlòhng; geihnéuih (M: go)

calligrapher N: syùfaatgà (M: go, wái)

calligraphy N: syùfaat

calling N: (profession) jīkyihp (M: júng)

callisthenics N: yàuhyúhn táichòu

callous VO: (of skin) héijám SV: mòuhchìhng ge

callow SV: móuhgìngyihm IE: yúh-chau-meih-gòn

callus N: jám (M: faai, gauh)

calm SV: ❶ (of person) jandihng; daahmdihng; ngònjihng ❷ (of weather) pìhngjihng ❸ (of sea) pìhngjihng; fùngpìhng lohng jihng

caloric N: yihtleuhng

calorie N: kà; kàlouhléih (M: go)

calumniate FV: jungsèung; dáiwái

calyx N: fàtok; fàtók (M: go)

Cambodian N: Gáanpòuh-jaaihyàhn/wá

Cambridge N: Gìmkìuh

camel N: loktòh (M: jek) * **camel-backed** SV: tòhbui ge

camellia N: sàanchàh fā; chàfā (M: déu, dó)

camera N: séunggèi; yíng-séunggèi (M: ga, bouh) * **camera-man** N: sipyíngsì (M: go) * **camera-plane** N: sip-yíng fèigèi (M: ga) * **in camera** A: sìhah; beimahtgám

camouflage FV: yímsīk; yímwuh

camp N: ❶ (tent) yìhng; yìhngmohk (M: go) ❷ (for soldiers) gwànyìhng (M: go) ❸ (people with the same ideas) jaahptyùhn; jahnyìhng (M: go) * **pitch a camp** VO: jaatyìhng * **break up camp** VO: bahtyìhng; chaakyìhng * **camp out** VO: louhyìhng * **in the same camp** IE: jìtùhng douhhahp * **camp bed** N: hàahnggwànchòhng (M: jèung) * **camp chair** N: jipyí (M: jèung) * **camp-fire** N: yìhngfó * **camp-stool** N: jipdang (M: jèung)

campaign N: ❶ (military) jinyìhk; jeung (M: chèuhng) ❷ (planned activites) wahnduhng (M: go) · *chìnggit ~*

camphor N: jèungnóuh *

camphor wood N: jèungmuhk * **balls of camphor** N: chauyún (M: nāp)

campus N: (university) haauhyùhn (M: go)

can AV: ❶ (know how to) wúih ❷ (be able to) hóyíh ❸ (able to) (V) dāk · *tái ~ gin* ❹ (not able to) m̀hóyíh, m̀ .(V) dāk · *~ heui · ~ heui ~* N: gun (M: go) * **canned** ... ATT.: guntáu * **as (SV) as can be** PH: jeuhn-hónàhng .SY.; jeuhn SV * **can only** A: jíyáuh; jí hóyíh * **cannot but** A: m̀ nàhngggaum̀ ...; bāt nàhng bāt ... * **can not help** A: bātgam; yánm̀jyuh * **can opener** N: guntáudōu (M: bá)

Canadian N: Gànàhdaaih yàhn (M: go)

canal N: wahnhòh (M: tìuh) * **canal-lock** N: séuijaahp (M: go, douh)

canary N: gàmsìjéuk (M: jek)

cancel FV: chéuisìu

cancer N: ngàahm; ngàahm-jìng; kènsàh; kènsá * **have cancer** VO: sàangngàahm

candid SV: táanbaahk; sēutjihk

candidate N: ❶ (for election) hauhsyúnyàhn (M: go) ❷ (of an examination) háausàng (M: go)

candle N: laahpjūk (M: jì) * **burn the candle at both ends** Adv. PH: yaht yíh gai yeh gám; (coll.) duhnghéi chòhng báan VO: (coll.) hòiyehchè * **candle light** N: jūkgwòng * **the game is not worth a candle** IE: dākbātsèuhng sāt

candy N: tóng (M: nāp) * **candy words** N/IE: tìhmyìhn mahtyúh

cane N: tàhngtíu (M: tìuh) * **sugar cane** N: je (M: pò, jì) * **cane sugar** N: je tòhng (M: gauh)

canine-tooth N: hyúnchí (M: jek)

canister N: gun (M: go)

canker N: kúiyèuhng

cannabis N: daaihmàh · *kāpsihk* ~

cannery N: (factory) jaigunchóng (M: gàan)

cannibal PH: ❶ sihkyàhnyuhk ge yàhn (M: go) ❷ sihk tùhng leuih ge yéhsau (M: jek)

cannon N: paau; daaihpaau (M: hám, jì)

cannonade FV: paaugwàng

cannot A: m̀ . . . dāk * **cannot blame him** PH: m̀ gwaai dāk kéuih * **cannot get it** RV: ló m̀ dóu * **cannot trust** RV: m̀ seun dāk gwo; seun m̀ gwo

canny SV: jèng

canoe N: duhkmuhkjàu (M: jek) VO: pàhduhkmuhkjàu

canon N: ❶ (church decree) gaaukwàt (M: tìuh) ❷ (principle) jéunjāk (M: go)

canonicals N: (of priests) faatyì (M: gihn) SV: gaaukwàige * **canonical books** N: gìngdín; gìngsyù (M: bún, bouh)

canopy N: pùhng (M: go)

cant N: ❶ (insincere talk) gáwah; gáwá (M: fàan) ❷ (jargon) seuhtyúh; yányúh; buihyúh (M: go, geui) FV: dájàk; fáanjàk * **thieves' cant** N: hākwá; hākyúh; ngamyúh (M: geui)

canteen N: ❶ faahntòhng; síumaaihbouh (M: gàan) ❷ (container) séuiwú (M: go)

canter N: làuhlohnghon (M: go) FV: maahnpáau

Canton N/PW: Gwóngjàu

Cantonese N: Gwóngjàuwá; Gwóngdùngwá; Yuhtyúh (M: geui)

canvas N: fàahnbou (M: jèung, faai) * **canvas cot** N: fàahnbou chòhng (M: jèung)

canvass VO: (for votes) làaipiu PH: ❶ chèuhngsai tóuleuhn ❷ (examine) chèuhngsai gímchàh

canyon N: haahpgūk (M: go)

cap N: ❶ (for the head) móu (M: déng) ❷ (for a bottle) koi; goi (M: go) VO: ❶ daaimóu ❷ kám (jèun) goi * **cap all** PH: lēkgwosaai; hóugwosaai * **cap the climax** Adj. PH: chiuchèut haahndouh, chèutfùhyiliuh jī'ngoih

capability N: nàhnglihk; chòihnàhng (M: júng)

capable SV: búnsih; yáuh búnsih

capacity N: ❶ yùhngleuhng ❷ (position) sànfán; jīkwaih (M: go) RV: (can hold) V dāklohk · *nīgo jèun jòng ~ yāt gùngsìng séui* * **in the capacity of** VO: yíh/yuhng . . . jì gaak/sànfán

cape N: ❶ (headland) gok, hóigok (M: go) ❷ (garment)

pèigìn; dáupùhng (M: gihn) *
The Cape of Good Hope N:
Hóu mohng gok

caper FV: tiu

capillary N: mòuhsaigún
(M: tìuh) SV: mòuhsaigúnjok
yuhngge

capital N: ❶ (city) sáudōu
(M: go) ❷ (alphabet) daaihsé;
daaihkáai (M: go) ❸ (money)
búnchìhn; jìbún (M: bāt) SV:
(excellent) méihmiuh *
capital offense N: séijeuih *
capital punishment N:
séiyìhng * **make capital of**
FV: leihyuhng

capitalism N: jìbúnjyúyih

capitalist N: jìbúngà (M: go)

Capitol N: Méihgwok gwokwúi daaihhah (M: joh)

capitulate VO: tàuhhòhng

capricious SV: fáanfūk

capsize FV: (boat) fáanjyun

capsule N: ❶ (of medicine)
gàaulòhng (M: go) ❷ (for a bottle) jēungoi (M: go) ❸ (receptacle for astronaut) taaihùng-
chōng (M: go) ❹ (dry seed-case)
haap (M: faai)

captain N: ❶ (of a ship)
syùhnjéung (M: go) ❷ (of a
team) deuihjéung (M: go) ❸
(Navy rank) seuhng gaau (M: go)
❹ (of a warship) laahmjéung (M:
go) ❺ (Army rank) seuhngwai
(M: go)

caption N: ❶ (short title)
bīutàih (M: go) ❷ (on a cinema
screen) jihmohk

captivation N: meihlihk;
muihlihk (M: júng)

captive N: fùlóuh (M: go) *
take captive FV: wuhtjūk;
gaamsàangjūk

captivity N: gàamgam;
fùlóuh; chūkbok

capture RV: jūkdóu; làaidóu
(people) FV: jimlíhng (place)

car N: ❶ (motor car) heichè
(M: ga) ❷ (tram car) dihnchè (M:
ga) ❸ (coach) fóchèkà; chèsēung (M: go) * **carport** N:
chèfòhng (M: go) * **car-park
(space)** N: chèwái (M: go)

carat M: kà

caravan N: ❶ (pilgrims)
chìuhsingjé (M: deuih) ❷ (of
persons making a journey) léuih
hàhngdéui (M: deuih) ❸ (of mer-
chants) sèungléuih (M: deuih)

carbon N: taan (M:gauh) *
carbon copy N: gwodái fubún
(M: jēung) * **carbon paper** N:
taanjí (M: jēung)

carbonite N: sìusyùn
gàmyàuh

carbonize FV: taanfa

carcass, carcase N: (of
animals) sìtái (M: go)

card N: kāt kātpín (M: jēung)
* **calling card** N: kātpín.
mìhngpín (M: jēung) * **invitation card** N: chéngtíp (M:
jēung) * **playing cards** N:
pēpáai (M: jēung) * **post card**
N: mìhngseunpín (M: jēung) *
record card N: jìlíu kāt;
géiluhkkāt (M: jēung) * **put
one's cards on the table** VO:
tàanpáai * **one's best cards**
N: wòhngpáai (M: jēung); jyuht-
jìu (M: jìu) * **have a card up
one's sleeve** PH: yáuh
gámlòhng miuhgai

cardboard N: ngaahng jí-báan (M: faai)

cardiac N: kèuhngsàmjài (M: fuhk) SV: sàmjohng ge

cardigan N: yèuhngmòuh-sāam; lāangsāam (M: gihn)

cardinal SV: jyúyiuge; gèibúnge N: ❶ hùhngyì jyúgaau; syùgèi jyúgaau (M: wái) ❷ (bright red) sínhùhngsīk

care FV: ❶ (feel interest) deui . . . gwàansàm ~ nígihnsih hóu ~ ❷ (be anxious) deui . . . joihfùh; dàamsàm ~ háausíh m ~ ❸ (love) ngoi; sek ❹ (look after) dáléih; jiugu; jiuliuh • bīngo bòng néih ~ saimānjái a? ❺ (pay attention) léih •kéuih m ~ ngóh góng mātyéh ✻ care about FV: gwàansàm; dàamsàm; léih ✻ care for FV: jùngyi; héifùn; séung ✻ have a care FV: bóujuhng; làuhsàm ✻ care of FV: chéng . . . jyúngàaubéi . . . ✻ take care SV: súisàm; làuhsàm ✻ take care of FV: jiugu; gwàanwàaih ✻ with care SV: síusàm; gánsahn

career N: ❶ (progress through life) gìnglihk; sàngngàaih ❷ (profession) jīkyihp (M: júng) ❸ (speed) chūkdouh (M: go) FV: fèichìh; fèipáau ✻ make a career PH: heung seuhng pàh

careerist N: yéhsàmgā (M: go)

careful SV: síusàm; jísai

careless SV: daaihyi; msíu-sàm

caress N/FV: ngoifú; yúngpóuh; sek; chànmáhn

caretaker N: hōn'gāang; gúnléihyùhn (M: go)

cargo N: fo; fomaht ✻ cargo boat N: fosyùhn (M: jek) ✻ cargo jet N: fogèi (M: jek, ga)

caricature N: maahnwá (M: fūk) VO: waahk maahnwá

caricaturist N: maahn-wágā (M: go)

carload SV: sèhngchège NuM-N: yātchè fomaht

carmine N: yèuhnghùhngsīk

carnage N: daaihtòuhsaat; chàahnsaat (M: chèuhng)

carnal SV: yuhktáige; sing-yuhkge ✻ carnal desire N: yuhkyuhk

carnation N: hòngnáaih-hìng (M: déu)

carnival N: gànìhnwàhwúi (M: go)

carnivorous SV: sihk-yuhkge

carol N: singdaangō (M: sáu)

carousal N: kwòhngfùnwúi (M: go)

carouse FV: kwòhngfùn

carp N: (fish) léihyú (M: tìuh) IE/FV: chèui-mòuh-kàuh-chì

carpenter N: daumuhklóu; daumuhksìfú (M: go)

carpentry N: daumuhk; muhkgùng

carpet N: deihjìn (M: jèung, faai)

carriage N: ❶ (vehicle pulled by horses) máhchè (M: ga) ❷ (of train) chèsèung (M: go) ❸ (cost of carrying goods) wahnfai (M: bāt) ✻ carriage way N:

chèlouh (M: tìuh) * **carriage paid** VO: béijó wahnfai

carrier N: ❶ (person) bùnwahn gùngyàhn (M: go) ❷ (support for luggage) hàhngléihgá (M: go) ❸ (person etc. that carries a disease) daaikwánjé (M: go) * **carrier pigeon** N: seungáap (M: jek) * **carrier rocket** N: wahnjoi fójin (M: jì)

carrot N: hùhng lòhbaahk; gàmséun (M: go)

carry FV: ❶ (in hand) nìng; nìk ❷ (in the arms) póuh ❸ (at two ends of a pole) dàam ❹ (on the back) mè, mèjyuh ❺ (in the pocket) doih; doihjyuh ❻ (on the head) díng; díngjyuh ❼ (on the palm) tokjyuh ❽ (on the shoulder) dàam (with a pole), tok, tòih ❾ (with both hands) búng; búngjyuh ❿ (bulky things with more than one person) tòih N: (range of a gun) sehchìhng * **carry away** FV: nìkjáu; nìngjáu; lójóheui * **be carried away** PH: béi . . . chùngfànjó tàuhnóuh, . . . lihng . . . sātheui léihji * **carry forward (of figures)** PH: jyún hah yāt yihp * **carry on** FV: gànjyuhjouh; gaijuhk * **carry out** FV: sahthàhng (a plan); léihhàhng (contract) * **carry over** FV: làuhdài

cart N: ❶ (pulled by horse) máhchè (M: ga). ❷ (pushed by people) sáutèuichē (M: ga) * **in the cart** Adj. PH: hái kwanging jìjùng * **put the cart before the horse** IE: bún muht dóu ji

cartel N: ❶ (combination of traders) tùhngyihp gùngwúi; tùhngyihp lyùhnmàhng (M: go) ❷ (letter of defiance) tiujinsyù (M: fahn) ❸ (written agreement for exchange of prisoners) gàauwuhn fùlóuh hipyíhsyù (M: fahn)

cartilage N: yúhngwāt (M: gauh)

carton N: jíháap; jípèihsèung (M: go)

cartoon N: ❶ (picture) maahnwá (M: fūk) ❷ (movie) kàtùngpín; duhngwá (M: tou) VO: waahkmaahnwá

cartridge N: ❶ (for blasting) jídáan (M: nāp) ❷ (head of a pick-up) cheungtáu (M: go) ❸ (film) fèilám (M: gyún) * **cartridge belt** N: jídáan dáai (M: tìuh) * **cartridge case** N: jí dáan hok (M: nāp, go) * **cartridge clip** N: jídáan gáap (M: go) * **cartridge pouch** N: dáanyeuhk háap (N: go)

carve FV: dìuhāk; hāk

cascade N: saige buhkbou (M: go; tìuh)

case N: ❶ (state of affairs) . chìhngyìhng (M: go) ❷ (medical) behnglaih (M: go) ❸ (legal) ngon; ngongín (M: gihn) ❹ (small box) háap; háapjái (M: go) ❺ (large box) sèung (M: go) ❻ (bag) dói (M: go) ❼ (covering) tou (M: go) · pèih ~ ❽ (cabinat) gwaih (M: go) * **in any case** Adv. PH: mòuhleuhndím; mòuhleuhn yùhhòh * **in case of** A: yùhgwó . . . (faatsàng) * **in the case of** A: yùhgwó; maahnyāt * **in the case of** A: deuiyù; yíh . . . làihgóng ~ nīgihnsih ~ * **in no case** A: yātdihng m̀ (hóyíh); yātdihng m̀ (hóu) * **lower case** N: síukáai; saisé (M: go) * **upper case** N: daaihkáai; daaihsé (M: go) * **case knife** N: chàandōu (M: bá) * **in that case** A: yùhgwó haih gám

cash N: yihnchín; yihngàm; yihnfún (M: bāt) FV: deuiyihn * **be short of cash, out of cash** VO: móuh yihngàm; móuhyihnchín * **cash desk** N: sàungánchyu; gwaihmín (M: go) * **cash in on** PH: kaau . . . jaahnchín; leihyuhng . . . * **cash on delivery** PH: fodou sàuchín * **cash register** N: sàungángèi (M: bouh, ga)

cashew N: yìugwó (M: nāp)

cashier N: sàungányùhn; chēutnaahpyùhn (M: go) VO: gaakjīk; chitjīk

cashmere N: kèsihmè

casing N: ❶ háap; tou; goi ❷ (of tire) ngoihtāai (M: go) ❸ (of sausages) chéungyī (M: faai)

casino N: dóuchèuhng; yùhlohkchèuhng (M: go, gàan)

cask N/M: túng; sêuitúng (M: go)

casket N: ❶ (for jewels) sáusīksèung (M: go) ❷ (for cremated ashes) gwātfùingāang; gwātfùijùng (M: go) ❸ (coffin) gùnchòih (M: fu, go)

casserole N: yáuhgoiwohk (M: go)

cassette N: háap (M: go) * **cassette tape** N: háapdáai; luhkyàmdáai (M: hahp, haahp) * **cassette tape recorder** N: háapdáai luhkyàmgēi (M: bouh, ga)

cassock N: ❶ (for priest) faatyī (M: gihn) ❷ (for buddhist monk or nun) gàsà (M: gihn)

cast FV: ❶ (throw) pàau; deng; diuh ❷ (form in a mould) jyu; jyujouh RV: (add) gàhéilàih PH: (give an actor a part in a play) paai . . . sīkyín . . . * **cast a ballot** VO: tàuhpiu * **cast the anchor** VO: pàau nàauh * **cast away** FV: dám; diuh * **cast about for** FV: wán; seiwàihmohng * **be cast down** SV: móuhsàmgèi * **cast off (a boat)** VO: gáailaahm * **cast off (in knitting)** VO: sàujàm * **cast on (in knitting)** VO: héijàm * **cast out** RV: dámchēutheui

caste N: gàaikāp (M: go)

castigate FV: bìndá; yìhmlaih jaakfaht

casting PH: jyu chēutlàih ge yéh (M: gihn) * **casting net** VO: saatmóhng

castle N: bóuléuih; sìhngbóu (M: go) * **castles in the air** IE/N: hùngjùng làuhgok

castor N: ❶ (wheel) lūkjái (M: go) ❷ (plant) bámàh ❸ (bottle) (yìhm, wùhjīufán, tòhng ge) jèunjái (M: go) * **castor bean** N: bámàhjí * **castor oil** N: seyàuh; bámàhyàuh

castrate FV: yìm; yìmgot

casual SV: ❶ (by chance) ngáuhyìhn; móuhyige ❷ (careless) m̀síusàm ❸ (informal) chēuihbín; kàuhkèih ❹ (irregular) làhmsìhge * **casual ward** N: làhmsìh sàuyùhngsó (M: gàan) * **casual wear** N: bihnjòng; bihnfuhk (M: tou)

casualty N: (persons killed) séisèung ge yàhn; sèungmòhng; séisèung

cat N: (animal) māau (M: jek) * **let the cat out of the bag** VO: sit lauh beimaht * **see which way the cat jumps** VO: gùnmohng yìhngsai * cats eyes N: màaungáahn sehk (M: nâp)

cataclysm N: ❶ (violent change) daaih binduhng (M: chèuhng) ❷ (flood) hùhngséui (M: chèuhng)

catacomb N: (deihdái ge) lìhng mouh (M: joh, go)

catafalque N: ❶ lìhngtòih (M: go) ❷ (vehicle) lìhngchè (M: ga)

catalogue N: muhkluhk (M: go) VO: pìnmuhk

catalyst N: chèuifajài (M: júng)

catamenia N: yuhtgìng

cataract N: ❶ (waterfall) daaihbuhkbou (M: go) ❷ (of eye) baahknoihjeung

catastrophe N: daaih-jòinaahn (M: chèuhng)

catch FV: ❶ (seize) jūk ❷ (intercept) làahnjiht ❸ (come upon sb. doing sth.) faatyihn; faatgok ❹ (get the meaning of) líhngwuih; mìhngbaahk ❺ (become infected with) yíhm; yíhmdóu; yáuh ~ behng RV: ❶ (snatch) jáaujyuh; jūkjyuh ❷ (be in time for) góndóu ~ fóchè ❸ (capture) jūkjyuh; jūkdóu N: ❶ (cunning device) gwáaigai (M: go) ❷ (of door) mùhnsēut (M: go) ✳ catch at FV/RV: jūkjyuh ✳ catch it PH: béi yàhn naauh ✳ catch on FV: ① léihgáai; líuhgáai; líhngwuih ② (become popular) làuhhàhng héiláih ✳ catch up FV: jèui; jèuiséuhng ✳ catch phrase N: miuhgeui (M: geui) ✳ catch word N: ① (of an article) biutàih (M: go) ② (slogan) bìuyúh; làuhhàhngyúh (M: geui) ✳ catch a ball VO:

jipbō; jipjyuh go bō ✳ catch a cold RV: láahngchàn FV: sèungfûng ✳ catch a disease VO: yáuhbehng; yíhmbehng

catching SV: ❶ (of disease) wúihchyùhnyíhm ge; yáuh chyùhnyíhmsing ge ❷ (of story) yáuhgámyíhmlihkge

catchy SV: ngāakyàhn ge; yáhnyàhn séuhngdong ge

catechism N: (about religion) gaauyih mahndaap gaaubún (M: bún, bouh)

categorical SV: jyuhtdeui; móuhtiuhgín ge

category N/M: leuih N: júngleuih; leuihyìhng; faahn-wàih (M: go)

caterer N: ❶ bàaufósihk ge yàhn (M: go) ❷ (of a canteen) faahntòhng lóuhbáan; faahn-tòhng sìhngbaahnsèung (M: go)

caterpillar N: mòuhchùhng (M: tiuh)

cathedral N: daaihgaau-tòhng (M: gàan)

catheter N: hàuh; douhgún (M: tiuh)

Catholic N: tìnjyúgaautòuh (M: go) SV: tìnjyúgaau (ge) ✳ catholic father N: sàhnfuh (M: wái, go)

cattle N: ngàuh (M: jek) ✳ cattle-man N: hòhngàuhjái (M: go) ✳ cattle-pen N: ngàuhlāan (M: go)

catty M: gàn

caucus N: kyutchaak wái-yùhnwúi; hahtsàm síujóu (M: go)

caught RV: jūkdóu

cauliflower FV: yèhchoifā (M: go, pò)

caulk FV: ❶ tihn; sāk ❷ (with sticky substance) mán

causal SV: yàngwó ge

causation N: yàngwó gwàanhaih

cause N: ❶ (reason) léihyàuh (M: go) ❷ (that produces an effect) yùhnyàn (M: go) ❸ (purpose) muhkbīu (M: go) FV: ❶ lihng, sáidou ❷ (induce) yáhnhéi * **cause of death** N: séiyàn (M: go) * **the immediate cause** N: gahnyàn (M: go) * **the underlying cause** N: yúhnyàn (M: go)

causeway N: tàih (M: tiuh)

caustic SV: ❶ (chemical) fuhsihksing ge ❷ (fig. — biting) hòhāk; hākbohk N: gōsihdīk

caution FV/N: (warning) gínggou (M: go) · faatchēut ~ * **for caution's sake** Adv. PH: waihjó gánsahn héigin

cautious SV: síusàm; gánsahn

cavalier N: (horseman) kèhsih; móuhsih (M: go, wái)

cavalry N: keibìng; kèhbìng; máhdéui; máhbìng (M: deuih)

cave N: sàanlūng (M: go) * **cave in** FV: ① bàng, lam ② (of person etc.) wātfuhk · heung . . . ~ * **the road caved in** N: deihhaahm * **cave-man** PH: jyuh hái sàanlūng ge yàhn; yuhtgèui ge yàhn (M: go)

cavern N: daaihsàanlùng (M: go)

caviar(e) N: yùhjíjeung (M: jèun) * **caviar(e) to the general** IE: (SV) kŭk-gòu-wohgwá; (N) yèuhng-chèunbaahk-syut

cavity N: ❶ lùng (M: go) · deih ~ · ngàh ~ ❷ (of body) hòng (M: go) · beih ~ · háu ~

caw N: wù'ngā giu sèng (M: bá) FV: wùngā giu

cease FV: tìhngjí * **cease fire** N/VO: tìhngfó

ceaseless A: m̀tìhng gám

cedar N: chaam; chaamsyuh (M: pò)

cede FV: ❶ gotyeuhng (land) ❷yeuhng; yeuhngchēut

ceiling N: tìnfābáan (M: go)

celebrate FV: ❶ hingjūk · ~ sàangyaht ❷ jaanyèuhng; gōjuhng ~ gódī waihgwokgà chēut lihk ge yìnghùhng * **celebrate a festival** VO: jouhjit

celebrated SV: chēutméng Patt: yíh . . . chēutméng

celebration N: hingjūkwúi (M: go)

celebrity N: mìhngyàhn PH: chēutméng ge yàhn (M: wái, go)

celery N: kàhnchoi (M: pò)

celestial SV: ❶ tìnge ❷ tìntái ge · yaht, yuht, sìngsàhn haih ~ yìhnjeuhng ❸ sàhnsing ge (see BF) BF: tìn- ~ gwok

celibate SV: duhksàn ge

cell N: ❶ (of prison) gàamfòhng; mahtsāt (M: go) ❷ (compartment in a larger structure) gèichàhng jóujīk (M: go) ❸ (of

a battery) dihnchìh (M: go) ❹
(of living matter) saibāau (M: go)
❺ (of a net) móhngngáahn (M:
go) ❻ (small box) háap (M: go)

cellar N: deihlòuh (M: go)

cellist N: daaihtàihkàhm sáu
(M: go, wái)

cello N: daaihtàihkàhm (M:
go)

cellophane N: bōlēijí (M:
jèung)

Celsius N: Sipsih ~ Nu
douh

cement N: séuinàih; hùhngmòuhnàih

cemetery N: fàhnchèuhng
(M: go)

cenotaph N: géinihmbèi (M:
go)

cense VO: sìuhèung

censer N: hèunglòuh (M: go)

censor FV: sámchàh; gímchàh N: sámchàhgùn; gím-
chàhyùhn (M: go)

censorious SV/IE: chèui-
mòuh-kàuh-chī

censure FV: hínjaak; jaakbeih

census N: yàhnháu diuhchàh; yàhnháu póuchàh (M: chi)

cent N: sìn (M: go) ✻ not
care a cent AV: m̀joihfùh ~
kéuih jouh mātyéh ✻ Nu per
cent Nu: baak fahn jī Nu

centaur N: bun yàhn máh
joh (N: go)

centenary N: baak jàunìhn
géinihm; yātbaak jàunìhn

center = centre

centigrade SV: sipsih(ge)

centigram(me) M: lèihhāk

centiliter M: lèihsìng

centimetre M: lèihmáih;
gùngfàn

centipede N: baakjūk (M:
tìuh)

central SV: jùnggàan(ge);
jùngyèung(ge) N: ❶ (telephone)
dihnwá júnggèi (M: go) ❷
(district in Hong Kong)
jùngwàahn; jùng kèui

centralism N: jùngyèung
jaahpkyùhn jai (M: júng, go)

centrality N: heungsàm-
sing

centralize FV: jaahpjùng

centre N: ❶ jùnggàan;
jùngsàm (M: go) · m̀hóu kéihhái
tìuh louh ~ ❷ (of football game)
jùngfùng (M: go) ❸ (place)
jùngsàm · sèungyihp ~ ❹ (in
politics etc.) jùnggàanpaai (M:
go) ✻ **centre of gravity** N:
juhngsàm (M: go)

centrifugal SV: lèihsàm
(ge) N: lèihsàmlihk

centripetal SV: heungsàm
(ge)

century N: saigéi (M: go) ✻
the 20th century N: yihsahp
saigéi

ceramic N: jaitòuh ngaihseuht; tòuhngaih SV: tòuhhei
(ge)

cereal SV: gūkleuih(ge) N:
gūkmaht

cerebellum N: síunóuh (M:
go)

cerebral SV: daaihnóuhge

cerebrum N: daaihnóuh (M: go)

ceremonial SV: jingsīk N: dínláih; yìhsīk (M: go) * **ceremonial dress** N: láihfuhk (M: tou, tyut)

ceremonious SV: lùhng-juhng ~ *ge yìhsīk*

ceremony N: dínláih; yìhsīk BF: -láih * **ceremony of baptism** N: sáiláih * **ceremony of burial** N: jongláih * **ceremony of ship launching** N: hahséuiláih * **stand on ceremony** SV: haakhei

certain SV: ❶ (sure) yāt-dihng(ge), hángdihng(ge) ❷ (not named) máuh ~ *yàhn* ~ *gihnsih* * **for certain** A: hángdihng * **make certain** FV: gáau chìngchó

certainly A: ❶ (without doubt) yātdihng (FV/VO) ~ *wúihsìhnggùng* ~ *dádihnwá béi néih* ❷ (really) jànhaih (SV/Adj. PH) · *ngóh* ~ *m̀jì nīgihnsih* · *kéuih* ~ *leng*

certificate N: jingsyù; jāp-jiu (M: jèung)

certify FV: jingmìhng

certitude N: bītyìhnsing

cervix N: jígùnggéng (M: go)

cessation N: tìhngjí

cesspit, cesspool N: wù-séuihàang; fanhàang; síhàang (M: tiuh, go)

chafe FV: ❶ (to get warmth) chaatnyúhn; chaatyiht ❷ (sore) chaattung; chaatsyún ❸ (make angry) gīknàu ❹ (be angry) faat-nàu; faatfó

chaff N: (of grain) gūkhòng; gūkhok VO: hòi wàahnsiu · . . . *tùhng* . . . ~

chafing dish N: fówò (M: go)

chain N: lín (M: tiuh) · *tit ~* · *géng ~* M: chyun SV/NuM: yātlìhnchyun · *nīgéi yaht ~ faatsàng ge sih* * **chain reaction** N: lìhnsó fáanying * **chain store** N: lyùhnhouh (ge poutáu) * **chain cable** N: nàauhlín

chair N: ❶ yí (M: jèung) ❷ (professor) gaausauh jīkwaih (M: go) ❸ (in meeting) jyújihk; góngjoh (M: go) * **in the chair** VO: jouh/dáamyahm jyújihk * **take the chair** VO: jyúchìh wuihyíh * **chair rail** N: (gin-jùk deihpùhn ge) wàihbáan (M: douh)

chairman N: jyújihk; wuih-jéung; yíhjéung (M: wái, go)

chalk N: fánbāt (M: ji) * **by a long chalk** Adv. PH: hóu dāk (chàdāk) hóu gányiu * **chalk out** FV: gaiwaahk; chitgai * **chalk up** VO: héiga RV: geidāi

challenge FV: ❶ tiujin · *jip-sauh* ~ · *heung . . . ~* ❷ (order) háulihng (M: go)

challenging Adj. PH: fu tiujinsing ge

chamber N: ❶ (room) fóng; sāt (M: go) ❷ (group of organized persons) wúi · *sèung* ~ · *yíh* ~ ❸ (of a gun) chèungtòhng; dáantòhng (M: go)

chameleon N: binsīklùhng (M: tiuh) PH: (fig.) fáanfūk mòuhsèuhng ge yàhn (M: go)

champagne N: hèungbān (jáu) (M: ji)

champion N: ❶ gungwàn (M: go) ❷ (person who supports another) yúngwuhjé; jīchìhjé; yúngdán (M: go)

championship N: gámbiuchoi (M: chèuhng)

chance N: gèiwuih (M: chi, go) FV: johnghâh; sihâh VO: pungwahnhei ✳ **by any chance** A: maahnyāt ✳ **by chance** A: ngáuhyìhn; yi ngoih gám ✳ **take a chance** FV· mouhhím; tàuhgèi ✳ **take one's chance** VO: pungwahnhei

chancellor N: ❶ (of a university) daaihhohk haauhjéung (M: wái, go) ❷ (chief minister of state) .sáuseung; júngléih (M: wái, go) ❸ (law officials) daaihsàhn; daaihfaatgùn

chancery N: (court of equity) pìhnghàhng faatyún (M: gàan); faattìhng (M: go, gàan)

chancre N: (medical) hahgàm

change FV: ❶ (alter, correct) gói ~ waaih jaahpgwaan ❷ (put in place of another) wuhn ~ sàam; ~ chín ❸ (means of transportation) jyun · deihtit heui m̀dóu sàngaai, yiu ~ fóchè ❹ (become different) bin · yihgā tìnhei ~ dākhóu láahng N: ❶ góibin; binfa · jiutàuhjóu tùhng yehmáahn ge tìnhei yáuh hóu daaih ge ~ ❷ (money in small units) seuingán (for coins); seuijí (for notes) ❸ (money that is the difference between the price and the amount offered in payment) jáaufàan/juhkfàan ge chín ✳ **change into** RV: binsèhng ✳ **change hands** VO: jyunsáu ✳ **change over** FV: diuhwuhn (waihji)

channel N: ❶ (stretch of water) hói haahp (M: go) ❷ (bed of stream) hòhchòhng (M: go) ❸ (waterway) hòhngdouh (M: tiuh) ❹ (of radio and television) pàhndouh; bōdyuhn (M: go) ❺ (fig.) tòuhging (M: tiuh) · yàuh nī tiuh ~ dākdóu hóudò siusīk FV: yáhndouh VO: hòikèuihdouh

chant N: jaanméihsī; singgō (M: sáu) FV: cheung; nihm ✳ **chant a liturgy** VO: nihmgīng ✳ **chant poetry** VO: yàhmsī

chaos N: wahnlyuhn johngtaai SV: wahnlyuhn

chaotic SV: lyuhnjòujòu PH: lyuhn chāt baat jòu; yāt taap wùhtòuh

chap N: ❶ (person) (coll.) yáujái; yáu (M: tiuh) ❷ (of animal) hahpàh (M: go) FV: (of skin) baauchaak

chapel N: láihbaaitòhng; gaautòhngjái (M: gàan, go)

chaperon N: néuihbuhn; buhnnéung FV: pùih

chaplain N: muhksī (M: wái, go)

chapter N/M: jèung; pìn; wùih ✳ **chapter and verse** PH: jìngkok yàhnjing N: koksaht ge chēutchyu (M: go)

char FV: sìusìhngtaan RV: sìunùng

character N: ❶ (mental or moral nature) singgaak; singchìhng ❷ (moral strength) bán'gaak ❸ (qualities which make a thing etc. different from others) dahkjāt; dahksing; dahkdím ❹ (well known person) mìhnglàuh; chēutméng ge yàhn ❺ (of novel, play etc.)

yàhnmaht; goksīk ❻ reputation) mihngyuh; sìngmohng ❼ (written symbol) jih • *Jùnggwok ~ ＊ in (out of) character* SV: (m̀) sīkhahp; (m̀) fùhhahp ＊ in the character of . . . FV: baahnyín

characteristic N: dahkjìng (M: go, júng)

charade N: gújih yàuhhei; jihmàih yàuhhei (M: go)

charcoal N: taan (M: gauh)

charge FV: ❶ (accuse) gou; hunggou ❷ (attack) jaahpgīk; gùnggīk ❸ (ask in payment) gai; yiu • *Nī dī yéh ~ géidōchín a?* ❹ (load) sēuhng; jòng (jídáan) ❺ (command) mihnglihng; jísih (M; go) VO: ❶ (make record of a debt) yahpsou; yahpjeung • *Nī chàanfaahn ~ ngóh ~* ❷ (of battery) chùngdihn ＊ **free of charge** SV: míhnfai(ge) ＊ **in charge** FV: fuhjaak; jyúgún ＊ **take charge of** FV: dàamyahm

chariot N: màhchè; jinchè (M: ga)

charitable SV: chìhsihnge

charity SV/N: (kindness) chìhbēi; bokngoi N: ❶ (organization) chìhsihn tyùhntái (M: go) chìhsihn gèigwàan (M: go) ❷ (philanthropy) chìhsihn sihyihp

charlatan N: wòhngluhk yīsāng (M: go) ATT: móuh pàaih(ge) ~ *yīsāng*

charm N: ❶ (attractivenss) meihlihk; mòlihk ❷ (words) jau; jauyúh (M: geui) ❸ (symbol) fùh (M: douh) FV: (attract) kāpyáhn VO: sī faatseuht; wahnyuhng mōfaat

charmer N: mōseuhtsī (M:

go)

charming SV: gìumeih; màihyàhn PH: lihngyàhn jeuhkmàih ~ *ge néuihjái*

chart N: ❶ (diagrams, curves etc.) tòuhbíu (M: go, jèung) ❷ (sea map) hòhnghói tòuh (M: fūk) VO: jaitòuh; jai tòuh bíu

charter N: dahkhéuijohng (M: jèung) FV: (hire) bāau; jòu ＊ **charter flight** N: bāaugèi (M: bāan) ＊ **chartered accountant** N: dahkhéui wuihgaisī (M: wái, go)

chase FV: jèui ＊ **give chase to** FV: jèuigón; jèuigīk ＊ **in chase of** FV: jèuijuhk ＊ **chase out** RV: gónchēutheui

chasm N: ❶ (crack) lihthàhn (M: tiuh) ❷ (fig.) lihthàhn'; fànkèih • *m̀tùhng ge yigin lihngdou gó léuhng go jingdóng jìgàan cháansàng ~*

chassis N: ❶ (of car) dáipún (M: go) ❷ (of aeroplane) fèigèigá (M: go) ❸ (of radio) dáigá (M. go)

chaste SV: ❶ jìnggit; sèuhngit ❷ (of style, taste) sèuhnpok

chastity N: jìngchòu

chastise FV: chìhngfaht; chìhnggaai

chat VO: kìnggái

chatter A/FV: ❶ (of a person) lōsō ❷ (of birds and children) jìjì jà jà N: ❶ (of person's teeth) kàhpkáp sèng • *dungdou ~ dá láahngjan* ❷ (of typewriter) dàahtdáat sèng

chatty Adj. PH: jùngyi kìnggái ge

chauffeur N: (automobile)

sīgēi (M: go)

chauvinism N: sàmàhn jyúyih; pàaihtà jyúyih * **male chauvinism** N: daaih nàahmyán jyúyih

cheap SV: pèhng; sèungyìh * **cheaper** SV: pèhngdī * **feel cheap** PH: gokdāk m̀syùfuhk; m̀hóu yisi; móuhmín * **make oneself cheap** VO: bíndài jihgéi

cheat FV: ❶ ngāak; hèipin VO: ❶ jokbaih ❷ (in an examination) jokbaih; (coll.) chēutmāau * **be cheated** VO: séuhngdong • séung jó kéuih dong PH: béi . . . ngāakjó

check FV: ❶ (examine) chàh; hahtdeui; chēk ❷ dím (a number) ~ háh dī chín ❸ (hold back) jaijí; jójí ❹ (restrain) hungjai; yeukchūk VO: ❶ (in chess game) jèunggwàn ❷ (in encirclement chess) giu sihk N: ❶ jì piu; chēk (M: jèung) ❷ (bill) jeungdāan; sàugeui (M: jèung) ❸ (bit of paper, wood or metal etc.) páai; hàhngléihpáai; pàaihjái (M: go) ❹ (the symbol ✓) tīk * **check in** FV: dànggei VO: baahn dànggei sáujuhk * **check out** VO: gitjeung; gitsou * **check list** N: chìngdāan (M: jèung) * **check up** N: gímchàh; hahtdeui N/VO: (physical) gímchàh sàntái * **check-book** N: jìpiubóu (M: bún) * **check-room** N: hàhngléih geichyùhn chyu; yìmóugàan (M: go) * **checkpoint** N: gímchàhjaahm (M: go) * **check-taker** PH: sàufèi ge yàhn

checker N: ❶ (person) gímchàhyùhn (M: go) ❷ (machine) chāaksigēi (M: ga)

cheek N: mihn (M: faai); mihnjyùdān (M: go) * **tongue in cheek** Adj. PH/IE: háu-sihsàm-fēi * **cheek-bone** N: kyùhngwāt (M: gauh)

cheer N: ❶ (gladness) héiyuht ❷ (shout of joy) fùnfù (M: jahn) PH: (food and drink) méih jáu gàai ngàauh FV: gúmóuh; fùnfù; hotchói * **cheer sb. on** SV: gīklaih; gúlaih * **cheer up** RV: gòuhing héilàih

cheerful SV: gòuhing; faailohk; yùhfaai

cheerless SV: yàmwāt ~ ge tìnhei

cheese N: jìsí (M: gauh)

chef N: daaihchyú; chyùhsī (M: go)

chemical SV: fahohk(ge) * **chemicals** N: fahohkbán

chemistry N: fahohk

chemist N: fahohkgā; yeuhkjàisī (M: wái, go)

cheque N: ❶ jìpiu (M: jèung) ❷ (pattern) gaakjái

cherish FV: ngoiwuh; fúyuhk VO: póuhjyuh hèimohng

cherry N: yìngtòuh (M: nāp) yìngtòuhsyuh (M: pò) SV: sìnhùhng ge * **cherry blossom** N: yìngfā (M: déu, dó) * **cherry-stone** N: yìngtòuhwaht (M: nāp)

cherub N: síutīnsí (M: go)

chess N: kéi (M: pùhn, pou) • jūk yāt pùhn ~ * **chess board** N: kèihpún (M: go) * **chess book** N: kèihpóu; kèihsyù (M: bún) * **chess man** N: kèihjí (M: jek) * **play chess** VO: jūkkéi

chest N: ❶ (box) sèung; háp; gwaih; lúhng (M: go) ❷ (breast) hùngbouh; sàmháu (M: go)

chestnut N: leuhtjí (M: nāp) SV: gafēsīk (ge); leuhtjísīk (ge)

chew FV: ❶ jiuh ❷ (consider) nám * **chewing-gum** N: hèungháugàau (M: gauh) * **chew the rag** VO: faat nòuhsòu/faat lòuhsōu

chicanery N: gwáigai; sáudyuhn (M: go)

chick N: ❶ gàijái (M: jek) ❷ (bird) jeukjái; chòníuh (M: jek) ❸ (small child) saimānjái

chicken N: gài; gàijái (M: jek) * **chicken broth** N: gài tòng (M: wún) * **chicken coop** N: gàilùhng (M: go) * **chicken feed** PH: gàiseui gamdō chín * **chicken-hearted** SV: móuhdáam; saidáam * **chicken pox** N: séuidáu • *chēut ~*

chide FV: gwaaijaak

chief N: (person) sáulíhng; a-táu (M: go) BF: − jéung SV: ❶ (principal) jyúyiu ge ❷ (first in rank) jeui gòukāp ge * **in chief** SV: jyúyiu ge ATT: júng - ~ *gùngchìhngsī* * **chief of staff** N: chàammàuhjéung (M: wái, go) * **chief executive** N: yùhnsáu; sáujéung (M: go) * **chief justice** N: daaih faatgún (M: wái, go) * **chief of a tribe** N: yàuhjéung (M: go) * **commander-in-chief** N: júng sī lihng

child N: ❶ saimānjái; sailóugó (M: go) ❷ (female) néuihjái; sailouhnéuih (M: go) * **with child** VO: wàaihyahn; yáuhjó bìhbī FV: yáuhjó * **child bearing** VO: sàang

saimānjái; sàang bìhbī

childhood N: tùhngnìhn sìhdoih; tùhngnìhn

childish SV: yaujih

childlike SV: tìnjàn; tìnjàn mòuhchèh

children N: (dī) saimānjái

Chilean, Chilian N: Ji-leihyàhn (M: go) SV: Jileih(ge)

chill N: (feeling of coldness) hòhnyi (M: jahn) VO: (shivering) faatláahng; dá láahng jan * **have a chill** VO: faatláahng; dá láahngjan

chilli N: (gòn) laahtjiu (M: jek)

chilly SV: ❶ hòhnláahng ❷ (fig.) láahngdaahm ~ *ge taaidouh*

chime NuM-N: yāttoujùng; yātjóujùng VO: dájùng * **chime in** VO: chaapjéui

chimes N: jùngsēng

chimney N: ❶ yìntùng (M: go, jì) ❷ (of oil lamp) dàngjaau; dàngtúng (M: go)

chimpanzee N: hāk sìng-sìng (M: jek)

chin N: hahpàh (M: go)

China N: ❶ Jùnggwok ❷ (articles) chìhhei * **China proper** N: Jùnggwok búntóu * **China town** N: Tòhngyàhn gāai (M: go)

chincough N: baakyahtkāt

Chinese N: ❶ Jùnggwok yàhn (M: go) ❷ Jùngmàhn SV: Jùnggwok ge * **Chinese characters** N: Jùnggwokjih;

Honjih (M: go) ✻ **overseas Chinese** N: wàhkìuh (M: go) ✻ **Chinese spoken language** N: Jùnggwok wá ✻ **Chinese cabbage** N: wòhngngàhbaahk (M: pò) ✻ **Chinese costume** N: tòhngjòng (M: tou, tyut)

chip N: ❶ (small piece broken off) seuipín (M: faai) ❷ (thin slice) pín ❸ (broken place as in a cup etc.) bàngháu ❹ (of games) chàuhmáh (M: go) VO: chitpín RV: jíngbàng FV: (shape) dahp; johk ✻ **chip off** RV: seukchēutlàih ✻ **dry as a chip** SV: fùchou

chirp, chirrup N: jìjìsèng

chisel N: jók; johk (M: go) FV: johk

chitchat VO: kìnggái

chivalry N: ❶ kèhsih; hòuhhaahp; móuhsih ❷ (qualities) móuhsih jìng sàhn

chlorine N: luhkhei

chloroform N: màhjeuijài; màhjeuiyeuhk; gōlòhfòng

chlorophyl(l) N: yihpluhksou

chock N: muhkjám; muhkjin (M: gauh)

chocolate N: jyùgūlīk (M: gauh)

choice N: syúnjaahk SV: jìngsyúnge ✻ **a great choice** N. PH: yáuh hóudō m̀tùhng ge syúnjaahk ✻ **at choice** PH: chèuihbín gáan ✻ **by choice** SV: jihsyún ge ✻ **make a choice** FV: gáan; tiusyún

choir, quire N: (of a church) singsībāan; sìgōbāan

choke FV: jahtsīk; juhk RV: (of breathing) juhkchàn N: (of car) chūk; jófùngmùhn (M: go) ✻ **choke off** VO: (fig.) put láahngséui · *kéuih ge pàhngyáuh heung kéuih ~ , lihng kéuih móuh hingcheui jouh gógihnsih* ✻ **choke up** RV: sākjyuh; sākmúhn

cholera N: foklyuhn

cholesterol N: dáamgusèuhn

choose FV: gáan; syúnjaahk ✻ **as you choose** PH: chèuihbín néih ✻ **cannot choose but** A: wàihyáuh; jíyáuh

choos(e)y SV: tiutīk; gáanjaahk

chop FV: ❶ (with an axe) pek ❷ (with a chopper) jáam ❸ (cut into small bits) deuk N: ❶ (seal) yan, tòuhjèung (M: go) ❷ (trade mark) pàaihjí; sèungbìu (M: go, jek) ❸ (meat) pàaihgwát (M: gauh) VO: dáyan, dámyan; kāptòuhjèung

chopper N: ❶ (for chopping meat) choidòu (M: bá) ❷ (for chopping wood) fútáu (M: bá)

chopping board N: jàmbáan (M: faai, go)

chopsticks N: faaijí (M: pair-deui, sèung; single-jek)

chop suey N: jaahpseui; jaahpgám VO/N: cháau jaahp gám

chord N: yìhn; yìhnsin (M: tìuh)

chore N: jaahpmouh; yahtsèuhng sósih

choreograph PH: móuhdouh chitgai

chorus N: hahpcheung tyùhn (M: deuih, go) ✴ **sing in chorus** FV: hahpcheung

Christ N: Gēidūk

christen VO: ❶ (baptize) sì sáiláih ❷ (give a name) mìhngmìhng; gói méng

Christian N: Gēidūktòuh (M: go) SV: Gēidūkgaau ge

Christianity N: Gēidūk-gaau

Christmas N: singdaanjit (M go) ✴ **Christmas box** N: singdaan láihmaht; singdaan-jit séungchín (M: fahn) ✴ **Christmas card** N: sing-daankāt (M: jèung) ✴ **Christmas eve** TW/N: sing-daan chìhnjihk (M: go) ✴ **Christmas tree** N: singdaan-syuh (M: pò) ✴ **Merry Christmas** PH: singdaan faailohk

chronic SV: ❶ (of disease) maahnsing(ge) ❷ (condition) chèuhngkèih ge

chronicle N: pìnnìhnsí (M: bún)

chronological SV: ngon nìhndoih seuhnjeuih

chronology N: ❶ (list) nìhnbíu (M: go) ❷ (science) nìhndoihhohk

chronometer N: jīngmaht gaisìhhei; tìnmàhnjùng; hòhnghóibíu (M: go)

chrysanthemum N: gūkfā (M: a flower — déu, dó; a plant — pò; a pot — pùhn)

chubby SV: fèihdyūtdyūt • *saimānjái ge mihnjái ~*

chuck FV: ❶ (throw) dám, diuh ❷ (abandon) fonghei ❸ (touch) mó VO: (dismiss) cháau yàuhyú PH: (móuhgài) gōkgōkgiu ✴ **chuck up** FV: fonghei

chuckle FV: mēimēijéuisiu

chum N: hóupàhngyáuh; tùhngfóng (M: go)

chump N: ❶ (wood) muhktàuh (M: gauh) ❷ (food) (coll.) bahndáan; chéunchòih (M: go)

chunk NuM: yātdaaihgauh

church N: ❶ (building) gaautòhng; láihbaaitòhng singtóng (M: gàan) ❷ (congregation) gaauwúi (M: go) ❸ (service) láihbaai • *jouh ~*

churn FV: gáaubuhn; gáau N: gáaubuhn gēi; gáaunáaihhei (M: ga)

cicada N: sìhm (M: jek)

cicatrice N: nā (M: daat)

cider N: pìhnggwójāp (M: bùi, jèun)

cigar N: syutgā; léuihsungyīn (M: jì, háu)

cigarette N: yìnjái (M: háu, jì) ✴ **cigarette butt** N: yìntáu (M: go, nāp)

cinch PH: sahp nàh gáu wán ge sih (M: gihn)

cinder N: mùihsí; mùihjà (M: dèui)

cinema N: heiyún; dihn-yíngyún (M: gàan)

cinematograph N: dihn-yíng sipyíng (fongyíng) gèi (M: ga, bouh)

cineprojector N: fongyíng-gēi (M: ga, bouh)

cinerama N: fut ngàhn-mohk dihnyíng (M: bouh)

cinerator N: ❶ (corpse) sìtái (M: go) ❷ (laahpsaap) fàhnfalòuh (M: go)

cinnabar N: jyùsà SV: jyùhùhng sīk ge

cinnamon N: yuhkgwai

cipher, cypher N: ❶ (zero) lìhng ❷ (secret writing) mahtmáh (M: go) ❸ (person) síu yàhn maht (M: go) ❹ (things) m̀dángsái ge yéh FV: gai VO: yihk mahtmáh

circle N: ❶ (ring) yùhnhyūn (M: go) ❷ (round shape) yùhnyìhng (M: go) ❸ (the curved line like a ring) yùhnjàu (M: go) BF: (persons having the same interests) -gaai • *gaauyuhk* ~ FV: pùhnsyùhn * **a large circle** M: daaihpài * **in a circle** PH: wàih sèhng yāt go yùhnhyūn

circuit N: ❶ (journey) chèuhnhàhng (M: chi) ❷ (electrical) dihnlouh (M: tiuh, go)

circuitous SV: gaanjipge; yùwùihge

circular SV: ❶ (round) yùhnyìhng(ge) ❷ (tour) chèuhn-wàahn(ge) N: ❶ (formal letter) tùngjìsyù; tùngjìseun (M: fùng) ❷ (advertisement) chyùhndàan (M: jèung) ❸ (announcement) tùnggou (M: jèung)

circulate FV: ❶ (go round continuously) chèuhnwàahn ❷ (spread out) chyùhnbo ❸ (move freely) làuhtùng • *fàahnwìhng sìhkèih, dìchín* ~ *dāk faai* ❹ faathòhng (publications)

circulation N: chèuhn-wàahn (M: go) * **in circulation** PH: làuhtùnggán

circumcise VO: gotbàau-pèih

circumcision N: gotláih

circumference N: yùhnjàu (M: go) jàugaai

circumnavigate PH: wàahnkàuh hòhnghàhng

circumscribe PH: háijàuwàih waahk yāt tiuh sin bìuchēut . . . ge faahnwàih (gaaihaahn) FV: (restrict) haahnjai

circumspect SV: jàu-chèuhng; sahnjuhng

circumstance N: ❶ chìhngfong; wàahngíng; chìhngyìhng ❷ (state of affairs) yìhngsai * **under all circumstances** Adv. PH: mòuhleuhn yùhhòh (mòuh-leuhndím) dōu . . . * **under no circumstances** Adv. PH: mòuhleuhn dím dōu m̀ . . .

circumstantial SV: ❶ (of description) chèuhngjeuhn ❷ (of evidence) ngáuhyìhn

circus N: ❶ (company) máhheiyùhn (M: go) ❷ (show) máhhei (M: chèuhng, chēut)

cistern N: chyúhséuichìh; séuichòuh (M: go)

citadel N: ❶ (sìhngbóu (M: go) ❷ (fig.) beihnaahnsó (M: go)

citation N: ❶ (statement) yáhnmàhn; yáhnjing (M: dyuhn) ❷ (for a brave act) jéungjohng (M: jèung) ❸ (in law) chyùhnpiu (M: jèung)

cite FV: ❶ (quote) yáhnjing; yáhnyuhng; yáhnseuht ❷ (in law) chyúhnseun ❸ (for a brave act) bòuyèuhng; bòujéung

citizen N: gùngmàhn; síhmàhn (M: go)

citizenship N: gwokjihk; gùngmàhn jìgaak (M: go)

citric SV: nìhngmūngsing(ge) * citric acid N: nìhngmūngsyùn

citrus N: gāmgwāt; gàmgāt (M: go)

city N: ❶ (a walled city) sèhng; sìhng (M: go) ❷ (municipality) síh (M: go) ❸ (in contrast with rural area) sìhngsíh; síhkèui (M: go)

civic SV: sìhngsíhge; síhmàhnge; gùngmàhnge

civics N: síhjinghohk; gùngmàhnhohk

civil SV: gùngmàhn (ge) * civil engineering N: tóumuhk gùngchìhng hohk * civil law N: màhnfaat (M: tiùh) * civil rights N: gùngmàhnkyùhn * civil servant N: gùngmouhyùhn (M: go) * civil war N: noihjin (M: chèuhng)

civilian N: pìhngmàhn (M: go)

civilization N: màhnmìhng

civilized SV: màhnmìhng ge

clad RV: pòumúhn

claim FV: ❶ (demand) yiukàuh ❷ (assert) sìngyìhn; singchìng; gùnghòi wah • kéuih ~ yáuh seunsàm yèhng nīchèuhng béichoi ❸ (deserve) jihk, jihkdāk ~ jyuyi ❹ (make a claim) yìhngléhng • nī

dī sātmaht móuhyàhn ~ * claim to be PH: jihgéi wah haih . . . * lay claim to FV: jyújeung, yiukàuh

claimant PH: tàihchēut yiukàuh ge yàhn (M: go)

clairvoyance N: ❶ (power of seeing at a distance) chìnléih ngáahn ❷ (exceptional insight) duhngchaatlihk

clam N: hín; póhng (M: jek)

clamber FV: pàhsèuhng

clamo(u)r FV: daaihsèng giu

clamorous Adj. PH: chòuhhyūn bàbai

clamp N: kím (M: bá, go); gáap; gíp (M: go) RV: gihpgán; gaahpgán

clan N: ❶ gàjuhk; sìhjuhk; jùngjuhk (M: go) ❷ (bloc) jaahptyùhn (M: go) * clan's association N: jùngchànwúi

clandestine SV: beimaht A: ngamjùng

clap VO: (applaud) paakjéung; paaksáu FV: (hèhnghēng) paak N: ❶ jéungsèng (M: jahn) ❷ (loud noise) pihkpihk paahk paahk; pàahkpáaksèng * clap eyes on RV: gindóu; táidóu

claptrap N: cheuktàuh (M: go) • chēut ~

clarify FV: chìhngchìng

clarinet N: syuhdék (M: jì)

clarity N: sèuhndouh; taumìhngdouh

clash FV: johng N: ❶ (conflict) chùngdaht • yigin yáuh ~ • sìhgaan seuhng yáuh ~ ❷ (sound) johnggīksèng

clasp RV: ❶ (hold tightly) póuhgán; jàgán ❷ (fasten) kaujyuh; ngàujyuh N: kau (M: go) * **clasp knife** N: jipdōu (M: bá)

class M: ❶ (sort, kind) leuih; tíng ❷ (grade) dáng • *tàuh ~* • *yih ~* ❸ (studying group) bàan ❹ (teaching period) tòhng N: (ranks in society) gāaikāp (M: go) * **class-mate** N: (tùhngbàan) tùhnghohk (M: go) * **classroom** N: fosāt; gaausāt; bàanfóng (M: go)

classic SV: gúdín

classical SV: gúdín(ge)

classics N: gúdín màhnhohk

classification N: fànleuih; leuihbiht (M: júng)

classified SV: ❶ fànleuih (ge) ❷ (officially secret) gèimaht(ge)

classify VO: fànleuih

clatter N: ❶ (of machine etc) kihkkihk kaahk kaahk sèng ❷ (of talk) gígí gwāgwā; jìjìjàjà

clause N: ❶ (of a treaty) tiuhfún (M: tiuh) ❷ (in grammar) fàngeui (M: go, geui)

claw N: jáau (M: jek) RV: jūkjyuh

clay N: nìmtóu; nàih

clean SV: ❶ gònjehng ❷ (fresh) sànsìn ❸ (innocent) chìngbaahk ❹ (pure) sèuhngit ❺ (well-formed) jíngchàih ❻ (even) wàhnching RV: ❶ (by washing) sái gònjehng ❷ (by wiping) maat gònjehng ❸ (by rubbing) chaat gònjehng * **clean up** FV: chìngléih; dásou * **clean-bred** SV: sèuhn-

júng(ge) * **clean-cut** SV: hóutái; lèuhnkok sìnmìhng * **clean-fingered (handed)** SV: lìhmgit; chìnglìhm

clear SV: ❶ (general) chìngchó ❷ (easy to see through) chìngchit • *dī hòhséui hóu ~* ❸ (easily heard) chìngsīk, héungleuhng ❹ (no obstacles) cheungtùng • *tiuh louh hou ~* ❺ (no dangers) ngònchyùhn mòuhjó FV: chìngchèuih * **clear away (off)** FV: chìngchèuih * **clear out** FV: tàhngchēut (deihfōng/ hùnggàan) * **clear up** RV: gáau chìngchó * **make things clear** RV: gáau chìngchó * **clear-sighted** SV: ngáahnleih * **clear of one's debt** RV-O: wàahnchìng jaai * **clear-headed** Adj. PH: tàuhnóuh chìngchó * **clear-cut** SV: chìngsīk

clearance N: ❶ (free space) hùngwái; hùnggàan ❷ (shipping) gitgwàan sáujuhk ❸ (certificate) chēut góng jing

clearing PH: ❶ (in a forest) sàmlàhm léuihbihn ge hùngdeih (M: faai, daat) ❷ (exchange of cheques, etc.) piugeui gàauwuhn * **clearing-house** N: piugeui gàauwuhnsó (M: gàan) * **clearing-hospital** N: jindeih yìyún; yéhjin yìyún (M: gàan)

cleat N: sip; sēut (M: go)

cleavage N: lihtháu (M: go)

cleave RV: ❶ (with an axe) pekhòi ❷ (split) lihthòi FV: (stick fast to) gínchìh * **cleave in two** PH: pekhòi léuhngbīn

clef N: (music) póuhouh; yàmbouh (M: go)

cleft N: ❶ la (M: tiuh) ❷ litháu; lihtháu (M: go) ✳ **in a cleft stick** IE: jeun-teui-wàih-gūk; jeun-teui-léuhng-nàahn

clement SV: ❶ (of person's temper) wànwòh ❷ (of weather) wòhnyúhn

clench RV: ❶ (with hands) jàsaht ❷ (with teeth) ngáauhsaht ✳ **clench one's teeth (jaws)** PH: ngáauh saht ngàh gàn

clergy(man) N: ❶ (protestant) muhksī (M: wái, go) ❷ (R. Catholic) sàhnfuh (M: wái, go)

clerical SV: ❶ (of the clergy) muhksīge ❷ (of a clerk) màhnsyù (ge)

clerk N: jīkyùhn; màhnyùhn; syùgei (M: go)

clever SV: ❶ (in learning) chùngmìhng ❷ (quick understanding) lìhngleih; lēk ❸ (skilful) lēk; jènglēk ❹ (smart) jìngmìhng • jouhsih hóu ~ ✳ **be clever at** A: sihnchèuhng

clew = clue N: sinsaak; sinsok (M: go)

click N: dāahkdāaksèng PH: kaahkkáaksèng héung

client N: ❶ (of a lawyer) sihjyú; wáitokyàhn (M: go) ❷ (at a shop) guhaak; haakjái (M: go)

cliff N: yùhnngàaih; chiubīk (M: go)

climate N: heihauh; sēuitóu

climax N: gòuchìuh (M:go) ✳ **come to a climax** VO: daahtdou gòuchìuh

climb FV: pàh ✳ **climb out** RV: sìnghéi ✳ **climb a moun-**tain VO: pàhsàan ✳ **climb up** RV: pàh séuhngheui

clinch = clench RV: láamjyuh

cling RV: chìhnjyuh; chìhn-saht ✳ **(a child) cling to its mother** SV: chìsàn • nīgo saimānjái hóu ~

clinic N: chánsó; chánliuhsó; yìmouhsó (M: gàan)

clip RV: ❶ gihpjyuh ❷ (cut to make short) jíndyún VO: dálūng N: gíp (M: go)

clippers N: jín (M: bá) ✳ **hair clippers** N: (fèifaat) mohjín (M: bá) ✳ **nail clippers** N: jígaap kím (M: go, bá)

clipping PH: jíndài ge yéh ✳ **newspaper clippings** N: jínbou (M: fahn)

clique N: paaihaih; jaahptyùhn; dóngpaai (M: go)

cloak N: ❶ (garment) dáupùhng; dáufùhng (M: gihn) ❷ (sth. to hide secret) yìm-sīkmaht; jēkoimaht (M: gihn) ❸ (pretext) jeháu (M: go) FV: yìm-sīk ✳ **under the cloak of** PH: yuhng . . . jouh jeháu ✳ **cloak-room** N: yìmóugàan; hàhngléih geichyùhn chyu (M: gàan)

clock N: jùng (M: go) ✳ **clock tower** N: (daaih) jùnglàuh (M: joh, go)

clockwise SV: seuhnsìhjàm fòngheung

clod M: gauh, peht ✳ **a clod of earth** NuM-N: yātgauhnàih; yātpehtnàih ✳ **clod-hopper** N: hèunghálóu; yātgeuk ngàuhsí ge yàhn (M: go)

clog N: ❶ (shoes with wooden

soles) kehk; muhkkehk (M: deui) ❷ (encumbrance) leuih-jeuih; fuhdāam (M: júng) RV: sākmúhn

cloister N: ❶ (convent or monastery) sàudouhyún; jihyún (M: gàan) ❷ (covered walk) chèuhnglòhng; wùihlòhng (M: tiuh) FV: yángeui VO: yahp sàudouhyún

close FV: ❶ (shut) sàan (doors, windows, etc.) hahp (mouth, eyes, etc.) kám (book, lid, etc.) ❷ (bring to an end) git (account) ~ sou/ ~ jeung git-chūk (situation) ~ nípùhn sàangyi; ~ tóuleuhnwúi ❸ (near) gahnjyuh, gahn • nīsyu ~ ngóh ngūkkéi RV: kámmàaih; hahpmàaih; sàanmàaih RVE: ❶ -màaih • hàahng ~ làih ❷ -káhn • hàahng ~ dī làih nībihn N: (end) hauhmēi; sàumēi; muhtméih • syù ge ~ gó bouhfahn sé dāk hóu SV: ❶ (near in space) káhn ❷ (with little space in between) maht • nīsyu dī láu hóu ~ ❸ (detailed) chèuhngjeuhn; jìngmaht; jéunkok ❹ (thorough) chitdái ❺ (intimate) chànmaht ❻ (of competitions) sai-gwàn-lihk-dihk ❼ (concealed) mahtsaht • kéuih go yàhn hóu ~ ❽ (of weather) ngaimuhn; ngaiguhk ✻ **close about** FV: bàauwàih ✻ **close down** FV/VO: sàanjómùhn; gitchūkjó; jāpjólāp • gógàan gùngchóng ~ ✻ **close in** PH: (days) yahttáu yuht làih yuht dyún FV: jipgahn; bīkgahn ~ yehmáahnhāk ✻ **close out** FV: pàausauh ✻ **close up** N: (photograph) káhngeng; daaih dahksé (M: fūk) ✻ **close shave** Adj. PH: hím gwo tai tàuh ✻ **fit close** FV: máhnhahp • . . . tùhng . . . ✻ **keep close** FV: yánchòhng

closet N: ❶ (cupboard) chyúhmahtgwaih (M: go) ❷ (store-room) chyúhmahtsāt (M: gàan) ❸ (private room) mahtsāt (M: gàan, go) ❹ (toilet) chisó (M: go) ❺ (the pan in a toilet) séuichi; máhtúng; chàuséui máhtúng (M:˙go)

closing SV: gitméihge; sāumēige

clot N: ❶ (of blood) hyutfaai (M: gauh, faai) ❷ (of other liquid) yìhnggitjó ge (yéh) (M: gauh) FV: yìhnggit PH: gitsìhng yāt gauhgauh

cloth N: bou; boulíu; yìlíu (M: faai)

clothe VO: jeuksàam, tùhng . . . jeuksàam FV: (cover) kám; kámjyuh

clothes N: sàam; yīfuhk (M: gihn, suit — tou, tyut) ✻ **clothes-horse** N: saaisàamgá; lohngsàamgá; yīgá (M: go) ✻ **clothes-line** N: lohngsàam-síng; saaisàamsíng (M: tiuh) ✻ **clothes-moth** N: jyuchúng (M: tiuh) ✻ **clothes-peg/pin** N: yīgíp; lohngsàamgíp (M: go) ✻ **bed-clothes** N: péihpōu; péihyúk (M: dī)

cloud N: wàhn (M: pin, gauh) M: ❶ (mass of things) jah • yāt ~ mahtfùng ❷ (mass of smoke, dust etc.) jahm, jahn • yāt ~ sà chàhn ❸ (patch) daat • yāt ~ laahttaatyéh ❹ (sth. that causes unhappiness) jahn • yāt ~ sàuhwàhn cháammouh ✻ **in the clouds** IE: sàm-bāt-joih-yīhn ✻ **under a cloud** VO: sauh wàaihyíh; sauh wáiwāt ✻ **cloud-built** SV: móhngséung ge ✻ **cloud-burst** PH: daaih jaauhyúh; kìng-pùhn-daaih-yúh

clouded SV: dòwàhn

cloudy SV: ❶ tìnyām; mahtwàhn ❷ (not clear) mòuhwùh

clough N: haahpgūk; sàmgūk (M: go)

clout FV: (knock) bōk; hàau; dá; kōk

clover ＊ in clover Adj. PH: sàngwuht séyi; sàngwuht ngònyaht

clown N: síucháu; cháugok (M: go)

club N: ❶ (a stick) gwan (M: jì, lūk) ❷ (group of people) kèui lohk bouh; wúi (M: go) ❸ (of cards) (hāk) mùihfā (M: jèung)

cluck FV: gōkgóksèng giu N: gōk góksèng; gòhkgóksēng

clue N: ❶ (of a crime) sinsok; sinsaak (M: tìuh) ❷ (of a puzzle) tàihsih (M: go) VO: béisinsok; tàihgùng sinsok

clump M: (of trees) chùhng; jah; dèui

clumsy SV: leuhnjeuhn

cluster M: ❶ (things) jah; jāp • yāt ~ tàuhfaat ❷ (persons) bàan; jah

clutch FV: màngjyuh; chéjyuh; jáaujyuh; chíjyuh N: (machine) lèihhahphei; gihklīkjí (M: go) M· (young chickens) dau

clutter N: sòulyuhn (M: chèuhng) RV: gáaulyuhn; jínglyuhn; dóulyuhn

coach N: ❶ (carriage pulled by horses) máhchè (M: ga) ❷ (railway) chèsēung; fóchèkā (M: go) ❸ (motor-bus) léuihyàuh bāsí; hòuhwàh bāsí; chèuhngtòuh heichè (M: ga) ❹ (instructor) gaaulihn (M: wái, go)

coagulate FV: yìhnggit; git

coal N: mùih (M: gauh) ＊ blow the coals FV: sòbáai; sinduhng ＊ call over the coals FV: (coll.) sáang; naauh ＊ coal breaker, coal cracker N: seuimùihgèi (M: ga) ＊ coal bunker N: mùihchòng (M: go) ＊ coal mine N: mùihkwong (M: go) ＊ coal-pit N: mùihhàang (M: go) ＊ coal tar N: mùihjiuyâuh; mùihyâuh ＊ coal gas N: mùihhei ＊ carry coals to Newcastle IE: dò-chíyāt-géui SV: dòyùh

coaling VO: séuhngmùih; jòngmùih

coalesce FV/RV: jiphahp; pinghahp; bokmàaih

coalition N: (union) lyùhnmàhng (M: go)

coarse SV: chòu; chòuchou

coast N: ngohn; hóingohn; ngohnbīn; hóipèih (M: go) FV: (slide) sinlohk (làih/heui) PH: yùhnjyuh hóingohn hòhnghàhng ＊ coast guard N: hóingohn chèuhnlòhdéui; hóingohn waihdéui (M: deuih) ＊ coast line N: hóingohn sin (M: tìuh)

coat N: (garment) lāu; daaihlāu; (gihn) M: (layer) jam; chàhng FV: (cover with) douh • níjì bāt haih ~ gàm ge

coax FV: ❶ tam (a child) ❷ tau; táuh (a fire)

cobble N: ngòhchēunsehk (M: gauh) FV: bóu ~ hàaih

cobbler N: bóuhàaihlóu (M: go)

cobra N: ngáahngéngsèh (M: tìuh)

cobweb N: jìjÿumóhng; kàhmlòuh sīmōng (M: go, dī)

coca-cola N: hóháu hólohk; hólohk (M: jì)

cock N: ❶ (fowl) gùngāi; gàigùng (M: jek) ❷ (water) jai (M: go) ❸ (hay) chóudèui (M: dèui, go) ❹ (balance) jíjàm (M: jì) RV: (erect) syuhhéi ~ tiuh méih ✳ at full cock PH: jéunbeihdāk hóu chùngfahn ✳ cock-crow VO: gāitàih; gùnggāi tàih ✳ cock-fighting N: daugāi (M: chèuhng) ✳ cock-pit N: daugāi chèuhng (M: go)

cockroach N: gaahtjáat (M: jek)

cockscomb N: ❶ gàigùn (M: go) ❷ (flower) gàigùnfà (M: déu)

cocktail N: gàiméihjáu ✳ cocktail party N: gàiméihjáu wúi (M: go) ✳ cocktail belt PH: gòuseuhng jyuhjaahkkèui (M: go)

coconut N: ❶ yèhjí (M: go) ❷ (coll.) (head) yèhhok (tàuh) (M: go)

cocoon N: ❶ gáan (M: go) ❷ (of a silkworm) chàahmgáan (M: go)

cod N: ❶ máhnyùh (M: tiuh) ❷ (of body) yàmlòhng (M: go) ✳ cod liver oil N: máhnyùhyàuh; yùhgònyàuh

coddle PH: gìusàang gwaan yéuhng ge yàhn (M: go)

code N: ❶ (of laws) faatdín (M: bouh) ❷ (principles) jéunjāk; kwàigéui (M: go) ❸ (signs) mahtmáh (M: go) ✳ code book N: dihnmáhsyù (M: bún)

codger N: gwaaiyàhn (M: go)

codify FV: pìnjyun ✳ codify the laws VO: pìnjyun faatdín

coeducation PH: nàahmnéuih tùhnghaauh ✳ coeducational school N: nàahmnéuih haauh (M: gàan)

coefficient N: ❶ (maths.) haihsou (M: go) ❷ (physics) léut; haihsou (M: go)

coerce FV: kéuhngbīk

coexist FV: tùhngsìh chyùhnjoih; guhngchyùhn ✳ peaceful coexistence PH: wòhpìhng guhngchyùhn; wòhpìhng guhngchyú

coffee N: gafē (M: cup — bùi) ✳ coffee-bean N: gafē dáu (M: nāp) ✳ coffee-pot N: gafē wú (M: go) ✳ coffee-stall N: gafē dong (M: go)

coffin N: gùnchòih; gùnmuhk (M: fu, go)

co-flyer N: fu fèihàhngyùhn (M: go)

cog N: ngá; lèuhnngá (M: go)

cogency N: seuifuhklihk

cogent PH: lihngyàhn seunfuhk ge SV: yáuhlihk ge

cognate SV: ❶ tùhngjuhk ge ❷ (ling.) tùhngyùhn

cognition N: yihngjī; yihngsīk

cognizance N: sámléihkyùhn; gúnhahtkyùhn (M: go, júng)

cohabit RV: jyuhmàaih FV: tùhnggèui • . . . tùhng . . . ~

coheir N: guhngtùhng gaisìhngyàhn (M: go)

cohere RV: nìhmmàaih; lìhnmàaih yátchái

coherent SV: ❶ nìhm màaih yátchái ge, ❷ (consistent) lìhngun, chìhnhauh yátji

cohesion N: fuhjeuhklihk; noihjeuihlihk

coiffeur N: fèifaatlóu (M: go)

coiffure N: faatyìhng (M: go)

coil FV/RV: gyúnmàaih N: (electric) sinhyūn (M: go)

coin N: ❶ (general) ngán (M: go) · *nǵh hòuhjí ~* ❷ (small change) ngánjái (M: go) ❸ (dollar coin) daaihbéng, daaihngán (M: go) · *léuhngmān ~* FV: jyujouh ✳ **coin money** FV: bouhfaat VO: jaahndaaihchín ✳ **pay sb. back in his own coin** IE: yíh kèihyàhn jìdouh, wàahnjih kèih yàhn jì sàn; yíh ngàh wàahn ngàh

coinage N: (words) sànjouh ge jih/chìh VO: jouh baih; jyujouh chìhnbaih

coincide FV: fùhhahp; sèungfùh . . . tùhng . . . sèungfùh ✳ **coincide with** Patt.: . . . tùhng . . .yátji

coincidence N: yátji; háauhahp ✳ **by coincidence** A: ngāamngāam; gònghóu ✳ **what a coincidence** PH: jànhaih ngāam laak!

coincidental Adj. PH: yáuh gam ngāam dāk gam kíu

coke N: ❶ jiutaan (M: gauh) ❷ (coca-cola) hóháu hólohk

cold SV: ❶ (temp.) láahng; dung ❷ (unfriendly) láahng-daahm ❸ (of colours) láahng · *fùi tùhng làahm haih ~ ge sìk*

N: (illness) sèungfūng; gámmouh ✳ **catch cold** RV: láahng chàn ✳ **in cold blood** SV: láahngjihng; (neg.) láahnghuhk ✳ **in the cold** FV: láahnglohk; béi . . . láahnglohk VO: chóh láahngbáandang ✳ **give the cold shoulder to** FV: deui . . . láahngdaahm; sòyúhn ✳ **cold storage** FV: láahngchòhng ✳ **cold war** N: láahngjin (M: chèuhng) ✳ **make one's blood run cold** PH: lihngyàhn mòuh-gwāt-súngyìhn; lihngyàhn sàmhòhn ✳ **cold-proof** SV: yuhhòhn ge; dáidāk láahng ge

colic N: gáau tóuhtung

collaborate FV: hahpjok; hahpjyu (books)

collaborator N: ❶ (of books) hahpjok jé; hahpjyujé (M: go) ❷ (of war) noihgàan (M: go)

collapse FV: ❶ (fall down or come to pieces) lam · *gàan ngūk ~ jó* ❷ (break down) (fig.) bàngkúi · *jì gwàndéui yuhdóu dihk yàhn jauh ~* RV/FV: (lose physical strength) behngdài · *kéuih ngàaihdāk sànfú dākjaih ~ jó* SV: (lose courage) tèuihsong · *kéuih sātbaaihjó bindāk hóu ~*

collapsible SV: jipdāk-màaih ge

collar N: ❶ (of a garment) léhng (M: tiuh) ❷ (of animal) génghyún (M: go) ❸ (of machine) juhkwàahn (M: go) VO: (seize) jāp jyuh tiuh léhng FV: ❶ (seize) jūkjyuh ❷ (take without permission) sàauh ✳ **slip the collar** RV: jáu lātjó

collar-bone N: sógwāt (M: gauh)

collate FV: gaauham; gaaudeui

collateral SV: fuhdaai ge; fuhsuhk ge N: pòhngchàn

collation N: chàhdím

colleague N: tùhngsih (M: go, wái)

collect FV: ❶ (gather together) sàujaahp ❷ (receive) sàu ❸ (obtain specimens) sáujaahp; chóijaahp ❹ (as a hobby) sàu chòhng ❺ (come together) jeuihjaahp · *dī yàhn ~ hái bāsí jaahm* ❻ (fetch) jip · *làih hohkhaauh ~ saimānjái* ❼ (get control of one's thoughts etc.) jaahpjùng · *~ jìngsàhn* ✻ collect oneself VO: sàusàm yéuhngsing; pìhngsàm jihnghei

collection N: (group of objects) sàuchòhngbán; chòhngbán (M: pài) M: ❶ dèui, jah · *yāt ~ laahpsaap* ❷ bāt (of money)

collector N: sàuchòhng gā (M: go) · *gúdúng ~* ✻ taxcollector N: sàuseuiyùhn (M: go) ✻ ticket collector N: sàufèiyùhn (M: go)

collective SV: guhngtùhng(ge); jaahptái(ge)

college N: ❶ hohkyún; syùyún (M: gàan) ❷ (university) daaihhohk (M: gàan)

collegian N: daaihhohksàang (M: go)

collide FV: ❶ (of car) johng ❷ (opinion, benefit) chùngdaht

collie N: muhkyèuhng gáu (M: jek)

colloquial SV: háuyúh ge ✻ colloquial expressions N:

juhkyúh; juhkwá (M: geui)

colloquialism N: háuyúh; juhkyúh (M: go, geui)

collusion FV: chyunmàuh; chyuntùng, ngâugit · *... tùhng ... ~*

colon N: ❶ (punctuation mark) mouh houh (M: go) ❷ (physical) git chèuhng (M: tiùh)

colonel N: seuhnggaau (M: go)

colonial SV: jihkmàhndeih (ge)

colonialism N: jihkmàhn jyúyih; jihkmàhndeih jyúyih

colonist N: jihkmàhndeih hòitokjé (M: go)

colonization FV: jihkmàhndeihfa

colonize VO: jihkmàhn FV: yìhjihk

colony N: jihkmàhndeih (M: go)

color, colour N: ❶ sīk; ngàahnsīk; sīkséui (M: jek, júng) ❷ (redness of the face) mihnsīk ❸ (race) fūsīk (M: júng) · *kéuih ge ~ haih wòhng ge* ❹ (in literature) sīkchói, fùng gaak (M: júng) · *deihfòng ~* ❺ (in music) yāmjāt; yàmsīk (M: jek) VO: jeuhksīk FV: yíhm ✻ change color PH: mihn binsaai sīk ✻ give color to PH: sáidou ... duhngting ✻ join the colors VO: yahpngh; chàamgwàn ✻ lose color PH: mihnsīk chòngbaahk ✻ show one's color VO: louhchēut jàn mihnmuhk ✻ under color of VO: je ... ge mìhngyih ✻ without color PH: móuh hyùnyíhm; móuh dahksīk ✻

color blindness N: sīkmàahng ✳ **color film** N: chóisīkpín (M: chēut) ✳ **color filter** N: leuihsīkgeng (M: go) ✳ **color T.V.** N: chóisīk dihnsih ✳ **color photo** N: chóisīkséung (M: fūk)

colors N: ❶ (materials used by artists) ngàahnlíu (M: júng) ❷ (symbol) fàihouh; fàijèung (M: go) ❸ (flag) kèih (M: jì)

colossal SV: geuihdaaih

colossus N: ❶ (statue) geuihjeuhng (M: go) ❷ geuihyàhn (M: go)

colt N: ❶ (horse) máhjái (M: jek) ❷ (fig.) sànsáu (M: go) '

column N: ❶ (pillar) chyúh (M: tiuh) ❷ (of soldiers) jùngdéui (M: go) M: ❶ (of characters) hòhng ❷ (in newspaper) làahn

columnist N: jyùnlàahn jokgà (M: go)

coma N: fànmàih johngtaai ✳ **in a coma** FV/SV: fànmèih; bātsíng yàhnsìh

comb N: ❶ (for hair) sò (M: bá, jek) ❷ (of bees) fùngfòhng; fùngchàauh (M: go) ❸ (of a cock) gàigùn (M: go) FV: ❶ sò (the hair) ❷ (search) sáusaak ✳ **comb the hair** VO: sòtàuh ✳ **comb out** FV: heuichèuih; chòihgáam

combat FV/N: jindau; dádau; bokdau; daujàng (M: chèuhng)

combatant N: jindauyùhn (M: go)

combative SV: houjin ge; houdau ge

combination N: githahp; lyùhnhahp; fahahp (M: júng) ✳ **combination lock** N: mahtmáhsó (M: go, fu)

combine RV: hahpmàaih FV: lyùhnhahp; githahp ✳ **combined operations (exercises)** N: lyùhnhahp jokjin/hàhngduhng (yínjaahp)

combustible SV: yihjeuhkfóge; yihyìhnsiuge; yihyìhnge PH: yihjeuhkfóge yéh; yihyìhnmaht (M: júng)

combustion N: (to burn) yìhnsiu; (to oxidize) yéuhngfa

come FV: ❶ làih ❷ (become) sìhngwàih ❸ (appear) chēutyìhn ❹ (happen) faatsàng ✳ **come about** FV: faatsàng ✳ **come across** FV: ngáuhyìhn yuhdóu, yuhdóu ✳ **come around** PH: fùifuhk jìgok; fùifuhkgìhnhòhng ✳ **come back** FV: fàanlàih ✳ **come by** FV: dākdóu; wohkdāk ✳ **come in** FV: yahplàih ✳ **come out** FV: chēutlàih ✳ **come up with** FV: gónséuhng

comedy N: héikehk (M: chēut; tou)

comedian N: héikehk yínyùhn (M: go)

comer PH: làihge yàhn; (slang) yáuh sìhnggùng hèimohngge yàhn (M: go) yáuh sìhnggùng hèimohng ge sih (M: gihn)

comet N: waihsīng (M: lāp)

comfort N: ngònwai; syùsīk (M: júng) FV: ngònwai PH: lihng . . . syùsīk

comfortable SV: ngònlohkge; syùsīkge; yuhfaaige

comfortably A: yuhfaai-gám

comforter N: waimahnge yàhn (waimahnjé); ngònwaige yàhn (ngònwaijé) (M: go)

comfrey N: jíchóufō jihkmaht; chògūk (M: pò)

comic SV: waahtkàige

comical SV: hóusiuge; waahtkàige; fùihàaihge

comma N: dauhdím (M: go)

command FV: mihnglihng; jífài; túngsēut N: mihnglihng(M: go) jífài; túngsēut * **at one's command** PH: tèng . . . fànfuh * **in command of** FV: jífài

commandant N: sìlihnggùn (M: go)

commander N: sìlihnggùn; jífàigùn (M: go) * **commander in chief** N: júngsìlihng (M: go)

commandment N: gaaimihng (M: go) * **the Ten Commandments** PH: sahpgaai

commemorate FV: géinihm

commemoration N: géinihm * **in commemoration of** PH: waih . . . géinihm

commemorative SV: géinihmsingge

commence FV: hòichí; héisáu

commencement N: hòichí; héisáu; (commencement exercises) bātyihp dínláih (M: go)

commend FV: chìngjaan; jaanyèuhng

commendable PH: ge; jihkdāk chìngjaan ge

commendation N: chìngjaan; jaanyèuhng (M: júng)

commensurable SV: yáuh tùhngleuhng ge; sèungching ge

commensurate SV: tùhngleuhngge; tùhngdaaihsaige; sèungchingge

comment N: ❶ pìhngleuhn ❷ (explanatory notes) jyugáai; jyusīk (M: go) FV: ❶ pìhngleuhn ❷ (to define) jyugáai; jyusīk

commentary N: (explanatory notes) jyugáai; jyusīk (M: go)

commentator N: sihsihpìhngleuhnnyùhn; sìhsihpìhngleuhngā; jyusīkjé (M: go)

commerce N: sèungyihp; mauhyihk (M: júng)

commercial SV: sèungyihpge PH: tùhng sèungyihp yáuhgwàange * **commercial bank** N: sèungyihp ngàhnhòhng (M: gàan) * **commercial college** N: sèunghohkyún; sèungyihp jyūnfō hohkhaauh (M: gàan)

commingle FV: wahnhahp; wahnjaahp

comminute FV: fánseui VO: jíngsèhng fánmut

commiserate FV: lìhnmáhn; tùhngchihng

commissary N: ❶ doihbíu; wáiyùhn (M: go) ❷ gwànlèuhngfu (M: gàan, go)

commission N: ❶ wáiyahm ❷ wáiyahmjohng (M: jèung) ❸

wáiyùhnwúi (M: go) ❹ (of sales)
yúnggām; FV: wáiyahm;
wáitok; sauhkyùhn ✻ on commission FV: sauhwáitok;
wáitok

commissioner N: jyùn-
yùhn; wáiyùhn (M: go)

commit FV: faahn (jeuih);
jouh (waaihsih); jèung . . .
wáitok; yìngsìhng

commitment N: hàhng-
wàih; wáitok; wáiyahm (M: go)
VO: faahnjeuih; héuinohk

committee N: wáiyùhnwúi
(M: go)

commodious SV: fùn-
chóng; fòngbihn ge

commodity N: sèungbán;
fomaht; mahtbán (M: júng)

commodore N: hóigwān
jéunjeung (M: go)

common SV: guhngtùhngge;
gùngguhngge; póutùngge N:
gùngyáuh deih (M: fùk)
pìhngmàhn (M: go) ✻ in common SV: guhngtùhng;
gùngyáuh ✻ The European
Common Market N: Ngāujāu
Guhngtùhng Síhchèuhng

commoner N: pìhngmàhn
(M: go)

commonplace SV: pìhng-
fàahnge; póutùngge PH:
póutùngge sih (M: gihn)

common sense N: sèuhngsīk

commonwealth N:
chyùhntái gwokmàhn; guhngwòhgwok; lyùhnbòng (M: go) ✻
**the British Commonwealth
of Nations** PH: Yìng
Lyùhnbòng

commotion FV:
bouhduhng; sòuduhng

communal SV: gùngséhge;
gùngguhngge; gùngyáuhge

commune PH: chànmaht
gàautàahm N: gùngséh (M: go)

communicate FV: chyùhndaaht; tùngjì; tùngseun

communication N: gàautùng; lyùhnlok (M: júng) VO:
chyùhndaaht sìusīk

communicator N: tùng-
seunyùhn (M: go)

communion FV/SV:
guhngyáuh; guhnghéung N:
gaauyáuh; gaauwúi (M: go) ✻
Holy Communion N: singchāan (M: go)

communiqué N: gùngbou;
gùnbou (M: fahn)

communism N: guhng-
cháanjyúyih

communist N:
Guhngcháandóngyùhn;
guhngcháanjyúyihjé (M: go) ✻
Communist party N:
Guhngcháandóng (M: go)

community N: tyùhntái;
séhwúi; (M: go) ATT: gùngjung

commutation FV: gàau-
wuhn; binwuhn N: (electricity)
jínglàuh (M: júng)

commutator N: jínglàuhhei; wuhnheunghei (M: go)

commute FV: gàauwuhn;
góibin ✻ **commute time** N:
fàangùng/fonggùng sìhgaan;
séuhngbāan/lohkbāan sìhgaan
(M: go)

commuter PH: yuhng
chèuhngkèih chèpiu ge yàhn
(M: go)

compact N: hahptùhng; hip-dihng; kaiyeuk (M: go) SV: gán-mahtge; gáangitge * **enter into a compact** VO: dingkai-yeuk; dinghahptùhng

companion N: tùhngbuhn; buhnléuih (M: go)

company NuMN: yātkwàhn yàhn N: haakyàhn; lòihbàn; gūngsī; sèunggaai * **for company** FV: pùihjyuh * **in company with** PH: tùhng . . . yāt-chàih * **keep company** FV: pùih; pùihbuhn * **keep company with** PH: tùhng . . . gitgàau * **part company with** PH: tùhng yàhn (lèihbiht) fànsáu * **company commander** N: lìhnjéung (M: go)

comparable PH: hóyíh béigaauge; hóyíh béidāk-séuhng ge

comparative SV: béi-gaauge N: béigaaukāp (M: go)

compare FV: béigaau; béiyuh; sèungbéi; béidāk-séuhng * **be compared to** FV: béijok * **beyond compare** PH: mòuh-yúh-lèuhn-béi * **compare with** PH: tùhng . . . béigaau

comparison FV/N: béigaau (M: go) * **by comparison** FV: sèungbéi

compartment N: ❶ gaan-gaak ❷ (of train) chèsèung (M: go)

compass N: jínàahmjām; lòhpùhn (M: go) FV: bàauwàih; wàihyíu

compassion FV/N: tùhng-chìhng; lìhnmáhn (M: júng)

compassionate SV: yáuh

tùhngchìhngsàm ge; chìhbèige FV: tùhngchìhng; lìhnmáhn; táisēut

compatibility PH: wòh-hàaih guhngchyú SV: wòhhàaih

compatible PH: hóyíh guhngchyúge; hóyíh guhng-chyùhn ge SV: sèungyùhngge; wòhhàaihge

compatriot N: tùhngbàau; tùhnggwokge yàhn (M: go)

compatriotic SV: tùhng-bàauge; tùhnggwokge yàhn ge

compeer N: tùhngbui; tùhngbuhn (M: go)

compel FV: kèuhngbīk; bīksí; bīklihng

compendious SV: gáan-gitge; gáanyiuge; ngāakyiuge; jaahkyiuge

compendium (compen-diums, compendia) N: koiyiu; gòngyiu; jaahkyiu; chyutyiu (M: go)

compensate FV: ❶ (for loss or injury) pùihsèuhng; bóusèuhng ❷ (for trouble) chàuhlòuh

compensation N: bóu-sèuhng; pùihsèuhng (M: go) chàuhgām; pùihsèuhnggām; (M: bāt) pùihsèuhngmaht (M: gihn); bouchàuh (M: go) * **in compensation for** PH: jokwàih . . . ge pùihsèuhng/ bouchàuh

compete FV: béichoi; gihng-jàng * **compete in** PH: hái . . . fòngmihn gihngjàng

competence (competen-cy) N: nàhnglihk; jìgaak; hahpfaatge kyùhnlihk (M: go);

sèungdòngge chòihcháan (M: bāt)

competent SV: nàhnggau sìngyahm ge; nàhnggonge; yáuhjīgaakge

competition FV/N: béichoi; gihngjàng; gokjuhk (M: chi, júng) * be (stand) in competiton with . . . for PH: tùhng . . . jàngdyuht

competitive SV: gihngjàngge; béichoige

competitor (competitress) N: gihngjàngge yàhn; dihksáu (M: go)

compilation N: pìnchāp (M: go); pìnchāpge syù (pìnchāpmaht) (M: júng)

compile FV: pìnchāp

compiler N: pìnchāpyàhn; pìnchāp (M: go)

complacence (complacency) N: jihmúhn; jihjūk; jihdāk

complacent SV: jihmúhnge; jihdākge; dākyige

complain FV: póuhyun; tàuhsou; soufú; hunggou; hungsou * complain of FV: póuhyun

complaint FV/N: soufú; hungsou; hunggou

complaisance N: yànkàhn; chànchit; bàn-bàn-yáuh-láih

complaisant SV: yànkàhnge; chànchitge; bàn-bàn-yáuhláih ge; wòhngói ge; hìmgùngge

complement N: bóujūkmaht; bóuchùngmaht; bóujohyúh; yùhgok; yùhwùh (M: go)

FV: bóuchùng; bóujūk

complete SV: yùhnchyùhnge; chyùhnbouhge; chitdáige; yùhnmúhnge; yùhnjíngge FV: yùhnsìhng

completion FV: yùhnsìhng SV: yùhnmúhn

complex SV: fūkjaahpge; jūnghahpge; fūkhahpge N: fūkjaahpge sihmaht (M: gihn) * a complex sentence PH: fūkhahpgeui

complexion N: mihnsīk; pèihfùge ngàahnsīk; heisīk; yìhngsai; guhkmihn; singchìhng; pèihhei (M: júng)

compliance FV: yìngsìhng; daapying; fuhkchùhng; seuhnchùhng

compliant SV: seuhnchùhngge; yìchùhngge; yìngwáhnge

complicacy SV: fūkjaahp N: fūkjaahpsing; fūkjaahpge sihmaht (M: júng)

complicate FV: lihngdou fūkjaahp; lihngdou gang waaih

complicated SV: fūkjaahpge

complication SV: fūkjaahp; wahnlyuhn N: (medicine): bingfaatjing (M: júng)

complicity FV: tùhngmàuh; chyuntùhng

compliment N: ❶ gùngwàih; chìngjaan; jaanméihge syutwah; ❷ (pl)(greetings) jiyi; mahnhauh; douhhoh (M: júng) FV: chìngjaan; gùngwàih; jūkhoh; mahnhauh * pay one's compliments to FV: mahnhauh

complimentary SV: jaan-méihge; mahnhauhge; jūk-hohge * **complimentary address** PH: jūkhohchìh; juhngchìh (M: pìn) * **complimentary ticket** N: jìudoihgyun; yàudoihgyun (M: jèung)

comply FV: seuhnchùhng; yìchùhng; * **comply with** FV: jèunsáu; jèunchùhng

component SV: jóusìhngge; sìhngfahnge N: sìhngfahn (M: júng)

compose FV: jóusìhng; kausìhng; jyu; jok; séjok; lìhng ngònjihng; jandihng; tiuhtìhng; wòhgáai; tìuhgáai (printing): pàaihjih * **be composed of** PH: yàuh . . . jóusìhng

composed SV: janjihngge; ngònjihngge; taaiyìhnjih-yeuhkge

composer N: jokkūkgā; jokgā; jyujokjé (M: go)

composing FV: jóusìhng; puihahp; (printing) pàaihjih * **composing frame** N: pàaih-jihgá (M: go) * **composing machine** N: pàaihjihgèi (M: ga) * **composing room** N. pàaih-jih fòhng (M: gàan, go) * **composing stick** N: pàaihjihpún (pàaihjihpùhn) (M: go)

composite SV: wahnhahp-sìhngge; hahpsìhngge; fūk-hahpge; N: hahpsìhngmaht; wahnhahpmaht (M: júng)

composition N: jóusìhng; sìhngfahn; wahnhahpmaht; singjāt (M: júng) jyujok; jok-mán; jokbán, màhnjèung (M: pìn) (printing) pàaihjih

compositor N: pàaihjih

compost N: wahnhahp fèihlíu; dèuifèih (M: júng)

composure SV: janjihng; chàhmjeuhk

compound FV: wahnhahp; tiuhtìhng; wòhgáai SV: hahp-sìhngge; fahahpge; fūkhahpge; wahnhahpge N: fūkhahpjíh; wahnhahpmaht; fahahpmaht (M: go) * **compound with some-meone** PH: tùhng máuhyàhn wòhgáai

comprador N: máaihbáan (M: go)

comprehend FV: líuhgáai; lìhngwuih; (include) bāaukwut; bàauhàhm

comprehensible SV: hó-yíh léihgáai ge; yih líuhgáai ge

comprehension N: léih-gáai; léihgáailihk

comprehensive SV: bàau-lòh fùngfu ge; jùnghahpge; gwóngfaan ge; gwóngbokge; yáuh léihgáailihk ge

compress FV: ngaatsūk; gánngaat; ngaatja N: bàngdáai (M: gyún, tìuh) ngaat-mìhn-sìhng-bàau ge gèihei (M: ga)

compression FV: ngaatja; ngaatsūk

compressive SV: yáuh-ngaatsūklihk ge; ngaatja ge

compressor N: ngaat-sūkgèi; ngaatsūkhei; ngaat-jahei (M: ga)

comprise (comprize) FV: bàaukwut; bàauhàhm; yáuh . . . jóusìhng

compromise FV: ❶ (settle a disagreement, quarrel, etc. by making a compromise) wòhgáai; tóhhip; jitchùng chyúléih; ❷ (bring sb. under suspicion by unwise behaviour, etc.) ngàihkahp; lìhnleuih; N: wòhgáai; tóhhip; hìpyíh (M: go) * **make a compromise** PH: jeunhàhng tóhhip

comptroller N: jyúgaijéung; sámgaiyùhn (M: go)

compulsion FV: kéuhngbīk; kéuhngjai * **by compulsion** A: kéuhngbīk gám

compulsory SV: kéuhngbīkge; kéuhngjaige; yihmouhge * **compulsory education** PH: yihmouh gaauyuhk

compunction FV/SV: hauhfui; noihgau; bātngòn PH: lèuhngsàm bātngòn

computation FV: gaisyun; gúgai PH: yuhng dihnjí gaisyungèi chòujok

computable SV: hóyíh gaisyunge; hóyíh tèuichāakge

compute FV: gaisyun; gúgai; (yuhng dihnjí gaisyungèi) gaisyun N: gaisyun; gúgai (M: go)

computer N: gaisyungèi; dihnjí gaisyungèi; dihnnnóuh (M: ga, go); gaisyunyùhn (M: go) * **computer-on-a-chip** N: mèihyìhng dihnnnóuh (M: ga, go)

comrade N: tùhngji; tùhngbuhn (M: go) * **comrade in arms** PH: móuhjōng tùhngji; jinyáuh (M: go)

Comtism N: Húngdākge hohksyut; Sahtjing jithohk

con FV: jingduhk; saisàm yuhtduhk; fáandeui N:

fáandeui; fáandeuijé; fáandeuige léihyàuh (M: go); fáandeui piu (M: jèung)

concave SV: nāpge N: nāpmín (M: go) * **concave lens** N: nāptaugeng (M: go, faai)

conceal FV: yánchòhng; yánnīk; deui . . . bóusáu beimaht

concealment FV/N: yánchòhng; yánnīk (M: chi) N: yánnīkge fòngfaat (M: go) yánnīkge deihfòng (M: daat)

concede FV: sihngyihng; yeuhngbéi; yeuhngbouh

conceit N: jihfuh; waahnséung (M: júng) * **in one's own conceit** PH: jih yíhwàihsih FV: jihkwà; séungjeuhng

conceited SV: jihkwàge; jihfuhge; waahnséungge

conceive FV: séungjeuhng; yíhwàih; sèungseun; póuh . . . séungfaat

conceivable SV: hóyíh séungjeuhng ge

concentrate FV: jaahpjùng; jyuyi; jyùnsàm; nùhngsūk * **concentrate on (upon)** PH: jaahpjùnghái; jyùnsàmhái

concentration FV/N: jaahpjùng; jyuyi; jyùnsàm; nùhngsūk (M: júng) * **concentration camp** N: jaahpjùng yìhng (M: go)

concentric SV: tùhng jùngsàmge; tùhng juhkge

concept N: koinihm; gùnnihm (M: go)

conceptual SV: koinihmge

conception N: koinihm; gùnnihm; séungjeuhng; séung-

jeuhnglihk; sèungfaat (M: go)
* **prevent conception** VO;
beihyahn

concern FV: tùhng . . . yáuh
gwàanhaih; gwàansàm; gwàanjyu; gwàanwàaih; sipkahp N:
gwàanhaih; gwàansàm; sih-
mouh (M: júng) sèunghóng;
sèungdim; gūngsī (M: gàan)
gúfán (M: fahn) * **as concerns**
CV: gwàanyù * **be concerned
about** FV: gwàansàm; gwàanwàaih; gwanihm * **be concerned in** FV: sipkahp * **concern oneself with** FV: jyuyi;
gwàansàm * **the persons
(parties) concerned** N:
dòngsihyàhn (M: go) * **as far
as . . . is concerned** CV:
gwàanyù, jiyù

concerned SV: gwanihm
ge; yàuleuihge; yáuhgwàange

concerning CV: gwàanyù

concert N: yàmngohkwúi
(M: go); yàtji; wòhhàaih (M:
júng) FV: hipyíh chitgai; hipyíh
jeunhàhng; hiptùhng gùngjok
* **in concert** A: yàtji; yàt-
chàih; guhngtùhng

concerted SV: hiptùhngge;
guhngtùhngge; yàtjige; wòhhàaihge; hiptiuhge

concerto N: hipjaukūk (M:
sáu)

concession N: yeuhngbouh;
dahkhéuikyùhn; (M: go) jòugaai
(M: go) jòudeih (M: faai)

conciliate FV: ngònfú;
fúwai; sàuhóu; wòhhóu;
wòhgáai; tiuhtìhng

conciliation FV: ngònfú;
fúwai; sàuhóu; wòhhóu;
wòhgáai

conciliator N: fúwaige

yàhn (fúwaijé); wòhgáaige yàhn
(wòhgáaijé) (M: go)

**conciliatory (concilia-
tive)** SV: fúwaige; ngònwaige; yuhnyi sàuhóuge; yáuh
wòhgáai chèuisai ge

concise SV: gáanmìhngge;
koikwutge

conclude FV: ❶ (come to an
end) gitchūk; yùhnbāt; ❷ (arrive
at a belief or opinion) tèuidyun;
dyundihng; ❸ (bring about; arrange) dinglahp; daigit; * **conclude with** PH: yíh . . . gitchūk

conclusion N: gitchūk;
gitleuhn; daigit; gitgwó (M: go)
dinglahp * **come to a conclusion** FV: goujùng; gitchūk *
draw the conclusion VO;
dākchēut gitleuhn * **in conclusion** A: jeuihauh; sāumēi;
gitchūk gójahnsí

conclusive SV: gitleuhn-
singge; kyutdihngsingge; jeuihauhge

concoct FV: ❶ (prepare by
mixing together) tiuhjai; ❷ (invent a story, excuse, etc.)
pìnjouh

concomitant SV: sèung-
buhnge; buhnchèuihge;
fuhchèuihge N: sèungbuhm-
maht; buhnchèuihge; fuh-
chèuihmaht (M: gihn)

concord N: wòhhàaih; yàtji;
hiptiuh * **in concord** SV:
wòhmuhk * **in concord with**
CV: yìjiu

concordance N: wòhhàaih;
yàtji; (index (of a book)) sokyáhn
(M: go)

concordant SV: wòhhàaihge; yàtjige

concordat N: hipdihng; hipyeuk; kaiyeuk (M: go)

concourse FV: jaahphahp; hahplàuh N: gwóngchèuhng (M: go)

concrete SV: geuihtáige; sahtjoihge; wahnyihngtóuge; séuinàihge; yìhnggitge N: wahnyìhngtóu; geuihtáimaht (M: júng) FV: yuhng wahnyìhngtóu pòu (louh); lihngdou yìhnggu

concretion N: yìhnggu; yìhnggumaht (M: júng) gitsehk (M: nāp)

concubine N: chipsih (chip); chìhngfúh (M: go)

concupiscence N: singyuhk

concupiscent SV: yuhkmohng kèuhngliht ge; singyuhk kèuhng ge; housīk ge; tàamlàahm ge

concur FV: tùhngsìh faatsàng; (agree) tùhngyi

concurence FV/N: tùhngsìh faatsàng; tùhngyi; jaantùhng

concurent SV: tùhngsìh faatsàng ge; wòhhàaihge; hahpjokge

condemn FV: hínjaak; (to confiscate) muhtsàu; chùnggùng

condemnation FV/N: hínjaak (M: go); VO:punjeuih; dihngjeuih

condense FV: láahngyìhng; ngaatsūk; yìhnggit; jaahpjeuih (light)

condenser N: láahngyìhnghei; yìhnggithei; jeuihgwòng-

hei; jeuihgwònggeng; dihnyùhnghei (M: go)

condescend FV: fújauh; gonggaak sèungchùhng; wātjyùn

condesension FV: wātjyùn N: yànkàhn; yànchi; hìmbēi (M: júng)

condiment N: tiuhmeihbán (M: júng)

condition N: ❶ (the present state of being) chìhngyìhng; chìhngfong; johngfong; ❷ (position in society) deihwaih; sànfán; ❸ (sth. on which another thing depends) tiuhgín; (M: go) FV: fanlihn; yíh . . . wàih tiuhgín ✳ in condition PH: gihnhòng chìhngyìhng lèuhnghóu ✳ in condition to do PH: sīkyìh jouh ✳ out of condition to do PH: m̀sīkyìh jouh ✳ on condition that PH: hái . . . tiuhgín jìhah; gásí ✳ on no condition PH: jyuhtdeui m̀hóyíh . . .

conditional SV: yáuh tiuhgín ge ✳ conditional clause PH: tiuhgín jígeui (M: go)

conditioned SV: yáuh tiuhgín ge; sauh tiuhgín haahnjaige ✳ conditioned reflex PH: tiuhgín fáanseh

conditioner N: tiuhjithei (M: go)

conditioning PH: (hùnghei) tiuhjit

condolatory SV: diuyihnge; ngòidouhge; diuwaige ✳ a condolatory letter N: waimahn seun (M: fùng)

condole FV: diuyihn; ngòidouh; diuwai; waimahn

condolence FV: diuyihn; ngòidouh; diuwai

condom N: beihyahntou; beiyahndói (M: go)

condominium N: guhng-yáuh-kyùhn; guhngtùhng-gúnhaht-kyùhn (M: go)

condonation FV: yùhn-leuhng; fùnsyu; semíhn

condone FV: yùhnleuhng; fùnsyu; semíhn * **condone an offence** VO: syujeuih

conduce FV: douhji; yáuh-johyù; yáhnhéi

conducive PH: deui . . . yáuhyīk ge; yáuhjohyù . . .

conduct N: hàhngwàih; jídouh; chyúléih; yáhndouh (M: júng) FV: yáhndouh; chyùhndouh; jífài; chyúléih

conductor N: jífàige yàhn; jífài (M: go) * **the conductor of an orchestra** N: ngohkdéui jífài (M: go)

conduit N: douhgún; séui-gún; yàuhgún (M: tiùh)

cone N: yùhnjēui; jēuimín; yùhnjēuitái; jēuiyìhngmaht (M: go) * **an ice-cream cone** N: tìhmtúng (M: go)

confab N: wuihtàahm; hàahntàahm (M: chi) FV: tàahmleuhn; tàahmsàm; wuihtàahm; hàahntàahm

confabulate FV: tàahm-leuhn; hàahntàahm; wuih-tàahm; tàahmsàm

confabulation FV: wuih-tàahm; hàahntàahm

confection N: tòhnggwó; dímsām; mahtjin (M: júng)

condolence FV: diuyihn; sìhmōuge néuihjōng (M: gihn, tou)

confectioner N: tòhnggwó sèungyàhn; maaih tòhnggwó tùhngmàaih béng ge sèung-yàhn (M: go)

confectionery N: tòhng-gwó (M: júng); maaih tòhnggwó ge poutáu (tòhnggwódim) (M: gàan)

confederacy N: tùhng-màhng; lyùhnmàhng; bòng-lyùhn (M: go)

confederate FV: gitmàhng; lyùhnhahp; tùhngmàhng ATT: tùhngmàhngge; lyùhnhahpge N: tùhngmàhngwok; lyùhn-màhngjé; lyùhnhahpjé (M: go)

confederation N: tùhng-màhng; lyùhnmàhng; bòng-lyùhn; tùhngmàhnggwok (M: go)

confer FV: ❶ (give or grant) chibéi; bàanbéi; ❷ (discuss) sèunglèuhng; sèungyíh

conference N: wuihyíh; tàahmpun; tóuleuhnwúi (M: go)

confess FV: sìhngyihng; gùngyihng; jihyihng; yihng-jeuih; chaamfui * **confess to** FV: sìhngyihng; yihngjeuih

confession FV: gùngyihng; gùngjohng; sìhngyihng; jihyihng; yihngjeuih; chaamfui; gougáai

confessor N: yihngchoge-yàhn; chaamfuigeyàhn (chaam-fuijé) (M: go)

confidant N: jìgéi pàhng-yáuh; jìgéi; mahtyáuh; sàmfūk-ge yàhn (M: go)

confide FV: seunyahm; seunlaaih; toulouh

confidence FV/N: seunyahm; seunlaaih; jihseun; N: seunsàm; beimaht (M: go) ∗ **in confidence** PH: beimahtgám ∗ **with confidence** PH: yáuhbá- ngāak gám ∗ **confidence game** N: hèija (M: go) ∗ **confidence man** N: pinjí (M: go)

confident SV: jihseunge; kokseunge; yùhnchyùhn sèungseun ge ∗ **be confident of** FV: kokseun

confidential SV: beimahtge; gèimahtge; wohkdāk seunyahm ge; sàmfùkge

configuration N: lèuhnkwok; ngoihmaauh; yìhngjohng; ngoihyìhng (M: go)

confine FV: ❶ (restrict within limits) haahnjai; ❷ (keep shut up) gàamgam; (to give birth) fànmíhn; N: gínggaai; bìngaai; gèunggaai (M: go) ∗ **be confined** FV: fànmíhn (sàang bìhbī) ∗ **confine to** CV: haahnjai . . .; haahnyù

confinement FV: haahnjai; gàamgam; fànmíhn (M: chi)

confirm FV: jingsaht; yìhnghó; (to give official approval for) pàijéun

confirmable SV: hóyíh kokdihng ge; nàhnggau jingsaht ge

confirmation FV/N: yìhnghó; jingsaht; gokdihng; pàijéun; jingmìhng

confiscable SV: hóyíh muhtsàu ge; yìnggòi chùnggùng ge

confiscate FV: muhtsàu; chùnggùng; jìngyuhng

confiscation FV: muhtsàu;

chùnggùng

conflagration N: daaihfó; fójòi (M: go, chi)

conflict FV: chùngdaht; jindau; jàngjāp; yígin chùngdaht N: jindau; jìnjàng; chùngdaht (M: chi)

conflicting SV: chùngdahtge; màauhtéuhnge; dáijūukge

confluence (conflux) N: (hòhlàuhge) hahplàuh; wuihlàuhge deihfòng (wuihlàuhchyu) (M: go)

confluent SV: hahplàuhge

conform FV: lìhng yātji; lìhng sèungchíh; lìhng seuhnying; jèunsáu; jèunchùhng

conformable SV: sèungchíhge; yātjige; sīkyingge; fuhkchùhngge

conformation N: kaujouh; yìhngtaai; jóusìhng; yātji (M: júng)

conformist N: seunfuhngge yàhn (seunfuhngjé); jèunfuhngge yàhn (jèunfuhngjé); Yìnggwok gwokgaautòuh (M: go)

conformity FV: sèungchíh; yātji; CV: yijiu; jèunjiu

confound FV: ❶ (fill with perplexity or confusion) lìhng wòhngwaahk; lìhng lòhngbui; wahnlyuhn; wahnngàauh; ❷ (defeat) dábaaih

confront FV: mihndeui; mihnlàhm; jòuyuh; ∗ **be confronted with (by)** FV: yuhdóu; mihnlàhm

confrontation FV/N: jòuyuh; deuikong (M: júng)

Confucius N: Húngjí

Confucian ATT: Húngjíge; Yùhgāge

confuse FV: gáaulyuhn; lihng wahnlyuhn; lihng fònglyuhn; màihwaahk

confusion SV: wahnlyuhn; lòhngbui; wahnngàauh; màihwaahk; wòhngwaahk (M: júng) * in confusion SV: wahnlyuhn; lòhngbui

confutation FV: bokdóu; bihnbok

confute FV: bokdóu

congeal FV: (lihng) dunggit; (lihng) yìhnggit

congee N: jūk (M: wún)

congenial SV: ❶ (of persons) (having the same or a similar nature, common interest, etc.) singgaak sèungtùhng ge; jicheui sèungtàuh ge; ❷ (of things, occupations, etc.) (in agreement with one's nature, tastes, etc.) sīkyige; sèungyìh ge

congenital SV: tìnsàangge sìntìnge; tìnfuge; yúh-sàngkèui-lòih ge

congest FV: chùngsāk; chùngmúhn; yúngsāk; chùnghyut

congestion FV: chùngmúhn; yúngsāk; chùnghyut

conglomerate FV: lihngdou sìhngtyùhn; sìhng kàuhyìhng; lihngdou sìhngwàih yùhnfaai SV: jeuihsìhng yāttyùhn ge; sìhng kàuhyìhng ge; sìhng tyùhn ge N: jaahpsìhngmaht; jeuihjaahpmaht

conglomeration FV: jeuihjaahp; yìhngjeuih N: jeuihjaahpmaht; tyùhnfaai (M: júng)

congratulate FV: gùnghoh; hoh; gùnghéi * congratulate on a birthday VO: hoh sàangyaht * congratulate on the new year VO: baainìhn

congratulation FV: jūkhoh; hinghoh N: jūkchìh; hohchìh (M: pìn)

congratulator N: jūkhohge yàhn (jūkhohjé); hinghohge yàhn (hinghohjé) (M: go)

congratulatory SV: hinghohge; jūkhohge; hingjūkge * congratulatory telegram N: hohdihn (M: fùng) * a congratulatory address N: hohchìh (M: pìn)

congregate FV: jaahphahp; jeuihjaahp

congregation FV/N: jaahphahp (M: chi); jaahpwúi (M: go) N: yàhnkwàhn (M: bàan)

congress N: gwokgà lahpfaat ge gèigwàan; Méihgwok gwokwúi; wuihyíh; jaahpwúi (M: go) * International Congress of Medicine PH: Gwokjai Yìhohk Wuihyíh

congressional SV: wuihyíhge; jaahpwúige; Méihgwok gwokwúige

congressman PH: Méihgwok gwokwúi yíhyùhn (M: go)

congruence (congruency) FV: sīkhahp; yātji chyùhndáng; fùhhahp

conic SV: yùhnjēuige; yùhnjēuiyìhngge N: yùhnjēui; yùhnjēuiyìhng (M: go); jēuisin yihchikūksin (M: tìuh)

conical SV: yùhnjēuige; yùhnjēuiyìhngge

conifer N: jàmyihpsyuh; chùhngpaakfō jihkmaht (M: pò)

coniferous SV: jàmyihpsyuhge; chùhngpaakfōge

conjecturable SV: hóyíh tèuichāakge

conjectural SV: tèuichāakge; chyúndohkge

conjecture FV/N: tèuichāak; chàaichāak (M: go)

conjugal SV: fùfúhge; fànyànge

conjugate FV: githahp; puihahp; lìhnjip; puideui; sìhngfàn SV: sìhngdeuige; tùhnggànge

conjugation FV/N: githahp; lìhnhahp; puihahp (M: júng) PH: duhngchìhge binfa yìhngsīk (M: go)

conjunction FV/N: lìhnjip; lìhngit; lìhnhahp N: lìhnjipchìh (M: go)

conjunctive SV: lìhngitge; lìhnjipge; yáuh lìhnjipjokyuhng ge N: lìhnjipchìh (M: go) * **conjunctive adverbs** PH: lìhnjip fuchìh (M: go) * **conjunctive phrase** PH: lìhnjip pinyúh (M: go) * **conjunctive pronoun** PH: lìhnjip doihmìhngchìh (M: go)

conjunctivitis N: gitmókyìhm

conjuncture FV/N: lìhnjip; githahp N: guhkmihn; sìhgèi; gányiugwàantàuh (M: go)

conjure FV: hánkàuh; VO: binheifaat

conjurer (conjuror) N: mòseuhtsì; hánkàuhge yàhn (M: go)

conjuring N: mòseuht (M: júng)

connect FV: lìhnjip; lyùhnhahp; githahp; lyùhnhaih; lyùhnsèung * **be connected with** PH: tùhng . . . sèung lìhnjip; tùhng . . . yáuh gwàanhaih * **connect . . . to** PH: jèung . . . jipdou . . . seuhngbihn * **in this connection** PH: hái nīyāt dím seuhngbihn

Connecticut PW: Hòngnáaihdìhkgaak

connection (connexion) FV/N: lìhnjip; lìhngit; lyùhnhaih N: gwàanhaih; chànchìk * **in connection with** CV: gwàanyù

connective SV: lìhnjipge; lyùhnhahpge; githahpge N: lìhnjipchìh (M: go)

connector N: lìhnjipgeyàhn; lìhnjipmaht; lìhnjiphei (M: go)

connivance FV/N: mahkhéui; jungyùhng; guhngmàuh

connive FV: jadai táimgin; mahkhéui; jungyùhng

connoisseur N: (ngaihseuhtbán ge) gaamdìhnggā; hòhnggā (M: go)

connote FV: ngamsih; hàhmyi; bàauhàahm

connubial SV: fànyànge; fùfúhge

conquer FV: jìngfuhk; hāakfuhk; gùngchéui; dábaaih; gīkbaaih

conqueror N: singleihjé; jìngfuhkjé (M: go)

conquest FV: jìngfuhk; jinsing; yèhngdāk N: singleihbán (M: júng)

consanguineous SV: tùhng hyuttúng ge; tùhng juhk ge; tùhng jóusīn ge; hyutyùhnge; hyutchànge

consanguinity N: hyutyùhn; hyutchàn; tùhng juhk; tùhng hyutyùhn

conscience N: lèuhngsàm (M: go) * **in all conscience** PH: pàhng lèuhngsàm góng A: dīkkok

conscientious SV: yihngjànge; jingjihkge; gánsahnge; jeuhnjaakge

conscious SV: gokdākge; jidouge; sàhnjichìngsíngge; yáuhjigokge; yáuhyisīkge

consciousness N: jìgok; jisīk; jihgok (M: júng)

conscript N: jìngjaahpyahpngǔhge bīngsih; yingjìngge bìng; sànbìng (M: go) FV: jingmouh; jìngjiuh ATT: beihjìng yahpngǔhge; jìngjiuhge

conscription FV/N: jìngbìng; jiumouh; jìngjaahp; (M: chi) * **conscription law** PH: bìngyihk faat

consecrate FV: fuhnghin; jyùnsùhng; fuhngwàih-sàhnsing

consecration PH: fuhnghin; fuhng-wàih-sàhn-sing; yahm singjīk ge yìhsīk; singjīk sauhyahm (M: chi)

consecutive SV: lihnjuhkge; lihngunge; gaijuhk bāt-

dyuhn ge

consensus N: (yigin) yātji; yātbùnge yigin; yùhleuhn (M: go)

consent FV: tùhngyi; yingsìhng; daapying N: tùhngyi; jéunhéui * **by common consent** PH: bāt-yeuk-yìh-tùhng

consenter N: jaansìhngge yàhn (jaansìhngjé) (M: go)

consequence N: ❶ (that which follows) gitgwó; ❷ (importance) juhngyiusing; (M: go) * **in consequence** A: yànchí; gitgwó haih . . . * **in consequence of** A: yàuhyù * **take the consequences** PH: jih-sihk-kèih-gwó

consequent PH: yàn . . . yìh héi ge; haih yàuhyù . . . N: gitgwó (M: go)

conservation FV/N: bóuchyùhn; bóuchòhng

conservatism N: bóusáu jyúyih; sáugauhsing (M: júng) Yìnggwok Bóusáudóng ge jyújeung tùhngmàaih jingchaak

conservative SV: ❶ (opposed to great or sudden change) bóusáuge; sáugauhge; ❷ (cautious) gánsahnge N: bóusáuge yàhn; sáugauhge yàhn; Yìnggwok Bóusáudóngyùhn (M: go)

conservatory N: (pùihyéuhng jihkmaht ge) wànsāt; nyúhnfòhng (M: gàan, go)

conserve FV: bóuchyùhn; chyúhchòhng N: mahtjinge gwóbán; mahtjin (M: júng)

consider FV: ❶ (think about) háauleuih; ❷ (regard as) yíhwàih; yihngwàih; ❸ (make allowances for) táileuhng * be considered as PH: beih yihngwàih haih . . .

considerable SV: jihkdāk háauleuih ge; jihkdāk jyuyi ge; juhngyiuge; hógùnge; m̀síuge

considerate SV: háauleuih jàudou ge; táileuhngge; táitipge

considering CV: jauh . . . yihleuhn; gaamyù; jiu . . . chìhngyìhng làih góng A: júng-yih-yihn-jí

consideration N: ❶ (quality of being considerate) táileuhng; ❷ (act of considering) háauleuih; ❸ (reward or payment) bouchàuh; (M: júng) * in consideration of A: háauleuihdou; yàuhyù * on no consideration A: kyut m̀ . . . * take into consideration FV: háauleuihdou; táileuhng * under consideration PH: jingjoih háauleuih jijùng; jingjoih yihngau jijùng

consign FV: wáitok; yìhgàau; geimaaih; sung; gei; chyùhndaih * consign . . . to FV: jèung . . . gàau béi

consignee N: sāugínyàhn; sàufoyàhn; sìhngsiuyàhn; doihmaaihyàhn; sauhtokyàhn (M: go)

consigner (consignor) N: geigínyàhn; wáitòkyàhn (M: go)

consignment FV/N: (fomaht ge) gàautok; geimaaih; wahnsung; wáitok N: gàautokge yéh; tokmaaihge fobán (M: júng)

consist PH: yàuh . . . jóusìhng; yàuh . . . sójouhsìhng * consist in CV: joihyù *

consist of FV: yàuh . . . jóusìhng * consist with FV: tùhng . . . yātji

consistence (consistency) SV: gìngu; gìnngahn N: gindouh; nùhngdouh; yātji; yātgun

consistent SV: yātjige; chìhnhauh yātgunge; m̀màauh-téuhnge; gìnguge

consolation FV/N: ngònwai; waimahn N: waijihk (M: júng)

console FV/N: ngònwai; waimahn N: jòngsīkyuhngge jichyúh (M: tiuh); lohkdeihjìgá (M: go)

consolidate FV: ❶ (make or become solid or strong) (linghdou) gìnkèuhng; (lihngdou) gúnggu; kèuhngfa; ❷ (unite or combine into one) túngyāt; hahpbing

consommé N: yuhng yuhk waahkjé gāi bòusèhng ge tòng (M: wún)

consonance N: hiptiuh; yātji; wòhhàaih; wòhyām; guhngmìhng (M: júng)

consonant N: jíyām; jíyām jihmóuh; fuhyām (M: go) SV: yātjige; wòhhàaihge

consort N: puingáuh; fù waahkjé chài (M: go); liuhsyùhn; liuhlaahm (M: jek) FV: pùihbuhn; gitgàau; tiuhwòh

consortium FV: hahpgú; hahpfó N: chòihtyùhn (M: go)

conspicuous SV: hínjyuge; hínmìhngge; yáhn-yàhn-jyumuhk ge; chēutjungge

conspiracy N: yàmmàuh

(M: go)

conspirator N: yàmmàuh-gā; guhngmàuhge yàhn (M: go)

conspire FV: tòuhmàuh; guhngmàuh

constable SV: gíngchaat; gínggùn (M: go)

constancy SV: gìndihng PN: gìndihng bātyìh

constant SV: gìndihngge; wíhnghàhngge; jùngsahtge N: sèuhngsou (M: go)

constellation N: sìngjoh; sìngkwàhn (M: go); Méihgwok sìngjohsīk haakwahn fèigèi (M: ga)

consternation SV: gìng-ngohk; húngbou; lòhngbui

constipate FV: lihngdou bihnbei; bihnbei

constipation FV: bihnbei

constituency N: syúngéui-kèui ge chyùhntái syúnmàhn; syúngéuikèui; jaanjohge yàhn (jaanjohyàhn) (M: go)

constituent SV: yáuh syún-géuikyùhn ge; jóusìhngge; yìhngsìhngge N: syúnmàhn; wáitokyàhn (M: go)

constitute FV: jóusìhng; kausìhng; yahmmihng; jaidihng

constitution N: hinfaat (M: bouh)

constitutional SV: hin-faatge; faatjihge; lahphinge

constrain FV: kéuhngbīk; ngaatjai; yīkjai

constraint FV/N:

kéuhngbīk; yīkjai (M: júng) *
by constraint FV: míhnkéuhng; kéuhngbīk

constrict FV: ngaatsūk; sàugán; lihngdou sàusūk

constriction FV: ngaatsūk; sàusūk

construct FV: ❶ héi (construct a house) ~ yātgàan ngūk ❷ jūk (construct a bridge) ~ jātdouh kiuh ❸ jouh (construct a sentence) ~ yātgeui géui

constructure N: ❶ (a building or structure) ginjūk ❷ (structure) gitkau; kaujouh

consul N: líhngsí (M: go) * **consul general** N: júng líhngsí (M: go)

consular SV: líhngsíge; líhngsígúnge; líhngsí jīkmouh ge; jāpjingge * **consular jurisdiction** PH: líhngsih chòihpunkyùhn (M: go)

consulate N: líhngsígún (M: gàan); líhngsíge jīkkyùhn waahkjé yahmkèih (M: go) * **consulate general** N: júng líhngsígún (M: gàan)

consulship N: líhngsíge jīkwaih; líhngsíge yahmkèih (M: go)

consult FV: chénggaau; jī-sèun; chàamháau; chàhyuht; sèunglèuhng; chòsèung * **consult with someone about something** PH: tùhng máuh-yàhn sèunglèuhng máuh sih

consultable SV: hóyíh sèunglèuhng ge

consultant N: gumahn; jī-sèunjé; gunghin yigin ge jyùngā (M: go)

consultee N: gumahn (M: go)

consulter N: tùhng yàhn sèunglèuhng ge yàhn; jìsèun ge yàhn (M: go)

consulting SV: jìsèunge; chénggaauge; jouh gumahn ge * **consulting engineer** N: gumahn gùngchìhngsī (M: go) * **a consulting room** N: chánjing sāt (M: go, gàan)

consultation FV: sèunglèuhng; chénggaau; jìsèun N: wuihyíh

consume FV: sìuhou; sìufai; wáimiht; sìuwái; sihksaai waahkjé yámyùhn; lohngfai; sìumòh * **comsumed with** PH: sām léuihbihn chùngmúhn

consumer N: sìufaijé; yuhngwuh (M: go) * **consumers' cooperative society** PH: sìufai hahpjokséh (M: go) * **consumers' goods** PH: yahtyuhng bītsèui bán (M: júng)

consummate FV: yùhnsìhng; lìhngdou yùhnméih SV: jeuhn-sihn-jeuhn-méih ge; yùhnmúhnge; mòuhseuhngge; yùhnchyùhnge

consummation SV: yùhnchyùhn; yùhnméih FV: yùhnsìhng

consumption FV: sìuhou; yuhngsaai; sìumìht N: sìuhouleuhng (faigithátbehng) (M: go)

consumptive SV: lohngfaige; sìuhousingge; sìufaige; faibehngge N: faibehngge yàhn (M: go)

contact FV/N: jipjūk; lyùhnhaih; lyùhnlok (M: chi) N:lìhnjiphei (M: go) PH: tùhng yàhn jipjūk; tùhng yàhn lyùhnlok * **come into contact with** PH: tùhng . . . jipjūk * **in contact with** PH: tùhng . . . lyùhnhaih * **make contact** VO: jiptùng dihnlouh * **contact lenses** N: yányìhng ngáahngéng (M: go, fu)

contagion N: chyùhnyíhmbehng FV: chyùhnyíhm

contagious SV: yáuh chyùhnyíhmsing ge; chyùhnyíhm jahtbehng ge; yìhgámyíhmge; maahnyìhnge

contain FV: bàauhàhm; jòng; yùhngnaahp

container N: sēung; gun; yùhnghei; fogwaih (M: go)

containment N: yīkjai; hìnjai jingchaak; jóngaat jingchaak (M: go)

contaminate RV: jínglaahttaat (jíngwùjòu) FV: yíhmwù; syúnhoih

contamination N: wùyíhm; wùwai; wùwaimaht; wùyíhmmaht; (language) wahnlyuhn (M: júng)

contemplate FV: jyusih; chàhmsì; mahkséung; dásyun

contemplation FV/N: jyusih; chàhmsì; háauleuih; kéihtòuh; kèihdoih (M: go)

contemplative SV: chàhmsìge; mahkséungge

contemporaneous ATT: tùhngsìhkèihge; tùhngsìhdoihge

contemporary ATT: tùhngsìhdoihge; tùhngnìhnlìhngge; tùhngyahtkèihge PH: tùhngsìhdoihge yàhn, tùhngnìhnlìhngge yàhn (M: go)

contempt FV: hìngsih; míuhsih N: chíyuhk (M: júng)

contemptible SV: bèipéige; hópéige

contemptibly A: bèipéigám; hahjihngám

contemptuous SV: hìngsihge; ngouhmaahnge; míuhsihge

contend FV: gihngjàng; jàngdau; jàngleuhn; gìnseun . . . haih sihsaht * contend with someone for something PH: waihjó máuhdī sih tùhng yàhn gihngjàng; waihjó máuhdī sih tùhng yàhn jàngleuhn

content N: yùhngleuhng; yùhngjīk; hàhmleuhng; noihyùhng; muhkluhk; múhnjūk (M: go) FV: lìhngdou múhnjūk; lìhngdou múhnyi; lìhngdou ngònsàm SV: múhnyige; múhnjūkge; ngònsàmge; yuhnyige; gàmyuhnge

contented SV: múhnjūkge; jìjūkge; múhnyige; ngònsàmge

contention FV/N: jàngleuhn; bihnleuhn; N: gihngjàng; jàngdau; jàngdyùn; jàngleuhndím; (M: go)

contentious SV: houjàngcháau ge; yáuh jàngleuhn ge; houbihn ge; jūkyíh yáhnhéi jàngleuhn ge

contents-bill N: sànmàhn tàihyiu (M: dyuhn)

conterminal (conterminous) SV: yáuh guhngtùhng bìngaai ge; lèuhnjipge; sèunglèuhnge

contest FV: jàngchéui; jàngdyuht; jàngbihn; jàngleuhn; gihngjàng; bihnbok; gihngchoi;

béichoi N: gihngjàng; béichoi; jàngdau; jàngleuhn; jàngbihn (M: go) * an oratorical contest PH: yíngóng béichoi (M: go)* to contest with a person FV: tùhng yàhn jàngleuhn; tùhng yàhn gihngjàng * a tug of war contest PH: bahthòh béichoi * to enter the contest VO: chàamgà béichoi * to contest an election FV: gihngsyún

context N: seuhnghahmàhn * in this contest PH: gwàanyù nīdím; jauh-chíyìh-leuhn

contiguous SV: jipgahnge; lèuhngahnge; lìhnjipge

continence (continency) FV: jihjai; jitjai; jityuhk

continent N: jàu; daaihluhk (M: go) SV: jihjaige; jityeukge * the Continent PW: Ngàu-jàu Daaihluhk

continental ATT: jàuge; daaihluhkge * continental climate PH: daaihluhksing heihauh (M: júng)

contingence (contingency) N: ngáuhyìhnsing; hónàhngsing; yingoih sihgu; ngáuhyìhnge sihgu (M: go)

contingent SV: ngáuhyìhnge; yingoihge; yáuh-hónàhngge PH: ngáuhyìhnge sih; yingoihge sih (M: gihn) síufàndeuih (M: deuih)

continual SV: m̀tìhngge; lìhnjuhkge; pàhnpàhnge

continuance A: lìhnjuhk; gaijuhk N: chìhjuhk kèihgàan (M: go)

continuation A: lìhnjuhk

FV: yihnchèuhng N: yihn-
chèuhngmaht; jànggàmaht ✻
continuation school PH:
bóujaahp hohkhaauh (M: gàan)

continue FV: gaijuhk; yihnchèuhng; lihnjuhk; yihnjuhk ✻
to be continued PH: meih-
yùhn-doih-juhk

continuity N: lihnjuhksing
(M: go)

continuous SV: lihnjuhkge;
bātdyuhnge

contort FV: náumé; náukūk;
lihngdou binsèhng wàankūk;
kūkgáai

contortion FV: náukūk;
wàankūk

contour N: lèuhnkwok;
ngoihyìhng (M: go); ngoihyìhng
gaaisin; jàusin (M: tìuh) VO:
waahk deihyìhngsin; waahk
lèuhnkwok ✻ contour line(s)
N: dánggòu sin (M: tìuh)

contraband VO: jáusì N:
jáusìge fobán; wàihgambán (M:
júng)

contrabass N: dàiyām
daaih tàihkàhm (M: go)

contraception VO: beih-
yahn N: beihyahnge faatjí
(beihyahnfaat) (M: júng)

contraceptive SV: beih-
yahnge N: beihyahnge yuhnggeuih; beihyahnyeuhk (M: júng)

contraclockwise
(counterclockwise) SV:
fáan-sihjām-fōngheung ge A:
fáan-sihjām-fōngheung gám

contract N: hahptùhng;
hahpyeuk (M: go) VO: dingyeuk
✻ to sign a contract VO:
chìmyeuk ✻ make a contract

VO: dáhahptùhng; dinghahptùhng ✻ by contract FV:
sihngbàau ✻ make a contract
with PH: tùhng . . . dingyeuk
✻ contract out PH: lahpkai-
yeuhk bàaugùng; teuichēut
hahpyeuk

contracted SV: sàusūkge;
jausūkge; sáangleuhkge; sūk-
dyúnge; yíhdingyeukge;
dinggwoyeukge

contractor N: lahpkai-
yeukge yàhn (lahpkaiyeuk-
yàhn); sìhngbàauyàhn; sìhngbaahnyàhn; sìhngjouhyàhn (M:
go)

contraction FV: sàusūk;
sūkdyún; sáangleuhk N: sáang-
leuhkjih (sáangleuhkchìh) (M:
go)

contradict FV: fáanbok;
fáuyihng; dáijūk SV/N:
màauhtéuhn

contradiction FV: fáan-
bok; fáuyihng; fáudihng; dáijūk SV/N: màauhtéuhn; (M: go)

contraposition FV: deui-
jiu; jàmdeui; deuiwuhn;
deuidiuh

contraption N: sàn faat-
mìhng ge yéh; kèihháauge
chitgai (M: júng)

contrariety SV/N: màauh-
téuhn FV: sèungfáan N:
deuilahpsing; deuilahpyànsou
(M: go)

contrarily (contrariwise)
A: sèungfáangám; fáandeuih-
gám

contrary SV: sèungfáange;
fáandeuige; màauhtéuhnge A:
sèungfáangám; fáandeuigám;
màauhtéuhngám FV: fáandeui;
sèungfáan SV/N: màauhtéuhn;
✻ by contraries A: sèung-

fáangám * on the contrary
A: jing sèungfáan; sèungfáan

contrast N: deuijiu; deuibéi;
chàbiht (M: go) FV: deuijiu;
deuibéi * by contrast with
FV: tùhng . . . béi * in contrast with (to) PH: tùhng . . .
yìhngsìhng deuibéi

contravene FV: ❶ (act in
opposition to) wàihfáan; dáijúk
❷ (dispute (a statement, etc.))
fáanbok

contravention FV: wàih-
fáan * in contravention of
PH: tùhng . . . sèung dáijúk

contribute FV: gunghin;
gyùnjoh; tàuhgóu * con-
tribute to PH: yáuhjohyù

contribution FV/N:
gunghin; VO: tàuhgóu; gyùnfún
N: dahkbihtseui (M: bāt); gyùn-
johge yéh (M: júng)

contributor N: gunghinge
yàhn; tàuhgóugeyàhn (tàuh-
góuyàhn) (M: go)

contributory SV: yáuh-
gunghinge; yáuhjohyù . . . ge

contrivance FV/N: faat-
mìhng; chitgai N: faatmìhngge
yéh; gwáigai; gēihaaih jōngji
(M: júng)

contrive FV/N: faatmìhng;
chitgai FV: tòuhmàuh; deuifuh

control FV: gúnléih; gún;
hungjai * be in control of FV:
hungjai; gúnléih * under control FV: sauh hungjai; sauhjan-
ngaat * without control A:
yahmyìgám * control chart
PH: (jātleuhng) hungjaitòuh

controller N: jyúgaiyùhn;
chàhjeungyùhn; chòujunghei;
jínglàuhhei; gúnléihyàhn (M:
go) * controller general N:

jyúgaijéung (M: go)

controversial SV: yáhnhéi
jàngleuhn ge; jàngleuhnge;
houjàngleuhnge

controversy FV/N:
jàngleuhn; bihnleuhn (M: chi)

controvert FV: bihnbok;
fáuyihng; fáudihng; jàngleuhn

contumacy FV: m̀fuhk-
chùhng; kongmihng

contuse RV: dásèung; johngsèung; chosèung

contusion RV: dásèung;
johngsèung; chosèung

convalesce FV: fùifuhk
gihnhòng; jihmjím hóufàan

convalescent SV: jìhngjoih
fùifuhk gihnhòng ge; yáuh-
yīkyù fùifuhk gihnhòng ge N:
jìngjoih fùifuhk gihnhòng ge
behngyàhn (M: go)

convection FV: chyùhn-
sung; chyùhndaih; deuilàuh

convene FV: jaahphahp;
jiuhjaahp; jiuhwuhn; jiuhhòi

convenience SV/N:
fòngbihn; bihnleih (M: go) * at
your earliest convenience
PH: yùhgwó fòngbihn, chéng
jeuhnjóu . . . * make a convenience of a person VO:
leihyuhng yātgo yàhn

convenient SV: fòngbihn-
ge; bihnleihge; hahpsīkge

convent N: sàuyún (sàu-
douhyún) (M: gàan); sàunéui
(waahkjé sàusih) ge tyùhntái
(M: go)

convention N: wuihyíh;
jiuhjaahp; gùngyeuk; gwaanlaih; jaahpjuhk; tiuhyeuk (M:

go) * **by convention** PH:
ngonjiu gwaanlaih

conventional SV: chyùhn-
túngge; jaahpgwaange; yàn-
jaahpge; yeukdihngge;
sèuhngkwàige

conventionalism PH:
yànjaahpjyúyih; mahksáu-
sìhngkwài; yìchùhng gwaanlaih

conventionalist N: yàn-
jaahpjyúyihjé; jèunsáu gwaan-
leih ge yàhn; mahksáu sìhngkwài ge yàhn (M: go)

conventionality N: yàn-
jaahpsing; gwaanlaih (M: go)
FV: yànjaahp

conventual ATT: néuih
sàudouhyún ge

converge FV: jaahpjùng;
jaahpjàng hái yātdím

convergent SV: jaahp-
jùngge; wuihjeuihge

conversant SV: jingtùng . .
. ge; suhksīk . . . ge; jìngtùngge; suhksīkge

conversation N: wuihwá;
tàahmwah; sēhgaau (M: go)

converse FV: tàahmwah;
yihngsīk; suhksīk N: tàahmwah; yihngsīk (M: go); sèungfáan ge sihmaht (M: júng) SV:
sèungfáange; dóujyunge

conversely A: sèungfáan
gám

conversion FV/N: jyúnbin;
binwuhn; góibin; bingàng;
deuiwuhn (M: júng)

convert FV: binwuhn; gànggói; jyúnbin; góibin; deuiwuhn;
gàauwuhn

converter N: jyúnwuhnge

yàhn; binlàuhhei; binngaathei;
jyúnfalòuh (M: go)

convertible SV: hóyíh
góibin ge; hóyíh deuiwuhn ge;
hóyíh jyúnwuhn ge

convex SV: dahtge; dahtchēutge N: dahtmín (M: go)

convey FV: wahnsung;
wahnsyù; chyùhndaih; chyùhndaaht; yeuhngbéi

conveyable SV: hóyíh bùn-
wahnge; hóyíh chyùhndaaht ge;
hóyíh jyúnyeuhng ge

conveyance FV: wahnsung;
wahnsyù; chyùhndaaht;
chyùhndaih; yeuhngyúh
(yeuhngbéi) N: gàautùng gùnggeuih (M: júng)

conveyer (conveyor) N:
wahnsungge yàhn; wahnsung-
gèi; bùnwahnhei (M: go); jyún-
wahndáai (M: tìuh)

convict FV: jingmihng yáuhjeuih; syùngou yáuhjeuih N:
jeuihyàhn; jeuihfáan (M: go)

conviction VO: (the convic-
ting of a person of crime) dihngjeuih; punjeuih; FV: (firm belief)
gìnseun; sàmseun

convince FV: seuifuhk;
lihngdou sèungseun; lihngdou
sàmseun * **be convinced of**
FV: kokhaih sèungseun;
sìhngyihng

convincible SV: hóyíh
lihngdou sèungseunge; hóyíh
seuifuhk ge

convincing SV: yáuh
seuifuhklihk ge; lihng yàhn
sàmfuhk ge; dīkkokge

convocation FV: jiuh-
jaahp; jaahpwúi N: wuihyíh (M:
go)

convoke FV: jiuhhòi (wuih-yíh); jiuhjaahp

convoy FV: wuhsung; wuh-waih; wuhhòhng; bóuwuh N: wuhsung; wuhwaih (M: chi) wuhsungdéui (M: deuih) * **convoy fleet** N: wuhhòhng laahmdéui (M: deuih)

convulse VO: chàugàn (of the muscles)

convulsion VO: chàugàn N: gīngfúngjing (in chinese herb medicine; convulsion or spasm suffered by a convalescent child)

cony (coney) N: tou (M: jek); toupèih (M: faai)

coo FV: (baahkgáap dáng-dáng) gūgù gám giu; tàahm-chìhng; saisaisèng góng syutwah

cook FV: jyú; pàangtìuh; ngaihjouh N: jyúfaahnge yáhn; chyùhjí; chyùhsì (M: go) * **cook up** FV: gaiwaahk; ngaih-jouh; nihpjouh * **cook book (cookery book)** N: sihkpóu; pàangyahm syù (M: bún)

cooker N: wohk (bōu); chèuigeuih (M: jek, go)

cookery N: pàangyahm; pàangyahmseuht (M: júng)

cookie (cooky) N: béng-gōn; kūkkèihbéng (M: faai)

cool SV: lèuhngge; lèuhng-sóngge; láahngjihngge; chàhm-jeuhkge; móuhláihge; daaih-dáamge FV: lihngdou láahng; binlèuhng; láahngkeuk; lihng-dou jandihng; pihngsīk N: lèuhngsóng; láahnghei (M: júng) lèuhngsóngge deihfòng (M: daat) * **keep cool** PH: bóu-chìh jandihng; m̀sái pa (m̀sái gèng) * **cool down** FV:

láahngkeuk * **cool one's heels** FV: dáng hóunoih

cooler N: láahngkeukhei; bīngsēung (M: go) chìnglèuhng-jāi; chìnglèuhngge yámbán (M: júng)

cool-headed SV: tàuhnóuh láahngjihngge; chàhmjeuhk ge

coolie (cooly) N: gūlēi; fúlihk; síugūng (M: go)

coop N: lùhng; pàahng; gàise (M: go) FV: wanhái (lùhng léuihbihn); kèuigam

co-op N: hahpjokséh; sìufai-hahpjokséh (M: go)

cooperate FV: hahpjok; hiplihk; hiptùhng

cooperation FV: hahpjok; hiplihk; hiptùhng * **in cooperation with** PH: tùhng . . . hahpjok

cooperative SV: hahp-jokge; hiptùhngge N: hahp-jokséh (M: go)

coordinate SV: tùhng-dángge; tùhnggaakge; deui-dángge; johbīuge N: tùhngdángge yàhn waahkjé mahtgín; johbīu (M: go)

coordination FV: tùhng-dáng; tùhnggaak; tùhngwaih; tiuhwòh; hipjok

cop FV: jūk; tàu N: gíngchaat (M: go) * **cop out** FV: tòuhbeih; jihsáu; tóhhip

copartner N: hahpjokge yàhn (hahpjokjé); hahpfóge yàhn (hahpfóyàhn) (M: go)

copartnership (partner-ship) FV: hahpjok; hahpfó N: hiptùhng

cope FV: deuifuh; yingfuh; deuikong; gihngjàng; kámjyuh N: chèuhngpòuh; dáupùhngsīkge chèuhngpòuh (M: gihn) ✻ **cope with** FV: deuifuh; hāakfuhk

copier N: chàausége yàhn (chàauséyùhn); mòuhfóngge yàhn (M: go)

copilot N: (fèigèige) fugēisī (fugasáiyùhn) (M: go)

copious SV: fùngfuge; yúngchèuhngge

copper N: tùhng; tùhngbaih; tùhnghei (M: júng); tùhngsīk FV: yuhng tùhng tòuhhái . . . SV: tùhngsīkge; tùhngjouhge

coppice (copse) N: ngái syuhchùhng; síugunmuhklàhm (M: go)

copula N: lìhnjipge yéh (lìhnhaihmaht) (M: gihn); lìhnhaih-duhngchìh (M: go)

copulate FV: jouhngoi; singgàau

copulative SV: lìhnhaihge; lìhnhaihchìhge; singgàauge N: lìhnhaihchìh; lìhnhaihlìhnjipchìh (M: go)

copy N: chàaubún; fubún; tàhngbún; fūkjaibún (M: fahn) góu (M: pìn) hàaubui (M: go) M: (for books; magazines; newspapers; etc.) báan; yìhp; fahn; bún; chaak FV: chàau; chàausé; mòuhfóng; fónghaauh ✻ **a copy of** NuM: yātfahn; yātchaak; yātbún ✻ **copy after** FV: fóngjìu ✻ **copy from** FV: làhmmòuh ✻ **copybook** N: jihtip (jihtíp); jaahpjihbóu (M: bún, bouh) ✻ **copygraph** N: yàuhyangèi (M: ga, go) ✻ **copy-money** N: góufai; báanseui (M: bāt) ✻ **copy-**

reader N: pìnchāp; gaaudingyàhn (M: go) ✻ **copyright** N: báankyùhn; jyujokkyùhn (M: go)

coquet (coquette) FV: (néuihyán) maaihluhng fùngchìhng; maaihchiu; hinmèih; wuhnluhng

coquetry VO: (néuihjí) wuhnluhng nàahmyán; maaihluhng fùngchìhng

coquettish SV: giuyihmge; maaihluhng-fùngchìhng ge

coral N: sàanwùh (M: gauh); sàanwùhjaibán (M: gihn) SV: sàanwùhsīkge; tòuhhùhngsīkge

cord N: síngjái (saige síng); sok; yìhn; saige dihnsin (M: tiuh) FV: bóng; kwánbóng; dèuijīk

cordage N: síhngsok (M: tiuh)

cordial SV: yihtsàmge; yihtsìhngge; jànsìhngge; yáuhsìhnge; hìngfáhnge; tàlhsàhnjibóuge N: hìngfáhnjāi; kèuhngsàmjāi (M: júng)

cordially A: yihtsìhnggám; sìhngjigám

cordon N: sīkdáai; gínggaaisin; saaubìngsin (M: tiuh)

core N: gwósàm; jūngsàm waahkjé jeui juhngyiu ge bouhfahn; hahtsàm (M: go) ✻ **to the core** A: chitdái

cork N: yúhnmuhkjāt; jēunjāt (M: go); yuhng yúhnmuhk jouhsìhng ge yéh (M: go) FV: yuhng jēunjāt sākjyuh; haahnjai; jójí

corn N: gūkmaht; síumahk;

yuhkmáih; bàausūk (yuhk-
suhksyú; sūkmáih); yuhksuhk-
syúnáp; gàingáahn (M: nāp) FV:
yuhng yùhngge yìhmséui yip

corn chandler N: lèuhngsihk lìhngsauhsèung (M: go)

corn-cob N: yuhksuhksyúge
seuihjuhk (M: tìuh)

cornea N: (ngáahnkàuhge)
gokmók (M: faai)

corner N: gok; pìnpīkge
deihfòng; kwangíng; FV:
lúhngdyuhn; tyùhnjīk lìhngdou
haahmyahp kwangíng ✻ cut
corners VO: hàahng káhnlouh;
jyuyi jìtyeuk ✻ turn the corner VO: jyunwāan; douhgwo
nàahngwàan; tyuthím ✻ the
four corners N: sahpjih
louhháu (M: go) ✻ corner boy
N: yàuhmàhn; yàuhdohngjé (M:
go) ✻ corner man N:
mòuhyíhp yàuhmàhn; yàuh-
dohngjé (M: go) ✻ corner-
stone N: chèuhnggeuksehk;
gèisehk (M: faai); gèichó (M: go)

corn-exchange N: lèuhngsihk gàauyihksó (M: go)

corn-field N: wòhtìhn;
mahktìhn (M: faai)

corn flour N: sūkmáihfán
(yuhksuhksyúfán)

corn-loft N: gūkchòng (M:
go)

corn-meal N: yuhksuhksyú
chòu fán; yuhkmáihpin;
yuhkmáihfán

corn mill N: mihnfángèi (M:
ga)

corn-plaster N: gàingáahn
gòuyeuhk (M: faai)

corn-stalk N: yuhksuhksyúge hàhng (M: jì)

corn-starch N: yuhksuhksyú dihnfán; yuhkmáihfán
(sūkmáihfán)

corolla N: fàgùn (M: go)

corona N: gùnjohngmaht (M:
gihn)

coronation N: gàmíhnláih
(M: go)

coroner N: yìhmsìgùn (M:
go)

coronet N: gùnmíhn; fàgùn
(M: go)

corporal SV: yuhktáige;
sàntáige N: luhkgwān hahsih
(seuhngdángbìng) (M: go)

corporality N: yìhngtái;
yuhksàn; yuhktái (M: go)

corporate SV: séhtyùhnge;
guhngtùhngge; tyùhntáige;
chyùhntáige

corporation N: tyùhntái;
gūngsī; séhtyùhn; faatyàhn (M:
go)

corporeal SV: yuhktáige;
mahtjātge; yáuhyìhngge

corps N: gwān; gwàntyùhn;
gwàndéui léuihbihn dahkjúng
bouhmùhn ge bouhdéui ✻
Marine Corps N: hóigwān
luhkjindéui (M: deuih) ✻
Signal Corps N: tùngseundéui
(M: deuih) ✻ Corps of
Engineers N: gūngbīngdéui
(M: deuih)

corpse N: sìtái (M: go) ✻ corpse candle (corpse-light) N:
lèuhnfó; gwáifó

corpulence (corpulency)
SV: fèih

corpulent SV: fèihge; fèihdaaihge

corpuscle (corpuscule) N: hyutkàuh (M: go)

corral N: chūklàahn; chèjahn (M: go)

correct FV: gói; góijing SV: ngāam; jingkokge; (proper) sīkdongge

correction FV/N: góijing; sàujing; gaaujing; chìhnggaai (M: júng) ＊ **house of correction** N: chìhnggaaisó; gámfayún (M: gàan) ＊ **under correction** PH: yáuh doih góijing

correction fluid N: tòuhgói-yihk (M: jēun)

corrective SV: góijìngge; gíujìngge N: góisihnge fòngfaat (M: go)

corrector N: góijingge yàhn (góijingjé); sàujingge yàhn (sàujingjé); gaaujingge yàhn (gaaujingjé) (M: go)

correlate FV: lihngdou wuhsèung gwāanlihn; gwāanlihn N: yáuh sèungwuh gwāanhaih ge yàhn waahkjé yéh

correlation N: sèungwuh gwāanlihn; gwāanlihn (M: júng)

correlative SV: gwāanlihnge; sèunggwāange; (mathematics) yihsou sehbinge N: gwāanlyùhnchìh; yáuh sèungwuh gwāanhaih ge yàhn waahkjé mahtgín

correspond FV: ❶ (be in harmony (with)) fùhhahp; ❷ (be similar (to)) sèungdòng; VO: (exchange letters (with sb.)) tùngseun

correspondence FV: fùh-hahp; yātji; sèungdòng; tùngseun N: seungín ＊ **by correspondence** PH: yuhng tùngseunge fòngfaat

correspondent N: tùngseunyùhn; geijé SV: fùhhahpge; sèungdòngge

corresponding SV: sèungyingge; fùhhahpge; tùngseunge

corridor N: jáulòhng (M: tiuh) deihdaai (M: go)

corrigendum N: yìnggòi góijing ge chongh; sèuiyiu góijing ge chongh; hamngh bíu (M: go)

corrigible SV: hóyìh góijing ge; yih gíujing ge

corroborate FV: lihngdou gúnggu; jingsaht

corroboration FV: kokdihng; kokjing; gìndihng; gúnggu

corrode FV: fuhsihk; chàmsihk

corrosion FV: fuhsihk; chàmsihk

corrosive SV: fuhsihkge; chàmsihkge N: fuhsihkmaht; fuhsihkjāi (M: júng)

corrugate FV: lihngdou héijaumàhn; héijaumàhn; lihngdou sìhngwàih bòjohng

corrupt SV: fuhbaaihge; tàamwùge; wùjuhkge FV: fuhfa; kwúilouh; fuhbaaih; lihngdou baaihwaaih; lihngdou dohlohk

corruptible SV: yih fuhbaaihge; yih wáiwaaihge; hóyìh kwúilouhge

corruption SV: fuhbaaih FV: tàamwù; fuhfa; dohlohk; kwúilouh

corsair N: hóidouh (M: go) hóidouhsyùhn (M: jek)

cortex N: ngoihpèih; pèihjāt; pèihchàhng

coruscate FV: símseuk; símgwòng

cosignatory SV: lìhnmìhng chìmchyúhge; lìhnchyúhge N: lìhnchyúhyàhn (lìhnchyúhjé); lìhnchyúhgwok (M: go)

cosily (cozily) A: syùsīkgám; wànnyúhn-yih-syùfuhkgám

cosine N: (mathematics) yùhyìhn

cosmetic(s) N: fajōngbán (M: júng) SV: fajōngyuhngge; jíngyuhngge; jōngsīksingge

cosmetology PH: jíngyùhngseuht (M: júng)

cosmic SV: yùhjauhge ∗ **cosmic dust** PH: yùhjauh chàhn ∗ **cosmic fog** PH: yùhjauh sìngwàhn ∗ **cosmic rays** PH: yùhjauh sin ∗ **cosmic rocket** PH: yùhjauh fójin (M: jì)

cosmo- ATT: taaihùng; yúhjauh; saigaai ∗ **cosmodom** N: taaihùngjaahm (M: go)

cosmodrome PH: yàhnjouh-waihsīng tùhng yúhjauhfèisyùhn faatsehchèuhng (M: go)

cosmopolis PH: gwokjai dòusíh; gwokjai sìhngsíh (M: go)

cosmopolitan PH: saigaai jyúyihjé (M: go) SV: saigaaijyúyihge; chyùhn saigaaige

cosmopolitanism N: saigaaijyúyúyih

cosmos N: yúhjauh; dihtjeuih; wòhhàaih (M: go); (jihkmaht) daaihbōsīgūk (M: pò)

cost N: (expense) faiyuhng; N/FV: (sacrifice) hèisàng FV: yiu *Nīgo bīu yiu géidō chín a?* ∗ **at all costs (at any cost)** A: mòuhleuhn yùhhòh; bātsīkyahmhòh-doihga ∗ **at the cost of** PH: yíh . . . doihga; hèisàng; songsāt ∗ **cost of living** N: sàngwuhtfai (M: bāt)

costive SV: bihnbeige

costly SV: ngòhnggwaige; gwaijuhngge

costume N: fuhkjōng; néuihngoihtou; (M: gihn, tou) fuhkjōngge sīkyeuhng VO: gùngkāp fuhkjōng ∗ **costume ball** N: fajōng móuhwúi (M: go) ∗ **a hunting costume** N: lihpjōng (M: gihn, tou) ∗ **costume play** N: gújōng kehk (M: chēut)

costumey SV: kèihjōng yihfuhk ge

costumer (costumier) N: yìfuhk sèungyàhn (M: go)

cosy, cozy SV: syùsīkge; wànnyúhnge; wànnyúhn yih syùsīk ge N: nyúhnjaau; bóuwànjaau (M: go)

cot N: ❶ (made of canvas) fàahnbouchòhng (M: jèung) ❷ (cot = cotangent) (mathematics) yùhchit

coterie N: síu hyúnjí; síu jaahptyúhn; paaihaih (M: go)

cottage N: nùhngse; màauhse; saige ngūk (síungūk) (M: gàan)

cotton N: mihn; mihnfà; mihnsin; mihnsà

cotton cake N: mihnjí béng (M: go)

cotton gin N: jaatmihngèi (M: ga, fu)

cotton mill N: sàchóng; fóngjīkchóng (M: gàan)

cottonseed oil N: mihnjí yàuh

cotton spinner N: fóngsà gùngyàhn; fóngjīk gùngyàhn; fóngjīkchóngge chóngjyú; gìngyìhng fóngjīkyìhp ge yàhn (M: go)

cotton-wood N: (jihkmaht) baahkyèuhng (M: pò)

cotton wool N: mihnfà; sàangmihn; tyutjì mihnfà

couch N: chòhng; fangaau yuhngge yí (seuihyí); chèuhng-yí; chèuhng sòfá (M: jèung) FV: (put (a thought) (in words)) chouchìh; bíudaaht

cough FV: kāt; kātsau; (cough up) kātchēut N: kāt; kāt-sau (M: sèng) ✻ **cough drop** N: kāttóng (M: nāp) ✻ **cough mixture** N: kātséui (jíkāt yeuhkséui) (M: jèun)

coulisse N: (heikehk) jākmihn bougíng; hauhtòih (M: go)

council N: wuihyíh; jing-mouhwúi; léihsihwúi; wái-yùhnwúi (M: go)

council chamber N: wuihyíhsāt (M: go, gàan)

councillor (councilor) N: (jàu; síh; jan dángdáng yíhwúige) yíhyùhn; pìhngyíh-yùhn; chàamjaan; gumahn (M: go)

counsel FV/N: sèungyíh; sèunglèuhng; hyungou; hyun-douh FV: jùnggūk; gínyíh

counselor (counsellor) N: gumahn; chàamsih; chàam-jaan; faatíeuht gumahn; leuhtsī (M: go)

count FV: ❶ sóu *Chéng néih sóuháh.* ❷ gai ❸ (include) bāau-kwut *Ṁgai saimānjái, nĭdouh yáuh sahpgo yàhn.* ❹ (rely on) kaau *Ngóhdeih chyùhn-kaau kéuih ge la.* N: (count = earl) baakjeuk (M: go) ✻ **count . . . as** PH: yìhng . . . haih (yìhng . . . wàih); jèung . . . dongjok ✻ **count for** SV: yáuh gajihk ✻ **count out** PH: ṁgaisyun joihnoih; dímsou ✻ **count up** RV: sóudou; sóuyùhn; júnggai ✻ **out of count** Nu: mòuhsouge ✻ **countess** N: baakjeuk fùyàhn; néuih baak-jeuk (M: go) ✻ **countless** Nu: mòuhsouge; bāt-gai-kèih-sou ge

countenance N: (face, including its appearance and expression) mihnbouh bíuchìhng; mihnsīk; mihnmaauh; yùhng-maauh FV: (support) jaanhéui; gúlaih; jaanjoh ✻ **keep one's countenance** PH: taai-yìhn-jih-yeuhk ✻ **put out of countenance** FV: lihngdou nàahnhàm

counter N: ❶ (small, round, flat piece of metal, plastic, etc. used for keeping count in games, etc.) chàuhmáh ❷ (table on which goods are shown, customers are serv ed, in a shop or bank.) gwaihmín (gwaihtói) SV: sèungfáange; fáandeuige A: sèungfáangám; fáandeui-gám FV: fándeui; wàahngīk ✻ **counter to** PH: tùhng . . .

sèungfáan FV: fáandeui * counter-attack FV/N: fáangùng; fáangīk * counter-balance FV: pìhnghàhng N: pìhnghàhng; pìhnghàhnglihk (M: go) pìhnghàhngmaht (M: júng) * counter-charge N/FV: fáangīk; fáansou * counter-claim N/FV: fáandeui yiukàuh; fáansou * counter-espionage N: fáangaandihp-wuhtduhng FV: chaakfáan * counter-evidence N: fáanjing (M: go) * counter-feit SV: gámouhge; mouhpàaihge FV: ngaihjouh; mòuhfóng N: ngaihjouhbán; ngaahnbán; gámouhge yàhn * counter-foil N: chyùhngàn; piugàn (M: jèung) * counter-intelligence N: (gwànsih) fáan chìhngbou; fáan-gaandihp-wuhtduhng * counter-mand FV: chitwùih waahkjé chéuisìu (yíhgìng faatchēut ge mihnglihng) chéuisìu; chitwùih; sâuwùih sìhngmihng * counter-part N: fubún (M: fahn); gihkjì sèungchíhge yàhn waahkjé mahtbán * counter-revolution N: fáan gaakmihng * counter-revolutionist N: fáan gaakmihng fahnjí (M: go) * counter-sea N: yihklohng (M: go) * counter-sign N: (gwànsih) háulihng; ngamhouh; fuchyúh; lìhnchyúh FV: fuchyúh; lìhnchyúh * counter-stroke FV/N: fáangīk; wàahngīk (M: go)

counteract FV: dáisìu; sìuchèuih; sìugáai

counteraction N: fáan-jokyuhng (M: go) PH: jokyuhng tùhng fáanjokyuhng.

counting FV/N: gaisyun * counting-house (counting-room) N: jeungfóng; wuihgaisāt (M: go) * counting

machine N: gaisyungèi (M: ga, go)

countrified (countryfied) SV: hèungtóuheige; chòujuhk ge; hēunghháyàhngge

country N: ❶ (land occupied by a nation) gwokgā ❷ (land in which a person was born) gàhèung; guhèung; hèunghá ❸ (region of open spaces, of land used for farming.) hēungchyūn; hèunggàan (M: go) ❹ (the people of a country) gwokmàhn M: gwok SV: hèunggàange; tìhnsege

country-dance N: tóufùngmóuh (M: júng)

country-folk N: hèunghá yàhn; tùhngbàau; gwokyàhn (M: go)

country-man N: hèunghá-yàhn; tùhngbàau (M: go)

country-rock N: móuh-ngàahm (M: faai)

country-seat N: hèung-gàange daaihhah; bihtséuih (M: gàan); (Yìnggwok) hèungsànge jyuhjaahk (M: gàan)

country-side PW: nùhng-chyūn; hèunggàan; hèung-chyùndeihfòng; nùhngchyūn-deihfòng N: hēungchyūnge gèuimàhn (M: go)

country-wide SV: chyùhn-gwoksingge; pinkahp chyùhn-gwok ge

country-woman N: chyūn-fúh; néuih tùhngbàau; néuih tùhnghēung (M: go)

county N: (Yìnggwok) gwahn (M: go); (Méihgwok) yún (yuhn) (M: go)

coup N: dahtyìhn yātgīk; chaakleuhk; (gwànsih) jingbin (M: go)

coup dé-tat N: jingbin *Gauhnìhn, Míhndihn faatsàng jingbin gójahnsí, séijó géi baak yàhn.*

coupe N: sèungjoh seilèuhn gíusìk máhchè; síugíuchè (M: ga)

couple N: ❶ (two persons, or things, seen or associated together) yātdeui ❷ (two persons (to be) married to one another) fùfúh FV: lìhngit; sìhngdeui; sìhngsèung

couplet N: léuhnghòhng sī; deuilyùhn; FV: (sī) deuigeui; sèungwahn

coupling N: lyùhngit; lyùhnjuhkjit; gwangāu; chèngāu (M: go)

coupon N: leihsīkdāan; jahnghyun (jahnggyun); sèunggàge yàudoihhyun (M: jèung)

courage N: yúhnghei (M: go) SV: yúhnggám

courageous SV: yúhnggámge

course N: ❶ (school work) gùngfo (M: mùhn) ❷ (routes, of an airline or shipping company) hòhngsin (M: tìuh) M: ❶ (of instruction) fō ❷ (of a meal) meih FV: jèuilihp; làuhduhng; jeunhàhng ✻ **in due course** A: kahpsìhgám; dousìhhauh (dousìh) ✻ **in the course of** A: hái . . . kèihgàan ✻ **of course** A: dòngyìhn

court N: ❶ (space with walls or buildings round it) tìhngyún; tìnjéng ❷ (place where law cases are heard) faattìhng ❸ (royal residence) gùngtìhng ❹ (for games) kàuhchèuhng FV: jèuikàuh; kàuhfàn; jàngchéui ✻ **out of court** FV: bātbeih háauleuih; beih bokwùih ✻ **play court to** FV: fuhngsìhng; tóuhóu; kàuhngoi ✻ **court day** N: sámpunyaht ✻ **courtesan** N: gòudáng (gòukáp) geihnéuih (M: go) ✻ **courtier** N: chìuhsàhn; fuhngsìhngjé (fuhngsìhngge yàhn) (M: go) ✻ **court-lady** N: gùngnéui (M: go) ✻ **court-martial** N: gwànsih faattìhng (M: go) FV: gwànsih sámpun

courteous Adj. PH: yáuh láihmaauh ge; hìmgùngge; yànkàhnge

courtesy N: láihmaauh; yànkàhn PH: láihmaauhge hàhngwàih; yànkàhnge géuiduhng (M: go)

court-ship FV: kàuhngoi

court-yard N: tìnjéng (M: go)

cousin N: ❶ (paternal uncle's elder son) sòtòhng agō ❷ (younger son) sòtòhng sailóu ❸ (elder daughter) sòtòhng ajé ❹ (younger daughter) sòtòhng amúi ❺ (a son of father's sister or of mother's brother or sister, who is older than oneself) bíugō ❻ (a son of father's sister or of mother's brother or sister, who is younger than oneself) bíudái ❼ (a daughter of father's sister or of mother's brother or sister, who is older than oneself) bíujé ❽ (a daughter of father's sister or of mother's brother or sister, who is younger than oneself) bíumúi (M: go)

cove N: saige hóiwāan (M: go)

covenant N: kaiyeuk; màhngyeuk (M: go) VO: daigitmàhngyeuk; dingmàhngyeuk

cover FV: kámjyuh (kám); pòu; yímsīk; yímwuh; (include) bàaukwut N: goi; tou; fūngmín; (M: go) * **be covered with** RV: pòumúhn * **under cover** SV: yánchòhngge; ngaihjòngge * **under (the) cover of** PH: yíh ... wàih jihkháu * **cover up** FV: yímsīk; yánchòhng * **cover crop** N: luhkfèih jokmaht (M: júng)

coverlet N: chòhngkám; péihdāan (M: jèung)

covert SV: yánchòhngge; yímbaige N: yímbaige deihfòng; yánfuhkge deihfòng (M: daat)

covet FV: móhngtòuh; móhngséung; tàam; VO: làuhháuséui

covetous SV: tàamlàahmge; tàamsàmge

covetously A: tàamlàahmgám; tàamsàm gám

covetousness SV: tàamlàahm; tàamsàm

covey PH: yātkwàhn jeukjái; yātkwàhn yàhn NuM: yātdeuih; yātpài

cow N: ngàuhná (móuhngàuh)FV: haak; húnghaak * **cow-boy** N: ngàuhjái (muhkyàhn) (M: go) * **cow-catcher** N: (fóchè gèichè chìhnbihn ge) pàaihjeunghei (M: go) * **cowfish** N: hóityùhn; hóingàuh (M: jek) * **cow-pea** N: làihdáu; ngàuhdáu (M: nāp) * **cow-pox** N: ngàuhdauh (ngàuhdóu) * **cow tree** N: yúhsyuh (M: pò)

coward N: móuhdáamge

yàhn; saidáamge yàhn; nohfù (M: go) SV: dáamhipge; saidáamge

cowardice SV: nohyeuhk; saidáam

cowardly SV: saidáamge; dáamhipge

cower FV: waisūk; teuisūk

cowl N: tàuhgān; tàuhbou (M: faai)

cox N: tòhsáu; tèhngjéung (M: go) VO: jouh tòhsáu; jéungtòh

coxcomb N: fàfàgùngjí (M: go); (plant) gàigùnfà (M: pò)

coxswain N: tòhsáu; tèhngjéung (M: go)

coy SV: pacháuge

crab N: ❶ háaih (M: jek); háaihyuhk ❷ (fruit of wild apple tree) (yéhsàangge) syùn pìhnggwó ❸ (a crane) héichúhnggèi (M: go) * **crab louse** N: yàmsāt; mòuhsāt (M: jek) * **crabbed** SV: gwàaileuihge; bouhchouge; lìuhchóu nàahntáige

crack FV: lihthòi; liht; jíngliht; N: la (M: tùh) SV: (firstrate; very clever) daihyātlàuhge; jìnglihnge * **crack down** PH: chóichéui yìhmlaih chousì; janngaat * **crack on** IE: (Yìnggwok) gàyáu; gaijuhk; (Méihgwok) yéhsiu; m̀tìhng gám daaihsiu * **crack up** FV: ① (lose strength) sàntái sèuiyeuhk; ② (praise highly) chìngjaan * **crack-brained** SV: dìnkwòhngge; jìngsàhncholyuhnge

cracked SV: jínglaahnge; polihtge; fùngkwòhngge

cracker N: ❶ (thin, hard, dry

biscuit) bohk yīh cheui ge béng-gōn (M: faai) ❷ (firework that makes a crack or cracks) paaujéung (M: go, chyun) PH: dálaahn . . . ge yàhn (M: go)

crackle VO: faatchēut pīkpāaksèng N: baauliht sèng

crackling N: pīkpāaksèng

cradle N: ❶ (small bed or cot, mounted on rockers, for a baby) yìuhlàahm ❷ (place where sth. is born or begins) faatyùhndeih (M: go)

craft N: gùngngaih; sáungaih (M: mùhn); (boat(s)) syùhn (M: jek); fèigèi (M: ga, jek) ✳ **craft brother** N: tùhnghòhng; hòhnggā (M: go)

craft carrier N: hòhnghùng móuhlaahm (M: jek)

crafty SV: gáauwaahtge

crag N: yùhnngàaih; chiubīk (M: go)

craggy SV: dòchiubīkge; kèikèuige

cram FV: tìhnsāk; chùngmúhn; sākmúhn

cramming PH: tìhnngaapsīkge gaauyuhk; ngoksingbóujaahp

cramp VO: chàugàn

cramped SV: chàugànge; (of space) haahpjaakge; (difficult to read) (jihtái) nàahnyihng ge

crampon N: hàaihdáidēng (M: ngáan); (yuhnglàih héichúhngge) titngāu (M: go)

crane N: ❶ (large waterbird with long legs and neck) hók (hohk) (M: jek) ❷ (machine for lifting heavy loads) héichúhng-gèi (M: ga) PH: yuhng héichúhnggèi làih bùn; (stretch out (the neck)) sànchèuhnggéng

crane fly N: daaih wūyīng; daaihmān (M: jek)

cranial SV: tàuhlòuhge; tàuhgoigwātge; tàuhgoige

cranium N: tàuhgoi (M: go)

crank N: (gèihaaih) kūkbeng

crank-shaft N: kūkjuhk (M: tìuh)

cranky SV: (of people) (odd) mjingsèuhngge; (of buildings) (unsteady) mwánge

crannied Adj. PH: yáuh la ge; yáuh lūngjáige

cranny N: la; lagwīk (M: tìuh)

crape N: jausì; jausà; jaucháu (M: fūk); (sòngyuhng) hāaksà (M: tìuh)

crash FV: pungjohng; máahngjohng; jeuihwái N: poseuisèng; ✳ **crash-dive** FV: (submarine) gāpchìhm ✳ **crash-land** PH: (airplane) kéuhngbīk gonglohk

crass SV: yùhchéunge; chòuchouge

crate N: báantiuhsēung (M: go) PH: jòngyahp daaih báantiuhsēung léuihbihn

crater N: fósàanháu (M: go)

cravat N: tāai (léhngtāai; léhngdáai); wàihgān (M: tìuh)

crave FV: hotmohng; hánkàuh

craven N: nohfù (M: go) SV: nohyeuhkge; móuhdáamge

crawl FV: pàh; pàhhàhng; maahnmáan hàahng

crawler N: pàhhàhngge yàhn (pàhhàhngjé) (M: go)

crayon N: yáuhsīkge fánbāt; laahpbāt (M: jì)

craze VO: faatdìn; faatsàhngìng; chìsin N: faatdìn; sàhngìng; chìsin

crazy SV: faatdìn (ge); dìnge; sàhngìng(ge); chìsin (ge)

creak FV: faatchēut jīyí jēkjēk sèng N: jījēksèng (M: go)

cream N: (of milk) geihlīm ✳ **ice cream** N: syutgōu (M: bùi) ✳ **cold cream** N: láahngsèung (M: hahp) ✳ **face cream** N: mihnsèung (M: hahp)

creamery N: náaihyàuhchóng (M: gàan)

crease N: jiphàhn (M: tìuh) FV: chàauh; bìnchàauh; jíngchàauh

creasy Adj. PH: yáuh jiphàhn ge; hóuchàauhge; yáuh hóudò jaumàhn ge

create FV: chongjouh; chongjok; cháansàng

creation FV/N: chongjouh; chongjok (M: go)

creative SV: yáuh chongjouhlihk ge; chongjouhge; chongjokge

creator N: chongjouhge yàhn (chongjouhjé); (religion) seuhngdai

creature N: sàngmaht; duhngmaht (M: jek)

crèche N: tokyìhsó (M: gàan)

credence N: seunsàm FV: seunyahm; sèungseun

credentials N: pàhngjing; jinggín

credible SV: hóseunge; hókaauge

credit N: (belief) seunyahm; (good name) seunyuh; (bouhgei) taaifòng; (unit, credit, or semester hour (of course work to meet degree requirements)) hohkfān (M: go) FV: sèungseun; seunyahm ✳ **be a credit to** PH: haih . . . ge gwōngwìhng ✳ **do credit to some person** PH: gwàigùng yù máuhmáuh yàhn ✳ **give credit to** FV: sèungseun; seunyahm ✳ **on credit** FV: sè; sèhim

creditable Adj. PH: mìhngyuhhóuge; jihkdāk jaanyèuhngge; jihkdāk chìngjaange

creditor N: jaaikyùhnyàhn; jaaijyú (M: go)

credo N: (religion) seuntìuh (M: go)

credulity N: hìngseun; yihseun

credulous SV: hìngseunge

creed N: gaautìuh; seunnihm (M: go)

creek N: (a rivulet) hòhjái (saige hòh) (M: tìuh)

creep FV: pàh; pàhhàhng

creeper N: pàhchùhng (M: tìuh)

creep-hole N: tokchìh; jihkháu (M: go)

creepy Adj. PH: mòuhgwātsúngyìhnge

cremate FV: (burn (a dead body) to ashes) fàhnfa; fójong

cremation FV: fójong; sìusèhngfùi

cremator N: sìusì gùngyàhn; fójonglòuh (M: go)

crematorium N: fàhnsìlòuh; fójongchèuhng (M: go)

crematory N: fójongchèuhng; fàhnsìlòuh (M: go) SV: fójongge

crepe, crêpe N: jausà; jaucháu (M: fūk); jaumàhnjí (jaují) (M: jèung)

crescendo Adv. PH: (music) jìhmkèuhnggám; jìhmchi gàkèuhnggám SV: jìhmkèuhngge; jìhmhéungge FV: jìhmhéung; jìhmchi gàkèuhng N: díngfūng

crescent N: ngòhmèihyuht; sànyuht; wàanyuht; sànyuhtyìhngge yéh (M: go) SV: sànyuhtyìhngge; jìhmjím jànggà ge

cress N: (plant) kàhn; kàhnchoi; séuikàhn (M: pò)

crest N: gùn; gàigùn; (M: go) PH: (get to the top of) doudaat . . . ge déng

crest-fallen SV: sèuihtàuhsongheige; jéuisongge; heinéuihge

crest table N: chèuhngmóu

cretin N: baahkchì (baahkchìbehng)

crevice N: la; lagwìk (M: tìuh)

crew N: séuisáu (M: go) PH: chyùhntái syùhnyùhn

crib N: ❶ (small bed for baby) bìhbīchòhng (M: jèung) ❷ (cattle pen) ngàuhlàahn (M: go)

cricket N: ❶ (of insects) sīksēut (M: jek) ❷ (of ball games) báankàuh (M: go) PH: wáan báankàuh yàuhhei

crier PH: daaihsèng giu ge yàhn; haam chēutsèng ge yàhn (M: go)

crime N: jeuih; jeuihhahng; jeuihngok (M: go)

crimeless SV: mòuhjeuihge

criminal SV: faahnjeuihge; faahnfaatge N: jeuihfáan (M: go)

criminology N: faahnjeuihhohk; yìhngsìhhohk

crimp FV: (make (e.g. hair) wavy or curly (as with a hot iron)) gyúnfaat; lìhngdou gyúnkūk N: bōmàhn; jipjau (M: go)

crimson N: sàmhùhngsīk SV: sàmhùhngsīkge FV: binsèhng sàmhùhngsīk

cringe FV: ❶ (move (the body) back or down in fear) waisūk; ❷ (be too humble) fuhngsìhng

crinkle N: jau; jaumàhn PH: lìhngdou jau; lìhngdou sūk

cripple N: bàige yàhn (M: go) PH: lìhngdou chàahnfai

crisis N: ngàihgèi; nàahngwàan; gányiu gwàantàuh (M: go)

crisp SV: cheuige

crisscross N: sahpjihyìhng; gāauchā (M: go) SV: sìhngsahpjihjohngge PH: wuhsèung gāauchā; yuhng sahpjih sin jouh geihouh; gāauchā sìhngwàih sahpjihyìhng

criterion N: bìujéun; chek-douh; jéunjāk (M: go)

critic N: pàipìhnggā; pìhng-leuhngā (M: go)

critical SV: ngàihgāpge; kyutdihngsingge

critically A: pàipìhnggám; ngàihgāpgám

criticism FV/N: pàipìhng; pìhngleuhn (M: go)

criticize (criticise) FV/N: pàipìhng IE: chèuimòuh kàuhchì

critigue FV/N: pàipìhng; pìhngleuhn (M: go)

crochet PH: yuhng ngāujām jīk N: ngāujām jīksìhngge yéh (ngāujām jīkmaht) (M: gihn)

crock N: ❶ (pot or jar made of baked earth.) ngáhchāang (M: go); seui ngáhpín (M: pin) ❷ (person who cannot work well because of bad health) chàahnfaige yàhn; móuhyuhngge yàhn (M: go) PH: lihngdou sihngwàih faimaht

crockery N: tòuhhei; ngáh-hei (M: gihn)

crocodile N: ❶ ngohkyùh (M: tiuh) ❷ gáchìhbèige yàhn (M: go)

crone N: ❶ lóuhtaaipòh (M: go) ❷ (of sheep) lóuhge yèuhngná (M: jek)

crony N: lóuh pàhngyáuh; chànmahtge pàhngyáuh (M: go)

crook N: ❶ (bend or curve) wàan; ngāu ❷ (stick with a rounded end) wàanbengge gwáaijéung; FV: wàankūk

croon FV: dàisìngcheung

crop FV/N: sàusìhng (harvest)

croquette N: jayuhkbéng (M: go)

cross N: sahpjihyìhng; sahpjihgá Adj. PH: (bad tempered) pèihhei mhóuge FV: (pass from one side to the other of) wàahnggwo; yuhtgwo; douhgwo ✴ **cross a person's path** PH: yuhgin máuh máuh yàhn ✴ **cross one's mind** FV: séunghéi ✴ **cross section** N: wàahngdyuhnmín; fáumíntòuh (M: go) ✴ **cross action** FV: (law) fáansou

cross-bar N: sàan; wàahngmuhk (M: tiuh)

cross-beam N: wàahnglèuhng; daaihlèuhng (M: tiuh)

cross-breed N: jaahpjúng FV: yìhjúng gàaupui; jaahpgàau

cross-country SV: wàahngchyùn chyùhngwokge; yuhtyéhge

cross-cut daaihgeu (M: bá)

cross-examination FV/N: púhnmahn; yìhmmaht sèun-mahn (M: chi)

cross-eye N: sehlēingáahn (M: jek, sèung)

cross-fertilize PH: lihng-dou yìhfā sauhjìng; lihngdou yìhtái sauhjìng

cross-fertilization PH: yìh-fā-sauhjìng

cross-fire N: gāauchā fó-lìhk FV: gāauchā sehgīk

crossing FV: wàahngyuht;

wàahngdouh N: gàauchādím

cross-legged SV: kíuh-
màaihgeukge; kíuhjyuhgeukge

cross-road N: gāauchālouh;
wàahnglouh (M: tìuh); sahpjihlouhháu (M: go)

cross talker N: góng
seungsīng ge yàhn (M: go)

cross-word puzzle PH:
tìhnjih-yàuhhei

crotchet N: (strange, unreasonable idea) gwaaiséung (M:
go)

crouch FV: màudài VO: dāpdàitàuh; wàanyiu PH:
màuháidouhge jìsai; wāansān

crow N: wù-ngà; ngà (M: jek)
N/FV: (gāi) tàih Jek gāigūng
jiutàuhjóu tàih. * as the crow
flies Adv. PH: bātjihkgám;
sìhngjihksin gám; * eat crow
PH: yánhei tānsèng; beih bīk
jouh hóu mjùngyi jouh waahkjé sàuchí ge sih; beih bīk
yìhngcho * as black as crow
SV: chāthāak * white crow
PH: jànkèihge mahtbán (M:
gihn) * crow's foot PH:
ngáahngokge jaumàhn;
yùhméihmàhn (M: tìuh)

crow-bar N: titbāt (M: jì,
tìuh)

crowd N: kwàhnjung; yàhnkwàhn FV: bīkmúhn; bīk; bīk-
yahpheui * a crowd of NuM:
yātkwàhn; yātdèui; hóudò * be
crowded with FV: bīkmúhn;
chùngmúhn

crown N: wòhnggùn (M:
déng) FV: gàmíhn * to crown
all PH: gang lihng yàhn
gòuhingge jauh haih . . ., gang
baihge jauh haih . . .

crowning SV: mòuhseuhngge; jigòuge

crucial Adj. PH: gàanfúge;
yáuhkyutdihngsingge; gihkjì
juhngyiu ge

crucible N: yùhnglòuh; hàm-
wò (M: go)

crucifix N: Yèhsōu sauh-
naahnjeuhng; sahpjihgá (M: go)

crucifixion N: huhkyìhng;
fúnaahn; jitmòh PH: dèng-
séihái sahpjihgásyu

crucify PH: dènghái sahpjihgá seuhngbihn FV: yeuhkdoih; lihngdou fúnóuh

crude SV: chòuchouge;
chòuge * crude workman-
ship N: chòuchouge sáugùng
* crude manners N: chòu-
lóuhge taaidouh

cruel SV: chàahnyánge

cruelty SV/N: chàahnhuhk
FV: yeuhkdoih; PH: chàah-
nyánge hàhngwàih; yéhmàahn-
ge hàhngwàih

cruet N: jòng tìuhmeihbán ge
jēun (M: go)

cruise FV: chèuhnhòhng;
hóiseuhng yàuhyihk; yàuhyihk

cruise missile N: chèuhnhòhng douhdáan (M: go)

cruiser N: chèuhnyèuhng-
laahm (M: jek); chèuhnlòhchè
(M: ga)

crumb PH: mihnbāauseui;
béngseui RV: jíngseui;
nihpseui

crumble RV: jíngseui; fánseui; bàngkwúi

crumbly SV: yihseuige;

cheuige

crumpet N: yātjúng sùng-cheuige yùhnge béng; háau-béng (M: go)

crumple RV: jaahkchàauh; jíngchàauh; jaahkseui; náukūk N: jauhàhn; jaumàhn

crunch PH: jìhjìhjaap-jaapsèng gám sihk

crusade N: Sahpjihgwān VO: gàyahp sahpjihgwān

crusader N: waihdouhjé (M: go)

crush FV: jaahkseui; ja; (embrace) yúngpóuh PH: yúngjàige yàhnkwàhn

crusher N: poseuigèi; ja-yàuhgèi (M: ga)

crust PH: mihnbāaupèih; ngaahngge ngoihhok; yuhng ngaahngpèih kámjyuh; git-sìhng ngaahngpèih

crustacean N: gaaphok-leuih duhngmaht (M: jek)

crusted Adj. PH: yáuh ngaahngpèihge; gauhge

crutch N: gwáaijéung (M: jì)

crux N: nàahntàih; jìnggit; gwàangihn; (M: go)

cry FV: haam; daaihgiu; daaihsèng fùgiu; giumaaih N: fùsìng; tàihsìng; yùhleuhn (M: go) * **cry down** FV: hìngsih; bíndài; dáiwái * **cry for** FV: hánkàuh; hātkàuh * **cry off** FV: chéuisìu; chitwùih * **cry out** FV: daaihgiu; daaihhaam * **cry up** FV: kwàjéung; tèuisùhng

crying SV: haamge; gán-gāpge;

crypt N: deihgaau; deihyuht (M: go)

cryptic (cryptical) SV: beimahtge; yánchòhngge; sàhnbeige

cryptogram N: mahtmáh; ngamhouh; ngamgei (M: go)

crystal N: séuijīng; jīngtái (M: go) PH: séuijīngjouh-sìhngge jòngsīkbán (M: gihn) SV: séuijīngge; taumìhngge

crystal-line SV: séuijīngge; taumìhngge N: gitjīngtái (M: go)

crystallize FV: gitjīng; geuihtáifa

crystallization FV/N: gitj-īng (M: go)

cub N: saige yéhsau * **bear cub** N: hùhngyánjái * **lion cub** sījíjái * **tiger cub** N: lóuhfújái (M: jek)

Cuba N/PW: Gúbā

Cuban N: Gúbāyàhn (M: go) SV: Gúbāge; Gúbāyàhnge

cube N: lahpfōng; lahpfōng-tái PH: lihngdou sìhngwàih lahpfōngtái

cubic (cubical) SV: lahp-fōngtáige; lahpfōngge

cubicle N: (school, hospital) saige seuihfóng (M: gàan, go)

cub-scout N: síulòhngdéui (M: deuih)

cuckold N: gàanfúhge jeuhngfù; chàijí tùhng yàhn tùnggàan ge nàahmyán (M: go) PH: tùhng (máuh yàhn ge) taaitáai tùnggàan

cuckoldry PH: tùhng yáuh

fù jì fúh sèunggàan; sìtùng (M: chi)

cuckoo N: (bird) douhgyūn (M: jek)

cucumber N: wòhnggwā (M: go, tìuh) * **cool as a cucumber** SV: láahngjìhng

cud N: fáanchòge sihkliuh; fáanchòge sihkmaht

cuddle FV: yúngpóuh PH: wàanjyuh sàntái fangaau

cuddlesome SV: hóyíh yúngpóuhge; hóngoige

cudgel N: chòudyúnge gwan; gwan (M: tìuh, jì) PH: yuhng chòudyúnge gwan dá

cue N: (hint) ngamsih; tàihsih (M: go) (cheukkàuhge) kàuhgōn (M: jì)

cuff N: jauhháu PH: yuhng sáujéung dá

cuisine N: pàangyahm; pàangyahmfaat; chyùhfóng (M: go) sihkbán (M: júng)

cul-de-sac N: gwahttàuh hóng; gwahttàuh louh (M: tìuh)

culminate FV: daahtdou díngdím; daahtdou jeuigòuchìuh

culmination N: díngdím; gihkdím; PH: jeuigòuchìuh (M: go)

culpable Adj. PH: yìnggòi sauhchyúfaht ge; yìnggòi sauh-jaakbeihge; yìnggòi sauhhín-jaakge

culprit N: faahnyàhn; jeuih-fáan; yìhmyìhfáan (M: go)

cult N: sùhngbaai; (religion) láihbaaige yìhsīk; màihseun (M: júng)

cultivate FV: ❶ (prepare (land) for crops by ploughing, etc.) gàangjung ❷ (give care, thought, time, in order to develop sth.) pùihyéuhng; jòipùih

cultivation FV: gàangjung; pùihyéuhng

cultivator N: gàangjungge yàhn (gàangjungjé) (M: go) gàangwàhngèih (M: ga)

cultural SV: gaauyéuhngge; màhnfaseuhngge; jòipùihge

culture N: màhnfa; FV/N: gaauyéuhng; jòipùih (M: júng)

cultured SV: yáuhgaau-yéuhngge; yáuhsàuyéuhngge

culvert N: ngamkèuih; pàaihséuikèuih (M: tìuh)

cumbersome SV: bahn-juhngge

cumquat N: (fruit tree) gàmgwāt (M: pò, go)

cumulate SV: leuihjīkge; dèuijīkge FV: leuihjīk; dèuijīk

cumulation FV: leuihjīk; dèuijīk

cumulative SV: jihmjím jàngdò ge (jihmjàngge); leuihjīkge

cumulus FV/N: dèuijīk; leuihjīk N: jīkwàhn

cunning SV: waahttáu; gáauwaaht; gwáimáh; gàanja; suhklihn

cup N: būi; jáubūi; ngàhnbūi; jéungbūi (M: jek) PH: lihngdou sìhngwàih būige yìhngjohng * **in one's cups** PH: yámjeui (jáu) gojahnsí

cupboard N: wúngwaih;

būigwaih (M: go)

cupidity SV: tàamsàm;
tàamlàahm; tàamchín

curable SV: hóyíh yìhóu ge;
hóyíh gíujing ge

curate N: (religion) fumuhk-
sī; johléih muhksī (M: go)

curator N: (museum, library)
gúnjéung (M: go)

curb N: máhlahk; máh-
hàahm; hungjai (M: go) FV:
hungjai; lahkjyuh

curd N: yìhngyúh   FV:
yìhnggit

curdle FV: yìhnggit; lihngdou yìhnggit

cure FV: (heal) yì; yìhóu; (as
meat,etc) yip; yìm *yip dī yuhk.*
＊ **cured ham** N: fótéui;
yìmyuhk ＊ **cure-all** N:
maahnlìhngyeuhk (M: júng);
baakbóudàan (M: nāp)

curfew FV/N: gaaiyìhm;
sìugam ~ *yíhgìng gáaichèuih
la*

curio N: gúdúng; gúwún; jàn-
bán (M: gihn)

curiosity N: houkèihsàm
(M: go); jànbán (M: gihn)

curious SV: houkèihge;
hèikèihge

curl FV: gyúnsèhng saige
hyūn; gyúnkūk PH: gyúnsèhng-
ge saihhyún; wàankūksìhng
gyūn yātyeuhng ge yéh ＊ **curl
up** FV: gyún; daihhéigeuk;
yìhngsyù; yātkyut bāt-jan ＊ **in
curl** SV: gyúnkūkge

curly SV: gyúnkūkge

currant N: sai yìh móuh-

waht ge pòuhtàihjígōn;
hùhngchouleuht (M: nāp)

currency N: ❶ (the money at
present in use in a country)
fobaih ❷ (being current)
làuhtùng; tùngyuhng

current SV: tùngyuhngge;
làuhhàhngge; dòngchìhnge
(yìhgāge) N: séuilàuh; heilàuh;
dihnlàuh; chèuiheung; chèuisai

curriculum N: fochìhng (M:
mùhn, júng)

currier PH: jaijouh pèihgaak
ge gùngyàhn (M: go)

curry N: galēi; galēifán;
galēijeung PH: yuhng galēijeung tìuhjai; jaijouh pèihgaak

curse N: jéuijau; wohgàn (M:
go) FV: jaumah; jéuijau;
(lihngdou) jòuyèung

cursive SV: chóusyùge;
chóusyùtáige N: chóusyù;
hàhngsyù; chóusyùtái

cursory SV: chòuleuhkge;
chóusēutge; chòngchyutge

curt SV: gáanleuhkge;
chóusēutge; fùyínlíuhsihge

curtail FV: jihtdyún; sūkdyún; seukgáam

curtain N: jeung; mohk;
chēunglím (M: jèung) FV: gwa
jèungjeung hái . . .; ＊ **curtain
call** PH: gùnjung yiukàuh
yínyùhn   chēut-chèuhng
jehmohk ge jéungsèng

curtsey, curtsy N: chíng-
ngōn (sàifòng néuihjí ge) wātsātláih PH: hàahng sàifòng
néuihyán ge wātsātláih

curvature N: wàankūk;
wùhdouh; kūkleuht

curve N: wàankūk; kūksin FV: Wàan; lihngdou wàankūk SV: wàankūkge

cushion N: kūséun; jin (M: go)

cuss FV/N: (chiefly American) jéuijau

cussed SV: hówuge; wàahngu ge

custodial SV: gàamgúnge; bóugúnge

custodian N: gúnléihyàhn (M: go)

custody FV: bóugún; hònsáu; kèuilàuh * **in custody** FV: beih kèuilàuh

custom N: fùngjuhk; jaahpgwaan; (pl) hóigwāan; gwàanseui

customary SV: sèuhnglaihge; gwaansèuhngge

customer N: guhaak; jyúgu (M: go)

custom house (custom office) N: hóigwāan (M: go) * **custom house broker** N: doihléih bougwàange yàhn (M: go); bougwàanhóng (M: gàan)

custom-made SV: dehngjouhge; dehngjaige

cut FV: ❶ (by slicing) chit ❷ (with a knife) got ❸ (with scissors) jín ❹ (with an ax) pek ❺ (with a sword) jáam ❻ (reduce) gáam; gáamsíu (to cut expenses) ~ *faiyuhng* N: sèungháu; sèunghàhn (M: go) · *sáujíge* ~ * **cut across** PH: hàahng káhnlouh wàahngchyùn gwoheui * **a short cut** N: jihtging (M: tiùh) * **cut down** RV: jáamlam (syuh); sūkdyún * **cut in** FV:

dahtyahp; chùngyahp; chaapjéui * **cut out for** FV: sīkhahpyù * **cut short** FV: dátyúhn; sūkgáam * **cut up** FV: chitseui; chìmmiht * **cut-and-dried** SV: yihnsìhngge; ngòihbáange * **cut-and-thrust** SV: jìmyeuihge; fùngleihge * **cut-back** FV: sàujín (syuhjí); seukgáam * **cut-in** PH: chaapyahpge yéh (M: gihn); syù waahkjé boují ge chaaptòuh (M: fūk); dihnyíng dahksé gengtàuh (M: go) * **cut-off** N: káhnlouh; jihtging (M: tiùh) * **cut-out** N: jínheui; (dihn) dyuhnlàuhhei (M: go) * **cut-throat** N: hùngsáu; chihaak (M: go) * **cut-water** PH: syùhntàuh polohng ge deihfòng

cute SV: dākyi; cheuiji

cuticle N: ngoihpèih; (dissect) wuhmók (M: faai)

cutie N: (American) méihyàhngyíh PH: hèipin hàhngwàih (M: go)

cutis N: (dissect) jànpèih; pèihfù (M: faai)

cutler N: jouh dōu ge yàhn (dōujeuhng); mòhdōuge yàhn (mòhdōujeuhng) (M: go)

cutlet PH: béi yàhn sìuháau waahkjé jìn ja yuhng ge bohkge yuhkpín

cutter N: ❶ chitgotgèi (M: ga); ❷ (movies) jínchápge yàhn; ❸ chòihjín sīfú (M: go)

cutting VO: chitpín; (movies) FV/N: jínjip SV: yeuihleihge

cuttlefish N: mahkyùh (M: jek)

cutty SV: dyúnge N: dyúnge yīndáu (M: go); dyúnge

chìhgāng (M: jek)

cybernation PH: dihnnóuh hungjai; dihnnóuhfa

cycle N: jàukèih; chèuhnwàahn (M: go); dāanchē (M: ga) FV: chèuhnwàahn VO: yáaidāanchē; cháaidāanchē

cycle-car PH: yātjúng sàamgo lūk waahkjé seigo lūk ge hìngbihn heichè (M: ga)

cycler (cyclist) N: yáaidāanchēge yàhn; cháaidāanchēge yàhn (M: go)

cyclone N: syùhnfùng (M: go)

cyclopedia (cyclopaedia) N: baakfōchyùhnsyù; baakfōchìhdín (M: bún)

cylinder N: yùhntúng; (gèihaaih) heigòng (M: go)

cymbal N: nàauhbaht (gúsìhge gwàn ngohkhei)

cynic N: jùngyi wàfúyàhnge yàhn SV: fáhnsai-jahtjuhk ge

cynical SV: fáhnsai-jahtjuhk ge; wuhnsaibātgùngge

Cynicism PH: Hyúnyùhjyúyih; Hyúnyùhjithohk (M: go)

cypress N: paaksyuh (M: pò)

cyst N: (sàngmaht) bāaulòhng; lòhng

cytoecology N saibāausàngtaaihohk

cytology N: saibāauhohk

Czech (Czekh) N: Jithāakyàhn; Jithāakmàhn Adj. PH: Jithāakyàhnge; Jithāakmàhnge

Czechoslovak N: Jithāakyàhn (Jithāaksílāaifúyàhn);

Jithāakmàhn (Jithāaksílāaifúmàhn) Adj. PH: Jithāakge (Jithāaksílāaifúge); Jithāakyàhnge (Jithāaksílāaifúyàhnge); Jithāakmàhnge (Jithāaksílāaifúmàhnge)

D

dab FV: hehnghēng paak N: taatsā (taatsāyú) (M: tìuh)

dabble FV: jíngsāp; jítsāp VO: wáanséui

dad N: bàhbā; dēdìh; adē (M: go)

daddy N: bàhbā; dēdìh; adē (M: go)

daffodil N: séuisínfā (M: pò)

daft Adj. PH: sòhge; fùngkwòhngge

dagger N: dyúngim (M: bá)

dahlia N: daaihlaihfā (M: pò)

daily Adj. PH: múihyahtge; yahtsèuhngge A: múihyaht; yahtyaht N: yahtbou (M: jèung, fahn)

dainty Adj. PH: yàuméihge; ngáhjige N: méihmeih (M: júng)

dairy N: ngàuhnáaihchèuhng; ngàuhnáaih gūngsī (M: go)

dairying PH: ngàuhnáaih jaibán yihp

dairy-maid N: ngàuhnáaihchèuhng néuihgūng (M: go)

dais N: gôujoh; góngtòih; yínjautòih (M: go)

daisy N: chògūk (M: pò) seuhngdáng fo (M: gihn)

dalliance FV: tiuhhei; heiluhng

dally FV: hèihei; tiuhhei; hàahndohng

dam N: séuijaahp; séuiba (M: go); tàih; ba (M: tiuh) VO: jūktàih; jūkba

damage FV: syúnwaaih; syúnhoih N: syúnhoih; syúnsāt (M: go)

damask N: gámdyuhn (M: fūk); fàdyuhn

dame N: fùyàhn (M: go)

damn FV/N: jaumah; jéuijau

damnable Adj. PH: gòiséige; tóuyimge

damnation FV/N: jíjaak; wáimiht

damned Adj. PH: gòiséige; tóuyimge

damp N: sāphei; sāpdouh SV: chiuhsāpge RV: jíngsāp

damp-proof SV: fòhngsāpge

damsel N: siunéuih; chyunéuih (M: go)

dance VO: tiumóuh N: tiumóuh; móuhdouh ✻ **dance attendance on** FV: fuhngsìhng ✻ **dancer** N: móuhnéuih; móuhdouhgā (M: go)

dandelion N: pòuhgùngyìng (M: pò)

dandle PH: jèung póuhjyuh

ge waahkjé jàihái jihgéige sāttàuhsyu ge bihbī seuhnghahgám yūkduhng

dandruff N: tàuhpèih (M: faai)

dandy N: fàfāgùngjí (M: go)

Dane N: Dàanmahkyàhn (M: go)

danger SV/N: ngàihhím

dangerous SV: ngàihhímge

dangle FV: yìuhbáai; yùhnbáai

Danish N: Dàanmahkyúh; Dàanmahkyàhn ATT: Dàanmahkge; Dàanmahkyàhnge; Dàanmahkyúhge

dank SV: yàmsāpge; chiuhsāp

dapple Adj. PH: yáuh bàandím ge N: bàanmàhn (M: tiuh) FV: (lihngdou) héi bàanmàhn

dare AV: gám

dare-devil PH: daaihdáam ge; dáamdaaih móhngwàih ge N: dáamdaaih móhngwàih ge yàhn; daaihdáam gwái (M: go)

daring PH: daaihdáamge; yúhnggámge N/SV: yúhnggám

dark SV: hāakngamge N: hāakngam ✻ **in the dark** A: beimaht gám PH: yāt-mòuhsó-jì

darken FV: jèngam; lihngdou yàmchàhm; bin hāakngam

darkly SV: ngam

darling N: ngoiyàhn (M: go) Adj. PH: sàmngoige

darn FV/N: jíkbóu; fùhngbóu

dart N: bīuchēung; bīu; jin (M: jī) FV: tàuhjaahk; faatseh

dash FV: chùngjohng; máahngjohng N: chùngjohng * **at a dash** PH: yāt-gú-jok-hei; yāt-hei-hò-sihng * **dash against** PH: tùhng . . . pungjohng

dash-board N: jènàih báan (M: faai)

data N: jīlíu; chòihlíu (M: júng) * **data bank** N: jīlíu fu (M: go)

date N: ❶ yahtkèih (M: go) ❷ (fruit) sàijóu;jóu (M: go) PH: jyumìhng nìhn yuht yaht * **date from** FV: wùihsoudou; jyumìhng yahtkèih * **out of date** SV: gwosìhge; chàhngauhge * **to date** PH: dou muhkchìhn wàih jí * **up (down) to date** PH: sìhmōuge; jeui sànsìkge * **date-mark** N: yahtcheuk (M: go)

daughter N: néui (M: go) * **daughter-in-law** N: sànpóuh (M: go)

daunt FV: húnghaak; haak

dauntless SV: daaihdáamge; yúhnggámge

dawdle FV: yàuhdohng

dawn A/FV: tìngwòng

day N: yaht; yātyaht; (day time) yahttáu * **day after tomorrow** TW: hauhyaht * **day by day** A: múihyaht; yahtyaht * **day in and day out** A: múihyaht; (often) sìhsìh * **from day to day** A: yahtyaht; yāt yaht yauh yāt yaht * **in days to come** A: jèunglòih * **some day** A: tàyaht * **day book** N: yahtgeibóu (M: bún) * **day**

break A/FV: tìngwòng * **daydream** N/FV: waahnséung (M: go) * **dayfly** N: fàuhyàuh (M: jek) * **in broad daylight** PH: hái yahttáu * **day laborer (day labourer)** N: sáangūng (M: go) * **daylight** N: yahtgwōng; (daytime) yahttáu * **day nursery** N: yahttok tokyìhsó; yahtgàan tokyìhsó (M: gàan)

daze PH: lìhngdou tàuhwàhn ngáahnfà N: màihlyuhn

dazzle PH: lìhngdou ngáahnfà * **dazzle lamp(s) (dazzle light(s))** N: heichè dāng (M: jáan)

deacon N: jāpsih (M: go)

deactivate PH: lìhngdou sātheui wuhtlihk

dead SV: séige; FV: séi A: yùhnchyùhn N: séijóge yàhn (séijé) (M: go) * **dead-alive (dead-and-alive)** SV: móuh jìngsàhnge * **dead-line** N: jihtjí sìhgaan (M: go) * **dead lock** N: tìhngdeuhn; gèungguhk (M: go)

deaden FV: gáamwuhn; gáamyeuhk

deadly Adj. PH: lómehngge; jimìhngge A: gìhkjì; fèisèuhng

deaf SV: lùhngge; yíhlùhngge * **deaf-mute** N: lùhng-ngá ge yàhn (M: go)

deafen PH: lìhngdou lùhng RV: janlùhng * **deafening** Adj. PH: lìhng yàhn yíhlùhng ge

deal FV: yingfuh; deuifuh N: sàangyi; gàauyihk (M: dàan) * **a good deal (a great deal)** ATT: daaihleuhng

dealer N: ❶ (in business) sèungyàhn; doihléih; ❷ (in playing cards) jōng; jònggà (M: go)

dealing N: deui yàhn ge taaidouh

dean N: gaaumouhjéung; gaaumouhjyúyahm (M: go)

dear Adj. PH: chànngoige; SV: (expensive) gwai N: chànngoige yàhn (M: go)

dearly A: sàmngoigám; yihtchitgám

dearth FV: kyutfaht; síu; (famine) gèifòng

death FV/N: séi; séimòhng VO: gwosàn * at death's door PH: hái séimòhngge bīnyùhn * to the death A: doudái * death-bed A: làhmjùng; làhm séi ge sìhhauh * death duty N: wàihcháanseui (M: bàt) * death rate N: séimòhngleuht (M: go) * death struggle PH: séimòhng jàngjaat; sèuihséi jàngjaat

debar FV: jójí; gamjí

debark VO: (soldiers) dàngluhk; séuhngngohn

debarkation VO: dàngluhk; séuhngngohn

debase FV: bíndài; gongdài VO: bínjihk

debatable SV: hó jàngbihn ge; sìhng mahntàih ge

debate FV/N: tóuleuhn; bihnleuhn

debauch FV: dohlohk; fongdohng

debauchery FV: fongdohng

debenture N: jaaihyun;

teuiseui-pàhngdāan (M: jèung)

debilitate FV: lihngdou hèuiyeuhk; lihngdou sèuiyeuhk

debility SV: hèuiyeuhk; sèuiyeuhk

debit N: jefòng; fuhjaai PH: dàngyahp jefòng; geiyahp jefòng

debris N: seuipín; chàahnhàaih

debt N: jaai; jaaimouh (M: bàt) * in debt VO: himjaai * out of debt VO: wàahnjaai * debtor N: jaaimouhyàhn; jaaijyú (M: go)

decadence SV: tèuihfai; wáiméih; (of morals) dohlohk

decadent Adj. PH: sèuilohkge; dohlohkge N: sèuilohkge yàhn (M: go)

decamp FV: chitteui; tòuhjáu

decanter N: bōlēi jáujēun (M: go)

decapitate VO: saattáu; jáamtáu

decathlon PH: sahphohng chyùhnnàhng wahnduhng

decay FV: laahn; fuhlaahn

decease FV/N: séi; séimòhng * the deceased N: séijé (M: go)

deceit FV: hèipin; hèija

deceitful Adj. PH: ngāakyàhnge; hèijage

deceivable Adj. PH: hóyíh hèipin ge; yih sauhpin ge

deceive FV: hèipin; hèija

decelerate FV: gáamchūk; gáamwuhn

December N/TW: sahpyihyuht

decency SV: dyùnjòng; jòngjuhng

decent Adj. PH: hahpsīkge; jingdongge

decentralize FV: fànsaan

decentralization PH: deihfòng-fànkyùhn

deception FV/N: hèipin

deceptive Adj. PH: ngāakyàhnge; hèipinge

decide FV: kyutdihng

decided Adj. PH: kokdihngge; mìhngkokge

deciduous Adj. PH: dihngsihlohkyihpge

decimal Adj. PH: sahpjeunge; sahpjeunjaige; síusouge N: síusou; sahpjeun síusou (M: go) * decimal fraction N: síusou (M: go) * decimal point N: síusoudím (M: go)

decimalization PH: fawàih sahpjeunwáijai

decimalize FV: góiwàih sahpjeunfaat; sahpjeunfa

decimeter (decimetre) M: gùngchyun (sahpfahnjī-yāt gùngchek)

decipher FV: yihkgáai (a secret code) (mahtmáh)

decision FV/N: kyutdihng (M: go)

decisive Adj. PH: kyutdihngsingge; gìnkyutge

deck N: gaapbáan; syùhnmín FV: jòngsīk * on deck PH: joih chèuhng * deck hand PH: hái gaapbáansyu jouhsih ge séuisáu (M: go)

declaim FV: ❶ hùhngbihn ❷ (to recite aloud) lóhngjuhng

declamation FV: hùhngbihn; (to give a speech) yínsyut

declaration FV/N: syùnbou; syùnyihn; sìngmìhng (M: go)

declare FV: syùnbou; (at customs) sànbou; bougwāan * declare for FV: jaansìhng * declare against FV: fáandeui * declare off FV: chéuisìu * declare war FV: syùnjin

decline FV: ❶ kéuihjyuht ❷ (refuse) tèuichìh ❸ (to slant) kìngchèh

decode FV: fàanyihk (telegram)

decoder N: yihkmáhyùhn (M: go)

decolonization N: fèijihkmàhnfa

decompose FV: fàngáai

decomposition FV: fàngáai

decontaminate VO: chìngchèuih duhkhei

decorate FV/N: jòngsīk; jòngsàu

decoration FV/N: jòngsīk N: jòngsīkbán

decorative Adj. PH: jòngsīkge; jòngwòhngge

decorum N: láihjit; láihyìh; láihmaauh

decoy N: hyūntou (M: go); yáuhleih (M: júng) FV: yáhnyáuh

decrease FV: gáamsíu; gáam ✻ **on the decrease** PH: jingjoih gáamsíu

decree N: ❶ faatling ❷ (by a court) punkyut (M: go) FV: mihnglihng; hahlihng

decrepit Adj. PH: sèui-yeuhkge; sèuilóuhge

decrepitude SV: sèuilóuh; lóuhyeuhk

decry FV: ❶ bíndài ❷ (to defame) dáiwái

dedicate FV: fuhnghin; hin-sàn ✻ **dedicate to** FV: hinbéi (hinkāp)

dedication FV/N: gùng-fuhng; fuhnghin

deduce FV: tèuileuhn; yínyihk

deduct FV: kauchèuih; gáamchèuih

deduction FV: kauchèuih PH: (deductive method) yínyihkfaat

deductive Adj. PH: tèui-dyuhnge; yínyihkge

deed N: ❶ (act) hàhngwàih ❷ (career) sihyihp ❸ (a written contract) kai; kaiyeuk (M: jèung) ✻ **in deed** A: jànjing; sihsahtseuhng

deep SV: sàm

deepen FV: gàsàm; binsàm

deep-laid PH: sàm-màuh-yúhn-leuih ge

deeply A: sahpfàn; fèi-sèuhng

deep-rooted IE: gàn-sàm-dai-gu ge

deep-seated IE: gàn-sàm-nàahn-yìh ge; gàn-sàm-dai-gu ge

deep-set Adj. PH: sàm-haahmge

deer N: lúk (luhk) (M: jek)

deer-skin N: luhkpèih (M: faai)

deface FV: syúnsèung; syúnwái

defame FV: dáiwái; fèi-póhng; jungsèung

defamation FV/N: dáiwái; fèipóhng

defamatory Adj. PH: dáiwáige; fèipóhngge

default VO: (a breach of contract) wàihyeuk; FV: (to be absent) kyutjihk ✻ **in default of** PH: yànwaih móuh . . .; hái kyutsíu . . . gójahnsí ✻ **make default** FV: kyutjihk

defeat FV: dábaaih *Ngóhdeih ~ dihkyàhn* FV/N: sātbaaih; baaihbāk

defeatism N: sātbaaihhjyúyih

defeatist N: sātbaaihhjyúyih-jé (M: go)

defect N: kyutdím; kyut-haahm; mòuhbehng (M: go)

defective Adj. PH: yáuh-kyutdímge; m̀yùhnméihge

defend FV: fòhngwaih; bóuwaih

defendant N: beihgou (M: go)

defense (defence) FV/N: bóuwuh; bóuwaih * **in defence of** FV/N: bóuwaih

defense-less Adj. PH: bātchitfòhngge; móuh fòhngbeih ge; bātnàhng bóuwaih jihgéi ge

defensive Adj. PH: fòhngwaihge; jihwaihge N: fòhngyuhmaht

defer FV: ❶ (to be postponed) yìhnkèih; jínkèih ❷ (to obey) fuhkchùhng

deference FV: fuhkchùhng; gingjuhng * **in deference to** FV: jyùnchùhng

deferential SV: gùnggingge; gùngseuhnge

defiance FV/N: (to challenge to battle) tiujin; (to look down upon) hìngsih * **in defiance of** FV: ❶ hìngsih ❷ (to disobey) m̀fuhkchùhng

defiant Adj. PH: tiujinge; tiuyahnge

deficiency FV: kyutfaht

deficient Adj. PH: m̀gauge; kyutfahtge (bātjūkge)

deficit FV/N: (to be in the red) kwàihùng N: [the red (in bookkeeping)] chikjih

defile FV: jíngwùjòu; jínglaahttaat

define FV: (to explain) gáaisīk VO: (to give a definition) hahdihngyih * **be defined as** FV: kwàidihngwàih

definite Adj. PH: mìhngkokge; koksahtge * **the**

definite article N: dihng gunchìh (M: go)

definitely A: mìhngkokgám; koksahtgám

definiteness SV: mìhngkok; koksaht

definition FV/N: (explanation) gáaisīk N: dihngyih (M: go)

deflate FV: fongchēut hùnghei * **to deflate a tire** PH: fong chētāaige hùnghei * **to deflate currency** PH: gánsūk tùngfo

deflation FV: fongchēut hùnghei (fonghei)

deflect PH: lihngdou pìnchèh; (change the direction) lihngdou jyúnheung

deflection (deflexion) FV: wàaichèh; wàaikūk

deflower VO: (to pluck flowers) jaahkfā FV: (to seduce and rape) gàanwù

defoliant N: tyutyihpjāi; lohkyihpjāi (M: júng)

deforest VO: chóifaht sàmlàhm; hòifaht sàmlàhm

deform VO: wáisèung táiyìhng

deformity ATT: (malformation) kèiyìhng; (disabled) chàahnfai

defraud FV: jachéui; pìnchéui

defrauder N: hèijage yàhn; hèipinge yàhn (M: go)

defray FV: béi; jìfuh

deft Adj. PH: lìhngháauge; suhklìhnge

defunct Adj. PH: séijóge; m̀chyùhnjoihge

defy FV: ❶ (in disregard of) m̀léih ❷ (to disobey) m̀fuhkchùhng

degeneracy FV: teuifa

degenerate FV: teuifa; (to regress) teuibouh

degeneration FV: teuifa; teuibouh

degenerative Adj. PH: teuifage

degradation VO: ❶ (to reduce in rank) gongkāp ❷ (deprive of office) gaakjīk

degrade VO: ❶ (to reduce in rank) gongkāp ❷ (to be dismissed from office) míhnjīk

degree M: (unit of measurement) douh N: (academic) hohkwái (ref. bachelor, master, Ph. D.) ✻ **by degrees** A: jihmjím, juhkjihm ✻ **to a certain degree** A: sèungdòng

deify PATT: jèung . . . sàhnfa; jèung . . . fuhng yeuhk sàhnmìhng

deign PH: gongdài jihgéige sànfán

deity N: sàhn; seuhngdai

deject PH: lihngdou jéuisong

dejected SV: baingai; sātyi

dejection SV: fùisàm; heinéuih; tèuihsong

delay FV: jóchìh; dàamgok ✻ **without delay** A: góngán; jīkhāak; lahphāak

delegate N: doihbíu (M: go) FV: sauhkyùhn; wáitok

delegation N: doihbíutyùhn (M: go); FV: (to appoint) wáipaai; (to authorize) sauhkyùhn

delete FV: sìuchèuih; sàanheui

deliberate PH: sahnjuhng háauleuih Adj. PH: sámsahnge

deliberative Adj. PH: sahnjuhngge

delicacy PH: hóu hóusihkge yéh

delicate Adj. PH: (as a situation) mèihmiuhge; (as the structure of body) gìuyeuhkge

delicatessen PH: jyúsuhkge sungchoi (M: júng); maaih jyúsuhkge sungchoi ge poutáu (M: gàan)

delicious Adj. PH: hóusihkge; hóu meihdouh ge

delight SV: gòuhing; N: (hobby) sihou PH: lihngdou fùnhéi

delightful Adj. PH: lihng yàhn gòuhing ge; hóngoige

delimit (delimitate) VO: dihnggaai; waahkgaai

delimitation VO: dihnggaai FV: kèuiwaahk

delineate FV: mìuhwaahk PH: waahkchèut ngoihyìhng

delinquency FV: sātjīk N: (faults) gwosāt

delinquent Adj. PH: sātjīkge N: sātjīkge yàhn (M: go)

delirious Adj. PH: fànmàihge; bātsíngyàhnsihge

delirium PH: (jaahmsihge) jìngsàhn kwòhnglyuhn; gihkdouhge hìngfáhn

deliver FV: (send, bring) sung; sungheui; sunglàih *
deliver a baby VO: jipsäng *
deliver oneself FV: jihsáu *
deliver a speech FV: yíngóng

deliverance FV: gauchëut; (to set free) sïkfong

delivery FV: sung; sungheui; sunglàih

delta N: (of river) sàamgokjàu (M: go)

delude FV: hèipin

deluge N: daaihséuijòi; hùhngséui FV: faanlaahm

delusion FV: hèipin

delusive Adj. PH: hèipinge

deluxe SV: hòuhwàhge

delve FV: waatgwaht N: yuht; hāang (M: go)

demand FV/N: yìukàuh (M: go) * **in demand** PH: yáuh sèuiyiu; sìulouhhóu * **on demand** PH: lòih chéui jík fuh

demarcation VO: waahkgaai

demean N: géuijí; hàhngwàih

demeanor (demeanour) N: hàhngwàih; géuijí

dement PH: lihngdou fùngkwòhng

demented Adj. PH: fùngkwòhngge

demerit N: kyutdím; gwosāt (M: go)

demilitarize VO: gáaichèuih móuhjōng

demobilization FV: (military) hínsaan; fuhkyùhn

demobilize (demob) FV: hínsaan; (military) fuhkyùhn

democracy N: màhnjyú jingjíh; màhnjyú

democrat N: màhnjyújyúyihjé; (America) Màhnjyúdóngyùhn (M: go)

democratic Adj. PH: màhnjyújyúyihge * **the Democratic Party** N: Méihgwok Màhnjyúdóng

democratization FV: màhnjyúfa

democratize FV: màhnjyúfa

demolish FV: wáiwaaih; powaaih

demolition FV: powaaih; wáiwaaih; N: (ruins) faihēui (M: go)

demon N: gwái; ngokmò

demonstrate FV: (to prove) jingmìhng; [to demonstrate (how a thing works, etc.)] sihfaahn PH: sihwàiyàuhhàhng

demonstration FV/N: (proof) jingmìhng PH: (public protest) sihwàiyàuhhàhng

demonstrative Adj. PH: jingmìhngge N: (grammar) jísihchìh (M: go)

demonstrator N: sihfaahnge yàhn (sihfaahnjé) (M: go)

demoralization PH: douhdāk baaihwaaih

demoralize PH: lihngdou douhdāk baaihwaaih; baaihwaaih (douhdāk)

demote VO: gongkāp PH: lihngdou gongkāp

demur FV: ❶ (to hesitate) chàuhchyúh ❷ (to oppose) fáandeui

demure Adj. PH: yìhmsūkge

den N: sauyuht; dau (M: go)

denary ATT: sahpge; sahpjeunge; sahppúihge

denial FV: fáuyihng

denigrate FV: tòuhhāak; tòuhwú

denominate VO: héiméng

denomination N: ❶ (name of a thing) mìhngchìng ❷ (of a religion) gaauwúi (M: go)

denominator N: (maths.) fahnmóuh

denote FV: ❶ (to instruct) jísih ❷ (to express) bíusih

denounce FV: hínjaak; jíjaak

dense SV: maht

density N: mahtdouh (M: go)

dent N: nāp; nāphàhn (M: go) RV: jíngnāp; nāpjó

dental ATT: ngàhfōge; ngàhchíge

dentist N: ngàhfōyīsāng; ngàhyī (M: go)

dentistry N: ngàhfō

denude RV: mōkgwòng

denunciation FV/N: chīkjaak; jíjaak

deny FV: fáuyihng ✳ **deny oneself** PH: hāakjai jihgéige yuhkmohng ✳ **deny oneself to** PH: kéuihjyuht wuihgin; jehjyuht wuihgin

depart FV: lèihhòi ✳ **depart from** PH: yàuh . . . chēutfaat

department N: ❶ (general) bouhfahn; bouhmúhn; bouh; chyu; ❷ (of the government) yún, bouh, tēng, chyu, etc., ❸ (of a university) haih (Department of History) *Lihksí Haih*

department store N: baakfo gūngsī (M: gàan)

departmentalism N: fànsaanjyúyih; búnwáijyúyih

departure FV: lèihhòi

depend FV: yìlaaih; yìkaau

dependable SV: hókaauge; kaaudākjyuhge

dependant N: (family) gyunsuhk ❷ (attendants) sihchùhng (M: go)

dependence FV: yìlaaih

dependency FV: (depend on) yìlaaih N: (accessory items) fuhsuhkmaht

depict FV: mìuhkwúi; mìuhsé

depicter (depictor) N: mìuhkwúige yàhn (mìuhkwúijé) (M: go)

deplete PH: lihngdou hùnghèui; yuhngjeuhn

deplorable Adj. PH: bèingòige; bèicháamge

deplore FV: ngòidouh SV: bèitung

deploy FV: (to use) síyuhng; (to disperse) saanhòi

depopulate PH: gáamsíu . . . ge yàhnháu

deport FV: (to drive out) kèuijuhk N: (conduct) géuijí

deportation FV: kèuijuhk N: géuijí

deportment N: (conduct) hàhngwàih; géuijí (M: go)

depose VO: míhnjīk; gaakjīk

deposit FV: chyùhn; chyùhnfong N: (money put in a bank) chyùhnfún; (a payment indicating trust) dehng; ngongām * on deposit ATT: geichyùhnge; chyùhnyahp ngàhnhòhngge

depositary N: bóugúnyàhn (M: go)

deposition VO: (to fire) gaakjīk; FV: (sedimentation) chàhmdihn

depositor N: chyùhnfúnyàhn (M: go)

depository N: bóugúnyàhn (M: go)

depot N: chòngfu (M: go)

deprave PH: lihngdou dohlohk; lihngdou baaihwaaih

depravity FV: dohlohk SV: fuhbaaih

depreciate VO: gáamga

depreciation VO: ditga

depredation FV: leuhkdyuht; gipleuhk

depress PH: lihngdou . . . hóu m̀ngònlohk

depression SV: m̀hòisàm

deprive FV: mōkdyuht * be deprived of FV: songsāt

depth N: sàmdouh * in depth PH: hái sàmdouhseuhng * depth bomb (depth charge) N: sámséui jadáan (M: go) * depth gauge N: sàmdouhgai (M: go)

deputation N: doihbíu; doihbíutyùhn (M: go)

depute PH: wáitok . . . jouh doihléih

deputy FV/N: doihléih (M: go)

derail VO: (train) chēutgwái

derange FV: yíulyuhn

derby N: (a horse-race) daaihchoimáh

derelict Adj. PH: beih pàauheige PH: beih pàauhei ge yàhn waahkjé mahtbán

deride FV: jàausiu

derider N: jàausiuge yàhn (M: go)

derision FV: jàausiu

derivation N: héiyùhn; yàuhlòih (M: go)

derivative PH: yáhnsànjih (M: go)

derive FV/N: héiyùhn * be derived from PH: yàuh . . . yìh lòih

derogate FV: syúnwái (wáisyún)

derogatory Adj. PH: wáisyúnge

descend FV: lohklàih; lohk * descend from PH: yàuh . .

. lohk làih

descendant N: hauhyeuih (M: go)

descent FV: gonglohk; lohk

describe FV: góngháh; yìhngyùhng * describe . . . as PH: jèung . . . góngsèhng

description FV/N: jeuih-seuht; mìuhsé

descriptive ATT.: jeuih-seuhtge; mìuhségé

desecrate FV: sitduhk; wùyuhk

desert Adj. PH: fòngmòuhge N: sàmohk (M: go) FV: fonghei; pàauhei

deserter N: tòuhbìng (M: go)

deserve PH: yìnggòi dākdóu

deservedly A: dòngyìhn

desiccate PH: lihngdou gòn; RV: jínggòn; bingòn

design FV/N: chitgai N: ❶ (drawing) tòuhyéung ❷ (pattern) tòuhngon (M: go) * design-er N: chitgaisī (M: go)

designate FV: jídihng Adj. PH: jípaaihóuge

designation FV: jídihng

desirable Adj. PH: hahpyige

desire FV/N: hèimohng N: yuhnmohng (M: go) * at somebody's desire (at the desire of somebody) PH: ying máuhyàhnge yiukàuh

desirous SV: hotmohngge

desist FV: tìhngjí

desk N: syùtói (M: jèung) *

desk study PH: jíseuhng tàahmbìng

desolate Adj. PH: fòng-lèuhngge PH: lihngdou fòngmòuh

despair FV/SV: sātmohng; FV: jyuhtmohng * in despair A: sātmohnggám; hái jyuhtmohng jìjùng

despairing Adj. PH: jyuht-mohngge

despatch (dispatch) FV: paaihín

desperate Adj. PH: sāt-mohngge; jyuhtmohngge

desperation VO/SV: (to take risks) mouhhím; FV: (hopeless) jyuhtmohng

despicable Adj. PH: bèipéi ge

despise FV: táisíu; táihèng

despite FV/N: jànghahn (M: go) CV: m̀léih; jungsí * (in) despite of (in spite of) CV: m̀léih

despoil FV: dyuhtchéui; leuhkdyuht

despondence (despondency) SV: jéuisong PH: yìjisìuchàhm

despondent Adj. PH: jéui-songge; yìjisìuchàhmge

despot N: jyùnjaigwànjyú; bouhgwàn (M: go)

despotic Adj. PH: jyùnjaige

despotism SV/N: jyùnjai N: jyùnjaijingfú; bouhjing (M: go)

dessert N: chāan hauh ge tìhmbán

dessertspoon N: (chāan hauh sihk tìhmbán yuhng ge) chìhgāng (M: jek)

destination N: muhkdīkdeih (M: go)

destine FV: jídihng; jyudihng ✻ **to be destined for** FV: ① jídihng *Nīdī syù haih ~ béi kéuih ge.* ② sáiheui *Gódī syùhn haih heui Gànàhdaaih ge.*

destiny N: mihngwahn; mehngséui

destitute SV/FV: kyutfaht

destitution SV/FV: kyutfaht SV: (poor) pàhnkùhng

destroy FV: wáiwaaih; wáimiht

destroyer N: kèuijuhklaahm (M: jek)

destruction FV: wáiwaaih; wáimiht

destructive Adj. PH: powaaihge ✻ **destructive to** PH: deui . . . yáuhhoih

destructor N: powaaihjé (M: go)

desultory Adj. PH: sáanmaahnge

detach FV: ❶ (to separate) fànhòi ❷ (to dispatch) paaihín

detachment FV: fànhòi; fànlèih

detail SV: chèuhngsai N: (details) saijit FV: chèuhngseuht ✻ **in detail** A: chèuhngsaigám

detain FV: kaulàuh; kaungaat

detect FV: faatyìhn; chàhchēut; faatgok

detective N: jìngtaam (M: go) Adj. PH: jìngtaamge; jìngchàhge

detention FV: gàamgam; kaulàuh

deter FV: jójí; jaijí

detergent Adj. PH: chìnggitge N: chìnggitjāi (M: júng)

deteriorate PH: lihngdou binwaaih FV: binwaaih

deterioration FV: binwaaih VO: binjāt

determinant Adj. PH: kyutdihngsingge

determinate Adj. PH: kokdihngge; mìhngkokge

determination N: kyutsàm (M: go)

determinative Adj. PH: kyutdihngge; haahndihngge PH: ❶ kyutdihng yànsou ❷ (grammar) jísih-doihmìhngchìh (M: go)

determine FV: kyutdihng N: kyutsàm

determined Adj. PH: yáuhkyutsàmge; gìnkyutge

determinism N: sūkmihngleuhn

deterrent Adj. PH: fòhngngoihge; jójíge N: jóngoihgeyéh; jaijígeyéh (M: gihn)

detest FV: tunghahn; jànghahn

detestable Adj. PH: gihkjì hóhahnge; gihkjì hówuge

dethrone FV: fai (gwàn-wòhng); failahp (gwànwòhng)

detonate FV: (lihngdou) dahtyìhn baauja; yìhnbaau

detonator N: lèuihgún (M: jì); jayeuhk

detour FV: yíudouh N: yíuhàahngge louh (M: tìuh)

detract FV: gáamsyún; wáisyún

detraction FV: wáisyún

detrain VO: lohkfóchè

detriment FV/N: syúnhoih; sèunghoih

detrimental Adj. PH: yáuh-hoihge; sèunghoihge

deuce FV: (tennis) dáwòh

devaluate PH: gongdài ... ge gajihk; lihngdou ngàhnjí (bank notes) bínjihk

devaluation FV: (economy) bínjihk

devastate FV: wáimiht; powaaih

devastation FV/N: wái-waaih; yàuhleuhn

develop FV: ❶ faatjín ❷ (of undertakings) jeunjín ❸ (grow) sihngjéung ❹ (of film) saai ＊ **develop into** PH: faatjín sihngwàih

developing Adj. PH: faat-jínjùngge FV: faatyuhk; sihngjéung

development FV/N: faat-jín; hòifaat

deviate FV: builèih; yuhtgwái

deviation FV: yuhtgwái N: pìnchà

deviationist N: (dóngnoih) yihdyùnfahnjí (M: go)

device FV/N: chitgai N: chaakleuhk (M: go)

devil N: mògwái FV: hei-luhng; jitmòh; jàauluhng ＊ **give the devil his due** PH: yātsihtùhngyàhn ＊ **raise the devil** PH: yáhnhéi daaih sòuyíu ＊ **the devil** A: gaugíng

devilish Adj. PH: kùhng-hùng gihkngokge; chàahn-huhkge A: gwodouhgám

devious Adj. PH: (improper) m̀jingdongge

devise FV/N: chitgai; FV: séungchēut N: wàihjahng; wàihjahngge chòihcháan

deviser N: faatmìhngge yàhn (faatmìhngjé); chitgaige yàhn (chitgaijé) (M: go)

devoid Adj. PH: kyutfahtge; hùngge; móuhge

devolve FV: yìhgàau

devote PH: jyùnsàm chùhng-sih FV: hinsàn

devoted Adj. PH: jùng-sahtge; jyùnsàmge ＊ **devoted to** FV: jùngyù; gunghinbéi

devotee N: seuntòuh (M: go)

devotion FV: hinsàn A/SV: jyùnsàm

devour FV: sihk; tànsihk

devout Adj. PH: kìhngingge; kìhnsìhngge

dew N: louh; louhséui (M: dihk)

dewdrop N: louhjyū (M: dihk)

dewy Adj. PH: daai louhséui ge; hóuchíh louh ge

dexterity SV: gèiháau; lìhngmáhn

dexterous Adj. PH: gèiháauge; lìhngmáhnge

diabetes N: tòhngniuhbehng

diabetic ATT: tòhngniuhbehngge; yáuh tòhngniuhbehngge N: yáuhtòhngniuhbehngge yàhn (M: go)

diabolic (diabolical) Adj. PH: chàahnhuhkge; chàahnyáhnge

diagnose FV/N: chándyuhn VO: táijing

diagnosis FV/N: chándyuhn

diagnostic ATT: chándyuhnge FV/N: chándyuhn N: chándyuhnhohk

diagonal Adj. PH: chèhge; chege N: deuigoksin (M: tiuh) ✲ **diagonal line** N: chèhsin (M: tiuh)

diagram N: tòuhgáai; tòuhbíu (M: go) PH: yuhngtòuh bíusih; yuhngtòuh gáaisīk

dial N: ❶ (sun dial) yahtkwāi ❷ (of a watch) bīumín VO: dádihnwá

dialect N: fòngyìhn; tóuwá (M: júng) ✲ **local dialect** N: búndeihwá

dialectic (dialectical) ATT: bihnjingge; bihnjingfaatge N: léihleuhn; lòhchāp (M: júng); bihnjingfaat

dialog (dialogue) FV/N: mahndaap; deuiwah

diameter N: jihkging (M: tiuh) ✲ **in diameter** PH: jihkging haih

diametrical ATT: jihkgingge

diamond N: jyunsehk (M: nāp)

diaper N: sípín; niuhpín (M: faai) PH: tùhng (bìhbījái) ngaap sípín Adj. PH: ngaapjyuhsípínge

diaphragm N: gaakbáan (M: faai) VO: jòng gaakbáan

diarrhea (diarrhoea) FV: tóuhngò; tóuhse; ngòleih

diary N: yahtgei (M: pìn, bún); yahtgeibóu (M: bún)

diatribe FV/N: fungchi; maahnmah (M: go)

dice N: sīkjái (M: nāp) PH: jaahksīkjái dóubok VO: jaahksīkjái (dóuchín)

dicey Adj. PH: mouhhímge

dictaphone N: luhkyàm dihnwágèi (M: go)

dictate FV: háusauh FV/N: mihnglihng (M: go); jífài

dictation VO; mahksyù

dictator N: duhkchòihjé (M: go)

dictatorship SV/N: duhkchòih FV/N: jyūnjing

diction N: yúhfaat; geuifaat; chouchìh

dictionary N: jihdín; chìhdín (M: bún) * to consult a dictionary VO: chàhjihdín

dictograph N: jìngtinghei; luhkyàmdihnwágèi (M: go)

didactic ATT: gaaudouhge; gaaufange

didactics N: gaauhohkfaat (M: go, júng)

die FV/N: séi; séimòhng * die a martyr FV: hèisàng * die off PH: sèunggai séimòhng * die out PH: juhkjihm sìumiht * die-away Adj. PH: móuhjìngsàhnge; tèuihsongge * die-hard N: wàahngu (bóusáu) fahnjí (M: go) SV: gwahtkéuhng

diesel N: noihyìhngèi; chàaihyàuhgèi (M: ga)

diet N: yámsihk; sihkmaht (M: júng) VO: gaaiháu

dietary ATT: yámsihkge N: sihkmaht; yámsihk

differ PH: tùhng . . . mtùhng SV: mtùhng * differ from PH: tùhng . . . mtùhng

difference SV: mtùhng N: fànbiht (M: go) * make a difference between PH: mtùhng deuidoih * split the difference FV: tóhhip

different Adj. Ph: mtùhngge * be different from PH: tùhng . . . mtùhng

differential Adj. PH: chàbihtge

differentiate FV: bihnbiht; kèuifàn

differentiation N: chàbiht; kèuibiht

difficult SV: kwannàahn;

nàahn

difficulty SV/N: kwannàahn; gàannàahn (M: go) * in difficulties PH: chyúgíng gaamgaai; gìngjai kwannàahn * make a difficulty FV: fáandeui

diffident Adj. PH: kyutfaht jihseun ge

diffuse FV: chyùhnbo; saanbou

diffusible Adj. PH: wúih kwongsaan ge

diffusion FV: kwongsaan

diffusive Adj. PH: kwongsaange

dig FV: gwaht * dig in (dig into) AV: nóuhlihk; yuhnggùng * to dig in one's books PH: yuhnggùng duhksyù * to dig into one's work PH: nóuhlihk gùngjok * to dig out FV: gwahtchèut

digest FV: ❶ (as food) sìufa; ❷ (understand) mìhngbaahk N: jaahkyiu * The Reader's Digest N: Duhkjé Màhnjaahk

digestion FV: sìufa N: sìufalihk

digestive Adj. PH: sìufage; bòngjoh sìufage N: bòngjoh sìufa ge yeuhk (M: júng)

digit N: soujih; (figures) soumuhkjih (M: go)

digital ATT: soujihge

dignify PH: lihngdou yáuh jyùnyìhm; gàyíh jyùnhouh

dignity N: jyùnyìhm

dignitary N: gòugwaige yàhn (M: go)

digress VO: lèihhòi búntàih; lèihhòi jyútàih

dike (dyke) N: tàih; ba; tàihba (M: tìuh)

dilapidate FV: syúnwái

dilapidated Adj. PH: wáiwaaihge; lamjóge

dilapidation FV: wáiwaaih; lamjó

dilate FV: pàahngjeung; kwongdaaih

dilemma PH: jeunteui léuhngnàahn

dilettante N: yihpyùh ngaihseuht ngoihoujé; màhnngaih ngoihoujé Adj. PH: ngoihhóngge

diligence SV: kàhnlihk

diligent SV: kàhnlihk

dilute FV: chùngtáahm; kàuhèi

dilution FV: chùngtáahm; kàuhèi

dim SV: ngam; (obscure) mùhngchàhchàh

dimmer N: mihtgwònghei (M: go)

dime N: yāthòuhjí ngán (M: go)

dimension N: mihnjīk (M: go) ✻ **in three dimensions** N: lahptái (M: go)

diminish FV: ❶ (lessen) gáamsíu ❷ sūksíu ❸ (make small) jíngsai

diminution FV: sūksai; binsai; gáamsíu

diminutive Adj. PH: saige; binsaige

dimple N: jáuwō; jáunāp (M: go)

din SV/FV: chòuh N: chòuhsèng; chòuhcháausèng

dine VO: sihkfaahn PH: chéng sihkfaahn ✻ **dine out** PH: chēutgāai sihkfaahn

diner N: ❶ sihkfaahnge yàhn (M: go) ❷ (Méihgwok) (fóchè seuhngbihn ge) chāanchè (M: ga)

dingy SV: laahttaat

dining N: jingchāan (M: chàan) ✻ **dining car** N: chāanchè (M: ga) ✻ **dining room** N: faahntēng (M: go) ✻ **dining hall** N: chāantēng (M: go)

dinner N: jingchāan (M: chàan) ✻ **dinner hour (dinner time)** N: sihkfaahn sìhgaan (M: go) ✻ **dinner jacket** N: móuhméihge máahnláihfuhk (M: tou) ✻ **dinner party** N: yinwuih (M: go)

dinosaur N: húnglùhng (M: tìuh)

dint N: nāphàhn (M: go) VO: dáchēut nāphàhn

dip FV: tíhm (dím) (to dip something in the soy sauce) ~ sihyàuh

diphtheria N: baahkhàuh; ngòhhàuh

diphthong N: (language) sēungyùhnyām

diploma N: màhnpàhng; bātyihpjingsyū (M: jèung)

diplomacy N: ngoihgàau; ngoihgàau sáuwún (M: júng)

diplomat N: ngoihgàaugùn (M: go)

diplomatic ATT: ngoihgàauge

diplomatist N: ngoihgàaugā (M: go)

dipper N: yáuhbengge hok (M: go)

dire Adj. PH: hópage; bèicháamge

direct FV: ❶ (oversee) jífài; ❷ (guide) jídouh; ❸ (lead) yáhndouh SV: (straight) jihk

direction N: fòngheung (M: go) ✻ **in all directions** PH: sei-mihn-baat-fòng ✻ **under the direction of somebody** PH: hái máuhmáuh yàhn ge jídouh jihah

directive N: jílihng (M: go) Adj. PH: jífàige; jídouhge

directly A: jihkjipgám

director N: ❶ jyúyahm ❷ (of a hospital, institute, etc.) yúnjéung ❸ (of a library, museum, etc.) gúnjéung ❹ (of a company) dúngsí (M: go) ✻ **board of directors** N: dúngsihwúi (M: go)

directorate N: dúngsihwúi (M: go)

directory N: yàhnméng jyuhjí bóu (M: bún) ✻ **telephone directory** N: dihnwábóu (M: bún)

dirge N: sòngkūk; wáangō (M: sáu)

dirk N: dyúngim; béisáu (M: bá) PH: yuhng dyúngim làih chi

dirt N: laahpsaap; nàih (M: dèui)

dirty SV: wùjòu; laahttaat; láhjá

disability FV: chàahnfai; mòuhnàhng

disabuse FV: gáujing (dáujing)

disaccord FV: mtùhngyi; myātji

disadvantage SV: bātleih FV/N: syúnhoih

disadvantageous SV: bātleih; yáuhhoih

disaffected Adj. PH: mmúhnyige

disaffection FV: mmúhnyi

disagree Adj. PH: yiginmtùhng; (unsuitable) msīkyìh

disagreeable Adj. PH: tóuyimge; lihng yàhn myuhfaai ge

disagreement SV: yiginmtùhng; msīkyìh

disallow FV: mjéun; (refuse) kéuihjyuht

disappear FV: sìusāt; sātjùng; mginjó

disappearance FV: sìusāt; sātjùng

disappoint PH: lihngdou sātmohng

disappointment SV: satmohng; souhing ✻ **to one's disappointment** PH: lihng yàhn sātmohng ge haih . . .

disapprove FV: mjéun N/FV: fáandeui

disarm VO: ❶ (to surrender arms) gíuhaaih ❷ gáaichèuih móuhjōng ❸ (to reduce the number of troops) chòihgwàn

disarmament VO: ❶ (to surrender arms) gíuhaaih ❷ (to reduce the number of troops) chòihgwàn ✳ **disarmament conference** N: chòihgwàn wuihyíh (M: go)

disarrange FV: yíulyuhn; jínglyuhn

disarrangement FV: jínglyuhn; yíulyuhn

disarray FV: (to disorder) jínglyuhn VO: (to remove one's clothing) chèuihsāam SV: (disorder) jaahplyuhn

disaster N: jòinaahn; jòiwoh (M: go)

disastrous Adj. PH: jòinaahnge; jouhsìhng jòiwoh ge

disbelief FV: m̀seun; m̀sèungseun

disbelieve FV: m̀seun; m̀sèungseun

disburden FV: báaityut PH: gáaichèuih fuhdàam

disburse FV: (to pay) jìchēut

disbursement FV/N: jìchēut (M: bāt)

disc (disk) N: yùhnpún (M: go); cheungpín (M: jek)

discard FV/N: pàauhei

discern FV: ❶ (distinguish) bihnbiht ❷ (make out) táichēut

discharge VO: (to unload cargoes) sefo FV: (to fire a person) gáaigu

disciple N: mùhntòuh (M: go)

disciplinarian Adj. PH: fanlihnge N: wàihchìh géileuht ge yàhn (M: go)

disciplinary ATT: fanlihnge

discipline N: fanlihn; chìhngfaht FV: ❶ (to train) fanlihn ❷ (to punish) chìhngfaht; faht

disclaim FV: ❶ (to deny) fáuyihng ❷ (to give up) fonghei

disclose FV: (as a secret) sitlauh

disclosure FV: kitfaat; sitlauh

discolor (discolour) VO: lātsīk

discomfit FV: dábaaih

discomfiture FV/N: sātbaaih (M: go)

discomfort SV: ❶ (of body) m̀syùfuhk ❷ (of mind) m̀ngònlohk

disconcert PH: lihngdou m̀ngònlohk

disconnect RV: chaakhòi; lihngdou fânhòi

disconsolate SV: m̀hòisàm; nàahngwo

discontent SV: m̀múhnyi

discontented SV: m̀jìjūk; (not satisfied) m̀múhnyi

discontinue FV: tìhngjí; tìhng

discontinuous Adj. PH: m̀lìhnjuhkge

discord FV: (to argue) jànggjāp; (not the same) m̀sèungtùhng

discordance SV: m̀wòh-hàaih; fànkèih

discordant SV: fànkèih

discothèque N: yìuhbáai-móuh; dīksihgòu

discount VO: dájittàuh; dá-jitkau N: jittàuh; jitkau (M: go)

discourage PH: lihngdou . . . fùisàm

discouragement SV: fùi-sàm

discourse FV/N: yíngóng; yínsyut (M: pìn)

discover FV: faatyìhn

discovery FV: faatyìhn

discredit FV/N: m̀seun-yahm; wàaihyíh

discreditable Adj. PH: móuhseunyuhngge

discreet SV: gánsahn; síu-sàm

discreetly A: síusàmgám; gánsahngám

discrepancy SV: m̀tùhng; N: (contrary) màauhtéuhn

discretion SV: síusàm; gánsahn

discriminate FV/N: kèihsih

discrimination FV/N: kèihsih * **racial discrimination** PH: júngjuhk kèihsih

discursive Adj. PH: sáan-maahnge

discus N: titbéng (M: go) * **the discus throw** VO: jaahk titbéng

discuss FV: ❶ tóuleuhn ❷ (consult about) sèungleùhng ❸ (talk about) kìngháh

discussion FV: tóuleuhn; sèunglèuhng * **under discussion**PH: jingjoih tóuleuhngán

disdain FV/N: hìngsih

disease FV/N: behng N: behngjing (M: júng) * **contagious disease** N: chyùhnyíhmbehng

diseased PH: yáuhbehng

disembark VO: séuhng-ngohn

disembody FV: tyutlèih

disengage VO: gáaiyeuk FV: (to sever one's relation with) tyutlèih

disengaged SV: jihyàuh; dākhàahn

disentangle RV: gáaihòi

disfavor (disfavour) FV: ❶ m̀jùngyi ❷ (to look down upon) hìngsih

disfigure PH: syúnwái . . . yìhngjeuhng FV/N: (to cause damage or loss) syúnhoih

disfigurement VO: wái-yùhng; poseung

disfranchise VO: chídyuht gùngkyùhn; mōkdyuht dahk-kyùhn

disfranchisement VO: chídyuht gùngkyùhn; mōk-dyuht dahkkyùhn

disgorge FV: touchēut; tou; ngáuchēut

disgrace N: (shame) chíyuhk VO: dīugá; dīu . . . ge gá

disgraceful Adj. PH: hóchíge; m̀mihngyuhge

disgruntle PH: lihngdou m̀gòuhing; lihngdou m̀múhnyi

disguise FV: gábaahn VO: (to masquerade) fajōng

disgust PH: lihngyàhntóu-yim SV/FV: tóuyim

dish N: ❶ díp (M: jek) ❷ (food) sung

dishcloth N: sáiwúnbou; wúnbou (M: faai)

dishearten PH: lihngdou fùisàm

dishevel SV: sùngsáan; lihnglyuhn

disheveled Adj. PH: lihng-lyuhnge

dishonest SV: m̀sìhngsaht; m̀lóuhsaht

dishonesty SV: m̀sìhngsaht; m̀lóuhsaht

dishonor (dishonour) N: chíyuhk (M: go) FV: móuhyuhk

dishonorable Adj. PH: m̀-mihngyuhge; hóchíge

disillusion FV: síngngh; goksíng

disincline PH: lihngdou m̀yuhnyi

disinfect VO: sìuduhk

disinfectant N: sìuduhkjāi; sìuduhk yeuhkséui (M: júng)

disinfection VO: sìuduhk

disinfest FV: chèuihheui

disinfestant N: saat-chùhngjāi (M: júng)

disinherit PH: mōkdyuht . . . ge gaisìhngkyùhn

disinheritance PH: mōk-dyuht gaisìhngkyùhn

disintegrate FV: bàng-kwúi; ngáhgáai

disintegration FV: bàng-kwúi; (to split) fànliht

disinterested Adj. PH: gùngpìhngge; gùngjingge

disjoint PH: lihngdou lātgaau VO: lātgaau

disjointed Adj. PH: lāt-jógaauge; móuhtiuhléihge; (disorderly) jaahplyuhnge

disk (disc) N: yùhnpún (M: go); cheungpín (M: jek)

dislike FV: m̀jùngyi; yìhm

dislocate PH: gwātgaau sùngjó; lātjógaau

dislocation VO: lātgaau SV: (confused or disorderly) fànlyuhn

dislodge FV: kèuijuhk; juhkchēut

disloyal SV: m̀jùngsàm; buibuhnge

disloyally SV: m̀jùngsàm

disloyalty SV: m̀jùngsàm FV: buibuhn

dismal SV: yàusàuh

dismay PH: lihngdou gèng; lihngdou m̀ngònlohk SV: gèng

dismember PH: gottyùhn seijī FV: ❶ (to apportion) gwàfàn ❷ (to divide up) fàngot

dismiss FV: ❶ (discharge, as an employee) cháau; gáaigu ❷

(expel from school) hòichèuih ❸ (as workman, for the day) fong-gùng * **dismiss the class** VO: lohktòhng * **dismiss the meeting** VO: saanwúi

dismissal FV: (expel from school) hòichèuih VO: (discharge, as an employee) cháau yàuhyú

dismount VO: ❶ (to dismount from a horse) lohkmáh ❷ (to get off from train, vehicle, etc.) lohkchè

disobedience FV/SV: m̀fuhkchùhng; m̀tèngwah

disobedient SV/FV: m̀-fuhkchùhng; m̀tèngwah

disobey SV/FV: m̀fuhk-chùhng; m̀tèngwah

disoblige FV: m̀tùngyùhng; (to offend) dākjeuih

disorder PH: móuh diht-jeuih; jaahplyuhn * **put into disorder** PH: lihngdou wahnlyuhn

disorderly Adj. PH: móuh-dihtjeuihge; wahnlyuhnge A: móuhdihtjeuihgám N: dóu-lyuhnfahnjí (M: go)

disorganize FV: yíulyuhn PH: lihngdou wahnlyuhn

disown PH: m̀sìhngyihng haih jihgéi sóyáuh ge FV: (to deny) fáuyihng

disparage FV: ❶ (to look down upon) hìngsih ❷ (to slander) wáipóhng

disparagement FV: hìng-sih; wáipóhng

disparity SV: m̀tùhng

dispassionate SV: gùng-pìhng

dispatch (despatch) FV: ❶ paai (to dispatch a messenger) ~ *sijé* ❷ faat (to dispatch a telegram) ~ *dihnbou* * **with dispatch** PH: chùhngchùk chyúléih * **dispatch box (dispatch case)** N: gùngmàhn daihsung sēung (M: go)

dispel FV: kèuisaan

dispensable Adj. PH: bāt-bītyiuge

dispensary N: yeuhkfòhng (M: gàan)

dispensation FV: fànpui; fànbéi

dispense FV: fànpui; fànbéi * **dispense with** FV: míhnchèuih

dispenser N: yeuhkjāisī (M: go)

disperse FV: fànsaan; saan-hòi

dispersion FV: fànsaan; saanhòi

dispirit PH: lihngdou hei-nèuih; lihngdou jéuisong

displace FV: doihtai

displacement FV: doihtai; chéuidoih

display FV/N: ❶ (exhibit) chàhnliht; jínláahm ❷ (manifest) bíuyihn * **make a display of** PH: jèung . . . kwàyiuh yātfàan * **on display** FV: jínláahm

displease FV: gīknàu; PH: lihngdou m̀hòisàm

displeasure SV: m̀gòuhing; m̀hòisàm

disposable Adj. PH: hóyíh jihyàuh chyúji ge; hóyíh chèuihyi síyuhngge

disposal FV: chyúléih; chyúji ✳ **at one's disposal** PH: tèng . . . ge jìpui

dispose FV: chyúléih; chyúji ✳ **to dispose of** FV: chyúji; chyúléih; jìpui

disposed AV: yáuhyi . . .; dásyun . . .

disposition N: ❶ singchìhng ❷ (temper) pèihhei FV: (to deal with) chyúji; chyúléih

dispossess FV: ❶ (to deprive one of) mōkdyuht ❷ (to occupy or take by force) bajim

dispossession FV: mōkdyuht; bajim

disproof FV: fáanbok; fáanjing

disproportion SV: m̀sèungching PH: lihngdou m̀sèungching

disproportionate SV: m̀sèungching

disprove FV: fáanbok; fáanjing

disputable Adj. PH: m̀jingkokge; yùhngyih yáhnhéi jàngleuhn ge

disputant N: chàamgà bihnleuhn ge yàhn; jàngleuhngeyàhn (M: go)

dispute FV: jàngleuhn; jàang ✳ **dispute on family property** VO: jàanggàcháan ✳ **beyond dispute** A: mòuhyìh; PH: mòuhhó jàngleuhn ✳ **in**

dispute PH: jingjoih jàngleuhn ge

disqualification PH: móuhjìgaak; chéuisiu jìgaak

disqualify PH: chéuisiu . . . ge jìgaak; lihngdou . . . . m̀hahpgaak

disquiet PH: lihngdou m̀ngònlohk FV/N: yàuleuih (M: go)

disquietude FV/N: yàuleuih SV: m̀ngònlohk

disquisition N: jyùntàih yíngóng; (a thesis) leuhnmàhn (M: pìn)

disregard FV: m̀léih; m̀gu ✳ **disregard one's life** A: m̀yiumehng gám ✳ **disregard one's reputation** PH: m̀gum̀hngyuh

disreputable Adj. PH: hahlàuhge

disrepute PH: wùmìhng; mìhngyuh m̀hóu

disrespect FV: m̀jyùnging SV: móuhláih

disrespectful Adj. PH: móuhláihge; bātgingge

disrupt PH: lihngdou fànliht; FV: ngáhgáai

disruption FV: fànliht; ngáhgáai

dissatisfaction SV/FV: m̀múhnyi

dissatisfy PH: lihngdou m̀múhnyi

dissect FV: gáaifáu; chithòi

dissection FV: chithòi; gáaifáu

dissemble FV: yímsīk

disseminate FV: saanbou; chyùhnbo

dissemination FV: saanbou; chyùhnbo

dissension FV/N: fànkèih; jàngleuhn

dissent PH: yigin m̀tùhng; FV: m̀tùhngyi

dissenter N: kongyíhge yàhn (M: go)

dissertation N: leuhnmàhn; hohkwái leuhnmàhn (M: pin)

disservice FV/N: ngàihhoih; syúnhoih (M: go)

dissimulate FV: yímsīk

dissipate FV: kèuisaan; sìusaan

dissipated FV: kèuisaan; sìusaan

dissociate FV: fànlèih

dissociation FV: fànlèih

dissoluble Adj. PH: hóyíh yùhnggáai ge; hóyíh fànlèih ge

dissolution FV/N: ❶ (to cancel) gáaichèuih ❷ (to dismiss) gáaisaan

dissolve FV: yùhng; yùhnggáai ＊ **dissolve a partnership** VO: chaakgú ＊ **dissolve phlegm** VO: fatàahm

dissonance SV: m̀hiptìuh; m̀tùihwòh

dissonant Adj. PH: m̀hiptìuhge; m̀wòhhàaihge

dissuade FV: hyunjó; hyungaai

distance N: kéuihlèih (M: go) FV: chiùgwo; yuhtgwo ＊ **at a distance** PH: gaakhòi yātdī ＊ **in the distance** A: hái yúhnchyu ＊ **keep a person at a distance** PH: láahngdaahm deuidoih yātgo yàhn

distant SV: yúhnlèihge; yúhn ＊ **distant view** N: yúhngíng (M: go)

distaste FV: m̀héifùn

distemper N: hyúnyihtbehng; behng PH: lihngdou behng

distend FV: kwongjèung; pàahngjeung

distill (distil) FV: jìnglauh

distillate N: jìnglauhmaht; jìnglauhyìhk (M: júng)

distillation FV: jìnglauh

distiller N: jìnglauhhei (M: go)

distillery N: jìnglauhsó; jáuchóng (M: gàan)

distinct SV: chìngchó

distinction (in examinations) N: yàu (yàudáng) (M: go) *Néih nīchi háausíh dākdóu géidō go yàu a?*

distinctive Adj. PH: dahksyùhge; yáuhdahksīkge

distinctively A: chìngchógám

distinguish FV: bihnbiht; fànbiht ＊ **distinguish right from wrong** VO: bihnbiht sihfēi ＊ **distinguish the true from the false** VO: bihnbiht jàngá

distinguished Adj. PH:

jyumìhngge; chēutméngge ＊
distinguished for (by) PH: yíh
. . . yih jyumìhng

distort FV: kūkgáai ＊ **to
distort the facts** VO: kūkgáai
sihsaht

distortion FV: kūkgáai; (to
twist or confuse (things, facts,
etc.) intentionally) wàaikūk

distract FV: ❶ (to fail to pay
full attention) fànsàm ❷ (to confuse) màihwaahk

distraction FV: fànsàm N:
(amusement) yùhlohk

distrain FV: kaungaat

distress N/SV: fàahnnóuh;
tungfú PH: lihngdou tungfú;
lihngdou nàahngwo ＊ **distress
call** N: yuhhím seunhou (s.o.s.)
(M: go)

distress gun N: yuhhím
seunhouh paau (M: mùhn)

distress warrant N: (law)
kaungaatlihng (M: go)

distributary FV: (of river)
jìlàuh (M: tìuh)

distribute FV: fàn; fànpui;
paai

distribution FV: fànpui; (to
be scattered over an area)
fànbou

distributive ATT: fàn-
puige; (individually) gobihtge

distributer (distributor)
N: fànpuigeyàhn (fànpuijé); (a
publisher) faathòhngyàhn (M:
go)

district N: kèui; deihkèui
(M: go)

distrust FV: mseun

disturb FV: ❶ yíulyuhn (to
disturb peace and order) ~
jihngòn ❷ gáaulyuhn Ḿhóu ~
ngóh dī yéh ❸ gáau Ḿhóu ~ dī
saimānjái ＊ **be distrubed** SV:
nàahngwo; sàmfàahn

disturbance FV: yíulyuhn
SV: mngònlohk

disunion FV/N: (to separate) fànlèih; (to split) fànliht

disunite PH: lihngdou
fànlèih; FV: fànlèih

disuse FV: tìhngyuhng;
myuhng

disyllable PH: sèung-
yāmjit-chìh; sèung-yāmjit-ge-
jih (M: go)

disyllabic Adj. PH: sèung-
yāmjit-chìh ge; sèung-yāmjit-
ge-jih ge

ditch N: kàu; kèuih;
kàukèuih (M: tìuh) VO:
gwahtkàukèuih

ditto FV: tùhngseuhng

dive VO: ❶ (to jump into the
water, to dive from a diving
board) tìuseuí ❷ (swim under
water) chìhmséui; meihséui

dive bomber N: fúchùng
gwàngjagèi (M: ga)

diver N: tiuséuige yàhn;
chìhmséuiyùhn (chìhmséuige
yàhn) (M: go)

diverge FV/N: fànkèih

divergence FV/N: fànkèih

divergency = divergence
FV/N: fànkèih

divergent SV: fànkèihge

divers SV: géigo; mtùhngge;

júngjúngge ✳ divers opinions PH: géijúng yigin

diverse Adj. PH: m̀tùhngge; yìhngyìhngsīksīkge

diversify PH: lìhngdou m̀tùhng; lìhngdou binfa

diversion FV/N: jyúnheung (the diversion of a stream) hòhlàuhge ~ FV: (to fail to pay full attention) fānsàm

diversity SV: m̀tùhng ✳ a great diversity of methods PH: gok júng m̀tùhngge fòngfaat

divert N/FV: (pastime) sìuhín

divest PH: chèuihjó . . . ge yìfuhk; FV: (to deprive one of) mōkdyuht

divestment PH: chèuih . . . jìfuhk FV: mōkdyuht

divide FV: fàn; fàngaai N: (Méihgwok) fànséuilèhng (M: go) ✳ be divided by PH: béi . . . chèuih; yuhng . . . chèuih . . . ✳ divide equally FV: pìhngfàn; deuifàn

dividend N: ❶ (arithmetic) beihchèuihsou ❷ (on stock) gúsīk; hùhngleih

divider N: fàngaakmaht (M: gihn)

dividers N: yùhnkwāi; léuhnggeukkwāi (M: go)

divine ATT: sàhnge N: sàhnhohkjé; muhksī (M: go) FV: yuhyìhn; tèuichāak

divinity N: ❶ sàhn ❷ (divine power) sàhnlihk ❸ (theology) sàhnhohk

divisible Adj. PH: chèuih-

dākjeuhn ge (hóyíh chèuihjeuhn ge) PH: 8 hóyíh yàuh 2 chèuihjeuhn

division N: ❶ (arithmetic) chèuihsou; chèuihfaat ❷ (segment) bouhfahn ❸ (army) sī ❹ (divisional commander) sījéung

divisional Adj. PH: (arithmetic) chèuihfaatge; (army) sīge

divisor N: (arithmetic) chèuihsou (M: go)

divorce VO: lèihfàn PH: lìhngdou lèihfàn; tùhng . . . lèihfàn ✳ be divorced from PATT: tùhng . . . lèihfàn

divulge FV: sitlauh ✳ to divulge a secret VO: sitlauh beimaht

divulgement (divulgence) FV: sitlauh

dizzy SV: tàuhwàhn FV: lìhngdou tàuhwàhn

do FV: jouh A: (as an emphatic word) jànhaih Ngóhdeih jànhaih sèuiyiu kéuih bòngmòhng ✳ Don't . . . AV: m̀hóu . . . Yìhgā m̀hóu heui ✳ do good VO: jouh hóusih ✳ do one's best A: jeuhnlihk ✳ do away with FV: chéuisiu Chéuisiu kwàijāk ✳ do without PH: móuh . . . dōu móuh mahntàih ✳ have something to do with PH: tùhng . . . yáuh gwàanhaih ✳ have nothing to do with PH: tùhng . . . móuh gwàanhaih (m̀gwàan . . . sih) Gógihn sih tùhng ngóh móuh gwàanhaih. Gógihn sih m̀gwàan ngóh sih ✳ do business VO: jouh sàangyi

docile SV: tēngwah; sèuhnleùhng

docility SV: wànseuhn;

sèuhnlèuhng

dock N: syùhnngou; (a wharf; a pier) máhtàuh (M: go) VO: yahpngou * **to moor a ship at the pier** VO: paak máhtàuh

docker N: syùhnngou gùngyàhn; máhtàuh gùngyàhn (M: go)

dockyard N: jouhsyùhnchóng; syùhnchóng (M: go)

doctor N: ❶ (medical) yīsāng; yīsī ❷ (academic) boksih (M: go) FV: yījih * **Doctor of Divinity** N: sàhnhohk boksih (M: go) * **Doctor of Science** N: léihhohk boksih (M: go) * **Doctor of Philosophy (Ph. D.)** N: jithohk boksih (M: go) * **Doctor of Laws** N: faathohk boksih (M: go) * **Doctor of Literature** N: màhnhohk boksih (M: go) * **Doctor of Medical Science** N: yihohk boksih (M: go) * **see a doctor** VO: tái yīsāng

doctorate N: boksihhohkwái (M: go)

doctrine N: ❶ (of a political party) jyúyih ❷ (of a school of thought; or a philosophy of a church) douhléih (M: go)

document N: gùngmàhn; màhngín (M: gihn)

documental Adj. PH: màhngínge

documentary Adj. PH: màhngínge N: géiluhkpín (M: tou)

dodder PH: (the aged) bàibàiháh gám hàahng

dodge FV: símbeih; dóbeih

doe N: (a roe dear) luhkná;

(rabbit) touná (M: jek)

dog N: gáu (M: jek) FV: jèuijùng; gànjùng * **go to the dogs** FV: binwaaih; dohlohk * **throw to the dogs** FV: pàauhei * **dog days** TW: daaihyihttīn

dogged Adj. PH: wàahnkèuhngge; wàahnguge; gujápge

dogma FV: móuhdyuhn N: (a doctrine) gaautiuh

dogmatic Adj. PH: gaautiuhge; móuhdyuhnge

dogmatism N: gaautiuhjyúyih

doldrums SV: m̀hòisàm; yàusàuh

dole N/FV: (to give to charity) sìsé N: (fate, lot) mihngwahn

doleful SV: bèingòi

do-little SV: láahn (ge) N: láahn (ge) yàhn (M: go)

doll N: gūngjái; yèuhngwàwà (M: go)

dollar M: mān (one dollar) *yātmān* N: ngàhnchín (M: go) (one dollar) *yātgo ngàhnchín*

dolly N: gūngjái; yèuhngwàwà (M: go)

dolomite N: wàhnsehk; daaihléihsehk (M: gauh, faai)

dolphin N: hóityùhn (M: jek)

dolt N: sòhgwā; sòhjái (M: go)

domain N: líhngtóu; líhngwihk

dome N: yùhndéng (M: go)

domestic SV: ❶ (family) gàtìhngge; ❷ (inside the country) gwoknoihge ✻ **domestic affairs** N: gàsih (M: gihn) ✻ **domestic expenses** N: gàyuhng ✻ **domestic animals** N: gàchŭk (M: jek) ✻ **domestic fowls** N: gàkàhm (M: jek) ✻ **domestic markets** N: gwoknoih síhchèuhng (M: go) ✻ **domestic products** N: gwokfo

domesticate PH: lihngdou héifūn gàtihng sàngwuht

domicile N: jyuhjaahk; jyuhsó (M: go) FV: dihnggèui; gèuijyuh

dominant Adj. PH: yáuh jìpuilihk ge; jeui yáuhsailihk ge

dominate FV: túngjih; jìpui

domination FV: túngjih; jìpui

domineer FV: ngaatjai IE: jok-wâi-jok-fūk

dominion N: ❶ (territory) líhngtóu ❷ (of the British Empire) jihjihlíhng ✻ **Dominion of Canada** PH: Gànàhdaaih jihjihlíhng

dominoes N: gwātpáai (M: fu, set; jek, piece)

donate FV: gyùn ✻ **donate blood** VO: gyùnhyut

donation VO/N: gyùnfún (M: bāt)

donkey N: lèuih; lèuihjái (M: jek)

donor N: gyùnjahngyàhn (sìjyú) (M: go)

doom N: ngâkwahn FV/N: séimôhng FV: jyudihng IE: mihng-jùng-jyu-dihng

doomsday N: saigaaimuhtyaht

door N: mùhn (M: douh) ✻ **next door to** PH: hái . . . ge gaaklèih A: gèifúh ✻ **doorbell** N: mùhnjūng; dihnjūng (M: go) ✻ **doorplate** N: mùhnpàaih (M: go)

doorcase (doorframe) N: mùhnkwāang (M: go)

doorkeeper N: táimùhnháuge yàhn (M: go)

doorman N: táimùhnháuge yàhn (M: go)

door money N: yahpchèuhngfai (M: bāt)

doorway N: mùhnháu (M: go)

dope N: màhjeuiyeuhk (M: júng)

dormant ATT: seuihmìhnjohngtaaige

dormer N: tìnchèung (M: go)

dormitory N: sūkse (M: go, gàan)

dose M: ❶ (medicine taken at one time) chi; fuhk ❷ (Chinese herbs) jài VO: ❶ puiyeuhk ❷ (to take medicine) sihkyeuhk ✻ **dose somebody with his own physic** PH: yíh-kèihyàhnjì-douh-wàahnjih-kèihyàhnjì-sàn

dot N: dím (síudím) VO: dá dímhouh ✻ **dotted line** N: hèuisin (M: tiuh)

dote RV: chúngwaaih *Kéuih chúngwaaih go jái*

double PH: gàdò yātpúih A/N: sèungpúih; gàpúih ✻ **double bed** N: sèungyàhn chòhng (M: jèung) ✻ **double room** N: sèungyàhn fóng (M:

gàan) * **double-face** N: ngaihgwànjí (M: go) * **double-faced** PH: háu-sih-sàm-fèi ge * **double-minded** Adj. PH: fáanfūk mòuhsèuhng ge; sàamsàm-léuhngyi ge

doubt FV/N: sìyìh; wàaihyìh * **beyond doubt (beyond a doubt)** A: hòuhmòuh yìhmahn; mòuhyìh * **in doubt** FV: wàaihyìh; meih kokdihng

doubtful Adj. PH: hóyìhge; meih kokdihng ge

doubtless A: mòuhyìh

douche FV: gunsái

dough N: sàang mihntyùhn * **dough-boy** N: tòngyún (M: go)

doughy ATT: bun-sàang-suhk ge

douse PH: jam. . . yahpheui séui leúhbihn

dove N: baahkgáp (M: jek)

dove-eyed Adj. PH: ngáahn-sàhn yàuhwòh ge

dowdy Adj. PH: yìsàam làahmláuh ge N: yìsàam làahmláuh ge néuihyán (M: go)

dowel N: muhkdēng (M: háu, ngáan)

dower N: gajòng VO: béi gajòng. . .

down A: heunghah FV: ❶ dábaaih (To down one's enemy) *Dábaaih dihkyàhn* ❷ dádóu (Down with the dictator!) *Dádóu duhkchòihjé!* * **come down** FV: lohklàih * **go down** FV: lohkheui * **please sit down** IE: chéngchôh * **write down** FV: sédài *Chéng néih hái nī-jèung jísyu sédài néihge deihjí*

* **down-and-out (down and out)** PH: kùhngkwan lóuhdóu (ge) * **upside down** PH: seuhnghah dìndóu * **down-pour** N: daaihyúh (M: chèuhng) * **down-stairs** PW: làuhhah A: hái làuhhah * **down-town** N: sèungyihpkèui (M: go) PH: heui sèungyihpkèui

dowry N: gajòng

doxy N: (a mistress) chìhngfúh (M: go)

doze VO: jùngngáahnfan

dozen M: dā (one dozen) *yāt-dā* * **dozens** Nu: géisahp PH: hóudò

drab SV: (monotonous) dàandiuh(ge)

draff N: (dregs) jà

draft N: ❶ (of a document) chóugóu ❷ (of a law) chóungon (M: go) ❸ (bill) wuihpiu; wuih-dāan (M: jèung) VO: héigóu; héichóu * **make a draft of** VO: héichóu; heigóu

draftman N: héichóuyàhn; waahkjīksī (M: go)

drag FV: (pull) làai; tò * **drag anchor** N: fàuhbīu (M: go) * **drag on (drag out)** FV: tòyìhn

draggle RV: tòwùjòu (tò-laahttaat); tòsāp

dragon N: lùhng (M: tìuh) * **dragon boat** N: lùhngsyùhn (M: jek) * **dragon boat festival** N: nǵhyuhtjit; dyùn-nǵhjit (M: go) * **dragon boat race** VO: daulùhngjāu, choilùhngsyùhn

dragonfly N: chìngtìhng; tòhngmēi (M: jek)

drain VO: pàaihséui N: (a

means of draining) kèuih (M: tìuh) * covered drain N: ngamkèuih (M: tìuh) * open drain N: mìhngkèuih (M: tìuh)

drainage VO: pàaihséui N: (sewers) hahséuidouh * drainage basin N: (river valley) làuhwìhk (M: go)

drama N: hei; heikehk (M: chēut) * drama school N: heikehk hohkhaauh (M: gàan)

dramatic Adj. PH: hei-kehkge

dramatist N: heikehkgā; kehkjokgā (M: go)

dramatize VO: pìnkehk; pìnsìhng kehkbún

drape FV: (to hang) gwa; yùhngwa

drapery N: (piece goods) boupāt

drastic SV: gīklìht * drastic measures PH: gīklìht sáudyuhn (M: go)

draught M: (yāt) móhng * A draught of fish PH: Yāt-móhng yú

draw FV: ❶ làai *Làai néih jèung yí màaihdī heui jèung tóisyu lā)* ❷ waahk (Draw pictures) *Waahkwá* ❸ (check, etc.) sé, hòi *séjìpiu; hòi jìpiu* * draw up VO: héichóu; héigóu * draw lots VO: jàpcháu; chāuchīm * draw-back N: kyutdím (M: go) * draw-bridge N: diukìuh (M: douh)

drawer N: ❶ gwaihtúng ❷ (painter) wágā (M: go)

drawing VO: (to paint pictures) waahktòuh N: (a painting) tòuhwá * drawing board N:

wábáan (M: faai) * drawing paper N: tòuhwájí (M: jèung) * drawing pen N: waahktòuh bāt * drawing pin N: tòuhdēng; gahmdēng (M: háu; ngáan) * drawing room N: (parlor) haaktēng (M: go)

dread FV: pa SV: hópa (ge)

dreadful SV: hópa(ge)

dreadfully A: gihkjì; dougihk

dream N: muhng (M: go) FV: (dream about) muhnggin VO: faatmuhng * dream-land N: muhnggíng; muhnghèung (M: go)

dreamy Adj. PH: hóuchíh muhng ge; (daydream) waahnséungge

dreary SV: chàhmmuhn (ge); mhòisàm (ge)

dredge FV: ❶ (in deep water) làauh ❷ (in shallow water) mò ❸ waat ~ nàih N: (a dredger) waatnàihgèi (M: ga)

dregs N: jà

drench RV: sápsaai; jíngsáp; FV: (to get wet in the rain) làhmsāp

dress VO: (put on clothes) jeuksāam N: (woman's garment in general) sāam-kwàhn (M: gihn) * dress-maker N: chòihfúng (M: go) * dress-stand N: yìgá (M: go)

dressing VO: jeuksāam; N: (spice, dressing material) tìuhmeihbán * dressing gown N: seuihyī (M: tou)

dribble VO: ❶ lauhséui; dihkséui (That faucet dribbles) *Gógo séuihàuh lauhséui* ❷ làuhháuséui *Dī bìhbī sìhsih dōu làuhháuséui* PH: (a drop) yātdihk; síusíu

dribblet (driblet) PH: yātdihk; síusíu

drift FV: (on or in water) pìulàuh

drill FV: lihn FV/N: lihnjaahp; (train or practice) fanlihn; FV: jyun VO: (to drill a hole) *jyunlūng*

drilling machine N: jyunchòhng; jyunlūnggèi (M: ga)

drill ship N: jyuntaamsyùhn (M: jek)

drink FV: yám VO: yámjáu N: yámgeyéh ✻ **drink to** PH: géuibūi jūkhoh *Jūk néih sàntái gihnhòng.* ✻ **be drunk** RV: yámjeuijó; yámjeuijáu

drip N: séuidihk FV: dihklohklàih

dripping N: dihklohklàihge yéh ATT: dihkséuige

drive FV: (vehicle) jà; sái (to drive a car) *jàchè; sáichè.* ✻ **drive a person to PW** Patt: chè yātgo yàhn heui PW ✻ **drive a pile** VO: dájòng

drivel VO: làuhháuséui

diver N: (of a car) sìgèi (sīgēi) (M: go)

drizzle N: yúhmēi (M: chèuhng) VO: lohkyúhmēi

droll VO: hòiwàahnsiu SV: yáuhcheuige; waahtkāige N: waahtkāige yàhn (M: go)

dromedary N: dāanfūng loktòh (M: jek)

drone N: hùhngfūng (M: jek)

PH: faatchēut wùngwùngsēng

droop FV: dàisèuih; hahsèuih

drop FV: ❶ (to fall or let fall) ditjó *Mhóu ditjó bún syù.* ❷ dihklohklàih *Dī yúh juhnghaih hái syuhseuhngbihn dihkgán lohklàih.* M: (a drop) (of liquid) dihk *yātdihk séui*

dropping FV: dihklohklàih; lohklohklàih N: dihk(lohk)lohklàihge yéh

dropsy N/SV: fàuhjúng N: séuijúng

dross N: fàuhjà; jaahpjāt

drought N: tìnhóhn; hóhnjòi

drown RV: (drown in water) jamséi ✻ **drown oneself in the sea** VO: tiuhói

drowse VO: jùngngáahnfan

drowsy SV: ngáahnfan (ge) Adj. PH: sēung fangaau ge

drub FV: dá; hàaudá

drudge VO: jouhfúgūng N: jouhfúgūngge yàhn (M: go)

drudgery N: fúgūng

drug N: yeuhk (M: júng)

druggist N: ❶ maaih yeuhk ge sèungyàhn ❷ (pharmacist) yeuhkjāisī (M: go)

druggy N: (Méihgwok) kāpduhkge yàhn; kāpduhkjé (M: go)

drug-store N: yeuhkfòhng (M: gàan)

drum N: gú (M: go) VO: **dágú** ✻ **drum-fire** PH: máahngliht (ge) paaufó

drummer N: gúsáu (M: go)

drunk Adj. PH: yámjeuige; yámjeuijáuge ✳ **drunkard** N: yámjeuijáuge yàhn; jeuimāau (M: go)

drunken Adj. PH: yámjeui (jáu) ge

drupe N: wahtgwó (M: go)

dry SV: (not wet) gòn; gòn-chou RV: ❶ (to dry in the air) lohnggòn ❷ (to dry in the sun) saaigòn ✳ **dry-boned** SV: hóu sau ge; gwāt-sau-yùh-chàaih ge ✳ **dry cell** N: gòn dihnchìh (M: go)

dry-clean (dry-cleanse) FV: gònsái

dry-nurse VO: jouh bóu-móuh N: bóumóuh (M: go)

dryer (drier) N: ❶ (a chemical substance that absorbs moisture) gònchoujái ❷ (an oven) gònchougèi

dual ATT: yihge; sèung-chùhngge; léuhngchàhngge; sèungge ✳ **dual-purpose** ATT: gìmyuhngge

dualism N: yihyùhnleuhn

duality N: léuhngchùhng-sing; yihchùhngsing

dub PH: sauh chìnghouh béi . . .; sauh fànjeuk béi . . .

dubious Adj. PH: hóyìhge; yàuhyùh bātkyut ge

duchess N: gùngjeuk fù-yàhn; néuih-gùngjeuk (M: go)

duchy N: gùngjeuk-líhng-deih

duck N: ngáap (ngaap) (M: jek)

duckling N: ngaapjái (M: jek)

duct N: gún; syùsunggún (M: tìuh)

ductile SV: yàuhyúhn(ge)

due PH: ❶ yìnggòi béi (paid) ge *Ngūkjòu yìnggòi géisí gàau a?* ❷ yìnggòi dou (arrive) ge *Ga fèigèi yìnggòi géisí dou a?* N: yìnggòi gàau ge chín (fai) *Ngóh yíhgìng gàaujó wúifai la.* ✳ **overdue** PH: gwokèih(ge) ✳ **due-bill** N: jegeui (M: jèung)

duel N/FV: kyutdau

duff VO: ngāakyàhn FV: hèipin N: (coal dust) mùihsit

duffer N: ❶ (a counterfeit) gáfo (M: gihn) ❷ (fool) bahnyàhn (M: go)

dugout N: ❶ (in battle field) jinhòuh (M: tìuh) ❷ (against air raid) fòhnghùnghòuh; fòhng-hùngduhng

duke N: gùngjeuk (M: go)

duke-dom N: gùngjeuk líhngdeih

dull SV: ❶ (monotonous) dàandiuh ❷ (not sharp) m̀leih; deuhn PH: ❶ (uninteresting) móuh cheuimeih ❷ (boring) lihng yàhn hāpngáahnfan ge

dullard N: bahndáan (M: go)

duly A: (at the right time) kahpsìh; (proper) sīkdong

dumb SV: ngáge; (stupid) chéun ✳ **dumb-bell** N: ngálihng (M: go) ✳ **dumb person** N: ① (man) ngálóu ② (boy) ngájái ③ (girl) ngámūi ④ (woman) ngápó (M: go)

dumb-found (dum-found)
PH: lihng yàhn gèngdou
mchēutdāksèng; haakngòihjó

dummy N: ❶ (a figure)
gáyàhn (M: go) ❷ (dummy gun)
gáchēung (M: jì) SV: gáge

dump FV: (empty out) dóu N:
laahpsaapdēui (M: go) ✳ **dump
rubbish** VO: dóulaahpsaap ✳
dump truck N: jihduhng sefo
kàchè (M: ga)

dumpling N: tòngyún;
gōutyún

dunce N: bahnyàhn; bahnge
hohksāang

**dunderhead (dunder-
pate)** N: daaihsòhgwā;
bahndáan (M: go)

dune N: sàyàu (M: go)

dung N: (manure) sí VO:
sífèih ✳ **dung beetle** N:
gèunglòhng (M: jek)

dungeon N: deihlòuh (M: go)

duologue N/FV: deuiwah N:
deuibaahk (M: dyuhn)

dupe FV: (to cheat) ngāak N:
yùhngyih béi yàhn ngāak ge
yàhn (M: go)

duper N: pinjí (ngāak yàhndeih ge yàhn) (M: go)

duplex ATT: sèungpúihge;
yihchùhngge N: sèunglyùhn-
faat (M: go)

duplicate N: ❶ (of document) chyùhndái ❷ (of check)
chyùhngàn (M: jèung) FV:
gàpúih; fūkjai Adj. PH:
yùhnchyùhn sèungtùhng ge;
fūkjaige ✳ **in duplicate** PH:
yātsīk léuhngfahn

duplication FV: gàpúih;
fūkjai; N: fubún (M: go)

duplicator N: ❶ (a copying
machine) fūkyangèi (M: ga) ❷
fūkbún jaijokyàhn (M: go)

duplicity FV/N: hèipin IE:
háu-sih-sàm-fèi

durable SV: (lasting) kàm

durability SV: kàm; gìngu

duration N: chìhjuhkge
sìhgaan; kèihgaan (M: go)

during CV: gójahnsí PATT:
hái . . . ge sìhhauh *Dájeung gójahnsí néih hái bīndouh a?* ✳
during the night PH:
máahntàuhhāak gójahnsí

durometer N: ngaahng-
douhbīu (M: go)

dusk TW/N: ngāaimāan
(wòhngfàn) (M: go)

dusky Adj. PH: (dim)
mèihngamge

dust N: fùichàhn; yìnchàhn
VO: dáfùichàhn; maatfùichàhn
✳ **dust-bin** N: laahpsaapsēung
(M: go) ✳ **dust-cart** N:
laahpsaapchè (M: ga) ✳ **dust
color** N: fūihotsīk; ngamhotsīk
✳ **dust-pan** N: búngèi (fangèi)
(M: jek) ✳ **dusty** Adj. PH:
dòfùichàhnge; pòumúhn
fùichàhn ge

duster N: (feather) gàimòuhsóu (M: bá)

dusting FV: dásou PH:
maatjó . . . ge fùichàhn

Dutch N: Hòhlāanyàhn;
Hòhlāanwá (Hòhlāanyúh) ATT:
Hòhlāanyàhnge; Hòhlāange;
Hòhlāanwáge

Dutch-man N: Hòhlāan-yàhn

dutiable Adj. PH: yìnggòi naahpseui ge

dutiful SV: ❶ jeuhnjaak ❷ (honest) jùngsaht

duty N: ❶ jaakyahm; jíkjaak; búnfahn (M: go) ❷ (tax) seui ✳ do duty for PH: dongjok . . . yuhng ✳ off duty VO: fonggùng; lohkbāan ✳ on duty VO: jihkbāan; fàangùng; séuhngbāan ✳ customs duties N: gwāanseui

duty-free Adj. PH: míhnseuige

dwarf N: ngáijái (M: go) PH: lihngdou ngáisai SV: ngáisaige

dwarfish SV: ngáisaige

dwell FV: jyuh; gèuijyuh

dweller N: gèuimàhn (M: go)

dwelling N: jyuhjaahk; yuhsó (M: gàan)

dwindle FV: sūkgáam; gáamsíu

dye FV: yíhm N: ngàahnliuh; yíhmliuh (M: jek, tíng)

dyer N: yíhmsīk geihsì; yíhmsīk gùngyàhn (M: go)

dye-stuff N: yíhmliuh (yíhmlíu) (M: júng, tíng, jek)

dye-works N: yíhmchóng; yíhmsīk gùngchèuhng (M: gàan)

dyeing VO: yíhmsīk

dying Adj. PH: jauhlàih séi ge; jèunggahn séige FV/N: séi; séimòhng

dyke (dike) N: ❶ (dike or levee) tàih ❷ (a ditch) kàu; hòuh (M: tìuh) VO: (to build a dike or embankment) jūktàih

dynamic Adj. PH: duhnglihkge; duhnglihkhohkge

dynamics N: duhnglihkhohk

dynamite N: jayeuhk RV: jawái

dynamo N: faatdihngèi (M: ga)

dynasty N: chìuhdoih; chìuh

dysentery N: leihjaht; hùhngleih

dysmenorrhea PH: yuhtgìng báttiùh; gìngtung

dyspepsia (dyspepsy) PH: sìufabātlèuhng

dyspeptic Adj. PH: sìufabātlèuhngge N: yáuh sìufabātlèuhngjing ge yàhn (M: go)

dystocia PH: nàahncháan

dystrophy PH: yìhngyéuhng bātlèuhng

E

each PN: gokjih SP: múih PN: múihyāt; múihgo; gogo; gokgo; gokyàhn; múihyàhn; gokjih ✳ each other A: wuhsèung; béichí ✳ each time TW: múihchi

eager AV: hóuséung; hotmohng

eagerness AV: hóuséung; hotmohng

eagle N: yīng; ngàhyīng (M: jek)

eaglet N: ngàhyīngjái (M: jek)

ear N: yíh; yíhjái (M: jek) ✻ **be all ears** IE: sái-yíh-gùng-tīng ✻ **fall on deaf ears** PH: meih sauh jyuyi; meih sauh juhngsih ✻ **lend an ear** FV: kīngting ✻ **turn a deaf ear** FV: m̀tēng; m̀jyuyi ✻ **ear-phone** N: yíhtúng (M: go) ✻ **ear trumpet** N: johtinghei; yíhlùhnggèi (M: go) ✻ **ear-wax** N: yíhsí (M: gauh)

earl N: baakjeuk (M: go) ✻ **earl-dom** N: baakjeukge jeukwaih (M: go); baakjeukge líhngdeih

early A/SV: jóu PH: hái chòkèih ✻ **as early as** PH: hóunoih jíchihn hái . . . ge sìhhauh ✻ **early or late** A: chìhjóu ✻ **earliness** A/SV: jóu A/BF: chò

earmark N: yíhcheuk (yíh-houh) (M: go) VO: gàyíhhouh

earn FV: ❶ (receive as pay or profit) wán (chín) ❷ (receive as profit in business) jaahn (chín) ✻ **earn one's bread (living)** FV: wánsihk; màuhsàng

earnest SV: yihngjànge; sihngjige ✻ **in earnest** A: yihngjàngám; jànsìhnggám

earning N: ❶ sàuyahp ❷ (income) yahpsīk ❸ (salary) sànséui

earth N: ❶ (the planet) deihkàuh ❷ (the world) saigaai ❸ (ground) deih ❹ (soil) nàih ✻ **come back to earth** PH: pàauhei waahnséung ✻ **on**

earth A: saigaaiseuhng; chyùhnsaigaai ✻ **earthnut** N: fāsāng (M: nâp) ✻ **earthquake** N: deihjan (M: chi) FV: deihjan ✻ **earth-worm** N: wòhnghyún (yàuyáhn) (M: tìuh)

earthly ATT: deihkàuhge; daaihdeihge

ease SV: syùsīk; jihjoih ✻ **with ease** Adv. PH: hóu yùhngyihgám

easily PH/A: hóu yùhngyih; hóu yih

east DW: dùng; dùngbouh; dùngbihn ATT: dùngbihnge; heungdùngge; yàuh dùngbihn làih ge A: heungdùng ✻ **in the east of** PH: hái . . . ge dùngbouh ✻ **on the east (of)** PH: hái (. . . ge) dùngbihn ✻ **(to the) east of** PH: hái . . . ge dùng bihn ✻ **the Far East** PW: Yúhndūng

Easter N: Fuhkwuhtjit

eastern ATT: dùngfòngge; dùngbihnge N: dùngfòngyàhn (M: go)

eastward A: heungdùng

easy A/SV: yùhngyih; yih; (comfortable) ngònlohk A: ngòn-sīkgám ✻ **go easy** IE: hìngsùngdī lā! m̀sái gánjèung ✻ **in easy street (on easy street)** PH: sàngwuht yàuyuh ✻ **take it easy** IE: hìngsùng dī; m̀sái gánjèung

eat FV: sihk VO: (to have a meal) sihkfaahn N: (eats) sihkmaht ✻ **eat one's words** FV: sihkyìhn ✻ **eat up** RV: sihksaai; yuhngsaai

eatable Adj. PH: hóyíh-sihkge; sihkdākge N: sihkmaht; sihkbán

eating FV: sihk N: sihkmaht
Adj. PH: sihkyuhngge

eaves N: ngūksihm (ngūk-
yìhm) (M: go)

eaves-drop FV: tàutèng

ebb FV: chìuhséuiteui;
séuiteui

ebony N: syūnjī; wùmuhk
ATT: syūnjījouhge; wùmuhk-
jouhge

eccentric SV: gúgwaaige N:
gúgwaaige yàhn

eccentricity SV: gwaaipīk;
gúgwaai

ecclesiastic N: muhksī;
chyùhngaausih (M: go) Adj. PH:
muhksīge; gaauwúige

ecclesiastical Adj. PH:
gaauwúige; muhksīge

echo N: wùihsìng PH: faatchēut wùihsìng

eclectic Adj. PH: jitchùngge;
jitchùngjyúyihge N: jitchùng-
paaige yàhn (M: go)

eclecticism N: jitchùng-
jyúyih

eclipse FV: sihk; jèbai ✳
lunar eclipse FV/N: yuhtsihk
✳ solar eclipse FV/N:
yahtsihk

ecliptic N: wòhngdouh ATT:
wòhngdouhge

ecology N: sàngtaaihohk ✳
ecologist N: sàngtaaihohkjé
(M: go)

economic Adj. PH: gìngjai-
hohkge; gìngjaige; gìng-
jaiseuhngge

economical N/SV: gìngjai

economics N: gìngjaihohk

economism N: gìngjaijyú-
yih

economist N: gìngjaihohk-
gā (M: go)

economize FV: jitsáang;
hàan

economy N: gìngjai

ecosystem N: sàngtaai-
haihtúng

ecstasy PH: fùnhéi dougihk;
(absorbed in) chēutsàhn

ecstatic PH: chēutsàhnge;
fùnhéi-dougihkge

eczema N: sāpchán

eddy N: syùhnwō (M: go) VO:
héisyùhnwō

Eden N: Yìdihnyùhn; lohkyùhn

edge N: (border) bīn ✳ edge
of a knife N: dōuháu (M: go) ✳
edge of a table N: tóibīn (M:
go)

edging VO: (to edge or hem
dress, handkerchief, etc.)
sēungbīn (kwánbīn)

edible Adj. PH: hóyíh sihk
ge; sihkdākge N: (pl.) hóyíh
sihk ge yéh; sihkmaht (M: júng)

edict N: faatlihng; bougou;
tùnggou (M: go)

edification FV/N: káifaat;
tòuhyéh; fàntòuh

edifice N: daaihhah; daaih
ginjūkmaht (M: joh)

edify FV: gaaudouh; káifaat;
fàntòuh

edit FV/N: pìnchāp (M: go)

edition N: báan * the fourth edition N: daihsei báan

editor FV/N: pìnchāp (M: go) * a chief editor (editor in chief) N: jyúpìn, júngpìnchāp (M: go)

editorial Adj. PH: pìnchāpge; séhleuhnge N: séhleuhn (M: pìn)

educate N/FV: gaauyuhk * an educated person N: sauhgwogaauyuhkge yàhn

education FV/N: gaauyuhk * moral education N: jiyuhk

educational Adj. PH: gaauyuhkge; gaauyuhkseuhngge

educationalist (educationist) N: gaauyuhkgā (M: go)

educator N: gaauyuhkgā; gaausì (M: go)

eel N: síhn (M: tiuh)

efface FV: chaatjó; maatjó; (to play down) chùngtáahm

effect N: ❶ (of function) gùnghaauh ❷ haauhgwó ❸ (result) haauhlihk ❹ (influence) yínghéung FV: ❶ (to realize)sahtyihn ❷ cháansàng (haauhgwó) * effects N: duhngcháan; gàchòih * give effect to FV: sahthàhng; sahtsì * in effect A: sihsahtseuhng FV: sànghaauh SV: yáuhhaauh * into effect FV: sahthàhng * of no effect FV: móuhhaauh; móuh gùnghaauh * to take effect FV: gingùng; sànghaauh

effective SV: yáuhhaauhge; yáuhlihkge

effectual SV: yáuhhaauhge

effectuate FV: sahthàhng; sahtyihn

effeminacy SV: wànyàuh; yàuhyeuhk

effeminate SV: (low and gentle, voice, etc.) (feminine) yàuhyeuhkge; tèuihfaige * effeminate art PH: tèuihfai ngaihseuht

effervesce FV: (boil) gwán SV: (excite) hìngfáhn

efficacious SV: yáuhhaauhge; lìhngyìhmge

efficacy N: gùnghaauh; haauhlihk (M: go)

efficiency N: haauhleuht; gùnghaauh (M: go)

efficient Adj. PH: yáuhhaauhleuhtge; haauhleuhtgòuge

effigy N: chiujeuhng; dìujeuhng (M: go)

effloresce VO: (to flower) hòifà FV: (in chemistry, efflorescence) fùngfa

efflorescence VO: hòifà FV: fùngfa

efflorescent Adj PH: hòifàge; fùngfage

effluence FV: faatchēut; làuhchēut

effluent Adj. PH: làuhchēutge; fongchēutge N: làuhchēutge yéh

effort SV/N/A: nóuhlihk * make an effort Adv. PH: jeuhn yātchai nóuhlihk * with effort A/SV: nóuhlihk; jeuhnlihk

effulgence SV/N: gwòngfài SV: chaanlaahn

effulgent SV: gwòngfàige; chaanlaahnge

effusion RV: làuhchēut; sechēut

effusive SV: làuhchēutge

egg N: dáan (M: go) FV: súngyúng; sinduhng

egg-plant N: ngáigwā; ké-gwā; ké (M: go)

ego N: (self) jihngóh SV: jihdaaih; (conceited) jihfuh ✻ **ego-ism** PH: jihngóhjyúyih; leihgéijyúyih ✻ **ego-ist** PH: leihgéijyúyihjé; jihngóhjyúyihjé ✻ **egoistic (ego-istical)** Adj. PH: leihgéijyúyihge; jihsì-jih-leih-ge

Egyptian N: Ngòikahpyàhn (M: go) ATT: Ngòikahpyàhnge; Ngòikahpge; Ngòikahpyúhge

eight Nu: baat

eighteen Nu: sahpbaat

eighteenth Nu: daihsahpbaatge; sahpbaatfahnjìyātge (1/18); daihsahpbaat

eighth Nu: daihbaatge; daih-baat; baatfahnjìyāt (1/8)

eightieth Nu: daihbaatsahpge; daihbaatsahp; baat-sahpfahnjìyātge (1/80)

eighty Nu: baatsahp

either A: (negative of also) yihk PATT: léuhng M jì yāt (one of) (léuhng go kèihjùng ge yāt go); (both) léuhng M dōu léuhng tiuh louh, néih hàahng bīntiuh dōu dāk. Léuhng go deui ngóh dōu sīkhahp. ✻ **either . . . or . . .** PATT: waahkjé . . . waahk-

jé . . .; m̀haih . . .jauh haih . . . . *Kéuih waahkjé hái Lèuhndēun waahkjé hái Bàlàih.*

eject RV: ❶ panchēut ❷ (to drive out, to expel) gónchēut

ejector N: pansehhei; pàaih-chēuthei (M: go)

elaborate PH: chèuhngsai syutmìhng; yuhngsàm jouh SV: jìngháauge

elaboration PH: fúsàm gìngyihng SV: (fine; exquisite) jìngjì

elapse FV: gwo; gwoheui

elastic Adj. PH: yáuh daahnsing ge N: jeuhnggànkwū

elasticity N: daahnsing; sànsūksing

elated PH: dākyiyèuhngyèuhngge; hing-gòu-chói-liht ge

elatedly Adv. PH: dākyi-yèuhngyèuhng gám; hing-gòu-chói-liht gám

elbow N: sáujàang (M: go) PH: yuhng sáujàang tèui ✻ **at one's elbow** A: hái pòhngbīn ✻ **out at the elbow (out at elbows)** Adj. PH: yìsàam-làahmléuihge (yìsàam-làahmláuh ge)

elder Adj. PH: chìhnbuige; nìhngéi-béigaaudaaih ge SV: (older) daaih N: ❶ (a senior, in age, standing, length of service, etc.) chìhnbui; ❷ (the senior generation) (pl) jéungbui

elderly Adj. PH: sēuhngjó nìhngéi ge; lóuhnìhnyàhnge

eldest SV: jidaaihge; jeui-daaihge ✻ **eldest brother** N: daaihgō (M: go) ✻ **eldest**

son N: daaihjái; jéungjí (M: go)
✻ **eldest daughter** N: daaihnéui; jéungnéui (M: go)

elect FV: syún; syúngéui Adj. PH: syúnchĕutge; beih syúndihngge ✻ **be elected** FV: dòngsyún

election FV/N: syúngéui FV: dòngsyún

elective Adj. PH: syúngéuige; syúnyahmge

elector N: syúngéuiyàhn (M: go)

electoral Adj. PH: syúngéuige

electorate N: syúnmàhn (M: go)

electric ATT: dihnge

electrician N: dihndānglóu (M: go)

electricity N: dihn

electrification FV: chùngdihn; dihnheifa

electrify FV: tùngdihn PH: lihngdou dihnheifa

electrize FV: dihnheifa

electrization FV/ATT: dihnheifa

electro- N/BF: dihn; dihnge

electrocute PH: sìyíh dihnyìhng

electrocution PH: sìyíh dihnyìhng

electrode N: dihngihk

electrograph N: chyùhnjàn dihnbou

electrolysis FV/N: dihn-

gáai

electromotor N: faatdihngèi (M: ga)

electron N: dihnjí

electronics N: dihnjíhohk

electronograph PH: dihnjí hínjeuhng; dihnjí hínjeuhnggèi; jihngdihn yanchaat

electroplate FV: dihndouh N: dihndouhge yéh (dihndouhge mahtbán) (M: gihn)

electrotheraphy FV/N: dihnlìuh N: dihnlìuhhohk

elegance (elegancy) SV: ❶ sìmàhn ❷ (of persons) màhnngáh; leng ❸ (of things) jìngji

elegant SV: sìmàhn (ge); màhnngáh (ge); jìngji (ge); lengge

element N: (chemical) yùhnsou; (essentials) yiusou

elemental ATT: yùhnsouge; yiusouge

elementary ATT: chòdángge; chòkápge; chòbouhge

elephant N: jeuhng; daaihbahnjeuhng (M: jek)

elephantine Adj. PH: jeuhngge; hóuchíh jeuhng ge

elevate FV: géuihéi; tàihgòu; tòihhéi

elevated SV: sìnggòuge; gòuhéige; (noble) gòuseuhngge

elevation N: gòudouh FV: (to put to a higher position) tàihgòu

elevator N: dihntài; sìnggonggèi (M: ga, bouh)

eleven Nu: sahpyāt

eleventh Nu: daihsahpyāt; sahpyātfahn jīyāt (1/11) ✳ **eleventh hour** TW: jeuihauhge sìhhāak; jeuihauh yāthāak

elf N: síugwái; yíujìng

elf fire N: gwáifó; lèuhnfó

elfish SV: ngokjokkehkge

elf-land N: mògíng; síuyíugwok (M: go)

elicit PH: lihngdou toulouh (jànchìhng)

eligible Adj. PH: hahpgaakge N: hahpgaakge yàhn (M: go)

eligibility N: hahpgaakge yàhn

eliminate FV: sìuchèuih; sìumiht

elimination FV: sìuchèuih; sìumiht

elixir N: chèuhngsàngbātlóuh yeuhk (M: júng)

elk N: mèihluhk; gokluhk (M: jek)

ellipse N: tóhyùhn; tóhyùhnyìhng (M: go)

ellipsis N: sáangleuhkfaat; sáangleuhkhouh (M: go)

elocution N: yínsyutseuht (M: go)

elongate FV: làaichèuhng; yìhnchèuhng

elope FV: sìbàn; tòuhjáu

elopement FV: sìbàn; tòuhjáu

eloquence N: háuchòih

eloquent Adj. PH: duhngyàhnge; yáuh háuchòih ge

else ATT: daihyihdī; kèihtàge A: fáujāk ✳ **or else** A: yùhgwó m̀haih; fáujāk ✳ **else than** Patt: chèuihjó . . . jìngoih

else-where A: hái daihyihsyu

elucidate FV/N: syutmìhng; gáaisīk

elude FV: dóbeih

elusion FV: dóbeih

elusive Adj. Ph: tòuhbeihge; (not easy to understand) nàahn mìhngbaahkge

emanate FV: faatchēut

emanation FV: faatchēut

emancipate FV/N: gáaifong

emancipation FV/N: gáaifong

emasculate FV: ❶ (castrate) yìm ❷ (to weaken) seukyeuhk (to weaken the force of an utterance or statement) *seutyeuhk yúhsai*. Adj. PH: yìmge; yàuhyeuhkge

embank VO: jūktàih; jūkba

embankment N: tàih; ba; tàihba (M: tìuh)

embargo FV/N: gamwahn

embark VO: séuhngsyùhn; lohksyùhn; chóhsyùhn ✳ **embark in (on, upon)** FV: chùhngsih; jeuhksáu

embarkation VO: chóhsyùhn

embarrass PH: lihngdou . . . nàahnwàihchìhng ✳ **embar-**

rassed SV: m̀hóuyisi

embarrassing Adj. PH: m̀hóuyisige; nàahnwàihchìhngge

embarrassment SV: nàahnwàihchìhng; m̀hóuyisi

embassy N: daaihsígún (M: gàan)

embed FV: màaihyahp; màaihhái

embellish FV: jòngsīk; bouji

ember PH: juhng yáuh fó ge lòuhfùi

embezzle FV: douhyuhng

embezzlement FV: douhyuhng

embitter PH: lihngdou tungfú

emblem N: jeuhngjìng (M: go)

emblematic (emblematical) ATT: jeuhngjìngge

embodiment VO/N: fasān

embody PH: geuihtái bíuyihn

embolden PH: lihngdou yáuhyúhnghei

embosom FV: wàahnyíu

emboss PH: gà fàuhdìu fàmàhn hái . . . seuhngbihn

embossment PH: gà fàuhdìu fàmàhn hái . . . seuhngbihn

embrace FV: ❶ (in the arms) póuh ❷ (include) bàauhàhm

embrasure N: (mùhnseuhngbihnge) fòhngdouh geng (M: go)

embroider FV: sau VO: saufā

embroidery N: chisau

embroil PH: lihngdou wahnlyuhn PH: (to get involved in a conflict, trouble, etc.) gyúnyahp syùhnwō

embroilment SV: wahnlyuhn PH: gyúnyahp syùhnwō

embryo PH: chòkèih; màhngngàh sìhkèih

emend FV: gaauding; sàujing

emendation FV: sàujing; gaauding

emerald N: féicheui; luhkbóusehk (M: nāp)

emerge FV: louhchēut; chēutyihn ✳ emerge from PH: yàuh . . . léuihbihn louhchēut; yàuh . . . chēutyihn

emergence FV: yihnchēut FV/N: chēutyihn

emergency N: gángāpge chìhngyìhng; gángāpge sih ✳ in an emergency PH: hái ngàihgáp gwáantàuh ✳ emergency door N: taaipìhngmùhn (M: douh)

emersion FV: yihnchēut; fàuhchēut

emery N: gàmgòngsà (M: nāp) ✳ emery cloth N: sàbou (M: faai) ✳ emery paper N: sàjí (M: jèung)

emigrant N: kìuhmàhn (M: go) ATT: kìuhmàhnge

emigrate FV: kìuhgèui; yìhgèui

emigration FV: kìuhgèui FV/N: yìhmàhn ✳ emigration

office N: yihmàhngúk

emigratory ATT: yihmàhnge

eminence SV: chēutméng

eminent SV: gihtchēutge; chēutméngge

emissary N: ❶ mahtsi ❷ (a spy) gaandihp (M: go) ATT: mahtsige; gaandihpge

emission FV: faatchēut; faatseh

emit FV: faatchēut

emotion N: chihnggám; gámchihng

emotional Adj. PH: chihnggámge; duhngyàhnge

emperor N: wòhngdai (M: go)

emphasis FV: jyujuhng; kèuhngdiuh

emphasize FV: jyujuhng; kèuhngdiuh

emphatic Adj. PH: yáuhlihkge; kèuhngdiuhge

empire N: daigwok (M: go)

empiric N: gìngyihmjyúyihjé (M: go) ATT: gìngyihmjyúyihge

empirical ATT: gìngyihmge

empiricism N: gìngyihmjyúyih

empiricist N: gìngyihmjyúyihjé (M: go)

employ FV: ❶ (to use, of persons or tools) yuhng ❷ (hire) chéng; guyuhng

employee N: guyùhn (M: go)

employer N: gujyú; sihtáu;

lóuhbáan (M: go)

employment N: jīkyihp ✳ employment agency N: jīkyihp gaaisiuhsó (M: go, gàan)

emporium N: sèungchèuhng; sèungyihp jūngsàm (M: go); baakfosèungdim (M: gàan)

empower FV: sauhkyùhn

empress N: néuihwòhng; wòhnghauh (M: go)

empty SV: hùngge RV: jínghùng; binhùng *Kéuih gōnbūi.* ✳ empty-handed ATT: hùngsáuge

emulate FV/N: gihngchoi Patt: tùhng . . . gihngjàng

emulation FV/N: gihngjàng; gihngchoi

emulative Adj. PH: gihngchoige; housingge

emulous Adj. PH: gihngjàngge; housingge

emulsion N: yúhgàau; yúhjāi

emulsive ATT: yúhgàauge; yúhjāige

enable PH: lihngdou nàhnggau; lihngdou hóyíh

enact PH/VO: jaidihng faatleuht FV: (to proclaim laws or regulations, orders, etc.) bàanbou

enactment FV: jaidihng; bàanbou N: (a general term for laws and regulations) faatlihng

enamel N: tòhngchìh; faatlòhngjāt; chìhchāt

enamor (enamour) PH: lihngdou kìngsàm; màihjyuh

encamp VO: louhyìhng; jaatyìhng

encampment VO: louhyìhng; jaatyìhng

encase PH: jònghái sēung léuihbihn FV: bàaujòng

enchain PH: yuhng lín sójyuh N: chūkbok

enchant FV/N: màihwaahk; PH: lihngdou jeuisàmyùh

enchantment FV/N: màihwaahk N: (sorcery) yíuseuht

enchantress N: néuihmòuh; yíufúh (M: go)

encircle FV: wàahnyíu; bàauwàih; wàihjyuh

enclose FV: ❶ wàihyíu ❷ wàihjyuh ❸ fuhgei *Kéuih fuhgei yātjèung jìpiu.*

enclosure FV/N: wàihyíu N: ❶ wàihchèuhng ❷ (an attachment of a letter, etc.) fuhgín

encompass FV: ❶ bàauwàih; ❷ (to contain) bàauhàhm

encore IE: joi cheung (yín) yātchi! PH: joi cheung; joi yín; (to perform for entertainment) yiukàuh joi yín; yiukàuh joi cheung

encounter FV/N: johngdóu; (to meet) yuhdóu

encourage FV/N: gúlaih

encouragement FV/N: gúlaih; jaanjoh; (to support) jìchìh

encroach FV: chàmjim; chàmfaahn

encroachment FV: chàmjim; chàmfaahn

encumber FV: fòhnghoih; FV/N: jóngoih

encumbrance N: jóngoih maht; FV/N: jóngoih

encyclop(a)edia N: baak fōchyùhnsyù (M: tou)

encyclop(a)edic Adj. PH baakfōchùhnsyùge

end N: ❶ tàuh; méih *gāa tàuh gāaiméih;* ❷ (result gitguhk ❸ (edge or side) bìhn FV: ❶ gitchūk; ❷ yùhngit; ❸ jùngjí * **at an end** FV yùhnbāt * **at one's wits' end** PH: hòuhmòuh baahnfaat * **draw (come) to an end** FV: gitchūk; yùhn la * **in the end** A: jeuihauh; jēutjì * **make an end of** FV: jùngjí * **make both ends meet** PH: jàujyún; leuhng-yahp-wàih-chēut * **put an end to** FV: gitchūk; jùngjí * **to no end** SV: tòuhlòuh; móuh gitgwó

endanger FV: ngàihhoi; ngàihkahp

endear PH: lìhngdou sauh héingoi

endearing SV: hóngoige

endearment FV/N: chúngngoi

endeavor (endeavour) N/A/FV: nóuhlihk A/FV: jeuhnlihk

endemic ATT: deihfòngsingge N: deihfòngsingge behng (M: júng)

ending N: gitméih; gitguhk (M: go)

endless Adj. PH: mòuhjeuhnge; mòuhjígíngge

endorse VO: chìmméng

endorsement VO: chìmméng

endow FV: gyùnjoh * to be endowed with FV: geuihyáuh

endowment FV/N: gyùnjahng; gyùnjoh

endurable Adj. PH: hóyíh yánsauh ge

endurance FV/N: yánnoih; N: noihsing * endurance limit PH: noihgáu haahndouh

endure FV/N: yánnoih FV: yánsauh; ngàaih; dáisauh * endure hardship VO: ngàaihfú * endure hunger PH: dáitóuhngoh * able to endure PH: ngàaihdākjyuh

enduring Adj. PH: chìhgáuge; chèuhnggáu bātbin ge

enema N: ❶ (clyster) gunchèuhngjái ❷ (a clyster pipe) gunchèuhnghei

enemy N: dihkyàhn; sàuhdihk (M: go) * an enemy warship N: dihklaahm (M: jek) * enemy troops N: dihkgwàn * an enemy plane N: dihkgèi (M: ga) * How goes the enemy? IE: Yìhgā géi dímjūng a?

energetic Adj. PH: yáuh wuhtlihk ge; jìngsàhn báaumúhn ge; jìnglihk chùngpui ge

energy N: ❶ (mental power) jìngsàhn ❷ (physical power) heilihk

enfold FV: láamjyuh

enforce FV: sahtsì; jāphàhng

enforceable Adj. PH: yáuh kéuhngjailihk ge; hóyíh sahtsì ge

enforcement FV: kéuhngbīk; sahtsì; jāphàhng

engage FV: (employ) chéng ~ gùng yàhn VO: (betroth) dihngfàn * be engaged in FV: mòhngyù; chùhngsihyù * engage for FV: bóujing

engagement N: yeukwuih VO: dihngfàn

engaging SV: duhngyàhnge; màihyàhnge

engender FV: cháansàng; faatsàng

engine N: faatduhnggèi; mōdá (M: go); gèihei (M: ga)

engine driver N: fóchè sìgèi (M: go)

engineer N: ❶ gùngchìhngsì ❷ (of a train) sìgèi ❸ (in military service) gùngbìng (M: go) FV: chitgai; chaakwaahk

engineering N: gùngchìhng; gùngchìhnghohk

English ATT: Yìnggwokge; Yìnggwokyàhnge; Yìngmàhnge N: Yìnggwokyàhn; Yìngmàhn

engraft FV: gunsyù

engrave FV: dìuhāak; hāak; tìu

engraving N: dìuhāakseuht; muhthāakwá

emgross PH: lìhngdou chyùhnsàhn gunjyu; FV: kāpyáhn

engulf FV: tànmuht; tànsihk

enhance FV: tàihgòu; jànggà

enigma N: màih (M: go)

enigmatic (enigmatical) Adj. PH: hóuchíh màih

yātyeuhng ge; sàhnbeige

enjoin FV/N: ❶ mihnglihng
❷ (to instruct or direct someone
to do something) fànfu

enjoy VO: (enjoy oneself)
héungfūk AV: héifūn; jùngyi
jùngyi yàuhséui ✳ enjoy
oneself FV: héunglohk VO:
taan saigaai; héungfūk

enjoyable Adj. PH: lihng
yàhn hòisàm ge; lihng yàhn
yuhfaai ge

enjoyment N: héungsauh;
lohkcheui (M: júng)

enkindle FV: gīkhéi; tiuhéi

enlarge FV: kwongdaaih; (a
photo) fongdaaih

enlargement FV: kwongjèung PH: fongdaaihge séung

enlarger N: fongdaaihgèi
(M: ga; go)

enlighten FV: káifaat;
káimùhng

enlightened Adj. PH:
màhnmìhngge; yáuhjisīkge

enlightenment FV/ATT:
káimùhng

enlist FV: (enroll) dànggei;
VO: jìngbìng

enmity N: sàuhhahn; yùn-
sàuh (M: go)

ennoble PH: fùng . . . wàih
gwaijuhk

enormity SV: chàahnbouh;
IE: kùhnghùng gihkngok

enormous SV: ❶ geuih-
daaihge ❷ pòhngdaaihge ❸
(cruel and violent) hùngbouhge

enormously SV: geuih-
daaih; pòhngdaaih Adv. PH:
hùngbouhgám

enough SV: jūkgau (ge); gau,
chùngjūk ✳ enough for PH
deuiyù . . . jūkgau . . . ge ✳
have enough to do PH: hóu
heklihk ✳ sure enough A: (exactly as one expected) gwóyìhn
(really) sahtjoih

enquire (inquire) FV:
sèunmahn; mahnmìhng

enrage RV: gīknàu

enrich PH: lihngdou fujūk;
lihngdou fèihyūk

enrichment PH: lihngdou
fujūk; lihngdou fèihyūk

enrol (enroll) VO: bou-
méng; jyuchaak

enrolment (enrollment)
PH: jyuchaak yàhn-sou VO:
jyuchaak

ensign N: kèih; gwànkèih
(M. jì)

enslave FV: nòuhyihk PH:
mōkdyuht . . . ge jihyàuh

ensnare FV: yáuhbouh;
haahmhoih

ensue PH: gànjyuh faatsàng
✳ ensue from PH: gànjyuh
faatsàng

ensure FV: bóujing; dàambóu

entail FV/N: sèuiyiu

entangle FV: lìhnleuih

entanglement FV/N:
hìnlìhn

enter FV: ❶ yahp ❷ (come into a place) yahplàih ❸ (go into
a place) yahpheui ❹ (to join an

organization) yahp; gàyahp

enterprise N: kéihyihp; (undertaking) sihyihp

enterpriser N: kéihyihpgā (M: go)

enterprising Adj. PH: yáuh sihyihpsàm ge; yáuh jeunchéuisàm ge

entertain FV: jiudoih; fúndoih

entertaining SV: yáuhcheuige

entertainment N: yàuhngaih; yùhlohk

enthral (enthrall) FV: màaihjyuh; kāpyáhn

enthrone PH: yúnglahp wàih gwokwòhng FV: jyùnsùhng; tèuisùhng

enthusiasm SV: yihtsàm

enthusiastic SV: yihtsàm (ge)

entice FV: yáhnyáuh; yáuhwaahk

entire SV/A: yùhnchyùhn; chyùhnbouh; (whole) sèhng M.N. *sèhng gàan ngūk*

entirely A: yātkoi; chyùhnbouh; yùhnchyùhn

entirety N: chyùhnbouh; A/SV: yùhnchyùhn ✳ **in its entirety** A: chyùhntái; chyùhnmìhngám

entitle PH: lìhngdou yáuh jìgaak; lìhngdou yáuhkyùhn ✳ **be entitled to** SV: yáuhjìgaak . . . ; yáuhkyùhn . . .

entity FV/N: chyùhnjoih

entomb FV: màaihjong

entomology N: kwànchùhnghohk

entomologist N: kwànchùhnghohkgā; kwànchùhnghohkjé (M: go)

entourage N: wàahngíng (M: go)

entrails N: noihjohng

entrain VO: séuhng fóchè; chóh fóchè

entrance N: yahpháu; mùhnháu (M: go) PH: lìhngdou chēutsàhn ✳ **entrance into (upon)** FV: jauhyahm; jauhjīk

entrant N: sàn wúiyùhn; (M: go)

entrap FV: yáuhbouh

entreat FV/N: hánkàuh; chéngkàuh

entreaty FV/N: hánkàuh; chéngkàuh

entrench PH: yuhng hòuh wàihyíu VO: gwahthòuh

entrenchment VO: gwahthòuh N: hòuh

entrepreneur N: kéihyihpgā (M: go)

entrust (intrust) FV: wáitok; seuntok

entry FV: yahp VO: (make an entry bookkeeping) yahpsou

entwine FV: chìhnjyuh; chìhnyíu

enumerate FV: sóu; dím

enumeration FV: gaisyun; sóu

enunciate FV/N: syùnbou

enunciation FV/N: syùnbou (M: go)

enuresis N: wàihniuhjing FV: wàihniuh

envelop FV: bàau; bàaujyuh

envelope N: seunfūng (M: go)

enviable Adj. PH: jihkdāk sihnmouh ge; lihng yàhn sihnmouh ge

envious Adj. PH: douhgeihge; sihnmouhge

environ FV: bàauwàih; wàahnyíu

environment FV: wàihyíu N: (surroundings, financial situation) wàahngíng (M: go)

envisage FV: jingsih; mihndeui

envoy N: sijé; dahksi; gùngsi (M: go)

envy FV: douhgeih; sihnmouh

enwrap FV: bàau

eon (aeon) N: sai; doih

epaulet (epaulette) N: gìnjēung (M: go)

epic N: jeuihsihsī (M: sáu)

epical Adj. PH: jeuihsihsīge

epicure N: gónggau yámsihk ge yàhn; héunglohkjyúyihjé (M: go)

epidemic (epidemical) N: làuhhàhngjing (M: go) ATT: làuhhàhngsingge; chùhnyíhmsingge

epigram N: gínggeui (M: geui); fungchi dyúnsī (M: sáu)

epilepsy N/FV: faatyèuhngdiu

epileptic N: faatyèuhngdiuge yàhn (M: go) ATT: faatyèuhngdiuge

epilog (epilogue) N: sàuchèuhngbaahk

episcopal ATT: jyúgaauge

episode N: chaapkūk (M: dyuhn)

episodic (episodical) ATT: chaapkūkge

epistle N: seun; syùseun

epitaph N: mouhjimìhng; mouhji (M: pìn)

epithet N: singjātyìhngyùhngchìh (M: go)

epitome N: daaihyiu; sūkyíng (M: go)

epoch N: sàngéiyùhn; sìhdoih (M: go)

equable SV: pìhngwánge; wándihngge

equal FV: sèungdáng; dángyù Adj. PH: sèungdángge; tùhngyeuhngge N: ❶ sèungdángge yéh ❷ (an opponent) deuisáu * **equal to** FV: dángyù * **without (an) equal** SV: mòuhdihk

equalitarian ATT: pìhngdángjyúyihge N: pìhngdángjyúyihjé (M: go)

equalitarianism N: pìhngdángjyúyih

equality FV/SV/N: pìhngdáng

equalization SV: gwàndáng; pìhnggwàn

equally A: tùhngyeuhng; FV: sèungdáng

equanimity SV: chàhmjeuhk; jandihng

equate PH: lihngdou pìhngdáng; lihngdou sèungdáng

equation N: fòngchìhngsīk (M: go) (2x + 5 = 11)

equator N: chekdouh (M: tìuh)

equatorial ATT: chekdouhge; gahnjyuh chekdouh ge

equilibrium FV: pìhnghàhng; gwànhàhng * in equilibrium FV: pìhnghàhng

equinoctial ATT: jauyehpìhngfànge

equip FV/N: jòngbeih; chitbeih * be equipped with FV: jòngbeihjó

equipment FV/N: jòngbeih; chitbeih

equitable Adj. PH: gùngpìhngge; gùngjingge

equitableness SV: gùngpìhng; gùngjing

equity SV: gùngpìhng; gùngdouh

equivalence (equivalency) N: dángga; dángjihk; dángleuhng * equivalence relation PH: dángga gwàanhaih

equivalent Adj. PH: sèungdángge; tùhngdángge N: sèungdángge yéh; tùhngdángge yéh * be equivalent to FV: dángyù; sèungdòngyù

equivocal Adj. PH: yiyih mmìhnghín ge; mòuhlihngléuhnghóge

equivocate VO: yuhng sèunggwàanyúh

equivoque (equivoke) N: sèunggwàanyúh

era N: géiyùhn; sìhdoih (M: go)

eradiate FV: fongseh; faatseh

eradicate FV: gànchèuih; pokmiht

erase FV: chaatjó

eraser N: ❶ (for pencil marks) gāauchaat; chaatjígāau (M: gauh) ❷ (for blackboard) fánbātcháat (M: go)

erasure FV: sàanchèuih; chaatjó

ere CV: hái . . . jìchìhn

erect ATT: jihklahpge; syuhhéige FV: ❶ (build) héi ❷ (establish) chitlahp; ginlahp

erection FV: syuhlahp, ginlahp

ermine N: dìu (M: jek); dìupèih (M: faai)

erode FV: chàmsihk; fuhsihk

erosion FV: fuhsihk; chàmsihk

erotic Adj. PH: sīkchìhngge N: housīkge yàhn (M: go)

erotica PH: sīkchìhng jokbán

erotical Adj. PH: sīkchìhngge

eroticism SV: sīkchìhng;

housīk

err FV: jouhcho; gáaucho

errand N: chàaisi; simihng (M: go)

errant SV: pìubokge

erratic SV: m̀wándihngge; (queer) gúgwaaige

erratum N: cho-ngh (M: go)

erroneous SV: cho-ngh ge

error N: cho-ngh; gwosāt; cho (M: go) ✳ **in error** FV: gáaucho

eruct (eructate) VO: dáyit; dángīk

erudite SV: bokhohkge; yáuhhohkmahnge

erudition SV: bokhohk

erupt FV: panchēut; baaufaat

eruption FV: panchēut; baaufaat

eruptive ATT: panchēutge; baaufaatge

escalator N: dihntài; jihduhng dihntài (M: ga)

escapade N: yuhtgwái hàhngduhng; ngokjokkehk

escape FV: tòuhjáu; (avoid) beihbòi; dóbeih VO: tyuthím; FV: tòuhmòhng; tòuhjáu ✳ **escape from** PH: yàuh . . . tòuhchēut; FV: beihmíhn

eschew FV: beihhòi; beihmíhn; yúhnlèih

escort FV: wuhsung; sung N: gíngwaihdéui; FV: wuhsung; FV/N: wuhwaih

Eskimo N: Ngoisìgèimòyàhn

(M: go) ATT: Ngoisìgèimòyàhnge

esophagus N: sihkdouh (M: tìuh)

especial SV: dahkbihtge ✳ **in especial** A: yàuhkèih; gaakngoih

especially A: yàuhkèihsih

espionage N: jìngtaam; gaandihp wuhtduhng

espouse FV: ga, chéui

esquire (esq. or esqr.) N: sìnsàang

essay N: mán; màhnjèung (M: pìn)

essayist N: síubánmàhn jokjé; sáanmàhngā (M: go)

essence N: búnjāt; yiusou; jìngwàh ✳ **in essence** A: (hái) búnjātseuhng

essential SV: bītyiuge; jyúyiuge; búnjātge N: yiusou; jìngséuih; búnjāt ✳ **essential to** PH: deui . . . haih bītyiu ge ✳ **in essentials** A: hái jyúyiu fòngmihn

essentiality N: búnjāt; juhngyiusing; yiudím (M: go)

establish FV: ginlahp; chitlahp; sihnglahp

establishment FV: ginlahp; N: (organization) gèigwàan; (factory) gùngchóng; (company) gūngsī; (shop) poutáu

estate N: cháanyihp; chòihcháan

esteem FV/N: jyùnjuhng; jyünging

esthesia FV/N: gámgok; N: jìgok (M: go)

esthetics N: méihhohk; sámméihhohk

estimable Adj. PH: jìhkdāk jyùnjuhng ge

estimate FV/N: gúgai

estimation FV/N: ❶ gúgai; gúga; ❷ (respect) jyùnging

estrange FV: sòyúhn; gaaklèih; yúhnlèih

estrangement FV: sòyúhn

estuary N: hóiwāan; góngwāan (M: go)

et cetera (etc.) N: dángdáng

eternal ATT: wíhnghàhngge; wíhnggáuge; wíhngyúhn (ge)

eternity SV: wíhnghàhng; mòuhkùhng; wíhngyúhn

ethane N: yuhtyùhn

ethanol N: yuhtsèuhn; jáujīng

ethereal (etherial) SV: tìnseuhngge; taaihùngge

ethical SV: lèuhnléihge; douhdākge

ethics N: lèuhnléihhohk

Ethiopia N/PW: Ngàaichoingòhbéinga; Yìsokpātnga

Ethiopian ATT: Ngàaichoingòhbéingage N: Ngàaichoingòhbéingayàhn (M: go)

ethnology N: yàhnjúnghohk

ethology N: yàhnsinghohk; sàngtaaihohk

ethyl N: yuhtgèi

ethylene N: yuhthèi

etiquette N: láihjit (M: go)

etymologic (etymological) ATT: yúhyùhnhohkge; chìhyùhnhohkge

etymology N: yúhyùhn; yúhyùhnhohk; chìhyùhn (hohk)

eucalyptus N: yáuhgàleihsyuh (M: pò)

eulogize FV: chìngjaan

eulogy N: juhngchìh

eunuch N: taaigaam (M: go)

euphemistic (euphemistical) SV: wáiyúnge

euphenics N: yàujúnghohk

euphonic (euphonious) SV: yuhtyíhge

Europe N/PW: Ngāujāu

European ATT: Ngāujāuge; Ngāujāuyàhnge N: Ngāujāuyàhn (M: go)

evacuate FV: sòsaan; (a place) chitteui; (a house) bùnhùng

evacuation FV: sòsaan; chitteui; bùnhùng

evacuee N: sòsaan ge yàhn; chitteui ge yàhn (M: go)

evade FV: tòuhbeih; wùihbeih; símbeih; dóbeih

evaluate FV/N: gúga; pìhngga; gúgai

evaluation FV/N: pìhngga; gúgai

evanesce FV: sìusāt; sìusaan

evanescence FV: sìusāt; sìusaan

evanescent SV: dyúnjaahmge; yihsìusaange; jaahmsìhge

evaporable Adj. PH: hóyíh jìngfaat ge; yáuh jìngfaatsing ge

evaporate FV: jìngfaat

evaporation FV: jìngfaat

evaporator N: gònchouhei; jìngfaathei (M: go)

evasion FV: tòuhbeih N: (an excuse) jihkháu

evasive SV: tòuhbeihge; (to make excuse) tèuiwáige

eve N: chìhnjihk

even SV: ❶ (regular) wàhnchèuhn; ❷ (level) pìhng; ❸ (numbers) sèung A: sahmji; lìhn . . . dōu; jīksí PH: lìhngdou pìhng; lìhngdou sèungdáng ✻ even if (even though) A: jīksí ✻ even so A: sèuiyìhn haih gám ✻ even-handed SV: gùngpìhngge ✻ even-minded SV: chàhmjeuhkge ✻ even-song N: máahntóu yìhsīk (M: go)

evening N/TW: máahntàuhhāak; yehmáahn; (dusk) ngāaimāan

event N: sih; daaihsih (M: gihn) ✻ in the event A: gitgwó; yùhgwó ✻ in the event of PH: ❶ yùhgwó . . . faatsàng; ❷ maahnyāt . . . ge sìhhauh ✻ eventful SV: dòsihge; juhngdaaihge

eventual ATT: jeuihauhge; gitgwóge; hónàhngge

eventually A: jeuihauh; jēutjì

eventuality PH: hónàhngsing; hónàhng faatsàng ge sih

ever A: (at any time) gwo Néih yáuh móuh heuigwo gódouh a? ✻ as . . . as ever A: júnghaih ✻ ever since MA: jihchùhng ✻ ever so (such) A: fèisèuhng ✻ for ever A: wíhngyúhn

everlasting Adj. PH: wíhnggáuge; wìhnghàhngge

evermore A: wíhnggáu; wíhngyúhn

every SV: múih; múihyāt ✻ every inch A: sahpjūk ✻ every now and then A: gáuṁgáu ✻ every once in a while A: gaanjùng; ngáuhyìhn ✻ every other A: múih gaak ✻ every way A: yùhnchyùhn; gokfòngmihn ✻ everybody, everyone N: gokyàhn; yàhnyàhn ✻ everyday SV: múihyaht; yahtsèuhng ✻ everything N: múihyeuhng yéh; yeuhngyeuhng yéh ✻ everywhere A: syusyu; seiwàih

evict FV: ❶ juhkchēut; kèuijuhk; ❷ (to recover what has been taken away illicitly) jèuiwàahn

eviction FV: ❶ juhkchēut; ❷ (to recover what has been taken away illicitly) jèuiwàahn

evidence N: jinggeui; pàhnggeui (M: go) FV: ❶ jingmìhng; ❷ (to indicate) hínsih

evident SV: mìhnghínge

evil SV: ngokge; waaihge; jeuihngokge N: ❶ chèhngok; ❷ bāthahng; ❸ jòiwoh (M: go)

evoke FV: wuhnhéi; yáhnhéi

evolution N: faatjín; jeunfa * **theory of evolution** N: jeunfaleuhn

evolutional (evolutionary) SV: jeunfage; jeunfaleuhnge

evolutionism N: jeunfaleuhn

evolve FV: faatjín; yínbin; jeunfa

ewe N: yèuhngná (M: jek)

exacerbate FV: ❶ ngokfa; ❷ gīknàu

exact SV: jìngkok; jéunkok N/FV: ❶ yìukàuh; ❷ sèuiyiu

exaction FV: lahksok; jachéui

exactitude SV: jingkok; jìngkok

exactly A: ngāamngāam; jinghaih

exaggerate FV: kwàjèung; kwàdaaih

exaggeration FV: kwàjèung; kwàdaaih

exalt FV: ❶ tàihsìng; ❷ (to glorify) jaanyèuhng

exaltation FV: tàihsìng; jaanyèuhng

exam VO/N: háausíh

examination VO/N: háausíh

examine FV: ❶ háau; ❷

(test) siyihm; ❸ (inspect) gímchàh; chàh; yihm VO: háausíh * **examine a patient** VO: gímchàh behngyàhn; gímyihm behngyàhn

examinee N: (one who participates in an examination) yingháauyàhn

examiner N: jyúháauyàhn; (inspector) gímchàhyùhn

example N: ❶ (precedent) laih; ❷ (model) bìujéun; ❸ (pattern) yéung (M: go) * **as an example** PH: géuilaih syutmìhng * **beyond (without) example** SV: móuh sìnlaih ge; hùngchìhnge * **by way of example** PH: géuilaih syutmìhng * **for example** A: peiyùh; laihyùh

excavate FV: waatgwaht; gwaht

excavator N: waatnàihgèi (M: ga)

exceed FV: chìugwo

exceeding A: fèisèuhng

excel FV: singgwo; chìugwo

excellence N: yàudím (M: go)

Excellency N: ❶ gokhah; ❷ daaihyàhn

excellent PH: hóu dougihk; gihkjì hóu

except CV: chèuihjó . . . jìngoih MA: (unless) chèuihfèi * **except for** PATT: chèuihjó . . . jìngoih

excepting CV: chèuihjó . . . jìngoih MA: chèuihfèi

exception FV/N: laihngoih * **with the exception of** CV:

chèuihjó . . . jìngoih ✻
without exception A: móuh
laihngoih

excerpt (excerption)
FV: jaahkluhk

excess FV: chìugwo; SV:
gwodouhge ✻ **in excess of** FV:
chìugwo; dògwo

excessive SV: gwodouhge

exchange FV: gàauwuhn;
diuhwuhn N: ❶ gàauwuhn; ❷
(trade) gàauyihk ✻ **exchange**
A for B PH: jèung A wuhn B
✻ **exchange A with B** PH:
tùhng B gàauwuhn A ✻
foreign exchange N:
ngoihwuih

exchangeable PH: hóyíh
gàauwuhn ge

excise N: fomahtseui VO: (to
collect taxes) sàuseui FV: got
got bíntòuhsin

excitable SV: yùhngyih
gīkduhngge

excitant ATT: chigīksingge
N: chigīkmaht; hìngfáhnjāi

excite FV: ❶ gīkduhng; ❷ (a
body of people) gúduhng; ❸ (a
body of people to sedition) sinduhng; PH: lihngdou hìngfáhn

excitation SV/FV/N:
chigīk FV: (to rejoice) gúmóuh

excitement SV: (stimulated)
hìngfáhn SV/FV/N: (to provoke) chigīk FV/N: (disturbance) sòuduhng

exclaim PH: daaihsèng
góng; daaihseng ngaai

exclamation N: gámtaanchìh

exclamatory SV: gìng-

taange; gámtaange

exclude FV: ❶ (not include)
m̀gai; ❷ (to expel) pàaihchīk ✻
exclude . . . from PH: jèung .
. . pàaihchèuih chēutheui

exclusion N: pàaihchīk; (to
refuse) kéuihjyuht ✻ **under**
the exclusion of PH: tùhng .
. . gaakjyuht

exclusionism N: pàaihtà-
jyúyih; pàaihngoihjyúyíh

exclusive SV: duhkyáuhge;
jyùnyáuhge

excrement N: pàaihsitmaht; fanbihn

excremental N: fanbihnge;
pàaihsitmahtge

excreta N: pàaihsitmaht;
fanbihn

excrete FV: pàaihsit; fànbei

excretion FV: pàaihsit;
fànbei N: pàaihsitmaht

excretive ATT: pàaihsitge;
fànbeige

excretory ATT: pàaihsitge;
fànbeige N: pàaihsit heigùn (M:
go)

excruciate FV: jitmòh;
lihngdou tungfú

excruciating SV: gihkjì
tungfúge

excruciation N: huhkyìhng
SV/N: tungfú

excursion FV: léuihhàhng

excursive SV: (incompact)
sáanmaahnge

excusable SV: hóyíh yùhnleuhng ge

excusably PH: hóyíh yùhnleuhng

excuse FV: yùhnleuhng; fùnsyu N: ❶ (reason) léihyàuh; ❷ (a pretext) jihkháu (M: go)

execrate FV: ❶ (to berate) daaihnaauh; ❷ (to incur dislike or disgust) tóuyim

execration N: tóuyimge yàhn; tóuyimge yéh

execute FV: ❶ jāpàhng; ❷ (to carry out) sahthàhng; ❸ (to shoot to death) chēungkyut; chēungbaih

execution FV: jāpàhng VO: jāpàhng sêiyìhng ✳ carry (put, bring) into execution (effect, practice) FV: sahthàhng; sahtyìhn ✳ do execution FV: ginhaauh; sànghaauh

executive SV: jāpàhngge; hàhngjingseuhngge N: ❶ hàhngjing yàhnyùhn; ❷ hàhngjing bouhmùhn

exegete N: pìhngjyugā (M: go)

exempt FV: míhnchèuih; míhn N: míhnseuiyàhn (M: go) SV: beih míhnchèuige

exercise N: ❶ (of the body) wahnduhng; ❷ (practice) lihnjaahp; ❸ (rights, etc.) hàhngsái; ❹ (in a lesson) lihnjaahp FV: ❶ hàhngsái; ❷ (to train) fahnlihn; ❸ wahngduhng ✳ exercise book N: lihnjaahpbóu (M: bún)

exert VO: chēutlihk; jeuhnlihk

exertion SV/A: nóuhlihk; VO: jeuhnlihk

exhale VO: táuhei

exhaust RV: yuhngjeuhn N: faihei

exhaustible PH: hóyíh yuhngjeuhn ge

exhaustion RV: yuhngjeuhn

exhaustive SV: chitdáige

exhibit FV: ❶ (as painting, etc.) jínláahm; ❷ (display, as goods) báai N: ❶ jínláahm; jínláahmbán; ❷ (as objects in a court) mahtjing

exhibition N: jínláahmwúi (M: go)

exhibitive SV: bíusihge

exhibitor (exhibiter) N: jínchēutjé

exhibitory SV: hínsihge; bíusihge

exhilarate PH: lihngdou gòuhing

exhilaration SV: gòuhing

exhort FV: hyungou; hyungaai

exhortation FV: hyungaai

exile FV: fongjuhk N: fongjuhk PH: beih fongjuhk ge yàhn

exist FV: chyùhnjoih; sàngchyùhn

existence FV: chyùhnjoih; PH: chyùhnjoihge yéh ✳ bring (call) into existence PH: lihngdou cháansàng ✳ come into existence FV: cháansàng ✳ in existence SV: yihnchyùhnge; yihnyáuhge

existent SV: dòngchìhnge; yìhnchyúhnge

exit ATT: chēutháu * **make one's exit** FV: teuichēut; teuichèuhng

Exodus N: Chēut-ngòikahp-gei

exonerate VO: míhnjeuih; gáaichèuih

exorbitant SV: gwogòuge; gwofahngge

exorcise (exorcize) FV: kèuichèh

exorcism FV: kèuichèh

exoteric SV: ❶ gùnghòige; ❷ (popular) tùngjuhkge

exotic ATT: ngoihlòihge PH: ngoihgwok chēutcháan ge N: ❶ (a term borrowed from a foreign language) ngoihlòihyúh; ❷ lòih-lóufo (lòihlóuyéh)

exotically SV: ngoihlòih

expand FV: ❶ (develop) kwongchùng; ❷ (to swell) pàahngjeung

expanse SV: (vast) gwóng-fut FV: pàahngjeung

expansion FV: pàahng-jeung; kwongjèung

expansionary SV: kwong-jèungge; pàahngjeungge

expansionism PH: kwong-jèungjyúyíh

expansionist PH: kwong-jèungjyúyíhjé; kwongjèung-jyúyíh fahnjí (M: go)

expansive SV: hóyíh kwongjèungge; gwóngfutge

expatiate FV: chèuhng-seuht (chèuhngsaigám góngháh)

expatriate PH: ❶ gón . . . lèihhòi búngwok; ❷ (to emigrate) yìhmàhn heui ngoihgwok PH: béi yàhn gón heui ngoihgwok ge yàhn; yìhmàhn heui ngoihgwok ge yàhn (M: go)

expatriation PH: béi yàhn gón heui ngoihgwok; yìhmàhn heui ngoihgwok

expect FV: ❶ (wait for) dáng; ❷ (count on someone for something) jíyi FV/N: (hope for) hèimohng * **be expecting** VO: yáuh sàngéi

expectance (expectan-cy) FV/N: kèihdoih; kèih-mohng (M: go)

expectant SV: kèihdoihge; kèihmohngge PH: jauhlàih sàang bìhbī ge

expectation N/FV: kèih-mohng; hèimohng (M: go) * **in expectation of** FV: kèih-mohng; (hope for) jímohng * **meet someone's expectation** IE: bāt-fuh-só-mohng

expectorate FV: kātchēut VO: toutàahm; (to spit) touháuséui

expectoration VO: tou-tàahm; touháuséui N: (phlegm) tàahm

expedience (expedien-cy) SV: fòngbihn; bihnleih

expedient SV: ❶ fòngbihn-ge; ❷ yáuhleihge N: ❶ baahnfaat; ❷ gaimàuh (M: go)

expedite PH: gàgán jeunhàhng SV: ❶ bihnleihge; ❷ seunchŭkge

expedition N: ❶ (for recreation) lĕuihhàhngtyùhn; ❷ (for scientific research) taamhímdéui ❸ (for military purposes) yùhnjinggwān

expeditionary SV: yùhnjìngge; taamhímge

expeditious SV: ❶ seunchŭkge; ❷ máhnjihtge

expel FV: ❶ (as from school) hòichèuih; ❷ (send away) gónjáu

expend RV: yuhngsaai FV: yuhng

expenditure N: faiyuhng; gìngfai (M: bāt) * **expenditure on armaments** N: gwànfai (M: bāt)

expense N: faiyuhng; fai * **household expenses** N: gàyuhng (M: bāt) * **at the expense of** PH: ❶ yàuh . . . béichín; ❷ yàuh . . . fuhdàam * **free of expense** PH: m̀sái chín

expensive SV: gwaige

experience FV/N: gìngyihm; gìnglihk (M: go)

experienced SV: yáuh gìngyihm ge; suhkhòhngge; lóuhlihnge * **experienced in** VO: yáuh . . . gìngyihm

experiment FV/N: sahtyihm; siyihm (M: go)

experimental SV: sahtyihmge; siyihmsingge

experimentation FV/N: sahtyihm; siyihm (M: go)

expert N: jyūngā; nàhngsáu SV: lóuhlihnge; suhkhòhngge

expiate FV: ❶ suhk (jeuih); ❷ dáisèuhng; bóusèuhng

expiation FV/N: ❶ bóusèuhng; ❷ suhkjeuih

expiration FV: (the term or period has expired) kèihmúhn; VO: (exhalation) fùhei

expiratory SV: fùheige; touheige

expire VO: ❶ fùhei; ❷ (to breathe one's last) tyúhnhei FV: kèihmúhn

explain FV/N: gáaisīk; syutmìhng * **explain away** Patt: jèung . . . gáaisīk mìhngbaahk

explanation FV/N: gáaisīk; syutmìhng (M: go)

explanatory SV: gáaisīkge; syutmìhngge

expletive N: hèuijih; johchìh; johyúhchìh (M: go)

explicable SV: hóyíh syutmìhng ge; hóyíh gáaisīk ge

explicate FV/N: gáaisīk; syutmìhng

explicative (explicatory) SV: gáaisīkge; syutmìhngge

explicit SV: mìhngkokge; chìngchóge

explode FV: baauja

exploder N: baaujajòngji; lèuihgún

exploit FV: ❶ (to develop) hòifaat; ❷ (to exploit people) mōkseuk N: gùngjīk; gùnglòuh (M: go)

exploitation FV: hòifaat; mōkseuk

exploiter N: mōkseukjé (M:

go)

exploration FV/N: taamchăak; FV: taamhím

**explorative (explora-
tory)** SV: taamhímge

explore FV: taamchăak;
taamhím; (to study and
research) yìhngau

explorer N: taamhímgā (M:
go)

explosion FV: baauja N:
baaujasèng

explosive SV: baaujage;
yihbaaujage N: jayeuhk

exponent N: ❶ gáaisīkge
yàhn ❷ (a model, a typical example) dínyìhng

export FV/N: chēutháu N:
(export commodity) chēutháufo

exportation FV/N:
chēutháu N: (export commodity) chēutháufo

expose FV: ❶ sái (expose a
film) sái fēilám; ❷ kitfaat, ❸
(expose a secret) kitchyùn; ❹
bouhlouh Hái kwongyéhsyu
gódī sihbīng bouhlouh hái
dihkyàhnge paaufó jihah. * be
exposed to FV: bouhlouhhái
* be exposed to view RV:
bouhlouh mòuhwàih

exposition FV/N: (explanation) gáaisīk N: (exhibition) jínláahmwúi (M: go)

expostulate N/FV:
hyungou

expostulation FV/N:
jùnggūk (M: go)

exposure FV: bouhlouh;
kitfaat

expound FV/N: gáaisīk

PH: chèuhngsai syutmìhng

express FV: bíusih; bíudaaht VO: gei faaiseun SV:
mìhngbaahkge; dahkbiht
faaige N: ❶ faaiseun; ❷
faaichè; ❸ (a special messenger)
jyùnchàai * **express train** N:
faaichè (M: ga)

expressible SV: hóyíh
bíudaaht ge

expression N: ❶ sàhn-
chìhng; sàhnhei; ❷ (facial)
bíuchìhng; ❸ chìhgeui dāanjih
tùhng chìhgeui. * **beyond expression** PH: móuh faatjí
bíudaaht; móuh faatjí
yìhngyùhng

expressive SV: ❶ fuyáuh
bíuchìhng ge; ❷ yáuh hàhmyi
ge

express-way N: gòuchūk
gùnglouh (M: tìuh)

expulsion FV: ❶ (to
dismiss, to fire) hòichèuih; ❷
(to drive out, to get rid of)
kèuijuhk

expulsive SV: kèuijuhkge;
hòichèuihge

exquisite SV: yàuméihge;
jìngjige

ex-service SV: teuiyihkge;
teuingħge

ex-serviceman N: teui-
yihk-gwànyàhn; teuingħ-
gwànyàhn (M: go)

extant SV: yihnchyùhnge;
meihsātge

extemporary SV: ❶ làhmsìhge; ❷ móuh jéunbeih ge

extempore A: ❶ làhmsìh;
❷ (on the spot) jīkjihk SV:
làhmsìh joksìhng ge

extemporize PH: jīkjihk yìngóng; jīkjihk joksìhng

extend FV: yìhnchèuhng

extended SV: yìhnchèuhng-ge

extendible (extensible) SV: ❶ hóyíh kwongjèung ge; ❷ hóyíh yìhnchèuhng ge

extension FV: ❶ yìhnchèuhng; ❷ kwongchùng N: (telephone extension) dihnwá fàngèi (M: go)

extensive SV: gwóngfutge; gwóngfaange

extent N: ❶ chìhngdouh; ❷ faahnwàih (M: go) * to the extent of Patt: dou . . . ge chìhngdouh

exterior SV: ngoihbouhge N: ngoihbouh (M: go)

exteriority (externality) N: ngoihbíu; ngoihyìhng (M: go)

exterminate FV: sìumiht

extermination FV: sìumiht

extern N: ❶ (students living outside the school) jáuduhk-sāng; ❷ fèijyuhyún yīsāng (M: go)

external SV: ngoihbouhge; ngoihmìhnge

externality N: ❶ hái ngoih-bihn ge yéh; ❷ (outward appearance) ngoihyìhng

extinct SV: yíhgìng sìumiht ge

extinction FV: sìumiht; mihtmòhng

extinguish FV: ❶ (as a light) sīk; ❷ (as a fire) jíngsīk; sìumiht; ❸ (destroy) wáimiht

extinguisher N: mihtfó-túng; mihtfóhei (M: go)

extol (extoll) FV: chìng-jaan; jaanméih

extolment FV: chìngjaan; jaanméih

extort FV: hàauja; lahksok

extortion FV: lahksok; hàauja

extortionate (extortion-ary) SV: lahksokge; hàau-jasingge

extortioner N: lahksokge yàhn (lahksokjé) (M: go)

extra SV: ❶ lihngngoihge; ❷ (additional) ngaahkngoihge; ❸ (special) dahkbihtge N: (of newspaper) houhngoih

extract FV: ❶ màngchēut-làih; ❷ (to make an extract of a report, article, document, etc.) jaahkluhk N: ❶ chàuchēut-làihge yéh; ❷ (outline) jaahkyiu

extraction FV: ❶ chàu-chēut; ❷ tàihchéui

extra-curricular activi-ties N: fo-ngoih wuhtduhng (M: júng)

extradite FV: yáhndouh

extradition VO: yáhndouh tòuhfáan

extraneous SV: móuh-gwàanhaihge; ngoihlòihge

extraordinary SV: fèi-sèuhngge; dahkbihtge

extrapolate FV: tèuidyuhn FV/N: tèuileuhn

extrapolation FV/N: tèuidyuhn N: ngoihtèuifaat

extraterritoriality N: jihngoihfaatkyùhn

extravagance (extravagancy) SV: chèchí; chèwàh

extravagant SV: chèchíge; chèwàh

extreme A: fèisèuhng PH: yùhnchyùhn sèungfáange yéh * go (run) to extremes FV: jáugihkdyùn * in the extreme A: fèisèuhng

extremely A: gihkjì; fèi sèuhng; dougihk

extremism N: gihkdyùnjyúyih

extremist N: gihkdyùnfahnjí; gihkdyùnjyúyihjé (M: go)

extremity N: ❶ gihkdím; ❷ jyuhtgíng (M: go)

extricate FV: ❶ gáaityut; ❷ gauchēut

extrinsic (extrinsical) SV: ngoihlòihge

extrude FV: jìtchēutlàih; PH: lihngdou panchēut

exuberance (exuberancy) SV: mauhsihng; fùngfu

exuberant SV: fàahnmauhge; mauhsihngge

exude FV: samchēut; lauhchēut

exult PH: fèisèuhng gòuhing; FV: kwòhngfùn

exultant SV: kwòhngfùnge

exultation (exultancy) FV: kwòhngfùn; fùntàhng

eye N: ngáahn (M: sèung) FV: tái * all eyes PH: muhk-bātjyúnjīng * an eye for an eye FV: boufuhk IE: yíh-ngáahnwàahn-ngáahn * catch somebody's eye PH: yáhn yàhn jyumuhk * have (keep) an eye on FV: hònjyuh; hâujyuh * see with half an eye IE: yāt-muhk-líuhyìhn

eye-ball N: ngáahnkàuh; ngáahnjyū

eye-brow N: ngáahnmèih; ngáahnmèihmòuh (M: tìuh)

eye-catcher PH: dahkbiht yáhn yàhn jyumuhk ge yéh

eye-ful N: múhnngáahn

eye-glass N: ngáahngéng (M: go, fu)

eye-hole N: ngáahnwò (M: go)

eye-lash N: jihtmòuh; ngáahnyāpmōu (M: tìuh)

eye-let N: ngáahnhúng; sihhúng (M: go) VO: hòingáahnhúng

eye-lid N: ngáahnpèih (M: faai)

eye-opener PH: lihngyàhn hòingáahngaai ge sànkèih faatyihn waahkjé sihmaht

eye-piece N: jipmuhkgeng (M: go)

eye-reach N: sihgaai; sihyéh (M: go)

eye-shot N: ngáahngaai; sihyéh (M: go)

eye sight N: sihlihk

eye-score N: nàahntáige yéh

eye-tooth N: hyúnngàh; hyúnchí (M: jek)

eye-wash N: tokchìh; wùh-yìhn (M: go)

eye-water N: ngáahnyeuhk-séui

eye-witness N: muhkgīkjé; ginjingyàhn (M: go)

F

fable N: yuhyìhn

fabric N: bou (M: pàt)

fabricate FV: ❶ nihpjouh; ❷ (to make) jaijouh

fabrication FV: nihpjouh; ngaihjouh

fabulous SV: ❶ chyùhnsyutge; ❷ yuhyìhnge

face N: ❶ mihn; mihnmaauh; ❷ (surface of anything) mín FV: heung (jyuh); deuijyuh * **face each other** PH: mihn deui mihn * **face off** FV: deuikong * **face to face** PH: mihn deui mihn A: dòngmín * **face value** PH: piumihn (bíumihn) gajihk (M: go)

facet N: (a precious stone) síupìhngmín Patt: hái . . . seuhngbihn hāak síu pìhngmín

facetious SV: ❶ waahtkàige; ❷ jùngyi hòiwàahnsiu ge

facial ATT: mihnbouhge; mihnbouhyuhngge PH: mihnbouh ngonmō

facile SV: ❶ yùhngyihge; ❷ (easy to get) yihdākge

facilitate PH: lihngdou yùhngyih

facility SV: yùhngyih N: (installation) chitbeih * **facilities** SV: bihnleih; fòngbihn

facsimile FV: fūkjai N: fūkjai (bán)

fact N: sihsaht (M: go) * **in fact** A: kèihsaht * **as a matter of fact** A: sihsahtseuhng

faction N: paaibiht; dóngpaai; paaihaih (M: go)

factious SV: ❶ dóngpaaisingge; ❷ dóngjàngge; ❸ noihhùhngge

factitious SV: ❶ yàhnwàihge; ❷ m̀jihyìhnge

factor N: ❶ yànsou; ❷ (reason) yùhnyàn (M: go)

factory N: gùngchóng; jaijouhchóng (M: gàan)

faculty N: ❶ chòihgon; ❷ (ability) chòihnàhng ❸ (teaching staff) gaaujīkyùhn

fad N: chiuhlàuh (M: go)

faddy (faddish) SV: làuhhàhngge

fade VO: làtsīk (the color fades) FV: jeh Dī fā jehjó la. * **fade away** FV: siusāt

fag VO: jouh fúgùng N: (hard labor) fúgùng

fag end N: móuhyuhngge yéh

Fahrenheit SV: Wàhsih (hòhnsyúbíu) ge N: Wàhsih hòhnsyúbíu (M: go)

fail FV/N: sātbaaih PH: lihngdou . . . m̀hahpgaak Go sìnsàang héi kéuih m̀hahpgaak. FV: m̀hahpgaak ＊ **fail to (do)** FV: móuh AV: m̀nàhnggau ＊ **never fail of** AV: yātdihng yiu ＊ **never fail to (do)** A: bītdihng; yātdihng ＊ **without fail** A: bītdihng; yātdihng ＊ **fail to pass an examination** FV: m̀hahpgaak (m̀kahpgaak)

failing N: ❶ kyutdím; ❷ (fault) gwosāt FV/N: sātbaaih (M: go) PH: yùhgwó móuh . . . SV: sātbaaihge

failure FV/N: sātbaaih

faint SV: ❶ (weak) yeuhk; ❷ (not bright) ngam; ❸ (not loud) mèihyeuhk FV: wàhn (tàuhwàhn)

faint-heart N: móuhdáamge yàhn; nohfù (M: go)

faint-hearted SV: móuh yúhnghei ge; dáamsíuge; móuhdáamge

faintly SV: ❶ (not clear) mòuhwùh; ❷ (weak) yeuhk (yúhnyeuhk)

fair SV: ❶ (in price) gùngdouh; ❷ (in dealing or game, etc.) gùngpìhng; ❸ (for grading) jūngtíng; ❹ (of weather) hóutin ❺ lóuhsaht (sìhngsaht); ❻ (clearly) chìngchó N: ❶ (market) síhchèuhng; ❷ (exhibition) jínláahmwúi (M: go) ＊ **fair and square** SV: jingjihk ＊ **fair deal** PH: gùngpìhng gàauyihk ＊ **fair play** N: gùngjing

fair-haired SV: gàmfaatge

fairly A: sèungdòng

fair-spoken SV: ❶ màhn-ngáh; ❷ yúnjyún

fair-way N: (route of a ship or airplane) hòhngdouh (M: tiuh)

fairy N: sīngū; sīnnéui (M: go) SV: sàhnsìnge

fairy-land N: sìngíng (M: go)

fairy tale N: sàhnsìn gusih; tùhngwá (M: go)

faith FV/N: seunyéuhng N: (a religion or belief) seunsàm (M: go) ＊ **have faith in** FV: sèungseun ＊ **in good faith** A: sìhngyigám

faithful SV: jùngsaht

faithless SV: m̀jùngsahtge

fake FV: ngaihjouh; ngaihjòng; mouhchūng SV: ngaihjouhge

falcon N: yīng; lihpyīng (M: jek)

fall FV: ❶ dit; ditlohklàih; ❷ (drop) ditlohkheui N: ❶ (America Autumn) chāutīn; ❷ bohkbou (The Niagara Falls. Nèih-a-gā-lāai daaih bohk bou.) ＊ **fall and hurt oneself** RV: ditchàn ＊ **fall down** FV: ditdài; ditdóu ＊ **fall of a city** FV: lèuhnhaahm; sāthaahm ＊ **fall for** FV: tàijung ＊ **fall guy** N: (America) taiséigwái (M: go) ＊ **fall into** FV: haahmyahp ＊ **fall off** FV: (to reduce) gáamsíu ＊ **fall on** FV: ❶ (to attack) jeungùng; ❷ (to take place) faatsàng

false SV: ❶ (dishonest) hèuingaih; ❷ (not true) gáge ＊ **be false to** Patt: deui . . . m̀jùngsaht ＊ **false teeth** N: gángàh (M: jek)

false-hood SV: hèuingaih; hèuigá

falsificiation FV: ❶ ngaihjouh; ❷ (to distort) wàaikŭk

falsify FV: ❶ ngaihjouh; ❷ (to distort) wàaikŭk

falter PH: (to limp) bàibàiháh gám hàahng; ❷ (to speak hesitatingly) tàntàntoutou gám góng

fame N: mìhngsìng; sìngmohng; sìngyuh PH: lihngdou chēutméng

famed SV: jyumìhng; yáuhméng; chēutméng ✻ **famed for** PH: yíh chēutméng

familiar SV: ❶ (of relations) chànmaht; ❷ (acquainted with) suhk FV: (to master) jìngtùng N: suhkyàhn; chànmahtge pàhngyáuh (M: go) ✻ **familiar to somebody** Patt: wàih . . . só suhksīk ✻ **familiar with** FV: suhksīk; jìngtùng

familiarity SV: chànmaht; suhksīk

familiarize PH: lihngdou chànmaht; lihngdou suhksīk

family N: ❶ (parents and children) gàtìhng; ❷ (one's wife and children) gàgyun; (the financial condition of a family) gàgíng; (family expenditure) gàyuhng; (a letter from home) gàseun; (family property) gàcháan

famine N: gèifòng

famous SV: chēutméngge; yáuhméngge; jyumìhngge ✻ **famous doctor** N: mìhngyì (M: go)

famously SV: jyumìhng; chēutméng

fan N: sin (M: bá) FV: put ✻ **movie fan** N: yíngmàih (dihnyíngmàih) (M: go) ✻ **an electric fan** N: dihnfùngsin (fùngsin) (M: bá)

fanatic N: kwòhngyihtjé (M: go) SV: kwòhngyihtge

fanatical SV: kwòhngyihtge; màahngseunge

fanaticism ATT: kwòhngyiht; màahngchùhng

fancy FV/N: ❶ séungjeuhng; ❷ (delusive imagination) waahnséung (M: go) FV: yíhwàih SV: fāyéungge; fàsīkge ✻ **have a fancy for** FV/N: ngoihou ✻ **take a fancy to (for)** FV: héingoi ✻ **take the fancy of** FV: kāpyáhn ✻ **fancy-ball** N: fajōng móuhwúi (M: go) ✻ **fancy-work** N: chisau

fang N: (dog, wolf, etc.) jìmngàh (M: jek)

fantastic (fantastical) SV: ❶ (strange) kèihyihge; ❷ (daydream) waahnséungge

fantasy (phantasy) FV/N: waahnséung (M: go) N: (music) waahnséungkūk (M: sáu, jì)

far SV/A: yúhn ✻ **far and near** A: dousyu; yúhngahn ✻ **so far so good** PH: dou muhkchìhn wàihjí dōu géi hóu ✻ **Far East** PW: Yúhndūng

farce N: siukehk; waahtkàikehk (M: chēut)

farcical Adj. PH: waahtkàikehkge; siukehkge

fare N: (freight charges) wahnfai; (fare for vehicles) chēfai; (fare for a voyage) syùhnfai

farewell IE: joigin FV:
lèihbiht SV: wahbihtge;
làhmbihtge * **farewell dinner** Patt: tùhng . . . jinhàhng *
farewell party N: fùnsungwúi
(M: go)

farm N: ❶ nùhngchèuhng; ❷
(cultivated land) tìhn VO:
gàangtìhn FV: gàangjung *
farm hand N: nùhngchèuhng
gùngyàhn * **farm-house** N:
nùhngse (M: gàan) * **farming**
N: nùhngyìhp; nùhngjok *
farmer N: nùhngmàhn;
nùhngyàhn; gàangtìhnlóu;
nùhngfù (M: go)

farrow NuMN: yāttòi jyùjái
VO: sàangjyùjái

far-seeing Adj. PH: yáuhyúhnginge; ngáahngwōng-
yúhndaaihge

far-sighted Adj. PH: ❶ (as
a physical defect) yúhnsìhge; ❷
yáuhyúhnginge

farther SV: juhngyúhn;
gangyúhn * **farther-most** SV:
jeuiyúhn

farthest SV: jeui yúhn * **at
(the) farthest** A: ❶ (at most)
jidò; ❷ (at latest) jichìh

farthing N: Yìnggwok yātjúng ngánjái (1/4 penny) (M: go)
* **not worth a farthing** PH:
hòuhmòuh gajihk

fascinate PH: lihngdou . . .
màihwaahk

fascination FV: màih-
waahk N: meihlihk

Fascism N: Faatsàisìjyúyih

Fascist N: Faatsàisìjyúyuihjé
(M: go) ATT: Faatsàisìjyúyihge

fashion N: ❶ (style) fún; ❷
(shape) yéung (M: go) * **new
fashion** N: sàn fún * **old
fashion** N: gauh fún * **after
the fashion of** FV: mòuhfóng
* **be in (the) fashion** SV:
làuhhàhng; sìhmōu * **out of
fashion** SV: m̀làuhhàhng

fashionable SV: sìhmōuge;
làuhhàhngge

fast SV: ❶ (quick) faai; ❷
(tight) gán; ❸ (firm) gán * **to
fast** VO: sáujàai FV: gamsihk;
jàaigaai. * **fast color** PH:
m̀làtsìk * **hold fast** FV: jàsaht

fasten FV: bóngjyuh *
fasten it tighter PH: bónggán-
dī * **fasten it with a nail** PH:
dèngsaht keúih * **fasten it
with string** PH: bóngsaht
kéuih

fastener N: kaugín * **a
paper fastener** N: syùdēng *
a snap fastener N: bāaknáu
(M: nāp) * **a zip (or slide)
fastener** N: làailín (M: tiuh)

fastening FV: (to fasten
tightly) kaugán; N: (shoelace,
button, lock, hook, etc.)
haihgitmaht

fastidious SV: yìmjìm

fat SV: fèih N: fèihyuhk PH:
lihngdou fèih; binfèih * **fat-
head** N: sòhgwā; bahndáan (M:
go) * **fat boy** N: fèihjái (M: go)
* **fat girl** N: fèih mūi; fèih
néui (M: go) * **fat man** N: fèih
lóu (M: go) * **fat woman** N:
fèih pòh (M: go)

fatal SV: jimihngge

fatalism N: sūkmihngleuhn

fatality N: mihngwahn (M:
go)

fate N: ❶ mihngwahn; wahn-sou; ❷ (destiny) mehng

fated SV: jíngdihngge; mihng-jùng-jyudihng ge

fateful SV: ❶ kyutdihng mihngwahn ge; ❷ jimihngge

father N: ❶ bàhbā; fuhchàn; lóuhdauh; ❷ (priest) sàhnfuh (M: go) ✳ **my father** N: gàfuh ✳ **my late father** N: sìnfuh ✳ **your father (polite term)** N: lihng jyùn; lihng jyùnyúng ✳ **the father of a country** N: gwokfuh ✳ **father and mother** N: fuhmóuh; bàhbā màhmā

father-hood N: fuhchànge sānfán

father-in-law N: ❶ (wife's father) ngoihfú (term used by husband); ❷ (husband's father) lóuhyèh; gāgūng (term used by wife)

father-land N: jóugwok (M: go) ✳ **fatherless** SV: móuh lóuhdauh(ge)

fathom M/N: chàhm; yìng-chàhm (= six feet) VO: lèuhng sàmdouh FV: ❶ (to understand) líuhgáai; ❷ (to infer; to predict) tèuichàak

fathomless PH: sàm-bāthó-chàak ge; móuh faatjí líuhgáai ge

fatigue SV: ❶ guih; ❷ sàn-fú PH: lihngdou guih

fatigue dress N: gùng-jokfuhk (M: tou)

fatigue duty PH: (done by soldiers) lòuhduhng fuhkmouh

fatten FV: yéuhngfèih; binfèih

fatty SV: jìfōngge; dò-jìfōngge N: fèihlóu; fèihjái (M: go)

fatuous SV: chéun (ge)

faucet N: séuihàuh (M: go)

fault N: ❶ cho; cho-ngh; ❷ (normal failing) gwosāt (M: go) ✳ **faultfinding** IE: chèui-mòuh-kàuh-chì ✳ **to find fault (with)** FV: tiutīk IE: chèui-mòuhkàuh-chì *Kéuih sìhsìh dōu chèui-mòuh-kàuh-chì* ✳ **in fault** PH: m̀ngāam; chojó

faulty SV: ❶ yáuh kyutdím ge; ❷ yáuh gwosāt ge

favor (favour) N: ❶ (kindness) (in statement) yàhnchìhng *Kéuih béi ngóhdeih yuhng gógàan ngūk hòichàhwúi haih yātgo hóu daaihge yàhnchìhng* ❷ (beg) (in questions) lòuhfàahn; kàuh *Lòuhfàahn néih bòng ngóh jouh yātgihn sih, hóu ma?* FV: jaansìhng; deui . . . yáuh-leih ✳ **ask a favor of** Patt: chéngkàuh . . . bòngmòhng ✳ **do someone a favor** VO: bòngmòhng yātgo yàhn ✳ **in favor** SV: làuhhàhng; hìng ✳ **out of favor** SV: m̀làuhhàhng; m̀hìng ✳ **in favor of** FV: jìchìh; jaansìhng

favorable SV: yáuhleihge; seuhnleihge ✳ **favorable wind** N: seuhnfùng ✳ **favorable opportunity** N: hóu gèiwuih (M: go)

favorably FV: jaansìhng SV: yáuhleih

favoring (favouring) SV: seuhnleihge; yáuhbòngjohge

favorite (favourite) SV: jeuijùngyi(ge); jìjùngyi(ge) N: ❶ jeuijùngyige yàhn (M: go); ❷ jeuijùngyìge yéh (M: gihn)

favoritism (favouritism)
FV: ❶ pìnngoi; ❷ pìntáan

fawn N: ❶ (deer) lúkjái (M: jek); ❷ chín wòhnghotsīk FV: bàgit; tóuhóu

fear FV: pa; gèng * **for fear of** FV: pa

fearful SV: hópage; hóbouge

fearless SV: ❶ mòuhwaige; ❷ yúhnggámge

feasible SV: hóhàhngge

feast N: (banquet) yinwuih VO: báaijáu; chéngyám

feat N: ❶ (skill, art) geihngaih; (meritorious records) ❷ gùngjīk (M: go)

feather N: yúhmòuh; jeukmòuh (M: tiuh) PH: yuhng yúhmòuh jòngsīk; chaap dī yúhmòuh hái . . . * **birds of a feather** IE: maht-yíh-leuih-jeuih * **feather bed** N: ngaapyùhngpéih (M: jèung) * **feather duster** N: gàimòuhsóu (M: tiuh, jì) * **feather fan** N: ngòhmòuhsin (M: bá)

feather-brained SV: hìngsēutge

feather-head N: ❶ hìngsēutge yàhn; ❷ yùhchéunge yàhn (M: go)

feather-headed SV: hìngsēutge

feather-weight N: ❶ gihkjì hèng ge yàhn (M: go); ❷ gihkjì hèng ge yéh (M: gihn) SV: hóuchíh yúhmòuh ge; hèng ge

feature N: ❶ (look, countenance) yùhngmaauh; mihnmaauh; seungmaauh; ❷

(characteristics) dahkjìng; dahksīk (M: go) Patt: yíh . . . wàih dahksīk

February TW/N: yihyuht (M: go)

Federal ATT: lyùhnbòngge; lyuhnhahpge * **federal government** N: lyùhnbòng jìngfú (M: go) * **federal state** N: lyùhnbòng

federate ATT: lyùhnmàhngge; lyùhnbòngge PH: jóusìhng lyùhnbòng FV: lyùhnmàhng

federation FV/N: lyùhnmàhng N: lyùhnbòng (M: go)

fee N: fai FV: gàaufai béi; gàaufai

feeble SV: ❶ hèuiyeuhkge; ❷ mèihyeuhkge * **feeble body** PH: sàntáiyeuhk * **feeble minded** PH: yìji bohkyeuhk

feebly SV: mèihyeuhk

feed FV: ❶ (to feed, to raise) wai; ❷ (to offer provisions, esp. to one's elders) (to feed one's children) gùngyéuhng; (animal feeds) jihlíu * **feed a baby** VO: wai bìhbī * **feed a bird** VO: wai jéuk * **feed a pig** VO: wai jyū * **feed cattle** VO: wai ngàuh

feeder N: (milk bottle) náaihjēun (M: go)

feeding FV: jihyéuhng; gùngyéuhng

feed bottle N: náaihjēun (M: go)

feel FV: ❶ (have feeling about) gin; gindāk; gokdāk; ❷ (touch) mò * **feel pain** PH: gintung * **feel cold** PH: gokdāk dung * to feel a person's pulse VO: bámahk

feeling N: ❶ (emotion) chìhnggám; ❷ (sensation) gámgok

feign FV: jadai * **feign death** FV: jaséi * **feign illness** FV: jabehng * **feign stupidity** FV: jasòh * **feign sleep** FV: jafan

feint FV: jadai IE: (feigning tactics) sìng-dùnggīk-sài

fellow N: yàhn (M: go) * **fellow countryman** N: tùhngbàau (M: go) * **fellow worker** N: tùhngsih (M: go) * **fellow student** N: tùhnghohk (M: go)

fellow-ship N: ❶ wúiyùhn jígaak; ❷ (friendship) gàauchìhng; yáuhyìh (M: go)

felon N: (a criminal) jeuihfáan (M: go)

felony N: chúhngjeuih (M: go)

female N: néuihyán; (female sex) néuihsing ATT: néuihsingge; chìsingge * **female teacher** N: néuih sìnsàang (M: go) * **female child** N: néuihjái (M: go)

feminine ATT: ❶ néuihsingge; ❷ yàmsingge

femininity (feminity) N: ❶ néuihsing; ❷ fúhnéuih

fence N: ❶ lèihbā (M: douh); ❷ wàihchèuhng (M: buhng) VO: jíng lèihbā; héi wàihchèuhng * **fence-sitter** N: kèhchèuhngpaai

fencing N: lèihbā (M: douh); wàihchèuhng (M: buhng)

ferment N: (yeast) hàaumóuh; háausou FV: faathàau; gīkduhng * **in a ferment** PH: jìngjoih sòuduhng

fermentation FV: faathàau; gīkduhng

fern N: yèuhngchíjihkmaht

ferny Adj. PH: (chíh) yèuhngchíjihkmahtge; dò yèuhngchíjihkmaht ge

ferocious SV: ❶ chàahnyánge; ❷ hùngmáahngge

ferocity SV: ❶ hùngmáahng; ❷ chàahnbouh; chàahnyán

ferry N: douhsyùhn; lèuhndouh (M: jek)

ferry-boat N: gwohóisyùhn; douhsyùhn (M: jek)

ferry-bridge N: ❶ douhkìuh; ❷ (pontoon bridge) fàuhkìuh (M: tiuh); ❸ wahnsung lihtchè ge douhsyùhn (M: jek)

ferry-man N: douhsyùhn gùngyàhn (M: go)

fertile SV: fèihyūk(ge) * **fertile in (of)** FV: fuyù * **fertile land** N: fèihtìhn (M: faai)

fertility SV: fèihyūk * **fertility rate** N: sàngyuhkleuht

fertilize FV: sìfèih PH: lìhngdou fèihyūk

fertilizer N: fèihlíu; fèihtìhnlíu (M: júng)

festal SV: ❶ jityahtge; ❷ (joy) fùnlohkge

fester VO: ❶ fanùhng; ❷ sàangnùhng N: nùhngchōng (M: go)

festival N: jityaht; jit (M: go)
SV: jityahtge * **the Spring festival** N: chèunjit (M: go) * **Dragon boat festival** N: Dyùnnghjit; Nghyuhtjit (M: go) * **Mid-autumn festival** N: Jūngchāujit; Baatyuhtjit (M: go)

festive SV: ❶ jityahtge; ❷ (joy) fùnlohkge

festivity N: hingjūk wuhtduhng (M: go)

fetch FV: nìnglàih; daailàih; ló * **fetch back** RV: ❶ lófàan; ❷ (to recall) sēunghéi

fetching ·SV: duhngyàhnge

fete N: ❶ hingjūk-dínláih; ❷ (feast) sìhngyìn (M: go) FV: sìhngyìn jiudoih; yinchíng

fetish N: ❶ mahtsàhn; ❷ (an idol) ngáuhjeuhng

fetishism N: baaimahtgaau (M: go)

fetter N: geukliuh PH: yuhnggeukliuh sójyuh

fetus (foetus) N: tòi; tòiyìh (M: go)

feud N: ❶ sūkyun; ❷ saisàuh (M: go) PH: saidoih gitsàuh

feudal SV: fùngginge * **feudal lord** N: jyùhàuh (M: go) * **feudal system** N: fùnggin jaidouh (M: go)

feudalism N: fùngginjaidouh (M: go)

feudalist N: fùngginjyúyihjé (M: go)

fever N: yiht VO: faatssìu; faatyiht * **scarlet fever** N: sìnghùhngyiht * **typhoid fever** N: sèunghòhn (jing) * **yellow feer** N: wòhngyihtjing

feverish SV: ❶ faatsìuge; ❷ (unreasonably enthusiastic) kwòhngyihtge

few SV: ❶ síusouge; hóusíuge; ❷ géi (go) N: síusou PH: hóusíuge yàhn; hóusíuge yéh * **a few** SV: síusou; PH: yáuh géigo * **a good few** PH: sèungdòng dò; msíu * **in a few words** A: júng yìhn jì; gáandàan làih góng * **quite a few** SV: hóudò; sèungdòng dò * **the few** N: síusou (yàhn)

fiancé N: meihfànfù (M: go)

fiancée N: meihfànchài (M: go)

fiasco FV: daaihbaaih; cháambaaih

fiat N/FV: mihnglihng; héuihó (M: go)

fib VO: góngdaaihwah

fiber (fibre) N: chìmwàih; chìmwàihjāt

fickle SV: ❶ dòbinge; ❷ (changeable) fáanfūkge

fickleness PH: dòbin; fáanfūk-mòuhsèuhng

fiction N: ❶ síusyut; ❷ gusih * **science fiction** N: fōhohk waahnséung síusyut (M: bún)

fictitious SV: gáge; hèuikauge

fiddle N: síutàihkàhm (M: go) VO: làaisíutàihkàhm

fidelity SV: ❶ jùngsaht; ❷ (accuracy) jìngkok

fidget PH: johlahpbātngòn; mtìhnggám yūk

fidgety SV: fàahnchouge

field N: ❶ (tract of land) deih; ❷ (cultivated) tìhn; (M: faai); ❸ (for playing) chèuhng (M: go) ∗ **athletic field** N: wahnduhng-chèuhng (M: go) ∗ **football field** N: jùkkàuhchèuhng (M: go) ∗ **field glasses** N: sèungtúng mohngyúhngeng (M: go) ∗ **field gun** N: yéhjinpaau; yéhpaau (M: hám, mùhn)

fiend N: mògwái (M: go, jek)

fiendish SV: hóuchíh ngok-mò ge

fierce SV: máahngliht(ge); kehkliht(ge)

fiery SV: fóge; hóuchíh fó ge

fifteen Nu: sahpnǵh; sahp-nǵhgo ∗ **fifteenth** Nu: daihsahpnǵh; sahpnǵhfahn jì yāt (1/15)

fifth Nu: daihnǵh; nǵhfahn jì yāt (1/5)

fiftieth Nu: daihnǵhsahp; nǵhsahpfahn jì yāt (1/50)

fifty Nu: nǵhshap N: nǵhsahp nihndoih; nǵhsahp-seui SV: hóudòge ∗ **fifty-fifty** IE: yih-yāt-tìm-jok-nǵh PH: pìhng fàn wàih léuhng fahn

fig N: mòuhfàgwó

fight VO: ❶ (between individuals, physically) dágāau; ❷ (to wage war) dájeung N: (a battle) jinyihk FV/N: (action, in military sense) jindau ∗ **fight against** FV: dáikong

fighter N: ❶ (a warrior) jin-sih (M: go); ❷ (a plane) jin-daugèi (M: ga)

fighting N: jinsih (M: go) SV: jindauge; jinjàngge ∗ **street fighting** N/FV: hohngjin ∗ **fighting spirit** N: jindau jìngsàhn; jindau yìji

figment PH: hèuikaugesih; mòuhkàijìtàahm

figuration VO/N: dihngyìhng

figurative SV: (metaphor) béiyuhge

figure N: ❶ (number) soumuhkjih; ❷ (of body) sàn-chòih; ❸ (form) yìhngjeuhng; ❹ (in art, human form) yàhnmaht PH: yuhng tòuh bíusih FV: ❶ (to estimate) gúgai; ❷ (to count) gaisyun; ❸ (to think) séung

file N: ❶ (tool) cho (M: bá); ❷ (for documents) dóngngon (fāailóu) (M: go) FV: ❶ (to file) cho; ❷ (put it on file) (term used in government organizations) gwàidong

filial SV: jínéuihge; haau-seuhnge ∗ **filial piety** SV: haauseuhn N: haausàm

filiation N: fuhjígwàanhaih (M: go)

Filipino N: Fèileuhtbànyàhn (M: go) ATT: Fèileuhtbànge

fill FV: ❶ (with dry things) jòng; ❷ (fill in a hole) tìhn; ❸ (a form) tìhn; bóu (fill a tooth. bóungàh.); (fill a vacancy. bóukyut.); (full) múhn N: (yuhnglàih) tìhnsāk ge yéh ∗ **fill it (the gasoline tank) up** PH: yahpmúhn kéuih ∗ **be filled with** RV: chùngmúhn

filling N: yuhnglàih tìhnsāk ge yéh; (anything serving as stuffing for dumplings, etc.) háam

film N: ❶ (photo) fēilám (M: gyún, tùhng); ❷ (thin skin) mók

(M: faai); ❸ (movie) yíngpín (M: tou) VO: ❶ paaksìhng dihnyíng; ❷ héi yātchàhng bohkmók * **film-fan** N: yíngmàih (M: go) * **film-strip (slide)** N: waahndāngpín (M: tou)

filter N: sāláu (M: go) FV: gwoleuih; leuih * **filter bed** N: leuihséuichìh (M: go) * **filter paper** N: leuihjí (M: jèung) * **filter tip** N: leuihjéui (yīnjái) (M: go)

filth SV: laahttaat; PH: laahttaatge yéh

filthy SV: laahttaatge

filtrate FV: gwoleuih; leuihchìng N: leuihyihk PH: gìnggwo leuihchìngge séui

fin N: yùhchi; kèih * **shark's fin** N: yùhchi

final SV: ❶ sāumēi (ge); ❷ (last) jeuihauh(ge) FV: (definite) dihngsahtjó; kyutdingjó N: ❶ (final examination) daaihháau; ❷ (the final game) kyutchoi (M: go)

finale N: ❶ (the result) gitguhk; ❷ (the end of a game, show, etc.) jùngchèuhng (M: go)

finality A: jeuihauh; N: gitguhk

finally A: ❶ sāumēi ❷ jeuihauh A/N: gitgwó

finance N: chòihjing VO: gùngkāp gìngfai; fuhdàam gìngfai

financial SV: ❶ chòihjingge; ❷ gàmyùhngge

financier N: chòihjinggā; gàmyùhnggā (M: go)

find FV: ❶ (search) wán; wándóu; ❷ (discover) faatyihn; ❸

(realize) faatgok; gokdāk ❹ (by investigating) chàhdóu * **find a clue to** VO: faatyihn . . . ge sinsok * **find oneself for** FV: bóuchìh * **find out** FV: ❶ faatyihn; ❷ chàhmìhng; ❸ séungchēut; ❹ yihngsīkdou * **find up** RV: wánchēut

finder PH: faatyihnge yàhn; wándóuge yàhn (M: go)

finding FV/N: faatyihn PH: faatyihnge yéh

fine SV: ❶ (minute) yausaige; ❷ (exquisite) jìngháauge; ❸ (nice or well) hóu N/VO: (a fine) fahtfún (M: bāt) PH: lìhngdou jìngméih FV: bìnhóu A: hóuhóu * **cut (run) it fine** VO: bá-ngāak sìhgaan

finger N: sáují (M: jek) PH: yuhng sáují mó (mò) * **burn one's fingers** IE: jih-chàhm-fàahnnóuh. * **by a fingers breadth** A: jāangdī; chādī * **finger-post** N: jílouhpáai (M: go) * **finger-print** N: jímàhn; jímòuh

finish RVE: yùhn (finish working.) *jouhyùhn.* FV: ❶ gitchūk *Jinjàng juhng meih gitchūk.* ❷ yùhn N: (result) gitguhk

finished SV: yùhnsìhngge

finisher PH: yùhnsìhngge yàhn (M: go)

finite SV: yáuhhaahnge

Finn N: Fànlàahnyàhn (M: go)

Finnish ATT: Fànlàahnge; Fànlàahnyàhnge; Fànlàahnyúhge N: Fànlàahnwá; Fànlàahnyúh

fir N: chùngsyuh (M: pò)

fire N: fó; fójūk VO: ❶ (to fire) hòichèung; ❷ cháau ... yàuhyú (hòichèuih) FV: (catch fire) jeuhkfó ✻ **on fire** FV: jeuhkfó ✻ **fire action** FV/N: paaujin (M: chèuhng) ✻ **fire alarm** N: fóging (M: go, chèuhng) ✻ **fire bomb** N: yìhnsíudáan (M: go) ✻ **fire-brigade** N: sìufòhngdéui (M: deuih) ✻ **fire cracker** N: paaujéung (M: go, chyun) ✻ **fire damp** N: jíuhei ✻ **fire engine** N: gaufóchè (M: ga) ✻ **fire escape** N: taaipìhngtài (M: douh) ✻ **fire-fly** N: yìhngfóchùhng (M: jek) ✻ **fire insurance** N: fójòi bóuhím ✻ **fire-man** N: sìufòhngyùhn; PH: gaufódéuige déuiyùhn (M: go) ✻ **fire-place** N: bīklòuh (M: go) ✻ **fire-plug** N: sìufósàan (M: go) ✻ **fire-proof** SV: fòhngfóge VO: jòng fòhngfó chitbeih ✻ **fire-wood** N: chàaih (M: tìuh) ✻ **fire-works** N: yìnfà

firm SV: ❶ saht; ❷ (solid) gitsaht; ❸ (steady) wánjahn; gìnngaahng PH: ❶ (firm ground) gìnngaahngge tóudeih ❷ lihngdou gìngu; ❸ lihngdou gindihng; ❹ binsìhng gìngu; ❺ binsìhng gindihng A: gindihnggám; sèunghóng (M: gàan)

firmament N: tìn; tìnhùng (M: go)

firmamental ATT: chòngtinge; tìnhùngge

first SV: ❶ daihyāt; ❷ (in time) jeuisìn; ❸ (the best) jeuihóuge A: daihyāt; jeuichò; sáusìn N: ❶ daihyātgo; ❷ (a contest) (champion) gun-gwān; daihyātmìhng; ❸ (beginning) hòichí PH: seuhngdángge yéh ✻ **at (the) first** A: héichò; jeuichò ✻ **at first sight (view)** A: yātgin jauh ✻ **first and**

foremost A: daihyāt; sáusìn ✻ **first of all** A: daihyāt; sáusìn ✻ **of the first importance** SV: tàuhdáng juhngyiu ge ✻ **first aid** FV: gāpgau ✻ **first-class** SV: jeuihóuge; tàuhdángge; seuhngdángge ✻ **first-hand** SV: ❶ jihkjipge; ❷ daihyātsáuge ✻ **first-rate** SV: jeui seuhngdáng ge; jeuihóuge ✻ **first-runner** N: tàuhlèuhn dihnyíngyún (M: gàan)

firstly A: daihyāt; sáusìn; jeuichò

fiscal SV: chòihjingge; wuihgaige N: gímchaatgùn (M: go)

fish N: yú (M: tìuh) VO: jūkyú; diuyú ✻ **fish for** FV: gaanjip dáting ✻ **fish in troubled waters** PH: wahnséui móyùh ✻ **fish out (up)** RV: làauhchēut ✻ **fish-pond** N: yùhtòhng; yéuhngyùhtòhng (M: go) ✻ **fish-works** N: séuicháan jaibánchóng (M: gàan)

fisher N: yùhyūng; yùhfù (M: go) yùhsyùhn (M: jek)

fisher-man N: yùhyàhn; yùhfù (M: go); yùhnsyùhn (M: jek)

fishery N: ❶ yùhyihhp; ❷ yùhchèuhng

fishing VO: ❶ diuyú; ❷ jūkyú PH: jūkyúge deihfòng

fishy ATT: yùhsèngmeihge; yúge

fist N: kyùhntàuh (M: go) ✻ **two-fisted** SV: jinglihk chùhngpui

fit PH: ❶ lihngdou sīkhahp ❷ lihngdou sīkying FV: sīkhahp SV: sīkdongge; sīkyihge; ngāamge PH: sīkhahpge yéh

fitful SV: dyuhn-dyuhn-juhk-juhk ge

fitful-ness SV: ❶ hāpdong; ❷ (health) gihnhòhng

fit-out N: jòngbeih; (léuihhàhngge) jéunbeih

five Nu: nǵh; nǵhgo

five-fold SV: nǵhpúihge; nǵhchùhngge A: nǵhpúih

fix FV: ❶ jíng; ❷ (establish) dihng RV: jíngfàan; jíngfàanhóu N: kwangíng (M: go) ✳ **fix on (upon)** FV: gudihng; kyutdihng ✳ **fix one's eyes on** FV: jyusih ✳ **fix up** FV: ❶ jíng; ❷ (arrange) ngònpàaih

fixation FV: ❶ gudihng; ❷ kyutdihng

fixed SV: gudihngge

fixer PH: ❶ lihngdou gudihng ge yàhn; ❷ lihngdou gudihng ge yéh

fixing FV: ❶ gudihng; ❷ jíng

fixture N: gudihng jòngji; gudihngmaht

fiz (fizz) VO: faatchēut sìsìsèng N: sìsìsèng

fizzle VO: faatchēut sìsìsèng N: sìsìsèng

flabbergast PH: haakjó yāt daaih gèng

flabby SV: ❶ sùngyúhnge; ❷ (weak) bohkyeuhkge

flag N: kèih (M: jì) VO: ❶ gwakèih; ❷ (to signal with a flag) dákèihhhouh; ❸ dákèihyúh

flagellate FV: bìndá SV:

yáuh bìnmòuh ge N: bìnmòuhchùhng (M: tìuh)

flagrant Adj. PH: jeuihngok chìujèung ge

flair N: ngáahngwōng

flak N: gòusehpaau (M: jì, mùhn)

flake N: bohkpín PH: lihngdou binsèhng bohkpín FV: (to come off, as a result of erosion) mōklohk

flam FV: ngāak (ngāakyàhn) FV/N: hèija SV: hèuingaih

flamboyace (flamboyancy) SV: yìhmlaih; chaanlaahn

flamboyant SV: chaanlaahnge; yìhmlaihge

flannel N: faatlāanyúng ATT: faatlāanyúngge; faatlāanyúng jouh ge

flap FV: ❶ (to tap lightly) paakdá; ❷ (to flutter) piuduhng N: paakgīksèng ✳ **flap-door** PH: heung hahhòige mùhn (M: douh) ✳ **flap-seat** N: jipyí (M: jèung) ✳ **the flap of a pocket** N: doihyím (M: go)

flare VO: ❶ (to flare up) faatpèihhei; faatfó; ❷ (to flash) símgwòng N: ❶ (flare bomb) jiumìhngdáan; ❷ símgwòngdáan (M: go)

flare-up VO: faatfó; faatpèihhei

flaring SV: símgwòngge

flash FV: (of light) sím VO: símgwòng SV: símgwòngge * **a flash in the pan** IE: tàahmfà yátyìhn * **by a flash** A: dahkyìhn; fātyìhn * **flash-bulb** N: símgwōngdāng (M: go) * **flash-lamp** N: símgwōng-dāng (M: go) * **flash-light** N: dihntúng (M: go, jì)

flask N: ❶ chèuhnggéngge jēun; ❷ sìupìhng (M: go)

flasket N: ❶ saige jēun; ❷ saige sìupìhng (M: go)

flat SV: ❶ (even) pìhng (ge); ❷ (of an object) bín(ge) N: pìhnggeyéh; (story) yātchàhng (láu) A: sēutjihkgám PH: lihngdou binpìhng; FV: binpìhng

flat-car N: pìhngbáanchè; PH: pìhngtòihyìhngge wahnfochè (M: ga)

flat-fish N: taatsā (taatsāyú) (M: tìuh)

flat-foot N: bínpìhnggeuk (M: jek)

flat-iron N; tongdáu (M: go)

flat-worm N: bínchùhng (M: tìuh)

flatten FV: jíngpìhng; jíngbín * **flatten out** FV: binpìhng

flatter VO: tokdaaihgeuk; paakmáhpei

flatterer PH: tokdaaihgeuk-ge yàhn; paakmáhpeige yàhn (M: go)

flavor (flavour) N: meih; meihdouh VO: tìuhmeih; gaaumeih

flavoring (flavouring) N: tìuhmeihbán; VO: tìuhmeih

flaw N: ❶ kyuthaahm; ❷ mòuhbehng (M: go) PH: ❶ lìhngdou yáuh hàhchì; ❷ lìhngdou yáuh kyuthaahm

flay VO: mōkpèih; mōk . . . ge pèih

flea N: sāt (M: jek) * **a flea in one's ear** FV/N: ❶ jaakbeih; ❷ fungchi * **skin a fea for its hide** IE: ngoi chòih yùh mihng * **flea market** N: gauhfo síhchèuhng (M: go) * **cat flea** N: māausāt (M: jek) * **dog flea** N: gáusāt (M: jek)

flee FV: ❶ tòuhjáu ❷ tòuhlèih P.W. ❸ (avoid) tòuhbeih; beihhòi ❹ (flee as a refugee) jáunaahn/beihnaahn Patt: ❶ . . . . jáunaahn làih/heui P.W. ❷ . . . . làih/heui (P.W.) beihnaahn

fleet N: ❶ laahmdéui (M: deuih) ❷ syùhndéui, chèdéui fèigèidéui (M: deuih) * **fleet of foot** PH: jáu dāk fèi faai

flesh N: ❶ yuhk ❷ (opp. to spirit) yuhktái * **make a person's flesh creep** PH: lìhng yàhn mòuhgwāt súngyìhn * **one's own flesh and blood** N: gwātyuhk; chànyàhn * **the spirit is willing but the flesh is weak** IE: sàm yáuh yùh yìh lihk bāt jūk

flexible SV: ❶ (of attitude or approach) lìhngwuht ❷ (adaptable) yih sīkying(ge) ❸ (of wire, tube) yih wāt(ge)

flight N: (flying) fèihàhng (M: chi) VO: fèihàhng sìhgaan (flying time) M: (of stairs) gyuht FV: tòuhjáu

flimsy SV: ❶ (of objects) cheuiyeuhk ❷ (of material) bohk PH: hèng yih bohk N: bohkjí (M: jèung)

flinch SV: waisūk FV: teuisūk

fling FV: deng, fihng, dám * **to have a fling** PH: jeuhn chìhng héungsauh; dìnháh * **flung out of the room** PH: chùngchēut gàanfóng

flint N: fósehk (M: gauh)

flip FV: daahn; tàahn * **flip over** fáanjyun

flirt VO: maaihluhng fùngchìhng FV: tiudauh; tiuhhei; lìuh (coll.)

float FV: fàuh; piu; pòuh N: ❶ (for fishing line) fàuhbīu ❷ (vehicle for festival parade) yàuhhàhng fāchè

flock M: kwàhn • yāt ~ jéuk * **flocks and herds** PH: yèuhngkwàhn tùhng ngàuh kwàhn

flog FV: ❶ dá ❷ (with whip) bīn; bìndá

flood N: séuijòi; daaihséui FV: séuijam * **in flood** PH: hùhngséui faahnlaahm * **floodlight** N: faahngwòngdāng (M: jáan, jì, pàaih)

floor N: ❶ deihhá ❷ (wooden) deihbáan (M: faai) M: (storey of a building) láu * **which floor?** PH: géi láu A? * **the third floor** NuM: seiláu

flop FV: tiuduhng N: (failure) cháambaaih

floss N: sīsin; chòusì (M: tiuh) * **dental floss** N: ngàhsin (M: tiuh)

flour N: mihnfán

flourish SV: ❶ (of city) fàahnwìhng; wòhng ❷ (of business) hìnglùhng; wòhng ❸

(of plant) mauhsihng FV: ❶ (wave) yìuhduhng; ❷ fàimóuh

flow FV: làuh * **flow in** D.C: làuh yahp (làih/heui) * **flow out** D.C: làuhchēut (làih/heui)

flower N: fā (M: déu, dó, jì, jaat-bunch) * **flower pot** N: fāpùhn (M: go) * **flower show** N: fājín (M: go)

flu N: làuhhàhngsing gámmouh

fluctuate FV: ❶ binduhng ❷ (price) bōduhng

fluent SV: làuhleih

fluid N: yihktái; làuhjāt

flunk FV: m̀hahpgaak

fluorescent VO: faatchēut yìhnggwōng * **fluorescent lamp** -N: yìhnggwòngdāng; yahtgwòngdāng (M: jáan) * **fluorescent tube** N: gwònggún (M: jì)

fluorine N: fāt

flurry M: jahn * **a flurry of wind** Nu-M-N: yātjahnfūng * **a flurry of rain** Nu-M-N: yātjahn jaauhyúh

flush VO: chùngchisó (tiolet) FV: (face) mihnhùhng

fluster PH: lihng subj gánjèung; lihng yàhn gánjèung SV: lòhngbui; fòngjèung

flute N: sìu (M: jì) * **to play a flute** VO: chèuisìu

flutter FV: pìupìuháh; yūkyūkháh VO: paakyihk (wing) SV: (annoyed) sàmfàahn * **go to the races and have a flutter** PH: heui máhchèuhng dóuháh

fly N: wū yīng (M: jek) FV: fēi * **to fly a kite** VO: fong jíyíu * **time flies** ① IE: gwòngyām chíhjin ② sìhgaan gwodāk hóu faai

flyer, flier N: fèihàhngyùhn (M: go)

foam N: póuh (M: go) VO: héipóuh * **foam rubber** N: faatpóuhgāau (M: faai)

focus N: jiudím (M: go) FV: jáahpjùng * **in focus** VO: deui (jéun) jiu (dím) * **focus one's attention on the problem** PH: jèung jyuyilihk jaahpjùng hái gógo mahntàih seuhngbihn

foliage N: (dī) yihp; (dī) syuhyihp * **foliage plant** N: séungyihp jihkmaht

folk N: ❶ yàhn ❷ (family) gāyàhn * **folk song** N: màhngō (M: sáu, jek, jì) * **folk dance** N: tóufùngmóuh (M: jek) * **folklore** N: màhngàan chyùhnsyut; màhngàan gusih * **country folk** N: hèunghá yàhn

follow FV: ❶ gàn (jyuh) ❷ (understand) mìhngbaahk ❸ (obey) jèunchùhng * **follow that road** PH: gānjyuh (seuhn- jyuh) gótìuh louh hàahng

folly SV: chéun; sòh N: sòhyéh

fond FV: jùngyi; (hóu) hou

food N: sihkmaht; sihkge yéh * **food street** N: sihkgāai (M: tìuh) * **French food** N: Faatgwok chāan (M: chàan) * **Sze chuan food** N: Seichyūn choi (M: chàan)

fool N: sòhgwā; (boy) sòhjái; (girl) sòhnéui; (man) sòhlóu; (woman) sòhpó; (M: go) FV: ngāak VO: wán bahn; wan subj. bahn * **Don't fool me** PH: m̀hóu ngāak ngóh; m̀hóu wán ngóh bahn

foolish SV: sòh; chéun; bahn

foot N: geuk (M: deui; jek) M: chek; yìngchek * **foot ball** N: jūkkàuh * **on foot** FV: hàahng VO: hàhnglouh * **to stand on one's own feet** IE: jihsihk kèihlihk; jihlihk gàngsàn

for CV: ❶ (in stead of) tai ❷ (on behalf of) tùhng; bòng; waih ❸ (with reference to) deui * **for example** MA: peiyùh * **for the sake of** MA: waihjó

forbear FV: yán; yùhngyán RV: yánjyuh * **to forbear one's enemy** VO: yùhngyán dihk yàhn * **to forbear to hit back** PH: yánjyuh m̀ wàahnsáu

forbid FV: gamjí * **forbid- den fruit** N: gamgwó (M: go) * **forbidden area** N: gamkèui (M: go)

force N: ❶ lihk ❷ (power) sailihk FV: kéuhngbīk; míhnkéuhng * **airforce** N: hùnggwàn * **policeforce** N: gíngdéui

forceps N: kím (M: go)

ford N: chíntāan (M: go)

fore ATT: chìhnbihn N: chìhnbouh * **to come to the fore** VO: chēutfùngtàuh PH: yéh yàhn jyu muhk

forbode N: yuhsiuh; yuhgám (M: go)

forecast FV/N: yuhchāak; yuhgou (M: go)

forefather N: jóusìn; jóujùng

forefinger N: sihkjí (M: jek)

forefront PW: jeuichìhnsin; jeuichìhnfòng

foreground N: chìhngíng (M: go)

forehead N: ngaahktàuh (M: go)

foreign ATT: ngoihgwok * **foregin student** N: ngoihgwok hohksàang (M: go) * **foreign policy** N: deuingoih jingchaak; ngoihgāau jingchaak

foreman N: gùngtáu; fōmán (M: go)

foremost ATT: jeuisìn; sáuyiu; jeuijuhngyiu

forensic ATT: faattìhng * **forensic ability** PH: (hái faattìhng) bihnleuhnge chòihnàhng * **forensic medicine** N: faatyīhohk

foreordain FV: jyudihng

foresee FV: yuhjī

foreshadow N: yuhsiuh (M: go)

foresight N: yúhngin IE: sìn gin jì mìhng

forest N: sàmlàhm (M: go)

forestry N: sàmlàhmhohk

foretaste FV: yuhsìn sèuhngsi * **a foretaste of suffering and enjoyment** PH: yuhsìn sèuhngsi dou fú yúh lohk

foretell FV: yuhyìhn

forethought RV: yuhsìnséunggwo; yuhsìnséunghàh

foretoken N: yuhsiuh (M: go)

forever A: wìhngyúhn

foreword N: jéui; yáhnyìhn (M: pìn)

forfeit FV: ❶ (property, things) muhtsàu ❷ (life, health) sātheui; songsāt

forge N: (furnance) yùhngtitlòuh (M: go) FV: (document, signature) gámouh VO: dátit * **forgery** N: gáyéh * **to forge three shoes for the horse** PH: bòng jek máh dájó sàamjek titjéung

forget FV: m̀gekdāk, mòhnggei

forgive FV: ❶ yùhnleuhng; fùnsyu ❷ (religions) semíhn * **forgive a sin** VO: sejeuih

forgiving SV: fùndaaih; daaihleuhng

forgo FV: fonghei

fork N: chā (M: jek)

forlorn SV: ❶ hólìhn ❷ (alone) gūlìnglíng ❸ (hopeless) jyuhtmohng

form N: ❶ (shape) yéung ❷ (document) bíu ❸ (class) bāan ❹ (style) gaaksīk; yìhngsīk FV: (organize) jóujīk RVE: FV. sìhng * **form good habits** PH: yéuhngsìhng hóuge jaahpgwaan * **form a family** PH: jóusìhng (jóujīk) yātgo gātìhng * **water form ice** PH: séui gitsìhng bìng * **form three** N: jùngsàam

formal ATT: jingsīk * **formal dress** N: láihfuhk (M: gihn, tou) * **formal party** N: lùhngjuhngge yinwuih (M: go) * **don't be so formal** PH: m̀hóu gam haakhei

formalism N: yìhngsīk-jyúyih (M: go)

formality N: ❶ (ceremony) láihjit; yihsīk (M: go) ❷ (procedure) sáujuhk (M: go)

formation N/RV: ❶ (committee) kausìhng; jóusìhng ❷ (character, idea) yìhngsìhng N/FV: (troops) pàaihlìht

former MA: yíhchìhn PH: (opp. of latter) chìhnjé; chìhnbihn gógo

formidable SV: ❶ (appearance) hópa; dākyàhngèng ❷ (task) gàannàahn ❸ (enemy, debt) nàahngáau ❹ (person) wàahnkèuhng; wàahngu

formula N: ❶ (in math.) gùngsīk (M: go) ❷ (in chem.) fòngchìhngsīk (M: go) ❸ (recipe) jaifaat (M: go)

formulate PH: ❶ yuhng gùngsīk làih bíusih ❷ hóuyáuh haihtúnggám bíusih; hóumìhngkok gám bíusih

forsake FV: ❶ (wife, girlfriend) pàauhei ❷ (wife, child) wàihhei ❸ (bad habits) gói; góichèuih

forswear FV: (smoking, drinking) gaai

fort N: paautòih; bóuléuih (M: go, joh)

for'te A: sìhnchèuhng; jeuilēk N: dahk chèuhng

forth A: heungchìhn * and so forth PH: dángdáng * from that day forth TW: yàuh gó yaht héi * to walk back and forth PH: hàahnglàih hàahngheui

forthright SV/A: táan-baahk; sēutjihk

fortieth Nu: daihseisahp * one fortieth Nu: seisahp-fahn jìyāt

fortification N: bóuléuih; diùbóu (M: go, joh) VO: jūk-bóuléuih; jūksìhngbóu

fortify FV: (courage, confidence) gàkeuhng (town, castle) PH: gàkeuhng fòhngwaih

fortitude SV: gòngngaih; yáuh ngaihlihk IE: bātwāt-bātlàauh

fortnight TW: léuhnggo láihbaai; léuhnggo sìngkèih * to be published fortnightly PH: gaakgo láihbaai chēut (báan)

fortress N: bóuléuih; paautòih (M: go, joh)

fortuitous A: ngáuhyìhn

fortunate SV: hóuchói; hóuwahn

fortune N: ❶ (fate) mìhng-wahn (M: go) ❷ (wealth) chòihcháan (M: bāt) * good fortune SV: hóuwahn * fortune teller N: syunmehnglóu (M: go)

forty Nu: seisahp

forum N: ❶ (place) gwóng-chèuhng (M: go) ❷ (public discussion) tóuleuhnwúi; johtàahmwúi; leuhntàahn (M: go)

forward A: heungchìhn N: (in football) chìhnfùng FV: ❶ (help) hipjoh; (plan) chūkjeun ❷ (pass on) jyún * come forward PH: hàahnglàih

chìhnbihn; hàahnchēutlàih! *
look forward to A/FV: paanmohng * **from this time forward** TW: chùhng chí jì hauh

fossil N: fasehk (M: gauh)

foster FV: ❶ (adopt) sàuyéuhng ❷ (raise) yéuhngyuhk
* **foster daughter** N:
yéuhngnéui (M: go) * **foster
father** N: yéuhngfuh (M: go)

foul SV: ❶ (smelly) chau ❷
(dirty) wūjōu * **foul play** VO:
(sport) faahn kwài FV: (crime)
ngamsaat

found FV: ❶ (establish)
chonglahp; chongbaahn ❷
(cast) jyu RV: wándóu

foundation N: ❶ (base)
deihgèi (M: go) ❷ (fund) gèigàm
(M: bāt) gèigàmwúi (M: go) ❸
(basis) gèichó; gàngèi * **foundation stone** N: gèisehk (M:
gauh) * **those rumours have
no foundation** PH: gódī
yìuhyìhn hòuh mòuh gàngeui

founder N: chongbaahnyàhn
(M: go)

foundling N: heiyìng (M: go)
* **foundling hospital** N:
yuhkyìngtóng (M: gàan)

foundry N: jyujouhchóng
(M: gàan) * **iron foundry** N:
jyutitchóng (M: gàan)

fountain N: ❶ (spring)
chyùhn; panchyùhn (M: go) ❷
(man-made) panséuichìh (M: go)
* **fountain pen** N:
mahkséuibāt (M: jì)

four Nu: sei

fourteen Nu: sahpsei

fowl N: fèikàhm; jeukníuh

fox N: wùhléi (M: jek)

fraction N: ❶ (part)
bouhfahn ❷ (for maths)
fahnsou

fracture RV: jíngtyúhn;
jíngseui N: tyúhnháu (M: go)

fragile SV: ❶ cheui; yìhseui
❷ (for health) hèuiyeuhk

fragment N: ❶ (for pottery)
seuipín (M: faai) ❷ (for conversation) bouhfahn; pindyuhn (M:
go)

fragmentary SV: lìhng-
lìhngseuiseui; m̀yùhnjíng

fragrance N: hèungmeih
(M: jahm)

fragrant SV: hèung

frail SV: cheuiyeuhk; dàan-
bohk

frame N: gá; kwàang (M: go)
FV: (trap) hahm hoih * **picture frame** ① (photo) séunggá
② gengá; gengkwàang; ③ (painting) wákwàang (M: go)

franc N: faatlòhng

franchise N ❶ (commercial)
jyùnleihkyùhn (M: go) ❷ (electoral) syúngéuikyùhn; tàuhpiukyùhn

frank SV/A: táanbaahk

frantic FV: faatdìn; faatkòhng

fraternal SV: yàuhngoi Adv.
PH: hóuchíh hìngdaih gám *
fraternal love IE: hìngdaih-
jìngoi; sáujùkjìchìhng *
fraternity N: (club) hìngdaih-
wúi (M: go)

fraud N: ❶ (person) pinjí (M:
go) ❷ (deception) pinguhk,
gwáigai (M: go)

fraught FV: chùngmúhn

fray N: (battle) daujàng (M: chèuhng) RV: mòhlaahn ✳ to fray a sleeve jauhháu mòhlaahnjó

freak N: gwaaimaht (M: go) SV: kèiyìhng

freckle N: mahksí; jeuk bàan (M: nāp)

free SV: ❶ jihyàuh ❷ (leisure) dākhàahn ✳ free way N: gòuchūk gùnglouh (M: tìuh) ✳ free port N: jihyàuh góng (M: go) ✳ free of charge VO: míhnfai ✳ to set free FV: sīkfong

freedom N: jihyàuh ✳ freedom of speech N: yìhnleuhn jihyàuh ✳ freedom of religion N: jùnggaau jihyàuh

freeze VO: gitbīng ✳ frozen chicken N: syutgāi; dunggāi (M: jek) ✳ freezing PH: hóu dung ✳ freezing point N: bīngdím

freezer N: ❶ bīnggaak (M: go) ❷ daaihbīngsèung (M: go) ❸ (refrigerator) syutgwaih (M: go)

freight N: ❶ (goods) fo, fomaht ❷ (fee) wahnfai (M: bāt)

French N/PW: Faatgwok N: ❶ (people) Faatgwokyàhn ❷ (Language) Faatgwokwá; Faatmàhn (M: geui)

frenzied SV: fùngkwòhng

frequent A: sìhsìh; jàusìh ✳ frequency N: pàhnléut (radio)

fresco N: bīkwá (M: fūk)

fresh SV: ❶ sànsìn ❷ (opp. of

tired) jìngsàhn ✳ fresh water N: táahmséui ✳ fresh man PH: daaihyātge hohksàang (M: go)

fricative ATT: mòhchaat N: mòhchaatyām

friction N: ❶ mòhchaat ❷ mòhchaatlihk; jólihk ❸ (conflict) chùngdaht

Friday TW: Láihbaaingh; Sìngkèihngh

friend N: pàhngyáuh (M: go) ✳ friendly SV: hóusèungyúh; yáuhsìhn PH: hóuhhóuyàhn

fridge N: syutgwaih (M: go)

frighten FV: ❶ haak ❷ (be frightened) gèng

frigid PH: (cold) hóudung SV: (attitude) láahngdaahm; láahng

frill N: kwánbīn; kwánbín (M: tìuh) VO: kwanbīn; kwánfābīn

fringe N: ❶ séuih (M: tìuh) ❷ (hairstyle) làuhhói

fro A: heunghauh ✳ walking to and fro PH: hàahnglàih-hàahngheui

frog N: tìhngāi (edible); chìngwā; gaapná (inedible) (M: jek) ✳ frogman N: wāyàhn (M: go)

frolic FV: wáan N: fùnlohkge jeuihwuih (M: go)

from CV: hái; yàuh ✳ from the beginning to the end PH: yàuh tàuh dou méih ✳ PW₁ is very far from PW₂ Patt: PW₁ lèih PW₂ hóu yúhn

front PW: chìhnbihn ✳ front door N: chìhnmún (M: douh) ✳ front page NuM:

daihyāt báan * in front of .
. . Patt: hái . . . chìhnbihn

frontier N: bīngíng; bīngaai;
bīngèung * **frontier spirit** N:
tokfòng jìngsàhn (M: go)

frost N: sèung * **frostbite**
N: dungchòng (M: go) * **a
frosted cake** PH: pòujó tòhngsèungge béng

frosty SV: ❶ (weather)
hòhnláahng ❷ (attitude)
láahngdaahm PH: hóudung

froth N: póuh (M: go) VO:
héipóuh

frown VO: jauhéi mèihtàuh

frozen VO: gitjóbìng *
frozen river PH: gitjóbìngge
hòh (M: tìuh) * **frozen assets**
VO/PH: dunggit jìcháan

frozen food N: láahngchòhng (syutchòhng) sihkmaht

frugal SV: hàan; hàangihm
* **to live in frugality** PH:
sàngwuht hóu hàangihm

fruit N: sàanggwó (M: go) VO:
gitgwó * **fruit juice** N: gwójāp

frustrate FV: (destroy)
powaaih SV: (emotion) máng;
mángjáng; SV/VO: gūkhei *
to frustrate an enemy's plan
PH: powaaih dihkyàhnge
gaiwaahk

frustration N: ❶ chojit (M:
go) ❷ (failure) sātbaaih ❸ (feeling) sauhchogám (M: júng)

fry FV: ❶ jìn ❷ (sauté) cháau
* **fried egg** N: jìndáan;
hòhbāaudáan (M: go) * **fried
rice** N: cháaufaahn

fudge N: (sweet) náaihyàuh-
jyūgūlīksùngbéng (M: gihn)

VO: (nonsense) lyuhnngāpyéh

fuel N: yìhnlíu * **to add fuel
to the flames** IE: fó seuhng gà
yàuh

fugitive N: ❶ tòuhmòhngjé;
tòuhmòhngge yàhn (M: go) ❷
(criminal) tòuhfáan (M: go) ❸
(refugee) naahnmàhn (M: go)

fulfil FV: ❶ yingyìhm (pro-
phesy) ❷ múhnjūk (expectation)
❸ jeuhn; yùhnsìhng (duty) ❹
sahtchín (promise)

full SV/FV: ❶ múhn ❷ (opp.
hungry) báau RVE: FV. múhn *
fullhouse VO: múhnjoh *
full-time teacher N:
jyùnyahm gaausì (M: go)

fumble Adj. PH: lyuhn mó;
lyuhn chaau RV: (of sports) jip
m̀dóu ~ *go bō (ball)*

fume N: ❶ yìn ❷ (smell)
yìnmeih (M: jahm) VO: chēutyìn
FV: (angry) nàu; faatnàu

fumigate FV: yìnfàn PH:
yuhng yìnfànfaat làih sìuduhk
(sterilize)

fun N: lohkcheui SV: hóu-
wáan •*ngóhdeih hóu ~* * **to
make fun of** FV: ① nánfa ②
wánbahn Patt: ① wán .PN.
bahn ② tùhng PN: hòiwàahnsiu

function N: ❶ jokyuhng;
gùngnàhng (M: go) ❷ (social)
dínláih; sihng wuih (M: go) ❸
(duty) jīkkyùhn; jīkjaak (M: go)

fund N: gèigàm (M: bāt) * **to
hold a bazaar to raise funds**
PH: hòi maaihmahtwúi
chàuhfún

fundamental ATT: gèibún;
jyúyiu N: ❶ gèibún yùhnléih
(principle) ❷ gèibún faatjāk
(rule)

funeral N: sòngláih; jongláih (M: go) VO: chēutban

fungus N: ❶ (general) kwán; kwánleuih ❷ (edible) wàhnyíh; muhkyíh ✳ **snow fungus** N: syutyíh

funk FV: gèng SV: húngbou N: (coward) nohfù (M: go)

funnel N: ❶ lauhdáu ❷ (for train, ship) yìntùng FV: jaahpjùng

funny SV: hóusiu

fur N: péi ✳ **fur coat** N: mòuhlāu; péi (M: gihn)

furious SV: fógwán Adv. PH: hóunàu; fèisèuhng nàu; nàudāk hóugányiu ✳ **a furious storm** IE: kwòhng fùng bouh yúh

furlough VO: yàuga

furnace N: ~~yèhnglòuh~~; fólòuh (M: go)

furnish FV: ❶ (supply) gùngkāp ❷ (equip) bouji N: ❶ chitbeih ·gàanngūk yáuhsaai ~ ❷ (furniture) gāsī

furniture N: gāsī (M: tou, gihn)

furrow N: nàihkàu; kwàih (lit.) ❷ gàangdeih (M: faai, fūk)

further Adj. PH: ❶ (far) yúhndī ❷ (more) dòdī ✳ **for further details** PH: yáuhgwàan chèuhngchìhng ✳ **further notice** PH: lihnghàhng tùngjì

furthermore A: yìhché; juhngyáuh

furthest Adj. PH: jeuiyúhn

fury PH: (angry) hóunàu SV: (fierce) máahngliht

fuse FV: yùhng; yùhngfa; yùhnghahp N: ❶ (electric) fiusí (translit); bóuhímsī (M: tiùh) ❷ (explosive) yáhngún; douhfógún; douhfósin (M: tiùh)

fuselage N: gèisàn (M: go)

fusible SV: yihyùhng

fusion FV: ❶ lyùhnhahp; githahp ❷ (chemical) yùhnghahp; yùhnggáai N: githahp ✳ **a fusion of interests** PH: leihyīkge githahp

fuss FV: fàahn ✳ **don't fuss over me** PH: m̀hóu fàahn ngóh IE: daaih gèng síu gwaai; síu tàih daaih jouh

fussy SV: ❶ (choosy) yìmjìm; dòsìh ❷ (weird) gúlihngjinggwaai

futile SV: móuhyuhng; mòuhwaih; sàaihei

futility SV: móuhyuhng; mòuhwaih; sàaihei PH: mòuhwaihge yéh; móuhgitgwóge sih

future TW: jèunglòih N: (prospect) chìhntòuh (M: go) ✳ **furtures** N: kèihfo

futurology N: meihlòihhohk

fuzz N: mòuh; yúngmòuh

G

gab FV: ngāp FV/SV: (talkative) jìjìjàjà * **have the gift of the gab** PH: háuchòih hóuhóu

gaff N: ❶ (fork) yùhchà (M: jì) ❷ (hook) yùhngàu (M: go)

gag VO: ❶ (deprive subj. of speech) kìhmjai yìhnleuhn; gamjí yìhnleuhn ❷ (of an actor) baautóuh N: ❶ sākháumaht ❷ (used by dentist) jèunghàuhei (M: go)

gage N: dáingaatbán (M: gihn)

gaiety SV: ❶ hòisàm; faai-lohk ❷ (gorgeous) wàhlaih; yìhmlaih PH: fùnlohkge heifàn

faily PH: hóu hòisàm gám

gain RV: (obtain) dākdóu FV: (reach) doudaaht; dáidaaht * **no pain, no gain** PH: m̀sànfú jauh móuh sàuwohk IE: hek dāk fú jùng fú; fòng wàih yàhn seuhng yàhn

gainsay FV: ❶ (oppose) fáandeui ❷ (deny) fáuyìhng

gait N: bouhfaat (M: go)

gala SV: hòisàm; faailohk N: ❶ (festival) jityaht (M: go) ❷ (party) sihngwuih (M: go)

galaxy N: ngàhnhòh (M: tìuh); ngàhnhòhhaih (M: go)

gale SV: daaihfùng N: kòhngfùng (M: jahm, jahn)

gall N: dáam (M: go) * **have the gall to do that** PH: (m̀jicháu) juhnggaudáam (gám) jouh

gallery N: ❶ jáulóhng (M: go, tìuh) ❷ (for theatre) làuhjoh * **art gallery** N: méihseuhtgún; wálòhng (M: go)

galley N: daaihyìhngge wàsyùhn (M: jek, sáu)

gallon M: gāléun

gallop SV: faai; faaicheui FV: (for horse) fèipáau * **to gallop through one's work** PH: hóu faai gám jèungdī yéh jouhyùhn

gallows N: ❶ (hanged) gáauyìhng ❷ (frame) gáauyìhnggá

gallstone N: dáamsehk (M: gauh, nāp)

galop N: ❶ (dance) faaibouh-yùhnmóuh (M: jek) ❷ (melody) faaibouh yùhnmóuhkūk (M: sáu, jì)

galore SV: fùngfu PH: hóudò

gamble VO: dóuchín FV: dóubok * **gambling house** N: dóugún; dóuchèuhng (M: go)

gambler N: dóutòuh (M: go)

gambol FV: tiu; tiutiuháh

game N: ❶ yàuhhei (M: go) ❷ (scheme) gwáigai; gaimàuh (M: go) · *jìngjih ~* ❸ (hunted animals or birds) lihpmaht M: ❶ (tennis . . .) chèuhng · *dá yāt ~ móhngkàuh* ❷ (chess . . .) pòu · *jūk yāt ~ kéi* * Olympic games N: Ngou (Ou)-wahnwúi (M: go) * **game over** PH: wáanyùhn (la)

gammon N: fànjyūtéui; fàntéui (M: jek, gauh, faai)

gandor N: ❶ ngòhgūng (M: jek) ❷ (fool) sòhgwā; chéunchòih (M: go)

gang M: ❶ bàan; kwàhn · *yāt ~ gùngyàhn jínggán louh* ❷ dóng; bòng * **triad gang** N: hākbòng * **14K triad gang** N: 14K dóng

gangrene VO: sàang jèuichùhng; sàangchùhng

gangster N: dáaitòuh; féi-tòuh (M: go)

gap N: ❶ (law) lauhduhng (M: go) ❷ (wall) la (M: tiuh) ❸ (fence) lūng (M: go) ✳ **generation gap** N: doihkàu

gape RV: (hole) lithòi PH: maakdaaihháu mohngjyuh

garage N: chèfòhng (M: go)

garb FV: jeuk; dábaan ✳ **to be elegantly garbed** PH: jeuk (dábaan) dāk hóu daaihfòng N: dábaan; jòngchūk (M: go)

garbage N: laahpsaap ✳ **garbage can** N: laahpsaap túng (M: go)

garden N: fāyún (M: go) ✳ **gardening** N: yùhnngaih

gardener N: fāwòhng (M: go)

garland N: fāwàahn (M: go)

garlic N: syuntàuh (M: go, nāp)

garment N: sāam; yīfuhk (lit) ✳ **garment factory** N: jaiyīchóng (M: gàan)

garnish FV: jòngsīk N: jòngsīkbán

garrison FV: jyusáu VO: jyugwān VO: gíngwaihbouhdéui (M: deuih)

gas N: mùihhei ✳ **gas station** N: dihnyàuh jaahm (M: go) ✳ **gas stove** N: mùihheilòuh (M: joh, go) ✳ **to gas up** VO: yahpyáu; gàyáu

gash N: sèunghàu (M: go)

gasify FV: heifa

gasket N: jinhyūn (M: go)

gasoline N: dihnyàuh

gasometer N: heileuhnggai (M: jì)

gasp VO: chyúnhei ✳ **to the last gasp** PH: dou séi gójahn

gassy Adj. PH: hóudò hei (tái) SV: kwàjèung; kwàdaaih

gastric N: waih; waihbouh ✳ **gastric juice** N: waihyihk ✳ **gastric ulcer** N: waih kúiyèuhng

gastritis N: waihyihm

gate N: ❶ daaihmùhn (M: douh) ❷ (entrace) daaihmùhn-háu (M: go)

gather FV: ❶ (people) jaahp-hahp; jeuihjaahp ❷ (flower, fruit) jaahk RV: jaahpmàaih ✳ **to gather things** PH: jèung dī yéh jaahpmàaih (kéuih) VO: (for skirt) dájaap ✳ **to gather oneself up** PH: janjok héilàih

gaudy SV: ❶ (flashy) chàahngngáan ❷ (vulgar) juhk; juhkhei Adj. PH: lengdāklàih hóu juhk

gauge FV: ❶ lèuhng; dohk ❷ (estimate) gúgai N: chāak-lèuhnghei; chāaklèuhngyìhhei (M: go)

gawk N: sòhlóu; chéunchòih; bahndáan (M: go)

gay SV: hòisàm; faailohk; faaiwuht N: (homosexual) gēilóu (tr.); tùhngsinglyúhnjé (M: go)

gaze RV: táijyuh; táisaht; mohngsaht

gazebo N: lèuhngtíng (M: go)

gazette N: hinbou (M: fahn, jèung) FV: gùngbou; syùnbou

gear N: chílèuhn (M: go) * to put in gear VO: yahpbō * second gear N: yihbō * gearshift N: bōgwan (M: jì)

geese N: ngó (M: jek)

gelatine N: ❶ (jelly) jēléi ❷ gàau; gàaujāt

gem N: bóusehk (M: gauh, nāp, faai)

gender N: sing * masculine gender N: yèuhngsing * feminine gender N: yàmsing * neuter gender N: jùngsing

gene N: gèiyàn; wàihchyùhn-yànjí (M: go)

genealogy N: gàpóu; jùngpóu (M: go) * genealogy of a clan N: juhkpóu (M: go)

general SV: póutùng; pìhngsèuhng ATT: yātbùn * generally speaking PH: yātbùnlàihgóng N: jèunggwān (M: go) * general manager N: júng gìngléih (M: go) * general meeting N: daaihwúi (M: go)

generality N: póupìnsing; koikwutsing

generalization IE: yāt koi yìh leuhn

generalize FV: gwàinaahp; koikwut; junghahp VO: hah gitléun; gwàinaahpchēut gitléun PH: koikwutlàihgóng; yātbùnsing gámgóng

generate FV: cháansàng RV: jouhsìhng; yìhngsìhng * hatred generated by racial differences PH: yàuh júngjuhk chàbiht só cháansàngge

sàuhhahn * to generate electricity from water power PH: yàuh séuilihk faatdihn

generation V: saidoih (M: go) M: doih

generator N: faatdihngèi (M: ga)

generic ATT: póutùng; yātbùn N/M: leuih • māau tùhng gáu mtùhng ~

generous SV: ❶ (noble) daaihleuhng ❷ (open-handed) daaihfòng; hóngkoi; futlóu

Genesis N: Chongsaigei

genetic ATT: wàihchyùhn (ge) * genetic code N: wàihchyùhn mahtmáh (M: go)

genetics N: wàihchyùhn-hohk

genial SV: wòhngói; wànwòh

genius N: tìnchòih (M: go)

genocide PH: júngjuhkmihtjyuht

genteel SV: yàungáh; yáuh láihmaauh; yáuhgaauyéuhng

gentle SV: ❶ sìmàhn ❷ (tender) wànyàuh

gentleman N: sìnsaang; sànsí (lit.) (M: go, wái)

gentlewoman N: ❶ néuihsih; suhknéuih (lit) ❷ (married) gwaifúh (lit.)

gently A: hehnghēng; maahnmáan PH: hóu sìmàhn gám

genuine SV: jàn; jànjing

geographer N: deihléihhohkgā (M: go, wái)

geography N: deihléih

geologist N: deihjàthohkgā (M: go, wái)

geology N: deihjàthohk

geometry N: géihòh

geophysics N: deihkàuh-mahtléihhohk

geriatrics N: lóuhyàhn-behnghohk; lóuhyàhnbehngfō

germ N: ❶ kwán; saikwán; behngkwán ❷ (microbe); mèih-sāngmaht ✳ **germ carrier** N: daaikwánjé (M: go) ✳ **germ cell** N: sàngjihksaibāau (M: go)

German PW/N: Dākgwok N: ❶ (people) Dākgwokyàhn (M: go) ❷ (language) Dākgwok-wá; Dākmàhn (M: geui)

germane SV: tipchit; hàap-dong

germanic ATT: Dākgwok; Yahtyíhmaahn

germicide N: saatkwánjài

gerund N: duhngmìhngchìh (M: go)

Gestapo N: ❶ Koisaitaaibóu (translit) ❷ Naahpséuih/Dāk-gwokge beimaht gíngchaat

gestation VO: wàaihyahn N: (period) wàaihyahnkèih FV: (for plan, idea) wàhnyeuhng

gesture N: ❶ (hand) sáusai (M: go) ❷ (face) bíuchìhng (M: go)

get FV: ❶ (fetch) ló ❷ (understand) mìhngbaahk RV: ❶ (obtain) dākdóu ❷ (receive) sàudóu ✳ **get on (transportation)** VO: séuhngchè ✳ **get off** VO: lohkchè ✳ **get sick** FV/VO:

behng (jó); yáuhbehng ✳ **get up** VO: héisàn ✳ **get along well** SV: kìngdākm̀aaih; gaap PH: sèungchyúhdāk hóuhóu

ghastly SV: ❶ (terrible) hópa; dākyàhngèng; húngbou ❷ (pale) chōngbaahk

ghetto N: pàhnmàhngwaht (M: go)

ghost N: gwái (M: jek)

giant N: geuihyàhn (M: go) SV: geuihdaaih

giddy SV: ❶ tàuhwàhn ❷ (not serious) hingtiu PH: wàhntòhtòh ✳ **a giddy young girl** PH: yātgo hingtiuge siunéuih

gift N: ❶ (present) láihmaht (M: fahn, gihn) ❷ (talent) tìn-chòih; tìnfu ✳ **a person of many gifts** PH: yātgo dò-chòih dò ngaih ge yàhn

gig N: ❶ (carriage) léuhng-léun (dàan) máhchè (M: ga) ❷ (boat) téhngjái (M: jek, ga) ❸ (fork) yùhchàh (M: jì)

gigantic SV: geuihdaaih PH: hóudaaih ✳ **gigantic appetite** PH: sihkleuhng hóudaaih

giggle FV: siu; gītgītsiu

gild VO: douhgām ✳ **a gild-ed watch** PH: douhgāmge bīu ✳ **to gild the lily** IE: waahk sèh tìm jūk

gill N: ❶ sòi (M: go)

gilt VO: douhgàm ✳ **a gilt-edged invitation card** PH: tongjógàmbīnge chéngtíp (M: go, jèung)

gin N: ❶ douh chùhng jí jáu; jìn jáu (translit) (M: jèun, jì) ❷ (machine) jaat mìhn gèi (M: ga, fu) VO: jaat mìhn

ginger N: ❶ gèung (M: gauh, faai, pin) ❷ (good spirits) wuhtlihk Patt: lihng . . . yáuh sàanghei; lihng . . . sàangduhng wuhtput ✳ **to ginger up a performance** PH: lihng bíuyín sàangduhng wuhtput

gingko, ginkgo N: baahkgwó (M: nāp)

ginseng N: yàhnsàm (M: jì)

gipsy, gypsy N: gātbūkchoiyàhn (M: go) ATT: gātbūkchoi

gird RV: bóngjyuh; jaatjyuh FV: ❶ (put on) puidaai ❷ (put round) wàihyíu

girdle N: yìudáai (M: tìuh)

girl N: ❶ (generally) néuihjái; síujé; gūnèuhng ❷ (daughter) néui (M: go) ✳ **girl school** N: néuihhaauh (M: gàan)

gist N: yiudím; juhngdím

give FV: béi ✳ **give back** RV: béifàan ✳ **give birth to** FV: sàang ✳ **give in** VO: yeuhngbouh ✳ **give up** FV: fonghei; gaai (vices) ~ jáu; ~ yìn; ~ dóu

giver N: ❶ béi yéh ge yàhn; sìyúh ge yàhn (M: go)

gizzard N: sàlòhng (M: go)

glacial SV: ❶ (cold) bìngdung; bìngláahng ❷ (of attitude) láahngdaahm ✳ **a glacial period** N: bìnghòhkèih (M: go)

glaciate VO: gitbìng; gitsìhngbìng FV: dunggit

glacier N: bìnghòh; bìng-

chyùn (M: tìuh)

glad SV: fùnhéi; hòisàm A: lohkyì ✳ **glad to meet you!** IE: hahng wuih! hanhng wuih!

glair N: dáanbáak; dáanbaahk VO: chàh dáanbáak

glamour N: muih/meihlihk; mōlihk SV: màih yàhn

glance RV: laapháh (hóufaaigám) táiháh PH: táiyāttái; mohngyātmohng ✳ **to take a glance at the newspaper** PH: laapháh jèung boují

gland N: sin ✳ **lymphatic gland** N: làhmbāsin ✳ **thyroid gland** N: gaapjohngsin

glare FV: sím VO: (a look) lūk daaih/héi sèung ngáahn ✳ **glaring neon sign** PH: símsímháhge gwònggún jiupàaih

glass N: ❶ bōlēi (M: faai) ❷ (drinking glass) bōlēibūi (M: jek) ✳ **glass house** N: wànsāt (M: gàan, go) ✳ **glass fibre** N: bōlēi chìmwàih ✳ **glasses** N: ngáahngéng (M: fu)

glaze VO: ❶ jòng bōlēi · *hái chēungsyu* ~ ❷ séuhngyáu; séuhngsīk ✳ **to glaze pottery** PH: tùhngdī tòuhchìhhei séuhngyáu N: yáu

gleam FV: sím; símsímháh N: gwòng; símgwòng ✳ **a gleam of hope** Nu-M-N: yāt sin hèimohng

glib SV: háuchí lìhngleih, yùhnwaaht; yúnjyún

glide FV: waahthàhng; waahtduhng ✳ **glide down** PH: waaht lohk làih/heui

glider N: waahtchèuhnggèi (M: ga)

glimmer N: gwòng; síusíugwòng * a glimmer Nu-M-N: yāt sin gwòng; yāt sī gwòngsin

glimpse RV: táigin; mohngdóu

glint FV: sím FV/ATT: símsímháh * the glint of sunshine PH: símsímháh ge yèuhnggwòng

glitter FV: sím FV/ATT: símsímháh N: gwòng; gwòngmòhng

gloat Adv. PH: ❶ hóu hòisàm/múhnjūk gám mohngjyuh ❷ hahngjòilohkwoh gám táijyuh ~ yàhndeihge bāthahng ❸ (with fixed eyes) ngáahn dihng dihng gám mohngjyuh

global ATT: ❶ kàuhyìhng (ge) ❷ chyùhnkàuhsing(ge) * a global war PH: chyùhnkàuhsingge jinjàng

globe N: deihkàuh (M: go) * desk globe N: deihkàuhyìh (M: go)

gloom SV: ngam; hāak (hāk) ngam N: yàuwāt * to chase her gloom away PH: sìuchèuih kéuihge yàuwāt

glorification N: jaanméih; chìngjaan

glorify FV: jaanméih; jaanyèuhng

glorious SV: ❶ gwòng wìhng ❷ chaanglaahn * glorious victory PH: gwòngwìhngge singleih; yèhng dāk hóu gwòngwìhng * glorious sunshine PH: chaanglaahnge yèuhnggwòng

glory N: gwòngwìhng; wìhngyiuh * glory be to God PH:

gwài wìhngyiuh yù Seuhngdai

gloss N: ❶ (shine) gwòngjaahk ❷ (footnote) jyugáai; jyusīk FV: (hide) yímsīk

glossary ❶ (dictionary) chìhdín (M: bún) ❷ chìhwuihbíu; jihwuih

glossy SV: gwòngwaaht

glove N: sáumaht; sáutou (M: deui, jek)

glow VO: ❶ faatgwòng (brightness) ❷ faatyiht (warmth) * cheeks with the glow of health on them PH: mihnsīk hùhngyeuhn; yùhnggwòngwuhnfaat

glowworm N: yìhngfóchùhng (M: jek)

glucose N: pòuhtòuhtóng

glue N: ❶ (paste) gàau ❷ (liquid) gàauséui FV: chì (jyuh)

glum SV: yàuwāt IE: muhn muhn bāt lohk

glut RV: chùngmúhn; chùngchīk (lit.) Adj. PH: dò gwotàuh; dò dākjaih

glutton SV: waihsihk N: waihsihkgwái; waihsihkmāau (M: go)

glycerine N: gàmyàuh

gnarled SV: ❶ (rough) chòu; chòuhàaih ❷ (twisted) lāklākkākkāk; wāanwāankūkkūk

gnash VO: ngáauhsahtdīngàh * to gnash the teeth IE: ngáauh ngàh chit chí

gnat N: mānyeuih (M: jek)

gnaw FV: ❶ (bite) ngáauh ❷ (torment) jitmòh

go FV: ❶ heui ❷ (leave) jáu ✳ **go by train** PH: chóh fóchè heui ✳ **go in** FV: yahpheui ✳ **go out** FV: chēutheui ✳ **go home** VO: fàanngūkhéi ✳ **go for a walk** PH: chēutheui-hàahngháh ✳ **go on** A: gaijuhk ✳ **go bad** RV: waaihjó; binwaaih ✳ **go out of fashion** VO: gwosih ✳ **go out of one's mind** RV: dìnjó VO: chìjósin

goal N: ❶ (generally) muhkbīu (M: go) • sàngwuhtge ~ ❷ (of a race) jùngdím (M: go) ❸ (of the soccer game) lùhngmùhn (M: go) M: fàn • dākdóu yāt ~ ✳ **win by three goals to one** PH: sàambéiyāt yèhngjó

goat N: sàanyèuhng; yèuhng-mē

gobble Adv. PH: (eat greedily) daaihdaahm daaihdaahm-gám sihk IE: lòhng tàn fú yin N: (sound) gòhkgóksèng

goblet N: gòugeukbūi (M: jek, go)

goblin N: yíugwaai; yíujìng (M: go)

God N: ❶ (generally) Sàhn ❷ (protestant) Seuhngdai ❸ (catholic) Tìnjyú (M: go, wái)

goggle VO: lūkdaaih sèungngáahn N: chìhmséuigeng (M: fu) ✳ **goggle-eyed man** N: dahtngáahn lóu (M: go)

gold N: ❶ gām; wòhng gām ❷ (color) gāmsīk; gām ✳ **gold coin** N: gāmbaih (M: go) ✳ **gold bar** N: gāmtíu (M: tìuh)

golf N: gòuyíhfūkàuh ✳ **golf links** N: gòuyíhfūkàuhchèuhng (M: go) ✳ **to play golf** VO: dá gòuyíhfūkàuh

gondola ❶ (boat) pìhngdái-syùhn (M: jek, ga) ❷ (cable car) diuchōng (M: go)

gong N: lòh (M: go, mihn)

good SV: hóu ✳ **have a good time** PH: wáandāk hóu hòisàm N: hóuchyu; yuhngchyu • yáuh mātyéh ~ nē? ✳ **good for nothing** SV: móuhyuhng; móuhgwáiyuhng ✳ **good will** N: hóuyi ✳ **for good** A: wíhngyúhn ✳ **good for . . .** Patt: deui . . . yáuhyīk ✳ **good at** ① A: jìngtùng • Kéuih ~ yìngmàhn ② PH: hóuhóu • Kéuihge yìngmàhn ~

goody N: tóng; tòhnggwó SV: (hypocrite) gájìnggìng; gádouhhohk

goose N: ngó (M: jek)

gooseflesh PH: mòuhgún-héi; mòuhgúnduhng

gorge N: haahpgūk (M: go) PH: lyuhn sihkyéh; sākbáaugo tóuh ✳ **the Yangtse gorges** N: Chèuhnggòng sàamhaahp

gorgeous SV: hòuhwàh; wàhlaih; leng

gorilla N: sīngsīng; daaih-sīngsīng (M: jek)

gosh IE: Baih la!; baihgāfó la!

gospel N: fūkyām ✳ **to preach the gospel** VO: chyùhn fūkyām

gossip VO: góngsìhfèi; góngwaaihwá SV/N: sìhfèi

gourd N: gwā (M: go) ✳ **bottle gourd** N: wùhlòuhgwā (M: go) wùhlóu ✳ **sponge gourd** N: sìgwā (M: go) ✳ **winter gourd** N: dūnggwā (M: go)

govern FV: ❶ (generally) gún; gúnléih ❷ (for country) túngjih;

jihléih ❸ (for one's temper) yīk-jai; hungjai

government N: ❶ (the governing body) jingfú ❷ (system) jingtái ❸ (ruling) gúnhaht; túngjih * **under the Dutch government** PH: hái Hòhlāan túngjih jihah

governor N: ❶ (generally) túngjihjé (M: go) ❷ (of a colony) júngdūk (M: go) ❸ (of Hong Kong) Góngdūk (M: go) ❹ (of a state) jāujéung (M: go)

gown N: chèuhngkwàhn (M: gihn) * **evening gown** N: máahnláihfuhk (M: gihn) * **nightgown** N: seuihpòuh (M: gihn)

grab RV: jàjyuh; lájyuh FV: (snatch) chéung

grace SV: sìmàhn; gòugwai; yàungáh N: ❶ (of God) yàndín; yànchi ❷ (prayer) jehyàntóugou * **sing grace** VO: cheung jehfaahn gō ·

gracious SV: ❶ (elegant) gòugwai; yàuméih; yàungáh ❷ (kind) wòhngói; chànchit

gradation N: dángkāp; chàhngchi (M: go) VO: fàn-dángkāp; fànchijeuih

grade N: ❶ (generally) dángkāp; dáng ❷ (class) nìhnkāp; nìhnbāan VO: ❶ fànkāp; fàndángkāp ❷ (for test paper) béifàn; dáfànsou * **grade three** N: sàamnìhnkāp

gradient N: ❶ (slope) chèhbō (M: go) ❷ (degree) bōdouh; chèhdouh SV: che

gradual A: jihmjím; juhkjím

graduate VO: bātyihp · jùnghohk ~ N: bātyihpsāng

(M: go) * **graduate school** N: yìhngauyún * **graduate student** N: yìhngausāng

graft VO: jipjì; bokjì FV: (for skin) yìhjihk SV/FV: (corrupt) tāamwū

grain N: gūk; nǵhgūk M: nāp * **a grain of wheat** Nu-M-N: yātnāp mahk

gram, gramme M: hāk, hāak; gùngfàn

grammar N: màhnfaat

grammarian N: yúhfaat-hohkgā (M: go, wái)

grammatical ATT: yúh-faatseuhng; màhnfaatseuhng * **grammatical errors** PH: màhnfaatseuhng ge chongh

gramophone N: làuhsìng-gèi (M: ga, fu) * **gramophone record** N: cheungpín; cheung-díp (M: jek, go)

granary N: gūkchōng; máih-chōng (M: go)

grand SV: ❶ (main) jyúyiu ❷ (splendid) jonglaih; hùhngwáih ❸ (elegant) gòugwai; gòu-seuhng * **grand piano** N: daaihgongkàhm (M: ga) * **grand child** N: syùn (M: go) * **grand father** N: ① (paternal) a yèh; ② (maternal) a gùng * **grand mother** N: ① (paternal) a màh; ② (maternal) a pòh

grandeur SV: jòngyìhm; wàhngwáih

granite N: màhsehk; fāgōng-sehk (M: gauh, faai)

grant FV: ❶ (permit) jéun; pàijéun (application) ❷ (agree) daapying N: ❶ (scholarship) johhohkgām ❷ (aid) bóu-

johgām * **take for granted**
IE: séungdòngyihn

granular ATT/N: nāpjohng
PH: yātnāpnāpgám (ge)

granule M: nāp PH: nāp-
johngge yéh

grape N: pòuhtàihjí (M: nāp-
piece; chàu-bunch) * **grape
wine** N: pòuhtòuhjáu (M: jèun,
jì)

grapefruit N: sàiyáu (M: go)

grapevine N: ❶ (tree) pòuh-
tàihjísyuh ❷ (rumour) yìuhyìhn;
síudouh sìusīk (lit.)

graph N: ❶ (curve) kūksin-
tòuh (M: fūk, jèung, go) ❷ (table)
tòuhbíu; tòuhgáai (M: fūk,
jèung, go)

graphite N: sehkmahk

grapple RV: (seize firmly)
wásaht; jáausaht FV: (struggle
closely) náudá; gaakdau

grasp FV: ❶ (hold) jà ❷
(understand) mìhngbaahk;
líuhgáai ❸ (fig.) bángāak * **to
grasp at an opportunity** PH:
bá ngāak gèi wuih RV: jàjyuh;
jàsaht; jáausaht

grass N: chóu (M: tìuh) *
grass roots N: chóugàngèi-
chàhng

grasshopper N: jamáang
(M: jek)

grassland N: ❶ (wild) chóu
yùhn (M: go, daat, faai) ❷
(pasture) muhkchèuhng (M: go)

grate N: ❶ (iron bar) tit làahn;
titsàan (M: douh) ❷ (window
bar) chēungfā VO: jòngtitlàahn
FV: (rub) pàauh; mòh (seui) RV:
(annoy) gīknàu

grateful FV: gámgīk; gámjeh

grating N: titlàahn; titjì (M:
jì)

gratitude FV: gámjeh; gámgīk N: jehyi * **to show my
gratitude** PH: bíusih ngóhge
jehyi

gratuity N: ❶ (tip) tīpsí ❷
(for retired employee) bouchàuh;
chàuhgām ❸ (for retired soldier)
teuinghgām

grave N: (tomb) fàhnmouh
(M: go) FV: (carve) dìuhhāk,
dìuhhāak SV: jòngyìhm; yìhmsūk; juhngdaaih * **grave
news** PH: juhngdaaihge sànmán * **a grave face** PH:
bíuchìhng yìhmsūk

gravel N: sehkjái (M: gauh,
nāp) VO: pòusehkjái

gravitation N: ❶ maahnyáuhyáhnlihk ❷ (inclination)
kìngheung

gravity N: deih sàmkāplihk;
maahnyáuhyáhnlihk SV: yìhmsūk; jòngyìhm * **centre of
gravity** N: juhngsàm *
specific gravity N: béichúhng
* **Newton's law of gravity**
Ngàuhdēunge deihsàmkāplihk
dihngleuht

gravy N: jāp

graze VO: ❶ sihkchóu ❷
fongngàuh (cattle) fongyèuhng
(sheep) RV: (scrape) gwaatsyún;
gwaatsèung; gwaatchàn

grazier N: muhkyàhn (M: go)
chūkmuhkjé (lit.)

grease N: ❶ (oil) yàuh ❷ (fat)
jìfòng VO: chàhyàuh FV: (bribe)
kúilouh

greasy SV: fèih; fèihneih; yàuhneih

great SV: daaih; wáihdaaih ✻ a great building PH: wáihdaaihge ginjūkmaht Patt: fèisèuhng .SV.; bātjìgéi SV .; .SV. dougihk ✻ that's great! PH: hóu dougihk! ✻ a great deal of, a great many PH: hóu dò

greatness SV: daaih; geuihdaaih; wáihdaaih

greedy SV: tàamsàm ✻ greedy for money SV/VO: tàamchín ✻ greedy for food SV: waihsihk

Greek N: ❶ Hèilihpyàhn (M: go) ❷ Hèilihpwá (M: júng, geui) ATT: Hèilihp ✻ It's Greek to .PN.IE: .PN yātdī dōu m̀ mìhngbaahk

green SV: luhksīk; luhk N: luhksīk ✻ green eyed FV: dougeih ✻ greens N: choi; chèngchoi

greenery N: luhkyihp; luhksīkge syuhmuhk

greenish SV: luhklúkdéi

greenhorn SV/N: sàangsáu (M: go)

greenhouse N: wànsāt (M: go)

greet FV: ❶ (welcome) fùnyìhng; jiufù ❷ (ask after) mahnhauh VO: (say hello to) dá jiufù · Kéuih tùhng ngóh ~

gregarious SV: hahpkwàhn ATT: kwàhngèui PH: jùngyigàaujai

grenade N: sáulàuhdáan (M: go)

grey, gray SV: fùisīk; fùi N: fùisīk

griddle N: ❶ (for baking cakes) chínwohk (M: go) ❷ (for selecting metals) sāi (M: go)

grief SV/N: yàusàuh; tungfú

grievance N: bātmúhn; yùnchìhng VO: soufú

grieve SV: sèungsàm

grievous SV/N: tungfú; bèitung SV: (serious) yìhmjuhng

grill N: ❶ (gridiron) sìuhàaugá ❷ (meat) sìuhàauyuhk; sìuhàausihkbán FV: ❶ sìu; sìuhàau ❷ (severe questioning) hàaumahn

grim SV: yìhmlaih; láahnghuhk; chàahnhuhk ✻ a grim expression PH: láahnghuhkge bíuchìhng

grimace N: gwáilíhm VO: baahngwáilíhm (in jest) PH: náumé faaimihn (in pain); fú màaih háu mihn

grime N: wūjōuyéh; wūgau RV: jíngwūjōu

grin FV: siu; daaihsiu ✻ to grin and bear it IE: yihk lòih seuhn sauh

grind FV: ❶ mòh ❷ (study hard) fúduhk; fúhohk VO: hahfúgùng ✻ to grind something to powder/pieces PH: jèungdīyéh mòhsìhng fán/mòh seui) ✻ to grind away at English studies VO: fúhohk/duhk yìngmàhn

grip RV: jàgán; jàsaht N: (hand luggage) léuihhàhngdói; sáutàihbāau (M: go) FV: ❶

(understand) mìhngbaahk;
líuhgáai ❷ (hold attention)
kāpyáhn

gripe RV: jágán; jàsaht FV:
(control) hungjai; jéungngāak
N: (stomachache) tóuhtung;
chéungtung VO: (complain)
soufú; faatlòuhsòu; faatyun-
yìhn

grisly SV: hópa; hùngngok ✳
a grisly monster PH: hópage
gwaaimaht

gritty VO: (sandy) yáuhsā;
hàhmsā SV: (brave) yúhnggám;
yáuh ngaihlihk

grizzle PH: fùisīkge
tàuhfaat; fùibaahkge tàuhfaat

groan FV: ngàhngngángsèng; ngàaihngáaisèng

grocer N: jaahpfosèung;
sihkbánsèung

grocery N: ❶ (shop) jaahpfo-
póu (M: gàan) ❷ (food) sung;
sihkbán ❸ (things) jaahpfo;
gātìhng yuhngbán

groom N: ❶ (servant in charge
of horses) máhfù (M: go) ❷
(bridegroom) sànlóng; sànlòhnggō (M: go) VO: waimáh;
jihyéuhngmáh FV: ❶ (tidy
oneself) sàusīk ❷ (prepare for)
jéunbeih; tèuigéui

groove N: ❶ (furrow) hàang
(M: tiuh) ❷ (habit) jaahpgwaan;
sèuhngkwài ✳ **get into a
groove** PH: yéuhngsìhng yātjúng jaahpgwaan VO: waat
hàang ✳ **groovy** IE: hóuyéh!
sàileih! miuhgihk!

grope FV: mó; lyuhnmó

gross A: júngguhng; chyùhnbouh N: ❶ júngsou (M: go) ❷
(12 dozen) sahpyìhdā SV:

(rough) chòujuhk ✳ **gross jest**
PH: chòujuhkge siuwá ✳ **in
the gross** PH: júngkwutlàih-
góng; daaihtáilàihgóng

grotesque SV: gúgwaai;
cháugwaai; gwaaidaan

grotto N: ngàahmduhng (M:
go)

grouch VO: faatpèihhei;
faatlòuhsōu N: lòuhsōu; bātmúhn FV/SV: nàu

ground N: ❶ (floor) deihhá
❷ (area) chèuhngdeih ❸ (surface) deihmín ❹ (reason)
léihyàuh • *yíh behng wàih* ~;
gàngeui ❺ (base) gēichó;
gàngèi ❻ (background) dái •
fūkbou baahk dái héi hùhngfā
FV: (of a ship) gokchín ✳
ground floor N: deihhá ✳
cover ground FV: sitkahp ✳
playground N: wahnduhng-
chèuhng (M: go) ✳ **groundless**
PH: hòuhmòuhgàngeui ✳ **hold
one's ground** VO: gìnchìh
lahpchèuhng

group M: kwàhn; bàan; jóu ✳
a group of people Nu-M-N: yāt
bàan yàhn

grow FV: ❶ (develop) jéung;
sàngjéung; sàang; daaih • *Go
sailouh* ~ *dāk hóu faai* ❷ (to
plant) jung ~ *mùihgwai* A:
jihmjím ~ *tìnhāak la!*

growl FV: ngaai; giu; hàaugiu; hòuhgiu N: lùhnglúngsèng

grown SV: sìhngsuhk ATT:
jéungdaaihjó ✳ **a grown man**
Nu-M-N: yātgo sìhngyàhn ✳ **a
full grown horse** Nu-M-N: yāt-
jek jéungdaaihjó ge máh

growth N: ❶ (of city, industry
. . .) faatjín ❷ (of population)
jànggā ❸ (of body, plant) sàngjéung ❹ (of disease) láu (M: go)

grub FV: gwaht; waat * **to grub weeds** VO: gwahthéidīchóu N: ❶ (larva of insect) jèuichùhng ❷ (food) sihkmaht VO: jouhfúgùng * **to grub for a living** PH: jouh fúgùng yìhngsàng

grubby SV: wūjōu; laahttaat VO: sàangchùhng

grudge FV: (envy) dougeih AV: (unwilling to) m̀sédāk N: yunhahn * **to bear a grudge** VO: wàaihhahn; geisàuh

gruesome SV: ❶ (frightful) hópa ❷ (horror) húngbou ❸ (disgust) tóuyim

gruff SV: ❶ (of voice) chòu; sà ❷ (of manner) chòu; chòulóuh

grumble VO: faatlòuhsōu FV: ngàhmngàhm chàhmchàhm; ngìhngī ngòhngòh

grunt FV: (of people) ngàhmngàhm chàhmchàhm; gìhlī gùhlùh FV/N: (of pigs) gùhgúsèng

guarantee FV: dàambóu; bóujing N: ❶ (guarantor) dàam bóuyàhn; bóujingyàhn (M: go) ❷ (written) bóujingsyù ❸ (security) dáingaatbán (M: gihn) * **guarantee to change** FV: bàauwuhn

guarantor N: dàambóuyàhn; bóujingyàhn (M: go)

guaranty N: ❶ dàambóu; bóujing ❷ (written) bóujingsyù ❸ (security) dáingaatbán; bóujingmaht (M: gihn) * **guaranty money** N: bóujinggàm

guard RV: ❶ sáujyuh; hònjyuh * **to guard prisons** PH: hònjyuhdī gāamdán/ faahn yàhn ❷ (protect) bóuwuh; bóuwaih * **to guard his life**

PH: bóuwuh kéuihge sàngmihng N: ❶ (sentry) waihbìng; saaubìng ❷ (of Royal Troops) gamwaihgwān; yuhlàhmgwān ❸ (warden) yuhkjēut; yuhkgíng * **bodyguard** N: bóubīu (M: go) * **on guard** VO: dōngbàan; jihkbàan * **to keep guard** VO: jaahmgòng; fongsaau * **rear guard** N: hauhwaih (M: go) * **advance guard** N: chìhnfūng (M: go) * **to guard against** FV: fòhngbeih; tàihfòhng; yuhfòhng * **guard of honour** N: yìhjeuhngdéui (M: deuih) * **security guard** N: wuhwaihyùhn (M: go)

guardian N: gāamwuhyàhn (M: go)

guerrilla N: yàuhgīkdéui; yàuhgīkdéui deuihyùhn (M: go, deuih — a band of.); * **guerrilla warfare** N: yàuhgīkjin (M: chèuhng)

guess FV: gú; chàai * **guess work** FV/N: tèuichāak FV: dyungú * **guess a riddle** VO: chàaimàihyúh * **guess right** RV: gújung * **guess wrong** RV: gúcho

guest N: haakyàhn; yàhnhaak (M: go, wái) * **guest house** N: bàngún (M: gàan) * **the guest of honour** N: jyúbàn; jyúhaak (M: go)

guidance N: jíyáhn; jídouh; líhngdouh

guide FV: daai; daailíhng; líhngdouh * **guidepost** N: louhpáai (M: go) * **guide book** N: yàuhláahm jínàahm (M: bún) * **tourist guide** N: douhyàuh (M: go)

guild N: hipwúi; tùhngyihp gùngwúi (M: go)

guile SV: gáauwaaht; gàanwaaht N: gwáigai; pinseuht

guise FV: (pretence) gájòng * **under the guise of friendship** PH: gájòng yáuhsihn N: (style of dress) dábaan; jòngchūk * **an old idea in a new guise** IE: sànpìhnggauhjáu

guitar N: gittā (M: go)

gulf N: hóiwāan; wāan (M: go) * **the gulf of Mexico** N: Mahksāigōwāan

gull N: (sea bird) hóingāu (M: jek) PH: (person) yíhjáiyúhnge yàhn; yùhngyi béiyàhn ngāakge yàhn FV: (cheat) ngāak

gullible SV: yíhjáiyúhn Adj. PH: yùhngyi séuhngdong; yùhngyi béiyàhn ngāak

gully N: séuikàu; kàukèuih; kèuih (M: tìuh)

gulp FV: tàn; RV: yámsaai; tànsaai * **to empty a glass at one gulp** PH: yātdaahm yámsaai (bùiyéh)

gum N: ❶ syuhgāau ❷ (of the mouth) ngàhyuhk FV: chì; nìhm; tip * **chewing gum** N: hèunghàugāau (M: tìuh, faai)

gun N: chēung; sáuchēung (M: bá, jì) VO: hòichēung * **machine gun** N: gèigwāanchēung (M: jì) * **air gun** N: heichēung * **to stick to one's guns** VO: gìnchìh lahp-chèuhng, gìnsáu gòngwái

gunboat N: paautéhng; paaulaahm (M: jek, sáu)

gunner N: paaubìng; paausáu; sehgīksáu * **gunnery** N: sehgīkhohk; chēungpaauhohk

gush FV: ❶ yúngchēutlàih; panchēutlàih ❷ (of talking) máahngggóng N: (oil well) panyàuhjéng (M: go)

gust M: jahn * **a gust of wind** Nu-M-N: yātjahnfùng

gut N: ❶ noihjohng; chéung ❷ (courage) yúnhghei; dáamleuhng ❸ (content) noihyúhng

gutter N: ❶ hàangkèuih; kèuih (M: tìuh) ❷ (poor district) pàhnmàhnkèui; pàhnmàhngwaht (M: go)

guttural N: hàuhyàm * **guttural consonants** PH: faatjìh hàuhlùhngge jíyàm * **a guttural language** PH: yātjúng yáuh hóudò hàuhyàmge yúhyìhn

guy N: yàhn (M: go); yáuhjái (slang) (M: go, tìuh) FV: (ridicule) siu; dai

guzzle Adj. PH: ❶ daaihyámdaaihsihk; ❷ máahngyám ~ bējáu ❸ maáhngsihk

gymnasium, gym N: táiyuhkgún (M: gàan) * **gymnastics** FV/N: táiyuhk; táichòu

Gypsy N: ❶ Gātbūkchoiyàhn (M: go) ❷ Gātbūkchoiwá (M: júng, geui)

gyrate FV: jyun; syùhnjyún; tàhmtàhmjyun ATT: yùhnyìhng

H

ha P: hà

habit N: ❶ jaahpgwaan (M: go) ❷ (of mind) sàmgíng ❸ (of body) táijāt ❹ (religious dress) sàunéuisāam (for nuns); wòhséunyépòuh (for monks) (M: gihn) * **fall into bad habits** PH: yéuhngsìhng waaihge jaahpgwaan * **get out of a bad habit** PH: gaaichèuih waaihge jaahpgwaan

habitual A/FV: jaahpgwaanjó; gwaanjó * **a habitual liar** PH: gwaanjó góngdaaihwah

hack FV: ❶ pek; jáam ❷ (cough) kāt; gònkāt ❸ (for rent) chēutjòu * **a hack horse** N: chēutjòuge máh

hades N: deihyuhk; deihfú; yàmgàan (M: go) * **Lord of hades** N: Yìhm Lòh Wòhng (M: go)

hag N: (witch) mòuhpòh; néuihmòuh; móuhyehchā (M: go) FV: jáam

haggard SV: chìuhséuih

haggle FV: (argue) ngaai; ngaau VO: (bargain) góngga

hail FV: fùnfù; gòufù N: bohk VO: lohkbohk * **hail Mary!** PH: maahn fūk Máhleihnga ! * **to hail to taxi** PH: giu dīksí * **to hail from?** PH: hái bīnsyu làih ga?

hair N: ❶ (on the human head) tàuhfaat (M: tìuh) ❷ (on the skin) mòuh (M: tìuh) ❸ (on the plant) yúngmòuh * **not worth a hair** PH: yātgo sīn dōu m̀ jihk * **to lose one's fair** VO: lāt tàuhfaat

hairdresser N: méihyùhngsī; fèifaatlóu (male) (M: go)

hale SV: jong, jonggihn Adv. PH: gaapngáanglàai

half Nu: bun ~ *go pìhnggwó* ~ *go yuht* N: yātbun * **two and a half years** PH: léuhngnìhnbun * **half-boiled egg** N: bun sàangsuhkdáan (M: go, jek) * **half-hearted** SV: (not enthusiastic) láahngdaahm; m̀yihtsàm PH: (not determined) móuh kyutsàm ge * **half price** N: bunga * **half blood** N: wahnhyutyìh; jaahpjúng

hall N: ❶ daaihtòhng (M: go) ❷ (auditorium) láihtòhng (M: go) ❸ (passage) tùngdouh; jáulóng (M: tìuh) * **dining hall** N: faahntòhng (M: go) * **lecture hall** N: yíngóngtēng (M: go) * **hall stand** N: yìmóugá (M: go) * **City Hall** N: Daaihwuihtòhng (M: go) * **a hall of residence** N: daaihhohksūkse (M: gàan)

hallmark N: yan; bīuji (M: go)

hallo P: ❶ (for answering the phone) wái; wéi ❷ (to attract attention) wai; wei

hallucination N: waahngok; chogok (M: júng, go)

halo N: gwònghyūn; gwòngwàahn (M: go) VO: wàihjyuhgwònghyūn/wàahn

halt FV: tìhng; tìhngjí

halter N: ❶ (for horse) máhgèung; gèungsíng (M: tìuh) ❷ (for hanging) gáauyìhng * **to halter a cow** PH: yuhngsíng toujyuh jek ngàuh

halve FV: ❶ pìhngfàn PH: fàn sìhng léuhngfahn • *Jèung-*

pìhnggwó ~ ❷ gáambun

ham N: fótéui (M: jek-whole, faai, pin — slice) PH: (poor acting) m̀sīkjouhhei; jouhdākhóujá

hamburger N: honbóubāau (M: go)

hammer N: chéui; chèuihjái (M: go) FV: dahp * **put under the hammer** FV: paakmaaih

hammock N: diuchòhng (M: jèung)

hamper N: láam; sihkmahtláam (M: go) FV: jójyuh; jóngoih

hand N: sáu (M: sèung, deui; jek) FV: gàaubéi; daihbéi · *Jèung dī yìhm* ~ *ngóh; daih dī yìhm béi ngóh* * **from hand to mouth** PH: ngàamǹgāam gau sái; jaahn yātgo yuhng yātgo * **give a big hand** PH: daaihlihk paaksáu * **handwriting** N: bātjīk; syùfaat * **hand brake** N: sáujai (M: go) * **hand down** PH: chyùhnlohk béi hauhyàhn * **hand in hand** PH: sáu làai sáu A: yātchái; (yātchàih) * **hand in** FV: gàau (béi) * **hands off** PH: m̀hóu dau; m̀hóu léih * **hands up** VO: géui sáu * **in the hands of** FV: chyúhléih; hungjai; jéungngàak * **made by hand** PH: yuhngsáujouhge; sáugùngjouhge * **out of hand** A: (at once) jīkhāak RV: (out of control) gáaum̀dihm

handful M: jah * **a handful of sweets** Nu-M-N: yātjahtóng

handicap FV/N: fòhngngoih N: jeungngoih

handicraft N: sáugùng; sáugùngngaih; gùngngaihbán

handicraftsman PH: jouh sáugùngngaihge yàhn N: gùngjeuhng (M: go)

handiwork N: sáugùng PH: sáugùngjouhge yéh

handkerchief N: sáugànjái (M: tìuh)

handle FV: ❶ (manage) chyúhléih ❷ (to buy and to sell) gìngsiu; máaihmaaih RV: gáaudihm N: ❶ (excuse) bábeng ❷ (title) hàahmtàuh (M: go) ❸ (of knife, broom) beng ❹ (of bucket) sáuwáan (M: go) ❺ (of cup, drawer) yíh (M: go) * **the cup handle** N: bùiyíh (M: go) * **the knife handle** N: dōubeng (M: bá)

handsome SV: ❶ (good looking) leng; yìngjeun (man only) * **a handsome building** PH: yātjoh hóulengge ginjūkmaht ❷ (generous) daaihfòng; futlóu · *hóu* ~ *gám gyùnchín.*

handy SV: ❶ (convenient) fòngbihn; leihbihn ❷ (deft) dáisáu; lìhngwuht

hang FV: ❶ gwa; gwahéi (picture, clothing . . .) ❷ lohng; lohnghéi (washing) ❸ tip; nìhm (wallpaper) * **get the hang of it** PH: jìdou kíumiuh; mìhngbaahk daaihyi; jūkdóu yuhngsàhn * **hang down** FV: dam lohklàih; diulohklàih * **hang on** PH: dángyātdáng (wait a minute) RV: jàgán; jàsaht (do not let go) * **hang up the phone:** VO: sàusin * **hang oneself** VO: diugéng * **hang around** FV: pùihwùih; yàuhdohng; hàahndohng

hanger N: sàamgá; yìgá (M: go) * **hanger-on** N: bohngyáu (M: go)

hanging N: gáauyìhng (M: go)

hank M: jaat * to wind a hank of wool into balls PH: jèung yāt jaat lāang kíuhsèhng géigo bō/lāangkàuh

hanker FV: hahn; hotmohng * hanker after fame VO: hahn chēutméng

haphazard A/SV: ngáuh-yìhn

hapless SV: m̀hóuchói; bāt-hahng; jaihwahn

happen FV: (take place) faat-sàng ~ *Jó mātyéh sih A?* A: (by chance) yuhngàam; gamngàam * happenings N: sih; sihgín

happiness N: fūkhei; fūkfahn

happy SV: hòisàm; faailohk; hahngfūk * happy-go-lucky IE: mòuhyàumòuhleuih * as happy as the day is long PH: fèisèuhng faailohk * Happy New Year! PH: sàn nìhn faai lohk!

harangue N: fanwah Patt: heung . PN. fanwah ~ *hohk-sàang* ~

harass FV: ❶ (trouble) sòu-yíu; fàahn ❷ (attack) chàmyíu

harbour N: ❶ (for ships) góng; góngháu; hóigóng (M: go) * a natural harbour N: tìnyìhngóng (M: go) ❷ (shelter) beihnaahnsó (M: go) FV: sàuchòhng; wōchòhng (criminal)

hard SV: ❶ (firm) ngaahng ❷ (difficult) nàahn ❸ (discomfort) fú; tungfú; sànfú ❹ (severe) yìhm ❺ (with great effort) jeuhnlihk; kàhnlihk * hard luck SV: jaihwahn; dóumùih *

hard hearted IE: mòuh-chìhngmòuhyih * hardworking SV: kàhnlihk * hardware N: ngaahnggín (M: tou) * hardheaded SV: gujāp

harden FV: ❶ ·ngaahngjó, ngaahngfa ❷ lihn; dyunlihn * to harden the heart VO: ngaahnghéi sàmchèuhng * to harden steel VO: lihngong * to harden the body VO: dyunlihn sàntái

hardly A: ❶ (not quite) m̀haihgéi ❷ (scarcely) hóusíu; gèifùh m̀/móuh ❸ (only, just) gángán * hardly enough PH: gángán gau

hardness SV: ❶ ngaahng; gìnngaahng ❷ (without sentiment) láahnghuhk N: ngaahng-douh

hare N: yéhtou (M: jek) * hare brained SV: hìngsèut; daaihyi; chòusò * hare hearted SV: saidáam

harm FV: hoih; sèunghoih

harmful SV: yáuhhoih * harmful to Patt: deui . . . yáuhhoih

harmless SV: móuhhoih

harmonic SV: wòhhàaih N: (music) wohyâm

harmonica N: háukàhm (M: go)

harmonious SV: ❶ wòh-hàaih; hiptiuh ❷ (for color) tiuhwòh ❸ (for family) wòhmuhk

harmony SV: ❶ wòhhàaih ❷ (color) tiuhwòh ❸ (between persons) yùhnghāp N: (music) wohsìng * in harmony SV: hiptiuh; yātji

harness N: máhgeuih VO: touséuhng máhgeuih ✻ **in harness** PH: jouhgán yahtsèuhng ge gùngjok; jāphàhnggán yahtsèuhngge yahmmouh ✻ **to die in harness** VO: sèun jīk

harp N: syuhkàhm (M: go) VO: tàahn syuhkàhm ✻ **harp on the same string** IE: gónglàih góngheui sàamfūkpéih

harpoon N: yùhchā (M: go); biuchēung (M: jì) ✻ **to harpoon a whale** VO: seh kìhngyùh

harrier N: (hound used in hunting rabbits) lihptougáu (M: jek)

harry FV: ❶ (plunder) chéung; chéunggip; gipleuhk ❷ (annoy) màhfàahn; jitmòh; kwanyíu

harsh SV: ❶ (rough) chòu; chòulóuh; hàaih (for material) ❷ (severe) yìhm; yìhmlaih ✻ **harsh to the ear** VO: chiyíh ✻ **a harsh system of government** PH: hō jing ✻ **harsh words** PH: hāak (hāk) bohkge syutwah

harvest N: sàuwohk; sàusìhng FV: sàugot ✻ **a succession of good harvests** N: lìhnjuhkge fùngsàu

hash RV: ❶ (cut up) chitseui ❷ (mess) gáaulyuhn; gáauwāang ✻ **make a hash of it** PH: gáaudou lahpláplyuhn; gáaudou lyuhn chāt baat jòu

haste SV: gāp; chùngmòhng; faai ✻ **make haste** PH: faaidī! gónfaai! ✻ **Haste makes waste** IE: yàn faai dāk maahn; yuhkchūk jāk bātdaaht

hasten A: gónjyuh FV: chèui; gàchūk ✻ **hasten him off to bed** PH: chèui kéuih heui fangaau ✻ **hasten the growth of plants** PH: gàchūk jihkmahtge sàngjéung

hasty SV: gāp Patt: hóufaaigám; hóu chùngmòhng gám ✻ **hasty preparations for flight** PH: chùngmòhng jéunbeih jáulóu

hat N: móu (M: déng)

hatch FV: ❶ bouh ✻ **to hatch eggs** VO: bouh dáan ❷ (to plot) chaakwaahk; N: (door) jaahpmùhn (M: douh, jek) ✻ **hatchway** N: chōngháu (M: go)

hatchet N: fútáu; fútáujái (M: go) ✻ **bury the hatchet** IE: góngwòh; yihn gwài yù hóu

hate FV: jàng A: hóu m̀séung; hóu m̀jùngyi ✻ **hateful** SV: hātyàhnjàng

hatred N: sàuhhahn; yunhahn

haughty SV: gìungouh; sàchàhn

have FV: yáuh ✻ **have to** AV: yiu; yātdihng yiu ✻ **have a walk** PH: hàahnghàh ✻ **have a seat** PH: chóhháh ✻ **have a baby** PH: yáuhjó; yáuhjó bìhbī; yáuhjó sàngéi ✻ **have a headache** N: tàuhtung ✻ **have (someone) on** FV: ngàak; ngàakgwái; jínggú ✻ **have a nice weekend** PH: jàumuht faailohk! ✻ **This have nothing to do with you** IE: m̀gwàan néih sih!

haven N: ❶ (harbour) góngháu (M: go) ❷ (shelter) beihnaahnsó (M: daat, go)

havoc　N: jòiwoh; houhgip (M: chèuhng)　FV: powaaih; sèunghoih

Hawaiian　N: ❶ Hahwāiyìhyàhn (M: go) ❷ Hahwāiyìhwá (M: júng, geui)

hawk　N: yìng; daaihmàhyìng (M: jek)

hawker　N: síufáan (M: go) ✳ **hawker control force** N: síufáan gúnléihdéui (M: deuih) ✳ **hawker's stall** N: síufáan dong (M: go, dong)

hay　N: gònchóu (M: tìuh) ✳ **make hay of** RV: gáaulyuhn ✳ **make hay while the sun shines** IE: dá tit chan yiht; bángāak gèiwuih

haystack　N: gònchóudèui

hazard　FV: ngàihhoih ✳ **smoking is a health hazard** PH: kāpyìn ngàihhoih gihnhòng SV: ngàihhím; mouhhím VO: mouhhím ✳ **to hazard one's life** PH: mouh sàngmihng ngàihhím

haze　N: ❶ (mist) bohkmouh; hàhmouh ❷ (confusion) yìhmahn; yìhwaahk FV: heiluhng; júkluhng

hazel　SV/N: (color) chín fē sīk ✳ **hazel tree** N: jēunsyuh (M: pò) ✳ **hazel nut** N: jēunjí (M: nāp)

H-bomb　N: hìngdáan (M: go)

he　PN: kéuih

head　N: tàuh; tàuhhohk ✳ **nod one's head** VO: ngahptáu ✳ **shake one's head** VO: nihngtáu FV: (lead) líhngdouh; sēutlihng ✳ **to head a revolt** VO: líhngdouh buhnlyuhn BF: -jéung　N: gàjéung (head of family) bāanjéung (of class) bouhjéung (of department) Patt: heung . . . hàahng ~ *nàahm* ~ ; ~ *jyuh ngūkkéi* ~ ✳ **keep one's head** PH: bóuchìh jandihng ✳ **lose one's head** PH: sātheui léihji SV: chùngduhng

headache　N: tàuhtung

headlight　N: chètàuhdāng (M: jáan)

headline　N: daaihbiutàih ✳ **headline news** N: tàuhtìuhsànmán

headmaster　N: haauhjéung (M: go) ✳ **headmistress** N: néuihhaauhjéung (M: go)

headphone　N: yíhtúnggèi (M: ga; fu)

headquarter　N: júngbouh (M: go)

heady　SV: ❶ (headstrong) wàahngu; yahmsing ❷ (impulse) lóuhmóhng; hìngsēut

heal　FV: yì; yìjih ✳ **heal all** N: maahnlìhngyeuhk (M: jek, júng)

health　SV: gihnhòng N: sàntái ✳ **healthy** SV: gihnhòng; jonggihn

healthful　SV: waihsàng; hahpwaihsàng ✳ **healthful diet** N: waihsàngchāan

heap　FV: dèui; dèuihéi M: dèui ✳ **heaps of** PH: hóudò; daaihbá

hear　RV: tènggin; tèngdóu ✳ **hear from** Patt: sàudóu (jipdóu) .P.N. ge seun ✳ **heard it said (hear that)** IE: tèngginwah; (tèngmàhnwah)

hearing　N: tìnggok FV: sám;

sámmahn; sámseun * to condemn without a hearing PH: m̀ sám jauh dihngjeuih * on hearing RV: tènggin; tèngdóu * hearing aid N: johtinghei (M: fu)

hearsay N: yiuhyìhn; yìuhchyùhn (M: go) FV/ATT: tèngfàanlàih; fùngmàhn

hearse N: gùnchòihchè (M: ga)

heart N: sàm; sàmjohng (M: go) * heart attack N: sàmjohngbehng * heart broken SV: sēungsàm; sàmseui * heart shape N: sàmyìhng * do not have the heart to A: m̀yánsàm * in the heart of PW: jùngsàm * kind hearted PH: hóu hóusàm; sàmdéi hóu * learn by heart RV: nihm-súhk; buihsuhk * soft hearted SV: sàmyúhn

hearten FV: gúmóuh; gúlaih PH: lihngyàhn hìngfáhn; lihngyàhn janfáhn • yātgo ~ ge siusīk

hearth N: ❶ (fireplace) bīk-lòuh (M: go) ❷ (family) gātìhng (M: go)

heartily A: sìhngsàmsìhngyi; chùngsàm * to thank him heartily PH: chùngsàm gámjeh kéuih * to eat heartily PH: hóu tungfaai gám sihk * to work heartily PH: hóu yiht sàm gám jouh

hearty SV: ❶ (of feelings) sìhnghán; yihtsàm ❷ (of health) gihnhòng ❸ (of meals) fùngfu

heat N: ❶ yihtlihk ❷ (hot air) nyúhnhei SV: yiht RV: jíngyiht • dī yuhk * heat stroke VO: jungsyú * prickly heat N: yihtfái (M: nāp)

heathen N: yihgaautòuh (M: go)

heating N: nyúhnhei * central heating system N: jùngyèung nyúhnhei chitbeih/ haihtúng

heave FV: ❶ (raise) géui; géuihéi ❷ (throw) pàau; dám ❸ (pull) làai; làaihéi; tō ❹ (up and down) héifuhk * heave ho! IE: chēutlihk làai lā

heaven N: ❶ tìn; tìnhùng ❷ (home of God) tìntòhng; tìngwok

heavenly ATT: tìn; seuhngtìn * heavenly bodies N: tìntái * Heavenly Father N: Tìnfuh

heavily SV: chúhng PH: hóu chúhng A: fèisèuhng; gihkjì * heavily taxed PH: chàuseui chàu dāk hóu chúhng * suffered heavily PH: gihkjì tungfú

heavy SV: chúhng * heavy food PH: nàahn sìufa ge sihkmaht; hóu nauhge sihkmaht * heavy heart IE: sàmchìhng chàhmjuhng * heavy rain VO: lohk daaihyúh * heavy weight boxer N: chúhngleuhngkāp kyùhnwòhng (M: go)

Hebrew N: ❶ Hèibaaklòihyàhn (M: go) ❷ Hèibaaklòihwá (M: júng, geui)

hectare N: gùngkíng

hectic SV: ❶ hìngfáhn; chigīk * a hectic life PH: chigīkge sàngwuht ❷ (red-like) hùhng * hectic cheeks PH: mihn hùhnghùhng

hedge N: lèihbā; syuhlèih PH: yuhnglèihbā wàihjyuh *

sit on the hedge IE/N.: kèhchèuhngpaai

hedonism N: héunglohkjyúyih

heed FV: jyuyi; làuhsàm ✻ **take no heed of what people say** PH: m̀ làuhsàm yàhndeih góng yéh

heel N: ❶ (of foot) geukjàang (M: jek) ❷ (of shoes) hàaihjàang (M: jek) VO: bóu hàaihjàang FV: (follow) gànjyuh RV: (lean over) jākmàaih yātbihn

hegemony N: bakyùhn

height N: ❶ gòudouh (M: go) ❷ (utmost degree) díngdím; gihkdím (M: go)

heinous PH: fèisèuhng chàahnbouh; gihkjì hùngngok

heir N: hauhyàhn; hauhdoih; sìhnggaiyàhn (M: go) ✻ **heir ship** N: sìhnggaikyùhn (M: go)

heirloom N: chyùhngàbóu

helicopter N: jihksīnggèi (M: ga, jek)

heliport N: jihksīnggèichèuhng (M: go)

helium N: hoih; hoihhei

hell N: deihyuhk (M: go)

hello P: ❶ wái; wéi (for answering the phone) ❷ wai; wei (to attract attention)

helm N: tòh (M: go) VO: jéungtòh; bátáaih FV: (lead) jífài; líhngdouh

helmsman N: tòhsáu (M: go)

helmet N: tàuhkwài (M: déng) ✻ **to wear a helmet** VO: daai tàuhkwài

help FV: bòng; bòngjoh VO: bòngsáu N: ❶ (assistance) bòngjoh; yùhnjoh ❷ (person who helps) johsáu; bòngsáu, gùngyàhn (servant) ✻ **help!** IE: gau mehng a! ✻ **help yourself!** IE: chèuihbín lā; jihbín lā! ✻ **can't help it** PH: móuh faat jí ✻ **can't help but** PH: yánm̀jyuh; móuhfaatjím̀ ✻ **helpmate, helpmeet** N: ① (companion) buhnléuih; tùhngbuhn (M: go) ② (husband or wife) puingáuh

helter-skelter SV: fòngsātsāt IE: sáumòhnggeuklyuhn

hem N: jipbīn; kwánbīn VO: lyùhnbīn; lyùhnmàaih dī bīn

hemisphere N: bunkàuh ✻ **northern and southern hemispheres** N: bākbunkàuh tùhng nàahmbunkàuh

hemp N: màh ✻ **hemp rope** N: màhsíng (M: tìuh) ✻ **hemp palm** N: jùngléuihsyuh (M: pò)

hen N: gàiná, móuhgài (M: jek)

henpecked VO/SV: pa lóuhpòh

hence PH: yàuh yìhgā héi; yàuh nīsyu héi yànchìh; sóyíh ✻ **hence forth** TW: chùhng gàm yíhhauh

henchman N: chànseun (M: go)

her PN: ❶ kéuih ❷ (possessive) kéuihge

herald N: ❶ (generally) sìnkèui ❷ (official who carries message) sijé ❸ (official who proclaims) chyùhnlihnggùn ❹ (person who proclaims) bouseunjé; tùngboujé FV: syùnbou; yuhgou; yuhbou

herb N: chóuyeuhk; jùng-yeuhk

herbivorous ATT: sihk-chóu

herd M: kwàhn FV: hòn; tái * **to herd cattle** VO: hòn (tái) ngàuh * **cowherd** N: hòn-ngàuhjái (M: go)

here PW: nīsyu; nīdouh * **here we are** PH: ngóhdeih dou la * **here and there** A: dousyu; syusyu * **here with** FV: fuhséuhng * **far from here** Patt: lèih nīsyu hóu yúhn * **here's to ... (a toast)** PH: waih ... gònbùi; jūk ... * **here's to your health!** PH: jūk néih gihnhòng! * **here's to our friendship!** PH: waih ngóhdeihge yáuhyìh gònbùi

hereditary FV: ❶ wàih-chyùhn; jóuchyùhn ❷ (of rank) saijaahp IE: doihdoihsèung-chyùhn

heresy N: chèhgaau; yìhgaau IE: yìhdyùnchèhsyut; pòhng-mùhnjódouh * **fall into heresy** PH: hahmyahp pòhngmùhn jódouh jìjùng

heretic N: yìhgaautòuh (M: go)

heritage N: wàihchsáan (M: fahn)

hermit N: yáhnsih (M: go)

hero N: ❶ yìnghùhng (M: wái, go) ❷ (in a play) nàahmjyúgok (M: go) * **hero worship** PH: yìnghùhng sùhngbaai

heroin N: hóilokyìng

heroine N: ❶ néuihyìng-hùhng (M: wái, go) ❷ (in a play) néuihjyúgok (M: go)

heroism N: ❶ yìnghùhng-jyúyih ❷ (of qualities) yìnghùhngheikoi

heron N: baahklouh (M: jek)

herring N: fèiyú; chèngyú (M: tìuh)

hers PN: kéuihge

herself PH: kéuih jihgéi; kéuih búnyàhn

hesitate SV: chàuhchyùh IE: yàuhyìhbātdihng A: mséung; myuhnyi

heterogeneous PH: m̀-tùhngge; m̀tùhng júngleuihge; wahnjaahpge

hew FV: ❶ (of woods) jáam ❷ (of stones) pīk, pek ❸ (of careers) chong * **to hew out a career** PH: chong yātfàansihyihp

hexagon N: luhkgokyìhng; luhkbīnyìhng (M: go)

hey P: wai; wei; hī!

hibernate FV: dùngmìhn VO: gwodùng

hibiscus N: daaihhùhngfā (M: déu, dó)

hiccup VO: dá sī'īk

hide FV: ❶ (conceal) sàu; sàumàaih ❷ (conceal oneself) nèi; nèimàaih ❸ (conceal secrets) yánmùhn; yímsīk ❹ (blocked) jèjyuh N: pèih; saupèih (animal) pèihfū (human) * **play hide and seek** PH: wáan jūk nèinèi; wáan jūk yìyán

hideous SV: dākyàhngèng; hópa; cháungok

hieroglyph N: jeuhngyìhngmàhnjih (M: go)

hierarchy N: ❶ gāaikāp jaidouh; gāaikāp jóujīk ❷ (organized priesthood) jàngléuih jóujīk; jàngléuihtúngjih

hi-fi N: cheunggèi (M: ga, fu, bouh) Adj. PH: gòudouh chyùhnjàn(ge); gòudouh chyùhnjànsing(ge)

high SV: gòu * **high official** N: gòukāp gùnyùhn (M: go, wái) * **high class** SV: gòukāp; gòu seuhng * **high handed** N: gòungaat sáudyuhn SV: jyùnjai * **high rise** N: gòulàuh daaihhah * **high blood pressure** N: gòuhyutngaat * **high jump** FV: tiugòu * **in high spirits** SV: gòuhing * **has a high opinion of** FV: puifuhk; jaanséung

highlight N: jìngwàh; gòuchiùh PH: jeui jìngchóige bouhfahn

highly Adj. PH: hóu gòu • *yàtgo sànséui ~ ge gìngléih* A: fèisèuhng; gihkjì • *yàtchēut ~ yáuhcheui ge dihnyíng* * **spoke very highly of** PH: fèisèuhng jaanséung

hijack FV: chéunggip; gipchìh * **to hijack a plane** VO: gipgèi * **to hijack a truck** PH: gipchìh ga fochè

hike FV/N: yúhnjūk FV: (rasie) tàihgòu * **a price hike** VO: tàihgòugachìhn; tàihgòu gagaak

hilarious SV: gòuhing; yihtnaauh; hóusiu

hilarity FV/ATT: kwòhngfùn SV/N: fùnlohk; yihtnaauh

hill N: sàan; sàanjái (M: go, joh) * **hill side** N: sàanbō;

sàanyìu; sàanbīn (M: go)

hilt N: beng; dōubeng (M: bá) * **up to the hilt** A: chitdái; chùngfahn; yùhnchyùhn * **armed to the hilt** PH: chyùhnfu móuhjòng

him PN: kéuih

himself PN: kéuih jihgéi; kéuih búnyàhn

hinder FV: jóngoih; jójí; fòhngngoih

hindermost, hindmost Adj. PH: jeuihauhge

Hindu N: ❶ (of people) Yandouhyàhn (M: go) ❷ (of religion) yandouhgaau

hindrance N: jeungngoih; fòhngngoih; jójaih

hinge N: ❶ (joint) gaau (M: go) ❷ (central principle) gwàangìhn; juhngdím (M: go) VO: jòng(òn) gaau

hint FV/N: ngamsih; tàihsih (M: go)

hip N: tyùhnbouh (M: go) * **hipbone** N: johgwāt

hippie, hippy N: hèipèihsih (M: go)

hippopotamus N: hòhmáh (M: jek)

hire FV: ❶ (employ) chéng ❷ (rent) jòu; giu * **hire purchase** FV: fànkèih fuhfún * **on hire** VO: chēutjòu * **to hire a car** VO: jòu / giu chè

his PN: kéuihge

hiss FV: ❶ hèu ~ *kéuih* ❷ sihsíseng • *dī sèh ~* VO: chàaihtòih

historian N: lihksíhohkgā; síhohkgā (M: wái, go)

history N: lihksí * **modern history** N: gahndoihsí * **history of China** N: Jùnggwoksí

hit FV: ❶ (to beat) dá ❷ (strike against something) johng; pung RV: johngchàn; pungchàn RVE: (strike the target) — jung N: dágík * **to be hit by a car** PH: béi ga chè pungchàn/johngchàn * **three hits and two misses** PH: sàamchi dájung, léuhngchi dá-m̀jung * **hit it off** PH: sèungchyùh dāk hóu hóu * **hit and run** PH: chēutsih / dájóyàhn jihauh jáugwáijó * **hit below the belt** PH: yuhng bèipéige sáufaat/sáudyuhn

hitch PH: (to pull quickly) hóu faai gám làai RV: ❶ (fasten with hook) ngàujyuh ❷ (with rope) bóngjyuh; toujyuh N: ❶ (stoppage) jóngoih; jeungngoih ❷ (knot) lit (M: go)

hither A: heung nīsyu * **hither to** MA: yātheung (dōu); douyìhgā

hive N: mahtfūngdau (M: go)

hoard RV: chóuhmàaih; jīkmàaih; chóuhhéi PH: chóuhmàaihge yéh; jīkmàaihge yéh * **a board of money** N: Jīkchūk PH: jīkmàaihge chín

hoarse SV: chòu; sà

hoax FV: ❶ (to play a trick) nánfa ❷ (to deceive) ngāak

hob N: titgá (M: go)

hobble A/FV: gaht (háh) gaht háh; bài (háh) bàiháh FV: (prevent) jójí; jóngoih

hobby N: sihou (M: go) * **hobby horse** N: muhkmáh (M: jek)

hock N: ❶ (of animal) hauhtéui gwàanjit ❷ (of ham) fótéui yuhk FV: (pawn) dong

hockey N: kūkgwankàuh

hoe N: chòhtàuh (M: go) FV: chòh; gwaht * **to hoe up weeds** PH: gwahthéui dī yéhchóu

hog N: ❶ jyū (M: jek) ❷ (greedy person) tàamsàmgwái (M: go)

hoist RV: sìnghéi; chéhéi; géuihéi N: héichúhnggèi; diugèi * **to hoist a flag** VO: sìngkèih

hold FV: ❶ jà (jyuh) ❷ (to embrace) láam (jyuh) ❸ (to cradle in one's arm) póuh (jyuh) ❹ (to contain) jòng ❺ (to stage) géuihàhng * **hold a meeting** VO: hòiwúi * **hold the audience's attention** PH: kāpyáhn gùnjungge jyuyi * **hold on!** PH: dánghàh! dángyātdáng! * **hold up** FV: dágip * **hold back one's temper** PH: yánjyuh m̀ faat pèihhei * **hold one's breath** PH: m̀hóu táuhei * **hold to one's promise** PH: gìnsáu nohkyìhn

holder N: chìhyáuhyàhn, chìhpiujé (M: go, wái) * **a share holder** N: gúdūng, gúpiu chìhyáuhyàhn (M: go, wái)

hole N: lūng (M: go) * **a square peg in a round hole** IE: gaakgaakbātyahp

holiday N: gakèih, gayaht (M: go) * **to have a holiday** VO: fongga * **summer holi-**

day N: syúga (M: go)

holiness SV: sàhnsing

hollow SV: ❶ (not solid) hùngge; jùnggàan hùngge ❷ (unreal) hùnghèui ❸ (false) hèuingaih * **hollow sympathy** PH: hèuingaihge tùhngchìhng ❹ (sunken) nāp N: ❶ (hole) lūng (M: go) ❷ (small valley) sàangūkjái RV: waathùng A: chitdái, yùhnchyùhn

holly N: dùngchìngsyuh (M: pò)

holocaust N: ❶ (burnt offering) fàahnjai ❷ (massacre) daaihtòuhsaat

holster N: chēungdói (M: go)

holy SV: sàhnsing * **Holy Bible** N: Singgìng (M: bún; bouh) * **Holy communion** N: Singchāan * **Holy Father** N: Singfuh (M: go) * **Holy Son** N: Singjí (M: go) * **Holy Spirit** N: Singlìhng (M: go)

homage FV: ❶ (respect) jyùnging ❷ (express loyalty to) haauhjùng N: gingyi (M: júng, fahn) * **to pay homage to the king** PH: heung wòhngseuhng haauhjùng

home PW: ngūkkéi; kéi * **home sick** VO: gwajyuh ngūkkéi; séunggà; sìgā * **make yourself at home** IE: m̀hóu haakhei * **home for the aged** N: lóuhyàhnyún (M: gàan) * **There is no place like home** IE: lùhngchòhng bātyùh gáudau

homely SV: ❶ (plain) poksou ❷ (not pretty) m̀leng; cháuyéung ATT: (ordinary) gàseuhng * **a homely meal** PH: gàseuhng bihnfaahn

homework N: gùngfo

homicide N: ❶ (killer) hùngsáu, saatyàhnhùngsáu (M: go) ❷ (case) hùngsaatngon (M: gihn; jùng) * **to commit homicide** VO: saatyàhn

homily VO: góngdouh N: (teaching) fanwah

hominid N: yùhnyàhn; yùhnchíyàhn (M: go)

homogeneous ATT: tùhngleuihge; sèungchíhge

homologous ATT: sèungtùhngge; sèungyingge; tùhnghaihge

homonym N: tùhngyàmyihyìhjih; tùhngyàmyiyìhchìh (M: go)

homosexual FV: tùhngsingnyún N: tùhngsingnyúnjé (M: go)

honest SV: sìhngsaht; lóuhsaht * **speak honestly** PH: lóuhsahtgóng

honey N: mahttòhng; fùngmaht * **honey comb** N: mahtfùngdau (M: go)

honeymoon N: mahtyuht VO: douhmahtyuht

honk VO: héungngòn (ōn); héunghōn; gahmngòn (ōn); gahmhōn FV: būt N: ❶ (of a car) héungngōnsèng ❷ (of a wild goose) ngaahnge giusèng

honorary SV: gwòngwìhng ATT/N: mìhngyuh * **honorary member** N: mìhngyuh wúiyùhn (M: wái; go)

honor, honour SV: wìhnghahng N: wìhngyuh FV: ❶ (respect) jyùnging; gingjuhng ❷ (accept) sìhngyihng * **to**

honour a signature VO: sìhngyihng chìmjí * **a first-class honours degree** PH: gaapkāp (yātkāp) wihngyuh hohkwái

hood N: ❶ (of clothing) móu, dàumóu (M: déng) ❷ (of car) chètàuhgoi (M: go)

hoof N: ❶ (of animal) tàih (M: jek) ❷ (of human) geuk (M: jek) FV: hàahng; jáu VO: (dance) tiumóuh

hook N: ngàu (M: go) RV: ngàujyuh * **hook nosed man** N: ngàubeihlóu (M: go) * **hook worm** N: ngàuchùhng (M: tiuh) * **fishhook** N: yùhngàu (M: go) * **crochet hook** N: ngàujām (M: jì) * **reaping hook** N: lìhmdōu (M: bá) * **by hook or by crook** IE: bāt jaahk sáudyuhn

hooligan N: fèijái; laahnjái (M: go)

hoop N: kū; hyūn (M: go) RV: kùjyuh

hoot N: ❶ (jeer) hēusèng; chàaihtòihsèng ❷ (of a horn) héungngònsèng; heidehksèng (steam whistle) ❸ (of an owl) māautàuhyìng giusèng * **don't care a hoot** IE: yātdī dōu m̀ joihfùh

hop FV: ❶ tiu ❷ (fly) fèi; fèihàhng VO: (dance) tiumóuh RV: tiugwo; tiuséuhng N: (plant) sèhmàhchóu * **hop it!** RV: jáuhòi! * **hop scotch** VO: tiu fèigèi * **hop, skip and jump** N: sàamkáp tiu (yúhn)

hope FV/N: hèimohng * **hopeless** VO: móuhhèimohng; jyuhtmohng * **to hope against hope** PH: póuh yātsin hèimohng

horde PH: yātdaaihkwàhn; yātdaaihbàan; yātdaaihdèui ~ *yàhn* N: (tirbe) yâuhmuhkbouhlohk

horizon N: ❶ deihpìhngsin (M: tìuh) ❷ (limit) faahnwàih; ngáahngaai; gaaihaahn * **horizontal line** N: séuipìhngsin (M: tìuh)

hormone N: hohyíhmùhng; gīksou; noihfànbei

horn N: ❶ gok (M: jek) ❷ (instrument) houhgok; labā (M: go) * **car horn** N: ngòn; on; hōn (M: go) * **a French horn** N: yùhnlabā; Faatgwokhouh (M: go) * **to sound a horn** VO: héungngòn (òn); gahmngòn (òn) * **horned cattle** PH: yáuhgokge ngàuh

hornet N: daaih wòhngfūng (M: jek)

horny ATT: gokjàtge; gokjouhge * **the horny layer** N: gokjàtchàhng (M: chàhng)

horoscope N: sìngseunghohk; jìmbūkseuht * **to cast a horoscope** VO: syunmehng

horrible SV: hópa; dākyàhngèng; hātyàhnjàng * **horror film** N: húngboupín (M: chèut)

horse N: máh (M: jek, pàt) VO: kèhmáh * **horse race** VO: páaumáh; choimáh * **horse power** N: máhlihk (M: pàt) * **to put the cart before the horse** IE: bún muht dóu ji; dóu gwó wàih yàn

horticulture N: yùhnngaih; yùhnngaihhohk * **horticulturist** N: yùhnngaihgā (M: wái, go)

hose N: ❶ (tube) hàuh (M: tìuh) ❷ (stockings) maht;

chèuhngtúngmaht (M: jek, deui)
FV: seh; fèh ✻ **pantyhose** N:
.mahtfu (M: tiuh) ✻ **fire hose**
N: mihtfóhàuh (M: tiuh)

hosiery N: ❶ (socks) maht
(M: jek, deui) ❷ (underwear)
dáisāam; noihyī (M: gihn)

hospitable SV: haakhei Adj.
PH: houhaak; hóujiufù

hospital N: yīyún (M: gàan)

hospitality SV: haakhei N:
fúndoih Adj. PH: hóujiufù;
houhaak

host N: ❶ jyúyàhn; jyúyán (M:
wái, go) ❷ (of T.V. programme)
jitmuhkjyúchìh (yàhn) (M: wái,
go) PH: hóudò ✻ **hostess** N:
néuihjyúyàhn / yán (M: go, wái)

hostage N: yàhnji (people);
dáingaatbán

hostel N: sūkse; jiudoihsó;
léuihgún (M: gàan)

hostile ATT: dihkdeui ✻
hostile attitude PH: dihkdeui
taaidouh ✻ **hostile army** N:
dihkgwàn

hostility ATT: dihkdeui N:
dihkyi ✻ **to feel no hostility
towards him** PH: deui kéuih
móuh dihkyi ✻ **hostilities** N:
jinjàng; jindau

hot SV: ❶ yiht ❷ (spicy) laaht
✻ **hot house** N: wànsāt (M: go,
gàan) ✻ **hot goods** N: chaahkjòng (M: gihn) ✻ **hot line** N:
yihtsin (M: tiuh) ✻ **hot spring**
N: wànchyùhn (M: go) ✻ **hot
blooded** SV: yihtchihng;
chùngduhng ✻ **hot headed**
SV: bouhchou; lóuhmóhng

hotel N: jáudim (M: gàan)

hound N: ❶ (dog) lihpgáu (M:

jek) ❷ (person) sèuiyàhn;
bèipéisíuyàhn (M: go) FV: jèui;
jèuibīk

hour N: jūngtàuh (M: go) M:
dímjūng ✻ **hour hand** N:
dyúnjām (M: jì) ✻ **office hours**
N: baahngūng sìhgaan ✻ **questions of the hour** PH: yìhgà /
muhkchìhn ge mahntàih ✻
hourly TW: múihgo jūngtàuh
A: sìhsìh; chèuihsìh

house N: ngūk (M: gàan) ✻
housewife N: jyúfúh; gàtìhng-
jyúfúh (M: wái, go) ✻ **house
work** N: gàmouh ✻ **fullhouse**
VO: múhnjoh ✻ **on the house**
VO: míhnfai ✻ **the housing
problem** PH: gèuijyuh (jyuh-
ngūk) ge mahntàih ✻ **the
house of representatives** N:
jungyíhyún (M: go) ✻ **the
house of Commons** N:
hahyíhyún (M: go) ✻ **the house
of Lords** N: seuhngyíhyún (M:
go)

household ATT/N: gàtìhng
✻ **household affairs** N:
gàmouh; gàsih ✻ **household
name** IE: gà chyùhn wuh híu ✻
the royal household N:
wòhngsāt (M: go) ✻
householder N: jyuhwuh;
wuhjyú (M: go)

hover FV: ❶ (of birds)
pùhnsyùhn ❷ (of persons)
pùihwùih VO: dàuhyūn ✻
hovercraft N: heijínsyùhn (M:
jek)

how A: ❶ (in what way) dím;
dímyéung ❷ (in what degree)
géi ✻ **how many, howmuch?**
A: géidō? ✻ **how often** A:
géinói; géinoih? ✻ **how SV
the . . . is!** Patt: . . . géi SV!

however MA: ❶ daahnhaih;
bātgwo ❷ (whatever way)
mòuhleuhn dím

howl FV: ngaai; hàaugiu N: hàaugiusèng • *jek gáuge ~*

hub N: ❶ (of a wheel) gūk ❷ (of activity) jùngsàm • *gùngyihp ~* ; jùngsyù (M: go)

hubbub SV: chòuh; chòuh-hyùnbàbai

huddle PH: (crowd together) sūkmàaihyātdèui; dèuimàaih-yātchàih ✳ **huddle up** RV: sūkhéi ✳ **huddled together** PH: sūkmàaihyātdèui

hue N: ❶ (color) sīk; ngàahn-sīk; sīkchói ❷ (outcry) giusèng; giuhaamsèng

huff VO: faat pèihhei SV/FV: nàu Adj. PH: nàubaaubaau

hug RV: (embrace) láamjyuh; póuhjyuh FV: (cling to) gìnchìh ✳ **hug oneself** (be very pleased with oneself) IE: jìmjìm-jihhéi

huge SV: daaih; geuihdaaih Adj. PH: hóudaaih

hulk N: ❶ (of ship) faisyùhn (M: jek) ❷ (of thing) pòhngyìhn-daaihmaht (M: gihn) ✳ **hulk-ing** SV: pòhngdaaih

hull N: ❶ (of ship) syùhnsàn; syùhnhok (M: go) ❷ (of fruit) pèih ❸ (husk) hok VO: heuipèih; heuihok

human ATT/N: yàhn; yàhn-leuih ✳ **human being** N: yàhn (M: go) ✳ **human nature** N: yàhnsing (M: go) ✳ **human weaknesses** PH: yàhnleuihge yeuhkdím

humane SV: yàhnchìh Adj. PH: yáuh yàhnchìhngmeih ✳ **humane studies** N: yàhn-màhnhohk (fō)

humanism N: yàhndouh-jyúyíh; yàhnmàhnjyúyíh

humanity N: ❶ (human race) yàhnleuih ❷ (human nature) yàhnsing SV: (kind) yàhnchìh; yàhnngoi

humanize FV: gámfa; gaau-fa PH: fuyúh yàhnsing; bindāk yáuh yàhnsing

humankind N: yàhnleuih

humble SV: ❶ (modest) hìmhèui; hìmbèi ❷ (of occupation) dàimèih; dàihah ❸ (of home) gáanlauh

humdrum SV: ❶ (dull) dàandiuh; mòuhlìuh ❷ (commonplace) pìhngfàahn ✳ **to live a humdrum life** PH: gwodī dàandiuhge sàngwuht

humid SV: sāp; chiuhsāp

humidity N: sāphei; sāp-douh (degree) ✳ **relative humidity** N: sèungdeui sāp-douh ✳ **high humidity** PH: sāpdouh hóugòu; sāphei hóu chúhng

humiliate FV: móuhyuhk VO: lohkmín ✳ **humiliation** N: chíyuhk

humility SV: hìmhèui; hìm-bèi; PH: hìmbèige hàhng-wàih

humming FV: hàng N: wūngwūngsèng PH: hahp-màaihháu cheungwoh SV: wuhtput; wuhtyeuk ✳ **humm-ing bird** N: fùngníuh (M: jek)

humorous SV: yàumahk; fùihàaih; waahtkài; hóusiu

humour SV: yàumahk; fùi-hàaih; waahtkài N: (temper) sàmchìhng FV: (gratify) jauh;

hump N: ❶ (of camel) tòh-fùng (M: go) ❷ (of people) láu (M: go) ❸ (hill) sāanjái (M: go, joh) RV: gúnghéi FV/SV/A: nóuhlihk; faatfáhn * **hump back** SV: tòhbui

hunch N: ❶ láu (M: go) ❷ (suspicion) yuhgám (M: go) * **hunch back** SV: tòhbui

hundred Nu/M: baak * **one hundred and one** Nu: yātbaak lìhng yāt Adj. PH: hóudò * **by the hundreds** IE: souyíhbaakgai * **three hundredfold** Nu. M: sàambaakpúih

Hungarian N: Hùngngàh-leihyàhn (M: go) Hùngngàhleih-wá

hunger SV: ngoh N: gēingoh FV: hotmohng * **hunger strike** FV/N: jyuhtsihk PH: jyuhtsihk kongyíh

hungry SV: ngoh; tóuhngoh FV: hotmohng

hunk PH: yātdaaihfaai * **a hunk of bread** PH: yāt-daaihfaai mihnbāau

hunt FV: ❶ dáilihp · heui ~ ❷ (search) wán; jèuichàh ❸ (chase away) gón * **hunter** N: lihpyàhn (M: go)

hurdle N: ❶ (fence) làahngòn ❷ (difficulty) jeungngoih (M: go) VO: tiulàahn

hurl FV: deng, dám

hurrah, hurray PH: hóu-yéh N: fùnfùsèng FV: (cheer) fùnfù

hurricane N: geuihfùng PH: daaihfùng; kfóudaaihfùng

hurry SV: chùngmòhng; gón A: gónjyuh FV: (rush) chèui ~ kéuih faaidī * **hurry up** PH: faaidī; faaidī lā! * **in a hurry** SV: pàhnlàhn; chùngmòhng

hurt SV: ❶ (pain) tung (of feeling) sèungsàm Patt: lihng . . . sèungsàm FV: (injure) sèunghoih; sèungjó VO: sauhsèung; sèungsàm RV: jíngchàn * **hurtful to** Patt: deui . . . yáuhhoih * **does it hurt?** tungm̀tung a?

hurtle FV: pung; johng N: chùnggīk * **hurtle down** PH: chùnglohklàih * **hurtle past** PH: chùnggwoheui

husband N: sīnsàang; jeuhngfù; ngoihjái; lóuhgūng (coll.) FV/SV: hàan * **animal husbandary** N: chūkmuhkhohk

hush P: syùh! PH: m̀hóu-chòuh!; m̀hóu chēutsèng!; jihngdī SV: jihng; nìhngjihng; ngònjihng * **hush up** FV: yán-mùhn * **hush money** N: ngámháufai (M: bāt)

husk N: hòng; hok VO: heui-hok; mōkhok * **husky voice** PH: sàngáge sìngyàm; sàsèng

hussy N: dohngfúh; jihnfo PH: hìngtiuge néuihjái (M: go)

hustle FV: tèui; ngúng; chèui * **hustle and bustle** SV: yihtnaauh

hut N: ❶ ngūkjái (M: gàan) ❷ (thatched house) màauhngūk; màauhlìuh (M: gàan)

hybrid N: jaahpjúng; wahn-hahpmaht; wahnhyutyìh (human) ATT: jaahpjúngge;

wahnjúngge

hydrant N: sìufòhnghàuh; séuilùhngtàuh (M: go)

hydraulic ATT: séuilihk * **hydraulic power plant** N: séuilihk faatdihnchóng (M: gàan) * **hydraulic press** N: séuingaatgèi (M: fu, bouh) * **hydraulics** N: séuilihkhohk

hydrogen N: hìnghei; hìng * **hydrogen bomb** N: hìnggheidáan (M: go)

hygiene N: waihsànghohk; bóugihnfaat SV: waihsàng

hymn N: jaanméihsī; singsī (M: sáu)

hypercritical SV: hòkàuh; hòhkàk; yìmjìm IE: chèui mòuh kàuh chī

hypertension N: gòuhyutngaat PH: gwodouh gánjèung

hyphen Nu. M: yātwaahk N: lìhnjìhhouh (M: go)

hypnosis N: chèuimìhnjohngtaai; chèuimìhnseuht * **hypnotism** N: cheùimìhnseuht * **hypnotize** VO: sì chèuimìhnseuht

hypocrite N: ngaihgwànjí PH: gámouhwàihsihnge yàhn (M: go) * **hypocrisy** PH: ngaihsihn; gáhóusàm

hypodermic ATT: pèihhah; pèihhahjyuseh N: pèihhahjyusehyeuhk * **hypodermic syringe** N: pèihhahjyusehjàm (M: jì)

hypothesis N/A: gáchit; gádihng

hysteria N: kitsīdáiléihjing * **to go into hysterics** FV: faatkòhng; faatdìn *

hysterical laughter PH: kwòhngsiu

I

I PN: ngóh

ice N: bìng; syut * **ice berg** N: bìngsàan (M: go, joh) * **ice box** N: syutgwaih; bìngsèung (M: go) * **ice cream** N: syutgòu * **ice skate** VO: làuhbìng * **break the ice** VO: dápo chàhmmahk; dápo muhnguhk PH: jeuhksáuheuijouh * **an iced wedding cake** PH: yáuh tòhngsèungge gitfàn láihbéng

icicle N: bìngchyúh; sèuihbìng (M: tiuh)

icon N: singjeuhng; wájeuhng (M: fūk, jèung)

icy SV: láahng, bìngláahng, láahngdaahm PH: pòumúhnsaai bìng * **icy wind** N: láahngfùng * **icy road** PH: pòumúhnsaai bìngge louh * **icy manner** PH: láahngdaahmnge taaidouh

idea N: ❶ (concept) koinihm; gùnnihm ❷ (plan) baahnfaat; faatjí; gaiwaahk ❸ (opinion) yigin ❹ (scheme) jyúyi • *yātgo sànge* ~ * **have no idea of** PH: yātdī dōu m̀jì; gúm̀dou

ideal N/SV: léihséung (M: go) N: (model) mòuhfaahn; dínfaahn (M: go) * **idealism** N: wàihsàmjyúyih; léihséungjyúyih

idealize FV: léihséungfa

identical ATT: tùhngyāt; ~ *yaht;* ~ *yàhn;* sèungdáng PH: tùhngyātyàhn PH: yùhnchyùhn sèungtùhng; yùhnchyùhn yātyeuhng

identification FV: jingmihng; gaamdihng; chàhmihng; yihngmihng PH: jingmihng sèungtùhng; sihwáihsèungtùhng

identify RV: yihngdākchēut; fàndākchēut FV: gaamdihng

identity ATT: tùhngyāt PH: yùhnchyùhn sèungtùhng; jyuhtdeui sèungtùhng N: sānfán * **identity card** N: sānfánjing (M: go)

ideological N/ATT: sìseungtáihaih; yisīkyìhngtaai (M: go) * **ideologist** N: sìséunggā; léihleuhngā (M: go)

idiom N: sìhngyúh (M: geui)

idiomatic ATT: gwaan-yuhngge; tùngseuhnge * **idionmatic phrases** N: gwaanyuhngyúh; sìhngyúh (M: geui)

idiosyncrasy N: ❶ dahk-jāt; fùnggaak; gosing ❷ (of medicine) dahkyihtáijāt; dahkyihfáanying

idiot N: baahkchì; sòhgwā; bahndáan (M: go)

idle SV: ❶ (of people) láahnsáan; láahndoh ❷ (useless) móuhyuhng; mòuhwaih; móuhyīk FV: lohngfai; sàai PH: (of engine) maahnmáanjyun * **to idle about** IE: mòuhsósihsih; yàuhsáuhouhàahn * **idle away one's time** PH: lohngfai sìhgaan

idol N: ❶ (image) ngáuhjeuhng (M: go) ❷ chúngyìh; chúngmaht

idolize VO: sùhngbaai ngáuhjeuhng FV: ngáuhjeuhngfa

idyl, idyll N: tìhnyùhnsī (M: sáu) * **idyllist** N: tìhnyùhnsīyàhn (M: wái, go)

if MA: yùhgwó; yeuhkkhaih Patt: (whether) pos. and neg. * **He asked me if I could help him.** Kéuih mahn ngóh hómhóyíh bōng kéuih. * **I don't know if she is busy.** Ngóh m̀jì kéuih dākm̀dākhàahn. * **as if** A: hóuchíh; chíhfùh * **even if** MA: jauhsyun; jīksí

ignite VO: dímfó; jeuhkfó FV: ❶ dím ❷ (excite) sinduhng RV: dímjeuhk ~ *fóchàaih*

ignoble SV: bēipéi; hahlàuh; dàijihn

ignoramus N: mòuhjìge yàhn; bahndáan (M: go)

ignorance SV/N: mòuhjì; yùhmuih FV: m̀jì; m̀jìdou

ignorant SV/N: mòuhjì; yùhmuih; ngoihhóng Adj. PH: móuhjìsīkge; móuhsauhgaauyuhkge

ignore FV: m̀léih; m̀chói * **to ignore rude remarks** PH: m̀léih dī mòuhléihge pàipìhng

ill FV/N: behng SV: m̀syúfuhk; m̀jingsàhn * **ill bred** SV: móuhgaauyéuhng * **ill fated** SV: fúmehng; m̀gātleih * **ill luck** PH: wahnhei m̀hóu * **ill mannered** SV: chòulóuh; móuhláihmaauh * **ill tempered** SV: bouhchou; PH: pèihhei hóu yáih * **ill treat** FV: yeuhkdoih

illegal ATT: fèifaatge; m̀-hahpfaatge; faahnfaatge VO: faahnfaat * **illegal act** PH: fèifaatge hàhngwàih

illegible SV: chóu; líu; líuchóu Adj. PH: hóunàahn táidākchēut; hóunàahnyihng

illegitmate ATT/SV: m̀-hahpfaat; m̀hahplòhchāp * **illegitimate child** N: sìsàngjí; yéhjái (coll.) yéhnéui (coll.)

illicit ATT: wàihfaatge; beihgamjíge

illiterate Adj. PH: m̀sīkjihge; móuhmàhnfage; meih sauhgwo gaauyuhkge * **illiterate person** N: màhnmàahng (M: go) * **illiterate tribes** PH: móuh màhnfage bouhlohk

illogical SV/VO: m̀hahplòhchāp; móuhdouhléih SV: lèihpóu; m̀tùng

illumine FV: ❶ jiu ❷ (enlighten) káifaat RV: jiujyuh Patt: jiudou . . . hóu gwōng

illusion N: chogok; waahnséung; waahnjeuhng (M: go)

illustrate FV/ATT: syutmihng N: chaaptòuh; tòuhgáai (M: go, fūk) PH: géuilaih syutmihng; yuhngtòuhbíu làih syutmihng * **a well-illustrated textbook** PH: yātbún chaaptòuh hóu fùngfuge gaaufōsyù

illustrious SV: chēutméng; gihtchēut; yàusau

image N: ❶ chiujeuhng (M: go) ❷ (idol) ngáuhjeuhng (M: go) ❸ (mental picture) yinihm; koinihm BF: -jeuhng · *faht* ~ FV: (reflect) fáanyíng (M: go) * **screen image** PH: ngàhn-

mohkseuhngge yîhngjeuhng * **spitting image of . . .** PH: hóuchíh . . .; haih . . . ge béngyan

imagination N: ❶ séungjeuhnglihk ❷ (illusion) waahngok FV: séungjeuhng

imagine FV: séungjeuhng; waahnséung

imbibe FV: ❶ yám ❷ kāpsàu * **imbibe beer** VO: yám bējáu * **imbibe knowledge** VO: kāpsàu jìsīk

imitate FV: mòuhfóng; hohk * **imitation** N: fóngjaibán (M: gihn) * **imitation diamonds** PH: fóngjai/jouh ge jyunsehk

immaculate SV: sèuhngit; gitjihng IE: gitjihng móuhhàh

immanent ATT: noihjoihge; yisīkjìnoihge

immaterial SV: (unimportant) m̀gányiu; m̀juhngyiu Adj. PH: (no substance) mòuhyìhngge; móuhsahtjātge

immature Adj. PH: meih faatyuhk hóu (peolpe); meih sìhngsuhk; meihdihngyìhng

immeasurable ATT: mòuhhaahnge ~ *seunsàm*

immediate A: (at once) jīkhāak SV/A: (direct) jihkjip * **immediate information** PH: jihkjip dāklàihge siusīk * **immediate family** N:jihkhaih chànsuhk

immemorial Adj. PH: mòuhfaatgeiyīkge; hóu noih tùhng hóu gauh ge

immense PH: gihkjì daaih; fèisèuhng daaih; daaih dougihk

immerse FV: jam • *jèung go tàuh ~ yahp séui léuihbihn* ✻ **immerse in thought** FV: chàhmsī ✻ **immerse in a book** PH: màaihtàuh táisyū ✻ **immerse in difficulties** PH: hahmyahp kwannàahn jìjùng

immigrant N: yìhmàhn (M: go) ✻ **immigration office** N: yìhmàhngúk (M: gàan)

imminent SV: bīkchit; gángáp; ngàihgáp PH: hóufaai jauhlàih

immobile FV: ❶ m̀yūk; gudihng ❷ (of money) m̀làuhtùng

immoderate Adj. PH: m̀jìjitjai; gwoleuhng • *yámsihk ~*

immodest SV: ❶ (rude) móuhláihmaauh; chòulóuh ❷ (impudent) móuhchí; bèipéi; m̀hnpèihháuh VO: móuhláihmaauh

immoral SV: ❶ m̀douhdāk; móuhdouhdāk ❷ (loose) m̀jingging; fòngyàhm; yàhmdohng

immortal PH: m̀wúihséige; bātnáuge; chèuhngsàngbātlóuhge IE: wíhng sèuih bāt náu ✻ **immoral poem** PH: bātnáuge sìpìn ✻ **immortal life** FV/N: wíhngsàng ✻ **the immortals** N: sàhnsīn (M: go, wái)

immovable ATT/FV: m̀yūkdāk; gudihng ✻ **immovable property** N: bātduhngcháan ✻ **immovable heart** IE: tit sehk sàm chèuhng

immune FV: míhn VO: míhnyihk (disease) ✻ **to be immune from taxation** VO: míhnseui ✻ **to be immune from smallpox** PH: deui tìnfā míhnyihk

immutable Adj. PH: bātbinge; bātyìhkge

impact N: chùnggīk; chùnggīklihk RV: jòngsaht; bīkgán; bīksaht; ngaatgán

impair FV: ❶ (damage) syúnhoih; sèunghoih ❷ (weaken) seukyeuhk

impale RV: ❶ (pierce through) gātchyūn ❷ (pin down) dèngjyuh PH: (punishment) sìyíh chiyìhng

impart FV: ❶ (give) béi; fàn(béi) ❷ (pass on) chyùhn; chyùhndaaht; tùngjì; chyùhnsauh (knowledge)

impartial SV: gùngpìhng IE: daaih gùng mòuh sī

impartible PH: m̀fàndākge; m̀hóyíh fàngotge

impassable RV: gwom̀dóu PH: móuhfaatjí tùnggwo

impasse N: gèungguhk; jyuhtgíng (M: go) séilouh (M: tìuh)

impassible SV: láahngdaahm; màhmuhk VO: móuhgámgok IE: mòuhduhngnyùjùng

impassion Patt: (arouse passons of) lihng ... gīkduhng; lihng ... gámduhng; gīkhéi ... yìhtchìhng

impatient SV: sàmgáp; singgáp; móuhnoihsing; m̀noihfàahn ✻ **impatient of** RV/A: yánm̀jyuh PH: bātnàhng yánsauh

impeach FV: ❶ (accuse) hunggou; gímgéui ❷ (question) jíjaak; jaakmahn ✻ **impeach a judge for taking bribes** PH:

gímgéuigo faatgùn sauhkwúi

impeccable SV: sèuhngit; yùhnsihn VO: móuhhàhchì; móuhgwosāt

impede FV: jóngoih; fòhngngoih

impel FV: ❶ (drive) tèuiduhng ❷ (force) bīksí; kèuisí ✳ **impeller** N: tèuiduhnghei; chèyíp (M: fu, ga)

impenetrable RV: yahpm̀dóu; chyùnm̀gwo ✳ **impenetrable darkness** Adj. PH: hākmahkmahk ✳ **impenetrable plot** PH: tèuichāakm̀dóuge yàmmàuh ✳ **men who are impenetrable to reason** PH: m̀góngdouhléihge yàhn

impenetrate RV: chyùnyahp; chyùngwo FV: samtau

impenitent SV: wàahngu; m̀góige IE: séisingbātgói

imperative SV: gángāp; gāpchit A/ATT: gāpsèui; bītsèui N: (command) mihnglihng (M: go) ✳ **imperative mood** N: mihnglihngsīk (M: go)

imperceptible SV: saimèih; hìngmèih PH: saidoum̀gokge

imperfect SV: m̀yùhnsihn; m̀yùhnchyùhn VO: yáuh kyutdím; yáuh hàhchì ✳ **imperfect tense** N: gwoheui jeunhàhngsīk (M: go)

imperial ATT: daigwokge; daiwòhngge SV: (magnificient) jòngyìhm; wàiyìhm; tòhngwòhng

imperialism N: daigwokjyúyih ✳ **imperialist** N: daigwokjyúyihjé (M: go)

imperil FV: ngàihhoih; ngàihkahp

imperishable ATT: bātmihtge; bātnáuge; wíhnghàhngge

impermanence N: jaahmsihsing; fèiwíhnggáusing

impersonal ATT: yātbùnyàhnchìngge; mòuhdahksyùhyàhnchìngge ✳ **impersonal remarks** PH: tùhng goyàhn mòuhgwàange pìhngleuhn ✳ **impersonal service** PH: fuhkmouh taaidouh hóu chà; fuhkmouh taaidouh him gàai

impersonate FV: ❶ (act) baahn; sīkyín; baahnyín ❷ (pretend) gábaahn ❸ (imitate) mòuhfóng ❹ (personify) yàhngaakfa

impertinent SV: (impolite) móuhláihmaauh; sātláih; chòulóuh VO: (not pertaining) lèihtàih; móuhgwàanlìhn; móuhgwàanhaih

impervious VO: m̀gwoséui; FV: (not moved by) m̀léih; m̀sauh . . . yínghéung RV: m̀samdākyahp

impetuous SV: gīkliht; chùngduhng; singgāp

impetus N: ❶ chùnglihk; duhnglihk ❷ (driving force) tèuiduhnglihk FV: tèuiduhng; gīklaih; chūkjeun

impinge N: chùnggīk FV: ❶ chùng; johng; gīkdá ❷ (interfere) chàmfaahn; chàmhoih

impious SV: ❶ (towards god) m̀kìhnsìhng (towards parents) m̀haauseuhn ❷ (wicked) chèhngok PH: m̀seunsàhn

implacable Adj. PH: hóunàahn wòhgáaige; hóunàahn fùnsyuge * **implacable hatred** IE: sàm sàuh daaih hahn

implant FV: ❶ (of idea) gunsyù; jyuyahp ❷ (medical) yìhjihk ❸ (of seed) jungjihk

implement N: (tool) gùnggeuih; heigeuih; gasàang (M: gihn) FV: (carry out) sahthàhng; léihhàhng; yùhnsìhng * **farm implements** N: nùhnggeuih

implicate FV: ❶ (involve) hìnlìhn; hìnsip; sipkahp ❷ (hint) ngamsih N: ngamsih; hàhmyi (M: go)

implicit SV: hàhmchūk A: (unquestionly) jyuhtdeui; (hóu) màahngmuhk (gám) IE: hòuh bāt wàaihyìh * **implicit promise** N: mahkkai (M: go) * **give implicit obedience** FV: màahngchùhng PH: jyuhtdeui fuhkchùhng

implore FV: ngài; kàuh

imply FV/N: ngamsih (M: go) Patt: hàhmyáuh . . . ge yisi

impolite SV: móuhláihmaauh; m̀haakhei; chòulóuh

import FV: wahnyahpháu; syùyahp ATT: yahpháu Patt: wahn . . .yahpháu N: ❶ yahpháufo ❷ (importance) juhngyiusing ❸ (significance) yiyih; yisi; hàhmyi * **import duty** N: yahpháuseui * **importer** N: yahpháusèung (M: go)

importance N: juhngyiusing SV: juhngyiu * **of great importance** PH: fèisèuhng juhngyiu; gihkjì juhngyiu

important SV: gányiu; juhngyiu

importunate RV: chìhnjyuh IE: chìhnyíubātyàu SV: (urgent) gāp; gángāp; gāpchit

importune FV: ngài; máahngngài A: haihyiu

impose FV: ❶ chàu * **impose tax** VO: chàuseui ❷ (make use of) leihyuhng ❸ (deceive) ngáak SV/FV: (force) míhnkéuhng VO: (of printing) jíngbáan; pingbáan

imposing SV: jòngyíhm; wàhngwáih IE: fulaih tòhngwòhng

impossible SV/A: m̀hónàhng; móuh hónàhng PH: mòuh faat yánsauh * **next to impossible** PH: gèifùh m̀hónàhng * **an impossible person** PH: yātgo lìhng yàhn mòuh faat yánsauhge yàhn

impostor N: gwònggwan; pinjí (M: go)

impotence Adj. PH: (of sex) yèuhngwái; singmòuhnàhng SV: (weak) hèuiyeuhk; móuhlihk

impound FV: ❶ muhtsàu; chùnggùng; kaungaat ❷ (shut in) wan RV: wanjyuh

impoverish Patt: lìhng (dou) . . . kùhng * **a country impoverished by war.** PH: jinjàng lìhngdou gwokgā hóu kùhng RV: yuhngsaai; yuhngjeuhn * **to impoverish the mind** IE: gáaujeuhn nóuhjāp

impracticable SV: m̀sahtjai RV: hàahngm̀tùng; jouhm̀dou

impregnable IE: gìndihngbātyìh PH: ❶ (of fortress) nàahn yíh gùngpo ❷ (of argument) nàahn yíh bokchīk

impregnation VO: wàaih-yahn; sauhjìng RV: (fill) jamtau; chùngmúhn FV: (saturate) báauwòh * **artifical impregnation** PH: yàhngùngsauhyahn

impress Patt: lihng . . . yáuh yātgo hóuge yanjeuhng; deui . . . ge yanjeuhng hóu sàm * **did not impress me much** PH: ngóh deui . . . móuhmāt yanjeuhng VO: dáyan; kāpyan

impression ❶ yanjeuhng ❷ (mark) yan M: (of print) báan * **second impression** Nu. M: daihyihbáan FV: gokdāk . . . * **I have the impression that . . .** PH: ngóh gokdāk . . . * **impressionism** N: yanjeuhngpaai; yanjeuhngjyúyih

impressive Adj. PH: lihng yàhn yanjeuhng hóu sàm; lihng yàhn nàahn mòhng

imprint RV: geisaht VO: (stamp) dáyan; kāpyan N: yan; hàhnjīk (M: go) * **the imprint of a foot** N: geukyan; jūkjīk (M: go)

imprison FV: wan; gàamgam VO: chóhgāam

improbability PH: meihbīt wúih yáuhge sih; móuhmāt hónàhngge; meihbītge

improbable PH: meihbītge; móuhmāt hónàhngge; bàthóseunge * **improbable story** móuhmāt hónàhngge gusih

impromptu Adj. PH: meih yáuh sihsìn jéunbeih hóu(ge); meih sihsìn ngònpàaih(ge) ATT/A: jīkjihk; làhmsìh * **impromptu party** PH: làhmsìhge jeuihwuih * **to speak**

impromptu PH: jīkjihk yíngóng

improper SV: ❶ (incorrect) m̀ngāam; m̀jingkok ❷ (not suitable) m̀hahpsīk ❸ (indecent) m̀jingdong; m̀douhdāk IE: m̀sàam m̀sei

impropriety SV: m̀sīkdong; m̀jingkok; m̀jingdong

improve RV: góilèuhng; góisihn; góijeun FV: ❶ (make use of) leihyuhng; sihnyuhng ❷ (progress) jeunbouh N: jeunbouh PH: (better) hóudī · *kéuihge sàntái ~ * **improve living conditions** PH: góisihn sàngwuht tìuhgín * **improve the occasion** PH: leihyuhng sìhgèi

improvise ATT: jīkhing(ge) A: jīkjihk; làhmsìh * **improvised musical performance** PH: jīkhìngge yínjau * **improvised repairs** PH: jīkjihksàuléih; làhmsìhsàuléih

impudent SV: ❶ (rude) chòulóuh; móuláihmaauh ❷ (shameless) mihnpèihháuh; mòuhchí

impulse SV: (of persons) chùngduhng FV: tèuiduhng; chūkjeun N: (of a force) tèuiduhnglihk * **give an impulse to trade** PH: chūkjeun mauhyihk

impulsive SV: chùngduhng

impunity VO: míhnjeuih; m̀sauhchìhngfaht; m̀sauhsyúnhoih

impure SV: m̀sèuhngit VO: yáuh jaahpjāt * **impure milk** PH: yáuh jaahpjātge ngàuhnáaih

impute FV: tèuiwái Patt:

jèung . . . gwàigauyù . . . • *ngóh
~ kéuihge sātbaaih ~
bāthahng*

in FV: hái Patt: ❶ hái . . .
léuihbihn (yahpbihn) ❷ .F.V.
yahp . . . leúihbihn (yahpbihn)
* in Asia PH: hái Ngajàu *
in the world PH: hái saigaaiseuhng * in two days TW:
léuhngyahtnoih; háiléuhngyaht
jínoih * in time SV: jéunsìh *
in detail SV/A: chèuhngsai *
in good health PH: sàntái hóu
hóu * in any case Patt:
mòuhleuhn dím . . . * in fact
A: sihsaht seuhng * in name
A: mìhngyihseuhng * in one
word A: júngjì; júngyìhnjì;
júngyìhyìhnjì * in place of
FV: tai; doihtai * in case MA:
maahnyāt; yùhgwó * put it in
the box PH: jàiyahp háp
léuihbihn * to write in
French PH: yuhng Faatmàhn
sé

inability SV: mòuhnàhng
VO/A: móuhnàhnglihk; móuhlihk; móuhlihkkleuhng * inability to help . . . PH: móuh
nàhnglihk bòng . . . * inability to stand PH: móuhlihk
kéihhéisàn

inaccessible PH: ❶ (of
place) m̀yahpdāk; nàahn-
heuidākdou ❷ (of things)
dākm̀dóu; nàahn yíh dākdóu ❸
(of persons) nàahn yíh jipgahn

inaccurate SV: m̀jéunkok;
m̀ngāam

inactive SV: láahnsáan;
chìhdeuhn; m̀wuhtput * inac-
tivity N: jihngjíjohngtaai

inadequacy SV: m̀sīkdong;
m̀chùngfahn; m̀yùhnchyùhn

inadmissible PH: móuhbaahnfaat sìhngyihng; móuh-

faatjí jipsauh * an inad-
missible proposal PH: yātgo
móuh faatjí jipsauhge ginyíh

inalienable PH: m̀hóyíh
jyúnyeuhngge; m̀hóyíh mōkdyuhtge; m̀fàngotdākge * inalienable rights PH: m̀hóyíh
mōkdyuhtge kyùhnleih

inanimate Adj. PH: ❶
(lifeless) móuhsàngmihngge ❷
(dull) móuhsàngheige; séihei-
chàhmchàhmge

inapplicable SV: m̀hahp-
yuhng; m̀sīkyuhng; m̀sīkyíh

inappreciable IE: mèih
bāt jūk douh; hòuh mòuh gajihk * an inapprecaible difference PH: saimèihdou táim̀-
chēut fànbiht(ge)

inapproachable Adj. PH:
❶ hóu nàahn jipgahn ge ❷ (incomparable) hóu nàahn béi-
dākséuhngge; nàahn yíh pāt-
dihkge

inappropriate SV: m̀sīk-
dong; m̀sīkhahp

inapt SV: ❶ m̀sīkdong;
m̀hahpsīk ❷ (unskilful)
m̀suhklihn; m̀suhksáu

inarticulate IE: háu chí bāt
lìhng

in as much A: ❶ (since)
geiyìhn ❷ (because) yànwaih;
yàuhyù

inattention FV: m̀jyuyi;
sòfāt SV: sòfāt IE: chòusàmdaaihyi

inaudible RV: tèngm̀gin;
tèngm̀dóu VO: móuhsèng

inauguration N: ❶ (of person to office) jauhjīkdínláih ❷
(of building) lohksìhngdínláih ❸

(of exhibition) hòimohkdínláih
(M: go)

inauspicious SV: m̀gātlcih;
m̀laihsih

inborn Adj. PH: tìnsàangge;
sàangchēutlàihge; sìntìnge;
wàihchyùhnge

inbred Adj. PH: tìnsàangge;
wàihchyùhnge N: (Bio.) gahnchànfàahnjihk

inbreeding N: gahnchàn-
gàaupui; gahnchànfàahnjihk

incalculable IE: ❶ (uncountable) sóujibātjeuhn;
bāthósìngsóu ❷ (uncertain)
jūkmóbātdihng PH: (unpredic-
table) móuhfaatjí yuhchāakge

incandescent Adj. PH:
fèisèuhng gwòng; hóu gwòng
PH: yuhdóu yiht jauh
faatgwòngge

incantation N: jauyúh;
fùhjau; yíuseuht VO: nihmjau

incapable SV: móuhyuhng
~ *ge gùngyàhn* AV/FV: m̀sīk
~ *góngdaaihwah* A: móuh-
nàhnglihk; móuhfaatjí ~ *jíng*;
~ *sàuléih*

incapacity A/VO: móuhnàhnglihk; móuhjìgaak

incarcerate FV: wan;
gàamgam RV: wanjyuh VO:
chóhgàam

incarnate PH: (in human
form) fasìhngyuhksàn N: fasàn
Patt: (into a real form) jèung . .
. geuihtáifa ✻ a devil incarnate PH: yātgo mōgwáige
fasàn

incendiary FV: sìnduhng
PH: sìnduhngge yàhn; fòngfó
geyàhn (M: go) ✻ incendiary

article PH: sìnduhngge màhnjèung ✻ incendiary bomb N:
yìhnsìudáan (M: go)

incense N: ❶ hēung (M: jì) ❷
(smell) hèungmeih RV: gīknàu
✻ incense burner N:
hèunglòuh (M: go)

incentive FV/N: gúlaih;
chigīk; gúmóuh N: gúduhng-
lihk

inception FV/A: hòichí;
héisáu

incessant A: m̀tìhng; bāt-
dyuhn

incest FV: lyuhnlèuhn

inch M: chyun PH: maahn-
máanhàahng; maahnmáan-
yìhduhng ✻ every inch IE:
chit tàuh chit méih PH: yàuh-
tàuh dou méih ✻ inch by inch
A: jihmjím Adj. PH: yātbouh
yātbouh

incident N: ❶ (event) sihgín
(M: gihn) ❷ (happening) sihbin
(M: chi) ❸ (of a play) chaapkūk
PH: (accident) ngáuhyìhngesih
✻ frontier incident PH:
bīngaai sihgín ✻ incidental
ATT: ngáuhyìhnge; fuhdaaige
✻ incidental expenses N:
jaahpfai

incinerate FV: sìu RV:
sìusaai ✻ incinerator N:
fàhnfalòuh (M: go)

incipient ATT: hòichíge;
chòkèihge ✻ incipient
disease PH: chòkèihge
behngjing

incise FV: ❶ (cut) got; chit ❷
(engrave) hāk; dìuhāk

incision N: chithàuh (M: go)

incisive SV: ❶ (of voice) jìm

❷ (of criticism) jìmyeuih **❸** (of mind) máhnyeuih ✻ **incisors** N: lòuhfúngàh; jìm mùhnngàh (M: jek)

incite FV: sinduhng; yáhnhéi

inclement SV: **❶** (of weather) hòhnláahng Adj. PH: (stormy) kwòhngfùngbouhyúh

incline FV/SV: (lean) che; jāk FV/N: kìngheung; ngoihou N: chelóu (M: tiùh) chèhbō (M: go) ✻ **inclined to** AV: séung; MA: jihmjím

include FV: bàaukwut RV: bàaumàaih; gaimàaih

inclusive PH: bàaukwutjoihnoih; bàaukwut . ﹑. joihnoih ~ leihsīk ~ ; bàau màaih saai

incognito IE: **❶** (with one's name concealed) yán sing màaih mìhng **❷** (travel in disguise) mèih fuhk chēut hàhng

incoherent SV: móuh tiùhléih; m̀lìhngun; sáansàusàu IE: (of speech) yúhmòuhlèuhnchi

income N: sàuyahp; yahpsīk ✻ **income tax** N: yahpsīkseui

incommunicable Adj. PH: móuhfaatjí chyùhndaahtge; móuhfaatjíbíudaahtge

incomparable PH: m̀ béi dāk séuhng; móuh faatjí béi gaau

incompatible SV: m̀hiptiuh; màauhtéuhn

incompetent SV: mòuhnàhng; m̀sīkhahp A/VO: m̀gau jìgaak

incomplete SV: m̀yùhnchyùhn; m̀yùhnsihn FV/ATT: meihyùhnsihng; meih héihóu

incomprehensible Adj. PH: móuhfaatjí léihgáai; móuhbaahnfaat mìhngbaahk

inconceivable IE: nàahnyíh séungjeuhng; bāt hó sìyíh

inconclusive Adj. PH: (of evidence, arguments . . .) móuh faatjí kokdihngge; móuh faatjí lìhng yàhn seunfuhkge **❷** (of effort) móuh gitgwóge

incongruity SV: m̀hahpsīk; m̀hiptiuh; m̀sèungching

inconsiderate Adj. PH: (thoughtless) m̀sīk waih yàhn jeuhkséung; m̀táileuhng yàhnge SV: (rude) lóuhmóhng; hìngsēut; m̀saisàm

inconsistency SV: m̀yātji; (chìhnhauh) màauhtéuhn; m̀hahpléih Adj. PH: yātsìhyātyeuhng

incontinent Adj. PH: móuh baahnfaat jih jai; móuh nàhnglihk hungjai(ge) ✻ **the incontinence of urine** PH: niuh sātgam

inconspicuous Adj. PH: m̀ yáhn yàhn jyuyi; m̀hínngáahn ge

incontrovertible Adj. PH: hóu mìhngkokge; móuh jàngleuhnnyùhdeihge; bātyùhngjiyihge

inconvenient SV: m̀fòngbihn

incorporate FV: hahpping; jóusìhng; pìngyahp; pìnyahp ✻ **This firm is incorporated with others.** Nīgàan gùngsī tùhng daihyihgàan hahppingjó.

incorporation FV: hahpping; githahp N: gùngsī (M: gàan) tyùhntái (M: go)

incorrect SV: m̀ngāam N/SV/RVE: cho

incorrigible RV: gói m̀ dóu IE: jīk jaahp nàahn gói

incorruptible SV: lìhmgit; chìnglìhm; m̀tàamwù Adj. PH: (of things) m̀yihlaahnge

increase FV: jànggà; gà PH: ❶ (become more) yuht làihyuht dò; dò hóudò ❷ (become greater) yuht làih yuht daaih * **increase of rent** VO: gàjòu * **increase of price** VO: gàga * **increase of salary** VO: gàsàn * **a steady increase in population** PH: yàhnháu bāt-dyuhn jànggà

incredible Adj. PH: hóu nàahn sèungseun ge IE: nàahn yíh ji seun

incredulity FV: m̀seun; m̀sèungseun; wàaihyìh

increment FV: jànggà; gà N: jànggàleuhng

incriminate FV: hunggou; lihnleuih; hìnlìhn PH: hìn-sihchēut . . . yáuhjeuih

incubate FV: ❶ fù ❷ (of germs) pùihyéuhng VO: fùdáan

incubation FV: fù VO: fù-dáan * **incubation period** N: chìhmfuhkkèih * **artificial incubation** PH: yàhngùng fùdáan

incubator N: ❶ (of egg) fù-dáanhei (M: go) ❷ (of baby) yuhkyìngsèung (M: go) ❸ (of germ) pùihyéuhnghei (M: go)

incumbent VO/A: yáuh-jaakyahm; yáuhyihmouh ATT: joihjīk; yihnyahm ~ haauhjéung

incur FV: jìuyéh; yéhhéi; mùhngsauh * **incur hatred** PH: jìuyéh sàuhhahn * **incur a loss** PH: mùhngsauh syún sāt * **incur his displeasure** PH: yéhhéi kéuihge bātyuht

incurable RV: yìm̀hóu; m̀yìdākhóu; móuhdākyì

indebted VO: himjaai; fuh-jaai; jàang . . . chín FV: (grateful) gámgīk * **heavily indebted** PH: himlohk hóudò chín (jaai)

indecent SV: ❶ (obscene) hahlàuh; wùisó; m̀jinggìng ❷ (improper) móuhláihmaauh PH: m̀ngāam kwàigéui

indecisive IE: yàuhyùh-bātkyut; géui kèih bāt dihng; sàam sàm léuhng yi

indeed A: koksaht; kokhaih; dīkkok; jànhaih

indefensible Adj. PH: ❶ (in war) móuh faatjí fòhngsáuge ❷ (in argument) móuh faatjí bihnwuhge

indefinite SV: m̀mìhngkok; hàhmwùh * **the indefinite article** PH: bātdihng gunchìh * **an indefinite time** PH: móuhhaahnkèih; móuhhaahn-ge sìhgaan

indelible Adj. PH: sáim̀lāt-ge; nàahnmòhngge * **indelible shame** PH: nàahnmòhng-ge chíyuhk

indent RV: jíngnāpjó VO: ❶ (of goods) dehngfo ❷ (of contract) dihng hahptùhng N: hahptùhng; kaiyeuk (M: fahn)

indenture N: hahptùhng; kaiyeuk (M: fahn)

independence FV/SV/N:

duhklahp FV: jihlahp * to live a life of independence PH: gwo duhklahpge sàngwuht

indescribable PH: nàahnyíh yihngyùhng RV: góngm̀chēut * indescribable beauty PH: góngm̀chēut gam leng

indestructible RV: Jíngm̀laahn PH: móuhfaatjí jínglaahn; móuh baahnfaat wáimiht

indeterminate PH: m̀kokdihngge; meihkyutdihngge SV: mòuhwùh; hàhmwùh * indeterminate color PH: sīkjaahk mòuhwùh

index N: ❶ (of a book . . .) sokyáhn ❷ (of statistics) jísou (M: go) ❸ (of an instrument) jíbiu; jíjàm (M: jì) * index finger N: sihkjí (M: jek)

Indian N: Yandouhyàhn ATT: Yandouhge * Indian corn N: sūkmáih (M: pò, gauh * Red Indian N: Yandaihngònyàhn (M: go)

indicate FV: bíusih; bíumìhng; jísih; jíchēut N: bíusih; jísih

indication FV/N: jísih; bíusih N: (sign) jīkjeuhng; yuhsiuh

indicative FV/N: jísih; bíusih ATT: jihkseuhtge; chàhnseuhtge * indicative mood N: jihkseuht yúhhei; jihkseuhtfaat

indicator N: ❶ (of machine) jísihhei (M: go) ❷ (of chemistry) jísihjài

indict FV: hunggou; héisou

indifferent SV: ❶ (cold)

láahngdaahm ❷ (not important) m̀gányiu ❸ (ordinary) pihngfàahn FV: ❶ (not care) m̀gwàansàm; m̀joihfùh ❷ (neutral) jùnglahp

indigestible Adj. PH: nàahn sìufage * indigestion PH: sìufa bātlèuhng

indignant FV/SV: nàu SV: fáhnnnouh SV: fáhnfáhnbātpìhng

indignity FV/N: móuhyuhk PH: sèunghoih . . . jihjyùnsàm

indirect A: gaanjip

indiscernible RV: fànm̀chēut; fànbihnm̀chēut

indiscreet SV: m̀gánsahn; hìngsēut

indispensable Adj. PH: m̀síudākge; bītsèuige; jyuhtdeui bītyiuge

indisposed SV: m̀syùfuhk; m̀jihyìhn AV: m̀séung; m̀yuhnyi

indisputable Adj. PH: bāt yùhng ji bihnge; bāthó wàaihyìhge

indistinct SV: m̀chìngchó; mòuhwùh

indistinguishable RV: fànm̀chēut

individual ATT: goyàhn; gobiht; jihgéi(ge) SV: duhkdahk * individual style PH: duhkdahkge fùnggaak * individualism N: goyàhn jyúyih; leihgéijyúyih

indivisible PH: ❶ m̀hóyíh fàngotge; m̀hóyíh fànlihtge ❷ (of maths.) chèuihm̀jeuhnge * indivisible atoms PH: m̀hóyíh fànlihtge yùhnjí

indolent SV: láahn; láahn-doh

indomitable PH: m̀wāt-fuhkge IE: bāt wāt bāt nàauh ~ *ge yúhnghei*

Indonesian N: Yannèih-yàhn; Yannèihwá

indoor ATT/PW: sātnoih * **indoor games** N: sātnoih yàuhhei * **indoor plants** N: sātnoih jihkmaht

induce FV: ❶ yáhn; yáhnyáuh; yáhnhéi ❷ (cause) lihng (dou); sáidou ❸ (persuade) hyun; yáuhdouh

induct FV: ❶ yáhndouh; yáhnlíhng; gaaisiuh ❷ (of reasoning) gwàinaahp ❸ (electrical) gámying PH: (of appointment) jingsīk jauhjīk * **induction** N: gwàinaahpfaat (M: go) * **induction coils** N: gámyinghyūn (M: go)

indulge FV: ❶ jung; jungyùhng; jauh; chìnjauh • *m̀hóu taaigwo ~ dī saimānjái* ❷ chàhmmàih ~ *dóubok*

induration FV: ngaahngfa SV: hánsàm; láahnghuhk; wàahngu

industrial ATT: gùngyihp (ge) * **industrial revolution** N: gùngyihp gaapmihng * **industrial estate** N: gùngyihp-chyūn * **industrialist** N: sahtyihpgā; gùngyihpgā (M: go) * **industrialize** FV: gùng-yihpfa

industrious SV: kàhnlihk

industry N: gùngyihp * **heavy industry**; N: chúhng-gùngyihp * **light industry** N: hìnggùngyihp

inebriate PH: lihngdou . . . jeui jó RV: yámjeui N: jáutòuh; jáugwái ; jeuijáugwái

inedible PH: m̀sihkdāk

ineffective PH: mòuh-haauh; móuh māt haauhyuhng SV: móuhyuhng * **indeffective medicine** PH: dī yeuhk móuh māt haauh

inefficient SV: móuhyuhng; m̀jùngyuhng PH: haauhléut hóu dài

ineligible A/VO: móuhjī-gaak

inequality SV: m̀pìhng-dáng; m̀gùngpìhng; m̀pìhng-gwàn N: (of maths) bātdángsīk

inequitable SV: m̀gùng-pìhng; m̀gùngjing

inequity SV: m̀gùngpìhng; m̀gùngjing PH: m̀gùngpìhngge yéh/sih

ineradicable PH: móuh baahnfaat gànjyuhtge IE: g̀an-sàmdaigu ~ *jaahpgwaan*

inert PH: móuh sàng-mìhngge; móuh wuhtduhng nàhnglihkge SV: láahndoh; chìhdeuhn

inertia N: gwaansing; doh-sing * **law of inertia** N: gwaansing dihngleuht

inestimable Adj. PH: móuh baahnfaat gúgaige; fèisèuhng jàngwaige * **a thing of inestimable value** PH: mòuhga (jì) bóu

inevitable Adj. PH: mòuhhó beihmíhnge; m̀míhndākge; yātdihng wúih faatsàngge

inexact SV: m̀jéunkok; m̀jingkok

inexcusable PH: bāt hó yùhnleuhngge; móuh baahnfaat yùhnleuhngge

inexhaustible Adj. PH: mòuhkùhngjeuhnge; chéuijibātjeuhnge; yuhngjibātyùhnge * **inexhaustible supply of coal** PH: mùihge gùngying, chéuijibātjeuhn, yuhngjibātyùhn

inexpensive SV: pèhng; sèungyìh

inexperience SV: móuh gingyihm; m̀suhksáu; m̀joihhòhng

inexplicable Adj. PH: móuh faatjí mìhngbaahkge móuh baahnfaat léihgáaige IE: mohk mìhng kèih miuh

inexplicit SV: m̀chìngchó; m̀mìhngkok; hàhmwùh; móuhwùh

inexpressible RV: góngm̀chēut PH: móuh faatjí bíudaaht; nàahn yíh yìhngyùhngge

inextinguishable Adj. PH: sìumihtm̀dóuge; móuh faatjí pokmihtge; móuh baahnfaat yìkjaige

infallible Adj. PH: wíhngyúhn m̀wúih choge; jyuhtdeui hókaau; jyuhtdeui koksaht

infamous SV: mòuhchí Adj. PH: bātmìhngyuhge IE: jeuihdaaihngokgihk * **infamous behavior** PH: bātmìhngyuhge hàhngwàih * **infamous traitor** PH: jeuihdaaihngokgihkge maaihgwokchaahk

infamy SV: hóchí; bātmìhngyuh N: chauméng PH: hóchíge hàhngwàih

infancy N: yaunìhn; yìngyìhkèih; chòkèih * **from infancy to old age** PH: chùhng yaunìhn dou lóuhnìhn * **the infancy of a nation** PH: yātgo gwokgā lahpgwokge chòkèih

infant N: bìhbījái; sòuhàjái; yìngyìh * **mortality rate** N: yìngyìh séimòhngléut

infantile ATT: yìngyìh (ge); síuyìh (ge); chòkèih (ge) SV: yaujih * **infantile paralysis** N: síuyìh màhbeijìng * **infantile mind** PH: yaujihge tàuhnóuh

infantry N: bouhbìng * **an infantry regiment** PH: yātgo bouhbìngtyùhn * **infantryman** N: bouhbìng (M: go)

infatuate FV: màihlyún ~ yātgo leng néui PH: lihngdou . . . wùhtòuh; lihngdou . . . màihwaahk

infeasible PH: m̀hónàhngge; baahnm̀douge; hàahngm̀tùngge

infect FV: ❶ (of disease) chyùhnyíhm; yéh (coll) ❷ (of excitement) gámyíhm * **infectious disease** N: chyùhnyíhmbehng

infer FV/N: tèuichāak; ngamsih N; tèuileuhn (M: go)

inference N: tèuileuhn; tèuiléih; gitleuhn (M: go)

inferior SV: ❶ (of quality) yáih ❷ (of position) dài; dàikāp N: sáuhah; hahsuhk; bouhhah * **inferior to** Patt: N1 dàikāpgwo N2; N1 yáihgwo N2 N1 bātyùh N2 * **inferiority complex** N: jihbēigám * **goods of inferior workmanship** PH: sáugùng béigaau yáihge fobán

infernal ATT: deihyuhkge SV: chàahnbouh; hùngngok; hātyàhnjàng * **infernal spirit** PH: deihyuhkge gwái * **infernal deed** PH: chàahnbouhge hàhngwàih

infest FV: sòuyíu; chàmyíu RV:múhnsaai; sàangmúhn (with lice)

infidelity SV: m̀jùngsaht; bātjùng PH: m̀jùngsahtge hàhngwàih; bātjùngge hàhngwàih * **conjugal infidelity** FV: tùnggàan

infiltrate FV: samyahp; samtau

infinite ATT: mòuhhaahnge; geuihdaaihge * **The Infinite** N: Seuhngdai (M: go, wái)

infinitive ATT: bātdihngge N: bātdihngsīk; bātdihngchih (M: go)

infirm SV: ❶ (weak) yeuhk; hèuiyeuhk ❷ (morally weak) nohyeuhk PH: yiji bohkyeuhk * **infirmary** N: yīliuhsāt; chánsó (M: gàan, go)

inflame FV: ❶ (of disease) faatyìhm ❷ (incite) sinduhng ❸ (burn) sìu RV: gīknàu; gīkhéi * **inflammation** FV: faatyìhm

inflammable Adj. PH: yùhngyih jeuhkfóge; yáhnfóge; yùhngyih gīkduhngge * **inflammable gas** N: yihyìhn heitái

inflate FV/ATT: pàahngjeung SV: ❶ (of language) kwàjèung ❷ (of pride) dākyi RV: chèuidaaih; chèuijeung ~ *go heikàuh*

inflation FV/ATT: pàahngjeung PH: (of money) tùngfo

pàahngjeung; mahtga bouhjeung

inflect VO/N: (of tones) binyàm; bindiuh PH: (of grammar) yùhméih binfa FV: wāt; ngáau

inflexible SV: gìndihng; kèuhngngaahng; bātwāt Adj. PH: m̀hóyíh góibinge

inflict CV: yúhyíh; gáyíh PH: gàhoihyù . . . VO: ❶ sauhfú (suffering) ❷ sauh chyúfaht (punishment) * **inflict a blow** PH: yúhyíh dágīk * **infliction** N: dágīk; sèunghoih

inflow FV/N: làuhyahp; jyuyahp; kāpyahp * **the inflow of the tide** PH: chiuhséuige làuhyahp

influence FV/N: yínghéung; gámfa N: (power) sailihk; kyùhnlihk * **have an influence on** PH: deui . . . yáuh yínghéung

influential SV: yáuh sailihk; yáuh yínghéunglihk

influenza N: làuhhàhngsing gámmouh

influx FV/N: làuhyahp; yúngyahp * **the influx of immigrants** PH: yìhmàhnge yúngyahp

inform FV/N: tùngjì FV: góng (béi) . . . jì/tèng * **well informed** SV: sìusīklìhngtùng

informal ATT: fèijingsīkge; m̀kèuiláihge

information FV/N: tùngjì; bougou N: ❶ (news) sìusīk ❷ (intelligence) chìhngbou; jìliu ❸ (knowledge) jìsīk * **ask for information** VO: dáting sìusīk * **for your information**

only PH: gán gùng chàamháau

infraction FV: wàihfáan; wàihbui VO: faahnfaat * **an infraction of treaty** VO: wàihfáan tiuhyeuk

infrared ATT: hùhngngoihsinge; hùhngngoihkèuige * **infrared ray** N: hùhngngoihsin

infrequent SV: hèisíu; hóngin * **infrequent visitor** N: hèihaak * **infrequently** A: ngáuhyìhn

infringe FV: chàmfaahn; wàihbui * **infringe a copyright** VO: chàmfaahn báankyùhn * **infringe an oath** VO: wàihbui saihyìhn

infuriate RV: gīknàu PH: lìhngdou . . . hóunàu Adj. PH: hóunàu; nàu dāk hóu gányiu

infuse FV: ❶ (pour) jyu (yahp) ❷ (incite) gúlaih; gúmóuh ❸ (of quality . . .) gunsyù ❹ (brew) paau; jam * **infuse tea leaves** VO: paauchàh

ingenious SV: ❶ chùngmìhng ❷ (of thing) jìn'gháau Adj. PH: (of a person) yáuh chongjoklihkge; yáuh chongjok tìnchòihge

ingenuity N: chongjouhlihk; chitgainàhnglihk; duhkchongsing

ingenuous SV: sēutjihk; táanbaahk; tìnjàn; dàansèuhn * **ingenuous smile** PH: tìnjànge mèihsiu

ingot N: jyumóu M: dihng * **gold ingot** N: gàmtíu (M: tìuh)

ingratiate FV: tóuhóu; bāgit VO: paakmáhpei (coll); tokdaaihgeuk (coll); chaathàaih (coll)

ingratitude IE: mòhngyànfuhyih

ingredient N: ❶ sìhngfahn; yiusou ❷ (of food) puilíu; chòihlíu

ingrown PH: heung noih sàang ge * **an ingrown toenail** PH: dáwàahng sàangyahp yuhkge geukgaap

inhabit FV: jyuh; gèuijyuh * **inhabitant** N: gèuimàhn (M: go)

inhale FV: kāp; kāpyahp VO: kāphei; sokhei

inherent PH: guyáuhge; sàangchēutge

inherit FV: ❶ (as an heir) gaisìhng; sìhngsauh ❷ (derive from ancestor) wàihchyùhn * **inheritor** N: gaisìhngyàhn (M: go)

inhibit FV: ❶ (hinder) gamjí ❷ (restrain) yīkjai; ngaatyīk * **an inhibited person** PH: yīkjai gámchìhngge yàhn

inhospitable SV: ❶ (of person) láahngdaahm; m̀yihtchìhng ❷ (of place) fònglèuhng

inhuman SV: móuhyàhnsing; chàahnyán; chàahnhuhk * **inhuman treatment** FV: yeuhkdoih

initial ATT: jeuichòge; héisáuge; hòitàuhge PH: (of a name) héisáuge jihmóuh VO: (sign) chìmméng * **initial stage** ATT/TW: chòkèih * **the initial letter of a word** PH: yātgo jih hòitàuhge jihmóuh

initiate FV: ❶ (give instruction) gaaudouh; yàhnjeun; chyùhnsauh ❷ (begin) hòichí; jeuhksáu ~ *yātgo gaiwaahk;*

faathéi PH: (introduce) jingsīk gaaisiuh

initiation FV: hòichí; faathéi; gáyahp VO: yahpwúi * initiation fee N: yahpwúifai * initiation ceremonies N: yahpwúi yìhsīk (M: go)

initiative ATT: chòbouhge; hòichíge N: jyúduhngsing; jīkgihksing

inject VO: dájām FV: jyuseh * injector N: ❶ jyusehhei; (M: jì) ❷ (of person) jyusehjé (M: go)

injure FV/N: sèunghoih; syúnhoih

injurious SV: yáuhhoih

injury FV/N: ❶ sèunghoih; syúnhoih ❷ (insult) móuhyuhk

injustice SV: m̀gùngpìhng; m̀gùngdouh; m̀jingyih

ink N: mahkséui (M: jèun, dihk) * ink fish N: mahkyùh (M: tiuh) * ink pad N: yannàih (M: hahp)

inkling FV/N: ngamsih (M: go) PH: leuhk jì yāt yih; jíjìdéi * to have an inkling of PH: leuhk yáuh só jì

inland PW: noihdeih

in-law N: yànchàn; ngoihchīk

inlay FV: sèung; ham ~ (dī) jyunsehk

inlet N: ❶ hóiháu; hóiwāan (M: go) ❷ (way in) tùngdouh; (M: tiuh) yahpháu (M: go)

inmate N: ❶ (of dwelling) tùhngngūkjyú ❷ (of person) gāamdáan ❸ (of hospital) behngyàhn (M: go) PH: tùhng-màaihjyuhge yàhn

inn N: haakjáan; léuihgún; jáudimjái (M: gàan)

innate ATT: tìnsàangge; tìnyìhnge

inner ATT: yahpbihnge; noihbouhge; noihsàmge * inner feelings PH: noihsàmge gámchìhng

innocent SV: tìnjàn; dàan-sèuhn VO: (not guilty) móuh-jeuih N/PH: tìnjànge yàhn; móuhjeuihge yàhn

innocuous ATT: móuhhoihge; móuhduhkge

innovate FV/N: góigaak FV/ATT: gaaksàn * innovator N: gaaksànjé; góigaakjé (M: go)

innuendo FV yíngseh; jung-sèung FV/N: fungchi; fúngchi; féipóhng

innumerable ATT: mòuh-souge Adj. PH: mòuhsou gam dò; sóum̀jeuhn gam dò

inobservance FV: m̀jyuyi; fātsih; m̀jèunsáu (rules)

inoculate VO: ❶ dá yuh-fòhngjām ❷ (small pox) jungdáu ❸ (of plant) jipngàh; jipmuhk

inoffensive Adj. PH: móuh-hoihge; móuhngoihge; m̀lihng-yàhn tóuyimge

inoperative Adj. PH: móuhhaauhyuhngge; móuhjok-yuhngge; móuhyīkge

inopportune SV: m̀hahp-sìh; m̀ngāam * inopportune visitor ❶ IE: bāt chūk jì haak ❷ PH: làihdāk m̀hahpsìh/m̀ ngāam ge yàhnhaak

inordinate Adj. PH: móuh-jitjaige; gwodouhge; móuh-kwàidihngge SV: lyuhn; móuh-kwàijāk ✳ **inordinate hours** PH: sìhgaan hóu lyuhn; sìhgaan móuh kwàidihng ✳ **inordinate request** PH: yiukàuh gwodouh

inorganic ATT: mòuhgèi (ge); mòuh sàngmahtge ✳ **inorganic matter** N: mòuhgèi-maht ✳ **inorganic chemistry** N: mòuhgèi fahohk

inpatient N: jyuhyúnbehng-yàhn (M: go)

input FV: syùyahp N: syù-yahpmaht; syùyahppleuhng

inquest FV/N: sámseun; sámpun ✳ **last inquest** PH: jeuihauh sámpun ✳ **coroner's inquest** VO: yihmsī

inquire FV: mahn; sèun-mahn; mahnkahp ✳ **inquire into** FV/N: diuhchàh

inquiry FV: sèunmahn FV/N: diuhchàh

inquisition FV/N: diuh-chàh; sámmahn ✳ **inquisitive** SV: houkèih; dōsih Adj. PH: hou gún hàahnsih

inroad FV/N: jaahpgīk; gùnggīk; chàmfaahn ✳ **inroads** FV/N: syúnhoih; chàmsihk

insane SV: dìn; sàhngìng FV: faatdìn ✳ **insane asylum** N: jìngsàhnbehngyún sàhn-gìngbehngyún (M: gàan)

insanitary SV: m̀waihsàng; m̀hahpwaihsàng

insanity SV: dìn; sàhngìng FV: faatdìn N: sàhngìngbehng

insatiable Adj. PH: fèi-sèuhng tàamsàm; tàam-dākmòuhyim

inscribe ❶ hāak; hāk ❷ (write) sé · *hái búnsyù seuhngbihn* ~ *go méng*; gei ❸ (dedicate) hin (béi) ✳ **inscribe a tomb with a name** PH: hāk go méng hái mouhbèi seuhngbihn

inscription N: (of a monument) bèimàhn; bèimìhng VO/N: tàihchìh; tàihjìh

inscrutable Adj. PH: bāthó-sīyìhge; bāthólèihgáaige; móuh faatjí chāakdohkge ✳ **Inscrutable are the ways of heaven** PH: tìndouh nàahn-chāak

insect N: chùhng; kwàn-chùhng (M: jek)

insecticide N: saatchùhng-jài; nùhngyeuhk

insecure SV: m̀ngònchyùhn; m̀wánjahn

insensible FV: ❶ (unaware) m̀jì; m̀gok ❷ (numb) màh-muhk; màhbei SV: láahng-daahm PH: (unconscious) bāt-síngyàhnsih; wàhnjó

insensitive VO: móuhgám-gok SV: m̀máhngám Adj. PH: gámgok chìhdeuhn

inseparable RV: fànm̀hòi; m̀fàndākhòi; lìhnm̀aaih

insert FV: ❶ chaap; chaap-yahp ❷ (of lace) sèung ✳ **insert an advertisement** VO: maaihgwónggou; dànggwóng-gou ✳ **insert a key in a lock** PH: chaap tiuh sósìh yahp bá sósyu

inset FV: chaap; chaapyahp;

ham; hamyahp N: chaaptòuh (M: fûk) chaapyihp

inside PW: yahpbihn; léuihbihn; léuihtàuh * **inside trouble** N: chèuhngwaihbehng * **inside out** FV: fáanjyunjó

insidious SV: yàmhím; gàanwaaht

insight N: gùnchaatlihk; ginsīk * **a man of insight** PH: yáuh ginsīkge yàhn

insignia N: fàijèung; fànjèung; biuji

insignificant SV: m̀juhngyiu; móuhyuhng; móuhyiyih IE: mèih bāt jūk douh

insincere SV: móuhsìhngyi; hèuingaih

insipid SV: táahm; móuhmeih

insist A: haih; haihwah FV: gìnchìh; kèuhngdiuh * **insist on** A: haihyiu; yātdihngyiu * **to insist on the importance of being punctual** PH: kèuhngdiuh sáusìhge juhngyiu

insolent SV: ❶ (rude) chòulóuh; móuhláihmaauh ❷ (arrogant) ngouhmaahn

insoluble Adj. PH: ❶ (of substances) m̀yùhnggáaige ❷ (of problems) móuhfaatjí gáaikyutge; nàahn yíh gáaisīkge

insolvent VO: pocháan Adj. PH: móuh nàhnglihk wàahnjaai * **insolvent debtor** N: pocháanjé; pocháange yàhn (M: go)

insomnia FV: sātmìhn N: sātmìhnjing

inspect FV: ❶ (of goods) gímchàh; gímyihm ❷ (of factory) sihchaat ❸ (of troops) gímyuht ❹ (of document) sámchàh

inspiration N: lìhnggám; káisih (M: go)

inspire VO: kāphei (air) FV: (encourage) gúmóuh; gīklaih PH: (fill with creative power) béi . . . lìhnggám; jyuyahp chongjouhlihk

instability SV: m̀wándihng; m̀ngòndihng N: bātwándihngsing

install FV: ❶ (of thing) jòng; ngòn; ngònjòng ❷ (of person) jauhjīk; jauhyahm; yahmmìhng * **ceremony to install a new principal** PH: sàn haauhjéung jauhjīk dínláih

installment FV: fànkèihfuhfún ATT: (of story) lìhnjoi NuM: yātkèih; yātpài; yātbouhfahn * **the first installment of goods** PH: daihyātpài fo * **a novel in installments** PH: lìhnjoi síusyut

instance N: laih; sahtlaih FV/N: chíngkàuh; ginyíh N: chìhngyìhng ; chìhngfong * **for instance** MA: peiyùh; laihyùh * **give an instance** VO: géuilaih * **in this instance** PH: hái nīgo chìhngyìhng jìhah

instant A: jīkhāak; lahphāak; góngán * **for an instant** TW: yātjahngāan * **to be in instant need of help** PH: gāp sèui bòngmòhng * **instant noodle** N: jīksihkmihn; gùngjáimihn * **instant coffee** PH: jīkchùngjīkyám gafē * **instant fame** PH: jīkhāak chēutméng

instantaneous A: jīkhāak; jīksih ∗ **instantaneous photograph** PH: jīk yíng jīk yáuh ge séung; faaiséung

instead FV: tai; doih; doihtai A: (yìh) m̀haih ∗ **You should be working instead of playing** Néih yìnggòi jouhyéh yìh m̀haih wáan

instigate FV: sinduhng; súngyúng

instill FV: gunsyù; jyuyahp; dihkyahp ∗ **instill knowledge** VO: gunsyù jìsīk

instinct N: jihkgok; búnnàhng; tìnsing

instinctive ATT: búnnàhngge; tìnsàangge; jihkgokge ∗ **instinctive movement** PH: búnnàhngge duhngjok

institute FV/N: chitlahp; jaidihng ~ *faatleuht* N: ❶ (of society) wúi; séh; wuihséh; hipwúi (M: go) ❷ (of school) hohkwúi (M: go) ❸ (of college) hohkyún (M: gàan) ∗ **an art institute** N: ngaihseuht hohkyún (M: gàan) ∗ **research institute** N: yìhngausó; yìhngauyún (M: gàan, go)

institution FV/N: chitlahp; jaidihng N: ❶ (of charity) gèikau; gèigwaan (M: go) ❷ (of society) wuihséh; hipwúi (M: go) ❸ (of school) hohkwúi (M: go) ❹ (of college) hohkyún (M: gàan)

instruct FV: ❶ (teach) gaau; gaausauh ❷ (inform) tùngjì ❸ (order) mihnglihng FV/N: gaaudouh; jídouh

instructor N: sìnsàang; gaausī; gaauyùhn (M: wái, go) ∗ **language instructor** N: yúhyìhn douhsī (M: wái, go)

instrument N: ❶ (tools) gùnggeuih; gachàang (coll.) (M: gihn) ❷ (apparatus) yìhhei (M: gihn) ❸ (of music) ngohkhei (M: gihn)

instrumentality N: gùnggeuih; mùihgaai; sáudyuhn ∗ **through/by the instrumentality of** PH: jihkjyuh/kaau . . . ge bòngjoh; yíh . . . wàih sáudyuhn

insubordinate Adj. PH: m̀tèngwahge; m̀fuhkchùhng seuhngsīge; m̀seuhnchùhng mihnglihngge

insufferable Adj. PH: nàahn yíh yánsauhge; lihng yàhn nàahnhàmge ~ *taaidouh;* ~ *syutwah*

insufficient FV/SV: m̀gau; m̀jūkgau

insulate FV: gaaklèih; gùlahp PH: lihng . . . jyuhtyùhn; lihngdou/sáidou . . . tùhng ngoihgaai jyuhtyùhn ∗ **to insulate an electric wire with rubber** PH: yuhngdī jeuhnggāau sáidou dī dihnsin tùhng ngoihgaai jyuhtyùhn ∗ **insulator** N: jyuhtyùhntái

insulin N: yìhdóusou

insult FV/N: móuhyuhk

insupportable Adj. PH: ❶ (unbearable) nàahn yíh yánsauhge ❷ (without logic) móuhléihyàuhge; móuh gàngeuige

insurance N: bóuhím; yinsō VO: bóuhím ∗ **insurance premium** N: bóuhímfai ∗ **life insurance** N: yàhnsauh bóuhím

insure VO: máaihbóuhím; máaihyinsō FV: bóujing;

kokbóu

insurgent FV: héiyih; bouhduhng; jokfáan; buhnbin N: bouhduhngjé; héiyihjé, buhnbinjé (M: go) ✳ **insurgent troops** N: buhngwān

insurmountable Adj. PH: móuh faatjí hākfuhkge; móuh faatjí gáaikyutge; nàahn yíh yuhtgwoge ✳ **insurmountable difficulty** PH: móuh faatjí hākfuhkge kwannàahn ✳ **insurmountable chain of hills** PH: nàahn yíh yuhtgwoge sàanmahk

insurrection FV/N: héiyih; buhnlyuhn; bouhduhng

intact SV: yùhnjíng PH: meih/móuh yūkgwo IE: yùhnfùngbātduhng ✳ **to live on the interest and keep the capital intact** PH: kaau leihsīk wàihchìh sàngwuht, móuh yūkgwo dī búngām

intake FV: yáhnyahp; naahpyahp; sipchéui N: ❶ (of place) yahpháu (M: go) ❷ (of quantity) naahpyahpleuhng

intangible Adj. PH: jūkmómdóuge; mòuhyìhngge

integral FV: jóusìhng SV: yùhnjíng ATT: ❶ bītsèuige; bītyiuge ❷ (of maths.) jíngsouge; jīkfànge ✳ **integral calculus** N: jīkfàn (M: go) ✳ **integral number** N: jíngsou (M: go)

integrate PH: sáidou/lihngdou . . . yùhnjíng; jèung . . . hahpyìhwàihyāt; jèung . . . hahpsìhng yātgo jíngtái N: jīkfàn; júngwòh

integrity SV: ❶ (upright) jingjihk; lìhmjing ❷ (complete) yùhnjíng

intellect N: ❶ jilihk; léihgáailihk; lìhngnghlihk ❷ (of person) jisīkfahnjí (M: go)

intellectual Adj. PH: hóuchùngmìhng; hóuyáuhjiwai N: jisīkfahnjí (M: go)

intelligence N: ❶ jilihk; chòihji ❷ (information) chìhngbou; sìusīk (M: go) ✳ **intelligence quotient (I.Q.)** jisèung ✳ **intelligence department** N: chìhngbougúk (M: go) ✳ **intelligence test** N: jilihk chāakyihm (M: go)

intelligentsia N: jisīkfahnjí (M: go)

intelligible Adj. PH: hóyíh léihgáaige; hóu yùhngyih mìhngbaahkge; hóu chìngchóge ✳ **intelligible explanation** PH: gáaisīk dāk hóu chìngchó

intend FV/N/AV: dásyun AV: sèung

intense SV: yihtliht; kèuhngliht; kehkliht; yihtchìhng; gánjèung ✳ **intense life** PH: gánjèungge sàngwuht ✳ **intense pain** PH: kehktung ✳ **intense young lady** PH: yihtchìhngge siunéuih

intensify RV: gàkèuhng; gàkehk; gàsàm ✳ **intensify hatred** PH: gàsàmjó sàuhhahn

intension N: ❶ kèuhngdouh ❷ (of logic) noihhàahm RV: gàkèuhng

intensity SV: kèuhngliht; kehkliht N: kèuhngdouh; sàmdouh

intensive RV: jàngkèuhng; gàkèuhng VO: (of grammar) gàkèuhng yúhhei SV: tauchit; jìngsàm SV/FV: jaahpjùng ✳

intensive reading PH: jīngduhk * intensive bombardment PH: jaahpjùng fólihk/paaufó * intensive care unit N: sàmchit jihlìuh bouh

intention N: kéihtòuh; muhkdīk; yisi * bad intention N: ngokyi * with the intention of A: guyi; dahkdáng; jyùndáng * without intention A: mòuhyi

inter FV: maaih; jong; màaih-jong * inter school ATT: haauhjai * inter school music competition N: haauh-jai yàmngohk béichoi

interact PH: wuhsèung yínghéung N: sèungwuhjok-yuhng

intercede FV: tiuhtìhng VO: jouhjùnggàanyán PH: doih . . . kàuhchìhng

intercept RV: jihtjyuh; jiht-tyúhn FV: jójí * interception N: tàutènghei (M: go)

interchange FV: gàauwuhn

intercom N: deuigónggèi (M: go, fu, bouh)

interconnect PH: wuh-sèung lyùhnhaih

intercontinental ATT: jàujaige * intercontinental ballistic missile N: jàu-jaidouhdáan (M: go)

intercourse FV: gàaujai; lòihwóhng; gàaulàuh * social intercourse ATT/N: séhgàau * sexual intercourse ATT/FV: singgàau * commercial intercourse ① FV: tùng-sèung ② PH: sàangyiseuhngge lòihwóhng * cultural intercourse N: màhnfagàaulàuh

intercross FV: ❶ gàaujīk ❷ (of breeding) gàaupui VO: dá kàauchà N: jaahpjúng

interdependence PH: wuhsèung yílaaih * the interdependence of capital and labour PH: lòuh jī sèungfòng wuhsèung yílaaih

interest N: ❶ hingcheui; cheuimeih ❷ (share) gúfán; kyùhnyīk ❸ (advantage) leihyīk ❹ (money return) leihsīk PH: yáuh leihhoih gwàanhaihge * interest party PH: yáuh leihhoih gwàanhaihge yātfòng * a book of no interest PH: yātbún móuh cheuimeihge syù * take an interest in FV: héifùn; gwàansàm * to be interested in PH: deui . . . yáuh hingcheui * common interest N: guhngtùhngleihyīk * to look after one's own interests PH: jíhaih gu jihgéige leihyīk * to pay 10% interest on a loan PH: jechín ge leihsīk haih yātlèih

interfere FV: gònsip; fòhngngoih; dágáau PH: tùhng . . . yáuh dáijùk * pleasure interferes with business PH: hingcheui tùhng sihyihp yáuh dáijùk

interference FV: gònsip; fòhngngoih FV/N: (of broadcasting) gònyíu

interim N: gwodouhsihkèih A/ATT: jaahmsìh; làhmsìh * interim certificate N: làhmsìhjingsyù (M: jèung)

interior, PW/ATT: ❶ (inside) léuihbihn(ge); noihbouh(ge) ❷ (inland) noihdeih(ge) ❸ (domestic) gwoknoih(ge) * interior decoration N: sāt-noihchitgai * interior trade PH: gwoknoih mauhyihk *

interior angle N: noihgok ∗ **traveling in the interior** PH: hái noihdeih léuihhàhng

interject FV: chaapyahp ∗ **interjection** N: gámtaanchìh (M: go)

interlope PH: ❶ chàmfaahn yàhndeihge kyùhnleih; gònsip yàhndeih ❷ (of business) mòuhpàaih gìngyìhng

interlude N: chaapkūk (M: jì, sáu)

intermediate ATT: jùnggàan(ge); jùngkáp(ge) N: (of person) jùnggàanyán (M: go) FV: tiuhgáai ∗ **intermediate stage** N: jùngdyuhn or jùng gàange gàaidyuhn ∗ **the elementary, intermediate, and advanced examination** PH: chòkāp; jùngkáp tùhng gòukāpge háausíh

intermedium N: mùihgaai; mùihgaaimaht

intermingle FV: wahnhahp RV: lòumàaih; kàumàaih

intermission FV: jaahmtìhng; jùngtyúhn; jùngjí PH: ❶ yàusīksìhgaan ❷ (of movie) jùngchèuhng yàusīk ∗ **without intermission** A: bāttìhnggám; bātdyuhngám ∗ **intermittent** N: jàukèihsing; gaanhitsing

internal N/ATT: noihbouh PW: léuihtàuh; léuihbihn ∗ **internals** N: noihjohng ∗ **internal injury** N: noihsèung ∗ **internal parts of the body** PH: sàntáige noihbouh ∗ **internal disturbances** N: noihlyuhn

international ATT: gwokjai ∗ **international law** N: gwokjaifaat; gwokjaigùngfaat ∗ **international phonetic**

alphabet N: gwokjaiyāmbīu ∗ **internationalism** N: gwokjaijyúyih

internment FV/ATT: kèuilàuh; gambai ∗ **internment camp** N: kèuilàuhsó; gambaiyìhng (M: go)

interpellate FV/N: jātmahn; jātsèun

interphone N: deuigónggèi (M: go, bouh, fu) noihbouh tùngseun dihnwá (M: go)

interplanetary ATT: sìngjai(ge) ∗ **interplanetary travel** PH: sìngjai hòhnghàhng

interplay N: sèungwuhjokyuhng

interpolate FV: ❶ (insert) chaap; chaapyahp ❷ (add) gà; gàtìm ❸ (alter) gói; chyúngói ∗ **interpolate a manuscript** PH: chyúngói màhngóu

interpose FV: chaapyahp; gaaiyahp; gònsip ∗ **interpose in a dispute** PH: gaaiyahp jàngcháau ∗ **interpose in this matter** PH: gònsip nīgihn sih

interpret FV: ❶ (explain) gáaisīk; gáaimìhng ❷ (translate) fàanyihk; chyùhnyihk (verbal) ❸ (perform) yín; bíuyín ❹ (consider) yihngwàih ∗ **interpreter** N: gónggáaiyùhn; fàanyihk; chyùhnyihkyùhn (verbal) (M: go)

interrelation N: sèungwuh gwàanhaih; sèunggwàansing FV: wuhsèung gwàanlihn; sèunggwàan

interrogate FV: jātmahn; sámmahn ∗ **interrogation mark** N: mahnhouh (M: go)

interrogative FV: jātmahn

N: yìhmahn; yìhmahnchìh ∗
interrogative sentence N:
yìhmahngeui (M: geui)

interrupt RV: dátyúhn FV:
dáyíu

intersect FV: ❶ chyùngwo;
wáahnggwo ❷ (of two lines)
sèunggàau · *Jihksin AB tùhng
CD ∼ yù E dím* ∗ **intersec-
tion** N: ❶ gàaudím ❷ (of roads)
louhháu; sahpjihlouhháu (M:
go)

intersperse FV: dímjyuht;
saanbou

interval PH: yàusīk sìhgaan;
sèunggaak sìhgaan FV: gaak;
sèunggaak ∗ **at short intervals** PH: gaak hóu dyúnge sìh
gaan ∗ **interval — 5 mins**
PH: yàusīk nģhfānjùng ∗ **at
intervals of 6 feet** PH: sèung
gaak luhkchek

intervene FV: ❶ (interfere)
gònsip; gònyuh ❷ (in a dispute)
tiuhtìhng

interview FV: ❶ (by employer . . .) gin; jipgin ❷ (by reporter)
fóngmahn VO: (by employee)
gingùng

interweave FV: gàaujīk;
wahnjaahp

intestine ATT: noihbouhge;
gwoknoihge N: chéung (M: tìuh)
∗ **the large intestine** N:
daaihchéung (M: tìuh)

intimacy SV: chànmaht;
mahtchit

intimate FV/N: ngamsih;
bíusih; tùngjì SV: chànmaht;
mahtchit; suhk ATT: (innermost) noihsàmge; sìyàhnge ∗
intimate friend PH: chànmahtge pàhngyáuh; hóusuhk-
ge pàhngyáuh ∗ **intimate**

feeling PH: noihsàmge gámchìhng ∗ **intimate one's approval** PH: bíusih jaansìhng

intimation FV/N: ❶ (hint)
ngamsih (M: go) ❷ (indicate)
bíusih ❸ (notify) tùngjì

intimidate FV/N: wàihip;
húnghaak

into RVE: -yahp; -
sìhng/sèhng DW: yahp- ∗ **to
go into the school** PH:
yahpheui hohkhaauh ∗ **walk
into the room** PH:
hàahngyahp gàan fóng ∗
translate into English PH:
fàanyihksìhng yìngmàhn ∗
divided into two rooms PH:
fànsèhng léuhnggàanfóng

intolerable Adj. PH: nàahnyíh yánsauh; dáisauhm̀dóu;
m̀yándāk A: dougihk ∗ **intolerable heat** PH: yiht-
dougihk

intonation N: sìngdiuh;
yàmdiuh (M: go)

intoxicant N: ❶ màhjeuijài
❷ (poison) duhkyeuhk ❸
(alcohol) jáujìng yámbán Adj.
PH: yámjeuiyàhnge; lìhng yàhn
tòuhjeuige

intoxicate PH: ❶ (get
drunk) lìhngyàhn yámjeui; yám-
jeuiyàhn ❷ (poisoning) lìhng
yàhn jungduhk ❸ (excite greatly) lìhng yàhn hìngfáhn; lìhng
yàhn tòuhjeui ∗ **to be intox-
icated with success** PH:
sìhnggùng lìhngyàhn hìngfáhn

intransitive ATT: bāt-
kahpmaht ∗ **intransitive
verb** N: bātkahpmahtduhng-
chìh (M: go)

intricate SV: fūkjaahp PH:
❶ (tangled) chojùngfūkjaahp;
dáuchìhnbātchìng; kíuhmàaih-

intrigue yātdèui ❷ (puzzling) hóunàahn mìhngbaahkge; hóu nàahn léihgáaige ✻ a novel with an intricate plot PH: chìhngjit fūkjaahpge síusyut

intrigue N: yàmmàuh (M: go) VO: chaakwaahkyàmmàuh FV: (of love affair) sìtùng PH: yáhnhéi . . . hingcheui • góbún syùge tàihmuhk ~ ngóhge ~ ✻ intrigue with a woman PH: tùhng yātgo néuihyán sìtùng

intrinsic ATT: noihjoihge; búnsànge; búnjātge ✻ the intrinsic value of a coin PH: yātgo ngán/chìhnbaih ge búnsàn gajihk

introduce FV/N: gaaisiuh FV: ❶ chyùhnyahp ❷ tàihchēut ✻ introduce a bill PH: tàihchēut faatngon

introduction FV/N: gaaisiuh N: (preface) jéui; yáhnyìhn BF: (elementary book) yahpmùhn ✻ a letter of introduction N: gaaisiuhseun (M: fùng) ✻ an introduction to English N: Yìngyúh yahpmùhn (M: bún, bouh)

introspect FV: fáansíng

introvert SV: noihheung PH: singgaak noihheungge yàhn (M: go)

intrude FV: chàmyíu; gwángáauu; dágáau ✻ intrude upon his privacy PH: chàmyíu kéuihge sì (yàhn) sàngwuht

intuition N: jihkgok

invade FV: chàmleuhk; chàmfaahn ✻ invader N: chàmleuhkjé (M: go)

invalid FV: mòuhhaauh; jokfai N: behngyàhn; chàahn-

faige yàhn (M: go) ✻ an asylum for invalids N: sèungchàahn liuhyéuhngyún (M: gàan)

invaluable SV: gwaijuhng; bóugwai N: mòuhga (jì) bóu (M: gihn)

invariable ATT: m̀binge N: (of maths.) sèuhngsou (M: go)

invasion FV/N: chàmleuhk; chàmfaahn; chàmhoih

invent FV: faatmìhng Adj. PH: jokchēutlàihge; hèuikauge ~ ge gusih ✻ inventor N: faatmìhnggā (M: wái, go)

inventory N: ❶ (stock) chyùhnfo ❷ (list) chìngdāan (M: jèung) ❸ (catalogue) muhkluhk (M: go) ✻ to make (draw up) an inventory VO: pìn muhkluhk; hòi chìngdāan ✻ check inventory VO: dímfo; pùhndím fomaht; chìngdím chyùhnfo

inverse ATT: sèungfáan FV: fáanjyun; diuhjyun ✻ inverse ratio N: fáanbéi

invert FV: diuhjyun; fáanjyun; doujyun

invertebrate Adj. PH: ❶ móuh jekgwāt ge; móuh jekjèuigwātge ❷ (fig.) móuh gwāthei ge; yiji bohkyeuhk ge ✻ invertebrate animal PH: móuh jekgwātge duhngmaht

invest VO/N: (put money in) tàuhjì FV: (surround) bāauwàih PH: (endow power) béi kyùhn lihk; sauhkyùhn béi . . .

investigate FV: ❶ (examine) diuhchàh; tìuhchàh ❷ (study) yìhngau ❸ (inquire into) sámchàh

invigorate FV: (encourage) gúmóuh; gīklaih PH: lihng . . . kèuhngjong; lihng . . . yáuh sàanghei * **invigorator** N: bóuyeuhk

invincible PH: mòuh dihkge; nàahn yih jìngfuhkge IE: jin mòuh bāt sing * **invincible army** N: sèuhngsìng gwān

inviolable SV: sàhnsing PH: bāthó chàmfaahnge * **inviolable sanctuary** N: singdihn (M: gàan, go)

invisible RV: táiṁgin ~ *kéuihdeih* PH: mòuhyìhngge; yányìhngge

invitation N: ❶ (card) chéngtíp (M: jèung, go) ❷ (request) yìuchíng * **an invitation tournament** N: yìuchíngchoi

invite FV: chéng

inviting FV/SV/N: yáuhwaahk IE: yáhnyàhnyahpsing

invoice N: faatpiu; dāan (M: jèung) VO: hòi faatpiu; hòidāan

invoke FV: kàuh; kèihkàuh; hánkàuh

involuntary PH: móuhsàmge; mòuhyige; bātjihgokge; ṁhaih jihyuhnge * **involuntary injury** PH: mòuhyige sèunghoih

involve FV: ❶ (implicate) lihnleuih; tòhleuih; hìnsip ❷ (include) bàaukwut ❸ (surround) bàauwàih

invulnerable PH: sèunghoih ṁdóuge IE: mòuhhaaih hógīk; dōuchēungbātyahp

inward ATT: noihjoihge; noihsàmge; jìngsàhnseuhngge * **inward happiness** PH: noihjoihge faailohk; jìngsàhnseuhngge faailohk * **inwardness** N: búnjāt

iodine N: dìnjáu; dīn

ion N: lèihjí * **a positive ion** N: yèuhng lèihjí * **a negative ion** N: yàm lèihjí

ionization N: dihnlèih SV/FV: lèihjífa

Iraqi N: Yìlàaihākyàhn; (M: go) Yìlàaihākwá

Iranian N: Yìlóhngyàhn (M: go) Yìlóhngwá

iris N: ❶ (of eye) hùhngchói; hùhngmók ❷ (of plant) yíuméihfā; wùhdihpfā (coll.) (M: déu, dó, jī)

Irish N: Ngoiyíhlàahnyàhn (M: go) Ngoiyíhlàahnwá

irk RV; fàahnséi PH: lihng . . . tóuyim; lihng yàhn tóuyim * **irksome** SV: hātyàhnjàng PH: fàahnséiyàhn

iron N: ❶ (metal) tit ❷ (for clothes) tongdáu (M: go) FV: tong SV: ❶ (undaunted) gìnkèuhng ❷ (cruel) chàahnhuhk; hòhhāk * **iron gate** N: titjaahp (M: go, douh) * **iron hearted** SV: mòuhchìhng * **iron works** N: gongtitchóng (M: gàan) * **electric iron** N: dihntongdáu (M: go) * **ironing board** N: tongsàambáan (M: faai) * **as hard as iron** PH: hóuchíh tit gam gìnngaahng * **to strike while the iron is hot** IE: dátit chan yiht

ironic FV/N: jàausiu FV/ATT/N: fungchi PH: lihngyàhn tàih siu gàai fèi

irony FV/ATT/N: fungchi FV/N: jàausiu; jàauluhng N: fáanwá; fáanyúh * **the irony of fate** PH: mihngwahnge jàauluhng; mihngwahn jàauluhng yàhn

irrational SV: móuhléihsing; m̀hahpléih * **irrational equation** N: mòuhléih fòngchìhngsīk

irreclaimable PH: sàum̀fàange; m̀lódākfàange; (of land) móuh faatjí góijouhge; móuh baahnfaat hòi hánge * **irreclaimable gift** PH: m̀lódākfàange láihmaht

irreconcilable PH: móuhfaatjí wòhgáaige; móuh faatjí tóhhipge; wuhsèung chùngdahtge

irrecoverable RV: yìm̀hóu; sàum̀fàan PH: móuh baahnfaat fùifuhkge; móuh faatjí wáahngauge * **irrecoverable debt** PH: dìjaai sàum̀fàan * **irrecoverable disease** PH: go behng m̀ yìdākhóu

irrefutable PH: móuh faatjí fáanbokge; bokm̀dóuge

irregular SV: ❶ bāt kwàijāk ❷ (uneven) m̀pìhngtáan ❸ (untidy) m̀ jíngchàih PH: (contrary to rules) m̀ hahp sèuhngkwàige; fèijingkwàige * **irregular troop** N: fèijingkwàigwān

irrelevant PH: móuhgwàanhaihge; lèihtàihge; m̀chittàihge; m̀jùngháng

irremediable PH: móuhfaatjí bóugauge; móuh faatjí wáahngauge RV: (of disease) yìm̀hóu * **irremediable faults** PH: móuh faatjí bóugauge gwosāt

irreparable PH: móuh

irreproachable PH: mòuhhófèiyíhge; móuhgwosātge; móuhdāktàahnge

irresistible PH: móuh faatjí dáikongge; bāthó kongkéuihge; móuh faatjí yīkjai/ngaatjai ge * **irresistible desire** PH: móuh faatjí ngaatjaige yuhkmohng

irrespective FV: m̀háauleuih; m̀gu; m̀kèui MA: bātleuhn * **irrespective of age** PH: bātleuhn nìhnlìhng * **irrespective of how much you donate** PH: gyùn géidō chín dōu m̀kèui * **irrespective of the consequences** PH: bāt/m̀ gu hauhgwó

irresponsible SV: ❶ m̀ fuhjaak; móuh jaakyahmgám ❷ (not trustworthy) m̀ kaaudākjyuh

irreversible PH: m̀ hóyíh dóujyungwolàihge; m̀ dìuhdākjyuntàuhge

irrevocable PH: m̀hóyíh góibinge; móuh faatjí chéuisiuge * **irrevocable treaty** PH: móuh faatjí chéuisiuge tiuhyeuk

irrigate FV: ❶ (of land) gunkoi ❷ (of wound) chùngsái VO: sàuséuileih

irritate FV: (provoke) gīk RV: ❶ (make angry) gīknàu ❷ (inflame) faatyìhm SV: (sore) tung; m̀syùfuhk

is EV: haih

Islam N: ❶ Wùihgaau; Yìsìlàahnggaau ❷ (follower) Wùihgaautòuh (M: go)

island N: dóu (M: go) ＊ **traffic island** N: ngònchyùhndóu (M: go)

-ism N: jyúyih (M: go)

isn't EV: m̀haih

isolate RV: ❶ gaakhòi; gaaklèih VO/ATT: (electricity) jyuhtyùhn FV: ❶ gūlahp ❷ (in chemistry) fāngáai ＊ **isolationism** N: gūlahpjyúyih

Israeli N: Yíhsīklihtyàhn; Yàuhtaaiyàhn (M: go) ATT: Yíhsīklihtge; Yàuhtaaige

issue FV: ❶ (of license, order . . .) faatchēut ❷ (flow) làuhchēut ❸ (publish) chēutbáan ❹ (put forth) faathòhng N: ❶ (problem) mahntàih ❷ (result) gitgwó; hauhgwó M: kèih ＊ **the issue of a new dollar note** PH: chēut sānngàhnjí; faathòhng sānngàhnjí ＊ **await the issue** PH: dánghauh gitgwó ＊ **this issue of the magazine** PH: nī yātkèih jaahpjí ＊ **force the issue** PH: jihngsih (nīgo) mahntàih

it PN: kéuih SP: (this) nī; (that) gó ~ *jek haih māau.*

Italian N: Yidaaihleihyàhn; (M: go) Yidaaihleihwá

italic ATT: chetái ＊ **italics** N: chetáijih (M: go)

itch SV: hàhn FV: (longing) hotmohng; hahn ＊ **have an itch for money** PH: hahn faatchòih ＊ **itchy** SV: hàhn

item N: hohngmuhk (M: go) M: hohng; tiuh ＊ **itemize** VO: fānhohng ＊ **the first item on the programme** PH: jitmuhk léuihbihn daihyāthohng

iterate FV/A: chùhngfūk

itinerant A/ATT: chèuhnwùih FV: chèuhnyàuh N: chèuhnwùih gūngjokjé (M: go) ＊ **itinerant performance** PH: chèuhnwùih bíuyín ＊ **itinerary** N: hàhngchìhngbíu (M: go)

its PH: kéuihge

itself PN: kéuihjihgéi

ivory N: jeuhngngàh

ivy N: sèuhngchèuntàhng

J

jab FV: ❶ (with sharp things) gāt ❷ (with ellow, etc) johng VO: (inject) dájām · *tùhng kéuih ~*

jack N: ❶ (machine) jīk (translit.); chìngàndíng (lit.) ❷ (of playing card) jīk ❸ (sailor) séuisáu (M: go) ❹ (flag) kèih (M: jī) ＊ **jack pot** PH: jeuidaaihjéung ＊ **jack of all trades** N: maahnnàhng boksih (M: go) ＊ **jack straw** N: douhchóuyàhn (M: go) ＊ **to jack up** RV: jīkhéi

jackal N: ❶ (wolf) wùhlòhng (M: jek) ❷ (of person) jáugáu; bònghùng (M: go)

jacket N: lāu; ngoihtou (M: gihn)

jade N: ❶ (stone) yúk; féicheui (lit.) (M: nāp, gauh, faai) ❷ (horse) lóuhmáh ＊ **jaded** PH: hóuguih

jag N: ❶ kyutháu ❷ (saw-like) geuichíyìhng * to go on a jag PH: yámjeuijáu * a jag of rock PH: yātfaai dahtchēutge ngàahmsehk

jail N: gàamyuhk; gàamfòhng * to break jail VO: yuhtyuhk; tòuhyuhk

jam N: jìm; gwójìm; gwójeung SV/FV: sāk RV: gihpchàn N: (of a machine) gujeung * traffic jam SV: sākchè * to jam one's clothes into the luggage PH: sākdī sāam yahp pèihgīpsyu * to jam one's finger PH: gihpchàn jek sáují * stoppage of a machine due to jamming PH: gèihei yànwaih faatsàng gujeung yìh tìhngdeuhn

janitor N: hòngàang; gúnléihyùhn (M: go)

January N: Yātyuht

Japan N: ❶ Yahtbún ❷ (varnish) chāt; chāthei

Japanese N: Yahtbúnyàhn (M: go) Yahtbúnwá

jar N: ❶ (of earthernware) ngáang; chìhng; ngung; gòng (rather big, barrel-like) (M: go) ❷ (of glass) bōlēingáang ❸ (sound) jaahpyām SV: (disharmony) mwòhhàaih; m'yātji VO: (quarrel) ngaaigāau FV/N: (shock) chigīk; janduhng; chùnggīk * a jarring note PH: chiyíhge yàmdiuh

jargon N: ❶ seuhtyúh; buihyúh PH: ❶ (of bad English) yèuhnggingbān yingmán ❷ (difficult to understand) nàahndúngge yúhyìhn

jasmine N: muhtléi * jasmine tea N: hèungpín (chàh)

jaundice N: wòhngdáambehng

javelin N: bīuchēung (M: jì) * to throw the javelin VO: jaahk bīuchēung

jaw N: ngàhgaau (M: go) SV: dòjéui * don't jaw PH: m̀hóu góng gamdō yéh * the upper jaw and the lower jaw PH: seuhngngohk tùhng hahngohk

jay N: ❶ (bird) gìnníuh * jay walker PH: lyuhn gwo máhlouhlge yàhn

jazz N: ❶ (music) jeuksih yàmngohk ❷ (dance) jeuksihmóuh SV: yihtnaauh PH: chòuhhyūnbābai

jealous FV: dougeih VO: (of love) haapchou

jeep N: gātbóuchè; jīpjái (M: ga)

jeer FV: dai; siu; jàausiu; nánfa

jelly N: jēléi * jelly fish N: ❶ (sea creature) baahk ja (M: jek) ❷ (sea food) hói jit

jeopardize FV: ngàihkahp PH: mouh . . . ge ngàihhím

jerk PH: ❶ (sudden push) (daaihlihk) yātjohng; (daaihlihk) yāttèui ❷ (sudden pull) (daaihlihk) yātché; hóu gāp gám làai FV: (of muscle) ginglyùhn * physical jerks N: táichòu; wahnduhng

jersey N: waihsāngyī; wahnduhngsāam (M: gihn)

jest N: siuwá (M: go) FV: siu VO: góngsiu; góngsíu

Jesus N: Yèhsōu

jet FV: pan; seh; panseh RV:

panchēut; sehchēut N: pansehháu; panjéui * jet plane N: pansehgèi (M: ga)

jetty N: ❶ (pier) máhtàuh (M: go) ❷ (breakwater) fòhngbōtàih (M: tìuh)

Jew N: Yàuhtaaiyàhn; Yàuhtaaigaautòuh (M: go)

jewel N: ❶ (collectively) jyūbóu; sáusīk ❷ (precious stone) bóusehk (M: nāp, gauh) * **jeweler** N: jyūbóusèung (M: go)

Jewish ATT: Yàuhtaaige; Yàuhtaaiyàhnge * **Jewish customs** N: Yàuhtaai fùngjuhk

jiffy TW: yātjahngāan; jáamháhngáahn * **in a jiffy** A: jīkhāak

jingle N: ❶ dìngdòngsèng ❷ (of advertisement) puingohk

jitter PH: sàhngìnggwo-máhn; sàhngìngjāt; sàhn-gìnggánjèung

job N: ❶ (employment) gùng-jok; jīkyihp; gùng ❷ (task) sih * **odd jobs** N: sáangùng; dyúngùng * **out of a job** VO: sātyihp * **to do a good job** PH: jouh yātgihn sih jouh dāk hóu hóu * **jobber** N: gúpiu gìnggéi (M: go) * **it's a good job!** PH: jànhaih hóuchói la!

jockey N: kèhsī (M: go) FV: (cheat) ngāak VO: (manoeuvre) sá sáudyuhn * **Jockey Club** máhwúi (M: go)

jocular SV: waahtkài; fùihàaih

jog PH: ❶ ngúngháh; johng-háh; tèuiháh ❷ (shaky) sàisàiháh; yìuhyìuhháh FV: (re-mind) tàihséng; ngamsih *

jogging VO: páaubouh PH: wùhnbouhpáau

join FV: ❶ (connect) bok (màaih); lìhnjip ❷ (meet) wuihhahp ❸ (add to) gàyahp ❹ (participate) chàamgà * **join two things together** PH: jèung léuhngyeuhng yéh bokmàaih * **join an island to the mainland** PH: jèung go dóu tùhng daaihluhk lìhnjip

joint N: gwàanjit; gwātjit ATT: lyùhnhahpge; guhng-tùhngge; guhngyáuhge FV: lìhnjip; jiphahp * **joint communique** N: lyùhnhahp gùngbou (M: go) * **joint statement** N: lyùhnhahp sìngmìhng (M: go) * **joint effort** VO: hahplihk * **joint venture** VO/ATT: hahpjī * **joint account** PH: lyùhnméng (hòige) wuhháu

joke N: siuwá (M: go) VO: góngsiu; hòiwàahnsiu

jolly SV: faailohk; faaiwuht; gòuhing * **a jolly Father Christmas** PH: yātgo faailohk-ge sìngdaan lóuhyàhn

jolt SV/FV: dan, chok

jostle FV: ngúng; johng; pung

jot N: yātdī PH: síusíu * **jot down** RV: sédài; geidài

journal N: ❶ (diary) yahtgei (M: bún) ❷ (magazine) jaahpji (M: bún, fahn) ❸ (newspaper) boují (M: jèung, fahn) ❹ (periodical) kèihhòn; dihngkèih hònmaht (M: fahn) * **journalism** N: sànmàhnhohk * **jornalist** N: geijé (M: go) * **the ladies' home journal** N: fúhnéuih gātìhng jaahpji (M: bún)

journey N: ❶ (trip) léuih-hàhng; hàhngchìhng ❷ (distance traveled) louhchìhng ✳ **a three days' journey** PH: sàamyahtge hàhngchìhng ✳ **to make a journey to Japan** PH: heui yahtbún léuihhàhng

joy SV: faailohk; gòuhing; fùnhéi ✳ **it gives me great joy to tell you . . .** PH: ngóh hóu gòuhing wahbéi néih tèng . . .

jubilant PH: lihngyàhn hòisàm; lihngyàhn héiyuht IE: héihei yèuhngyèuhng

jubilee N: gāaijit; kwòhng-fùnjit ✳ **golden jubilee** PH: gàmhèi géinihm; nǵhsahp jàunihn géinihm ✳ **silver jubilee** PH: ngàhnhèi géinihm; yihsahpnǵh jàunihn géinihm

Judaism N: Yàuhtaaigaau

judge N: ❶ (in a court) faatgùn (M: go, wái) ❷ (in a contest) pìhngpun; pìhngpunyùhn; chòihpunyùhn (M: go, wái) ❸ (in Hebrew history) sihsī FV: ❶ sámpun · *Seuhngdai jèung-wúih ~ sóyáuhge yàhn* ❷ (estimate) dyundihng; gaamdihng; pundyun ✳ **don't judge a man by his looks** PH: m̀hóu yíh maauh chéui yàhn ✳ **judgement** N: pundyunlihk e.g. (a) (sound judgement) PH: pundyunlihk hóu kèuhng (b) (faulty judgement) PH: pundyunlihk hóu yeuhk

judicial ATT; sīfaatge; faat-yúnge ✳ **judicial proceedings** N: sámpun chìhng-jeuih; soujuhng sáujuhk ✳ **Judicial Yuan** N: Sīfaatyún (M: go)

judicious SV: yìhnmìhng; sámsahn ✳ **judicious parents**

PH: yìhnmìhngge fuhmóuh

jug N: ❶ (vessel) wú; ngāang (M: go) ❷ (coll.) (prison) gāamyuhk (M: go)

juggle VO: (to do tricks) wáan báhei; bin heifaat FV: (deceive) ngāak ✳ **juggle the figures** PH: wuhnluhng soujih làih ngāakyàhn ✳ **to juggle with balls** PH: yuhng bō làih wáan báhei ✳ **juggler** N: wáan báhei/jaahpsá ge yàhn (M: go) N: (trickster) pinjí (M: go)

juice N: jāp ✳ **lemon juice** N: nìhngmūngjāp ✳ **juicy** PH: hóudōjāp

July N: Chātyuht

jumble SV: wahnlyuhn; lyuhn FV: lòulyuhn ✳ **jumble up** PH: lyuhn jòujòu dèui màaih yātchàih ✳ **jumble sale** PH: jaahpfo paakmaaih; daaih pèhngmaaih

jumbo SV: daaih; geuihdaaih PH: hóudaaih; fèisèuhngdaaih ✳ **jumbo jet** N: jànbóu haakgèi (M: ga, jek)

jump FV: tiu PH: (sudden rise) bouhsìng; dahtyìhngāan gòujó; dahtyìhngāan sìngjó; dahtyìhngāan dòjó ✳ **jump up and down** PH: tiu sèuhng tiu lohk ✳ **a jump in exports** PH: chēutháu dahtyìhngāan dòjó ✳ **price jumped** PH: mahtga bouhsìng ✳ **high jump** FV: tiugòu ✳ **long (broad) jump** FV: tiuyúhn ✳ **jumpy** Adj. PH: sàhngìnggwomáhn; sàhngìng-jāt

junction N: ❶ gàaugaai-chyu; gàauchàdím ❷ (cross-road) sahpjihlouhháu (M: go) ✳ **Junction Road** PW/N: Lyùhn-hahpdouh (M: tìuh)

juncture N: ❶ sìhhāk; sìhgèi; gwàantàuh ❷ (meeting point) jìphahpdím ✳ **at this juncture** PH: hái nīgo sìhhāk/gwàantàuh

June N: Luhkyuht

jungle N: sàmlàhm (M: go)

junior SV: ❶ (younger in age) hauhsāang; sai ❷ (lower in rank) dàikāp ATT: chōkāp N: ❶ (subordinate) hahsuhk (M: go) ❷ (of university) daaihhohk sàamnihnkāp; daaihsàam ✳ **junior class** N: chōkāpbāan (M: bàan) ✳ **John Jones Junior** N: Síu Yeukhohn Jūngsī

junk N: ❶ (sailing vessel) fàahnsyùhn; daaih ngáahngāi (slang) ❷ (rubbish) laahpsaap; laahntùhng laahntit

Jupiter N: Muhksīng (M: go)

jurisdiction N: chòihpunkyùhn; sīfaatkyùhn; gúnhahtkyùhn

jurisprudence N: faathohk; faatléihhohk ✳ **medical jurisprudence** N: faatyīhohk

jurist N: faatléihhohkgā; faatleuhtgā; faathohkkkyùhnwài (M: go, wái)

jury N: ❶ (of law) pùihsámtyùhn (M: go) ❷ (of competition) pìhngpun wáiyùhn wúi (M: go) ✳ **juryman** N: pùihsámyùhn (M: go)

just SV: gùngdouh; gùngpìhng; gùngjing; hahpléih A: ❶ (a moment ago) ngāamngāam; jingwah ❷ (exactly) jauh ❸ (only) jí; jíhaih ❹ (simply) jànhaih · *Tìnhei ~ hóu* ✳ **to be just to a person** PH: deui yàhn gùngjing ✳ **just as** PH: chíhjūk; jànhaihchíh ✳ **just then**

PH: jingdòng . . . gójahnsí ✳ **just about** MA: ngāamngāam; ngāamngāamhóu A: chàbātdò

justice N: (judge) faatgùn (M: go, wái) SV: jingyih; gùngdouh; gùngpìhng; jingdong ✳ **to do justice to** PH: gùngpìhng deuidoih ✳ **to bring to justice** PH: gwàaingon sauhsám ✳ **a court of justice** N: faattìhng (M: go) ✳ **to have a sense of justice** PH: yáuh jingyihgám ✳ **Justice of the Peace (J.P.)** N: Taaipìhng Sànsí (M: wái, go)

justification FV: bihnwuh N: (reason) léihyàuh (M: go) ✳ **in justification of** PH: waih . . . bihnwuh ✳ **in justification of his behavior** PH: waih kéuihge hàhngwàih bihnwuh

justify FV: bihnwuh PH: ❶ (be a good reason for) waih . . . jokjing; waih . . . bihnwuh ❷ (show that . . . is right) jingmìhng . . . haih ngāam ge; yihngwàih . . . haih jingdongge; yihngwàih móuhjeuih ✳ **justified the killing as self-defence** PH: waih jihwaih saatyàhn yìh bihnwuh

jut RV; dahtchēut (làih); sànchēut (làih)

juvenile N/ATT: chìngsiunìhn ✳ **juvenile delinquent** N: chìngsiunìhn jeuihfáan (M: go)

K

kaleidoscope N: maahnfātùhng (M: go) ✳ **kaleidoscopic**

IE: chìn bin maahn fa

kangaroo N: doihsyú (M: jek)

kapok N: muhkmìhn; muhkmìhnfā (M: déu, dó) * **kapok tree** N: muhkmìhnsyuh (M: pò)

keel N: ❶ (framework) lùhnggwāt ❷ (boat) pìhngdáisyùhn (M: jek) * **to lay down a keel** VO: ngòn lùhnggwāt PH: hòichi jouhsyùhn * **keep over** FV: fáanjyun

keen SV: ❶ (sharp) leih; jìmyeuih (fig.) ❷ (of the mind) jìngmìhng; chùngmìhng; jèng ❸ (enthusiastic) yihtsàm ❹ (fierce) gīkliht FV: ❶ (eager) hotmohng ❷ (fond of) héifùn; jùngyi ❸ (wail) haam * **a knife with a keen edge** PH: bá dōujái hóu leih * **a keen criticism** PH: jìmyeuihge pàipìhng * **a keen sportsman** PH: yātgo yihtchùng yù wahnduhng ge yàhn * **a keen competition** PH: gīklihtge béichoi

keep FV: ❶ làuh (fàan); bóulàuh * **keep it for oneself** PH: làuh (fàan) béi jihgéi ❷ sàu (màaih) · *Néih ~ dīchín hái bīn a?* ❸ sáu * **keep goal** VO: sáu lùhngmùhn * **keep a secret** VO: sáu beimaht * **keep a promise** VO: sáuseun; sáu seunyuhng ❹ yéuhng * **keep a bird** VO: yéuhngjéuk ❺ dáléih * **keep a shop** VO: dáléih poutáu ❻ hingjūk * **keep Thanksgiving Day** VO: hingjūk Gámyànjit ❼ gei * **keep accounts** VO: geijeung * **keep ... from** FV: fòhngjí * **keep an eye on** RV: hònjyuh; hàujyuh * **keep in mind** RV: geijyuh * **keep in touch** PH: bóuchìh lyùhnlok * **keep on** A: gaijuhk * **keep off**

grass PH: m̀hóuyáai chóudéi * **keep to the right** PH: kaau yauh hàahng * **keep the change** PH: m̀sái jáau * **please keep quiet!** PH: chéng néihdeih jihngdī; chéngnéihdeih bóuchìh ngònjihng!

keg M: túngjái * **a keg of brandy** PH: yāt túngjái baahklāandéi

kennel N: gáungūk (M: gàan)

kernel N: ❶ gwóyàhn ❷ (fig.) jùngsàm; hahtsàm; yiudím M: nāp * **the kernel of a walnut** N: hahptòuhyuhk; hahptòuhgwóyàhn * **a kernel of wheat** Nu-M-N: yātnāp mahk * **the kernel of the whole matter** PH: nīgihn sihge yiudím

korosene, kerosine N: fóséui

ketchup N: kéjāp

kettle N: chàhbōu; séuibōu (M: go)

key N: ❶ sósìh (M: tìuh, chàubunch) ❷ (answer) màihdái; daapngon ❸ (of piano) kàhmgihn ❹ (scale of notes) diuh ATT: jyúyiuge * **the key of C major** PH: C daaih diuh * **the key industries of a nation** PH: yātgwok jeui jyúyiuge gùngyihp

khaki N: ❶ (color) nàihwòhngsīk; wòhnghotsīk ❷ (cloth) kākèihbou (M: faai, fūk) ❸ (uniform) kākèihbou jaifuhk; (military) kākèihbou gwānjòng

kick FV: ❶ tek ❷ (expel) gón ❸ (give up) gaai SV: (excited) hìngfáhn; hòisàm * **kick him out** PH: gón kéuih chēutheui * **to kick a bad habit** PH: gaaijódī waaih jaahpgwaan * **kick off** VO: hòikàuh; hòibō *

to kick the bucket FV: (slang)
dèngjó; séi jó * to get kick-
ed out (sacked) VO: cháauyàuhyú

kid N: ❶ (child) saimānjái;
sailóugō (M: go) ❷ (goat)
sàanyèuhngjái (M: jek) VO:
góngsiu; hòiwàahnsiu * whiz
kid N: sàhntùhng (M: go) *
kid sister N: saimúi (M: go)

kiddy N: ❶ (child) saimānjái
(M: go) ❷ (goat) sàanyèuhngjái
(M: jek)

kidnap FV: (abduct) gwáai;
gwáaidaai VO: (for ransom)
bìusàm; bóngga; bóngpiu *
kidnapper N: gwáaijílóu;
bóngféi (M: go)

kidney N: sahn; sahnjohng
(M: go) * duck's kidney N:
ngaapsáhn (M: go) * kidney
machine N: sáisahngèi (M: ga,
fu)

kill FV: séi RVE: -séi RV: (put
to death) ❶ (by being stabbed)
gātséi ❷ (usually people only)
saatséi ❸ (hit by car) chèséi ❹
(by drowning) jahmséi ❺ (by
hand or holding materials) dáséi
❻ jíngséi * to kill a pig VO:
tòngjyú * to kill time PH:
siumòh sìhgaan * dressed to
kill PH: dábaan dāk hóu leng;
jeukdāk hóu leng * Thou
shalt not kill PH: bāt hó
saatyàhn * to kill two birds
with one stone IE: yātgéui
léuhngdāk; yātsehk yihníuh

kiln N: yìuh (M: go) FV: sìu

kilo BF: gùng; chìn * kilo-
gramme M: gùnggàn; chìnhāk
* kilometre M: gùngléih;
chìnmáih * kilolitre M:
gùngsìng; chìnsìng

kilocycle N: chìnjàu

kin N: chànchīk; chànsuhk
PH: (to be related to somesome)
yáuh chànchīk gwàanhaih

kind SV: hóu; hóuyàhn; hóusèungyúh yàhnchìh (lit.) M:
júng, leuih * a kind of fruit
PH: yātjúng sàanggwó *
mankind N: yàhnleuih * be
kind to him PH: deui kéuih
hóudī * a kind heart PH: hóu
hóusàm; sàmdéi hóuhóu * a
kindmother N: chìhmóuh (M:
go) * kind of N: yáuhdī; yáuh
síusíu * something of the
kind PH: leuihchíh ge yéh

kindergarten N: yaujihýún
(M: gàan)

kindle FV: dím RV: dím
jeuhk VO: dímfó RV: (rouse)
yáhnhéi * kindle the in-
terest of an audience PH:
yáhnhéi tìngjung (gùnjung) ge
hingcheui

kindly SV: yàhnchìh; wòh-
ngói; chànchit * in a kindly
manner PH: taaidouh hóu
wòhngói/chànchit

kindness N: hóuyi SV:
yàhnchìh; wòhngói; chànchit *
out of kindness PH: chēutyù
hóuyi * do him a kindness
PH: bòngkéuih; bòngkéuih-
mòhng

kindred N: chànchīk PH:
yáuh chànchīk gwàanhaih ATT:
tùhngleuihge; tùhngjúng;
tùhngjuhk

kinetic ATT: duhnglihk-
hohkge; wàhnduhngge *
kinetic energy N: duhng
nàhng * kinetic friction N:
duhngmōchaat * kinetics N:
duhnglihkhohk

king N: ❶ (ruler) gwok-
wòhng; wòhng ❷ (tycoon)

daaihwòhng ✳ an oil king N:
sehkyàuh daaihwòhng ✳ king
size N: dahkdaaihmáh PH:
dahkdaaihge ✳ kingfisher N:
cheuiníuh, yùhgáu, diuyùh-
lòhng (coll.) (M: jek)

kingdom N: ❶ wòhnggwok
❷ (realm) líhngwihk ✳ the
United Kingdom N: Daaih
Yìng Daigwok ✳ the kingdom
of thought PH: sīséunggge
líhngwihk

kingly ATT: gwokwòhngge
SV: gòugwai PH: hóuchíh
gwànwòhnggám ✳ kingly
bearing PH: yáuh gwàn-
wòhngge fùngfaahn; yáuh
wòhngjé jì fùng

kink RV: kíuhmàaih; náumàaih; gyúnmàaih ✳ kink
cough N: (whooping cough)
baakyahtkāt ✳ kinky PH: ①
(mentally) gúgú gwaaigwaai;
gwaaigwáaidéi ② (twisted)
náumàaih yātdèui; kíuhmàaih
yātdèui

kinsfolk N: chànchīk (M: go)

kinship PH: chànchīk-
gwàanhaih SV: (similar)
sèungchíh

kiss FV: sek; sekháh; máhn
(lit.) ✳ to blow a kiss VO:
fèimáhn

kit N: ❶ (equipment) jòngbeih
❷ (tools) gùnggeuih; yuhnggeuih ❸ (bucket) muhktúng (M:
go) ✳ kit bag N: fàahnboudói
(M: go) ✳ skiing kit PH:
waahtsyut jòngbeih

kitchen N: chyùhfóng;
chèuih fóng (M: go, gàan) ✳ kitchen ware PH: chyùhfóng
yuhnggeuih

kite N: jíyíu (M: jek) ✳ to fly
a kite VO: fongjíyíu PH: (fig.)

si . . . háufùng; si . . . fáanying

kitten N: māaujái (M: jek)

knapsack N: builòhng (M:
go)

knave N: ❶ mòuhláai; pinjí
(M: go) ❷ (poker) jīk ✳ the
knave of hearts PH:
hùhngsàm jīk

knavery PH: mòuhláaige
hàhngwàih; gàanjage hàhngwàih

knavish SV: gàanja; m̀-
sìhngsaht; SV/N: mòuhláai

knee N: sāttàuhgō (M: go) ✳
kneecap N: wuhsāt (M: go) ✳
to go on one's knees RV:
gwaihdài

kneel FV: gwaih ✳ kneel
down RV: gwaihdài

knickknack N: (ornament)
síu báaichit; síu sīkmaht (M:
gihn)

knife N: dōu (M: bá, jèung) ✳
pocket knife N: dōujái (M: bá,
jèung) ✳ table knife N: chāan-
dōu (M: bá, jèung)

knight N: ❶ móuhsih;
kèhsih (M: wái, go) ❷ (title)
jeuksih ❸ (chess) máhtàuhkéi;
máh ✳ knight errant N:
yàuhhahp; hahpsih (M: wái, go)
✳ knight qualities N:
móuhsih heikoi ✳ knight er-
rantry N: haahpyìh hàhng-
wàih; kèhsih jokfùng

knit FV: ❶ jīk (sweater) · ~
lāangsāam ❷ jau (brows) · ~
mèihtàuh RV: jipfàanhóu
(broken bones) · ~ dī seuigwāt
✳ knitting needle N: jīkjām
(M: fu)

knob N: ❶ (lump) láu; kīk (M:

go) ❷ (handle) châusáu (M: go)
dīk (round-shaped) (M: nāp) ❸
(of radio) jai ✳ **a knobbly tree**
PH: pò syuh yáuh hóudo kīk

knock FV: ❶ (hit) dá ❷ (tap)
hâau, paak ✳ **knock at a door**
VO: hâau (paak) mùhn ✳
knock down FV: ① (tear)
chaak ② (sell) maaih VO: (of
price) gáamga RV: (strike with
a blow) johngdóu; pungdóu;
dádài

knot N: ❶ lit; kīk (M: go) ❷
(difficulty) kwannàahn (M: go)
VO: dálit; dákīk M: hóiléih ✳
a vessel of 20 knots PH:
sihchūk yihsahp hóiléihge
syûhn ✳ **to tie oneself into
knots** PH: hahmyahp kwannàahn jijùng ✳ **knotty** PH:
hóudòlit; hóudòkīk; hóudo
kwannàahn

know ❶ jì; jídou ❷ (be acquainted with; be able to) sīk ✳
know . . . from RV: fàndākchēut ✳ **know the ropes**
PH: sīksaaidī kíumiuh ✳
know all PH: mātdōusīk N:
maahn sih tùng (M: go)

knowing SV: ❶ yáuh
hohkmahn; bokhohk ❷ (cun-
ning) gáauwaaht; gèigíng;
lóuhlihn ✳ **a knowing
scholar** PH: bokhohk jìsih ✳
knowingly A: guyi

knowledge N: ❶ jìsīk; jisīk
❷ (information) sìusīk ❸ (learning) hohkmahn ✳ **have no
knowledge of** FV: m̀jì;
m̀líuhgáai ✳ **to my knowledge** PH: geui ngóh só jì

known FV: jì SV: chēutméng
✳ **be known as** PH: ① yíh . .
. chēutméng; yíh . . . jyuching
② (is called) giujouh ✳ **it is
well known that** PH: yàhn
yàhn dōu jì IE: Jung só jâu-

jì; yàhn só guhng jì

knuckle N: sáujíjit; sáují-
gwāanjit (M: go, jit) ✳ **pig's
knuckle** N: jyūsáu (M: jek)

kodachrome N: chóisīk-
dihnyíng gāaupín (M: jèung)

kodak ATT: ōdaaht PH:
(camera) síuyìhng séunggèi;
ōdaaht pàaih síuyìhng séunggèi
(M: go, bouh) PH: yuhng
síuyìhng séunggèi yíngséung

Koran N: Hólàahngìng (M:
bún, bouh)

Korean N: Hòhngwok yàhn
(M: go) Hòhngwokwá ATT:
Hòhngwok (ge)

kowtow VO: kautàuh

Kremlin N: Hākléihmóuh-
làhmgùng (M: go, gàan, joh)

Krugerand N: Fugaaklàhm
gàm baih (M: go)

Ku Klux Klan N: sàam K
dóng (M: go)

kumquat N: gàmgāt; gātjái
(M: go)

Kuomintang N: Gwok-
màhndóng

L

lab. N: sahtyìhmsāt (M: go,
gàan)

label N: ❶ (of products)
jìupàaihjí; sèungbìu; māktàuh
(M: go) ❷ (specimen) bìuchìm ❸
(tag) bìugei PH: (fig.) wah . . .

haih; jí . . . wàih * **plant label**
N: jihkmaht bìuchìm * **properly labelled luggage** PH: dī
hàhngléih tiphóu bìugei la *
**to label him as an oppor-
tunitist** PH: wah kéuih haih
gèiwuih jyúyihjé

labial ATT: (of the lips)
sèuhn(ge) * **libial sounds** N:
sèuhnyàm

laboratory N: sahtyihmsāt
(M: go, gàan) * **language
laboratory** N: yúhyìhn
sahtyihmsāt (M: go, gàan)

laborious SV: ❶ sànfú;
gàanfú ❷ (hard working)
kàhnlihk ❸ (not fluent)
m̀làuhleih

labour, labor FV/N: gùngjok N: gùngyàhn; dágùngjái;
lòuhgùng (M: go) FV: ❶
lòuhduhng ❷ (childbirth) fànmíhn * **to labour for the
happiness of mankind** PH:
waih yàhnleuihge hahngfūk yìh
lòuhduhng * **labour union** N:
gùngwúi (M: go) * **the Labour
Party** N: Gùngdóng (M: go) *
labor and capital PH:
lòuhgùng tùhng jìbúngā; lòuh-
jì sèungfòng * **Labor Day** N:
Lòuhduhngjit (M: go)

labyrinth N: ❶ màihgùng;
màihjèun (M: go) ❷ (fig.)
kwangíng (M: go)

lace N: fàbīn (M: tìuh) *
shoes laces N: hàaihdáai (M:
tìuh) * **to lace up one's shoes**
PH: bónghóu hàaihdáai

lacerate RV: ❶ jíngsèung;
(by sharp things) gotsèung; (by
claws) wásèung FV: sèunghoih

lack FV: kyutsíu; kyutfaht

lackadaisical SV: láahnsáan PH: láahn yèuhngyèuhng

lacklustre SV: ngamdaahm
PH: móuh gwòngjaahk; móuh
sàanghei

lacquer, lacker N: ❶ (varnish) chāt ❷ (articles) chāthei
VO: panchāt; séuhngchāt

lactic BF: náaih; yúh * **lactic acid** N: yúhsyùn

lad, laddie N: hauhsàangjái
(M: go) * **my lads** PH: ngóhge
lóuhyáuh

ladder N: tài (M: bá)

lade FV: ❶ (load) jòng; joi ❷
(ladle) bāt; fāt; yíu

lady N: ❶ (married woman)
taaitáai; (formal address)
fùyàhn ❷ (female) néuihsih;
(formal) suhknéuih (M: wái) BF.:
néuih * **lady teacher** N:
néuih sìnsàang (M: go, wái) *
young lady N: síujé (M: go,
wái) * **ladies (toilet)** N:
néuihchi (M: go) * **ladies and
gentlemen** PH: gokwái
lòihbàn; gokwái sìnsàang,
gokwái néuihsih

lag SV: chìh N: (criminal)
faahnyàhn; gàamdán (M: go) *
to lag behind FV: lohkhauh *
a time lag of one month PH:
chìh yātgo yuht

lagoon N: hàahmséuiwùh;
jiuwùh (M: go)

lair N: dau; yuht (lit.) (M: go)
* **lion's lair** N: sījídau (M: go)
* **tiger's lair** N: fúyuht M: go)

laissez-faire PH: fongyahm
jingchaak; jihyàuh gìngjàng;
bātgònsip jyúyih

laity N: ❶ (layman) juhkyàhn;
fàahnyàhn (M: go) ❷ (not of a
profession) ngoihhóng

lake N: wùh (M: go) *

lakelet N: wùhjái (M: go)

lama N: lāmàh (M: go) * **Dalai Lama** N: Daahtlaaih- lāmàh * **Lamaism** N: Lāmàhgaau

lamb N: yèuhngjái; yèuhng- mējái; (used in bible) gòuyèuhng

lame SV: bài; bàigeuk * **lame duck** N: bàigeukngáap (M: jek) * **to be lame in the left leg** PH: jó geuk bàijó

lament SV: bèisèung FV: ngòidouh; yúnsīk N: (song) wáahngō * **lament for a friend** PH: waih pàhngyáuh bèisèung

lamp N: dāng (M: jáan) * **lamp post** N: dāngchyúh (M: jī) * **lamp shade** N: dāngjaau (M: go)

lampoon FV: fungchi; jàau- siu PH: fungchige màhnjèung

land FV: (of an aeroplane) gonglohk VO: (disembark) séuhngngohn N: ❶ (ground) deih; tóudeih ❷ (contrasted with sea) luhkdeih (M: faai) * **landlord** N: ngūkjyú; fòhng- dūng; yìhpjyú; deihjyú (M: go) * **landmine** N: deihlèuih (M: go) * **landslide** PH: sàan nàih kìng se

landing VO: séuhngngohn; dàngluhk FV: (of an aeroplane) gonglohk * **landing craft** N: dàngluhktéhng (M: jek)

landscape N: fùnggíng * **landscape painting** N: fùng- gíngwá (M: fūk, jèung) * **Chinese landscape painting** N: Jùnggwok sāanséuiwá (M: fūk, jèung)

lane N: ❶ (alley) hóng (M: tiuh) ❷ (route) hòhngsin (M:

tiuh) * **the inside lane** N: noihsin * **the outside lane** N: faaisin

language N: wá; yúhyìhn; yúhmàhn * **language centre** N: yúhyìhn jùngsàm; yúhmàhn yìhnjaahpsó (M: gàan) * **finger language** N: sáuyúh * **body language** N: sàntái yúhyìhn

languid SV: guih; móuh jìngsàhn; móuhlihk

lank Adj. PH: ❶ (of person) yauh gòu yauh sau ❷ (of hair) yauh pìhng yauh jihk; jihk làaihlàaih

lantern N: dānglùhng (M: go)

lap N: (round) hyūn (M: go) PH: sāttàuhgō seuhngbihn; wàaihpóuh (lit.) FV: ❶ (with the tongue) láai; líhm ❷ (wrap) bàaujyuh; bàaugwó ❸ (overlap) chùhngdihp ❹ (of water) paak * **lap strap** N: ngòn- chyùhndáai (M: tìuh)

lapse N: (error) gwocho; gwosāt (M: go) VO: (of law) sāthaauh FV: ❶ (decay) dohlohk ❷ (to tail off) siusāt FV/N: (of time) làuhsaih * **the lapse of time** PH: sìhgaange làuhsaih * **a lapse of the tongue** VO: sātyìhn * **a moral lapse** PH: douhdākseuhngge gwosāt

larceny N: tàusit jeuih PH: (theft) fèifaat chàmjim

lard N: jyūyàuh

large SV: daaih * **at large** SV: jihyàuh; sìuyìuh * **by and large** A: daaihjiseuhng; gèibúnseuhng * **a large sum of money** PH: yāt daaih bāt chín

lark N: baaklìhngníuh; wàhnjéuk (M: jek)

larva N: yauchùhng (M: tìuh)

larynx N: hàuhlùhng (M: go); sèngdáai (M: tìuh) * **laryngitis** PH: hàuhlùhng faatyìhm

lase VO: fongseh gīkgwòng

laser N: gīkgwòng; lèuihseh gīkgwòng

lash N: ❶ (of eyes) ngáahnyāpmōu; ngáahnjitmòuh (M: tìuh) ❷ (of a whip) pèihbīn (M: tìuh) FV: ❶ (strike) bīn; dá; bīndá ❷ (fasten) bóng PH: (fiercely criticize) gīkliht hínjaak

lass; lassie N: ❶ (girl) siunéuih; gùnèuhngjái (M: go) ❷ (sweet heart) ngoiyàhn (M: go)

lasso N: sìhngsok; tousok (M: go) PH: yuhng tousok làih jūk

last PH: jeuihauh; jeuisāumēi A: (most recent) jeuigahn FV: chìhjuhk; wàihchìh RVE: -dou · díchìn hóyíh yuhng ~ Láihbaaiyāt * **the last man I wanted to see**. PH: ngóh jeui m̀séung gin ge yàhn * **at last** MA: jēutjí; jùngyú * **the last chance** PH: jeuihauhge gèiwuih * **last judgement** PH: jeuihauh sámpun * **last supper** PH: jeuihauh máahnchāan * **last letter** PH: jeuigahn gó fūng seun * **last news** PH: jeuigahnge sìusīk * **last night** TW: kàhmmáahn; johkmáahn; chàhmmáahn * **last year** TW: gauhnín; gauhnìhn * **last week** TW: seuhnggo láihbaai * **last time** TW: seuhngchi; seuhngyātchi * **last resort** PH: jeuihauhge baahnfaat; jeuihauhge sáudyuhn * **at long last** MA: jēutjí * **the last word in** PH:

hóu dou móuh dāk joi hóu; jeui hóuge; jeui sānsīkge ~ sàuyàmgèi

lasting SV: kàm; kàmyuhng ATT: chìhgáu; wíhnggáu * **lasting peace** PH: wíhnggáuge wòhpìhng * **long lasting** Adj. PH: hóukàm; hóu kàmyuhng

latch FV/N: sēut (M: go) * **latch the door** PH: jèung douh mùhn sēuthóu

late SV: chìh · Kéuih sìhsìh dōu ~ dou; ngaan (usually in the morning or day-time); yeh (at night) * **to stay up late** PH: hóu yeh fangaau * **lately** MA: jeuigahn; gahnlòih; gahnlói * **at the latest** MA: jeuichìh; jichìh * **sooner or later** A: chìhjóu * **see you later** PH: joigin

latency FV/ATT: chìhmfuhk; chìhmjoih PH: chìhmjoih yànsou

latent ATT: chìhmfuhkge; chìmjoihge; chìhmfuhksingge * **latent disease germs** PH: chìhmfuhksingge behngkwán

lateral ATT: jākbīngè PH: sàanghái jākbīnge * **lateral sounds** N: bīnyām * **lateral buds** PH: sàanghái jākbīn ge fālām

latex N: jāp; gāaujèung * **rubber latex** N: gāaujèung; gāaujāp; jāp

lath PH: hóu jaakge báan N: báantìuh * **as thin as a lath** IE: sau gwāt yùh chaàih

lathe N: chèchòhng (M: fu)

lather N: ❶ póuh; fàangáanpóuh ❷ (of a horse) hohn VO: ❶ héipóuh ❷ chàh faàngáanpóuh ❸ (of a horse) chēuthohn * **lather one's chin before shaving** PH: taisòu jìchìhn chàhdī fàangáanpóuh hái hahpàh sìn

Latin N: ❶ (of people) Lāaidìng màhnjuhk ❷ (of language) Lāaidìngwá; Lāaidìngmàhn * **Latin America** PW/N: Làaidìng Méihjàu

latitude N: wáihdouh; wáihsin * **latitudes** N: deihkèui (M: go) * **north latitude** N: bākwáih

latrine N: chisó; gùngguhng chisó; mòuhhāang (lit) (M: go)

latter ATT: hauhbihnge; hauhbihn gógo N: hauhjé

lattice N: gaakjái PH: dáchege gaakjái; lìhngyìhngge gaakjái

laud FV: jaan; chìngjaan; jaanméih

laugh FV: siu * **laugh at** FV: siu; jàausiu * **laughter** N: siusèng * **laughable** SV: hóusiu

laughing SV: hóusiu PH: daaijyuh siuyùhng * **laughing faces** PH: mihndaai siuyùhng; múhnmihn siuyùhng * **laughing stock** N: siubeng * **to burst out laughing** PH: fātyìhngàan siuhéiséuhnglàih

launch VO: (of a ship) lohkséui FV: ❶ (of a missile) faatseh; fongseh ❷ (get started) chongbaahn; hòibaahn ❸ (of an attack) faatdung N: fósyùhnjái; heitéhng (M: ga; jek) * **launch an attack upon the enemy** PH: heung dihkyàhn faatduhng gùngsai * **launch a new business enterprise** PH: chongbaahn yātjúng sàn

kéihyihp * **launch picnic** PH: yàuhsyùhnhó * **launch out into** FV/A: hòichí * **launch out into extravagance** PH: hòichí fàifok * **launching ceremony** N: hahséuiláih (M: go)

laundry N: ❶ (shop) sáiyìdim; sáiyìpóu (M: gàan) ❷ (clothes) sāam (M: gihn)

laurel N: ❶ (shrub) yuhtgwaisyuh (M: pò) ❷ (wreath) gwaigùn (M: déng) * **laurels** N: wìhngyuh * **the poet laureate** N: gwaigùn sīyàhn (M: go)

lava N: yùhngngàahm

lavatory N: chisó (M: go)

lavender N: ❶ (plant) fànyìchóu ❷ (color) chínyísīk

lavish SV: (generous) daaihfòng; hóngkoi FV: (waste) lohngfai A: (excessive) gwodouh * **lavish praise** PH: gwodouh chìngjaan * **to be lavish with money** PH: lohngfai gàmchìhn

law N: ❶ (legal) faatleuht ❷ (of nature . . .) faatjāk (M: go) ❺ (of a game . . .) kwàijāk (M: go) BF: -faat * **law court** N: faattìhng (M: go) * **law suit** N: soujuhng * **lawful** VO: hahpfaat * **criminal law** N: yìhngfaat * **international law** N: gwokjaifaat (M:go) * **law abiding** VO/SV: sáufaat * **lawbreaking** VO: faahnfaat; wàihfaat * **Newton's Law** PH: Ngàuhdēundihngleuht * **the laws of supply and demand** N: gùngkàuhleuht (M: go)

lawless PH: ❶ wàihfaatge; bātfaatge ❷ (not having laws) móuh faatleuhtge * **lawless**

acts PH: bātfaatge hàhngwàih

lawn N: chóudéi; chóudeih (M: faai) * **lawn mover** N: cháanchóugèi (M: ga)

lawyer N: leuhtsī (M: go, wái)

lax SV: ❶ (free) sùng; m̀yìhmgaak ❷ (negligent) sòfāt; m̀síusàm FV/N: (of the bowels) tóuhngò; tóuhse * **lax behaviour** PH: sòfātge hàhngwàih

laxative N: seyeuhk; hìngsejài

laxity FV/SV: sùngchìh SV: (behavior) láahnsáan; sòfāt; daaihyi

lay FV: ❶ (put) jài; fong ❷ (produce) sàang ❸ (spread) pòu * **lay bricks** VO: chaijyún * **lay aside** RV: jàimaàih FV: (give up) fonghei * **lay on** FV: ngònpàaih; jóujīk * **lay by** N: beihchèchyu (M: go) * **lay off** FV: gáaigu VO: cháauyàuhyú (slang) * **layman** N: ❶ (opp. priest) juhkyàhn (M: go) ❷ (not expert) ngoihhóng (M: go) * **lay a floor with a carpet** PH: jèung deihjīn pòuhái deihbáansyu

layer M: chàhng VO: (of gardening) ngaattìuh; ngaatjì * **a layer cake** N: gaapsàm daahngòu (M: go)

lazy SV: láahn; láahndoh * **lazy bones** N: láahngwàttàuh (M: go)

leach FV: gwoleuih N: gwoleuihhei (M: go) * **leach out** PH: gwoleuih chēutlàih

lead N: (metal) yùhn FV: ❶ (guide) daai ❷ (act as chief) líhngdouh; sēutlíhng (army) ❸ (of road) tùngheui * **lead the**

choir PH: líhngdouh sīgōbāan cheunggō * **lead the fashion** VO: hòi fùnghei; chong sìhseuhng * **All roads lead to Rome** IE: Tiuhtiùh daaihlouh tung Lòhmáh * **lead a dog's life** PH: gwodī gàanfúge sàngwuht

leaden ATT: yùhnjouhge SV: ❶ (color) sàmfùisīk ❷ chàhmjuhng; chàhmmuhn * **leaden air** PH: hùnghei hóu chàhmmuhn * **leaden heart** PH: sàmchìhng hóu chàhmjuhng

leader N: líhngdouhyàhn; líhngjauh; líhngdéui; a táu; tàuhtáu (coll.) * **under the leadership of** PH: joih (hái) . . . ge líhngdouh jìhah * **the leader of the choir** PH: sīgōbāange jífài * **the leader of an expedition** PH: taamhímdéuige líhngdéui

leading Adj. PH: ❶ líhngdouh ge ❷ (most important) jeui jyúyiuge

leaf N: yihp; syuhyihp (M: faai, pin) M: (of books) pìn; jèung

leaflet N: chyùhndāan (M: jèung)

league N: wúi; hipwúi; lyùhnhahpwúi (M: go) VO/N: tùhngmàhng; lyùhnmàhng VO: gitmàhng PH: gàyahp tùhngmàhng * **in league with** Patt: tùhng . . . lyùhnhahp/ lyùhnmàhng

leak FV: lauh (electricity, water etc.) N: lauhduhng (M: go)

lean FV: ❶ (sloping) kìngchèh ❷ ngàai; bahng SV: ❶ (thin) sau ❷ (not productive) pàhnfaht

leap FV: tiu * **leap over** FV:

tiugwo * by (with) leaps and bounds IE: dahtfèimáahngjeun * leap-year N: yeuhnnihn

learn FV: hohk; hohkjaahp RV: tèngdóu * learn of PH: tèngginwah * learn sth by heart FV: buih; nihm; gei * learned in PH: jìngtùng . . . ge * learned Adj. PH: yáuhhohkmahn ge * learning N: hohkmahn; hohksīk

lease FV: jòu N: ❶ jòuyeuk (M: fahn) ❷ (rights given) jòujekyùhn

leash N: pèihdáai (M: tiuh)

least PH: jisíu; jeui síu

leather N: pèih; péi (M: faai) * leather belt N: pèihdáai (M: tiuh) * leather shoes N: pèihhàaih (M: deui)

leave FV: ❶ jáu ❷ lèihhòi (PW) ❸ (departure of a train, ship etc.) hòi; hòisàn RV: ❶ (intentionally) làuhdài ❷ (unintentionally) lauhdài N: (vacation) ga VO/N: yàuga * ask leave VO: chéngga; gouga

leaven N: hàaumóuh FV: (fig.) yínghéung

leavings N: ❶ jà ❷ (of a meal) sungméih

lecture N: yíngóng (M: pìn)

lecturer N: (at a university) góngsī (M: go)

ledge N: (chèuhngsyu ge) gá (M: go)

ledger N: júngjeung; fànleuihjeung

leech N: kèhná; kèihná; séuijaht (M: jek)

leek N: gáuchoi (M: pò , tiuh) * not worth a leek PH: hòuhmòuhgajihk

leer N: chàubò PH: chèhngáahn gám tái VO: sung chàubò

leeway FV/N: (of a ship) pìnhòhng N: lìhngwuhtsing

left DW: jó * left-handed Adj. PH: yuhng jósáu ge PH: (coll.) jóyàau * leftist Adj. PH: jópaai ge PH: jópaai yàhnsih * leftover (food) PH: gaakyehsung; sihkjihng ge sung * left-wing N: jóyihk; jópaai

leg N: ❶ (lower part) geuk (M: jek) ❷ (thigh) béi; daaihbéi (M: jek) * leg-man PH: chóifóng geijé (M: go) * leg-pull FV: yùhluhng * leg-work PH: chóifóng gùngjok

legacy N: wàihcháan

legal Adj. PH: ❶ faatleuht (seuhng) ge ❷ (lawful) hahpfaat ge ❸ (fixed by law) faatdihng ge * legal adviser PH: faatleuht gumahn (M: go)

legality N: hahpfaatsing PH: (faatleuht seuhngge) yihmouh

legalize FV: pàijéun; hahpfaatfa

legation N: gùngsigún (M: gàan)

legend FV/N: chyùhnsyut (M: go)

legibility PH: jihjīk (yanchaat) chìngchó

legible Adj. PH: yihduhk ge; jihjīkchìngchó ge

legion N: gwàntyùhn (M: go)

legislate VO: lahpfaat

legislation VO: lahpfaat N: faatkwài; faatleuht (M: tìuh)

legislative Adj. PH: lahpfaatge * **legislative assembly** N: lahpfaatyún * **legislature** PH: lahpfaatgèigwàan; lahpfaatbouh

legislator N: yíhyùhn (M: go)

legitimate Adj. PH: (lawful) hahpfaat ge; jingtúng ge

legume N: ❶ (dauh) haap (M: tìuh) ❷ dáu (M: nāp)

leisure SV: dākhàahn

lemon N: nìhngmūng; lihngmūng * **lemonade** N: nìhngmūngséui (M: bùi) * **lemon-drop** N: nìhngmūngtóng (M: nāp) * **lemon squash** N: nìhngmūng séui

lend FV: je . . . béi; jebéi * **lend an ear to** PH: làuhsàmtēng

length SV: chèuhng N: chèuhngdouh * **at full (considerable) length** Adv. PH: chèuhngsai gám; chùngfahn gám

lengthen RV: ❶ (by pulling out) làaichèuhng ❷ (by adding something) bokchèuhng FV: (extend) yìhnchèuhng

lengthy PH: chèuhnggwotàuh; chèuhngdākjaih

lenience (-ency) SV: fùndaaih; yàhnchìh

lenient SV: fùndaaih; yàhnchìh FV: fùnyùhng

Lenin N: Lihtnìhng * **Leninism** N: Lihtnìhng jyúyih * **Leninist** N: Lihtnìhng jyúyihjé (M: go)

lens N: (of a camera) gengtàuh (M: go)

leopard N: paau (M: jek)

leprosy N: màhfūngbehng * **show signs of leprosy** VO: faatfūng

leper N: ❶ màhfūngbehngyàhn (M: go) ❷ (coll.) màhfūnglóu; faatfūnglóu (M: go) * **leper asylum** N: màhfūngbehngyún (M: gàan)

lesion FV/N: syúnhoih; syúnsèung N: mòuhbehng

less PH: ❶ (in quantity) síudī ❷ (in size) saidī FV: (minus) gáam * **less than** PH: síugwo; saigwo FV: (not in comparison) m̀gau * **none the less** A: yìyìhn

lessen FV: ❶ gáamsíu; gáamhèng ❷ (cause sth. to appear smaller, less important) sūksai; bíndài

lesson M: (learning unit) fo N: ❶ (instructive experience) gaaufan ❷ (homework) gùngfo

lest A: míhnji PH: yùhgwó m̀haih jauh . . .

let FV: ❶ (allow) béi; yáu ❷ (for rent) chēutjòu * **let me see** PH: ❶ (to look at) dáng ngóh táiháh ❷ (to think over) dáng ngóh séungháh * **let go one's hold** FV: fongsáu * **let oneself go** IE: chìhngbātjihgam * **let-down** FV: ① (disappointed) sātmohng ② (lower) hahgong

lethal Adj. PH: jiséi ge

lethargic SV: (sleepy) hóu ngáahnfan SV: (uninterested) láahngdaahm PH: (want of energy) móuhsànghei

letter N: ❶ (message) seun (M: fùng) ❷ (alphabet) jihmóuh (M: go) ❸ (word) jih (M: go) ∗ **letter box** N: seunsèung (M: go) ∗ **letter carrier** N: yàuhchàai (M: go) ∗ **letter sheet** N: seunjí (M: jèung) ∗ **letter of introduction** N: gaaisiuhseun (M: fùng)

lettered Adj. PH: yáuh hohkmahn ge; yáuh màhnfa ge

lettuce N: sàangchoi (M: pò)

level N: ❶ séuipìhng ❷ (rank) kāpbiht; deihwaih SV: pìhng FV: jíngpìhng ∗ **level ground** N: pìhngdeih (M: faai, daat)

lever N: gòn; gunggòn (M: jì)

levis N: ngàuhjáifu (M: tìuh)

levitate FV: pìufàuh (hái hùngjùng)

levity SV: hìngsèut; hìngfàuh PH: binfa mòuhsèuhng

levy FV: ❶ chàu (tax, etc.) ❷ jìngyuhng; jìngjaahp (troops) ❸ kaungat (one's property) VO: ❶ (of tax) chàuseui; jìngseui ❷ (of troops) jìngbīng

lewd SV: yàhmdohng; hahlàuh

lexicon N: chìhdín; jihdín (M: bún, bouh)

liability N: ❶ (responsibility) jaakyahm; (obligation) yìhmouh ❷ (debt) jaai FV/N: kìngheung

liable Patt: ❶ (for) deui ... yìngfuh jaakyahm ge ❷ (to) yáuh ... kìngheung ge; yùhngyih ... ge

liaison FV/N: ❶ (connexion) lyùhnlok ❷ (illicit and intimate relationship) sìtùng

liar N: (coll.) daaihpaauyáu (M: go)

libel FV: dáiwái; wáipóhng

liberal SV: (generous) hóngkoi; daaihfòng Adj. PH: ❶ (free from prejudice) móuh pìngin ge; gùngjing ge ❷ (free, casual) jihyàuh, chèuihbín ge PH: ❶ hòitùng ge yàhn (M: go) ❷ jihyàuh jyúyihjé (M: go)

liberalism N: jihyàuhjyúyih; jihyàuhfongyàhmjyúyih

liberality SV: gùngjing; daaihfòng PH: sàmhùngfut

liberate FV/N: gáaifong ∗ **liberation army** N: gáaifonggwān (M: deuih)

liberation FV/N: gáaifong

libertine N: lohngjí (M: go) SV: fongdohng

liberty SV/N: jihyàuh SV: mouhmuih N: dahkkyùhn ∗ **at liberty** SV/N: jihyàuh PH: yáuh kyùhn SV: dākhàahn ∗ **set at liberty** FV: sīkfong

library N: toùhsyùgún (M: gàan) ∗ **librarian** N: ❶ (head) toùhsyùgún gúnjéung (M: go) ❷ toùhsyùgúnyùhn, toùhsyùgúnléihyùhn (M: go)

Libyan Adj. PH: Leihbéinga ge N: Leihbéinga yàhn (M: go)

licence, license N: pàaihjiu; jāpjiu (M: go) SV: (wrong use of freedom) fongsi FV: pàijéun; héuihó

licentious SV: fongsi; fongdohng

lichen N: ❶ (plant) deihyì; sehkyíh ❷ (medical) sín

lick FV: láai; lím

licorice N: gàmchóu

lid N: goi (M: go) * **to put on a lid** RV: kámjyuh VO: kámgoi

lie RV: fandài FV: fanhái; buhkhái VO: (deceive) góng daaihwah N: daaihwah (M: go) * **as far as in me lies** PH: jeuhn ngóh ge lihkleuhng * **lie at the mercy of** Patt: sauh .. . jìpui * **lie in the way** FV/N: fòhnghoih; jóngoih

lieutenant N: ❶ (army) luhkgwàn jùngwai (M: go) ❷ (navy) hóigwàn seuhngwai (M: go)

life N: ❶ mehng; sàngmihng; singmihng (M: tìuh) ❷ (span) sauhmihng ❸ (biography) jyuhngei FV/N: (way of living) sàngwuht PH: (the extent in time one lives) yātsàng; yāt-saiyàhn * **life-and-death** IE: sàngséiyàuhgwàan * **life belt** N: ngònchyùhndáai (M: tìuh) * **life-boat** N: gausàngtéhng (M: jek) * **life buoy** N: gausànghyùn (M: go) * **life jacket** N: gausàngyī (M: gihn) * **life guard** N: gausàngyùhn (M: go) * **life-long** Adj. PH: jùngsànge * **life-style** PH: sàngwuht fòngsīk * **life-work** PH: bātsàng ge sìhyihp * **life imprisonment** PH: mòuh kèihtòuhyìhng; jùngsàn gàamgam * **life-insurance** N: yàhnsauh bóuhím; yàhnsauhyinsō

lift RV: ❶ (raise) nìnghéi ❷ (with two hands) tòihhéi; chàuhéi ❸ (above the shoulder) géuihéi ❹ (of raising a cover) kínhòi N: (elevator) dihntài; (tr.) līp (M: bouh)

ligament N: ❶ haihdáai ❷ (of bones) yahndáai

light SV/N: gwòng N: ❶ gwòngsin ❷ (source of artificial illumination) dāng (M: jáan) FV: ❶ dím (lamp) ❷ tau (stove) SV: ❶ (of colour) chín ❷ (of weight) hèng * **light bulb** N: dāngdáam (M: go) * **light house** N: dāngtaap (M: go) * **light year** N: gwòngnìhn * **light-headed** PH: tàuhwàhn-ngáahnfā * **light-hearted** PH: mòuhyàu mòuhleuih * **light-minded** SV: hìngfàuh; hìngsēut

lighten FV: ❶ (reduce the weight of) gáamhèng Patt: (make bright) sái PW gwòngsaai

lighter N: (for cigarette) dáfógèi (M: go)

lightly A: hehnghēng

lightness SV: hèng; hìng-yìhng

lightning VO: símdihn * **lightning conductor (or rod)** N: beihlèuihjām (M: jì)

lignite N: mùih (M: gauh)

likable SV: hóngoi

like FV: ❶ jùngyi ❷ (indicating opinion) gokdāk FV/SV: ❶ fùnhéi ❷ (similar to) chíh FV/A: hóuchíh * **should (would) like to do** AV: séung; yuhnyi; hèimohng * **and such (the) like** PH: dángdáng; jyùyùhchíleuih * **something like** PH: yáuhdīchíh A: daaihyeuk * **likelihood** PH: hónàhngsing

likely Adv. PH: hóu hónàhng A: daaihkoi; daaihkói AV: (may be) wúih * **as likely as not** Adv. PH: hóu hónàhng PH: góngmdihng * **likely enough** A: dòsou * **not likely** PH: m̀gindāk

liken Patt: jèung . . . béijouh

likeness SV: sèungchíh N: (picture) wájeuhng (M: fūk) * **in the likeness of** PH: go yéung chíh

likewise Adv. PH: jiu yéung gám A: dōu; yìhché

liking N: hingcheui; sihou * **have a liking for** FV/SV: fùnhéi * **to sb's liking** PH: hahp . . . ge waihháu

lilac N: ❶ jídīnghēung (M: pò déu, dó) ❷ (of colour) chínjísīk

lily N: baakhahpfā (M: déu, dó) * **water lily** N: lihnfā; hòhfā (M: déu, dó) * **white lily** N: yuhk jāamfā (M: déu, dó) * **lily-livered** SV: saidáam * **lily-white** Adj. PH: sèuhnbaakge; sèuhngit ge

limb N: (of the body) jītái (M: go) PH: (of trees) daaih syuhjī (M: jì) * **the four limbs** PH: sei jī

limber Adj. PH: yàuhyúhnge; yáuh daahnsing ge N: (military) paauchìhnchè (M: ga)

lime N: ❶ sehkfūi ❷ (fruit) chèngnìhngmūng (M: go) * **limelight** N: (on stage) fùigwōngdāng; séuingāhndāng (M: jáan) PH: jungyàhn jyumuhk ge jùngsām * **limestone** N: sehkfūisehk (M: gauh)

limit N: gaaihaahn; haahndouh; haahnjai FV: haahnjai * **limited** SV: yáuhhaahn * **limited to** PH: haahnyù * **within the limits** Patt: hái . . . faahnwàih noih * **limitless** Adj. PH: mòuhhaahn ge * **limited company** PH: yáuhhaahn gūngsī (M: gàan)

limousine PH: daaih fóngchè (M: ga)

limp PH: bàiháh bàiháh; gahtgahtháh Adj. PH: yàuhyúhnge; móuhlihkge

line N: ❶ (mark) sin; gaaisin (M: tìuh) ❷ (of battle) jinsin ❸ (of business, occupation) hòhngyihp (M: go) ❹ (on face) jaumáhn (M: tìuh) M: ❶ (of writing) hòhng ❷ (series of objects) laaht; pàaih * **telephone line** N: dihnwásin (M: tìuh) * **line of defense** N: fòhngsin (M: tìuh) * **line up** VO: pàaihdéui; pàaih chèuhnglùhng * **come into line** PH: ❶ sihngwàih yāt pàaih ❷ (unanimous) yātji FV: tùhngyi * **in line with** Patt: tùhng . . . yātji FV: fùhhahp

lineal Adj. PH: jihkhaihge; jingtúngge

linear Adj. PH: ❶ jihksin ge ❷ (of length) chèuhngdouh ge

linen N: màhbou (M: fūk, faai)

liner N: ❶ (of ships) yàuhsyùhn; bàansyùhn (M: ga) ❷ (of aircraft) bàangèi (M: ga)

linesman N: pòhngjing (M: go)

linger FV: pùihwùih; dauhlàuh; tòyìhn

lingo N: ❶ (foreign language) fàanwá; ngoihgwokwá ❷ hòhngwá; ngamyúh

lingual Adj. PH: ❶ leih ge ❷ (of languages) yúhyìhn ge N: (of linguistics) leihyām

linguistics N: yúhyìhnhohk * **linguist** N: yúhyìhnhohkgā (M: go)

lining N: (of clothes) léih; sāamléih

link FV: lìhnmàaih; lìhnjip N: lyùhnhaih * **link arms** PH: kíuhjyuhsáu

linoleum N: chātbou (M: fūk, faai)

linotype N: pàaihjihgèi (M: fu)

lion N: sī; sìjí (M: jek) * **lion dance** VO: móuhsī * **the lions' share** PH: chyùhnbouh; daaihbouhfahn * **lion-hearted** SV: yúhnggám; yúhngmáahng

lip N: háusèuhn; jéuisèuhn * **lipstick** N: háusèuhngōu; sèuhngōu (M: jì) * **lip-deep** PH: bíumihnseuhng ge; móuh sihngyi ge * **lip service** PH: háutàuh seuhng hóutèng ge syutwah; yingchàuhwá

liquefy FV: yihkfa * **liquefier** N: yihkfahei (M: go)

liquid N: yihktái Adj. PH: ❶ (not solid) làuhjāt ge (food) ~ **sihkmaht** ❷ (transparent) taumìhngge ❸ (of sounds) làuhcheung ge ❹ (easily changed) yihbin ge * **liquidity** N: làuhduhngsing

liquidate RV: ❶ wàahnchìng (debts) ❷ sūkchìng (rebels, etc.) FV: (of a business company) chìngpún

liquidation RV: wàahnchìng (debts) * **go into liquidation** PH: tìhngyihp chìngléih VO/FV: pochàan

liquor N: ❶ jāp ❷ (alcoholic drink) jáu (M: jèun) * **liquor store** N: jáupóu (M: gàan) * **a man's capacity for liquor** N: jáuleuhng

liquorice N: gāmchóu

lisp PH: háuchímlìhngleih

list N: ❶ (bill) dāan (M: jèung) ❷ (form) bíu (M: jèung, go) ❸ (of names) mìhngdāan (M: jèung) ❹ (of items) muhkluhk (M: go) VO: lihtbíu

listen FV: tèng * **listener** N: tingjung (M: go, wái)

listless PH: móuh sāmgèi; móuh jìngsàhn; láahn yèuhngyèuhng gám

literacy VO: sīkjih PH: ❶ yáuh màhnfa; jìngtùng màhnhohk ❷ yuhtduhk tùhng séjok ge nàhnglihk

literal Adj. PH: jihmín ge (meaning) ~ **yisi** * **literally** PH: jiu jìhyih * **in the literal sense of the word** it is PH: jiu jihmín gáai nī go jih ge yisi haih . . . * **literal translation** FV: jihkyihk

literary Adj. PH: màhnhohkge; syùbún ge

literate PH: yáuh màhnfa ge (yàhn); nàhnggau séjok ge (yàhn); yáuh hohkmahn ge (yàhn)

literature N: ❶ màhnhohk ❷ màhnhin PH: màhnhohk jokbán

litre M: sìng; gùngsìng

litter N: ❶ (stretcher) dàamgá ❷ (couch) kíu (M: déng) ❸ (rubbish) laahpsaap M: (of animals) dau FV: lyuhndám RV: jínglyuhn

little SV: ❶ (of size and age) sai ❷ (of quantity) síu ❸ (short in time, distance) dyún BF: -jai • (little cat) *māau* ~ N/M: (yāt)

dī Nu/PH: sèsíu; síusíu ✻ a
little while TW: yātjahngāan
✻ a very little Nu: dīgamdēu
✻ a little better SV: hóudī ✻
little by little Adv. PH: yātdī
yātdī gám; juhk dī juhk dī gám

livable PH: ❶ (of houses,
weather etc.) jyuhdāk ge ❷ (of
life) gwodākheui ge ❸ (of people) yùhngyíh sèungchyú ge

live FV: ❶ (dwell) jyuh ❷
(pass) gwo (one's days or life)
FV/N: ❶ (be alive) sàngchyùhn
❷ (spend one's life) sàngwuht
PH: (of broadcast) yihnchèuhng
jyúnbo ✻ a live fish PH:
yàuhséui yú (M: tìuh) ✻ as I
live PH: dīkdīkkokkok ✻ live
by Patt: kaau . . . wàih sàng ✻
live it up FV: kwòhngfūn;
kòhngfūn ✻ live up to FV:
sahtchìhn RV: jouhdou

livestock N: gàchūk; sàngchūk

livelihood FV/N: sàngwuht
N: sànggai FV: màuhsàng

lively SV: ❶ wuhtput ❷ (of
colour) sìnmìhng ❸ (life like)
sàangduhng PH: chùngmúhn
wuhtlihk (ge)

liver N: ❶ (of man) gòn (M: go)
❷ (of animal) yéun; gòn ✻
liver-colour N: jyùgònsīk ✻
liver-complaint N: gònbehng

livid Adj. PH: yùhnsīk ge;
chèngfùisīk ge

living FV/N: sàngwuht;
sàngchyùhn Adj. PH: ❶ yáuh
sàngmihng ge ❷ (existent)
yìhgā chyùhnjoih ge ❸ (active)
wuhtput ge ✻ living-room N:
haaktēng (M: go)

lizard N: yìhmsé (M: tìuh)

load FV: ❶ joi; jòng (a cargo)

❷ yahp (cartridge or film) FV/N:
❶ fuhdàam ❷ (of care and electricity etc.) fuhhoh ✻ loads of
PH: hóu dò; daaihleuhng

loaf PH: ❶ yāttìuh mihnbāau
❷ (waste time) lohngfai
sìhgaan; wahn yahtjí

loan VO: jechín; taaifún ✻
loan office N: taaifúnchyu ✻
loan-word N: ngoihlòihyúh ✻
loan sharks PH: daaihyíh-
lūng; gwailéiwòhng (M: go)

loath AV/FV: m̀yuhnyi FV:
yìmwu ✻ nothing loath PH:
hóu lohkyi ✻ loathsome Adj.
PH: tóuyim ge; hówu ge

loathe FV: jànghahn; yìmwu

lob PH: ❶ (cricket) hahsáubō;
dàibō ❷ (tennis) gòu bō VO: diu
gòubō

lobby N: daaihtòhng; yàusīksāt (M: go); mùhnlòhng PH:
(group of people) yíhyún ngoih
wuhtduhng jaahptyùhn

lobe N: (of the ear) yíhjyū (M:
jek) BF: (of lungs etc.) -yihp

lobster N: lùhnghā (M: jek)

local Adj. PH: búndeih ge;
guhkbouh ge PH: ❶ (of people)
búndeih yàhn ❷ (of news)
búndeih sànmàhn; búndeih
sànmán ✻ local authority
PH: deihfòng dòngguhk ✻
local court PH: deihfòng faatyún ✻ local anaesthesia PH:
guhkbouh màhjeui ✻ local
congestion PH: guhkbouh
chùnghyut

localism PH: ❶ deihfòng
gùnnihm; deihfòngjyúyih ❷ (of
dialect) fòngyihn; tóuwá

locality N: deihfòng; waihji;
deihkèui (M: go)

localize PH: guhkbouhfa; deihfòngfa FV: guhkhaahn; taamchāak

locate FV: chitji FV/CV: hái PH: wánchèut . . . ge waihji; kokdihng deihdím

location N: ❶ (place) deihdím (M: go) ❷ (position) waihji (M: go)

lock N: ❶ só (M: bá) ❷ (of a canal or river) syùhnjaahp (M: douh) ❸ (of a gun) gāi FV: só (door etc.) ✻ **locksmith** N: sósìhlòu (M: go) ✻ **lock up** RV: sómàaih; wanjyuh

locker PH: (yáuh só ge) chyúhmahtgwaih (M: go)

locomotion FV/N: wahnduhng FV: yìhduhng

locomotive N: fóchètàuh; gèichè Adj. PH: gèiduhng ge

locus N: ❶ waihji; deihdím (M: go) ❷ gwáijīk (M: tiuh)

locust N: wòhngchùhng; máang (M: jek)

lode N: ❶ kongmahk ❷ séuilouh; pàaihséuikèuih (M: tiuh)

lodge N: ❶ mùhnfóng ❷ (small hotel) sai ge léuihgún (M: gàan) ❸ (branch of a society) fànwúi (M: go) FV: ❶ (live) jyuh ❷ jài; chyùhn (money etc.) ❸ tàihchèut (protest etc.) RV: (of bullets etc.) dáyahp ✻ **lodger** N: fòhnghaak (M: go)

lodg(e)ment N: ❶ (dwelling) yuhsó ❷ (sth. accumulated) jīk; chàhmdihn FV: (of a complaint etc.) tàihchèut

lodging PH: chēutjòu ge fóng (M: gàan) N: sūkse (M: gàan) FV: geisūk

loft N: goklàu (M: chàhng) VO: (of golf) dá gòubō

lofty Adj. PII: ❶ (of great height) fèisèuhng gòu ge ❷ (of thoughts etc.) sùhnggòu ge; gòuseuhng ge SV: gòungouh; gìungouh; ngouhmaahn

log N: ❶ (wood) muhk; muhktàuh (M: gauh) ❷ (apparatus of a ship) chāakchìhngyìh (M: go) PH: (record book of a ship) hòhnghói yahtji (M: bún)

logarithm N: deuisou

logic N: lòhchāp (hohk) PH: lòhchāpsing FV/N: tèuiléih

logistic Adj. PH: lòhchāp ge; hauhkàhn ge PH: gaisyunseuht; souléih lòhchāp

loin N: yìu; yìugwāt; yìuyuhk

loiter FV: yàuhdohng; dohngdohnghá PH: sìumòh sìhgaan

lollipop N: ❶ tòhnggwó ❷ bòbáantóng (M: jì)

lone SV: jihkmohk; gùduhk

lonely SV: ❶ gùdàan; jihkmohk ❷ (of places) pìnpīk

long SV: ❶ (in space) chèuhng ❷ (in time) noih PH: (of time) chèuhng sìhgaan FV: (for sth.) hotmohng ✻ **before long** PH: móuh géinoih; móuh géinòi ✻ **long before** PH: hóu noih yíhchìhn ✻ **long-hand** PH: póutùng sèfaat ✻ **long-headed** SV: jìngmìhng ✻ **long-lived** Adj. PH: chèuhngmehng ge ✻ **long-sighted** Adj. PH: yáuh yúhngìn ge ✻ **long-standing** Adj. PH: chèuhng sìhgaan ge ✻ **long-suffering** Adj. PH: gìnyán ge

longevity SV/PH: chèuhngmehng; chèuhngsauh

longing FV: hotmohng

longitude N: gīngsin; gīngdouh * **east longitude** N: dūnggīng * **west longitude** N: sāigīng

longshore Adj. PH: hóingohnbīn ge * **longshoreman** PH: máhtàuh jòngse gùngyàhn (M: go)

look FV: tái PH: (appear, seem) táigin hóuchíh N: ❶ mihnsīk ❷ yéung * **look like** FV: chíh * **look after** FV: ❶ (to guard) hòn (place, people etc.) ❷ (to take care of) chau (children) ❸ jiugu (people needed help) RV: hònjyuh; táijyuh * **look down upon** RV: tái mhéi; táisíu * **look for** FV: wán * **look forward to** FV/N: paanmohng * **look around** PH: seiwàih táiháh * **look into** FV: diuhchàh * **looking glass** N: geng (M: mihn, faai) * **look out** FV: jyuyi; làuhyi * **look-over** PH: daaihkói táiháh * **look-see** FV: diuhchàh * **look-up** FV: chàh (dictionary etc.)

looker N: gùnjung (M: go) * **looker-on** N: pòhnggùnjé (M: go)

lookout FV: jyuyi; làuhyi N: ❶ (place to watch) liuhmohngtòih (M: go) ❷ (prospect) chìhntòuh * **on the lookout for** FV: jyuyi; gínggaai

loom N: (weaving machine) jīkbougēi (M: ga) PH: mùhnglùhng chēutyihn FV: bīkgahn

loony N: kòhngyàhn; dīnlóu; chìsīnlóu (M: go) SV: sòh; dīn; chìsīn * **loony-bin** N: sàhngīng behngyún; jīngsàhn behngyún (M: gàan)

loop N: (of a rope) hyūn (M: go) VO: dá gwàandáu PH: jíngsìhnghyūn; yuhng hyūn hyùnjyuh * **loop-hole** N: ❶ chēungngáahn (M: go) ❷ (fig.) lauhduhng

loose SV: (not tight) sùng Adj. PH: ❶ saanhòi ge ❷ (of behaviour etc.) m̀yìhmgánge; fongdohng ge ❸ (not strict) m̀yìhmgaak ge RV: fongsùng; gáaihòi * **at a loose end** IE: bātjìsóchou PH: móuhjeuhklohk * **play (at) fast and loose** IE: fáanfūk mòuhsèuhng * **loose-leaf** Adj. PH: wuhtyihp ge

loosen RV: fongsùng; sūnghòi; gáaihòi

loot N: ❶ (of thieves) jòngmaht ❷ (of soldiers) jīnleihbán FV: (plunder) chéung

lopsided PH: yātbihn gōu yātbihn dāi ge; m̀pìhnghàhng ge

loquacious SV: dòháu; dòjéui

loquat N: ❶ (plant) pèihpàh (M: pò) ❷ (fruit) pèihpàhgwó (M: go)

lord N: ❶ jyú ❷ (noble) gwaijuhk (M: go) * **lordly** PH: hóuchíh gwaijuhk gám SV: (haughty) gòungouh * **lordship** PH: gwaijuhk sànfán * **Lord's day** N: Jyúyaht * **Lord's prayer** PH: Jyútóu màhn

lore N: jìsīk; hohkmahn PH: háutàuh chyùhnsyut

lorry N: fochē (M: ga)

lose FV: ❶ (of objects) sātjó; m̀ginjó ❷ (in a game or gambling) syūjó * **lose one's labour**

PH: tòuhlòuh; sàai sàamgèi *
lose oneself RV: dohngsàtjó
VO: (engrossed) yahpmàih *
lose face PH: diugá; móuhmín; làtsòu (vulgar) * **lose
hope** FV/SV: fūisàm * **lose
weight** FV: saujó * **lose one's
temper** VO: faat pèihhei *
lose in business VO: sihtbún

loss FV/N: syúnsàt; sàtbaaih
* **at a loss** IE: bātjísóchou *
without (any) loss of time A:
jīkhāak

lost VO: (in one's way)
dohngsàtlouh RV: (of com-
prehension) gànm̀dóu Adj. PH:
sàtheui ge; sàtbaaih ge * **be
lost to** RV: gámgok m̀dóu

lot N: ❶ (of land) deih (M: faai,
daat) ❷ (as fate) mihngwahn;
mehng ❸ (to draw) chīm (M: jī);
cháu (M: go, tiùh) PH: (much)
hóudò; daaihbá * **draw lots**
VO: jāpcháu; chāuchīm * **lots
and lots (of)** PH: hóudò hóudò
(ge)

lotion N: ❶ (for cleansing) git-
fūlouh (M: jèun) ❷ (for moistur-
ing) yeuhnfūlouh (M: jèun)

lottery N: chóipiu; jéung-
gyun (M: jèung) PH: (fig.)
m̀hóyíh yuhchāak ge sih

lotus N: lìhn; hòh * **lotus
flower** N: lìhnfā; hòhfā (M:
déu, dó) * **lotus roots** N: lìhn-
ngáuh (M: jī, gauh) * **lotus
seed** N: lìhnjí (M: nāp) * **lotus-
eater** PH: tàam ngònyaht ge
yàhn (M: go)

loud SV: daaihsèng *
loudspeaker N: kongyāmgèi
(M: go)

lounge N: yàusīksàt; wuih-
haaksàt; haaktēng (M: go) FV:
hàahndohng PH: láahnyèuhng-
yèuhnggám chóhháh, kéihháh

louse N: sāt; sātná (M: jek)
VO: jūksāt; jūksātná RV:
gáauwaaih

lousy Adj. PH: sàangsāt ge
SV: (bad) chā; yáih; waaih

lovable Adj. PH: hóngoi ge

love FV/N: (between persons,
general) ngoi AV/FV: (of people
and things) jùngyi N: ❶
ngoichìhng ❷ (a person)
chìhngyàhn (M: go) FV: ❶ (between elders and children involving close relationship) sek ❷
(between children and parents)
haauseuhn ❸ (of an action)
ngoihou ❹ (strong like of an action) yìhtngoi PH: ❶ hóu jùngyi
❷ (in games) lìhngfàn * **love
child** N: sìsàngjí (M: go) *
love each other PH: béichí
sèungngoi * **love letter** N:
chìhngseun (M: fùng) * **love-
lorn** FV: sātlyún * **love-sick**
PH: (yáuh) sèungsibehng

lovely Adj. PH: ❶ hóngoi ge
❷ yuhfaai ge

lover N: ngoiyàhn; chìhngyàhn (M: go)

loving Adj. PH: chànngoi ge;
ngoi ge

low SV: ❶ dài ❷ (of price) dài;
pèhng ❸ (vulgar) bèijihn; chòujuhk Adj. PH: (of humble rank)
dàihah PH: ❶ (of voice) saisèng
❷ (of tide) séui teui * **low-
born** PH: chēutsàn dàimèih *
low-bred Adj. PH: hahjihn ge
* **low-brow** PH: màhnfasàu-
yéuhng dài ge yàhn (M: go) *
low-down SV: bèipéi N:
noihmohk; jànseung * **low-
key(ed)** PH: dàidiuh ge * **low-
minded** SV: hahlàuh * **low-
spirited** SV: tèuihsong

lower PH: hahkáp ge; dàikáp
ge RV: gongdài

loyal SV: jùngsàm; jùngsìhng * **loyalist** N: jùngsàhn (M: go)

lozenge N: lìhngyìhng (M: go)

lubricant N: waahtgèiyáu; gáiyáu

lubricate VO: séuhngyáu * **lubricator** N: waahtgèiyáu; gáiyáu

lubrication PH: yeuhnwaaht jokyuhng VO: séuhngyáu

lucid SV: ❶ (clear) chìngchó ❷ (of mind) chìngsíng Adj. PH: mìhngbaahk ge

lucidity SV: mìhnglóhng; chìngsíng FV: mìhngbaahk

lucifer N: mògwái; Saatdaahn

luck N: wahnhei SV: hahngwahn * **good luck** PH: ❶ (a wish) jūk néih seuhnleih ❷ wahnhei hóu * **by luck** A: hóujoih * **in luck** VO: hàahngwahn * **hard luck, bad luck** PH: wahnhei mhóu; jaihwahn; dóumùih * **luckily** Adv. PH: hahngwahn gám; hiuhahng gám * **luckless** SV: bāthahng

lucky VO: hàahngwahn A/SV: hóuchói PH: wahnhei hóu

lucrative Adj. PH: yáuh leih ge; jaahnchín ge

lucre N: wàahngchòih (M: bāt)

ludicrous SV: fòngmauh; fòngtòhng; hóusiu

lug PH: yuhng lihk tò làai IE: jònghùng joksai

luggage N: hàhngléih (M: gihn)

lukewarm PH: ❶ nyúhnnyúndéi ge ❷ (fig.) mǐyihtchìhng ge

lull FV: sìuchèuih (fears) SV/FV: pìhngjihng (wind, storm etc.) Patt: ngam PN (saimānjái) fan

lullaby N: chèuimìhnkūk (M: sáu)

lumbago PH: yīugwāttung

lumber N: muhkchòih; muhklíu PH: (of sound) lùhnglúngsèng FV/N: lyuhndèui * **lumber-jack** PH: geumuhk/wahnmuhk gùngyàhn (M: go) * **lumber-mill** N: geumuhkchóng (M: gàan) * **lumber-room** N: jaahpmahtfóng (M: gàan) * **lumber-yard** N: chyúhmuhkchèuhng (M: go)

luminary N: ❶ (in the sky) faatgwòngtái; (sun) taaiyèuhng; (moon) yuhtgwòng (M: go) ❷ dänggwòng PH: (fig.) (of a person) gihtchèutyàhnmaht (M: go)

luminous Adj. PH: ❶ faat gwòng ge ❷ (fig.) chìngchó ge; yìhmìhng ge

lump M: gauh PH: ❶ hóu leuhnjeuhn ge yàhn (M: go) ❷ kìhngmàaih yāt gauh ❸ (put together) gaapmàaih yātchàih

lumpy PH: ❶ yāt gauh yāt gauh ge ❷ (of waves) bòlohnghéifuhk ge

lunacy PH: sàhngìngcholyuhn SV: dìn; chìsin * **become a lunatic** VO: faatdìn * **lunatic asylum** N: jìngsàhnbehngyún

lunar PH: yuht ge * **lunar calendar** N: yàmlihk; gauhlihk

lunch N: ngaanjau; ngaanjaufaahn (M: chàan)

lung N: fai (M: go)

lunge FV: ❶ (with a sword) chaap, chì ❷ (of the body) chùng; máahngchùng

lurch PH: ❶ (of a person) pêhháhpéhháhgám hàahng ❷ (of a ship) fātyìhn kìngchèh

lure N: meihlihk; yáuhwaahklihk FV: yáhnyáuh

lurid SV: ❶ (pale) chòngbaahk ❷ (frightful) hópa PH: (overdone) gwofahnhyùnyíhmge

lurk FV: chìhmfuhk; màaihfuhk

luscious Adj. PH: ❶ (of taste and smell) hóu hèung ge; hóu meih ge ❷ (of music, writing etc.) wàhlaih ge ❸ (of women) yuhkgám ge; singgám ge

lush SV: ❶ (of grass and vegetation) mauhsihng ❷ (of taste) hóumeih

lust N: yuhkmohng; sīkyuhk FV: hotmohng ✳ **lustful** Adj. PH: hou sīk ge; yàhmdohng ge

luster, lustre N: ❶ gwòngjaahk; gwòngchói ❷ (glory) gwòngwìhng SV: (fig.) chēutsīk

lustrous Adj. PH: ❶ yáuh gwòngjaahk ge ❷ (fig.) chēutsīk ge

lusty Adj. PH: kèuhngjong ge; yáuh jìngsàhnge

lute N: pèihpàh (M: go) VO: tàahn pèihpàh

luxuriant SV: ❶ (strong in growth) mauhsihng ❷ (of literary style) wàhlaih; wàhméih

luxury SV: chèchí; chèwàh

N: chèchíbán

lye N: gáanséui

lying PH: ❶ (telling lies) góng daaihwah ge ❷ fanháidouh ge ✳ **lying-in** FV: sàngcháan VO: sàang bìhbī

lymph N: làhmbā

lynch N: sìyìhng VO: hàhng sìyìhng

lyre N: chātyìhnsyuhkàhm (M: go)

lyric N: ❶ syùchìhngsī (M: sáu) ❷ gōchìh SV: syùchìhng

M

Macao/Macau PW: Oumún; Ngoumún

macaroni N: tūngsàmfán; tùngfán

machine N: gèihei; heihaaih ✳ **machine-gun** N: gèigwàanchēung (M: jì) ✳ **machine rifle** N: jihduhng bouhchēung (M: jì)

machinery N: ❶ gèihei; heihaaih ❷ (methods) fòngfaat ❸ (organization) jóujīk; gèikau (M: go)

machinist N: gèihaaihsī; gèihaaihgùngyàhn (M: go)

mackerel N: chèngyú; chèngfāyú (M: tìuh)

mackintosh PH: ❶ (cloth) fòhngséui gàaubou (M: faai) ❷

(raincoat) gàaubou yúhyī (M: gihn)

macrobiotics PH: lóuhnihnbóugihn; chèuhngsauhfaat

macrocosm PH: daaih saigaai; daaih yúhjauh; jíngtái

mad SV: ❶ (angry) nàu ❷ (crazy) dìn; fùngkòhng FV: faat nàu; faatngok Adj. PH: (much excited) kòhngyihtge; kòhng fùn ge * **mad-cap** SV: lóuhmóhng; chùngduhng PH: kòhngmóhng ge yàhn (M: go)

madam N: fùyàhn; néuihsih; taaitáai (M: wái)

madame N: taaitáai; fùyàhn; néuihsih (M: wái)

made Adj. PH: dahkjai ge; hèuikauge RV: (done) jouhhéi Patt: (manufactured) haih . . . jouh ge * **made up of** Patt: yàuh . . . jóu sìhng * **made-up** Adj. PH: yàhngùng ge * **made to order** FV: dehngjouh

magazine N: ❶ (pamphlet) jaahpji (M: bún) ❷ (store for arms) fóyeuhkfu (M: go) * **magazinist** PH: jaahpji; jaangóuyàhn; kèihhón/kèihhòn pìnchàp (M: go)

maggot N: jèui (M: tìuh) * **maggoty** PH: (fig.) séungyahp fèifèi (ge)

magic N: ❶ mòseuht; mòuhseuht; faatseuht ❷ (charm) mòlihk * **magic hand** PH: gèihaaihsáu * **magic lantern** N: waahndāng * **magic lantern slide** N: waahndāngpín (M: jèung)

magician N: mòseuhtsī; seuhtsih (M: go) * **a performance by a magician** VO: wáanbáhei; luhng faatseuht

magistrate N: faatgùn (M: go) PH: deihfòng hàhngjìnggùn (M: go)

magnanimous SV: daaihleuhng

magnate N: fuhòuh (M: go) N/BF: daaihwòhng * **oil magnate** PH: mùihyàuh daaihwòhng

magnesium N: mèih

magnet N: chìhsehk; sipsehk (M: gauh, faai) PH: (fig.) yáuh kāpyáhnlihk ge yàhn/yéh * **magnetometry** N: chāakchìhhohk

magnetism N: chìh (lihk); chìhhohk PH: (fig.) kāpyáhnlihk

magnetize FV: chìhfa; kāpyáhn

magnificent SV: jonglaih; wàhngwái; sùhnggòu

magnify FV: ❶ (make sth. appear larger) fongdaaih; kongdaaih ❷ (extol) tèuisùhng; jaanméih (God) FV/SV: (exaggerate) kwàdaaih

magnifier N: fongdaaihgeng (M: go)

magnitude N/BF: leuhng PH: (size) daaihsai SV: ❶ geuihdaaih ❷ (important) juhngdaaih

magpie N: hèijéuk (M: jek) PH: (fig.) dòjéui ge yàhn (M: go)

mahjong N: màhjeuk; màhjéuk (M: fu) * **play mahjong** VO: dámàhjeuk; dá màhjéuk

mahogany N: hùhngmuhk

maid N: ❶ gùnèuhng; siunéuih (M: go) ❷ (servant)

gùngyàhn (M: go) * **old maid**
PH: lóuhgùpòh; lóuhchyúh-
néuih (M: go)

maiden N: chyúhnéuih;
siunéuih (M: go) PH: chòchige
* **maiden-hair tree** N:
ngàhnhahngsyuh (M: pò) *
maiden-head N: chyúh-
néuihmók

mail N: ❶ yàuhjing; yàuhgín
❷ (letter) seun (M: fùng) ❸ (ar-
mour) hóigaap (M: fu) FV: gei *
mail carrier N: yàuhchàai (M:
go) * **mailbox** N: seunsēung
(M: go) * **mail order** FV:
yàuhkau

maim FV: ❶ (to injure)
sèunghoih ❷ (handicapped)
chàahnfai PH: sauh chúhng-
sèung

main BF: ❶ jing-; daaih-
(door, road etc.) ~ *mùhn,*
louh ❷ júng- (office, shop etc.)
~ *gúk,* ~ *gùngsī* Adj. PH:
jyúyiu ge; jeui juhngyiu ge N:
❶ (physical force) heilihk;
lihkleuhng ❷ (principal wire)
gonsin (M: tìuh) PH: jyúyiu
bouhfahn A: dòsou * **main
point** N: yiudím (M: go) * **in
the main** PH: gèibún seuhng;
daaihtáiseuhng * **with (all
one's) might and main** IE:
kitjeuhnchyùhnlihk * **main
body** N: jyúlihk * **mainland**
N: daaihluhk * **main-spring**
PH: jyúyiu duhnggèi * **main-
stay** N: gwātgon

maintain FV: ❶ wàihchìh
(order, peace etc.) ❷ bóuchìh
(temperature etc.) ❸ (assert as
true) gìnchìh; jyújèung FV/N:
(keep in good repair) bóuyéuhng

maintenance FV: wàihchìh
FV/N: bóuyéuhng PH: sàng-
wuhtfai

maize N: sūkmáih (M: nāp)

majestic SV: hùhngwáih;
jòngyìhm

majesty SV/N: wàiyìhm;
jyùnyìhm N: ❶ (to a king)
baihhah ❷ (power) wòhng-
kyùhn

major FV: (in college) jyúsàu
N: ❶ (army officer) luhkgwān
siugaau (M: go) ❷ (adult)
sìhngnihnyàhn (M: go) PH: ❶
(greater or more important)
béigaau daaihge, béigaau
juhngyiu ge ❷ (mainly) jyúyiu
ge ❸ (older in age) nìhnjéung ge

majority PH: ❶ daaihdòsou; gwo bunsou; daaihbouhfahn ❷ (of age) sìhngnìhn

make FV: ❶ (construct) jouh;
jíng ❷ (manufacture) jaijouh ❸
(cause) lihng * **make a motion** FV: tàihyíh * **make in-
quiries** FV: dátìngháh *
make friends VO: gàau
pàhngyáuh * **make money**
VO: wánchín * **make out a
list** VO: hòidāan * **make tea**
VO: chùngchàh * **make the
bed** VO: pòuchòhng * **make
up one's mind** FV: kyutyi PH:
lahpdihngjyúyi * **make use of**
FV: yuhng * **make-believe**
FV: jadai * **make-shift** IE:
kyùhnyìhjígai * **make-up** N:
① (structure) kaujouh ②
(cosmetics) fajōngbán ③
(character) singgaak VO/N:
(printing) pàaihbáan FV/N: fajōng FV: bóu, nèihbóu,
bóuchùng

making FV/N: jaijok N:
chòihlíu PH: sìhnggùng yùhnyàn * **be in the making** PH:
hái faatjín jùng, meih
yùhnsìhng ge * **have the
makings of** PH: yáuh . . .
tìuhgín, yáuh . . . singjāt

maladjustment FV: sāt-tiuh; PH: m̀sīkying wàahngíng

maladministration PH: gúnléihbātsihn; gúnléihdāk m̀hóu

malady N: jahtbehng, baih-behng

malaria N: yeuhkjaht FV: faatláahng

Malay N: ❶ (language) Máh-lòihwá ❷ (people) Máhlòihyàhn (M: go)

Malaysia N: Máhlòihsàinga

malcontent FV: bātmúhn PH: bātmúhnfahnjí; fáanbuhn ge yàhn (M: go)

male N: nàahmyán (M: go) BF: ❶ (human) nàahm - (teacher etc.) ❷ (animals) - gūng, hùhng - ✳ **male dog** N: gáugūng (M: jek)

malice N: ❶ ngokyi ❷ (of law) yuhmàuh

malicious ' SV: hāksàm

malign Adj. PH: yáuhhoih ge, ngokyi ge FV: wáipóhng

malignant SV: yàmduhk; ngokduhk Adj. PH: (of illness) ngoksing ge ✳ **malignant tumor** N: duhkláu (M: go)

malinger VO: jabehng

mall N: syuhyàmlouh (M: tiuh)

mallet N: muhkchèuih, muhkchéui (M: go, jì)

malnutrition PH: yìhng-yéuhngbātlèuhng

malpractice PH: ❶ (legal) bātfaathàhngwàih ❷ (of medi-cal treatment) jihlìuhbātdong

malt N: ❶ mahkngàh ❷ (liquors) mahkngàhjáu, bējáu (M: jì) VO: faat (mahk) ngàh

Malta PW: ❶ (island) Máhyíh-tàdóu ❷ (country) Máhyíhtà

maltreat FV/N: yeuhkdoih FV: (over use) láahmyuhng

mamma N: màhmā

mammal N: bouhyúhduhng-maht

mammon N: ❶ (money) chìhnchòih ❷ (with capital let-ter) chòihsàhn ❸ (biblical) máhmùhn

mammoth N: máahngmáh-jeuhng (M: jek) Adj. PH: pòhngdaaih ge

man N: ❶ (human being) yàhn (M: go) ❷ (human race) yàhn-leuih ❸ (male) nàahmyán (M: go) ❹ (adult) daaihyàhn (M: go) PH: (supply with) waih . . . puibeih yàhnyùhn ✳ **manful** SV: yúhnggám ✳ **manhood** N: sìhngyàhn PH: jeuhngfù heikoi ✳ **man-made** Adj. PH: yàhn-jouh ge

manacle N: sáukau; sáulìuh (M: fu)

manage FV: ❶ (control) chyúléih; gúnléih; chòujung ❷ (succeed; contrive) yùhnsìhng; chitfaat RV: gáaudihm; gáau-dākdihm ✳ **manage with** PH: yuhng . . . gáaudihm ✳ **manage without** PH: móuh . . . dōu gáaudākdihm

manageable PH: yihchyú-léih ge; yihgúnléih ge; hóyíh chòujung ge

management FV/N: gúnléih PH: ❶ (collective) gúnléih-chyu; gìngléihbouh ❷ (skill) gìngyìhng chòihnàhng

manager N: gìngléih (M: go) * **general manager** N: júng-gìngléih (M: go)

Manchu N: ❶ (people) Múhnjàu yàhn; Múhnjuhk yàhn (M: go) ❷ (language) Múhnjàu wá

mandarin N: ❶ (language) gwokyúh; póutùngwá; Bāk-gìngwá ❷ (fruit) gām (M: go) * **mandarin duck** N: yìnyèung; yùnyèung (M: jek)

mandate N: mihnglihng; fanlihng FV/N: wáiyahm; tokgún

mandatory PH: ❶ fanlihng ge; sauh wáitok ge ❷ (obligatory) kèuhngbīksing ge ❸ (of country) sauh tokgúngwok

mane N: (of animals) jùng-mòuh PH: (of man) yauh dò yauh háuh ge tàuhfaat

mangel (-wurzel) PH: ngàuh sihk ge tìhmchoi

manger N: ❶ (for horses) máhchòuh (M: go) ❷ (for cows) ngàuhchòuh (M: go)

mangle FV/N: syúnwaaih N: gáauyuhkgèi (M: ga)

mango N: mònggwó (M: go)

mania SV: (mad) dìnkòhng; fùngkòhng SV/N: (enthusiasm) kòhngyiht PH: (mental illness) choukòhngjing * **maniac** Adj. PH: fùngkòhng ge N: (coll.) dìnlóu; sàhngìnglóu (M: go)

manifest FV: bíumìhng; jingmìhng; hínsih * **manifest oneself** FV: hínsih FV/N: chēutyihn

manifestation FV: bíu-mìhng FV/N: bíuyihn PH: gùnghòi sìngmìhng

manifesto FV/N: sìng-mìhng N: syùnyìhn PH: faatbíu syùnyìhn/sìngmìhng

manifold PH: ❶ dòjúng yuhngtòuh ge; dò fòngmihn ge ❷ (make copies) gwo Nu fahn dái

manikin N: ❶ ngáiyàhn (M: go) ❷ (dwarf) jyùyùh (M: go) PH: ❶ yàhntái mòuhyìhng ❷ (fashion model) sìhjōng mòuhdahkyìh (M: go)

Manila N: Máhnèihlāai

manipulate FV: ❶ (operate) sáiyuhng; chyúléih; chòujung ❷ (manage or control) chòujung; hungjai; leihyuhng ❸ (cope with) yingfuh

manipulation FV: chòu-jung; yingfuh FV/N: chòujok

mankind N: ❶ yàhnleuih; yàhn ❷ (male sex) nàahmsing

manna N: (biblical) máhnàh PH: (fig.) jìngsàhn sihklèuhng; gàmlouh

manly Adj. PH: ❶ hùhngdáu-dáu ge; yúhnggámge ❷ (of a woman) yáuh nàahmjí heikoi ge ❸ (of things) sīkhahp nàahm-yánge

manned PH: joiyàhn ge; yàhn chòujung ge

mannequin, mannikin PH: ❶ (fashion model) sìhjōng mòuhdahkyìh ❷ yàhntái mòuhyìhng (M: go)

manner N: ❶ (way) fòngsīk; fòngfaat ❷ (behaviour) taaidouh; géuijí ❸ (habits and

customs) jaahpgwaan; fùngjuhk ❹ (social behaviour)
láihmaauh; kwàigéui ❺ (style
in literature or art) fùnggaak;
jokfùng ✻ after the manner
of PH: hohk . . . ge yéung ✻ in
a manner PH: hái máuhjúng
yìyìhseuhng; yáuhdī ✻ in like
manner (wise) PH: tùhng-
yéung; tùhngyêung gám

man(o)euvre FV/N: (mili-
tary) diuhduhng; yínjaahp N: ❶
(lit.) chaakleuhk; (M: go) ❷
(coll.) gái; gáijái (M: go)

manor N: (lit.) jòngyún (M:
go) PH: fàyún daaih ngūk (M:
gàan)

mansion N: daaihhah;
daaihngūk (M: gàan)

mantis N: tòhnglòhng (M:
jek)

mantle N: dáupùhng (M:
gihn) FV/N: jaau; tou PH: (of
the face) mihnhùhng

manual PH: sáugùng ge;
táilihk ge N: (instruction
booklet) syutmihngsyù; sáuchaak (M: bún) BF: jínàahm

manufactory N: gùng-
chóng; jaijouhchóng (M: gàan)

manufacture FV: ❶ jai-
jouh ❷ (invent) hèuikau PH:
daaihleuhng sàngcháan N:
cháanbán; jaibán (M: gihn)

manure N: ❶ (for cultivation)
fèihlíu; fanfèih ❷ fan; (coll.) sí
VO: sífèih

manuscript N: yùhngóu;
chàaubún

many SV: dò PH: hóu dò ✻
a good (great) many PH: hóu
dò; fèisèuhng dò; mòuhhaahn
gam dò ✻ one too many for

FV: hóugwo; sìnggwo ✻ how
many Nu: géidò ✻ many-
minded IE: sàamsàmléuhngyi
(ge) ✻ many-sided PH: dò
fòngmihn ge IE: (of capabilities)
dò chòih dò ngaih (ge)

map N: deihtòuh (M: fūk) PH:
yuhng deihtòuh bíusih; waahk
. . . ge deihtòuh ✻ map out
VO: dihng gaiwaahk FV/N:
ngònpàaih; chitgai

maple N: fùngsyuh (M: pò)

mar FV: syúnhoih; wáiwaaih
RV: (coll.) gáauwàang

Marathon PH: Máhlāai-
chùhng choipáau

maraud FV: chéunggip (people); chàmleuhk (country)

marble N: ❶ wàhnsehk;
daaihléihsehk ❷ (play thing) bō-
jí (M: nāp) ✻ play marbles VO:
dábōjí

March TW: sàamyuht

march FV: chòu VO: (mili-
tary) hàhnggwàn N: (piece of
music) jeunhàhngkūk (M: jì)

mare N: chìmáh; (coll.)
máhná

margarine N: yàhnjouh
ngàuhyàuh

margin N: ❶ bīn; bīnyùhn ❷
(of a page) yihpbīn ❸ (commerce) yìhngyùh

marijuana, marihuana
N: daaihmàh

marine PH: ❶ hòhnghói ge;
hóicháan ge ❷ (sea trade)
hóiwàhnyìhp ❸ (military)
hóigwānluhkjindéui deuiyùhn
(M: go) ✻ marine products N:
hóicháan ✻ marine police N:
séuigíng (M: go) ✻ marine

corps PH: hóigwānluhkjindéui

mariner N: séuisáu; hóiyùhn (M: go)

marital Adj. PH: ❶ (of a husband) jeuhngfù ge ❷ (of marriage) fànyàn ge

mark N: ❶ (symbol) geihouh; geiyìhng; fùhhóu (M: go) ❷ (stain) hàhnjīk ❸ (on the body) dahkjīng (M: go) ❹ (indication of a quality etc.) bīuji (M: go) ❺ (target) muhkbīu (M: go) ❻ (fame) mìhngsīng; mìhngyuh ❼ (of German currency) máhhāk ❽ (grade) fānsou VO: ❶ (to grade) béi fānsou ❷ (a price on goods) bīu gachìhn FV: (pay attention) jyuyi * **marked** Adj. PH: chìngchóge; hínjyuge * **to make a mark** PH: jouh go geiyìhng (geihouh); tīkhéi * **below (up to) the mark** PH: dàigwo (daahtdou) bīujéun FV: m̀hahpgaak (hahpgaak) * **beyond the mark** PH: gwodouh; gwofahn * **get off the mark** FV: chēutfaat; hòichí * **mark down** RV: geidài VO: (sale) gáamga PH: (of price) bīudài gachìhn * **mark up** PH: (the price) bīugòu gachìhn * **marker** N: ❶ (a person) geifānyùhn (M: go) ❷ (a tool) geifānhei (M: go, ga) ❸ (bookmark) syùchìm (M: go)

market N: ❶ (place) gāaisíh; síhchèuhng (M: go) ❷ (demand for goods) siulouh ❸ (price) hòhngchìhng * **supermarket** N: chīukāpsíhchèuhng (M: gàan) * **market value** N: síhga

marksman N: sehsáu; sàhnchēungsáu (M: go)

marmalade N: cháangjīm; cháangjēm (M: jèun)

maroon N: ❶ (colour) jí-

hùhngsīk ❷ (firework) paaujéung (M: go)

marriage VO: gitfàn N: ❶ (married life) fānyàn ❷ (wedding) fānláih * **marriageable** PH: dou gitfàn nìhnlìhngge * **marriage certificate** PH: gitfànjingsyù; fānsyù * **marriage engagement** VO: dihngfàn * **marriage guidance** PH: fànyàn fuhdouh

married Adj. PH: gitjófànge PH: gitjófàn ge yàhn (M: go) * **married couple** PH: léuhng fùfúh; (coll.) léuhng gùngpó * **married man** PH: yáuh fúh jì fù * **married woman** PH: yáuh fù jì fúh

marrow N: ❶ (of bones) gwātséuih ❷ (fig.) jingwàh ❸ (gourd) gwā (M: go)

marry VO: gitfàn Patt: tùhng PN gitfàn (of a man) FV: chéui VO: chéui lóuhpòh Patt: chéui PN jouh lóuhpòh (of a woman) FV: ga VO: ga lóuhgùng Patt: ga béi PN

Mars N: fósīng

marsh N: jíujaahk; jíudeih * **marsh-gas** N: jíuhei

marshal N: ❶ (officer of highest rank) yùhnseui (M: go) ❷ (M.C.) sìyìh (M: go) ❸ (head of police) gíngchaatguhkjéung (M: go) FV/N: pàaihliht; ngònpàaih; yàhndouh

martial Adj. PH: ❶ (of war) jinjàngge; gwànsih ge ❷ (fond of fighting) houjinge * **marshal law** N: (regulation for army) gwànfaat PH: gaaiyìhmlìhng * **proclaim marshal law** FV: gaaiyìhm

Martian Adj. PH: fósīng ge N: fósīng yàhn (M: go)

martyr N: (for a country) lihtsih (M: go) PH: ❶ (for a religion) sèundouh ge yàhn; sèungaau ge yàhn (M: go) ❷ (for a cause other than country or religion) sèun naahn ge yàhn (M: go) ❸ (of illness) chèuhngkèih sauh tungfú ge yàhn (M: go) FV: chàahnsaat; jitmóh

marvel Adj. PH: gìngkèih ge N: kèihjīk; kèihgùn FV/SV: gìngkèih; chayìh

marvellous PH: gìngkèih-ge; bāthósìyíh ge; líuhbāthéi ge

Marxian (Marxist) PH: máhhāaksí jyúyìh ge; máhhāaksí jyúyìh jé (M: go)

Marxism PH: Máhhāaksí jyúyìh * **Marxism-Leninism** PH: Máhhāaksí Lihtnìhngjyúyìh

mascot (te) N: fūksàhn (M: go) PH: gātchèuhng ge yéh

masculine N: nàahmyán (M: go) Adj. PH: ❶ nàahmyán ge ❷ yáuh nàahmjí heikoi (ge) * **masculine gender** N: nàahmsìng

mash N: (for cattle) jihlíu RV: mòhlaahn; jùnglaahn PH: mòhlaahn ge yéh

mask N: ❶ mihngeuih; mihnjaau (M: go) ❷ (sanitary) háujaau (M: go) PH: (fig.) . . . gá mihngeuih VO: (to wear) daai mihngeuih FV: (to conceal) yímsīk; jèyím * **gas mask** PH: fòhngduhk mihngeuih

mason PH: ❶ (bricklayer) nàihséuisìfú (M: go) ❷ (stonemason) dásehksìfú (M: go)

masquerade PH: (a ball) fajōngmóuhwúi (M: go) FV: ❶ fajōng ❷ (fig.) mouhchùng; baahnjouh

mass Nu M: (a lump) yātgauh N: ❶ (people) kwàhnjung ❷ (of physics) leuhng PH: hóu dò FV/N: jaahphahp * **in the mass** PH: daaihtáiseuhng; júngkwut làih góng * **the (great) mass of** PH: daaihbouhfahn; daaihdòsou * **mass meeting** PH: kwàhnjung daaihwúi (M: go) * **mass production** PH: daaihleuhng sàngcháan * **mass wedding** PH: jaahptái gitfàn

Mass N: (Roman Catholic service) nèihsaat * **high Mass** PH: daaih nèihsaat

massacre PH: daaih tòuhsaat FV: chàahnsaat

massage FV/N: ngonmò N: tèuinàh

massive Adj. PH: ❶ hóudaaih ge; geuihyìhng ge ❷ (substantial) gitsaht ge

mast N: ngàihgōn; chyúh (M: jì) VO: jòng ngàihgōn

master N: ❶ (of a household) jyúyán; jyúyàhn (M: go) ❷ (principal) haauhjéung (M: go) ❸ (teacher) sìnsàang; lóuhsī (M: go) ❹ (in a business) sìhtáu; lóuhbáan (M: go) ❺ (of an apprentice) sìfú (M: go) ❻ (academic degree) sehksih (M: go) FV: ❶ (control) hungjai ❷ jingtùng (a subject or a skill) * **master copy** N: làahmbún; jingbún * **master key** N: baakhahpsih (M: tiuh) * **masterly** Adv. PH: háaumiuh gám; gòumìhng gám * **master-mind** PH: jinòhng yàhnmát (M: go) * **masterpiece** N: gihtjok

masterful SV: jyùnwàahng

mastery FV: ❶ (control)

hungjai ❷ jìngtùng (a subject or a skill)

mat N: jehk (M: jèung) N/BF: jin (M: faai, go) • *yí* ~ VO: pòujehk

match N: ❶ (to make fire with) fóchàaih; fócháai (M: jì, 'stick'; hahp, 'box') ❷ (person met as one's equal) deuisáu; dihksáu FV/N: (a contest) béichoi RV: (be equal to) paakdākjyuh FV: ❶ (a well suited pair) dāngdeui; hahpchan • *PN1 tùhng PN2 hóu* ~ ❷ (corresponding with) pui; chan * **matchless** Adj. PH: mòuhdihkge; mòuhbéige

matchmaker N: mùihyán (M: go)

mate N: ❶ (fellow-workman) fógei; tùhngsih (M: go) ❷ (partner in marriage) puingáuh ❸ (ship's officer); daaihfu (M: go) ❹ (helper) johsáu (M: go) RV: (in chess) jèungséi * **running mate** PH: gìhng syún paakdong (M: go) * **schoolmate** N: tùhnghohk (M: go)

material Adj. PH: ❶ mahtjāt ge ❷ (essential) jyúyiu ge; juhngyiu ge N: ❶ (for building; sewing etc.) chòihlíu ❷ (for writing) jílíu ❸ (raw) yùhnlíu ❹ (tool) yuhnggeuih (M: gihn)

materialism N: ❶ wàihmahtjyúyih; wàihmahtlèun ❷ (over-valuation of material things) mahtjāt jyúyih

materialist PH: ❶ wàihmahtjyújihjé (M: go) ❷ mahtjātjyúyihjé (M: go) * **materialistic** Adj. PH: ❶ wàihmaht ge ❷ mahtjāt ge

materialize FV/N: sahtyihn PH: sìhngwàih sihsaht; geuihtáifa

maternal Adj. PH: móuhchàn ge; móuhhsing ge

maternity VO: wàaihyahn * **maternity hospital** N: cháanfō yìyún; làuhcháansó (M: gàan) * **maternity ward** N: cháanfō behngfóng (M: gàan)

mathematical Adj. PH: souhohkseuhng ge; jìngkok ge

mathematician N: souhohkgā (M: go)

mathematics N: souhohk

matinee PH: yahtchèuhng

matriculation PH: daaihhohk yahphohk (háau) si

matrimony N: fànyàn

matrix N: ❶ (of anatomy) jígùng (M: go) ❷ (mould) móu; mòuhyìhng (M: go)

matron N: ❶ (of a hospital) wuhsihjéung (M: go) ❷ (of a dormitory) séhgāam (M: go) PH: (married woman) gitjófàn ge néuihyán (M: go)

matter N: ❶ (affair) sih; sihgon; sihchìhng (M: gihn) ❷ (substance) mahtjāt ❸ (pus) nùhng SV: (important) gányiu; juhngyiu * **what's the matter?** PH: jouh māyéh a? * **as a matter of fact** A: kèihsaht PH: sihsahtseuhng * **in the matter of** CV: gwàanyù * **it doesn't matter** PH: ṁgányiu * **it makes (is) no matter** PH: mòuhgwàan juhngyiu; mòuhgwàangányiu * **no matter how** Patt: mòuhleuhndím . . . * **matter-of-course** A: dòngyìhn * **matter-of-fact** Adj. PH: ❶ sahtsihkàuhsihge ❷ (unimaginative) pìhngdaahmge

matting N: ❶ chóujehk; jehk (M: jèung) ❷ (for packing) màhbāaudói; màhbāaudoih (M: go)

mattress N: jinyúk (M: jèung)

maturate FV: ❶ (of pus) fanùhng ❷ (fully developed) sìhngsuhk

mature FV: (fully developed) sìhngsuhk VO: (of bills) doukèih

maturity FV: sìhngsuhk VO: doukèih PH: jongnihnkèih

mausoleum N: lìhngmouh (M: go)

maxim N: gaakyìhn (M: geui)

maximize PH: jànggà dou jeui daaih haahndouh; chùngfahn juhngsih

maximum N: gihkhaahn PH: jeui daaih haahndouh; jeui gòu ge soumuhk Adj. PH: jeui daaih ge; jeui gòu ge

May TW: ńgh yuht ✻ **May day** PH: ńgh yāt lòuhduhng jit

may AV: ❶ (be allowed or permitted) hóyíh ❷ (possibly will) hónàhng A: waahkjé ✻ **as the case may be** PH: tái chìhngyìhng ✻ **may as well (had better)** Patt: jeui hóu . . .; juhnghaih . . . hóu ✻ **may I ask** PH: chéngmahn

maybe A: waahkjé; daaihkói; dòsou AV: hónàhng

mayor N: ❶ síhjéung (M: go) ❷ (of a town) janjéung (M: go) ✻ **mayoress** N: ❶ néuih síhjéung (M: go) ❷ (wife of a mayor) síhjéung fùyàhn (M: wái)

maze SV: màihmóhng; kwan-

waahk IE: bātjì sóchou N: (labyrinth) màihgùng (M: go)

me PN: ngóh

meadow N: chóudeih (M: faai, daat); muhkchèuhng (M: go)

meagre (meager) SV: ❶ (thin) sau ❷ (insufficient; poor) m̀gau; pàhnfaht PH: ❶ (lacking in flesh) pèihbāaugwāt ❷ (scanty) fèisèuhng síu

meal M/N: chāan N: ❶ (of grain) chòufán ❷ (oatmeal) mahkpín; mahkpèih

mealy Adj. PH: ❶ chòufán ge; hóuchíh fán gámge ❷ (of complexion) chòngbaahk ge

mean N: yisī; yisi PH: ❶ yisī haih ❷ yáuh yi FV: (design) yuhdihng; dásyun SV: ❶ (discreditable) bèipéi ❷ (not generous) gùhòhn N: (method) fòngfaat; sáudyuhn PW: (middle) jūnggāan ✻ **by all means** A: yātdihng; chìnkèih ✻ **by any means** Patt/PH: mòuhleuhn dím ✻ **by fair means or foul** IE: bātjaahk sáudyuhn ✻ **by means of** FV: yuhng . . .; kaau . . . ✻ **by no means** PH: máih yíhwàih . . .; yātdī dōuṁ . . .; gànbún móuh

meander VO: kìnggái FV: saanbouh

meaning N: yisī; yisi; yiyìh PH: yáuh yiyìh ge ✻ **with meaning** PH: yáuh yisī (gám) ✻ **meaningful** PH: hóu yáuh yisī ge ✻ **meaningless** PH: móuh yiyìh ge ✻ **meaningly** Adv. PH: yáuh yisī gám; guyi gám

meanly Adv. PH: gùhòhn gám; míuhsih gám

meant ✻ **be meant by** PH:

yisī haih; yisi haih

meantime; meanwhile
A: tùhngsìh; dòngsìh

measles N: màhchán; fùngchán; (coll.) má * **to have
measles** VO: chēutmá;
chēutchán

measurable PH: sīkdouh
ge

measure FV: dohk; lèuhng
N: ❶ chekchyun ❷ (unit) dàanwái (M: go). ❸ (extent)
chìhngdouh; bìujéun ❹ (pl.,
method) sáudyuhn; baahnfaat
❺ (of grammar) leuhngchìh *
adopt or take measures IE:
chói chéui chousi * **by
measure** PH: ngon chekchyun
* **in a (some) measure** Nu/A:
dòsíu PH: yáuh géifàn * **in
any measure** PH: hái
yahmhòh chìhngdouh seuhng
* **set measures to** N/FV:
haahnjai; yeukchūk * **take
measure of** FV: chāakdihng *
within measure PH: sīkdouh
* **without measure** PH:
gwodouh

measurement FV: dohk;
lèuhng; chāaklèuhng N: ❶ (of
length) chèuhngdouh ❷ (of
width) futdouh ❸ (of depth)
sàmdouh PH: daaih sai

meat N: yuhk (M: faai; gauh)
* **meatball** N: yuhkkyún (M: go)
* **easy meat** PH: yihjouh ge
sih

Mecca PW: Mahkgà PH:
(fìg.) heungwóhng ge muhkbīu

mechanic N: geihgùng;
gèigùng; (coll.) gèiheijái;
gèiheilóu (M: go)

mechanics N: lihkhohk;
gèihaaih gùngchìhng

mechanical Adj. PH: gèihaaih ge; lihkhohk ge

mechanism N: gèikau;
gèigau PH: gèihaaih jokyuhng;
gitkau fòngsīk

**mechanize/mechaniza-
tion** PH: gèihaaihfa *
mechanized unit PH:
gèihaaihfa bouhdéui

medal N: jéungjēung; fàn-
jēung (M: go) * **the reverse
side of the medal** PH:
mahntàih lihng yāt mihn;
sihchìhngge fáanmihn

meddle FV ❶ gònsip (in) ❷
lyuhngáau (with) PH: gún-
hàahnsih

medi(a)eval Adj. PH: jùng-
gú ge; jùng saigéi ge

medial Adj. PH: ❶ (in the
middle) jūnggāan ge ❷ (of
average size) pìhnggwàn ge;
daaihsíu sīkjūng ge

median Adj. PH: jūnggāan
ge PH: jùngwáisou

mediate FV/N: tìuhtìhng;
tìuhgáai Adj. PH: gaanjip ge

mediation FV/N: tìuhtìhng;
tìuhgáai

mediator N: ❶ wòhsihlóuh;
jūnggāanyàhn/yán (M: go) ❷
(Jesus Christ) jùngbóu (M: go)

medical Adj. PH: yìhohk ge;
yìhohkseuhng ge; yìlìuh ge N:
(student) yìfō hohksāang (M:
go)* **medical school** N:
yìhohkyún (M: gàan) * **medical fee** N: yìyeuhkfai *
medical science N: yìhohk;
yìfō * **medicated spirits** N:
yeuhkjáu (M: jēun)

medicine N: ❶ (of science)

yìhohk; yìfō ❷ (hospital department) noihfō ❸ (drug) yeuhk ❹ (fluid) yeuhkséui (M: jèun) ❺ (ointment) yeuhkgōu (M: jì; hahp 'box') ❻ (pill) yeuhkyún (M: nāp) ❼ (plaster) gōuyeuhk (M: faai) ❽ (herb) yeuhkchòih * **take medicine** VO: sihkyeuhk

mediocre SV: póutùng; pìhngfàahn

mediocrity SV: pìhngfàahn; pìhngyùhng PH: pìhngfàahn ge yàhn (M: go)

meditate FV ❶ (consider) háauleuih ❷ (give oneself up to serious thought) chàhmsì; mahkséung FV/N: (plan) gaiwaahk

medium N: mùihgaai; gùnggeuih PH: (surrounding) sàngwuht wàahngíng Adj. PH: jùngdáng ge; jūnggāan ge * **medium size** PH: jùngmáh; jùnghouh

medley FV: wahnjaahp N: wahnhahpmaht

meek SV: wànwòh; hìmwòh

meet FV: ❶ (welcome, greet) jip; yìhngjip ❷ (make the acquaintance of) ginháh ❸ wuihgin (reporters etc.) ❹ múhnjūk (needs) RV: (come upon) yuhdóu; yuhgin N: jaahpwúi * **make both ends meet** PH: sáidou sàujì pìhnghàhng * **meet the ear (eye)** PH: hóyíh tèngdóu (gindóu) * **meet together** FV/N: jaahpphahp; wuìhhahp * **meet with** FV/N: (experience) jòuyuh RV: ❶ sauhdóu/sauhdou ❷ (come upon) yuhdóu; pungdóu

meeting N: wúi; wuihyíh; jeuihwuih; jaahpwúi FV: wuihgin * **meeting place** N:

wuihchèuhng; wúichèuhng (M: go)

megalopolis PH: dahk daaih ge sìhngsíh (M: go)

megaphone N: labàtúng (M: go)

melancholy SV/N: yàuwāt; bèingòi N: (illness) yàuwātjing

mellow SV: ❶ (ripe and tender) nàhm ❷ (of people) lóuhsìhng ❸ (of music, colour, light etc.) yàuhwòh ❹ (of land) fèihyūk ❺ (genial) gòuhing SV/FV: (matured) sìhngsuhk

melody N: (of music) syùhnléut; kūkdiuh PH: hóutèng ge yàmdiuh

melodious SV: hóutèng

melon N: gwà (M: go) * **water melon** N: sàigwà (M: go) * **melon cutting** VO: (coll.) fànjòng; fànhùhng (leih)

melt FV ❶ yùhng; yùhngfa; yùhnggáai; ❷ (of a person; heart; feelings) yúhnfa PH: (go slowly away) juhkjím sìusāt

melting PH: ❶ yùhngfa ge; ❷ (fig.) sái yàhn gámduhng ge * **melting point** N: yùhngdím

member N: ❶ wúiyùhn; séhyùhn (M: go) ❷ (of a church) gaauyáuh ❸ (of political party) dóngyùhn ❹ (of a team) deuihyùhn ❺ (of a committee) wáiyùhn ❻ (of parliament or government council) yíhyùhn * **membership** PH: ❶ wúiyùhn sànfán ❷ (of number) wúiyùhn yàhnsou

membrane N: ❶ mók; bohkmók (M: chàhng) ❷ (of paper) yèuhngpèihjí (M: jèung)

memento N: geinihmbán
(M: go, gihn) PH: lìhng yàhn
wùih yīk ge yéh

memorable Adj. PH: jihkdāk geinihmge; nàahn mòhng
ge

memoir N: ❶ (life-history)
jyuhngei (M: bún; pìn) ❷
(academic essay) hohkseuht
leuhnmàhn (M: pìn) ❸ (person's
written account of his own life)
wùihyīklúk (M: bún)

memorandum (memo)
N: ❶ beihmòhnglúk (M: bún;
go; jèung) ❷ (informal letter)
bihnhàahm (M: fùng) FV/N:
geiluhk (M: go)

memorial Adj. PH: yáuh-
geinihmsing ge N: ❶ (sth to remind people of) geinihmbán;
géinihmbán (M: gihn, go) ❷
(statement to make a request or
protest) chíngyuhnsyù (M: fùng)
❸ (historical records) pìnnìhnsí
* **memorial arch** N:
pàaihlàuh (M: go) * **memorial
day** N: géinihmyaht *
memorial hall N: géinihm-
tòhng (M: gàan, go) *
memorial service N: jèui-
douhwúi; gùngjai * **memorial
stone** N: géinihmbèi (M: go)

memorize FV: (to record)
geiluhk RV: nihmsuhk; geijyuh

memory N: ❶ geising; geiyīk; geiyīklihk ❷ (of a calculator) chyúhchyùhnhei FV/N:
géinihm (a person, an event etc.)

menace FV: húnghaak;
wàihip

mend FV: ❶ bóu (clothes,
shoes etc.) ❷ jíng; sàuléih (appliances) ❸ (free from errors)
gói; góijing; góisihn RV: (regain
health) hóufàan; yìhóu

menial Adj. PH: bèijihn ge;
nòuhbuhk ge N: nòuhbuhk (M:
go)

meningitis N: nóuhmók-
yìhm

menses N: yuhtgìng *
menstrual period N: gìngkèih

mental Adj PH: jìngsàhn ge;
sìséung ge; jìlihkge; sàmléih ge
* **mental debility** PH: sàhngìng sèuiyeuhk * **mental
disease** N: sàhngìngbehng;
jìngsàhnbehng * **mental
hospital** N: jìngsàhnbehngyún (M: gàan)

mentality N: jìlihk; sàmléih
PH: sàmléih johngtaai

mention FV: tàihkahp;
gónghéi * **don't mention it**
PH: ❶ (thanks for a gift) síu yisi
jē ❷ (thanks for a favour) m̀sái
haakhei

menu N: choidāan (M: jèung);
choipáai; chāanpáai (M: go)

mercenary Adj. PH: waih-
chín ge; chéng fàanlàih ge N:
(soldiers hired) guyùhngbìng (M:
go)

merchandise N: fo; fomaht; sèungbán FV: gìngsèung

merchant N: (formal) sèungyàhn; (coll.) sàangyilóu (M: go)
* **merchantman** N: sèung-
syùhn (M: jek, ga)

mercury N: ❶ séuingàhn ❷
(the planet) séuisīng

mercy SV: yàhnchìh; chìhbèi
FV/N: lìhnmáhn FV: fùnsyu

mere A: jí; bātgwo * **merely** A: jíhaih

merge FV: hahpbìng; tànbìng

meridian N: jínghsin TW: jingngh

merit N: yàudím; gajihk; gùnglòuh PH: gùnggwo; sih-fèikúkjihk FV: jihkdāk; yìngdāk

meritorious PH: yáuh gùng(lòuh) ge; jihkdāk jaan ge

mermaid N: méihyàhnyùh (M: tiuh)

merrily Adv. PH: (hóu) faailohk gám; faaiwuht gám

merriment SV/N: fùnlohk FV: daaihsiu

merry SV: gòuhing; faaiwuht * merry-go-round N: syùhn-jyún muhkmáh * Merry Christmas PH: Singdaan faailohk

mesh N: móhngngáahn; móhnglūng (M: go) PH: (to catch e.g. fish) yuhng móhng jūk

mesmerism N: chèuimihn-seuht

mess SV/FV: wahnlyuhn PH: lyuhn chāt baat jòu N: (of meals) fósihktyùhn; faahntòhng (M: go) RV: (upset) gáaulyuhnsaai

message N: ❶ (news) sìusīk (M: go) ❷ (errand) chàaisih (M: gihn) FV/N: (of a prophet) yuhyihn; gaaufan FV: tùngjī * to leave a message VO: làuh jèung jihtiuh * any message for me? PH: ① (for a written message) yáuh móuh yàhn wángwo ngóh a? PN yáuh móuh làuhdài jihtiuh béi ngóh a? ② (of a call) yáuh móuh yàhn dádihnwá béi ngoh a? (PN) yáuhmóuh góngdài mātyéh a?

messenger N: seunchàai (M: go)

Messiah N: Nèihchoinga; gausaijyú

metabolism PH: sànchàhn-doihjeh

metal N: ❶ gàmsuhk; ngh-gām ❷ (of a train) louhgwái (M: tiuh)

metallurgy N: yéhgām-hohk; yéhgāmseuht

metamorphosis VO: bin-yìhng; binjāt; bintaai

metaphor N/FV: yányuh

metaphysical Adj. PH: yìhngyihseuhnghohk ge * metaphysics PH: yìhngyih seuhnghohk

meteor N: làuhsīng (M: go, nāp) * meteoric Adj. PH: hóuchíh làuhsīng gám ge; símseuk ge * meteoritics N: làuhsīnghohk * meteoroid N: làuhsīngtái (M: go)

meteorite N: wáhnsehk (M: faai, gauh) wáhnsīng (M: go, nāp)

meteorology N: heijeuhng-hohk * meteorological observatory N: heijeuhngtòih (M: go)

meter/metre M: máih; gùngchek BF/N: bīu (M: go) * electric meter N: dihnbīu (M: go) * gas meter N: mùihheibīu (M: go) * water meter N: séuibīu (M: go) * metric system N: sahpjeunjai

methane N: jíuhei

method N: ❶ faatjí; fòng-faat (M: go) ❷ (orderliness) tiuhléih; dihtjeuih

meticulous PH: jísai ge; jìngkok ge

metonymy FV/N: wuhn-yuh; jyúnyuh

metro N: deihtit; deihhah-titlouh

metrology N: gailèuhng-hohk; gailèuhngjai

metropolis PH: daaihsìhng síh; daaihdōuwuih (M: go)

metropolitan Adj. PH: daaih sìhngsíh ge PH: daaih sìhngsíh ge yàhn (M: go) N: (bishop) daaih jyúgaau (M: go)

mettle N: heijāt; yúhnghei; noihlihk *✻* **mettlesome** Adj. PH: yáuh jìngsàhnge; yúhng-gámge

mew N: ❶ (sea-gull) hóingāu (M: jek) ❷ (of horses) máhfòhng (M: go); (of cars) chèfòhng PH: (of a cat) mīumīu Patt: (to shut up) jèung . . . sómàaih

Mexican N: Mahksāigō yàhn (M: go)

mica N: wàhnmóuh

mice N: lóuhsyú (M: jek)

mickey N: gìuhei; jìngsàhn *✻* **Mickey Mouse** N: máihkèih lóuhsyú (M: jek) PH: (fig.) taai gáandàange; chàhngauh faht-meih ge

microbe N: mèihsàngmaht; saikwán

microbiology N: mèih-sàngmahthohk

microcosm PH: mèihgùn saigaai

microfilm PH: sūkyíng gāaupín (M: tùhng, gyún)

micrometer N: chāakmèih-gai (M: go)

micron M: mèihmáih

microphone N: māi; kwongyāmhei (M: go)

microray/microwave N: mèihbō

microscope N: hínmèih-geng (M: go)

mid PH: jùnggāan ge *✻* **mid-day** TW: jingngh *✻* **midnight** TW: bunyeh PH: bunyeh sāamgàang *✻* **midsummer** TW: juhnghah; hahji *✻* **mid-way** PH: bunlóu *✻* **midwife** N: johcháansih; jipsāngpó (M: go) *✻* **midwifery** N: cháanfō *✻* **mid-term exam.** PH: kèihjùngháau(síh)

middle PW: jùnggāan *✻* **middle-aged** PH: jùngnìhn *✻* **middleman** PH: gìnggéi (yàhn) jùnggāanyán (M: go) *✻* **middle class** PH: jùngcháan/jùngdáng gāaikāp; jùngchàhng séhwúi *✻* **middle-of-the-road** PH: m̀jáu gihkdyùn SV: wángihn; wànwòh

middling Adj. PH: jùngdáng ge; yìhlàuh ge N: ❶ (of goods) jùngdángfo ❷ (of wheat) chòumìhnfán

midget N: ngáiyàhn; jyùyùh (M: go) ATT: síuyìhng; jauhjāan

midst PW: jùnggāan

mien N: fùngdouh; taaidouh; ngoihbíu

might N: ❶ (power) kyùhn-lihk ❷ (strength) lihkleuhng *✻* **might as well** A: bātfòhng *✻* **with all one's might** IE: chyùhnlihk yíhfuh; kìng-chyùhnlihk

mighty Adj. PH: ❶ kèuhng-daaih ge (nation) ❷ (biblical)

yáuh daaih nàhng(lihk) ge ❸
(massive) geuihdaaih ge;
houhdaaih ge A: fèisèuhng

migrant N: ❶ (of birds)
hauhníuh (M: jek) PH: yìhgèui
ge yàhn/duhngmaht

migrate FV: yìhgèui; chìnyìh

migration FV: chìnyìh N: (of
people) yìhmàhn (M: go)

mild SV: ❶ (of manner)
sìmàhn ❷ (of character) wànwòh; wànyàuh ❸ (of disease and
medicine) hèng ❹ (of food)
táahm ❺ (of climate) wànwòh

mildew N: mòu VO: faatmòu

mile M: léih; yìngléih ✻
mileage PH: léihsou; léih-
chìhng ✻ **milepost** PH: léih-
chìhngbīu ✻ **milestone** N:
léihchìhngbèi; PH: juhngdaaih
sìhgín

militant Adj. PH: houjin ge
N: jinsìh (M: go)

militarism PH: gwàngwok
jyúyíh; seuhngmóuh jīngsàhn

military BF: gwànsìh N:
gwànfòng; luhkgwàn; móuh-
jōngbouhdéui ✻ **military law**
N: gwànfaat ✻ **military man**
N: gwànyàhn (M: go) ✻
military officer N: gwàngùn
(M: go) ✻ **military service** N:
bīngyihk ✻ **to be in military
service** VO: fuhk bīngyihk ✻
military strategy N: jinleuhk

militia N: ❶ màhnbīng (M:
go, deuih) ❷ (British) gwok-
màhngwàn (M: go, deuih) ❸
(American) gwokmàhn gíng
waih déui (M: deuih)

milk N: ❶ (general) náaih (M:
jèun, 'bottle'; hahp 'box') ❷ (of a
cow) ngàuhnáaih VO: jànáaih

✻ **milk-and-water** Adj. PH:
móuhmeihge; móuhlihkge ✻
milkmaid PH: jànáaih néuih-
gùng (M: go) ✻ **milksop** N:
nohfù (M: go)

milky Adj. PH: ❶ hóuchíh
ngàuhnáaih gám ge ❷ (of colour) náaihbaahk sīk ge ❸ (of liquid) hóu juhkge; mchìng ge ✻
Milky way N: Ngàhnhòh

mill N: ❶ (of grinding grain)
mòhfángèi (M: ga); mòhfánchòng; mòhfòng (M: gàan) ❷
(factory, workshop) gùngchóng
(M: gàan) ; gùngchèuhng (M: go)
FV: mòh ✻ **miller** PH:
mòhfòngjyú; mòhfánchòng
chóngjyú (M: go) ✻ **water mill**
N: séuichè

millennium PH: ❶ yātchìn-
nìhn ❷ (fig.) taaipìhng sìhngsai

millet N: síumáih; sūk

milligram M: hòuhhāk

millilitre M: hòuhsīng

millimetre M: hòuhmáih

million Nu: baakmaahn ✻
ten million Nu: chìnmaahn ✻
hundred million Nu: maahn-
maahn; yīk ✻ **millionaire** N:
baakmaahn fuyūng; fuhòuh

mime FV: mòuhfóng N: ❶
(play) waahtkài hei (M: chèut) ❷
(clown) cháugok (M: go)

mimeograph N: yàuhyangèi (M: ga) FV: yàuhyan

mimic FV: mòuhfóng VO:
hohkyéung PH: ❶ (actor)
héikehk yínyùhn (M: go) ❷
(coll.) hóu sīk baahnyéh ge
yàhn (M: go)

mince FV: deuk RV: deuk-
seui VO: ❶ deukyuhk ❷ (fig.)

mind N: ❶ (that feels, knows) sàm; sàmgèi; jìngsàhn ❷ (that thinks) tàuhnóuh; nóuhgàn ❸ (opinion) yigin ❹ (mental ability) jìnàhng ❺ (memory) geiyīk FV: ❶ (be troubled by) gaaiyi ~ m̀ ~ ngóh sihkyīn a? ❷ (take care of) jiugu; jiuliuh RV: ❶ (pay attention to) gujyuh (e.g. cars) ❷ (take care of) táijyuh; gujyuh (háh) * **bear in mind** RV: geijyuh * **bring (call) to mind** RV: séunghéi; wùihyìkhéi * **make up one's mind** FV: kyutdihng VO: hah kyutsàm * **never mind** PH: m̀gányiu; hóuhàahnjē * **mind your own business** PH: m̀hóu léih yàhndeih gam dò sih

(put on airs) jokjohng PH: tàntàntoutou gám góng * **mincer** N: ❶ (machine) gáauyuhkgēi (M: ga) ❷ (person) jokjohng ge yàhn (M: go)

mine Adj. PH: ngóh ge N: ❶ (pit) kong; kwong ❷ (military, of land) deihleùih; (of water) séuileùih VO: ❶ hòikong/ hòikwong ❷ bouleùih; fong deihleùih; fong séuileùih * **mine clearance** N: souleùih * **miner** N: ❶ konggùng/ kwonggùng (M: go) ❷ (soldier) deihleùih gùngbīng (M: go) * **minefield** N: bouleùihkèui

mineral N: kongmaht/ kwongmaht * **mineral products** N: kongcháan/kwongcháan * **mineral water** N: kong/kwongchyùhnséui

mineralogy N: kongmahthohk/kwongmahthohk

mingle RV: kàumàaih FV: wahnhahp

mini Adj. PH: fèisèuhng sai ge N: (skirt) dyúnkwàhn (M: tìuh)

miniature Adj. PH: mèihyìhngge; síuyìhngge N: jauhjànwá; sūktòuh (M: fūk) FV: sūkyíng

minibus N: síubā (M: ga)

minimize PH: gáamdou jeui síu; sūkdou jeui sai; gúgai jeui dài

minimum PH: jisíu; jidài; jeui síu; jeui dài

mining VO: chóikong/chóikwong; hòikong/hòikwong N: kongyihp/kwongyihp

minister N: ❶ (in a government) bouhjéung (M: go) ❷ (in a monarchy) daaihsàhn (M: go) ❸ (as a diplomat) gūngsi (M: go) ❹ (pastor) muhksī (M: go) FV: bòngjoh; fuhksih * **prime minister** N: sáuseung (M: go)

ministry BF: -bouh N: (chyùhntái) bouhjéung; (cabinet) noihgok PH: ❶ jìngfú gokbouh ❷ bouhjéungjīkwaih

minor PH: ❶ béigaau sai ge; síusou ge; mòuh gwàan juhngyiu ge ❷ (legal) meih sìhngnìhn ge yàhn (M: go)

minority PH: meih sìhngnìhn; síusou; síusoumàhnjuhk * **in the minority** PH: jim síusou

mint N: ❶ (herb) bohkhòh ❷ (factory) jouhbaihchóng (M: gàan) FV: jyu; jyujouh (coins)

minus FV: gáam N: (sign) gáamhouh; fuhhouh; fuhsou BF: fuh- ~ yāt

minute M: (of time) fàn (jùng) FV/N: (record) geiluhk; gēiluhk PH: (of a meeting) wuihyìhgeiluhk / gēiluhk Adj. PH: ❶ (very small) mèihsaige; jìngmaht ge;

❷ (detailed) chèuhngsai ge ✳ **in a minute** A: jīkhāak; máhseuhng ✳ **to the minute** A/PH: jéunsih ✳ **wait (just) a minute** PH: dáng yātjahngāan

minutiae PH: saijit; sósih

miracle N: kèihjīk; sàhnjīk; kèihsih

miraculous PH: hóuchíh kèihjīk gám ge; sàhnkèih-mohkchāakge

mirage N: waahnséung PH: hóisíhsàhnlàuh

mire N: nàih; nàihjíu; jíudeih VO: hahmyahp nàihjíu ✳ **find (stick) oneself in the mire** IE: hahmyahp kwangíng; chūksáu mòuhchaak

mirror N: geng (M: mihn, faai) FV: ❶ fáanseh ❷ (fig.) fáanyíng

mirth SV/N: fùnlohk SV: faaiwuht

miry Adj. PH: múhnsaai nàihbaahnge; wùjòu ge

misadventure SV/N: bāthahng N: jòinaahn

misapply/misapplication FV: láahmyuhng RV: yuhngcho

misapprehend FV: nghgáai RV: tèngcho

misappropriate FV: láahmyuhng; douhyuhng; sītàn (e.g. public funds) ~ *gùngfún*

misbehave PH: hàhngwàih m̀hóu ✳ **misbehaved** PH: m̀kwàigéui ge

miscarriage FV: ❶ (of plans etc.) sātbaaih ❷ (of letters etc.) nghsung ❸ (abortion) síucháan

❹ (of justice) nghpun

miscellaneous PH: goksīkgokyeuhngge; wahnjaahp ge; jaahphohng ✳ **miscellaneous goods** N: jaahpfo

miscellany N: ❶ jaahpmaht; wahnhahpmaht ❷ (of writings) jaahpluhk (M: bún)

mischief FV/N: syúnhoih; sèunghoih PH: (of playing tricks) ngokjokkehk; (of people) ngokjokkehk ge yàhn ✳ **play the mischief with** PH: jèung ... gáaudou lyuhnchātbaatjòu ✳ **mischief-maker** PH: tìubuht lèihgaan ge yàhn (M: go)

mischievous SV: baakyim; tiupèih Adj. PH: (harmful) yáuh hoihge

misconceive FV: nghgáai; nghwuih

misconception FV: nghgáai N: chogok

misconstrue FV: nghgáai ✳ **misconstruction** FV: nghgáai; kūkgáai

misdeal PH: faatchopáai

misdeed N: ngokhahng; jeuihhahng

miser N: gùhòhngwái; sáuchòihnòuh (M: go)

miserable SV: ❶ (very unhappy) chàilèuhng; hólìhn ❷ (bad or unpleasant) yáih

misery SV/N: tungfú; bāthahng SV: pàhnkùhng

misfire RV: ❶ (of a gun) dámchēut ❷ (of an engine) hòim̀jeuhk; hòim̀yūk PH: dám̀jung yiuhoih

misfit FV: ❶ m̀sīkhahp (PN)
❷ m̀sèungching · *tùhng PN ~*

misfortune SV: jaihwahn
SV/N: bàthahng N: jòinaahn

misgiving FV/N: wàaihyìh;
yàuleuih

misguide PH: jídouh chongh
IE: nghyahpkèihtòuh

mishap N: jòiwoh PH:
bàthahng ge sih

misinform RV: boucho PH:
boucho sīusīk FV: nghchyùhn

misinterpret FV/N:
nghgáai RV: chyùhncho;
yihkcho

misjudge RV: táicho PH:
gúgai chongh

mislead PH: daai cholouh;
sáidou . . . nghgáai; chongh
yáhndouh

mislike FV: yimwu

mismanage PH: chyúléih
chongh; gúnléih bàtsihn

misname RV: giucho (méng)

misnomer PH: yuhngchìh
bàtdong; yuhng jih chongh

misplace RV: jàicho PH: ❶
jàicho/fongcho deihfòng ❷ (of
love, affection) ngoichoyàhn;
seunchoyàhn

misprint RV: yancho

mispronounce PH/VO:
faatcho yām; duhkcho yām

misread RV: duhkcho;
táicho; gáaisīkcho

misrepresent FV: ngh-
chyùhn; wàaikūk PH: chyùhncho syutwah

miss N/BF: ❶ (unmarried
woman) síuyé (M: wái) ❷ (married and unmarried) néuihsih (M:
wái) FV: ❶ (lose) sātjó; m̀ginjó
❷ (be lonesome without)
séungnihm, wàaihnihm ❸ (fail
to put in) lauhjó RV: ❶ (fail to
catch a train, etc.) daapm̀dóu ❷
(fail to meet someone at the station) jipm̀dóu ❸ (fail to see)
táim̀dóu ❹ (fail to hit) dám̀jung
✳ **miss out** FV: sáangjó;
sáangleuhk; lauhjó ✳ **miss the
mark** PH: meihjung muhkbīu;
móuh daahtdou muhkbīu ✳
missing FV: m̀ginjó FV/VO:
sāt(jó) jūng ✳ **miss an opportunity** VO: chogwo gèiwuih

missile N: douhdáan; fèidáan; tàuhsehhei (M: go)

mission N: ❶ (diplomatic)
doihbíutyùhn; gùngjoktyùhn;
sijittyùhn (M: go) ❷ (religious)
chàaiwúi; sityùhn (M: go) ❸
(task) simihng; yahmmouh FV:
paai VO: chyùhngaau; boudouh

missionary N: chyùhngaausih; syùngaausih (M: go)

misspell RV: chyuncho;
pingcho

mist N: mouh; hàhmouh ✳
misty PH: (of weather) yáuhdī
bohkmouh; yáuhmouh

mistake FV/N: cho; nghwuih
FV: nghgáai RV: gáaucho;
táicho; yihngcho N: chongh;
gwosāt ✳ **and no mistake** A:
mòuhyìh; dīkkok ✳ **by
mistake** A: m̀gokyi ✳ **make a
mistake** RV: jouhcho VO:
faahncho(ngh) ✳ **mistake for**
Patt: yihngcho . . . jouh/haih .
. . ✳ **mistaken** PH: chongh ge

mister N/BF: sìnsàang (M:
go, wái) BF: -sàang

mistress N: ❶ (of a household) jyúfúh; néuih jyúyán (M: go) ❷ (teacher) néuih gaausī, néuihsinsàang (M: go) ❸ (concubine) chìhngfúh (M: go)

mistrust FV/N: wàaihyìh FV: m̀seunyahm

misunderstand FV/N: nghwuih FV: nghgáai RV: tèngcho

misuse FV: ❶ (use wrongly) nghyuhng; láahmyuhng ❷ (treat badly) yeuhkdoih

mite PH: (of donation) síu gyùnfún N: (child) saimānjái; sailóugō (M: go)

mitigate FV: wuhnwòh; gáamhèng; janjìhng

mitt N: sáutou (M: deui)

mix FV: ❶ (stir) gáau ❷ (of persons) gitgáau PH: (blended) kàumàaih yàtchàih * be mixed up with sb (in sth.) PH: tùhng . . . yáuh hìnlìhn * mix up (in identity) RV: gáauchosaai; fànm̀chēut * mix up (disarrange) RV: gáaulyuhn * mixed up (emotionally confused) PH: sàm lyuhn * mixer N: (machine) gáaubuhngèi (M: ga) * mixture N: wahnhahpmaht FV: wahnhahp

mnemonic(al) PH: bòngjoh geiyīkge * mnemonics PH: geiyīkfaat

moan FV ❶ sànyàhm ❷ (for the dead) ngòidouh PH: ngàhngngángsèng

moat N: hòuhkàu (M: tiuh)

mob N: ❶ bouhtòuh (M: go, 'group' kwàhn) ❷ (the masses) màhnjung FV: bàauwàih IE: jeuihjungsàngsih PH: sèhng-kwàhnyàhn háisyu sòuyíu

mobile PH: ❶ gèiduhngge ❷ (easily changing) yìhbinge N: chè; heichè (M: ga)

mobility PH: gèiduhngsing; binduhngsing

mobilize FV: duhngyùhn

mock FV: (ridicule) gèisiu; jàausiu Adj. PH: gáge; mòuhfóngge * mock-modesty PH: gá haakhei * mock-up N: (sahtmaht) daaih mòuhyìhng (M: go)

mockery FV: jàausiu N: siubeng

modal PH: yìhngsīkseuhng ge; fòngsīkseuhngge; yúhhei ge

mode N: fòngsīk; yéung; fún; yìhng; fùnghei

model N: ❶ (form for imitation or copying) yéung (M: go) ❷ (imitation of a structure) mòuhyìhng (M: go) ❸ (person who poses) mòuhdahkyìh (M: go) ATT/N: mòuhfaahn FV: mòuhfóng PH: jouh . . . ge mòuhyìhng * after (on) the model of FV: hohk; fónghaauh Patt: yíh . . . jouhmòuhfaahn * model after (on, upon) FV: fónghaauh; fóngjai

moderate Adj. PH: ❶ yáuh jitjai ge; sīkdouh ge ❷ (personality) wángihn ge; wànwòh ge PH: wángihn ge yàhn (M: go) FV: wuhnwòh; jitjai * in moderation PH: sīkdouh; sīkjūng; yáuh jitjai * moderatism N: wànwòhjyúyìh; wángihnjyúyìh * moderatist N: wànwòhjyúyìhjé (M: go) * moderator N: juhngchòihyàhn; wuihyìh jyújihk

modern Adj. PH: ❶ (present)

yihndoih ge ❷ (up-to-date)
mōdāng ge; sìhmōuge PH:
yihndoih yàhn (M: go)

**modernize/moderniza-
tion** PH: yihndoihfa

modest SV: ❶ (of attitude)
hìmhèui ❷ (of dress) poksou ❸
(showing care in manners)
jòngjuhng

modification FV ❶ (make
less severe) wuhnwòh;
gáamhēng ❷ (make changes)
gói; gànggói; sàugói ❸ (of grammar) sàusīk FV/N: (to limit)
haahnjai

modify FV: ❶ (make less
severe) wuhnwòh; gáamhēng ❷
(make changes) gói; gànggói;
sàugói ❸ (of grammar) sàusīk
FV/N: (to limit) haahnjai *
modifier N: sàusīkyúh

modish SV: sìhmōu SV/FV
/ATT: làuhhàhng

modulate VO: binyām; bindiuh; jyundiuh

module N: mòuhsou; haihsou; (mèihyìhng) jóugín

Mohammedan N: (a follower) wùihgaautòuh; yīsīlàahn
gaautòuh (M: go) * **Mohammedan mosque** N: wùihgaau
jí (M: gàan) * **Mohammedani-
sm** N: wùihgaau; yīsīlàahngaau

moist SV: sāp; chìuhsāp

moisten RV: jíngsāp; binsāp

moisture SV: chìuhsāp N:
sāphei; séuihei; sāpdouh

molar N: (tooth) daaihngàh
(M: jek) Adj. PH: mòhseui ge

molasses N: mahttòhng

mold N: móu (M: go)

mole N: ❶ (on the skin) jì;
mák (M: nāp) ❷ (rat) yínsyú (M:
jek) ❸ (wall built in the sea)
fòhngbōtàih

molecular Adj. PH: fahnjí
ge

molecule N: fahnjí

molest FV: ❶ sòuyíu ❷
tiùhhei (woman)

molten Adj. PH: ❶ (melted)
yùhngjó ge; yùhngfa ge ❷ jyujouh ge

moment TW: yātjahngāan *
at any monemt A: chèuihsìh
* **at moments** A: sìhsìh * **for
the moment** MA: jaahmsìh
TW: muhkchìhn * **the (very)
moment** Patt: . . . yāt . . . jauh
. . . * **this (very) moment** TW:
yìhgā * **to the (very) moment**
PH: ngāamsaai la * **momen-
tary** PH: ❶ dyúnjaahm ge ❷
(at every moment) chèuihsìhge;
sìhsìhhākhāk ge

momentous Adj.   PH:
juhngyiuge; yìhmjuhng ge

momentum N: chùnglihk;
lihkleuhng

monarch N: gwànjyú;
daaihwòhng (M: go)

monarchy PH: ❶ gwànjyújingtái ❷ (country) gwàn-
jyúgwok (gà) (M: go)

monarchic(al) Adj. PH:
gwànjyújingtái ge; gwànjyújai
ge

monastery N: ❶ sàudouhyún; sàuyún (M: gàan) ❷ (Buddhist) jí; jihyún (M: gàan) ❸
(taoist) douhgun (M: gaàn)

Monday TW: láihbaaiyāt;
sìngkèihyāt

monetary Adj. PH: fobaih ge; chín ge; gàmyùhng ge ✳ **monetary system** N: baihjai (M: go) ✳ **monetary unit** PH: fobaih dàanwái

money N: ❶ chín ❷ fobaih ✳ **moneyed** Adj. PH: (rich) yáuhchínge; gàmchìhnseuhng ge ✳ **money order** N: wuihpiu (M: jèung) ✳ **money-changer** N: ① (a merchant) deuiwuhnsèung (M: go) ② (a shop) jáauwuhndim (M: gàan)

monger N: sèungyàhn; (hawker) síufáan (M: go) BF: -sèung, (hawker) -fáan FV: maaih; faanmaaih

Mongol N: (people) mùhnggúyàhn (M: go); (race) mùhnggújuhk; (language) mùhnggúwá ✳ **Mongolia** N: Mùhnggú

mongolism PH: mùhnggújing; sìntìnyùhyìhng SV/N: baahkchì (M: go) ✳ **mongoloid** SV/N: baahkchì

mongrel Adj. PH: jaahpjúng ge N: ❶ (dog) jaahpjúng gáu (M: jek) ❷ (person) wahnhyutyìh; (boy) jaahpjúngjái; (girl) jaahpjúngmūi (vulgar) (M: go)

monitor N: ❶ (in school) bāanjéung (M: go) ❷ (person employed) gàamtingyùhn; gàamsihyùhn (M: go) ❸ (machine) gàamsihhei (M: go) FV: gàamting; gàamsih

monk N: ❶ (Buddhist) wòhséung (M: go) ❷ (Catholic father) sàhnfuh; (brother) sàusih (M: go)

monkey N: ❶ máhlāu (M: jek) ❷ (child) wàahnpèihjái (M: go) FV: heiluhng (PN) FV/SV: wùhnaauh

monogamy PH: yātfū yāt-

chāi jai

monograph N: jyùntàih leuhnmàhn; jyùnmàhn (M: pìn)

monologue PH: ❶ duhkbaahk ❷ (dramatic composition) duhkgeukhei kehkbún

monopolist -lizer N/PH: lùhngdyuhnjé; jyùnleihjé (M: go)

monopolize FV/N: ❶ (the sale of certain merchandise) jyùnleih ❷ (the market) lùhngdyuhn; duhkjim FV: duhkjim

monopoly FV/N: jyùnleih; lùhngdyuhn N: ❶ (the right) jyùnleihkyùhn ❷ (merchandise) jyùnleihbán

monosyllable N/PH: dàanyàmjih; dàanyàmjitchìh (M: go)

monotone N/SV: dàandiuh

monotonous Adj. PH: dàandiuhge

monotony N: dàanyàm N/SV: dàandiuh

monoxide N/PH: yātyéuhngfamaht

monsieur (messieurs) N: sìnsàang (M: go)

monsoon N: gwaihauhfùng

monster N: gwaaimaht (M: jek) PH: (of people) chàahnyán ge yàhn (M: go)

monstrous Adj. PH: ❶ kèihyìhng gwaaijohng ge ❷ (fearful) hópa ge ❸ (absurd) fòngmauh ge

montage PH: (of films, tr.) mùhngtaaikèih FV: jínchāp; jínjip

month N/BF: yuht * **last month** TW: seuhnggo yuht * **next month** TW: hahgo yuht * **this month** TW: nīgo yuht

monthly PH: múih(go) yuht yātchi N: yuhthón; yuhthón (M: bún, bouh)

monument N: géinihmbèi (M: go) PH: (of writing) bātnáujyujok

moo PH: ngàuhgiu (sèng)

mood N: ❶ (state of mind) sàmchihng; chìhngséuih ❷ (of language) yúhhei * **be in the mood for** AV/FV: séung (yiu) PH: yáuhyi

moody Adj. PH: ❶ chìhngséuihfa ge ❷ (gloomy) yàuwāt ge ❸ (bad-tempered) chaupèihheige

moon N: ❶ yuhtgwōng; yút (M: go) ❷ (astronomical) yuhtkàuh FV: hàahndohng * **moon light** N: yuhtgwōng * **moon cake** N: yuhtbéng (M: go) * **eclipse of the moon** PH: yuhtsihk * **moonblindness** N: yehmàahngjing * **a blue moon** PH: m̀hónàhng ge sih * **moonlit** Adj. PH: yuhtmìhng ge * **moon shine** N: yuhtgwōng N/FV: (foolish ideas) hùngséung

moor N: fòngyéh; jíujaahk FV: tìhngbohk; tìhngpaak

moose N: tòhlúk; mèih (M: jek)

moot FV: ❶ tóuleuhn ❷ tàihchēut (question) Adj. PH: meih gáaikyut ge (question)

mop N: ❶ (for the floor) deihtō (M: go) ❷ (for bowls) sáiwúnchaat (M: go) FV: chaat; maat

mope SV: fàahnmuhn; yàuwāt

moral Adj. PH: douhdāk (seuhng) ge; douhyih (seuhng) ge SV/N: douhdāk FV/N: gaaufan N: ❶ bánhahng; lèuhnléih ❷ (lesson) yuhyi * **moral support** PH: jìngsàhn seuhng ge jìchìh

morality SV/N: douhdāk * **commercial morality** PH: sèungyihp douhdāk

moralize FV/VO: syutgaau FV: gaaufa

morale N: sihhei; seunsàm; douhyih

morass N: ❶ nàihbaahn; jíujaahk ❷ (fig.) hahmjihng

moratorium PH: yìhnkèihwàahnjaai FV: (of activities) jaahmtìhng

morbid Adj. PH: ❶ behngtaai ge; m̀gihnchyùhn ge ❷ (fearful) hópa ge

more A: juhng; joi P: tìm PH: dōdī Adj. PH: béigaau dō ge; juhngdōge; gangdō ge * **more or less** A: gamseuhnghá; jóyáu; yeukmók; chàmdò Patt: ... dò gwo ... * **more than ten** PH: sahp géi go * **more than enough** PH: dōdākjaih * **more than probable** IE: sahpjì baat gáu * **more and more** Patt: yuht làih yuht ... * **the more ... the...** Patt: yuhtdò ... yuht ... * **the more ... the more ...** Patt: yuht ... yuht ... * **(and) what is more** A: lìhngngoih PH: gang juhngyiu ge haih

moreover A: yìhché; bihngché; fongché

morning TW: jìutàuhjóu;

jiujóu; seuhngngŃh

moron PH: dàihnàhng ge
yàhn (M: go) N/SV: dàinàhng

morphia, morphine N:
māfē; mōfē

mortal Adj. PH: ❶ (which
must die) bītséi ge ❷ (causing
death) jimihng ge ❸ (lasting until death) jùng sàn ge ❹ (accompanying death) làhmséi ge ❺
(extreme) gihkdouh ge N: yàhn;
fàahnyàhn (M: go) ✻ **mortal-
ly** Adv. PH: jimihng gám A:
fèiseuhng ✻ **mortal wound**
PH: jimihngsèung ✻ **mortal
sin** N: daaihjeuih (M: gihn)

mortality PH: ❶ bītséising
❷ (number of deaths) séimòhng-
sou(muhk) ❸ (death rate)
séimòhngléut

mortar N: ❶ (for building)
hùhngmòuhnàih; fūisà; fūinàih
❷ (for pounding) jùnghám (M:
go) ❸ (military) bīkgīkpaau (M:
go)

mortgage FV/N: dáingaat
PH: (agreement) dáingaat
kaigeui (M: jèung)

mortification N: ❶ fú-
hahng ❷ (shame) chíyuhk

mortify FV: ❶ (control) hākjai ❷ (of shame) sàuyuhk
SV/FV: (decay) laahn VO: (of
lust) gamyuhk

mortuary N: líhmfòhng;
tìhngsìfòhng (M: go)
mosaic PH: sèunghahm
saigùng (ge)

moslem, moslim N: wùihgaautòuh; yīsīlàahn gaautòuh
(M: go) ✻ **moslemism** N:
yīsīlàahngaau; wùihgaau

mosque N: chìngjànjí; wùih-

gaaují (M: gàan)

mosquito N: mān (M: jek) ✻
mosquito net N: mānjeung
(M: tòhng) ✻ **mosquito
boat/craft** N: faaitéhng (M:
jek) ✻ **mosquitocide** N:
mihtmānyeuhk ✻ **mosquito
hawk** N: chìngtìhng

moss N: chèngtòih

most A: jeui; ji Adj. PH: jeui
dò ge; jeui daaih ge; jeui gòu ge
PH: daaih dòsou; daaih bouhfahn ✻ **at (the) most = the
very most** PH: jeuidò; jidò ✻
make the most of PH:
chùngfahnleihyuhng ✻ **most
of all** A: jeui daaih ✻ **most
probably** A: daaihkoi; daaihkói ✻ **mostly** A/ATT/PH:
dòsou A: gèifùh dōu

mote N: ❶ chàhnngòi; mèih-
nàp ❷ (fig.) hàhchì; (biblical) chi

motel N: heichè léuihgún (M:
gàan)

moth N: fèingòh; dāngngòh
(M: jek) ✻ **moth ball** N:
chauyún (M: nàp)

mother N: ❶ (formal term)
móuhchàn ❷ (more intimate
term) màhmā; amā FV: ❶ (to
take care of) jiugu ❷ (to adopt)
líhngyéuhng ✻ **mother-in-law**
N: ❶ (wife's mother) ngoih-
móuh; ngoihmóu ❷ (husband's
mother) gàpó; nàaihnáai ✻
stepmother N: hauhmóuh;
gaimóuh ✻ **motherland** N:
jóugwok ✻ **mother tongue** N:
móuhyúh ✻ **motherly** SV:
chìhngoi

motif N: jyújí; jyútàih (M: go)

motion N: (gesture) sáusai
FV/N: ❶ (moving) wahnduhng
❷ (suggestion to be voted on)
tàihyíh; duhngyíh VO: dásáu-

sai; sihyi * **motion picture** N: dihnyíng (M: chēut) * **second a motion** VO: wohyíh * **a motion is passed** FV: tùnggwo * **go through the motions of** IE: fûhínsākjaak

motivate VO: yáhnhéi duhnggèi FV: yáuhdouh; gīkfaat

motivation N: duhnglihk PH: duhnggèi yìhngsìhng

motive N: duhnggèi; nihmtàuh; muhkdīk (M: go) Adj. PH: faatduhng ge

motley Adj. PH: jaahpsīkge; wahnjaahp ge N: ❶ (of cloth) jaahpsīkbou (M: fūk, faai) ❷ (clown) síucháu (M: go) ❸ (dress) chóiyì (M: gihn)

motor N: ❶ mōdá (M: go); faatduhnggèi (M: go, ga) ❷ (car) chè; heichè PH: ❶ (muscle) wahnduhnggèi ❷ (nerves) wahnduhng sàhngìng VO: chóhchè; chóh heichè * **motorbike/motor cycle** N: dihndàanchè (M: ga) * **motorboat** N: dihnsyùhn; dihnsyùhnjái (M: ga) * **motor car** N: chè; heichè (M: ga)

motto N: gaakyìhn; johyauhmíhng; tàihchìh (M: geui)

mo(u)ld N: ❶ móu; mòuhyìhng (M: go) ❷ (fungi) mōu PH: (soil) gàangjung ge nàih VO: ❶ (to have fungi) faatmōu ❷ (give a shape to) jouhyìhng FV: soujouh

moulder RV: (decay) fuhlaahn FV: sèuiteui

moulding FV: mòuhjai; mòuhjouh; soujouh VO: jouhyìhng

mouldy Adj. PH: ❶ faatmōu

ge ❷ (out-of-date) gwosìh ge; gauhsìkge ❸ (tasteless) fahtmeih ge

mo(u)lt VO: ❶ (of birds) wuhnyúhmòuh ❷ teuipèih FV: (fig.) chèuihheui

mound M/BF: dèui; dēui (of earth) nàih ~ ; SP ~ nàih RV: dèuihéi

mount FV: ❶ (of picture) bíu ❷ (of jewelry) sèung ❸ (of plays) séuhngyín ❹ (to install) ngònjòng ❺ (to increase) jànggà; seuhngsìng VO: (get on a horse) séuhngmáh N: ❶ (mountain) sàan (M: go, joh) ❷ (for mounting) johgá (M: go); tokbáan (M: faai) ❸ (for pictures) bíuwájí (M: jèung)

mountain N: sàan (M: go, joh) PH: (a lot) daaihdèui; daaihleuhng * **mountain chain** N: sàanmahk * **mountain range** N: sàanmahk; sàanlíhng; sàanléhng * **mountaineering** VO: pàhsàan * **mountain top** N: sàandéng (M: go) * **mountain path** N: sàanlouh (M: tìuh) * **mountain cave** N: sàanlūng (M: go) * **mountainous** Adj. PH: ❶ dòsàan ge ❷ (huge) geuihdaaih ge

mourn FV: ngòidouh SV/FV: bèisèung

mouse N: lóuhsyú (M: jek) * **Mickey Mouse** N: máihkèih lóuhsyú (M: jek) * **mouse-trap** N: lóuhsyúgíp; lóuhsyúlùhng (M: go)

moustache N: sòu

mouth N: háu; jéui (M: go) RV: góngchēut FV/SV: (boast) kwàháu FV: ❶ (eat) sihk ❷ (kiss) sek * **give mouth to**

RV: góngchēut * **make a mouth** PH: jíng gwaai yéung * **mouth-organ** N: háukàhm (M: go) * **mouth piece** N: ❶ (of a tobacco pipe) yīnjéuiháu (M: go) ❷ (of musical instrument) chèuihháu (M: go) ❸ (-muffle) háujaau (M: go) ❹ (a person) doihyìhnyàhn; faatyìhnyàhn (M: go) * **mouthful** PH: múhnháu; yātdaahm; síuleuhng

movable Adj. PH: wúihyūkge; yūkdākge; wuhtduhng ge N: duhngcháan

move FV: ❶ (change one's position) yūk ❷ (change the position of sth.) bùn ❸ (propose) tàihyíh ❹ (affect emotionally) gámduhng ❺ (in chess or games) hàahng ~ yāt bouh kéi FV/N: (as troops) diuhduhng PH: (take action) chóichéui hàhngduhng

movement FV/N: wahnduhng N: duhngheung

movie N: ❶ dihnyíng (M: chēut) ❷ (theatre) dihnyíngyún (M: gàan) * **movie star** N: dihnyíng mìhngsīng (M: go)

moving Adj. PH: (affect emotionally) duhngyàhn ge; gámyàhnge * **moving picture** N: dihnyíng (M: chēut)

mow FV: ❶ (with a scythe) got ❷ (with a machine) cháan ❸ (destroy) cháanchèuih; souchèuih; chèuiwái N: (gòn) chóudēui; wòhdēui * **mower** N: (lawn-) cháanchóugèi; jínchóugèi (M: ga) PH: (a person) got chóu ge yàhn (M: go)

Mrs. BF: -táai BF/N: ❶ taaitáai (M: go, wái) ❷ (a polite address for the wife of a teacher, minister) sīmóuh ❸ (for the wife of a prominent man) fùyàhn (M: wái)

Ms BF/N: néuihsih (M: wái, go)

much Nu: géidō PH: hóudò; taai dò A: (of time) sìhsìh * **as much . . . as** Patt: tùhng . . . yātyeuhng gamdò * **as much as** Patt: . . . géidō, jauh . . . géidō * **be too much for** RV: sauhm̀jyuh * **have much to do with** Patt: tùhng . . . hóu yáuh gwàanhaih * **much more** A: hòhfong * **much too** PH: gwofahn; sahtjoih taai . . . * **so much as** A: sahmji (yù)

muck N: ❶ (dung) sí; fan ❷ (manure) fanfèih; fèih ❸ (dirt) wùjòuyéh; laahpsaap VO: sí(fan) fèih PH/RV: (make dirty) jíng wùjòu

mucus N: ❶ (of the eye) ngáahnsí ❷ (of the nose) beihtai * **mucus running from one's nose** VO: làuh beihtai

mud N: nàih (jèung); nàihbaahn PH: hàaidóu nàihbaahn * **muddy** Adj. PH: ❶ múhnsaai nàihbaahn ge ❷ (of colour) nàihsīkge ❸ (fig.) wùhtòuhge; wahnlyuhn ge * **mudguard** N: dóngnàihbáan (M: faai)

muddle SV: lyuhn; wahnlyuhn RV/PH: gáaulyuhn; gáauwùhtòuh PH: wahn yahtjí * **muddle-headed** Adj. PH: tàuhnóuh wùhtòuh ge

muff N: ❶ (gloves) sáumaht (M: deui) ❷ nyúhnsáudói; pèihsáutúng (M: go) PH: (of a person) leuhnjeuhn ge yàhn (M: go) RV: (of a ball) jipm̀dóu; FV: sātjó (go bō)

muffle RV: ❶ bàaujyuh; kámjyuh ❷ (of mouth, eyes)

ngámjyuh * **muffler** N: ❶ (scarf) génggān; wàihgān (M: tiùh) ❷ (gloves) háuhsáutou (M: deui) ❸ (of sound) mihtsìnghei (M: go)

mug N: ❶ daaihbūi (M: jek, go) ❷ (mouth) jéui (M: go) ❸ (face) mihn (M: faai) ❹ (simpleton) chéunyàhn (M: go) FV: (study hard) fúduhk

muggy Adj. PH: muhnyihtge; yauh sāp yauh yiht ge

mule N: lèuih (M: jek) PH: ❶ (of people) gujáp ge yàhn (M: go) ❷ (slippers) móuhjāang ge tòháai (M: deui)

mulish Adj. PH: wàahngu ge; jápngaau ge

multilateral Adj. PH: dòbìnge; dògwok chàamgà ge * **multilateralism; multilateral trade** PH: dòbìn mauhyihk; dògwokmauhyihk

multiple Adj. PH: dòyeuhng ge; fūkjaahpge N: púihsou PH: dòlouhhaihtúng * **multiplex** Adj. PH: dò bouhfahn ge; dò yihngsīk ge

multiplication N: (maths.) sìhngfaat; sìhngsou FV/N: púihjáng; fàahnjihk

multiplicity FV: chùhngfūk PH: dòyeuhngsing

multiply FV: (maths.) sìhng FV/N: ❶ (increase) jànggà ❷ (by procreation) fàahnjihk; jàngjihk

multitude N: (the masses) kwàhnjung; yàhnkwàhn Nu: daaihpài; daaih kwàhn; daaihleuhng M: kwàhn *yāt ~ yàhn*

mum N: màhmā; amā Adj.

PH: chàhmmahk ge FV/N: jàmmahk; gàammahk

mumble SV: ngàhmchàhm PH: ngàhmngàhmchàhmchàhm

mummy N: muhknáaihyī (M: go); gēungsī (M: tiùh)

mumps N: jasòi * **have the mumps** VO: sàangjasòi

mundane Adj. PH: saijuhkge; saigāange

municipal Adj. PH: síhjingge; síhlahp ge * **municipal area** N: síhkèui * **municipality** N/BF: síh PH: síhjingfú; jihjih (deíh) kēui

munificent SV: hóngkoi; fùnháuh

munition PH: gwànsèuibán; gwànyuhngbán

mural Adj. PH: chèuhngbīkseuhngge N: bīkwá (M: fūk) * **muralist** N: bīkwágà (M: go)

murder FV: ❶ (kill) màuhsaat; saat(séi) ❷ (massacre) tòuhsaat * **murderer** N: hùngsáu (M: go) * **murderous** Adj. PH: saatyàhnge; hùngngok ge

murky Adj. PH: yàmngamge; mùhnglùhngge

murmur FV: (complain) ngàhm SV: ngàhmchàhm PH: (utter in a low voice) saisènggóng

muscle N: gèiyuhk; táilihk

muscular Adj. PH: gèiyuhk faatdaaht ge; jonggihnge

muse FV: chàhmsì; mahkséung; míhngséung

museum N: bokmahtgún; bokmahtyún (M: gàan)

mush N: jaahpsèng FV/N: gònyíu

mushroom N: dūnggū; sīngū; chóugū PH: (grow rapidly) sàngjéung seunchūk; (develop rapidly) seunchūkfaatjín * **spring up like mushrooms** IE: hóuchíh yúhhauh chēunséun gám yúngyihn

music N: ❶ yàmngohk; ngohkkūk ❷ (written notes) ngohkpóu (M: bún) * **face the music** PH: yúhngyù sìhngdàam hauhgwó; m̀pa gàannàahn * **music hall** N: yàmngohktēng (M: go) * **music stand** N: ngohkpóugá (M: go)

musical Adj. PH: (sīk) yàmngohkge; hóutèng ge; ngoi hou yàmngohk ge N/PH: (film) yàmngohkpín; (comedy) yàmngohk héikehk (M: chēut) * **musical instrument** N: ngohkhei (M: gihn)

musician N: yàmngohkgā; jokkūkgā (M: go)

musing FV: chàhmsī; míhngséung

musk N: sehhēung * **muskdeer** N: sehhēunglúk (M: jek) * **musk-melon** N: tìhmgwā; hēunggwā (M: go)

musket N: ❶ (gun) waahttòhngchēung; gauhsīk bouhchēung (M: jì) ❷ (bullets) bouhchēungjídáan (M: nāp)

muslin N: (mìhn) bou

muss SV/FV/N: wahnlyuhn RV: jínglyuhn; jíngwùjòu

mussel N: hín (M: jek)

must A.AV: yātdihng yiu; bītdihng yiu * **must not** A. AV: yātdihng m̀hóu; chìnkèih m̀hóu

mustard N: ❶ gaailaaht ❷ (plant) gaaichoi * **mustard powder** N: gaaimuht

muster FV/N: jaahphahp; jiuhjaahp FV: janjok * **muster up** FV/N: jaahphahp FV: janjok * **pass muster** FV: hahpgaak * **muster book/muster roll** N: dímméngchaak; mìhngchaak (M: bún)

musty Adj. PH: faatmōuge; chàhngauhge

mutable Adj. PH: yihbin ge; sàamsàm léuhngyi ge

mutant Adj. PH: binyihge; binyih só yáhnhéi ge

mutation FV/N:. binfa; jyúnbin; (of a sudden) dahtbin

mute Adj. PH: ❶ ngá ge ❷ (of a letter in a word) móuhyām ge N: ❶ ngábā; (boy) ngájái (M: go) ❷ (of music) yeuhkyāmhei Patt: gáamyeuhk ge sīngyām/sēng

mutilate RV: jíngtyúhn (arms or legs) FV: chàahnfai

mutineer N: buhnbīng; buhngwān (M: go, deuih)

mutiny FV/N: buhnbin; fáankong

mutter SV: ngàhmchàhm PH: gīlīgūlū; ngàhmngàhm chàhmchàhm

mutton N: yèuhngyuhk * **eat mutton cold** IE: sauhyàhnbaahkngáahn * **mutton-head** N: bahndáan (M: go)

mutual A: wuhsèung Adj. PH: guhngtùhng ge * **mutual**

agreement PH: sēungfòng
tùhngyi ✱ **mutual aid** PH:
wuhsèungbòngjoh; wuhjoh ✱
mutualism N: wuhjohleuhn ✱
mutuality PH: sèungwuh-
gwàanhaih

muzzle N: ❶ (mouth) háu;
jéui; (nose) beih ❷ (on a dog
etc.) háujaau; háulāp (M: go) ❸
(of firearm) chēungháu; paau-
háu (M: go) VO: daaiháujaau;
séuhngháujaau

my Adj. PH: ngóhge

myopia N: gahnsih PH: (fig.)
kyutfaht yúhngin; kyutfaht-
bihnbihtlihk

myriad Nu/PH: mòuhsou

myself PN: ngóhjihgéi

mysterious Adj. PH: sàhnbei ge

mystery SV: (mysterious)
sàhnbei N: ❶ ngoubei (M: go)
❷ (secret) beimaht (M: go)

mystic Adj. PH: sàhnbei ge;
ngoubei ge; ngoumiuh ge PH:
sàhnbei jyúyihjé (M: go); (a
religious group) ngoubei paai ✱
mysticism PH: sàhnbei jyúyih

mystify SV: màihwaahk;
kwanwaahk FV: sàhnbeifa

myth N: sàhnwá (M: go) PH:
hèuikau ge gusih (M: go) ✱
mythic(al) Adj. PH: hèuikau
ge

mythology N: ❶ sàhnwá
(M: go); (a study) sàhnwáhohk
❷ (collection of) sàhnwájaahp
(M: bún)

N

nab FV: daihbouh

nag PH: sai ge máh (M: jek)
FV: lòsò

nail N: ❶ (of metal) dēng (M:
háu) ❷ (of fingers) sáugaap ❸
(of toes) geukgaap FV: dēng ~
N hái PW ✱ **hit the nail on
the head** PH: yāt jàm gin hyut
✱ **nail securely** RV: dèngsaht;
dènggáng ✱ **nail to the cross**
PH: dènghái sahpjihga seuhngbihn ✱ **nail up** RV: dèngmàaih

naive SV: tìnjàn; poksaht

naked SV: lótái; bouhlouh
PH: (of men) chēuihdaaih chek
laak ✱ **the naked eye** PH:
yuhk ngáahn

name N: mēng (M: go) FV:
(nominate) tàihmìhng VO: (give
a name to) hēiméng • tùhng PN
~ ✱ **call a person names**
PH: yuhng nàahn tèng ge syutwah naauh yàhn ✱ **full name**
N: singmìhng ✱ **in the name
of** FV: doihbíu PH: yíh . . . ge
mìhngyih ✱ **nickname** N:
fàméng (M: go) ✱ **pen name** N:
bātméng (M: go) ✱ **trade
name** N: pàaih; māktàuh (M:
go)

nameless PH: ❶ (of letters
etc.) móuh méng ge; līkmìhng
ge ❷ (indescribable) nàahn
yíhyìhngyùhng ge

namely A: jīkhaih; jauhhaih

nap ✱ **have (take) a nap**
VO: fan ngaangaau PH: hāp
yātjahngāan ngáahnfan

nape N: géngbui

naphthalene N: jèung-
nóuhyún; chauyún (M: nāp)

napkin N: chāangān (M: faai, tìuh)

narcissus N: séuisīnfā (M: déu)

narcotic N: (drug) màhjeuiyeuhk (M: jek, júng)

narrate FV: góng; góngseuht

narrow SV: jaak FV: binjaak · tìuh louh ~ jó * **narrow down** FV: binjaak; sūkgáam * **a narrow escape** PH: gáu séi yāt sàng * **narrow-minded** SV: síuhei; sàmhùngjaak

nasal N: beihyām * **nasal cavity** N: beihgōlūng (M: go)

nascent SV: chòsàng ge; chòkèih ge

nasty SV: ❶ (dirty) wùjòulaahttaat (ge) ❷ (low in morality) hahlàuh ge * **a nasty smell** N: chaumeih (M: jahm)

natal SV: chēutsàng ge

natality PH: chēutsàng léut

nation N: ❶ (country) gwok; gwokgà ❷ (people) màhnjuhk

national Adj. PH: gwokgà ge; màhnjuhk ge N: gwokmàhn * **national anthem** N: gwokgō (M: sáu) * **national day** N: gwokhing (yaht) * **national defense** N: gwokfòhng * **national flag** N: gwokkèih (M: jì)

nationalism N: màhnjuhk jyúyih; gwokgà jyúyih

nationalist N: màhnjuhkjyúyihjé (M: go)

nationality N: gwokjihk; màhnjuhk (M: go)

nationalization VO: yahp-

jihk PH: sàugwàigwokyáuh

nationalize FV: gwokyáuhfa

native SV: búndeih ge N: búndeih ge; tóuyàhn (M: go) * **native dialect** N: búndeihwá (M: júng) * **native goods** PH: búndeih fo (M: júng) * **native products** N: tóucháan (M: júng)

nativity FV: chēutsàng; daansàng

natty SV: ❶ (clean) gònjehng ge ❷ (agile) máhnjiht ge

natural SV: ❶ (not artificial) tìnyìhn ge ❷ (innate) tìnsàang ge ❸ (unaffected) jihyìhn ❹ (normal) jingsèuhng ge

naturalization FV: gwàifa

naturally A: (of course) dòngyìhn

nature N: ❶ jihyìhn; jihyìhngaai ❷ (inborn nature) tìnsing; búnsing ❸ (characteristic, of something other than a person) dahksing; singjāt * **by nature** PH: búnsing seuhng; sàngsing * **in nature** PH: singjāt seuhng; sahtjaiseuhng * **true to nature** SV: bīkjàn

naught N: (mathematics) lìhng * **bring (come) to naught** PH: fa wàih wùyáuh FV: sātbaaih * **set at naught** FV: hìngsih (a person) ~ *yàhn*

naughty SV: yáih; ngànpèih; baakyim

nauseate FV: ❶ séungngáu; jokngáu; jokmuhn ❷ yimwu (people, things, jobs)

nautical SV: hòhnghói ge * **nautical mile** M/N: hóiléih

naval SV: hóigwān ge ✳ **naval base** N: hóigwān gèideih (M: go) ✳ **naval blockade** PH: hóiseuhng fùngsó ✳ **naval flag** N: hóigwānkèih (M: jì) ✳ **naval officer** N: hóigwāngwāngùn (M: go) ✳ **naval port** N: gwāngóng (M: go) ✳ **naval warfare** N: hóijin (M: chèuhng)

navel N: ❶ tóuhchìh ❷ (umbilical cord) chìhdáai (M: tìuh)

navigate FV: ❶ (a ship or airplane) sái ❷ hòhnghàhng

navigation N: hòhnghóiseuht

navigator N: hòhnghóigā; líhnghòhngyùhn (M: go)

navy N: hóigwān (M: deuih, jì)

Nazi N: naahpseuihfahnjí (M: go) ✳ **the Nazis** N: naahpseuihdóng

near FV: gahnjyuh SV: (closely related) gahnbohng Patt: lèih . . . káhn • *PW1* ~ *PW2* hóu/géi ~ ✳ **a near escape** PH: gáu séi yāt sàng ✳ **far and near** PH: dousyu; yúhngahn ✳ **nearby** PW: jógán; fuhgahn ✳ **nearsighted** N: gahnsih ✳ **to near PW** PH: jauhlàih dou PW la

nearly A: jìpgahn; daaihyeuk; gèifùh ✳ **not nearly** PH: yúhnbātkahp; jàangdākyúhn

neat SV: kéihléih; jíngchàih ✳ **neat and tidy** SV: jíngchàih PH: jíngjíngchàihchàih

nebula N: ❶ panmouhjāi (M: júng) ❷ (of astronomy) sīngwàhn

necessarily A: bītdihng; dòngyìhn ✳ **not necessarily** PH: meihbīt; m̀yātdihng

necessary SV: bītsèui ge ✳ **it is necessary to** A: sihbīt

necessaries N: bītsèuibán ✳ **daily necessaries** N: yahtyuhngbán (M: júng)

necessity N: ❶ (needs) sèuiyiu ❷ bītsèuibán ❸ (poverty) pàhnkùhng

neck N: géng (M: tìuh) ✳ **a stiff neck** SV: ngaahngggéng ✳ **necklace** N: génglín (M: tìuh) ✳ **necktie** N: tāai; léhngtāai (M: tìuh)

nectar N: ❶ (honey) fāmaht ❷ (drinks) hóu yám ge yámbán

need N: ❶ sèuiyiu; kyutfaht ❷ bītsèuibán FV: sèuiyiu ✳ **be in need of** PH: bīkchitsèuiyiu ✳ **meet needs** PH: múhnjūksèuiyiu ✳ **need not** CV: m̀sái ✳ **needless to say** PH: m̀sáigóng

needle N: jām (M: háu) ✳ **eye of a needle** N: jāmngáahn (M: go) ✳ **look for a needle in a stack of hay** PH: hóidáilàauhjām ✳ **needlework** N: jāmjí

negate FV: ❶ fáudihng ❷ (cancel) chéuisiu

negative N: (photo) séungdái (M: jèung) SV: (opp. to positive, constructive) siugihk ✳ **negative electricity** N: yàmdihn ✳ **negative sign** N: fuhhouh (M: go)

neglect FV: fātleuhk; m̀léih

negligent SV: sòfāt; chòusàmdaaihyi

negotiate FV/N: tàahmpun

negotiation FV/N: tàahmpun

negro N: hākyàhn (M: go)

neigh PH: máhgiu

neighbo(u)r N: gaaklèihlèuhnséh; gāaifōng * neighbouring PW: gaaklèih * neighbouring village N: gaaklèihchyūn * next-door neighbour N: lèuhngèui (M: go) * neighbouring country N: lèuhngwok (M: go) * in the neighbourhood of PH: hái fuhgahn; daaihyeuk

neighbo(u)rly SV: muhklèuhn; yáuhngoi

neither * neither... nor Patt: ❶ (yauh) m̀ ... (yauh) m̀ ... • yauh m̀ gòu, yauh m̀ leng ❷ m̀haih ... yauh (or yihk) m̀ haih ... • m̀ haih géi gòu, yihk m̀ haih géi leng * neither of the two PH: léuhnggo dōu m̀haih

neon sign N: gwònggún; ngàihhùhngdāng (M: ji)

neophyte PH: ❶ (religious) sānyahpgaau ge; sàngàyahp ge (yàhn) ❷ chòhohk ge (yàhn)

nephew N: ❶ (brother's son) ját (M: go) ❷ (sister's son) ngoihsāng (M: go) ❸ (son of wife's brother) noihját (M: go)

nepotism FV: pìntáan PH: juhngyuhng chànchīk; kwàhndaai gwàanhaih

Neptune N: (planet) hóiwòhngsīng

nerve N: ❶ sàhngìng ❷ (being bold) dáamleuhng PH: (sensitive) sàhngìng gwomáhn; sàhngìngját * be all nerves PH: sàhngìnggánjèung * get on sb's nerves PH: sái ... sàmfàahn * nerve oneself PH: gúhéi yúhnghei

nervous SV: gánjèung PH: sàhngìng gwomáhn Adv. PH: fòngsātsāt gám * nervous system N: sàhngìng haihtúng (M: go) * nervous breakdown SV/N: sàhngìng sèuiyeuhk * nervous disorder FV: sàhngìngcholyuhn

nest N: dau (M: go) * bird's nest N: jeukdau; jeukchàauh (M: go)

net N: móhng (M: go) * net amount N: sahtsou * net price N: sahtga * net profit N: jihngleih; sèuhnleih * net weight FV: jihngchúhng * to fish with a net VO: jūkyú; dáyú * to throw a net VO: saatmóhng

nether Adj. PH: hahbihn ge * netherworld N: (Hell) yàmgàan; deihyuhk PH: (society) hahchàhngséhwúi

nettle N: chàhmmàh RV: gīknàu * nettle rash N: chàhmmàhchán; fùngchán

network N: ❶ móhng (M: go) ❷ (broadcasting) gwóngbomóhng; (of television) dihnsihmóhng * a network of railways N: titlouhmóhng

neural SV: sàhngìng ge; sàhngìng haihtúng ge

neuralgia N: sàhngìngtung

neuritis N: sàhngìngyihm

neurology N: sàhngìngbehnghohk

neurotic Adj. PH: ❶ sàhngìngbehng ge ❷ (sensitive) sàhngìnggwomáhn ge N: (yáuh) sàhngìngbehng (ge) yàhn

neuter SV/N: ❶ (linguistics) jùngsing(chìh) ❷ (animals) mòuhsing ge

neutral SV: jùnglahp neutral country PH: jùnglahp gwokgà (M: go) ✳ **neutral zone** PH: jùnglahp deihdaai ✳ **remain neutral** PH: bóuchìhjùnglahp

neutron N: jùngjí (M: nāp, go) ✳ **neutron bomb** N: jùngjí dáan (M: go)

never Adv. PH: ❶ (in past time) chùhnglòih meih; chùhnglòih móuh ❷ (habitually, present and future) joiṁ; wìhngṁjoi; wìhngyúhn dōuṁ ✳ **better late than never** IE: chìhjouh júng béi ṁjouh hóu; chìhdou hóugwo móuh dou ✳ **never mind** PH: ṁgányiu

nevertheless Patt: sèuiyìhn haih gám . . . juhnghaih . . .

new SV: sàn; sànge ✳ **new born baby** N: sōuhàjái, bìhbījái (M: go) ✳ **newcomer** PH: sànlàih ge (yàhn) (M: go) ✳ **new-fashioned** SV: sànfún ge; sànsīk ge ✳ **new hand** SV: sàangsáu ✳ **New Testament** N: Sànyeuk chyùhnsyù ✳ **New Year** N: sànnìhn ✳ **Happy New Year** IE: Sànnìhn faailohk; Gùnghoh sànhèi ✳ **New Year's Eve** PH: nìhnsàahmáahn; chèuihjihk ✳ **New Zealand** PW: Sànsàilàahn; Náusàilàahn

newly MA: sàngahn; jeuigahn ✳ **newly arrived** Adj. PH: sàndou ge ✳ **newly bought** Adj PH: sànmáaih ge ✳ **newly married couple** N: sànfànfùfúh PH: sàngahngitfàn ge

news N: ❶ (in a newspaper) sànmán; sīusīk ❷ (personal) yàmseun; sīusīk ✳ **news agency** N: tùngseunséh (M: go) ✳ **newsreel** N: sànmàhnpín

(M: chēut) ✳ **news stand** N: boujídong; boutāan (M: go)

newspaper N: boují (M: jèung, fahn) ✳ **morning paper** N: jóubou; yahtbou (M: jèung, fahn) ✳ **evening paper** N: máahnbou (M: jèung, fahn) ✳ **newspaperman** N: sànmàhn geijé (M: go) ✳ **newspaper office** N: bougún (M: gàan)

next SP: ❶ (used with a measure of time or things) daihyih ❷ hah . . . ✳ **the next time** TW: hahchi; hahyātchi ✳ **the next week** TW: hahgo láihbaai ✳ **the next month** TW: hahgo yuht ✳ **the next year** (like school year etc.) TW: hahyātnìhn ✳ **next year** TW: chēutnín; mìhngnìhn PW: pòhngbīn A: (after that) yìhnhauh ✳ **who is next?** PH: dou bīngo a?

nib N: bātjīm

nibble PH: hehnghēng ngáauh

nice SV: hóu ✳ **nice-looking** SV: hóutái; leng

nicety SV: (of observation etc.) jéunkok; jìngkok

niche N: (for religious images) sàhnngàm (M: go)

nick N: lihtháu; kyutháu (M: go)

nickel N: ❶ nihp; nīp ❷ nihp baih; nīpbaih (M: go)

nickname N: fàméng (M: go)

nicotine N: nèihgúdìng

niece N: ❶ (brother's daughter) jahtnéui ❷ (sister's daughter) ngoihsàngnéui

niggard PH: síuheigwái (M: go) SV: gùhòhn; síuhei

night TW: yehmáahn; máahnhāk; máahntàuhhāk; yehmáahnhāk * **all night** Nu M: sèhngmáahn * **good night** PH: jóutáu * **last night** TW: kàhmmáahn; chàhmmáahn; johkmáahn * **tomorrow night** TW: tìngmáahn * **night before last** TW: chìhnmáahn * **night after tomorrow night** TW: hauhmáahn * **night after night** MM: máahnmáahn * **every night** TW: múih máahn * **night duty** N: yehbāan VO: jihkyé * **night school** N: yehhohk; yehhók; yehhaauh * **night and day** PH: yaht yíh gai yeh * **overnight** VO: gwoyé * **night blindness** N: yehmàahngjing * **night-club** N: yehjúngwúi (M: gàan) * **nightfall** N: wòhngfàn * **nightlong** TW: tùngsīu * **nightmare** N: ngokmuhng (M: go)

nightingale N: yehngāng (M: jek)

Nihilism N: hèuimòuhjyúyih

nil Nu: lìhng FV: móuh

nimble SV: máhnjiht; gèigíng

nimbus N: ❶ (weather) yúhwàhn ❷ (religious) gwònghyūn; gwòngwàahn (M: go)

nincompoop N: sòhyàhn; sòhlóu (M: go)

nine Nu: gáu * **nineteen** Nu: sahpgáu * **ninety** Nu: gáusahp * **ninety nine** Nu: gáusahpgáu; gáuahgáu * **nine to five (office hours)** PH: jìu gáu máahn ńgh

nip RV: ❶ (pinch) nìmjyuh ❷

(with an instrument) gihpjyuh; kìhmjyuh * **nip up** RV: nìmhéi; gihphéi; kìhmhéi

nippers N: kímjái (M: go)

nipple N: ❶ náaihtàuh (M: go) ❷ (plastic) náaihjéui (M: go)

nitric acid N: kéuhngséui; sìusyūn

nitrogen N: daahmhei

no P: (in answering a question) m̀; meih * **have no, there is (or are) no** FV: móuh * **no . . .-ing** FV: m̀jéun; bātjéun ~ sihkyīn * **no longer** Patt: m̀ . . . la · m̀ hái Hèunggóng la * **nobody** PH: móuh yàhn * **no entry** PH: m̀jéun yahp; bātjéun sáiyahp * **no matter (how, if, what etc.)** MA: mòuhleuhn (dím / géi; mātyéh . . .) * **no means** PH: móuh faatjí * **no more** PH: móuh la * **no need** CV/AV: m̀sái * **no parking** PH: m̀jéun tìhngchè * **there is no rain** PH: móuh yúh * **no use** SV: móuhyuhng * **no wonder** PH: m̀gwaaidāk

nob N: ❶ (head) tàuh (M: go) ❷ seuhnglàuhyàhn (M: go)

Nobel prizes N: Nohkbuiyíh jéunggām

nobility SV: gòugwai; gòuseuhng N: gwaijuhk

noble SV: gòugwai; chìnggòu N: gwaijuhk * **noble-minded** SV: gòuseuhng

nobody PH: móuh yàhn

nocturnal SV: yeh Adj. PH: yehgāan ge

nod ❶ VO: dímtàuh; ngahptáu ❷ PH: (doze) hāp ngáahnfan

Noel N: Singdaanjit

nog N: ❶ muhkdēng (M: háu)

noggin PH: sai būi (M: jek, go)

nohow Patt: yātdī dōu m̀

noise N: sèng * make a noise FV: chòuh; chòuhcháau

noisy SV: chòuh

nomad PH: yàuhmuhk màhnjuhk

nominal PH: mìhngyihseuhng ge; yáuh mìhng mòuh saht ge

nominate FV: tàihmìhng; jídihng; tèuijin

nominative ATT/N: jyúgaak

nominee PH: beih tàihmìhng ge yàhn; beih yahmmìhng ge yàhn (M: go)

non P: m̀; bāt; fēi; mòuh * non-aligned Adj. PH: bāt git màhng (ge) * non-attendance FV: kyutjihk * non-effective Adj. PH: mòuh haauh ge * non-essential Adj. PH: m̀juhngyiu ge * non-member N: fēi wúiyùhn * non-metal N: fēi gàmsuhk * non-stop ATT/SV: jihktùng(ge) PH: jùngtòuh m̀tìhngge

nonchalant Adj. PH: mohk bāt gwàansàm ge; láahngdaahmge

none FV: mòuh PH: yātdī dōu mòuh * none the less A: juhnghaih

nonintervention FV: m̀gònyuh (noihjing)

nonproductive PH: m̀nàhnggau sàngcháan ge;

fèisàngcháansing ge

nonsense N: faiwá * talk nonsense VO: faat ngāpfūng; faat ngahmwah

nonsuit VO: chitsiusoujuhng

noodle N: ❶ (of people) chéunyàhn (M: go) ❷ mihn

nook N: goklōk (M: go)

noon TW: ngaanjau (M: go) * the noon of life N: jongnìhn

noose N: tousok (M: go)

nor see neither

norm N: kwàifaahn; bìujéun

normal SV: ❶ (natural) jingsèuhng ❷ (usual) pìhngsèuhng * a normal school N: sīfaahn hohkhaauh (M: gàan) * normal temperature N: jingsèuhng wàndouh

north DW/BF: bāk * North America N: Bākméih (jàu) * North China N: Wàhbāk * North Pole N: Bākgihk * northward(s) CV/FV: heungbāk * northwinds N: bākfūng

northeast DW: dùngbāk * a northwest wind N: dùngbākfūng

northern ATT/PW: bākfòng(ge) * northern regions PW: bākfòng * northern side DW: bākbihn * northern climate N: bākfòngheihauh * northernspeech N: bākfòngwá (M: júng) * northerner N: bākfòngyàhn (M: go); bākfònglóu (vulgar); ngoihgōnglóu (vulgar)

northwest DW: sàibāk

Norwegian Adj. PH: Nòh-wāi ge N: ❶ Nòhwāiyàhn (M: go) ❷ Nòhwāiwá

nose N: beihgō (M: go) ✻ **running nose** VO: làuh beihséui; làuh beihtai ✻ **stuffed nose** N/FV: beihsāk ✻ **turn up one's nose at** RV: táiṁhéi ✻ **nose bleed** VO: làuhbeihhyut

nosy SV: jyùsih; baatgwa

nostalgia N: sìhèungbehng VO/SV: wàaihgauh

nostril N: beihgōlūng (M: go)

not A: ṁ ✻ **not very** Adv. PH: ṁhaihgéi ✻ **do not** AV: (imperative) ṁhóu ✻ **not much** PH: móuhmāt ✻ **not yet** P: meih ✻ **not a bit** Patt: yātdī dōu ṁ (FV/SV) ✻ **not certain** A: ṁyātdihng ✻ **not for sale** N: fēimaaihbán ✻ **not only . . . but also . . .** Patt: ṁjí . . . juhng . . . ✻ **not to be used for, not to be taken** Patt: ṁhaih ngoilàih . . . ge ✻ **not to speak of** PH: ṁsái góng ✻ **not at all (don't mention it)** PH: ṁsái haakhei ✻ **not used to sth.** PH: ṁjaahpgwaan . . .; meih jaahpgwaan . . .

notable Adj. PH: jyumìhng ge PH: jìmìhng yàhnsih (M: wái) N: mìhngyàhn (M: go)

notary N: gùngjing yàhn (M: go)

notation N: fùhhóu (M: go; tou)

note N: ❶ (short letter) jihtìuh (M: jèung) ✻ **drop me a note** PH: làuh jèung jihtìuh béi ngóh ❷ bātgei ✻ **take notes** VO: gei bātgei ✻ **make a note of** RV: geidài ✻ **notebook** N: bātgeibóu; bóujái (M: bún, bouh) ❸

(paper money) ngàhnjí (M: jèung) ❹ (musical sound) yām ❺ (written musical symbol) yām fùh (M: go) FV/N: (comment) jyugáai FV: (observe) jyuyi

noted Adj. PH: jyumìhngge; jìmìhng ge ✻ **be noted for . . .** PH: yàn . . . jyumìhng

noteworthy SV: hínjyu (ge)

nothing PH: móuhyéh ✻ **nothing to do** Patt: móuh yéh jouh ✻ **nothing to wear** Patt: móuh sāam jeuk ✻ **come to nothing** PH: sìhngwàih paauyíng FV: sātbaaih ✻ **for nothing** A: baahkbaahk PH: ṁsái chín SV: mìhnfai ✻ **have nothing to do with** PH: tùhng . . . móuh gwaanhaih ✻ **nothing but** PH: jíyáuh; jí bātgwo

notice N: ❶ (notification) tùngjì; tùngjísyù ❷ (posted announcement) tùnggou; bougou FV: jyuyi; làuhsàm(dou) ✻ **take no notice of** FV: ṁjyuyi; ṁléih ✻ **notice-board** N: bougoubáan (M: faai)

noticeable SV: yihgin ge; hínjyu ge

notification N: tùnggou; tùngjídāan; bougousyù

notify FV: tùngjì

notion N: yigin; gingáai; gùnnihm

notorious IE: sìngmìhng-lòhngjihk (ge)

notwithstanding MA: sèuiyìhn

nought Nu: lìhng FV: móuh ✻ **bring to nought** IE: fawàihwùyáuh

noun N: mìhngchìh (M: go)

nourish FV: (to raise) yéuhngyuhk SV: jìyéuhng; jìbóu PH: yáuh yìhngyéuhng ✻ **nourishing food** N: bóubán

nourishment N: sihkmaht; yìhngyéuhngbán

novel SV: sànwihng; sànkèih N: síusyut (M: bún)

novelist N: síusyutgā (M: go)

novelty SV: sànkèih; sànwihng PH: sànkèih ge sihmaht

November TW: sahpyāt yuht

novice SV/N: sàangsáu PH: chòhohk ge yàhn (M: go); chògō; sànjái

noviciate (novitiate) PH: chòhohkkèih; ginjaahpkèih

now TW: yìhgā; muhkchìhn; yihnjoih ✻ **from now on** PH: yàuh yìhgā hòichí; chùhng gàm jihauh ✻ **just now** MA: ngāamngāam ✻ **up to now** PH: dou yìhgā ✻ **now and then** PH: sìhbātsìh; noihbāt-nói; gáuﬂgáu ✻ **now or never** IE: (lit.) mahtsātlèuhngèi; gèiwuihnàahnjoi

nowadays TW: yìhgā; sìh-hah

noway(s) Patt: yātdī dōu ﬂ

nowhere PH: ❶ móuh deihfòng ❷ (unknown place) ﬂjìdou ge deihfòng ✻ **be nowhere** FV: syù PH: yāt mòuh só dāk ✻ **get nowhere** PH: yāt sih mòuh sìhng

noxious Adj. PH: yáuh hoih ge; yáuh duhk ge

nozzle N: gúnjéui; panjéui

(M: go)

nuance PH: (of shade, of meaning, opinion, colour etc.) saiméih ge chàbiht

nub, nubble PH: (small tumour) sai ge láu (M: go) N: (coll.) (of a story, affair) yiudím (M: go)

nuclear Adj. PH: hahtsàm ge; yùhnjíhaht ge; hahtjí ge ✻ **nuclear bomb** N: hahtjídáan (M: go) ✻ **nuclear energy** N: hahtnàhng ✻ **nuclear free zone** PW: mòuhhahtkèui ✻ **nuclear weapon** PH: hahtjí móuhhei

nucleus N: haht; hahtsàm; hahtjí (M: go)

nude ATT: lótái ✻ **picture of a nude** N: lótáiwá (M: fūk) ✻ **statue of a nude** N: lótái-jeuhng (M: go) ✻ **in the nude** PH: cheklóló ge

nudge PH: hehnghēng tèuiháh

nudist N: lótáiwahnduhngjé (M: go)

nugget N: gàmfaai; kongfaai (M: gauh)

nuisance PH: màhfàahn sih; tóuyim ge yàhn/yéh

null Adj. PH: mòuhhaauh ge ✻ **null and void** SV: (legal) mòuhhaauh

nullify FV: faihei; chéuisīu

numb SV: bei; màhbei Adj. PH: màhmuhk ge; móuh gámgok ge

number N: ❶ (how many) sou; soumuhk ❷ (of telephone, lottery etc.) houhmáh SP (M: (number) daih . . . (houh) VO:

geihouhsou; pìnhouhmáh * **a
large number of** SV: **hóudò** *
a hot number PH: yìhtmún fo
* **house number** N: (door
plate) mùhnpàaih (M: go) *
wrong number PH: ❶
houhmáh m̀ngāam; houhmáh
chojó ❷ (in answering a wrong
telephone call) daapchosin

numberless PH: mòuh sou
gam dò; bāthósìngsóu (ge)

numeral N: soumuhkjih (M:
go)

numerous SV: hóudò;
daaihpài PH: mòuh haahn gam
dò

numskull N: bahnyàhn (M:
go)

nun N: ❶ (Catholic) sàunéui
(M: go) ❷ (Buddhist) nèihgū;
sīgū (M: go)

nunnery N: ❶ (Catholic)
sàu(néui)yún (M: gàan) ❷ (Buddhist) sīgūngām (M: gàan)

nuptial Adj. PH: fànyàn ge
* **nuptials** N: fànláih VO:
gitfàn

nurse N: ❶ (looking after patients) wuhsih; hònwuh (M: go)
❷ (looking after babies)
bóumóuh (M: go) VO: (to feed a
baby) waináaih FV: ❶ (hold)
póuh (children) ❷ hònwuh;
wuhléih (patients) ❸ pùihjihk
(plants) * **headnurse** N:
wuhsihjéung (M: go) * **nursemaid** N: bóumóuh (M: go)

nurs(e)ling N: yìngyih; bìhbī (M: go)

nursery N: tokyìhsó (M:
gàan)

nurture FV: yéuhngyuhk;
gaauyéuhng N: yìhngyéuhngbán (M: júng)

nut N: (with shell) ngaahng-
hokgwó (M: go); gwóyàhn *
chestnut N: fùngléut; leuhtjí
(M: nāp) * **peanut** N: fāsāng
(M: nāp) * **walnut** N:
hahptòuh (M: go) * **a hard nut
to crack** PH: ❶ (thing) gīksáu
ge sih ❷ (person) nàahn
deuifuh ge yàhn

nutrient Adj. PH: yáuh
yìhngyéuhngge N: yìhng-
yéuhngbán (M: júng)·

nutriment N: yìhngyéuhngbán

nutriology N: yìhngyéuhng-
hohk

nutrition N: yìhngyéuhng
(jokyuhng); yìhngyéuhngbán
(M: júng) * **want of nutrition**
PH: yìhngyéuhngbātjūk; kyutfaht yìhngyéuhng

nutritious Adj. PH: yáuh
yìhngyéuhng ge

nutritive Adj. PH: yáuh
(gwàan) yìhngyéuhngge N:
yìhngyéuhngbán (M: júng)

nutshell N: ngaahnggwóhok
(M: go) * **in a nutshell** PH: yāt
geui syutwah jauh haih . . .;
gáandàan gám góng

nylon N: nèihlùhng

nymph N: ❶ (in old Greek
and Roman stories) néuihsàhn;
sìnnéui (M: go) ❷ (lit.)
méihnéuih

O

o P: aìhyàh, òh

oaf SV/N: baahkchì (M: go) N: ❶ (awkward lout) chòuyàhn (M: go) ❷ (stupid person) chéun yàhn (M: go)

oak N: jeuhngsyuh (M: pò)

oakum N: màhsī (M: tiùh)

oar N: jéung, syùhnjéung (M: jì); lóuh (M: tiùh) FV: pàh (boat) ~ *téhng*

oasis N: luhkjàu (M: go)

oat(s) N: yinmahk ✳ **oat meal** N: mahkpín; mahkpèih

oath N: saih; saihyeuk (M: go) VO: saihyuhn FV/N: jaujo ✳ **make an oath** VO: saihyuhn; faatsaih ✳ **take an oath** VO: syùnsaih ✳ **ceremony of taking an oath** N: syùnsaihláih

obedience FV: fuhkchùhng ✳ **in obedience to** FV: jèunjiu

obedient SV: (children to adult) tèngwah FV: ❶ seuhnchùhng (superior) ❷ haauseuhn (parents)

obese PH: hóu fèih SV: chìfèih

obey FV: fuhkchùhng ✳ **obey orders** PH: fuhkchùhng mihnglihng ✳ **obey the teacher** PH: tèng sìnsàang wah ✳ **obey my instruction** PH: tèng ngóh ge fànfu

obituary (notice) N: fuh-màhn (M: fahn, dyuhn)

object N: ❶ (thing) yéh (M: gihn) ❷ (purpose) muhkdīk (M: go) ❸ (of linguistics) bànyúh FV/N: (oppose) fáandeui; kongyíh

objection FV/N: fáandeui; kongyíh ✳ **no objection to** FV: m̀fáandeui ✳ **make an objection to** PH: bíusih fáandeui

objective SV: haakgùn N: muhkbìu; muhkdīk (M: go)

oblation N: jaimaht; gung-maht; fuhnghin

obligation N: yihmouh

obligatory Adj. PH: (required by law, rule or custom) bītsèui (jouh) ge

oblige FV: ❶ yiukàuh (PN to do sth.) · *Ngóh ~ kéuih béifàan dī chín ngóh* ❷ (compelled) beihbīk ✳ **be obliged** FV: gámgīk; gámjeh ✳ **be obliged to (do)** PH: yātdihng yiu (jouh)

obliging Adj. PH: chànchit ge; gwàansàm yàhn ge

oblique SV: (sloping) che A: (indirectly) gaanjip

obliterate FV: ❶ chèuih-heui; sàanheui ❷ (destroy) sìumiht

oblivion FV: (forgotten) beihwàihmòhng; màaihmuht

oblivious FV: mòhnggei (one's surroundings) ~ *jàuwàih ge wàahngíng* SV: gihnmòhng

oblong Adj. PH: chèuhng-fōng ge

obnoxious Adj. PH: lihng yàhn tóuyim ge

oboe N: (music) sèungwòhng-gún (M: jì)

obscene SV: ❶ (of a man) hàahmsāp ❷ (of a woman) yàhmdohng

obscure PH: ❶ mùhng chàh chàh ❷ (not well known) mchèutméng ge

obsequies N: jongláih; sòngláih (M: go)

observation FV: gùnchaat N: ❶ gùnchaatlihk ❷ (opinion) yigin * **under observation** PH: béi yàhn gàamsih (gán)

observatory N: tìnmàhntòih; heijeuhngtòih

observe FV: gùnchaat; tái * **observe the law** PH: jèunsáu faatleuht * **observer** N: gùnchaatgà; pìhngleuhnyùhn (M: go)

obsess FV: kwanyíu; chìhnjyuh

obsolete Adj. PH: gwosìhge; gwohei ge

obstacle N: jeungngoih * **obstacle race** PH: jeungngoih choipáau

obstetrics N: cháanfō

obstinate SV: wàahngu; gujàp; gwahtkéuhng

obstruct FV: jóngoih; jójyuh

obstruction N: jeungngoih FV: fùngsó

obtain RV: dākdóu

obtrude PH: bīkyàhn jipsauh

obtuse SV: deuhn; chìhdeuhn

obviate FV: pàaihchèuih; sìuchèuih (dangers, difficulties etc.)

obvious SV: mìhnghín; chìngchó

obviously A: hínyìhn

occasion N: ❶ (situation) chèuhnghahp (M: go) ❷ (thing) sih (M: gihn) ❸ (time) sìhhauh (M: go) * **big occasion** N: daaihsih (M: gihn) * **happy occasion** N: (as a wedding, birthday etc.) héisih (M: gihn) * **as occasion offers** PH: yāt yáuh sìhgèi * **for the occasion** A: làhmsìh * **give occasion to** FV: yáhnhéi * **on occasion** MA: yáuhsìh * **take occasion** CV: sìhnggèi

occasional Adj. PH: ngáuhyìhn ge * **occasionally** A: ngáuhyìhn

occident ATT/PW: sàifòng

occlude FV: baisāk; jósāk

occult Adj. PH: ❶ (mysterious) sàhnbei ge ❷ (supernatural) chìu jihyìhn ge

occupant PH: jimyáuh yàhn; háisyu jyuh ge yàhn

occupation FV: ❶ jimyáuh ❷ (by army) jimlíhng N: (business or work) jīkyihp (M: júng)

occupy FV: ❶ jimjó; yuhngjó (time or space) ❷ jimlíhng (a place by military action) * **occupied** PH: (place) yáuh yàhn SV: (busy) mdākhàahn

occur FV: ❶ (take place or happen) faatsàng ~ mātyéh sih a?/yáuh mātyéh sih ~ a ? ❷ (come to one's mind) séungdou; séunghéi ❸ (be found) chēutyìhn

occurence N: sih; sihgon (M: gihn) * **common occurence** PH: pìhngsèuhng ge sih

ocean N: yèuhng; daaihhói; hóiyèuhng (M: go) * **Pacific Ocean** N/PW: Taaipìhngyèuhng * **Atlantic Ocean** N/PW: Daaihsàiyèuhng * **Indian Ocean** N/PW: Yandouhyèuhng

o'clock M: dím; dímjūng * **five o'clock** TW: ńgh dímjūng * **at what o'clock?** PH: géi dímjūng a?

octagon N: baatbīnyìhng (M: go)

octagonal Adj. PH: baatgokge

octave N: ❶ (music) daihbaatyām ❷ (poetry) baathòhngsīgeui

October TW: sahpyuht

octopus N: baatjáauyùh; jèungyùh (M: jek, tìuh)

oculist N: ngáahnfō yīsāng (M: go)

odd N: (number) dàansou (Maths.) gèisou Adj. PH: (extra, not matching) dāandīng ge SV: (peculiar) gúgwaai * **at odd times** PH: dākhàahn gójahnsìh * **odd job** N: sáangūng (M: fahn)

oddity SV: kèihgwaai N: ❶ (person) gwaai yàhn (M: go) ❷ (thing) kèihsih (M: gihn)

odds PH: (chances) hónàhng ge gèiwuih SV: (not even) m̀pìhnggwàn N: (betting) chàngáak * **at odds** FV: jàngjāp; bātwòh * **make odds even** RV: làaipìhng * **odds and ends** PH: lìhngseui jaahpmaht; sápsìng ge yéh * **the odds are** A: daaihkoi; hónàhng

ode N: juhnggō; fu (M: sáu)

odious SV: tóuyim; cháungok

odometer N: léihchìhngbíu (M: go)

odo(u)r N: meih (M: jahm) * **bad odour** N: chaumeih (M: jahm) * **good odour** N: hèungmeih (M: jahm)

of P: (belonging to) ❶ (N) ge (N) • *Sàhn ~ ngoi* (the love of God) ❷ (N) dī (pl.N) • *ngóh pàhngyáuh ~ saimānjái* (the children of my friend) CV: ❶ (location) hái . . . (ge) . . . PW1 hái PW2 (ge) DW • *Gànàhdaaih hái Méihgwok bākbihn* ❷ (concerning) gwàanyù Patt: (expressing time before the hour) jàang . . . -dím • *(4:45) ~ sahpńgh fānjūng ńgh ~* * **a table of wood** PH: yāt jèung muhk tói * **a cup of tea** PH: yāt būi chàh * **know of** FV: jìdou * **of course** PH: gánghaih lā * **of late** MA: gahnlòih

off FV: ❶ chèuihjó (clothings) ❷ sàan(jó) (TV, radio, tap etc.) ❸ lātjó (buttons) Patt: juhng jàang . . . jauhhaih . . . ~ *sàamyaht ~ háausih (la)* * **be well off** SV: yáuhchìhn * **off and on** Patt: yáuhsìh . . . yáuhsìh . . . * **off duty** VO: fong(jó) gùng * **right off** A: jīkhāak

offal BF: (of a chicken, pig etc.) -jaahp • *gāi ~* , *jyū ~*

offence (offense) N: gwocho * **no offence** PH: m̀hóu gingwaai

offend FV: dākjeuih * **offender** N: faahnyàhn (M: go)

offensive Adj. PH: ❶ tóuyimge ❷ (not well-behaved) móuh láihmaauhge N: gùngsai * **assume the offensive** PH:

chóichéui gùngsai

offer FV: ❶ chēut (a price) ❷ tàihchēut; bíusih (to help PN) ❸ fuhnghin (to God) ✳ **make an offer** FV: tàihyíh

offering FV: tàihgùng N: ❶ (sacrifice) jai (M: go) ❷ (money offered in church) fuhnghin; hìngǎm ✳ **a burnt offering** N: (biblical) fàahnjai

offhand A: jīksìh; jīkjihk SV: (rude) tòhngdaht; chòulóuh

office N: sējihlàuh; baahngùngsāt; baahnsihchyu (M: go) ✳ **office boy** N: hauhsāang (M: go) ✳ **office building** N: baahngùng daaihlàuh (M: joh) ✳ **office hours** PH: baahngùng sìhgaan ✳ **office supplies** N: màhngeuih ✳ **the Foreign Office** N: (British) Ngoihgāaubouh

officer N: ❶ (of govt.) gùnyùhn; gùngmouhyùhn ❷ (of company, society, etc.) jīkyùhn ❸ (of army) gwàngùn ✳ **officer in charge** N: jyúyahm (M: go) ✳ **commanding officer** N: jífàigùn; sìlihnggùn (M: go)

official N: ❶ (of government) gùnyùhn (M: go) ❷ (administrator) hàhngjingyàhnyùhn (M: go) Adj. PH: ❶ (formal) jingsīk ge ❷ (public, not personal) gùnggā ge ✳ **official circle** N: gùnchèuhng; jinggaai ✳ **official gazette** N: hinbou ✳ **official interpreter** N: fàanyihkgùn (M: go) ✳ **official letter** N: gùngmàhn (M: fahn) ✳ **official receipt** PH: jingsīk sàugeui (M: jèung) ✳ **official report** PH: gùnfòng bougou (M: fahn) ✳ **official title** N: gùnhàahm (M: go)

officiate FV: ❶ dàamyahm

(a post, e.g. a chairman) ❷ jyúchìh (a meeting or a ceremony)

offset FV: dáisìu; nèihbóu N/FV: (printing) gàauyan; òsīk

offshore PH: heunghói; gahnhói ✳ **offshore fisheries** PH: gahnhói yùhyihp

offspring N: jísyùn; hauhdoih

often A: sìhsìh; jàusìh; sìhsèuhng ✳ **how often** PH: géinoih yāt chi

ogre PH: sihkyàhn (yíu)mò (M: go)

oh P: ò; àihyàh

oil N: yàuh (M: jēun, gun) VO: chàhyàuh; gàyáu ✳ **lubricating oil** N: gèiyáu; waahtgèiyáu ✳ **peanut oil** N: fàsāngyàuh (M: jēun, gun) ✳ **oil-mill** N: yàuhchóng (M: gàan) ✳ **oil-painting** N: yàuhwá (M: fùk) ✳ **oil field** N: yàuhtìhn (M: faai) ✳ **oil plant** N: lìhnyàuhchóng (M: gàan) ✳ **pour oil on fire** PH: fóseuhng gà yàuh ✳ **strike oil** PH: gwahtchēut sehkyàuh; faatjóchòih

oily SV: yàuhneih

ointment N: yeuhkgōu (M: hahp, jì, jēun)

okay (ok, o.k.) P: dāk AV: hóyíh ✳ **get an ok** PH: dākdóu tùhngyi

old SV: ❶ (not young) lóuh ❷ (not new) gauh ❸ (ancient) gúlóuh ❹ (long known) lóuh (friend) Adj. PH: (former) gauhsìh ge (colleagues, students) ✳ **(five) years old** (Nu) M: (ńgh) seui ✳ **how old are you?** PH: néih géidō seui a? * **old-fashioned** SV: gúlóuh ge * **old hand** N/SV: lóuhsáu * **old man** N: baakyēgūng (M: go) * **old woman** N: baakyēpó (M: go) * **old people's home** N: lóuhyàhnyún (M: gàan) * **Old Testament** N: Gauhyeuk (chyùhnsyù)

oleander N: gaapjūktòuh (M: pò)

oleomargarin(e) N: yàhnjouhngàuhyàuh (M: hahp)

olive N: ❶ (tree) gaamláamsyuh (M: pò) ❷ (fruit) baahkláam; láam (M: nāp)

Olympics N: Ngoulàhmpāthāk wahnduhngwúi; Ngouwahnwúi; Saiwahnwúi (M: go, chi)

omega N: ❶ (the end) jùngguhk ❷ (biblical) ngòhmùihngaat

omelette N: (tr.) ngāmliht

omen N: yuhsiuh (M: go) PH: hínchēut . . . ge yuhsiuh

ominous Adj. PH: yuhsiuh ge; bātchèuhng ge

omission FV: ❶ (intentionally) sáangleuhk ❷ (unintentionally) wàihlauh

omit FV: sáangheui; lauh

omnibus N: gùngguhngheichè (M: ga)

omnipotence PH: chyùhnnàhng; mòuhhaahn ge lihkleuhng

omnipotent Adj. PH: mòuhsóbātnàhngge; chyùhnnàhngge; maahnnàhng ge

omnipresent Adj. PH:

mòuhsóbātjoih ge

omniscient Adj. PH: mòuhsóbātjì ge

omnivorous Adj. PH: jaahpsihk ge; mātyéh dōu sihkge

on PH: ❶ (resting on top of) hái (N) seuhngbihn ❷ (indicating time) hái TW CV: ❶ (about) gwàanyù ❷ (close to) gahnjyuh PW CV/N: (expressing the basis for sth) gàngeui CV/FV: (indicating direction) heung * **and so on** PH: dángdáng * **be well on** PH: jeunhàhng seuhnleih * **on and on** Adv. PH: gaijuhkbātdyuhn gám

once NuM: (one time) yātchi A: ❶ (in the past) chàhnggìng ❷ (even for one time) yāt daan * **once more** PH: joi yāt chi * **at once** A: jīkhāk/jīkhāak * **not even once** PH: yāt chi dōu meih sigwo * **all at once** A: dahtyìhn; fātyìhn * **once and again** Adv. PH: joi sàam gám * **once for all** PH: yātlòuhwíhngyaht * **once in a while** MA: gaanjùng * **once upon a time** A: chùhngchìhn

oncology N: júngláuhohk (M: fō)

oncoming Adj. PH: ❶ làihgán ge; jipgahn ge ❷ (promising) yáuh chìhntòuh ge

one Nu: yāt (M) * **one-act play** N: duhkmohkkehk (M: chēut) * **all in one** PH: chyùhntái yātji * **for one thing** MA: sáusìn * **in one word** PH: júngyìhyìhnjì; júngjì * **no one** PH: móuh yàhn * **one after another** PH: yāt go yāt go gám; luhkjuhkgám * **one by one** PH: yāt go yāt go

gám * **one half** N: yātbun *
one man exhibition PH: go
yàhn jínláahmwúi (M: go) *
one or two PH: yātléuhng go
* **oneself** N: jihgéi * **one
tenth** PH: sahpfahnjiyāt *
oneness A/SV: yātji SV: yùhnjíng * **by one's own hand** A:
chànsáu * **one and only** Adj.
PH: wàihyāt ge * **one
another** A: wuhsēung; béichí
* **one-sided** Adj. PH: dàan-
fòngmihnge; pinmihn ge *
one-way ATT/N: dàan-
chìhng

onerous Adj. PH: màhfàahnge; fàahnjuhng ge * **for
onerous** PH: waih jihgéi

oneself N: jihgéi A: chànjih
* **of oneself** Adv. PH: jihfaat
gám

onion N: yèuhngchūng (M:
go) * **green onion** N: chūng
(M: tìuh)

onlooker N: muhkgīkjé;
pòhnggùnjé (M: go)

only Adj. PH: ❶ (one, single)
wàihyāt ge ❷ (best) jeui hóuge;
jeui sīkhahpge A: ❶ (no more
than) jíhaih ❷ (only if) chèuihfēi
BF: (only existing one) duhk-
~ jí * **only if** Patt: daahn-
yuhn * **not only ... but (also)**
Patt: ... m̀jí ... juhng ... *
only just MA: ngāamngāam

onrush FV: máahngchùng
FV/N: gāplàuh

onset FV: gùnggīk PH: yáuhlihkge hòichí

onslaught FV/N: dahtgīk;
máahnggùng

onto PH: séuhngdou . . .
seuhngbihn

onward(s) A: heungchìhn

FV: chìhnjeun

oolong N: wùlúngchàh

ooze FV: samchēut; sitlauh
N: (on the riverbed) nàihjèung;
yúhnnàih

opal N: màaungáahnsehk (M:
nāp)

opaque Adj. PH: ❶ m̀tau-
mìhng ge ❷ (dull) chìhdeuhn ge

open SV/FV: (public) gùnghòi
SV: (frank) táansēut; táanbaahk
Adj. PH: ❶ (not settled) meih
gáaikyut ge (problem) ❷ (not
protected) bātchitfòhng ge (city) RV: dáhòi (window, door,
book etc.) VO: (ready for daily
business) hòimùhn * **open
(start) a meeting** VO: hòiwúi
* **open a lottery** VO: hòichói
* **open fire** VO: hòifó * **open
letter** N: gūnghòiseun (M: fùng)
* **open up waste land** FV:
hòifòng * **open your eyes
wide** PH: maakdaaih sèung
ngáahn * **be open to** PH: deui
. . . hòifong * **in open** SV/FV:
gùnghòi * **in the open (air)**
ATT: louhtin ATT/PW: wuh-
ngoih * **open up** FV: hòifaat
* **open sea** N: gùnghói *
open-armed Adj. PH:
yìhtsìhng ge * **open-book** Adj.
PH: hòigyún ge * **open-
handed** SV: hóngkoi * **open-
hearted** SV: táanbaahk;
sìhnghán

opening N: ❶ (position vacant) hùngkyut (M: go) ❷ (open
space) háu (M: go) FV/N: (beginning) hòichí VO: (opening of a
shop) hòimohk

openly Adv. PH: gùnghòi
gám; táanbaahk gám

opera N: ❶ (Cantonese)
daaihhei (M: chēut) ❷ (European) gòkehk (M: chēut) *
opera house N: gòkehkkyún

(M: gàan)

operate FV/N: chòujok FV: hòiduhng VO: (surgical) duhng sáuseuht ✻ **operate on** SV: ginhaauh VO: (surgical) hòidōu

operation N: ❶ (working) jokyuhng; chòujok ❷ (piece of work) gùngjok (M: gihn) ❸ (surgical) sáuseuht (M: go) VO: (military) jokjin PH: gwànsihyínjaahp ✻ **bring operation into** PH: tàuhyahp sàngcháan ✻ **come (go) into operation** PH: hòichísahthàhng; sànghaauh

operator N: chòujokyùhn; gùngjokjé (M: go) ✻ **telephone operator** N: (dihnwá) jipsinsàng (M: go)

opthalmic Adj. PH: ngáahn ge; ngáahnfō ge

opthalmologist N: ngáahnfō yīsāng (M: go)

opiate N: ngàpinjāi; màhjeuijāi

opinion N: ❶ yigin (M: go) ❷ (estimation) pìhngga N/FV: jyújèung (M: go) ✻ **be of (the) opinion that** FV: yíhwàih; sèungseun ✻ **give one's opinion on** PH: deui . . . faatbíu yigin ✻ **have a bad (good) opinion of** PH: deui . . . pìhngga dài (gòu) ✻ **in my opinion** PH: jiu ngóh ge yigin ✻ **opinion poll (survey)** N: màhnyichāakyihm (M: chi, go)

opinionated PH: jihyíhwàihsih; gujāpgéigin

opium N: ngàpin; ngàpinyīn ✻ **opium war** N: ngàpin jinjàng

opponent Adj. PH: deuikong ge; fáandeui ge N:

fáandeuijé; deuisáu (M: go)

opportune Adj. PH: ❶ (just right) ngāamngāam hóu ge ❷ (in time) kahpsìh ge

opportunism N: gèiwuihjyúyih ✻ **opportunist** N: gèiwuihjyúyihjé (M: go)

opportunity N: gèiwuih; sìhgèi (M: go) ✻ **get an opportunity** PH: dākdóu gèiwuih ✻ **take an opportunity** PH: leihyuhnggèiwuih; je (chan) nīgo gèiwuih

oppose FV: ❶ fáandeui (e.g. one's suggestion) ❷ fáankong (e.g. government) ✻ **as opposed to** PH: tùhng . . . sèungfáan

opposite PW: (facing) deuimihn ATT: (different, reverse) sèungfáan ✻ **be opposite to** PH: ❶ (be against) tùhng . . . deuilahp ❷ hái . . . deuimihn

opposition FV: ❶ fáandeui ❷ deuikong (enemies, government) ✻ **opposition party** N: fáandeuidóng (M: go); fáandeui paai

oppress FV: ngaatbīk; ngaatjai (e.g. people) ✻ **be oppressed with (anxiety)** PH: béi (yàuleuih) sókwan ✻ **the oppressed** PH: beihngaatbīkjé (M: go)

oppression FV: ngaatbīk SV: chàhmmuhn ✻ **oppressor** N: ❶ ngāatbīkjé (M: go) ❷ (tyrant) bouhgwàn (M: go)

opt FV/N: syúnjaahk; kyutjaahk

optician N: ❶ yihmgwōngsī (M: go) ❷ (merchant) ngáahngéngsèung (M: go)

optics N: gwònghohk

optimism SV: lohkgùn; lohktìn N: lohkgùnjyúyih

optimistic SV: lohkgùn Adj. PH: yáuh hèimohng ge

optimum PH: jeui gàai tiuhgín Adj. PH: jeui hóu ge; jeui sīkhahp ge

option N/FV: syúnjaahk PH: ❶ (right of choosing) syúnjaahk-kyùhn ❷ (thing that is chosen) syúnjaahkmaht ❸ (commercial use) máaihmaaih ge dahk-kyùhn ✳ **at one's option** PH: chèuihyi; chèuih (bín) . . . lā ✳ **have no option but to (do)** PH: chèuihjó . . . jìngoih, móuh daihyihdī baahnfaat; fèi . . . bāthó ✳ **make one's option** PH: jeunhàhng syúnjaahk

optional PH: chèuih néih syúnjaahk; chèuih néih yiu m̀ yiu N: (course) syúnsàufō (M: fō)

opulence SV: fuyuh; fùngfu

opus N: jyujok; ngohkkūk (M: sáu)

or A: ❶ (only used in answers) waahkjé ❷ (between choices in questions) dihng; yīkwaahk ✳ **either . . . or . . .** Patt: waahkhaih . . . waahkhaih . . .; yáthaih . . . yáthaih . . . ✳ **or else** MA: yeuhkm̀haih; fáujāk ✳ **or so** A: daaihyeuk

oracle N: sàhnyuh; káisih; yuhyihn (M: go)

oral Adj. PH: ❶ háutàuh-seuhng ge; háugóng ge ❷ (anatomy) háubouhge ✳ **oral report** PH: háutàuh seuhng ge bougou ✳ **oral examination** N: háusi; háusíh (M: chi, go)

orange N: ❶ cháang (M: go) ❷ (colour) cháangsīk ✳

Sunkist N: (tr.) sànkèihsih cháang (M: go) ✳ **orange juice** N: cháangjāp

oration N/FV: yínsyut (M: pìn)

orator N: yínsyutgā (M: go)

oratory N: ❶ (art of making speeches) yíngóngseuht ❷ (small chapel) síuláihbaaitòhng (M: gàan, go)

orb N: tìntái (M: go)

orbit N: gwáidouh (M: tiuh)

orchard N: gwóyùhn (M: go)

orchestra N: gúnyìhn-ngohktyùhn (M: go) gúnyìhn-ngohkdéui (M: deuih) ✳ **a symphony orchestra** N: gàauhéungngohktyùhn (M: go)

orchid N: ❶ làahnfā (M: déu; jì 'stem'; pùhn'pot') ❷ (colour) chínjísīk

ordain FV: ❶ (destine) jyudihng ❷ fùngwàih; lahp-wàih (minister etc.) Patt: fùng . . . wàih; lahp . . . wàih (minister etc.) ~ PN ~ N

ordeal PH: yihmgaakháauyihm FV/N: jitmòh

order N: ❶ chijeuih ❷ (discipline; lawful conduct) dihtjeuih; jihngòn ❸ (written direction to pay money) wuihpiu (M: jèung) ❹ (list of things wanted) dehngdāan; dehngfodāan (M: jèung) ❺ (tr.) ōdá N/FV: (command) mihnglihng FV: ❶ dehng (goods) ❷ (in a restaurant) giu (dishes) ✳ **be out of order** FV: (of machines) waaihjó SV: lyuhn ✳ **be in order** SV: jíngchàih PH: ngonseuhnjeuih; yìchijeuih ✳ **made to order** PH: dehngjouh ge ✳ **in order to**

PH: jauhhaih waih yiu * **carry out an order** PH: jāphàhng-mihnglihng * **order book** N: dehngfobóu (M: bún, bouh) * **order cheque** N: geimihng-jipiu (M: jèung)

orderly Adj. PH: yáuh diht-jeuih ge; jíngchàihge N: ❶ (army) chyùhnlihngbīng (M: go) ❷ (military hospital) kàhnmouh-yùhn; fuhkmouhbīng (M: go)

ordinal N: jeuihsou Adj. PH: seuhnjeuihge

ordinance N: ❶ (law) faat-lihng (M: go, tiuh) ❷ (regulation) tiuhlaih (M: go, tiuh)

ordinarily MA: tùngsèuhng

ordinary Adj. PH: pìhng-sèuhng ge; póutùng ge * **ordinary events** PH: pìhng-sèuhng ge sih * **ordinary meal** N: bihnfaahn (M: chàan) * **in ordinary** Adj. PH: sèuhngyahm ge * **out of the ordinary** Adj. PH: m̀pìhng-sèuhng ge

ordination N/FV: yahm-mihng PH: (religious) singjīk-sauhyahm

ordnance N: daaihpaau; gwànhaaih

ore N: kongsehk; kongmaht * **iron ore** N: titkong * **silver ore** N: ngàhnkong * **tin ore** N: sekkong * **ore-bed** N: kongchòhng

organ N: ❶ (a part of the body) heigūn (M: go) ❷ (muscial instrument) fùngkàhm (M: go, ga) * **five sense organs** PH: ńgh gūn * **internal organs** N: noihjohng * **administrative organ** PH: hàhngjing gēigwàan

organic Adj. PH: heigūn ge;

yáuhgēi ge * **organic chemistry** N: yáuhgēi fahohk

organism N: yáuhgēitái; sàngmahttái (M: go)

organization N: tyùhntái; jóujīk (M: go)

organize FV: jóujīk; chong-baahn * **organize a political party** PH: jóujīk jingdóng * **organize a club** PH: jóujīk yāt go wúi

orgie, orgy FV/N: kòhng-fūn FV/SV: fongdohng

orient N/PW: dùngfòng; ngajāu; yúhndūng

oriental N/ATT: dùngfòng (ge) * **oriental art** PH: dùngfòng ngaihseuht * **oriental culture** PH: dùngfòng-màhnfa

orientate Patt: sáidou . . . heung dùng; waih . . . dihngfòngheung

origin N/FV: (beginning) héiyùhn N: (cause) yùhnyàn; héiyàn * **the origin of a quarrel** PH: ngaaigāau ge héiyàn * **be of . . . origin** PH: héiyùhn yù . . .

original Adj. PH: ❶ (first) jeui chò ge; yùhnlòih ge ❷ (new, novel) sànyìhng ge; yùh-jungbāttùhng ge * **original draft** N: yùhngóu (M: fahn) * **original sin** N: yùhnjeuih * **original text** N: yùhnmàhn * **the original** Adj. PH: jàn ge

originally MA: búnlòih

originality N: chonggin; chongjouhlihk

originate FV: faathéi; chongbaahn * **originate from**

(in) PH: héiyùhn yù * **originator** N: chongjokjé; faathéi yàhn (M: go)

oriole N: wòhngngāng (M: jek)

ornament N: jōngsīkbán (M: gihn) FV/N: jōngsīk

ornamental Adj. PH: jōngsīkge; sāusīk ge * **ornamental moulding** PH: ngaihseuht jouhyìhng

ornate Adj. PH: jōngsīk ge; wàhlaih ge

orphan N: gùyìh (M: go)

orphanage N: gùyìhhyún (M: gàan)

orthodox Adj. PH: jingtúng ge; N: (religion) jinggaau

orthography N: jingjihfaat; bíuyàmfaat (M: go)

orthop(a)edics N: (medical) gíuyìhnghohk; gíuyìhngseuht

oscillate FV: báaiduhng; jandohng

osier N: láuhsyuh (M: pò) * **osier-bed** N: láuhyùhn (M: go)

osmosis FV: samtau PH: samtau jokyuhng

osophone; otophone N: johtinghei (M: go)

ossification FV: ❶ ngaahngfa ❷ (of thoughts) gèungfa

ostensible Adj. PH: ngoihbíu ge; bíumihn ge

ostentation FV/N: kwàyiuh N: fùngtàuhjyúyih

osteology N: ❶ (medical) gwāthohk ❷ gwātgaak

ostracize FV: làuhfong; pàaihchīk

ostrich N: tòhníuh (M: jek) * **an ostrich policy** PH: tòhníuh jingchaak

other SP. M: (more, additional) daihyihdī Adj. PH: (remaining) kèihtà ge; kèihyùh ge * **the other** SP. M: daihyihgo * **every other** CV: gaak . . . * **and others** PH: dángdáng * **at other times** MA: pìhngsìh * **each other** A: béichí; wuhsèung * **in other words** PH: wuhngeuiwahgóng * **on the other hand** PH: lihngyātfòngmihn * **other than** MA: chèuihjó

otherwise PH: yùhgwó m̀haih; yeuhkm̀haih; fáujāk * **and otherwise** PH: dángdáng * **or otherwise** PH: waahkjé sèungfáan

otic Adj. PH: yíhge

otolaryngology N: yíhbeihhàuhfòhohk

otter N: séuichaat (M: jek)

Ottoman N: Tóuyíhkèihyàhn (M: go)

ought AV: yìnggòi; yìngdòng; yìngfahn * **ought not** AV: m̀yìnggòi

ounce M: ōnsí; ōn

our Adj. PH: ngóhdeih ge

ours Adj. PH: ngóhdeih ge

ourselves PH: ngóhdeih jihgéi

oust FV: ❶ gónjáu (a person) ❷ (from office) chitjīk

out PW: (outside) ngoihbihn FV: (extinct) sīk PH: (out of)

móuhsaai FV + out: FV + chēutlàih/chēutheui · *bùn* ~ * **all out** PH: chyùhnlihk * **out size** PH: dahkdaaihyìhng * **out of date** Adj. PH: gwosih ge * **out-of-the-way** Adj. PH: pìnpìkge; síugìn ge * **out-of-control** PH: sātheui hungjai; bātnàhng hungjai

outbalance FV: gwochúhng

outbid FV: chéungsìn PH: (at an auction) chēutga gòugwo daihyihdī yàhn

outbound Adj. PH: (of a ship) hòi heui ngoihgwok ge; lèihhòi góngháu ge

outbrave FV: ❶ (resist) dáikong ❷ (despise) hìngsih

outbreak FV: ❶ (of a war etc.) baaufaat ❷ (of illness) faatjok

outburst FV: (volcano, emotion etc.) baaufaat

outcast Adj. PH: (driven out from home or society) béi gàtìhng waahkjé séhwúi wàihhei ge PH: (homeless) mòuhgàhógwài ge yàhn (M: go)

outclass PH: yúhnsìnggwo; yúhnchìugwo

outcome N/A: gitgwó (M: go) N: sìhnggwó; gitguhk (M: go)

outcry PH: ❶ (scream) daaihsèng ngaai; daaihsèng giu ❷ (public protest) gùnghòi fáandeui

outdistance FV: faaigwo

outdo FV: singgwo; hóugwo

outdoor Adj. PH: wuhngoih ge; sātngoihge * **outdoor exercises** PH: wuhngoih

wuhtduhng

outdoors PH: hái wuhngoih

outer Adj. PH: ngoihbihn ge * **outer space** PH: sìngjaihùnggàan * **the outer world** PH: ngoihgaai * **outermost** Adj. PH: jeui ngoih ge; jeui yúhn ge

outfit PH: chyùhntou jòngbeih N: yuhnggeuih (M: gihn) FV: jòngbeih; gùngkāp

outflank FV: bàauwàih; yíugwo

outgo PH: jáudāk yúhngwo; jáudākfaaigwo FV/N: jìchēut; hòisìu

outgoing Adj. PH: chēutfaat ge; lèihhòi ge * **outgoings** FV/N: hòijì

outgrow PH: ❶ sàangdāk taai daaih ❷ (leave behind bad habits etc. as one grows older) yànwaih jéungdaaih yìh fonghei (yāt dī waaih jaahpgwaan, hingcheui dángdáng)

outgrowth N: (offshoot) fànjì; jītiuh N/A: (result) gitgwó

outing N: léuihhàhng (M: chi) * **go on an outing** PH: chēutheui ngoihbihn yàuhláahm

outlandish Adj. PH: ❶ chēutkèih ge; gúgwaai ge ❷ (foreign) ngoihgwok heipaai ge

outlast Patt: béi ... noih; béi ... wuhtdāk chèuhng

outlaw N: (bad people) waaih yàhn (M: go); dáaitòuh (M: go)

outlay N: faiyuhng N/FV: fàfai; hòijì

outlet N: ❶ chēutlouh (M: tiuh); chēutháu (M: go) ❷ (commerce) sìulouh FV: faatsit (feelings, energy etc.)

outline N: ❶ (of shape or boundary) ngoihyìhng; lèuhnkok ❷ (statement of chief facts, points etc.) yiudím; daaihgòng ❸ (a general sketch of a plan etc.) daaihyi PH: waahkchēut . . . ge lèuhnkok ✳ in outline Adv. PH: koikwut gám

outlive Patt: béi . . . chèuhngmehng FV: douhgwo

outlook N: ❶ (view) gíngsīk ❷ (prospect for the future) jínmohng; chìhntòuh ❸ (person's way of looking at sth.) táifaat; gùndím ✳ the world outlook PH: saigaai gùn

outlying Adj. PH: yúhnlèihjùngsàm ge

outmatch FV: chìugwo; singgwo

outmoded Adj. PH: gwosìhge; m̀làuhhàhng ge

out number PH: souleuhng daaihgwo Patt: béi . . . dò

out-of-date SV: gwosìh; m̀hahpsìh

outpatient PH: m̀uhnchánbehngyàhn (M: go); (coll.) gāaijing (behngyàhn) (M: go)

outpost N/ATT: chìhnsaau

outpace PH: hái chūkdouh seuhng chìugwo FV: singgwo

output N: cháanleuhng; cháanbán

outrage N: (violence) bouhhahng FV: ❶ (assault sexually) kèuhnggàan; wùyuhk ❷ (treat violently) yeuhkdoih; chàmhoih

outrageous Adj. PH: gìng-

yàhn ge; chàahnbouh ge

outreach Patt: chìuchēut . . . faahnwàih PH: jim seuhngfùng FV: sànchēut

outride PH: kèhseuht hóugwo; kèhmáh faaigwo

outright SV: ❶ (completely) yùhnchyùhn ❷ (openly) táansēut

outrun FV: chìugwo Patt: béi . . . jáudāk faai

outset FV: hòichí PH: jeuichò

outshine Patt: jiudāk béi . . . gang gwòngleuhng

outside PW: ngoihbihn ✳ at the (very) outside PH: jeuidò; chùngkèihleuhng ✳ from the outside PH: chùhng ngoihbíu tái ✳ outside and in PH: léuihléuih ngoihngoih ✳ outside of Patt: hái . . . jingoih

outsider N: ngoihyàhn; guhkngoih yàhn (M: go)

outskirt(s) N/PW: gàaungoih; bīngaai

outspoken SV: sēutjihk; táanbaahk

outspread Adj. PH: jèunghòi ge; kongsaange

outstanding Adj. PH: ❶ (obvious) hínjyu ge ❷ (of performance) gihtchēut ge; bīuchēng ge ❸ (of unsolved problems) meih gáaikyut ge

outstretched Adj. PH: kongjèung ge; sànjín ge

outvote PH: piusou dògwo

outward Adj. PH: ngoihbihn ge; bíumihn ge ✳ outward eye PH: yuhkngáahn ✳ out-

ward things PH: jàuwàih saigaai * **to outward seeming** PH: chùhng bíumihn tái

outwear Patt: (last longer than) béi ... kàm (jeuk) RV: (wear out) jeuklaahn; yuhnggauh

outweigh FV: chúhnggwo; singgwo Patt: béi ... gang yáuh gajihk

outwit FV: jìsing PH: sái PN sèuhngdong * **outwit one's enemy** PH: dauji sìngdihk

outwork PH: ❶ (outdoor work) wuhngoihgùngjok ❷ (of reporters etc.) ngoihkàhngùngjok

outworn Adj PH: (of poetry) yíhfai ge; gwosihge

oval Adj PH: tóhyùhnyìhng ge * **oval face** PH: gwàjíháu-mihn

ovary N: léunchàauh (M: go)

ovation PH: yihtlihtfùn-yìhng; daaihsèngfùnfù

oven N: guhklòuh (M: go)

over FV: ❶ (more than) dògwo; chìugwo ❷ (across) gwo; FV + gwo · hàahng ~ Patt: (above) hái ... seuhng-bihn * **over sixty years old** PH: chìugwo luhksahp seui; luhksahp seui yíhseuhng; luhksahp géi seui * **go over** FV: yìhngau * **over and over** PH: yāt chi yauh yāt chi; joisàam * **do it over** PH: joi jouh yāt chi * **over an hour** PH: dím géi jūng; go géi jūngtàuh * **knock over** RV: pungditjó * **all over the world** PH: pinkahp chyùhnsai-gaai * **be over** PH: yùhn la; gwoheui la * **over all** PH:

seimihnbaatfòng * **over here (there)** PH: hái nīdouh/gódouh

overact PH: yíndākgwofó; jouhdāk gwofahn

overage Adj. PH: chìulìhng ge; gwolóuhge

overall Adj PH: chyùhn-mihnge

overalls N: ❶ (trousers) gùngyàhnfu ❷ (apron) wàih-gwán

ovebalance FV: chúhng-gwo; chiugwo PH: sātheui pìhnghàhng

overbear FV: ngaatfuhk; hākfuhk; chiugwo

overbearing Adj. PH: ngouhmaahnge; jyùnwàahngge

overboard PH: ditlohkséui

overbold SV: lóuhmóhng

overbridge N: tìnkiuh (M: tìuh)

overburden PH: jòng-joigwodò; fuhdàamgwodouh

overcast SV: ❶ (of the sky) yàmngam ❷ (fig.) sàuhmuhn

overcharge PH: (ask a high price) hòidaaihga

overcloud PH: wùwàhn-múhnbou

overcoat N: daaihlàu (M: gihn)

overcome FV: ❶ hākfuhk (difficulties) ❷ dábaaih (enemies)

overcrowd PH: bīkdākjaih

overdo PH: jouhdāk taai gwofahn

overdose PH: gwoleuhng

overdraw FV: taujì

overdress PH: jeukdāk gónggau; gwofahnjōngsīk

overdrink PH: yámdāk taai dò

overdue Adj. PH: gwokèihge; chihdou ge

overdye PH: yíhmdāk taai sàm

overeat PH: sihk dāk taai báau

overestimate PH: gúgaigwogòu

overfall N: gāplàuh; yahtséuidouh (M: tìuh)

overflow PH: múhngwotàuh FV: faanlaahm

overfulfil(l) PH: chiungáak yùhnsìhng

overfull PH: taaimúhn; taaidò

overgrowth SV: fàahnmauh PH: sàngjéunggwodouh FV/N: (medical) jàngsàng

overhand Adv. PH: géuisáugwogìnge ATT: seuhngsáu (ball) ~ bō/kàuh

overhang Patt: diuhái . . . seuhngbihn FV: (threaten) wàihip

overhasty Adj. PH: gwoyùsinggāpge SV: hìngsēut

overhaul PH: jísaigímchàh; daaihsàujíng

overhead PH: hái tàuhdéng seuhngbihn Adj. PH: gahùng ge N: (business) gúnléihfai

overhear RV: tēngdóu FV: (on purpose) tàutèng

overjoy PH: hòisàmdougihk

overland Adj. PH: luhkseuhng ge; luhklouh ge Adv. PH: gìngluhklouh

overlap FV: chùhngfūk

overlay FV: bàau; douh PH: sai tóibou (M: faai)

overleap FV: tiugwo PH: (fig.) kéihtòuh taaidò

overload FV: chiujoi PH: (of electricity) gwoleuhngfuhdihn

overlook SV: sōfāt FV: fātleuhk

overmuch PH: taai dò; gwodouh

overnight TW: (the night before) chìhn yāt máahn A/PH: tūngsīu

overpass FV: tùnggwo; yuhtgwo N: tìnkìuh (M: tìuh)

overpower FV: ❶ dá baaih (enemies) ❷ hākfuhk (difficulties)

overproduction PH: sàngcháangwosihng

overrate FV: gòugú PH: gúgaigwogòu

overreach FV: (get the better of) singgwo PH: (damage one's own interests by being too ambitious) yàn chòujìgwogáp yìh syúnsāt ✳ **overreach oneself** IE: luhnghgáaufáanjyuht

override FV: míuhsih; m̀léih

overrule FV: pàibok; fáukyut; faijí

overrun FV: ❶ (spread over) maahnyihn ❷ (occupy) jimlihng ❸ (go beyond) yuhtgwo ❹ (injure) chàmhoih

oversea(s) ATT: hóingoih ✳ **overseas Chinese** N: wàhkìuh (M: go)

oversee FV: gàamdūk; gàamsih

overseer N: gùngtáu; gàamgùng (M: go)

overset FV: fàanjyun

overshadow RV: jèjyuh

overshoes N: touhàaih (M: jek, deui)

overshoot FV: yuhtgwo PH: ❶ (shoot over a mark) sehdākgòugwotàuh ❷ (fig.) (go too far) gwofahn ✳ **overshoot mark** IE: gwosahmkèihchìh

overside Adv. PH: yàuh syùhnbīn

oversight FV: ❶ (watch over) gàamdūk; hòngún ❷ (failure to notice sth.) sòfāt; sātchaat

oversize PH: ❶ taai daaih ❷ dahkdaaihmáh

oversleep PH: fangwolùhng

oversleeve N: jauhtou (M: jek, deui)

overspend RV: yuhngjeuhn FV: chìujì

overstate FV: kwàjèung IE: yìhngwokèihsaht

overstep FV: chìugwo

overstrain PH: ❶ (use too much strength) yuhnglihkgwodouh ❷ (overtired) gwodouh-

pèihlòuh ❸ (too tense) gwodouhgánjèung

overstrung Adj. PH: gwodouhgánjèung ge; sàhngìnggwomáhnge

overt Adj. PH: gùnghòi ge

overtake FV: (catch up with, outstrip) jèuiséuhng; chìugwo PH: (come upon suddenly) dahtyìhn làhmdou (a person)

overtax PH: chàuseui gwochúhng

overthrow FV: tēuifàan; dīnfūk (a government)

overtime PH: gàbàan sìhgaan; gàbàan

overtone N: (music) faanyām

overture FV: tàihyíh N: (music) jeuihkūk

overturn FV: ❶ tēuifàan; dīnfūk (a govenment) ❷ fàanjyun (an object e.g. a boat)

overvalue PH: gwoyù juhngsih FV: gòugú

overview PH: yātbùngùnchaat

overweight FV: gwochúhng; chìuchúhng

overwhelm FV: ❶ ngaatdóu (an opponent) ❷ gīkkwúi (the enemy) ❸ (e.g. by a flood) yìmmuht

overwhelming Adj. PH: ngaatdóu yātchai ge; saibāthódóng ge

overwork PH: gùngjok gwodouh FV: gwolòuh

overwrought Adj. PH: ❶

(too nervous) gwodouh gán-jèung ge; sàhngìngjāt ge ❷ (overtired) gwolòuhge

overzeal PH: gwofahn yihtsàm

oviduct N: syùléungún (M: tiuh)

ovum N: léun; léun saibāau (M: go)

owe FV: him, jàang

owing * owing to MA: yànwaih

owl N: māautàuhyīng (M: jek)

own Adj. PH: jihgéi ge FV: yáuh * hold one's own PH: gìnchìhjihgéi ge (gùndím) * of one's own PH: suhkyù (máuhyàhn) jihgéi ge * on one's own A. PH: dàanduhk gám; jyúduhng gám

owner N: mahtjyú (M: go) * owner of a car N: chèjyú (M: go) * owner of a factory N: chóngjyú (M: go) * owner of a house N: ngūkjyú (M: go) * owner of a ship N: syùhnjyú (M: go) * owner of land N: deihjyú (M: go) * owner of lost property N: sātjyú (M: go) * ownership N: yihpkyùhn; sóyáuhkyùhn

ox N: ngàuh; gùngngàuh (M: jek)

Oxford N: ❶ (city) Ngàuhjēun ❷ (university) Ngàuhjēun daaihhhohk

oxygen N: yéuhng; yéuhnghei

oyster N: hòuh; sàanghòuh (M: jek) * dried oysters N: hòuhsí (M: jek) * oyster shell N: hòuhhok (M: go)

P

pace M: bouh * walk in a longer pace PH: hàahng daaih bouhdī * at a steady pace PH: wánbouh * keep pace with RV: gāndākséuhng; paakdākjyuh

Pacific Adj. PH: wòhpìhng ge * the Pacific Ocean N: Taaipìhngyèuhng

pacification SV: jandihng FV: pìhngdihng

pacificism, pacifism N: wòhpìhng jyúyih; fáanjinjyúyih * pacificist, pacifist N: wòhpìhng jyúyih jé (M: go)

pacify FV: ❶ (soothe) ngònwai ❷ (quieten one's anger) hyun ❸ (put down an uprising) pìhngdihng

pack M: ❶ (yāt) bāau (things) ❷ yāt kwàhn (wolves) ❸ yāt fu (cards) FV: jāp; jòng; bàau RV: sākmúhn (people) * a pack of cigarettes PH: yāt bāau yīn * a charge for packing PH: bāaujòngfai * pack in FV: tìhngjí * pack off FV: dáfaat * pack up PH: jāphàhngléih

package M: bàau N: bàaugwó (M: go) FV: bàaujòng

packer PH: bàaujòng gùngyàhn (M: go)

packet M: hahp N: (sai gihn ge) bàaugwó * packet ship N: (dihngkèih) yàuhsyùhn

pact N: ❶ (contract) hahptùhng ❷ (between countries) tiuhyeuk * gùngyeuk

pad FV: jin * shoulder pad N: jinbok (M: go) * pad of paper N: paakjíbóu (M: go, bún)

paddle N: jéung (M: jì) FV: pàh ✻ **paddle a boat** VO: pàhtéhng ✻ **paddle a dragon-boat** PH: pàhlùhngsyùhn

paddock N: (sai ge) muhk-chèuhng (M: go)

paddy N: tìhn; wòhtìhn (M: faai)

padlock N: só (M: bá)

padre N: gaausih; sàhnfuh (M: go)

paean N: hóigō; jaanméihgō (M: sáu)

paediatric Adj. PH: yìhfō-hohk ge; síuyìhfō ge ✻ **paediatrician** N: yìhfōyīsāng (M: go) ✻ **paediatrics** N: yìhfōhohk; síuyìhfō

pagan N: yìhgaautòuh (M: go) ✻ **paganism** N: yìhgaau

page M: ❶ (one side of a leaf of a book) yìhp ❷ (one leaf of a book) pìn N: (boy servant in uniform) sihjái (M: go) ✻ **in the first page** PH: hái daihyātyìhp ✻ **page after page** Adv. PH.: yāt yìhp yāt yìhp gám

pageant N: ❶ hingdín ❷ (outdoors) louhtìnhei (M: chèuhng)

pagoda N: taap (M: joh)

paid FV: béijó

pail M/N: túng (M: go)

pain SV: tung ✻ **pain in the stomach** N: tóuhtung; waihtung ✻ **at pains** VO: jeuhnlihk; hahfúgùng ✻ **be in pain** PH: hái tungfú jìjùng ✻ **take pains** VO: jeuhnlihk

painful SV: tung; tungfú; sànfú

painkiller N: jítungyeuhk (M: jek, júng)

painstaking PH: hóu sāai sāmgèi ge Adv. PH: hóu yuhng sāmgèi gám; hóu fúsàm gám

paint N: yàu; yàuhchāt (M: jek, júng) FV: ❶ yàuh ❷ (of pictures) waahk VO: (of pictures) waahkwá ✻ **wet (fresh) paint** PH: yàuhchātmeihgòn ✻ **paint brush** N: wábāt (M: jì)

painter N: ❶ (artist) wágā (M: go) ❷ (artisan) yàuhchātlóu (M: go)

painting N: wá (M: fūk) ✻ **oil painting** N: yàuhwá (M: fūk) ✻ **watercolour painting** N: séuichóiwá ✻ **to paint a Chinese landscape painting** PH: waahk sàanséuiwá

pair M: ❶ deui; sèung ❷ (for glasses) fu ❸ (for trousers) tìuh ❹ (for scissors) bá ✻ **in pairs** Adv. PH: sìhngsèung sìhng deui gám ✻ **pair off** PH: fàn-sìhng léuhnggo yàhn yāt jóu

pajamas N: seuihyī (M: tou)

pal PH: hóu pàhngyáuh

palace N: gùngdihn (M: go)

palatable Adj. PH: hóu-meihdouhge; hóusihkge

palate N: ❶ ngohk ❷ (taste) meihgok

palaver N: ❶ (idle talk) hùngtàahm ❷ tàahmpun; gàausip

pale SV: chèng; chòngbaahk

palebuck N: lìhngyèuhng (M: jek)

paleolith N: gauhsehkhei

Palestinian N: Bàlahksītáan yàhn (M: go)

palette N: ❶ tiuhsīkbáan (M: faai) ❷ (used by a painter) ngàahnlíu

paling N: làahngōn (M: douh)

palingenesis FV/N: joisàng; sànsàng; lèuhnwùih

palisade N: làahngōn (M: douh)

pali(s)sander N: hùhngmuhk

pall N: ❶ gùnjaau ❷ (fig.) mohk PH: (of food) móuh meih

pallet N: ❶ chóuchòhng; deihpòu ❷ (for goods) tokbáan

palliate FV: ❶ gáamhèng; wùhnwòh (pain, disease) ❷ yímsīk (crime etc.)

pallid SV: chèng; chòngbaahk

palm N: ❶ (tree) jùnglèuihsyuh (M: pò) ❷ (of hand) sáujéung (M: jek) ✳ **bear (carry off) the palm** VO: dākjéung FV: dāksing ✳ **yield the palm to somebody** PH: syùbéi máuhyàhn ✳ **palm-oil** N: jùnglèuihyàuh

palmist N: sáuseunggā (M: go)

palpable Adj. PH: módākchēutge

palpitation FV/N (of heart) sàmtiu

palsy FV: jungfùng; táan SV: màhbei

paltry Adj. PH: mèihbātjūkdouh ge; m̀juhngyiu ge

pamper FV: jung; jungyùhng

pamphlet N: síuchaakjí (M: bún)

pan N: (pihngdái) wohk (M: go) ATT: (all) faahn ✳ **pan out** A/N: gitgwó N/SV: sìhnggùng

panacea N: maahnlìhngyeuhk (M: júng, jek)

Panamanian N: Bànàhmáh yàhn (M: go)

Pan-American ATT: faahnmèih; faanmèih Adj. PH: chyùhnmèihjàuge

panavision PH: futngàhnmohk dihnyíng; futngàhnmohkdihnsih

pancake N: bohkjìnbéng (M: go)

panchromatic Adj. PH: chyùhnsīkge ✳ **panchromatic film** PH: chyùhnsīkgàaupín

pancreas N: yìh; yìhsin

panda N: hùhngmāau (M: jek)

pandemic Adj. PH: làuhhàhng ge; chyùhnyíhmsing ge (illness)

pandemonium N: ❶ (disorder) daaihwahnlyuhn; sòuduhng (ge chèuhngmín) ❷ kwàhnmòdihn (M: go)

pane PH: chēung seuhngbihn ge bōlēi (M: faai)

panegyric N: juhngchìh ✳ **a panegyric on somebody** FV: juhngyèuhng

panel N: ❶ hahmbáan (M: faai) ❷ (group) jyùnjaak síu jóu (M: go)

pangolin N: chyùnsàangaap
(M: jek)

panic SV: gèng; húngfòng *
don't panic PH: m̀hóu gèng

panoply N: chyùhnfu kwàigaap; láihfuhk

panorama N: chyùhngíng;
chyùhnmaauh

pansy N: sàamsīkjílòhlàahn
(M: pùhn, pò)

pant VO: sokhei; chyúnhei
SV: sokhei

pantaloon N: ❶ (pants)
máhfu (M: tiùh) ❷ (clown)
cháugok (M: go)

pantelegraph N: chyùhnjàndihnbou (M: fùng)

panther N: paau (M: jek)

pantomime N: ❶ ngákehk
(M: chēut) ❷ (gesture) sáusai
(M: go)

pantry N: chāangeuihsāt;
sihkbánsāt

pants N: fu (M: tiùh) * **a
pair of pants** PH: yāt tiùh fu

pap N: (nipple) náaihtàuh PII:
(semi-liquid food) bun làuhjātsihkmaht

papa N: bàhbā

papacy PH: lòhmáhgaauwòhng ge jīkwaih; tìnjyúgaau
jaidouh

papal Adj. PH: lòhmáhgaauwòhng ge; tìnjyú gaau ge

papaya N: muhkgwā (M: go)

paper N: ❶ jí (M: jèung) ❷
(newspaper) boují (M: jèung) ❸
(of examination) háaugyún (M:
fahn) ❹ (academic) leuhnmàhn

(M: pìn) ❺ (document) màhngín
(M: fahn) * **papers** N: (identification) jìnggín * **paper-
back** N: pìhngjòngbún *
paper-cut VO/N: jínjí *
paper-knife N: chòìhjídōu (M:
bá) * **paper-mill** N: jouhjíchóng (M: gàan) * **paper-
pulp** N: jíjèung * **paper-
weight** N: jíngaat; syùjan; jíjan; màhnjan (M: go)

papilla N: yúhtàuh (M: go)

paprika N: hùhnglaahtjìu
(M: jek)

par PH: ❶ (average or normal
amount) pìhnggwàn/jìngsèuhng souleuhng ❷ (normal
performance) sèuhngtaai * **not
feeling up to par** PH: ❶ (of
performance) móuh pìhngsih
gam hóu ❷ (not feeling well)
yáuh dī m̀syùfuhk

parable N: yuhyìhn; béiyuh
(M: go)

parachute N: gonglohksaan
(M: go) * **parachutist** N: tiusaanyàhn; saanbìng (M: go)

parade FV: ❶ (march in procession) yàuhhàhng ❷ (of
troops) gímyuht ❸ (display)
kwàyiuh * **parade-ground** N:
yuhtbìngchèuhng (M: go)

paradigm PH: chíhyìhngbinfabíu (M: go)

paradise N: (of Christians)
tìntòhng; tìngwok; lohkyùhn
PH: (of Buddhists) sàifòng gihk
lohk saigaai

paradox PH: chíhsihyìhfēi
ge yíhleuhn; fáanleuhn

paraffin(e) N: sehklaahp

paragon N: (model of excellence) dínyìhng; mòuhfaahn

PH: (perfect person) yùhnméih ge yàhn (M: go)

paragraph N: dyuhn; jit

parallel SV: pìhnghàhng * without parallel IE: mòuh yúh lèuhn béi

parallelogram N: pìhnghàhngseibīnyìhng

paralyzed FV: táanjó * paralyzed on one side of body PH: bunsànbàtseuih

paralysis N/FV: táanwuhn SV: màhbei * infantile paralysis PH: síuyìhmàhbeijing

paralytic Adj. PH: màhbei ge; jungfùng ge PH: jungfùng behngyàhn (M: go) * paralytic stroke VO: jungfùng

paramount Adj. jeui gòu ge; jiseuhng ge; sáuyiu ge N: yùhnsáu (M: go)

paramour N: chìhngyàhn; chìhngfù (M: go)

parapet N: ❶ (railing) làahngòn (M: douh) ❷ (low wall) ngáichèuhng (M: buhng) ❸ (military) hùngchèuhng; wuhchèuhng

paraphernalia N: douhgeuih N/FV: jòngji PH: chèuihsàn yuhnggeuih

paraphrase FV: yiyihk

parasite N: ❶ (worm) geisàngchùhng (M: tìuh) ❷ (plant) geisàngchóu; geisàngjihkmaht * parasitology N: geisàngchùhnghohk * parasitosis N: geisàngchùhngbehng

parasol N: taɛ iyèuhngsaan (M: bá) * a Chinese parasol N: nǧhtùhng (M: pò)

paratroop N: saanbīng (M: go) * paratroops N: saanbīngbouhdéui (M: deuih)

par avion ATT: hòhnghùng

parboil PH: ❶ jyúsihng bunsuhk ❷ (fig.) yihtdāk nàahnsauh

parcel N: bàaugwó; yàuhbāau (M: go, gihn) VO: dábàau

parch RV: honggòn SV: (of thirst, the sun etc.) yìhmyihtgònchou

parchment N: yèuhngpèihjí (M: jèung) PH: yèuhngpèihjí seuhngbihn ge sáugóu

pardon FV: ❶ (excuse) yùhnleuhng; yiuhsyu ❷ (of sin or crime) semíhn * I beg your pardon PH: chéng yùhn leuhng; deuimjyuh * beg pardon/pardon PH: chéng néih joi góng yāt chi

pare FV: ❶ pài (fruit skin) ❷ sàu; jín (nails etc.) ❸ (fig.) seuk gáam (expenses)

parent N: fuhchàn; móuhchàn; jóusìn * parents N: fuhmóuh

parentage N: chēutsàn; mùhndaih; gànbún PH: fuhmóuh sànfán

parenthesis PH: ❶ chaapyahpyúh ❷ (brackets) kwutwùh * by way of parenthesis Adv. PH: fuhdaai gám

pariah N: ❶ (Indian) jihnmàhn (M: go) ❷ (fig.) làuhlohngjé; mòuhláai (M: go)

parish N: gaaukèui (M: go)

parity N/SV: pìhngdáng SV: tùhngdáng

park N: ❶ (public garden) gùngyún (M: go) ❷ (plaza) gwóngchèuhng (M: go) ❸ (for cars) tìhngchèchèuhng (M: go) FV: paak (cars) ✻ **parking lot** N: tìhngchèchèuhng (M: go) ✻ **parking metre** PH/N: tìhngchèsàufaibiu; (coll.) lóuhfúgēi (M: go) ✻ **parking is prohibited** PH: bātjéun paakchè; m̀jéun paakchè

parlance PH: juhkyúhsówaih; jiu yāt bùnge góngfaat

parley N: tàahmpun; wuihtàahm

parliament N: yìhwúi; gwokwúi

parlo(u)r N: ❶ (at home) haaktēng (M: go) ❷ (in a school or office) yàusīksāt; jipdoihsāt (M: go) ✻ **beauty parlour** N: méihyùhngyún (M: gàan)

parlous Adj. PH: ngàihhím ge

parochial Adj. PH: ❶ gaaukèui ge ❷ (fig.) haahp-ngaai ge

parody PH: ❶ fungchi sìmàhn (M: pìn) ❷ (weak imitation) mòuhfóng dāk hóu chà

parole N: saihyìhn FV: (of a prisoner) gásīk PH: dahkbiht háulihng (M: go)

parotitis N: sòisinyìhm; jasòi

paroxysm FV: ❶ (of illness) faatjok ❷ (of emotion) gīkfaat ✻ **a paroxysm of laughter** PH: yātjahn daaihsiu

parquet N: sèungmuhk deihbáan

parricide PH: ❶ (killer) saat fuhmóuh waahkjé gahnchàn ge

yàhn (M: go) ❷ (of sin) buhnyihk jeuih

parrot N: ❶ yìngmóuh; ngànggō (M: jek) ❷ (fig.) yingsìngchùhng (M: tiuh)

parry FV: dónghòi; beihhòi

parse FV: fànsīk

parsimonious SV: gùhòhn; síuhei

parsley N: (yèuhng) yùhnsāi; hèungchoi (M: pò)

parson N: gaaukèui muhksī; muhksī (M: go)

part N/M: (portion) bouhfahn N: ❶ (piece of a machine) lìhnggín ❷ (role in a play) goksīk (M: go) ❸ (music) sìngbouh (M: go) ❹ (region) kèuiwihk (M: go) M: ❶ (length) gyuht; dyuhn ❷ (unit measurement) fahn ✻ **act (play) a part** Patt: héi . . . jokyuhng; baahn . . . goksīk ✻ **take part in** FV: chàamgà; chàamyúh ✻ **part with** FV: séhei

partake FV: chàamgà; chàamyúh; fànhéung; fàndàam

partial Adj. PH: (forming only a part) bouhfahn ge SV: (showing too much favour) pìnsàm FV: pìntáan

participant PH: chàamgà ge yàhn; chàamgàjé (M: go)

participate FV: chàamyúh; chàamgà

participle N: fànchìh (M: go)

particle N: ❶ mèihnáp (M: náp) ❷ (of linguistics) síubánchìh; hèuichìh (M: go)

parti-coloured Adj. PH:

jaahpsīk ge

particular SV: ❶ (distinct from others) dahksyùh ❷ (special) dahkbiht ❸ (very exact, scrupulous) jìngkok; yìhmgán SV/FV: tiutīk * **be particular about** Patt: deui . . . gónggau * **go into particulars** PH: chèuhngsai góngseuht

particularly A: yàuhkèihsih; dahkbihthaih

parting Adj.ʹ PH: làhmbiht ge; jeui hauh ge VO/N: (of hair) fàngaai * **at the parting of the ways** PH: sahpjih louhháu; kyutjaahk gwàantàuh

partisan N: ❶ dóngyàhn (M: go) ❷ (guerrilla) yàuhgīkdéuiyùhn (M: go)

partition FV: gwàfàn FV/N: (of a house) gaangaak

partly PH: yātbouhfahn N: yáuhdī

partner N: ❶ hahpfó yàhn; hahpjokjé; pāatná (M: go) ❷ (husband or wife) jeuhngfù; taaitáai ❸ (of dancing) móuhbuhn (M: go)

partnership PH: hahpgú sàangyi

partridge N: jegū (M: jek)

part-time . Adj. PH: bouhfahn sìhgaan ge; gímyahmge

party N: ❶ (group) tyùhntái (M: go) ❷ (political group) jìngdóng; dóng (M: go) ❸ (gathering) jeuihwuih (M: go) ❹ (one side in a legal agreement or dispute) (yāt) fòng * **a dancing party** N: móuhwúi (M: go) * **a tea party** N: chàhwúi (M: go) * **a party member** N:

dóngyùhn (M: go) * **(the) Communist Party (of China)** N: (Jùnggwok) Guhngcháandóng * **Chinese Nationalist Party** N: (Jùnggwok) Gwokmàhndóng

pass FV: ❶ (go by) gìnggwo ❷ (of an examination in school) hahpgaak; kahpgaak ❸ (approve) tùnggwo; pàijéun N: (permit) chēutyahpjìng; tùnghàhngjìng (M: go) * **come to pass** FV: faatsàng; sahtyihn * **pass away** FV: gwosàn * **pass out** FV: (faint) wàhnjó

passage FV: (act of passing) tùnggwo N: ❶ (a way to go through) louh; tùnglouh (M: tiuh) ❷ (corridor) láahnghòng (M: tiuh) M: (paragraph) jit; dyuhn

passbook N: ngàhnhòhng chyùhnjip (M: bún)

passenger N: daaphaak; sìhnghaak; léuihhaak (M: go) * **passenger car** N: haakchè (M: ga)

passer PH: ❶ gwolouh yàhn (M: go) ❷ (of an examination) háausíh hahpgaak/kahpgaak ge yàhn (M: go) * **passer-by** PH: gwolouh yàhn (M: go)

passing Adj. PH: gìnggwo ge; dyúnjaahmge; muhkchùhn ge * **passing-bell** N: songjìng

passion N: ❶ (capacity for emotion) chìhng; chìhnggám ❷ (desire) yuhkmohng; chìhngyuhk SV: yihtchìhng FV/N: (love) ngoi

passionate Adj. PH: hóu yùhngyih gīkduhng ge

passive SV: (negative) siugihk Adj. PH: (acted upon) beih duhng ge

passkey N: baakhahpsih (M: tiuh)

passport N: wuhjiu (M: go, bún)

password N: háulihng; háuhouh (M: go)

past FV: (gone by in time) gwojó Adj. PH: gwoheui ge N: wóhngsih; gìnglihk

paste N: jèungwùh FV: nihm; chi; tip

pasteboard N: jíbáan (M: faai)

pastel N: ❶ (drawing pencils) chóisīkfánbāt; laahbāt (M: jì) ❷ (picture) fánbātwá (M: fūk) ❸ (light colour) táahm ngàahnsīk

pasteurize FV: sìuduhk

pastime N: sìuhín; yùhlohk

pastor N: muhksī (M: go)

pastry N: gōubéng; dímsām (M: gihn)

pasture N: ❶ (grassland for cattle) muhkchèuhng (M: go) ❷ (grassland) chóudéi; chóudeih (M: faai)

pasty Adj. PH: ❶ jèungwùh gám ge ❷ (pale) mihnsīkchōngbaahk ge

pa system = public-address system PH: kongyām jòngbeih; yáuh sin gwóng bo

pat PH: hehnghēng paak ✳ **stand pat** PH: gìnchìhjyújèung

patch FV: bóu N: (over a wound) gòuyeuhk; gàaubou (M: faai) ✳ **patch-work** PH: pingchau ge (yéh) (M: gihn)

pate N: tàuh; nóuh (M: go)

patent Adj. PH: mihnghín ge; sáuchong ge; jyùnleihge N: jyùnleihkyùhn; jyùnleihbán ✳ **patent letters** N: jyùnleihjing (M: go) ✳ **patent leather** N: chātpéi (M: faai)

pater N: fuhchàn; bàhbā

paternalism PH: wànchihngjyúyih; gàjéungjai

paternity N: ❶ (fatherhood) fuhsing ❷ (being a father) fuhjīk ❸ (fig.) (source) lòihyùhn

path N: louhjái (M: tiuh) ✳ **a beaten path** N: sèuhngkwái; gwaanlaih ✳ **foot path** N: louhjái; (on a hill) sàanlouh (M: tiuh)

pathetic Adj. PH: bēicháam ge; hólìhnge; gámchìhng seuhng ge

pathfinder PH: taamhím ge yàhn; taamlouh ge yàhn (M: go)

pathless PH: móuhlouh ge

pathology N: behngléihhohk

pathos FV: tùhngchìhng FV/N: lihnmáhn SV: bēingòi; sèunggám

pathway N: louhjái; síuging (M: tiuh)

patience FV/N: yánnoih N: noihsing FV/SV: yùhngyán ✳ **have no patience with** PH: bātnàhng yùhngyán; m̀yándāk

patient FV/N: yánnoih SV: yáuhnoihsing N: behngyàhn (M: go)

patio N: tìnjéng; yún (M: go)

patriarch N: gàjéung; juhkjéung; fuhlóuh ❷ (Catholic) daaihjyúgaau (M: go)

patricide VO: ❶ (kill father) saatfuh ❷ (kill kinsfohk) saatchàn ❸ (kill a king) saat gwànwòhng PH: saatfuh, saatchàn, saat gwànwòhng ge yàhn (M: go)

patrimony N: wàihcháan; jóuyihp PH: (of church) gaauwúi chòihcháan

patriot PH: ngoigwok ge yàhn; ngoigwokjé (M: go) ✳ **patriotic** Adj. PH: ngoigwok ge

patriotism PH: ngoigwok jyúyih; ngoigwoksàm

patrol FV: chèuhnlòh; chèuhnchàh N: ❶ (of unit) chèuhnlòhdéui (M: deuih) ❷ (of ship) chèuhnlòhténg (M: jek)

patron N: ❶ (customer) haakjái (M: go) ❷ (of a society) jaanjohyàhn (M: go)

patronize FV: ❶ (a shop) bòngchan ❷ (to sponsor) jaanjoh

patter PH: ❶ (of sound) daahpdaahp gám héung ❷ (speak quickly) hóu faai gám góng ❸ (rapid talk of a performer) gāpháulihng

pattern N: ❶ (design) fún; yéung (M: go) ❷ (of linguistics) geuiyìhng

patty N: béngjái (M: go)

paucity SV/N: síuleuhng SV: hèisíu

paunch N: tóuhnáahm PH: daaih tóuhnáahm (M: go)

pauper N: kùhngyàhn (M: go)

pause FV: jaahmtìhng; tìhngdeuhn PH: tìhng yātháh

pave FV: pòu; pòuchit ✳ **pave the way for (to)** Patt: waih . . . pòu louh

pavement N: hàhngyàhnlouh (M: tiuh)

pavillion N: ❶ (for spectators) tòih (M: go) ❷ (for resting) tíng; lèuhngtíng (M: go)

paw N: jáau; jéung (M: jek)

pawn FV: dong; dáingaat ✳ **pawn-shop** N: dongpóu (M: gàan) ✳ **pawn ticket** N: dongpíu (M: jèung)

pay VO; ❶ (make payment for something) béichín ❷ (give salary or wage) chēutlèuhng; jì yàhngùng FV: ❶ (spend for buying) máaihjó; máaih ❷ (of payments as rents, electricity etc.) gàau ❸ (of damages) pùih ❹ (of taxes etc.) naahp; gàau RV: (debts, loans) wàahnfàan (béi) SV: (beneficial) jeuhksou AV: (be worthwhile) jìhkdāk N: (salary, wages) sànséui; yàhngùng ✳ **pay a visit to** FV: fóngmahn; chàamgùn ✳ **pay attention (to)** FV: jyuyi; làuhsàm ✳ **pay back** FV: ① sèuhngwàahn (debts); ② boudaap (one's kindness); ③ (revenge) boufuhk ✳ **pay-bill** N: sàngàmdāan (M: jèung)

payee N: sàufúnyàhn (M: go)

payer N: fuhfúnyàhn (M: go)

paymaster N: chēutnaahpyùhn (M: go)

payment VO; béichín; gàaufai FV/N: ❶ (reward) bouchàuh ❷ (punishment, what one deserves) bouying

pea N: chèngdáu; hòhlāan

dáungàhn (M: nāp) * **pea pod** N: hòhlāandáu (M: tìuh) * **as two peas** PH: sahpfān chíh; fèisèuhng chíh * **pea green** PH: chínluhksīk; chèngdáu sīk * **pea-souper** PH: wòhngsīk nùhngmouh

peace SV/N: ❶ (national) wòhpìhng; (SV) taaipìhng ❷ (domestic) pìhngngòn SV: (between people) wòhmuhk * **at peace** SV: pìhngjihng * **make peace with** Patt: tùhng . . . wòhhóu * **hold (keep) one's peace** PH: bóuchìh chàhmmahk * **peacemaker** PH: tìuhgáai yàhn; wòhsihlóu (M: go) * **R.I.P. (Rest in peace)** PH: ❶ (lit.) sīklòuh; wàhngwàitìngwok ❷ (lit.) (for christians) sīklòuhgwàijyú; Jyúwàaih ngònsīk; mùhngjyúchúngjiuh

peaceful SV/N: wòhpìhng SV: ngònjihng * **peaceful coexistence** PH: wòhpìhng guhngchyúu

peach N: tóu (M: go) * **peach blossoms** N: tòuhfā (M: jì, pò)

peacock N: húngjéuk; húngjeuk (gūng) (M: jek)

peafowl N: húngjeuk; húngjéuk (M: jek)

peahen N: húngjeuk (ná) (M: jek)

peak N: (of a mountain) sàandéng (M: go) * **peak hours** PH: (of traffic) fàahnmòhngsìhgaan

peal PH: lùhnglúngsèng

peanut N: fāsāng (M: nāp) * **peanut oil** N: fāsāngyàuh

peapod N: dauhhaap; dauhgaap (M: tìuh)

pear N: ❶ léi (M: go) ❷ (tree) léisyuh (M: pò)

pearl N: jànjyū; jyū (M: nāp) * **cultured pearl** N: yéuhngjyū (M: nāp) * **cast pearls before swine** IE: mìhngjyū ngamtàuh PH: (Biblical) jèung jànjyū dìujoih jyūchìhn * **pearl-diver** PH: chìhmséui chóijyū ge yàhn (M: go)

peasant N: ❶ nùhngmàhn; nùhngfù (M: go) ❷ (coll.) gàangtìhnlóu (M: go)

peat N: nàihtaan

pebble N: ❶ sehkjái (M: nāp) ❷ (oval and smooth) ngòhchēunsehk (M: nāp)

peck M: dáu FV: dèung * **pecker** N: deukmuhkníuh (M: jek)

pectoral Adj. PH: hùngbouhge; (yì) hùnghōng/fai behng ge

peculate FV: ❶ douhyuhng; chàmtàn (money placed in one's care) ❷ douhyuhng (things placed in one's care)

peculiar A/SV: (special) dahkbiht; (special) SV: ❶ dahksyùh ❷ (strange) gúgwaai; kèihgwaai

peculiarity N: dahksing; dahksīk

pecuniary Adj. PH: gàmchìhn ge

pedagog(ue) PH: ❶ (primary school master) síuhohk sìnsàang (M: go) ❷ (pedantic teacher) maaihluhng hohkmahn ge sìnsàang (M: go)

pedagogy N: gaauyuhkhohk; gaauhohkfaat

pedal FV: daahp N: (geuk) daahpbáan (M: faai)

pedant N: hohkgau (M: go) PH: syùdāaijí (M: go) ✻ **pedantic** Adj. PH: yùfuh ge

peddler N: síufáan (M: go)

peddling Adj. PH: m̀juhngyiu ge; sóseui ge

pedestal N: tòih; gá; chyúhgèi

pedestrian N: hàhngyàhn (M: go) Adj. PH: ❶ bouhhàhng ge ❷ (prosaic) pìhngdaahm ge

pedicab N: sàamlèuhnchè (M: ga, bouh)

pedigree N: ❶ gàhaih; gàpóu ❷ (of linguistics) chìhyùhn N/VO: chēutsàn

peek FV: tàutái

peel N: gwópèih; pèih (M: faai) FV: ❶ (with hands only) mīt (oranges etc.) ❷ (with a knife) pài (apple etc.) VO: mītpèih; pàipèih

peep FV: tàutái; jòng

peer N: ❶ (aristocracy) gwaijuhk (M: go) ❷ (equal) tùhngbui PH: (equal) gahnchíh ge yàhn ✻ **peerless** Adj. PH: mòuhbéi ge; géuisaimòuhsèungge

peevish SV: bouhchou; gāpchou

peg N: ❶ (of wood) muhkdēng (M: háu) ❷ (of bamboo) jūkdēng (M: háu) ❸ (of clothes) sāamgáap; sāamgíp (M: go) ✻ **peg away at** PH: m̀tìhng gám gùngjok ✻ **take somebody down a peg (or two)** PH: cho PN ge yeuihhei (ngouhhei) ✻ **hat-peg** N: gwamóudēng (M: háu)

Pekinese Adj. PH: Bākgìng (yàhn) ge N: ❶ Bākgìng yàhn (M: go) ❷ (language) Bākgìngwá ❸ (dog) hàbàgáu (M: jek)

Peking N/PW: Bākgìng

Pekingman PH: Jùnggwok yùhnyàhn/Bākgìng yàhn

pellet N: ❶ (slug of small shot) jídáan (M: nāp) ❷ (pill) yeuhkyún (M: nāp)

pellmell SV: wahnlyuhn PH: lyuhnchātbaatjòu

pellucid SV: taumìhng; chìng (chit)

pelt N: mòuhpèih (M: faai) FV: dám; deng (stones etc.) PH: (of rain etc.) lohkdāk hóu faai; lohkdāk hóu daaih

pelvis N: gwātpùhn

pem(m)ican N: (American) ngàuhyuhkgōn; gònyuhkbéng (M: faai)

pen N: ❶ (Chinese brush) mòuhbāt (M: jì) ❷ (fountain pen) mahkséui bāt (M: jì) ❸ (enclosure) lāan (M: go) ✻ **penname** N: bātméng (M: go)

penalize PH: syùnbou yáuh jeuih VO: punyìhng FV: chyúfaht ✻ **penal law** N: yìhngfaat

penalty N: (punishment) yìhngfaht FV: chyúfaht FV/N: chìhngfaht N: (fine) fahtfún

penance FV/N: chaamfui VO: suhkjeuih

penchant FV/N: kìngheung; ngoihou; sihou

pencil N: yùhnbāt (M: jì) ✻ **pencil sharpener** N: yùhnbātpáau (M: go)

pencraft N: syùfaat PH: séjok geihháau

pendant (pendent) Adj. PH: dìujyuh ge; hahsèuih ge

pending PH: ❶ meih kyutdihng ge ❷ hái . . . kèihgàan; hái . . . yìhchìhn; jihkdou

pendulous Adj. PH: dìujyuh ge; yìuhbáai bātdihngge

pendulum N: jūngbáai (M: go) ✳ the swing of the pendulum PH: ❶ jūng báaiduhng ❷ (fig.) sihngsèui

penetrate FV: (spread through) samtau RV: ❶ samyahp ❷ (pierce) chaapyahp ❸ (see through) táichyūn

penguin N: kéihngó; kéihngòh (M: jek)

penholder N: ❶ bātgòn (M: jì) ❷ bātgá (M: go)

penicillin N: (tr.) pùhnnèihsàilàhm

peninsula N: bundóu (M: go)

penis N: yàmging

penitence FV: hauhfui; chaamfui

penitentiary N: ❶ gaauyéuhngsó (M: gàan) ❷ (American) gàamlòuh (M: go)

penknife N: dōujái (M: bá)

penman FV/N: chàausé N: syùfaatgà (M: go) ✳ penmanship N: syùfaat; jaahpjih

pennant N: ❶ (flag) kèih; sàamgokkèih (M: jì) ❷ (of a ship) syùhn seuhng yuhng ge seunhouh kèih

penniless PH: yāt go sīn dōu móuh; kùhngdou nùhng

penny N: ❶ (in England) bihnsih (M: go) ❷ (U.S. or Canadian) sīn (M: go) ✳ in for a penny, in for a pound IE: yāt bāt jouh, yih bāt yàu ✳ penny wise and pound foolish IE: síu sih chùngmìhng, daaih sih wùhtòuh ✳ turn (earn) an honest penny PH: jaahn jingdong chín

penology PH: jeuihfáan gaauyuhkhohk; yìhngfahthohk; gàamyuhkhohk

pension N: ❶ (after retirement) teuiyàugām; chèuhnglèuhng ❷ (of social service) yéuhnglóuhgām

pensive Adj. PH: chàhmsi ge; jiuleuih ge

pentagon N: nǵhbīnyìhng; nǵhgokyìhng (M: go)

pentagram N: nǵhgoksīngyìhng (M: go)

Pentecost N: Nǵhchèuhnjit

penthouse N: jèpùhng PH: héiháidaaihhah ngūkdéng ge ngūk

penurious SV: ❶ (poor) pàhnkùhng ❷ (stingy) gùhòhn SV/FV: kyutfaht

peon N: ❶ (in Latin America) yahtgùng; nùhngchèuhng gùngyàhn (M: go) ❷ (in India) sihchùhng; bouhbīng; chyùhnlihngbīng (M: go)

peony N: máauhdāan; cheukyeuhk (M: déu)

people N: ❶ (persons) yàhn (M: go) ❷ (others) yàhndeih ❸ (electorate) yàhnmàhn; màhnjung ❹ (race) júngjuhk; màhn-juhk (M: go)

pep N: jīngsàhn; wuhtlihk ✳ **peppy** Adj. PH: fuyáuh sànghei ge

pepper N: wùhjīu(fán) VO: sámwùhjīufán FV: ❶ (pelt) lyuhndá ❷ (question) jātmahn

peppermint N: bohkhòh ✳ **peppermint candy** N: bohkhòhtóng (M: nāp)

peptic Adj. PH: sīufa ge; johsīufa ge N: gihnwaihjài

per SP: múih CV: yàuh ✳ **per annum** PH: múih nìhn ✳ **per post** PH: yàuh yàuhgúk

perambulate FV: chèuhn-sih; maahnbouh; pùihwùih

percapita PH: ngon yàhn-háu gaisyun; múihyàhn

perceive RV: ❶ (see) táigin ❷ (see clearly into) táichēut FV: ❶ (understand) mìhngbaahk; jì ❷ (comprehend) líuhgáai

percent, per cent PH: baak fahn jì . . . ✳ **five percent** PH: baakfahn jì ńgh

percentage PH: baakfahn-béi; baakfahnléut M: (proportion) sìhng

perception FV: léihgáai N: ❶ (instinctive) jigok ❷ (comprehension) léihgáailihk

perch N: lòuhyùh; lòuhyú (M: tìuh) FV: ❶ (of birds) lohk (hái) ❷ (of a person) chóhhái (sth. high)

percolate FV: gwoleuih RV: (seep out) samchēut ✳ **percolator** N: gwoleuihhei; (of coffee) gafēwú (M: go)

percussion FV: hàau; gīk; janduhng

perdition FV: wáimiht PH: wìhngyúhn chàhmlèihn

perdurable Adj. PH: wìhng-gáu ge

peremptory Adj. PH: jyùn-wàahng ge; kéuhngjai ge

perennial Adj. PH: ❶ (throughout the whole year) seigwaibātdyuhnge ❷ (lasting for a very long time) chìhgáu ge PH: (plant) dònìhn sàng jihkmaht

perfect SV: ❶ (complete) yùhnchyùhn ❷ (without fault) yùhnméih ❸ (exact) jéunkok PH: (of linguistics) yùhnsìhng-sīk ✳ **be perfect in** FV: jīngtùng

perfection RV: yùhnsìhng SV: yùhnméih; yùhnmúhn IE: dàngfùngchouihk

perfidious Adj. PH: mjùng-saht ge IE: buiseunheiyih ge

perforate VO: dálūng

perforator N: dálūnggèi (M: go)

perforce A: bītsèui FV: kèuhngbīk PH: bātdākyíh

perform FV: ❶ léihhàhng (a contract, obligation etc.) ~ hahpyeuk ❷ jāphàhng (a duty) ~ jīkmouh FV/N: ❶ (on a stage) bíuyín ❷ (of music) yín-jau ✳ **performer** N: ① yínjau-jé (M: go) ② (actor) yínyùhn (M: go)

perfume N: ❶ (liquid) hèungséui (M: jèun) ❷ hèunglíu

perfunctory Adj. PH: fùhínge; māfù ge

pergola N: fāpàahng (M: go)

perhaps A: waahkjé; hónàhng Patt: waahkjé . . . dōu m̀díng

peril SV/N: ngàihhím FV: mouhhím

perimeter N: jàuchèuhng; jàugaai A: jàuwàih

period N: (stretch of time) sìhkèih; sìhdoih PH: yātdyuhn sìhgaan M: (class hour) tòhng

periodical N: kèihhòn; kèihhón (M: bún) PH: dihngkèih hònmaht/hónmaht (M: bún)

periphery N: yùhnjàu (M: go)

periscope N: chìhmmohnggeng (M: go)

perish FV: mìhtmòhng SV: yihfuhbaaih ge PH: yihfuhbaaih ge sihkmaht

peritonitis N: fūkmókyìhm

periwig N: gáfaat (M: go)

perjure VO: faatgásaih PH: faatgásaih ge yàhn (M: go)

perk FV: ❶ janjok ❷ dábaan N: jéunggām (M: go)

perky SV: ❶ wuhtput ge ❷ hìngsēut ge

permanent SV: m̀bin ge; wíhnggáu ge

permeate FV: ❶ samyahp ❷ chùngmúhn

permission N: jéunhéui (M: go) * **ask (beg) permission** FV: chéngkàuh * **with PN permission** PH: hái PN jéunhéui jì hah . . .

permit FV: jéun N: héuihójing (M: go, jèung)

permutation N: ❶ gàauwuhn; wuhwuhn (M: júng) ❷ (Mathematics) pàaihliht; seuhnliht

pernicious SV: yáuhhoih ge; ngoksing ge

pernickety SV: (coll.) ngoi tiutīk ge; chèuimòuhkàuhchì ge

perorate VO: lohk gitleuhn

perpendicular SV: sèuihjihk ge; jihklaahp ge N: sèuihjihk sin (M: tiuh) * **perpendicular to** PH: sìhng jihkgok

perpetration VO: ❶ hàhnghùng; ❷ faahnjeuih

perpetrator N: faahnyàhn; jeuihfáan (M: go)

perpetual SV: wíhnggáu ge; jùngsàn ge

perplexity N: wahnlyuhn; kwanwaahk

perquisite N: ❶ làhmsìhjēuntip ❷ jéunggām; ❸ ngaahkngoih sàuyahp

persecute FV: ❶ bīkhoih ❷ yeuhkdoih

perseverance N: gindihng; ginchìh

persevere FV: ❶ ginyán ❷ ginchìh

Persian PH: ❶ Bōsī ge ❷ Bōsī yàhn ge N: Bōsīwá

persimmon N: ❶ làhmchí (M: go) ❷ làhmchísyuh (M: pò)

persist FV/SV: ginchìh; gujāp

person N: ❶ yàhn (M: go) ❷ sàntái (M: go) ❸ yàhnmàt (M: go) ✳ **in person** A: chànjih ✳ **in the name of** PH: doihbíu . . ✳ **person to person** PH: mihn deui mihn; go yàhn deui go yàhn; dòngmín

persona N: ❶ (Latin) yàhn (M: go) ❷ goksīk; yàhnmát (M: go) ✳ **persona (non)grata** PH: sauh (m̀sauh) fùnyìhng ge yàhn (M: go)

personal SV: goyàhn ge; sìyàhnge; chànjihge ✳ **personal affairs** N: sìsih ✳ **personal beauty** N: yìhbíuméih ✳ **personal abuse** PH: yàhnsàn gùnggīk

personality N: gosing; yàhngaak

personate FV: baahnyín; mouhchūng

personification N: yàhngaakfa; dínyìhng

personnel N: ❶ chyùhntái yàhnyùhn ❷ yàhnsih (bouhmùhn) (M: go)

perspective N: ❶ tausihwá (faat) ❷ mohngyúhngeng (M: go) ✳ **in perspective** Adj. PH: (gùnchaat) jingkok gám

perspex N: gaaidihn yáuh gèi bōlēi (M: júng)

perspicuity SV: chìngchó

perspire VO: chēuthohn; làuhhohn (perspire freely) biuhohn

persuade FV: hyunfuhk (a person)

pert SV: lóuhmóhng ge; chòulóu ge; móuhlaihge (of manners and talk)

pertain FV: (pertain to) suhkyù

pertinacious SV: ❶ (opinion, method) gínchìh ❷ (of a person) gujàp

pertinent SV: hāpdong ge (of questions and examples) ~ mahn tàih; ~ laihjí

perturbation N: yíulyuhn; fàahnlyuhn

peruse FV: ❶ saiduhk; jìngduhk ❷ gùnchaat (of matter) ~ sihchìhng

Peruvian N: Beilóuhyàhn (M: go) SV: ❶ Beilóuhge ~ sàngwuht; ~ séungfaat; ❷ Beilóuhyàhn ge

pervade FV: pìnbou (of certain smell) ~ chaumeih

perversion N: (of the truth, history) dìndóu; wīkūk ~ sihsaht; ~ lihksí

perversity N: chèhngok ❶ (of behavior) ~ hàhngwàih ❷ (of thinking, idea) ~ sìséung

pervert FV: ❶ dìndóu (of the truth) ~ sihfēi ❷ laahmyuhng (of company's money) ~ gùngfún PH: (sexual) dōhlohk ge yàhn (M: go)

pervious PH: (of liquid) hóyíh tùnggwo ge

pesky SV: ❶ (American IE) màhfàahnge ❷ tóu yim ge

Peso N: (the money unit of Spain, Philippine and the country in Latin America) Péisok

pessimism N: ❶ bēigùn jyúyih (sìu gihk jyúyih) ❷ bēigùn paai

pessimist N: bēigùnleuhnjé

(M: go)

pessimistic SV: bèigùn ge

pest N: ❶ yihkbehng ❷ hoihchùhng (M: jek) PH: (disgusting person) tóuyim ge yàhn (M: go) ✳ **pest hole** PW: wànyihk kèui (M: go) ✳ **pest house** N: chyùhnyíhmbehng yìyún (M: gàan)

pester PH: lihng PN fàahnnóuh ge FV: dáuchìhn

pestiferous SV: ❶ chyùhnyíhmsing ge ❷ yáuh hoih ge

pestilence N: ❶ syúyihk ❷ làuhhàhngbehng

pestilent SV: (to the society) ❶ yáuh hoih ge; ❷ jimihng ge

pet N: chúngmaht (M: jek) PH:chúngngoi ge yàhn (M: go) FV: ngoi ✳ **a pet cat** N: chúngmāau (M: jek) ✳ **a pet dog** N: chúnggáu (M: jek)

petal N: (plant) fāfáan (M: faai)

petard N: (in ancient time used to bambard a city) jayeuhk túng ✳ **be hoist by one's own petard** PH: bùn sehktàuh jaak jihgéi ge geuk

petition N: chíngyuhn; chíngkàuh; sànchíng (M: go, júng) FV: (of matter) chíngkàuh

pettioner N: ❶ chíngyuhnyàhn (M: go) ❷ sànchíng lèihfànjé (M: go)

petrel N: hóiyin (M: jek)

petrify FV: ❶ gèungfa ❷ faatngòih

petrochemical SV: sehkyàuhfahohk ge N: sehkyàuhfahohkcháanbán ✳ **petrochemi-**

cal industry N: sehkyàuhfahohk gùngyihp

petrol N: heiyàuh (M: jek)

petroleum N: sehkyàuh (M: jek)

petticoat N: dái kwàhn (M: gihn; tiùh)

pettifog PH: ❶ chùhng sih sóseui ge faatleuht sihmouh ❷ yíhgwáija ge sáudyuhn chùhngsih faatleuht sihmouh

pettifoger N: síu leuhtsī (M: go)

pettish SV: yih nàu ge; yih faatpèihhei ge

petty SV: ❶ sóseui ge (of matter) ❷ sàmhùng jaak ge (of person) ✳ **petty cash** N: lihngyuhngchín ✳ **petty officer** N: hóigwàan gwàngùn (M: go)

petulance - ancy SV: ❶ singgāp ❷ bouchou

petunia N: lábāfā; hìnngàuhfā (M: déu, dó)

pew N: gaautòhng johwái (M: jèung, go)

pewter N: sekhei

phantom N: gwáigwaai; yàulihng (M: jek) ✳ **a phantom ship** N: gwái syùhn (M: jek) ✳ **a phantom king** PH: yáuh mihng mòuh saht ge gwokwòhng

pharaoh N: ❶ (Ancient Egyptian king) Faatlóuh (M: go) ❷ bouhgwàn (M: go)

pharisee N: ❶ Faatleihchoiyàhn (M: go) ❷ ngaihgwànjí (M: go)

pharmaceutist (pharmacist) N: yeuhkjàisī; jaiyeuhkjé (M: go)

pharmacology N: yeuhkmahthohk; yeuhkléihhohk (M: mùhn)

pharmacy N: ❶ yeuhkkhohk ❷ yeuhkfòhng (M: gàan)

pharynx N: (anatomy) hàuhlùhng (M: go)

phase N: ❶ gàaidyuhn (M: go) ❷ fòngmihn

pheasant N: yéhgāi (M: jek)

phenomenon N: ❶ yihnjeuhng (M: go) ❷ jinghauh (M: go)

philander VO: wuhnluhng yihsing

philanthropic SV: ❶ bokngoi ge ❷ yàhnchìh ge ✻ **philanthropism** N: bokngoi jyúyi ✻ **philanthropist** N: ❶ bokngoi jyúyihjé (M: go) ❷ chìhsihngā (M: go)

philately N: jaahpyàuh ✻ **philatelist** N: jaahpyàuhgā (jé) (M: go)

Philippines SV: Fèileuhtbān (yàhn) ge

Philistine SV/N: ❶ síhkwúi (M: go) ❷ Fèilihksī yàhn (M: go) SV: ❶ dàikáp ge ❷ móuh gaauyéuhng ge

philology N: yúhyìhnhohk; yúhmàhnhohk ✻ **philologist** N: yúhyìhnhohkgā (M: go)

philosopher N: ❶ jithohkgā; sìséunggā (M: go) ❷ hohkjé (M: go)

philosophic(al) SV: jithohk seuhng ge Adj. PH: yáuh

jithohk yi meih ge

philosophy N: ❶ jithohk ❷ yàhnsànggùn

phlegm N: tàahm (M: daahm) SV: láahngdaahm ge (attitude)

phlox N: chóugaapjūktòuh (M: pò)

Phoebe N: ❶ (girl's name) Fèibéi ❷ (Greek Goddess) Hèilaahp néuihsàhn (M: go)

phoenix N: fuhngwòhng (M: jek)

phone N: ❶ dihnwá; dihnwágèi (M: go) ❷ yìhgēi (M: go) VO: dádihnwá

phonetician N: yúhyìhnhohkgā (M: go)

phonetics N: yúhyāmhohk; faatyāmhohk (M: mùhn)

phonevision N: dihnwádihnsih (M: ga)

phon(e)y N: pinjí (M: go) SV: gá ge; ngaihjouh ge

phonics N: ❶ sìnghohk ❷ gèichói yúhyām gaauhohkfaat

phonogram N: ❶ cheung pín (M: jèung) ❷ yāmbiu màhnjih ❸ dihnwá dihnbou

phonograph N: cheunggēi (M: ga)

phonology N: yàmwàhnhohk (M: mùhn)

phonorecord N: cheungpín (M: jèung)

photo N: séung (M: fūk, jèung) VO: yíngséung N: (physics) gwòngdihnchìh ✻ **photoflash** N: símgwòngdāng (M: go) ✻ **photogram** N:

chyùhnjàn dihnbou (M: fùng) *
photographer N: sipyíngsī (M:
go)

photostat N: ❶ jihkjip
yíngyangēi (M: ga, fu) ❷ fūksé-
jiuseung gēi (M: ga, fu) PH:
yuhng jihkjip yíngyangēi
paaksip

phrase N: chouchìh; dyún-
geui (M: geui) * **phrasal verb**
SV: duhngchìh chìhjóu

phraseology N: yuhngyúh;
seuhtyúh

physiatrics N: mahtléih-
jihlìuhfaat

physic N: yeuhk (M: jek)

physical SV: ❶ mahtjāt ge
❷ mahtléihhohk (seuhng) ge *
physical science N: jihyìhn
fōhohk (M: mùhn) * **physical
examination** N: táigaak gímchàh (M: chi) * **physical exercise** FV/N: táichòu (M:
tòhng; chi)

physician N: ❶ yīsāng (M:
go) ❷ noihfō yīsāng (M: go)

physicist N: mahtléih
hohkgā (M: go)

physics N: mahtléihhohk
(M: fō, mùhn)

physiognomy N: seung-
mihnseuht (M: júng) *
physiognomist N: tái-
seunglóu (M: go)

physiology N: sàngléih
hohk (M: fō, mùhn)

phisique N: táigaak

pianist N: gongkàhmgā (M:
go)

piano N: gongkàhm (M: go,
fu, ga)

piazza N: ❶ (U.S.A.) jáulòhng (M: tìuh) ❷ (Italy) gwóng
chèuhng (M: go)

piccalilli N: gaailaahtchoi
(M: pò) syùnlaahtpaauchoi

piccloo N: dyúndék (M: jì)

pick FV: ❶ jaahk (fruit;
vegetables) ~ *sàanggwó*; ~
choi ❷ syúnjaahk N: syúnjaahk
(M: júng, go) * **pick at** Adj. PH:
tiutik ge * **pick holes** IE:
chèui mòuh kàuh chì ge *
pick out FV: tìusyún * **pick
up** PH: jihgéi hohk wúih ge *
beware of pickpockets N:
tàihfòhng síusáu; tàihfòhng
pàhsáu PH: gujyuh béi yàhn dá
hòhbāau bo!

pickaback PH: kèhhái bui
seuhngbihn ge

pickerel N: saigáuyú (M:
tìuh)

picket N: ❶ saaubīng (M: go)
❷ dáuchaatyùhn (M: go) FV:
dáuchaat

pickle N: ❶ chou (M: jèun;
daahm) ❷ paau choi (M: pò)

picklolck N: ❶ giuhsó geui
(M: bá) ❷ giuhsó chaahk;
síutàu (M: go)

pick-me-up N: ❶ hìngfán
yámbán (M: júng) ❷ hìngfánjài
(M: júng)

pickpocket N: pàhsáu (M:
go)

pickup Adj. PH: tìusyún ge

picnic N: yéhchāan VO: heui
yéhchāan

pico- (kauchìh sìhngfahn)
bíusih "mèihmèih"

pictograph N: ❶ jeuhngyìhngjih (M: go) ❷ túnggai tòuhbíu (M: go)

picture N: ❶ tòuhwá (M: fūk, jèung) ❷ séung (M: fūk; jèung) ❸ dihnyíng (hei) (M: tou, chēut) FV: ❶ mìuhsé ❷ séungjeuhng * be in the picture N: sihnggùng * come into picture PH: yàhnyàhn jùngyi * out of the picture N: tàihngoih * picture book N: tòuhwá syù (M: bún)

picturesque SV: sàangduhng ge

picul N: daam = yātbaakgàn * picul-stick N: daamtiu (M: tiuh, jì)

pidgin N: wahnjaahp yúhyihn * pidgin English PH: m̀sèuhnjing ge yìhnyúh

pie N: pài (M: go, gihn, faai)

piebald SV: hākbaahkbàan ge N: bàanmáh (M: jek)

piece M: faai, pin gihn, jèung, tiuh, dyun, bouhfahn, hòhng, jì, pin, sáu FV: ❶ bóu ❷ lìhnjip * a piece of M: yāt-jèung (gihn; pin; fūk; sáu) * in pieces FV: chaaksáan * piece work PH: gai gihn gùngjok

piecemeal SV: lìhngseui; PH: yātgihn yātgihn

pied SV: jaahpsīk ge

pier N: ❶ máhtàuh (M: go) ❷ fòhngbōtàih (M: tiuh, go)

pierce FV: ❶ gāt chyūn ❷ samtau

piercing RV: gātchyūn

piety N: ❶ kìhnsìhng ❷ (parents) haauseuhn

piffle VO: jouh mòuhlìuhsih

N: faiwá (M: fàan)

pig N: ❶ jyū (M: jek) ❷ sàangtit (M: júng) ❸ (U.S.A. coll.) gíngchaat (M: go) VO: sàang jyùjái * pig bed N: jyùlāan (M: go) * pig-tail N: bīn (M: tiuh)

pigeon N: ❶ baahkgáap (M: jek) ❷ sòhjái (M: go) ❸ (U.S.A.) néuihjái (M: go)FV: fànleuih * pigeon-breasted SV: gáihūng ge * pigeon-hearted SV: dáamsíu ge; pacháu ge * pigeon-hole N: ❶ saifóng (M: gàan) ❷ fànleuihgá (M: go)

pigment N: ❶ ngàahnlíu ❷ (biology) sīk sou

pigsty N: jyūhyūn (M: go)

pike N: ❶ (long weapon) màauh (M: jì) ❷ (fish) gáuyú (M: tiuh) ❸ tùnghàhngseui * turn pike N: gwàankā (M: go)

pilchard N: sàdīnyú (M: tiuh)

pile M: dèui; daahp N: haht fáanyingdèui FV: ❶ dèuijīk ❷ bīkyahp * a pile of PH: yāt daaih dèui (daahp, pài, kwàhn) * pile it on PH: kwàjèung * pile up FV: jīk jeuih * pile-driver N: dájònggèi (M: ga)

pilfer FV: tàu N: jòngmaht (M: gihn)

pilferer N: pàhsáu (M: go)

pilgrim N: làuhlohngjé (M: go) PH: heui singdeih chiuhbaai ge yàhn (M: go)

pill N: yeuhkyún (M: jeun, nāp) PH: tóuyihm ge yàhn (M: go)

pillage N/FV: chéunggip (M: dàan, jùng, gihn)

pillar N: chyúh (M: tiuh) PH:

yuhng chyúh jìchìh * **form pillar to post** PH: jáutàuh mòuh louh * **pillar-box** * N: yàuhtúng (M: go)

pill box N: yeuhkyúnháp (M: go)

pillory N: géngsáugá FV: jàausiu

pillow N: jámtàuh (M: go) PH: jam hái jámtàuh seuhngbihn * **pillow-case** N: jámtàuhdói (M: go)

pilot N: líhnghòhng yùhn; gasáiyùhn; fèihàhngyùhn (M: go) FV: ❶ sái ❷ daai louh * **pilot boat** N: líhnggóngsyùhn (M: jek)

pimple N: (medical) ngamchōng (M: nāp)

pin N: ❶ sàmháujām (M: go) ❷ dēng (M: háu) RV: dèngjyuh * **not care a pin** Adj. PH: yātdī dōu mjoihfùh * **pin on** RV: ❶ dèngjyuh ❷ kaujyuh * **safty pin** N: kaujām (M: go)

pinafore N: ❶ wàihkwán (M: tiùh) ❷ háuséuigìn (M: tiùh, go)

pincers N: kím (M: go, bá)

pinch FV ❶ mīt ❷ jitmòh * **at a pinch** Adj. PH: ❶ gányiu gwàantàuh ❷ bītyiusìh

pine N: ❶ chùhngsyuh (M: pò) ❷ chùhngmuhk (M: gauh, faai) FV: ❶ sau * **pine to do** Adj. PH: hotmohng jouh

pineapple N: ❶ bòlòh (M: go; faai, gihn) ❷ sáulàuhdáan (M: go)

pinery N: ❶ chùhnglàhm (M: go) ❷ bòlòhyùhn (M: go)

ping-pong N: bìngbāmbō (M: go)

pinion N: ❶ yihk (M: jek) ❷ sáukau (M: go) FV: jíntyún yihk RV: bóngjyuh

pink N: ❶ sehkjūk ❷ fánhùhng sīk SV: táahmhùhng sīk ge PH: binjó fáahùhngsīk ge * **in the pink** Adj. PH: sahpfàn gihnhòng

pinnacle N: ❶ saijìmtaap (M: go) ❷ sàandéng (M: go) PH: jài hái gòn ge deihfòng

pint N: bántyut = 1/8 gāléun)

pioneer N: taamhímjé (M: go) FV: hòitok (a place)

pious SV: ❶ kìhnsìhng ge ❷ haauseuhn ge

pip N: júngjí (M: nāp) ❷ dím (páai seuhngbihn ge) VO: jungdáan

pipe N: ❶ gún (M: tiùh) ❷ yīndáu (M: go) FV: chèui (musical instruments) ~ **dék** * **pipe down** FV: máihchòuh ~ mhóu chēutsèng * **pipe-layer** N: pòugún gùngyàhn (M: go) * **pipe-line** N: syùyàuhgún (M: tiùh)

piper PH: chèuidék ge yàhn (M: go)

piquancy N: ❶ (food) laaht ❷ chigīk

pique FV ❶ nàu ❷ sinduhng (the mass) ~ *yàhnkwàhn*

pirate N: ❶ hóidouh (M: go) ❷ hóidouhsyùhn (M: jek) PH: chàmfaahn báan kyùhn ge yàhn FV: fèifaat fàanyan (publication) ~ *syù*; ~ *màhnjèung*

piscatology N: bouhyùhhohk (M: mùhn)

pisciculture N: ❶ yéuhng-yùhhohk (M: mùhn) ❷ yéuhng-yùhyihp

piss N: niuh (coll.) (M: dihk); síubihn VO: ngòniuh

pistol N: sáuchēung (M: bá, jì) VO: hòicheūng

pit N: ❶ (nullah) hāang (M: go) ❷ (trap) haahmjehng (M: go) VO: johkhāang ✻ **pit-head** hāang (M: hāangháau) ✻ **pit-man** N: konggùng (M: go)

pit-A-pat Adj. PH: pīk pīk pāak pāak gám

pitch FV: ❶ dám (balls) ~ bō ❷ daap (tents) ~ jeungmohk ❸ jaat ~ yìhng ❹ pòu (road) ~ louh ❺ (music) yàmgòu ✻ **make a pitch for** (coll.) tai PN-góng hóu wá ✻ **pitch into** RV: tàuhyahp

pitcher N: ❶ daaih séuigun (M: go) ❷ (base ball) tàuhsáu

pitfall N: ❶ haahm jehng (M: go) ❷ yauhwaahk (M: go, júng) ❸ hyūntou (M: go)

pith N: ❶ (trees) muhkséuih ❷ (human body) jekséuih ❸ (articles) jìngséuih

pity N: ❶ tùhngchìhng ❷ lìhnmáhn ❸ wàih hahm FV: hólìhn ✻ **have pity on** FV: lìhnmáhn ✻ **what a pity!** Adj. PH: jànhaih hó sīk la!

pivot N: ❶ syùyán ❷ yiudím PH: jài hái juhk seuhngbihn

placard N: ❶ jiutip (M: jèung, go) ❷ hóibou (M: jèung, go) FV/VO: tip jiutip

placate FV: ngònwaih; ngònfú

place N: ❶ deihfòng (M: daat, go) ❷ chèuhng só (M: go) ❸ bouhwaih (M: go) FV: ❶ fong; jài ❷ ngònji ❸ tàuhjì (business) ~ deih cháan ✻ **all over the place** A: dousyu ✻ **give place to** PH: yeuhngwaih (wái) béi PN ✻ **in place of** FV: doihtai ✻ **in the first place** AV/FV: sáusīn ✻ **take place** FV: ❶ géuihàhng (a ceremony) ❷ faat-sàng (to happen)

placenta N: (animal) tòipún (M: go)

placer N: tàuhjìjé (M: go) ✻ **placer-gold** N: sàgàm

placid SV: ❶ ngònjihng ge (place) ❷ daahmdihng ge (person)

plagiarism N: douhsit

plagiarist N: douhsitjé (M: go)

plagiarize FV: chàaujaahp (articles) ~ màhnjèung

plague N: wànyihk FV: jit-mòh PH: ❶ tóuyihm ge yàhn ❷ sái (lihng) dou PW/PN dāk dóu wànyihk ✻ **black plague** N: hākséibehng ✻ **plague spot** N: wànyihkkèui (M: go)

plaid N: gaakjáibou; fònggaakbou (M: fūk; faai)

plain SV: ❶ pìhngtáan ge ❷ poksou ge (clothes) ~ sāam ❸ táanbaahk ge (words) ~ syut-wah ❹ nàahn tái ge (face) ~ yéung N: pìhngyùhn (M: go) ✻ **as plain as day light** PH: yāt-chìng yihchó ✻ **plain with** PH: deui PN jihk góng

plaint N: ❶ (poem) bēitaan ❷ (law) hunggou

plaintiff N: (law) yùhngou

(M: go)

plait N: ❶ jaap (M: go) ❷ (hair) bīn (M: tìuh) FV/VO: ❶ dájaap ❷ banbīn; sòbīn

plan N: ❶ gaiwaahk (M: go) ❷ fòngngon (M: go) ❸ dásyun (M: go) ❹ chóungon (M: go) FV: ❶ chitgai ❷ gaiwaahk * **plan on** FV: dásyun

plane N: ❶ (flat) pìhngmín (M: go) ❷ (sea surface) séuipìhng ❸ fèigèi (M: jek, ga) FV: waahthàhng * **plane tree** N: (tree) Faatgwok ǹghtùhng (M: pò)

planer N: pàauhchòhng (M: jèung)

planet N: hàhngsīng (M: go)

planetarium N: ❶ tìn-jeuhng yìh (M: go) ❷ tìn-màhngún (M: gàan)

planing N: páau (M: go) * **planing-machine** N: pàauhchòhng (M: jèung) * **planing-work** N: pàauhgùng (M: go)

plank N: ❶ báan (M: faai) ❷ jìnggòng (M: go) ❸ tìuhfún VO: pòubáan

plant N: ❶ jihkmaht (M: pò; pùhn) ❷ (factory) gùngchóng (M: gàan) FV: ❶ jung (jihk) (trees) ❷ chaap

plantation N: ❶ daaih-nùhng chèuhng (M: go) ❷ jung-jihkyùhn (M: go) ❸ jihkmàhn-deih (M: daat, go)

planter PH: ❶ jungjihk ge yàhn (M: go) ❷ bojúnggèi (M: ga) ❸ jihkmàhnjé (M: go)

plaque ❶ bíu (M: go) ❷ sīkmaht (M: gihn) ❸ fàijèung

(M: go) ❹ (medical) bàandím (M: nāp)

plash N: ❶ jīkséui hàang (M: tìuh) fàhfásèng ❷ wà wà sèng (water) FV: chínbuht

plasm N: ❶ (anatomy) hyut-jèung ❷ (biology) làhmbāyihk

plaster N: ❶ suhksehkgōu ❷ gōuyeuhk (M: jek) VO: tip gōuyeuhk * **plaster-stone** N: (biology) sehkgōu

plastic SV: ❶ yih binfa ge ❷ (medical) jíngyìhng ge N: sougàau (sokgàau) (M: jek)

plate N: ❶ díp; dihp (M: jek) ❷ (commericial sign) jiupàaih (M: go) ❸ (medical) gámgwòng-báan (M: go, faai) FV: douh (metal) ~ gām; ~ ngán * **plate glass** N: bōlèibáan (M: faai) * **plate iron** N: titbáan (M: faai)

plateau N: ❶ gòuyùhn; gòudeih (M: go) ❷ tokpún (M: go)

platform N: ❶ tòih (M: go) ❷ (speech) góngtòih (M: go) ❸ (train) yuhttòih ❹ (political) jìnggòng (M: go) * **platform bridge** N: tìnkìuh (M: go, tìuh)

plating N: (dihn) douh

platinum N: ❶ (chemistry) bohk ❷ baahkgām

platitude N: pìhngfàahn

platonism N: Paaklāaitòuh jithohk (M: mùhn)

platoon M: (military) pàaih * **platoon leader** N: pàaih-jéung (M: go)

plausibility PH: ❶ hóuchíh jàn ge; ❷ hóuchíh yáuh douhléih ge

play FV: ❶ wáan ❷ yàuhhei ❸ baahnyín (in play, drama, movie) ❹ bofong (tape recorder) ❺ chèui; jau; tàahn (musical instruments) chèui dék (flute) jau ngohkhei (instruments) tàahn kàhm (piano) N: ❶ yàuhhei (M: go) ❷ kehkbún (M: bún, go) ❺ wahnduhng (M: júng) * **bring into play** FV: faatfài * **come into play** PH: hòichí héi jokyuhng * **in full play** PH: chùngfahn faatfài * **play on (upon)** FV: leihyuhng * **TV play** N: dihnsih kehk (M: go) * **play-back** FV: chùhngyín * **play-day** N: yàuga yaht * **play-ground** N: wahnduhng-chèuhng (school) (M: go) * **play-house** N: ❶ heiyún (M: gàan, go) ❷ yìhtùhng yàuhhei sāt * **play-thing** N: wuhngeuih (M: go) * **play-writer** N: kehkjokgā (M: go) * **play football** VO: dájúkkàuh; tek júk-kàuh * **play piano** VO: tàahn gongkàhm * **play a joke** VO: hòi wàahnsiu

player N: ❶ (in sports) syún-sáu (M: go) ❷ (in play, movie) yínyùhn (M: go) ❸ cheunggèi (M: ga)

playing N: ❶ yàuhhei (M: go) ❷ béichoi (M: go) * **play/cards** N: jípáai (M: jèung; halp) * **play field** N: ❶ wahnduhng-chèuhng (M: go) ❷ yàuhhei-chèuhng (M: go)

plead FV: ❶ hánkàuh ❷ bihnwuh

pleader N: bihnwuhyàhn (M: go)

pleasant SV: ❶ yùhngyih sèungchyú ge ❷ hóngoi ge ❸ chìhng lóng ge (weather)

please FV: ❶ gòuhing ❷ chéng * **as you please** PH: chèuih néih ge yisi lā

pleased SV: ❶ hòisàm ge ❷ múhnyi ge * **be pleased to (do)** PH: lohkyi yù . . .

pleasure N: ❶ faailohk ❷ lohkcheui (M: go) * **at one's pleasure** PH: chèuihbín * **for pleasure** PH: waihjó siuhín * **with pleasure** Adj. PH: lohkyi gám * **pleasure ground** N: yàuhlohkchèuhng (M: go)

pleat N: ❶ jaap (M: go) ❷ pìnjīk FV: ❶ dájaap ❷ pìnjīk VO: dájaap

plebeian N: pìhngmàhn PH: póutùng ge yàhn (M: go) SV: pìhngmàhn ge

plebiscite N: gùngmàhn tàuhpiu

pledge N: ❶ bóujing ❷ dái-ngat (bán) (M: gihn) FV: dáijingat (things) ~ yātgàan ngūk

plenary SV: ❶ mòuhhaahn ge ❷ jyuhtdeui ge ~ kyùhnlihk * **a plenary session or meeting** N: chyùhntái wuihyíh (M: go)

plenipotentiary N: chyùhnkyùhn daaihsi (M: go) PH: yáuh chyùhn kyùhn ge

plenty PH: hóudò ge * **in plenty** SV: daaihleuhng * **plenty of** PH: hóudò ge

pliability N: yihwāan (sing)

pliers N: kím (M: bá)

plight N: fànyeuk (M: go) FV: bóujing VO: faatsaih

plimsolls N: gàaudái fàahn-bou hàaih (M: deui, jek)

plod Adj. PH: hóu guih gám

hàahng

plot N: ❶ yàmmàuh (M: go) ❷ (plan) gaiwaahk (M: go) ❸ (drama, novel) chìhng jit (M: go) ❹ (area) deih kèui (M: go, daat) FV: chaakwaahk ✳ **a plot of** PH: yātfaai deih

plough, plow N: ❶ làihtàuh (M: go) ❷ gàngdeih (M: faai, fūk) FV: ❶ gàng (field) ~ tìhn ❷ hòi (road) ~ louh ✳ **plough up** VO: chèuihchóu ✳ **plough-man** N: nùhngfù; nùhngyàhn (M: go) ✳ **plough-share** N: làihtàuh (M: go)

pluck FV: ❶ māng (grass, feather) ~ chóu, ~ mòuh ❷ jaahk ❸ làai

plucky SV: ❶ yáuh yúhnghei ge ❷ daaihdáam ge

plug N: ❶ sāk (M: go) ❷ (electric) chaapsōu (M: go) FV: ❶ sāk ❷ chaap

plum N: ❶ léi (M: go) ❷ léih syuh (M: pò) ❸ múi (M: go) ❹ mùih syuh (M: pò)

plumage N: ❶ yúhmòuh (M: tìuh) ❷ leng sāam (M: tou, gihn)

plumb N: yùhnjèui (M: go) SV: jìngkok ge FV: táichyùn ✳ **out of plumb** PH: m̀sèuih jihk

plumber N: (water, gas pipe) sàugún gùngyàhn (M: go)

plump SV: jeungmúhn ge; báaumúhn ge PH: lihngdou hóu báaumúhn

plunder FV: tàu; chéunggip N: jòngmaht (M: gihn)

plunge FV: chaapyahp N: màahngmuhk tàuhjì (land) (M: júng) ✳ **take the plaunge** PH: mouhhím sèuhngsi

plural SV: fūksou ge, juhngsou ge

plus N: gàhouh (M: go)

plush N: chèuhngmòuhyúng; háuhyúngbou (M: fūk, faai)

ply PH: ❶ m̀tìhng gám sái yuhng ❷ m̀tìhng gám mahn FV: ❶ chùhngsih ❷ (traffic) lòihwóhng N: (wire, rope) háuhdouh (M: go) ✳ **ply-wood** N: gaapbáan (M: faai)

pneumonia N: faiyìhm SV: faiyìhm ge

poach FV: ❶ (steal) tàudāk ❷ séuijyú N: bōdáan (M: jek)

poacher N: tàulihp jé (M: go)

pock N: dauhpèihjái (M: go) ✳ **pock-marked (or)- pitted** PH: yáuh dauhpèih

pocket N: ❶ dói (M: go) ❷ sāamdói (M: go) SV: jauhjàn ge; síuyìhng ge FV: yánchòhng (feeling) ~ gámchìhng ✳ **pick a pocket** N: pàhsit ✳ **pocket-book** N: ① jauhjànbún (M: bouh, bún) ② bātgeibóu (M: bouh, bún) ✳ **pocket-money** N: lìhngyuhngchìhn; lìhngyuhngchín

pod N: dauhgók; dauh gok (M: tìuh)

podgy SV: fèihngái ge

poem N: ❶ sì (M: sáu) ❷ wáhnmàhn (M: pìn)

poet N: sìyàhn (M: go)

poetess N: néuihsìyàhn (M: go)

poetry N: ❶ sì (N: sáu) ❷ sìjaahp (M: bún)

poignant SV: sèungsàm ge

poignancy N: sàmhāak; sàmhāak

point M: dím N: ❶ (mathematics) síusoudím ❷ (competition) fàn FV: ❶ jíheung ❷ bíumíhng ✳ a full point N: geuihouh (M: go) ✳ at the point of A: jèunggahn ✳ catch the point of PH: bángāak yiudím ✳ come to the point PH: góngdou yiudím ✳ point out RV: jíchēut ✳ off the point FV: lèihtàih ✳ point of view N: gùndím (M: go)

pointed SV: ❶ (things or words) jìmyeuih ge ❷ (words) sēutjihk ge

pointer N: ❶ jísihmaht (M: gihn) ❷ yātjúng lihpgáu

pointless SV: ❶ deuhn ❷ móuh yiyih ge

poise FV: bóuchìh gwànhàhng N: chàhmjeuhk

poison N: duhkyeuhk FV: duhkhoih ✳ poison-gas N: (military) duhkhei

poisoning VO: jungduhk

poisonous SV: jungduhk ge

poke FV: ❶ (use pointed thing) gāt ❷ gònsip ❸ gīklaih ✳ poke one's nose into VO: gún hàahn sih FV: gòn yuh

poky SV: ❶ yáuh haahn ge ❷ mòuhlìuh ge ❸ chìh'deuhn ge

polar SV: ❶ nàahmgihk ge ❷ bākgihk ge ❸ deihgihk ge N: (mathematics) gihksin

polaris N: (astronomy) bākgihksīng (M: nāp)

pole N: ❶ chyúh (M: tiuh) ❷ pàahng (M: jì) ❸ gòn (M: jì) ✳

pole-jump(ing) N: chàang gòntiu ✳ pole-star N: ❶ bākgihksīng (M: nāp) ❷ jídouhyàhn (M: go)

pole N: Bōlàahnyàhn (M: go)

polemic N: ❶ jàngleuhn ❷ gùnggīk SV: jàngleuhn ge

police N: ❶ gíngchaat; chàaiyàhn (M: go) ❷ gíngchaat gèigwàan; gíngchaatgúk (M: go, gàan) ❸ gùngngòn bouhmùhn (M: go) FV: gúnhaaht

policeman N: gíngchaat; chàaiyàhn (M: go)

policlinic N: mùhnchánbouh (M: go)

policy N: ❶ jingchaak (M: júng, go) ❷ fòngjàm ✳ domestic (foreign) policy N: gwoknoih (ngoihgāau) jingchaak ✳ carry out a policy FV/VO: jāphàhng jingchaak ✳ follow the policy of PH: fuhnghàhng . . . jingchaak ✳ policy-maker N: kyut chaak yàhn (M: go)

Polish SV: (people, language) Bōlàahn ge N: Bōlàahnwá

polish FV: ❶ yàuh (shoes) ~ hàaih ❷ dálaahp (floor, funiture) ✳ polish off PH: hóu chùngmòhng gám jouh yùhn

polite SV: ❶ yáuh láih (maauh) ge ❷ yáuh gaauyéuhng ge ❸ sìmàhn ge ✳ polite greeting N: haaktou

politeness N: láihmaauh

politic SV: ❶ jingmìhng ge ❷ yáuh chaakleuhk ge

political SV: jingjih ge PH: hàhngjingseuhng ge ✳ political activities N: jingjih wuhtduhng * political conception N: jingjih sīséung * political economy N: jingjih gìngjai hohk * political party N: jingdóng (M: go) * political policy N: jingchaak (M: go) * political power N: jingkyühn * political prisoner (criminal) N: jingjihfáan (M: go) * political situation N: jingguhk (M: go)

politician N: ❶ jingjihgā (M: go) ❷ jinghaak (M: go)

politics N: ❶ jingjih ❷ jingjihhohk (M: mùhn) ❸ jinggin ❹ chaakleuhk * play politics VO: gáau jingjih

poll N: ❶ (ancient time) yàhntàuh (M: go) ❷ tàuhpiu chyu (M: go) FV: (election) syúngéui VO: tàuhpiu * polling distric N: syúnkèui (M: go) * poll tax N: yàhntàuhseui * poll parrot N: yìngmóuh (M: jek)

pollen N: (plant) fàfán

pollute FV: ❶ gáau wùjòu ❷ wùyuhk N: (medical) wàihjīng

pollutant N: wùyíhm mahtjāt

pollution N: wùwai; wùyíhm * air pollution N: hùnghei wùyíhm * noise pollution N: chouyām

polo N: máhkàuh * water polo N: séuikàuh (M: go)

polygamy N: ❶ dòpuingáuhjai ❷ yātchàidòfùjai ❸ yātfùdòchàijai

polyglot PH: ❶ (people) sīk géijúng yúhyìhn ge (yàhn) (M: go) ❷ (books) yuhng géijúng sésìhng ge (syù) (M: bún)

polygragh N: ❶ dòcháan jokgā (M: go) ❷ fūkséhei (M: ga) ❺ chāakfōnggèi (M: ga)

polysyllable N: dòyàmjitchìh

polytechnic PH: dòjúng gùngngaih ge N: ❶ gùngngaih hohkhaauh (M: gàan) ❷ gùngyihp daaihhohk (M: gàan)

polytheism N: dòsàhnleuhn

pomade (pomatum) N: faatyàuh (tàuhyàuh) (M: jèun) VO: chàh faat (tàuh) yàuh

pomegranate N: sehkláusyuh (M: pò)

pomelo N: lūkyáu; sàtìhnyáu; sòng-màhyáu (M: go; káai)

pommel N: (top of a knife) ngontàuh (M: go) FV: ngàudá

pomp N: jonggùn; wàhlaih (M: go)

pond N: chìhtòhng; yàhngùngwùh (M: go) VO: héi (jūk) chìh * pond life N: chìhsàng duhng maht

ponder FV: nám; jísaiháauleuih (problem, difficulty, etc) * ponder on (over) FV: fáanfūk sīháau

ponderous SV: ❶ bahnjuhng ge ❷ pòhngdaaih ge PH: ❶ lìhng yàhn yimgyuhn ge ❷ chúhng dougihk ge

pontiff N: ❶ gaauwòhng; gaaujūng (M: wái, go) ❷ jyúgaau (M: wái, go) ❸ (ancient Roman) gòujàung; gaaujéung (M: wái, go) ❹ (old Jewish) daaihjai sī (M: wái, go)

pony N: ❶ máhjái (M: jek) ❷ choimáh * pony tail N: ❶

(hair) máhméih (M: tìuh) ❷faatyìhng

poodle N: sijígáu; chèuhng gyúnmòuh gáu (M: jek)

pool N: ❶ séuitòhng (M: go) chìh (M: go) ❸ tàahm (M: go) FV: lyùhnyìhng; hahpfógingyìhng; hahpbaahn ✻ **a swimming pool** N: yàuhséuichìh; yàuhwihngchìh (M: go)

poop N: ❶ syùhnméih gaapbáan ❷ syùhnméih (M: go) ❸ (people) sòhjái (M: go) VO: fongpei

poor SV: ❶ kùhng; móuhchín ❷ (in quality) yáih; m̀hóu ❸ (worthy of pity) hólìhn ✻ **the poor** N: kùhng yàhn ✻ **poor spirited** SV: yúhnyeuhk ge; móuhheilìhk ge

poorly PH: m̀syùfuhk ✻ **think poor of** FV: dàigú

pop PH: ❶ faatchēut baaulihtsēng ❷ dahtyìhn hàhngduhng VO: hòichēung N: ❶ chēungsēng ❷ (coll.) heiséui; bējáu (M: jèun) ❸ (music) làuhhàhng yàmngohk; làuhhàhng gōkūk (M: sáu) ✻ **popcorn** N: paaugūk (M: nāp) ✻ **pop-gun** N: heichēung (M: bá, jì) ✻ **pop wine** N: heijáu (M: jèun)

pope N: Lòhmáh gaauwòhng (M: wái)

poplar N: baahkyèuhng; yèuhngmuhk (M: pò)

poppy N: ❶ (American sl.) bàhbā (M: go) ❷ (plant) ngàngsūk; ngàngsūkfā (M: pò) ✻ **poppy-cock** N: faiwá

populace N: pìhngmàhn; daaihjung

popular SV: ❶ làuhhàhng ge; sìhhìng ge ❷ yáuh mìhngmohng ge Adj. PH: ❶ dī yàhn jùngyi ge ❷ (of style of writing or speaking) tùngjuhk syù sédāk hóu . . . ❸ (of people) yàhnmàhn ✻ **popular with** Patt: sauh N ge fùnyìhng ge

population N: ❶ yàhnháu ❷ chyùhntái gèuimàhn ✻ **population explosion** PH: yàhnháu fātyìhn jànggàjó

populous SV: yàhnháu chàuhmaht ge N: yàhnháu hóudò

porcelain N: chìh; chìhhei (M: gihn, go) SV: jìngméih ge ✻ **porcelain wares** N: chìhhei (M: gihn)

porch N: ❶ yahpháuchyu (M: go) ❷ jáulòhng; jáulóng (M: tìuh)

procupine N: jinjyū (M: jek)

pore N: mòuhgún; mòuhhúng (M: go) FV: ❶ suhkduhk ~ yāt-bún syù ❷ mahkséung ✻ **sweat from every pore** Adj. PH: hìngfáhn dougihk

pork N: jyùyuhk (M: gauh, faai, gihn) ✻ **pork-pie** N: jyùyuhkbéng (M: gihn) ✻ **pork chop** N: jyùpá (M: gihn, faai) ✻ **pork ribs** N: pàaihgwāt (M: gihn, gauh)

porker N: yúhjyū (M: jek)

pork-ling N: jyùjái (M: jek)

porky SV: fèih ge

pornography N: ❶ sīkchìhng màhn hohk (M: bún) ❷ sīk chìhngwá (M: fūk, jèung)

porous SV: dòlūng ge PH: hóyíh samséui ge

porpoise N: kìhngyùhjái (M: tìuh)

porridge N: ❶ (rice congee) jūk (M: wún) ❷ mahkpèihjūk; mahkpínjūk (M: wún) ✳ **porridge with fish** N: yùhsàangjūk (M: wún) ✳ **porridge with pork** N: jyùyuhkjūk (M: wún) ✳ **porridge with beef** N: ngàuhyuhkjūk (M: wún)

port N: ❶ góng; gónghàu (hóiháu) (M: go) ❷ gèichèuhng (M: go) ❸ beihfùnggóng (M: go) ❹ hòhnghùngjaahm (M: go) ❺ (town) fauh; fauhtàuh (M: go) ❻ géuijí; taaidouh; jìsai ❼ hùhngpòuhtòuhjáu (M: jèun; bùi) VO: jàchēung ✳ **put into port** VO: yahpgóng ✳ **port authority (office)** N: góngmouhguhk (M: gàan) ✳ **port charge** N: yahpgóngseui ✳ **naval port** N: gwàngóng (M: go) ✳ **port clearance** N: chēutháují (M: jèung) ✳ **port wine** N: būtjáu (M: jèun; bùi)

portable SV: ❶ yihdaai ge; hìngbihn ge ❷ sáutàih ge ✳ **portable typewriter** N: sáutàih dájihgēi (M: ga)

portent N: ❶ yuhsiuh; jìngsiuh ❷ ngoksiuh; hùngsiuh

porter N: ❶ gūlēi (M: go) ❷ (luggage carrier) bùnwahngùngyàhn (M: go) ❸ (train) lihtchèyùhn (M: go) ❹ hàkbējáu (M: bìu)

portfolio N: gùngmàhndói; gùngsihdói (M: go) ✳ **minister without portfolio (British)** N: bātgúnbouh daaihsàhn (M: go)

porthole N: ❶ syùhnchēung (M: go) ❷ chōnghàu (M: go) ❸ paaumùhn (M: go)

portion N: ❶ bouhfahn (M: go) ❷ (share) fahn ❸ gajòng FV: fânpui

portly SV: ❶ fèih ge ❷ gihnsehk ge

portrait N: ❶ séung; chiujeuhng (M: fūk) ❷ mìuhsé ❸ mùihseuht

portray FV: ❶ waahk ❷ baahnyín

portrayal N: chiujeuhng (M: fūk)

Portuguese N: Pòuhtòuhngàhyàhn; sàiyèuhngyàhn (M: go)

pose N: (bodily attitude) jìsai (M: go) FV: ❶ jònghùngjoksai ❷ tàihchēut

position BF: (location) — syu; — douh N: (posture) ❶ waihji ❷ jìsai (M: go, júng) ❸ (situation) chìhng yìhng (M: go) ❹ (social position) deihwaih (M: go) ❺ (job) jīkwaih; sànfán (M: go) ❻ (attitude and position) yigin; gingáai (M: go) PH: jài hái sīkdong ge waih ji ✳ **in a position to (do)** PH: nàhnggau . . . ✳ **in (out of) position** PH: hái (m̀haih hái) sīkdong ge waihji ✳ **people of position** N: jùngseuhngchàhng gàaikàp

positive SV: ❶ móuh mahntàih ge; koksaht ge; hángdihng ge ❷ jīkgihk ge ❸ (electricity) yèuhngsing ge ❹ (mathematics) jing ge ✳ **positive electricity** N: yèuhngdihn

positivism N: (philosophy) sahtjingjyúyih; sahtjingleuhn

posse N: (police) yātdeuih; yāttyùhn ~ gíngchaat ✳ **in posse (law)** A: hónàhng gám

possess FV: ❶ (own, of property) yáuh; geuih yáuh ❷ hungjai; jìpui (people, family finance) ~ *yàhn;* ~ *gàtìhng ge gìngjai; béi PN/N* ~ ❸ hākjai (feeling) ~ *gámchìhng* N: ❶ jimyáuh ❷ sóyáuhkyùhn (M: go) ✳ **possessed by a devil** PH: gwái séuhngsàn

possessor N: chìhyáuhyàhn (M: go) ✳ **possessor of property** N: yihpjyú (M: go)

possibility N: hónàhngsing (M: go) ✳ **by any possibility** PH: mòuhleuhn dím . . . A: maahnyāt ✳ **by some possibility** A: waahkjé

possible SV: ❶ hónàhng yáuh ge; hónàhng ge; jouhdākdou ❸ hahpléih ge PH: lìhngyàhn mùhnyi ge ✳ **as possible as** PH: jeuhn hónàhng ✳ **in possible** PH: yùhgwó yáuh hónàhng ✳ **possible candidate** PH: sīkdong ge hauhsyúnyàhn (M: go)

possibly SV: hónàhng gám A: ❶ waahkjé ❷ jeuhn hónàhng

post N: ❶ jīkwaih; sih (job) (M: go) ❷ (of a fence) chyúh (M: tiúh, jì) ❸ seun; yàuhgín (M: fūng) ❹ yàuhguhk; yàuhgúk (M: gàan) ❹ yàuhtúng; yàuhsēung (M: go) ❻ yihkjaahm (M: go) FV: ❶ gei (letter) ❷ dènghái; gwahái ❸ tip hái; nihm hái VO: gwojeung ✳ **post-box** N: seunsēung (M: go) ✳ **parcel post** N: yàuhbāau (M: go) ✳ **post card** N: mìhngseunpín (M: jēung, go) ✳ **post free** PH: m̀sái béi yàuhfai ge ✳ **post office** N: yàuhguhk; yàuhgúk (M: gàan) ✳ **post-man** N: paaiseunlóu; yàuhchàai (M: go) ✳ **post-paid** PH: yàuh fai yíhgìng béijó ge ✳

post test PH: hohkkèih méih ge chāakyihm ✳ **post-dated check** N: kèihpiu (M: jèung) ✳ **post master** N: yàuhjìngguhk-jéung (M: go) ✳ **post mortem examination** VO: yihmsì ✳ **post meridian (p.m.)** TW: hahjau

postage N: yàuhfai ✳ **postage stamp** N: yàuhpiu (M: go)

postal PH: yàuhguhk ge; yàuhjing ge N: mìhngseunpín (M: go, jèung) ✳ **postal matter** N: yàuhgín (M: gihn)

poster N: ❶ (printed bill) goubaahk; gāaijiu ❷ gwóng-gouwá (M: fūk) PH: tipchyùhn-dāan ge yàhn (M: go) ✳ **post a poster** VO: tip goubaahk; tip gāaijiu; tip gwónggouwá; tip hóibou

posterior SV: ❶ hauhmihn ge ❷ gaauchìh ge N: (of the body) tyùhnbouh; hauhbouh (coll.) peigú; lōyáu (M: go)

posterity N: jísyùn; hauhdoih

postgraduate N: yìhngau-sāng (M: go) PH: ❶ yìhngauyún ge ❷ daaihhohk bātyihphauh gaijuhk yìhngau ge ✳ **postgraduate course** N: yìhngau fōmuhk ✳ **postgraduate school** N: yìhngauyún; yìhngausó (M: gàan)

posthumous PH: ❶ wàih-jok ge; ❷ séihauhchēut báan ge ❸ bàhbā séijó jihauh chēut-sai ge; wàihfūkge ✳ **a posthumous book** N: wàih-jok; wàihjyu (M: bún, bouh) ✳ **posthumous fame** PH: séijó jihauh ge sìngyuh ✳ **a posthumous son** N: wàihfūkjí (M: go)

postmeridian TW/N: ❶ jùngngh (ngaanjau jihauh ge) ❷ hahjau (abb. P.M. waahkjé p.m.)

postpone FV: yìhnkèih; jínkèih; tèuichìh

postponement N: yìhnkèih

postscript N: ❶ (to a letter) joijé (Abb. P.S.) ❷ (to a periodical) fuhkái ❸ (to a book) fuhkái

postulate FV: ❶ jyújèung ❷ yiukàuh ❸ peiyuh; gádihng N: ❶ gádihng ❷ tiuhgín (M: go) ❸ gèibún yùhnléih (M: go)

posture N: ❶ jìsai (M: go) ❷ chìhngfong (M: go) ❸ taaidouh (M: go)

postwar SV: jinhauhge TW: jinhauh

posy NuM: yātjaat fā

pot M: ❶ wùh ❷ bōu ❸ gun N: ❶ wohk (M: go) ❷ (coll.) yātbāt chín ❸ kèigām jíngngáak (M: bāt) ❹ daaih yàhnmát (M: go) ❺ ngàhnbūi (M: jek) ✳ **go to pot** PH: bèi yàhn jíngwaaihjó ✳ **flower pot** N: fāpùhn (M: go) ✳ **teapot** N: chàhwú (M: go) ✳ **waterpot** N: séuigòng (M: go)

potato N: syùhjái; hòhlāansyú (M: go) ✳ **sweet potato** N: fàansyú (M: go) ✳ **potato chips** N: syùhpín

potential SV: hónàhng ge N: ❶ chìhmlihk (M: júng) ❷ dihnsai

potion Nu M: (of Chinese medicine) yātjài

potter N: ❶ tòuhgùng (M: go) ❷ mòuhsìhmòhng PH: jouh gòngngáh ge yàhn (M: go) FV: mòuhsihmòhng Adj. PH: maahnmáan gám hàahng

pottery N: ❶ tòuhhei; gòngngáh ❷ tòuhheijaijouhseuht (M: mùhn) ❸ tòuhheichèuhng; tòuhheichóng (M: gàan)

potty SV: m̀juhngyiu ge; sóseui ge N: niuhwú (M: go)

pouch N: ❶ doih (M: go) ❷ yīndói (M: go) ❸ (kangaroo) tóuhdói (M: go) PH: jòngyahp dói léuihbihn ✳ **a postman's pouch** N: yàuhdói (M: go)

poult N: ❶ (gāi; ngaap; fógāi dáng dáng) gàkàhm PH: maaihgàkàhmgeyàhn (M: go)

poulterer N: gāingaaplóu (M: go)

poultry N: gāingaap ✳ **poultry shop** N: gāingaap póu (M: gàan)

pounce FV: (sudden quick action) máahngpok

pound M: (weight) bohng (= 16 ōnsí; Abb: lb) N: ❶ (British: unit of money) yìngbohng; yìngbóng ❷ yùhtòhng (M: go) FV: dám; paak (to hit) ✳ **pound on the door** VO: dámmùhn; paakmùhn ✳ **pound on the table** VO: dám tói; paaktói ✳ **pound into small pieces** FV: dámseui ✳ **pound with a pestle** FV: jùng ✳ **pound rice** VO: jùngmáih

poundage N: bohngsou; bohngchúhng

pounder PH: ❶ yātbohng chúhng ge yéh (e.g. yú) ❷ yáuh Nu bohng ge yéh N: gwan (M: tiuh, jì)

pour FV: ❶ (heavily) dóu ❷ (gently) jàm N: kìngpùhn daaihyúh ✻ **pour cold water on** PH: heung PN put láahngséui ✻ **pour oil on the fire** IE: fóséuhng gàyàuh ✻ **pour out water** VO: dóuséui ✻ **pour the water out** PH: dóujó dī séui kéuih

pout PH: ❶ (angry or unhappy) dyūthéi go jéui ❷ m̀gòuhing VO: dyūtjéui

poverty SV: ❶ kùhngfú ❷ kyutfaht PH: m̀jūkgau ✻ **poverty of the soil** Adj. PH: sau tóudeih

powder N: ❶ (fine particles) fán (M: ngàang, jèun, hahp) ❷ yeuhkfán (M: jèun) ❸ fóyeuhk FV: ❶ mòhseui ❷ (sprinkle with) sám VO: chàhfán (the face) ✻ **medicinal powder** N: yeukfán; yeuhksáan (M: jèun) ✻ **gunpowder** N: fóyeuhk (M: júng) ✻ **keep one's powder dry** PH: sihsih dōu yuhbeih gán ✻ **powder blue** N: chínlàahmsīk ✻ **powder and shot** N: jídáan (M: nāp) ❷ gwànyuhngbán ✻ **powder mill** N: fóyeuhkchóng (M: gàan) ✻ **powder magazine** N: fóyeuhk fu (M: gàan) ✻ **powder puff** N: fánpok (M: go)

powdered PH: yáuh hóudò bàandím ge ✻ **powdered milk** N: náaihfán (M: gun) ✻ **powdered sugar** N: fántòhng

power N: ❶ (energy) lihk; táilihk ❷ (ability) lihk; lihkleuhng ❸ (electronic) duhnglihk ❹ (authority) kyùhn; kyùhnlihk ❺ (influence) sai lihk (M: go) ✻ **beyond (out of) power** PH: nàhnglihksónàhnggau dou ge SV: (authority) sātsai ge ✻ **come into power**

VO: jāpjing ✻ **in full power** PH: hòijūkmáhlihk ✻ **power house (power plant; power station)** N: faatdihnchóng (M: gàan) ✻ **power transmission** VO: syúdihn ✻ **in power** SV: dòngkyùhn ge; dāksai ge ✻ **out of power (office)** VO: lohktòih; sātsai ✻ **power politics** N: kèuhngkyùhn jingjih ✻ **the powers that be** N: dòngguhkjé (M: go, wái) ✻ **power of attraction** N: kāpyáhnlihk ✻ **power of resistance** N: dáikonglihk ✻ **power of imagination** N: séungjeuhnglihk (M: go) ✻ **political power** N: jingkyùhn (M: go)

pox N: ❶ (medical) dáu; séuidáu (M: nāp) tìnfā ❷ (medical) mùihduhk

practical SV: ❶ sahtjai ❷ sáidāk ❸ saht-yuhng PH: ❶ sahtsih kàuhsih ge ❷ gìngyihmfùngfu ge ✻ **practical nurse** N: chōkāp-wuhléihyùhn (M: go)

practice(d) N: ❶ sahthàhng; sahtchín ❷ (perform repeatedly) lihnjaahp; sahtjaahp FV: ❶ sahthàhng ❷ lihnjaahp; sahtjaahp ~ séjih; ~ tàahnkàhm ✻ **in practice** A: saht jaiseuhng ✻ **practice makes perfect** IE: suhknàhng sàngháau ✻ **put in (into) practice** FV: sahthàhng; sihhàhng ✻ **practice teacher** N: sahtjaahp gaausī (M: go) ✻ **make a practice to (of)** FV: gwaanjó MA: heunglòih

pragmatic SV: ❶ jihfuh ge ❷ (philosophy) sahtyuhng jyúyih ge PH: jùngyi léih hàanhnsih ge

prairie N: ❶ daaihchóuyùhn (M: go) ❷ muhkchèuhng (M: go)

praise N: ❶ jaanméih; chìng-jaan ❷ jaanchìh (M: pìn) FV: jaan ~ *PN lēk* ❷ jaanméih ~ *seuhngdai* ❸ kwàjéung * **praise-worthy** Adj. PH: jihkdāk jaange

pram N: yìngyihchè (M: ga) ❷ pìhngdáisyùhn (M: jek) PH: sungngàuhnáaih ge sáutèui chè (M: ga)

prance FV: (happy action) tiu PH: daaihbouhhàahng

prank VO: hòiwàahnsiu N: ngokjokkehk FV: jōngsīk; dábaan

prate FV/N: ❶ lòsō ❷ hùngtàahm

prawn N: (seafood) hā; lùhnghā; deuihā (M: jek) VO: jūkhā

pray FV: ❶ chíngkàuh; kàuh ❷ kèihtóu; tóugou

prayer PH: ❶ chíngkàuh ge yàhn (M: go) ❷ tóugou ge yàhn (M: go) N: ❶ kèihtóu ❷ kèihtóumàhn (M: pìn) * **prayer book** N: kèihtóumàhn (syù) (M: bún) * **lord's prayer** N: jyútóumàhn (M: pìn) * **prayer meeting** N: kèihtóuwúi (M: go)

preach VO: chyùhngaau; chyùhndouh; góngdouh * **preach the gospel** VO: chyùhfūkyām

preacher N: chyùhndouh yàhn (M: go)

preact N/FV: tàihchìhn; chìuchìhn

preamble N: jeuih; douh-yìhn; hòichèuhngbaahk (M: pìn)

prearange FV: yuhsìn ngòn-

pàaih; yuhdihng

preassembled PH: yuhsìn ngònjòng ge

preassigned PH: yuhsìn jídihng ge; yuhsìn fànpui ge

precarious SV: ❶ m̀kokdihng ge ❷ ngàihhím ge ❸ m̀wándihng ge

precaution N: ❶ síusàm ❷ gíngtīk ❸ yuhfòhng; fòhngbeih * **take precaution against** FV: yuhfòhng

precede FV: ❶ joihsìn; sìn (in time) ❷ hàahngsìn (go in front of) Patt: bèi — lìhngsìn

precedent N: ❶ chìhnlaih; sìnlaih; laih (M: go) ❷ gwaanlaih (M: go) SV: ❶ chìhnbihn ge ❷ yàusìn ge

preceding SV: chìhnbihn ge PH: seuhngbihn sógóng ge * **the preceding day** PH: chìhn yātyaht

precept N: ❶ gaakyìhn (M: geui) ❷ gaaufan (M: go) ❸ (technical) kwàifaahn

preceptor N: ❶ gaaudouhjé (M: go) ❷ gaausī (M: go) ❸ haauhjéung (M: go)

precinct N: gínggaai; hahtkèui (M: go)

precious SV: jàngwai ge; gwaijuhng ge; bóugwai ge A: fèisèuhng * **precious blood** N: bóuhyut (M: dihk) * **precious stone** N: bóusehk (M: nāp) * **precious sword** N: bóugim; bóudōu (M: bá) * **precious things** N: bóubui; jànbóu; bóumaht * **precious words** IE: gàmyuhk lèuhngyìhn

precipice N: sàanngàahm; yùhnngàaih; chiubik (M: go)

precipitant SV: ❶ hímjeun ❷ dahtyìhn ge ❸ gāpchou ge N: chàhmdihnjāi

precipitate RV: ❶ dámlohk ❷ jeuihlohk FV: chūkjeun

precis N: (law) jaahkyiu; tàihyiu VO: ❶ jaahk yiudím; ❷ jouh daaihgōng

precise SV: ❶ jìngkok ge; ❷ koksaht ge; ❸ yìhmgaak ge ✳ be precise PH: kokchit gám góng

preclude FV: ❶ pàaihchèuih (doubt) ~ yìhleuih ❷ jójí ❸ fòhngngoih

precocious SV: jóusuhk ge

preconception N: ❶ yuhséung ❷ pìngìn; sìhnggin

precondition N: ❶ chìhntàih ❷ sìnkyut tiuhgín PH: yuhsìn jéunbeih

predatory SV: ❶ chéungdyuht sing ge ❷ (animal) sihkyuhk ge

predecessor N: ❶ chìhnyàhm (office) (M: go) ~ júngtúng ❷ chìhnyàhn ❸ chìhnbui ❹ jóusìn PH: yùhnlòih yíhgìng yáuh ge sihmaht

predestinate FV: yuhdihng PH: mihngjùng jyudihng SV: jyudihng ge; jíngdihng ge

predestination N: ❶ mihngwahn (M: go) ❷ sàhndihngleuhn; sūkmihngleuhn

predetermine FV: ❶ yuhdihng; sìndihng ❷ jyudihng

predicament N: ❶ chyú-

gíng (M: go) ❷ (tragic suffering) fúgíng (M: go) ❸ (danger) hímgíng (M: go) ❹ (embarrassment) kwangíng ❺ (logic) faahnchàuh (M: go)

predicate N: ❶ (language) waihyúh ❷ (grammar) seuhtchìh; seuhtyúh ❸ (logic) bànchìh FV: ❶ sìngmìhng ❷ yimeihjyuh

predict FV: (prophecy) yuhyìhn; yuhgou; yuhbou; yuhchāk (yuhchāak)

predilection N: pìnngoi; pìnhou; ngoihou

predisposition N: ❶ soujāt ❷ kìngheung ❸ pīksing ❹ (medical) souyàn

predominance N: dahtchēut; yàuyuht; cheukyuht

predominant SV: ❶ jyúyiu ge ❷ dahtchēut ge ❸ yáuh yínghéung ge ❹ yáuh sailihk ge ❺ gihtchēut ge

predominate FV: jìpui

preeminence N: gihtchēut ge

preeminent SV: ❶ yàusau ge ❷ yàuyuht ge IE: chēutleuih bahtséuih ge

preengage FV: ❶ yuhyeuk; ❷ dāksìn; jimsìn

preestablish PH: yuhsìn chitlaahp; yuhsìn jaidihng FV: yuhdihng

preexist FV: ❶ sìnchyùhn (joih)

preexistence N: ❶ sìnchyùhn (joih) ❷ chìhnsai

prefabricate FV: yuhchāk (yuhchāak) PH: yuhsìn kauséung

preface N: (of a book or speech) jéui; jeui chìhnyìhn (M: pìn, go) VO: séjéui; séjeui FV: hòichí

prefect N: ❶ (ancient Roman, France or Italy) deihfòng hàhngjing jéunggùn (M: go) sìlìhnggùn (M: go) ❷ (class prefect) kāpjéung; bāanjéung (M: go)

prefecture PH: deihfòng jéunggùn ge jīkwaih (M: go) N: sáang; jàu (M: go)

prefer A: nìhngyún; chìhngyún AV: béigaau jùngyi (héifùn) FV: ❶ tàihchèut ❷ tàihsìng Patt: gokdāk . . . hóudī * prefer . . . above all others Patt: jeui jùngyi . . . * prefer . . . to . . . Patt: chìhngyún (nìhngyún) . . . daahnhaih (yìh) m̀ . . . * prefer to die rather than surrender IE: nìhngséi bātwāt

preference N: ❶ syúnjaaht (M: go) ❷ yàusìnkyùhn (M: go)

prefigure FV: ❶ yuhséung; ❷ yuhsih

prefix N: (language) chìhtàuh; jìhsáu Patt: jàihái . . . jìchìhn

preform PH: ❶ yuhsìn yìhngsìhng ❷ yuhsìn kyutdihng ❸ chòbouh gàgùng (of products) ~ ge jaisìhngbán

pregnancy N: wàaihyahn (M: chi)

pregnant PH: wàaihyahn ge SV: (full of meaning) fuyáuh yiyìh ge VO: yáuh sàngéi

prehistoric SV: síchìhn ge

prehistory N: ❶ síchìhnsí

❷ síchìhnhohk (M: mùhn)

prejudg(e)ment N: ❶ yuhkyut ❷ yuhdyuhn

prejudice N: ❶ pìngin; sìhnggin ❷ sèunghoih ❸ syúnhoih Patt: deui N yáuh ~ PH: chyùhn yáuh pìngin (sìhnggin) * in prejudice of A: bātleihyù * racial prejudice PH: júngjuhk kèihsih * without prejudice PH: móuh pìngin; móuh syúnhoih; deui N móuh pìngin

prelate N: ❶ gòukāp gaausih (M: go) ❷ jyúgaau; daaihjyúgaau (M: go)

preliminary SV: chòbouh ge; hòichí ge N: ❶ yuhsi ❷ yuhchoi PH: (pl.) chòbouh ge hàhngduhng, chousì dángdáng * preliminary announcement N: yuhgou (M: go) * preliminary expense N: hòibaahnfai (M: bāt) * preliminary hearing N: (law) yuhsám (M: go) * preliminary matches N: yuhchoi (M: go) * preliminary measure FV/N: chòbouh gaiwaahk * preliminary remarks N: yuhyìhn (M: pìn, go)

prelude N: ❶ jeuihyìhn (M: pìn) ❷ jeuihmohk (M: go) ❸ (music) jeuihkūk; chìhnjau (kūk) (M: sáu) PH: ❶ waih N ge jeuihmohk (chìhnjau) ❷ waih PN séjéui

premature SV: ❶ jóusuhk ❷ meih sìhngsuhk * premature birth N: síucháan ❷ premature death SV: dyúnmehng * premature opinion PH: m̀sìhngsuhk ge yigin

premedical PH: yìfō daaihhohk yuhfō ge * premedical student N: yìyuhfō hohksāang

(M: go)

premeditate PH: ❶ yuhsìn gaiwaahk ❷ yuhsìn séunggwo

premier N: ❶ (monarchical government) júngléih (M: go) ❷ (prime minister) sáuseung (M: go) ❸ (in America) gwokmouhhìng (M: go) ❹ (in China) hàhngjing yúnjéung (M: go) PH: ❶ jeui gányiu ge ❷ daihyāt ge ❸ jeui jóu ge * premier of the state council N: gwokmouhyún júngléih (M: go)

premiere N: ❶ (France) sáuchi (daihyātchi) (of dramma, opera) gùng yín (M: chi) ❷ néuihjyúgok (M: go)

premise N: (in logic) chìhntàih (M: go) PH: yuhsìn góng * the major premise N: daaih chìhntàih (M: go) * the minor premise N: síu chìhntàih (M: go)

premises N: ❶ hòichèuhng-baahk (M: pìn) ❷ fòhngcháan

premium N: ❶ bouchàuh ❷ jéunggām (M: bāt) ❸ jéungbán (M: fahn, go) ❹ (of insurance) bóuhímfai; yinsō (M: bāt) ❺ hohkfai (M: bāt) * at a premium PH: sauhdou juhngsih * put a premium on FV/SV: ❶ jéunglaih ❷ juhngsih

premonition N: ❶ yuhgou (M: go) ❷ sìnsiuh (M: go) ❸ yuhgám (M: go) * premonition of failue PH: sātbaaih ge sìnsiuh

premonitory PH: yuhsìn gínggou ge

preoccupation N: ❶ sìn-dāk ❷ sìnjim ❸ sìnjyuh ❹ pìngin (M: go) PH: chyùhnsàhn gunjyu

preordain PH: yuhsìn jyudihng FV: yuhdihng

prep N: ❶ (of students) sìn-sàubāan; bóujaahpbāan (M: bāan) ❷ jihsàn ❸ gātihng jokyihp (M: bún, bouh; yihp) * a prep school N: yuhbeih hohkhaauh; bóujaahp hohk-haauh (M: gàan)

preparation N: ❶ yuhbeih; jéunbeih ❷ yeuhkjai * in preparation PH: jéunbeihgán * make preparation for Patt: waih N jouh jéunbeih

preparatory SV: ❶ yuhbeih ge ❷ chòbouh ge N: yuhfō * preparatory class N: yuhbeihbāan (M: bāan) * preparatory school N: yuhbeih (yuhfō) hohkhaauh (M: gàan) * preparatory measures (training) N: chòbouh chousì (fanlihn)

prepare FV: ❶ yuhbeih; jéunbeih ❷ jyú; jíng (in cooking) ~ faahn; ~ sung ❸ puijai (medicine) ❹ jaidihng * prepare a drug VO: puiyeuhk * prepare someone for something FV: hòideuh

prepared PH: jéunbeih hóu ge * be prepared to (do) Patt: jéunbeih hóu . . .

preparedness N: ❶ yuhbeih; yáuh jéunbeih ❷ (in military) gwànbeih; jìnbeih * preparedness averts peril IE: yáuh beih mòuh waahn

prepay FV: yuhsìn béichín VO: gàau seuhngkèih; béi seuhngkèih

preponderance N: (in number, weight, strength) yàusai

preponderant PH: (in weight) jim yàusai ge SV: jyúyiu

ge; juhng yiu ge

preponderate Adj. PH: ❶ (in number) soumuhk chiugwo ❷ (in weight) chúhngleuhng singgwo ❸ (in strength) lihkleuhng daaihgwo ❹ (in influence) yínghéunglihk singgwo

preposition N: (grammar) chihnjichìh; gaaichìh

prepositional PH: chihnjichìh ge; gaaichìh ge * **prepositional phrase** N: gaaihaihchìh pinyúh

prepossess PH: ❶ lihngdou yáuh (affection; thinking) ~ gámchìhng; ~ sìséung ❷ lihng dou sìn yáuh (hóugám waahkjé fáangám) FV: ❶ yínghéung ❷ gunsyù

prepossesing SV: kāpyáhnyàhn ge PH: lihngdou yàhn yáuh hóugám ge

prepossession N: ❶ pìnhou; pìnngoi ❷ pìngin ❸ sìndāk; sìnjim

preposterous SV: ❶ fáansèuhng ge ❷ fòngmauh ge

prepotency N: ❶ yàusai ❷ (biology) yàusìn wàihchyùhn; wàihchyùhn yàusai

prepequisite SV: bītyiu ge PH: bitsèui yuhsìn geuihbeih ge N: bītyiu tiuhgín; sìnkyut tiuhgín * **be prerequisite to** Patt: deui N haih bītyiu ge

prerogative N: dahkkyùhn (M: go) SV: yáuh dahkkyùhn ge * **the royal prerogative** PH: dai wòhng ge dahkkyùhn * **the prerogative of mercy** N: semíhnkyùhn (M: go) * **prerogative court** N: (law) daaih jyúgaau faattìhng (M: go) * **a prerogative writ** N:

gángāplihng (M: go)

presage N: yuhgám; yuhsih; sìnsiuh; yuhjì (M: go) FV: yuhgám; yuhjì; yuhyìhn; yuhchāak

presbyopia N: yúhnsihngáahn; lóuhfā

presbyterian SV: jéunglóuhwúi (jai) ge N: jéunglóuhwúigaauyáuh * **presbyterian church** N: (Gèidūkgaau) jéunglóuhwúi

presbyterianism N: jéunglóuhwúijai PH: jéunglóuhwúi ge gaauyih

preschool SV: hohkchìhn ge N: yauyìhyún (M: gàan)

prescribe FV: ❶ kwàidihng; jídihng ❷ jisih ❸ mihnglihng VO: hòiyeuhkfòng

prescript N: ❶ mihnglihng; faatlihng; faatleuht ❷ kwàidihng SV: ❶ mihnglihng ge ❷ kwàidihng ge

prescription N: ❶ jísih; kwàidihng (M: go) ❷ yeuhkfòng; chyúfòng (M: jèung) * **write a prescription** VO: hòi yeuhkfòng

prescriptive SV: ❶ kwàidihng ge ❷ gwaanlaih ge

presence FV: háisyu; joihchèuhng; chēutjihk PW: mihnchìhn N: ❶ yihyùhng (M: go) ❷ fùngdouh * **in the presence of** Patt: ① hái PN ge mihnchìhn ② dòngjyuh PN ge mihnchìhn * **presence of mind** SV: jandihng * **saving your presence** PH: deuimjyuh * **your presence is requested** PH: chéng néih chēutjihk

present SV: ❶ chēutjihk ge; joihchèuhng ge; yìhgā ge ❷ muhkchìhn ge; yìhgā ge ❸ jīkhāak ge TW: muhkchìhn; yìhgā N: láihmaht (M: gihn, fahn) Patt: sung ~ béi PN FV: ❶ gaaisiuh ❷ tàihchēut ❸ séuhngyín (play, drama) ~ wákehk ✳ **present a report** FV: chìhngbou ✳ **present at meeting** VO: chēutjihk ✳ **present circumstances** PH: muhkchìhn ge wàahngíng ✳ **present condition** PH: yìhgā ge chìhngyìhng ✳ **present credentials** PH: chìhngdaih gwoksyù ✳ **present political situation** PH: (muhkchìhn ge) sìhguhk ✳ **be present in a meeting** VO: chēutjihk wuihyíh ✳ **for the present** TW: jaahmsìh; muhkchìhn ✳ **up to the present** PH: jihkdou muhkchìhn ✳ **present prices** N: sìhga, yihnga ✳ **by these presents** PH: gàngeui nīdī màhngín

presentable PH: ❶ sīkhahp sung béi yàhn ge ❷ hóyíh tèuijin ge ❸ chíhyéung ge ✳ **a presentable gift** PH: yātfahn nīkdāk chēutlàih (sungdāk chēutheui) ge láihmaht ✳ **a presentable play** PH: yātchēut hóyíh séuhngyín ge hei ✳ **presentable clothes** Adj. PH: leng ge sāam ✳ **to look quite presentable** PH: go yéung sèungdōng leng

presentation N: ❶ jahngsung ❷ gaaisiuh ❸ chēutjihk ❹ tàihchēut ❺ (drama) yínchēut

presentiment N: yuhgám (unlucky) (M: go)

presently A: ❶ mouhgéi-noih (nói); yātjahngāan ❷ jīkhāak

preserve FV: ❶ bóuchyùhn;

chyùhchyùhn (food) ~ sihkmaht ❷ wàihchìh ❸ bóujuhng (health) ~ sàntái ❹ bóuwuh (eyes) ~ sèungngáahn N: ❶ mahtjìn; mahtjìn tòhnggwó ❷ gamlihpkèui (M: go) ❸ yùhtòhng (M: go) ✳ **preserved dates** N: mahtjóu (M: nāp, go) ✳ **preserved fruits** N: mahtjingwó (M: go) ✳ **preserved ginger** N: tòhnggēung (M: gauh) ✳ **duck eggs preserved in lime** N: pèihdáan (M: jek) (thousand years egg)

preside VO: jouh jyújihk FV: ❶ túnghaht ❷ jífài (military) ~ gwàndéui ❸ jyúchìh (company) ~ gùngsī

president N: ❶ (Repubic) júngléih; daaihjúngtúng (M: go) ❷ (of a republic governed by a committee) jyújihk (M: go) ❸ (of a company) dúngsihjéung (M: go) ❹ (of a college in the university) yúnjéung (M: go) ❺ (of a school) haauhjéung (M: go) ❻ (of a business concern) gìngléih; júnggìngléih (M: go) ❼ (of a bank) hòhngjéung; júnggìngléih (M: go) ❽ (of a society or association) wuihjéung (M: go) ❾ (of a newspaper) séhjéung (M: go) ✳ **vice president** BF: fu — (plus any of the above terms)

presidium N: jyújihktyùhn (M: go)

press FV: ❶ (exert physical pressure) ngaat (fruits) ❷ gahm (with finger and hand) ❸ (with foot) yáai; daahp ❹ (apply weight to) jaak ❺ jài ❻ kéuhngbīk (people) ~ PN jouhsih ❼ yīkjai (feeling) ~ gámchìhng ❽ tong (clothes) ~ sāam N: ❶ ngaatlihk (M: go) ❷ ngaatjagèi (M: ga, fu) ❸ yanchaatgèi; yanjihgēi (M: fu, ga) ❹ sànmáhngaai; bougaai ❺ chēutbáan gaai ❻ bouhón (M: fahn) ❼ yanchaatgún (M: gàan) ∗ be pressed for FV: kyutsíu ∗ go (come) to press FV: fuhyan ∗ in press PH: fuhyangán ∗ off the press PH: yíhgìng faathàhngjó ∗ out of press PH: maaihsaai la ∗ press conference N: geijéjiudoihwúi (M: go) ∗ press for PH: gángāp yiukàuh ∗ press home PH: jīkgihk jyújèung ∗ press on (forward) with PH: kyutsàm gaijuhk ∗ press up N: jéungseuhngngaat (M: háh) ∗ press-photograph N: sànmàhnsipyíngyùhn (M: go) ∗ press gallery N: sànmàhngeijéjihk ∗ press law N: chēutbáanfaat (M: tìuh) ∗ press reader N: gaaudeuiyùhn (M: go)

pressman N: yanchaatgùngyàhn (M: go)

pressure N: ❶ ngaat; ngaatlihk (M: go) ❷ dihnngaat ❸ ngaatbīk ❹ gàannàahn ∗ put pressure on PH: sìgā ngaatlihk ∗ under (the) pressure of Patt: hái N ngaatlihk jìhah ∗ work at high pressure PH: gánjèunggám jouhsih ∗ a pressure gauge N: ngaatlihkgai (M: go) ∗ a pressure cooker N: ngaatlihkbōu (M: go) ∗ the blood pressure N: hyutngaat ∗ pressure group N: ngaatlihk tyùhntái (M: go)

prestige N: ❶ sìngmohng; mìhngyuh; mìhngmohng (M: go) ❷ wàiseun ❸ sailihk (M: go)

presto A: ❶ (music) gāpchūk gám ❷ (music) jyúnngáahngāan SV: faaipaakjí ge (music) PH: (music) gāpchūk ge ngohkkūk waahkjé ngohkjèung

presume FV: gú CV: yíh-

wàih; gádihng; yihngwàih

presumption N: ❶ tèuichāak; gádihng ❷ (in manner) jyùnwàahng

presumptive SV: gádihng ge; tèuichāak ge ∗ the heir presumptive PH: gádihng sìhnggaiyàhn

presumptuous PH: ❶ jihyíhwàihsih ge ❷ fongsi ge

presuppose FV: yuhliuh; gádihng; tèuichāak ∗ effects presuppose causes IE: yáuhgwó bīt yáuhyàn

presupposition N: ❶ yuhliuh (M: go) ❷ chìhntàih (M: go)

pretend FV: ja; jadai ∗ pretend to N PH: jih yíhwàih haih N ∗ pretend to be ill FV: ja behng ∗ pretend to be mad FV: jadìn IE: jadìn baahnsòh ∗ pretend to sleep FV: ja fan

pretender PH: ❶ móhngséung ge yàhn (M: go) ❷ mouhchùng ge yàhn (M: go)

pretentious SV: ❶ chùngdaaihtói; chùnghàhngsaai ❷ jihfuh ge ❸ gìungouh ge ❹ jouhjok ge

preternatural SV: ❶ chìujihyìhn ge ❷ kèihgwaai ge

pretext FV/N: jihkháu (M: go) FV: jagàyì ∗ on (under) the pretext FV/N: jihkháu, jeháu (M: go)

pretty SV: ❶ hóuyéung; leng ❷ hóutèng ❸ hóu ❹ jùngyi ge A: ❶ sèungdòng ❷ sahpfàn ∗ pretty good PH: sèungdòng hóu ∗ pretty much A: fèisèuhng ∗ pretty soon A: jīkhāak ∗ sit pretty PH: hóu wàahngíng * **pretty late** PH: hóu yeh la

prevail FV: ❶ singgwo; hóugwo ❷ làuhhàhng; sihnghàhng ❸ jinsing (people) ~ jihgéi; ~ dihkyàhn * **prevail against** FV: singgwo; ngaatdóu * **prevail on (upon, with)** FV: hyundouh; hyunfuhk

prevaricate Adj. PH: yìhyìngòhngòh * **don't prevaricate** PH: góng lóuhsaht ge syutwah

prevent FV: ❶ jójí ❷ yuhfòhng; fòhngjí (keep something from occuring) ❸ fòhngngoih * **prevent from** FV: jójí

preview, prevue N: ❶ (movie) siyíng ❷ yuhgoupín (M: chēut) ❸ yuhyín ❹ yuhjín ❺ yuhjaahp

previous PH: ❶ yíhchìhn ge ❷ seuhngyātchi ge * **previous to** Patt: hái N yíhchìhn (jìchìhn)

prewar PH: jinchìhn ge

prey PH: béi (beih) yàhn jūk ge duhngmaht N: hèisàngbán (M: jek) FV: bouhsihk * **be a prey to** FV: beihbouh * **prey on (upon)** FV: bousihk

price N: ❶ gachìhn; gagaak (M: go) ❷ doihga (M: go) ❸ gajihk VO: biuga; dihngga * **at a price** PH: béi (fuhchēut) hóu daaih ge doihga * **at any price** PH: bātsīk yahmhòh doihga * **at the price of** Patt: yíh N ge doihga * **beyond (above, without) price, priceless** PH: mòuhga ge * **set high (little) price on** FV/SV: juhngsyih (mjuhngsih) * **price current** N: síhgabíu (M: go)

price-cutting VO: gáamga * **price-list** N: dihnggabíu; gamuhkbíu (M: jèung) * **price-work** N: gaigihn gùngjok * **fixed price** N: sahtga * **price has fallen** VO: ditga * **retail price** N: lìhnggûga; lìhngsauhga * **wholesale price** N: pàifaatga PH: faathòhng ge gachìhn * **price is going up** VO: hēiga

prices N: mahtga

priceless SV: mòuhga ge PH: gwaijuhng dougihk ge

prick N: chi; lahk (M: tìuh) FV: gāt * **prick up** RV: syuhhéi * **prick so that it pains** PH: gātdāk yàhn hóu tung

pricker N: ❶ jàm (M: háu) ❷ yèui (M: go)

prickle N: ❶ (thistle) lahk ❷ (thorn) chi (M: tìuh) PH: gokdāk chitungjó FV: chi

pride N: ❶ giungouh ❷ jihhòuh ❸ jihjyùn (sàm) (M: go) SV: ❶ dākyi ❷ jihfuh PH: jihkdāk jihhòuh ge yàhn (M: go) M: kwàhn (animals) FV: jihhòuh * **pride oneself on** Patt: yíh N jihngouh * **take (a) pride in** Patt: yíh N jihhòuh

priest N: ❶ (Roman Catholic) sàhnfuh (M: go) ❷ (Protestant) muhksī (M: go) ❸ gaausih (M: go) ❹ (Buddist) wòhséung (M: go) ❺ (Taoist) douhsí (M: go) * **become a priest** VO: chēutgà * **quit the priesthood** VO: wàahnjuhk

priestess N: ❶ nèihgù (M: go) ❷ néuihgaausih (M: go) ❸ néuih jaisī (M: go)

priesthood PH: gaausih ge jīkwaih N: gaausih (M: go)

priggish SV: jihfuh ge Adj.
PH: ❶ jih mìhng dākyi ge ❷
yātbún jinggìng gám

prim Adj. PH: ❶ jingjinggìng-
gìng gám ❷ jingsīk gám ❸ yātbún jinggìng ge yéung

prim (primary, primitive)
SV: ❶ daihyāt ge ❷ jyúyiu ge

primacy N: sáuyui PH:
(religion) daaih jyúgaau ge
(gaauwòhng ge) jīkjaak waahkjé kyùhnlihk

primary SV: ❶ chòbouh ge;
jeuichò ge ❷ sáuyiu ge ❸
gèibún ge N: ❶ jyúyiu sihmaht
❷ yùhnsīk ❸ (America) chòsyún ❹ (Astronamy) jyúsìng (M:
nāp) ✳ **primary election** N:
chòsyún (M: chi) ✳ **primary
school** N: síuhohk (M: gàan) ✳
primary assembly N: ❶
gùngmàhn daaihwúi (M: go,
chi) ❷ yuhsyúnwúi (M: chi, go)
✳ **primary election** N: yuh-
syún (M: chi) ✳ **primary
evidence** PH: gànbún jinggeui
✳ **primary meeting** N: yuh-
syún wúi (M: go) ✳ **primary
products** N: nùhngcháanbán
✳ **primary tenses** PH: (grammar) yihnjoih sìhtaai; jèunglòih
sìhtaai tùhng yùhnsìhng sìhtaai

primate N: ❶ daaih jyúgaau
(M: go) ❷ (pl.) (animal) lìhng-
jéungmuhk (yàhn, máhlāu,
dáng dáng)

prime SV: ❶ jeuichò ge ❷
sáuyiu ge ❸ jeuihóu ge;
yātlàuh ge ❹ (mathematics) jāt-
sou ge PH: jeui hóu ge
bouhfahn waahkjé sihkèih N:
❶ chēuntīn ❷ jùngnìhn;
jongnìhn FV: jéunbeih RV:
sākmúhn Adj. PH: jeui hóu
gám ✳ **the prime minister** N:
① (of a Republic) júngléih (M:
go) ② (Ancient term) jóiseung

(M: go) ❸ (modern term) sáuseung (M: go) ✳ **of prime importance** PH: ji (jeui) gányiu
ge ✳ **in the prime of life** PH:
hái hauhsāang gójahnsí ✳
prime cost N: yùhnga ✳
prime mover N: ① yùhn-
duhnglihk (M: júng) ② faathéiyàhn (M: go)

primer N: ❶ sīkjih fobún (M:
bún, bouh) ❷ lèuihgún,
yáhnfósin (M: tiuh) PH:
jòngfóyeuhk ge yàhn (M: go) ✳
a primer of phonetics PH:
yúhyàmhohk yahpmùhn

primeval SV: gúlóuh ge PH:
yùhnchí sìhdoih ge

priming N: yáhnfóyeuhk;
héibaaujài (M: júng)

primitive SV: ❶ yùhnchí ge;
taaigú ge ❷ chòu ge ❸ lóuhsīk
ge ❹ gáandàan ge ❺ gèibún ge
N: ❶ yùhnchí yàhn (M: go) ❷
(language) yùhnchìh ✳
primitive weapons PH: gáandàan ge móuhhei ✳ **primitive
colors** N: yùhnsīk

primogenture N: ❶ jéungjí sànfán ❷ (law) jéungjí
gaisìhngjai (M: go) ✳ **the right
of primogeniture** N: jéungjí
gaisìhnghkyùhn

primordial SV: ❶ yùhnchí
ge; jeuichòge ❷ gànbún ge ✳
primordial customs PH:
yùhnchí sìhdoih ge fùngjuhk
jaahpgwaan ✳ **primordial
cell** N: yùhnchí saibāau

primrose N: ❶ (plant)
yìngchòu (fā) (M: déu, dó) ❷
chínwòhngsīk SV: ❶ yìngchòu
ge ❷ gòuhing ge ❸ chín-
wòhngsīk ge ✳ **to follow the
primrose path** Adj. PH:
jèuikàuh héungsauh

prince N: ❶ (ruler) wòhng; chànwòhng (M: go) ❷ (son of a king) wòhngjí (M: go) ❸ (crown prince) taaijí; wòhngchyúh ❹ geuihjí; geuihtàuh (M: go) SV: ❶ gòugwai ge ❷ gwànjyú ge * **merchant prince** N: sèungyihp geuihjí (M: go) * **prince consort** N: wòhngfù (M: go) * **prince of darkness** N: mōgwái (M: go) * **prince of peace** N: Yèhsōu Gèidūk * **prince regent** N: sipjingwòhng (M: wái, go) * **prince royal** N: daaihtaaijí (M: wái, go) * **prince of the blood** N: wòhngjuhk

princess N: ❶ gùngjyú (M: go) ❷ wòhngfèi (M: go) ❸ (ancient) néuihwòhng (M: go)

principal SV: ❶ jyúyiu ge; sáuyiu ge ❷ jíbún ge N: ❶ (school) haauhjéung (M: go) ❷ (law) dòngsihyàhn (M: go) ❸ sáujéung (M: go) ❹ jyúgok (M: go) ❺ jíbún; búnchihn (M: bāt) ❻ jyúfáan (M: go) * **principal and interest** PH: lìhnbún daai leih (búnleih) * **principal clause** PH: jyúyiu jígeui

principle N: ❶ (as of physics) yùhnléih (M: go) ❷ (of person) yùhnjāk ❸ jyúyi (M: go) ❹ yiusou ❺ lòihyùhn; gànyùhn ❻ (of conduct) dākhahng; ❼ douhléih (M: go) * **in principle** A: tùhngsèuhng * **on principle** PH: gàngeui jihgéi ge seunnihm * **the principles of democracy** N: màhnjyú yùhnjāk

print FV: ❶ yan; yanchaat ❷ (photographic positive) saai (séung) ❸ chēutbán ❹ koi (yan) PH: yuhng jingkáai sé N: ❶ yanchaatbán (M: bún, fahn) ❷ yanjéung (M: go) ❸ yanfābou (M: fūk, faai) ❹ báanbún (M: go)

❺ séung (M: fūk, go) * **in print** PH: yíhgìng chēutbáan hóyíh maaihchēut * **put into print** PH: hóyíh nīk heui yan * **print works** N: yanfāchóng (M: gàan) * **printed patterns** N: yanfā tòuhngon (M: go) * **printed cost** N: yanchaatfai (M: bāt) * **printed cotton cloth** N: fābou (M: fūk) * **printed matter** N: yanchaatbán (M: bún, fahn) * **the print of a foot** N: jūkyan * **finger prints** N: jíyan; sáujímòuhyan; jímòuh * **out of print** N: jyuhtbáan (M: bún, bouh) * **printed shop** N: yanchaatsó; yanchaatgún; yauchaatpóu (M: gàan)

printer N: ❶ yanchaatjé (M: go) ❷ pàaihjihgùngyàhn (M: go) ❸ yanfāgùng ❹ yanchaatgèi (M: ga)

printing N: ❶ yanchaat (seuht) (M: júng) ❷ yanchaatyihp (M: hòhng) * **printing ink** N: yàuhmahk * **printing press** N: yanchaatgèi (M: ga)

prior SV: yàusìn ge PH: gang juhngyiu ge N: sàudouhyún fu yúnjéung (M: go, wái) * **prior to** Patt: ❶ hái N jìchihn ❷ béi N yàusìn

priority N: ❶ yàusìn (kyùhn) (M: go) ❷ juhngdím PH: jài (fong) hái chihnbihn * **according to priority** PH: ngon jìgaak (sìhgaan) ge chijeuih * **take (give, have) priority of** Patt: ❶ béi N yàusìn ❷ dāk N ge yàusìnkyùhn

priory N; sàudouhyún (M: gàan)

prism N: ❶ (sàam) lìhnggeng (M: go) ❷ (mathematics) lìhngchyútái

prismatic(al) Adj. PH: ❶ lihng-chyú (yìhng) ge ❷ ńghgwòngsahpsīk ge

prison N: ❶ gàamfòhng; gàamyuhk (M: go, gàan) ❷ kèuilàuhsó (M: go, gàan) ❸ gàamgam ✻ **in prison** VO: chóhgàam ✻ **cast (put, take) into prison** Patt: béi N làaiyahp gàamyuhk syu ✻ **prison breaker** N: yuhtyuhk-jé (M: go) tòuhyuhkjé

prisoner N: gàamfaán; faahnyàhn; chàuhfáan (M: go) ✻ **prisoner of war** N: jinfù; fùlóuh (M: go) ✻ **prisoner at the bar** N: yìhngsih beihgou (M: go) ✻ **prisoner of state** N: gwoksihfáan (M: go)

pristine SV: ❶ chòkèihge ❷ yùhnchí ge ❸ sèuhnjīng ge

privacy N: ❶ yángèui (M: júng) ❷ beimaht (M: go)

private SV: ❶ jihgéi ge; go yàhn ge; sìyáuh ge ❷ sìyìhng ge (company) ❸ bóumaht ge; sìhah ge ❹ (individual owned) sìgà ge ❺ sìlahp ge (school) N: bīng (M: go) ✻ **in private** SV: ❶ sìhah ❷ ngamjùng ✻ **private affair** N: sìsíh ✻ **private life** N: sìsàngwuht PH: go yàhn ge sàngwuht ✻ **a private secretary** N: sìyàhn bei syù (M: go) ✻ **private letter** N: sìyàhn seungín (M: fùng) ✻ **private opinion** N: go yàhn yigin (M: dím) ✻ **a private citizen** N: pìhngmàhn (M: go) ✻ **some private corner** PH: pìnpīk ge deihfòng ✻ **private enterprise** N: sìyàhn kéihyihp (M: júng) ✻ **private view** PH: fèigùnghòi jínláahm

privation N: ❶ kyutfaht (daily necessity) ❷ kùhngfú

privilege N: ❶ kyùhnleih (M: júng, go) ❷ dahtkyùhn (M: júng, go) ❸ dahkbiht doihyuh FV: dahkjéun SV: dahkkyùhn ge Patt: béi N dahkkyùhn ✻ **privilege and duty** PH: kyùhnleih tùhng yihmouh

prize N: ❶ (material) jéungbán (M: go) ❷ (money) jéunggām (M: bāt) ❸ jinleihbán (M: go) ❹ fùlóuh (M: go) RV: giuhhòi PH: yihngwàih yáuh daaih ge gajihk ✻ **prize fighting** N: jīkyihp kyùhngīk ✻ **prize-ring** N: kyùhngīk cheùhng (M: go) ✻ **the prizes of life** PH: yàhnsàng ge muhkdīk ✻ **a prize scholarship** N: jéunghohk gām (M: go, bāt) ✻ **prize fighter** N: jīkyihp kyùhnsáu (M: go)✻ **prize man (winner)** N: dākjeúngjé (M: go)

pro N: ❶ jaansìhngpiu (M: jèung) ❷ jaansìhngpiujé (M: go) A: jingmín (mihn) gám SV: jaansìhng ge ✻ **the pros and cons of the matter** PH: deui yātgihn sih ge jaansìhng tùhng fáandeui ge yíhleuhn ✻ **pro forma** A: yìhngsīkseuhng ✻ **pro pata** Adv. PH: ngon (jiu) béilaih

probability N: ❶ hónàhng-sing (M: go) ❷ gèiwuih (M: go) ❸ (mathematics) koiléut ✻ **in all probability** PH: sahpjì baatgáu; hóu hónàhng ✻ **the probability is that** PH: hóu hónàhng haih . . .

probable SV: hónàhng ge; daaihkói ge PH: hóu yáuh hèimohng ge

probably A: waahkjé; daaihkói; hóu hónàhng

probation N: ❶ siyuhng; ginjaahp (person) (M: júng) ❷ siyihm (M: go) ❸ (law) wuhnyìhng * to be on probation PH: siyihm (siyuhng) jùng * a probation official N: siyuhnggùn (M: go) * probation officer N: gámfagùn (M: go)

probational (probationary) SV: ❶ siyuhng ge; ginjaahp ge ❷ wuhnyìhng ge

probationer N: ❶ sahtjaahpsāng (M: go) ❷ wuhnyìhng fáan (M: go) ❸ (school) siduhksāng (M: go)

probe N: ❶ (medical) taamjām (M: jì) ❷ taamjí (M: go) ❸ taamchāakhei (M: ga) FV: ❶ taamchàh (use needle) ❷ diuchàh (case) ~ yātgihn sih

problem N: ❶ mahntàih (M: go, tìuh) ❷ jaahptàih (M: tìuh) ❸ nàahntàih (M: go) PH: faatsàng kwannàahn ge * a problem child N: mahntàih yìhtùhng (M: go)

problematic(al) SV: ❶ sìhng mahntàih ge ❷ nàahn deuifuh ge

proboscis N: jeuhngbeih; chèuhngbeih (M: tìuh)

procedure N: ❶ sáujuhk (M: go) ❷ gwochìhng (M: go) ❸ bouhjaauh; chìhngjeuih (M: go)* **legal procedure** N: sou juhng chìhngjeuih (M: júng) * **code of civil (crimival) procedure** N: màhnsih(yìhngsih) soujuhngfaat (M: tìuh)

proceed FV: ❶ gaijuhk ❷ jeunhàhng; yuhsìn ❸ héisou (case) ~ yātgihn ngon PH: heung chìhnjeun * **proceed from** Patt: ① hái (yàuh) PW héichìhng ② yàuh N yáhnhéi * **proceed on** Patt: jiụ N jeunhàhng * **proceed to the**

degree of PH: (M.A.) dākdóu (sehksih) hohkwái * **proceed with** PH: gaijuhk jeunhàhng * **to proceed against (a person)** FV: hungsou

proceeds N: sàuyahp (M: go) RV: dākdóu (degree) ~ hohkwái

proceeding N: ❶ hàhngduhng (M: go, júng) ❷ chìhngjeuih (M: go)

proceedings N: ❶ soujuhng chìhngjeuih (M: go) ❷ wuihyíh géiluhk (M: bún) ❸ wuihhón (M: bún) ❹ chyùhnpiu (M: jèung) ❺ soujuhng . . . (M: go) FV: ❶ chyúléih ❷ héisou * **in process** PH: jingjoih jeunhàhngjùng * **in (the) process of** Patt: hái . . . gwochìhng jìjùng

process N: ❶ (method) fòngfaat (M: go) ❷ (procedure) sáujuhk (M: go) ❸ gwochìhng; bouhjaau (M: go)

procession N: ❶ yàuhhàhng (M: go) ❷ deuihngh (M: go) ❸ hòhngliht * **a funeral procession** PH: sungjong hòhngliht * **to march in procession** PH: lihtdéui jeunhàhng

processor N: ❶ jaijouhjé (M: go) ❷ gàgùngjé (M: go) ❸ (electric) seunsīk chyúléihgēi (M: ga, fu)

proclaim FV: ❶ syùnbou ❷ (as a law) gùngbou ❸ hínsih * **proclaim marital law** VO: syùnbou gaaiyìhm * **proclaim war** FV: syùnjin; heung N syùnjin

proclamation N: ❶ syùnbou ❷ gousih (M: go, jèung) ❸ gùnbou (M: go) ❹ sìngmìhng

(M: go) * **issue a proclamation** VO: chēut gousih N:
syùnyìhn (M: go, geui, fahn)

proclivity N: ❶ kìngheung
❷ pèihhei (M: go) ❸ pīksing

proconsul N: jihkmàhndeih
júngdūk (M: go)

pro-consul N: doihléih
líhngsí (M: go)

procrastination FV:
tòyìhn

procreate FV: ❶ sàngjihk
❷ sàngyuhk ❸ cháansàng

proctor N: ❶ doihléihyàhn
(M: go)❷ (law) doihsouyàhn (M:
go) ❸ fandouhjéung; fandouh
jyúyahm (M: go)

procurator N: ❶ doihléihyàhn (M: go) ❷ (law) doihsouyàhn (M: go) * **public procurator** N: gímchaatgùn (M:
go) * **public procurator
general** N: sáujihk gím-
chaatgùn (M: go)

procure RV: ❶ wándóu (job)
~ *gùngjok* ❷ dākdóu * **to
procure a person's death** PH:
chūksihng PN ge séi mòhng

prod FV: ❶ (needle) gāt ❷
dūkchūk ❸ yáhnhéi N: jām (M:
jì, háu, ngáan) * **to prod one's
memory** PH: yáhnhéi PN
geidāk

prodigal SV: ❶ lohngfai ge
❷ fàifok ge N: baaihgàjái (M:
go) * **play the prodigal** FV:
yàuhdohng * **prodigal entertainment** PH: chèchí ge
jiudoih * **to play the prodigal** PH: gwo fongdohng ge
sàngwuht

prodigality SV: ❶ lohngfai
❷ chèchí

prodigious SV: ❶ pòhngdaaih ge❷ gìngyàhn ge

prodigy N: ❶ kèihjìk (M: go)
❷ tìnchòih ❸ sàhntùhng (M:
go)

produce FV: ❶ chēut ❷
faatsàng ❸ gitgwó ❹ cháan-
léun ❺ saàng (jái) ❻ (factory)
jaijouh ❼ yáhnhéi ❽ (articles)
chongjok N: ❶ (farm products)
chēutcháan; nùhngcháanbán ❷
sihnggwó (M: go)

producer N: ❶ (of a movie)
jaipínsèung ❷ sàncháanjé (M:
go) ❹ (machine) faatsànghei
(M: ga)

product N: ❶ (industrial)
chēutbán; jaijouhbán (M: gihn)
❷ mahtcháan ❸ chongjok (M:
pìn) ❹ sihnggwó (M: go) * **the
products of genius** PH: tìnchòih ge cháanbán *
agricultural product N:
nùhngcháanbán * **local product** N: tóuchaán

production N: ❶ (factory)
jaijouh; sàngcháan ❷ (written
article) jokbán (M: pìn) * **make
a production (out) of** (coll)
síutàih daaihjouh * **put N into production** VO: tàuhyahp
sàngcháan

productive SV: ❶ sàngcháan ge ❷ fèihyūk ge (land) *
a productive farm PH:
fèihyūk tùhng chēut cháan
fùngfu ge nùhngchèuhng * **a
productive writer** N: dòcháan
jokgā (M: go)

productivity N: ❶ sàng-
cháanlihk ❷ sàngcháanleuht

profane SV: ❶ saijuhk ge ❷
sitduhk ge FV: sitduhk * **profane language** PH: sitduhk
sàhnsing ge syutwah * **profane literature** N: saijuhk

màhnhohk

profess FV: ❶ gùnghòi
sìhngyihng ❷ gaausauh ~
lihksí PH: bíusih seunyéuhng
A: bíumihnseuhng Patt: yíh N
wàih jīkyihp

profession N: ❶ jīkyihp ❷
tùhnghòhng ❸ jyùnyihp
tyùhntái (M: go) ❹ sìngmìhng
(M: go) ❺ bíubaahk ✳ by profession Patt: yíh N wàih
jīkyihp

professional SV: jīkyihp
ge; jyùnyihp ge N: ❶ noihhóng
❷ jyùnyihp yàhnyùhn ✳ professional soccer player N:
jīkyihp jūkkàuhyùhn (M: go) ✳
professional man N: jyūngā
(M: go) ✳ professional politician N: jìnghaak (M: go) ✳
professional school N: jyùnmùhn hohkhaauh (M: gàan)

professionalism N: ❶
jyùnyihpfa ❷ jyùnyihp jyúyih

professor N: ❶ gaausauh
(M: go) ❷ jyūngā (M: go) ❸
gaausī; sìnsàang (M: go) ✳
assistant professor N: fu
gaausauh (M: go) ✳ associate
professor N: (America) jéun
gaausauh (M: go)

proficiency N: jìngtùng;
suhklihn

proficent SV: suhklihn ge;
jìngtùngge N: jyūngā (M: go,
wái) ✳ be proficent in (at)
Patt: deui N hóu jìngtùng
(suhklihn)

profile N: ❶ jākmín (mihn)
❷ lèuhnkok (M: go) ❸
ngoihyìhng ❹ séjiu Patt: ❶
waahkPN/N ge jākmín (mihn)
❷ deui N sé yàtdī yéh ✳ in
profile N: jākmín

profit N: ❶ leihchìhn ❷
leihyīk FV: yáuhleih Patt: deui
N yáuh yīk ✳ make a profit
VO: jaahnchín ✳ gross profits
N: mòuhleih ✳ net profits N:
jìhngleih ✳ make one's profit of FV: leihyuhng

profitable SV: yáuhleih ge;
yáuhyīk ge A: yáuh leih gám

profiteer N: ❶ tàuhgèi
sèungyàhn (M: go) ❷ gàan-
sèung (M: go) PH: dākdóu
bouhleih ✳ a war profiteer
PH: faat jinjàng chòih ge yàhn
(M: go)

profiteering N: tàuhgèi
wuhtduhng

profitless SV: móuh yuhng
ge PH: mòuhleihhhótòuh ge ✳
a profitless business PH:
jaahnm̀dóu chín ge sàangyi ✳
a profitless task PH: móuh
leihyīk ge gùngjok

profligacy SV: fongdohng
PH: m̀gímdím ge hàhng wàih

profligate SV: fongdohng
ge PH: ❶ hàhngwàih m̀gímdím
ge ❷ lyuhn sái chín ge N:
lohngjí (M: go) ✳ a profligate
life PH: fongdohng ge
sàngwuht

profound SV: ❶ sàm ge ❷
sàmngou ge ✳ a profound
sleep PH: fandāk hóu lahm ✳
profoundly grateful PH:
feìsèuhng dòjeh ✳ profound
regrets (apologies) PH:
feìsèuhng deuim̀jyuh ✳ a profound book PH: sàmngou ge
syù (M: bún) ✳ a profound
thinker PH: sàmngou ge sìséunggā (M: go)

profusion SV: ❶ daaihleuhng ❷ fùngfu ❸ lohngfai

progenitor N: ❶ jóusīn (M: go) ❷ chìhnbui (M: go)

progeny N: jísyùn

prognosis N: yuhchãak (M: go) PH: (medical) behngjohng ge yuhsìn dyundihng

program(me) N: ❶ (entertainment) jitmuhk (M: go) ❷ (plan) gaiwaahk (M: go) ❸ syutmìhngsyù (M: fahn, jèung) ❹ daaihgòng (M: go, pìn) ❺ (time table) sìhgaanbíu (M: go) FV: ❶ gaiwaahk (future) ~ jèunglòih ge sih ❷ ngònpàaih ❸ chitgai * what's on the program? PH: yáuh mātyéh jitmuhk a? * what's the program for today? PH: gàmyaht yáuh mātyéh wuhtduhng a? * a concert program N: yàmngohkwúi jitmuhkbíu (M: jèung, fahn) * a business program N: sèungyihp gaiwaahk (M: go)

programmer PH: ❶ pìnpàaih jitmuhkbíu ge yàhn (M: go) ❷ ngònpàaih jitmuhk ge yàhn (M: go) ❸ gaiwaahk ge yàhn (M: go)

progress N: ❶ jeunbouh ❷ jeunjín (M: go) ❸ (kings) chèuhn hàhng (M: go) FV: ❶ jeunhàhng ❷ faatjín * in progress PH: ❶ jingjoih jeunhàhng jìjūng ❷ jingjoih faatjín jóng * has made progress PH: yáuh jeunbouh * no progress PH: móuh jeunbouh * the progress of science PH: fōhohk ge jeunbouh * progress in civilization PH: màhnmìhng ge jeunbouh

prohibit FV: ❶ gamjí; gam ❷ jójí * smoking prohibited PH: gamjí sihk yīn

prohibiter PH: ❶ gamjí ge yàhn (M: go) ❷ jójí ge yàhn (M: go) ❸ jeungngoihmaht (M: gihn)

prohitition N: ❶ gamlihng (M: tiuh) ❷ gamjáulihng (M: tiuh)

prohibitionist N: gamjáu jyúyih jé (M: go)

project FV: ❶ gaiwaahk ❷ chitgai ❸ sehchēut ❹ tàuhseh; tàuhyíng N: ❶ gaiwaahk (M: go) ❷ chitgai (M: go) ❸ sihyihp; kéihyihp (M: go) * project on Patt: jèung N tàuhseh (tàuhyíng) dou N * project oneself PH: daht chēut jihgéi * to project a missile VO: faatseh fèidáan

projector N: ❶ chitgaijé (M: go) ❷ (movie) fongyínggēi (M: ga) ❸ taamjiudāng (M: jáan)

prolapse N: (medical) tyutchēut (jing) tyutsèuih FV: tyutchēut; tyutsèuih * a prolapsed rectum PH: tyutchēut ge jihkchéung

proletariat(e) N: mòuhcháan gàaikāp; nòuhduhng gàaikāp

proliferate FV: ❶ (physiology) (lihngdou) jàngjihk; (lihngdou) fàahnjihk (cells) ~ saibāau ❷ (lihngdou) kongsaan

proliferation N: kongsaan * neuclar proliferation PH: gwaht kongsaan

prolific SV: ❶ daaihleuhng sàngcháan ge ❷ dōcháan ge ❸ fùngfu ge * prolific author N: dōcháan jokgā (M: go)

prolix ❶ chèuhng ge ❷ lòsò ge

prologue N: ❶ jeuihyìhn; jeuihchìh (M: pìn) ❷ hòi-

chèuhngbaahk (M: pìn) ❸
jeuihmohk (M: go)

prolong FV: ❶ yìhnchèuhng
(time) ~ sìhgaan ❷ jínkèih ❸
jíngchèuhng; màngchèuhng
làaichèuhng (things, pronunciation) ~ dī mihn ~ gógo yām *
to prolong a visit VO:
yìhnchèuhng fóngkèih * to
prolong one's life VO:
yìhnchèuhng tiuh mehng

promenade N: ❶ saanbouh
❷ yàuhhàhng (M: go) ❸
daaihohksāang móuhwúi PH:
❶ saanbouh ge deihfòng ❷
hòichè dàufùng VO: saanbouh
* promenade concert N:
sìuyìuh yàmngohkwúi (M: go)

prominence N: ❶ daht-
chèut ❷ gihtchèut SV/VO:
chèutméng PH: dahtchèut ge
yéh * give prominence to
N/FV: dahtchèut * a prominent novelist PH: gihtchèut
ge síusyutgā (M: go)

promiscuity N: ❶ wahnlyuhn ❷ (for man and woman)
lyuhnfàn; lyuhngàau; jaahpgàau * promiscuity in racial
relations PH: màhnjuhk
gwàanhaih ge wahnjaahp

promise N: ❶ nohkyìhn ❷
yeukwaih (M: go) FV: yìngsìhng
❷ yeukdìhng SV: yáuh hèi-
mohng ❷ yáuh chìhntòuh;
yáuh chēutsīk * of promise
SV: yáuh chēutsīk ge * make
a promise FV: yìngsìhng *
give a promise VO: tàihchèut
yātgo yeukwuih * keep a promise VO: sáuyeuk * break a
promise VO: ① wáiyeuk ②
sātseun ③ sātyeuk * a writer
of promise PH: yáuh
hèimohng ge jokgā * the pro-
mised land N: ① (bible)
Gānàahm ② tìntòhng (M: go)

promisee N: (law) sauhyeuk-
jé (M: go)

promiser (promisor) N:
yeukchūkjé; dihngyeukjé;
hahpyeukjé (M: go)

promising SV/PH: ❶ yáuh
hèimohng ge ❷ yáuh faatjín
chìhntòuh ge * a promising
young man PH: yáuh
hèimohng ge hauhsàangjái (M:
go)

promissory SV: ❶ yeukdìhng ge ❷ yáuh yeuk-chūk ge
* a promissory note N:
kèihpiu; búnpiu (M: jeùng)

promontory N: hóigok RV:
(anatomy) dahthéi

promote FV: ❶ sìng (in
rank) ❷ tàihchèung (as arts,
etc) ❸ gúlaih; jéunglaih (as industry) ❹ jàngjeun; chūkjeun
❺ faathéi ❻ tèuisìu VO: ❶ (in
rank) sìngkāp ❷ (government
office) sìnggùn * promoted
world peace VO: jàngjeun
saigaai wòhpìhng * to promote the development of
recources of backward
countries PH: tàihchèung
faatjín lohkhauh gwokgā ge
jìyùhn * to promote a
scheme VO: tàihchèung yātgo
gaiwaahk * to promote
health VO: jàngjeun gihnhòng
* to promote peace VO:
chūkjeun wòhpìhng * pro-
moted a new company PH:
chongbaahnjó yātgàan sàn ge
gùngsī

promoter N: ❶ faathéiyàhn
(M: go) ❷ tèuisìusēung (M: go)
❸ sinduhngjé (M: go) ❹ (charity) jaanjohjé (M: go) ❺ (company, school etc) chongbaahnyàhn ❻ (chemistry) chèuifajài
(M: júng) * promotor of
disorder PH: daaitàuh jok-

fáanjé (M: go)

prompt SV: seunchūk A: máhseuhng; jīkhāak N: chèuifúndāan (M: jèung) * a prompt reply PH: seunchūk ge daapfūk

promptor PH: ❶ gúmóuh ge yàhn (M: go) ❷ tàihtòihchìh ge yàhn (M: go)

promulgate FV: ❶ (law) syùnbou; bàanbou ❷ chyùhnbo ❸ syùnchyùhn * to promulgate news VO: gùngbou sìusīk * to promulgate a new form of religion PH: chyùhnbo yātjúng sàn ge jùnggaau yihngsīk * to promulgate official secret VO: sitlauh gùnfòng gèimaht

pone PH: ❶ yáuh N ge kìngheung ❷ yùhngyih yù . . . ge ❸ kìngheung . . . RV: pàdāi

prong N: ❶ chā (M: jek) ❷ jìmtàuh FV: gāt

pronoun N: (language) doih (mìhng) chìh

pronounce FV: ❶ syùnbou ❷ duhk (utter sounds) ❸ faatyām ❹ punkyut * pronounce against VO: bíumìhng fáandeui * pronounce . . . on FV: bíutaai

pronunciation N: faatyām (faat)

proof N: ❶ (evidence) pàhnggeui; jinggeui; jingmìhng ❷ góu (M: go, pìn) ❸ siyihm (M: go) ❹ (printing) gaauyéung (M: yihp, pìn) ❺ (mathematic) jingfaat ❻ (law) jingchìh ❼ jingmìhng màhngín (M: fahn) ❽ noihlihk PH: ❶ yáuh noihlihk ge ❷ mhóyíh chyùngwo ge * bring (put) to proof FV: siyihm, siyuhng * give proof

on PH: géuilaih jingmìhng * in proof of Patt: jouh N ge jinggeui * proof-reader N: gaaudeuiyùhn (M: go) * proof sheet N: gaauyéung (M: yihp, pìn) * proof-spirit N: biujéun jáujing * proof-gold N: sèuhngām (M: gauh, nāp)

prop N: ❶ jìchyú (M: tiuh) ❷ jìchìhjé (M: go) ❸ jìchìhmaht (M: gihn) ❹ douhgeuih (M: gihn) FV: ❶ wàihchìh ❷ díngjyuh * prop up FV: chàangjyuh * a clothes-prop N: saaisàamjūk (M: jì) * the main prop of a state PH: gwokgā ge duhnglèuhng

propaganda N: ❶ syùnchyùhn ❷ syùnchyùhn gèikau (M: go) ❸ syùnchyùhn fòngfaat (M: go) ❸ syùnchyùhn jóujīk (M: go)

propagate FV: ❶ (pass on) chyùhn ❷ syùnchyùhn ❸ chyùhnbo ❹ fàahnjihk * propagate doctrine FV/VO/N: chyùhndouh

propagation N: ❶ fàahnjihk ❷ chyùhnbo

propel FV: ❶ tèuiduhng ❷ tèuijeun

propeller N: ❶ lòhsyùhnjéung (M: jì) ❷ tèuijeunhei (M: ga)

propensity N: ❶ kìngheung (M: go) ❷ jaahpgwaan (M: go) ❸ sihou (M: go)

proper SV: ❶ sīkdong ge ❷ yáuh láihmaauh ge ❸ jànjing ge ❹ jiu kwài géui ❺ ngāam kwàigéui ge ngāam * proper to PH: ❶ jyùnwaih . . . ge ❷ . . . dahkyáuh ge * proper noun N: (language) jyùnyáuh mìhngchìh * proper time TW: kahpsìh * China proper

PW/N: Jùnggwok búnbouh * **Japan proper** PW/N: Yahtbún búnbouh

properly A: ❶ síkdong gám ❷ jingdong gám * to speak properly (properly speaking) PH: ❶ yìhmgaak gám góng ❷ lóuhsaht góng * properly done Adj. PH: jouhdāk hóu tóhdong * properly said PH: góngdāk hóu ngāam * do it properly PH: hóu hóu déi jouh * not properly said PH: góngdāk m̀hngāam

property N: ❶ chòihcháan (M: bāt) ❷ sóyáuhkyùhn (M: go) ❸ (attribute) singjāt ❹ (stage) douhgeuih (M: gihn) ❺ (possessions) yéh (M: gihn; yeuhng) ❻ (family possessions) gādong ❼ (real estate) cháanyihp ❽ (land only) deih; deihcháan (M: faai, fūk) ❾ ngūk; fòhngcháan * personal property N: sīyáuh chòihcháan; duhngcháan * real property N: bātduhngcháan

prophecy N: ❶ yuhyìhn (M: go, geui) ❷ yuhyìhn nàhnglihk

prophet N; sìnjì; yuhyìhnjé (M: go)

prophetical SV: yuhyìhn ge

prophylactic PH: yuhfòhng jahtbehng ge N: ❶ yuhfòhngyeuhk (M: jek) ❷ yuhfòhngfaat (M: go)

prophylacticaxis N: ❶ yuhfòhngfaat (M: go) ❷ beigyahn yuhngbán (yeuhk-maht) (M: gihn)

propitiate FV: hyúngáai VO: màuhkàuh wòhgáai Patt: tùhng PN . . .

propitiatory SV: ❶ hyun-gáai ge ❷ tiuhgáai ge

propitious SV: ❶ seuhnleih ge ❷ chìhchèuhng ge ❸ gāt-chèuhng ge * propitious omens N: gātsiuh (M: go)

proportion N: ❶ béilaih (M: go) ❷ béileuht (M: go) ❸ pìhnghàhng; gwānhàhng ❹ (part) bouhfahn (M: go) ❺ (the relations between parts) wàhnchèuhn; dahng ching

proportions N: ❶ daaihsíu (length, width, thickness) ❷ yùhngjīk PH: ❶ lìhngdou wàhnchèuhn (dahngching) ❷ lìhngdou gwànhàhng * in direct (inverse) proportion to Patt: tùhng N sìhng jing (fáan) béilaih * in proportion to Patt: ❶ tùhng N sìhng béilaih ❷ tùhng N sèungching

proportable PH: hóyíh sáidou sèungching ge

proportional SV: sìhng (síkdong) béilaih ge; pìhng-hàhng ge N: (mathematics) béilaihsou

proportionate SV: ❶ síkdong ge ❷ béilaih ge PH: ❶ lìhngdou wàhnchèuhn ❷ lìhngdou sìhng béilaih

proposal N: ❶ tàihyíh; gínyíh (M: go) ❷ (motion) sān-chíng; tàihngon (M: go) ❸ (of marriage) kàuhfàn ❹ gaiwaahk (M: go)

propose FV: ❶ tàihyíh ❷ sānchíng ❸ tèuijin ❹ kàuhfàn * be proposed as Patt: beih (béi) tàihmìhng wàih N * propose a toast to Patt: ① tàihyíh waih PN yám (yāt) bùi ② ging PN yātbùi

propietor N: ❶ yihpjyú (M: go) ❷ sihtáu; lóuhbáan (M; go)

proprietorship N: sóyáuhkyùhn (M: go)

proprietress N; néuihyihp-jyú (M: go)

propriety SV: ❶ sīkdong ❷ dāktái N: ❶ láih; láihjit (M: go) ❷ kwàigéui (M: go)

propulsion N: ❶ (ship, airplane etc) tèuijeun (lihk) ❸ tèuijeunhei (M: go, ga)

propulsive SV: yáuh tèuijeunlihk ge

prorate PH: ngon (jiu) béilaih fànpui FV: tàanfàn * **to proprate dividends** PH: ngon (jiu) béilaih fànhùhng

prorogation N: (British Parliament) baiwúi; yàuwúi

proscribe FV: ❶ fongjuhk (a person) ~ *yātgo yàhn* ❷ pàaihchīk ❸ gamjí VO: ❶ chùnggwàn ❷ mōkdyuht gùngkyùhn (yàhnkyùhn)

prose N: ❶ sáanmán (sáanmàhn) (M: pìn) ❷ pìhngfàahn SV: ❶ dàandiuh ❷ sáanmàhn ge PH: móuh séungjeuhnglihk ge

prosecute FV: ❶ héisou ❷ (sue) hunggou; gou ❸ jeunhahng (investigate, research) * **prosecuting attorney** N: gímchaatgùn (M: go)

prosecution N: ❶ jāp-hàhng; ❷ jeunhàhng ❸ héisou (M: go) ❹ gímgéui

prosecutor N: ❶ yùhngou (M: go) ❷ héisouyàhn (M: go) * **public prosecutor** N: gímchaatgùn (M: go)

proselyte N: jyúnbinjé (M: go) PH: góibin seunyéuhng ge yàhn (M: go)

prosody N: ❶ wáhnleuhthohk (M: mùhn) ❷ joksīfaat

prospect N: ❶ hèimohng (M: go) ❷ chìhntòuh ❸ fùnggíng; gíngsīk (M: go) FV: ❶ (geography) hamtaam ❷ wán (coalmines) ~ *kong* * **in prospect of** PH: N joihmohng * **prospect for** FV: hamtaam

prospective SV: ❶ yáuh hèimohng ge ❷ yáuh yuhkèih ge

prospectus N: ❶ (of a business enterprise) jèungchìhng (M: fahn, yihp) ❷ (of a plan, device) yiginsyù (M: fahn, bún) ❸ gaiwaahksyù (M: bún) ❹ (of new books, magazines etc) noihyúhng syutmìhng (syù); gáangaai

prosper FV: (of a business enterprise) hìngwohng; wohng Adj. PH: ❶ lihngdou fàahnwìhng ❷ lihngdou sìhnggùng

proserity N: ❶ fàahnwìhng ❷ hahngwahn ❸ sìhnggùng

prosperous SV: ❶ fàahnwìhng ge ❷ sìhnggùng ge ❸ seuhnleih ge ❹ hìngwohng ❺ faatdaaht ❻ hóu saigaai

prostitute N: geihnéuih; chēunggéih (coll.) lóuhgéui (M: go) FV: ❶ maaihyàhm ❷ maaihsàn ❸ laahmyuhng VO: maaihsàn

prostrate PH: ❶ pà hái deihhásyu ❷ lihngdou sèuiyeuhk SV: sèuiyeuhk ge

prostration N: ❶ sèui-yeuhk (M: júng) ❷ (medical) hèuityut * **nervous prostration** N: sàhngìng sèuiyeuhk * **general prostation** PH: yātbún ge hèuiyeuhk

protagonist N: ❶ jyúgok (M: go) ❷ jyúyàhngùng (M: go) PH: tàihchèung ge yàhn (M: go)

protect FV: ❶ bóuwuh ❷ fòhngjí ❸ (defend) fòhngwaih; fòhngsáu ❹ (of the gods) bóuyauh ✳ **protect from** Patt: ① bóuwuh N míhngji N ② míhnji N

protectionism N: ❶ (economics) bóuwuh (mauhyihk) jyúyih (M: júng) ❷ bóuwuh jingchaak (M: go)

protector N: ❶ bóuwuh-yàhn (M: go) ❷ bóuwuh jòngji ✳ **a chest protector** N: wuh-hùng ✳ **point protector** N: bāttou (M: go)

protectorate N: ❶ sipjing jingtái ❷ bóuwuhgwok (M: go) ❸ bóuwuh jaidouh

protégé PH: beih bóuwuhjé (for male) (M: go) N: mùhntòuh (M: go)

protein N: dáanbaahkjāt

protest FV: ❶ kongyíh ❷ fáandeui N: ❶ sìngmìhng (M: go) ❷ kongyíh (syù) (M: bún) ❸ fáandeui ✳ **make (lodge, enter) a protest against** Patt: deui PN tàihchēut kongyíh ✳ **under protest** PH: m̀yuhnyi douģihk FV: bātfuhk

Protestant N: ❶ Gèidūk-gaau ❷ Gèidūktòuh; sàngaautòuh (M: go) SV: sàngaautòuh ge ✳ **Protestant reformation** N/FV: jùngggaau góigaak (M: júng) ✳ **Protestant Episcopal Church** N: (religion) Singgùngwúi (M: go)

protocol N: ❶ yíhdihngsyù (M: bún) ❷ chóuyeuk; chóu-ngon (M: go) ❸ ngoihgàauláih-

jit (M: júng) PH: yíhdihng tiuhyeuk chóungon

prototype N: ❶ yùhnyìhng ❷ dínyìhng; mòuhfaahn ❸ (bilolgy) yùhnyìhng

protract FV: ❶ yìhn-chèuhng (war) ~ jìnjàng ❷ sànchēut (paws) ~ dī jáau

protraction N: ❶ jaitòuh ❷ yìhnchèuhng ❸ kongjèung

protractor N: ❶ lèuhng-gokhei (M: ga) ❷ fàndouhkwài ❸ (anatomy) hìnyáhngèi PH: lihng (sìhgaan, hàhngduhng) tòchèuhng ge yàhn waahkjé mahtgín

protrude RV: (stick out) dahtchēut; sànchēut ✳ **protruding eyes** PH: dahtngáahn

protuberance RV: daht-héi; dahtchēut PH: dahtchēut ge yéh; dahtchēut ge bouhfahn N: láu (M: go)

protuberant A: ❶ dahthéi ge; dahtchēut ge ❷ hínyu ge

proud SV: ❶ (haughty) giungouh; sàchàhn ❷ (conceited) jihgòu jih daaih ❸ jihhòu ge PH: gámdou gwòngwìhng ge ✳ **be proud of** Patt: yíh PN/N wàih wìhng

proudly A: ❶ dākyi gám ❷ fàiwòhng gám

prove FV: ❶ jingmìhng (haih) ❷ siyihm ❸ gímyihm ❹ jingsaht ❺ (law) chàhyihm (will) ~ wàihjūk ❻ yùhnlòih haih ✳ **prove (oneself) to be** PH: jingmìhng (jihgéi) haih ✳ **prove out** PH: jingmìhng haih sīkahp ge

provenance N: (arts) chēut-chyu; héiyùhn (M: go)

provender N: ❶ (for household animals) gònjihlíu ❷ (coll.) sihkmaht

proverb N: ❶ yihmyúh; gaakyìhn (M: geui) ❷ wahbeng ❸ juhkyúh; juhkwá (M: geui) * **as the proverb goes (says)** PH: juhkwá wah * **to a proverb** PH: jung só jàujì * **the book of proverbs** N: (Old Testament) Jàmyìhnpìn * **there is a proverb which says** PH: yáuh geui juhkwá wah; juhkwá (juhkyúh) yáuh wah

provide FV: ❶ (supply) chēut ~ léuihfai ❷ (stipulate) kwàidihng ❸ gùngkāp; gùngying ~ sihmaht ❹ tàihgūng (non-material) ~ jìlíu * **provide against** FV: yuhfòhng * **provide with** FV: ① tàihgūng ② gùngying ③ jòngbeih ④ béi * **provide for** FV: ① jéunbeih ② gùngkāp ③ gukahp

provided, providing MA: ❶ jíyiu ❷ yùhgwó; gáyùh; yeuhkhaih * **provided that** . . . . Patt: ① yùhgwó . . . ② yíh N wàih tìuhgín

providence N: ❶ seuhngdai (M: go) ❷ tìnyi (M: go) ❸ yúhngin * **have trust in providence** IE: tìngtìn yàuhkmihng

providential SV: ❶ seuhngdai ge ❷ tìnyi ge PH: seuhngtìn jyudihng ge

provider N; ❶ gùngkāpjé (M: go) ❷ fósihk sìhngbaahnyàhn (M: go) * **universal provider** N: baakfosèung (M: go)

province N: ❶ sáang (M: go) ❷ jàu (M: go) ❸ (sphere) faahnwàih ❹ bouhfahn (M: go)

provincial SV: ❶ deihfòng ge ❷ sáang ge ❸ chòujuhk ge N: hèunghálóu (M: go) * **provincial capital** N: sáangsèhng (M: go) * **provincial government** N: sáangjingfú (M: go) * **chairman of provincial government** N: sáang (jing) fú jyújihk (M: go))

provincialism N: ❶ hèungháhei ❷ fòngyìhn ❸ deihfòng gùnnihm; hèungtóu gùnnihm

provision N: ❶ gùngying ❷ yuhbeih ❸ (food) lèuhngsihk; sihkbán VO: gùngkāp sihkmaht * **make provision against** FV: fòhngbeih

provisional SV: ❶ jaahmsìh ge ❷ làhmsìh ge * **a provisional governor** N: làhmsìh jàujéung (M: go) * **a provisional agreement** N: làhmsìh hipdihng (M: go) * **provisional arrangement** PH: làhmsìh ge baahnfaat * **provisional government** N: làhmsìh jingfú (M: go)

proviso N: ❶ (treaty) fuhmàhn (M: pìn) ❷ (law) daahnsyù ❸ fuhdaai tìuhgín

provoke FV: ❶ gīknàu (of person; animal etc) ~ gógo yàhn ❷ lìuh ❸ chigīk ❹ sinduhng (people) ~ dī yàhn * **to provoke a riot** PH: gīkhéi bouduhng

provoking PH: lìhngyàhn nàu ge

provost N: ❶ (Oxford; Cambridge univerity) yúnjéung (M: go) ❷ (Scotland) sìhjéung (M: go) ❸ (religion) sàudouh yúnjéung (M: go) ❹ (military) hinbìng gwàngùn (M: go) * **provost marshal** N: hinbìng sìlìhng (M: go) ✳ **provost marshal department** N: hinbing sìlihngbouh (M. go)

prow N: ❶ syùhntàuh (M: go) ❷ (airplane) gèitàuh (M: go)

prowess SV: yúhngmáahng N: búnlíhng PH: m̀pìhngfàahn ge geihnàhng

prowl N/FV: ❶ sáusok ❷ chèuhnlòh VO: wánsihk ✳ **on the prowl** FV: chìhmhàhng

proximity N: ❶ jipgahn ❷ gahnchíh ❸ chàngahn ✳ **in (close) proimity to** Patt: tùhng N (hóu) jipgahn ✳ **in the proximity of** Patt: hái N fuhgahn ✳ **proximity of blood** N: ❶ gahnchàn ❷ gwātyuhk jìchàn

proxy N: ❶ doihléih (kyùhn) (M: go) ❷ doihléihhyàhn (M: go) ✳ **to stand (be) proxy for . . .** Patt: ❶ jouh N ge doihléih ❷ doihbíu . . .

prudence N: ❶ sínsàm (M: júng) ❷ gánsahn (M: júng) ❸ jìngmìhng (M: júng) ✳ **in common prudence** PH: léihsó dòngyìhn

prudent SV: ❶ (wisely, careful) sahnjuhng ge; síusàm ge; gánsahn ge; sámsahn ge ❷ jìngmìhng ge ❸ saisàm ge ❹ (of money) hàan ge

prudish SV: ❶ yātbún jìnggìng ge ❷ jòngmòh jokyeuhng ge

prune FV: ❶ sàujín (branches of tree) ~ *syuhjì* ❷ sàangói (essay) ~ *màhnjèung* N: sàimúi (M: go)

pry FV: ❶ jìngchàh (secret) ~ *yātgo yàhn ge beimaht* ❷ dáting ❸ giuhhéi ❹ dáhòi N:

gunggōn (M: jì)

psalm N: ❶ singgō (M. sáu, jì) ❷ jaanméihsī; jaanméihgō (M. sáu)

psalmody N: ❶ jaanméih sìjaahp (M: bún) ❷ (Christian) singgōjaahp (M: bún)

pseudo SV: ❶ gá ge ❷ mouhchùng ge

pseudonym . N: ❶ (writer) bātméng (M: go) ❷ gáméng (M: go)

psyche N: ❶ lìhngwàhn (M.: go) ❷ sàmlìhng (M: go) ❸ jingsàhn

psychia-ter, - trist N: jìngsàhnbehng yìsàng (M: go)

psychiatry N: ❶ jìngsàhnbehnghohk (M: mùhn) ❷ jìngsàhnbehng jihliuhfaat

psychics N: ❶ sàmléihhohk (M: mùhn) ❷ sàmléih yìhngau

psycho N: ❶ (sl.) jìngsàhn fànsīkhohk (M: mùhn) ❷ sàhngìngbehngwaahnjé (M: go) ❸ sàmléihbehngyàhn (M: go)

psychoanalyst N: jìngsàhn fànsīkhohk gā (M: go)

psychology N: ❶ sàmléihhohk (M: mùhn) ❷ sàmléih (M: go)

psychopath N: ❶ jìngsàhnbintaaijé (M: go) ❷ sàmléihbehngyàhn (M: go)

psychopathic PH: yáuh jìngsàhnbehng ge

psychopathist N: jìngsàhnbehng yìsàng (M: go)

psychopathology N: ❶ sàmléihbehngléihhohk (M:

mùhn) ❷ bintaaisàmléihhohk
(M: mùhn, fò)

psychosis N: ❶ jìngsàhnbehng ❷ jìngsàhnbintaai ❸
behngtaaisàmléih

pub N: ❶ (English sl.)
léuihgún; jáudim

puberty N: ❶ faatchìhng-
kèih ❷ chìngchèun kèih ❸
(plant) hòifākèih

pubescence N: ❶ chìng-
chèunfaatduhngkèih ❷
(aminal, plant) yúhnmòuh

public SV: ❶ gùngguhng ge;
gùngjuhng ge ❷ gùnghòi ge ❸
chyùhngwok ge N: gùngjuhng;
màhnjuhng * **in public** A:
dòngjuhng; gùnghòi gám; PH:
hái yàhn mihnchìhn * **make
public** FV: ❶ faatbíu ❷
gùngbou * **open to the
public** Patt: yahmyàhn FV *
public office N: ① jinggaai ②
jìngfú gèigwàan (M: go) ③
jìngfú yahpbihn * **public
health** PH: gùngguhng
waihsāng * **public organ** N:
gùngguhng gèigwàan (M: go) *
public school N: gùnglahp
hohkhaauh (M: gàan) * **public
telephone** N: gùngyuhng
(gùngguhng) dihnwá * **public
welfare** N: gùngyīk * **public
officer** N: gùngmouhyùhn (M:
go) * **public enemy** N:
gùngdihk (M: go) * **public
park** N: gùngyún (M: go) *
public opinion N: yùhleuhn *
public servant N: gùngbuhk
(M: go) * **public relations** N:
gùngguhng gwàanhaih *
public utility N: gùngguhng
sihyihp * **public spirit** PH:
waih gùngjuhng fuhkmouh ge
jìngsàhn * **the public debt** N:
gùngjaai * **the reading
public** N: duhkjé (M: go) * **the
public** N: gùngjung

publicly A: ❶ gùnghòi ❷
dòngjuhng

publication N: ❶ (periodicals, journals) hónmaht (M: bún)
❷ (that which is published)
chēutbáanmaht (M: bún) PH:
(of one's work) faatbíugwo ge
jokbán

publicist N: ❶ gwokjai
faathohkgā (M: go) ❷ jing-
leuhngā (M: go)

publicity N: ❶ gwónggou
(M: go) ❷ syùnchyùhn VO:
chēutfùngtàuh

publish FV: ❶ (promulgate)
gùngbou ❷ (as in a news paper)
faatbíu ❸ syùnchyùhn ❹
faathòhng ❺ (a book,
periodicals) chēutbáan ❻ (announce) syùnbou

publisher N: ❶ chēutbáan-
jé (M: go) ❷ faathòhngyàhn (M:
go) ❸ faatbíujé (M: go) ❹
chēutbáan gùngsī (M: gàan)

publishing FV: chēutbáan
* **publishing business** N:
chēutbáanyihp * **publishing
house** N: chēutbáanséh (M:
gàan) * **publishing world** N:
chēutbáangaai (M: go)

puce SV: jíhot sīk ge N:
sàmhot sīk

puck N: ❶ jeuhnggàaujai
yùhnpún (M: go) ❷ bìngkàuh
(M: go)

pucker FV: ❶ jipjaap VO:
jaumèihtàuh N: ❶ jaap (M: go)
SV: ❶ chàauh ❷ gīkduhng

pudding N: ❶ boudīn (M:
go, bùi) ❷ hèungchéung (M:
tiuh) * **pudding faced** PH:
yauh fèih yauh yùhn daahnhaih
móuh bíuchìhng ge mihn *
pudding-headed SV: chéun ge

N: sòhgwā (M: go)

puddle N: ❶ séuihāang (M: tìuh) ❷ nàihhāang (M; tìuh) ❸ nàihjèung FV: gáauwàhn

pudgy, pudsy SV: ❶ ngáifèih ge ❷ dyúnchòu ge

puerility N: yaujih; sailouhhei

puff N: ❶ yātchèui (pan) ❷ chèui (pan) sèng) ❸ kwàjeúng ❹ fánpok (M: go) VO: ❶ chèuihei ❷ panhei ❸ chyúnhei ✳ **puff out (away)** VO: ❶ chèuihei ❷ chèuihòi ✳ **puff box** N: fánháp (M: go)

puffy SV: ❶ pàahngjeung ge ❷ fèihge ❸ kwàdaaih ge ❹ chyúnhei ge

pug N: ❶ hàbāgáu (M: jek) ❷ sìjíbeih (M: go) ❸ sai fóchètàuh (M: go) ❹ kyùhnsí; kyùhngīkgā ❺ geukyan (M: go) FV: gáau (mud) ~ nàih ✳ **pug-mill** N: ❶ gáaunàihgèi (M: ga) ❷ gáaubuhngèi (M: ga)

pugilism N: kyùhngīk; kyùhnseuht

pugilist N: kyùhngīkgā; jīkyihp kyùhnsí (M: go)

pugancious SV: ❶ houdau ge ❷ houjin ge PH: jùngyi ngaai gàau ge

pugnacity N: houdau

puisne N: ❶ (law) máahnbui ❷ hahkāp gaaudài ge PH: jīkwaih gaaudài ge

puissant SV: ❶ (ancient poem) yáuh kyùhnlihk ge ❷ kèuhngdaaih ge

puke FV: ngáutou PH: ❶ touchēutlàih ge yéh ❷ (American sl.) lihngyàhn jokngáu ge

yàhn (yéh)

pull FV: ❶ (draw) màng; làai ❷ (extract) màng; baht; mōk (teeth) ~ ngàh ❸ (tear, rip) chaak (houses) ~ ngūk ❹ tò (vehicles) ~ chè ❺ ché (hair) ~ tàuhfaat N: ❶ làai ❷ tò ❸ ché ❹ básáu ✳ **give a pull at** FV: ❶ làai ❷ tò ✳ **have the pull of (over)** FV: singgwo; kèuhnggwo ✳ **pull apart** RV: ❶ làaihòi ② làaityúhn ③ mànghòi ✳ **pull in** VO: ① (car) doujaahm ② (ship) doungohn FV: gánsūk ✳ **pull off (on)** FV: ① chèuih (jeuk, daai) ② mànglāt ✳ **pull out** FV: ① (vehicles) sáichēut ② (articles) màngchēut ③ hòi ④ lèihhòi ✳ **pull over** PH: làaigwolàih ✳ **pull (a person) round** PH: (sáidou) fùifuhk gihnhòng ✳ **pull together** PH: tùhngsàm hiplihk ✳ **pull through** RV: hóufàan; hóudākfàan VO: douhgwo nàahngwàan ✳ **pull the cork out** PH: mànggo jēut chēutlàih ✳ **pull tight** FV: mànggán; màngsaht ✳ **pull to pieces** PH: chéseuisaai ✳ **to pull a long face** PH: làaichèuhng go mihn; m̀gòuhing

puller N: ❶ làaijé (M: go) ❷ kím (M: go)

pullet N: ❶ móuhgàijái (M: jek) ❷ (American sl.) gùlèuhng (M: go)

pulley N: ❶ waahtchè (M: ga) ❷ waahtlèuhn (M: go) ❸ pèihdáailèuhn (M: go)

pulmonary PH: ❶ tùhng fai yáuh gwàanhaih ge ❷ faibouh ge chìhngyìhng ge

pulp N: ❶ (of a melon) nòhng ❷ gwóyuhk ❸ gwójeung ❹ jèungjāp ❺ (anatomy) ngàh

séuih PH: ❶ dàikāp cheuimeih ge jaahpji (M: bún) ❷ fasìhngjeung

pulper N: gáaubuhngèi (M: ga)

pulpit N: ❶ hungjaisāt (M: gàan) ❷ (church) góngtàahn (M: go) ❸ gaausih (júngchìng) (M: go)

pulsate FV: ❶ mahtbohktiu ❷ (as the heart) sàmjohngtiu

pulse N: ❶ (the regular throbbing of the arteries) mahkbok; mahk ❷ dáu (M: nāp) FV: mahktiu ✳ **feel PN'S pulse** Patt: tùhng PN bámahk ✳ **to stir one's pulse** PH: gīkhéi PN ge gámchìhng

pulverize FV: ❶ ngàahnseui ❷ fánseui (enemy) ~ *dihkyàhn*

pulverizer N: fánseuigēi (M: ga)

puma N: (animal) Méihjàu sàanpaau

pummel = plmmel PH: yuhng kyùhntàuh lìhnjuhk gám dá

pump N: ❶ bām (M: go) ❷ jèuimahn FV: ❶ bàm ❷ jèuimahn ❸ pùhnmahn ✳ **be pumped out** A: guih dougihk PH: seuhnghei m̀jip hahhei ✳ **pumped out** RV: bàmchēutlàih ✳ **pump up** FV: dáhei

pumpkin N: fàangwā (M: go)

pun N: sèunggwàanyúh (M: geui) PH: góng sèunggwàan yisi ge syutwah

punch N: ❶ dálūnggèi (M: go) ❷ lihkleuhng ❸ cháugok (M: go) PH: yuhng lìhngmūng;

tòhng; jáu dángdáng ge yéh kàumàaih ge yámbán VO: dálūng FV: kyùhndá ✳ **pull one's punches** VO: bêimín ✳ **punch in (out)** PH: dá fàan (fong) gūng ge kākpín

puncheon N: ❶ ngáichyúh (M: jì) ❷ dáyangèi (M: go) ❸ daaihtúng (M: go)

puncher N: ❶ dálūng gèi (M: go) ❷ fuhkmouhyùhn (M: go)

punctual SV: sáusìh ge; jéunsìh ge ✳ **puntual to the minute** SV: jéunsìh PH: yātfànbātchà

punctuality N: jéunsìh; sáusìh

punctuate PH: ❶ gà bìudím hái . . . ❷ bātsìh dátyúhn (daihyihdī yàhn ge syutwah) FV: gàchúhng

punctuation N: ❶ bìudím ❷ bìudím faat (M: go) ✳ **punctuation marks** N: bìudím fùhhouh

puncture N: lūng (M: go) RV: gātchyùn FV: wáiwaaih VO: ❶ lauhhei ❷ chyùn lūng

pungency N: chigīk (M: go)

pungent SV: ❶ chigīksing ge ❷ gùngbeih ge ❸ jìmsyùn hākbohk ge

punsih FV: ❶ faht; chyúfaht; chìhngfaht ❷ tunggīk

punishment N: ❶ chìhngfaht; chyúfaht ❷ (legal and physical) yìhngfaht

punk PH: ❶ yáhnfó ge yéh (M: gihn) ❷ mòuhlìuh ge syut wah (M: geui) ❸ mòuhjì ge yàhn (M: go) SV: ❶ móuhyuhng ge ❷ waaih ge ❸ m̀gihnhòng ge N: ❶ faimaht (M: gihn) ❷ (sl.) a fèi (M: go)

punt N: pìhngdáisyùhn (M: jek) PH: yuhng júkgòu làih chàang FV: ❶ dóubok ❷ tek (football) ~ *jūkkàuh*

puny SV: ❶ yeuhksíu ge ❷ sai ge ❸ saimèih ge ❹ m̀juhngyiu ge

pup (abv. of: puppy) N: ❶ gáujái (M: jek) ❷ wùhléijái (M: jek) ❸ (sl.) hohksāang (M: go) PH: gìungouh ge hauhsàangjái (M: go)

pupa(e) N: yúng (M: go)

pupal SV: yúng ge

pupil N: ❶ (of a student) hohksāang (M: go) ❷ síuhohksāang (M: go) ❸ (of the eye) tùhnghúng

pupil(l)age N: hohksāang sànfán PH: saimānjái gójahnsí

pupillary SV: ❶ (anatomy) tùhnghúng ge * **pupillary membrane** N: tùhnghúngmók

puppet N: ❶ muhktàuhgùngjái; muhkngáuh (M: go) ❷ faailéuih (M: go) * **puppet-play; puppet show** N: muhktàuhgùngjáihei; muhkngáuhhei (M: chēut) * **puppet government** N: faailéuih jingfú (M: go)

puppetry N: muhktàuhgùngjáihei; muhkngáuhhei (M: chēut) PH: muhktàuhgùngjái (muhkngáuh) ge duhng jok

purblind FV: ❶ bunmàahng; gahnsih ❷ chìhdeuhn

purchase FV: ❶ máaih ❷ kaumáaih RV: dākdóu N:

kaumáaih PH: kaumáaih dóu ge yéh * **make a purchase** VO: máaihyéh

purchaser N: máaihjyú (M: go)

pure SV: ❶ (unmixed) sèuhnjihng ge; sèuhnséuih ge ❷ (of person) dàansèuhn ge ❸ (sheer) yùhnchyùhn ge ❹ (in heart) sèuhngit ge ❺ (unpolluted) gònjehng * **pure gold** N: júkgām; sèuhngām * **pure white** N: sèuhnbaahk * **pure mathematics** N: léihleuhnsouhohk (M: fō)

purely A: ❶ sèuhnséuih gám ❷ tìnjàn gám

purgation N: ❶ jihngfa ❷ chìnggit ❸ (sihk seyeuhk) tùngbihn VO: jingmìhng móuhjeuih

purgative SV: tùngbihn ge * **purgation medicine** N: seyeuhk (M: jèun)

purgatory N: ❶ (Catholic) lihnyuhk ❷ (Buddist) jihngtóu

purge FV: ❶ chìngchèuih ❷ se ❸ chìngsyun ❹ sūkchìng; jíngsūk (Party) N: ❶ sūkchìng; jíngsūk ❷ chìngsyun ❸ seyeuhk VO: chìngdóng * **vomiting and purging** PH: yauh ngò yauh ngáu * **to purge a political party** VO: chìngdóng * **to purge the members of a political party** N: jíngsūk

purify PH: lihngdou gònjehng VO: sáichèuih jeuihngok FV: jìnglihn

Puritan PH: chìnggaautòuh (M: go)

puritan PH: yìhmgán ge yàhn (M: go)

puritic(al) SV: ❶ chìnggaautòuh ge ❷ yìhmgaak ge

puritanism N: chìnggaau jyúyih (gaauyíh)

purity SV: ❶ sèuhnséuih ❷ chìngbaahk

purl VO/FV/N: ❶ saubīn ❷ fáanjāmjīk

purloin FV: tàu(sit)

purple N: ❶ jísīk ❷ jípòuh (M: gihn) ❸ wòhngwaih (M: go) ❹ wòhngjuhk; gwaijuhk * **reddish purple** N: jíhùhngsīk

purport N: yiují; jyújí (M: go) FV: ❶ sìngchìng ❷ yìmeihjyuh

purpose N: ❶ (intention) muhkdīk; yisi (M: go) ❷ yitòuh; yiheung (M: go) FV: ❶ séung; dásyun ❷ kyutsàm * **answer the purpose** VO: fùhhahp muhkdīk * **for the purpose** Patt: waihjó . . . * **on purpose** Patt: waihjó . . . A: ① guyi gám ② jyūndāng gám; dahkdāng gám * **to the purpose** A: jùhnghàhng gám SV: chittàih ge * **with the purpose of** Patt: yíh . . . wàih muhkdīk * **serve a purpose** SV: ② yáuh yuhng ② yáuh hóuchyu * **to little (no) purpose** PH: gèi fùh (yātdī dōu) móuh gitgwó * **to some purpose** PH: ① yáuhdī gitgwó ② yáuhdī sàuwohk

purposely A: guyi gám

purr FV/N: māaugiu PH: faatchēutdī dài tùhng múhnjūk ge sèng

purse N: ❶ ngàhnbāau (M: go) ❷ chìhndói (M: go) ❸ jéunggām (M: bāt) FV: chàugán VO: dyūtjéui * **a common purse** N: gùngguhng gèigām (M: bāt) * **a heavy purse** SV: fuyuh;

yáuh chín * **put up a purse** FV: yùhséung * **the public purse** N: gwokfu (M: go) * **purse one's lips** Adj. PH: dyūt (míu) héi go jéui

purser N: (of ship, airplane) sìhmouhjéung (M: go)

pursue FV: ❶ (chase) jèui (gón) ❷ (to seek to accomplish) jèuikàuh ~ faailihk ❸ gaijuhk

pursuer N: ❶ jèuibouhjé (M: go) ❷ jèuikàuhjé (M: go) ❸ (law) yùhngou (M: go)

pursuit N: ❶ jèuibouh ❷ jèuijuhk ❸ jèuijuhk ❹ yìhngau ❺ kèuijuhkgèi (M: ga) * **in pursuit of** FV: chàhmkàuh

purvey FV: gùngkāp; gùngying VO: baahnfósihk

purveyance N: ❶ gùngkāp; gùngying ❷ fósihk

purveyor N: sihkbángùngyingsèung (M: go) PH: baahnfósihk ge yàhn (M: go)

pus N: nùhng * **to gather pus** VO: fanùhng

push FV: ❶ tèui ❷ ngúng ❸ chùng ❹ jài ❺ tèuijeun (matter) ~ yātgihn sih ° bīk (bāak) ❼ gahm (button) ~ jai N: ❶ tèui ❷ (coll.) lihkleuhng; nàhnglihk ❸ gonging * **at a push** PH: gángāp gójahnsí * **come to the push** PH: beih yìhmgaak háauyihm * **make a push** FV: fánfaat; jeungùng VO: gàyáu * **push against** FV: tèuijohng * **push apart** RV: tèuihòi * **push button** VO: gahmjai * **push off** RV: chàanghòi * **push through** FV: chūksihng * **push up** FV: ① tèuiséuhng ② jànggà * **push-cart** N: ① sáutèuichē (M: ga) ② bihbíchè (M: ga) * **push someone**

around FV: hà

pusher N: ❶ tèuiduhnghei (M: ga) ❷ tèuijeunsīk fèigèi (M: ga) PH: tèui ge yàhn (M: go)

pushful SV: ❶ yáuh jeunchéui sám ge ❷ yáuh chùngging ge

puss N: ❶ māaujái (M: jek) ❷ néuihjái (M: go) ❸ (British) yéhtou (M: jek)

put FV: ❶ (place) jài; fong; báai ❷ góngmìhng; bíubaahk ❸ jòng ❹ yingyuhng (skill) ~ geiseuht ❺ (ship) sáiheung ❻ gúgai ❼ tàuhjī (business) ~ jouh sàangyi ❽ faatngàh ✳ **put across** PH: ① lìhngdou daahtsìhng ② lìhngdou yùhngyih jipsauh ✳ **put all one's eggs in one basket** (coll.) gùjyu yātjaahk ✳ **put an end to** FV: ① gitchūk ② siumiht ✳ **put aside** PH: dámmàaih yātbihn ✳ **put back** RV: fongfàan ✳ **put down** RV: ① fongdài ② geidài; sédài FV: ① janngaak (people) ~ dī yàhn ② jaijí ✳ **put forward** RV: ① tàihchēut ② buhtfaai (clock; watch) ~ go jūng (bíu) ❸ tèuigéui ✳ **put in** VO: ① chaapwah ② yahp góngháu ✳ **put into** RV: ① dámyahp; fongyahp ② fàanyihksìhng ✳ **put off** FV: ① chèuih (clothes) ~ sàam ② yìhnkèih ③ tèuiwái (responsibility) ~ jaakyahm ④ báaityut ⑤ tòyìhn ❻ fùyín (person) ~ kéuih ✳ **put on** FV: ① jeuk (articles of clothing) ~ sàam; hàaih ② daai (hats, gloves, onaments) ~ sáusīk ③ jadai ④ jànggà ⑤ séuhngyín (movie) ~ yātchēut hei ✳ **put out** FV: ① miht (fó); sīk; jíngsīk ② sòuyíu ③ faathòhng ✳ **put up with** FV: yùhngyán; yándāk; m̀gaigaau ✳ **put in**

FV: (of time) yuhng;. jouh ✳ **put (things) in order** RV: júngdihm; gáaudihm ✳ **put through** FV: dátùng; jiptùng (telephone) ~ jó dihnwá PH: seuhnleih jouhhóu ✳ **put to good use** PH: hóu hóu déi yuhng ✳ **put up** FV: héi ✳ **to put in black and white** RV: geidài; sédài IE: baahkjí hākjih ✳ **to put in order** Patt: ngon (jiu) . . . chijeuih pàaihliht ✳ **to put into practice** FV: sahthàhng; sìhàhng

put; putt PH: dá gòuyíhfùkàuh yahp lūng

putative FV: ❶ gádihng ❷ séungjeuhng

putrefy FV/SV: ❶ fubaaih ❷ dohlohk

putter PH: ❶ jàiyéh ge yàhn (M: go) ❷ tàihchēut ge yàhn (M: go) ❸ (golf) dábō ge yàhn (M: go) ❸ wùhwùh wahnwahn gwo yahtjí FV: tàuláahn

putty N: yàuhfùi PH: ❶ yùhngyih sauh yínghéung ge yàhn (M: go) ❷ yuhng yàuhfùi jiphahp

puzzle N: ❶ màih (M: go) ❷ nàahntàih (M: go) FV: wàihmàahn PH: lìhngyàhn nàahngáai

puzzlement SV: ❶ m̀mìhngbaahk ❷ màihmóhng

pygmy PH: ❶ ngáisai ge yàhn (M: go) ❷ sai dougihk ge N: jyùyúh (M: go)

pyjamas N: seuihyìfu; fangaausāam (M: tou)

pylon N: ❶ tittaap (M: joh) ❷ taapyìhng ginjúkmaht (M: joh)

pyorrhoea N: ❶ (medical)

chígànnùhngyaht jing ❷ nùhnglauh

pyramid N: ❶ gàmjihtaap (M: joh) ❷ gokjèui PH: (lihngdou) sìhng taapyìhng

pyramidal Adj. PH: ❶ gàmjihtaapyìhng N: (anatomy) jèuigwāt

pyramidic(al) Adj. PH: ❶ jèuiyìhng ge ❷ jìmtaapyìhng ge

pyre PH: ❶ sìuyéh yuhng ge daaihdèui muhklíu ❷ (fójong yuhng ge) chàaihdèui

python N: ❶ móhngsèh (M: tìuh) ❷ yuhyìhnjé (M: go)

pyxis (pl. pyxides) N: ❶ fajònghháp (M: go) ❷ bóusehkháp (M: go) ❸ sēungjái (M: go) ❹ saiháp; hápjái (M: go)

Q

quack N: ❶ ngáap (ngaap) giusèng ❷ wòhngluhk yìsàng (M: go) PH: ❶ mòuhfóng ngaapgiu ❷ daaihsèng góng móuh yisi ge syutwah ✻ **quack medicine** N: gáyeuhk

quarangle N: ❶ seigok-yìhng ❷ seihahpyún (M: go)

quadrant N: ❶ seifahn jìyāt yùhnjàu ❷ (mathematics) jeuhnghaahn ❸ (astronomy) jeuhnghaahnyìh (M: go)

quadraphony N: sei-singdouh lahptáising

quadrate PH: ❶ jingfòng-

yìhng ge ❷ chèuhng fòng yìhng ge N: ❶ fòngyìhng ❷ chèuhngfòngyìhng FV: ❶ sīkhahp ❷ yātji

quadrennial PH: múih seinìhn yātchi ge (sìhgín) N: daihsei jàunìhn NuM: seinìhn PH: seinìhngàan ge

quadric NuM: (mathematics) léuhngchi

quadrilateral Adj. PH: sei-bīnyìhng ge N: (mathematics) seibīnyìhng; seigokyìhng

quadruped N: (animal) seigeuk duhngmaht (M: jek) PH: yáuh seijek geuk ge

quadruple Adj. PH: ❶ seipúih ge ❷ seichùhng ge

quadruplet N: seigihn yāttou

quadruplets N: seibàautòi

quaff FV: tungyám

quag, quagmire N: ❶ nàihjíu ❷ kwangíng (M: go)

quail N: ❶ ngāmchēun (M: jek) FV: waisūk

quaint SV: ❶ gúgwaai ge ❷ kèihmiuh ge ❸ leng ge

quake FV: janduhng N: ❶ deihjan ❷ janduhng

qualification N: ❶ jìgaak (M: go) ❷ tìuhgín (M: go) ❸ haahnjai tìuhgín ✻ **without qualification** SV: móuh tìuhgín

qualified SV: ❶ yáuh jìgaak ge ❷ gau jìgaak ge; hahpgaak ge ❸ sìngyahm ge ❹ yáuh bóulàuh ge ✻ **qualified teacher** N: gímdihng gaausī (M: go) ✻ **qualified test** N:

gímdihng háausíh (M: chi)

quality N: ❶ jātleuhng ❷ singjāt (M: go) ❸ bánjāt (M: go) ❹ sèuhnhohkseuht syùbou (M: bún) ❺ bánjúng (M: go) ❻ (characteristics) deihfòng ❼ (grade) jātdéi ✻ quality of life PH: gèibún sàngwuht tiuhgín ✻ good quality N: hóuchyu ✻ bad quality N: waaihchyu ✻ of good quality SV: hóu jātdéi ge ✻ of superior quality N: seuhngdáng jātdéi ✻ of medium quality N: ① jùngdáng jātdéi ② jùngtíng ✻ of poor quality N: hahdáng jātdéi SV: yáih ge

quantity N: ① leuhng. síu ~ ; daaih ~ ❷ souleuhng (M: go) ❸ fahnleuhng ❹ dihngngáak (M: go) ✻ a quantity of SV: daaihleuhng ✻ in quantity N: daaihhleuhng ✻ an unknown quantity N: meih jìsou

quantum N: ❶ dihngleuhng ❷ fahnngáak ❸ (physics) leuhngjí ❹ júngleuhng ✻ quantum theory N: leuhngjí leuhn

quarantine N: ❶ gaaklèihkèui (M: go) ❷ gímyihk (kèihgaan) FV: ❶ gímyihk ❷ gaaklèih ✻ in (under) quarantine N: gaaklèih gímyihk ✻ out of quarantine PH: chitsìu làuhyihm

quarrel N: ❶ ngaaigàau (M: chi) ❷ màaihyun FV: ngaai; chòuh VO: ngaaigàau ✻ in a good quarrel PH: waaihjó jingyih làih jàang

quarrelsome PH: jùngyi ngaaugéng; jùngyi dínggéng; jùngyi tùhngyàhn ngaaigàau

quarry N: ❶ chóisehk-

chèuhng (M: go) ❷ sehkkong (M: go) ❸ lihngyìhng (waahkjé fòngyìhng) bōlēibáan (M: faai) VO: ❶ chóisehk ❷ wán jìlíu

quart N: ❶ kwàtyut ❷ yāt kwàtyut yùhnghei ✻ put a quart into a pint pot PH: baahnm̀dou (dóu) ge sih

quarter N: ❶ (one fourth) yātgo gwāt; seifahn jìyāt ❷ yātgwai ❸ kèui; síhhèui (M: go) ❹ (America, Canada) léuhng hòuhbun FV: ❶ jyuhsūk ❷ (army) jyujaat PH: fèisèuhng m̀ yùhnchyùhn ge ✻ a quarter of N: seifahn jìyāt ✻ come to close quarters PH: yuhkbok ✻ first (last) quarters PH: yuht ge seuhng (hah) yìhn ✻ from a safe quarter PH: hái hókaau fòngmihn ✻ in all quarters A: dousyu ✻ industrial quarter N: gùngyihpkèui ✻ servants' quarters N: gùngyàhnfóng (M: gàan) ✻ quarter-master N: ① (sea) tòhsáu (M: go) ② (military) gwànsèuigùn (M: go)

quarterly PH: yātnìhn seichi ge A: yātnìhn seichi N: gwaihón (M: bún)

quartet(te) N: ❶ seichùhngcheung ❷ seiyàhn yātjóu

quartz N: (mineral) sehkyìng

quaver FV: jan VO: faat janyàm N: ❶ janyām ❷ (music) baatfàn yàmfùh

quavery SV: ❶ jan ge ❷ dò janyām ge

quay N: máhtàuh (M: go)

quayage N: máhtàuh sáiyuhngfai; paaksyùhnfai (M: bāt)

queasy SV: m̀wándihng ge PH: lihng yàhn jokngáu ge;

lihng yàhn m̀syùfuhk ge

queen N: ❶ (wife of king) wòhnghauh (M: go) ❷ (reigning) néuihwòhng PH: jeui ngoi ge néuihjái (M: go) VO: laahp néuihwòhng ✻ **queen mother** N: wòhngtaaihauh (M: go) ✻ **queen size** N/SV: daaihhouh

queenship PH: ❶ néuihwòhng sànfán (M: go) ❷ néuihwòhng túngjih kèihgāan

queer SV: ❶ kèihgwaai ge ❷ (odd) gúgwaai ❸ hóyìh ge ❹ m̀syùfuhk ge ❺ ngáahnfà ge ❻ gá ge FV: ❶ jòutaat ❷ powaaih ✻ **in queer street** PH: jaai tòuh gòujūk ge ✻ **to queer a person's pitch** PH: jihngjíng powaaih PN ge gaiwaahk

queerish SV: yáuhdī gúgwaai ge

quell FV: ❶ janngaak (riot, rebellion) ~ buhnlyuhn ❷ ngaakjai ❸ pìhngsīk ❹ gáamhèng

quench FV: ❶ (put out) jíngsīk (fire) ~ fó ❷ yīkjai PH: sáidou PN tìhngháu ✻ **quench the thirst** FV: jíhot; gáaihot

quenchable PH: hóyíh sīkmiht ge

quern N: sáutèuimòh (M: go) ✻ **quern-stone** N: mòhsehk

query N: ❶ jātmahn ❷ yìhmahn (M: go) ❸ sèunmahn FV: ❶ jātmahn ❷ sèunmahn ✻ **to raise a query** FV: faatmahn

quest N: ❶ taamkàuh ❷ chàhmkàuh FV: ❶ wán ❷ taamsok ✻ **in search of** FV: taamkàuh

question N: ❶ (matter of doubt) mahn tàih (M: go) ❷ jāt-

sèun; jātmahn ❸ yíhtàih; tàihngon (M: go) ❸ leuhndím (M: go) ❺ jàngleuhn (M: go) ❻ bíukyut FV: ❶ mahn (questions) ~ *mahntàih* ❷ sèunmahn; jātmahn ❸ sámmahn ❹ wàaihyìh ✻ **beside the question** PH: tùhng búntàih móuh kwàanhaih ✻ **beyond (out of, past, without) question** PH: hòuhmòuh yìhmahn ✻ **call in question** VO: bíusih wàaihyìh ✻ **in question** PH: yíhleuhnjùng ge ✻ **out of the question** PH: ① m̀ hóyíh sahthàhng ge ② m̀sái jíyí ✻ **question at (in) issue** N; yùhnngon (M: gihn) ✻ **put a question to** FV: jātmahn; jātsèun ✻ **put the question** PH: yàuh tàuhpiu gáaikyut FV; bíukyut ✻ **to the question** A: chittàih gám ✻ **to put to the question** FV: ① hàaumahn ② yìhngfaht bīkgùng ✻ **without question** A: gáng ✻ **to question a person** VO: sámmahn yātgo yàhn

questionable SV: hóyìh ge

questioningly A: jātmahn gám; sèunmahn gám

questionmark N: mahnhouh (M: go)

question(n)aire N: (ask for opinions) mahntàihbíu; diuhchàhbíu (M: go, fahn)

queue N: ❶ bīn (M: tìuh) ❷ hòhngliht VO: ❶ sòbīn ❷ pàaihdéui ✻ **jump the queue** PH: ① m̀jiu sìnhauh pàaihdéui ② séung chéungsìn máaih yéh ③ dájìm ✻ **queue up for** PH: pàaihdéui dáng

quick SV: ❶ faai ge; faaicheui ge ❷ faaisáu ge; lìhngmáhn ge ❸ gèilìhng ge ❹ singgāp ge N: gámgok máhnyeuih bouhwaih (M: go) ✻

in quick succession FV: gán-jipjyuh * quick as lighting Adj. PH: símdihn gam faai * quick at figures PH: gaisyun dāk faai * quick of sight SV: ngáahnleih ge * to the quick VO: jūkkahp yiuhoih SV: bīkjàn * quick ear Adj. PH: yíhjái lìhngmáhn * quick-eyed Adj. PH: ngáahnlihk máhnyeuih ge * quick freeze FV: gāpdung * quick-line N: sàangsehfùi * quick-sand N: làuhsà * quick-silver N: séuingàhn * quick-tempered SV: singgáp ge; bouhchou ge * quick-witted Adj. PH: ① yáuh gāpji ge ② chòihsì máhnjiht ge * the quicker the better Patt: yuht faai yuht hóu

quicken FV: ❶ gón faai ❷ gàchūk ❸ gúmóuh

quickly SV: faai

quiescence N: ❶ jihngjí ❷ jihngjihk

quiescent Adj. PH: ❶ jihngjí ge ❷ mýūk ge

quiet SV: ❶ jihng ge ❷ (of a place) chìngjihng ❸ (of a person) màhnjihng ge ❹ ngamjùng ge; beimaht ge ❺ (of the sea) pìhngjihng ❻ (of a country) taaipìhng N: ❶ ngòn jihng ❷ (of a person) chàhmjihng FV: ❶ jihng ❷ ngònwai * be quiet PH: chéng jihngdī * on the quiet A: jihngjíng gám; beimaht gám

quill N: ❶ yúhmòuhgún ❷ ngòhmòuhbāt (M: jì)

quilt N: péih; mìhnpéih (M: jèung); lyùhnpéih FV: ❶ jíntip ❷ pìnchàap * quilted garments N: mìhnnaahp (M: gihn) * quilted gown N: mìhnpóu (M: gihn)

quinine N: (medicine) gàm-gàingaahpsēung

quinsy N: bíntòuhsin (faat) yìhm

quintessence N: ❶ jìngwàh ❷ dínyìhng ❸ sahtjāt ❹ jáujìng

quinte(te) N: (music) ńghbouhkūk; ńghchùhngjau PH: ńghyàhn yātjóu

quintuple Adj. PH: ńghpúih ge N: ńghpúih PH: lìhngdou sìhngwáih ńghpúih

quip = quibble N: ❶ fungchiwá (M: geui) ❷ miuhyúh (M: geui) ❸ sèunggwàanyúh (M: geui) ❹ gwaaisih (M: gihn)

quirk N: ❶ gāpnáu; gāpjyun ❷ gwaaipīk ❸ (writing) fātái

quisling N: ❶ (of a country) maaihgwokchaahk (M: go) ❷ (of a company; organization) noihgàan

quit FV: ❶ lèihhòi ❷ teuichēut ❸ tìhngjí ❹ fonghei ❺ chìngchèuih ❻ (office work) chìhjīk ❼ (labour work) chìhgūng VO: chìhjīk; chìhgùng * be (get) quit of FV: báaityut * quit cost FV: ① jìfuh ② sèuhngwàahn * quit office FV: chìhjīk * quitting-time N: (America) fonggùng sìhgaan * quit drinking VO: gaaijáu

quite A: ❶ yùhnchyùhn gám ❷ sahpfàn ❸ sèungdòng ❹ jànsaht gám ❺ géi; pó * be quite the thing SV/FV: làuhhàhng; sìhmōu * not quite proper PH: mhaih géi jingdong * quite long Adj. PH: sèungdòng chèuhng ge * quite another thing PH: yùhnchyùhn mtùhng ge * quite right Adj. PH: yùhn-

chyùhn ngāam; hóuhóu; géi
ngāam * quite so Adj. PH:
haih la; m̀cho * quite up-to-
date Adj.PH: jeui sànsīk ge *
not quite PH: juhng meih dāk
* it's quite unexpected RV:
gúm̀dóu * the price is quite
reasonable PH: gachihn géi
sèungyìh

quiver FV: jan N: ❶ jan-
duhng ❷ jindói (M: go) *
quiver with fear Adj PH:
gèngdoujan

quiz N: ❶ síuchāakyihm ❷
ngokjokkehk ❸ (broadcast)
mahndaap béichoi (M: chi) ❹
jilihk chāakyihm (M: chi) FV: ❶
wàfú (person) ~ yàhn ❷
chāakyihm * quizzes on
general knowledge N:
sèuhngsīk chāakyihm

quizzical SV: ❶ jàausiu ge
❷ houkèih ge ❸ waahtkài ge

quod N: (English sl.) gāamyuhk (M: gàan, go) * quod
vide VO: chàamjiu gòitiuh

quoit N: ❶ tithyūn (M: go) ❷
sìhnghyūn (M: go)

quoits PH: jaahk tithyūn
yàuhhei

quondam MA: ❶ yíhchìhn
❷ gwoheui

quorum N: faatdihng yàhn-
sou * form a quorum VO:
yìhngsìhng faatdihng yàhnsou

quota N: ngáak; haahn-
ngáak; dihngngáak * the
quota system N: dihng ngáak
fànpuijai (M: go) * the quota
of immigrants N: yìhmàhn-
ngáak (M: go)

quotation N: ❶ yáhnjing ❷
yáhnyuhng ❸ yáhnmàhn (M:
pìn) ❹ yúhluhk (M: geui, pìn) ❺

hòhngchìhngbíu (M. jèung) *
quotation marks N: yáhn-
houh (M: go)

quote FV: ❶ yáhnyuhng ❷
yáhnjing VO: hòiga N: ❶
yáhnyuhnggeui (M: geui) ❷
yáhnyuhngmàhn (M: pìn) *
quote from RV: yáhnjih *
quote a precedent VO:
yáhnyuhng chìhnlaih * quote
from the classics IE: yáhn-
gìng geuidín * quote . . . to
prove Patt yáhn (yuhng) . . .
làih jingmìhng

R

rabbit N: ❶ toujái; tou (M:
jek) ❷ toumòuh ❸ toupèih (M:
faai) ❹ dáamsíugwái (M: go)
VO: dá toujái; lihptou * go
rabbiting PH: heui dá toujái
* rabbit fever N: (medical)
touyiht

rabble IE: wùhahp jìjuhng N:
❶ hahdángyàhn (M: go) ❷
gáaubuhnhnei (M: ga) * the
rabble N: jihnmàhn (M: bàan)

rabies N: (medical) fùnggáu-
jing; dìngáujing

race N: ❶ (a contest of speed
and competition) béichoi (M: go,
chi) ❷ choipáau ❸ gāplàuh ❹
séuidouh (M: tiuh) ❺ (species)
yàhnleuih ❻ (people of the same
ancestry) júngjuhk (M: go) ❼
(biology) juhkleuih; júngjuhk
(M: go) ❽ hyuttúng ❾ gàhaih ❿
mùhndaih VO: béichoi FV: dau;
béichoi Patt: tùhng PN/N
choipáau * race cup N: ①
singleihbūi (M: jek) ② jéungbūi

(M: jek) * **race meeting** N: choimáhwúi; páaumáhwúi (M: go) * **race course** N: ① (choi) máhchèuhng; páaumáhdéi (M: go) ② choisyùhn séuidouh * **race track** N: páaudouh (M: tiuh) * **race between persons** FV: ① daujáu ② daufaai * **horse race** N/VO: choimáh; páaumáh * **white race** N: baahkjúngyàhn (M: go) * **yellow race** N: wòhngjúngyàhn (M: go)* **black race** N: hākjúngyàhn (M: go) * **red race** N: hùhngjúngyàhn (M: go) * **the winged race** N: níuh leuih * **the race of fishes** N: yùh leuih * **race discrimination** N: júngjuhk kèihsih

racial PH: ❶ yàhnjúng ge ❷ júngjuhk ge * **racial prejudice** N: júngjuhk pìngin * **racial revolution** N: júngjuhk gaakmihng (M: chi) * **racial traits** N: júngjuhk dahkjing (M: go) * **racial dislike** N: júngjuhk jàngwu

racialism N: ❶ júngjuhk jyúyih (M: go) ❷ màhnjuhk jyúyih (M: go) ❸ màhnjuhk jingsàhn

rack N: ❶ (frame, shelf) gá (M: go) ❷ tòih (M: go) ❸ yìhngtòih (M: go) ❹ síupáau (M: chi) ❺ powaaih ❻ wáimiht FV: ❶ hàaumahn ❷ jitmòh VO: gáaunóuhjáp * **be on the rack** VO: sauh huhkyìhng * **go to rack and ruin** PH: gwàiyù wáimiht * **put to (on) the rack** FV: hàaumahn * **rack one's brains** VO: gáaujeuhn nóuhjáp

racket N: ❶ (móhng) kàuhpáak (M: go) ❷ syuthàaih (M: deui) ❸ cháaunaauh ❹ fèifaat máaihmaaih PH: ❶ fèisèuhng fàahnmòhng ge gàaujai

yingchàuh ❷ tàungāak gwáaipin ge hàhngwàih FV: chòuh * **be in on a racket** VO: chàamyúh hàauja * **stand the racket** PH: gìngdākhéi háauyihm * **racket court, racket ground** N: móhngkàuhchèuhng (M: go)

racketeer PH: ❶ tàungāak gwáaipin ge yàhn (M: go) ❷ dáaitòuh (M: go) FV: ❶ lahksok ❷ húnghaak

racy SV: ❶ bóuchìh yùhnmeih ge ❷ sànsin ge ❸ sàangduhng ge ❹ (books, articles) yàhmsit ge * **a racy style** PH: wuhtput ge fùnggaak * **a racy novel** PH: yàhmsit ge síusyut (M: bún)

radar N: ❶ lèuihdaaht ❷ mòuhsindihn dihngwái * **radar astronomy** N: lèuihdaaht tìnmàhn hohk * **radarscope** N: lèuihdaaht hínsihhei (M: ga)

RADCM (radar counter measures) PH: fáan lèuihdaaht chousī

radiance radiancy N: gwòngfài

radiant PH: ❶ faatgwòng ge ❷ fūkseh ge N: gwòngdím

radiate VO: ❶ faatgwòng ❷ fongseh yihtlihk FV: ❶ chyùhnbo ❷ gwóngbo

radiator N: ❶ fūksehtái ❷ nyúhnheilòuh (M: go) ❸ saanyihthei (M: ga) ❹ láahngkeukhei (M: ga) ❺ faatseh tìnsin

radical SV: ❶ chitdái ge ❷ gànsàang ge A: gànbúnseuhng N: ❶ gīklihtfahnjí; gīkjeunfahnjí ❷ (chemistry) gèi ❸ (mathematics) gàn; ❹ bouhsáu

(M: go) * radical difference
PH: gànbúnsenhng ge chàbiht
* radical treatment N: (of
disease) gànbún jihlìuh

radicalism N: gīkjeun
jyúyih

radio N: ❶ mòuhsindihn
(bou, wá, gwóngbo) ❷
sàuyàmgèi (M: ga, go) ❸
mòuhsindihn chitbeih ❹
mòuhsindihn gwóngbo sihyihp
PH: ❶ yuhng mòuhsindihn
faatsung waahkjé gwóngbo ❷
yuhng sehsin yíngséung
waahkjé jihlìuh * English by
radio N: gwóngbo Yīngyúh
gaauhohk * radio Beijing N:
Bākgìng gwóngbo dihntòih *
radio-broadcast; radio-cast
FV: mòuhsindihn gwóngbo *
radio-detector N: mòuhsindihn taamchāakhei lèuihdaaht
(M: go, ga) * radio-element N:
fongsehsou yùhnsou * radio-
gram N: ① X gwòng jiupín (M:
fūk, jèung) ② mòuhsin dihnbou
(M: go) ③ sàuyàm dihncheung
léuhngyuhng gēi (M: ga) *
radio-news N: gwóngbo sànmàhn * radio-phone N:
mòuhsin dihnwá (gèi) (M: ga) *
radio-phonograph N: sàuyàm
dihncheung léuhng yuhnggèi
(M: ga) * radio-photo (gragh)
N: mòuhsindihn chyùhnjàn *
radio-rator N: gwóngbo
yínyùhn (M: go) * radio-scope
N: fongsehgeng (M: go) *
radio-telegram N: mòuhsin-
dihnbou (M: go) * radio-
therapy N: fongseh jihlìuhfaat
* radio-torial N: gwóngbo
pìhngleuhn * radio broad-
casting station N: dihntòih;
gwóngbo dihntòih; mòuhsin
dihntòih (M: gàan, go) * radio
wave N: dihnbō; mòuhsin
dihnbō

radiology N: fongsehhohk

(M: mùhn)

radiologist N: fongseh-
hohkgā (M: go)

radionics N: dihnjíhohk (M:
mùhn)

radish N: lòhbaahkjái;
hùhnglòhbaahkjái (M: pò, go)

radius (pl = dü) N: ❶
bunging ❷ fūkseh gwòngsin
(M: go) ❺ faahnwàih (M: go)

raffish SV: (of people)
fongdohng ge

raffle PH: chàuchìm maaih
yéh ge fòngfaat N: faimaht VO:
chàuchìm

raft N: ❶ muhkpàaih ❷
gausàngtéhng (M: jek) N/ATT:
daaihleuhng; PH: yuhng faht
wahnsung

rag N: ❶seuibou (M: faai) ❷
laahnbou (M: faai) ❸ sáugān
(M: tìuh) ❹ boují (M: jèung;
fahn) ❺ kèih (M: jì) ❻ ngàhnjí
(M: jèung) FV: ❶ naauh ❷
heiluhng; yéh * cooked to
rags PH: jyúdou laahn * rag
baby PH: yuhng seuibou jouh
ge gùngjái (M: go) * rag-fair
N: guyì síhcheùhng (M: go) *
rag-man PH: sàumáaih
laahnsāam ge yàhn * rag-
paper N: faijí (M: jèung) *
rag trade N: (sl.) fuhkjōngyihp

ragamuffin PH: yìsāam
polaahn ge yàhn (M: go)

rage PH: ❶ nàudāk hóu
gányiu ❷ (coll.) làuhhàhng ge
N: yihtchìhng SV/FV: ❶ nàu ❷
làuhhàhng ❸ fùnghàhng * be
(all) the rage PH: làuhhàhng
yātsìh * in a rage A: hóu nàu
gám * the rage of the wind
N: fùngbouh (M: go)

ragged SV: ❶ polaahn ge ❷ lāpdaht bātpihng ge ❸ chiyíh ge

raid N: ❶ (miditary) jaahpgīk; dahtgīk ❷ (of police) sáuchàh ✳ **air raid** N: hùngjaahp (M: chi) ✳ **air raid alarm** N: fòhnghùng gíngbou (M: go)

rail N: ❶ làahngōn (M: tìuh, jī) ❷ titgwái (M: tìuh) ❸ titlouh (M: tìuh) VO: pòutitlouh FV: ❶ naauh ❷ hàihlohk ❸ tìutīk ✳ **off the rails** VO: chēutgwái ✳ **on the rails** PH: ① hái jìngsèuhng ge gwáidouh seuhngbihn ② seuhnleih jeunhàhng

railing N: ❶ làahngōn (M: tìuh, jī) ❷ kongyíh (M: chi; go) PH: màaihyun ge syutwah

railery FV: wàfú PH: sihnyi ge jàausiu

railroad N: ❶ (America) titlouh ❷ titlouh bouhmùhn (M: go) ❸ (company) titlouhgúk (M: gàan) ❹ (company) titlouhgúk (M: gàan) ❹ (train) fóchè (M: ga) PH: yuhng titlouh heui wahnsyū ✳ **railroad track** N: titgwái (M: tìuh) ✳ **railroad station** N: fóchèjaahm (M: go) ✳ **railroad ticket** N: fóchèfēi (M: jèung)

railway N: ❶ (British) titlouh (M: tìuh) ❷ titlouh bouhmùhn ❸ titlouh haihtúng (M: go) PH: chóh fóchè heui léuihhàhng ✳ **at railway speed** A: fèifaai gám ✳ **railway carriage** N: (British) fóchè chèkā; fóchè chèsēung (M: go)

rain N: yúh (M: nāp) PH: lohkyúhtīn (M: go) VO: lohkyúh ✳ **a heavy (light) rain** VO: lohk daaih (sai) yúh ✳ **rain or**

shine PH: mòuhleuhn hóutīn yīkwaahk lohkyúhtīn ✳ **rainbow** N: chóihùhng (M: tìuh) ✳ **rain-coat** N: yúhyī; yúhlāu (M: gihn) ✳ **rain-fall** N: yúhleuhng ✳ **rain glass** N: chìhngyúhbíu (M: go, jèung) ✳ **rain proof** PH: fòhngyúh ge ✳ **rain storm** N: bouhfūng yúh (M: go) PH: ① lohk daaihyúh ② yauh dá fùng yauh lohkyúh ✳ **rain-worm** N: yàuyáhn (M: tìuh) ✳ **light rain** N: yúhmēi

rainy SV: dò yúh ge ✳ **rainy season** N: yúhgwai (M: go)

raise FV: ❶ (grow) jung ~ syùhjái ❷ (of farm animals) yéuhng ~ gāi ❸ géui (héi) (limbs) ~ sáu ~ geuk❹ ginlahp ❺ tàihgòu (voice) ~ sìngyàm ❻ syuhhéi ❼ chàuhjaahp (money) ~ yātbātchín ❽ jòipùih (person) ~ yātgo yàhn ❾ tàihchēut (question) ~ mahntàih ❿ gà (wages, salary) ~ yàhngūng; ~ sànséui RV: ❶ (America) géuihéi ❷ dahthéi ❸ tàihhéi (spirit) ~ jìngsàhn ✳ **raise a dust** Adj PH: yáhnhéijó sòulyuhn ✳ **raise a laugh** PH: yáhnhéi siuséng ✳ **raise an army** VO: yéuhngbìng✳ **raise money** VO: ① gyún (chín) ② chàuh (chín) ③ gaap (chín) ✳ **raise a flag** VO: ① sìngkèih (hoist) ② gwakèih (hang) ✳ **raise a price** VO: héiga ✳ **raise one's head** VO: dàamgòu go tàuh

raised PH: (America coll.) sauhgwo gaauyuhk ge

raisin N: pòuhtàihjígōn (M: nāp)

rake N: ❶ pá (M: go) ❷ laahnjái (M: go) ❸ kìngchèh FV: ❶ pàh ❷ (ship) kìngchèh ✳ **rake up** FV: sáujaahp VO: chùhngtàih gauhsih ✳ **rake**

the lawn PH: pàhháh go
chóudéi

radish PH: chŭkdouh hóu-
chíh hóu faai gám SV: ❶
sìhmōu ge ❷ fongdohng ge

rally FV: ❶ sàujaahp ❷
jaahphahp (military) ~
gwàndéui ❸ chùhngjíng ❹
jàausiu N: ❶ fùifuhk ❷
kwàhnjuhng daaihwúi (M: go)
❸ jaahpwúi (M: go)

ram N: ❶ (male sheep)
yèuhnggŭng (M: jek) ❷ johng-
gĭkgēi (M: ga) FV: ❶ johng ❷
sāk ❸ gunsyù

ramble VO: saanbouh FV: ❶
tàahmwah ❷ maahnyìhn

rambling SV: ❶ sáanmaahn
ge ❷ jaahplyuhn ge PH:
hàahntàahm ge

ramification N: ❶ fànjì ❷
jìlàuh ❸ saijit ❹ fànjìfaat (M:
go)

ramp PH: (lion) yuhng
hauhgeuk kéihhéi sàn FV: ❶
máahngpok ❷ maahnyìhn ❸
máahngchùng N: ❶ húnghaak
❷ (sl.) hèipin

rampage N: ❶ boutiu ❷
lyuhnchùng PH: wàahngchùng
jihkjohng

rampageous SV: boulyuhn
ge PH: hóu nàahn yīkjai ge

rampart N: fòhngyuhmaht
(M: gihn) FV: ❶ fòhngyuhb ❷
bóuwuh PH: héi chèuhng heui
bóuwuh

ramshackle Adj.   PH:
jauhlàih dóulam gám SV: ❶
kingchèh ge ❷ (person) yahmsing ge

ranch N: ❶ (America) daaih-

nùhng chèuhng (M: go) ❷
(horses, cows) daaihmuhk
chèuhng (M: go) PH: hái
nùhngchèuhng jouh gùng ge
yàhn (M: go) VO: jyúchìh nùhng
chèuhng

rancid SV: ❶ fuhbaaih ge ❷
yáuh chaumeih ge

ranco(u)r N: ❶ sàmsàuh ❷
jīkyun (M: chi)

ramdom PH: ngáuhyìhn ge
hàhngduhng N: chèuihbín SV:
❶ chèuihbín ge ❷ chèuih yi ge
* at ramdom A: ❶ chèuihbín
gám ❷ yahmyi gám

range FV: ❶ pàaihliht ❷
fànleuih ❸ mìuhjéun N: ❶
faahnwàih (M: go) ❷ fūkdouh
(M: go) ❸ sàanmahk (M,: tìuh)
❹ fànboukèui (M: go) ❺
muhkchèuhng (M: go) ❻
báchèuhng; sehgīk chèuhng
(M: go) ❼ lòuhjou (M: go) ❽
(distance) kéuihlèih (M: go) *
a range of M: ① yātdaaihpin
② yātpàaih ③ yāthaihliht *
out of one's range PH:
nàhnglihk sóbātkahp ge * out
of (in, within) range N:
sehchìhng jìngoih (noih) Patt:
hái N ge faahnwàih ngoih (noih)
* range from ... to Patt: fànbou hái N faahnwàih noih

ranger PH: ❶ hàahnglàih
hàahngheui ge yàhn (M:go) N:
❶ (U.S.A.) yùhnlàhm hònsáu
yàhn (M: go) ❷ chèuhnlòh
déuiyùhn (M: go) ❸ yàuhgīk
déuiyùhn (M: go)

rank M: ❶ liht ❷ pàaih N: ❶
deuihngh (M: go) ❷ dángkáp
(M: go) ❸ sànfán (M: go) ❹
séhwúi gàaichàhng (M: go) ❺
(position, title) gàaikáp (M: go)
FV: ❶ pàaihliht ❷ fànleuih
VO: fàn dángkáp SV: ❶

fàahnsihng ge ❷ (coll.) gwahtkéuhng ge ✻ **break ranks** SV: lohknǵh VO: diuhdéui ✻ **close ranks** Adj. PH: gánmaht tyùhngit ✻ **in the front rank** PH: ① hái daihyātpàaih ② hái chìhnliht ✻ **rank with** Patt: tùhng N bihnglìht ✻ **the first (highest) rank** N: daihyātlàuh ✻ **the rank and file** N: ① póutùng sihbīng (M: go) ② póutùng sìhngyùhn (M: go)

ranking SV: ❶ gòukáp (waih) ge ❷ biuchèng ge ❸ chēutméng ge

rankle FV: ❶ yunhahn ❷ tungjúng VO: faatyìhm PH: lìhngyàhn sàmtung

ransack PH: dousyu sáusok FV: chéunggip

ramsom N: suhkgām; suhkfún (M: bāt) FV: ❶ suhk ❷ lahksok RV: suhkfàan

rant PH: ❶ kwàdaaih só góng ge syutwah ❷ hóu nàu gám giu (ngaai)❸ daaihsèng gám góng syutwah N: daaihgiusèng VO: góngdaaihwah FV: lyuhngiu

rap N: ❶ hàaumùhnsèng (M: háh) ❷ yìhmlaih pàipìhng ❸ síusíu ❹ tùhngchìhng ❺ wòhmuhk FV: ❶ hàau ❷ chéunggsuk ❸ màihjyuh ❹ yìhntóu PH: ❶ dahtyìhn góng ❷ jeunhàhng táansēut sìhnghán ge tàahmwah ✻ **rap out** Adj. PH: yìhmlaih gám góng

rapacious PH: chéunggip ge SV: tàamsàm ge

rapacity N: ❶ tàamlàahm ❷ tàamyuhk

rape N: ❶ pòuhtòuhjà ❷ gwoleuihhei (M: ga) ❸ (people) kèuhnggàan ❹ yàuhchoi FV: ❶

kèuhnggàan ❷ sáigip ✻ **rape cake** N: choijí (M; nāp) ✻ **rape oil** N: choiyàuh ✻ **rape-seed** N: yàuhchoijúng (M: nāp)

rapid SV: ❶ faai ge ❷ seun-chūk ge ❸ gāp ge ❹ (thinking) máhnjiht ge ✻ **rapid transit** N: gòuchūk gàautùng ✻ **rapid-fire, rapid firing** N: chūkseh

rapids N: ❶ gāplàuh ❷ tāan (M: go)

rapier N: hènggim; dyúngim (M: bá) SV: lìhngmáhn gèiji ge

rapine N: chéunggip

rapport N: ❶ (France) gwàanhaih (mahtchit) (M: go) ❷ yùhngháp ❸ lyùhnhaih (M: go)

rapprochement PH: ❶ (France) fùifuhk bònggàau ❷ ginlaahp yáuhhóu gwàanhaih ❸ gwokjaigàan ge wòhgáai

rapture N: ❶ kòhnghéi ❷ chyùhsàhn gunjyu

raptures Adj. PH: fùntìnhéideih

rare SV: ❶ (seldom met with) hèiyáuh ge; hèihón ge ❷ (wonderful) hèikèih ge ❸ jàngwai ge ✻ **in rare cases** MA: ngáauhyìhn ✻ **on rare occasions** SV: nàahndāk PH: m̀haih sìhsìh

rarely A: ❶ hèihón gám ❷ jàngwai gám ❸ hónyáuh gám ❹ hóngin gám SV: nàahndāk

rascal N: waaihdáan (M: go, jek) SV: ❶ bèipéi ge ❷ jihngaak ge

rash SV: ❶ (impetuous) lóuhmóhng ge ❷ singgáp ge ❷ (acting hastily) pàhnlàhn ❸ m̀síusàm ge N: (skin) chán (M: nāp)

rasher N: hàahmyuhk bohkpín (M: faai)

rasp N: cho (M: bá) FV/SV: jiuchou PH: ❶ yuhng cho làih cho yéh ❷ faatchēut chiyíhsèng lihng sàhngíng sauhdou chigīk

rasper N: chogeuih

raspberry N: sàanmúi (M: nāp)

rat N: lóuhsyú (M: jek) PH: ❶ tóuyim ge yàhn (M: go) ❷ buhnbin ge yàhn (M: go) ❸ bèipéi ge yàhn (M: go) VO: ❶ jūk lóuhsyú ❷ goumaht * **like a drowned rate** Adj. PH: sāpdou hóuchíh lohktòng gāi gám

rats PH: (sl.) lyuhngóng! ngóh m̀seun * **rat-face** PH: (U.S.A.) gàanhím ge yàhn (M: go) * **rat-trap** N: ① jūksyúgēi (M: go) ② kwangíng (M: go) * **rat poison** N: lóuhsyúyeuhk

ratable PH: ❶ hóyíh gúga ge ❷ yìnggòi jingseui ge ❸ ngon (jiu) béilaih ge

rate N: ❶ léut ❷ (proportion) béiléut; béilaih (M: go) ❸ (goods) gagaak (M: go) ❹ dángkāp (M: go) ❺ (charge or fees) gachihn (M: go) ❻ (degree) chihngdouh (M: go) ❼ (degree of speed) chūkdouh (M: go) ❽ (of exchange) hòhngchìhng (M: go) BF: (class, grade) làuh; dáng; daihyātlàuh; tàuhdáng VO: ❶ gúga ❷ dihngdángkāp FV: ❶ lihtwàih ❷ naauh * **a birth rate** N: chēutsàngléut (M: go) * **a death rate** N: séimòhngléut (M: go) * **at a great rate** PH: yuhng gòu chūkdouh * **at all rates** Patt: mòuhleuhn dím . . . dōu . . .

at that (this) rate Patt: mòuhleuhn dím . . . dōu . . . * ❶ jiu gám ge chihngyìhng làihtái (góng) ② yùhgwó haih gám * **at the rate of** Patt: ① ngon (jiu) . . . béilaih ② yíh . . . chūkdouh * **at the current rate of exchange** PH: síhmihnseuhng ge deuiwuhn ga * **postage rate** N: yàuhjí; yàuhfai (M: bāt) * **special rate** N: jittàuh (M: go)

rather A: ❶ nìhngyún; chìhngyún ❷ yáuhdī ❸ sèungdòng ❹ (a little) dōugéi ❺ chíhfùh * **had rather . . . (than)** Patt: nìhngyún . . . (yìhm̀) . . . * **. . . rather than** Patt: . . . kèihsaht haih; . . . m̀syundāk haih . . . * **would rather** A: ① chìhngyún ②, dōuhaih

ratification N: pàijéun (M: go)

ratify FV: ❶ pàijéun ❷ sihngyihng

rating N: ❶ kāpbiht (M: go) ❷ dihngngáak (M: go) ❸ seunyuhng chihngdouh (M: go) ❹ gúga (M: go) ❹ pìhng ga (M: go)

ratio N: ❶ béi ❷ béileuht (M: go) ❸ béilaih (M: go) PH: ❶ ngon béilaih fongdaaih ❷ yíh béileuht biusih * **the ratio of (three) to (five)** Patt: (sàam) tùhng (ńgh) jìbéi

ratiocinate FV: ❶ tèuileuhn ❷ tèuiléih

ration N: ❶ dihngngáak (M: go) ❷ dihngleuhng (M: go) ❸ puikāpleuhng (M: go) * **an iron (emergency) ration** N: ① nùhngsūk sihkmaht ② gwànyuhng gònlèuhng

rations N: (food) ❶ fósihk ❷
lèuhngsihk ✻ on short ra-
tions PH: puikápleuhng
m̀jūkgau ✻ put on rations
VO: sahthàhng puikáp
gùngyingjai

rational SV: ❶ yáuh léihsing ge ❷ hahpléih ge

rationalism N: wàihléih-
leuhn

rationalist N: léihsing-
leuhnjé; wàihléihleuhnjé (M:
go)

rationality N: ❶ hahpléih-
sing ❷ tèuiléihlihk

rationalize SV: hahpléihfa

ratsbane N: saatsyúyeuhk

rattan N: ❶ tàhng (M: tìuh)
❷ tàhngjèuhng (M: jì) ✻ rattan
chair N: tàhngyí (M: jèung) ✻
rattan mat N: tàhngjehk (M:
jèung) ✻ rattan ware N:
tàhnghei

rattle Adj. PH: dihkdihk-
daahpdaahp héung Adj. PH:
lihngdou yàhn gánjèung ✻
rattle-box PH: yáuh héung-
sèng ge wuhngeuih ✻ rattle-
brain, -head, -pate N:
wùhtòuhchùhng (M: go) ✻
rattle-snake N: héungméihsèh (M: tìuh) ✻ rattle-trap N:
laahnchè (M: ga) PH: polaahn
ge yéh (M: gihn)

rattler N: ❶ héungméihsèh
(M: tìuh) ❷ fowahn lihtchè (M:
ga) PH: yáuh sèng ge yéh

rattling PH: ❶ fùngchèui ge
sèng ❷ fèisèuhng faai ge ❸
hóu dougihk ge A: fèisèuhng

ravage N: ❶ powaaih ❷

fòngfai FV: ❶ powaaih ❷
wáiwaaih

rave PH: ❶ lyuhngóng syutwah ❷ daaihsèngggiu ❸ sìnmìhng ge jínláahm

ravel FV: ❶ gáaichèuih ❷
dáuchìhn RV: chaakhòi PH:
lihngdou yáuh dáuchìhn N:
dáugit ✻ ravel out FV: ①
léihching ② sìuchèuih

raven N: (crow) wùngà (M:
jek) SV: wùhāak ge FV: ❶
chéung ❷ bouhsihk PH:
sihkdāk fèisèuhng faai

ravenous PH: ❶ ngohdou-
gihk ge ❷ tàamsàm ge

ravine N: ❶ haahpgūk (M:
go) ❷ sàangaan (M: tìuh) ❸
sàmgūk (M: go) ❹ sàangūk (M:
go)

ravish FV: ❶ chéung ❷
kèuhnggàan PH: lihngdou
fùnhéidāk hóu gányiu

ravishing SV: yáhnyàhn
yahpsing ge

ravishment SV/N: sìu-
wàhn

raw SV: ❶ (uncooked) sàang
ge ❷ m̀sìhngsuhk ge ❸ móuh
gingyìhm ge PH: ❶ meih
gàgùng ge ❷ meih gìnggwo
fanlìhn ge N: chaatsèungchyu
(M: go) ✻ in the raw SV:
m̀yùhnsìhn ge ✻ raw-boned
Adj. PH: gwātsau yùhchàaih ge
✻ raw material N: yùhnlíu ✻
raw silk N: sàangsī (M: fūk) ✻
raw cotton N: mìhnfà

ray N: (of light) gwòngsin FV:
❶ fongseh ❷ símyìhn

rayon N: ❶ yàhnjouhsī ❷
yàhnjouh chìmwàih

raze, rase FV: ❶ cháan-pìhng ❷ yìhpìhng (mountain) ~ *go sàan* ❸ sìuchèuih ❹ wáimiht

razor N: ❶ taidōu (M: bá) ❷ sōupáau (M: go) * **as sharp as a razor** SV: laihhoih ge; sàileih ge * **on a razor's edge** PH: ❶ hái taidōu bīnyùhn ❷ hái ngàihhím gwàantàuh * **razor edge** N: dōuháu * **razor strop** N: mòhdōu pèihdáai (M: tìuh) * **razor-thin** Adj. PH: bohkdougihk ge * **razor-blade** N: dōupín (M: faai)

reach RV: ❶ daahtdou ❷ sànchèut ❸ wán(dāk) dóu FV: ❶ daihbéi ❷ (arrive at) dou ❸ (without much effort) ngàhm RVE: (extend to) dou PH: hóyíh dou ge faahnwàih N: làuhchìhng * **as far as the eye can reach** PH: sèung ngáahn hóyíh táidóu ge * **beyond (out of, above) one's reach** PH: nàhnglihk mjouh-dākdou ge * **lower (upper) reaches of a river** PH: hòh ge seuhng (hah) yàuh * **reach after (at, for)** PH: jeuhnlihk séung daahtdou

reach-me-down SV: (British) yihnsìhng ge; yihnsíng ge

reaches-me-down N: sìhngyì (M: gihn; tou)

react FV: ❶ fáanying ❷ fáankong ❸ joijouh ❹ chùhngyín * **react on (upon)** Patt: ① deui N yáuh fáanying ② deui N héijokyuhng * **react to** Patt: deui N yáuh fáanying * **react against oppression** FV: fáankong

reaction N: ❶ fáanying (M: go) ❷ fáan jokyuhng (M: go) ❸ fáanduhng

reactionary SV: ❶ fáan-duhng ge ❷ bóusáu ge N: (of a person) fáanduhng fahnjí (M: go)

reactor N: ❶ fáanyingjé (M: go) ❷ fáanduhngjé (M: go) ❸ (electricity) dihnkonghei (M: ga) ❹ fáanyingdèui

read FV: ❶ (aloud or study) duhk ❷ lóngduhk ❸ mahk-duhk ❹ jísih ❺ yìhnduhk ❻ gáaisīk ❼ (silently) tái RV: yihkchèut N: yuhtduhk * **read aloud** FV/N: lóngduhk * **read between the lines** PH: hái jih léuihbihn wán yihnngoih jìyi * **read out** FV: ① syùnduhk ② lóngduhk; duhk chēutsèng * **read PN's hand** VO: tái (sáu) jéung * **read up** FV: gùngduhk

readable SV: yihduhk ge PH: ❶ sédāk yáuhcheui ge ❷ jihkdāktái ge

readdress PH: ❶ joi jichìh ❷ joi gói singmìhng tùhng deihjí

reader N: ❶ (of a newspaper etc.) duhkjé (M: go) ❷ (lecturer) góngsī (M: go) ❸ (textbook) duhkbún (M: bún, bouh)

readily A: ❶ yùhngyih gám ❷ lohkyi gám ❸ máhnjihtgám; seunchūk gám ❹ sóngfaai gám

readiness SV: ❶ yùhngyih ❷ seunchūk * **in readiness** PH: jéunbeih hóu

reading N: ❶ yuhtduhk ❷ duhkmaht (M: bún) ❸ gáaisīk (M: go) ❹ táifaat (M: go) PH: yuhtduhk ge * **reading book** N: duhkbún (M: bún) * **reading-room** ① yuhtduhksāt (M: gàan) ② syùfóng (M: gàan)

readjust PH: ❶ joi jíngléih ❷ joi tiuhjíng

ready PH: ❶ yáuh jéunbeih ge ❷ yuhbeih hóu ge ❸ lohkyi ge ❹ yihnsīhng ge N: yihngām (M: bāt) * **be ready at** Patt: ① jìngyù . . . ge ② sihnyù . . . ge * **make (get) ready** RV: jéunbeih hóu * **ready at hand** PH: hái sáutàuh * **ready-for-service; ready-made** SV: ❶ yihnsíng ge ❷ jouhhóu ge * **ready estate** N: bātduhngcháan * **ready money; ready cash** N: yihngām; yihnchín; yihnfún; yihnngán * **ready-to-wear** SV: ① yihnsíng ge ② sihngyì (M: tou, gihn)

reaffirm FV: chùhngsàn PH: ❶ joi hángdihng ❷ joi jingsaht

reagent N: ❶ siyeuhk (M: jèun) ❷ fáanyinglihk(M: go) ❸ fáanyingmaht (M: gihn)

real SV: ❶ jàn ge ❷ jànjing ge ❸ yihnsaht ge ❹ sahtjai ge PH: bātduhngcháan ge * **real estate** N: sahtyihp * **real thing** N: jingfo * **real sunkist** N: jing gām sāan cháang (M: go)

really A: ❶ jànjing gám ❷ jìnsaht gám ❸ sahtjoih * **really and truly** A: jànjing gám

realism N: ❶ yihnsaht jyúyih (M: go) ❷ sésaht jyúyih (M: go) ❸ sahtjoihleuhn

realistic SV: ❶ yihnsaht jyúyih ge ❷ bīkjàn ge PH: chùhng sahtjai chēutfaat ge

reality N: ❶ (state of being real) jànsaht ❷ yihnsaht ❸ sahtjai ❹ (fact) sihsaht (M: go) ❺ yihnsahtsing * **bring PN back to reality** PH: lihngdou

PN mihndeui yihnsaht * **in reality** MA: sihsahtseuhng

realization N: ❶ sahtyihn ❷ yihngsīk ❸ líhngwuih (M: go) ❹ binmaaih

realize FV: ❶ líuhgáai ❷ sahtyihn ❸ táiwuih

realm N: ❶ wòhnggwok (M: go) ❷ líhngwih (M: go) ❸ faahnwàih (M: go)

realty N: bātduhngcháan

ream M: nīm; līm

reanimate PH: ❶ sáidou (lihngdou) fuhksòu ❷ sáidou (lihngdou) yáuh sàanghei SV/FV: ❶ gúmóuh ❷ gīkduhng

reap FV: ❶ (cut) got ❷ sàugot ❸ sàuwohk ❹ dākdóu * **reap what (as) one has sown** IE: ① jihsihk kèihgwó ❷ bātlòuh yìhwohk * **reaping hook** N: lìhmdōu (M: bá) * **reaping machine** N: sàugotgēi (M: ga) * **reap rice** VO: gotwòh

reaper N: ❶ sàugotyàhn (M: go) ❷ sàugotgēi (M: ga)

reappear PH: ❶ joi chēut- yihn ❷ joi faat

rear PW: hauhbihn BF: hauh — N: ❶ hauhfòng (M: go) ❷ hauhbouh ❸ buihauh SV: ❶ hauhfòng ge ❷ hauhbouh ge FV: ❶ syuhlaahp ❷ ginlaahp (a monument) ~ geinihmbèi ❸ jihyéuhng (poultry) ~ gàkàhm ❹ jòipúih (a person) ~ yātgo yàhn * **at (in) the rear of** Patt: hái N jihauh * **front and rear** PW: hái chìhn hauh * **in (the) rear** PW: ❶ hái buihauh ❷ hái hauhfòng * **rear ad-miral** N: hóigwàn siujeung (M: go) * **rear guard** N: hauhwaih

(M: go)

rearm PH: ❶ chùhngsàn (chùhngjíng) móuhjòng ❷ chùhngsàn bouji

rearmament N: ❶ chùhngsàn móuhjòng ❷ chùhngjíng gwànbeih

rearmost PH: ❶ jeui hauhbihn ge ❷ jeui hauh ge ❸ jeui méih ge

rearrange PH: ❶ chùhngsàn báaigwo (furniture) ~ *dī gàsì* ❷ chùhngsàn pàihlihtgwo (as index cards etc.) ~ *dīkāt*

rearward PH: ❶ hái hauhfòng ❷ jeui méih ge A: heung hauhbihn gám N: ❶ hauhfòng (M: go) ❷ buihauh

reason N: ❶ (cause) yùhnyàn (M: go) ❷ (ground) léihyàuh (M: go) ❸ (of person) léihji ❹ léihsing ❺ douhléih (M: go) FV: ❶ tèuileuhn ❷ bihnleuhn VO: góngdouhléih ＊ bring PN to reason Patt: lihngdou (sáidou) PN mìhngbaahk douhléih ＊ by reason of Patt: ① waihjó . . . ② yàuhyù . . . ＊ for reasons of Patt: yànwaih . . . ＊ for some reason Patt: yàuhyù máuhjúng yùhnyàn ＊ in reason SV: ① hahpléih ② yáuh douhléih ＊ reason out RV: tèuileuhnchèut

reasonable SV: ❶ góngléih ge ❷ (logical, sensible) hahpléih ge ❸ (fair and just) gùngdouh

reasonably A: hahpléih gám

reasoning N: ❶ tèuiléih (M: go) ❷ leuhnjing (M: go)

reasonless SV: ❶ ṁgóngléih ge ❷ ṁhahpléih ge

reassemble PH: ❶ joi jaahphahp ❷ chùhngsàn jòngpui

reassert PH: ❶ joi jyújèung ❷ joi góngmìhng

reassume PH: ❶ joi chóichéui ❷ joi chitséung ❸ joi gádihng ❹ joi jipsauh

reassure PH: ❶ joi bóujing ❷ joi bóuhím ❸ lihngdou ngònsàm

rebate FV: ❶ jit (kau) ❷ gáamsíu N: jitkau

rebel N: ❶ (as a person) buhntòuh (M: go) ❷ héiyihjé (M: go) ❸ fáankongjé (M: go) FV: ❶ fáanbuhn ❷ jouhfáan

rebellion N: ❶ buhnlyuhn (M: chi) ❷ jouhfáan (M: chi) ❸ deuikong ❹ fáankong

rebind PH: ❶ joi bóng ❷ chùhngsàn dèngjòng

rebirth PH: joi sàang N: ❶ fuhkwuht (M: chi) ❷ gàngsàng ❸ fuhkhìng

reborn PH: ❶ joi sàang ge ❷ fuhkhìng ge ❸ chùhngsàng ge

rebound Adj. PH: daahnfáan jyuntàuh N: ❶ bouying (M: go) ❷ fuhkhìng

rebuff N/FV: ❶ (of plans, hope etc) chojit (M: go) ❷ làahnjó ❸ kèuijuhk PH: (for request etc.) yùhnchyùhn gám kéuih jyuht

rebuild, rebuilt FV: ❶ chùhnggin ❷ góijouh PH: ❶ chùhngsàn héigwo ❷ joi héigwo

rebuke FV/N: ❶ jaakbeih (M: chi) ❷ jíjaak (M: go) ❸ chìhnggaai (M: chi)

recalcitrant SV: ❶ fáankong ge ❷ m̀fuhkchùhng ge N: fáankongjé (M: go) PH: m̀fuhkchùhng ge yàhn (M: go)

recall RV: ❶ séung (dāk) héi ❷ geihéi FV: ❶ jiuhwùih (an ambassador) ~ daaihsíh ❷ diuh N: ❶ chitsìu ❷ fùifuhk ❸ wùihyīk (M: go) * **beyond (past) recall** RV: geim̀héi PH: m̀hóyíh wáahnwùih * **to one's mind** RV: séunghéi

recant FV: ❶ fonghei (religion, opinion) ~ seunyéuhng ❷ chitsìu PH: gùnghòi yihngcho

recantation N: chéuisìu (M: chi)

recapitulate PH: ❶ ngāakyiu joigóng ❷ jaahkyiu góngmìhng

recapture PH: ❶ joi dākdóu ❷ lófàan ge yéh RV: ❶ geihéi ❷ sàufàan; lófàan FV: jìngfuhk (of a country) ~ yātgo gwokgā

recast PH: ❶ joi jyujouh ❷ joi gaisyun FV: góijìng; góisé (articles, paper, words etc.) ~ màhnjèung VO: (play, movie) gàngwuhn goksīk

recede FV: ❶ hauhteui ❷ teuichēut (certain field) ~ nīgo hyùnjí ❸ chitwùih (army) ~ gwàndéui ❹ dit ❺ gwàiwàahn (land) ~ líhngtóu PH: (of problem, people) sātjó juhngyiusing

receipt N: ❶ (a written statement) sàutiuh; sàugeui (M: jèung) ❷ (money received) sàuyahp RV: (act of receiving) sàudóu; jipdóu VO: ❶ béi sàutiuh ❷ sé sàugeui * **be in receipt of** RV: sàudóu * **on receipt of** Patt: dòng sàudóu N gójahnsí (ge sìhhauh)

receive RV: (accept something offered) sàudóu; jipdóu FV: ❶ yùhngnaahp ❷ jipsàu (electric waves) ~ dihnbō ❺ jipgin (receive a person) ~ yàhn ❸ fúndoih (welcome and entertain guest) ~ yàhnhaak ❺ sauh (suffering) ~ tungfú * **received from (of)** PH: yìhgā sàudóu N * **be received into** PH: beih (béi) jipsauh gàyahp * **receive baptism** VO: líhngsái; sauhsái * **received command from a superior officer** VO: fuhngmihng * **received a prize** VO: líhngjéung * **received in full** FV: sàuchìngsaai

received PH: ❶ gùngyihng ge ❷ beih póupin jipsauh ge SV: pìhngfàahn ge

receiver N: ❶ (of a letter) sàuseunyàhn (M: go) ❷ (of a telephone) tèng túng; yíhtúng (M: go) ❸ sàusauh jé (M: go) ❹ (receive stolen goods) jipjòngjé (M: go) ❺ sàufúnyàhn (M: go)

receiving N: ❶ líhngsauh ❷ jipsàu ❸ sàuchéui PH: ❶ líhngsauh ge ❷ sàuchéui ge ❸ sàubou ge * **receiving aerial** VO: jipsàu tìnsin * **receiving set** N: jipsàugēi; sàubougēi (M: ga) * **receiving station** N: (wireless) jipsàujaahm (M: go)

recent PH: ❶ jeuigahn ge; sàngahn ge ❷ gahndoih ge * **in recent times** PH: hái gahndoih * **in recent years** PH: jeuigahn (nī) géinìhn * **until recently** PH: jihkji (dou) jeuigahn

recently A: gahnlói; gahnlòih; sàngahn * **very recently** A: jeui gahn; nīpáai

receptacle N: ❶ yùhnghei (M: go) ❷ fātók (M: go) ❸ (spittoon) tàahmtúng (M: go)

reception N: ❶ jipgin ❷ jipdoih ❸ jipsàu ❹ jiudoihwúi (M: go) ❺ fùnyìhngwúi (M: go) ❻ chàhwúi (M: go) ✻ **reception-room** N: jipdoihsāt; wuihhaaksāt (M: gàan; go) ✻ **afternoon tea reception** N: chàhwúi (M: go)

recess N: ❶ yàusīk ❷ yàuwúikèih (M: go) ❸ yàuyihpkèih (M: go) FV: ❶ yánchòhng ❷ yàusīk VO: yàuga ✻ **in recess** PH: ① yàusīk ge sìhgaan ② yàuwúi gójahnsí ✻ **take a ten-minute recess** PH/VO: yàusīk sahpfànjūng

recession N: ❶ yáhnteui ❷ yáhnbaichyu (M: go) ❸ bouhdit ❹ bātgínghei; sìutìuh

recessive SV: ❶ teuihauh ge ❷ (language) yihkhàhng ge ❸ (biology) yánsing ge

rechannel PH: lihngdou (sáidou) góidouh

recharge PH: ❶ joi chùngdihn ❷ joi mìhnglihng ❸ joi wáiyahm ❻ joi jòngjoi

recheck PH: joi gímchàh

recipe N: ❶ (medicine) yeuhkfōng; chyúfōng (M: tìuh, jèung) ❷ sihkpóu (M: bún) ❸ jaifaat (M: go) ❹ pàangyahmfaat (M: go)

recipient SV: ❶ yùhngnaahp ge ❷ jipsauh ge N: ❶ jipsauhjé (M: go) ❷ sauhwaihjé (M: go) ❸ yùhnghei (M: go) ✻ **recipient of goods** N: sàufoyàhn (M: go)

reciprocal PH: ❶ wuhsèung ge ❷ wuhwaih ge PH: béichí sèungfáan ge N: ❷ (mathematics) fáansēung; dóusou ❸ (language) sèungwuh doihchìh (M: go)

reciprocate FV: ❶ wuhwuhn ❷ gàauwuhn ❸ chàuhdaap ❹ wùihbou; boudaap

recital N: ❶ lóhngjuhng (M: pìn) ❷ duhkjauwúi (M: go) ❸ duhkcheungwúi (M: go) ✻ **a piano recital** N: gongkàhm duhkjauwúi (M: go)

recite FV: ❶ (from memory) buih; nihm ❷ lóhngjuhng ✻ **recite incantation** VO: nihmjau ✻ **recite lessons** VO: nihmsyù; buihsyù ✻ **recite litanies** VO: nihmging

reckless SV: ❶ (without care) m̀siúsàm ge ❷ lóuhmóhng ge ❸ m̀guhauhgwó ge

reckon FV: ❶ sóu ❷ gaisyun (expenses) ~ faiyuhng ❸ syunjeung ❹ yihngwàih ❺ gúgai ❻ yílaaih ✻ **reckon for** FV: ① yihngwàih ② gukahp· ③ táileuhng ✻ **reckon on** FV: ① yílaaih ② jímohng ✻ **reckon with** Patt: tùhng PN syunjeung RV: háauleuihdou

reckoner N: ❶ gaisyunjé (M: go) ❷ gaisyunhei (M: go) ❸ gaisyun sáuchaak (M: bún)

reclaim FV: ❶ hòihán (land) ~ tóudeih ❷ dáujing; gíujing (mistake) ~ chongh ❸ gámfa (people) ~ yàhn RV: lófàan (houses; money) ~ gàan ngūk; ~ dī chín

reclaimable PH: ❶ hóyíh sàufàan ge (lófàan) ge ❷ hóyíh góijing ge ❸ hóyíh hòihán ge

recline FV: ❶ kaau ❷ fan hái ❸ seunlaaih

recluse SV: yángèui ge N: yánsih (M: go)

recognition N: ❶ yihngsīk ❷ séungsīk ❸ jiufù (M: go; chi)

* **beyond recognition** PH: ❶ yihngṁchēut ❷ mihnmuhk chyùhnfèi

recognizance N: ❶ sìhng-yihng ❷ (law) bóujingsyù; geuigit ❸ (law) bóusīkgām (M: bāt)

recognize PH: ❶ (by looking) yihngdākchēut ❷ (by listening) tēngdāk chēut FV: ❶ yihngsīk ❷ sìhng yihng (degree, a new state) ~ *hohkwái;* ~ *sàn jìngfú* ❸ gùngyihng ❹ chaatgok; jyuyi (danger) ~ *ngàihhím*

recoil N: ❶ teuisūk ❷ fáan-jokyuhng FV: ❶ teui ❷ waisūk

recollect RV: séunghéi FV: janjok PH: ❶ joi sàujaahp ❷ joi jaahphahp ❸ lihngdou jan-dihng ✻ **as far as I can recollect** PH: jauh ngóh só geidāk ge

recollection N: geiyīklihk ✻ **beyond (past) recollection** RV: séungṁhéi ✻ **in one's recollection** FV: geidāk

recommend FV: ❶ (for employment) tèuijin; gaaisiuh (a person) ~ *yātgo yàhn* ❷ gaaisiuh (a book) ~ *yātbún syù* ❸ hyungou ❹ gàautok; tokfuh

recommendation N: ❶ tèuijin ❷ hyungou ❸ (of job and person) gaaisiuhseun (M: fūng) ❹ (of job) tèuijinsyù (M: fahn)

recompense N/FV: ❶ (to reward for service) chàuhbou; bouchàuh (M: go) ❷ (to repay a favor) boudaap; daapjeh ❸ pùihsèuhng; bóusèuhng N: chàuhgām (M: bāt)

reconcile FV: ❶ (other parties who disagree) tiuhtìhng ❷ (become friendly again) wòhgáai;

fuhkgāau PH: ❶ lihngdou hóu-fâan ❷ lihngdou yātji ❸ lihngdou yàhn seuhnchùhng

recondition FV: ❶ sàujíng; sàuléih ❷ góigaak ❸ gíujing (a matter) ~ *yātgihn chojó ge sih*

reconnaissance N: ❶ (military) jìngchaat ❷ sáusok (sáusaak) ❸ (of situation) ham-chàh ✻ **reconnaissance plane** N: jìngchaatgèi (M: ga)

reconnoiter, -tre FV: ❶ jìngchaat (the situation of the enemy) ~ *dihkchìhng* ❷ ham-chaat; jìngchaat

reconsider PH: ❶ chùhng-sàn háauleuih; joi háau-leuihháh ❷ (of meeting) chùhngsàn tóuleuhn

reconstruct FV: chùhng-gin; héigwo (a building etc) ~ *gāan ngūk* PH: chùhngsàn jíng-gwo; góijouhgwo

reconstruction N: chùhngginmaht; góiginmaht (M: joh)

record N: ❶ géiluhk (M: chi) ❷ (history) geijoi (M: go) ❸ luhkyām (M: dyuhn) ❹ dóng-ngon (M: go) ❺ léihlihk ❻ (phonograph disk) cheungpín; cheungdíp (M: jèung) ❼ (financial) soumuhk (M: go) PH: ❶ luhkjó yàm ge chihdáai ❷ beih luhkyām ❸ jeunhàhng luhk-yām FV: ❶ géiluhk; geiluhk ❷ dànggei ❸ (of temperature) jísih; hínsih ~ 40°C ❹ (on disks) gun ❺ (on tape) luhkyàm ✻ **a matter of record** PH: yáuh ngondái hóyíh chàh ge sih ✻ **beat (break, cut) the record** VO: dápo géiluhk ✻ **hold the world's record** VO: bóuchìh saigaai géiluhk ✻ **on record** PH: ① làuh yáuh

recorder N: ❶ géiluhkyùhn; syùgei (M: go) ❷ géiluhkhei (M: ga) ❸ dihnbougēi (M: ga) ❹ luhkyāmgēi (M: ga)

recording N: ❶ géiluhk (M: go) ❷ luhkyāmdáai (M: gyún, béng) ❸ cheungpín; cheungdíp (M: jèung)

recount FV: ❶ miuhseuht (a matter) ~ *yātgihn sih* ❷ lihtgéui

recount FV: ❶ joisóu (votes) ~ *syúnpiu* ❷ chùhngsàn gaisyun (gwo) N: chùhnggai (M: chi)

recoup FV: ❶ kauchèuih ❷ pùihsèuhng (loss) ~ syúnsāt PH: chyùhngsàn dākdóu ❷ bóusèuhng (nèihbóu) syúnsāt

recourse N: ❶ yílaaih ❷ kàuhjoh ✻ have recourse to FV/N: yíkaau

recover FV: ❶ fùifuhk ❷ fuhkyùhn ❸ wáahnwùih ❹ nèihbóu ❺ (as a captured city) sàufuhk RV: ❶ (from sickness) hóufàan ❷ (get back) wánfàan

recovery N: ❶ fùifuhk ❷ fuhkyùhn ✻ wish PN a quick recovery PH: hèimohng PN jóudī hóufàan

recreant A/N: ❶ nohyeuhk ❷ buhntòuh (M: go) ❸ maaihgwokchaahk (M: go)

recreat(e) FV: ❶ yàuyéuhng ❷ sìuhín; yùhlohk ✻ recre

at(e) oneself with PH: yíh N yùhlohk (jihyùh)

recreation N: ❶ (past-time) sìuhín ❷ (amusement) yùhlohk ❸ yàuyéuhng ❹ (sport) wahnduhng ❺ góijouh PH: joi chongjouh ✻ for recreation PH: waihjó sìuhín ✻ recreation ground N: ① yùhlohkchèuhng (M: go) ② (for games) wahnduhngchèuhng (M: go) ✻ recreation room N: yùhlohksāt (M: gàan)

recreational PH: ❶ yùhlohk ge ❷ sìuhín ge ✻ recreational activities N: màhnyùh wuhtduhng

recriminate FV: ❶ (law) fáanhunggou ❷ fáanjaakbeih PH: wuhsèung hunggou

recruit FV: ❶ bóuchùng ❷ jìngmouh; jìumouh ❸ (lihngdou) fuhkyùhn N: ❶ (military) sànbīng (M: go) ❷ sànwúiyùhn (M: go) ❸ sànohksàang (M: go) ❹ bóukāpbán (M: pài) ✻ recruit soldiers VO: jìngmouh sànbìng; jìubing

recruitment N: ❶ jìumouh sànbìng ❷ bóuchùng VO: fùifuhk gìhnhòng

rectangle N: ❶ (mathematics) géuiyìhng ❷ chèuhngfòngyìhng

rectification N: ❶ (political party) jìngdeuhn ❷ (political party) jìngfùng ❸ gáujìng; góijìng; gíujìng ❹ (chemistry) jìnglauh

rectifier N: ❶ gáujìngjé; góijìngjé (M: go) ❷ gíujìnghei (M: ga) ❸ (electricity) jìnglàuhhei (M: ga) ❹ (chemistry) jìnglauhhei (M: ga)

record breaker N: ❶ chongsàn géiluhkjé (M: go) ❷ dápo géiluhkjé (M: go) ✻ off the record PH: ① m̀hóyíh geiluhk waahkjé yáhnyuhng ge ② m̀hóyíh gùnghòi ge ③ fèi jìngsīk ge tàahmwah

rectify FV: ❶ (put right) gíujing ❷ (put straight) jíngjing ❸ (chemistry) jínglauh ❹ (wireless) gímbō RV: (adjust) jínghóu

rectilineal; rectilinear SV: jihksin ge

rectitis N: (medical) jihkchéungyìhm

rectitude N: ❶ jingjihk ❷ sìhngsaht PH: jingjihk ge hàhngwàih waahkjé bánnahng

rector N: ❶ gaaukèuijéung (M: go) ❷ sàudouhyún yúnjéung (M: go) ❸ (university) haauhjéung (M: go) ❹ fuhjaakyàhn (M: go)

recumbent PH: ❶ yàusīkgán ge ❷ wàahngfan ge jītaai

recuperate FV: ❶ fùifuhk (health) ~ *gihnhòng* ❷ yàuyéuhng VO: nèihbóu syúnsāt

recurrence N: ❶ chùhngfūk; fáanfūk ❷ chèuhnwàahn

recusant PH: ❶ m̀fuhkchùhng kyùhnwāi ge ❷ m̀fuhkchùhng gwokgaau ge

recycle PH: (lihngdou) joi chèuhnwàahn

red SV: hùhng ge PH: ❶ làuhkyut ge ❷ gaakmihng ge N: ❶ hùhngsīk ❷ (financial) chekjih (M: go) FV: (financial) kwàihūng * **in the red** FV/N: kwaisyún (M: go) PH: chēutyihn chekjih * **see red** VO: faatnàu * **turn red in the gills** VO: faatnàu * **red alert** N: (bombard) gánggāp gíngbou (M: go) * **red handed** SV: chàahnyán ge * **red-hot** SV: ① kèuhngliht ge ② jeuisàn ge * **redwood** N: séuichaam; hùhngsyuh (M: pò) * **red-dish** SV:

hùhngsīk ge PH: sáauwàih hùhngge * **red cross (society)** N: hùhngsahpjih wúi (M: go) * **red corpuscle** N: hùhnghyutkàuh

redact FV: ❶ pìnsé ❷ yíhdihng ❸ pìnchāp ❹ chóuyíh (government ordinance) ~ *jingfú kwàilaih*

redaction N: ❶ pìnchāp ❷ gaaudihng ❸ sàudihng (bún)

redactor N: pìnchāpjé (M: go)

redden VO: binhùhng PH: lihngdou hùhngjó

redeem FV: ❶ suhk ❷ wáahnwùih ❸ léihhàhng (an obligation) ~ *yihmouh* ❹ nèihbóu chínggau (the people) ~ *saiyàhn* RV: ❶ suhkfàan (a mortage) ~ *dáingaatbán* ❷ suhkchēut (a slave) ~ *yātgo nòuhdaih*

redeemer N: ❶ suhkwùihjé (M: go) ❷ chínggaujé (M: go) ❸ suhkjeuihjé (M: go) * **the redeemer** N: gausaijyú (Yèhsōugèidūk)

redemption N: ❶ suhkfàan ❷ suhksàn ❸ suhkjeuih ❹ sèuhngwàahn ❺ bóugau * **beyond redemption** PH: mòuhhó gauyeuhk

redeploy FV: ❶ diuhhín (military) ~ *gwàndéui* ❷ diuhpui (manpower etc) ~ *yàhnlihk* PH: chùhngsàn bouhchyùh

rediffusion N: ❶ jyúnbo ❷ bosung * **rediffusion on the wire** N: yáuhsin gwóngbo

redirect VO: ❶ góidouh ❷ gànggói singmìhng deihjí

redivide PH: ❶ chùhngsàn fànpui ❷ joi waahkfàn

redo (-did, -done) FV: ❶ joi jouh ❷ chùhng jouh ❸ chùhng yín PH: chùhngsàn jòngsīk

redolent SV: ❶ hèung ge ❷ yáuh heimeih ge PH: lihngyàhn séunghéi N ge

redouble FV: ❶ gàpúih ❷ jàngtìm ❸ gàkèuhng ❹ chùhngfūk

redoubtable PH: lihngyàhn waigeuih ge (debater) ~ bihnleuhnjé SV: ❶ yúhnggám ge ❷ gihtchēut ge

redound FV: ❶ jànggà ❷ tàihgòu PH: yáuh johyù

redress N: ❶ gáujing; sàujing; góijing ❷ pùihsèuhng ❸ tiuhjíng ~ gáujing; sàujing; góijing ~ baidyùn ❷ pùihsèuhng (damages) ~ syúnsāt ❸ tiuhjíng (salary) ~ sànchàuh * seek redress VO: yìukàuh pùihsèuhng

redress PH: ❶ joi jeukfāan ❷ joi jínggéih ❸ joi chyúléih

reduce FV: ❶ gáamsíu; sūkgáam (expenses) ~ faiyuhng ❷ gáamdāi (speed) ~ chūkdouh ❸ gwàinaahp ❹ gáamchūk ❺ (mathematics) gáamfa; yeuk ❻ (chemistry) wàahnyùhn PH: ❶ lihng PN sihngwàih PN (beggar) ~ hātyì ❷ lihng N binsìhng N * reduce to PH: ① lihngdou sihngwàih ② gáamfawàih RV: gáamdou * reduce to practice FV/N: sahtsi * reduce the price VO: gáamga; gáamdài gachìhn * reduce the penalty VO: gáamhèng go jeuih * reduce the fine VO:

gáamhèng fahtfún * reduce the swelling VO: siujúng

redundance, -cy SV: ❶ (population) gwodō; ❷ leuihjeuih ❸ dòyùh PH: dòyùh ge yéh

reduplicate FV: ❶ gàpúih ❷ chùhngfūk ❸ (language) chùhngdihp A: ❶ gàpúih ❷ chùhngfūk

reed N: ❶ séuichòu (M: pò) ❷ lòuhwáih (M: pò) ❸ (musical instrument) wòhng ngohkhei (M: gihn) ❹ jin (M: jì) * a broken reed PH: m̀hóyíh seunlaaih ge yàhn waahkjé yéh

reedy SV; ❶ dò lòuhwáih ge ❷ saichèuhng ge

reeducate PH: joi gaauyuhk

reef N: ❶ chìuhsehk (M: gauh; dèui) ❷ ngamchìuh ❸ kongmahk ❹ dihpfàahn bouhfahn VO: sàufàahn

reek N: ❶ yīn ❷ séuijìnghei ❸ ngokchau; chaumeih (M: jahm) ❹ sāphei VO: ❶ faatchēut yīnmouh ❷ faatchēut chauhei ❸ faatchēut jìnghei

reel N: ❶ fóngchè (M: ga) ❷ (babbin of thread) sinlūk (M: go) ❸ (a spool on which a film is wound) gyúntúng ❹ (movie) gyúnpùhn (M: go) FV: ❶ gyún ❷ fóng ❸ syùhnjyún Adv. PH: m̀tìhng gám góng yéh * off the reel Adv. PH: ① m̀tìhng gám góng yéh ② lihnjuhk bāt-dyuhn * reel in RV: gyúnséuhng * reel out RV: fongchēut * reel off RV: chàuchēut * reel up RV: gyúnséuhng

reelect FV: chùhngsyún; joisyún

reenforce, reinforce
FV/N: ❶ jàngwùhn ❷ jàng-kèuhng

reenter PH: ❶ joiyahp ❷ joi gàyahp ❸ joi geiyahp; joi dànggei

reestablish FV: ❶ chùhng-gin ❷ fùifuhk

reeve VO: chyùngwo tiuh síng RV: bóngjyuh N: deihfōng-gùn (M: go)

reexamination N: ❶ joi siyihm ❷ joi diuhchàh (tiuhchàh) ❸ joi sámmahn

reexamine PH: ❶ joi siyihm ❷ joi diuhchàh (tiuhchàh) ❸ joi sámmahn (the witness) ~ *jingyàhn*

reexport PH: ❶ joi syúchēut ❷ joi syúchēut ge fomaht (M: pài)

refection N: ❶ síusihk ❷ dímsàm (M: dihp) ❸ chàhdím

refectory N: ❶ (in church, university etc.) sihktòhng; faahntòhng ❷ yàusīksāt (M: gàan)

refer FV: ❶ wáitok ❷ ngam-sih ❸ (go for information) chàh ❹ chàamjiu; chàamháau ~ *jihdín* ❺ sipkahp ❻ tàihgàau ❼ (to a person for information or decision) mahn ~ *haauhjéung* ❽ (recommend) gaaisiuh ❾ (relate, point) góng ~ *bīngo a?* ∗ **refer to** FV: ❶ sipkahp ❷ chàamháau CV: gwàanyù ∗ **refer to somebody as** Patt: ① chīng PN jouh ② giu PN jouh

referee N: ❶ (umpire) chòih-punyùhn (M: go) ❷ juhngchòih-jé (M: go) ❸ (sports) kàuhjing (M: go) FV: chòihpun

reference N: ❶ tàihkahp ❷ chàamháau ❸ yàhnjing ❹ jyu ❺ jingmìhng ❻ jīkkyùhn faahnwàih (M: go) ❼ jing-mìhngyàhn; bóujingyàhn (M: go) ❽ bóujingsyù; gaaisiuhsyù ∗ **in (with) reference to** CV: gwàanyù ∗ **without reference to** FV: ① mìléih ② bātgún MA: mòuhleuhn ∗ **reference book** N: chàamháausyù (M: bún)

referendum N: ❶ yàhn-màhn tàuhpiu ❷ fúkkyutkyùhn (M: go) ❸ chíngsihsyù (M: fùng)

refill PH: ❶ joi jòngmúhn ❷ joi tìhn

refine FV: ❶ tàihlihn; lihn (gold, oil, etc) ~ *gām* ~ *yàuh* ❷ deukmòh ❸ jingjai PH: ❶ lihngdou màhnngáh (speech) ❷ lihngdou jingméih

refined SV: ❶ jinglihn ge ❷ màhnngáh ge ❸ jingmaht ge ❹ (as in manner) sìmàhn; màhn-ngáh ∗ **refined sugar** N: baahktòhng (M: hahp; bàau; gàng) ∗ **refined tastes** Adj. PH: gòuseuhng ge bánmeih ∗ **refined measurements** Adj. PH: jingkok ge chāak lèuhng

refinement N: ❶ jinglihn ❷ tàihlihn ❸ sèuhnjihng ❹ (manner) yàungáh

refiner PH: jingjai ge yàhn (M: go) N: jingjaigēi (M: ga)

refinery N: jingjaichòhng; jinglihnchòhng (M: gàan) ∗ **an oil refinery** N: lihnyàuhchòhng (M: gàan)

refit FV: ❶ sàuléih (ship) ~ *jek syùhn* ❷ góijòng (ship) ~ *jek syùhn* PH: chùhngsàn jòngpui

reflect FV: ❶ fáanseh (light) ~ *dī gwōng* ❷ fáanyíng

(behavior) ~ *bánhahng;* ~
hàhngwàih ❸ jìuji ❹ fáansíng
❺ siháau PH: jísai séunghǎh ✳
reflect on FV: háauleuih RV:
séungfàan

reflection; reflexion N:
❶ fáanseh; fáanseh jokyuhng
❷ (reflected image) fáanyíng (M:
chi) ❸ yíngjeuhng (M: go) ❹
(serious consideration) gám-
séung (M: go) ❺ yigin (M: go) ❻
(of light) fáangwòng ✳ **cast a
reflection on (upon)** FV: ① jíjaak ② jaakgwaai; gwaai

reflector N: ❶ fáansehhei
(M: ga, go) ❷ fáansehgeng (M:
go, faai) ❸ bíudaaht yiginjé (M:
go) ✳ **reflector lamp** N:
fáangwōngdāng (M: jáan)

reflex SV: ❶ fáanseh ge ❷
fáanyíng ge ❸ fáabsíng ge N:
❶ (light) fáanseh ❷ fáanyíng ❸
yíngjeuhng (M: go) ❹ dóuyíng
(M: go) ❺ fūkjaibán (M: gihn)
FV: fáanseh

reflexive SV: ❶ fáanseh ge
❷ (language) fáansàn ge ✳
reflexive pronoun N: fáansàn
doihmìhngchìh ✳ **reflexive
verb** N: fáansàn duhng chìh
(M: go)

reflux N: ❶ wùihlàuh ❷
yihklàuh ❸ teuichìuh

reform FV: ❶ góigaak
(political condition) ~ *séhwúi;*
~ *jingjih* ❷ góilèuhng (a situation) ~ *chìhngyihng* ❸ góijouh
(a person) ~ *yātgo yàhn* ❹
gaaksàn (a policy) ~ *yātgo
jaidouh* ✳ **reform school** N:
(siunìhn) gaauyéuhngyún (M:
gàan)

reformation N: ❶ góijouh
❷ góigaak ❸ góilèuhng PH:
chùhngsàn jouhsìhng

reformatory N: gámfayún;

gaauyéuhngyún (M: gàan) SV:
❶ gámfa ge ❷ góijouh ge

reformism N: góilèuhng
jyúyih (M: go)

reformist N: góigaakgā; góigaakjé; gaaksànjé; góilèuhng
jyúyihjé (M: go)

refract FV: ❶ jitseh ❷
(chemistry) fànsīk

refraction N: (physics)
jitseh; jitseh jokyuhng

refractory SV: ❶ (of a person) gwahtkéuhng ge ❷ (of a
person) gujàp ge ❸ nàahnyì ge
❹ nàahnyùhngfa ge

refrain FV: ❶ (keep oneself
from doing something) gaai (liquor; cigarette) ~ *jáu;* ~ *yīn*
❷ yánjyuh (laugh) ~ *siu* ❸ yīkjai
(anger) ~ *fáhnnouh* N: (poetry)
dihpgeui ✳ **refrain from
(laughing/smoking)** PH: yánjyuh m̀ (siu/sihkyīn)

refresh PH: ❶ lihngdou
chīngsàn ❷ lihngdou fùifuhk
pèihlòuh FV: ❶ tàihsàhn ❷
janjok ❸ gàngsàn ❹ bóuchùng
VO: ❶ sihk dímsàm ❷ yám yéh

refresher N: ❶ jáu (M: jèun,
jì, bùi) ❷ yámbán (M: bùi) ❸
fūkjaahp ❹ (scientific technician) jeunsàu duhngtaai FV:
jeunsàu ✳ **refresher course**
N: wànjaahp fochìhng; jeunsàu
fochìhng

refreshment SV: sóngfaai
✳ **refreshment room** N: (in
railway station) yámsihkdìm;
chāansàt síusihkbouh (M: gàan)

refreshments N: ❶ chàhdím (M: dihp) ❷ yámbán (M:
bùi) ✳ **take some refreshments** VO: sihk (yám) dī yéh

refrigeration N: láahng-chòhngfaat VO: (medical) siuyiht; gáaiyiht SV/ATT: bìngdung; láahngdung

refrigerator N: ❶ syut-gwaih (M: go) ❷ bīngsēung (M: go) ❸ láahngdunggēi (M: ga) ❹ láahngchòhng fu (M: gàan)

refuge VO: beihnaahn N: ❶ beiwuhjaahm (M: go) ❷ beihnaahnsó (M: gàan) * **take refuge in** Patt: hái PW beihnaahn PH: tòuh(naahn) dou

refugee N: ❶ naahnmàhn (M: go; pài, bàan) ❷ tòuh-mòhngjé (M: go) * **refugee camp** N: ❶ naahnmàhnyìhng (M: go) ❷ naahnmàhn sàu-yùhngsó (M: gàan)

refund RV: ❶ teuifàan ❷ gwàiwàahn; sèuhngwàahn VO: (of goods) teuichín

refurnish PH: ❶ joi gùng-kāp ❷ chùhngsàn jòngsāu

refusal N: ❶ kéuihjyuht (M: chi) ❷ jehjyuht (M: chi) ❸ (yàusìn) chéuisékyùhn (M: go) * **to take no refusal** FV: gínchìh

refuse FV: ❶ kéuihjyuht (a proposal) ~ *yiukàuh* ❷ tèuichìh; jehjyuht (an invitation) ~ *chàamgà máahnwúi* ❸ m̀háng; m̀jai (for doing something) N: ❶ laahpsaahp (M: túng; dèui; bàau) ❷ faimaht

refute FV: ❶ fáanbok; bok ❷ bohchīk

regain RV: ❶ dākfàan ❷ fàandou FV: ❶ fùifuhk ❷ sàufuhk (lossland) ~ *sātdeih*

regal PH: ❶ gwokwòhng ge ❷ wòhngsāt ge ❸ jòngyìhm ge

regale FV: fúndoih PH: ❶ yihtchìhng jiudoih ❷ lihngdou yàhn dākdóu héungsauh ❸ lihngdou yàhn hòi sàm N: sihngyin (M: chāan)

regalia N: ❶ wòhngkyùhn; dahkkyùhn (M: júng) ❷ fāi-jēung (M: go) PH: leng ge sāam (M: gihn)

regalias N: wòhngwai bìuji (wòhnggùn; wòhngjeuhng dáng dáng)

regard FV: ❶ (considered as) dong (jok); yihngwàih ❷ (respect or obey) jyùnjuhng; jyùnging ❸ jyuyi; gwàansàm (other's feeling) ~ *daihyih dī yàhn ge gámgok* ❹ háauleuih N: ❶ háauleuih ❷ gwàansàm ❸ jyùnjuhng * **have a regard for** FV: ① jyùnging ② juhngsih * **in (with) regard to (of)** CV: gwàanyù; deuiyù * **in this regard** PH: hái nīyātdím seuhng * **regard N as** PH: ① yihngwàih haih ② dong(jok) haih * **be well regarded** Adj. PH. mìhngmohng hóu hóu

regards FV: mahnhauh * **as regards** CV: ① gwàanyù ② jiyìu RV: góngdou * **with best (kind) regards** PH: chéng mahnhauh

regardful SV: ❶ làuhsàm ge ❷ bíusih gìngyi ge

regarding CV: gwàanyù

regardless SV: ❶ m̀jyuyi ge ❷ m̀gwàansàm ge ❸ m̀léih (consequences) ~ *hauhgwó* A: m̀léih dím * **regardless of** Patt: m̀léih N dím

regatta N: choisyùhnwúi (M: go)

regency N: ❶ sipjing ❷ sip-jing sìhkèih (M: dyuhn)

regeneration N: ❶ (religion) joisàng; gàngsàng; sànsàng ❷ góigaak; gaaksàn ❸ (physiology) saibāau jóujīk ge joisàng ❹ (physics) joisàng yìhnjeuhng

regent SV: sipjing ge N: ❶ sipjingwòhng (M: go) ❷ gàamdūkyàhn (M: go) ❸ dúngsih; dúngsí (M: go)

regime N: ❶ jaidouh (M: go) ❷ (form of government) jingkyùhn; jingjai; jingtái; túngjih fòngsīk; túngjih haihtúng ❸ sipjingfaat (M: go)

regiment N: (unit of troop) tyùhn (M: go) VO: pìnsìhng tyùhn PH: yìhmgaak yìhché túngyāt gám gúnléih * regiment commander N: tyùhnjéung (M: go)

regiments M: daaihkwàhn NuM: dòsou

regimental SV: tyùhn ge

regimentals N: gwànfuhk (M: tou; gihn)

regimentation N: tyùhn ge pìnjai

region N: ❶ (section or part of a country) deih fòng (M: daat) ❷ deihkèui (M: go) ❸ deihwihk (M: go) ❹ (body) sàntái bouhwaih ❺ faahnwàih (M: go) ❻ chàhng ❼ lìhngwihk (M: go) * in the region of Patt: hái N jóyáu * the upper regions N: ① tìn (M: go) ② tìngwok (M: go) * tropical regions N: yìhtdaai deihfòng * abdominal region N: fūkbouh * the region of the breast N: hùngbouh * the region of the equator N: chekdouh kèuiwihk

regional SV: ❶ deihfòng ge ❷ guhkbouh ge N: (America) deihkèui gàauyihksó (M: gàan)

register N: ❶ mìhngdāan (M: jèung) ❷ (of names) méngbóu; mìhngchaak (M: bún) ❸ dànggei ❹ jyuchaak ❺ (as in hospital) gwahouh ❻ (official) dànggeibóu (M: bún) ❼ geiluhkhei (M: ga) ❽ (music) yàmwihk (M: go) VO: ❶ (in official register) jyuchaak; dànggei ❷ (at a clinic; hospital) gwahouh ❸ bíuyihn (surprise; happiness; sadness) ~ *dāk hóu pa (hòi sàm; sèungsàm)*

registered PH: ❶ dànggeigwo ge ❷ jyugwochaak ge ❸ gúnfòng gaamdihnggwo ge * a registered letter N: gwahouhseun (M: fùng) * registered trademark N: jyuchaak sèungbīu (M: go) * registered letter with return receipt N: sèung gwahouhseun (M: fùng)

registrar N: ❶ dànggeiyùhn (M: go) ❷ (of school) jyuchaak jyúyahm (M: go)

registration N: ❶ geiluhk; géiluhk ❷ dànggei ❸ jyuchaak ❹ chìmdou ❺ gwahouh

registry N: ❶ geiluhk; géiluhk (M: go) ❷ gwahouhchyu ❸ dànggeichyúh; jyuchaakchyúh ❹ jīkyihp gaaisiuhsó (M: gàan) ❺ dànggeibóu; géiluhkbóu (M: bún) * registry office N: (birth, death, marriage) dànggeichyúh (M: gàan)

regress FV: ❶ wùihgwài ❷ teui fa ❸ teuihauh ❹ fuhkgú

regression N: ❶ fuhkgwài ❷ sèuiteui ❸ dóuteui

regressive SV: teuifa ge

regret N/FV: ❶ (say that one is sorry for) póuhhip ❷ (feel sorry) hósīk ❸ (repent) hauhfui ❹ wàihhahm ❺ fuihahn ✳ **express regret for** Patt: yànwaih ... bíusih póuhhip ✳ **much to my regret** PH: ngóh hóu póuhhip ✳ **with regret** A: ① wàihhahm gám ② póuhhip gám ✳ **to have no regrets** PH: ① móuh wàihhahm ② yāt-dī dōu m̀hauhfui

regular SV: ❶ (normal customary) jingsèuhng ge ❷ (orderly) kwàigéui ❸ yáuh kwàileuht ge ❹ dihngkèih ge ❺ jaahpgwaansing ge ❻ jíngchàih ge ❼ hahpgaak ge; yáuh fanlihn ge ❽ (rascal) sahpjúk ge N: ❶ sèuhngbeih-gwàn; jingkwàigwàn (M: deuih) ❷ sèuhnghaak (M: go) ❸ sàusih (M: go) ✳ **regular army** N: Méihgwok jingkwàigwàn (M: deuih) ✳ **regular customer** N: suhkhaakjái (M: go)

regularly A: ❶ kwàijāk gám ❷ jingjīk gám ❸ sahpfàn

regularize PH: ❶ (proceedings) lihngdou yáuh kwàijāk ❷ (marriage) lihngdou hahpfaatfa FV: tiuhjíng

regulate FV: ❶ (adjust a mechanism) gaaujéun ❷ (put in good order) jíngléih ❸ gúnléih (one's conduct) ❹ gúnjai (traffic) ~ *gàautùng* ❺ tiuhjit (temperature) ~ *wàndouh*

regulation N: ❶ (rule) jèungchìhng (M: bún) ❷ (order or law) faatlihng (M: tìuh; go) ❸ kwàijāk (M: go; tìuh) ❹ gúnléih ❺ tiuhjíng SV: ❶ jingsīk ge ❷ kwàidihng ge ✳ **traffic regulation** N: gàautùng kwàijāk (M: tìuh)

regulator N: ❶ tiuhjíngjé

(M: go) ❷ tiuhjínghei; tiuhjithei; gaaujínghei (M: go) ❸ biujéungjūng (M: go)

regulatory = regulative SV: ❶ kwàidihng ge; haahnjai ge ❷ tiuhjíng ge

rehabilitation FV: ❶ fuhkyùhn ❷ fùifuhk ❷ fuhkhìng

rehash PH: ❶ joi chyúléih PH: ❷ yuhng sàn ge yìhngsīk chyúléih gauh ge chòihlíu ❸ gusih sānpin

rehearsal N: ❶ buijuhng ❷ chùhngseuht ❸ (play) pàaihyín

rehearse FV: (as a play etc) pàaihyín; siyín; yuhyín PH: chèuhngsai góng

rehouse Patt: tùhng PN ngònpàaih sàn ge ngūk

reign N: ❶ gwànjyú (M: go) ❷ túngjih ❸ jīpui ❹ chìuhdoih (M: go) FV: ❶ túngjih ❷ sìhnghàhng ✳ **a reign of terror** N: húngbou túngjih; húngbou sìhdoih (M: go)

reimburse FV: bóuseuthng RV: béifàan

rein N: ❶ gēung; máhgèung (M: jì, tiuh) ❷ gayuh ❸ túngjih ❸ kèuichūk FV: ❶ gayuh ❷ hungjai ❸ jíjyun ❹ fongmaahn ✳ **rein in on the brink of a precipice** IE: yùhnngàaih lahkmáh ✳ **give rein to** PH: lihngdou hàhngduhng jihyàuh

reincarnate PH: ❶ joi fuhyúh yuhktái ❷ lihngdou joi sāang ❸ tàuhtòi joi sàang ge

reindeer N: sèuhnlúk (M: jek)

reinforce FV: ❶ jàngwùhn

reinforce the troops PH: paai bìng jàng wùhn VO: jàng bìng ✳ **reinforce an argument** VO: gàkèuhng léihyàuh ✳ **reinforced concrete** N: gonggwāt séuinàih

reinforcement N: ❶ jàngwùhn ❷ (additional troops) wùhnbīng; gaubīng (M: deuih)

reinstate PH: ❶ lihngdou fuhkyùhn ❷ lihngdou fuhkjīk

reinsure PH: joi bóuhím

reinsurance N: joi bóuhím

reintegrate PH: ❶ lihngdou chùhngsàn yùhnjíng ❷ lihngdou chùhngsàn túngyāt

reissue PH: joi faathòhng (books) N: ❶ joi faathòhng ❷ joi báan

reiteration FV: ❶ fáanfūk ❷ chùhngsàn PH: chùhngfūk ge syutwah (M: fàan)

reject FV: ❶ kéuihjyuht (a proposal; a suggestion) ~ yātgo jìkwai ~ yātgo ginyíh ❷ fáukyut ❸ dám (spotted apples) ~ dī laahn pìhnggwó ❸ ngáu ❺ bokwùih (a petition) Patt: jèung N dáfàan jyuntàuh (goods etc) PH: ❶ beih kéuihjyuht ge yàhn (M: go) ❷ beih dám ge yéh (M: gihn)

rejection N: ❶ kéuihjyuht (M: chi) ❷ pàaihsit ❸ pàaihchīk (sing)

rejoice FV: fùnhéi SV: gòuhing ✳ **rejoice in** FV: hèung yáuh

rejoicing N: ❶ héiyuht ❷ fùnlohk

rejoicings N: ❶ fùnfù ❷

hingjūk (M: chi) ❸ lyùhnfùn (M: chi)

rejoin PH: ❶ joi jiphahp ❷ joi gàyahp; joi chàamgà FV: (people) chùhngjeuih ❹ daapbihn; yingdaap

rejuvenate, -nize Adj. PH: ❶ lihngdou yàhn fáanlóuh wàahntùhng ❷ lihngdou yàhn chùhngmúhn chìngchēun wuhtlihk

rekindle PH: ❶ joi dímfó ❷ joi gīk héi ❸ joi janjok

relapse N/FV: ❶ (of sickness) fuhkfaat ❷ dohlohk IE: gutaai fuhkmàhng

relate FV: ❶ (of problems) sèunggwaan; gwàanhaih ❷ jeuihseuht; góng ❸ sipkahp ❹ fùhhahp ✳ **relate to** Patt: tùhng N yáuh gwàanhaih ✳ **relating to** CV: gwàanyù

related PH: ❶ yáuh chànchīk gwàanhaih ge ❷ yáuh gwàan ge ✳ **be related to** Patt: ① tùhng N yáuh gwàan ② tùhng PN yáuh chànchīk gwàanhaih

relation N: ❶ bougou (M: go) ❷ jeuihseuht ❸ gwàanhaih ✳ **have relation to (with)** FV: yáuhgwàan Patt: tùhng N yáuh gwàanhaih ✳ **in close relation with** Patt: tùhng PN yáuh mahtchit gwàanhaih ✳ **make relation to** RV: ① tàihkahp N ② tàahmdou N

relations N: ❶ gàauwóhng ❷ chànsuhk (M: go) ✳ **break off relations** VO: ① tyúhnjyuht gwàanhaih ② (friends) jyuht gàau ② (countries) tyúhnjyuht ngoihgàau gwàanhaih

relationship N: ❶ chànsuhk gwàanhaih ❷ gwàanhaih

relative SV: ❶ yáuh gwàanhaih ge ❷ sèungdeui ge ❸ béigaau ge ❹ sèungying ge N: ❶ chānchīk; chànsuhk (M: go) ❷ (language) gwàanhaih chìh ✻ **relative to** Patt: tùhng N sèung deuiying

relatives N: ❶ (kin; members of the same family) ngūkkéiyàhn ❷ (not in the same household) tùhngjùngge; tùhngjuhk ge ❸ (by marriage) chānchīk ✻ **relatives and friends** N: chānchīk pàhngyáuh; chānyáuh

relatively A: ❶ sèungdeui gám ❷ béigaau gám

relativism N: ❶ sèungdeuileuhn ❷ sèungdeuising ❸ sèungdeui jyúyih

relativity N: ❶ sèungdeuising ❷ sèungwuh yìchyùhn ❸ (physics) sèungdeuileuhn

relax FV: ❶ sùngchìh (nerves) ~ *sàhngìng* ❷ fongsùng (muscles, mood) ~ *gèiyuhk,* ~ *sàmchìhng* ❸ wuhnwòh ❹ yàusīk ❺ (in hospital) yàuyéuhng ✻ **relax in one's efforts** FV: fongsùng ✻ **relax one's attention** FV/SV: ① sòfāt ② daaihyi

relaxation N: ❶ (for nerves) sùngchìh ❷ (for rules) gáamhèng ❸ (for enjoyment) sìuhín; yùhlohk

relay FV: ❶ (a message) chyùhndaaht ❷ taiwuhn ❸ (broadcast) jyúnbo PH: taiwuhn ge máh waahkjé gáu N: ❶ wuhnbāan ❷ mahtjì bóuchùng ❸ (electric) gaidihnhei (M: ga) ❹ jiplihkchoi ✻ **relay race** N: jiplihkchoi (páau)

relay (-laid, -laying) PH: ❶ joi pòuchit ❷ joi ngònji ❸ joi jìngsàu

release FV: ❶ (set at liberty) fong; sīkfong; fongjó (prisoner) ~ *faahnyàhn* ❷ gáaichèuih (from a promise) ~ *sihngnohk* ❸ fonghei (rights) ~ *kyùhnleih* ❹ faatbou sànmàhn ❺ faathòhng (movies etc.) ~ *dihnyíng* ❻ dám (bombs) ~ *jadáan* ❼ faatbíu (articles) ~ *màhnjèung* ❽ sīkfong ❾ gáaichèuih ❿ míhnchèuih RV: ❶ gáaihòi ❷ fonghòi ❸ fongsáu N: ❶ faathòhngmaht ❷ sīkfong jòngji

relegate FV: ❶ bínyuht ❷ fongjuhk; kèujuhk ❸ pàauhei; dám ❹ yìhgàau ❺ gwàileuih

relent PH: ❶ bin wànwòh ❷ lìhnmáhn ✻ **to relent toward a person** Patt: deui PN yáuh lìhnmáhnsàm

relentless SV: mòuhchìhng ge

relevance, -cy N: ❶ tipchit; jungháng ❷ hāpdong

relevant SV: ❶ yáuh gwàan ge ❷ chittàih ge ❸ junghcháng ge PH: deui muhkchìhn juhngdaaih mahntàih gwàanjyu ge ✻ **relevant to** Patt: tùhng N yáuh gwàan ✻ **relevant details** PH: yáuh gwàan ge saijit

reliable SV: ❶ kaaudākjyuh ❷ koksaht ge

reliance N: ❶ seunyahm ❷ yìkaau ❸ seunsàm (M: go) PH: só seunlaaih ge yàhn waahkjé mahtgín ✻ **place reliance on/in** Patt: seunlaaih N yìh

relic N: ❶ (ancient time) wàihmaht (M: gihn) ❷ géinihmmaht (M: gihn) ❸ wàihjīk ❹ (of church) singmaht (M: gihn) ❺ wàihgwāt (M: fu) ❻ gúmaht (M: gihn)

relief N: ❶ gaujai ❷ (pain, worries, difficulties) gáaichèuih ❸ (pain, worries) gáamhèng ❹ wùhngau ❺ gaujaibán (M: pài) ❻ wuhnbāan ❼ lèuhnbāanjé; jiptaijé (M: go) SV: sìnmihng; sàngduhng; hínjyu ＊ **in relief** A: ❶ sahpfàn sìnmihng gám ❷ fèisèuhng hínjyu gám ＊ **on relief** N: jipsauh gaujai ge ＊ **relief map** N: laahptái deihtòuh (M: go) ＊ **relief value** N: ngònchyùhnmóhng (M: go)

relieve FV: ❶ gau ❷ gaujai (refugees; poor; people from disaster etc) ~ naahnmàhn ❸ gáaichèuih ❹ gáamhèng ❺ tiuhjài VO: jipbāan ＊ **be received of** FV: báaityut CV: míhnyù ＊ **relieve oneself (nature)** FV: daaihsíubihn ＊ **relieve guard or work** VO: wuhnbāan

religion N: gaau; jùnggaau; seunyéuhng (M: go) ＊ **enter into (be in) religion** VO: chēutgā

religious SV: ❶ jùnggaau ge ❷ (devout) kìhnsìhng ge; sàhn sàm ge ❸ yìhm gán ge N: ❶ (for Buddist monk) wòhséung (M: go) ❷ (for Buddist nun) sìgù ❸ (for Catholic brother) sàusih (M: go) ❻ (for Catholic sister) sàunéui (M: go) ＊ **religious education** N: jùnggaau gaauyuhk ＊ **religious question** N: jùnggaau mahntàih (M: go, tiuh) ＊ **a religious house** N: sàudouhyún (M: gàan)

relinquish FV: ❶ (give up) fonghei (a claim, hope) ~ yiukàuh; ~ hèimohng ❷ chitwùih ❸ yeuhngbéi RV: fonghòi ＊ **relinquish rights or privileges** VO: fonghei kyùhnleih; heikyùhn

relish N: ❶ méihmeih; jìmeih ❷ tiuhmeihbán; hèunglíu ❸ sìhou (M: go) FV: ngoihou; héihou

relive PH: ❶ joi sàang ❷ joi táiyihm ~ gwoheui ge sàngwuht ❸ chùhngsàn gwo N sàngwuht FV: fuhkwuht

reluctuance, -ancy FV/SV: míhnkéuhng N: (physics) chìhjó

reluctant SV: ❶ m̀yuhnyi ge ❷ nàahn deuifuh ge ❸ nàahn chyúléih ge

rely FV: ❶ yíkaau; yílaaih (financial support or decision making) ~ kéuih ge gòhgō wàihchìh sàngwuht ❷ (put faith in someone to do something) seunlaaih; seunyahm ~ yātgo yàhn jouh gógihn sih ＊ **rely on (upon)** FV: ❶ yíkaau ❷ seunlaaih

remain FV: ❶ (stay) làuh ❷ yìhngyìhn haih ❸ bóuchìh ❹ gokyi RV: ❶ (be left over) jihngfāan ❷ làuhdài (properties) ~ chòihcháan ＊ **remain with** FV: gwàiyù; suhkkyù Patt: hái N ge kyùhnlihk noih

remainder PH: ❶ (the part that is left) jihngfāan gódī; jihngfāan ge ❷ yùhsou (M: go) ❸ chyùhnfo (M: pài) ❹ wàihjūk (M: go) ❺ sìhngyùh ge; ❻ jihngyùh ge RV: (a number found by subtracting) jihngfāan FV: ❶ lihmga chēutsauh; pèhngga maaihchēut

remains N: ❶ (that which is left or not used) yuhngjihng ge ❷ (for food) sihk jihng ge ❸ (things left by the dead) wàihmaht (M: gihn) ❹ (corpse) wàihtái; sìtái (M: go) ❺ (ancient ruins) faihèui (M: go) ❻ (last will) wàihjūk (M: fahn)

remand N/FV: ❶ wàahn-ngaat ❷ fūksám; chùhngsám RV: sungfàan

remark FV: ❶ jyuyi ❷ gùn-chaat ❸ pìhng leuhn ❹ góng RV: gónghéi N: ❶ jyuyi ❷ pìhngleuhn ❸ tàahmwah (M: chi) ✻ **as remarked above** PH: hóuchíh seuhngbihn sógóng ge ✻ **make a remark upon** Patt: jauh N bíusih yigin ✻ **make remarks** FV: ① pìhngleuhn ② yíngóng ③ tàahmwah; góng ✻ **remark on (upon)** N: ① pìhngleuhn ② pàipìhng

remarkable PH: ❶ jihkdāk jyuyi ge ❷ fèisèuhng chēutsīk ge; fèisèuhng chēutjung ge SV: ❶ cheukyuht ge ❷ m̀pìhng-sèuhng ge ✻ **a remarkable change** PH: hínjyu ge binfa

remarkably A: hínjyu gám

remarry PH: ❶ joi fàn ❷ (for man) joi chéui ❸ (for woman) joi ga

remedial SV: ❶ jihlìuh ge ❷ bóugau ge ❸ gíujing ge

remedy N: ❶ yeuhkmaht ❷ jihlìuhfaat (M: go) ❸ bóugau-faat (bóugau ge fòngfaat) (M: go) FV: ❶ (correct or make right) gójing; gójeng (pronunciation) ~ *faatyàm* ❷ dáujing (a mistake) ~ *chongh* ❸ sàuléih (a leak in a pipe) ~ *séuihàuh ge lauhháu* ❹ bóusèuhng (loss) ~ *syúnsāt*

remember FV: geidāk; gei-jyuh RV: geihéi ✻ **remember me to** PH: chéng doih ngóh heung PN mahnhauh; doih ngóh mahnhauh PN

remembrance N: ❶ geiyīk

❷ geinihmbán (M: gihn, fahn) ✻ **call to remembrance** RV: séunghéi ✻ **in remembrance of** PH: waih (jó) geinihm

remembrances FV: mahn-hauh

remind PH: ❶ lìhngdou séunghéi ❷ lìhngdou geihéi FV: tàihséng ✻ **remind PN of** Patt: tàihséng PN

reminder N: ❶ tàihséngjé (M: go) ❷ geinihmbán (M: gihn, fahn) PH: bòngjoh yàhn geihéi ge yéh

reminiscence N: ❶ wùih-yīk ❷ wahgauh

reminiscences N: wùihyīk-luhk (M: bún, bouh) ✻ **remini-scences of the war** N: daaih-jin wùihyīkluhk (M: bún, bouh)

remiss SV: ❶ (duty) sòfāt ge; m̀síusām ge ❷ mòuhjìng dáchói ge

remission N: (sins) semíhn FV: ❶ míhnchèuih (debts, of-fences) ❷ gáamhèng; gáamteui (pain; labour etc.)

remit FV: ❶ wuih (gei) (money) ~ *chín;* ~ *fún* ❷ gáamhèng; wuhnwòh (anger) ~ *nouhhei* ❸ fùnsyu; se (a sin) ~ *jeuih* VO: geichín; wuihfún RV: ❶ sungfàan (prison) ~ *gàamyuhk* ❷ sungheui

remittance N: wuihfún (M: bāt) PH: jìfuh ge gāmngáak (M: bāt)

remittee N: (wuihpiu) sàufúnyàhn (M: go)

remitter N: ❶ wuihfúnyàhn (M: go) ❷ semíhnjé; fùnsyujé (M: go)

remmant N: ❶ chàahnyùh ge ❷ jihngfaan ge fomaht (M: pài) ❸ lihngtáubou * the rem-nant of the bandits PH: chaahkdóng ge chàahnyùh

remodel PH: joi jouh ❶ sàugói ❷ góipin (army) ~ *gwo ge gwàndéui*

remonstrate FV: ❶ kong-yíh ❷ jùnggúk * (advise) kwàihyun; hyungaan VO: bíusih m̀tùhng ge yigin

remorse N: ❶ (crime) hauhfui; fuihahn ❷ tùhng-chìhngsàm (M: júng) * with-out remorse PH: móuh fuiyi

remorseful SV: hauhfui ge

remorseless SV: ❶ m̀jì hauhfui ge ❷ mòuhchìhng ge ❸ chàahnyán ge

remote SV: ❶ (distance) yìuhyúhn ge ❷ (people) sòyúhn ge ❸ saimèih ge * remote control FV: yìuhhung * remote times N/TW: seuhnggú sìhdoih (M: go, dyuhn) * a remote relative N: yúhnchàn (M: go) * a remote ancester N: yúhnjóu (M: go)

remould = remold FV: ❶ góijouh ❷ chùhngjyu

remount PH: ❶ joi séuhng (horse, car etc) ~ *máh; ~ chè* ❷ joi pàhséuhng (mountains) ~ *sàan* ❸ joi ngònjòng (canon) ~ *paau* ❹ taiwuhn ge máh (M: jek) FV: jèuisok (antiquity) ~ *yúhngú* N: sànmáh (M: jek)

remove FV: ❶ chèuih (hat or other garments) ~ *hàaih; móu; sàam* ❷ jínglāt (of stains, ink, spots etc.) ~ *dī mahkséui* ❸ bùn (objects from some place) ~ *dī yéh* ❹ chaak (of instal-

latiions, as a telephone) ~ *dihnwá* ❺ got (a growth, an ap-pendix etc) ~ *láu; ~ màahngchéung* ❻ hòichèuih (students) ~ *hohksàang* ❼ saatséi (a person) ~ *yātgo yàhn* ❽ dek; gón (a person) ~ *yātgo yàhn chēutheui* VO: (an official) gaakjīk; mìhnjīk; chitjīk N: ❶ gàaidyuhn (M: go) ❷ chìhngdouh (M: go) ❸ (school) sìngkāp * remove N from Patt: jèung N yàuh PW bùnheui FV: pàaihchèuih * remove oneself RV: jáuhòi FV: lèihhòi * remove pain VO: jítung * remove prohibitions VO: hòigam * remove a restric-tion VO: hòigam * remove a tooth VO: tyutngàh; mōkngàh

removed SV: ❶ yúhnchàn ge ❷ mòuhgwaan ge

remover N: ❶ bùnwahn gùngyàhn (M: go) ❷ chèuijīkjāi (M: jèun)

remuneration N: ❶ bou-chàuh; chàuhbou; chàuhboufai (M: bāt) ❷ bóusèuhng (M: chi) * remuneration for contributors of articles N: góufai (M: bāt) * remuneration for loss N: pùihsèuhngfai (M: bāt)

renaissance N: ❶ fuhk-hìng; fuhkwuht (M: chi) * the renaissance N: (revival of art, literature and learning) màhn-ngaih fuhkhìng

renal PH: sahnjohng ge * renal calculus N: (medical) sahngitsehk

rename PH: chùhngsàn béi méng; joi góiméng

rencounter PH: ngáuhyìhn johnggin; ngáuhyìhn yuhdóu N/FV: ❶ chùngdaht (M: go; chi) ❷ kyutdau ❸ háaihhauh

rend RV: sìseui (the clothes) ~ dī bou

render FV: ❶ (help) boudaap ❷ tàihchēut ❸ béi (help) ~ bòngjoh ❹ (to the conqueror) naahpgung ❺ béi (certain role) ~ yātgo goksīk ❻ (accident) lihngdou ~ PN móuh baahnfaat ❼ fàanyihk (into English) ~ sihng yìngmàhn ✱ **render an account of** FV: góngmìhng ✱ **render good for evil** IE: yíhdāk bou yun ✱ **render help to** FV: wùhnjoh ✱ **render up** FV: ① yeuhngbéi ② fonghei

rendering N: ❶ bíuyín (M: go, chi) ❷ fánchaat (M: chi) ❸ fuhkjai

rendezvous N: ❶ yeukwuih (M: go) ❷ jeuihwuih (M: go) ❸ jaahphahpdeih PH: hái jídihng ge deihfòng jaahp hahp

rendition N: ❶ (music) gáaisīk ❷ fàanyihk ❸ sàngcháanleuhng

renegade FV: binjit PH: ❶ buhngaau ge ❷ binjit ge N: ❶ buigaaujé (M: go) ❷ buhntòuh (M: go)

renew FV: ❶ wuhn (liscence) ~ pàaihjiu ❷ fùifuhk (youth) ~ chìngchèun ❸ chùhngdìhng (a contract) ~ hahptùhng ❹ juhk (a subscription) ~ dehngyuht hónmaht ❺ bóuchùng (provisions) ~ lèuhngsihk

renewable PH: ❶ hóyíh gàngsàn ge ❷ hóyíh joi hòichí ge

renminbi (abb. RMB) N: (China's money) yàhnmàhnbaih (M: jèung)

renounce FV: ❶ fonghei (a privilege) ~ kyùhnleih ❷ fáuyihng ❸ tyúhnjyuht; tyutlèih (a relationship) ~ gwàanhaih ✱ **to renounce the world** PH: heijyuht chàhnsai FV: sàudouh

renovate FV: ❶ sàujínggwo (house) ~ ngūk ❷ gaaksàn ❸ chaatsàn (policy) ~ jingchaak

renown N: ❶ mìhngmohng (M: go) ❷ sìngyuh (M: go)

renowned SV: chēutméng ge

rent N: ❶ (payment) jòu ❷ jòugàm (M: bāt) ❸ lihtháu (M: go) FV: ❶ jòu (a house) ~ gàan ngūk ❷ jòubéi; chēutjòubéi ~ nùhngyàhn ✱ **for rent** SV: chēutjòu ge ✱ **rent-a-car** N: jòuyahm heichè (M: ga) ✱ **rent-free** SV/A: m̀sàu jòugàm ge ✱ **house rent** N: ngūkjòu ✱ **rent payment in advance** N: seuhngkèihjòu ✱ **rent collector** N: sàujòuyàhn; sàujòulóu (M: go) ✱ **house for rent** N: gàtngūk chēutjòu

rentable PH: hóyíh chēutjòu ge

rental N: jòugàmngáak (M: bāt) PH: jòuyuhng ge

renter N: chēutjòuyàhn (M: go)

renunciation N: ❶ (rights, title) fonghei; heikyùhn ❷ fáuyihng ❸ jihjai; hākgéi

reopen PH: ❶ joi hòi ❷ joi hòichí

reorganization N: ❶ góijóu ❷ góijouh ❸ jíngléih

reorganize FV: ❶ góijóu ❷ góipin (an army) ~ gwàndéui ❸ jóigaak

repair FV/N: ❶ sàuléih; sàu- jíng (car) ~ *ga chè* ❷ sàuchāp (a house) ~ *gàan ngūk* ❸ bóu- fàan (shoes) ~ *deui hàaih* ❹ jāplaúh (a leak) ❺ bóugau ❻ bóusèuhng (loss) ~ *syúnsāt* ✻ **under repair** PH: sàuléihgán

repairable PH: hóyíh sàu- léih ge

repairs N: sàuléih gùng- chìhng

reparation N: ❶ pùih- sèuhng ❷ bóugau

reparations N: ❶ wàihsàn- gùngjok ❷ pùihfún (M: bāt)

repartee PH: mánjit ge deuidaap

repartition N/FV: ❶ fàn- pui ❷ waahkfàn PH: joi fàn- pui; chùhngsàn fànpui

repast N: ❶ yámsihk ❷ chāan (M: go) ✻ **a light repast** N: dímsàm (M: dihp; lùhng) ✻ **a rich repast** PH: fùngfu ge chāan

repatriate FV: hínfáan PH: ❶ hínsung fáangwok ❷ beih hínsung fáangwok ge yàhn

repay FV: ❶ (money) wàahn ❷ sèuhngwàahn ❸ (requite) boudaap ❹ (indemnify) pùih) RV: ❶ wàahnfàan ❷ pùihfàan ✻ **repay debt** VO: wàahnjaai ✻ **repay money** VO: wàahnchín

repayment N: ❶ sèuhng- wàahn; pùihsèuhng ❷ boudaap ❸ bouchàuh

repeal FV/N: ❶ chéuisiu ❷ chitsiu (a grant) ~ *johhohkgām* ❸ faichèuih

repeat PH: ❶ joijouh ❷ joi

góng ❸ (for words) gànjyuh góng FV: (performance) chùhngyín ❷ chùhngfūk

repeal FV: ❶ gīkteui (an enemy) ~ *dihkyàhn* ❷ kéuih- jyuht (an invitation) ~ *yātgo yiuchíng* ❸ pàaihchīk (similar electric charges) PH: ❶ lihng yàhn fáangám ❷ lihng yàhn m̀hòisàm

repellent PH: juhkteui ge SV: ❶ fòhngséui ge ❷ tóuyim ge

repent FV: ❶ hauhfui ❷ chaamfui ✻ **repent a fault** FV: fuigwo ✻ **repent and reform** FV: fuigói

repentance N: fuihahn

repentant SV: fuihahn ge

repercussion RV: daahn- fàan N: ❶ wùihsèng ❷ (light) fáanseh ❸ fáanying

repertoire N: ❶ kehkmuhk ❷ sèuhngyín jitmuhk ❸ (com- puter) jílihngbíu (M: go)

repertory N: ❶ chōngfu (M: gàan) ❷ bóufu (M: gàan) ❸ muhkkluhk; muhkluhkbíu (M: fahn, go)

repetition N: ❶ chùhngfūk ❷ chùhng góng ❸ chùhng jouh ❹ fubún (M: fahn) ❺ fūkjaibán (M: gihn)

replace FV: ❶ (take the place of) doihtai ❷ gwàiwàahn ❸ fuhkjīk ❹ gàngwuhn PH: jài- fàan hái yùhnlòih ge waihji ✻ **replace by (with)** Patt: yíh N doihtai

replaceable PH: ❶ hóyíh taiwuhn ge ❷ hóyíh jàifàan háiyùhnlòih ge deihfòng ge

replacement N: ❶ doihtai ❷ jiptai ❸ (soldiers) bóuchùng

replay FV/N: chùhngchoi; joichoi

replenish PH: joi jòngmúhn FV: ❶ tìmmúhn (wine) ~ *bùi jáu* ❷ bóuchùng (the stock of goods) ~ *fomaht*

replenishment N: ❶ joi jòngmúhn ❷ bóuchùng

replete PH: ❶ jòngmúhn ge ❷ sihkbáau ge SV: chùngjùk ge

repletion N: ❶ chùngmúhn ❷ báaumúhn ❸ chùngjùk ❻ (medical) dòhyut; chùnghyut

replica N: ❶ fùkjaibán (M: bún, jeung) ❷ làhmmòuhbún ❸ (music) chùhngfùk

reply N: daapfūk (M: go) FV: ❶ (verbal) daap; wùihdaap ❷ daapfūk ❸ daapbihn VO: wùihseun ✻ **in reply to** Patt: waihdaapfūk N ✻ **make a reply** FV: (jok) daap ✻ **reply for somebody** Patt: doihbíu PN daapfūk ✻ **reply to** FV: daap

report FV: ❶ (formal) bougou ❷ boudouh ❸ goufaat ❹ boudou ❺ (of reporter) chóifóng ❻ hunggou N: ❶ gùngbou ❷ mìhngyuh; sìngyuh ✻ **it is reported that** Patt: ① geui bougou ② geui chyùhnmàhn ✻ **of good (ill) report** PH: sìngyuh hóu (m̀hóu) ✻ **report on (upon)** Patt: jok N bougou ✻ **hear a report that** FV: (rumour) tèngmàhnwah; tèngginwah ✻ **report card** N: ① gàtìhng bougoubíu (M: go) ② sìhngjīkdāan (M: jèung)

reportage N: ❶ boudouh ❷ bougou màhn hohk

reporter N: ❶ (of news) gei-

jé; sànmàhn geijé (M: go) ❷ tùngseunyùhn (M: go)

reports N: ❶ punkyutsyù ❷ geiluhk ❸ baaujasèng

repose N/FV: ❶ yàusīk ❷ seunlaaih

repository N: ❶ fufòhng (M: gàan) ❷ chyúhchòhng sāt (M: gàan)

reprehend FV: naauh

represent FV: ❶ (act for, politically, symbolize) doihbíu ❷ (in court) chēuttihng ❸ bíuyihn ❹ baahnyín (role) ~ *yātgo goksīk* ✻ **represent N to oneself** PH: sàm léuihbihn séungjeuhng N ✻ **represent by signs (letters)** PH: yuhng fùhhouh (màhnjih) bíusih

representation N: ❶ doihbíu (M: go) ❷ jeuhngjìng ❸ wá (M: fūk) ❹ kongyíh ❺ yínchēut (M: chi)

representative PH: ❶ doihbíu ge ❷ mìuhsé ge ❸ doihyíhjai ge N: ❶ doihbúi (M: go) ❷ yíhyùhn (M: go) ❸ dínyìhng (M: go) ✻ **be the representative of** Patt: ① doihbíu N ❷ búisih N ✻ **diplomatic representatives** N: ngoihgàau gùnyùhn (M: go) ✻ **the house of representatives** N: (America) jungyíhyún

repress FV: ❶ janngaat (revolt) ~ *bouhlyuhn* ❷ ngaatjai (one's feelings, actions) ~ *yātgo yàhn ge gámchìhng; yātgo yàhn ge chìhngséuih* ❸ yīkjai (cough) ✻ **repress a laugh** FV: yánjyuhsiu ✻ **repress anger** VO: yánhei

repression N: ❶ janngaat ❷ jaijí ❸ yīkjai

reprieve N: (law) wuhn yìhng PH: ❶ jaahmsìh gáamsíu ❷ jaahmsìh m̀chyúkyut

reprimand FV: (reprove) naauh; wah N: chìhnggaai PH: yìhmlaih gám heui naauh

reprint N: ❶ (a second printing) joibáan ❷ chùhngyanbún (M: bouh) FV: ❶ joiyan; joibáan ❷ fàanyan

reprisal N: ❶ (retaliation) boufuhksing ❷ boufuhk hàhngwàih IE: yíhngah wàahnngah ✳ to make reprisals Adj. PH: chóichéui boufuhk sáudyuhn

reproach N: chíyuhk FV: (scold) naauh PH: lihngdou móuhmín

reprobate FV: ❶ kéuihjyuht ❷ naauh SV: dohlohk ge PH: dohlohk ge yàhn (M: go) N: mòuhláai (M: go)

reproduce FV: ❶ joisàang ❷ fūkjai (picture) ~ tòuhpín ❸ fàanyan (books) ~ dī syù ❹ (biological) sàngjihk; fàahnjihk ❹ (a printed article) jyúnjoi Patt: yuhng N FV chēutlàih

reproductive PH: ❶ joisàang ge ❷ sàngjihk ge ❸ dòcháan ge ✳ reproductive organs N: sàngjihkhei (gùn) (M: go)

reprogram FV: góipin (dihnnóuh chìhngjeuih)

reprography N: dihnjí fàanyan (seuht)

reprove FV: (scold) naauh; wah

reptile PH: ❶ pàhhàhng ge ❷ hahjihn ge yàhn (M: go) SV: bèipéi ge N: ❶ pàhchùhng ❷ pàhhàhng duhngmaht (M: jek)

republic N: ❶ (a nation) guhngwòhgwok (M: go) ❷ tyùhntái (M: go) ✳ the People's Republic of China N: Jùngwàh Yàhnmàhn Guhngwòhgwok

republican PH: ❶ guhngwòhgwok ge ❷ guhngwòh jingtái ge ✳ the republicans N: (America) guhngwòhdóngyùhn (M: go) ✳ the republican party N: guhngwòhdóng (M: go)

republicanism N: ❶ guhngwòh táijai (M: go) ❷ guhngwòhgwok jingfú (M: go)

republish PH: ❶ joi chēutbáan ❷ joi yan ❸ chùhngsàn faatbíu ❹ (law) joidihng; joisé (last will) ~ wàihjūk

repudiate FV: ❶ fáuyihng (wrong deed) ~ jouh cho sih ❷ kéuihjyuht (a gift) ~ sàu láihmaht ❸ wàihhei (a son) ~ yātgo jái ✳ to repudiate a debt VO: laaihjaai

repudiation N: ❶ kéuihjyuht ❷ fáuyihng

repugnance, -ancy N: ❶ yimwu ❷ màauhtéuhn ✳ a repugnance for Patt: deui N ge yimwu

repugnant PH: lihngyàhn tóuyim ge SV: ❶ sèungfáan ge ❷ dihkdeui ge

repulse FV/N: ❶ gīkteui (an enemy) ~ dihkyàhn ❷ kéuihjyuht (help) ~ bòngjoh

repulsion N: ❶ gīkteui ❷ kéuihjyuht ❸ yimwu ❹ (physics) chīklihk

repulsive SV: ❶ tóuyim ge

❷ láahngdaahm ge ❸ (physics) pàaihchīk ge

reputation N: ❶ mìhng yuh (M: go) ❷ sìngyuh (M: go) ❸ sìngmohng (M: go) ✳ **of good (light) reputation** SV: yáuh mìhngmohng ge ✳ **to live up to one's reputation** PH: mìhngsaht sèungfùh ✳ **bad reputation** PH: m̀hhóu mìhngsìng

repute N: ❶ mìhngyuh (M: go) ❷ mìhngsìng (M: go) FV: yìhngwàih (somebody as a scholar) ~ *kéuih haih hohkjé*

reputed SV: chēutméng ge PH: chyùhnsyut ge

request FV: ❶ chéng; yìuchéng (participate in the party) ~ *heui chàam gà móuhwúi* ❷ (demand) yìukàuh (financial assistance) ~ *dòdī jèun tip* ❸ (pleading) chíngkàuh (a loan) ~ *jefún* ❹ (beg) kàuh (a favour) ~ *PN jouh yātgihn sih* N: ❶ chíngkàuh (M: go) ❷ yìukàuh (M: go) ❸ sèuiyiu (M: go) ❹ yìuchíng (M: chi) ✳ **at somebody's request** Patt: yìng PN ge yìuchíng ✳ **by request** FV: yìngyìu ✳ **in great request** PH: fèisèuhng sèui yiu ✳ **make a request to** VO: tàihchēut chíngkàuh

require FV: ❶ (demand something) sái (give deposit) ~ *m̀ ~ béi dehng a?* ❷ yiu; kwàidihng (an examination) ~ *háausi* ❸ sèuiyiu (more help) ~ *dòdī wùhnjoh* ❹ yìukàuh; kwàidihng (keep silent) ~ *m̀hhóu chēutsèng* ✳ **require of** FV: sèuiyiu

requirement PH: ❶ sèuiyiu ge tìuhgín ❷ sèuiyiu ge jìgaak ✳ **meet the requirement of** VO: ① múhnjūk

sèuiyiu ② fùhhahp tìuhgín

requisite SV: bītsèui ge N: ❶ (things) bītsèuibán (M: gihn) ❷ (circumstances) yiusou; tìuhgín (M: go) ❸ (courses) bītsàufō (M: mùhn; fō)

requisition N: ❶ (formal) yìukàuh (M: go) ❷ sànchíng (syù) ❸ (supply) jìngyuhng FV: ❶ jìngyuhng ❷ saakchéui

requite FV: ❶ boudaap (an obligation) ~ *yànwaih* ❷ boufuhk ✳ **to requite evil with good** IE: ① yíh sihn bou ngok ② yíh dāk bou yun

rescind FV: ❶ faichèuih (a law) ~ *yāttiuh faatleuht* ❷ chéuisìu; chitsìu (a resolution) ~ *yātgo kyutyíhngon* ❸ gáaichèuih

rescript N: ❶ jílihng; mìhnglihng; faatlihng ❷ gùnggou

rescue N: ❶ chínggau ❷ gaujoh FV: ❶ chínggau ❷ gaujoh ❸ gaujai (poverty; famine; disasters etc) ~ *jòimàhn* ✳ **come (go) to the rescue** VO: heui yìhnggau ✳ **rescue from** Patt: yàuh N gau

rescuer N: ❶ gausìng (M: go) ❷ gaujohjé (M: go)

research N/FV: ❶ yìhngau ❷ tìuhchàh; diuhchàh ❸ háauchaat ✳ **a research worker** N: yìhngauyùhn (M: go) ✳ **operations research** N: ① wahnchàuhhohk (M: mùhn) ② wahnyuhng yìhngau ✳ **reasearch-on-research** N: fōhohk gúnléih (M: mùhn)

researches N: hohkseuht yìhngau ✳ **make scientific researches** VO: jeunhàhng fōyìhn gùngjok

resemblance N: ❶ sèung-chíh (jìchyu) ❷ ngoihbíu (M: go) ❸ fubún (M: jèung; fahn) ✳ **bear a resemblance to** FV: leuihchíh Patt: tùhng PN/N sèungchíh

resemble FV: ❶ hóu-sèungchíh ❷ hóuchíh (mother) ~ màhmā

resent FV: ❶ nàu ❷ m̀jùngyi (criticism) ~ pàipìhng ❸ bātmúhn

resentful SV: ❶ fáhnhahn ge ❷ nàu ge

resentment N: fáhnhahn

reservation N: ❶ bóulàuh ❷ (of hotels, restuarants, theatres) yuhdehng

reserve RV: ❶ làuhfàan (a day) ~ nīyaht FV: ❶ dehng; yuhdehng (books, seats) ~ syù; ~ wái ❷ bóulàuh (talking) ~ yātdī syutwah ❸ chyúhchòhng (food) ~ sihkmaht ❹ chyúhbeih (money) ~ jūkgau ge chín N: ❶ bóulàuh ❷ hauhbeih gwān (M: jì; deuih) ❸ gùngjīkgám (M: bāt) ❹ jyùn-yuhngdeih (M: faai) ❺ haahndouh SV: ❶ chyúhbeih ge ❷ hàhmchūk ge ✳ **in reserve** SV: ① yuhbeih ge ② chyúhbeih ge ✳ **with reserve** A: ① yáuh bóulàuh ge ② hàhmchūk ge ✳ **without reserve** A: mòuh tìuhgín gám ✳ **to accept without reservation** PH: mòuh tìuhgín gám jipsauh

reserved SV: ❶ bóulàuh ge ❷ yuhdihng ge ❸ gaammahk ge ❹ yáuh jitjai ge

reservist N: ❶ yuhbeihbìng (M: go) ❷ hauhbeihbìng (M: go)

reservoir N: ❶ séuitòhng (M: go) ❷ chūkséuichìh (M: go) ❸ chyúhchòhng fu (M: go) ❹ séuifu (M: go) ✳ **Ming Tomb's reservoir** N: sahpsàamlìhng séui fu

reset PH: ❶ (reset) joichit ❷ chùhngjóu ❸ (machinery) chùhngjòng ❹ (rearrange) chùhngpàaih ❺ (jewellery) chùhngsèung

reshape Patt: béi N sàn ge yìhngsīk VO: ❶ joi dihng sàn fòngjām ❷ jíngyìhng PH: joijouh

reshaper N: jíngyìhnghei (M: ga)

reshuffle PH/N: ❶ (cards) joisáipáai ❷ (of the cabinets, government) gói jóu (M: chi)

reside FV: ❶ (dwell) jyuh ❷ (power) gwàiyù PH: chyùhnjoih hái

residence N: ❶ (abode) jyuhjáak; jyuhgā ❷ jyujaat ❸ gùnggún (M: gàan) ✳ **fixed residence** N: gudihng jyuhsó (M: gàan) ✳ **official residence** N: gùndái (M: gàan)

resident PH: ❶ gèuijyuh ge ❷ gèuilàuh ge ❸ jyujaat ge N: ❶ gèuimàhn (M: go) ❷ jyu ngoihgwok ge doihbíu (M: go) ✳ **resident at** PH: jyuh hái ✳ **resident population** N: ① gèuijyuh wuhháu ② gèuimàhn yàhnháu ✳ **foreign residence** N: kìuhmàhn; ngoihkìuh (M: go)

residential PH: ❶ jyuhjáak ge ❷ gèuijyuh ge ✳ **residential area** N: jyuhjaahkkēui (M: go) ✳ **residential dwelling** N: jyuhgā'ngūk (M: gàan)

residual SV: ❶ chàahnyùh ge ❷ sihngdài ge N: ❶ chàahnyùh ❷ sihngyùh ❸ chùhngyín báankyùhn fai (M: bāt) ❹ hauhwàihjing (M: go) * **residual property** N: (law) sihngyùh chòihcháan; yùhcháan * **residual products** N: fucháanmaht

residue N: ❶ chàahnyùh; sihngyùh ❷ (law) sihngyùh chòihcháan; yùhcháan ❸ jàjí ❹ (mathematics) chàahnsou

residuum (pl. residua) N: ❶ chàahnyùh ❷ (chemistry) chàahnjà; fucháanmaht ❸ (mathematics) nghchà ❹ séhwúi hahchàhng

resign VO: (as office) chìhjik PH: joi chìmméng FV: ❶ fonghei; séhei ❷ seuhnchùhng; tèngchùhng

resignation N: ❶ chìhjiksyù; chìhjiksèun (M: fūng) ❷ háusauh ❸ seuhnchùhng

resilience; -ency N: ❶ daahnlihk; daahnsing ❷ jingsàhn fùifuhklihk; fuhkyùhnlihk ❸ seuhnyinglihk

resilient SV: ❶ yáuh daahnsing ge ❷ wuhtput ge

resin N: ❶ syuhjì (M: tiuh) ❷ chùhnghèung

resist FV: ❶ dáikong (an attack; enemy; disease; temptation) ~ *gùnggīk*; ~ *dihk yàhn*; ~ *jahtbehng*; ~ *yáuhwaahk* ❷ jódóng ❸ deuikong ❹ yánjyuh (laughing) ~ *siu*

resistance N: ❶ (to an attack) dáikong ❷ (to disease) dáikonglihk ❸ jólihk ❹ (electricity) dihnjó * **a line of least resistance** PH: jólihk jeuisai (síu) ge fòngheung

resistant SV: dáikong ge * **resistant to** Patt: dáikong N ge

resistivity N: (physics) dihnjóleuht; kongsing

resistless SV: ❶ mhhóyíh dáikong ge ❷ móuh dáikonglihk ge

resistor N: (electric) dihnjóhei (M: ga)

resit N: (an examination) bātsíh bóuháau

resolute SV: ❶ (resolved) gìnkyut ge ❷ yúhnggám ge

resolution N: ❶ (resoluteness; firmness) kyutsàm (M: go) ❷ gìnkyut ❸ gáaikyut ❹ (adopted by a meeting) yíhkyut (ngon) (M: go) ❺ fàngáai ❻ kyutdyunlihk (M: go) ❼ (medical) siut
eui * **made (come to, take) a resolution** VO: hah kyutsàm * **pass a resolution** VO: tùnggwo kyutyíh

resolve FV: ❶ gáaikyut (difficulty) ~ *kwannàahn* ❷ kyutdihng (a matter) ~ *yātgihn sih* ❸ kyutsàm ❹ gáaidaap (problem) ~ *mahntàih* ❺ (chemistry) fàngáai ❻ siuchèuih ❼ yùhnggáai N: ❶ kyutsàm; kyutyi (M: go) ❷ gìndihng * **be resolved to (go)** FV: kyutsàm (heui) * **resolve into** RV: ① fàngáaisihng ② gwàigitwàih * **resolve a chemical compound** FV: fàngáai * **resolve by vote** FV: bíukyut

resolved SV: kyutsàm ge

resonance N: ❶ guhngmìhng ❷ fáanhéung ❸ guhngjanjí * **vocal resonance** N: sìngyàm fáanhéung

resonant SV: guhngmìhng

ge

resort N: ❶ beihsyú singdeih (M: go, daat) ❷ pàhngje ❸ sáudyuhn (M: go) PH: sìhsìh heui ge deihfòng FV: ❶ sìhsìh heui ❷ kàuhjoh ❸ yíkaau * **in the last resort** PH: jokwàih jeuihauh ge sáudyuhn * **a summer resort** N: beihsyú-deih (M: go, daat)

resound FV: ❶ guhngmìhng ❷ wùihhéung ❸ chyùhnbo ❹ chēutméng

resounding SV: ❶ guhng-mìhng ge ❷ héungleuhng ge ❸ kèuhngliht ge

resource N: ❶ (accommodate, help, relief) lòihyùhn ❷ (of a person) gèiji ❸ sìuhín

resources N: ❶ (of a country) fuyùhn; jìyùhn; chòihyùhn ❷ (financial means) chòihlihk * **natural resources** N: jihyìhn jìyùhn

resourceful SV: ❶ (of a person) jūkji dòmàuh ge ❷ (of a country) jìyùhn fùngfu ge ❸ yáuh baahnfaat ge; yáuh bápau ge

respect N: ❶ (as person) jyùnging; gingyi ❷ (as others' right) jyùnjuhng ❸ juhngsih ❹ fòngmihn FV: ❶ jyùnging (an honest man) ~ *sìhngsaht ge yàhn* ❷ jyùnjuhng (others) ~ *yàhndeih* ❸ jyuyi ❹ gwàanyù * **in all respects; in every respect** PH: hái gokfòngmihn * **in respect that . . .** RV: háauleuihhdou * **in (with) respect to (of)** CV: gwàanyù Patt: jauh N làihgóng * **in this respect** PH: hái nīfòngmihn * **without respect to** PH: m̀yuhnyi

respectable SV: ❶ hóging

ge ❷ yáuh hóu mìhngyuh ge ❸ m̀síu ge

respectful SV: ❶ bíusih jyùnging ge ❷ yáuh láihmaauh ge

respecting CV: gwàanyù

respective SV: ❶ gobiht ge ❷ gokgo ge

respectively A: ❶ fànbiht gám ❷ gobiht gám

respiration N: fùkāp VO: táuhei * **artificial respiration** N: yàhngùng fùkāp

respirator N: ❶ háujaau (M: go) ❷ fùkāphei (M: go) ❸ fòhngduhk mihngeuih (M: go)

respire FV: fùkāp RV: faatchēut (heimeih)

respite N/FV: ❶ yìhnkèih (M: chi) ❷ wùhnyìhng (M: chi) ❸ jaahmtìhng ❹ yàusīk (M: chi)

resplendent SV: ❶ fàiwòhng ge ❷ chaanlaahn ge

respond FV: ❶ (answer) wùihdaap; daap (question) ~ *mahntàih* ❷ fáanying ❸ fuhjaak (damage) ~ *syúnsāt* * **respond to** FV: héungying * **to respond to kindness** FV: gámyàn

responsibility N: ❶ jaakyahm (M: go) ❷ (debt) fuhdàam ❸ jīkjaak (M: go) ❹ yahmmouh (M: go) * **bear (take) the responsibility for** Patt: fuhhéi PN/N ge jaakyahm * **bear responsibility of** VO: fuhjaak * **sense of responsibility** N: jaakyahmsàm; jaakyahmgáam (M: go)

responsible SV: ❶ yáuh jaakyahm ge ❷ fuhjaak ge ❸

(trust worthy) **hókaau** ge ∗ **responsible for** FV: **dàamfuh** Patt: deui PN/N fuhjaak

ressentiment N: (law) bātpìhnggám (M: go)

rest N: ❶ yàusīk ❷ jihngjí ❸ séi ❹ jichihmaht FV: ❶ táu; yàusīk ❷ fong (hái) ❸ fan ❹ seunlaaih; yíkaau ❺ gwàiyù ∗ **among the rest** A: kèihjùng ∗ **and the rest** PH: kèihtà dáng dáng ∗ **at rest** FV: ① yàusīk ② pìhngjihng ∗ **for the rest** PH: jiyù kèihyùh ge ∗ **rest on (upon)** A: gèiyù Patt: waih PN/N sójichìh FV: ① saanbouh hái ② (eyes) ngáahn dihngdihng ∗ **take a rest** FV: yàusīk yātjahnggāan; yàusīkháh ∗ **rest against** FV: ① (for people) ngàai hái ② (for things) baahng hái ∗ **rest assured that** FV/SV: fongsàm ∗ **to put a person's mind at rest** PH: lihngdou yàhn ngònsàm

restaurant N: ❶ faahndim (M: gàan) ❷ choigún (M: gàan) ❸ (western food) chāangún; chāansāt; chāantēng (M: gàan) ❹ (chinese food) jáulàuh; jáugā (M: gàan) ❺ (tea house) chàhgēui; chàhlàuh; chàhsāt (M: gàan)

restful SV: ❶ pìhngjihng ge ❷ nìhngjihng ge

restitution N: ❶ pùihsèuhng ❷ gwàiwàahn ❸ (physics) fùifuhk

restive SV: ❶ gwahtkéuhng ge ❷ m̀ngòndihng ge

restless SV: ❶ m̀ngòndihng ge ❷ móuh yàusīk ge; móuh fan ge

restorative SV: fùifuhk gihnhòng ge N: ❶ hìngfáhn

yeuhk (M: nāp) ❷ fùifuhkjài ❸ bóuyeuhk (M: wún)

restore FV: ❶ fùifuhk ~ dihtjeuih ❷ sàuléih ~ ngūk RV: ❶ (sickness, relationship) hóufàan ❷ (money) gàaufàan ❸ (order) fùifuhkfàan VO: fuhkjīk ∗ **restore to the former condition** VO: fùifuhk yùhnjohng ∗ **restore friendship** VO: fùifuhk gámchìhng ∗ **restore diplomatic relations** VO: fùifuhk ngoihgàau gwàanhaih; fùifuhk bònggàau ∗ **restore to the throne** VO: fuhkwaih

restrain FV: ❶ (control) yeukchūk (freedom) ~ PN ge jihyàuh ❷ gúnchūk (child) ~ saimānjái ❸ yánjyuh (laughing) ~ siu ❹ gàamgam (a person) ~ yātgo yàhn ❺ jaijí; gamjí (curiosity) ~ houkèihsàm

restraint N: ❶ yīkjai ❷ haahnjai ❸ yeukchūk ❹ gàamgam

restrict FV: ❶ (limit) haahnjai ❷ (as one's vision) jèjyuh ❸ jaijí

restriction N: ❶ haahnjai ❷ haahndihng ❸ yeukchūk

restrictive SV: ❶ haahnjai ge ❷ yeukchūk ge ❸ haahndihng ge

result N: ❶ (consequence) gitgwó; gitguhk ❷ (of an experiment, analysis examinations etc) sìhngjīk (M: chi) ❸ (of medicine) gùnghaauh ❹ gaisyun gitgwó FV: ❶ cháansàng; héiyù; yàuhyù ❷ douhji ❸ gitgwó haih ∗ **as a result** MA: ① sóyíh ② gitgwó ∗ **in result** N: ① gitguhk (M: go) ② gitgwó (M: go) ∗ **result from** FV: héiyù; yàuhyù ∗ **result in** A/N: ①

gitguhk (M: go) ② gitgwó (M: go) * **without result** Adv. PH: hòuhmòuh gitgwó gám

resume FV: ❶ (recommence) fùifuhk ❷ joi hòichí ❸ gaijuhk RV: sàufàan * **the work resumes** VO: fùifuhk gùngjok; fuhkyihp * **the train resumes** PH: fóchè gaijuhk hòihàhng * **to resume one's office** VO: fuhkjīk

résumé N: ❶ (France) jaahkyiu ❷ koileuhk ❸ goyàhn gáanlihk

resurrect FV: ❶ fuhkhìng ❷ gaijuhk ❸ fuhkwuht RV: (coll.) gwahthéi; gwahtchēut (an old bone) ~ *yātgauh gwāttàuh* PH: ❶ lihngdou sòuséng ❷ lihngdou fuhkwuht

Resurrection N: ❶ fuhk-wuht (M: chi) ❷ sòuséng ❸ fuhkyuhng * **the resurrection** N: Yèhsōu fuhkwuht jit * **the resurrection of Jesus** PH: Yèhsōu fuhkwuht

resuscitate FV: ❶ sòuséng ❷ fuhkhìng N: (medical) fuhksòuhei (M: ga)

retail N: lihng sauh SV: lihnggù ge; sáanmaaih ge A: lihngmaaih; lihng gù FV: ❶ sáanmaaih; lihnggù ❷ chyùhnbo * **at retail** A: lihngsìng gám * **retail business** N: lihngsauhsàangyi; sáanmaaih sàangyi * **retail price** N: sáanmaaih ge gachìhn; lihngsauh ge gachìhn * **the retail department** N: lihngmaaihbouh (M: go)

retailer N: lihngsauhsēung; lihngùsēung (M: go) PH: chyùhn bo làuhyìhn ge yàhn (M: go)

retain FV: ❶ (continue to hold) bóulàuh (old custom) ~ *gauh ge jaahpjuhk* ❷ bóuchìh ❸ geijyuh (the facts) ~ *sihsaht* ❹ chéng; pingchíng (lawyer) ~ *leuhtsī* N: (keep back) làuhfàan * **retain in office** FV: làuhyahm * **retain heat** FV: bóunyúhn

retainer N: ❶ sihchùhng (M: go) ❷ mùhnhaak (M: go) ❸ bóulàuhkyùhn (M: go) ❹ leuhtsīfai (M: bāt)

retake PH: ❶ joi ló ❷ (movies, films) joi sipyíng ❸ joi lófàan ❹ joi dyuht fàanlàih

retaliate FV: boufuhk VO: (to fight back with hands) wàahnsáu

retard FV/N: ❶ (delay) jóchìh; yihnchìh ❷ (impede) fòhngngoih; jóngoih ❸ gáam-chūk * **retard progress** VO: fòhngngoih jeunbouh * **mentally retarded child** N: baahkchìjái (M: go)

retardation N: ❶ jóngoih ❷ jójaih

retch FV: ngáu; jokngáu

retell PH: joi góng

retention N: ❶ bóulàuh ❷ bóuchìhlihk ❸ geiyīklihk ❹ kaulàuh ❺ (medical) làuhjaih; baijí * **retention of urine** N: bainiuhjing

retentive SV: ❶ bóuchìh ge ❷ geiyīklihkkèuhng ge ❸ yihchìuhsáp ge

reticence N: chàhmmahk

reticulate SV: móhngjohng ge PH: ❶ lihngdou yáuh móhng ge yìhng johng ❷ fànsìhng sai fònggaak

retina N: (anatomy) sih-móhngmók; ngáahnkàuh móhngmók

retinal PH: sihmóhngmók ge

retinue N: ❶ chèuihyùhn (M: go) ❷ sihchùhng (M: go)

retire FV: ❶ (from service) teuijīk ❷ (on account of age) goulóuh; teuiyàu ❸ chìhteui RV: sàufàan (stocks etc) ~ gúpiu PH: ❶ (go to bed) heui fangaau ❷ (military) lihngdou chitteui; lihngdou yáhnteui ✲ retire on a pension PH: léhng yéuhnglóuhgām teuiyàu

retired SV: ❶ yáhnteui ge ❷ yàujihng ge ❸ tihngyihp ge ❹ teuijīk ge ✲ retired pay N: teuiyàugām (M: bāt)

retirement N: ❶ teuiyán ❷ teuijīk ❸ yàujihng deihfòng (M: daat)

retort N: ❶ fáanbok ❷ náu jyun ❸ (chemistry) jìnglauhhei (M: ga) FV. ❶ fáanbok ❷ náujyun

retouch FV/N: ❶ (printing) yeuhnsīk ❷ (photo, negative) sàumìuh

retrace PH: ❶ joi taamchàh ❷ fàanfàan jyuntàuh ❸ hàahn-fàan yùhnlòih gótìuh louh

retract FV: chéuisìu PH: sūkfàan yahpheui RV: sàufàan

retractable PH: ❶ hóyíh chitwùih ge ❷ hóyíh sàusūk ge

retractation N: ❶ (opinion) chéuisìu ❷ chitsìu

retreat FV: ❶ teui ❷ (of an army) chitteui ❸ yáhnteui VO: ❶ (of an army) teuibīng N: ❶ yàuyéuhngdeih ❷ yánbeihsó (M: gàan) ✲ beat a retreat VO: dá teuitòhnggú ✲ retreat from Patt: hái N teui chēut ✲ retreat into RV; teuiyahp ✲ retreat to a position and make a stand Patt: teuisáu PW

retrench FV: ❶ jitsáang (expenses) ~ jìchēut ❷ sàanchèuih; sáangleuhk (privileges) ~ dahkkyùhn ❸ gánsūk ❹ chòihgáam

retrenchment N: ❶ jitsáang ❷ sáangleuhk ❸ (military) hòuhkàu (M: tiuh) ❹ (military) bóuléuih (M: go)

retribution N: ❶ chìhngfaht ❷ bouying ❸ boufuhk ❹ bouchàuh

retrieve FV: ❶ fùifuhk (fortunes) ~ chòihcháan ❷ nèihbóu; bóugau (a loss or defeat) ~ syúnsāt waahkjé sātbaaih RV: wánfàan

retroact FV: ❶ fáanduhng ❷ (law) jèuisou

retrocede FV: ❶ gàauwàahn; gwàiwàahn (land) ~ líhngtóu ❷ (medical) noihgūng

retrograde SV: ❶ dóuteui ge; hauhteui ge ❷ yihkhàhng ge ❸ dìndóu ge FV: ❶ teuifa ❷ sèuilohk ❸ (astronomy) yihkhàhng VO: teuibouh A: ❶ yihkhàhng gám ❷ dóulàuh gám

retrogression N: ❶ dóuteui ❷ teuibouh ❸ sèuiteui ❹ (biology) teui fa ❺ (anatomy) yihkhàhng wahnduhng

retrogressive SV: ❶ teuibouh ge ❷ teuifa ge ❸ sèuiteui ge ❹ dohlohk ge

retroject PH: ❶ heung hauh (bihn) pàau ❷ heung hauhtàuhseh ❸ séungfàan jyuntàuh RV: dámfàan

retrorse PH: ❶ heung hauh wàan ge ❷ heung hah wàan ge ❸ hauh wàan ge

retrospect FV/N: ❶ wùihgu ❷ jèuisou ❸ geiwóhng

retrospection N: ❶ wùih-gu ❷ jèuiséung

retrospective PH: ❶ wùihgu ge ❷ jèuiséung ge

return FV: ❶ fàanlàih (home) ~ *ngūkkéi* ❷ fàan heui ❸ wàahn (articles) ~ *syù;* ~ *chín* ❹ wùihfuhk (old customs) ~ *gauh jaahpgwaan* ❺ wùihdaap (question) ~ *mahntàih* ❻ fáanseh ❼ syúngéui (members in the council) ~ *yíhyùhn* N: ❶ fuhkfaat ❷ wùihchìhng ❸ boudaap ❹ fûifuhk ❺ bougou (M: go) ❻ leihyeuhn (M: bāt) * **in return** PH: jokwàih boudaap * **in return for** FV: taiwuhn PH: jokwàih boudaap * **many happy returns (of the day!)** PH: (sàangyaht, jityaht) jūk néih chèuhngsauh * **return address** N: wùihseun deihjí (M: go) * **return like for like** IE: yíh ngàh wàahn ngàh * **to return** (coll.) yìhn'gwài jingjyún

reunion PH: ❶ joi githahp ❷ joi túngyāt ❸ chùhng jeuih N: tyùhnyùhn

Reuter(s) N: (British) Louhtauséh (Reuter's News Agency)

revamp FV: ❶ bóujyuht ❷ sàujíng ❸ fàansàn

reveal FV: ❶ (let out secret) sitlauh; sitlouh ~ *beimaht* ❷ (indicate display or show) hínchēut; hínsih ❸ jínyihn ❹ (by a deity) káisih N: chēungjāk * **to reveal oneself** VO: hínsih sànfán

revel FV: ❶ fùnyin ❷ joklohk ❸ chàhmmàih (books) ~ *syùbún* N: ❶ jáuyin ❷ kòhng fūn

revelation N: ❶ kitlouh ❷ hínsih (M: chi) ❸ káisih (M: go) * **Book of Revelations** N: káisihluhk (M: bún)

revenge N/FV: bousàuh; boufuhk * **be revenged on somebody; have (take) revenge on (upon) somebody** Patt: heung PN bousàuh * **in revenge** A: boufuhk gám

revengeful SV: ❶ geisàuh ge ❷ boufuhk ge

revenue N: ❶ (of an individual) sàuyahp; jeunghohng yahpsīk ❷ (of the state) seuisàu ❸ (customs) gwàanseui ❹ seuimouhchyúh (M: gàan) ❺ seuimouhgùn (M: go) * **revenue office** N: seuimouhgúk (M: gàan) * **revenue stamp** N: yanfā (M: go)

reverberate FV: ❶ fáanhéung ❷ (light, heat etc) fáanseh ❸ fáanwùih

revere FV: jyùnging; jyùnsùhng (sacret things) ~ *sàhnsing sihmaht*

reverence N: ❶ jyùnging ❷ gingyi ❸ gūkgùng (M: go) ❹ jyùnyihm (M: go) FV: jyùnging * **make a reverence** VO: gūk yātgo gùng * **show reverence to (a person)** FV: jyùnging * **show reverence (to god)** FV: gingwai . . . * **show reve-**

rence (to parents) FV: haauging

reverend PH: yìnggòi dāk-dóu jyùnging ge N: muhksī (M: go)

reverent SV: ❶ jyùnging ge ❷ kìhnsìhng ge

reverie, revery N: ❶ hùngséung; waahnséung (M: go) ❷ (music) waahnséungkūk (M: sáu)

reverse FV: ❶ dìndóu (order) ~ *chijeuih* ❷ dóujyun (the bottle) ~ *go jèun* ❸ dóuteui ❹ chéuisiu (a decision) ~ *kyutdihng* ❺ tanhauh (the car) ~ *ga chè* SV: ❶ sèungfáan ge ❷ dìndóu ge ❸ (coin) fáanmihn ge; buimihn ge N: ❶ (idea) sèungfáan ❷ fáanmihn ❸ dìndóu ❹ chojit (M: go) ✻ **in reverse** N: sèungfáan ✻ **in reverse order** VO: dìndóu chijeuih ✻ **quite (just) the reverse = the very reverse** PH: ngāamngāam sèung fáan

reversion N: ❶ fuhkyùhn (M: chi) ❷ fáanjyun ❸ gaisìhngkyùhn (M: go) ✻ **reversion to type** N: fáanjóu

revert VO: fùifuhk yùhn-johng FV: ❶ gwàisuhk ❷ dìndóu ✻ **revert to** RV: fàandou FV: gwàisuhk

revertant N: fáanjóuwàih-chyùhnjé (M: go)

review FV/N: ❶ gímchàh (the fleet) (M: chi) ~ *laahm déui* ❷ háauchaat ❸ gímyuht (military) ~ *gwàndéui* ❹ (for newspaper) pìhngleuhn (M: pìn) ❺ wànjaahp (a lesson) ~ *yātfo syù;* ~ *gùngfo* ❻ wùihgu (the past) ~ *gwo heui* ❼ gùnchaat (the situation) ~ *guhksai* ✻ **in**

(under) review PH: hái gímchàh (jì) jùng ✻ **pass in review** PH: ① sauh gímyuht ② beih gímchàh FV: wùihgu ✻ **review a matter** VO: gímtóu yātgihn sih ✻ **reveiw troops** FV/N: gímyuht VO/N: yuht-bìng ✻ **to come under review** VO: jipsauh gímchàh PH: beih háauleuih ✻ **to reveiw one's opinion** VO: góibin yigin

revile FV: ❶ féipóhng ❷ naauh

revise FV: ❶ (manuscript) gaujing; sàudihng; sàujing; gaaudihng; sàugói ❷ (British) wànjaahp (gùngfo) N: (printing) yìhgaauyéung (M: fahn) ✻ **revised edition** N: gaaujing-báan; gaaujingbún; góidihng-báan (M: fahn; bún)

reviser N: ❶ gaaudingjé (M: go) ❷ (printing) gaaudeuiyùhn (M: go)

revisionism N: sàujing jyúyih

revival N: ❶ (of people) sòu-síng ❷ fuhkwuht ❸ (of religion, art, learning etc) fuhkhìng ❹ (energy, health) wùihfuhk ✻ **the revival of classical music** PH: gúdín yàmngohk ge fuhkhìng

revive FV: ❶ fuhkwuht ❷ fùifuhk ❸ fuhkhìng ❹ (recover life) fàansàang PH: chùhngyíng (old film) ~ *gauh hei* RV: (from a faint) séngfàan

revocation N: ❶ (of law) chitsiu ❷ gáaichèuih

revoke FV: ❶ chéuisiu faijí (order, right, treaty etc) ~ *faatlihng* ❷ chitsiù ❸ jiuhwùih

revolt N/FV: ❶ jouhfáan ❷ bouhduhng (M: chi) ❸ héiyih

(M: chi) ❹ buhn lyuhn (M: chi) ❺ jàngwu ❻ fáangám * **to raise a righteous revolt** N/FV: héiyih (M: chi)

revolution N: ❶ (political) gaakmihng ❷ syùhnjyún ❸ (of seasons) chèuhnwàahn ❹ (of a planet) gùngjyún ❺ góigaak; daaih gói bin * **the American Revolution** N: Méihgwok duhklaahp jinjàng * **the great October Socialist Revolution** N: wáidaaih ge sahpyuht séhwúi jyúyih gaakmihng

revolutionary SV: ❶ gaakmihng ge ❷ syùhnjyún ge ❸ góigaaksing ge N: ❶ gaakmihnggâ (M: go) ❷ góigaakjé (M: go) * **revolutionary party** N: gaakmihngdóng (M: go) * **revolutionaries** N: gaakmihngdóng yàhn (M: go)

revolutionist N: ❶ (member) gaakmihngdóng yùhn (M: go) ❷ gaakmihngjé (M: go)

revolutionize FV: ❶ gaakmihngfa ❷ gaaksàn RV: tèuifàan

revolve FV: ❶ (rotate) jyun ❷ wàahnyíu ❸ chèuhnwàahn * **revolve round** Patt: yíu N jyun

revolver N: ❶ lihnfaat sáuchēung (M: bá, jì) ❷ jóléun (M: bá, jì) ❸ syùhnjyunsīk jòngji

revulsion RV: sàufàan; làaifàan N: ❶ (mood) dahtbin ❷ (medical) yáuhdouhfaat

reward N: ❶ bouchàuh ❷ jéung (M: go) ❸ bouying ❹ chàuhlòuhgám; séunggám; jehgám (M: bāt) FV: ❶ boudaap ❷ chàuhlòuh; chàuhjeh (service) ❸ jéungséung ❹ chìhng-

faht ❺ (by an institution or government) bàanjahng (a prize) ~ *yātgo jéung* ❻ (by a master to a servant) dáséung * **in reward for** PH: waih chàuhdaap * **get a reward** VO: dākjéung * **give a reward** VO: (for the recovery of something lost, for the capture of fugitives) chēut fā hùhng * **reward the troops** VO: (after a campaign) wailòuh gwàndéui

rewarding PH: boudaap ge PH: jihkdāk jouh ge

rewardless SV: ❶ móuh bouchàuh ge ❷ tòuhlòuh mòuhgùng ge

reword PH: joigóng (story) FV: góigóng

rework FV: ❶ góijóu ❷ sàujing

rewrite FV: ❶ góisé ❷ ségwo ❸ syùmín daapfūk PH: kòhngyiht ge yìhnleuhn waahkjé sī

rhapsody N: ❶ jeuihsihsī (M: sáu;pìn) ❷ (music) kòhngséungkūk (M: sáu) ❸ kòhnghéi

rhetoric N: ❶ sàuchìhhohk (M: mùhn) ❷ sàuchìhhohk syùjihk (M: bún) ❸ hèuisīk chyìhjóu

rhetorical SV: ❶ sàuchìh ge; (yuhng sàuchìhfaat ge) ❷ kwàjèung ge ❸ chìhjóu leng ge

rhetorician N: ❶ sàuchìhhohkgā; sàuchìhhohkjé (M: go) ❷ hùhngbihngā

rheumatic PH: fùngsāpjing ge N: fùngsāp behngyàhn (M: go) * **rheumatic pains** N: fùngsāptung

rheumatism N: fùngsāp

(jing)

rhinitis N: (medical) beih-yihm

rhinoceros N: sàingàuh (M: jek)

rhinology N: beihfōhohk

rhomb N: ❶ lìhnggok; lìhngyìhng ❷ chèhfōngyìhng

rhyme; rime N: ❶ wáhn ❷ wáhnmàhn ❸ sī (M: sáu) ❹ ngaatwáhnsī (M: sáu, pìn) VO: ngaatwáhn

rhythm N: ❶ jitjau ❷ wáhnleuht

rhythmic(al) SV: ❶ wáhn-leuht ge ❷ yáuh jitjau ge

rib N: ❶ (anatomy) lahkgwāt (M: tìuh) ❷ (of meat) pàaihgwāt (M: faai) ❸ (of leaves) yihpmahk ❹ (of umbrella, fan) gwāt (M: jì) ❺ (of cloth, knitting wear) lìhngsin

ribbon N: ❶ sìdáai (M: tìuh) ❷ (of typewriter) dájihgèisīk-dáai (M: tìuh) ❸ (medal) sauhdáai (M: go)

rice N: ❶ (growing in the field) wòh ❷ (rice grain) gūk (M: nāp) ❸ (hulled) máih (M: nāp, jah, doih, bāau) ❹ (cooked) faahn (M: wún, bòu) ❺ (well hulled rice) baahkmáih ✳ **rice paper** N: syùnjí (M: jèung, faai; daahp)

rich SV: ❶ yáuh chín ge ❷ (productive, minerals) fùngfu ge ❸ jàngwai ge; gwaijuhng ge ❹ mauhsihng ge ❺ (soil) fèihyūk ge ❻ (voice) gau daaihsēng ge ❼ (smell) meihnùhng ge ❽ (clothes) wàhgwai ge; wàhlaih ge ❾ hóusiu ge; yáuh cheui ge ❿ (generous in spending money) fut cheuk ge ✳ **rich in** Patt:

yáuh hóudò N ge ✳ **the rich** N: ① yáuhchínlóu (M: go) ② futlóu (M: go)

rick N: ❶ wòhdēui (M: dèui) ❷ gònchóudēui (M: dèui) VO: dèuisìhng chóudēui

rickets N: ❶ (medical) yúhngwātbehng ❷ kaulàuh-behng

ricksha(w) N: chèjái; yàhnlihkchè (M: ga)

ricochet FV: ❶ (cannon ball; bullet; stone) wùihtiu ❷ tiufèi N: (military) tiudáan (M: nāp)

rid FV: ❶ míhnchèuih; gáai-chèuih (debt) ~ jaaimouh ❷ chèuihheui ✳ **be (get) rid of** FV: báaityut ✳ **rid oneself of** FV: ① báaityut ② chèuihheui

riddle N: ❶ gú (M: go) ❷ màih; màihyúh (M: go) ❸ chòusài (M: go) PH: hóu nàahn jūkmō ge yàhn (M: go) VO: ❶ gáaimàih ❷ chēutmàih ❸ chyùnlūng RV: bokdóu

ride FV: ❶ kèh (horse, etc.) ~ máh ❷ chóh (carriage; bus etc) ~ chè ❸ yáai (bicycles) ~ dàanchē; ~ sàamlèuhnchē ❹ (of vehicles) hàahng N: ❶ léuihhàhng (M: chi) ❷ gàautūng gùnggeuih ✳ **ride in a race** FV: choimáh ✳ **ride down** PH: kèhmáh gónséuhng FV: ① chíndaahp ② jìngfuhk RV: gīkdóu ✳ **ride high** PH: seuhnleih dougihk ✳ **ride off on (side issue)** PH: yuhngjìjit mahntàih wùihbeih yiu dím ✳ **ride out** PH: ngònyìhn douh gwo; pìhngngòn douhgwo

rider PH: kèhmáh ge yàhn (M: go) N: ❶ fuhjāk; fuhmàhn ❷ (mathematics) yingyuhng tàih (M: tìuh)

ridge N: ❶ (animal) bui; jek (M: go) ❷ lihng ❸ (roof) ngūk-jek (M: go) ❹ (mountain) sàan-jek (M: go) ❺ (nose) beihlèuhng PH: ❶ dahthéi ge bouhfahn ❷ sáidou sihngwàih jekjohng ✻ **ridge-beam, -piece, -pole** N: ① (house) jinglèuhng (M: tìuh) ② (tent) wàahng muhk (M: tìuh) ✻ **ridge-way** N: sàanjeklouh (M: tìuh)

ridicule N: ❶ jàausiu ❷ hàihlohk FV: dai (people) ~ yàhn

ridiculous SV: ❶ hóusiu ge ❷ waahtkài ge ❸ fòngmauh ge

rife SV: ❶ làuhhàhng ge ❷ sihnghàhng ge ❸ dò ge

riffraff N: ❶ bouhtòuh (M: go; bāan; kwàhn) ❷ deihmāu (M: go; bāan, kwàhn) ❸ làuhmàhn (M: go; bāan) ❹ faimaht; jàjí

rifle N: bouhchēung; lòihfūk-chēung (M: jì) PH: yuhng bouhchēung sehgīk FV: ❶ chēung gip ❷ tàu (sit)

rifles N: lòihfūk chēungbīng (M: go, deuih)

rift N: ❶ lihtháu (M: go) ❷ la (M: tìuh, go) RV: ❶ pekhòi; paakhòi ❷ tyúhnliht

right SV: ❶ yauh ge ❷ (matter) jingdong ge ❸ (conduct) hóu ge; móuh sih ge ❹ seuhnleih ge ❺ jihk ge ❻ (post) hahpsīk ge ❼ jànjing ge ❽ (words) ngāam ge; jànsaht ge ❾ (time, words, person) sīkdong ge A: ❶ ngāam dougihk ❷ (of good weather) hóu ❸ (correct, proper of a size) ngāam ❹ (immediately) jauh ❺ (completely) yātjihk ❻ m̀cho ❼ heung yauh N: ❶ yauh ❷ yauhmihn ❸

yauhpaai ❹ jingyih ❺ (privilege; legal) kyùhn (leih) (M: go) FV: ❶ dáujing; góijing (errors) ~ cho ngh ❷ jingléih (room) ~ fóng ❸ fùhjing (a ship) ~ jek syùhn ❹ gùngjing (to the oppressed) ~ doih beih ngaatbīk ge yàhn PH: lihngdou fùifuhk jing sèuhng ✻ by **right(s)** A: hahpléih gám ✻ in the right SV: yáuhléih ✻ right about (face) PH: (military) heung hauhjyun ✻ right off (now) A: jīkhāak ✻ to rights FV: jingléih PH: fùifuhk jing-sèuhng ge chìhngyìhng ✻ to the right A: heung yauh ✻ right-handed PH: ① yauh sáu ge ② heung yauh; ③ syùhnjyún ge ✻ right-minded SV: gùngjing ge ✻ right on A: jingkok dougihk ge ✻ right-ward(s) A: heung yauh (ge) ✻ right of ownership N: sóyáuhkyùhn (M: go) ✻ right of priority N: yāusìnkyùhn (M: go) ✻ right to vote N: syúngéuikyùhn; tàuhpiukyùhn (M: go)

righteous SV: ❶ (conduct) jingjihkge ❷ jingyih ge ❸ jingdong ge ❹ sīk dong ge ❺ (upright) jùngjihk ge ❻ (equitable) gùngjing ge

righteousness N: jingyih

rigid SV: ❶ (stiff) gáng ge ❷ (strict rules) yìhm (gaak) ge ❸ (physics) gòngsing ge

rigidity N: ❶ gèungfa ❷ (manner, opinion) gòngjihk ❸ hākbáan

rigor N: ❶ faatláahng ❷ yìhmhòhn ❸ (mortis) gèung-ngaahng

rigorous SV: ❶ (harsh) yìhmlaih ge ❷ (climate) láahng dougihkge ❸ (stern discipline) yìhm; yìhmgaak

rigo(u)r N: ❶ yihmlaih ❷ hòhāk ❸ yihmmaht

rile FV: ❶ (coll.) yéh ❷ gīknàu PH: lihngdou fàahnchou

rill N: ❶ hòhjái (M: tiùh) ❷ kàijái (M: tiùh)

rim N: ❶ (hats, cups, wheels) bīn (M: tiùh) ❷ kwāang (M: go) ❸ séuimín (M: go) PH: ❶ jòngbīn hái ❷ gàbīn hái ❸ sèungbīn hái

rind N: ❶ (fruit) gwópèih (M: faai) ❷ (vegetable) choipèih ❸ (tree) syuhpèih (M: faai) ❹ (animal) saupèih (M: faai) ❺ (external appearance, person and thing) ngoihgùn; ngoihbíu (M: go)

ring N: ❶ hyūn; wàahn (M: go) ❷ gaaijí (M: jek) ❸ (gang) dóng; móhng (M: go) ❹ yùhnyìhng (gìnggeih) chèuhng (M: go) ❺ jūng (M: go) ❻ lìhngsing ❼ héungsing ❽ sìngdiuh (M: go) M: yātbòng; yātkwàhn ✳ **lead the ring** A: sáusìn ✳ **ring at the door** VO: gahm mùhnjūng ✳ **ring down** VO: baimohk ✳ **ring off** VO: gwatyùhn dihnwá ✳ **ring the bell** VO: gahmjūng SV: sìhnggùng ✳ **ring up** VO: dá dihnwá ✳ **jade ring** N: yuhk gaaijí (M: jek) ✳ **engagement ring** N: dihngfàn gaaijí (M: jek) ✳ **earring** N: yíhwáan (M: deui; jek) ✳ **key ring** N: sósìhhyūn (M: go) ✳ **the ring of blackmarketers** N: wòhngngngàuhdóng (M: bàan) ✳ **a spy ring** N: gaandihpmóhng (M: go) ✳ **ring upon ring** A: chàhngchàhng ✳ **ring-leader** N: jeuihfùi; wohsáu (M: go) ✳ **ring-let** N: ① hyūnjái (M: go) ② wàahnmóuh ③ gyúnfaat ✳ **ring-lock** N: mahtmáh jihhòisó (M: go) ✳ **ring-master** PH: máhheityùhn

gúnléihyàhn (M: go) ✳ **ring-way** N: wàahnyìhnglouh (M: tiùh) ✳ **ring-worm** N: (gāmchìhn) sín ✳ **have ring-worm** VO: sàangsín ✳ **ring-ster** N: (America) jaahptyùhn sìhngyùhn (M: bàan; go)

ring FV: ❶ bàauwàih ❷ wàahnyíuh ❸ (sound) héung ❹ wàihyíuh (enemy) ~ *dihkyàhn* VO: ❶ gahmjūng ❷ dá dihnwá ❸ (bull) daai wàahn ❹ mōkpèih ✳ **ring at the door** VO: gahm mùhnjūng ✳ **ring down** VO: baimohk ✳ **ring off** VO: sàujó dihnwá ✳ **ring up** VO: dá dihnwá PH: yuhng dihnwá lyùhnlok

ringer N: ❶ hàaujùngyàhn (M: go) ❷ yìuhlìhngyàhn (M: go) ❸ titwàahn (M: go) ❹ héifongàu (M: go)

rink N: làuhbìngchèuhng (M: go) VO: làuhbìng

rinse FV: ❶ piusái ❷ chìngsái (clothes) ~ *dī sāam* ❸ lóng (mouth) ~ *háu* ❹ yíhmfaatyihk (M: jèun) PH: yuhng séui tànsihk

riot N: ❶ naauhsih ❷ bouhlyuhn; bouhduhng (M: chi) ❸ sòuduhng (M: chi) ❹ fongdohng FV: ❶ sòuyíu ❷ fùnnaauh ❸ sòuduhng

rioter N: bouhtòuh; bouhduhng fahnjí (M: go)

rip RV: ❶ (by tearing with light action) sihòi; chaakhòi (letter) ~ *fùng seun* ❷ (by tearing with strong action) chéhòi ❸ mōkhòi ❹ (use knife) pekhòi (the firewood) ~ *dī chàaih* ❺ lihthòi FV: ❶ (sl.) tàu ❷ (sl.) chéung N: ❶ lihtháu (M: go) ❷ lohngjí ❸ lyutmáh (M: jek) ❹ faimaht (M: dèui) ✳ **rip off** N: ①

chéung ② ja

ripe SV: ❶ sìhngsuhk ge ❷ lóuhlihn ge ❸ sīkhahp sihk ge ❹ (fruit) suhk ge PH: jéunbeih hóu ge * **a person of ripe years** N: sìhng nìhnyàhn; sìhng yàhn; daaihyàhn (M: go) * **soon ripe, soon rotten** IE: jóusuhk jóulaahn

ripple N: ❶ (of water) bòmàhn; lihnyí ❷ (of hair) bòmàhn (M: go) ❸ sìnglohng (M: go) ❹ (America) chín VO: héi bòmàhn

rise VO: ❶ héisàn; héichòhng ❷ (get up from sitting) kéih héi sàn ❸ (move upward) sìngséuhng heui; fèiséuhng heui FV: ❶ (of the sun) chēut ❷ (of the prices) héi; ~ *ga* ❸ (of water) jeung; séui daaih ❹ tàihgòu ❺ fuhksòu ❻ (river) héiyùhn ❼ janfáhn (spirit) ~ *jìngsàhn* ❽ (of temperature) gòu N: ❶ (ballon) seuhngsìng ❷ gòudeih (M: daat) ❸ tàhnggwai ❹ sìngkāp * **give rise to** PH: lihngdou sìngkāp FV: douhji * **on the rise** FV: seuhngsìng; jàngséung * **take its rise in** FV: faatyùhnyù * **the rise and fall** N: ① hingmòhng ② sihngsèui * **rise to fame** VO: sìhngmìhng

risk N: ❶ (danger) ngàihhím (M: go) ❷ mouhhím (M: chi) ❸ bóuhím gàmngáak (M: bāt) ❹ ngàihhím fahnjí (M: go) * **at risk** PH: ① ngàihhgèi seifuhk ge ② mbeihyahn ge Patt: mouh N ge ngàihhím * **at any risk** PH: bātsīk mouh yātchai ge ngàihhím; bātgu yātchai Patt: mòuhleuhn dím dōu . . .* **at the risk of** PATT: mouh N ge ngàihhím * **run risks, take a risk** VO: mouhhím * **risk one's life** VO: ① mouhhím ②

pìngmehng

rite N: ❶ yìhsīk (M: go) ❷ (dín) láih (M: go) ❸ gwaanlaih (M: go, tiuh) * **funeral rites** N: sòngláih (M: go)

ritual PH: ❶ yìhsīk ge ❷ dínláih ge N: yìhsīk

rituals PH: yìhsīk ge géuihàhng

rival N: gingjàngjé; deuisáu; dihksáu (M: go) FV: ❶ gingjàng ❷ deuikong * **rival in love** N: chìhngdihk (M: go) * **without a rival** PH: ① mòuhdihk ② jeui hóu

rivalry N: ❶ gingjàng ❷ dihkdeui

river N: ❶ hòh (M: tiuh) ❷ gòng (M: tiuh) ❸ geuihlàuh (tiuh) * **down (up) the river** PH: heung hah (seuhng) yàuh sái * **river-bed** N: hòhchòhng; hòhdái (M: go) * **river-head** N: hòhyùhn * **river-horse** N: (animal) hòhmáh (M: jek) * **river-side** N: hòhbīn; gòngbīn (M: go) * **Yellow River** N: Wòhnghòh (M: tiuh) * **Yangtze River** N: Chèuhnggòng; Yèuhngjígòng (M: tiuh) * **Pearl River** N: Jyūgōng (M: tiuh) * **river valley** N: làuhwihk (M: go) * **river water** N: hòhséui

rivers PH: daaihleuhng

rivulet N: ❶ hòhjái (M: tiuh) ❷ kàiláuh (M: tiuh)

road N: ❶ louh; gāaidouh; douhlouh (M: tiuh) ❷ (thoroughfare) máhlouh (M: tiuh) ❸ (highway) gùnglouh (M: tiuh) ❹ (main road) daaihlouh (M: tiuh) ❺ (side road) síulouh; louhjái (M: tiuh) * **in the road** VO: dóngjyuh louh SV: jólouh ge * **on the road** PH: (America) hái tòuhjùng * **road-block** N: douhlouh jeungngoih * **road-book** N: léuihhàhng jínàahm (M: bún) * **road-side** N: louhpòhng (M: go) * **road-way** N: chèhàhng louh (M: tìuh) * **roadster** N: ① hòipùhngchè (M: ga) ② dàanchè (M: ga) * **road sign** N: louhbīu (M: go) * **to get out of the road** VO: yeuhnglouh

roam N/FV: làuhdohng * **roaming from place to place** PH: dousyu làuhlohng; làuhlèih lóngdohng

roar PH: ❶ daaihsèng gám giu ❷ (with laughter) daaihsèng gámsiu FV: (of animals) giu * **the roar of cannon** PH: paausèng lùhnglùhng * **the roar of thunder** PH: lèuihsèng lùhnglùhng

roast FV: ❶ sìu; hàau ❷ buih (coffee beans) ~ gòn gafēdáu ❸ jyú; bòu (coffee) ~ gafē ❹ jūkluhng (person) ~ yàhn ❺ hòjaak PH: lìhngdou nyúhnwòh SV: ❶ sìuhàau ge ❷ buih ge N: ❶ hàauyuhk; sìuyuhk (M: gauh; faai) ❷ sìuhàau * **roast duck** N: sìungáap (M: jek) * **roast pig** N: sìujyū (M: jek) * **roast goose** N: sìungó (M: jek)

roaster N: ❶ sìuhàaujé (M: go) ❷ sìuhàau yuhnggeuih (M: gihn) ❸ (chicken, duck) hàaumaht (M: jek)

rob FV: ❶ chéung ❷ dágip ❸ mōkdyuht (human right) ~ yàhn ge kyùhnleih

robber N: chaahk; cháak (M: go) * **robber's den** N: chaahk dau (M: go)

robbery N: ❶ chéunggip (M: chi) ❷ douhsit (M: chi) ❸

chéunggipjeuih (M: tìuh)

robe N: ❶ pòuh (M: gihn) ❷ yuhkyì (M: gihn) ❸ pèigìn (M: gihn)

robes N: ❶ láihfuhk (M: gihn, tou) ❷ faatyì (M: gihn) ❸ jaifuhk (M: gihn; tou) FV: jeuk * **royal robes** N: wòhngfuhk (M: gihn, tou) * **a robe of office** N: gùnfuhk (M: gihn, tou)

robot N: ❶ gèihaaihyàhn (M: go) ❷ mòuhyàhn gwàngjagèi (M: ga) ❸ jihduhnggèi (M: ga)

robotics N: ❶ yìuhhung-hohk (M: mùhn) ❷ gèihaaih-yàhnhohk (M: mùhn)

robust SV: ❶ (strong and sturdy) fèihjong ge ❷ (health) kèuhngjong ge; jonggihn ge ❸ chòujong ge ❹ gìnkèuhng ge

rock N: ❶ sehk (tàuh) (M: gauh, faai) ❷ ngamsehk ❸ ngamjìu FV: ❶ yìuhduhng ❷ janduhng * **on the rocks** VO: ① jūkjiu ② pocháan FV: wáiwaaih * **rock and roll** N: yìuhbáaimóuh VO: tiu yìuhbáaimóuh * **rock oil** N: sehkyàuh (M: túng, gun) * **rock salt** N: sehkyìhm * **rock-tar** N: chúhngyàuh; sàang sehkyàuh * **rock wool** N: sehkmìhn * **rock-work** N: ① chòusehkgùng ② gásàan (M: go) ③ pàhngàahmseuht

rockery N: gásàan (M: go)

rocket N: ❶ fójin (M: jì) ❷ fójin faatduhnggèi (M: ga) VO: faatseh fójin FV: fèichùk seuhngsìng; heungseuhng jihk chùng * **rocket-drome** N: fó-jin faatsehchèuhng (M: go) * **rocketeer** N: fójin jyùngā (M: go) * **rocketery** N: fójinhohk (M: mùhn)

rocking SV: yìuhduhng ge; yìuhbáai ge PH: lūklàih lūkheui N: yìuhduhng * **rocking chair** N: yìuhyí (M: jèung)

rod M: jì N: ❶ (clothes line) gòn (M: jì) ❷ (walking stick) jéung (M: jì) * **fishing rod** N: diuyùhgōn (M: jì) * **iron rod** N: titjì (M: jì) * **spare the rod and spoil the child** IE: saimānjái bātdá bātsìhngchòih

roe N: ❶ (fish eggs) yùhchēun (M: gauh) ❷ lúkjái (M: jek)

rogue N: ❶ dáaitòuh (M: go, bàan) ❷ làuhmàhn (M: go) ❸ mòuhláai (M: go) ❹ gwònggwan (M: go)

role N: ❶ (play) goksīk (M: go) ❷ yahmmouh; jīkfahn ❸ jokyuhng (M: go) * **fill the role of** PH: dàamdòng N ge yahmmouh * **play the role of** PH: ① baahnyín N goksīk ② héi N jokyuhng * **title role** N: jyúyiu goksīk (M: go) * **the leading role** N: jyúyúgok (M: go)

roll FV: ❶ (turn over and over and move ahead) lūk ❷ (making thin by rolling something over it) ngàahn ❸ (of a ship) ngòuh ❹ (eyes) jyunduhng RV: ❶ (shape a flat thing into a spiral) gyún héi (map, rug) ~ faai deihjīn ❷ (sleeves or pant legs only) ngaaphéi (sleeves) ~ sàamjauh N: ❶ yātgyún ❷ yāttyùhn ❸ yìuhbáai ❹ lùhnglúngsèng ❺ mihngdāan (M: fahn) ❻ ngongyún ❼ jínngaatgèi (M: ga) * **on the roll** PH: hái mìhngchaak seuhng * **roll about** FV: gwánduhng * **roll call** VO: dímméng * **roll off** RV: ① gwaatdóu ② lūklohklàih * **roll on** PH: gaijuhk chìhnjeun * **roll out** RV: jíngpìhng VO: héisàn PH: fèigèi waahkjé sàn cháanbán sáuchi jínláam

* **roll up** RV; gyúnséuhng FV: jīkleuih; jànggā

Roman SV: Lòhmáh ge N: ❶ Lòhmáhyàhn (M: go) ❷ Tìnjyú gaautòuh (M: go) ❸ Lòhmáhjih (M: go) * **Roman Empire** N: Lòhmáh daaigwok (M: go) * **Roman numerals** N: Lòhmáh soujih (M: go)

romanization N: Lòhmáh pìngyām

romance N: ❶ (fiction) lohngmaahn síusyut (M: bún) ❷ jyuhnkèih (M: bún) ❸ ngoichìhnggusih (M: go) ❹ jyuhnkèih màhnhohk ❺ (music) lohngmaahnkūk (M: sáu) ❻ (love affair) lòhmaahnsí; lohngmaahnsí VO: sé jyuhnkèih FV: ❶ hyùnyím ❷ jèuikàuh PH: tàahmchìhng syutngoi * **The Romance Of The Three Kingdoms** N: Sàamgwok (yínyih)

romantic PH: jyuhnkèih síusyut ge SV: ❶ lèihkèih ge ❷ fùnglàuh ge ❸ lohngmaahn jyúyih ge * **romanticism** N: (arts) lohngmaahn jyúyih * **romanticist** N: ① lohngmaahn jyúyih jok gā (M: go) ② lohngmaahn jyúyihjé (M: go)

romp N: wàahnpèih ge yàuhhei FV: yàuhhei

roof N: ❶ (of a house) ngūkdéng; ngūkmín (M: go) ❷ (of a building) làuhdéng (M: go) ❸ (of a car) chèdéng ❹ ngūkkéi VO: pòu ngūkdéng FV: beiwuh * **hit the roof** Adj. PH: nàudāk hóu gányiu * **the roof of the mouth** N: seuhngngngohk (M: go) * **the roof of the world** N: saigaai ngūk jek * **under PN's roof** Patt: hái PN ngūkkéi jouh yàhnhaak * **roof garden** N:

tìntói fàyún (M: go)

roofed   PH: yáuhdéng ge

roofless   PH: ❶ móuh ngūk-déng ge ❷ móuh ngūkkéi ge

rooftree   N: ❶ ngūkdéng ge lèuhngmuhk (M: tìuh) ❷ ngūkdéng (M: go)

rook   N: ❶ baahkjéuingā (M: jek) ❷ pinjí (M: go) VO: ❶ hàau-jūkgong ❷ (gamable) pinchín

rookery   N: ❶ baahkjéuingā; kéihngó dáng dáng ge chàauh (M: go) ❷ pàhnmàhngfāt (M: go) M: kwàhn

room   N: ❶ fóng (M: gàan) ❷ (space, place) deihfòng ❸ (seat) wái (M: go) ❹ chèuhngsó (M: go) ❺ gēiwuih (M: go) FV: jyuhsūk VO: làuhsūk ✻ **give room** PH: teuiyeuhng béi ✻ **in PN's room** PH: ① jiptai máuh yātgo yàhn ② chyúyù máuh yātgo yàhn ge deihwaih ✻ **leave room for** Patt: waih PN làuh yùhdeih ✻ **make room for** PH: yeuhngwaih béi ✻ **no room to turn in** FV: haahp-jaak PH: móuh wuhtduhng ge yùhdeih ✻ **room and board** N: (gùng) sihnsūk ge deihfòng (M: daat)

roomed   PH: yáuh Nu gàan fóng ge

roomer   N: ❶ fòhnghaak; jyuhhaak (M: go) ❷ geisūkjé (M: go)

roomful   SP/N: sèhnggàan-fóng

roommate   N: tùhngfóng (M: go)

roomy   SV: ❶ fùnchóng ge ❷ gwóngdaaih ge

roost   N: ❶ chàimuhk (M: gauh) ❷ jeukchàauh (M: go) ❸ yàusīk ge deihfòng (M: go) ❹ seuihfóng (M: gàan) FV: táu VO: tàuhsūk ✻ **curses come home to roost** IE: hoih yàhn fáan hoih géi

rooster   N: ❶ gāigūng (M: jek) ❷ (America) kòhngmóhng jih daaih ge yàhn

root   N: ❶ (of plant; tooth etc) gàn (M: tìuh) ❷ gànbún ❸ (of matter) gànyùhn ❹ gàngēi (M: go) ❺ bītsèui ge bouhfahn (M: go) ❻ (language) chìhgàn (M: go) ❼ (mathematic) gànsou VO: ❶ sàanggàn FV: ❶ gudìhng ❷ (U.S.A. sl.) púngchèuhng ❸ gúhéi PH: (pigs) yuhng beih jèung nàihtóu fàan héi ✻ **at the root** A: gànbúnseuhng ✻ **go to (get at) the root of** VO; jèuigau gànyùhn ✻ **root and branch** A: ① yùhnchyùhn ② chitdái gám ✻ **root up (out away)** FV: gànchèuih ✻ **take (strike) root** VO: sàanggàn ✻ **root-crop** N: gànchoi jokmaht

rooted   SV: ❶ sàangjó gàn ge ❷ gànsàm ge

rope   N: ❶ síng (M: tìuh) ❷ gáausok (M: tìuh) NuM: yāt-chyun PH: ❶ yuhng síng kwán-bóng ❷ (U.S.A.) yíh yáuh sàang lit ge síng jūk máh, ngàuh dáng dáng ✻ **rope-dancer** N: jáu gongsokjé (M: go) ✻ **rope-way** N: sokdouh (M: tìuh)

ropes   N: ❶ noihchìhng (M: go) ❷ kwàijāk (M: go, tìuh) ✻ **know the ropes** VO: suhksīk noihchìhng, kwàijāk dáng ✻ **on the high ropes** FV: hìngfáhn SV: dākyì VO: faat-nàu ✻ **on the ropes** PH: jauhlàih mdāk ✻ **ropes PN in** Patt: yáhnyáuh PN yahp N

rose N: ❶ (flower) mùihgwai
(fā) (M: déu; jì) ❷ chèuhngmèih
(M: déu; jì) ❸ (colour) sàm-
fánhùhngsīk ❹ yùhnfāchēung
(M: jek; douh)❺ (medical) dàanduhk ＊ **not all roses** PH:
mhaih yùhn chyùhn yùhnmèih
＊ **rose-bay** N: (plant) gaapjūktòuh; sehknàahm (M: pò) ＊
rose-bit N: (machine) mùihfāsó
(M: go) ＊ **rose-bud** N:
mùihgwai fālām (M: go) PH:
leng ge néuihjái (M: go) ＊ **rose-
drop** N: jáuchòuhbeih (M: go)
＊ **rose-window** N: yùhnfāchēung (M: douh) ＊ **rose-
wood** N: hākwòhngtàahn

rosin N: ❶ syuhjì; chùhngjì
❷ chùhnghēung

roster N: ❶ mìhngchaak (M:
bún) ❷ mìhngdāan (M: fahn;
jèung) ❸ dànggei bóu (M: bún)

rostrum N: ❶ gímyuhttòih
(M: go) ❷ sìhng làuh (M: go) ❸
syùhntàuh; syùhnjéui (M: go) ❹
jéui (M: go)

rosy SV: ❶ mùihgwai sīk ge
❷ hùhngyeuhn ge ❸ méihhóu
ge ❹ gwòngmìhng ge PH: yuhng
chèuhngmèih jòngsīk ge ＊
rosy prospects PH: lohkgùn
ge chìhntòuh

rot FV: ❶ (as wood) laahn ❷
(as metal; meat) mùih ❸ fùwái
❹ (for people) sèuiyeuhk ❺ (use
words) hei luhng; jàauluhng ❻
yeuhkdoih N: ❶ fuhsihk;
fuhlaahn ❷ (plant) fuhsihkjing
(M: go) (coll.) wùhsyut;
lyuhngóng SV: mòuhliuh

rotary PH: ❶ jyun ge ❷
syùhnjyun wahnhàhng ge gèi
hei (M: ga) ＊ **rotary action**
FV: jyun ＊ **rotary club** N:
fùhlèuhnséh (M: go)

rotate FV: ❶ (of a wheel)

syùhnjyun; syùhnjyún ❷
lèuhnláu ❸ lèuhn jihk ❹
chèuhnwàahn ❺ (farming)
lèuhnjok

rotation N: ❶ syùhnjyun;
syùhnjyún ❷ (earth) jihjyún ❸
chèuhnwàahn ❹ (physics)
syùhngwòng NuM: yāt hyūn ＊
in rotation A: gàautai gám ＊
make a part of a rotation
PH: jyun géi fahn jì yāt hyūn ＊
in rotation FV: lèuhnláu;
gàautai ＊ **to do something in
rotation** FV: lèuhnláu jouh

rote N: ❶ séigei; kéuhng gei
❷ gèihaaih fòngfaat (M: go) ＊
by rote A: gèihaaih gám

rotten SV: ❶ (decay) laahn
ge❷ (very bad) yáih ge ❸
(government) fuhbaaih ge ❹
chau ge ❺ (luck) waaih ge ❻
yeuhk ge ❼ (coll.) móuh yuhng
ge

rotter N: ❶ (English sl.)
mòuhláai (M: go) ❷ faimaht
(M: gihn) PH: ❶ hówu ge yàhn
(M: go) ❷ móuh yuhng ge yàhn
(M: go)

rotund SV: ❶ yùhn ge ❷
fèih dyūt dyūt ge ❸ sìngyàm
héung leuhng ge

rotunda N: ❶ yùhnyìhng
ginjūkmaht (M: joh) ❷
daaihhah (M: joh)

r(o)uble N: (USSR monetary
unit) Lòuhbou

rouge N: ❶ yìnjì (M: hahp) ❷
sèulhngòu (M: jì) ❸ hùhngtit-
fán VO: ❶ chàh yìnjì ❷ chàh
sèuhn gòu

rough SV: ❶ (not smooth-
surfaced) hàaih ❷ (sketchy)
daaihji (ge) ❸ (severe, difficult)
màhfàahn ❹ chòuchou ❺
(road) nāpdaht ge ❻ mpìhng ge

❼ dòmòuh ge ❽ kòhngbouh ge
❾ (manners, words) chôulóuh
ge ❿ (words) nàahntèng ge ⓫
(life) gàanfú ge A: ❶ chòuchou
gám ❷ (action) chòubouh gám
❸ chòuleuhk gám N: ❶
chòuchoumaht (M: gihn) ❷
chòu bouh ge yàhn (M: go) ❸
meih gàgùng ge yéh (M: gihn)
PH: ❶ lihngdou chôulóuh ❷
lihngdou ṁpìhng FV: ❶ chòujai ❷ chóuyíh ✳ be rough on
SV: chòu ✳ have a rough
time PH: lihkjeuhn gàan sàn ✳
in the rough SV: ① meih
gàgùng ge ② meih yùhngùng
ge ③ chôulóuh A: daaihyeuk ✳
over rough and smooth VO:
lihkjeuhn gàmfú ✳ rough it
VO: gwo gàanfú sàngwuht ✳
rough-and-ready SV:
lóuhchóu sākjaak ge ✳ rough-
and-tumble SV: lyuhn chāt
baat jòu ge N: wahn jin (M: chi)

roughly A: ❶ chòubouh gám
❷ chòuchou gám ❸ koileuhk
gám

round SV: ❶ yùhn ge ❷
kàuhyìhng ge ❸ wùhyìhng ge
❹ (number) yùhnjíng ge ❺
jíngsou ge ❻ làuhcheung ge ❼
(words) sēutjihk ge ❽ (voice)
yùhnyeuhn ge N: ❶ yùhn
(yìhng) maht ❷ hyūn ❸ (fight)
wùihhahp ❹ (for man)
chèuhnsih (M: chi) ❺ guhk ❻
wàahnyìhng (M: go) ❼ tàikáp ❽
yùhn móuh ❾ (human know-
ledge) faahnwàih A: ❶ seichyu
gám ❷ jàuwàih gám ❸
yíuhdouh gám ❹ juhkyāt gám
❺ (hái) fuhgahn gám Patt: hái
. . . ge seijàu PH: ❶ lihngdou
yùhn ❷ lihngdou yùhnmúhn
yùhnsìhng ❸ yíuh N làih
hàahng FV: ❶ chèuhnsih ❷
binyùhn ❸ jeunjìn ✳ all
(right) round A: ① syusyu ②
jàuwàih ✳ all the year round
PH: yātnìhn doutauh N/SP:

sèhngnìhn ✳ look round FV:
① wùih gu ② chàamgùn
yàuhláahm ✳ make one's
rounds; go the rounds FV:
chèuhnsih VO: chàhfóng ✳ go
the round of FV: chyùhn pin
✳ round about A: daaihyeuk
✳ round and round A:
goksyu Adj. PH:
syùhnjyún
ṁtìhng ✳ round off (out) FV:
① yùhnsìhng ② yùhnmúhn gitchūk ✳ round up FV: ① kèui-
jaahp ② dàubouh ✳ round
trip ticket N: lòihwùih fēi (M:
jèung) ✳ round and round Adj
PH: tàhm tàhm jyun ✳ round
worm N: wùihchùhng (M: tìuh)

rounder N: ❶ chèuhnhàhng
jé (M: go) ❷lohngjí (M: go)

roundly A: ❶ yùhnyún déi
❷ chyùhnmín gám ❸ sēutjihk
gám ❹ yìhmlaih gám

rouse FV: ❶ (disturb; make
up) gáauséng ❷ (stir up and
make angry) gīknàu ❸
giuséng
❹ janfáhn ❺ gáau N: (ancient)
jáuwúi; jáuyin (M: go)

roust FV: ❶ kèuijuhk ❷
sáubou ❸ (coll.) kàhn faai
gùngjok

roust-about N: (U.S.A.)
máhtàuh gùngyàhn (M: go)

rout N: ❶ kwúibaaih (M: chi)
❷ máahnwúi (M: go) FV: ❶
dábaaih ❷ gwaht ❸ kéuhngbīk

route N: ❶ louh (M: tìuh) ❷
louhsin (M: tìuh) ❸ louhchìhng
(M: go) ❹ hòhngsin (M: tìuh) ❺
hàhnggwàn mìhnglihng (M: go)
VO: kwàidihnglouhsin PH:
ngon (jiu) louhsin faatsung ✳
take one's route to Patt: dou
PW heui ✳ air route N:
hòhnghùng louhsin (M: tìuh) ✳
sea route N: séuilouh (M: tìuh)

routed FV: ❶ (defeated) dásyújó (as in games) ~ *nīchèuhng béichoi* ❷ dábaaih-jó (as in battle) ~ *nīchèuhng jeung* ✻ **completely routed** IE: yātbaaih tòuhdeih

routine N: ❶ laihhàhng gùngsih (M: gihn) ❷ yaht-sèuhng gùngjok (M: gihn) ❸ sèuhngkwài (M: go) SV: ❶ yahtsèuhng ge ❷ laihhàhng ge

rove N/FV: ❶ làuhlohng ❷ pùihwùih ❸ (weaving) chàusà VO: (weaving) chàusà PH: ❶ (eyes) jyunlàih jyunheui ❷ (love affairs) sihsìh góibin; pìufàt bātdihng

rover N: ❶ yàuhlihkjé (M: go) ❷ làuhlohngjé (M: go) ❸ hóidouh (M: go) ❹ hóidouh-syùhn (M: jek)

row N: ❶ pàaih ❷ hòhngliht (M: go) ❸ gāai (M: tiuh) ❹ jaauhsyùhn (M: jek) ❺ laaht; hòhng FV: jaauhsyùhn ✻ **a hard row to hoe** N: ① kwannaahn ge mahntàih (M: tiuh, go) ② màhfàahn ge sih (M: gihn) ③ gàangeuih yahmmouh (M: gihn) ✻ **a row of** Nu M: yāthòhng (pàaih, liht)

row N: ❶ jàngcháau (M: chi) ❷ ngaaigàau (M: chi) FV: ❶ cháaunaauh ❷ jàngleuhn PH: naauhdāk hóu gányiu

rowdy N: ❶ chòubouh ge yàhn (M: go) ❷ mòuhláai (M: go) SV: ❶ chòubouh ge ❷ hou cháaunaauh ge

royal SV: ❶ daiwòhng ge; wòhnggā ge ❷ gòugwai ge ❸ jòngyìhm ge ❹ sìhngdaaih ge ❺ gihkdaaih ge ✻ **the Royal Navy** N: Yīnggwok Hóigwān (M: deuih) ✻ **the Royal Society** N: (Yīnggwok) Wòhnggā

Hohkwúi (M: go) ✻ **Royal Air Force** N: Wòhnggā Hūnggwān (M: deuih) ✻ **Royal Family** N: Wòhngsāt (M: go) ✻ **royal palace** N: wòhnggùng (M: joh)

royalist N: bóuwòhngdóng (yùhn) (M: go)

royally A: ❶ jòngyìhm gám ❷ gòugwai gám

royalty N: ❶ wòhngkyùhn (M: go) ❷ wòhngwaih (M: go) ❸ wòhngjuhk (M: go) ❹ dahk-kyùhn gàaichàhng (M: go) ❺ báanseui (M: bāt) ❻ jyūnleih kyùhnseui (M: bāt)

rub FV: ❶ (out, off) chaat, maat ❷ mòchaat ❸ chàai ❹ chàh ❺ chò (clothes) ❻ lín; ngonmō ❼ jēut (eyes, alcohol, clothes) ~ *ngáahn;* ~ *fójáu;* ~ *sāam* N: ❶ mòchaat ❷ jeungngoih ❸ fúngchi (M: go) ❹ mòhdōusehk (M: gauh) ✻ **rub down** FV/N: ngonmō ✻ **rub in (into)** RV: chaatyahp FV: fáanfūk góng ✻ **rub off (out)** RV: ① mòhheui ② chaatlāt ✻ **rub up** RV: ① chaatjehng ② giuséng FV: wànjaahp

rubber N: ❶ mòchaatjé (M: go) ❷ chòucho (M: bá) ❸ jeuhngpèih (M: faai) ❹ jeuhng-gàau; syuhgàau ❺ gàaujouh ge gùnggeuih (M: gihn) ❻ lèuhntòi (M: go) ❼ (eraser) gāaucháat (M: gauh) ✻ **rubber-stamp** N/FV: (kāp) jeuhngpèih tòuhjēung (M: go) ✻ **rubber band** N: jeuhng-gàn (M: tiuh)

rubbers N: ❶ séuihàaih (M: deui) ❷ jeungngoih (M: go) VO: chàh jeuhng gàau

rubbish N: ❶ (refuse) laahpsaap (M: dèui, bàau) ❷ faimaht (M: gihn) ❸ mòuh-

rubble N: ❶ seuisehk (M: náp) ❷ seuijyùn (M: dèui, gauh) ❸ ngáh līk (M: dèui) * **rubblework** N: mòuhsehkgùng (chìhng) (M: gihn)

rubella N: (medical) fùngchán

rubicund SV: (face) hùhngyeuhn ge

ruble = rouble N: (Russian money) Lòuhbou

rubric N: ❶ hùhngjih (M: go) ❷ hùhngjih biutàih ❸ sihngkwài (M: go) ❹ ngonyúh (M: geui)

ruby N/PH: ❶ hùhngbóusehk (ge) (M: náp) ❷ sìnhùhngsīk (ge) ❸ hùhng pòuhtòuhjáu (ge) (M: jèun, bùi) * **ruby lips** N: hùhng jéuiseuhn (M: go) * **ruby wine** N: hùhngjáu (M: jèun, bùi)

rucksack N: fàahnbou buidói; fàahnbou builòhng (M: go)

rudder N: ❶ syùhntòh; syùhntáaih (M: go) ❷ (plane) fòngheungtòh (M: go) ❸ jídouh yùhnjàk (M: ji) ❹ jíjàm (M: ji) ❺ líhngdouhjé; jéungtòhjé (M: go) * **rudder-fish** N: jèuisyùhn yú (M: tìuh)

rudderless SV: ❶ móuhtòh ge; móuh táaih ge ❷ móuh líhngdouhyàhn ge

ruddy SV: ❶ hùhng ge ❷ (healthy) heisīk hówu ge ❸ (coll.) hówu ge ❹ tóuyìhm ge

rude SV: ❶ (lacking delicacy) chòulóuh ge ❷ (impolite) móuh-láih ❸ (awakening) dahtyìhn ge ❹ (tools) chòujai ge ❺ (forefathers) meih hòifa ge ❻ (health) chòujong ge ❼ m̀jouhjok ge

rudimental, -tary SV: ❶ gèibún ge ❷ chòbouh ge ❸ (biology) faatyuhk m̀ gihnchyùhn ge

rueful SV: ❶ bèingòi ge; bèisèung ge ❷ fuihahn ge ❸ hólìhn ge ❹ baingai ge

ruffian N: ❶ bouhtòuh (M: go) ❷ móuhláai (M: go)

ruffle FV: ❶ jíngchàauhjó ❷ binchàauh; héijaumàhn ❸ jìyíu VO: faatnàu SV: ngouhmaahn N: ❶ jipbīn (M: go, tìuh) ❷ géngmòuh ❸ bōmàuh; mèihbō ❹ sòuduhng (M: chi) * **without ruffle** PH: bātfòng bātmòhng

rug N: ❶ (used when travelling) háuh mòuhjīn (M: jèung) ❷ háuh deihjīn (M: jèung, faai) ❸ fáan lèuihdaaht gònyíu faatsehgēi (M: ga)

rugby, rugger N: (British) gaamláamkàuh (M: go)

rugged SV: ❶ fùhngsùngmòuh ge ❷ (as mountain road) kēikèui ge ❸ chòuyéh ge ❹ (person) yìhmlaih ge ❺ (U.S.A.) chòujong ge; kèuhngjong ge

ruin N: ❶ wáimiht ❷ bàngkwúi ❸ wohgàn (M: go) FV: ❶ (destroy) wái waaihsaai; powaaih ❷ (spoil) jíngwaaih (health) ~ sàntái ❸ (spoil) jòutaatsaai (material) ~ chòihlíu ❹ muhtlohk

ruined PH: lihngdou pocháan SV: dohlohk ge

ruins N: ❶ (ancient remains)

gújīk; wàihjīk (M: go) ❷ faihèui (M: go) ❸ syúnsāt (M: chi)

rule N: ❶ (regulation) kwàigéui; kwàijāk (M: go, tiùh) ❷ jèungchìhng (M: fahn, bún) ❸ sèuhngkwài (M: go) ❹ (act of ruling) túngjih ❺ chek (M: bá) FV: ❶ túngjih ❷ gúnléih ❸ kwàidihng ❹ chòihdihng ❺ (yuhngchek) waahksin * **as a rule** A: ① tùngsèuhng ② jiulaih * **by rule** PH: jiu kwàidihng A: gèihaaih gám * **hard and fast rule** PH: ngaahngsing gám kwàidihng * **make it a rule** PH: jaahp yíh wàih sèuhng * **rule out** FV: ① pàaihchèuih ② m̀jipsauh * **rule over** FV: jìhléih * **as a rule** A: ① tùngsèuhng ② jiulaih * **according to rule** PH: jiu kwàigéui * **detailed rules** N: saijāk (M: go) * **fundamental rule** N: yùhnjāk (M: go) * **supplementary rule** N: fuhjāk (M: go)

ruler N: ❶ (country) túngjihjé (M: go) ❷ (organization) gúnléihjé (M: go) ❸ chek; gaanchek (M: bá) ❹ (sovereign) yùhnsáu (M: go) ❺ (king) wòhng (M: go) ❻ (emperor) wòhngdai (M: go)

ruling PH: túngjih ge SV: ❶ jyúdouh ge ❷ làuhhàhng ge N: ❶ túngjih ❷ jìpui ❸ chòihpun * **ruling price** N: sìhga

rum N: ❶ tòhngjáu (M: jèun; bùi) ❷ tihmjáu (M: jèun; bùi) ❸ (U.S.A.) jáu (M: jèun; bùi) SV: (English) gúgwaai ge

Rumanian SV: Lòhmáhnèihnga (yàhn; wá) ge N: Lòhmáhnèihnga yàhn (wá) (M: go)

rumble N: ❶ lùhnglúngsèng ❷ chòuhcháausèng ❸ chè-

méihsēung (M: go) Adj. PH: ❶ lùhnglúngsèng ❷ gùhgúsèng FV: (English sl.) táichyùn

ruminate PH: ❶ joi ngáauh ❷ jísai séung chìngchó

rummage FV: ❶ lyuhnchaau ❷ sáuchàh PH: jísai gímchàh N: ❶ fàanchàh (M: chi) ❷ jaahpmaht (dèui) (M: dèui)

rumo(u)r N: ❶ yìuhyìhn ❷ chyùhnmàhn FV: ❶ yiuchyùhn ❷ chyùhnsyut * **it is rumoured that** FV/N: geuisyut * **start (spread, spike) a rumour** VO: jouhhyiuh

rump N: ❶ (animal) tyùhnbouh (M: go) ❷ méihbouh (M: go) ❸ jà ❹ yùhdóng * **rump steak** PH: hauh téuibouh ge yuhkpáai

rumple FV: ❶ jíngchàauh ❷ gáaulyuhn

run FV: ❶ (go fast on foot) jáu ❷ (be in operation) hàahng ❸ (flow, as water, etc.) làuh ❹ (an apparatus or machine) sái ❺ (as in business) jouh ❻ hàhngsái (right) ~ kyùhnleih ❼ jáusí ❽ (coll.) hèifuh ❾ gìngyìhng (business) ~ sàangyi ❿ (hìng) baahn (school; hospital etc.) ~ hohkhaauh; ~ yìyún ⓫ gúnléih ⓬ mouhhím ⓭ gìngsyún (presidency) ~ júngtúng N: ❶ (competition) choipáau (M: chi) ❷ (outing) léuihhàhng (M: chi) ❸ (continuous) lihnjuhk ❹ (run on the bank) jài tàih ❺ (popular selling object) cheungsiu ❻ (route) hàhngchìhng (M: chi) ❼ (transportation route) hòhngsin (M: tiùh) ❽ (music) gāpjau * **get the run of** FV: suhksīk * **have a good run** PH: ① hóu sauh fúnyìhng ② sahpfàn

làuhhàhng * **in the long run**
PH: chùhngchèuhngyùhn làih
góng * **keep the run of** PH:
① gingsèuhng líuhgáai ②
bóuchìh jipchūk * **run across**
PH: ngáuhyìhn yuhdóu * **run
after** FV: jèuichàhm * **run
back** FV: ① wùihgu ② jèuisou
* **run counter to** FV: wàihbui
* **run down** FV: ① tìhng ②
yuhngyùhn RV: ① johngdóu ②
chàhchēut Adj. PH: guih
dougihk * **run in** RV: ①
jáuyahp ② bóuyahp VO: sichè
* **run off** PH: làuhjó heui
VO: ① lèihtàih ② chēutgwáai ③
jeunhàhng kyutchoi RV: yan-
chēut SV: làuhleih * **run out**
RV: ① làuhchēut ② kèihmúhn
FV: yuhngsaai * **run over** RV:
múhnsé FV: ① gwomuhk ②
lūkgwo ③ jíngwo Adj. PH: ①
leuhkléuk góng ② múhnsaai
chēutlàih * **run short** FV:
kyutfaht PH: jauh faai
yuhngyùhn * **run through**
FV: ① sáisaai ② samtau ③
ngàusiu ④ chyùngwo * **run to
an extreme** Adj. PH: jáu gihkdyùn * **run up** PH: ① heung
seuhng jáu ② seunchūk sìhng-
jéung FV: jeung RV: hìnghéi *
run up to RV: ① jáudou ②
daahtdou * **run-in** N: ①
cháaunaauh ② sichè ③ bóugá
bouhfahn * **run-up** N: ①
fèigèi faatduhnggèi siyihm ②
jeuihmohk ③ chìhnjau ④
jeungga * **run around** FV:
gokchín * **run along** PH:
hàahnghòi lā * **run away
with** PN VO: jáulóu * **run by**
FV: jáugwo * **run PN down**
FV: ① (struck down) pungchàn
② (speak ill of) pàipihng; naauh
* **run dry** FV: gòn * **run for
an office** FV: gingsyún * **run
low** PH: yuht làih yuht síu *
run to a place FV: tùng (dou)
PW * **a run** M: (trip) chi

runabout N: ❶ làuhlohngjé

(M: go) ❷ síuyíhng yihyàhn
heichè (téhng) (M: ga; jek)

runaround N: ❶ (U.S.A.)
jeháu ❷ míuhsih

runaway N: ❶ tòuhmòhngjé (M: go) ❷ sìbàn (M: chi) SV:
❶ tòuhjáu ge ❷ sìbàn ge PH:
tyutgèung ge máh (M: jek)

runlet, runnel N: hòhjái
(M: tìuh)

runner PH: jáu ge yàhn (M:
go) N: ❶ choipáaujé (M: go) ❷
jáusìjé (M: go) ❸ (U.S.A.)
tèuisìuyùhn (M: go) ❹
waahthàhng jòngji (M: gihn) *
runner-up N: ❶ (athletics)
ngagwàn (M: go) ❷
daihyihmihng

running SV: ❶ jáu ge ❷
làuhduhng ge ❸ lihnjuhk ge N:
❶ choipáau (M: chi) ❷
gìngyìhng ❸ gúnléih ❹ syùhnjyún * **in (out of) the running** PH: yáuh (móuh) dākdóu
singleih ge gèiwuih * **running
dog** N: jáugáu (M: go, jek)

runt PH: faatyuhk myùhn-
sìhn ge ngáisai duhngjihkmaht
N: ❶ saijúng ge ngáuh (M: jek)
❷ ngáiyàhn (M: go)

runway N: ❶ (for airplane)
páaudouh (M: tìuh) ❷
hòhchòhng (M: go) ❸ hòhdouh
(M: tìuh) ❹ waahtdouh (M. tìuh)
❺ síuging (M: tìuh)

rupee N: (Indian money)
lòuhbéi

rupture N: ❶ poliht❷
kyutliht ❸ (medical) poliht ❹
(burst) litháu (M: go) RV: lìhthòi
FV: (relation) dyuhnjyuht * **a
rupture of diplomatic relations** VO: dyuhnjyuht
bònggàau

rural SV: ❶ hèunghá ge ❷ nùhngchyùn ge ❸ tìhnyùhn ge nùhngyihp ge ✻ **rural area** N: hēungchyùnkēui hèunghá (M: go) ✻ **rural life** N: hēungchyùn sàngwuht ✻ **rural scenery** N: hēungchyùn fùnggíng

rush FV: ❶ chùng ❷ jáu ❸ jaahpgīk ❹ chéungkau RV: chùngyahp ❶ chùnggīk ❷ gīkjàng ❸ yātjúng béichoi ❹ (fuhksihk màhjeuibán ge) faaigám ❺ dàngsàmchóu SV: ❶ gāpsèui ge ❷ chùngmòhng ge ✻ **not worth a rush** PH: yātdī gajihk dōu móuh ✻ **rush hours** N: (traffic) jàisāk sìhgaan ✻ **rush to conclusion** PH: hóufaai lohk gitleuhn ✻ **with a rush** A: ① dahtyìhn ② chùngchūk gám

rusk N: ❶ mihnbāaugōn (M: faai) ❷ cheuibénggōn (M: faai)

russet SV: ❶ jyùgònsīk ge ❷ sáujīk ge N: jyùgònsīk

Russian PH/N: ❶ Ngòhgwok ge; Sòulyùhn ge ❷ Ngòhlòhsiyàhn (ge); Sòulyùhnyàhn (ge) ❸ Ngòhyúh ge

rust N: ❶ sau ❷ tìhng jaih VO: sàangsau FV: bìndeuhn

rustic SV: ❶ (rural) hèunghá ge ❷ (simple and plain) poksou ❸ chòuyéh ge ❹ (artless) lóuhtóu

rusticate VO: hahhēung PH: ❶ sungheui hèunghá ❷ (British) mihnglìhng tìhnhohk N: ❶ hèunghàyàhn (M: go) ❷ nùhngyàhn (M: go)

rustiness N: sàangsau

rustle N/FV: sàhsásèng

rustler N: ❶ wuhtyeukfahn--jí (M: go) ❷ tàuh sàngchūk ge

chaahk (M: go)

rusty SV: ❶ sàangsau ge ❷ fuhsihkjó ge ❸ chàhngauh ge ❹ chìhdeuhn ge ❺ (flesh) fuhlaahn chaujó ge ✻ **be (turn) rusty** PH: ❶ hái syu faat pèihhei ❷ faat pèihhei ge ✻ **cut up rusty** FV: nàu

rut N: ❶ sèuhngkwài; gwaanlaih (M: tìuh) ❷ nāp-chòuh (M: go)

ruttish SV: housīkge

rutty SV: yáuh chè chit ge

rye N: ❶ (grain) hākmahk (M: nāp) ❷ (wine) lómahkjáu (M: jèun)

S

sabbath N: ngònsīkyaht (M: go) ✻ **keep the sabbath** VO: sáu ngònsīkyaht

sabbatic(al) ATT: ❶ ngònsīkyaht ge ❷ ngònsīk ge ✻ **sabbatical year, sabbatical leave** N: yàuganìhn (M: nìhn)

saber = sabre N: (knife) gwàndōu (M: bá) PH: (to strike with) yuhng gwàndōu jáam

sable N: ❶ (mink) hāakdīu (M: jek) ❷ (mourning dress) sòngfuhk (M: gihn)

sabotage N: (damaging) powaaih hàhngduhng (M: chi; júng) FV: (damage) powaaih VO/FV: (sit-in strike) tóihgūng

sack M: (a bag of) doih N: dói

(M: go) (made of hemp)
màhbàaudói (M: go) PH: (to put
sth. in) jòngyahp dói léuihbihn
* **sack-cloth** N: ① (coarse
hempen fabrics) chòu màhbou
(M: faai, fūk) ② (mourning dress)
sòngfuhk (M: gihn) * **knapsack** N: builòhng (M: go) * **get
the sack** VO: cháau yàuhyú

sacrament N: (ceremony)
singláih PH: (of things) sàhnsing ge yéh (M: gihn) * **holy
sacrament** N: singchāan (M:
chi) * **to receive or take the
sacrament** VO: sáu singchāan
* **sacramental wine** PH: sáu
singchāan só yuhng ge
pòuhtòuhjáu (M: būi; dihk)

sacred SV: ❶ (with religion)
sàhnsing ❷ (solemn) yìhmsūk,
lùhngjuhng Adj. PH: fuhnghin-
béi sàhn ge * **sacred book** N:
singgìng (M: bún, bouh) *
sacred music N: singngohk
(M: sáu) * **sacred place**
PW/N: singdeih (M: daat) *
sacred service N: láihbaai (M:
chi)

sacrifice N: ❶ (ceremony)
jailáih, hinjai ❷ (thing offered)
jaibán (M: gihn; júng, yeuhng)
FV: jai, jaijih (to a god, to one's
ancestors) ~ **sàhn**, ~ **jóusīn**
FV: (give up) hèisāng *
sacrifice one's life PH:
hèisāng singmihng *
sacrifice oneself PH: hèisāng
jihgéi * **sacrifice money** PH:
hèisāng gàmchìhn

sacrilege FV: (disrespectful
to) sitduhk; duhksing

sacrosanct Adj. PH: sàhnsing bāthó chàmfaahn ge

sad SV: ❶ (of feeling) nàahngwo, mngònlohk ❷ (of colour)
ngamdaahm

sadden PH: lihng yàhn
nàahngwo

saddle N: ❶ (horse)
máh'ngōn (M: go) ❷ (bicycle)
johwái (M: go) VO: (get on a
horse) séuhngmáh * **put a
saddle on a horse** PH: jèung
máhngōn   jònghái   máh
seuhngbihn * **in the saddle**
VO: kèh(gán)máh

sadiron N: tongdáu (M: go)

sadism N: ❶ (loosely) yeuhkdoihkwòhng ❷ (sexual) sing
yeuhkdoihkwòhng

sadness N/SV: bèisèung,
yàusèung

safe SV: ❶ (no danger) ngònchyùhn ❷ (not harmed)
pìhngngòn, móuh sih ❸
(reliable) wánjahn A: (certain)bītdihng N: (a box) gaap-
maahn (M: go) * **safe-deposit
(locker)** N: bóuhímsèung (M:
go) * **safeguard** FV: bóujeung
* **safe-keeping** FV: bóugún *
on the safe side Adv. PH:
waihjó wánjahn héigin IE: yíh
fòhng maahnyāt * **safe and
sound** Adj. PH: pìhngngòn
mòuhsih, (in good health) móuh
behng móuh tung

safety N: ngònchyùhn *
safety first PH: ngònchyùhn
daihyāt * **safety-lock** N:
bóuhímsó (M: bá, go) * **safety-
pin** N: ngònchyùhn kaujàm (M:
go) * **be in safety** Adj. PH:
pìhngngòn mòuhsih * **safety
belt** N: ngònchyùhn dáai (M:
tìuh)

sag SV: (sink down) nāpjó,
nīpjó FV: (price) (hah)dit

saga N: ❶ bākngàu yìnghùhng síusyut (M: bún) ❷ (of a
family) gàsai síusyut (M: bún)

sagacious SV: chùngmìhng, jìngmìhng

sage N: sìngyàhn, (of wisdom) jìtyàhn, sìngyìhn (M: go, wái)

Sahara, the N/PW: (desert) Saathālàai sàmohk

Saigon N/PW: (in Vietnam) Sàigung

sail N: (canvas) fàahn (M: faai) FV: (move) sái, hòhnghàhng * **sail-cloth** N: fàahnbou (M: faai, fūk) * **sailing-boat** N: fàahnsyùhn (M: jek) * **set sail** VO: hòisyùhn, hòisàn * **hoist the sails** PH: chéhéi fàahn * **go for a sail** VO: yàuh syùhn hó

sailor N: séuisáu, hóiyùhn (M: go)

saint N: sìngyàhn, (christian) sìngtòuh (M: go, wái)

sake N: yùhngu (M: go) * **for the sake of** Adv. PH: waihjó . . . ge yùhngu * **for someone's sake** Adv. PH: waihjó, (out of respect for) tái PN fahn seuhng

salaam VO: gūkgūng · heung PN gūk yàtgo gūng

salable Adj. PH: (fit for sale) hóyíh maaih ge

salacious ATT: (of books, pictures) sīkchìhng

salad N: sāléut (M: júng; go, dihp, pùhn) * **salad-dressing** N: sāléut jeung (M: jēun) * **salad-oil** N: sāléut yàuh (M: jēun, gāng)

salamander N: fólùhng (M: tìuh)

salary N: sànséui, yàhngùng * **monthly salary** N: yuhtsàn * **yearly salary** N: nìhnsàn * **the salaried classes** N: sauhsàn gàaikāp; dágūngjái (M: go)

sale FV: (selling) maaih N: (business) sàangyi, sìulouh * **for sale** FV: maaih, chēutsauh * **for sale by auction** FV: paakmaaih * **on sale** VO: gáamga N: daaih gáamga (M: chi) * **sales department** N: mùhnsíhbouh (M: go)

salesman N: sauhfoyùhn (M: go)

saleswoman N: néuih sauhfoyùhn (M: go)

salient SV: ❶ (obvious) hínjyu, mìhnghín ❷ (pointing out) dahtchēut FV: (shape) dahtchēutge bouhfahn N: (angle) dahtgok (M: go)

saliferous Adj. PH: yáuh yìhmfahn ge

salify PH: lìhng yātdī yéh binsìhng hàahmge

salinity N: yìhmfahn

saliva N: háuséui (M: daahm; dūk)

salivary * **salivary glands** N: teuyihksin (M: tìuh)

salivate VO: làuh háuséui

sallow PH: ❶ (skin) fùsīk hóu wòhng ❷ (face) mihnsīk hóu wòhng N: (tree) láuhsyuh (M: pò)

sally PH: (humourous remark) fùihàaihge syutwah (M: geui)

salmon N: sàammàhnyú (M: tìuh)

salon N: (exhibition of pictures) wájín (M: go; chi) sàlùhng (tr.) (M: go)

saloon N: (fóchège) chāankā (M: go) * **hair-dressing saloon** N: fèifaatpóu, mèihyùhngyún (M: gàan)

salt N: yìhm (M: jēun; nāp; gāng) PH: ❶ (to season) gà (dī) yìhm ❷ (to preserve) yuhng yìhm yip * **salt water** N: hàahmséui (M: dihk) * **salt and peper** PH: yìhm tùhng wùhjìufán

salted Adj. PH: yuhng yìhm yip ge * **salted black beans** N: dauhsih (M: nāp; bāau) * **salted egg** N: hàahmdáan (M: jek) * **salted fish** N: hàahmyú (M: tìuh)

salty SV: hàahm

salubrious Adj. PH: deui sàntái yáuhyīk ge, yáuhyīk gihnhòng ge

salutary SV: yáuhyīk Adj. PH: deui sànsàm yáuhyīk ge

salute VO: ❶ (for soldiers) hàahng gingláih ❷ (bow) gūkgūng ❸ (greet) dá jìufù

Salvador N/PW: Saatyìhngáhdò

salvage FV: ❶ (for crew) chéunggau ❷ (for ship or cargo) dálàauh PH: (for waste material) faimaht leihyuhng

salvation N: gauyàn, gausuhk

salve N: (on wounds or sores) yeuhkgōu (M: hahp; jì)

salver N: tokpún (M: go)

salvo FV: (applause) hotchói

same SV: yātyeuhng, sèungtùhng · *N1 tùhng N2 ~* * **the same** N SP: (identical) tùhngyāt A: (the old one) yùhnlòih ge * **the same day** A: jīkyaht * **same size** PH: yātyeuhng gam daaih/sai * **at the same time** A: tùhngsìh * **born in the same year** FV: tùhngnìhn · *PN1 tùhng PN2 ~* * **the same way** Patt: yātyeuhng gam · *N1 tùhng N2 ~ SV* * **in the same boat** IE: tùhng behng sèung lihn * **all the same** A: (still) yìhngyìhn Patt: (no matter how) mòuhleuhn dím... PH: (of one kind) tūngtūng yātyeuhng, (no difference) móuh fànbiht * **go to the same school** N: tùhnghohk (M: go) * **work in the same place** N: tùhngsìh (M: go) * **live in the same room** N: tùhngfóng (M: go) * **come from the same town or village** N: tùhnghēung (M: go)

sampan N: téhng (jái), sàanbáan (M: jek)

sample N: báan, yeuhngbún (M: go)

sanatorium = sanitarium N/PW: liuhyéuhngyún (M: gàan)

sanatory = sanative Adj. PH: deui sàntái yáuhyīk ge, yáuh yīk gihnhòng ge

sanctify PH: sái N/PN sìhngsing

sanctimonious Adj. PH: gájòng sàhnsing ge

sanction FV/N: (approval) pàijéun, (agree) tùhngyi

sanctity SV: singgit, sàhnsing

sanctuary N/PW: ❶ (altar) jaitàahn (M: go) ❷ (holy place) singsó ❸ (Jewish) jisingsó ❹ (shelter) beiwùhsó, beihnaahnsó (M: gàan, go)

sand N: sà (M: nāp; jah) *
sandbag N: sàbāau (M: go) *
sandpaper N: sàjí (M: jèung) *
numberless as the sands IE:
hàhnghòh sàsou

sandal N: ❶ (with thongs)
lèuhnghàaih (M: deui; jek) ❷
(slipper) tōháai (M: deui; jek)

sandalwood N: tàahn-
hēungmuhk (M: gauh; faai)

San Diego N/PW: Sing-
deihngàhgō

sandwich N: sàammàhnjih
(M: gihn, faai; go) PH: (insert)
chaapyahpheui jùnggàan PH:
(situation) gaahpái jùnggàan
* **make sandwich** VO: jíng
sàammàhnjih * **sandwich**
spread N: sàammàhnjih jeung
(M: jèun)

sandy Adj. PH: hóudò sà ge,
yáuh sà ge, N: (quality) sàjāt

sane PH: (not mad) jìngsàhn
jìngsèuhng

San Francisco N/PW:
Sàamfàahnsíh, Gauhgāmsāan

sanguinary N/SV: (bloody)
hyutsèng SV: (cruel) chàahnyán, chàahnbouh

sanguine N: (colour) hyut-
hùhngsīk PH: (complexion)
mihnsīk hùhngyeuhn

sanitarian N: (specialist)
waihsānghohkgā (M: go, wái)

sanitary N: waihsāng SV:
hahp waihsāng * **sanitary**
towels N: waihsānggān (M:
tiuh; hahp) * **sanitary inspec-**
tor N: waihsāng bòngbáan (M:
go)

sanitation N: ❶ (environment) wàahngíng waihsāng ❷

(equipment) waihsāng chitbeih
(M: júng)

sanitize FV/VO: (sterilize)
sìuduhk

sanity PH: (not mad) jìngsàhn jìngsèuhng

San Salvador N/PW: Sìng-
saatyíhngáhdō

Santa Claus N: Sìngdaan
Lóuhyàhn (M: go)

sap N: ❶ (liquid) syuhjáp ❷
(energy) wuhtlihk VO: (dig a tunnel) waat deihdouh, gwaht
deihdouh PH: (destroy faith)
powaaih yàhndeih ge seunsàm

sapless Adj. PH: ❶ (exhausted) guihdou séi ❷ (tree)
móuh syuhjáp

sapling N: ❶ (plant) syuh-
mìuh (M: pò) ❷ (teenager) hauh-
sāangjái (M: go)

sapper N: gùngbìng (M: go)

sapphire N: làahmbóusehk
(M: nāp; kà)

sappy Adj. PH: ❶ (energetic)
jìnglihk chùhngpui ge, wuhtlihk
chùhngpui ge ❷ (liquid) hóudò
syuhjáp ge

Sarawak N/PW: Sàlòuyuht

sarcastic FV: fungchi/fúng-
chi; dai Adj. PH: yáuh fungchising ge

sardine N: sàdīnyú (M: tiuh;
gun) * **packed like sardines**
PH: bīkdou hóuchíh sàdīnyú
gám

sardonic Adj. PH: yáuh
fungchising ge

sash N: ❶ (scarf) léhnggān
(M: tiuh) ❷ (round waist)

yìudáai (M: tìuh) ❸ (window frame) chēungkwàang (M: go)

Satan N: (tr.) Saatdaahn, mōgwái

satanic PH: hóuchíh mōgwái gám

satchel N: (of school children) syùbāau (M: go) (in general) dói (M: go)

satellite N: ❶ (planet) waihsing (M: go) ❷ (artificial) yàhnjouh waihsing (M: go)

satiate Patt: FV dou yim

satin N: dyuhn (M: faai, pāt)

satire N: ❶ (literature) fungchi màhnhohk ❷ (writing) fungchimàhn (M: pìn) N/FV: fungchi/fúnghci

satiric Adj. PH: yáuh fungchising ge

satirist PH: ❶ (author) fungchimàhn ge jokjé (M: go) ❷ dai yàhndeih ge yàhn (M: go)

satirize FV: fungchi/fúnghci; dai PH: (by writing) sé dī yéh fungchi yàhn

satisfaction FV/SV: múhnyi PH: (sth. that satisfies) lihng yàhn múhnyi ge yéh/sih (M: dī, gihn) N: (compensation) pùihsèuhng ✳ **give satisfaction** Adj. PH: lihng yàhn múhnyi ✳ **demand satisfaction** PH: yìukàuh douhhip ✳ **with satisfaction** Adv. PH: hóu múhnyi gám

satisfactory Adj. PH: lihng yàhn múhnyi ge

satisfied PH: gokdāk múhnyi ✳ **be satisfied with** PH: deui N/PN hóu múhnyi

satisfy FV/SV: ❶ múhnyi · *lihng PN* ~ ❷ (contented) múhnjūk FV/N: (compensate) pùihsèuhng FV: sèuhngwàahn (debt) ~ *himjaai*

saturate RV: (soak thoroughly) jamtau, (make very wet) sāptau SV: (chemical) báauwòh

Saturday TW: láihbaailuhk, sìngkèihluhk

saturn N: (planet) tóusing (M: nāp)

satyr N: ❶ (myth) sàmlàhmjìsàhn ❷ (man) sīklòhng (M: go)

sauce N: (seasoning) jeung, jeunglíu (M: jēun) ✳ **soy sauce** N: sihyàuh, sàangchāu (M: jēun; gāng) ✳ **apple sauce** N: pìhnggwó jeung ✳ **white sauce** N: baahkjāp (M: dī; gāng) ✳ **brown sauce** N: hùhngjāp (M: dī; gāng) ✳ **tomato sauce** N: fàanké jeung, kéjāp (M: jēun; dī) ✳ **add sauce to** PH: gà dī jeunglíu tiuhmeih

saucepan PH: yáuh goi tùhngmàaih yáuh beng ge bōu (M: go)

saucer N: (for teacup) chàhbūidíp (M: jek, go) ✳ **flying saucer** N: fèidíp (M: go)

Saudi Arabia N/PW: Sàdeihalàaibaak

saunter VO: saanbouh

sausage N: (Chinese style) laahpchéung (M: tìuh; gàn) (Western style) hēungchéung (M: tìuh; bohng)

sauté FV: ❶ (fry) jìn ❷ (with constant stirring) cháau

savage SV: ❶ (wild) yéhmàahn ❷ (cruel) chàahnyán

Adj. PH: (uncivilized) meih hòifa ge N/PH: (uncivilized people) sàangfàan, yéhmàahnyàhn; meih hòifa ge yàhn (M: go) PH: (cruel person) hóu chàahnnyán ge yàhn (M: go)

savannah N/PW: yihtdaai chóuyùhn (M: go)

savant N: (scholar) hohkjé (M: go, wái) PH: (scientist) daaih fōhohkgā, hóu chēutméng ge fōhohkgā (M: go, wái)

save FV: ❶ (rescue) gau, (Christian) chínggau, (Buddhist) chìudouh ❷ (collect) chóuh (money, stamps) ~ chín, ~ yàuhpiu ❸ (thrifty) hàan (money) ~ chín ❹ (not spend) hàan (time, material) ~ sìhgaan, ~ jí (paper) AV: (no need to) m̀sái, m̀sèuiyiu * save up VO: chóuhchín * save one's skin PH: míhn sauh syúnsāt

saver N: (person) gausìng, (Christian) chínggaujé (M: go) PH: (instrument) hóyíh hàan sìhgaan waahkjé hàan yàhnlihk ge yuhnggeuih (M: gihn)

saving N: jīkchūk * savings bank N: chyúhchūk ngàhnhòhng (M: gàan) * savings account N: chyúhchūk wuhháu (M: go)

saviour N: (Christian) gau (sai)jyú (M: go)

saw N/FV: geu, geui (M: bá) * sawdust N: muhkhòng (M: dī) * saw-mill N: geuimuhkchóng (M: gàan) * saw off RV: geuityúhn * saw up RV: geuihòi, geuisèhng

say FV: góng, wah * say a prayer FV: kèihtóu * say good-bye FV: chìhhàhng ·

heung PN ~ VO: góng joigin · tùhng PN ~ * say the word VO: faat mihnglihng * that is to say PH: wuhnyìhnjì, jīkhaihwah * it is said that PH: tèngmàhnwah, tènggóngwah, tèngyàhngóng * it is hard to say PH: hóu nàahn góng * have nothing to say PH: móuh wah hóu góng

saying N: gaakyìhn (M: geui) * common saying N: juhkyúh, juhkwá (M: geui) * as the saying goes IE: juhkyúhwah, (jing)sówaih

scab N: yím (M: faai) * form a scab VO: gityím

scabbard N: chiu (M: go) (for sword) gimchiu, (for dagger) dōuchiu

scaffold N: ❶ (construction) ginjūk pàahnggá; pàahng (M: go) ❷ (for execution) dyuhntàuh tòih (M: go) * set up a scaffold VO: daappàahng

scald FV: luhk RV: ❶ (hurt) luhkchàn · béi gwánséui ~ ❷ (cooked) luhksuhk

scale N: ❶ (covering) lèuhn, (of fish) yùhlèuhn (M: faai) ❷ (weighing machine) tìnpìhng (M: go) (Chinese scale) ching (M: bá) (for pounds) bóng (M: go) ❸ (proportion) béilaih (M: go) (on a map) béilaihchek (M: go) ❹ (marks for measurement) douhsou (M: go) ❺ (grade) dángkāp (M: go) ❻ (music) yāmgāai (M: go) VO: (fish) dálèuhn Patt: (weight) yáuh Nu M chúhng * put on the scale FV: bohngháh, chingháh * on a large scale A: daaih kwàimòuh * scale down PH: jiu béilaih gáam * scale up PH: jiu béilaih gà * pay scale N: sànkāpbíu (M: go) * scaling-ladder N: wàhntāi (M: bá)

scaled Adj. PH: hóuchíh yùhlèuhn gám, yáuh lèuhn ge

scallop N: (sea food) daaijí (M: jek); (dried) gònyìuhchyúh (M: nāp)

scallywag N: làuhmàhn, mòuhláai (M: go)

scalp N: tàuhpèih (M: faai) VO: (ticket) cháaufēi

scalpel N: gáaifáudōu (M: bá)

scamp N: (person) làuhmàhn, mòuhláai (M: go) PH: (work) móuh sàmgēi jouhyéh, jouhyéh hóu lásài

scamper FV: jáu, bīu

scan PH: (carefully) hóu jísai gám tái FV: (glance) laapháh N: (medical) soumìuh

scandal FV: (gossip) féipóhng PH: (gossip) góng yàhn waaihwá N: (shameful behaviour) cháumàhn (M: gihn)

scandalize FV: (gossip) féipóhng, jungsèung PH: (gossip) góng yàhn waaihwá

scandalous SV: (shameful) móuhmín, diugá Adj. PH: (of a person) hóu jùngyi góng yàhn waaihwá ge

Scandinavia N/PW: Sīhàamdīknàhwàiha Bundóu, bākngāu

Scandinavian PH: (people) Sīhàamdīknàhwàiha yàhn, bākngāu yàhn (M: go)

scant FV: m̀gau, kyutfaht SV: kyutfaht

scanty FV: m̀gau, kyutfaht

SV: kyutfaht

scapegoat N: taisèigwái (M: go) PH: (Christian) doih jeuih gòuyèuhng (M: go)

scapegrace N: (good-for-nothing) faahntúng (M: go) PH: (naughty) hóu baakyim ge saimānjái (M: go)

scar N: (of skin) nà (M: go, daat); (a long one) hán (M: tìuh) FV: (of furniture) fàjó

scarce Adj. PH: (few, little) hóusíu, (rare) hóu hèihón ge, SV/FV: kyutfaht

scarcely A: hóusíu Adv. PH: fèisèuhng síu

scare FV: haak RV: haakchàn • béi PN/N ~ * scare one to death PH: haakséi yàhn * don't be scared PH: m̀hóu gèng

scarecrow N: douhchóuyàhn (M: go)

scarf N: ❶ (round the neck) génggān (M: tìuh) ❷ (round the head) tàuhgān (M: tìuh) * wear a scarf VO: laahm génggān, bóng tàuhgān

scarify VO: (for cultivation) sùngtóu PH: (to hurt by criticism) yuhng yìhmlaih ge pàipìhng sèunghoih yàhn

scarlet N: daaihhùhngsīk, sìnhùhngsīk * scarlet fever N: sìnghùhngyiht

scarp N/PW: (cliff) yùhnngàaih (M: go)

scathe FV: (hurt) sèunghoih

scathing SV: yìhmlaih, máahngliht

scatology N: (literature)

sīkchìhng màhnhohk (M: júng)

scatter FV: (toss or sprinkle) saat RV: ❶ (break up by force) jíngsáan ❷ (break up and go in different directions) saanhòi

scattered SV: sáan

scavenge PH: dóugònjehng dī laahpsaap, (of scavenger) sou gònjehng tiuh gāai

scavenger N: ❶ (on streets) chìngdouhfù, sougāaige (M: go), ❷ (in buildings) laahpsaaplóu, (woman) laahpsaappó (M: go)

scenario N: kehkbún (M: go)

scene N: ❶ (view) fùnggíng (M: dī) ❷ (on the stage) bougíng (M: go; júng; chèuhng) N/PW: (place at which anything occurs) yihnchèuhng, chēutsih deihdím, faatsàng deihdím M: (parts of a play) chèuhng ✳ a change of scene PH: wuhnháh wàahngíng ✳ behind the scenes Adv. PH: hái mohkhauh, (secretly) hóu beimaht gám A: (secretly) ngamjūng ✳ come on the scene FV: chēutyihn ✳ make a scene VO: faat pèihhei

scenery N: ❶ (landscape) fùnggíng ❷ (on the stage) bougíng (M: go; júng; chèuhng)

scenic PH: (of landscape) fùnggíng hóu leng ✳ a scenic spot N/PW: fùnggíng kèui

scent N; ❶ (smell) meih (M: jahm, buhng) ❷ (pleasant smell) hèungmeih (M: jahm, buhng) ❸ (perfume) hèungséui (M; dī, jēun, dihk) RV: (to smell) màhndóu ✳ put scent on PH: sá dī hèungséui hái N seuhngbihn

scented Adj. PH: ❶ (of plea-

sant smell) yáuh hèungmeih ge ❷ (with perfume) sájó hèungséui ge

sceptic PH: deui N yáuh wàaihyìh ge yàhn (M: go)

scepticism N: wàaihyìh jyúyih

sceptre PH: wòhngdai ge kyùhnjeuhng (M: jì)

schedule N: (timetable) sìhgaanbíu (M: go) PH: (arrangement) sìhgaanseuhng ge ngònpàaih (M: go, júng) FV: (arrange) ngònpàaih ✳ make a schedule VO: pìn sìhgaanbíu ✳ a progress schedule N: jeundouhbíu (M: go) ✳ be scheduled to do something PH: ngònpàaihhóu/dihngjó géisìh géiyaht jouh yātgihn sih ✳ on schedule SV/A: jéunsìh ✳ (according) to schedule Adv. PH: jiujyuh sìhgaanbíu ✳ ahead of schedule A: tàihchìhn ✳ behind schedule FV: lohkhauh

scheme N/FV: ❶ (plan) gaiwaahk (M: go) ❷ (design) chitgai (M: go)

schism FV: fànliht

schizophrenia N: jìngsàhn fànliht jing (M: go, júng)

scholar N: (learned man) hohkjé (M: go, wái)

scholarship N: (financial aid) jéunghohkgām (M: go; bāt)

scholasticism N: fàahnsó jithohk

school N/PW: ❶ hohkhaauh (M: gàan) ❷ (division of a university) hohkyún (M: gàan, go) (of liberal arts) màhnhohkyún (of natural sciences) léihhohkyún (medical school) yìhohkyún N: (academic group) hohkpaai (M: go) M: (for fish) dèui, kwàhn ✻ **primary school, grade school, elementary school** N/PW: síuhohk (M: gàan) ✻ **secondary school, high school, middle school** N/PW: jùnghohk ✻ **graduate school** N/PW: yìhhgauyún (M: gàan) ✻ **schoolmate** N: tùhnghohk (M: go) ✻ **school uniform** N: haauhfuhk (M: gihn, tou) ✻ **school work** N: gùngfo (M: yeuhng) ✻ **no school** FV/VO: tìhngfo PH: m̀sái fàanhohk

schooling N/FV: gaauyuhk (M: júng)

sciatica N: (disease) johgwātsàhngìngtung

science N: fòhohk (M: júng) ATT: léihhohk ~ *boksih* (doctor) ✻ **natural science** N: jihyìhn fòhohk ✻ **social science** N: sèhwúi fòhohk

scientific ATT: fòhohkseuhng ge SV/FV: fòhohkfa ✻ **scientific method** PH: fòhohk fòngfaat (M: go) ✻ **scientific instruments** PH: fòhohk yìhhei (M: gihn; júng)

scientist N: fòhohkgā (M: go)

scintilla N: (spark) fófà (M: dím)

scintillate PH: (sparkle) faatchēut fófā

scientology N: seunyéuhng jìhliuh faat

scissor PH: yuhng gaaujín jín FV: jín

scissors N: gaaujín (M: bá)

sclerosis FV: ngaahngfa ✻ **vascular sclerosis** PH: hyutgún ngaahngfá

scoff FV: (laugh at) siu, gèisiu, jàausiu

scold FV: naauh

scoop N/M: (spoon) hok (M: go) FV: ❶ (to ladle) bāt, fāt, yíu ❷ (to dig) waat

scooter N: ❶ (for adults) dihndàanchè (M: ga) ❷ (for children) daahpbáanchè (M: ga)

scope N: (sphere) faahnwàih (M: go) ✻ **beyond the scope of** PH: hái nīgo faahnwàih jìngoih/yíhngoih ✻ **within the scope of** PH: hái nīgo faahnwàih jìnoih/yíhnoih

scorch RVE: (make burnt or withered) nùng ✻ **scorched by the sun** PH: bêi taaiyèuhng saainùngjó ✻ **scorch while ironing** RV: tongnùngjó

score M: (points in a game) fān Nu: (twenty) yihsahp N: ❶ (record in a game) dākfān géiluhk (M: go) ❷ (musical) ngohkpóu, gōpóu, póu (M: go) VO: ❶ (keep a record) geifān ❷ (make points) dākfān FV: (make points) yèhng

scorer N: (= score keeper) geifānyùhn PH: (player who scores) dākfān ge deuihyùhn

scorn RV: (regard lightly) táim̀héi FV: (laugh at) siu

scorpion N: kit, kitjí (M: jek)

Scot N: Sòugaaklàahnyàhn (M: go)

Scotch ATT: ❶ (of the country) Sòugaaklàahnge ❷ (of the people) Sòugaaklàahnyàhnge

N: ❶ (people) Sòugaaklàahn-yàhn (M: go) ❷ (whisky) wàisihgéi(jáu) (M: jēun)

scotch ＊ **hop scotch** N: tiu fèigèi · *wáan* ~

scot-free VO: (tax-free) míhnseui

Scotland N/PW: Sòugaak-làahn

scoundrel N: mòuhláai, gwònggwan, waaihdáan (M: go)

scour RV: (make clean) chaat gònjehng, (make bright) chaat-ling FV: (rub) sáang

scourge N: ❶ (whip) bīn (M: tiuh) ❷ (calamity) jòiwoh (M: chèuhng, chi) FV: ❶ (to flog) bīn-dá ❷ (to punish) chìhngfaht

scout PH: dátaam chìhng-yìhng ＊ **boy scouts** N: tùhng-jígwān (M: deuih, go) ＊ **girl scouts = girl guides** N: néuihtùhnggwān (M: deuih; go) ＊ **scout master** N: tùhnggwān deuihjéung (M: go)

scowl IE: (a sad look) sàuhmèih fúmihn, sàuhyùhng múhnmihn PH: (a sad look) jaumàaih mèihtàuh

scrabble FV: (scrawl) lyuhn-sé, lyuhnwaahk PH: (look for) màudàai hái deihhá wán

scramble FV: ❶ cháau (egg) ~ *dáan* ❷ (climb) pàh

scrap N: faimaht (M: dī) ＊ **scrap iron** N: laahn tit (M: dī, gauh) ＊ **scraps** N: (left-over rice) láahngfaahn (M: dī) PH: (left-over food) láahngfaahn choijáp (M: dī) ＊ **scraps of cloth** N: bouseui (M: dī) ＊ **scraps of paper** N: jíseui, jihjí (M: dī)

scrape FV: (remove) gwaat, sáang (pans) ~ *wohk* ＊ **scrape off** RV: gwaatlát, sáanglát

scraper N: gwaatdōu (M: bá)

scrapper N: (boxer) kyùhn-gīksáu (M: go)

scrappy PH: (made up of bits) yuhng seuilíu jouh ge

scratch FV: ❶ ngàau, wá (an itching spot) ~ *hàhn* ❷ (with claws) wá RV: (mark with something sharp) kaatfà, kaat-chàn N: (mark) hán (M: tiuh) ＊ **scratch out** PH: waahkjó kéuih ＊ **scratch pad** N: paak-jíbóu (M: bún) ＊ **from scratch** PH: chùhng tàuh joi jouhgwo

scratchy SV: ❶ (of writing) líuchóu ❷ (of pen) kaatjí ❸(of cloth) dūksàn Adj. PH: (feeling) lihng yàhn gokdāk hóu hàhn ge

scrawl PH: (write) séjih sédāk hóu líuchóu RV: (draw) waahkfà PH: (handwriting) sédāk hóu líuchóu ge jih

screak PH: daaihsèng gám ngaai

scream PH: daaihsèng gám ngaai, daaihsèng gám giu ＊ **scream with laughter** PH: daaihsèng gám siu, siudou tóuh dōu tungjó, siudou lūkdéi ＊ **scream oneself hoarse** PH: ngaaidou sèngdōu sàjó ＊ **a scream** PH: yáuh yàhn daaihsèng gám ngaai

screech N: (sound, voice) jìmgiusèng (M: bá)

screen N: ❶ (standing) pìhngfùng (M: go) ❷ (hanging) lím (M: douh, faai, tòhng) ❸ (of a cinema) ngàhnmohk (M: go) ❹ (of a TV) yìhnggwòngmohk (M: go) FV:

(hide) jèjyuh * **screen play** N:
dihnyíng kehkbún (M: go) *
screen window N: sāchēung
(M: go) * **smoke screen** N:
yīnmohk (M: go)

screw N: (nail) lòhsī, lòhsī-
dēng (M: nāp) FV: (turn) náu,
nihng * **screw-driver** N:
lòhsīpāi (M: go, bá) * **air-
screws** PH: fèigèi ge lòhsyùhnjéung (M: go) * **screw tight**
RV: nihnggán, nihngsaht *
screw in a screw PH: náusaht
nāp lòhsī * **screw out a
screw** PH: náusùng nāp lòhsī
* **fasten with a screw** VO:
séuhng lòhsī

scribble PH: séjih sédāk
hóu líuchóu PH: (handwriting)
sédāk hóu líuchóu ge jih

scribe N: ❶ (in Bible)
màhnsih (M: go) ❷ (Catholic)
gìngsì (M: go) FV: (copy)
chàausé * **be a scribe** PH:
jouh chàausé

scrimmage PH: dágàau
dádou m̀chìngm̀chó

scrimp PH: hàan dākjaih

scrip N: (paper) saige jí, jíjái
(M: jèung)

script N: ❶ (Chinese cursive
writing) chóusyù ❷ (draft) góu
(M: pìn)

scripture PH: jùnggaau ge
gìngsyù (M: bún) * **the holy
scriptures** N: singgìng (M:
bún)

scroll M: ❶ (paper, writing)
gyún ❷ (cloth) pāt * **a pair of
scrolls** N: (Chinese) déui,
deuilyùhn (M: deui, fu)

scrub FV: (rub) chaat RV:
chaat gònjehng * **scrubbing-
brush** N: ngaahngmòuhcháat

(M: go)

scrubby Adj. PH: (small and
short) hóu ngáisai ge * **a
scrubby chin** PH: sàangsaai-
sòu ge hahpàh (M: go)

scruff N/PW: (of the neck)
géng hauhbihn

scrumptious Adj. PH: hóu
hóusihk ge

scrunch RV: ❶ (by pressure)
ngàahnseui ❷ (by biting)
ngáauhseui, ngáauhlaahn

scruple SV/FV: (hesitate)
chàuhchyùh FV/N: (worry)
gugeih (M: dī) * **without scruple** IE: mòuhsógugeih

scrupulosity SV: (careful)
síusàm, gánsahn

scrupulous Adj. PH: ❶
(careful) fèisèuhng síusàm ge ❷
(serious) hóu yihngjàn ge ❸
(worried) hóudò guleuih ge

scrutineer N/FV: gāampiu
(M: go) * **be a scrutineer** PH:
jouh gāampiu

scrutinize PH: hóu jísai
gám gímchàh

scuff FV: hàahnglouh
mohháh mohháh

scuffle PH: dágàau dádou
m̀chìngm̀chó

scull N: (oar) jéung (M: jì, jek)

sculptor N: dìuhāakgā (M:
go, wái)

sculpture FV: dìuhāak N: ❶
(carving) dìuhāak (M: júng) ❷
(work) dìuhāakbán (M: gihn)

scum N: ❶ (of boiling water)
pōk (M: go) ❷ (foam) póuh (M:
dī)

scurf N: (on the scalp) tàuhpèih (M: faai)

scurry PH: hàahngdāk hóu faai, hóu chùngmòhng gám jáu Adj. PH: chùngchùngmòhng-mòhng gám

scurvy N: (disease) waaih-hyutjing SV: (mean) bèipéi, hahlàuh

scutcher N: ❶ (for cotton) dámihngèi (M: ga, fu) ❷ (for hemp) dámàhngèi (M: ga, fu)

scythe N: daaih lìhmdōu (M: bá)

sea N: hói (M: go) ✳ **sea food** N: hóisīn (M: júng) ✳ **sea-gull** N: hóingāu (M: jek) ✳ **sea level** N: hóipìhngmín ✳ **seaman** N: (sailor) hóiyùhn, séuisáu (M: go) (in the Navy) séuibīng (M: go) ✳ **seaquake** N: hóisiu (M: chi) ✳ **seasick** VO: wàhn (syùhn) lohng SV: wàhnlohng ✳ **above sea level** ATT: hóibaht ~ *10,000 chek* ✳ **between the devil and the deep sea** IE: jeunteui léuhngnàahn ✳ **the high seas** N/PW: gùnghói (M: go) ✳ **the South China Sea** N/PW: Nàahm Jùnggwokhói ✳ **rough sea** PH: (hói seuhngbihn) fùnglohng hóu daaih

seal N: ❶ (sea-animal) hóipaau (M: jek) ❷ (wax) fóchāt, fùnglaahp ❸ (chop, stamp) yan, tòuhjèung (M: go) FV: (close tightly) mahtfùng, fùngjyuh VO: (mark with a stamp) kāpyan, kāp tòuhjèung RV: (close tightly) fùngsaht, fùngmàaih, fùnghóu ✳ **a personal seal** N: sijèung, yan (M: go) ✳ **the imperial seal** N: sáai, gwoksáai, (Chinese) yuhksáai (M: go)

sealing-wax N: fóchāt, fùnglaahp (M: dī)

seam N: (in garment) gaapháu (M: go) FV: (sew) lyùhn ✳ **seam it up** PH: lyùhnmàaih kéuih

search FV: ❶ wán; chaau (person) · ~ sàn ❷ (look for something concealed) sáu, sáuchàh, chaau ❸ (investigate) diuhchàh ✳ **search out** RV: wándóu, sáudóu, chaaudóu ✳ **search-warrant** N: sáuchàh-lihng (M: jèung)

season M/BF: gwai · (spring) *chēun ~* , (summer) *hah ~* (fall) *chāu ~* , (winter) *dūng ~* N: (period of the year) sìhhauh, gwaijit (M: go) ✳ **holiday season** N: gakèih PH: fongga ge sìhhauh ✳ **in season** FV: (fruit, vegetable) dòngjouh SV: (fruit, vegetable, fish) hahpsìh ✳ **out of season** SV: m̀hahpsìh, gwosìh ✳ **rainy season** N: yúhgwai (M: go) ✳ **seasoning** N: tiuhmeihbán (M: júng)

seasonable SV: (suitable, at the right time) hahpsìh A: (not late) kahpsìh

seasonal Adj. PH: yáuh gwaijitsing ge

seat N: wái (M: go) RV: (capacity) chóhdāklohk ✳ **book a seat** VO: dehngwái ✳ **seatbelt** N: ngònchyùhndáai (M: tìuh) ✳ **take a seat** PH: chéng chóh RV: chóhdài ✳ **win a seat** FV: dòngsyún

Seattle N/PW: Sàingáhtòuh

seaward Adj. PH: heung hói ge

secede FV: teuichēut, tyut-lèih

seclude FV: ❶ (keep away

from) lèihhòi, gaaklèih ❷ (for
a person) yángèui

secluded SV: (of a place)
yàujihng

second Nu: daihyih; (of floor)
yih ~ *láu* N: (of a month)
yihhouh M: (of time) míuh FV:
(of a proposal) fuhyíh, jaansihng
∗ **second coming** PH: Yèhsōu
Gèidūk joilàih ge sìhhauh ∗
second-class ATT: yihdáng,
yihkāp, yihlàuh ∗ **secondhand** ATT: yihsáu SV: gauhge
∗ **secondhand** N: (in watches
and clocks) míuhjām (M: jì) ∗
second lieutenant N: siuwai
(M: go) ∗ **second teeth** N:
hàhngchí (M: jek) ∗ **in a few
seconds** Adv. PH: hóu faai TW:
yātjahngāan, géimíuhjūng
jinoih ∗ **in the second place**
A: daihyih, kèihchi, yihlòih,
yihlàih

secondary ATT: jùngkāp,
jùngdáng N: (agent) doihléihyàhn (M: go) Adj. PH: (of importance) móuh gam gányiu ge ∗
secondary education N:
jùngdáng gaauyuhk ∗ **secondary school** N/PW: jùnghohk
(M: gàan)

seconder N: fuhyíhyàhn (M:
go)

secondly A: daihyih, kèihchi, yihlòih, yihlàih

secrecy N: beimaht (M: go)
VO: (keep a secret)(bóu)sáu
beimaht ∗ **in secrecy** Adv.
PH: beimaht gám A: ngam-
jùng, jihngjíng

secret N/SV: beimaht (M: go)
N: ❶ (mystery) oubei (M: go) ❷
(hidden cause) beikyut (M: go)
SV: (of a place) yàujihng ATT:
(not obvious) ngam ~ *mùhn*
(door) ∗ **secret agent** N:

dahkmouh, gaandihp (M: go) ∗
secret code N: mahtmáh (M:
go) ∗ **secret plot** N: yàmmàuh
(M: go) ∗ **an open secret** N:
gùnghòi ge beimaht (M: go) ∗
in secret Adv. PH: beimaht
gám A: ngamjùng, jihngjíng ∗
keep a secret VO: sáu
beimaht ∗ **keep something
secret from somebody** PH:
m̀béi yātgo yàhn jìdou yātgihn
sih ∗ **let out a secret** PH:
sitlauh beimaht

secretariate N: beisyù-
chyúh

secretary N: beisyù, (female)
néuih beisyù (M: go) ∗ **private
secretary** N: sìyàhn beisyù (M:
go) ∗ **the secretary of state**
N: (England) gwokmouh daaihsàhn (U.S.A.) gwokmouhhìng
∗ **secretary of the treasury**
N: chòihjing bouhjéung ∗
secretary-general N: beisyù-
jéung, júng syùgei

secrete RV: sàumàaih
(things) ~ *dī yéh* FV: (produce)
fànbei

secretion N: fànbeimaht
(M: dī, júng)

secretive A: (secretly) jē-
jēyímyím gám PH: (to make
more secretion) chūkjeun
fànbei

sect M: paai N: jùngpaai (M:
go) (of religion) gaaupaai (M: go)
(academic) hohkpaai (M: go)

sectarian Adj. PH: (between
sects) paaihaih jìgàan ge

sectarianism N: jùngpaai
jyúyih (M: júng)

section M/N: ❶ (part)
bouhfahn (M: go) ❷ (area) kèui
(M: go) M/BF: (subdivision) jóu
N: (parts) lìhnggín (M: gihn) M:

❶ (of writing) jit **❷** (one length) dyuhn, gyuht, jiht

sectional Adj. PH: (of a place) deihkèuising ge

sector N: **❶** (shape) sinyìhng (M: go) **❷** (branch, department) bouhmùhn (M: go)

secular PH: **❶** (worldly affairs) saijuhk ge sih (M: dī) **❷** (people in the world) saijuhk ge yàhn (M: go)

secularize FV: saijuhkfa

secure SV: **❶** (firm) wánjahn **❷** (reliable) kaaudākjyuh **❸** (safe) ngònchyùhn FV: (guarantee) dàambóu, bóujing FV: (succeed in getting) dākdóu ✳ **feel secure about** PH: deui N yáuh ngònchyùhngám

security SV/N: (safe) ngòn-chyùhn N: (self-confidence) bángaak • deui N yáuh ~ ✳ **sense of security** N: ngòn-chyùhngám ✳ **in security** Adv. PH: ngònchyùhn gám ✳ **security council** N: (of the United Nations) ngònchyùhn léihsihwúi ✳ **security company** N: wuhwaih gùngsī (M: gàan) ✳ **security guard** N: wuhwaihyùhn (M: go)

sedan N: gíu • chóh ~ (M: déng) ✳ **carry a sedan-chair** VO: tòihgíu ✳ **sedan-chair bearers** N: tòihgíulóu, gíufù (M: go)

sedate SV: **❶** (calm) daahm-dihng **❷** (serious) yìhmsūk

sedative VO: (for pain) jítung N: **❶** (medicine to relieve pain) jítungyeuhk (M: júng) **❷** (medicine to calm) janjihngjài (M: júng)

sedentary PH: (sit) chóhhái-

syu hóunoih

sediment N: jà (M: dī)

sedition PH: sinduhng buhnlyuhn ge yìhnleuhn

seditious Adj. PH: yáuh sin-duhngsing ge

seduce PH: **❶** (persuade to do wrong) yáhnyáuh yàhn jouh waaihsih **❷** (tempt into crime) yáhnyáuh yàhn faahnjeuih FV: (immorality) ngāuyáhn

seductive Adj. PH: hóu kāpyáhn yàhn ge

sedulous Adv. PH: (persevering) hóu yáuhhàhngsàm gám Adj. PH: (hard-working) hóu kàhnlihk

see FV: **❶** (look at) tái, (look!) táiháh **❷** (meet and talk) gin **❸** (understand) mìhngbaahk, mìhng **❹** (know) jídou RV: **❶** táigin, yùhnlòih haih gám **❷** (make certain) táichìngchó ✳ **as far as I can see** PH: jiu ngóh sójì ✳ **be seen** PH: béi yàhn táigin ✳ **Oh, I see!** PH: (find out the truth) óh, yùhnlòih haih gám ✳ **see a doctor** VO: tái yìsāng ✳ **see if, see whether** Patt: táiháh SV/FV m̀SV/FV ✳ **see off** FV: (at airport, railway station) sung ✳ **see over** FV: (check) táiháh, chèkháh ✳ **see somebody home** PH: sung PN fàanngūkkéi ✳ **see somebody out** PH: sung PN chēut-mùhnháu ✳ **see through** RV: (not be deceived) táichyūn SV: (of clothes) taumìhng ✳ **see the sights** PH: yàuhláahm mìhng-sing FV: gùngwòng ✳ **see to** FV: (take care) chyúhléih RV: gáaudihm ✳ **see in a dream** FV: muhnggin ✳ **holy see** N: (Catholic) lòhmáh gaautìhng

seed N: ❶ (of a plant) júngjí (M: nāp) ❷ (inside the fruit) waht, wát (M: nāp) ❸ (of melon) gwājí (M: nāp) * **sow with seed** VO: bojúng, saatjúng * **seedtime** N: bojúngkèih * **seeded player** N: júngjí syúnsáu (M: go)

seedling N: yaumìuh (M: jì, pò)

seeing FV: gin, tái RV: gindóu, táidóu, táigin * **seeing that** A: yànwaih * **sightseeing** FV: yàuhláahm, gùngwòng * **seeing is believing** IE: baakmàhn bātyùh yātgin

seek FV: ❶ (look for) wán ❷ (ask for) kàuh, chéng * **seek a livelihood** VO: wánsihk * **seek a quarrel** PH: wángàau ngaai * **seek advice** FV: chénggaau * **seek employment** PH: wángùng jouh * **seek ones fortune** VO: wánchín * **seek opinions** PH: jìngkàuh yigin

seem A: hóuchíh, chíhfùh FV: (to someone) gokdāk

seemingly A: bíumihnseuhng

seep FV: ❶ lauh (liquid) ~ séui ❷ sam (water, rain) ~ yúh RV: lauhchēutlàih, samchēutlàih

seer N: sìnjì, yuhyìhngā

seesaw N: ngaht(ngaht)báan yìuhyìuhbáan (M: go) · wáan ~

seethe SV: (agitated) gīkduhng RV: (boil) jyúgwán

segment M: ❶ (section) dyuhn, gyuht, jit ❷ (piece) pin, faai ❸ (of a citrus fruit) káai, gauh

segregate FV: fànhòi, gaaklèih * **racial segregation** N: júngjuhk gaaklèih

seismograph, seismometer N: deihjanyíh (M: go)

seize FV: ❶ (hold) jūkjyuh (person or thing), lájyuh (thing) ❷ (arrest) jàujyuh · béi gíngchaat ~ ❸ bángāak (opportunity) ~ gīwuih ❹ (take possession of by law) muhtsàu, fùng, chàhgùng, chùnggùng ❺ (take possession of by force) bajim, jimgeui, jim ❻ (take possession of by enemy) jimgeui, jim

seizure FV: ❶ (take possession of by force) bajim, jimgeui, jim ❷ (take possession of by law) muhtsàu, fùng, chàhfùng, chùnggùng * **seizure of contraband by customs officers** PH: hóigwāan jíkyùhn muhtsàu wàihgambán

seldom A: hóusíu

select FV: gáan, syún PH; (chosen from among) yàuh/hái yāt bāan yàhn jìjung syúnchēutlàih

self- PN: jihgéi, jihgēi * **myself, yourself, himself etc.** PN: PN jihgéi · ngóh ~, néih ~ * **by oneself** A: (alone) jihgéi, jihgēi Adv. PH: (alone) yātgo yàhn, jihgéi yātgo yàhn, yātgo yán

self- Prefix: jih ATT: jihngóh * **self-confidence** N: jihseunsàm * **self-control** FV: jihjai * **self-defence** FV: jihwaih * **self-support** FV: jihlahp

selfish SV: jihsì Adj. PH: jihsì jihleih

selfishness N: jihsìsàm

sell FV: maaih * **sell out** RV:

maaihsaai FV: (betray) chēut-maaih * **sell well** PH: hóudò yàhn máaih, hóu maaihdāk * **sell at $ 10 for one** PH: yātgo maaih sahpmān

seller PH: maaihyéhge yàhn

semantics N: yúhyihohk, yúhyihhohk

semblance N: (superficial) ngoihbíu, bíumihn PH: (likeness) sèungchíh ge deihfòng FV: (look like) sèungchíh, hóuchíh * **put on a semblance of** FV: jadai * **bear the semblance of an angel but have the heart of a devil** IE: yàhnmihn sausàm

semen N: jìngyihk (M: dihk)

semester N: hohkkèih (M: go)

semi- Prefix: bun * **semi-colon** N: fànhouh (M: go) * **semi-final** N: jéunkyutchoi (M: chi, chèuhng) * **semi-tropical** N/PW: ayihtdaai

seminar N: yìhntóuwúi (M: go; chi)

seminary N: (theological) sàhnhohkyún (M: gàan)

senate N: (upper house) chàamyíhyún, seuhngyíhyún (M: go) N: (in university) daaihhohk pìhngyíhwúi (M: go)

senator N: chàamyíhyùhn (M: go, wái)

send FV: ❶ (deliver, of gift) sung ❷ (mail) gei ❸ (with a mission) paai ❹ dá (telegraph) ~ *dihnbou* CV: (send PN VO) sái * **send king regards** FV: mahnhauh * **send out** FV: faat ~ *chéngtíp* (invitation card) * **send N off** FV: geichēut

* **send PN for it** PH: sái yàhn làih ló

seniority N: (in rank) nìhnjì

sensation N: (feeling) gám-gok (M: júng) PH: (things that cause excitement) gwàngduhng ge sih

sensational SV: (exciting) gwàngduhng (frightening) dāk-yàhngèng PH: (arousing deep feeling) lihng yàhn gīkduhng

sense BF: ❶ -gám · (of duty) *jaakyahm* ~ ; (of humour) *yàumahk* ~ ; ❷ -gok · (of hearing) *ting* ~ ; (of sight) *sih* ~ ; (of smell) *chau* ~ ; (of taste) *meih* ~ ; (of touch) *jùk* ~ N: ❶ (feeling) gámgok (M: júng) ❷ (meaning) yisi ❸ (reason) douhléih FV: (feel, aware of) gokdāk * **common sense** N: sèuhngsīk (M: dī) * **come to one's senses** RV: (out of a faint) sèngfàan FV: (understand) Mìhngbaahk * **have a sense of** FV: gokdāk, gámgokdāk * **in a sense** PH: joih yātfòngmihn làih góng * **make sense** SV: yáuhyisi * **make sense of** FV: mìhngbaahk * **out of one's sense** FV: dìnjó, sàhngìng

senseless PH: ❶ (meaningless) móuh yisi ❷ (unconscious) móuhjó jìgok ❸ (fainted) bātsíng yàhnsih

sensibility N: ❶ (power of feeling) gámgoklihk ❷ (susceptibility) chìhnggám N/SV: (sensitive) máhngám

sensible Adj. PH: ❶ (reasonable) mìhngbaahk sihléih ge ❷ (that can be felt) hóyíh gámgokdóu ge

sensitive SV: máhngám ·

deui N ~ Adj. PH: (of feeling) sàhngìng gwomáhn

sensitivity N: ❶ (nature) máhngámsing ❷ (degree) máhngámdouh

sensory PH: hái gámgok fòngmihn, hái gámgokseuhng

sensual PH: ❶ (of body) hái yuhktái fòngmihn ❷ (sexual) hái sīkyuhk fòngmihn

sensuality N: sīkyuhk

sensuous PH: ❶ hái gámgokseuhng, hái gámgok fòngmihn ❷ (of pictures) lihng yàhn gokdāk hóu leng ❸ (of music) lihng yàhn gokdāk hóu hóutèng

sentence N: ❶ (words) syutwah (M: geui) ❷ (judgement) punkyut FV: (in court) punkyut, pun M: (of words) geui ✳ **under sentence of death** PH: beihpun séiyìhng ✳ **sentence to imprisonment** PH: PN1 pun PN2 chóhgāam

sentfrom SV: ❶ (short and witty) gáangit ❷ (dull) muhn

sentiment N: (mental feeling) gámchìhng ✳ **a man of sentiment** PH: gámchìhng fùngfu ge yàhn

sentimental Adj. PH: ❶ (of personality) dòsàuh sìhngám ❷ (in doing things) gámchìhng yuhngsih SV: (for things) sèunggám ~ ge síusyut (novel)

sentry N: saaubìng (M: go) ✳ **sentry-box** N/PW: saaugōng (M: go)

Seoul N/PW: Honsìhng

separate FV: ❶ (divide) fàn,

fànhòi • *jèung N1 tùhng N2* ~ • *PN1 tùhng PN2* ~ ❷ (divide by putting something in between) gaakhòi ❸ (pull apart) làaihòi VO: ❶ (say good-bye) fànsáu • *PN1 tùhng PN2* ~ ❷ (in marriage) fàngèui • *taaitáai tùhng sìnsàang* ~ RV: ʹ (divide) fànsèhng

separately A: ❶ fànhòi ❷ (not joined) gokyáuhgok, gokjih

separation FV: (divide, not together) fànhòi VO/N: (in marriage) fàngèui

September N: gáuyuht

septic VO: hahmnùhng, fanùhng PH: yáuh nùhng

Septic(a)emia N: baaihhyutjing

sepulcher N: fàhnmouh (M: go)

sepulchral SV: ❶ (deep and gloomy) yàmsàm ❷ (low) yàmchàhm ~ *ge sìngyàm* (voice)

sequel N: ❶ (end of story, film) gitguhk (M: go) ❷ (result) gitgwó ❸ (of what will happen) hauhgwó (M: go) ✳ **in the sequel** A: hauhlòih, (as a result) gitgwó

sequence N: (order) chijeuih (M: go) ✳ **in sequence** Adv. PH: jiujyuh chijeuih ✳ **a sequence of** A: yātlìhn, lìhnhei

serenade N: síuyehkūk (M: sáu)

serene Adj. PH: (of weather) hóu hóutìn SV: ❶ (of weather) chìhnglóhng ❷ (calm) pìhngjihng ❸ (peaceful) ngònchèuhng ~ *ge siuyùhng* (smile)

serf N: nùhngnòuh (M: go)

serfdom N: nùhngnòuh jaidouh (M: go)

sergeant N: ❶ (police-officer) sàjín (M: go) ❷ (in army) jùngsih (M: go)

serial ATT: lìhnjuhk A: lìhnjyuh, lihnjuhk ✳ **TV serial** N: dihnsih (lìhnjuhk) kehkjaahp (M: chēut)

series A: yātlìhn, lìhnhei, lìhnjuhk ✳ **in series** Adv. PH: seuhnjyuh chijeuih A: seuhnjeuih

serious SV: ❶ (adverb of degree) gányiu, yìhmjuhng ❷ (the way one works) yìhngjàn ❸ (stern) yìhmsūk, jinggìng ❹ (of illness) yìhmjuhng ❺ (true) jànge PH: (not joking) m̀haih góngsiu

seriously A: (earnestly) jànhaih, jànge Adv. PH: (not casually) hóu yìhngjàn gám PH: (not joking) m̀haih góngsiu, m̀haih góng wáan

sermon VO: (preach) góngdouh (léih) N/FV: (instruction) gaaufan (M: go)

serpent N: ❶ (snake) sèh, daaihsèh (M: tìuh) ❷ (venomous) duhksèh (M: tìuh)

serpentine Adj. PH: ❶ (of shape) wāanwāankūkkūk ❷ (cunning) hóuchíh sèh gam gáauwaaht

serum N: hyutchìng (M: dī)

servant N: gùngyàhn • (female) néuih ~ ,(male) nàahm ~ (M: go) ✳ **civil servant** N: gùngmouhyùhn (M: go) ✳ **part-time female servant** N: jùngdím (néuih) gùngyàhn (M: go)

serve FV/N: ❶ (work for) fuhkmouh • waih PN/N ~ ❷ jiufù (customers) ~ yàhnhaak, ~ haakjái ❸ (supply) gùngying FV: ❶ (like a servant) fuhksih ❷ (treat) deui, deuidoih ❸ sung (a notice) • ~ yātjèung tùngjì VO: ❶ (of food) séuhngchoi ❷ (of a ball) faatkàuh ❸ (in army) dòngbìng ❹ (of a prison term) chóhgāam ✳ **serve PN right** SV: dái PH: dáiséi, dái kéuih, dái kéuih séi

server N: ❶ fuhkmouhyùhn (M: go) ❷ (in Chinese restaurant) fógei (M: go) ❸ (in restaurant, hotel) sihjái (M: go) ❹ (of a ball) faatkàuhyùhn (M: go) ❺ (at Mass) fuhjai (M: go) ❻ (tray) tokpún (M: go) PH: (for salad) sihk sāléut yuhng ge chā tùhng gāng (M: fu)

sevice N/FV: ❶ fuhkmouh ❷ (to customers in restaurants) jiufù ❸ (help) bòngjoh ❹ (contribute) gunghin ❺ (maintain after sale) bóuyéuhng ❻ (repair) sàuléih, jíng ✳ **church services** N: láihbaai • sáu ~ , jouh ~ (Catholic) nèihsaat • mohng ~ , chàamyúh ~ ✳ **serve military service** VO: fuhk bìngyihk, (coll.) dòngbìng ✳ **10% service charge** PH: gàyāt síujeung

serviceable SV: (of use) yáuhyuhng, ngāamyuhng

serviette N: chāangān (M: tìuh)

servility PH: nòuhdaih ge singgaak

servitude VO: (labour) jouh fúgùng N: (punishment from court) tòuhyìhng

sesame N: jìmàh (M: nāp)

session N: (term) hohkkèih (M: go) BF: ❶ -bāan, -haauh ·*hahngh* ~ (afternoon session) ❷ -bouh · *sìuhohk* ~ (primary session) ✳ **summer session** N: syúkèihbāan

set FV: ❶ (put) jài, báai, fong ❷ dihng (time) ~ *sìhgaan, yahtjí* ❸ (inlay) sèung ❹ (become solid) kìhng ❺ gaau (watch, alarm clock) ~ *bīu,* ~ *naauhjūng* M: (for things) tou, fu VO: ❶ (for hair) sèutfaat ❷ (bear fruit) gitgwó ❸ (for bone) bokgwāt N: ❶ (style) fúnsīk (M: go, júng) ❷ (posture) jìtaai, jìsai (M: go, júng) ❸ (scenery on stage) bouging (M: go, júng) CV: ❶ (with, by use of) yuhng, yíh ❷ (make, cause) lihng, sái ✳ **off set** N: (printing) ōsīk yanchaat ✳ **set lunch** N: haakfaahn, touchāan (M: go) ✳ **set aside** RV: ① (save) chóuhmàaih ② (put) báaimàaih, sàumàaih ✳ **set a thief to catch a thief** IE: yíh duhk gùng duhk ✳ **set down** FV: fongdài ~ ✳ **set forth** FV: ① (start journey) chēutfaat ② faatbíu (opinion) ~ *yigin* VO: (start journey) héichìhng ✳ **set free** FV: sīkfong ✳ **set sail** VO: hòisyùhn, hòisàn ✳ **set up** FV: ① (establish) ginlahp, chitlahp ② hòi (shops) ~ *poutáu*

settee N: (sofa) sōfáyí (M: jèung; tou) PH: saige sōfáyí

setter N: (one who installs) ngònjòng gùngyàhn (M: go) PH: (one who inlays jems) sèung sáusīk ge yàhn (M: go) ✳ **type-setter** N: pàaihjih gùngyàhn (M: go)

setting N: ❶ (furnishings) chitbeih (M: dī) ❷ (on stage) bouging (M: go; júng) ❸ (surrounding) wàahngíng (M: go; júng) ❹ (of jewellery) sèungfaat (M: júng; go)

settle FV: ❶ (make a permanent home) dihnggèui · *hái PW* ~ ❷ (go to live) jyuh ❸ (sit down) chóhdài ❹ (rest) yàusīk ❺ (sink) chàhm ❻ (solve) gáaikyut ❼ (decide) kyutdihng RV: ❶ (move) bùnhóu ngūk ❷ (conclude by agreement) dihnghóu ❸ (pay a bill in full) wàahnching ❹ (arrange) ngònpàaihhóu ❺ (get fixed) gáaudihm ✳ **settle down** RV: (live) jyuhdihng, jyuhlohk PH: ① (calm down) pìhngjihng lohklàih ② (after restless movement) ngòndihng lohklàih ③ jihmjím jaahpgwaan (new situation) ~ *sànge wàahngíng* ✳ **settle with somebody** PH: tùhng PN syunjeung

settlement FV: (solve) gáaikyut N: (solution) gáaikyut ge baahnfaat (M: go) PW/N: ❶ (colony) jihkmàhndeih (M: go) ❷ (foreign settlement at a treaty port) jòugaai

settler PH: (for people) yìhgèui PW ge yàhn, kìuhgèui PW ge yàhn (M: go)

settling N: jà (M: dī)

seven Nu: chāt ✳ **seven-fold** N: chātpúih ✳ **seven seas** PH: saigaai chāt daaih hóiyèuhng N: chāthói

seventeen Nu: sahpchāt

seventeenth Nu: daih sahpchāt TW: (day of month) sahpchāthouh

seventh Nu: daihchāt TW: (day of month) chāthouh

seventy Nu: chātsahp ✳

seventy times seven PH: (in Bible) chātsahpgo chātchi

sever RV: (cut) chittyúhn, gottyúhn (with a chopper) jáamhòi FV: (break) tyúhn

several Nu: géi

severe SV: ❶ (stern) yìhmsūk ❷ (strict) yìhm ❸ (difficult to be sustained) yìhmgaak ❹ (for pain, illness) gányiu, sàileih ❺ (for event, illness) yìhmjuhng

sew FV: ❶ lyùhn ❷ (by machine) chè ❸ dèng (button) ~ náu

sewage N: ❶ (water) hàangkèuihséui, wùjòuséui (M: dī) ❷ (refuse) laahpsaap, wùjòuyéh (M: dī)

sewer N: hàangkèuih (M: tìuh)

sewerage N: ❶ (water) hàangkèuihséui, wùjòuséui (M: dī) ❷ (refuse) wùjòuyéh, laahpsaap (M: dī)

sewing N: (as a subject) fùhngyahn · hohk ~ ∗ sewing-machine N: yìchè (M: ga) ∗ sewing needle N: lyùhnsāamjām, jām (M: ngáan, jì)

sex N: singbiht ∗ sex appeal SV: singgám

sextant N: luhkfànyìh (M: go)

sextet(te) N: ❶ (of players) luhkchùhngcheung ❷ (of instruments) luhkchùhngjau

sexual Adj. PH: yáuh sing ge ∗ sexual desire N: singyuhk (M: dī) ∗ sexual equality PH: nàahmnéuih pìhngdáng ∗ sexual organ N: sing heigùn,

sàngjihkhei (M: go)

shabby SV: chàahngauh PH: (in dress) laahnsàn laahnsai IE: (dress) yìsàamlàahmláuh / yìsàamlàahmléuih

shack N: (hut) muhkngūkjái (M: gàan)

shackle N: (of hands) sáukau (M: fu, deui) (of foot) geuklìuh (M: fu, deui) PH: (to a prisoner) yuhng sáukau / geuklìuh sójyuh VO: (to put on) daai sáukau

shade PH/PW: yàmge deihfòng N: ❶ (of tree) syuhyàm ❷ (of painting, picture) yàmyíng bouhfahn PH: (of colour) ngàahnsīk ge sàmchín FV: (to screen) jèjyuh VO: ❶ (to draw) waahk yàmyíng ❷ (change colour) binsīk ∗ lamp-shade N: dāngjaau (M: go) ∗ windowshade (blind) N: chēunglím (M: douh, tòhng)

shadow N: yíng (M: go) FV: (follow) gànjùng PH: (watch secretly) ngamjūng gàamsih ∗ eye shadow N: ngáahnyíng · waahk ~ (M: dī) ∗ shadow boxing N: taaigihk (kyùhn) · dá ~ ∗ shadows round the eyes N: (not enough sleep, ill) hāak ngáahnhnyūn

shadowy Adj. PH: ❶ (having shade) yáuh yàmyíng ge ❷ (of woods, trees) yáuh hóudò syuhyàm ge SV: (not clear) mòuhwùh, (coll.) mùhngchàhchàh

shady Adj. PH: (having shade) yáuh yàm ge SV: (and cool) yàmlèuhng

shaft N: ❶ (handle) beng (M: jì, go) ❷ (of arrow) (jin) gòn (M: jì) ❸ (of elevator) dihntàichòuh, sìnggonggèijéng (M: go)

shag PH: ❶ (of hair) hóu chòuhàaih ge mòuh (M: dī) ❷ (of tobacco) hóu chòu ge yīnsī (M: dī)

shaggy SV: ❶ (of hair) pùhngsùng ❷ (rough and coarse) chòumaht ✻ **shaggy eyebrows** N: chòumèih (M: douh, hòhng) PH: chòumaht ge ngáahnmèih, chòumaht ge mèihmòuh

shake FV: ❶ ngòuh (bottle, tree) ❷ (quiver) jan ❸ (up and down) ngòuh, chok ❹ (hold one end and shake up and down) yéung, dan ❺ (move) yūk RV: (to mix) ngòuhwàhn, chokwàhn ✻ **milk-shake** N: náaihsīk (M: būi) ✻ **shake hands with** PH: tùhng PN ngāaksáu ✻ **shake off** FV: lāt RV: ① ngòuhlāt ② (by throwing away) fihnglāt ③ gaailāt (a bad habbit) ~ *waaih jaahpgwaan* ✻ **shake up** RV: ① (to mix) ngòuhwàhn ② (shock) haakséi ✻ **shake with cold** PH: dungdou dá láahng jan, dungdou jan

Shakespeare N: Sàsihbéia

Shakespearian Adj. PH: ❶ Sàsihbéia ge ❷ (style) Sàsihbéia fùnggaak ge PH: yìhngau Sàsihbéia ge yàhn/hohkjé (M: go, wái)

shaky FV: ❶ (hands) sáujan ❷ (legs) geukjan Adv. PH: ❶ (hands) sáujanjan gám ❷ (legs) geukjanjan gám ❸ (voice) sèngjanjan gám Adj. PH: (unsafe) wúihyūk ge

shall A: ❶ wúih, yiu ❷ (should) yìnggòi Adv. PH: (be required) yātdihng yiu ✻ **shall I ....?** PH: sái m̀sái .... a? PH: (after a suggestion) .... hóu ma?

shallop N: tèhngjái (M: jek)

shallot N: dūngchūng (M: go)

shallow SV: (not deep) chín

sham SV: (pretend) jadai, ja-FV • (sleep) ~ *fan*, (sick) ~ *behng*, (dead) ~ *séi* SV: (false) gá

shambles N/PW: ❶ (scene of killing) tòuhchèuhng (M: go) ❷ (scene of confusion) faihèui (M: go)

shame SV: (disgrace) cháu, SV/N: sàuchí ✻ **have no shame** PH: m̀ji cháu, móuh sàuchísàm ✻ **shame on you** PH: jànhaih diugá la!

shameful SV/VO: diugá

shameless PH: m̀ji cháu, mihnpèihháuh / háuhmihn-pèih

shammy, shamoy N: lìhngyèuhng(jái) (M: jek)

shampoo VO: sáitàuh N: (liquid) sáitàuhséui (M: jēun; jek) ✻ **shampoo and set** PH: sáitàuh sēutfaat

Shanghai N/PW: Seuhng-hói

Shangri-La N/PW: ❶ (Utopia) saingoih tòuhyùhn (M: go) ❷ (hotel) Hèunggaakléihlàai Jáudim (M: gàan)

shank N: ❶ (of leg) geukgwā-lōng (M: go) ❷ (of stockings) mahttúng (M: jek)

shanty PH: (hut) hóu gáanlauh ge ngūkjái (M: gàan)

shape N: ❶ yìhngjohng, ngoihyìhng (M: go) ❷ (feature) yéung (M: go) ❸ (model) mòuhyìhng (M: go) ❹ (condition) chìhngyìhng (M: go; júng)

❺ (kind) júngleuih (M: júng) BF:
yìhng • (square) seifòng ~;
(round) yùhn ~; (triangle)
sàamgok ~ ✳ **in good shape**
SV: tóhdong RVE: -hóu ✳ **put
into shape** FV: jíngléih

share M: ❶ (part) fahn ❷
(part ownership, stocks) gú N:
(part ownership) gúfán (M: gú)
FV: ❶ (divide) fàn ❷
fànhéung (good things) ~
faailohk (happiness) ❸ fàndàam (bad things)
~ yàuleuih (worry) A: ❶ (use in
common) gaapfán ❷ (have in
common) dōu ✳ **pay one's
own share** PH: jihgéi chēut
jihgéi gófahn ✳ **share a table
(in restaurant)** VO: daaptói ✳
share certificate N: gúpiu (M:
jèung) ✳ **shareholder** N:
gúdūng (M: go)

shark N: sàyú (M: tiuh) ✳
shark's fin, shark's fin soup
N: yùhchi • sihk ~ (M: faai;
gàn; go; wún)

sharp SV: ❶ (pointed) jìm ❷
(not blunt) leih ❸ (for clock time)
jeng, jing • yātdím ~ ❹ (clear)
chìngchó ❺ (smart) chùng-
mìhng ❻ (for sound) chiyíh ❼
(for a turn) gāp

sharpen FV: ❶ (with a knife)
pài ❷ pàauh (pencil) ~
yùhnbāt ❸ mòh (knife) ~ dōu
❹ (to a point) seuk RV: pàauhjìm, mòhleih, seukjìm

sharpener PH: yuhnglàih
pàauhjìm waahkjé seukjìm ge
yéh ✳ **pencil sharpener** N:
yùhnbātpáau (M: go) ✳ **knife
sharpener** N: mòhdōusehk
(M: gauh; faai)

shatter RV: (for glass)
dáseui, dálaahn FV: (in vain)
fánseui • ~ hèimohng (hope)
N: (broken pieces) seuipín (M:
faai)

shatterproof ATT: bātseui

shave VO: (for beard) taisòu
FV: (cut a little) pàauh

shawl N: pèigīn (M: faai, tiùh)

she PN: kéuih

sheaf M: jaat

shear VO: (cut off wool) jín
yèuhngmòuh N: ❶ daaih gaaujín (M: bá) ❷ (machine) jíngèi
(M: ga)

sheath N: ❶ (for sword) gimchiu, gimtou (M: go) ❷ (for
knife) dōuhok (M: go)

sheathe PH: (put into a
sheath) (jèung gim) chaapyahp
gimchiu léuihbihn

sheave FV: (tie) bóngjyuh,
jaatjyuh N: waahtlèuhn (M: go)

shed FV: ❶ làuh (tears, blood)
~ ngáahnleuih, ~ hyut ❷
(send out) faatchēut PW/N: ❶
(a building) pàahng (M: go) ❷
(little house) ngūkjái (M: gàan)
✳ **aeroplane shed** N: fèigèifu
(M: go)

sheen SV: ling

sheep N: yèuhng, mìhn-
yèuhng (M: jek) ✳ **sheep-dog**
N: muhkyèuhng gáu (M: jek) ✳
sheep-fold N/PW: yèuhng-
làahn (M: go)

sheepish Adj. PH: hóuchíh
yèuhng yātyeuhng gam sèuhn
SV: ❶ (shy) pacháu ❷ (self-
conscious) m̀jihjoih, m̀jihyìhn

sheer A: ❶ (completely)
yùhnchyùhn ❷ (absolute)
jyuhtdeui SV: (transparent)
taumìhng Adj. PH: (steep) hóu
che

sheet M: ❶ (for paper) jèung

❷ faai N: **❶** (for paper) jí (M: jèung) **❷** (for bed) chòhngdāan (M: jèung) **❸** (for person) péih (M: jèung) * **answer sheet** N: daapngonjí (M: jèung)

Sheik(h) N: (Arab chieftain) Alàaibaak yàuhjéung (M: go)

shelf N: gá (M: go) (for books) syùgá (M: go) (in kitchen) chyùhgá (M: go)

shell N: **❶** (hard outer covering) hok (M: go) **❷** (projectile) paaudáan (M: go) VO: (remove shell) mōkhok, mīthok RV: (remove) mōkhòi, mīthòi

shelter N/PW: **❶** beihnaahnsó (M: go) **❷** (for charity) sàuyùhngsó (M: go) PH/PW: (safe place) ngònchyùhn ge deihfòng (M: daat, go) FV: **❶** beiwuh **❷** (take care) jiugu, jiuliuh * **air raid shelter** N/PW: fòhnghùngduhng (M: go) * **find a shelter from rain** VO: beihyúh * **take shelter** FV: (hide) nèimàaih VO: (from trouble) beihnaahn * **typhoon shelter** N/PW: ① (for boats) beihfūngtòhng (M: go) ② (for people) tòihfùng beiwuhjaahm (M: go)

shelve PH: jèung N jàihái gá seuhngbihn

shepherd N/PH: muhk-yèuhngyàhn, hònyèuhng ge yàhn (M: go) FV: **❶** (take care) jiugu **❷** (guide) yáhndouh * **the good shepherd** N: (Jesus) sihnmuhk PH: hóu muhkyàhn

shield N: téuhnpàaih (M: go) FV: **❶** (resist) dóngjyuh **❷** (cover) jējyuh **❸** (protect) bóuwuh * **wind shield** N: (in a car) dóngfùng bōlēi (M: faai)

shift BF/M: (of working time)

gāang, bāan FV: **❶** (change) gói, jyun **❷** (move) yūk, yìh **❸** tong (gear) ~ *bō* * **change shift** VO: **❶** wuhnbāan **❷** (for bus, taxi) gāaugāang * **on day shift** VO: fàan yahtbāan, jouh yahtbāan PH: (for bus, taxi) dòng yahtgāang * **on night shift** VO: fàan yehbāan, jouh yehbāan PH: (for bus, taxi) dòng yehgāang * **work in shifts** A/VO: lèuhnbāan

shiftless RV: (no ability of doing things) jouhm̀dóu yéh PH: (cannot work) m̀jouhdāk yéh SV: (no use) móuhyuhng, m̀jùngyuhng

shifty SV: **❶** (unreliable) kaaum̀jyuh **❷** (cunning) gáauwaaht

shilling M/N: sīlíng (M: go)

shimmer FV: sím

shin PH: seuhng ng̀hchyun hah ng̀hchyun ge deihfòng * **shin beef** N: ngàuhjínyuhk (M: gauh) * **shin bone** N: geukgwāt (M: tìuh)

shindig PH: hóudaaih ge móuhwúi (M: nāp)

shine FV: **❶** (give light to) jiu **❷** (dazzle) chàahng **❸** (polish) chaat (shoes) ~ *hàaih;* sáang (like silver) ~ *ngàhnhei* **❹** (like star) sím RV: (polish) chaatling, sáangdou ling VO: (give out light) faatgwòng * **sunshine** N: yèuhnggwòng, yahttáu (M: dī)

shingle N: **❶** (pebbles) yùhn-sehkjái (M: nāp; gauh) **❷** (piece of wood) muhkbáan (M: faai) **❸** (signboard) jiupàaih (M: faai) PH: (on roofs) muhkge ngáhmín (M: faai)

shining SV: símsímling, sím

Adj. PH: (like flashes) símháh símháh VO: (give out light) faatgwòng

ship N: ❶ syùhn (M: jek) ❷ (for war) laahm, jìnlaahm, gwànlaahm (M: jek) FV: ❶ (send by freight) yuhng syùhn wahn ❷ (dispatch, as troops) paai ✻ **ship building** VO: jouhsyùhn ✻ **ship launching** N: hahséuiláih (M: chi, go) ✻ **ship wreck** PH: chàhmsyùhn yingoih ✻ **ship yard** N/PW: syùhnngou (M: go)

shipment PH: jèung dī fo jònghái syùhn seuhngbihn wahnheui daihyihsyu VO: lohkfo FV: jòngwahn

shipper PH: ngònpàaih jòngwahn fomaht ge yàhn (M: go)

shipping FV: wahn (goods) ~ *fo* PH: yuhng syùhn wahn ✻ **shipping company, shipping agency** N: wahnsyù gùngsī, fowahn gùngsī (M: gàan)

shire N: gwahn (M: go)

shirk FV: ❶ (run away) (jihngjíng) jáujó ❷ (avoid) tòuhbeih (responsibility) ~ *jaakyahm* ✻ **shirk school** VO: tòuhhohk ✻ **shirk work** VO: tàuláahn

shirt N: sēutsāam (M: gihn). (long sleeves) *chèuhngjauh* ~ (M: gihn) (short sleeves) *dyúnjauh* ~ (M: gihn) (Hawaii style) *hahwāiyìh* ~ (M: gihn) ✻ **sport shirt** N: tīsēut, bōsēut, wahnduhngsēut (M: gihn) ✻ **terry cloth shirt** N: mòuhgānsēut (M: gihn)

shiver VO: (tremble) dá láahngjan PH: ❶ (from cold) dungdou dá láahngjan ❷ (from fear) gèngdou dá láahngjan

N/BF: (broken pieces) seuipín, -seui

shoal M: (for fish, people) dèui PH/PW: (shallow place) chín séui ge deihfòng

shock N: (as by bad news) dágīk, chigīk (M: go) PH: (of grain) yātjaat yātjaat ge wòh PH: (by electricity) béi dihn dihnchàn SV/VO: (surprised) ngohkyìhn FV: (shake) jan FV/SV: (frightened) gèng ✻ **it gives me a shock** PH: N haakjó ngóh yāttiu

shocking PH: ❶ (very frightening) lihng yàhn janging ❷ (greatly surprising) lihng yàhn ngohkyìhn SV: (frightening) dákyàhngèng, hópa

shoddy N: (goods of poor quality) chifo

shoe N: hàaih (M: deui, jek) ✻ **tennis shoes** N: wahnduhnghàaih (M: deui; jek) ✻ **shoehorn** N: hàaihchāu (M: go) ✻ **shoelace** N: hàaihdáai (M: tiuh) ✻ **cobble shoes** VO: bóuhàaih

shoot VO: ❶ (with a gun) hòichēung ❷ (sprout) faatngàh ❸ (injection) dájām ❹ (take pictures) yíngséung ❺ (football) sehmùhn; sehkàuh; sehbō (basketball) sehlàahm, sehkàuh; sehbō ❻ (hunt) dálihp FV: ❶ (as for arrow) seh ❷ (with a gun) (hòichēung) seh N: (sprout) ngàh (M: go) (of bamboo) (jūk) séun (M: tiuh, jì) Adv. PH: hóu faai ✻ **shoot a fishnet** VO: saatmóhng ✻ **shoot down** RV: dálohk; sehlohk ✻ **shoot out** FV: sehchēut; (throw) pàauchēut

shooting N: sehgīk FV: seh (arrow) ~ *jin* ✻ **shooting**

gallery N/PW: lihnbáchèuhng (M: go) * **shooting star** N: làuhsīng (M: nāp) * **executed by shooting** FV: chēungbaih

shop N/PW: poutáu (M: gàan) BF: -póu (for books) · *syù ~* ; (for haircut) *fèifaat ~* ; (pawn) *dong ~* (M: gàan) VO: máaihyéh * **shop around** PH: juhkgāan poutáu táiháh sìnji máaih * **shop hours** N: yìhngyihp sìhgaan * **shop window** N: sīkgwaih; chēungchyùh (M: go) * **set up a shop** VO: hòipoutáu PH: hòichí jouh sàangyi * **shut up shop** VO: sàanmùhn; séuhngpou; (in market) sàusíh; (for stalls) sàudong

shopping VO: máaihyéh * **window shopping** VO: hàahng gùngsī * **shopping centre** N/PW: kaumaht jùngsàm (M: go) * **shopping mall** N/PW: sèungchèuhng (M: go)

shore N/PW: ngohn; ngohn-bīn (M: bīn) * **go on shore** VO: séuhngngohn

short SV: ❶ (in length) dyún ❷ (in height) ngái * **short cut** N: jihtging (M: tìuh) * **short of** FV: m̀gau SV/FV: kyutfaht; kyutsíu * **short-sighted** N/SV/ATT: gahnsíh Adj. PH: (in doing things) ngáahngwòhng dyúnsíu * **short-tempered** Adj. PH: pèihhei m̀hóu SV: cháu pèihhei, (impatient) gāpchou * **for a short time** TW: yātjahngāan; V suffix: -háh * **for short** N/FV: ① (in speaking) gáanchìng ② (in writing) gáansé; súksé * **in short, make a long story short** A: júngjì Adv. PH: júngyìhyìhnjì * **in a short time** TW: (soon) yātjahngāan Adv. PH: (soon)

hóufaai * **the long and short of it** PH: yātchai(ge) gìnggwo * **cut short** RV: ① (by cutting) jíndyún ② (shorten) súkdyún

shortage FV/SV: kyutfaht; kyutsíu FV: m̀gau

shortcoming N: kyutdím (M: go); dyúnchyu

shorten RV: ❶ súkdyún (time, distance) *~ sìhgaan; ~ kéuihlèih* ❷ (make short) jíngdyún ❸ (become short) bindyún

shorthand N: chūkgei

shortly TW: (soon) yātjahngāan

shorts N: (in uniform) dyúnfu (M: tìuh) PH: (for sport) dyúnge wahnduhngfu (M: tìuh)

shot N: ❶ (sound of gun) chēungsèng (M: háh) (sound of cannon) paausèng (M: háh) ❷ (that which is fired from a gun) paaudáan (M: go) ❸ (in movie) gengtàuh (M: go) FV: ❶ (with a gun) (hòichēung) seh; (hòichēung) dá ❷ seh (arrow) *~ jin* VO: ❶ (with a gun) hòichēung ❷ (injection) dájām ❸ (football) sehmùhn; sehkàuh; sehbō (basketball) sehlàahm; seh-kàuh; sehbō * **like a shot** Adv. PH: hóufaai A: jīkhāak * **shot-gun** N: (for hunting) lihpchēung * **shot put** N: tèui yùhnkàuh * **give PN a shot** PH: tùhng PN dájām

should AV: yìnggòi; yìng-dòng

shoulder N: boktàuh (M: go, bihn) FV: ❶ (carry on one side) tok ❷ (with a pole weighted on each end) dàam * **shoulder responsibility** FV: fuhjaak

shout PH: daaihsèng ngaai

/ giu ✳ **shouts of joy** N: fùn-
fùsing (M: dī)

shove FV: tèui

shovel N: cháan (M: go) ✳
shovel up FV: cháanhéi

show PH: (for someone to
look at) béi N PN táiháh; (by
pointing out) jíbéi PN tái; (by
demonstration) jouhbéi PN tái;
(by giving the way) daai PN
táiháh FV: ❶ (display) báai;
chàhnliht ❷ (for a film) fongyíng ❸ (express) bíusih ❹ (exhibit) jínláahm ❺ (boast) yín N:
(exhibition) jínláahmwúi VO: ❶
(boast) yínyéh ❷ (for a movie)
jouhhei · gógàan heiyún ~
mātyéh ~ a? N: ❶ (in TV) jitmuhk (M: go) ❷ (performance)
bíuyín (M: go) ❸ (movie) dihnyíng; hei (M: chēut) M: (for
movie, performance) chèuhng;
chēut ✳ **to show that** PH:
yuhnglàih syutmìhng; yuhnglàih bíusih ✳ **show oneself,
show up** FV: (at a meeting)
chēutjihk; dou; làih ✳ **show
someone in/out** PH: daai PN
yahplàih/chēutheui

shower N: jaauhyúh (M:
jahn) PH: yātjahn yúh ✳ **take
a shower** VO/PH: chùng-
lèuhng; yuhng fàsá chùng-
lèuhng

shown PH: bíusih chēutlàih
✳ **as shown** PH: hóuchíh
sóbíusih chēutlàih ge gám

showy Adj. PH: taai leng;
lengdākjaih

shred VO: (cut) chitsī RV:
(cut) chitsìhng sī; chitsìhng yāt
tìuh (yāt) tìuh

shredded Adj. PH: (cut) chitsìhng sī ge; chitsìhng yāttìuh
(yāt) tìuh ge BF: -sī. (of ginger)
gēung ~ (of pork) yuhk ~ (of

chicken) gāi ~

shrew N: (woman) putfúh (M:
go)

shrewd SV: (smart and
clever) jènglēk ✳ **shrewd-
headed** Adj. PH: tàuhnóuh
jìngmìhng ✳ **shrewd with
money** PH: hóu wúih dá syunpùhn; (very thrifty) hóu sīk hàan

shrewish PH/Adv. PH: (as
for woman) hóuchíh putfúh gám
PH: (scolding) hóu jùngyi
naauhyàhn Adj. PH: (sharp-
tongued) ngàhjìm jéuileih

shriek PH: (scream) gwáijà
hàuhlùhng gám ngaai (or giu)
N: (of a person) jìmgiusèng

shrill PH: hóu jìm (ge) SV:
chiyíh

shrimp N: hā (M: jek) ✳
shrimp dumpling N: hāgáau
(M: jek; lùhng) ✳ **light boiled
shrimp** N: baahkcheukhā (M:
gàn; jek)

shrine N: sàhnngām (M: go)
(Chinese) sàhnwái (M: go)

shrink FV: sūk; sàusūk
(decrease) gáamsíu VO: (as
cloth) sūkséui RV: ❶ (become
smaller) sūksai; sūksíu ❷
(become narrow) sūkjaak ✳
shrink with cold PH:
láahngdou sūkmàaih yātgauh

shrinkage FV: sūk; sàusūk
(decrease) gáamsíu VO: (as
cloth) sūkséui

shrivel PH: lihng N fùgòn

shroud N: líhmbou; gwósìbou (M: faai) (Chinese) sauhyī
(M: gihn; tou) PH: ❶ (to wrap)
yuhng líhmbou / gwósìbou
kámjyuh sītái ❷ (Chinese)
tùhng séiyàhn jeuk sauhyī

shrub N: ngái syuh (M: pò)

shrug PH: sūkháh go boktàuh

shuck N: (shell) hok (M: go) VO: (remove the shell) mōkhok

shudder VO: (shiver) dá láahngjan Adj. PH: (extremely frightened) mòuhgún duhng ✻ **shudder with cold** PH: dungdou dá láahngjan

shuffle VO: (for cards) sáipáai M: dèui, (for paper) daahp

shun FV: ❶ (avoid) beihmíhn ❷ (stay away from) beihhòi ❸ (in a command) lahpjing

shunt VO: (for train) jyungwái FV: láahnglohk (a person)

shunter PH: fuhjaak jèung fóchè jyungwái ge titlouh gùngyàhn (M: go)

shut FV: ❶ sàan (door, window, drawer) ❷ (with a latch) sēut (jyuh) ❸ (imprison) wan (héi); wan (jyuh) RV: ❶ sàanmàaih; sàanhóu; (tightly) sàansaht ❷ hahpmàaih (book) VO: (for office) sàanmùhn ✻ **shutin** PH: sóhái léuihbihn ge yàhn (M: go) ✻ **shut off** PH: tihngjí gùngying; móuh N làih ✻ **shut one's ears to all advice** PH: m̀tèng yàhn góng / hyun ✻ **shut out** FV: (shade) jējyuh ✻ **shut up** PH: (stop talking) m̀hóu góng la! hóu tihngháu la bo! FV: ❶ (hide) sàumàaih ❷ (imprison) wan(héi); wan(jyuh) ✻ **shut up a house** PH: jèung ngūk léuihbihn sóyáuh ge mùhn chēung dōu sàanhóu

shutter N: ❶ (venetian blind) baakyihpchēung (M: douh, tòhng) ❷ (in camera) faaimùhn (M: go)

shuttle N: sō (M: go) ✻ **space shuttle** N: taaihùng chyùnsōgèi (M: ga) ✻ **shuttle bus** N: chyūnsō básí (M: ga) ✻ **shuttle light bus** N: chyūnsō síubà (M: ga)

shuttlecock N: yín (M: go) · tek ~

shy SV: ❶ pachàu ❷ (modest) haakhei FV: (throw) deng; dám

Siberia N/PW: Sàibaakleiha

Siberian N: (people) Sàibaakleiha yàhn (M: go) Adj. PH: Sàibaakleiha ge

sibyl N: ❶ (in ancient times) néuih yuhyihngā; néuihsìnjì (M: go) ❷ (witch) néuihmòuh (M: go) PH: (fortune-teller) syunmehng ge (yàhn) (M: go)

Sicilian N: (people) Sàisàiléihdóu yàhn Adj. PH: Sàisàiléihdóu ge

Sicily N/PW: Sàisàiléihdóu

sick FV/N: behng (M: go; júng) SV: (unwell) m̀syùfuhk; m̀jingsàhn ✻ **air sick** PH: wàhn fèigèi lohng ✻ **home sick** N: sīhēungbehng FV: sīhēung gwajyuh ngūkkéi ✻ **sea sick** VO: wàhnlohng ✻ **make one sick** SV: hātyàhnjàng PH: lihng yàhn tóuyim ✻ **sick leave** N: behngga (M: yaht) ✻ **sick of / tired of** RV: FV: dou yim(saai) FV: yim

sickle N: lìhmdōu (M: bá)

sickly Adj. PH: ❶ (always sick) hóudò behng ge; sihsìh behng ge ❷ (causing sickness) lihngyàhn jokngáu ge SV: ❶ (pale) mìhnchèng ❷ (weak) hèuiyeuhk

side BF/M: -bihn; -mihn; -bīn

M/N: ❶ (surface) mihn ❷ (line) bīn (M: tìuh) ❸ (aspect) fôngmihn FV: bòng (jyuh) ✳ **side door** N: wàahngmún; jākmùhn (M: douh) ✳ **side effect** N: fujokyuhng (M: júng) ✳ **side walk** N: hàhngyàhnlouh (M: tìuh) ✳ **right side** N: jingmihn; (for cloth) mín ✳ **wrong side** N: fáanmihn; (for cloth) dái ✳ **side by side** A: paakjyuh

sidle PH: ❶ jākjāksàn hàahng ❷ (stealthily) gwáigwáisyúsyú gám hàahng

siege FV: (to a fortified place) bàauwàih

siesta N: ngaangaau VO: fan ngaangaau

sieve N/FV: sài (M: go) RV: sàichēutlàih

sift FV/N: sài (M: go) RV: sàichēutlàih

sigh VO: taanhei

sight RV: táigin; táidóu; gindóu N: ❶ (places) mìhngsing (M: go, douh) ❷ (opinion) yigin (M: go) ✳ **at sight** Patt: yāt táigin / táidóu / gindóu jauh . . . ✳ **fall in love at first sight** IE: yāt gin jùngchìhng ✳ **far-sighted** N/ATT: yúhnsih ✳ **in sight** RV: mohnggin; mohngdóu ✳ **lose one's sight** FV: màahngjó PH: táimgin yéh; táimdóu yéh ✳ **out of sight, out of mind** IE: ngáahn bāt gin; sàm bāt séung ✳ **sight-seeing** N/FV: yàuhláahm; gùn'gwòng

sign N: ❶ (mark) fùhhouh; fùhhóu (M: go) ❷ (of wood) pàaih; páai (M: go) ❸ (of the hand) sáusai (M: go) ❹ (omen) yitàuh (M: go) ❺ (trace) jùngjīk

(M: dī) ❻ (news, hope) sènghei (M: dī) VO/N: (write ones name) chìmméng; chìmjí ✳ **road sign** N: louhpáaih; gousihpáai (M: go)

signal N: seunhouh; (of the hands) sáusai • *dá ~* ✳ **traffic signals** N: gàautùng seunhouh (M: júng; go)

signalize PH: ❶ (by use of signals) yuhng seunhouh tùngjì ❷ (make noteworthy) lìhng yàhn jìdou; lìhng yàhn jyuyi

signatory N: (person) chìmyeukjé; (country) chìmyeukgwok VO: (of a treaty) chìmyeuk

signature N/VO: chìmméng; chìmjí (M: go)

signboard N: jīupàaih (M: go)

signet N: tòuhjēung; síjēung (M: go) VO: kāp tòuhjēung; koiyan

significance N: ❶ (special meaning) yiyih (M: go) ❷ (importance) juhngyiusing (M: go)

significant SV: (meaningful) yáuhyiyih PH: (important) yáuh juhngyiusing

signify FV: (mean, express) bíusih PH: (what significance) yáuh mātyéh yisi; yáuh mātyéh yiyih

signpost N: louhpáaih; gousihpáai (M: go)

silence SV: jihng ✳ **in silence** Adv. PH: hóu jihng gám; m̀chēutsèng gám ✳ **silence!** PH: ① chéng gokwái jihngdī ② (don't make noise) m̀hóu chòuh ③ (don't talk) m̀hóu chēutsèng ✳ **silence a baby's crying** VO: jíhaam PH:

sái bìhbī m̀haam * **silence is golden** IE: chàhmmahk sih gàm

silent SV: jihng * **be silent about** PH: móuh góngdou; móuh tàihkahp

silently Adv. PH: ❶ hóu jihng gám; jihngjíng gám ❷ (without saying a word) m̀chēutsèng gám; m̀sèng m̀hei gám

silents N: mahkpín (M: chēut)

silhouette N: jínyíng (M: go)

silk N: ❶ sī (M: tìuh) ❷ (material) sīchàuh; sīfaat (M: faai; pāt) PH: (made of) yuhng sī (chàuh) jouh ge * **raw silk** N: sàangsī (M: tìuh)

silkworm N: chàahmchúng (M: tìuh)

sill N: ❶ (of window) chēungtòih (M: go) ❷ (of door) mùhncháahn; mùhncháahm (M: go)

silly SV: ❶ (foolish) sòh; bahn ❷ (stupid) chéun N: (people) sòhyàhn; bahnyàhn; chéunyàhn (M: go) * **don't be silly** PH: m̀hóu gam sòh lā!

silo N/PW: (basement) deihlòuh (M: go) N: (underground barn) deihhah chōngfu (M: go)

silt N: (sand) nàih; yúnàih (M: dī) FV: (stopped with sand) sākjyuh PH: (blocked with sand) béi dī nàih sākjyuh

silver N: ngàhn PH: (made of) ngàhn jouh ge * **silver medal** N: ngàhnpàaih (M: go) * **silver plate** PH: douhjó ngán ge yéh (M: gihn) VO: douhngán * **silver wedding** N: ngàhnfàn

PH: gitfàn yahngh jàunihn

silversmith PH: ❶ jouh ngàhnhei ge yàhn (M:go) ❷ (seller) maaih ngàhnhei ge yàhn (M: go)

silverware N: ❶ (knife and fork) dōuchā (M: fu, tou) ❷ (vessels) ngàhnhei (M: gihn) PH: (table silver) ngàhnjouh ge chāangeuih (M: gihn, fu, tou)

silvery Adj. PH: hóuchíh ngàhn gám ge

simian N: ❶ (ape) yùhn; yàhnyùhn; yùhnhàuh (M: jek) ❷ (monkey) hàuhjí; máhlāu (M: jek) Adj. PH: (like) hóuchíh yùhnhàuh gám

similar Adj. PH: hóu sēungchíh • *N1 tùhng N2 ~* SV: (same) yātyeuhng • *N1 hóuchíh N2 ~*

similarity PH: sēungchíh ge deihfōng (M: dím, douh, go)

simile N: béiyuh (M: go)

similitude SV: (similar) sēungchíh FV: (look like) hóuchíh N: ❶ (outlook) yéung (M: go) ❷ (simile) béiyuh (M: go) PH: ❶ (similar things) sēungchíh ge yéh ❷ (look like each other) sēungchíh ge yàhn

simmer PH: ❶ (cook) yuhng maahnfó jyú ❷ (cook for a longer time) maahnmáan jyú

simper FV: sòhsiu

simple SV: ❶ (not complicated) gáandāan ❷ (easy) yùhngyih ❸ (plain, not luxurious) poksou ❹ (naive) dàansèuhn * **simple minded** PH: tàuhnóuh gáandāan

simplicity SV: ❶ (simple)

gáandàan ❷ (not luxurious) **poksou ❸** (naive) **dàansèuhn ❹** (childish) **tìnjàn**

simplify FV: **gáanfa · jèung** N ~ PH: **lihng N gáandàandī**

simplistic PH: (too simple) **taai (gwo) gáanfa** A: (not from all sides) **pinmihn**

simply A: **❶** (only) **jíhaih ❷** (merely) **bātgwohaih; mòuhfèihaih; bātngoihhaih ❸** (completely, no doubt about it) **gáanjìhk; jihkchìhng**

simulation FV: (pretend) **jadai** (imitate) **mòuhfóng; hohk** RV: (in disguise) **dábaahnsèhng; fajòngsèhng**

simulator N: (machine) **mòuhyíhhei** (M: ga) (equipment) **mòuhyíh jòngji** (M: dī; júng)

simultaneous A: **tùhngsih** Adv. PH: **tùhngyātgo sìhgaan ✳ simultaneous translation** N: **jīksìh chyùhnyihk**

sin N: **jeuih, jeuihngok** (M: júng) VO: **faahnjeuih**

Sinai N/PW: **❶ Sàinoih bundóu ❷** (the mountain) **Sàináaihsàan ❸** (the wilderness) **Sàináaih kwongyéh / kongyéh**

since MA: **❶ jihchùhng ❷** (seeing that) **geiyihn ❸** (because) **yànwaih** Patt: **❶** (of something still going on) **jihchùhng . . . yíhlòih; jihchùhng . . . héi ❷** (at some time and after that) **jihchùhng . . . jihauh ✳ ever since** Patt: **jihchùhng TW héi yātjihk dou yìhgā**

sincere SV: **❶** (honest) **lóuhsaht; sìhngsaht ❷** (desire) **yáuh sìhngyi ❸** (real, from a**

sincere heart) **jànsàm**

sinecure PH: **m̀sái jouhyéh baahk ló yàhngùng ge gùngjok**

sinew N: (tendon) **gàn** (M: tìuh)

sinewy Adj. PH: **❶** (having sinews) **hóudò gàn ge ❷** (tough) **hóu ngahn ge**

sinful Adj. PH: **yáuh jeuih ge; faahnjó jeuih ge**

sing VO: (person, birds, kettle) **cheunggō** FV: **❶** (birds) **cheung, giu, tàih ❷** (kettle) **héung ✳ sing up** PH: **daaihsèng cheung**

Singapore N/PW: **Sìnggabō**

singe RV: **❶** (by burning) **sìu nùng (jó) ❷** (by ironing) **tongnùng (jó)**

singer PH: **❶** (the person) **cheunggō ge yàhn ❷** (birds) **hóu wúih cheunggō ge jeukjái** N: **❶** (in public) **gōsáu** (M: go, wái) **❷** (very famous) **gōsīng** (M: wái, go)

single N: (one) **yātgo** PH: (marital status) **dàansàn; meih gitfan** ATT: **dàanyàhn** ~ **fóng** (room); ~ **chòhng** (bed) FV: (select) **gáan; syún ✳ singleminded** Adv. PH: **yātsàm yātyi ✳ single ticket** N: **dàanchìhng piu** (M: jèung) **✳ remain single** PH: **juhng haih dàansàn; juhng meih gitfàn**

singlet N: **❶** (undershirt) **dáisāam** (M: gihn) **❷** (vest) **buisàm** (M: gihn)

singsong PH: **❶** (of friends) **pàhngyáuh jeuihjaahp hái yātchái ge gōcheungwúi** (M: go) **❷** (impromptu vocal concert) **jīkhing ge gōcheungwúi** (M: go) SV: (monotonous) **dàandiuh**

singular N: (number) dàan-sou

sinister Adj. PH: (bad omen) m̀hóu yìtàuh SV: ❶ (bad omen) m̀gātchèuhng ❷ (fierce) hùngngok ❸ (ill will) yàmhím

sink FV: ❶ (ship) chàhm ❷ (become lower) hahgong ❸ (foundations) hahhahm RV: (to make it sink) dáchàhm ~ *jek syùhn* N: (in kitchen) sìngpùhn (M: go)

sinless PH: (no sin) móuh jeuih; mòuhjeuih SV: (innocent) mòuhgù

sinner PH: faahn (jó) jeuih ge yàhn N: jeuihyàhn (M: go)

sinologist N: honhohkgā (M: go, wái)

sinology N: honhohk

sinuous SV: wāankūk Adj. PH: wāanwāankūkkūk

sip FV: jyut M: daahm * **take a sip** PH: jyut yātdaahm

siphon N: ❶ (tube)wāangún; hùhngkāpgún (M: jì, tiùh) ❷ (bottle) hùhngkāppìhng; ngaatlihkpìhng (M: go) PH: (draw out) yuhng hùhngkāpgún kāpchēutlàih

sir N: ❶ (gentleman) sìnsàang (M: wái) ❷ (honorable title) jeuksih (M: wái) PH: (polite form of 'you') gokhah

sire N: (founder) chongchíyàhn

siren N: ❶ (alarm) gíngbou (M: go) ❷ (the instrument) gíngbouhei (M: go) ❸ (on ship) heidehk (M: go) ❹ (the sound of fire-engine) fójūkchèsèng; (of policecar) gíngchèsèng

sister N: ❶ (of same parents) jímuih (M: go); (elder ones) gājē (M: go); (younger ones) mùihmúi (M: go) ❷ (catholic nun) sàunéui; gūnèuhng (M: go) * **sister-in-law** N: ① (husband's elder sister) daaih/yìh/sàam gūnāai ② (husband's younger sister) gūjái (M: go) ③ (wife's elder sister) daaihyìh (M: go) ④ (wife's younger sister) yìjái (M: go) ⑤ (elder brother's wife) a sóu (M: go) ⑥ (younger brother's wife) daihfúh (M: go)

sit FV: chóh ~ *hái PW* * **sit down!** PH: chóhdài * **sit for an examination** PH: chàamgà háausíh * **sit up** PH: chóh héisàn

site N: ❶ deihdím (M: go) ❷ (of construction) deihpùhn (M: go) ❸ (of occurence) yihnchèuhng; deihdím PH: (find a place) dihng yātgo deihdím; dihng yātdaat deihfòng

sitting N: (seat) johwái (M: go) PH: ❶ (of Parliament) hòiwúi ge sìhgaan ❷ (of court) hòitìhng ge sìhgaan RV: (can seat) chóhdāklohk Adv. PH/PH: chóhháisyu * **sitting room** N: haaktēng (M: go)

situate FV: hái

situation N: ❶ chìhngyìhng (M: go; júng) ❷ (place) waihji; deihdím (M: go)

six Nu: luhk * **at sixes and sevens** PH: lahplahplyuhn; lyuhnsaai daaihlùhng

sixteen Nu: sahpluhk

sixteenth Nu: daihsahpluhk

sixth Nu: daihluhk

sixtieth Nu: daihluhksahp

sixty N: luhksahp

size N: ❶ (largeness or smallness) daaihsai; chekchyun (tr.) sāaisí ❷ (figure) sànchòih (M: júng) ❸ (of clothes or shoes) máh (M: go) ✳ **same size** PH: yātyeuhng gam SV ✳ **what size** PH: mātyéh máh a? géidō houh a? géi SV a?

skate VO: (sport) yáai syutkehk N: ❶ (sport) làuhbìng ❷ (shoe) làuhbìnghàaih; syutkehk (M: jek, deui) ✳ **skating rink** N/PW: làuhbìngchèuhng (M: go)

skein M: ❶ (coiled) gauh ❷ (bundle) jaat FV: kíuh (wool, thread) ~ *lāang*, ~ *sin*

skeleton N: ❶ (of mankind) fùlòuhgwāt; hàaihgwāt (M: fu; gauh) ❷ (of animal) (duhngmaht ge) hàaihgwāt (M: fu; gauh) ❸ (bone) gwāt; gwāttàuh (M: gauh; tìuh) ❹ (of building) gwātgá; gwātgon (M: go) ✳ **skeleton key** N: maahnnàhng sósìh (M: tìuh) ✳ **thin as a living skeleton** PH: saudou dāk pàahng gwāt

skeptic N: (person) wàaihyìhjé; wàaihyìhleuhngjé (M; go)

sketch N: ❶ (draft) góu (M: pìn) ❷ (outline) daaihgōng (M: go) ✳ **make a sketch** FV: ① (drawing) sésàng; soumìuh; chūksé ② (designing) chitgai VO: (painting) waahkwá ✳ **sketch-book** N: tòuhwábóu (M: bún) ✳ **sketch-map** N: chóutòuh (M: fūk, jèung)

skew SV: (not straight) mé; che

skewer PH: (fork) sìuyéhsihk yuhng ge chā (M: jì) N: (wooden or metal pin) chyùnyuhkjām;

chā (M: jì)

ski VO: waahtsyut N: (shoe) waahtsyutkehk (M: deui; jek)

skid FV: (of skate) sin VO: (of vehicles) sintáai PH: (for the wheel) yuhnglàih sipjyuh chèlūk ge yéh

skiff N: téhngjái (M: jek)

skilful SV: ❶ (showing skill) lēk ❷ (experienced) suhklihn

skill N: ❶ (technique) geih seuht (M: júng) ❷ (workmanship) gùngfù ❸ (to make a living) sáungaih; geihnàhng (M: mùhn; júng) ✳ **skilled worker** N: suhklihn gùngyàhn (M: go)

skim VO: beiyàuh FV: bei ✳ **skim-milk** N: tyutjìnáaih

skin N: ❶ (of a person) pèihfū (M: faai) ❷ (of fruits, vegetables, animals) pèih (M: faai) VO: (take away) mōkpèih; mītpèih ✳ **skin and bone** PH: (very thin) saudou pèih bàau gwāt ✳ **have a thick skin, thick-skinned** Adj. PH: háuh mihnpèih; mihnpèih háuh ✳ **wet to the skin** PH: chyùhnsàn sāpsaai ✳ **skin-deep** SV: fùchín

skinny PH: pèih bàau gwāt; saudou pèih bàau gwāt; saudou dāk pàahng gwāt

skip FV: (jump, omit) tiu VO: (a game) tiusíng

skirmish N: síu chùngdaht (M: chi)

skirt N: (garment) kwàhn (M: tìuh)

skit N: ❶ (article) fúngchi dyúnmàhn (M: pìn) ❷ (play) waahtkài dyúnkehk (M: chēut) M: dèui

skittish Adj. PH: ❶ (easily frightened) hóu yùhngyih haakchàn ge ❷ (difficult to control) hóu nàahn hungjai ge SV: (of woman) fùngsòu

skull N: ❶ (top of the head) tàuhhok ❷ (bone of the head) tàuhgwāt; tàuhkoigwāt (M: go)

skunk N: (animal) wòhngsyúlòhng; yàuhsyú (M: jek) PH: (person) hahlàuh ge yàhn (M: go)

sky N: ❶ tìn (M: go) ❷ (weather) tìnsīk ✳ **sky-high** PH: hóuchíh tìn gam gòu ✳ **sky scraper** N: mōtìn daaihhhah (M: joh)

slab N: ❶ (of wood) muhkbáan (M: faai) ❷ (of stone) sehkfaai (M: faai) M: faai

slack SV: ❶ (lazy) láahn ❷ (no energy) móuh jìngsàhn PH: (no energy) móuh hei móuh lihk

slacken FV: ❶ (make loose) fongsùng ❷ (for speed) gáammaahn ❸ (weaken) gáamyeuhk PH: ❶ (slow down) maahnjó ❷ (become weak) yeuhkjó

slag N: kongjà (M: dèui; dī)

slake FV: ❶ (satisfy) múhnjūk ❷ (get rid of) sìuchèuih PH: (of lime) gàséui lihng sehkfùi suhkfa

slam PH: ❶ (shut noisily) bàahng yātsèng sàanmàaih ❷ (shut violently) daaihlihk sàanmàaih Adv. PH: (with a bang) bàahng yātsèng

slander FV: dáiwái; féipóhng

slang N: (words) chòuwá (M: geui)

slant RV: jíngche N: (slope) chèhbō (M: go)

slap FV: (hit) gwaak; dá PH: (hit) gwaak yātbā; dá yātbā Adv. PH: (with a slapping noise) pàahk yātsèng

slash FV: ❶ (cut) jáam ❷ (with a whip) bīndá ❸ (strike) dá ❹ (condemn) naauh VO: (make gashes) hòichā

slat N: ❶ (of wood or metal) báan (M: tiuh; faai) ❷ (rib) laahkgwāt; lahkgwāt (M: tiuh) ❸ (sound) pìhkpìhk pàahk-pàahksèng FV: (hit) dá PH: (throw) chēutlihk dám; chēutlihk deng

slate N: (for writing) sehkbáan (M: faai)

slaughter FV: ❶ tòng (animal) ~ jyū (pig) ❷ saat (human beings) FV/N: (massacre) tòuhsaat (M: chi)

Slav N: Sìlàaifùyàhn (M: go)

slave N: (person) nòuhdaih (M: go) VO: (labour) jouh fúgūng ✳ **make a slave of PN** PH: jèung PN dongjouh lòuhdaih / nòuhdaih

slaver N: (saliver) háuséui (M: dī; dūk) VO: (spit) làuhháuséui PH: ❶ (trader) fáanmaaih nòuhdaih ge yàhn (M: go) ❷ (ship) wahn nòuhdaih ge syùhn (M: jek)

slavery N: ❶ (hard work) fúgūng ❷ (system) nòuhdaih jaidouh (M: júng; go)

slavish Adj. PH: hóuchíh nòuhdaih gám

Slavonic Adj. PH: ❶ (of the people) Sìlàaifùyàhn ge ❷ (of the language) Sìlàaifùwà ge N:

(language) Sìlàaifūwá

slay FV: ❶ (kill) saat ❷ (murder) màuhsaat RV: ❶ (put to death) jíngséi ❷ (kill) saatséi

sleave N: saisī (M: tìuh) PH: (make into threads) fànsìhng saisī

sled N: syutchè (M: ga)

sledge N: ❶ syutchè (M: ga) ❷ (hammer) daaih titchèuih (M: go)

sleek Adj. PH: (smooth and soft) gwōngwaaht yàuhyúhn

sleep VO: fangaau FV: (place for sleeping or living) fan; jyuh N: seuihmìhn ✻ **get to sleep, fall asleep** RV: fanjeuhk ✻ **sleep like a log** PH: fandāk hóu nahm; fandou hóuchíh jek jyū gám ✻ **sleep soundly** PH: fandou gēuhgéusèng ✻ **sleepwalker** PH: yáuh muhngyàuhbehng ge yàhn (M: go) ✻ **sleep with PN** PH: tùhng PN fan (gaau); tùhng PN séuhngchòhng

sleeper N: ❶ (on railway track) jámmuhk (M: tìuh) ❷ (on road) louhgúng (M: go) ❸ (in train) ngohchè (M: kā) ngohkā (M: go) ✻ **heavy sleeper** PH: fandāk hóu nahm ge yàhn (M: go)

sleeping VO: fangaau N: seuihmìhn ✻ **sleeping-bag, sleeping-sack** N: seuihdói (M: go) ✻ **sleeping-car, sleeping-carriage** N: (in a train) ngohkā (M: go) ngohchè (M: kā) ✻ **sleeping-pill** N: ngònmìhnyeuhk (M: nāp)

sleepless FV: sātmìhn RV: fanm̀jeuhk PH: fanm̀jeuhk gaau; fanm̀dóu gaau ✻ **sleepless night** PH: sèhng-

máahn móuh fangaau; sèhng-máahn (dōu) fanm̀jeuhk

sleepy SV: ngáahnfan

sleeve N: ❶ jauh; sāamjauh (M: jek, go) ❷ (for a disc) cheungpíntou (M: go) ✻ **sleeve link** N: jauhháunáu (M: deui, fu; nāp)

sleeveless Adj. PH: móuh-jauh ge

sleigh N: syutchè; syutcheui (M: ga) VO: (ride on) chóh syut-chè; chóh syutcheui

slender SV: ❶ (of figure) míuhtíuh ❷ (thin) yau ❸ (thin and long) yauchèuhng ❹ (scanty) síu

sleuth N: ❶ (police) gínghyún (M: jek) ❷ (for hunting) lìhphyún (M: jek)

slice VO: chitpín PH: jèung N chithòi yāt faaifaai M: (piece) faai; pin

slide FV: sin; waaht N: ❶ (for children) waahttài (M: go) ❷ (picture) waahndāngpín (M: jèung; tou) PH: (of land) sàannàih kìngse ✻ **play slide** VO: sèuh waahttài ✻ **slide fastener** N: làailín (M: tìuh) ✻ **let things slide** IE: seuhn kèih jihyìhn; tìngkèih jihyìhn

sliding PH: (that can slide) hóyíh waahtduhng ge ✻ **sliding door** N: tongmùhn (M: douh) ✻ **sliding scale** N: gai-syunchek (M: bá)

slight PH: ❶ (very little) hóu síu ❷ (not important) m̀gányiu ge SV: ❶ (not serious) hìngmèih ❷ (of figure) míuhtíuh FV: (neglect) doihmaahn; láahng-lohk ✻ **not in the slightest** PH: yātdī dōu m̀ / móuh

slim SV: (of figure) míuhtíuh FV: (lose weight) gáamfèih

slime N: ❶ (sticky mud) nìmtóu (M: dī) ❷ (from snails) nìmyihk (M: dī)

sling N: ❶ (for throwing stone) tàuhsehkhei (M: go) ❷ (band, strap) diudáai (M: tìuh) FV: (throw) dám

slip A: (secretly) jihngjíngdéi; tàutàudéi PH: (sneak away) jihngjíng sùngyàhn FV: ❶ (slide) sin ❷ (fall) dit ❸ (untie, unlock) gáai; hòi RV: (slide and get hurt) sinchàn N: ❶ (of paper) jítìuh; jíjái (M: jèung) ❷ (under a dress) dáikwàhn (M: tìuh) ❸ (for baby) háuséuigīn (M: tìuh) ❹ (pillowcase) jámtàuhdói (M: go) VO: ❶ (of plant) jipjì ❷ (of bones) làtgaau * **slip-cover** N: gàsìtou (M: go) * **slip-knot** N: sàanglit (M: go) * **slipover** N: gwotàuhlāp (M: gihn) * **slip-on** N: (shoe) láahnlóuhàaih (M: deui; jek) * **deposit slip** N: chyùhnfúndāan (M: jèung) * **withdrawal slip** N: tàihfúndāan (M: jèung) * **let an opportunity slip** PH: chogwo yātgo gèiwuih

slipper N: tōháai (M: deui; jek)

slippery SV: ❶ (will easily fall) waaht; sin ❷ (not safe) m̀wánjahn

slipup N: ❶ (error) chongh (M: go, chi) ❷ (negligence) sòfāt (M: chi, go) PH: (unfortunate thing) bàthahng ge sih (M: gihn; chi)

slit N: ❶ la (M: tìuh) ❷ (of letterbox) seunsèungháu (M: go) RV: (to cut open) gothòi; gaaihòi PH: (cut into long pieces) chìthòi yāttìuh (yāt) tìuh

slither PH: hóu m̀wánjahn gám waahthàhng FV: (of snakes) làan; pàh

sliver M: faai N: ❶ (thin pieces) bohkpín (M: faai) ❷ (small pieces) saipín (M: faai) ❸ (broken pieces) seuipín (M: faai) PH: (cut into pieces) jèung N chitsìhng bohkpín RV: (cut) chithòi

slobber VO: (drool) làuh háuséui N: (saliver) háuséui (M: dī; dihk; dūk) PH: ❶ (in speaking) góngyéh chīleihgán ❷ (wet with saliva) yuhng háuséui jíngsāp

slog PH: ❶ (hit) chēutlihk dá ❷ (work hard) kàhnlihk jouhgùng

slogan N: háuhouh (M: go) (written) bìuyúh (M: jèung; geui)

slope N/PW: chèhbō; sàanbō (M: go)

sloping SV: che

sloppy SV: (poor) séuipèih PH: (in doing things) jouhyéh hóu lásài; jouhyéh kàuhkàuh kèihkèih Adj. PH: (dirty with rain) hóudò nàihbaahn ge

slot N: la (M: tìuh) * **slot-machine** N: jihduhng sauhfogèi (M: ga)

sloth SV: (lazy) láahn N: (animal) syuhlaaih (M: jek)

slouch Adv. PH: (in low mood) móuh sàhn móuh hei gám; móuh lèih sàmgèi gám PH: (clumsy) leuhnjeuhn ge yàhn

slough PH: (swamp) yāttàhm nàih; yáuh nàihbaahn ge deihfòng VO: (of snake) tyutpèih FV: (fall off) làt

slow SV: ❶ (of speed) maahn ❷ (of movement) chìhdeuhn ❸ (dull) muhn ATT: maahnsing · ~ *duhkyeuhk* (poison) ✻ **slowdown** PH: (slower) maahndī FV/N: (of workers) tóihgūng (M: chi) RV: (of speed) gáammaahn

slowly SV: maahn A: maahnmáan; maahnmáan Adv. PH: hóu maahn gám

sluggard SV: láahn N: (of person) láahnyàhn (M: go)

sluggish SV: ❶ (lazy) láahn ❷ (slow) maahn ❸ (of market) sìutìuh ❹ (not active) chìhdeuhn

sluice N: ❶ (water gate) séuijaahp (M: go) ❷ (water channel) pàaihséuidouh (M: tìuh) PH: (water) làuhchēutlàih ge séui FV: ❶ (wash) chùngsái ❷ (flow) làuhchēut

slum N/PW: (area) pàhnmàhnkēui (M: go)

slumber VO: (sleep) fangaau PH: (sleep) fan yātjahn

slump FV: (of price) daaihdit SV: ❶ (of business) daahm ❷ (of market) sìutìuh PH: (of market) bātgínghei

slush N: ❶ (mud) laahnnàih; nàihbaahn (M: dī) ❷ (melting snow) bun yùhngsyut (M: dī) PH: (get wet) béi jīthěi ge séui jíngsāp

sly SV: ❶ (cunning) gáauwaaht ❷ (stealthily) gwáaisyú A: (secretly) ngamjūng; jihngjíng; tàutàudéi

smack N: (taste) meihdouh; meih PH: ❶ (boat) jūkyú ge fàahnsyùhnjái ❷ (kiss) jyūt yātdaahm; sek yātdaahm ❸ (hit) chēutlihk dá; daaihlihk dá FV:

❶ (hit) paak ❷ (hit with hand) gwaak

small SV: ❶ (of size, area, age) sai ❷ (of quantity) síu ❸ (not important) m̀gányiu ❹ (miscellaneous) sāpsāpseui ❺ (mean) bèipéi N suffix: (diminutive) -jái RVE: seui PH: (of social status) deihwaih dàimèih ✻ **small change** N: sáanngán; sáanjí; seuijí (M: dī) ✻ **small finger** N: mĕijí (M: jek) ✻ **small-minded** SV: síuhei ✻ **small-pox** N: tīnfā ✻ **small talk** PH: kìnghàahngái ✻ **small token of appreciation** PH: síu yisi jē; bātsìhng gingyi ✻ **feel small** PH: gokdāk hóu míuhsíu

smart SV: ❶ (clever) lēk; jènglēk; chùngmìhng ❷ (quick brain) sìngmuhk ❸ (good-looking) leng ❹ (fashionable) sìhmōu ❺ (light-hearted) hìngsùng ❻ (of pain) tung PH: (pain like sting) hóuchíh jāmgat gam tung

smarten PH: (in dress) jeukdāk lengdī ✻ **smarten up** FV: lengjó

smash RV: ❶ jíngseui ❷ (by striking) dáseui; dálaahn FV: (hit together) johng ✻ **smash-up** VO: johngchē

smatter IE: (slight knowledge) yātjì bungáai · *deui* N ~

smear FV: ❶ (spread) chàh ❷ (defame) jungsèung RV: (make dirty) jíngwùjòu N: (stain) wùjīk; jīk (M: dī); (of blood) hyutjīk (M: dī); (of paint) yáujīk (M: daat) PH: (stain) wùjòu ge deihfòng

smell FV/RV: (with nose) màhn; màhndóu; màhngin SV/FV: (rotten) chau N: (scent) meih; heimeih; chèuih (M: jahm) PH: (give out scent) faat-chēut SV meih; yáuh SV meih ∗ **bad smell** SV: chau; nàahnmàhn ∗ **good smell/ smell good** SV: hèung; hóumàhn ∗ **smell around** PH: (inquire) seiwàih dáting sìusīk ∗ **fishy smell** N: sèngmeih (M: jahm)

smelly SV: chau

smelt FV: ❶ (melt) yùhng ❷ (refine) lihn

smelter N: ❶ (furnace) yùhnglòuh (M: go) ❷ (factory) lihn N chóng (M: gàan)

smile FV: siu; mēimēisiu; siumēimēi ❷ N: (appearance) siuyùhng ∗ **wear a smile** SV: hóusiuyùhng

smirk FV/N: (silly) sòhsiu

smith N: dátit gùngyàhn (M: go)

smithereens N: seuipín (M: faai)

smoke N: yīn (M: dī) VO: ❶ (of pipe) sihk yīndáu ❷ (of cigarette) sihkyīn ❸ (of opium) sihk ngāpin; kāpduhk ❹ (give out smoke) chēutyīn FV/prefix: (of food) fàn- PH: (have smoke) yáuh yīn chēut ∗ **smoke-bomb** N: yīnmohkdáan (M: go) ∗ **smoke lobby door** N: fòhngyīnmùhn (M: douh) ∗ **smoke screen** N: yīnmohk (M: go) ∗ **smoke stack** N: yīntūng (M: go) ∗ **no smoke without fire** IE: mòuh fùng bāthéi lohng

smoking VO: chēutyīn PH: yáuh yīn chēut Adj. PH: ❶ yáuh yīn chēut ge ❷ (very hot) yiht laaht laaht ge ∗ **no smoking** PH: m̀jéun sihkyīn; (slogan)

gamjí kāpyīn

smooth SV: ❶ (not rough) waaht ❷ (of surface) pìhngwaaht ❸ (and shining) gwòngwaaht ❹ (in handling things) yùhnwaaht ❺ (of sea) pìhngjihng ❻ (for riding or flying) dihng ❼ (no difficulty) seuhnleih ❽ (of temper) wàn-wòh ∗ **smooth away** FV: sìuchèuih ∗ **smooth down** PH: (of sea) pìhngjihng lohklàih RV: (by ironing) tongpìhng

smother RV: (breathless) guhkséi FV: (breathless) jahtsīk PH: (of fire) kámsīk dī fó

smoulder FV: (burn) fàn PH: (of feelings suppressed) yīkngaathái sàm léuihbihn

smudge RV: (make dirty) jíng wùjòu N: (stain) wùjīk (M: daat) (of ink) mahkséuijīk (M: daat)

smuggle VO: jáusī FV: tàuwahn ~ *wòhnggàm* (gold); ~ *gwànfó* (weapon)

smut N: ❶ (from coal) mùihsí (M: dī) ❷ (language) chòuháu (M: geui) PH: (get dirty) béi mùihsí jíngwùjòu

snack N: ❶ (pastry) dímsàm; síusihk (M: júng; lùhng; dihp) ❷ (fastfood) faaichāan (M: júng)

snail N: wòⁿngàuh; ló (M: jek) (of fresh water) tìhnló (M: jek)

snake N: sèh (M: tìuh) PH: (of person) yàmhím ge yàhn ∗ **snake in** FV: wātsèh ∗ **snake soup** N: sèhgāng (M: wún, go)

snap FV: ❶ (bite) ngáauh ❷ (snatch) chéung ❸ (of string) tyúhn RV: ❶ (to twig) ngáautyúhn ❷ (of string) màngtyúhn Adv. PH: (with a sharp sound) pāak yātsèng PH:

(bite hard) daaihlihk ngáauh N:
(crisp cake) cheuibéng (M: faai)
* **snap-shot** N: faaiséung (M:
fūk, jèung)

snappish PH: (like to bite)
jùngyi ngáauhyàhn; jùngyi
ngáauhyéh PH/Adj. PH: (in
speech) ngàhjìm jéuileih

snappy SV: ❶ (quick) faai ❷
(smart) chùngmìhng ❸ (active)
wuhtput ❹ (swift) máhnjit Adv.
PH: (with a sound) pīkpīkpāak-
pāak; pìhkpìhkpàahkpàahk

snare N: ❶ (pit, trap) hahmjihng (M: go) ❷ (net) móhng (M:
go) FV: ❶ (catch) jūk ❷ (harm)
hahmhoih

snarl FV: ❶ pàauhhàau ❷ (of
dog) faih PH: (chaotic)
lyuhnsaai daaihlùhng

snatch FV: ❶ (grab) chéung
❷ (hold tightly) jàsaht VO: (take
a chance) chan gèiwuih PH:
(take a chance) bángāak gèiwuih

snazzy SV: (modern) sìhmōu;
mōdāng PH: (extremely pretty)
fèisèuhng leng

sneak PH: (go quietly) jìhngjíngdéi sùngyàhn Adv. PH:
(stealthily) tàutàudéi; gwáaigwái-
syúsyú gám

sneer FV: (ridiculing) siu;
jàausiu

sneeze VO: dá hātchì N: hātchì (M: go)

sniff FV: ❶ (smell) màhn ❷
(inhale) kāp, sok FV/N:
(breathe) fùkāp (M: chi, háh)

snigger FV: (sort of laugh)
tàusiu PH: (laugh at) tàutàudéi
siu

snip FV: (cut) jín PH: (cut with
scissors) yuhng gaaujín jín

snipe N: (bird) sàjèui; waht;
leuht (M: jek) FV: (kill) saat

sniper N: jèuigīksáu (M: go)

snippet N: ❶ (broken pieces)
seuipín (M: faai) ❷ (of information) pìndyuhn (M: go)

snitch FV: (steal) tàu; pàh
FV: (inform) goumaht PH: (person who inform) goumaht ge
yàhn

snivel FV: (pretend to cry)
jahaam VO: (have running nose)
làuh beihtai PH: (complain)
yātmihn haam yātmihn góng

snob SV: saileih PH: saileih
ge yàhn IE: gìngòu baai; gìn dài
cháai

snooker N: cheukkàuh · *dá*
~

snoop SV: (of character) jìsih
PH: (of character) houléih
hàahnsih FV: (look for information) taamting

snooze VO: hāp ngáahnfan
PH: hāp yātjahn

snore N: beihhòhn; beihhòhnsèng (M: dī) PH: yáuh
beihhòhnsèng

snot N: (of the nose) beihtai
(M: dūk)

snout N: (of pig) jyūjéui (M:
go)

snow N: ❶ (like ice) syut (M:
dī; gauh) ❷ (on TV) syutfā (M:
dī) VO: lohksyut * **snowball**
N: syutkàuh (M: go) *
snowflake N: syutfā (M: pin)
* **snowman** N: syutyàhn (M:
go) * **snow-slide** N: syutbēng
(M: chèuhng, chi) * **snow-
storm** N: daaih fùngsyut (M:
chèuhng, chi) * **snow-white**

SV: syutbaahk PH: baahksyūt-
syūt * **be snowed up** PH: béi
daaihsyut jójyuh

snowy PH: yáuh syut; dò
syut SV: (white) syutbaahk *
snowy weather PH: lohksyut
ge sìhhauh

snub RV: (of cigarette) jíngsīk
FV: (in treating people) m̀léih;
láahnglohk * **snub nose** N:
(like lion) sìjíbeih (M: go); (flat)
bínbeih (M: go)

snuff N: ❶ (tobacco) beihyīn
❷ (of candle) dāngsàm (M: tìuh)
FV: (inhale) sok; (smell) màhn
VO: (cut) jín dāngsām * **snuff-
box** N: beihyīnháp (M: go)

snuffle VO: (when having a
cold) sokbeih N: (nasal sound)
beihyàm

snug Adj. PH: ❶ (warm and
comfortable) yauh nyúhn yauh
syùfuhk ❷ (clean and neat) gònjehng kéihléih

snuggery PH: ❶ (bar)
léuihgún léuihbihn ge jáubā ❷
(warm and comfortable) yauh
nyúhn yauh syùfuhk ge
deihfòng

snuggle RV: (embrace) láamsaht; láamjyuh PH: ❶ (to coil)
sūkmàaih yātgauh ❷ (to make
warm) lihng PN gokdāk yauh
nyúhn yauh syùfuhk

so A: ❶(of degree) gam ❷ (in
this way, and so, well) gám ❸
(also) dōu; yihkdōu ❹ (really)
jànhaih ❺ (therefore) sóyíh ❻
(extremely) fèisèuhng * **so-so**
PH: màhmádéi lā; syunhaih
gám lā * **so-and-so** N: (of person) máuhmáuhyàhn; (of thing)
máuhmáuh sih * **so be it** PH:
jauh gám lā; haih gám lā * **so-
called** ATT: sówaih * **so far
as I know** PH: jiu ngóh só jì *

so far so good PH: jihkdou
yìhgā dōu hóuhóu * **so long as**
A: jíyiu * **so to say, so to
speak** PH: hóyíh góng * **and
so on** A: dángdáng * **or so** A:
jóyáu * **it so happened that**
A: yuh'ngāam Adv. PH: yáuh
gam ngāam dāk gam kíu

soak FV/VO: (put in water)
jam; jamséui; RV: (make wet)
jamsāp; jamtau FV: kāp; sok
(liquid) * **be soaked to the
skin** PH: sèhngsàn sāpsaai

soap N: ❶ fàangáan (M: gauh)
❷ (fine) hèunggáan (M: gauh) *
soap-bubble N: fàangáanpóuh
(M: dī) * **soap-suds** N:
gáanséui

soar PH: ❶ (of birds) fèidāk
hóu gòu ❷ (of price) gwaijó hóu
dò Adj. PH: (very high) hóu gòu
FV: (rise) gòujeung

sob FV: (cry) haam PH: (utter
with sobs) yātmihn haam yātmihn góng

sober, sobriety SV: ❶
(awake) chìngsíng ❷ (calm) jandihng; láahngjihng ❸ (serious)
yìhmsūk ❹ (simple) poksou PH:
(not drunk) meih jeui; móuh
jeui * **as sober as a judge**
PH: (not drunk) meih jeui;
móuh jeui SV: chìngsíng

soccer N: (Yìnggwok) jūkkàuh

sociability/sociable Adj.
PH: ❶ hóu sīk gàaujai
yìngcháuh ❷ (showing friend-
liness) hóu yáuhsihn ge

social ATT: (of the society)
sèhwúi; sèhwúising PH: (fond
of the company of others) jùngyi
gàaujai yìngcháuh * **social
club** N: lyùhnyìhwúi (M: go) *
social climber PH: heung
seuhng pàh ge yàhn IE: lihk-

jàng seuhngyàuh ✳ **social engagement** PH: gàaujai yìngchàuh ✳ **social intercourse** N/ATT: sèhgàau ✳ **social-minded** PH: gwàansàm séhwúi ✳ **social worker** N: séhwúi gùngjokjé (M: go) ✳ **social security** N: séhwúi bóujeung gaiwaahk ✳ **social standing** N: séhwúi deihwaih; sànfán ✳ **social welfare** N: séhwúi fúkleih (M: júng)

socialism N: séhwúi jyúyih

socialist N: (of person) séhwúi jyúyihjé (M: go, wái) ATT: séhwúi jyúyih ~ *jaidouh* (system) ✳ **socialist party** N: séhwúidóng (M: go)

society N: ❶ (community) séhwúi (M: go) ❷ (association) wúi (M: go) ❸ (organization) jóujīk (M: go) ❹ (group) tyùhntái (M: go) ❺ (in school) hohkwúi (M: go) ✳ **red cross society** N: hùhng sahpjih wúi ✳ **pests of society** IE: hoihkwàhnjìmáh

sociologist N: séhwúihohkgā (M: go, wái)

sociology N: séhwúihohk

sock N: (to put on) maht; dyúnmaht (M: deui, jek)

socket N: ❶ (for electricity) chaapsōu (M: go) ❷ (hole) lūng (M: go) ❸ (of eye) ngáahnkwāang

Socrates N: Sòugaaklàaidái

sod VO: (of grassland) pòu chóupèih N: (grassland) chóupèih (M: faai)

soda N: ❶ sōdá (M: dī) ❷ (for cooking) sōdáfán (M: dī) ❸ (drink) heiséui (M: jèun; gun) ✳ **soda-cracker** N: sōdá bénggōn (M: faai; hahp)

soever A: ❶ (no matter) mòuhleuhn ❷ (any) yahmhòh

sofa N: sōfá (yí) (M: jèung; tou)

soft SV: ❶ (not hard) yúhn; yàuhyúhn ❷ (smooth) yúhn-waaht ❸ (of light) yàuhwòh ❹ (of noise) saisèng ❺ (of voice) wànyàuh ❻ (easy) yùhngyih ❼ (light) hìngsùng ❽ (feeble) yúhnyeuhk ❾ (not clear) mòuhwùh ✳ **soft drinks** N: heiséui tùhng gwójāp ✳ **soft-boiled** Adj. PH: bun sàangsuhk ge ✳ **soft-hearted** Adj. PH: sàmchèuhng yúhn ✳ **software** N: (of computer) yúhngín (M: gihn)

soften RV: (make soft) jíngyúhn FV: (become soft) binyúhn; yúhnfa

soggy SV: (wet) sāp

soil N: (ground) tóudeih; nàihtóu (M: faai) RV: (make dirty) jíngwùjòu; jínglaahttaat ✳ **rich soil** PH: faai deih hóu fèih

sojourn FV: (stay) dauhlàuh

solace FV/N: (comfort) ngònwai

solar ATT: yèuhng-; taaiyèuhng - ✳ **solar calendar** N: yèuhnglihk; sànlihk; sàilihk ✳ **solar energy** N: taaiyèuhng-nàhng ✳ **solar system** N: taaiyèuhnghaih

solarium N/PW: yahtgwòngyuhksāt (M: go)

solarize FV: (under the sun) saai VO: ❶ (stay in the sun) saai taaiyèuhng ❷ (of film) jáugwòng

solder N: (for metal) laatgāi (M: go) FV: (to join) sìuhón PH:

(a tool) yuhnglàih sìuhón ge yéh

soldier N: (in general) gwànyàhn; (coll.) gwànlóu (M: go) PH: dòngbìng ge * go soldiering VO: dòngbìng

soldierly Adj. PH: (like a soldier) hóuchíh gwànyàhn gám SV: (brave) yúhnggám; yìngyúhng

soldiery N: ❶ gwànyàhn (M: go); (troop) gwàndéui (M: deuih) ❷ (training) gwànsih fanlihn (M: júng)

sole VO: (of shoe) wuhn hàaihdái N: ❶ (of shoe) hàaihdái (M: go) ❷ (of foot) geukbáan(dái) ❸ (flatfish) béimuhkyùh; taatsàyú (M: tìuh) A: (only) wàihyāt; duhkyáuh ATT: duhkgā ~ doihléih (agent)

solemn SV: ❶ (causing respect) jòngyìhm ❷ (grave) lùhngjuhng

solemnize PH: ❶ (make solemn) sái N lùhngjuhng ❷ (celebrate) lùhngjuhng hingjūk

solicit FV: ❶ (request) chíngkàuh ❷ (ask for) jìngkàuh VO: (of a prostitute) làaihhaak

solicitor N: (lawyer) leuhtsī (M:go)

solicitous FV/SV: (worry) dàamsàm FV: ❶ (long for) hotmohng ❷ (worry) gwajyuh PH: (long for) hóu séung

solicitude N: (worry) yàuleuih; dàamsàm

solid N: ❶ (not liquid nor gas) gutái (M: go) ❷ (cube) lahpfòngtái (M: go) Adj. PH: (not hollow) sahtsàm ge SV: ❶ (of body, flesh) gitsaht ❷ (unanimous) yātji ❸ (safe) wánjahn ❹ (dependable) hókaau A: (exactly) jūkjūk * solid gold N: sèuhngām (M: gauh) * solid colour N: jihngsīk

solidarity FV/PH: (unite) tyùhngit; tyùhngit yātji

solidify FV: (become solid) kìhng RV: (become hard) binngaahng PH: (to make unite) sái PN tyùhngit

soliloguy IE: (speak to oneself) jihyìhn jihyúh N/FV: (in drama) duhkbaahk

solitary SV: ❶ (alone) gùduhk ❷ (lonely) jihkmohk ❸ (of place) pìnpīk A: (only) wàihyāt

solitude SV: ❶ (alone) gùduhk ❷ (of place) pìnpīk

solo N/FV: ❶ (vocal) duhkcheung ❷ (instrumental) duhkjau

Solomon N: Sólòhmùhn

solstice N: jidím * the summer solstice N: hahji * the winter solstice N: dūngji

solubility N: (degree) yùhnggáaidouh

soluble Adj. PH: ❶ (can be dissolved) wúih yùhng ge ❷ (of a problem) hóyíh gáaikyut ge

solution PH: (of a difficulty) gáaikyut ge baahnfaat N: ❶ (answer) gùhngyihk (M: go) ❷ (liquid) yùhngyihk (M: dī) ❸ (medicinal) yeuhkséui (M: júng; jēun)

solve FV: ❶ (of difficulty) gáaikyut ❷ (answer) gáaidaap ❸ chàai (riddle) ~ màihyúh ❹ wáan (cross-word puzzle) ~ tìhnjih yàuhhei PH: (of debts) wàahnchìng dī jaai

solvent Adj. PH: (the power of dissolving) hóyíh jèung daihyihdī yéh yùhnggáai ge

sombre SV: (gloomy) yàuwāt PH: ❶ (of colour) ngàahnsīk hóu chàhm ❷ (of weather) tīnsīk yàmchàhm

some N: ❶ (for a subject) yáuhdī ❷ (for an object) yātdī; dī ❸ (of people) yáuhdī yàhn Nu: géi PH: (remarkable) fèisèuhng hóu A: (about) daaihkói; daaihyeuk; yeukmók * **some more** PH: joi FV yātdī * **some other day** TW: daihyihyaht * **for some time** A: (for the time being) jaahmsìh PH: (quite a long time) yātdyuhn sìhgaan

somebody N: ❶ yáuh yàhn ❷ (VIP) daaih yàhnmát (M: go) * **somebody else** PH: daihyihgo yàhn

someday Adv. PH: (eventually) jēutjì yáuh yātyaht; júng yáuh yātyaht

somehow A: ❶ (must) yātdihng ❷ (anyhow) júngjì

someone PH: (as subject) yáuh yàhn N: (as object) yàhn (M: go) * **someone else's** PH: daihyihgo yàhn ge

somersault N: gwàandáu (M: go) * **turn a somersault** VO: dá gwàandáu

something N: yáuhdī yéh; dī yéh * **something else** PH: daihyihdī yéh * **something like** PH: yáuhdī chíh * **have something to do with** PH: N1 tùhng N2 yáuh gwàanhaih * **make something of** FV: leihyuhng

sometime A: ❶ (other day) daihyihyaht ❷ (in future)

jèunglòih ❸ (have before) chàhnggìng MA: (before) yíhchìhn PH: (find a time) wán go sìhgaan

sometimes MA: yáuhsìh

somewhat A: yáuhdī Adv. PH: yáuh dòsíu

somewhere PH/PW: yātdaat deihfòng Adv. PH: (nowhere) mjì hái bīndouh * **somewhere about** PH: hái N fuhgahn

somnambulism N: muhngyàuhbehng

somniferous PH: chèuimihn ge

somnolence SV: ngàahnfan PH: hóu séung fan

somnolent Adj. PH: hóu ngàahnfan ge; hóu séung fan ge

son N: ❶ jái (M: go) ❷ (pl.) jísyùn * **your son** N: néihge jái (polite form) lìhnglóng; néih gùngjí * **son-in-law** N: néuihsai (M: go) * **son of a bitch** N: chūksàng * **the son of god** PH: sàhndīk yihjí; seuhngdai dīk yihjí N: (Catholic) tìnjyújí

sonar N: ❶ (an apparatus in general) séuidái taamchàak haihtúng (M: júng) ❷ (sound navigation ranging) sìngbō douh hòhng yúh chàak kéuih haihtúng (M: go) ❸ (locating underwater objects) sìngbō dihngwaih yìh (M: go) ❹ (for detecting fish) yùhkwàhn taamchàakhei (M: go) ❺ (for detecting submarine) chìhmtéhng taam chàakhei (M: go)

sonata N: jaumìhngkūk (M: sáu)

song N: gō (M: sáu, jì, jek) (pl.) gōkūk (M: sáu, jì, jek) BF: -gō; -kūk ✳ **folksong** N: màhngō (M: sáu, jì, jek) ✳ **pop song/hit song** N: làuhhàhnggō; làuhhàhngkūk (M: sáu, jì, jek); (pl.) làuhhàhng gōkūk ✳ **Cantonese operatic songs** N: yuhtkūk (M: sáu, jì, jek) ✳ **marching song** N: jeunhàhngkūk (M: sáu, jì) ✳ **song-bird** PH: wúih cheunggō ge jeukjái (M: jek) ✳ **song writer** N: gōkūk jokjé (M: wái)

songster gōcheunggā (M: wái)

songstress N: néuih gōcheunggā (M: wái)

sonic Adj. PH: (have sound) yáuh sìngyām ge ✳ **sonic speed** N: yàmchūk ✳ **supersonic** N/ATT: chìuyàmchūk

son-in-law N: néuihsai (M: go)

sonorous SV/FV: héung

soon TW: (in a short while) yātjahngāan PH: (before long) móuh géinói SV: ❶ (early) jóu ❷ (quick) faai A: (in a short while) hóufaai ✳ **as soon as/no sooner than** Patt: yāt . . . jauh . . . ✳ **as soon as possible** A: jeuhnfaai Adv. PH: yáuh gam faai dāk gam faai ✳ **sooner or later** A: chìhjóu ✳ **the sooner, the better** PH: yuht faai yuht hóu

soot N: mùihyīn PH: (made dirty) béi mùihsí jíng wùjòu

soothe FV: (comfort) ngònwai PH: (of pain) gáamhēng tungfú; móuh gam tung ✳ **soothe a crying baby** VO: ngam bìhbī

sooty Adj. PH: ❶ (very dark) hāakmàngmàng ❷ (having soot)

yáuh mùihyīn ge ❸ (made dirty) béi mùihyīn jíng wùjòujó ge

sophisticated/sophistication SV: ❶ (complicated) fūkjaahp ❷ (having lost simplicity) saigu ❸ (supreme) gōukāp

sophomore PH: (in university) daaihhohk yih nìhnkāp ge hohksāang (M: go)

soporific N: (that produces sleep) chèuimìhnjài Adj. PH: (producing sleep) wúih chèuimìhn ge

soppy Adj. PH: (soaked) jamtau ge; (all wet) sāptau ge

soprano N: néuih gōuyām (M: wái, go)

sorcerer N: (witch) mòuhsī (M: go); (magician) mōseuhtsī (M: go)

sordid Adj. PH: (dirty) wùjòu laahttaat SV: ❶ (of behaviour) bèipéi ❷ (selfish) jihsī

sore SV: tung; syùntung N: (injured spot) sèungháu (M: go, daat)

sorority N: ❶ (women's society) fúhnéuihwúi (M: go) ❷ (in college) daaihhohk néuihsāng lyùhnyìhwúi (M: go)

sorrel N: (color) fèhùhngsīk

sorrow SV: ❶ (sad) nàahngwo ❷ (heart-broken) sèungsàm ❸ (tragic) chàilèuhng SV/N: (trouble) fàahnnnóuh PH: ❶ (misfortune) bāthahng ge sih ❷ (sad things) sèungsàm ge sih ❸ (tragic things) chàilèuhng ge sih

sorrowful SV: (upset) baingai

sorry PH: (apology) deuimjyuh; mhhóuyisi SV: (sad) nàahngwo SV/FV: (regret) hauhfui * **feel sorry for PN** PH: waih PN gokdāk hóu nàahngwo; (pity) **waih PN gokdāk hóu hósīk**

sort M: júng; yeuhng; leuih; tíng FV: (separate) jíngléih; gáan VO: fànleuih RV: fànhóu * **sort of** Adj. PH: dōu géi SV * **sort out N1 from N 2** PH: jèung N1 tùhng N2 fànhòi * **of a sort** PH: tùhngyāt leuih

sorter PH: (in post-office) gáanseun ge jīkyùhn

S O S N: kàuhgau seunhouh

so-so PH: gwodākheui lā; màhmádéi lā; syunhaih gám lā

soul N: (spirit) lìhngwàhn; wàhnpaak (M: go) * **heart and soul** Adv. PH: chyùhnsàm chyùhnyi * **not a soul** PH: yātgo yàhnyíng dōu móuh

soulless Adj. PH: (no soul) móuh lìhngwàhn ge SV: (selfish) jihsī

sound N: (noise) sìngyàm; sèng FV: (make noise) héung PH: (feeling) tènghéiséuhnglàih SV: ❶ (healthy and good) gihnchyùhn ❷ (reliable) hókaau; kaaudākjyuh ❸ (safe) wánjahn ❹ (of sleep) lahm ❺ (reasonable) hahpléih * **soundproof** ATT: gaakyàm * **sound-wave** N: yàmbō; sìngbō * **sound-effects** N: yàmhéung haauhgwó

soundly A: ❶ (completely) yùhnchyùhn ❷ (real) jànjing SV: ❶ (legally) hahpfaat ❷ (healthy and good) gihnchyùhn

soundless Adj. PH: ❶ (no sound) móuh sìngyàm ge ❷

(quiet) hóu jihng ge ❸ (deep) hóu sàm ge

soup N: tòng (M: wún; go) BF: (thick) -gāng (M: wún; go)

sour SV: (taste) syūn RV: (become sour) binsyūn FV: (of not fresh food) sūkjó * **sourpepper soup** N: syūnlaahttòng (M: wún; go)

source N: ❶ (of river) héiyùhn; faatyùhndeih ❷ (where it comes from) lòihyùhn (M: go) ❸ (literary material) jīlíu FV: (of river) héiyùhnnyù; faatyùhnnyù * **light source** N: gwòngyùhn (M: dī)

south N/PW: ❶ (direction) nàahm ❷ (side) nàahmbihn ❸ (area) nàahmbouh; nàahmfòng Adv. PH/PH: (towards) heung nàahm * **south pole** N/PW: nàahmgihk * **in the south of PW** PH: hái PW ge nàahmbihn

South Africa, Republic of N/PW: Nàahmfēi Guhngwòhgwok

South America N/PW: Nàahmméih(jàu)

southeast N/PW: dùngnàahm (bihn) * **Southeast Asia** N/PW: Nàahmyéung

southwest N/PW: sàinàahm (bihn)

southerly Adv. PH: (towards) heung nàahm Adj. PH: (of wind) hái nàahmbihn chèuilàih ge

southern Adj. PH: ❶ (facing south) heung nàahm ge ❷ (in the south) hái nàahmbihn ge; hái nàahmbouh ge * **southern hemisphere** N/PW: nàahm bunkàuh

souvenir N: geinihmbán (M: gihn); (as gift) sáuseun (M: dī)

sovereign N: ❶ (ruler) yùhnsáu (M: go) ❷ (emperor) gwànjyú (M: go) PH: (of a country) yáuh jyúkyùhn ge

sovereignty N: ❶ (emperor) gwànjyú (M: go) ❷ (of a country) jyúkyùhn; túngjihkyùhn

sovietologist N: Sòulyùhn mahntàih jyùngā (M: go, wái)

Soviet Union N/PW: Sòulyùhn

sow VO: bojúng; saatjúng N: (of pig) jyūná (M: jek) ✻ **as a man sows, so shall he reap** IE: junggwā dāk gwā; jungdauh dāk dauh

soy N: baahkdáu; wòhngdáu ✻ **soy sauce** N: sihyàuh (M: jēun; dī)

soybean N: baahkdáu; wòhngdáu ✻ **soybean milk** N: dauhjèung (M: wún)

spa N/PW: wànchyùhn (M: go)

space N/PW: ❶ (place) deihfòng (M: daat) ❷ (vacancy) wái; hùngwái (M: go) ❸ (outer space) taaihùng N: (extension) hùnggàan N: ❶ (distance) kéuihlèih (M: dyuhn) ❷ (interval) gaangaak PH/PW: (blank) hùngbaahk ge deihfòng ✻ **space-ship** N: taaihùngsyùhn (M: jek) ✻ **space shuttle** N: taaihùng chyùnsōgèi (M: ga) ✻ **parking space** N: chèwái (M: go) PH: paakchè ge deihfòng

spacious SV: (roomy) fut; futdaaih

spade N/M/FV: (of tool) cháan (M: go) PH: (with a spade) yuhng cháan cháan N: (of cards) hāaktòuh (M: jèung)

spaghetti N: yidaaihleihfán (M: tìuh)

Spain N/PW: Sàibāanngàh

span M: ❶ (of distance) laam ❷ (of time) dyuhn N: (of bridge) kìuhgúng (M: go) FV: (cross) laamgwo N: (to measure) yuhng sáují laamháh; yuhng sáují dohkháh

Spaniard N: Sàibàanngàhyàhn (M: go)

spaniel N: chèuhngyíhgáu (M: jek)

Spanish N: ❶ (people) Sàibàanngàhyàhn (M: go) ❷ (language) Sàibàanngàhmàhn Adj. PH: ❶ (of the people) Sàibàanngàhyàhn ge ❷ (of the language) Sàibàanngàhmàhn ge

spank VO: (slap on the buttocks) dá lōyáu; dá sífāt

spanner N: (tool) sihbālá (M: go)

spare Adj. PH: ❶ (superfluous) dòyùhge ❷ (in reserve for use) hauhbeihge; sihbēge ~ *tāai* (tyre) ❸ (very little) hóusíu SV: (of figure) sau AV: (refrain from using) m̀sái RV: (refrain from using) hàanfàan FV: ❶ (give) yeuhng ❷ (leave unharmed) fongsàang ✻ **spare time** FV/SV: dākhàahn PH: dākhàahn ge sìhhauh

sparerib N: pàaihgwāt (M: tìuh; faai)

spark N: fófā; fósīng (M: dī) PH: (give out sparks) faatchēut fófā

sparkle FV: ❶ (gleam) sím ❷ (shining) faatgwòng PH: (give out sparks) faatchēut fófā N: ❶ (spark) fófā; fósīng (M: dī) ❷ (of light) símgwòng (M: dī)

sparrow N: màhjéuk (M: jek)

sparse SV: ❶ (few) síu ❷ (not dense) sō

Spartan N: (Greek people) Sibādaahtyàhn (M: go) SV: (style of life) hāakfú

spasm FV: chāugān M: (of sudden movement) jahn

spatial Adj. PH: (of space) hùnggàan ge

spatter FV: (splash) jīt M: (of rain) jahn

spatula N: (for cooking) gwaat; gwáat (M: go)

spawn N: (of fish) yùhchēun (M: go)

speak FV: góng VO: góng syutwah; góngyéh FV/N: (make a speech) yíngóng (M: pìn) * **speak for PN** PH: waih/tai/doihbíu PN góngsyutwah * **speak the truth** VO: góng jànwá * **speak up** PH: daaihsèng góng * **speak ill of a person** PH: góng PN waaihwá * **speak of** FV: góngkahp; góngdou

speaker PH: góng syutwah ge yàhn; (one who gives a speech) yíngóng ge yàhn * **loud-speaker** N: kwongyàmhei (M: go)

speaking VO: góng syutwah Adj. PH: gónggán syutwah ge * **speaking of** FV: góngdou * **generally speaking** PH: yāt-būn làih góng * **strictly speaking** PH: yìhmgaak làih

góng

spear N: ❶ màauh (M: jì) ❷ (with metal head) chēung (M: jī) ❸ (for fish) yùhchā (M: jì) FV: (to pierce) gāt * **spear-head** N: màauhtàuh; chēungtàuh (M: go)

special SV: ❶ (unusual) dahkbiht; dahksyùh ❷ (extra) ngaahkngoih ❸ (expert) jyùnmùhn A: ❶ (on purpose) dahkdāng; dahkbiht ❷ (exclusive) jyùnmún; jyùnmùhn ATT: (exclusive) jyùnfō * **special train** N: jyùnchè (M: bàan) * **special agent** N: ① dahkbiht doihléih (M: go) ② (spy) dahkmouh (M: go)

specialist N: jyùngā (M: go, wái)

speciality SV: (skilful) nàhsáu N: ❶ (skill) jyùnchèuhng (M: júng) ❷ (characteristic) dahksing; dahkdím (M: go) ❸ (product) dahkcháan (M: júng) Adj. PH: (good at) jeui lēk ge PH: (make special study of) jyùnmún yìhngau

specialize PH: ❶ (make special study of) jyùnmún yìhngau ❷ (become a specialist) sìhngwàih jyùngā ❸ (point out clearly) chèuhngsai gám jíchēutlàih FV: (become special) jyùnmùhnfa

specially A: (on purpose) dahkbiht; dahkdāng; jyùndāng

specie N: ngaahngbaih (M: go) * **payment in specie** VO: béi ngaahngbaih

species N: júngleuih M: júng

specific SV: ❶ (clear) chìngchó ❷ (detailed) chèuhngsai ❸ (special) dahkbiht * **specific remedy** N: dahkhaauhyeuhk

specification PH: chèuhngsai ge syutmìhng N: (instruction) syutmìhngsyù (M: jèung; fahn)

specify PH: hóu chèuhngsai/chìngchó gám syutmìhng FV: (mention definitely) jídihng

specimen N: bīubún (M: go; júng)

speck N: hāakdím (M: go) (stained spot) wùdím (M: go)

spectacles N: (eye-glasses) ngáahngeng (M: go, fu)

spectacular PH: ❶ (to look at) hóudò yàhn tái ge ❷ (attracting) hóu kāpyáhn yàhn ge

spectator N: ❶ (on looker) pòhnggùnjé (M: go) ❷ (audience) gùnjung (M: go)

spectre N: (ghost) gwái (M: jek)

speculate FV/SV: tàuhgèi

speculator N: tàuhgèijé (M: go)

speech FV/N: yíngóng (M: pìn) PH: (words) góngge syutwah * **speech day** N: bāanjéung dínláih (M: go, chi)

speechless PH: góng m̀chēut syutwah SV: (dumb) ngá

speed N: chūkdouh; (per hour) sìhchūk SV: (fast) faai * **speed up/down** PH: faaidī/maahndī * **speed-boat** N: faaitéhng (M: jek) * **speed-limit** N: chūkdouh haahnjai * **more haste, less speed** IE: séung faai dāk maahn

speedy Adj. PH: hóu faai ge

spell FV: (of letters) chyun; ping VO: (of letters) chyunjih

TW: (period of time) yāt-jahngāan M: (of time) jahn N: (as a charm) fùhjau (M: go) jauyúh (M: geui) * **spell-bound** SV: (be attracted) yahpmàih PH: ❶ (by a charm) béi fùhjau janjyuh ❷ (be attracted) béi . . . màihjyuh

spend FV: ❶ (of money) sái; yuhng ❷ (kill time) sìuhín ❸ gwo (holidays) ~ *singdaan* (Christmas) * **spend time with PN** VO: pùih PN

spendthrift PH: hóu jùngyi sáichín ge yàhn

spent PH: móuhsaai

sperm N: ❶ (liquid) jìngyihk ❷ (cell) jìngjí

spew FV: ngáu

sphere N: ❶ kàuh; kàuhtái (M: go) ❷ (range) faahnwàih (M: go) ❸ (globe of the earth) deihkàuhyìh (M: go)

spheroid PH: tóhyùhn ge kàuhtái

Sphinx N: (in Egypt) Sìsàn yàhnmihn jeuhng (M: go)

spice N: hèunglíu (M: júng)

spick-and-span PH: ❶ (all new) chyùhnsàn ge ❷ (tidy) gònjehng kéihléih

spicy PH: gàjó / yáuh hèunglíu ge

spider N: (insect) jìjyū (M: jek) * **spider's web** N: jìjyūmóhng (M: go)

spike N: (of shoes) hàaihdēng (M: nāp) * **spiked running-shoes** N: dènghàaih (M: deui; jek)

spill FV/RVE: sé RV: dóusé

spin FV: ❶ jyun, dàhmdàhm-jyun, dàhmdámjyun ❷ nihng (top) ~ tòhló ❸ (make it turn) fìhng ❹ (make yarn) fóngjīk VO: (make yarn) fóngsā ✱ **spin drier** N: gònyìgèi (M: ga) ✱ **spin cocoons** VO: tousī ✱ **spin a coin** PH: dengngánjái kyutdihng

spinach N: bōchoi (M: pò)

spindle N: ❶ (in spinning) fóngchèuih (M: go) ❷ (axle) juhksàm (M: go)

spine N: ❶ (backbone) buijekgwāt (M: tiuh) ❷ (of the neck) génggwāt (M: tiuh) ❸ (of plants or animals) chi (M: tiuh)

spineless PH: ❶ móuh buijekgwāt ❷ (of plants) móuh chi ❸ (cowardly) móuh yúhnghei

spinner N: fóngsā gùngyàhn (M: go)

spinning VO: fóngsā FV: fóngjīk ✱ **spinning machine** N: fóngsāgèi (M: ga)

spinster N: lóuhgùpòh (M: go) PH: móuh gitfàn ge néuihyán

spiral A: dàhmdàhmkwāak N: lòhsīsìn; lòhsīmàhn (M: tiuh) FV: dàhmdàhmjyun

spire N: (top) jìmdéng PH: (of church) gaautòhng ge taapjìm

spirit N: ❶ (energy) jìngsàhn ❷ (mind) sàmlìhng ❸ (as from body) lìhngwàhn; wàhnpaak ❹ (ghost) yàulìhng; yíujìng (M: go) ❺ (alcohol) jáujìng ❻ (alcoholic drinks) jáu ❼ (real meaning) jànjing yiyih; jìngsàhn ✱ **in high spirits** PH: ① (good health) jìngsàhn hóuhóu ② (exciting) hìnggòu chóiliht ✱ **in poor (low) spirits** PH: ①

móuhlèih sàmgèi ② (mood) sàmchìhng m̀hóu ✱ **Holy Spirit** N: singlìhng, sìng sàhn

spiritual Adj. PH: ❶ (of spirit) jìngsàhnseuhngge ❷ (of soul) sàmlìhngseuhngge ❸ (supernatural) chìujihyìhnge

spit VO: ❶ (of saliva) tou háuséui ❷ (of sputum) toutàahm FV: (send out from mouth) léu; lèu N: (for roasting) hàauyuhkchā (M: jek)

spite N: (ill will) ngokyi FV: (hate) jànghahn ✱ **in spite of** A: sèuiyìhn

spittle N: ❶ (saliva) háuséui (M: dūk; dī) ❷ (sputum) tàahm (M: dūk; dī)

spitton N: tàahmgun (M: go)

splash PH: jīthéi dī séui FV: (sprinkle) sá

splatter PH: (of speech) góngyéh lauháu

splay RV: (spread out) jìngmé; jìngche ✱ **splay-foot** N: baatjihgeuk (M: deui)

spleen N: (organ) pèih; pèihjohng (M: go)

splendid PH: ❶ (extremely good) hóu dougihk ❷ (best) jeui hóu SV: (magnificent) gasai

splendour SV: ❶ (magnificent) gasai ❷ (of brightness) fàiwòhng

splint N: (strip of wood) gaapbáan (M: faai)

split FV: ❶ lithòi; lihthòi ❷ (of nation, party) fànliht

splurge FV: (show off) yín VO: (show off) yínyéh

spoil FV: ❶ (of food) laahn ❷ (ruin) powaaih RV: (of children) jungwaaih N: ❶ (stolen things) chaahkjōng (M: gihn) ❷ (military) jinleihbán (M: gihn)

spoken Adj. PH: ❶ góngge; ❷ (not written) háuyúhfa ge

spokesman N: faatyihnyàhn (M: go)

sponge N: (animal) hóimìhn (M: gauh) PH: (soak, wipe) yuhng hóimìhn sok, yuhng hóimìhn maat ✳ **sponge cake** N: daahngōu (M: go; gauh)

spongy Adj. PH: ❶ (like sponge) hóuchíh hóimìhn gám ge ❷ (many holes) yáuh hóudò lūng ge ❸ (loose) hóu sùngge

sponsor FV: ❶ (guarantee) dàambóu ❷ (of a proposal) faathéi ❸ (of a programme) jaanjoh N: ❶ (guarantor) dàambóuyàhn (M: go) ❷ (of a proposal) faathéiyàhn (M: go) ❸ (of a programme) jaanjohyàhn (M: go)

spontaneous Adj. PH: hóu jihyìhn ge; jihyìhn faatsàng ge

spook N: (ghost) gwái (M: jek)

spooky Adj. PH: (haunted) yáuh gwái ge SV: (strange) gúgwaai PH: (strange) gúlìhng jìnggwaai

spool N: lūk · (of thread) sin ~ (M: go)

spoon M/N: gāng; sìhgāng; chìhgāng (M: go) ✳ **serving spoon** N: gūnggāng (M: go, jek)

sporadic SV: lìhngsìng

sport FV/N: wahnduhng (M: júng) PH: táiyuhk wahnduhng ✳ **sports car** N: páauchè (M:

ga) ✳ **sports day** VO: hòi wahnduhngwúi

sporting Adj. PH: ❶ (connected with sports) tùhng wahnduhng yáuh gwàanhaih ge ❷ (willing to lose) yáuh táiyuhk jìngsàhn ge

sportsdom N: táiyuhkgaai

sportsman N: wahnduhngyùhn; (expert) wahnduhnggā (M: go, wái)

sportswoman N: néuih wahnduhngyùhn; (expert) néuih wahnduhnggā (M: go, wái)

sportswriter N: táiyuhk jyùnlàahn jokgā (M: wái)

spot M: (dot) dím; daat N: ❶ (round) yùhndím (M: go) ❷ (place) deihfòng; deihdím (M: daat, go) ❸ (on skin) ji (M: nāp) N: (dirty ones) wùdím (M: go, daat) PH: (dirty place) wùjòu ge deihfòng FV: (recognize) yìhngchēut ✳ **on the spot** PH: (be there) hái yihnchèuhng A: (immediately) jīkhāak, dòngtòhng ✳ **spot-check** N: dahtgīk gímchàh (M: chi)

spotless Adj. PH: (clean) hóu gònjehng; fèisèuhng gònjehng

spotlight N: sehdāng (M: jáan)

spouse N: (husband or wife) puingáuh (husband and wife) fùchài (M: deui)

spout FV: (of liquid) pan; yúng N: (of a teapot) chàhwújéui (M: go)

sprain FV: náuchàn; wātchàn

sprawl PH: ❶ (lie) tāanhòisaai sáugeuk fan ❷ (lie like

swimming) pàháisyu fan FV: ❶ (of plants) lāan ❷ (spread) maahnyìhn

spray FV: pan; jīt N: ❶ (of waves) lohngfā (M: dī) ❷ (sprayer) panmouhhei (M: go)

sprayer N: panmouhhei (M: go)

spread FV: ❶ (put on) pòu ❷ (of butter, ointment) chàh ❸ (extend) kwongjín ❹ chyùhnbo (disease, knowledge) ~ *jahtbehng*; ~ *jìsīk* ❺ (of cancer) maahnyìhn N: jeung • (for sandwich) *sàammàhnjìh* ~ (M: jèun) ✻ **bed spread** N: chòhngkám (M: jèung)

sprig PH: (small twig) saige syuhjì

spring N: (season) chēuntīn, chēungwai N/PW: (water source) chyùhn; séuichyùhn (hot one) wànchyùhn (M: go) FV: (jump) tiu, daahn ATT/N: (elastic metal device) daahngūng ~ *chòhng* (bed)

springlet N/PW: síuséuichyùhn (M: go) síukāi (M: tìuh)

sprinkle FV: ❶ sá (water) ~ *séui* ❷ (scatter) saat ❸ (of powder) sám N: (rain) mèihyúh; mèimēiyúh (M: jahn) Adj. PH: ❶ (very little) hóu síu ❷ (handful) yātjah

sprinkler N: panséuiwú (M: go)

sprint FV: (at the end of a race) chùngchi PH: (run at speed) chyùhnchūk dyún páau

sprinter N: dyúnpáaugā (M: wái)

sprite N: (ghost) yíugwaai (M: go, jek)

sprout VO: faatngàh; chēut ngàh N: (of plant) ngàh, miùh (M: jì) ✻ **bamboo sprout** N: jūkséun ✻ **bean sprout** N: ngàhchoi (M: tìuh; gàn)

spry SV: (quick) máhnjit

spur N: (on boot) máhchi (M: go) FV: (of horse) kèuichaak ✻ **spur of the moment** Adv. PH: (without consideration) yātsìh chùngduhng

spurn FV: (step on) cháai FV: (kick) tek PH: (kick) yàtgeuk tekhòi

spurt FV: ❶ (burst out) panchēutlàih; yúngchēutlàih ❷ (at the end of a race) chùngchi

sputter N/Adv. PH: (sound) pàhkpáksèng

sputum N: tàahm (M: dūk; dī)

spy N: gaandihp; gàansai (M: go) VO: jouh gàansai; jouh gaandihp FV: ❶ (inquire about) dátaam ❷ (observe) jìngchaat ~ *waihsìng* (spy-in-the-sky)

squabble VO: ngaaigàau FV: jàang

squad N: síudéui (M: deuih) síujóu (M: go)

squadron N: kèhbìngdéui (M: deuih)

squall PH: (of baby) daaihsèng haam N: (storm) bouhfùng; kwòhngfùng (M: chèuhng)

squander FV: sàai; lohngfai

squanderer N: lohngjí (M: go)

square ATT: ❶ (of shape) seifòng; fòng ❷ (measurement) pìhngfòng; fòng N/PW: (place)

gwóngchèuhng SV: (honest)
lóuhsaht N: (shape) jingfòng-
yìhng (M: go)

squash RV: (press flat)
jaahkbín (press and ruin)
jaahklaahn N: ❶ (sport) bīk-
kàuh ❷ (juice) jēunjōng gwójāp
(M: jēun)

squat FV: (bend the knee)
māu; māudài Adj. PH: (fat and
short) fèihfèih ngáingái

squatter PH: (one who
squats) māudài / māuháisyu ge
yàhn VO: (in water) gaangsēui
∗ **squatter area** N/PW:
muhkngūkkèui (M: go)

squeak N: ❶ (of mouse) jī-
jìsèng ❷ (of hinge) ngītngītsèng
❸ (shrill) jīmgiusèng FV: (inform) goumaht

squeal PH: (scream) gwáijā
hàuhlùhng gám giu FV: ❶
(complain) màaihyun ❷ (inform)
goumaht

squeamish PH: ❶ (feel sick)
sēung ngáu ❷ (delicate
stomach) go waih hóu
máhngám ❸ (easily angry) hóu
yih nàu

squeeze FV: ❶ (press) ngaatja ❷ (hold) jàsaht ❸ (sandwich)
gaahpsaht ❹ (close together)
bīk N: (money) hāakchín

squib N: ❶ (firework) paau-
jéungjái (M: jì; pàaih) ❷ (written) fúngchi dyúnmàhn (M: pìn)

squid N: yàuhyú (M: jek, tìuh)

squint N: (cross-eyed) dau-
gāingáahn (M: deui)

squire N: ❶ (landowner)
hèungsàn deihjyú (M: go, wái)
❷ (man) gùnyàmbìng (M: go)

squirm PH: ❶ (uneasy)
jàusàn m̀jihyìhn ❷ (move)
yūkháh yūkháh

squirrel N: chùhngsyú (M:
jek)

squirt FV: (jet) pan; jīt N:
(toy) séuichēung (M: jì)

stab FV: (pierce, and get hurt)
gāt, gātchàn RV: (pierce
through) gātchyùn ∗ **stab in
the back** IE: ngamjin
sèungyàhn

stability, stabilization
SV: ❶ ((of job, currency) wándihng ❷ (safe) wánjahn

stabilize PH: ❶ (of job) wándihng lohklàih ❷ (of currency)
lihng N wándihng ❸ (make safe)
lihng N wánjahn

stabilizer N: pìhnghàhnghei
(M: go)

stable SV: ❶ (of job, currency) wándihng ❷ (safe) wánjahn
N: (of horse) máhfòhng (M: go)
∗ **stableman** N: máhfù (M: go)

staccato A: dyuhndyuhn-
juhkjuhk; N: tyúhnyàm

stack N: ❶ (of grass)
chóudeuī (M: dèui) ❷ (for books)
syùgá (M: go) ❸ (chimney) yīntūng (M: go)

stadium N: wahnduhng-
chèuhng (M: go) (for ball games)
kàuhchèuhng (M: go)

staff N: ❶ (stick) gwan;
gwáaijéung (M: jì) ❷ (person)
jīkyùhn (M: go) ❸ (official sign)
kyùhnjeuhng (M: jì) ❹ (for flag)
kèihgōn (M: jì) ❺ (music)
ńghsinpóu (M: go; bún)

stag N: luhkgùng (M: jek)

stage N: ❶ (for performance) móuhtòih; tòih (M: go) ❷ (period) gàaidyuhn; sìhkèih (M: go) ✻ **stage by stage** A: juhkbouh Adv. PH: yātbouh yātbouh ✻ **stage play** N: móuhtòihkehk (M: chēut)

stagger PH: hàahnglouh séung dit gám; hàahnglouh gahtháh gahtháh N/SV: (of eye) ngáahnfā Adj. PH: (dizzy) wàhnwándéi

stagnate PH: (of water) m̀yūk SV: (of market) jaihsíh

stain PH: (make dirty) jíng wùjòu N: (spot) wùdím (M: go) (flaw) hàhchì (M: dím) VO: (color) yíhmsīk

stainless ATT: (no rust) bāt-sau ~ *gong* (steel) PH: m̀wúih sàangsau Adj. PH: (flawless) móuh hàhchì ge

stair N: làuhtàikāp; tàikāp (M: kāp) (pl.) làuhtài (M: douh, tòhng, tìuh)

staircase N: làuhtàiháu (M: go) làuhtài (M: douh, tòhng, tìuh)

stake N: ❶ jōng (M: go) ❷ (in betting) dóujyu (M: jyu) FV: (bet) tàuhjyu; dóu

stalactite N: jūngyúhsehk (M: gauh; faai)

stalagmite N: sehkséun (M: gauh; jì)

stale PH: ❶ (not fresh) m̀sàn-sìn; gaakyeh ❷ (lose taste) móuh meih VO: (of animal) ngòliuh N: (urine) liuh (M: dūk)

stalemate PH: (in chess) wòhngkéi sauhkwan N: (situation) gēungguhk (M: go)

stalk N: (of plants) gìng; hāng

(M: jì) M: (of plants) pō PH: ❶ (walking) daaihbouh hàahng ❷ (get near) jihngjíng jáumàaih-heui

stall N: (in market) dongháu (M: go, dong) M/BF: (in market) -dong M: (in stable) gaak BF: (in cinema) -joh • (front) *chìhn* ~ VO: (for time) tò sìhgaan

stallion N: máhgūng (M: jek)

stamina Adj. PH: hóu ngàaihdāk

stammer PH: góngyéh lauháu

stamp N: ❶ (mark) yan; tòuh-jēung (M: go) ❷ (on letters) yàuhpiu (M: go) ❸ (on documents) yanfā (M: go) VO: ❶ (to mark) kāpyan; dáyan; kāp tòuh-jēung ❷ (on letters) nìhm yàuhpiu; tip yàuhpiu ❸ (on documents) tip yanfā; nìhm yanfā ✻ **stamp duty** N: yanfāseui

stampede PH: bokmehng-jáu

stanch VO: (of blood) jíhyut

stancher N: jíhyutyeuhk (M: júng)

stanchion N: (post) chyúh (M: tìuh)

stand FV: ❶ (not sit) kéih ❷ (make something upright) duhng ❸ (bear) yánsauh; yán N: ❶ (position) lahpchèuhng (M: go) ❷ (stall) dong • (for magazine) *boují* ~ (M: go) ❸ jaahm • (for taxi) *dīksí* ~ ❹ (for audience) hontòih (M: go) ❺ (support) gá (M: go) ✻ **stand-point** N: lahp-chèuhng; gùndím ✻ **stand up** PH: kéihhéisàn ✻ **stand still** PH: m̀yūk ✻ **stand aside** PH: kéihmàaih yātbihn IE: jauhsáu

pòhnggùn * **stand on ceremony** SV: haakhei * **stand by** PH: (be ready) chèuihsìh jéunbeih * **stand clear** PH: m̀hóu kéihgahn * **stand for** FV/N: doihbíu (M: go)

standard N: ❶ (level) bīujéun; séuijéun (M: go) ❷ (of flag) kè̀ihhouh ATT: johdeih ~ dāng (lamp) (M: jáan); (fan) ~ fùngsin (M: bá)

standardization, standardize FV: ❶ (become standard) bīujéunfa ❷ (unify) túngyāt

standing FV: (upright) jihklahp PH: (not sit) kéihháisyu N: ❶ (position) deihwaih; sànfán ❷ (financial) wàahngíng

stanza M: ❶ (of poem) jit ❷ (of game) guhk; chèuhng; pùhn

staple N: (for papers) dèngsyùdēng PH: (to bind) yuhng dèngsyùgéi dènghóu PH: (chief product) jyúyiu cháanbán SV: (chief) jyúyiu; juhngyiu

stapler PH: saige dèngsyùgéi N: dèngsyùgéi (M: go)

star N: ❶ (in sky) sìng (M: nāp) ❷ (fate) mihngwahn ❸ (sign) sìngfùh (M: go) ❹ (of movie or TV) mìhngsìng (M: go)

starch N: ❶ (substance) dihnfánjāt ❷ (for clothes) jěungfán

stare FV: mohngjyuh; mohngsaht PH: ngáahn gàmgàm gám mohngjyuh

stark SV: (in death) gēungngaahng A: (completely) yùhnchyùhn PH: (naked) móuh jeuksāam

start AV/FV: hòichí; héisáu VO: (of journey) héichìhng FV: ❶ hòi (vehicles) ~ chè ❷ (manage) baahn ❸ (establish) ginlahp

starting AV/FV: hòichí; héisáu * **starting-point** N: héidím (M: go)

startle PH: (shock) sèhnggo jaathéi PH: (frightening) lihng yàhn hóu gèng SV: (frightening) dākyàhngèng; hópa

starvation N/SV: gēingoh * **die of starvation** RV: ngohséi

starve PH: ❶ (hungry) hóu tóuhngoh ❷ (no food) móuh yéh sihk RV: (die of) ngohséi

stash PH/PW: nèimàaih ge deihfòng

state N: ❶ (nation) gwokgā (M: go) ❷ (in U.S.) jàu (M: go) ❸ (government) jingfú (M: go) ❹ (condition) chìhngyìhng (M: go; júng) ❺ (rank) gàaikáp (M: go; júng) Adj. PH: (of the nation) gwokgā ge ATT: ❶ (established by state government) jàulahp ❷ (formal) gùnsīk; jingsīk FV: (definite) jímihng; jídihng PH: ❶ (express fully) hóu chèuhngsai gám góngchèutlàih ❷ (to do with politics) tùhng jingjih yáuh gwàanhaih ge * **lie in state** PH: jìmyéuhng wàihyùhng * **state-craft** N: jingjih chòihnàhng

stately SV: ❶ (solemn) jòngyìhm ❷ (splendid) tòhngwòhng ❸ (elegant) gòugwai

statement N: ❶ (announcement) sìngmìhng (M: pìn) ❷ (bill) dāan · (monthly) yuhtgit ~ (M: jèung) N/FV: (narration) jeuihseuht

statesman N: jingjihgā (M: wái, go)

static PREFIX: jihng ~ *dihn* (electricity) PH: (not move) m̀yūk ge

station N: ❶ jaahm · (railway) *fóchè* ~ (M: go) ❷ (of broadcasting) dihntòih; gwóngbo dihntòih (M: go) (TV) dihnsihtòih (M: go) ❸ (position) deihfòng; waihji (M: go) ❹ (base) gèideih (M: go) BF: -guhk; -gúk · (fire) *siufòhng* ~ (M: go) · (police) *gíng* ~ (M: go) FV: (sent by government) paaijyu

stationary Adj. PH: ❶ (fixed) gudihng ge ❷ (not moving) m̀yūk ge ❸ (not changing) m̀binge; bātbinge

stationery N: ❶ (materials) màhngeuih (M: júng) ❷ (letter paper) seunji (M: jèung)

statist N: túnggaihohkgā (M: wái, go)

statistician N: túnggaihohkgā (M; wái, go) (technician) túnggaiyùhn (M: go)

statistics N: túnggaihohk

statuary N: ❶ (art) dìusou ngaihseuht ❷ (person) dìusougā (M: wái, go)

statue N: jeuhng (M: go)

statuette PH: saige jeuhng

stature N: ❶ (figure) sànchòih (M: júng) ❷ (height) gòudouh ❸ (condition) gínggaai (M: júng)

status N: ❶ (position) sànfán; deihwaih ❷ (state) chìhngyìhng (M: júng) ❸ (condition) johngfong · (marital) *fànyàn* ~

statute N: faatlihng (M: tìuh)

statutory A: faatlihngseuhng; faatdihng

stanuch VO: (of blood) jíhyut

stave N: ❶ (of a barrel) túngbáan (M: faai) ❷ (staff) ngohkpóu (M: pìn; bún) VO: (make a hole) chyùnlūng RVE: chyūn

stay FV: ❶ (settle down) jyuh ❷ (for a short period) dauhlàuh ❸ (not going on) tìhnglàuh ❹ (remain there) làuh ~ *háisyu* ✳ **stay away** PH: m̀hóu hàahngmàaihlàih / heui

stead ✳ **in stead of** FV: doihtai Patt: . . . . yìhm̀ . . .

steadfast SV: ❶ (fixed) gudihng ❷ (firm) gíndihng

steadily Adv. PH: hóu wánjahn gám

steady SV: ❶ (firm) wánjahn ❷ (regular) wándihng

steak N: ngàuhpá (M: faai)

steal FV: tàu VO: tàuyéh

stealth N: ❶ (secret) beimaht (M: go) ❷ (action) beimaht hàhngduhng (M; go, chi)

stealthy Adj. PH: hóu beimaht ge

stealthily A: tàutàudéi; ngamjùng; jìhngjíngdéi

steam N: (vapour) jìnghei; hei FV: (in cooking) jìng PH: (hot) yihtdou chēutyìn

steamer N: ❶ (ship) lèuhnsyùhn (M: jek) ❷ (for cooking) jìnglùhng (M: go)

steel N: (material) gong • (stainless) *bātsau* ~ Adj. PH: (made of) yuhng gong jouh ge

steep SV: che N/PW: yùhnngàaih chiubīk (M: go) FV: (soak) jam

steeple N: jìmdéng; jìmtaap (M: go) * **steeple chase** N: yuhtyéh choimáh

steer FV: (of boat, car) jà; gasái N: (animal) ngàuhgùng (M: jek)

steerage VO: (on ship) jéungtòh N: (for passengers) póutùngchōng (M: go)

steering FV: jà; gasái * **steering wheel** N: (of vehicle) táaih; táaihpùhn (M: go); (of ship) tòh (M: go)

steersman N: tòhsáu (M: go)

stem N: ❶ (of plants) gwáang; ging; hāng (M: jì) ❷ (of things) beng N/PW: (of ship) syùhntàuh * **stem from** FV: héiyùhnyù

stench N: chaumeih (M: jahm, buhng) PH: yáuh chaumeih

stencil N: (for printing) laahpjí; yàuhyanjí (M: jèung; daahp)

stenographer N: chūkgeiyùhn (M: go)

stenography N: chūkgei

step M: ❶ (of walking) bouh ❷ (of stairs) kāp N: ❶ (of walking) geukbouh; (sound of) geukbouhsèng ❷ (of action) bouhjaauhFV: (walk) hàahng; jáu PREFIX: (relationship) hauh • (father) ~ *fuh;* (mother) ~ *móuh* Adj. PH: ❶ (of same father) tùhng fuh yih móuh ge

❷ (of same mother) tùhng móuh yih fuh ge * **step by step** Adv. PH: yātbouh yātbouh (gám)

steppe N/PW: chóuyùhn (M: go)

stepping-stone N: daahpgeuksehk (M: gauh); (device) sáudyuhn (M: júng)

stere M: lahpfòngmáih

stereo ATT: (of broadcasting) lahptáising; sànlihksing

stereotype N: ❶ yùhnbáan (M: faai) ❷ (printing) yùhnbáan yanchaat

sterile, sterility PH: ❶ (of plants) m̀gitgwó ge ❷ (of childbirth) móuh jái sàang ge ❸ (no germs) móuh kwán ge

sterilization VO: (of germs) saatkwán; sìuduhk FV: (of childbirth) jyuhtyuhk

sterilize VO: (of germs) saatkwán; sìuduhk FV: (of childbirth) jyuhtyuhk

sterling N: (money) yìngbóng PREFIX: (of silver) sèuhn ~ *ngán*

stern SV: ❶ (appearence) yìhmsūk ❷ (strict) yìhmgaak N/PW: (of ship) syùhnméih N: (tail) méih (M: tiuh)

sternum N: hùnggwāt (M: tiuh)

stethoscope N: tèngtúng (M: go)

stew FV: ❶ mān ❷ (like steaming) dahn

steward N: ❶ (servant) sihyingsāng; sihjái (M: go) ❷ (housekeeper) gúngā (M: go)

stewardess N: nêuih sih-ying (M: go)

stick N: ❶ (rod) gwan; (tr.) sihdīk (M: jì) ❷ (branch) syuhjī (M: jì) FV: ❶ (glue) tip; nìhm; chì ❷ (fail to get out) kīkjyuh ❸ (put in) chaap ❹ (prick) gāt

sticker N: ❶ (label) bīuchīm (M: go) ❷ (plaything) tipjí (M: jèung)

sticking PH: yuhnglàih chìyéh ge yéh

sticky Adj. PH: chìchì nahpnahp; hóu chì

stiff SV: (hard) ngaahng ＊ **stiff-necked** PH: (from sleeping) fanlái géng

stiffen RV: binngaahng PH: lihng N binngaahng

stifle PH: lihng yàhn jahtsīk; lihng yàhn fùkāp kwannàahn FV: (of rebellion) janngaat

stigma N: ❶ (shame) chíyuhk (M: júng) ❷ (mark) sèunghàhn (M: go; douh)

still A: juhng; yihngyìhn (more) ganggā PH: ❶ (no movement) m̀yūk ge ❷ (no sound) móuh sèng ge; hóu jihng ge N: (of liquors) jìnglauhhei (M: go)

stimulant Adj. PH: (exciting) hóu chigīk ge; lihng yàhn hóu hìngfáhn ge N: (drug) hìngfáhnjài

stimulate FV/N: ❶ (excite) chigīk (M: júng) ❷ (encourage) gúlaih AV: (quicken) chūkjeun

stimulation N/FV: ❶ (excitement) chigīk (M: júng) ❷ (encouragement) gúlaih

stimulus N/FV/SV: chigīk

sting FV/N: (of bee) jām; chi (M: jì) N: ❶ (of plants) chimòuh (M: tìuh) ❷ (of pain) chektung PH: (by a swindler) béi yàhn wánbahn

stingily, stingy SV: (mean) gùhòhn

stink PH: (smell) yáuh chaumeih SV: (smell) chau

stint FV: haahnjai; jitjai; gánsūk

stipulate FV: yeukdihng; kwàidihng

stipulation FV: (state) yeukdihng; kwàidihng N: ❶ (contract) hahptúhng (M: fahn, jèung) ❷ (item) hohngmuhk (M: go)

stir FV: ❶ (move) gáau ❷ (excite) gáau; gúduhng ＊ **stir up trouble** PH: gáausih gáaufèi

stitch FV: lyùhn VO: (medical) lyùhnjām N: (way of sewing) jāmfaat M: jām ＊ **stitch up** PH: lyùhnmàaih kéuih

stock N: ❶ (ancestry) hyuttúng ❷ (of goods) chyùhnfo ❸ (investment) gúpiu (M: júng; jek; jèung) FV: ❶ (store) chyúhchyúhn ❷ (supply) gùngkāp ＊ **laughing-stock** N: siubeng ＊ **stock breeding** N: chūkmuhkyihp (M: júng) ＊ **out of stock** PH: móuh fo RV: móuhsaai

stocking N: chèuhngmaht (M: deui, jek)

stocky PH: ngái yìh gitsaht ge

stoic N: gamyuhkjyúyihjé (M: go)

stomach N: (organ) waih (M: go) FV: (endure) yán; yánsauh ＊

stomachache N: (of abdomen) tóuhtung * **stomach-warmer** N: yihtséuidói (M: go)

stomp VO: dahmgeuk

stone N: (stone in kidney or bladder) sehk (M: gauh; nāp) M: (for weight) sehk ATT: sehkhei ~ sihdoih (age) * **stone-pit** N/PW: sehkkong (chèuhng) (M: go) * **kill two birds with one stone** IE: yātsehk yihlíuh

stony Adj. PH: ❶ (many stones) dò sehk ge ❷ (of stone) sehkjāt ❸ (hard) ngaahngge * **stony-hearted** Adj. PH: titsehk sāmchèuhng

stooge N: ❶ (clown) cháugok (M: go) ❷ (spy) gàansai (M: go) VO: ❶ (clown) jouh cháugok ❷ (spy) jouh gàansai

stool N: ❶ (for sitting) dang; dangjái (M: jèung) ❷ (in toilet) johchipùhn (M: go) VO: (excrement) daaihbihn; ngòsí N: daaihbihn; sí (M: dūk; chi)

stoop PH: ❶ (bend the body) wàandài sàn ❷ (of head) dāpdàitàuh N: (of back) tòhbui

stop FV: ❶ (not going on) tìhng; tìhngjí ❷ (prevent) jójí ❸ (put an end) gitchūk ❹ (close up) sākjyuh AV: (not going on) m̀ N: jaahm‥ (for bus) bāsí ~ (M: go) * **full stop** N: geuihouh (M: go) * **stop watch** N: míuhbīu (M: go)

stopper N: sāk; jāt (M: go)

storage FV: ❶ (put aside) jàimàaih; sàumàaih ❷ (save) chóuhmàaih ❸ (stock) chyúhchyùhn

store FV: ❶ (save) chóuhmàaih ❷ (stock) chyúhchyùhn

❸ (put aside) jàimàaih; sàumàaih N/PW: ❶ (shop) poutáu; sihdōpóu (M: gàan) ❷ (for goods) fochōng (M: go, gàan) * **department store** N/PW: baakfo gùngsī (M: gàan) * **store-room** N/PW: sihdōfóng; chyúhmahtsāt (M: go, gàan)

storey M: chàhng

stork N; baahkhók (M: jek)

storm PH: dá daaihfùng lohk daaihyúh; daaihfùng daaihyúh N: fùngbouh (M: chèuhng) * **storm-troops** N: dahtgīkdéui (M: deuih)

story N: ❶ (tale) gusih; gújái (M: go) ❷ (novel) síusyut (M: go; pìn; bún) ❸ (lie) daaihwah (M: go) ❹ (things happened) gìnggwo ❺ (of one's life) sàngpìhng

stout PH: (fat and big) yauh fèih yauh daaih SV: ❶ (strong) kèuhngjohng ❷ (brave) yúhnggám

stove N: fólòuh (M: go)

stow FV: (pack) jòng; bàaujòng; (as in a ship) joi N: (packing) bàaujòng

stowage N/FV: (pack) bàaujòng FV: (as in a ship) jòngjoi

stowaway PH: tàudouh ge yàhn (M: go)

straddle PH: maakhòigeuk kéih

straight SV: ❶ (not bend) jihk ❷ (honest) jingjihk A: (one direction) yātjihk * **straight face** PH: báanhéi go mihn; hāakhéi go mihn * **straight away** A: jīkhāak; màhseuhng * **straight forward** SV: (personality) sóngjihk; táanbaahk IE: (in speaking or writing) hòimùhn gínsàan PH: (in speaking or writing) mjyunwāan mutgok ✳ **get straight** RV: gáaudihm; gáauchingchó ✳ **straight out** PH: táanbaahk góng chēutlàih

straighten RV: jíngjihk; binjihk

strain FV: ❶ (pull tightly) làaigán ❷ (hold tightly) láamsaht ❸ (stretch the meaning) kūkgáai ❹ (force) mîhnkéuhng ❺ (twist) náuchàn PH: ❶ (unnatural) mjihyìhn ❷ (too much strength) taai jeuhnlihk M: (breed) júng N: (breed) bánjúng (M: go)

strainer N: gaak • (for tea) *chàh ~* (M: go)

strait SV: (narrow) jaak N/PW: (gulf) hóihaahp (M: go)

strand N/PW: (sandy shore) sàtāan; sāngohn (M: go) FV: (of a ship) gokchíhn M: (bundle of) jaat; (string of) tìuh PH: (of a person) lihngyàhn yātchàuh mohkjín

strange SV: ❶ (surprising) kèihgwaai ❷ (new) sàangbóu

stranger N: sàangbóuyàhn (M: go)

strangle FV: (kill) laahkséi (by hanging) diugéngséi

strap N: dáai; pèihdáai (M: tìuh) PH: yuhng pèihdáai dá FV: (tie) bóng

strapper N: daaihjeklóu (M: go)

strapping SV: daaihjek Adj. PH: gòudaaih wàimáahng

strategic N: jinleuhkseuhng; bīngfaatseuhng

strategist N: jinleuhkgā (M: wái; go)

strategy N: jinleuhkkhohk

stratify N: yìhngsìhngchàhng

straw N: ❶ (plant) douhchóu (M: tìuh) ❷ (for drinking) yámtúng (M: ji) Adj. PH: (cheap) mjihkchín ge

strawberry N: sihdōbēléi (M: go)

stray VO: (lose way) dohngsātlouh

streak N: (line) sintìuh; tìuhmàhn (M: tìuh) VO: (draw) gà sintìuh; gà tìuhmàhn

stream N: (brook) kāi (M: tìuh) FV: (flow) làuh ✳ **down stream** A: seuhnlàuh ✳ **up stream** A: yihklàuh

street N/PW: gāai; (pl.) gāaidouh (M: tìuh) ✳ **street car** N: dihnchè (M: ga) ✳ **street walker** N: geihnéuih; gāi (M: go) ✳ **street-sleeper** N: (man) làuhlohnghon; louhsūkjé (M: go) PH: fangāai ge

strength N: ❶ (physical) lihk (M: júng, dī) ❷ (power) lihkleuhng (M: júng, dī)

strengthen FV: gàkèuhng RV: (become strong) binkèuhng

strenuous Adj. PH: (hardworking) hóu kàhnlihk ge

strenuously Adv. PH: (hard-working) hóu kàhnlihk gám

stress FV: ❶ (emphasize) kèuhngdiuh ❷ (regard highly) jyujuhng N: ❶ (of a syllable) chúhngyām (M: go) ❷ (essential point) juhngdím (M: go) PH:

(read) yuhng chúhngyám duhk

stretch FV: (make wider) sàn RV: (make longer, tighter, wider by pulling) làaichèuhng; làaigán; làaifut PH: (extend) yàuh PW1 yātjihk heuidou PW2 FV/SV: (loose after washing) wéh ∗ **stretch out** PH: sàn chēutlàih/chēutheui

stretcher N: **❶** (for carrying person) dàamgáchòhng (M: jèung) **❷** (a device) kwongjèunghei (M: go)

strew FV: **❶** (scatter) saat ~ júng (seeds), ~ fā (flower) **❷** (cover) jējyuh

striate Adj. PH: **❶** (striped) yáuh tìuhmàhn ge **❷** (furrowed) yáuh hāangmàhn ge

strict SV: **❶** (not loose) yìhm; yìhmgaak **❷** (clear and exact) mìhngkok ∗ **in the strict sense of a word** Adv. PH: yìhmgaak làih góng

strictly Adv. PH: hóu yìhm gám; hóu yìhmgaak gám ∗ **strictly prohibited** PH: yìhmgam • (of smoking) ~ kāpyīn

stride PH: **❶** (of walking) daaihbouh jáu **❷** (of step) yāt daaihbouh

strident N: (shrill) jìmsèng (M: bá)

strife VO: (quarrel) ngaaigāau N: (conflict) chùngdaht (M: chi)

strike FV: **❶** (hit) dá **❷** (collide) johng **❸** (with a hammer) dahp **❹** (attack) gùnggīk **❺** (of a clock) hàauhéung **❻** waahk (match) ~ fóchàaih **❼** jyu (coins) ~ ngaahngbaih **❽** (cancel) cháh **❾** (take down) chaak **❿** (of instrument) tàahn VO/N: (of work) bahgūng (M: chi) VO: **❶** (of ship) jūkchìuh **❷** (of root) sàanggàn PH: **❶** (of clock) faatchēut bousìh seunhouh **❷** (of impression) lìhng yàhn yáuh hóu sàmhāak ge yanjeuhng **❸** (by claws or bite) béi N wásèung; béi N ngáauhsèung ∗ **strike while the iron is hot** IE: dátit chan yiht ∗ **go on strike** VO: bahgūng (M: chi) PH: jeunhàhng bahgūng ∗ **hunger strike** FV/N: jyuhtsihk

striker PH: (worker) bahgūng ge gùngyàhn N: **❶** (worker) bahgūngjé (M: go) **❷** (of a clock) jūngchèuih (M: go) **❸** (of a gun) johngjām (M: jì)

striking Adj. PH: (attracting attention) hóu kāpyáhn yàhn ge; hóu yáhn yàhn jyuyi ge

string N: **❶** (thread) sin (M: tìuh) **❷** (rope) síng (M: tìuh) **❸** (of instrument) yìhn; sin; yìhnsin (M: tìuh) M: (string of) chyun FV: (with a string) chyun; chyunmàaih; chyunhéi ∗ **string up** RV: diuséi

stringent SV: (strict) yìhm PH: **❶** (of money market) ngàhngàn hóu gán **❷** (difficult to make ends meet) jàujyún kwannàahn

strip FV: chèuih; mōk (clothes) ~ sāam VO: (of milk) jà ngàuhnáaih N: **❶** (of paper) jítiuh (M: jèung) **❷** (foreshow) tyutyīmóuh (M: chèuhng) ∗ **strip cartoon** N: lìhnwàahntòuh (M: jèung; bún)

stripe N: (pattern) tìuhmàhn (M: tìuh) M: (of rank) waahk; wáak FV: (with a whip) bīndá ∗ **the stars and stripes** N: Méihgwok gwokkèih; sìngtìuhkèih

stripling N: ❶ (youth) hauh-sāangjái; nìhnhèngyàhn (M: go) ❷ (tree) syuhjái (M: pò)

strive FV: ❶ (struggle) fáhndau ❷ (make great effort) nóuhlihk ✻ **strive for** FV: jàngchéui

stroke FV: ❶ (of a blow) dá ❷ (touch gently) mó ❸ (knock) hàau PH: (rub) hehnghēng sou BF: (breast stroke) -sīk • (breast stroke) wā ~; (free style) jihyàuh ~ M: (of writing) bāt; waahk N: (of writing) bātwaahk VO: (illness) jungfùng

stroll VO: saanbouh; hàahng-gāai FV: hàahnghháh

strong SV: ❶ (of figure, health) kèuhngjong; jong ❷ (much strength) daaihlihk; yáuhlihk ❸ (of character) gìnkèuhng ❹ (of faith) gìndihng ❺ (of a country, power) kèuhng; kèuhngdaaih ❻ (of alcohol) sàileih; kang ❼ (of tea, coffee) nùhng; yùhng ❽ (of building) gìngu ❾ (firm) gaulihk; wánjahn

structural Adj. PH: ❶ (of framework) gitkauseuhng ge ❷ (of building) ginjùkseuhng ge

structure N: ❶ (way of organizing) gitkau; kaujouh (M: júng) ❷ (building) ginjùkmaht (M: joh, duhng)

struggle FV: ❶ (as in a fight) jàngjaat ❷ (strive) fáhndau ✻ **struggle for** FV: jàngchéui

strum FV: lyuhntàahn N: (the sound) lyuhntàahnsèng

strut PH/IE: (of walking) hàahnglouh hóu sàchàhn; jígòu heiyèuhng N: (of building) jìchyúh (M: tiuh)

stub SUFFIX: ❶ -táu • (of cigarette) yīn ~ ; -tàuh • (of pencil) yùhnbāt ~ ❷ -méih • (of ticket) piu ~ ; fēi ~ N: (of cheque) dái (M: jèung)

stubble N: (beard) dyúnsōu (M: dī; jáp) PH: (of grain plants) gotjihng ge bouhfahn

stubborn SV: (personality) ngaahnggéng; gújáp Adj. PH: (difficult to deal with) hóu nàahngáau ge

stubby Adj. PH: yauh chòu yauh dyún ge

stud N: ❶ (horse) júngmáh (M: jek) ❷ (nail) daaihtàuhdēng (M: háu) ❸ (button) jōngsīknáu (M: nāp)

student N: hohksāang (M: go) ✻ **students' union** N: hohksāangwúi (M: go)

studio N/PW: ❶ (of an artist) wásāt (M: gàan) ❷ (for photos) yíngséungpóu (M: gàan) ❸ (of film making) pínchèuhng (M: go, gàan) ❹ (of radio broadcasting) boyāmsāt (M: go) ❺ (of TV broadcasting) boyíngsāt (M: go)

studious SV: kàhnlihk

study VO: (with books) duhksyù FV: ❶ (with books) duhk ❷ (research, make a study of) yìhngau ❸ (learn) hohk; hohkjaahp PH: (read carefully) jísai táiháh ✻ **study abroad** FV/VO: làuhhohk

stuff N: (material) chòihlíu; yéh (M: dī, júng) FV: (fill) tìhn; sāk RV: (fill) tìhnmúhn; sākmúhn

stuffing N: (for cooking) háam (M: dī, júng)

stuffy SV: (of ventilation) guhk

stumble PH: ❶ (cause to fall) béi N gwaandái ❷ (discover) ngáuhyihn faatyihn ❸ (in speaking) góngyéh háujahtjaht

stump N: (of a tree) syuhtàuh (M: gauh) VO: (to cut) jáam syuhjì FV: (speech) yínsyut PH: (in walking) hàahnglouh gahtháh gahtháh

stun RV: (by a blow) dáwàhn PH: (by a shock) ngòihsaai

stunning Adj. PH: ❶ (splendid) hóu sàileih ge ❷ (ravishing) lihng yàhn wàhntòhtòh ge

stunt N: ❶ (skill) dahkgeih (M: júng; dī) ❷ (in advertising) cheuktàuh (M: dī) ❸ (of people) ngáiyàhn (M: go) ❹ (of tree) ngáisyuh (M: pò) PH: (slow growth) faatyuhk chìhwuhn ✻ **stuntman** N: taisàn (M: go)

stupefy PH: (not stirring) lihng yàhn màhmuhk

stupendous SV: ❶ (amazing) gìngyàhn ❷ (tremendous) geuihdaaih

stupid SV: chéun; bahn

stupor PH: góngyéh lauháu

sty N/PW: (of pig) jyūlāan (M: go) N: (illness) ngáahntiujàm (M: nāp)

style N: ❶ (of clothing) fún; fúnsīk (M: go; júng) ❷ (attitude) jokfùng (M: júng) ❸ (of an artist) fùnggaak (M: júng) ❹ (of writing) màhntái; táichòih (M: júng) ✻ **out of style** SV: gwosih PH: m̀làuhhàhng

stylist N: (designer) chitgaisì • (of hair) *faatyìhng* ~ (M: go)

stylistic Adj. PH: ❶ (of writing) táichòihseuhng ❷ (of an artist) fùnggaakseuhng

stylus N: ❶ (in pick-up) cheungjām (M: jì) ❷ (for writing) titbāt (M: jì)

stymie N: (situation) kwanging

styptic N: (medicine) jíhyutyeuhk (M: dī) Adj. PH: (stop bleeding) hóyíh jíhyut ge

suave SV: (mild) wòhngói; wànwòh

subagent N: fu doihléihyàhn; fànsìusēung (M: go)

subaquatic, subaqueous ATT: séuidái

subatomic Adj. PH: ayùhnjí ge

subcommittee N: síujóu wáiyùhnwúi; suhkwúi (M: go)

subconscious Adj. PH: hahyisīk ge

subcontinent N/PW: chidaaihluhk

subcontract PH: punbéi daihyihdī yàhn jouh N: (contract) fànkai (M: jèung)

subcutaneous ATT: pèihhah

subdivide FV: joifàn

subdivision PH: joi fànsihng ge bouhfahn

subdue FV: ❶ (overcome) jìngfuhk ❷ (control) hàakfuhk ❸ (make softer) gáamyeuhk; gáamdài VO: (of pain) jítung

subedit N: fupìnchāp (M: go, wái) VO: jouh fupìnchāp

subgroup N: ❶ síujóu (M: go) ❷ (chemistry) juhk (M: go)

subheading N: síubīutàih; fubīutàih (M: go)

subject N: ❶ (topic) tàihmuhk (M: go) ❷ (people) jímàhn; gwokmàhn; (M: go) ❸ (in grammar) jyúchìh; jyúyúh (M: go) ❹ (of conversation) wahtàih (M: go) M/N: (in school) fō FV: (subdue) jìngfuhk ✻ **subject matter** N: (of book, music) jyútàih ✻ **subject to** PH: yiu gìnggwo N/FV1 sìnji hóyíh FV2

subjection FV: ❶ (subdue) jìngfuhk ❷ (encounter) jòusauh; sauh FV/N: (rule) túngjih

subjective N/SV: (of feeling) jyúgùn Adj. PH: (of subject) jyúchìh ge

subjugate FV: ❶ (subdue) jìngfuhk ❷ (conquer) janngaat

subjunctive PH: gáchit yúhhei Adj. PH: gáchit ge

sublet FV: (rent) fànjòu ~ béi PN

sublieutenant N: (army) luhkgwàn siuwai (M: go, wái) (navy) hóigwàn jùngwai (M: go, wái)

sublime SV: ❶ (supreme) sùhnggòu ❷ (great) wáihdaaih ❸ (solemn) jòngyìhm FV: (chemistry) sìngwàh

sublimity N: (extreme) gihk (M: go) SV: see sublime

submachine-gun N: chùngfùngchēung (M: jì)

submarine ATT: (in water) séuidái; hóidái N: chìhmséuitéhng (M: jek)

submerge VO: (of sub-

marine) chìhmséui FV: (cover with water) jam PH: ❶ (go into water) chìhmyahp séuidái ❷ (cover with water) jam hái séui léuihbihn

submissive FV: (obedient) fuhkchùhng SV/VO: (obedient) tèngwah

submission FV: ❶ (give in) tàuhhòhng ❷ (obey) fuhkchùhng N: (opinion) yigin; táifaat (M: go)

submit FV: ❶ (give in) tàuhhòhng ❷ (obey) fuhkchùhng; seuhnchùhng ❸ (suggest) tàihyíh ❹ tàihchēut (opinion) ~ yigin ❺ (hand to superior) chìhnggàau ❻ (hand) gàau; tàihgàau

subnormal Adj. PH: dàiyù jingsèuhng ge

subordinate N: (junior) hahsuhk, bouhhah, sáuhah (M: go) Adj. PH: ❶ (dependent) fuhsuhk ge ❷ (less important) chiyiu ge ✻ **subordinate to** N daihsuhk (yù) N jìhah

subpoena N: chyùhnpiu (M: jèung)

subscribe VO/N: (sign) chìmmèng (M: go) FV: (donate) gyùn ✻ **subscribe to** FV: ❶ dehng (magazine, newspaper) ~ jaahpji; ~ boují ❷ (of opinion) tùhngyi

subscriber N: ❶ (of magazine, newspaper) dehngwuh (M: go) ❷ (of telephone) dihnwá yuhngwuh (M: go) PH: ❶ (of signature) chìmmèng ge yàhn ❷ (donator) gyùnchín ge yàhn

subscription VO/N: (sign) chìmmèng FV: (donate) gyùn N: ❶ (donation) gyùnfún (M: dì, bāt) ❷ (of magazine) dehngyuht fai

subsequence PH: (what will happen) hauhlòih faatsàng ge sih N: (as a result) hauhgwó (M: go)

subsequent A: hauhlòih Adj. PH: gànjyuh làih ge

subservient SV: (useful) yáuhyuhng FV: (flatter) fuhngsìhng

subside FV: ❶ (sink) chàhm ❷ (go back) teui PH: (of sea) pìhngjihng lohklàih

subsidiary Adj. PH: (dependent) fuhsuhk ge

subsidize FV/N/ATT: (of school) jìjoh; jèuntip

subsidy FV: (as an aid) jèuntip; jìjoh N: (money) jèuntipngáak; jìjohngáak; bóujohgàm (M: bāt)

subsist, subsistence FV: (exist) sàngchyùhn PH: (living) wàihchìh sàngwuht

subsoil N: hahchàhngtóu PH: fàanhéi . . . dáitóu

substance N: ❶ (matter) mahtjāt (M: júng) ❷ (importance) yiuyih (M: go)

substantial SV: ❶ (real) jànsaht; sahtjoih ❷ (firm) wánjahn

substantiate FV: ❶ (of a job) sahtyàhm ❷ (proof) jingmìhng; jingsaht ❸ (make it not so abstract) geuihtáifa

substation N/PW: (branch) fàngúk (M: gàan)

substitute FV: (replace) doihtai VO: (in school) doihfo N: ❶ (teacher) doihfo sìnsàang

(M: go) ❷ (worker) taigūng (M: go) ❸ (things) doihyuhngbán (M: júng)

substitution FV: ❶ (replace) doihtai ❷ (of things) doihyuhng

substratum N: ❶ (level) hahchàhngtóu ❷ (foundation) gèichó

substruction, substructure N: ❶ (foundation) gèichó (M: go) ❷ (building) deihhah ginjūk (M: joh) ❸ (of road) louhgèi

subterfuge N: ❶ (trick) gwáigai (M: go, júng) ❷ (excuse) jihkháu (M: go)

subtitle N: ❶ (of movie) jihmohk; jihmók ❷ (of a book) síubīutàih (M: go)

subtle, subtlely SV: ❶ (wonderful) mèihmiuh ❷ (not thick) hèi ❸ (sensitive) máhngám ❹ (cunning) yàmhím

subtotal FV/N: (calculate) síugai (M: go)

subtract FV: ❶ gáam ❷ (deduct) kau ✳ subtract 1 from 2 PH: 2 gáam 1

subtraction N: gáamfaat

subtropical Adj. PH: ayihtdaai ge

suburb(s) N/PW: gàaukèui (M: go)

suburban Adj. PH: (of suburb) gàaukèui ge PH: (people) jyuhhái gàaukèui ge yàhn

subvention N: jèuntip; bóujohgàm (M: dī, bāt)

subversion FV: ❶ (overturn) dìnfūk ❷ (destroy)

powaaih

subway N/PW: seuihdouh (M: tiuh) N: (in U.S.A.) deih (hah) tit

succeed N/FV/SV: (not fail) sìhnggùng (M: chi) FV: ❶ (inherit) gaisìhng; sìhngsauh ❷ (go on) gaijuhk

success N/SV/FV: sìhnggùng (M: chi) * **failure is the mother of success** IE: sātbaaih náaih sìhnggùng jì móuh

successful SV/N/FV: sìhnggùng (M: chi)

succession FV: ❶ (go after) gaijuhk ❷ (inherit) gaisìhng; sìhngsauh A: (in order) lìhnjuhk

successive A: lìhnjuhk

sucessor N: gaisìhngyàhn (M: go)

succinct SV: (simple and clear) gáangit

succour FV: gaujoh; gaujai

succumb FV: ❶ (surrender) wātfuhk ❷ (die) séi

such A: ❶ (for a SV) gam ❷ (for a FV) gám; gámyéung Adj. PH: (for a N) gámyéung ge * **as such** Adv. PH/PH:hóuchíh gám (yéung) * **such as** FV: hóuchíh PH: hóuchíh . . . jìléui * **and such** N: dángdáng

suchlike PH: hóuchíh . . . jìléui ge yéh/yàhn

suck FV: ❶ (by mouth) jyut ❷ (by tongue) láai ❸ (absorb) kāp-sàu VO: (of milk) jyutnáaih * **sucking-pig** N: yúhjyū (M: jek)

sucker PH: (baby) sìhknáaih ge bìhbī N: ❶ (tube) kāpgún (M: jì) ❷ (slang) lóuhchan

suckle VO: wai yàhnnáaih

suckling PH: (baby) sìhknáaih ge bìhbī Adj. PH: (for young people) yúhchau meih gòn

sucrose N: jetòhng (M: dī)

suction FV: ❶ (suck) kāp ❷ (remove) chāu

sudden SV/A: dahtyìhn * **all of a sudden** A: dahtyìhn (gāan); fātyìhn (gāan)

suds N: (of soap) fàangáanpóuh (M: dī)

sue FV: (claim) gou; hunggou * **sue for** FV: kàuh; chíngkàuh * **sue out** PH: dākdóu semíhn

Suez Canal N/PW: Sòuyìhsih Wahnhòh (M: tiuh)

suffer VO: ❶ (of pain) sauhfú ❷ (of loss) sauh syúnsāt ❸ (of hardship) ngàaihfú FV: (tolerate) sauhdāk; yánsauh; ngàaih PH: (of great pain) gokdāk hóu tung * **suffer from . . . disease** PH: yáuh . . . behng

sufferer PH: ❶ (of pain) sauhfú ge yàhn ❷ (of disease) yáuh behng ge yàhn

sufferance FV: (tolerate) yán; yánsauh; sauhdāk * **on sufferance** FV: mahkhéui

suffering N: (pain) tungfú

suffice SV/FV: (enough) gau; jùkgau

sufficiency SV: chùngjùk; jùkgau; gau FV: gau

sufficient SV: chùngjùk; jùkgau; gau FV: gau

suffix N: jihméih; chìhméih (M: go) VO: gà chìhméih

suffocate FV: (of breath) jahtsīk RV: (of fire) jíngsīk

suffrage VO: (vote) tàuhpiu N: ❶ (ballot) jaansìhngpiu (M: jèung) ❷ (right) tàuhpiukyùhn; syúngéuikyùhn

suffuse FV: (full of) chùngmúhn

sugar N: tòhng (granulated) sàtòhng (M: dī); (cube) fōngtòhng (M: nāp, gauh); (brown) pìntòhng (M: gauh); (rocks) bīngtòhng (M: gauh) ✳ **sugar cane** N: je (M: tiuh, gauh, lūk)

suggest FV/N: (propose) tàihyíh (M: go) FV: ❶ (of hint) ngamsíh ❷ (remind) tàihséng PH: ❶ (of hint) yáuh . . . ge yisi ❷ (remind) lihng yàhn séunghéi

suggestion N/FV: tàihyíh (M: go)

suggestive Adj. PH: yáuh ngamsíhsing

suicide FV: jihsaat ✳ **commit suicide** FV: jihsaat ✳ **suicide squad** N: gámséidéui (M: deuih)

suit M: ❶ (of clothing) tou ❷ (of cards) fu N: ❶ (of clothing) toujōng (M: tou) ❷ (for men) sàijōng (M: tou) ❸(of law) ngongín, ngon (M: gihn) FV: (fit) sīkhahp, ngáam PH: (fit) deui PN hóu hahpsīk FV: (ask for) chíngkàuh ✳ **bring a suit against PN** PH: gou PN; hunggou PN

suitable SV: sīkhahp; hahpsīk; ngáam ✳ **suitable for PN** PH: deui PN hóu hahpsīk; hóu sīkhahp PN

suitcase N: pèihgīp (M: go)

suite M: tou N: (of rooms) toufóng (M: go, gàan)

sulk SV/FV: (angry) nàu

sullen PH: (facial) hāakmàaih háumihn; hāakháu hāakmihn SV: (of weather) yàmchàhm

sully RV: (make dirty) jíng wù jòu PH: (of reputation) powaaih mìhngyuh

sulphur N: làuhwòhng (M: dī)

sulphurate ATT: làuhfa-

sulphuric PH: yáuh làuhwòhng ge ✳ **sulphuric acid** N: làuhsyūn

sultry SV: ❶ (of weather) ngaiyiht ❷ (of person) yihtchìhng ❸ (impatient) singgāp

sum M: bāt N: ❶ (calculation) sou (M: tiuh) ❷ (figure) soumuhk (M: go) ❸ (total) júngsou ✳ **sum up** A: júngjì

summarize FV/N: júnggit; gáanseuht (M: go)

summary N: jaahkyiu; daaihgōng; júnggit (M: go)

summer N: ❶ (weather) hahtīn ❷ (season) hahgwai ATT: ❶ syúkèih ~ *bāan* (summer course) ❷ hahlìhng ~ *yìhng* (summer camp)

summit N: ❶ (peak) sàandéng (M: go) ❷ (point) díngdím (M: go) ✳ **summit conference** N: gòufùng wuihyíh (M: go)

summon FV: ❶ (call) chyùhn; jiuh; chyùhnjiuh ❷ (of God) jiuhwuhn ❸ (of chairman) jiuhjaahp ❹ jiuhhòi (meeting) ~ *wuihyíh*

summons N: (document) chyùhnpiu (M: jèung)

sumptuous SV: ❶ (luxurious) chèchí ❷ (costly-looking) hòuhwáh

sun N: taaiyèuhng; yahttáu (M: go) ＊ **sunbathe** VO: saai taaiyèuhng; saai yahttáu ＊ **sun-dried** PH: (béi taaiyèuhng) saaigòn ge ＊ **sun flower** N: heungyahtkwàih (fā) (M: déu, dó) ＊ **sun-light** N: yèuhnggwòng ＊ **sunrise** FV/N: yahtchēut ＊ **sunset** FV/N: yahtlohk

sunburnt RV: saaihāakjó

Sunday TW/N: sìngkèihyaht; láihbaaiyaht; láihbaai; (Christian) jyúyaht ＊ **sunday school** N: jyúyahtthohk

sunder FV: fànhòi; gaakhòi

sundry PH: (things) sāpseui ge yéh N: (expense) jaahpfai

sunglow N: ❶ (morning) jiuhàh ❷ (evening) máahnhàh

sunny SV: ❶ (bright) gwòng; gwòngmáahng ❷ (cheerful) hòisàm N/SV: (weather) hóutìn

sunstroke VO: jungsyú

sup FV: ❶ (drink) yám ❷ (suck) jyut VO: (take supper) sihk máahnfaahn N: (small amount) saidaahm, síusíu, dīgamdēu

super ATT: ❶ (of size) dahkdaaih ❷ (highest) jeuigòu N: (actor) kēlēfē (M: go)

superabundance PH: gwo dò

superannuate VO: (give pension) béi yéuhnglóuhgām PH: (dismiss) giu jīkyùhn teuiyàu

superannuation N: (pension) teuiyàugām (M: bāt)

superb SV: wàhngwáih; jonglaih

supercharge VO: jàngngaat PH: jànggà ngaatlihk

supercilious SV: ngouhmaahn

superficial A: bíumihnseuhng

superfluity PH: (too many) gwo dò SV: (not necessary) dòyúh

superhighway N/PW: gòuchūk gùnglouh (M: tìuh)

superhuman Adj. PH: chìuyàhn ge

superintend FV: ❶ (supervise) gāamdūk ❷ (manage) gúnléih

superintendent N: ❶ (supervisor) gāamdūk (M: go, wái) ❷ (man in charge) jyúgúnyàhn (M: go, wái)

superior SV: (of rank) gòukāp N: ❶ (boss) seuhngsī (M: go) ❷ (abbot) sàudouhyún yúnjéung (M: go) SV: ❶ (excel) yàusing ❷ (in quality) seuhngdáng; yàujāt

superiority SV: (excellence) yàusing; yàuyuht N: (state) yàusai (M: júng)

superjet N: chìuyàmchūk pansehgèi (M: ga)

superlative Adj. PH: jeui gòukāp ge

superman N: chìuyàhn (M: go)

supermarket N/PW: chìukāp síhchèuhng (M: go, gàan)

supernatural Adj. PH:

chiùjihyihn ge SV: (wonderful) sàhnkèih

supernormal SV: chìu-sèuhng; yihsèuhng

superpower N/PW: chiù-kāp daaihgwok (M: go)

superscription VO: (write) tàihjih PH: (name and address) singmihng deihjí

supersede FV: doihtai

supersonic Adj. PH/ATT: chìuyàmchūk

superstition N/SV: màih-seun (M: júng)

superstitious SV/N: màih-seun (M: júng)

superstructure N: seuhngchàhng ginjūk (M: dī)

supertax N: fuhgāseui

supervene Adj. PH: yàt-chàih faatsàng ge

supervise FV/N: gàamdūk (M: go, wái)

supervision N/FV: gàam-dūk (M: go, wái)

supervisor N/FV: gāamdūk (M: go, wái) * **school supervisor** N: haauhgāam (M: go, wái)

supper N: máahnfaahn; máahnchāan (M: chàan)

supplant FV: ❶ (supersede) doihtai ❷ (take the place) chéuidoih

supple SV: (soft) yàuhyúhn RV: (soften) jíngyúhn

supplement, supplementary N/FV/ATT: (addition)

bóuchùng Adj. PH: (additional) bóuchùngsing ge

supplicate FV: ❶ (beg) hánkàuh ❷ (pray) kèihkàuh

supply FV/N: gùngkāp; gùngying FV: (with money) gùng

supplies PH: yahtsèuhng yuhng ge yéh

support FV/N: (back up) jìchìh FV: ❶ wàihchìh (living) ~ sàngwuht ❷ (living of somebody else) yéuhng ❸ (of music) buhnjau ❹ yúngwuh (a power, a powerful man)

supportive PH: deui PN hóu yáuhbòngjoh; deui PN yáuh hóu daaih ge bòngjoh

suppose FV: ❶ (assume) gáyùh ❷ (think) yíhwàih AV: (expect) yìnggòi

supposition N: gáséung; gáchit FV: gáchit

suppress FV: ❶ (put an end by force) janngaat ❷ (prevent) jójí

supremacy Adj. PH: (highest) jigòu mòuh seuhng ge PH: (power) jigòu mòuh seuhng ge kyùhnlihk

supreme Adj. PH: ❶ (highest) jigòu mòuh seuhng ge ❷ (greatest) jeui daaih ge ATT: jeui gòu ~ faatyún (court); ~ túngseui (commander)

surcharge N: ❶ (payment in addition) ngaahkngoih fuhgāfai (M: dī) ❷ (as penalty) fahtfún (M: dī) FV: (overlaod) chìujoi

sure SV: ❶ (clear) chìngchó ❷ (certain) hángdihng ❸ (real) koksaht ❹ (dependable) kaau-dākjyuh; wánjahn ❺ (confident)

surf N: lohng (M: dī) VO:
(sport) waahtlohng ✳ **surf
board** N: waahtlohngbáan (M:
faai)

yáuh bángāak A: ❶ (really)
jànhaih ❷ (certainly) yātdihng
PH: (as a promise) hóu! ✳ **make
sure** RV:gáau chìngchó; tái
chìngchó

surface N/M: (side) mihn N:
❶ (outlook) ngoihbíu ❷ (top)
bíumihn BF: (top) -mín · (of
table) *tói ~* ✳ **surface mail** N:
pìhngyàuh

surfy PH: ❶ (having surf)
yáuh lohngfā; ❷ (like surf)
hóuchíh lohngfā gám Adj. PH:
(having surf) yáuh lohngfā ge

surge N: (big wave) daaih
lohng (M: go) VO: (have big
wave) héi daaihlohng

surgeon N: ngoihfō yīsāng
(M: go, wái)

surgery N/ATT: (the science)
ngoihfō N: (treatment) ngoihfō
sáuseuht (M: júng) N/PW:
(operating room) sáuseuhtsāt
(M: go, gàan)

surgical Adj. PH: ❶ (of
surgery) ngoihfō ge ❷ (used in
surgery) ngoihfō yuhng ge;
sáuseuht yuhng ge ✳ **surgical
operation** N: ngoihfō sáuseuht (M: júng)

surly SV: ❶ (bad-tempered)
cháu pèihhei ❷ (rude) chòulóuh

surmise FV: tèuichāak; gú

surmount FV: (overcome)
hāakfuhk PH: (have on top)
dēng seuhngbihn yáuh

surmountable Adj. PH:
(overcome) hóyíh hāakfuhk ge

surname N/FV: (family
name) sing (M: go)

surpass PH: singgwo; hóugwo

surplus N: (money) yìhngyùh
(M: dī; bāt) FV: (in excess)
gwosìhng

surprise SV/N: (feeling)
gìngkèih PH: (feeling) lihng
yàhn gìngkèih PH: (amaze)
gokdāk kèihgwaai FV: (to
enemy) dahtjaahp

surprising Adj. PH: lihng
yàhn gìngkèih ge

surrealism N: chìuyìhnsaht
jyúyih

surrender FV: ❶ (to enemy)
tàuhhòhng ❷ (to police) jihsáu
· *heung gíngfòng ~* ❸ (give up)
fonghei

surrogate N: ❶ (agent)
doihléihyàhn (M: go) ❷ (things)
doihyuhngbán (M: júng) PH:
(agent) jídihng PN jouh doih
léihyàhn

surround FV: ❶ (like a circle) wàihjyuh ❷ (as by enemy)
bāauwàih

surrounding A/PW:
seiwàih PH: (environment)
seiwàih ge wàahngíng

surtax N: fuhgāseui

surveillance FV/N:
gāamsih

survey FV: ❶ (investigate)
diuhchàh ❷ (measure) chāaklèuhng ❸ (observe) háauchaat
❹ (of views) fúham

surveyor N: (of land) tóudeih
chāaklèuhngyùhn; lèuhngdeih-
gùn (M: go)

survival FV/N: sàngwàahn (M: chi) PH: (not die) móuh séidou; séim̀heui; m̀séidāk

survive PH: ❶ (still exist) juhng sàngchyùhn ❷ (not die) móuh séidou; séim̀heui; m̀séidāk

survivor N: sàngwàahnjé (M: go) PH: móuh séidou ge yàhn; yihngyìhn sàngchyùhn ge yàhn

susceptibility N/SV/FV: (sensitive) máhngám • deui N ~

susceptible see susceptibility

suspect FV: sìyìh; wàaihyìh; gú N: (person) yìhmyìh yàhn (M: go)

suspectable, suspected SV: hóyìh

suspend FV: ❶ (hang) diu; gwa ❷ (delay) yìhnchìh ❸ (stop for a time) jaahmtihng ❹ (stop) tìhngjí VO: (fo job) tìhngjìk

suspender(s) N: (for trousers) diudáai (M: tiuh)

suspense PH: (uncertainty) yùhn yìh meih kyut SV: (of film) yùhnyìh

suspension FV: see suspend PH: see suspense ✳ **suspension bridge** N: diukìuh (M: tiuh)

suspicion N: yìhsàm FV: sìyìh

suspicious SV: (causing suspicion) hóyìh

sustain FV: ❶ (keep from falling) jìchàang ❷ (keep up) jìchìh ❸ (maintain) wàihchìh ❹ (con-tinue) gaijuhk A: ❶ (keep on) yātlouh ❷ (without stop) bāt-dyuhn; bāttìhng

sustenance N: ❶ (food) sihkmaht ❷ (drink) yámbán ❸ (nutrition) yìhngyéuhng ❹ (liv-ing) sàngwuht FV: ❶ (keep up) jìchìh ❷ (maintain) wàihchìh

suture VO: (of wounds) lyùhnsin PH: (thread) lyùhn sèungháu yuhng ge sin N: (thread) sin (M: tiuh)

swab N: (of mop) deihtō (M: go) PH: (to clean) yuhng deihtō tōdeih ✳ **cotton swab** N: mìhnfākàuh (M: go)

swagger PH: (put on airs) báai gají VO: (boast) chèui-ngàuh SV: (selfimportant) jihdaaih

swallow N: (bird) yinjí (M: jek) FV: (of food) tàn

swamp N/PW: (land) jíujaahk (M: go) PH: (cover with water) béi séui jamjó

swan N: (bird) tìnngòh (M: jek)

swap FV: (exchange) gàauwuhn

swarm M: (of insects) jah; dèui ✳ **move in a swarm** PH: yúngmàaihlàih/heui

swathe N: (bandage) bàng-dáai (M: tiuh); sàbou (M: faai) PH: (to wrap) yuhng bàngdáai/ sàbou bàaujyuh/jaatjyuh

Swatow N/PW: Saantàuh

sway PH: (move) yúklàih yúkheui FV: ❶ (of influence) yínghéung ❷ (rule) túngjih ❸ (control) hungjai; jìpui

swear VO: saihyuhn FV: ❶ (for an oath) syùnsaih ❷ (swear) faatsaih

sweat VO: (perspire) chēut-hohn N: (perspiration) hohn (M: dī)

sweater N: (of wool) lāang-sāam (M: gihn)

Swede N: (people) Seuihdín-yàhn (M: go)

Sweden N/PW: Seuihdín

Swedish Adj. PH: ❶ (of the country) Seuihdín ge ❷ (of people) Seuihdínyàhn ge ❸ (of the language) Seuihdínwá ge N: (language) Seuihdínwá

sweep RV: (clean with a broom) sou gònjehng FV: ❶ (pass) leuhkgwo ❷ (with a broom) sou ✻ **street sweeper** N: chìngdouhfū (M: go) ✻ **sweep up** FV/N: daaih souchèuih (M: chi)

sweet SV: ❶ (of taste) tìhm ❷ (of smell) hèung ❸ (of sound) hóutèng SV: (lovely) hóngoi Adj PH: (lovely) yàhn gin yàhn ngoi N: ❶ (candy) tóng (M: nāp) ❷ (dessert) tìhmbán (M: júng) ✻ **sweetheart** N: chìhngyàhn; ngoiyàhn (M: go) ✻ **sweet and sour** ATT: tìhmsyùn ~ pàaihgwāt (pork-ribs) Adj. PH: (of taste) syùnsyùn tìhmtìhm

swell FV: ❶ (of infection) júng ❷ (become bigger) jeung RVE: (of infection) -júng

swelling PH: (swollen place) júngjó ge deihfòng ✻ **swelling gone away** VO: sìujúng

swelter VO: (suffer from heat) jungsyú

swerve FV: (change) góibin

PH: (turn suddenly) dahtyìhn-jyun

swift SV: ❶ (of speed) faai; faaijit ❷ (of movement) máhnjit

swim VO: yàuhséui

swimming ATT: yàuhwihng (suit) ~ yī/wihngyī (M: gihn); ~ fu (pants) (M: tiuh); ~ chìh (pool) (M: go)

swindle FV: ngāak; pin

swindler N: ❶ pinjí (M: go) ❷ (in gambling) lóuhchìn (M: go)

swine N: ❶ (animal) jyū (M: jek) ❷ (abuse) jyūlō (M: go) ✻ **swine-herd** PH: yéuhngjyū ge yàhn

swing N: (in playground) chìn-chāu (M: go) VO: (to play) dá chìnchāu FV: (like a pendulum) fìhng

swirl VO: (of water, air) dá-jyuhn FV: (of water) gyún N: (eddy) syùhnwō (M: go)

Swiss N: (people) Seuihsih-yàhn (M: go) Adj. PH: ❶ (of the country) Seuihsihge ❷ (of the people) Seuihsihyàhn ge

switch N: (for electrical appliances) dihnjai (M: go) BF: (for electrical appliances) -jai (of light) dāng ~ (of fan) fùngsin ~ FV: ❶ (change) góibin ❷ (shift) jyun ✻ **switch on** FV: hòi RV: hòijeuhk ✻ **switch off** FV: sīk; sāan ✻ **switch board** N: (of telephone) dihnwá júng-gèi (M: go)

Switzerland N/PW: Seuihsih

swivel FV: (turn) jyun; dàhmdàhmjyun ✻ **swivel chair** N: jyunyí (M: jèung) PH:

hóyíh jyun ge yí

swollen Adj. PH: júngjó
RVE: -júng • (by beating) *dá* ~

swoon FV: (faint) wàhn

swoop FV: ❶ (snatch)
chéungjáu ❷ (attack) dahtjaahp

swop = swap FV: (exchange)
gàauwuhn

sword N: ❶ dōu (M: bá) ❷
(double-edged) gim (M: bá) ✻
sword-play N: gimseuht (M:
júng)

swordsman N: gimhaak;
gimgīkjé; gimhaahp (M: go)

sycophant PH: tokdaaihgeuk ge yàhn

syllable N: yàmjit; yàm (M:
go)

syllabus N: fochihng (M: go)

symbol N/FV: ❶ (sign)
jeuhngjìng (M: júng) ❷ (to represent) doihbíu (M: go) N: (mark)
fùhhóu (M: go)

symbolize FV/N: ❶ (as a
sign) jeuhngjìng (M: júng) ❷
(represent) doihbíu (M: go) PH:
(by use of mark) yuhng fùhhóu
bíusih

symmetrical Adj. PH: deui-
chìnggge

symmetry N/SV: deuiching

sympathize FV/N: tùhngchìhng

sympathy N: ❶ (feeling)
tùhngchìhngsàm; ❷ (pity)
lìhnmáhn

symphony N: gàauhéung-
ngohk; gàauhéungkūk (M: sáu;
jì)

symposium N: ❶ (of essays)
leuhnmàhnjáap (M: bún) ❷
(meeting) tóuleuhnwúi (M: go,
chi)

symptom N: jingjohng;
behngjìng (M: júng, go)

synagogue N/PW: yàuh-
taaigaau wuihtòhng (M: go)

synchronize PH: (happen at
the same time) tùhngsìh faatsàng VO: (of the clock) deuisìh

syndic N: ❶ (officer) síhjing-
gùn (M: wái, go) ❷ (manager)
gìngléih (M: go, wái) ❸ (agent)
doihléih (M: go)

syndicate N: (committee)
léihsihwúi (M: go)

synonym N: tùhngyihchìh
(M: go)

synopsis N: ❶ (of a film)
heikíu (M: jèung) ❷ (outline)
daaihgōng (M: go)

synopsize VO: ❶ (of a film)
sé heikíu ❷ (outline) jouh / sé
daaihgōng

synoptic Adj. PH: ❶ (summary) jaahkyiu ge ❷ (of
weather) tìnhei ge

syntax N: geuifaat (M: go,
júng)

synthesis N/FV: jùnghahp

synthesize see synthesis

synthetic(al) Adj. PH: ❶
jùnghahp ge ❷ (manmade)
yàhnjouh ge

syphilis N: mùihduhk

Syria N/PW: Jeuihleiha

Syrian N: (people) Jeuihleihayàhn (M: go) Adj. PH: ❶ (of the

country) Jeuihleiha ge ❷ (of the people) Jeuihleihayàhn ge

syringe FV: (inject) jyuseh N: ❶ (for injection) jyusehhei; jāmtúng (M: go, jì) ❷ (in garden) panséuihei (M: go)

syrup N: tòhngjēung; (for cough) kātséui

system N: ❶ haihtúng · (digestive) *siufa* ~ (M: go); (of nerves) *sàhnging* ~ (M: go) ❷ jaidouh · (political) *jingjih* ~ (M: go); (education) *gaauyuhk* ~ (M: go) ❸ (way) fòngsīk (M: júng)

systematic SV: (orderly) yáuh haihtúng

systematization FV/N: (well arranged) haihtúngfa

Szechuan N/PW: Seichyūn

T

tabernacle N: ❶ jeung pùhng; jyuhsó (M: go) ❷ (in the Bible) láihbaaitòhng (M; go) singmohk (M: go)

table N: ❶ (furniture) tói (M: jēung) ❷ (form) bíugaak, bíu (M: go) ❸ (food) jáu choi (M: wàih) ❹ (in the Bible) sehkbáan (M: faai) màhnhin (M: pīn) FV: gok ji ✳ **table cloth** N: tói bou (M: jēung) ✳ **table tennis** N: bīngbōngbō (M: go) ✳ **table ware** N: chāan geuih (M: tou) ✳ **timetable** N: sìhgaanbíu (M: go) ✳ **table of contents** N: muhk luhk (M: go) ✳ **turn the table(s) on sb.** PH: náujyún

yìhng sai ✳ **table a motion;** (a bill) PH: gokji duhngyíh N: tònggàng gūnggàng (M: jek)

tablet N: ❶ (pill) yeuhkpín (M: pin) yeuhkyún (M: nāp) ❷ (flat surface withwords) bín (M: go); bín (M: faai) bínngáak (M: faai) ❸ (writing paper) paakjí bóu (M: go)

tabular Adj. PH: bíu gaak yìhng sīk ge

tabulate VO: lihtbíu

tabulator N: jaibíugèi (M: go)

tack N: daaih tàuh dèng (M: háu) FV: ❶ dèngjyuh ❷ jūkjyuh

tackle N: ❶ (for sailing) syùhn geuih (M: fu) ❷ (for fishing) yùhgeuih; diugeuih (M: fu) FV: deuifuh; yingfuh; chyúhléih

tact SV: lóuhlihn; gèigíng; yùhnwaaht

tactical SV: ❶ jinseuhtge ❷ sihn yù ying bin ge ✳ **tactical exercises** N: jin seuht yín jaahp (M: chi) ✳ **tactician** N: bìngfaat gà (M: go)

tactics N: jinseuht; (M: júng); chaakleuhk (M: júng)

tactile SV: jūk gok ge; hójūkmódóu ge

tactless SV: ṁgèiji; ṁyùhnwaaht

tadpole N: fódáu (M: tìuh)

tael N/M: (Chinese Ounce) leúng

tail N: méih (M: tìuh) FV: gànjùng (a person) ✳ **tail coat** N: yinméih fuhk (M: tou) ✳ **tail light** N: méih dāng (M: jáan) ✳

tail light N: méih dāng (M: jáan) * **the tail of the eye** N: ngáahn gok

tailor N: chòihfúng (M: go) FV: jínchòih

taint N: ❶ fuhbaaih; gám yíhm (M: júng) ❷ wūdím (M: go) FV: gámyíhm; fuhbaaih

take FV: ❶ (carry, bring etc) ló; nīk; nīng; jā ❷ (accept, receive) jipsauh; sàu ❸ sihk (medicine) ❹ yám (drinks) * **take a break** FV: yàusìk; táuháh * **take a nap** VO: fan ngaahngaau (at noon time) * **take a walk** FV: saanbouh; hàahnghàh * **take care of** FV: jiugu; dáléih * **take off** (of a plane) FV: héifēi * **take off** (clothing, shoes etc) FV: chèuih * **take over** FV: jipgún * **take part in** FV: chàamgà; chàamyúh * **take turns** FV: lèuhnláu * **take for granted** Adv. PH: yíhwàih haih yìngfahn ge * **take it easy** Adv. PH: maahnmáan làih; m̀sáigāp

taking N: sàuyahp SV: duhngyàhn; màihyàhn

talcum-powder N: sóngsànfán (M: hahp, gun)

tale N: ❶ (story) gújái; gusih (M: go) ❷ (report, account) yìuhyìhn; chyùhnmàhn (M: go) * **tale-bearer** N: góng sihfēi ge yàhn (M: go)

talent N: chòihnàhng; búnsih; tìnchòih

talisman N: ❶ wuhsànfùh (M: douh) ❷ beihchèh ge yéh (M: júng)

talk FV: góng VO: kìnggái; góngsyutwah N: tàahmwah; yíngóng * **have a talk with** somebody Patt: tùhng yātgo yàhn kìnggái * **talk back** FV: bokjéui

talkative SV: ❶ (positive meaning) gihntàahm ❷ (negative meaning) dòjéui

talking N: góngwah; tóuleuhn SV: yáuh bíuchìhng * **talking machine** N: làuhsìnggèi (M: bouh)

tall SV: ❶ gòu ❷ gwofahn; kwàjèung * **tall story** N: kwàjèung ge gújái (M: go)

tallow N: duhngmaht jīfòng * **tallow faced** Adj. PH: mihnsīk chòngbaahk

tally N: ❶ dākfàn ❷ chàuhmáh (M: go, fu) FV: geifàn; gaisou

talon N: jáau (M: jek)

tambourine N: lìhnggú; sáugú (M: go)

tame SV: ❶ (of animal) sèuhnfuhk ❷ (of a person) móuh jìngsàhn; seuhnchùhng ❸ (of story) chàhmmuhn; dàandiuh

tamer N: sèuhn sausì (M: go)

tamper FV: ❶ gònsip ❷ chýúngói

tan N: gútùhng sīk

tang N: dahksyùh ge heimeih (M: júng)

tangible SV: ❶ jànsaht ge ❷ hóyíh módóu ge

tango N: taamgwòmòuh (M: jek)

tank N: ❶ táanhāakchè (M: ga) ❷ (for liquid) sèung; túng (M: go) * **petrol tank** N: (hei) yàuh sèung (M: go) ✻ **tank ship** N: yàuh syùhn (M: jek)

tankard N: daaih (bē) jáubūi (M: jek)

tanner N: ❶ (of money) luhkbihnsí ❷ jaipéi gùngyàhn (M: go) ❸ pèihgaakchóng (M: gáan)

tantamount EV: sèungdòngyù

tantrum VO: faat pèihhei

Tao N: douh; douhgaau ✻ **Tao-ism** N: douhgaau ✻ **taoist** N: douhsí; douhgaautòuh

tap N: ❶ séui hàuh (M: tìuh, go) ❷ sāk (M: go) ✻ **tap room** N: (in the hotel) jáubā (M: gàan)

tape N: ❶ (for recording) luhkyàmdáai (M: hahp) ❷ (for measuring) yúhnchek (M: bá) FV: ❶ luhkyàm ❷ bóng ✻ **tape recorder** N: luhkyàmgèi (M: ga, bouh) ✻ **scotch tape** N: gàaují (M: gyún) ✻ **red tape** N: sáujuhk (M: júng)

taper N: sai laahpjūk (M: jì) Adj. PH: juhkjím binjim / sai

tapestry N: gwa jin; fā jin (M: faai, jèung)

tar N: laahpchēng; paakyàuh VO: pòulaahpchēng

tardiness SV: wùhnmaahn FV: yìhnchìh

tare N: jaahpchóu (M: júng, pò)

target N: ❶ muhkbīu (M: go) ❷ (for shooting) bá (M: go) ✻ **be dead on target** VO: sehjung muhkbīu

tariff N: ❶ gwàanseuibíu (M:

go, jèung) ❷ dihnggabíu (M: go, jèung) ❸ seui léut

tarnish Adj. PH: sātjó gwòngjaahk

taro N: wuhtáu (M: go)

tarpaulin N: fòhngséui fàahnbou (M: faai)

tarry FV: ❶ dauhlàuh ❷ dáng ❸ dāamgok

tart SV: ❶ (food) syūn ❷ (manner) jìmsyùn N: ❶ (food) tāat (M: go) ❷ geihnéuih (M: go)

task N: gùngjok; yahmmouh (M: gihn) ✻ **taskmaster** N: gùngtáu (M: go)

tassel N: séuih (M: tìuh)

taste N: ❶ meihdouh (M: júng) ❷ bánmeih VO: simeih

tasty SV: hóumeihdouh

tatter N: laahnbou; seuibou (M: faai) FV: sìlaahn

tattle N: hàahntàahm VO: kìnggái

tattoo N/VO: màhnsàn (M: júng)

taunt FV/N: móuhyuhk (M: júng) FV: jàausiu

taurus N: gàmngàuhjoh

taut SV: gán

tavern N: haakjáan; jáudim (M: gàan)

tawdry SV: yùhngjuhk

tawny SV: fēwòhngsīk; chàhsīk

tax N: seui (M: júng) VO: dáseui; chàuseiu; jingseui ✻ **tax free** VO: mîhnseui ✻ **tax**

payer N: naahpseuiyàhn (M: go) * **income tax** N: yahpsīk seui

taxi N: dīksí (M: ga, bouh)

tea N: chàh (M: júng) * **tea ceremony** N: chàhdoulı * **tea pot** N: chàhwú (M: go)

teach FV: gaau

teacher N: gaauyùhn; sīnsàang; lóuhsì; gaausī (M: go) * **teacher training college** N: sīfaahn hohkyún (M: gàan)

teaching N: gaaudouh; gaaufan

teakwood N: yàumuhk (M: faai)

teal N: ❶ séuingaap (M: jek) ❷ yéhngaapjái (M: jek)

team N: déui (M: júng) M: deuih * **team spirit** N: tyùhntái jìngsàhn (M: júng)

tear N: ngàahnleuih (M: dihk) FV: silaahn; maaklaahn

tease FV: lìuh; siu

teaser N: jùngyi lìuh yàhn ge yàhn (M: go)

teat N: náaihtàuh (M: go)

technical Adj. PH: geihseuhtseuhng ge; jyunmùhn ge * **technical school** N: gùngyìhp hokkhaauh (M: gàan) * **technical term** N: jyùnmùhn mìhngchìh

technicality N: ❶ geihseuhtseuhng ge saijit (M: go) ❷ jyùnmùhn seuhtyúh (M: júng)

technician N: geihsī; geihseuht yàhnyùhn (M: go)

technicolor N: ❶ chóisīk

dihnyíng (M: bouh) ❷ sìnyihm ge sīkchói (M: júng)

technics N: gùngngaih (hohk) (M: mùhn)

technique N: geihseuht; gaihháau (M: júng)

technologist N: gùngngaihhohkgā; geihseuht jyùngā (M: go)

technology N: gùngngaihhohk; gùnghohk

tedious SV: chàhmmuhn; dāandiuh

teenager N: chìngsiunìhn; siunìhnyàhn (M: go)

teens N: chìngsiunìhn; siunìhnyàhn (M: dī)

teeter N: yìuhyìuhtbáan (M: faai) VO: wáan yìuhyìuhbáan

teeth N: ngàh (M: jek) * **flase teeth** n: gángàh (M: jek)

telecamera N: dihnsih sipyínggèi (M: ga, bouh)

telecast N: ❶ dihnsihgwóngbo ❷ dihnsih jitmuhk (M: go) VO: yuhng dihnsih bosung

telecommunications N: dihnseun

telecontrol N/FV: yìuhyúhn hungjai

telegram N: dihnbou (M: fùng) VO: dá dihnbou

telegraph N: ❶ dihnbougèi (M: bouh, ga) ❷ dihnbou (M: fùng) * **telegraph code** N: dihnmáh * **telegrapher** N: dihnbouyùhn (M: go) * **telegraph register** N: sàubougèi (M: bouh, ga) * **telegraph transmitter** N:

faatboujèi (M: bouh, ga)

telepathy N: sàmlìhnggámying (M: júng)

telephone N: dihnwá (M: go) VO: dá dihnwá

telephonograph N: dihnwá luhkyàmgèi (M: bouh, ga)

telephoto N: chyùhnjàn dihnbougèi (M: bouh, ga)

telephotograph N: yúhnkéuihlèih sipyíng

telescope N: mohngyúhngeng (M: go)

televise FV: dihnsih bosung

television N: dihnsih; dihnsihgèi (M: ga, bouh, go)

televisor N: dihnsih gwóngboyùhn (M: go)

telex N: jyùnyuhng dihnbou; yuhngwuh dihnbou

tell FV: ❶ (say or speak) góng ❷ (order) giu, fànfu ❸ (know) jìdou

teller N: chēutnaahpyùhn (M: go)

telling SV: yáuhhaauh; sàangduhng

telltale N: ❶ góngsihfèi ge yàhn (M: go) ❷ sitlouh beimaht ge yàhn (M: go)

tellurion N: deihkàuhyíh (M: go)

temper N: ❶ (disposition) singchìhng; pèihhei ❷ (of steel) ngaahngdouh ✻ lose temper VO: faatpèihhei

temperament N: heijāt; singchìhng

temperance FV/N: jitjai VO: gaaijáu

temperate SV: ❶ yáuh jitjai ❷ wànwòh

temperature N: ❶ (of a person) táiwān; yiht douh ❷ (of the weather) heiwān ✻ take one's temperature Patt: tùhng N taamyiht

tempest N: ❶ (of weather) bouh fùngyúh (M: chèuhng) ❷ duhnglyuhn (M: chèuhng)

temple N: ❶ míu; jihmíu (M: gàan) ❷ (pressure point) taaiyèuhngyuht (M: go)

tempo N: jitpaak; jitjau

temporality N: ❶ dyúnjaahmsing ❷ (pl. form) gaauwúi chòihcháan

temporary SV: jaahmsìh; làhmsìh

temporize FV: tòyìhn

tempt FV: yáhnyáuh

temptation N: yáuhwaahk; yáhnyáuh (M: go, júng)

ten Nu: sahp

tenacious FV: gīnchìh SV: gujāp

tenancy N: ❶ jòuyuhngkèih (M: dyuhn) ❷ jòuyahm

tenant N: jyuhhaak; jòuwuh (M: go)

tend FV: ❶ jiugu; dáléih ❷ kìngheung

tendency N: kìngheung; chèuisai (M: júng)

tender SV: ❶ (kind) hóusàm ❷ (gentle) wànyàuh ❸ (delicate) cheuiyeuhk; nyuhn ❹ (of meat) nàhm

tendon N: gàn (M: tìuh)

tenement N: ❶ jyuhjáak (M: go, gàan) ❷ (legal) bātduhngcháan

tenet N: ❶ (doctrine) jyúyih (M: júng) ❷ (principle) seuntìuh (M: go) ❸ (belief) gaautìuh (M: tìuh)

tennis N: móhngkàuh (M: go) * **tennis court** N: móhngkàuhchèung (M: go) * **tennis racket** N: móhngkàuhpáak (M: go)

tenor N: ❶ (music) nàahm-gòuyàm (M: go) ❷ daaihyi

tense SV: gánjèung FV: làaigán N: sìhsīk; sìhtaai

tension N: ❶ gánjèung-johngtaai ❷ jèunglihk; ngaatlihk

tensity N: gánjèungchìhng-douh

tent N: jeungmohk (M: go)

tentacle N: jūkgok (M: jek); jūksòu (M: tìuh)

tentative SV: siyihmsing; jaahmsìhsing

tenth Nu: daihsahp

tenure N: ❶ sáiyuhngkèih (M: go) ❷ (of office) yahmkèih (M: chi)

tepid SV: ❶ (of liquids) nyúhn ❷ m̀yihtsàm

term(s) N: ❶ (in office) yahmkèih (M: chi) ❷ (in school) hohkkèih (M: go) ❸ (conditions) tìuhgín (M: go) ❹ (relations) gwàanhaih ❺ (technical name) mìhngchìh; seuhtyúh (M: go, júng)

terminal N: ❶ júngjaahm (M: go) ❷ jùngdím

terminate FV: jùngjí; gitchūk

terminology N: jyùnmùhn mìhngchìh; seuhtyúh (M: júng)

terminus N: júngjaahm (M: go)

termite N: baahkngáih (M: jek)

ternace N: ❶ tòih (M: go) ❷ (field) tàitìhn (M: faai)

terrain N: ❶ deihyìhng (M: júng) ❷ (geography) ngàahm-chàhng (M: chàhng)

terrible SV: ❶ dākyàhn-gèng; húngbou ❷ (extreme) gányiu; gàaugwàan

terrific SV: ❶ hópa; dāk-yàhngèng; húngbou ❷ (wonderful) hóugihk

terrify FV: haak

territorial BF: líhng * **territorial land** N: líhngtóu (M: faai) * **territorial air** N: líhnghùng (M: pin) * **territorial water** N: líhnghói (M: go)

territory N: ❶ (of a nation) líhngtóu; báantóuh (M: faai) ❷ (land, district) deihfòng (M; daat) faahnwaih; kèuiwihk (M: go)

terror N: húnggeuih (M: júng) * **terrorism** N: húngbou-jyúyih (M: júng) * **terrorist** N: húngbou fahnjí (M: go)

terse SV: jìnggáan

tertiary N: daihsàamkāp; daihsàamwaih

test N/FV: chāakyihm; háaujihm; fayihm; gímyihm N: (examination) háausíh; chāakyihm ✳ **test tube** N: sigún (M: jī)

testament N: wàihjūk (M: fahn) ✳ **Old Testament** N: Gauhyeuk ✳ **New Testament** N: Sânyeuk

testicle N: gòuyún (M: go)

testify FV: jokjing; jingmìhng

testimonial N: ❶ (of a person's abilities) tèuijin seun (M: fùng) ❷ (of a person's merits) jéungjohng (M: jèung)

testimony N: ❶ (given in court) jinggùng; háugùng ❷ (proof) jinggeui (M: júng)

testy SV: bouhchou; singgāp

tetanus N: posèungfùng

text N: ❶ yùhnmàhn; jingmàhn ❷ (Bible) gīngmàhn ✳ **text book** N: gaaufōsyù (M: bún)

textile N: fóngjīkbán BF: fóngjīk ✳ **textile factory** N: fóngjīk chóng; jīkjouh chóng (M: gàan)

texture N: ❶ (in a textile fabric) màhnléih ❷ (arrangement) gitkau ❸ (tissue) jóujīk

than Patt: ❶ A béi B SV ❷ A SV gwo B

thank FV: dò jeh; gámjeh ✳ **Thanks giving** N: Gámyànjit

that SP: gó -M ~ go yàhn (that person) A: (to such a dagree) gam-SV ~ gwai (that expensive) ✳ **that's tough** Adj. PH: jànhaih kiksáu la

thatch N: wòhgónchóu; màauhchóu (M: tìuh)

thaw FV: gáaidung

the SP: gó -M, nī -M the . . . the Patt: yuht . . . yuht; yuht faai yuht hóu (the sooner the better)

theatre/theater N: heiyún; kehkyún

theatrical SV: (of manner) heikehksing

theft N: tàusit; douhsit

their PH: kéuihdeih ge

theirs N: kéuihdeihge (yéh)

theism N: yātsàhnleuhn; yáuhsàhnleuhn

them PN: kéuihdeih

theme N: ❶ (topic) tàihmuhk (M: go) ❷ (music) jyútàih; jyúyiu syùhnléut

themselves PH: kéuihdeihjihgéi

then TW: (at that time) gójahnsí MA: (afterward) sāumēi; hauhlòih A: (in that case) gám ✳ **now and then** A: sìhbātsìh; gáuṁgáu

theocracy N: sàhnkyùhn jingjih (M: júng)

theology N: sàhnhohk ✳ **theological seminary** N: sàhnhohkyún (M: gàan)

theorem N: dihngléih; yùhnléih

theoretical SV: léihleuhnge; tèuiléihge

theorist N: léihleuhngā (M: go)

theory N: léihleuhn; hohksyut (M: go)

therapy N: jihlìuh (M: júng)
* **physio therapy** N:
mahtléih jihlìuh * **radio
therapy** N: fongsehjihlìuh

there PW: gósyu; gódouh

thereafter TW: jìhauh

thereby A: yànchí

therefore MA: sóyíh; yànchí

thereof A: yàuhchí

thereupon A: yànchí; yùsih

thermal SV: yiht N: yiht
heilàuh (M: gú)

thermodynamics N:
yihtlihkhohk

thermometer N: ❶ wān-
douhgai (M: jì); hòhnsyúbíu (M:
go) ❷ (for measuring one's
temperature) taamyihtjām (M:
jì)

thermos N: nyúhnséuiwú
(M: go)

these N: nīdī

thesis N: leuhnmàhn / mán
(M: pìn)

they PN: kéuihdeih

thick SV: ❶ (in dimension)
háuh ❷ (in consistency) giht ❸
(in density) maht

thickhead N: sòhgwà;
bahndáan (M: go)

thickness N: ❶ (of dimension) háuhdouh ❷ (of consistency) nùhngdouh ❸ (of density)
mahtdouh

thief N: cháak; chaahk (M:
go)

thigh N: daaihbéi *
chicken thigh N: gāibéi (M:
jek)

thimble N: díngjām (M: go)

thin SV: ❶ (in dimension)
bohk ❷ (of consistency) hèi ❸
(lean) sau

thing N: ❶ (indefinite material
objects) yéh ❷ (indefinite non-
material entities) sih (M: gihn)

think FV: ❶ (conceive) séung
❷ (meditate, ponder) nám ❸
(believe likely or possible) tái ❹
(to hold as an opinion) yíhwàih
❺ (to consider) yihngwàih *
think tank N: jilòhng tyúhn
(M: go)

thinking N: ❶ sìséung ❷
séungfaat (M: go)

third Nu: daihsàam

thirst N: háuhot; génghot

thirsty SV: háuhot; génghot

thirteen Nu: sahpsàam

thirteenth Nu: daihsahp-
sàam

thirtieth Nu: daihsàamsahp

thirty Nu: sàamsahp

this SP: nī

thong N: pèihdáai; pèihbīn
(M: tìuh)

thorax N: hùngbouh (M: go)

thorn N:chi (M: tìuh); lahk (M:
tìuh)

thorny SV: yáuhchi; yáuh-
lahk

thorough SV: ❶ (doing all
that should be done) jàudou ❷

yihngjàn (with seriousness) ❸ (fully executed) chitdái

those N: gódī

though MA: sèuiyihn ✳ even though MA: jīksí

thought N: ❶ (thinking) sìséung; nihmtàuh ❷ (opinion) yigin (M: go)

thousand M/Nu: chìn

thrash FV: bīndá

thread N: sin (M: tiuh) ✳ thread a needle VO: chyūnjàm

threadbore SV: chàahngauh; laahn

threat FV/N: wāihip FV: húnghaak

threaten FV: húnghaak

three Nu: sàam

thresh FV: dá ✳ thresh grain VO: dáwòh

threshold N: mùhncháahm (M: douh)

thrice Nu-M: sàamchi

thrift SV: hàan; hàangihm

thrill SV: hìngfáhn; gīkduhng

thrive SV: wohng; sìhnggùng

throat N: hàuhlùhng (M: go)

throb N: (of the heart, pulse) tiuduhng

throe(s) N: (sharp pain esp of childbirth) kehk tung; jahntung

throne N: wòhngwaih; daiwaih (M: go)

throng N: yàhnkwàhn (M: kwàhn)

through CV: gìnggwo P: (across to, over) ~ gwo ✳ walk through FV: hàahnggwo

throughout PH: yàuh chí ji jùng ✳ throughout the day / night A/SP-V sèhngyaht / sèhngmáahn

throw FV: diuh; dám ✳ throw up FV: ngáu

thrust FV: chaap N: (in war) dahkgīk; dahtgīk

thrusting SV: badouh

thug N: hùngtòuh; ngokba (M: go)

thumb N: sáujígùng (M: jek) ✳ thumbtack N: gahmdèng (M: háu)

thump FV: chèuih; dahp

thunder VO: hàahnglèuih N: lèuihsèng ✳ thunder and lightening PH: hàahnglèuih símdihn

thunderstorm N: lèuihbouh; bouh fùngyúh (M: chèung)

Thursday TW: láihbaaisei; sìngkèihsei

thus A: ❶ (in this way) gámyéung ❷ (so, this) gám MA: (therefore) sóyíh

thwart FV: jóngoih; fáandeui

tick N: ❶ (of a clock or watch) dihkdaahtsèng ❷ (small mark) geihouh (M: go) FV: tīk

ticker N: ❶ sàubougèi (M: bouh, ga) ❷ jùngbáai (M: go)

ticket N: ❶ fēi; piu (M: jèung) ❷ (for admission) yahpchèunggyun (M: jèung) ❸ (giving information about something) bīuchìm (M: jèung) * **aeroplane ticket** N: gēipiu (M: jèung) * **round trip ticket** N: lòihwùih fēi (M: jèung) * **ticket office** N/PW: sauhpiuchyu (M: go) * **parking ticket** N: tihngchèjing (M: jèung)

tickle FV: jīt N: hàhnyéuhng

ticklish SV: ❶ (of a person) pa jīt ❷ (of a problem) kīksáu

ticktack N: dihkdaaht sèng

tide N: ❶ chiuhséui; chiuhlàuh ❷ (of public opinion) chèuisai

tidings N: sìusìk; yàmseun (M: go)

tidy SV: jíngchàih; kéihléih * **tidy up** FV: jāp (sahp) hóu

tie FV: bóng, jaat N: tāai (M: tiuh)

tiff N: jàngjàp

tiffin N: ngaanjau

tiger N: lóuhfú (M: jek)

tight SV: ❶ gán ❷ (not fit) jaak ❸ (small) sai

tigress N: lóuhfúná

tile N: ❶ (for roof) ngáh (M: pin, faai) ❷ (for floor) gāaijyún (M: faai)

till Patt: ..... dou, jidou ....jí N: chìhngwaih (M: go) FV: làih (tìhn, deih)

timber N: muhkchòih; muhklíu (M: pài)

timbrel N: lìhnggú; sáugú

(M: go)

time N: ❶ sìhgaan; sìhhauh ❷ (time consumed) géinói ❸ (hour of day) dímjūng ❹ (era, age) sìhdoih (M: go) ❺ (rhythm) paakjí M: ❶ (occasion) chi; tong ❷ (doubling, tripling etc.) púih * **time table** N: sìhgaanbíu (M: go)

timer N: ❶ gaisìhhei (M: go) ❷ (person) gaisìhyùhn (M: go)

times FV: sìhng * **two times two is four** PH: yih sìhng yih dángyù sei

timid SV: saidáam, nohyeuhk

timpano N: tùhnggú (M: go)

tin N: ❶ sek ❷ (canned food) guntáu

tinder N: douhfósin (M: tiuh)

ting N: dīng dīng sèng; līnglīng sèng

tingle SV: ❶ chektung; chek ❷ hìngfáhn

tinker N: bóuwohklóu (M: go)

tinkle N: dīng dīng sèng; līng līng sèng

tinsel N: gàmsuhkpín (M: faai, pin)

tint N: táahmsīk

tiny SV: hóusai, dīgamdāai, dīgamdēu

tip N: ❶ (end) jīm ❷ (money given for service) tīpsí FV: (give money for service) dáséung * **tip off** N: ngamsih, gínggou (M: go)

tipsy SV: bunjeui, jeuijéuidéi

tiptoe N: geukjíjìm FV: gaht-heí jek geuk

tiptop N: díngdím (M: go) SV: yātlàuh; chēutsīk

tirade N: chèuhng pīn gīkliht ge yìhnleuhn (M: pìn)

tire SV: guih N: tāai, chētāai (M: go)

tired SV: guih

tireless SV: m̀guih

tiresome SV: tóuyìmge; lihng yàhn yìmgyuhn ge

tissue N: ❶ (of woven fabric) sījiik maht, bohkgyun ❷(of muscle) gēiyuhk jóujīk ❸(paper) jígàn

tit FV: hehng hèng dá ✳ **tit for tat** PH: jàm fùng sèungdeui

titanic SV: geuihdaaih; lihk daaih mòuh béi

titbit N: jànbán, jànmàhn (M: gihn)

tithe N: (tax) sahpyāt seui Nu: sahp fahn jì jāt

titivate FV: ❶ dábaan (person) ❷ jòngsīk (place)

title N: ❶ (name of thing) méng (M: go) ❷ (topic) tàihmuhk (M: go) ❸ (rank, status) hàahmtàuh (M: go)

titter FV: sòhsiu; tàusiu

tittle Nu: dītgamdēu

titular PH: ❶ yáuhkyùhn chìhyáuh ❷ yáuh mìhng mòuh saht

to FV: heui (place) ✳ **give N to PN** Patt: beí N PN ✳ **T spent to T when** Patt: jàang Tsp

(dou) TW ✳ **like to FV** Patt: jùngyi FV

toad N: kàhmkéui (M: jek) ✳ **toad stool** N: duhk kwán (M: déu)

toady N: daaihgeuk yáu (M: go) FV: ngòyùh; fuhngsìhng

toast N: dōsí; hongmihnbāau (M: faai) FV: ❶ hong (bread) ❷ (for a drink) gingjáu ✳ **toast master** N: jūkjáuyàhn (M: go)

toaster N: dōsílòuh (M: go)

tobacco N: yìnchóu; yìnyíp; yìnsī

tocology N: cháanfōhohk

today TW: gàmyaht ATT: yìhndoih

toddle PH: hàahng m̀wán N: hohk hàahng ge saimānjái

toddler PH: chò hohk hàahng ge saimānjái (M: go)

toe N: geukjí (M: jek) ✳ **toenail** N: geuk (jí) gaap ✳ **from top to toe** PH: chùhngtàuh dougeuk, SV/A: chitdái

toffee, toffy (U.S.A. taffy) N: tōféitóng; ngàuhnáaihtóng (M: júng, nāp)

tog FV: dábaan ✳ **togs** N: sàam (M: gihn)

together A: yātchàih; yātchái

toil N: sànlòuh; fúgùng FV: sànfúgùngjok

toilet N: ❶ chisó; sáisáugàan (M: go, gàan) ❷ fajòng; dábaan ✳ **toilet paper** N: chijí; chóují (M: jèung, gyún) ✳ **toilet set** N: fajòng yuhnggeuih (M: tou)

toilful, toilsome SV: sànfú

toils N: hahmjihng; hyūntou (M: go)

token N: ❶ (souvenir) géinihmbán (M: gihn) ❷ (sign) geihouh (M: go) SV: jeuhng-jingsīk

tolerance N: yùhngyán

tolerant SV: yùhngyán ge

tolerate FV: yùhngyán; yán

toll N: ❶ (payment required for the use of a road, bridge ....) fai; gwolouhchihn; seui ❷ (fig. something paid, lost, or suffered) doihga, syúnsāt, hēisāng ✻ **toll of the roads** N: gàautūng yingoih sèungmòhng yàhnsou

tomato N: fàanké (M: go) ✻ **tomato catsup** N: kéjáp (M: jēun) ✻ **tomato juice** N: fàankéjáp (M: bùi, gun)

tomb N: fàhnmouh (M: go) ✻ **tomb stone** N: mouhbēi (M: faai)

tomorrow TW: tìngyaht

ton M: dēun

tone N: ❶ (sound) sèngyàm; yàmjāt ❷ yàmdiuh; yúhdiuh ❸ (of colour) sīkdiuh ❹ (of light) gwòngdouh

tongs N: kím (M: go)

tongue N: ❶ leih (M: tìuh) ❷ (language) wá; yúhyìhn ✻ **tongue tied** SV: chàhmmahk

tonic SV: tàihsàhn; jìbóu N: (medicine) bóuyeuhk

tonight TW: gàmmáahn

tonsil N: bíntòuhsin; diujūng

✻ **tonsillities** N: bíntòuhsin-yihm

too A: ❶ taai SV ❷ SV dāk-jaih; gwotàuh ❸ (also) dōu; yihk; yihkdōu

tool N: ❶ gùnggeuih; gasāang ❷ (person used by powerful interests) faailéuih

tooth N: ngàh (M: jek) ✻ **toothache** N: ngàhtung ✻ **tooth paste** N: ngàhgōu (M: jì) ✻ **tooth pick** N: ngàhchìm (M: jì)

top BF: déng N: (toy) tòhló (M: go) SV: ❶ jeui gòu ❷ jeui juhngyiu ✻ **at the top of** PH: hái ... déng ✻ **on top of** PH: hái ... jìseuhng ✻ **top coat** N: ngoihtóu (M: gihn) ✻ **top-drawer** SV: jeuigòukáp ge ✻ **top hat** N: gòuláihmóu (M: déng) ✻ **top secret** N: jeuigòubeimaht

topic N: tàihmuhk; bīutàih (M: go)

topical SV: sìhsìh ge

topography N: ❶ deih-yìhng ❷ deihyìhnghohk

topple FV: lam SV: yìuhyìuh yuhk jeuih

topsoil N: bíutóu; bíutóu-chàng

topsy-turvy SV: wahn-lyuhn; wūlēi dāan dōu

torch N: ❶ fóbá (M: bá) ❷ (flashlight) dihntúng

toreador N: daungàuh yúhngsih (M: go)

torment N: kehktung; fúnóuh FV: jitmòh

tornado N: syùhnfùng;

lùhnggyúnfùng (M: jahn)

torpedo N: yùhlèuih; séui-lèuih (M: go) ✳ **torpedo boat** N: yùhlèuihtéhng (M: jek)

torque N: génglín (M: tiuh)

torrent N: gāplàuh ✳ **mountain torrents** N: sàanhùhng

torrid SV: yìhmyiht

tortoise N: gwāi (M: jek)

torture FV/N: yeuhkdoih; jitmòh

tory N: bóusáupaai

toss FV: deng; diuh ✳ **toss a coin** VO: jaahk ngánjái

tot N: saimānjái (M: go) FV: (add) gà

total N: júngsou A: hahm-baahnglaahn; yātguhng FV: gàmàaihyātchái

totalitarian SV: gihk-kyùhnjyúyih ge N: gihkkùhn-jyúyihjé (M: go) ✳ **totalitarianism** N: gihkkyùhn jyúyih

totality N: júngsou; chyùhn-tái

tote FV: bùnwahn; nīk N: (abbrev of totalizator) dóugámgai-syungèi (M: bouh, ga)

totter PH: hàahngdāk péh péh háh

touch FV: ❶ (feel with fingers) mó ❷ (lay hands on) dau ❸ (strike lightly) dìm ❹ (evocative of emotion) gámduhng N: ❶ jip-chūk ❷ (one of the senses) chūkgok ✳ **a touch of** SV: yātdī dī ✳ **in touch with** PH: tùhng . . . jipjūk ✳ **keep in**

touch with sb PH: tùhng . . . bóuchìh lyùhnlok ✳ **touch-and-go** SV: ngàihím ge

touchy SV: bouhchou

tough SV: ❶ (meat) ngahn ❷ (rough) chōulóuh; ngàuhjìng ❸ (difficult) nàahn N: ngokgwan (M: go)

tour FV: léuihhàhng; yàuh-lihk N: (group) léuihhàhng-tyùhn

tourist N: yàuhhaak (M: go) ✳ **tourist class** N: gìngjai-chōng

tournament N: béichoi; gámbíuchoi; lyùhnchoi (M: chèuhng)

tousle FV: jínglyuhn; gáau-lyuhn

tout VO: dàusàangyi

tow FV: tò

toward(s) CV/FV: (direction) heung FV: (to) deui A: (of time) jèunggahn

towel N: mòuhgān (M: tiuh) ✳ **towel horse** N: mòuhgāngá (M: go)

tower N: taap; bóuléuih (M: joh) ✳ **tower operator** N: seunhouhyùhn (M: go) ✳ **bell tower** N: jūnglàuh (M: go)

town N: jan; síhjan; sèhng (M: go)

towns folk N: síhmàhn

townsman N: tùhng sìhng síhmàhn; gāaifōng

toxic SV: yáuhduhk ✳ **toxicology** N: duhkléihhohk; duhkmahthohk

toy N: wuhngeuih (M: gihn); gùngjái (M: go) FV: wuhnsá; wáan   *   **toy shop** N: wuhngeuihdim (M: gàan)

trace N: (mark) hàhnjīk; yìhngjīk FV: ❶ diuhchàh; gānjùng ❷ (through tin paper) mìuh; yan * **trace back to** FV: jèuisok dou * **traceable** SV: hóyíh jèui jùng ge

trachea N: heigún (M: jì)

trachoma N: sāngáahn

track N: ❶ hàhnjīk; jùngjīk ❷ (foot prints) geuk yan (M: go) ❸ (of a railroad) titgwái; louh gwái (M: tiuh) ❹ (for running, racing) páaudouh (tiuh) ❺ (course) louhsin (M: tiuh) FV: jèuijùng * **on the track** SV: hahptàih * **off the track** SV: lèihtàih * **track field** N: tìhngingwahnduhng chèuhng (M: go) * **track meet** N: wahnduhng wúi; tìhnging choi (M: go) * **track and field** N: tìhnging choi * **track suit** N: wahndung jōng

tract N: ❶ (area) kèuiwihk (M: go) ❷ (shortessay) dyúnmàhn (M: pīn) síuchaakjí (M: bún)

traction N: hìnyáhnlihk

tractor N: tōlāaigēi (M: ga)

trade N: sàangyi; gàauyihk; mauhyihk FV: gàauyihk; jouhsàangyi * **trading company** N: mauhyihkgùngsī (M: gàan) * **trade mark** N: māktàuh; sēungbīu (M: go) * **trade union** N: gùngwúi (M: go) * **trade in** PH: yuhng gauhyéh wuhn sànyéh

tradition N: chuùhntúng (M: go)

traditional SV: chyùhntúng (ge)

traffic N: gāautùng; wahnsyù * **traffic light** N: gāautùngdāng; hùngluhkdāng (M: jáan) * **traffic sign** N: gāautùngbīuji (M: go) * **traffic in illegal drugs** N: fèifaat duhkbán máaihmaaih

traffic congestion, jam N: gāautùng jāisāk; sākchè

tragedy N: ❶ (event) cháamsih (M: gihn) ❷ (drama) bèikehk (M: chēut)

tragic SV: bèicháam; chàilèuhng

tragicomedy N: bèihéikehk (M: chēut, tou)

trail N: ❶ (mark) hàhnjīk ❷ (path) síuging (M: tiuh) FV: ❶ (pull) tò ❷ (follow) jèuijùng

train N: fóchè (M: ga) FV: fanlihn M: chyun * **express train** N: faaichè * **local train** N: maahnchè (M: ga)

training N: fanlihn (M: júng)

trait N: dahkdím; dahksing (M: go)

traitor N: maaihgwokchaahk; buhntòuh (M: go)

trajectory N: gwáidouh (M: tiuh)

tram N: dihnchè (M: ga) * **tramlines** N: dihnchèlouh (M: tiuh)

tramp FV: bouhhàhng N: làuhlohngjé; lohngyàhn (M: go)

trample FV: yáai; daahp

trance SV: jìngsàhn fóngfāt

tranquil SV: nìhngjihng; pìhngjihng

tranquillizer N: jandihngjài (M: júng) jítungyeuhk (M: nàp)

transact FV: baahnléih; chyúléih

transalantic SV: hái Daaihsàiyèuhng béi ngohn ge; wàahngdouh Daaihsàiyèuhng ge

transcend FV: chìuyuht

transcontinental SV: wàahnggun daaihluhk ge

transcribe FV: chàau; chàausé

transcript N: fubún; chàaubún (M: bún)

transfer FV: ❶ (to another school) jyunhohk; jyunhaauh ❷ (to another post) diuh; diuhyahm ❸ (hand over) yìhgàau; gàau ❹ (to another bus, train) jyunchè FV: ❺ (something) jyúnyeuhng ❻ (stocks) gwowuh

transfiguration VO: binyihng FV: góigùn

transfix FV: gātchyùn

transform FV: ❶ (character or personality) góibin ❷ (shape) binsèhng; binwàih

transfuse FV: syù; gunsyù ✳ **blood transfusion** VO: syùhyut

transgress FV: ❶ (limit or bound) chìugwo ❷ (law, agreement) wàihfáan

transient SV: jaahmsìhge; dyúnjaahm ge N: gwolouhhaak (M: go)

transistor N: ❶ (radio) sàuyàmgèi (M: go) ❷ jìngtái; bundouhtái

transit FV: ❶ (goods) wahnsyù ❷ (from PW1 to PW2) gwoging

transition N: jyúnbin; binchìn (M: go) ✳ **transitional period** N: gwodouh sìhkèih (M: go)

transitive SV: kahpmaht ✳ **transitive verb** N: kahpmaht duhngchìh (M: go)

translate FV: fàanyihk; yihk

translator N: fàanyihk; fàanyihkyùhn (M: go)

transliterate FV: yihkyàm

translucent SV: buntaumìhng

transmit FV: ❶ chyùhn (electricity, heat) ❷ chyùhnbo (disease)

transmutation FV: ❶ (of shape) binyìhng ❷ (of nature) binjät

transparent SV: taumìhng

transpire FV: ❶ (of an event; or secret) sitlauh ❷ (of the body; plants) saanfaat; ❸ (of moisture, vapour) jìngfaat

transport FV: wahnsyù; wahn

transportation N: gàautùng; wahnsyù

transpose FV: ❶ diuhwuhn ❷ (music) bindiuh

transsexual N: yàmyèuhng yàhn (M: go)

trans-sonic SV: chìuyàmchük

transubstantiation VO: binjāt N: (in Bible) fatái

transverse SV: wàahng fong ge

trap N: hahmjehng; hyùntou (M: go) ✻ **mouse-trap** N: lóuhsyú gáap (M: go)

trappings N: jòngsīkbán; jòngsīkmaht (M: go)

trash N: laahpsaap; faimaht

travail N: (pains of childbirth) jahntung (M: jahn)

travel FV/N: léuihhàhng; yàuhlihk

traveller N: léuihhaak (M: go)

travelog(ue) N: ❶ (lecture) léuihhàhng gùngám ge yín góng (M: go) ❷ (film) léuihhàhng geiluhkpín (M: chēut)

traverse FV: gìnggwo; waàhnggwo N: jeungngoih-maht (M: go)

travesty FV/N: wāaikūk

trawl N: tòmóhng (M: go) FV: tò (fish)

tray N: tokpún (M: go) ✻ **ash-tray** N: yīnfùidíp (M: jek) yīn fùigōng (M: go)

treacherous SV: hèui-ngaih; gáauwaaht

treachery N: buibuhn hàhngwàih (M: júng)

tread FV: cháai; yáai

treason FV: ❶ (betrayal of one's country or ruler) buhngwok; jokfáan ❷ (disloyal-ty) buiseun

treasure N: bóumaht; jàn-bán (M: gihn) FV: ❶ (store up) jànchòhng ❷ (value highly) juhngsih; jànjuhng ✻ **treasure house** N: bóufu (M: go)

treasurer N: sīfu; chòihjing (M: go)

treasury N: ❶ (department) chòihjingbouh (M: go) ❷ (of a country) gwokfu (M: go) ❸ bóu-johng; bóufu (M: go)

treat FV: ❶ (act toward) deui; doih ❷ (give medical attention (to) yì; tái ❸ (pay for someone else) chéng ❹ (consider) dong; dongwaih; dongjouh ❺ (supply with food, drink) jiudoih ❻ (discuss) tàahmpun ❼ (process) chyúléih; chyúji ✻ **it is a real treat** PH: jànhaih gwoyáhn la! jànhaih yātdaaih lohksih la! ✻ **treat of** FV: yìhngau; taamtóu

treatise N: leuhnmán (M: pìn)

treatment N: ❶ (particular way) deuidoih; doihyuh (M: júng) ❷ (medical) jihlìuh (M: júng)

treaty N: ❶ (between nations) tiùhyeuk (M: tiùh) ❷ (between persons) tàahmpun; hipyíh (M: go)

treble N: sàampúih

tree N: syuh (M: pò) ✻ **fami-ly tree** N: juhkpóu; gàpóu (M: bún)

tremble SV: ❶ (shaking) jan ❷ (worried) yàusàm N: jan

tremendous SV: ❶ (very great) hóudaaih ❷ (powerful) máahngliht

tremor N: jan; janduhng SV: gīkduhng; hingfáhn

tremulous SV: ❶ (trembling) jan ❷ (timid) saidáam; dáam síu

trench VO: ❶ (for protection) waathòuh ❷ (for draining) waat kèuih/kàu N: ❶ (for protection) hòuh (M: tìuh) ❷ (for draining) keùih / kàu (M: tìuh)

trend N: ❶ (tendency) chèuisai (M: júng) ❷ (direction) chèuiheung FV: kìngheung

trepang N: hóisām (M: gauh)

trepidation N: húnggeuih

trespass FV: chàmfaahn; mouhfaahn

trestle N: geukgá (M: go)

triad N: ❶ sàamgo yātjóu ❷ (secret society) sàamhahpwúi (M: go)

trial N: ❶ (test) siyihm (M: go) ❷ (in court) sámseun

triangle N: ❶ (shape) sàamgokyìhng (M: go) ❷ (for drafting) sàamgokchek (M: bá) ❸ (a love affair involving a group of three) sàamgoklyúnngoi

tribe N: júngjuhk; bouhlohk (M: go) M: juhk

tribulation N: fúnaahn; yāuwaahn

tribunal N: faattìhng; sámpuntyùhn (M: go)

tribune N: ❶ (platform for speech) góngtòih (M: go) ❷ (popular leader) màhnjunglíhngjauh (M: go)

tributary N: ❶ (of a state) suhkgwok (M: go) ❷ (of a river) jìlàuh (M: tìuh)

tribute N: ❶ (regular tribute) gungmaht ❷ (to show respect or admiration) jaanmèihchìh (M: pìn)

trick N: ❶ (to deceive) gwáigai (M: go) ❷ (mischievous act) ngokjokkehk ❸ (to amuse people) báhei FV: (deceive) ngāak; pin

trickle FV: dihk; làuh

trickster N: pinjí (M: go)

tricky SV: ❶ (deceptive) gáauwaaht ❷ (difficult, complicated) laahtsáu; kīksáu

tricolo(u)r SV: sàamsīk N: sàamsīkkèih (M: jì)

tricycle N: sàamlèuhnchè (M: ga)

tried SV: gìnggwo siyihm ge; gìnggwo háauyihm ge

trifle N: síusih; sósih (M: gihn) FV: hìngsih; wuhnnuhng

trigger N: yáhnfaatgèi (M: go)

trigonometry N: sàamgok

trilateral SV: sàambīn ge

trill N: janyàm VO: faat janyàm

trilogy N: sàambouhkūk

trim FV: ❶ (by cutting) sàujín ❷ (decorate) sàusīk SV: jíngchàih; jínggit

trimming N: jōngsīk (M: júng)

trinity N: ❶ (group of three) sàamyàhn yātjóu ❷ (in christian teaching) sàamwaihyāttái

trinket N: síusīkmaht (M: gihn)

trio N: ❶ (group of three) sàamyàhnyātjóu ❷ (in music) sàamchùhngjau

trip N: léuihhàhng; yúhnjūk FV: ❶ (stumble) gwaanchàn ❷ (cause to stumble) sin ❸ (walk with quick, light steps) faaibouh hàahng

tripe N: ngàuhpaakyihp (M: faai) ngàuh tóuh (M: go)

triple SV: sàampúih; sàamchùhng VO: gàsàampùih * **triple jump** (athletics) N: sàamkāptiu

triplet N: ❶ (pl) sàambāautòi ❷ (set of three) sàamgo yātjóu

triplicate SV: yātsīk sàamfahn

tripod N: sàamgeukgá (M: go)

trite SV: pìhngfàahn; yūfuh

triumph N/SV: singleih; sìhnggùng FV: jinsing

trivial SV: ❶ (of small value) sóseui ❷ (commonplace) pìhngfàahn mòuhlìuh ❸ (of a person) hìngtiu; chínbohk

trolley, trolly N: ❶ (handcart) sáutèuichē (M: ga) ❷ (for serving food) yáuhlūk ge tóijái (M: jèung) ❸ (British tram) mòuhgwái dihnchè (M; ga)

troop N: (soldiers) gwàndéui (M: deuih) M: deui; kwàhn FV: gitdeuih; lyùhnkwàhn

trooper N: kèhbīng; kèhgíng (M: go)

trophy N: ❶ (prize) jéungbán (M: fahn) ❷ (captured arms) jīnleihbán ❸ (a silver cup as prize) ngàhnbūi (M: joh) ❹

(memorial or memento) géinihmbán (M: gihn)

tropic(s) N: ❶, wùihgwàisin ❷ (pl) yihtdaai

trot FV: síupáau N: síupáau; páaubouh

trouble FV: màhfàahn; lòuhfàahn N: màhfàahn; fàahnnóuh * **be in trouble** PH: baihgàfó la * **fish in troubled water** PH: wahnséui móyùh * **look for trouble** PH; jáaufuihei * **a troublemaker** N: jìsihjé (M: go)

trough N: chòuh (M: go)

troupe N: kehktyùhn; máhheityùhn (M: go) FV: chèuhnwùih yínchēut

trousers N: fu (M: tiuh)

trousseau N: gajōng (M: fahn)

trowel N: ❶ (for spreading mortar) fùichìh (M: go) ❷ cháanjái (M: go)

truant N: ❶ (stay away from school) tòuhhohk ge yàhn (M: go) ❷ (avoid duty) tòuhbeih jaakyahm ge yàhn (M: go)

truce FV: tìhngjin; yāujin

track N: fochè; kāchè (M: ga)

true SV: ❶ (factual) jàn ❷ (genuine) jànjingge * **come true** PH: sìhngwàih sihsaht * **true to one's word** SV: sáunokyihn; sáuseun * **truelove** N: ngoiyàhn (M: go) * **true-hearted** SV: jànsàm ge

truism IE: lóuhsāng sèuhngtàahm

truly SV: sìhngsaht; jànsaht

trump N: ❶ (in card game) wòhngpáai (M: jèung) ❷ (colloq) hóu hóu sìnsàang (M: go) VO: chēut wòhngpáai

trumpet N: labā (M: go)

trunk N: ❶ (of a tree) syuhsàn (M: pò) ❷ (of an elephant) jeuhngbeih (M: go) ❸ (a suitcase) lúhng (M: go) ✳ **trunk call** N: chèuhngtòuhdihnwá (M: go)

trust FV: ❶ (have faith) seunyahm; sèungseun ❷ (entrust) tok; wáitok N: seunyahm ✳ **in trust** VO: sauh wáitok ✳ **trust with** FV: wáitok

trustee N: sauhwáitokyàhn; dúngsí (M: go)

trustworthy SV: hókaau; jihkdāk seunyahm

truth N: ❶ sihsaht; jànseung (M: go) ❷ (as in the Bible) jànléih ✳ **tell the truth** PH: ~ jiusahtgóng; góngchēut jànseung

try FV: ❶ (attempt) si ❷ (before a judge) sám ✳ **try one'a best** PH: jeuhnlihk yìhwàih ✳ **try sth on** FV: si jeuk

trying SV: nàahnhām; lìhngyàhn tungfú ✳ **a trying person to deal with** N: nàahn yíh sèungchyú ge yàhn

tub N: pùhn; túng ✳ **bathtub** N: yuhkgōng (M: go)

tube N: ❶ (in general) gún (M: jì) ❷ (a radio part) jànhùnggún (M: jì) ❸ (inner part of a tire) noihtāai (M: go) ❹ (London underground) deihhahtitlouh (M: tìuh) M: tùhng

tuberculosis N: faibehng; faigithaht; failòuh

tuck N: ❶ (in a garment) jaap (M: go) ❷ (cakes, pastry) tòhnggwó; dímsàm ✳ **tuck in** FV: siphóu ✳ **tuck up** FV: ngaaphéi ✳ **tuck shop** N: tòhnggwópóu; dímsàmpóu (M: gàan)

Tuesday TW: sìngkèihyih; láihbaaiyih

tug FV: tò; làai ✳ **tug boat** N: tòsyùhn (M: jek) ✳ **tug of war** N: chédaaihlaahm béichoi; bahthòh béichoi (M: chèuhng)

tuition N: ❶ (fee) hohkfai ❷ (instruction) gaausauh

tumble FV: ❶ (fall) ditdóu; ditdài ❷ (move in a disorderly way) lūklàihlūk heui ✳ **tumble down** PH: yìuhyìuhyuhkjeuih

tumbler N: ❶ (a drinking glass) bōlēiséuibūi (M: jek) ❷ (toy) bātdóuyūng (M: go)

tumo(u)r N: láu (M: go) ✳ **malignant tumo(u)r** N: duhkláu (M: go) ✳ **brain tumo(u)r** N: nóuhjúngláu (M: go)

tumult N: sōulyuhn (M: chèuhng)

tuna N: tànnàhyú; gàmchēungyú (M: tìuh)

tune N: ❶ (melody) kūk (M: jek) ❷ sìngdiuh FV: gaauyām ✳ **out of tune** SV: m̀tiuhhip

tung-oil N: tùhngyàuh

tunnel N: ❶ (passage underground) seuihdouh ❷ (through a mountain) sāanlūng (M: go)

turban N: tàuhgān (M: tìuh)

turbine N: wōlèuhngēi (M: go)

turbulent SV: kwòhngliht; wahnlyuhn

truf N: ❶ (gress) chóupèih; chóudéi ❷ (race-course) máhchèuhng (M: go) ❸ (peat) nàihtaan (M: gauh) VO: pòu chóupèih

Turk N: Tóuyíhkèihyàhn (M: go)

Trukey N: (fowl) fógāi (M: jek) N/PW: Tóuyíhkèih

turmoil N: sōudung; wahnlyuhn (M: chèuhng)

trun FV: ❶ (change position of the body) nihngjyunmihn ❷ (change direction) jyun ❸ (a chance, opportunity) lèuhnláu ❹ (become) binsèhng ❺ (switch on) hòi ❻ (switch off) sàan; sīk N: ❶ (act of turning) jyúnduhng (M: chi) ❷ (change of direction) wāan (M: go) * **trun-back** FV: fàan jyuntàuh * **turn something over** FV: diuhjyun; fáanjyun * **turn a somersault** VO: dágwàandáu * **trun-table** N: cheungpún (M: go) * **turning point** N: jyungēi; jyúnlihtdím

turnip N: lòhbaahk (M: go)

turpentine N: ❶ chùhngjī ❷ (used in medicine) chùhngjityàuh

turtle N: gwāi (M; jek) * **turtle neck** N: jēunléhng lāangsāam (M: gihn)

tusk N: chèuhngngngàh (M: jek) * **elephant tusks** N: jeuhngngngàh (M: jek)

tussle N/FV: daujāng; jāngdau

tutelage N: gaaudouh; bóuwuh; gàamwuh

tutor N: ❶ sìnsàang (M: go) ❷ douhsī (M: go) ❸ (private teacher) bòujaahp sìnsàang (M: go) FV: gaaudouh; jídouh

tutorial N: douhsāutòhng (M: tòhng)

tweak FV: náu; níng

tweezers N: gípjái; kímjái (M: go)

twelve Nu: sahpyih

twenty Nu: yihsahp

twice Nu-M: léuhngchi N: léuhngpúih * **think twice** FV: háauleuih

twiddle FV: nán; wáan (a ring on one's finger)

twig N: syuhjī (M: jì) FV: (colloq) míng; mìhng

twilight TW: tìnmùngggwòng N: ❶ (before sunrise) chyúhgwòng; syúhgwòng ❷ (after sunset) bohkmouh; wòhngfàn

twill N: ❶ (cloth) chébou; chèhmàhnbou ❷ (pattern) chèhmàhn; tòuhngon

twin SV: mā (ge) * **twin brothers** N: mājái (M: deui) * **twin sisters** N: mānéui (M: deui)

twinge N: kehktung (M: jahn)

twinkle FV: ❶ (light) símsímháh ❷ (move rapidly) jáamjáamháh N: símlīk VO: jáamngáahn * **in a twinkle** PH: jáamngáahn jìgàan; jáamháhngáahn

twirl FV: jyúnduhng; náu N: syùhnjyún

twist FV: ❶ chò (threads) ❷ pīnjīk (garland) ❸ níng; nihng (cap, cloth) ❹ náuchàn (ankle) ❺ wāaikūk (meaning)

twit FV/N: ❶ (tease) jàausiu; wàfú ❷ (scold) jaakbeih

twitch FV: chāugàn

two Nu: yih; léuhng * put two and two together PH: gàngeui sihsaht tèuileuhn * two edged SV: ❶ (of a sword) sèungfùng ge ❷ (of an argument) sèungchùhng yiyih * two sided SV: léuhngmihn ge * two ply SV: sèungchàhng ge

type N: (example of a class) dínyìhng; mòuhfaahn M: tíng VO: dájih

typewriter N: dájihgèi (M: ga)

typhlitis N: màahngchéung yihm

typhoid N: sèunghòhn; chèuhngyihtjìng

tyhoon N: tòihfùng (M: chèuhng) VO: dá (daaih) fùng

typical SV: dínyìhng; yáuhdoihbíusing

typist N: dájihyùhn (M: go)

typography N: yanchaatseuht

tyrannize FV: yeuhkdoih VO: sìbouhjing

tyranny N: bouhjing; bouhhahng

tyrant N: bouhgwàn; ngokba (M: go)

tyre N: chētāai (M: go)

U

ubiquitous SV: mòuhchyubātjoih

u-boat N: chìhmséuitéhng (M: jek)

ugly SV: ❶ (unpleasant to look at) cháauyéung; nàahntái ❷ (unpleasant) hātyàhnjàng; tóuyim

ulcer N: kwúiyèuhng

ulterior SV: beimaht; yánbei

ulterior motive N: yánbai bātmìhng ge duhnggèi (M: go)

ultimate SV: ❶ (last) jeuihauh ❷ (basic) gèibún

ultimatum N: jeuihauhtùngdihp (M: fùng, go)

ultramarine SV: ❶ (colour) sàmlàahm ❷ hóingoih ge N: sàmlàahmsīk

ultra SV: gwodouh; gihkdyūn

umbrage N: yunfáhn; yūnwāt

umbrella N: jē (M: bá)

umpire N: gùngjingyàhn; pìhngpun; chòihpunyùhn (M: go) FV: pìhngpun; chòihpun

un- Pref: m̀; móuh

unabashed SV: háuh mihnpèih

unable AV: m̀nàhnggau; m̀hóyíh; m̀wúih

unacceptable SV: m̀hóyíhjipsauhge

unaccompanied SV: móuhpúhn

unaccomplished SV: meihyùhnsìhng(ge)

unaccountable SV: móuhfaatjígáaisīk (ge)

unaccustomed FV: m̀jaahpgwaan

unacknowledged SV: meihbeihsìhngyihng ge

unaffected SV: ❶ (sincere) jànsàmge ❷ (not affected) m̀sauhyínghéung ge

unaided SV: mòuhjohge

unalterable SV: m̀góidāk

unanimous SV: yātji ge

unanswered SV: meihdaapfūkge; móuhfáanying ge

unapproachable SV: nàahn jipgahn

unasked SV: meihgìngyìukàuh; jyúduhng

unassuming SV: hìmhēui

unattached SV: duhklahp

unattainable SV: dākm̀dóu; jouhm̀dóu

unattended SV: móuhyàhnjiugu; móuhpúhn

unavailable SV: móuhhaauh

unaware FV: m̀jì

unawares A: ❶ (unexpectedly) dahtyìhn ❷ (unconsciously) m̀gokyi

unbalance SV: ❶ sàtpìhnghàhng; lyuhn ❷ (of a person) m̀jingsèuhng

unbearable SV: hounàahnnyán; hóunàahndái

unbecoming SV: m̀hahpsīk; m̀ngāam

unbelievable SV: hóunàahnsèungseun

unbend FV: sūngchìh (one's mind) SV: chèuihwòh

unbiased SV: gùngjing; móuhpìngin

unbind FV: gáaihòi VO: gáailit

unblamable SV: móuhcho

unblemished SV: chìngbaahk

unbolt FV: dáhòi

unborn SV: meihdaansāngge; meihlòih ge

unbreakable SV: m̀yihdálaahn; dám̀laahn ge

unbridled SV: m̀sauhyeukchūk

unbroken SV: ❶ (of a horse) m̀sèuhnfuhk ❷ (not interruped) yùhnjíng ❸ (of records) meihdápo

unburden VO: gáaichèuihfuhdāam

unbutton VO: gáaihòinápnáu; gáain> náu

uncanny SV: gwaaidaan; sàhnbei

unceasing A: bātdyuhn; bāttìhng; m̀tìhnggám

uncertain SV: m̀kokdihng; wahm̀dihng

uncharitable SV: hāakbohk; mòuhchìhng

uncivil SV: móuhláihmaauh; sātláih

uncivilized SV: yéhmàahn

unclassified SV: móuh-fànleuih

uncle N: ❶ (father's elder brother) baakfuh ❷ (father's younger brother) asūk ❸ (mother's brother) káuhfú ❹ sūksūk; a-baak

unclean SV: m̀gònjehng

uncomely SV: m̀jingpaai; m̀sīkdong

uncomfortable SV: m̀syùfuhk

uncommon SV: ❶ (unusual) dahkbiht; bātpìhngfàahn ❷ (rare) síuyáuh; hèihón

uncompromising SV: m̀tóhhip; gìndihng

unconcerned SV: ❶ (free from anxiety) mòuhyàumòuhleuih ❷ (not concerned) m̀gwàansàm; láahngdaahm

unconditional SV: mòuhtìuhgínge

unconfirmed SV: meihjingsaht ge

unconnected SV: m̀sèunglìhn; m̀sèunggwàan

unconquerable SV: m̀hóyíhhāakfuhk ge

unconscious SV: bātsíngyàhnsih

unconstitutional SV: wàihfáanhinfaat ge

uncontrollable SV: móuhfaatjíhungjai ge

uncooked SV: meihjyúdāksuhkge; sàangge

uncountable SV: sóum̀dóu ge

uncouth SV: chōulóuh; bahn

uncover FV: ❶ (remove a cover) kínhòi ❷ (disclose) powohk; kitlouh

unction N: (religious rite) tòuhyàuhláih IE: (insincere earnestness in speaking) tìhm yìhn maht yúh

uncultivated SV: ❶ (land) meihhòihán ❷ (manners) móuhgaauyéuhng

undated SV: móuhdihng-kèih; móuhjyumìhng yahtkèihge

undaunted SV: daaihdáam; yúhnggám

undecided SV: meihkyutdihng ge

undefined SV: meihkokdihng ge

undemocratic SV: m̀màhnjyú

undeniable SV: m̀hóyíhfáuyihng ge; koksaht

under Patt: hái . . . hahbihn; hái . . . (hah) dái FV: ❶ (in the process of) jingjoih . . . gán ❷ (by the provisions of) yìjiu; gàngeui SV: (lower in rank) hahkāp ＊ **from under** Patt: hái . . . yíhhah ＊ **under one's charge** PH: yàuh . . . gúnléih ＊ **under one's eye** IE: hín yìh yìh gin

underbred SV: ❶ (person) móuhláihmaauh ❷ (animal) lyutjúng

underclothes N: dáisàamfu (M: tou)

undercover SV: beimaht ✻ **undercoveragent** N: mahttaam; gaandihp (M: go)

undercurrent N: ngamlàuh (M: gú)

underdevelop SV: meihchūngfahnfaatjín

underdog N: sātbaaihjé; sauhbīkhoihjé (M: go)

underestimate FV: gúgaigwodài

underexposure N: bouhgwòngm̀gau ge dáipín

undergarment N: dáisàam (M: gihn)

undergo FV: gīnglihk

undergraduate N: daaihhohksàang (M: go)

underground ATT: ❶ deihhah – ❷ beimaht – ✻ **underground organization** N: beimahtjóujīk (M: go) ✻ **underground subway** N: deihhahtitlouh; deihtit

underhand SV: beimaht; gáauwaaih

underlie Patt: ❶ (under) hái . . . jihah ❷ (from the basis) wàih . . . ge gèichó

underline Patt: (word) hái jih hahmihn waahksin

underling N: sáuhah (M: go)

undermentioned SV: hahseuht ge

undermine FV: (weaken) powaaih

underneath Patt: hái . . . hahbihn

underpants N: dáifu (M: tiuh)

underpay RV: béisíujó yàhngùng

underpopulated SV: yàhnháuhèisíu

underprivileged SV: pàhnfúge; deihwaih dàihah ge

underproduction SV: sàangcháanbātjūk

undernate FV: táidài; gúdàijó

undersecretary N: fubouhjéung; chigùn (M: go)

undersell FV: jihnmaaih

undersign N/VO: chìmméng

undersized SV: m̀gaudaaih

undershirt N: dáisāam (M: gihn)

understand FV: ❶ (get the meaning of) mìhngbaahk ❷ (have heard that) tèngginwah ❸ (be thoroughly acquainted with) líuhgáai ✻ **make oneself understood** PH: bíudaaht jihgéi ge yisi ✻ **come to an understand with N** PH: tùhng N daahtsìhng hipyíh

understate V PH: góngm̀gausou; góngm̀chùngfahn

understudy N: hauhbóu yàhnyùhn; hauhbeih yàhnyùhn (M: go)

undertake FV: dàamyahm; fuhjaak

undertaken N: (one who prepares the dead for burial) m̀ghjohklóu (M: go)

undertone N: ❶ dàiyàm; dàidiuh ❷ chínsīk

undervalue FV: táisíu; táidài

underwear N: noihyì; dáisàamfu (M: tou)

underweight SV: m̀gauchúhng

underworld N: ❶ (Hades) deihyuhk ❷ (the place of departed souls) yàmgàan ❸ (the debased, criminal portion of humanity) hahlàuh séhwúi

underwriter N: bóuhímsēungyàhn (M: go)

undescribable SV: nàahn yíh bātmahk yìhngyùhng (ge)

undesirable SV: bātsauhfùnyìhng; tóuyim ge

undetermined SV: meihkyutdihng ge

undeveloped SV: ❶ m̀faatdaaht ge ❷ (land) meih hòihán ge

undiluted SV: meih chùngtáahm ge; sèuhnjing (ge)

undistinguishable SV: nàahnfànbihn; móuhdahtsīk

undisturbed SV: móuhsauhgònyíu; nìhngjihng

undivided SV: móuhfànhòige; yātji ge

undo FV: (untie) gáaihòi

undock FV: káihòhng

undoubted SV: móuhyìhmahn; hángdihng

undress VO: ❶ (to strip) chèuih saai sāam ❷ (to take the dressing from the wound) gáai bāngdáai

undue SV: (excecusive) gwodouh; gwofahn

undying SV: wíhnghàhng ge

unearned IE: bātlòuhyìhwohk

unearth FV: faatgwaht; faatyìhn

unearthly SV: chìujihyìhn ge; sàhnbei (ge)

uneasy SV: ❶ (uncomfortable) m̀syùfuhk; m̀jihjoih ❷ (anxious) m̀ngònlohk

uneducated SV: meih sauh gaauyuhkge; móuhjì ge

unemployed SV: sātyihp (ge) N: sātyihpjé (M: go)

unemployment N: ❶ sātyihp ❷ (amount of unused labour) sātyihpyàhnsou

unending SV: ❶ (everlasting) wíhngyúhn ❷ (unceasing) bāttìhng; móuhjeuhn

unequal SV: ❶ (not fair) m̀pìhngdáng ❷ (not uniform) m̀sèungdáng; chāamchì ge

unerring SV: jéunkok

uneven SV: ❶ (not even) m̀pìhng ❷ (not the same size) m̀kwàijāk

unexceptionable SV: móuhkyutdímge; yùhnméih ge

unexpected SV: séungm̀dou; chēutfùhyiliuhjingoih; dahtyìhn

unfailing SV: ❶ (never coming to an end) móuhjígíng ge ❷ (meeting one's expectations) fùhhahpkèihmohng ge ❸ (loyal) jùngsaht (ge)

unfair SV: m̀gùngpìhng; m̀gùngdouh

unfaithful SV: m̀sìhngsaht; m̀lóuhsaht

unfamiliar SV: m̀suhksīk; sàangbóu

unfashionable SV: gúlóuh; gwosìh

unfasten FV: gáaihòi; fongsùng

unfavourable SV: bātleih; yáuhhoih

unfeeling SV: chàahnhuhkge; mòuhchìhng ge

unfetter VO: chèuih geukliuh

unfinished SV: meihyùhnsìhng ge

unfit SV: m̀ngāam; m̀sīkhahp

unfold FV: ❶ (open out) dáhòi ❷ (reveal) bíumìhng

unforeseen SV: yuhliuhm̀douge; yingoih

unforgettable SV: nàahnmòhng ge

unforgiving SV: mòuhchìhng (ge)

unfortunate SV: m̀hóuchói; bāthahng

unfortunately PH: hóusèuim̀sùi

unfounded SV: hòuhmòuhgàngeui

unfreeze FV: gáaidung

unfriendly SV: yáuhdìhkyi; m̀yáuhsihn

unfurl FV: dáhòi

ungainly SV: ❶ (clumsy) leuhnjeuhn ❷ (ungraceful) nàahntái

ungenerous SV: gùhòhn

ungovernable SV: nàahnhungjai

ungracious SV: chòulóu

ungrateful IE: mòhngyānfuhyih

ungrounded SV: móuhgàngeui; móuhgàngèi

unguarded SV: m̀síusàm; daaihyi

unhappy SV: m̀hòisàm; m̀faailohk

unhealthy SV: m̀gihnhòng; m̀waihsāng

unheard IE: chìhnsómeihmàhn

unholy SV: chèhngok; yáuhjeuih

unhuman SV: bātyàhndouh; yéhmàahn

unicorn N: kèihlèuhn (M: jek)

unification N: túngyāt

uniform SV: yātleuhtsèungtùhng; jíngchàih N: jaifuhk (M: tou) ✻ **school uniform** N: haauhfuhk (M: tou)

unify FV: túngyāt

unilateral SV: dāanfòngmihnge; pinmihnge

unimpeachable SV:

mòuhhhówàaihyìh; hókaau;
mòuhhó jíjaak ge

unimportant SV: m̀gányiu;
m̀juhngyiu

uninformed SV: ❶ (of a
person) móuhjìsīk ❷ meihjip-
dou tùngjì

unintelligible SV: nàahn-
mìhngbaahk

uninterested SV: móuh-
hingcheui; m̀gwàansàm

union N: (association) gùngwúi (M: go) FV: lyùhnhahp SV:
tyùhngit

unique SV: duhkdahk; wàih-
yātge

unison N: wòhhàaih (M: júng)

unit N: ❶ dāanwái (M: go) ❷
(in army) bouhdéui

unite FV: ❶ (form a union)
lyùhnhahp ❷ (cause to form a
union) túngyāt

United States N/PW:
Méihgwok

unity N: túngyāt

universal SV: chyùhn
saigaai ge; póupin

universe N: ❶ (the creation)
yùhjauh ❷ (the world) saigaai
* **Miss Universe** N: Saigaai
síujé (M: wái)

university N: daaihhohk
(M: gàan)

unjust SV: m̀gùngpìhng;
m̀gùngdouh

unkampt SV: m̀gònjehng-
kéihléih

unkind SV: hāakbohk

unknown SV: meihjìge;
m̀suhksīkge

unlace VO: gáaihòi tiuh dáai

unlawful SV: m̀hahpfaat;
faahnfaat ge

unlearned SV: móuhmàhnfage; móuhginsīk ge

unless MA: chèuihfèi

unlike SV: m̀tùhng

unlimited SV: mòuhhaahn
ge

unload FV: ❶ (remove a load)
se ❷ (get rid of) gáaichèuih *
unload cargo VO: sefo

unlock VO: hòisó

unloose FV: ❶ gáaihòi ❷
(make free) sīkfong

unlucky SV: m̀hóuchói;
bāthahng

unmannerly SV: chōulóuh;
móuhláihmaauh

unmarried SV: meihfàn;
dāansàn

unmatchable SV: móuh-
dākbéi

unmeaning SV: móuhyi-
sìge; móuhmuhkdīkge

unmerciful SV: mòuh-
chìhng

unmistakable SV: mìhnghín; chìngchó

unmixed SV: sèuhnjing ge

unnatural SV: ❶ m̀jihyìhn
❷ (abnormal) fáansèuhng ge

unnecessary SV: m̀sèuiyiu;
móuhbītyiu

unnerve FV: lihng (yàhn) sātsèuhng

unnoticeable SV: táimchēutge

unobtrusive SV: hìmhèui

unoccupied SV: móuhyàhnjyuh ge; hūng ge

unofficial SV: ❶ (not authoritative) fèigūnfōng ge ❷ (not formal) fèijingsīk ge

unpack FV: ❶ (open) dáhòi; chaakhòi ❷ (take out things packed) nīk . . . chēutlàih Patt: (take things out of) hái . . . ló chēutlàih ✻ unpack a trunk VO: hòisèunglóyéh

unpaid SV: meih béichínge; móuhbouchàuh ge

unparalleled SV: hùngchìhn ge; móuhdākbéi ge

unpleasant SV: ❶ (feeling) mhòisàm; tóuyim ge ❷ (weather) msóng

unpopular SV: msauh fūnyìhng; mdākyàhnsàm

unpractical SV: msahtjai

unprecedented SV: hùngchìhn ge

unprejudiced SV: gùngjing ge; móuhpìngin ge

unprepared SV: móuhyuhbeih ge

unpretending SV: hìmhèui; mgìungouh

unprincipled SV: mòuhchí; móuhyùhnjāk

unproductive SV: móuhsàngcháan ge

unprofessional SV: mhahphòhngkwài ge

unprofitable SV: móuhyīkge; mòuhleihhhótòuh ge

unpromising SV: móuhchìhngtòuh; móuhhèimohng

unprotected SV: móuhfòhngwaih; móuhbóuwuh

unqualified SV: ❶ (not qualified) mhahpgaak; mgaujìgaak ❷ (not limited) mòuh haahnjai ge; jyuhtdeui ge

unquenchable SV: jímjyuh ge

unquestionable SV: koksaht ge

unquiet SV: duhngdohng

unravel FV: ❶ (separate) gáaihòi; chaakhòi ❷ (make clear) gáaisīk; syutmìhng

unread SV: meihduhkgwo ge; meihtáigwo ge

unready SV: ❶ meihjéunbeihhóu ge ❷ (not prompt) mlìhngmáhn ge

unreal SV: gá ge; mjànsaht ge

unreasonable SV: móuhpóu ge

unrecognized SV: ❶ meih béiyàhn yìhngchēut ge ❷ meih béiyàhn sihngyìhng ge

unrelenting SV: ❶ myeuhngbouh ❷ mòuhchìhng

unreliable SV: mhókaau; kaaumjyuh

unremitting SV: bātdyuhn ge

unreserved SV: móuh bóulàuh ge; táanbaahk ge

unresolved SV: meih gáaikyut ge

unrest N: duhnglyuhn; bātngòn * **political unrest** N: jingjih bātngòn

unrestrained SV: móuh haahnjai ge

unrighteous SV: m̀gùngjing ge; bātyih ge

unripe SV: meihsuhk

unrival(l)ed SV: mòuhdihk ge; móuhdākbéi ge

unroll FV: gyúnhòi

unruly SV: nàahn hungjai; m̀sáu kwàigéui

unsafe SV: m̀wánjahn; m̀ngònchyùhn

unsanitary SV: m̀hahpwaihsàng (ge)

unsatisfactory SV: m̀lihngyàhn múhnyi; m̀dākyàhnsàm

unsatisfied SV: meihmúhnjūk; m̀múhnyi

unsavo(u)ry SV: (food) nàahnsihk ge IE: (reputation) sìngmìhnglòhngjihk * **unsavoury scandals** N: cháumàhn (M: gihn)

unscrew FV: níngsùng (screw)

unscrupulous SV: mòuhchí; m̀góngdouhléih

unsealed SV: móuhfùnghháu ge * **unsealed letter** N: hòiháu seun (M: fùng)

unseasonable SV: m̀hahpsìh ge

unseemly SV: (of behaviour etc) m̀hápdong ge; diugá ge

unseen SV: táimgin ge * **the unseen** N: jìngsàhn saigaai

unselfish SV: ❶ m̀jihsì ❷ (generous) futlóu

unsettle FV: yíulyuhn; gáaulyuhn

unshaken SV: gìndihng (ge)

unskilled SV: ❶ m̀suhklihn; móuhgìngyihm ❷ m̀sáigeihhháau ge

unskillful SV: móuh geihhháau ge; bahnjyuht ge

unsolvable SV: ❶ (problem) nàahn gáaikyut ge ❷ (liquid) m̀hóyíh yùhnggáai ge

unsophisticated SV: dāansèuhn

unsound SV: m̀gihnchyùhn * **unsound mind** PH: jìngsàhncholyuhn

unsparing SV: ❶ m̀hàan; futlóu ❷ (show no mercy) yìhmlaih

unspeakable SV: nàahnyíh yìhngyùhng

unspotted SV: (of reputation) chìngbaahk ge; móuhhàhchì ge

unstable SV: m̀wánjahn; m̀gudihng * **unstable job** N: m̀gudihng ge gùngjok (M: fahn)

unsteady SV: m̀wándihng; yìhbin ge

unstressed SV: ❶ (point) m̀kèuhngdiuh ge ❷ (sound)

móuhchúhngyàm ge

unsubstantial SV: m̀gitsaht; m̀gìngu

unsuccessful SV: m̀sìhnggùng

unsuitable SV: m̀ngāam; m̀sīkhahp

unsuspected SV: móuhyìhmyìh

unthinkable Adj. PH: bāthósìyíh

unthinking SV: móuhsìséung; hìngsēut

untidy SV: ❶ (of things) láaugaauh; lyuhn ❷ (of persons) léhe; léhféh

untie FV: gáai; gáaihòi

until Patt: ❶ yātjihk . . . dou ❷ (from . . . till . . ., to) yàuh . . . ji (dou) . . . ✽ **not until** Patt: ① . . . jìchìhn . . . m̀ ② . . . jihkdou . . . sìnji . . . ✽ **until now** PH: jihkdouyihnjoih; jigàm ✽ **until then** PH: jihkdougójahnsí

untimely SV: m̀hahpsìhyíh ✽ **an untimely remark** N: m̀hahpsìhyíh ge syutwah

untold SV: sóum̀chingchó ge; gaim̀dóu ge ✽ **untold wealth** N: sóum̀ching ge chòihfu

untouchable SV: daahtm̀dou ge N: (lowest caste) jeuidàigàaikāp ge yàhn (M: go)

untoward SV: ❶ (of person) gwahtkéuhng ❷ màhfàahn; kwannàahn

untraceable Adj. PH: nàahnyíh yìhngyùhng ge; nàahnyíh chaatgok ge

untrained Adj. PH: móuhsauhgwo fanlihn ge

untried SV: ❶ meihsiyihm ge ❷ (case) m̀sámseun ge ✽ **leave nothing untried** VO: yuhngjeuhn baahnfaat

untrue SV: m̀haih jàn ge; gá ge

untrustworthy SV: m̀kaaudākjyuh; kaaum̀jyuh

unused SV: meihyuhnggwo ge FV: (not accustomed) m̀ (jaahp) gwaan

unusual SV: m̀pìhngsèuhng (ge); duhkdahk (ge)

unusually A: m̀chàhmsèuhng

unutterable Adj. PH: nàahnyíhyìhngyùhng ge; góngm̀chēut ge

unveil VO: chēuih mihnsā FV: kitlouh; hínlouh

unwarrantable SV: m̀hahpfaat ge

unwearied IE: bātgwāt bātnáau

unwelcome SV: m̀sauh fùnyìhng FV: m̀fùnyìhng

unwell SV: m̀syùfuhk

unwholesome SV: móuhyīk ge; m̀waihsàng ge

unwieldy SV: ❶ (awkward to move) bahnjuhng ❷ (awkward to control) nàahn chōujung ge

unwilling SV: m̀háng; m̀yuhnyi

unwise SV: bahn; chéun

unwitting SV: mòuhsàm

ge; m̀gokyi ge

unworthy SV: m̀jihkdāk

unwrap FV: chaakhòi
(parcel, gift . . .)

unwritten SV: bātsihng-
màhn ge; háuchyùhn ge * an
unwritten law N: bāt-
sihngmàhn faat (M: tiuh)

unyielding SV: ❶ (obstinate) gujáp; gwahtkéuhng ❷
(not easily bending) m̀yih-
wāankūk ge

up FV: ❶ (of a person) héisàn
❷ (above the ground) chēut
(làih) ❸ (stand) kéihhéisàn ❹
(increase) jànggà ❺ (lift)
géuihéi; tòihhéi SV: ❶
seuhngmihn ge ❷ heung-
seuhng ge * all up (with) FV:
gitchūk * up against N:
mihnlàhm (difficulty) * up on
(in) FV: suhksīk; jingtùng *
up-and-down Adj. PH: ① (to
and fro) lòih lòih wùih wùih ②
(rise and fall) seuhng hah héi
fuhk * up-to-date SV:
jeuigahnge; jeuisànge * up to
someone A: yàuh * up to A:
jihkdou (now, then) * up with
FV: yúngwuh * up-and-
coming Adj. PH: yáuh jeunchéuisàm (ge)

upbraid FV: jaakbeih;
hínjaak

upbringing N: gaauyéuhng

upcoming Adj. PH: jīkjèung
lòihlāhm ge

upcountry N: noihdeih SV:
noihdeih ge

update Patt: sái N yihndoihfa N: ❶ yihndoihfa ❷ (information) jeuisànjìlíu

upheaval N: binfa; bin-

duhng * a volcanic
upheaval N: fósàan baaufaat
* a political upheaval N:
jingjih binduhng

uphill VO: séuhng chelóu
SV: ❶ (sloping upward) heung
seuhng che ❷ (difficult) gàannàahn ge * an uphill task N:
yāt gihn gàannàahn ge gùngjok

uphold FV: ❶ (support)
jichìh; yúngwuh ❷ (approve)
jaansìhng ❸ (confirm) jingsaht
* upholder N: jichìhjé;
yúngwuhjé (M: go)

upholster VO: ❶ jòngsīk
fòhnggàan (with carpets, cur-
tains etc) ❷ gàyíjín; gàyítou *
upholstery N: sātnoihjòngsīk

upkeep N: bóuyéuhng fai;
wàihsàu fai FV: bóuyéuhng;
wàihsàu

upland N: ❶ gòudeih ❷
(mountainous) sàandeih

uplift FV: ❶ (spirtually or
emotionally) janfáhn; gúmóuh
❷ gòugéui N: gúmóuh (M: júng)

upon Patt: (on PW) hái PW
seuhngbihn * once upon a
time MA: chùhng chìhn *
upon my word IE:
jyuhtmòuhhèuiyìhn

upper SV: seuhngmihn;
seuhngbihn * upper classes
N: seuhnglàuh séhwúi (M: go)
* upper floors PW: làuh-
seuhng * upper lip N:
seuhngsèuhn * uppermost
SV: jeuigòu ge * upper part
of a shoe N: hàaihmín (M: faai)
* upper part of the body N:
seuhngsàn * have the up-
perhand of SV: hóugwo

upright SV: ❶ (honest) jingjihk; lóuhsaht ❷ (erect) jihkge;
sèuihjihk ge; jíkjihk N: jihk-

chyúh (M: tìuh)

upriver SV: ❶ hái seuhng-yàuh ge ❷ heung seuhngyàuh ge

uproar N: sōuduhng; chòuh-chaáau; gúchou SV: chòuh Adj. PH: chòuhhyūnbābai

uproot VO: lìhn gàn bahthéi FV: gónjáu

upset FV: ❶ (turnover) fūkjyun ❷ (trouble) yíulyuhn; sòuyíu SV: (disturbed, worried) m̀ngònlohk

upside PW: seuhngbihn/mihn ✻ **upside down** RV: doujyuntàuh ✻ **turn . . . up-side down** PH: gáaudou lyuhnsaai

upstage SV: gìungouh; jihfuh; jihdaaih

upstanding SV: ❶ (standing erect) kéihjihk ge ❷ (strong and healthy) gihnhòng ge

upstairs PW: làuhseuhng

upstart N: bouhfaatwuh (M: go) ✻ **upstart officials** N: sàngwai (M: go)

upstream PH: heung seuhngyàuh yàuh IE: yihk làuh yìh séuhng

upsurge N: ❶ (of emotion) gīkfáhn ❷ (of tide) gòuchiùh FV: gòujeung; jàngjéung

upturn N: hóujyún ✻ **an up-turn in business** PH: yìhng yihp chìhngfong hóujyún

upvalue Patt: ❶ jèung (currency) sìngjihk ❷ tòihgòu (sth) ge gajihk

upward VO: heung seuhng ✻ **the upward trend of**

prices PH: mahtga seuhngsìng ge chèuisai ✻ **ten years up-ward** PH: sahpnìhn yíhseuhng

uranium N: yáu

Uranus N: Tīnwòhngsìng (M: nāp)

urban SV: sìhngsíhge; dōu-síh ge ✻ **Urban Council** N: síhjing gúk

urbane SV: yáuhláihmauh; sìmàhn

urbanize SV/FV: sìhngsíhfa

urchin N: ❶ hóuyáihge saimānjái (M: go) ❷ (zool) hóidáam (M: jek)

urge FV: ❶ (request earnest-ly) ngài ❷ (persuade) hyun N: bīkchit ge yuhkmohng (M: go) ✻ **an urge to do sth** Patt: fèi (yiu) . . . bāt hó

urgent SV: gángàp (ge) ✻ **in urgent need of** FV: gāpsèui

urinate FV: síubihn VO: ngò/ò niuh

urine N: niuh; síubihn

urn N: ❶ (for holding ashes of a person whose body has been cremated) gwātfùi ngáang (M: go) ❷ (for making or keeping tea or coffee) chàhséui wùh (M: go)

us PN: ngóhdeih

usable SV: ngāamyuhng ge

usage N: ❶ (way of using sth) yuhngfaat (M: júng) ❷ (custom) jaahpgwaan (M: go)

use FV: yuhng N: yuhng; yuhngchyu; yuhngtòuh ✻ **come into use** PH: hoichí sáiyuhng ✻ **for the use of** PH: gùng . . . yìngyuhng ✻ **make**

use of FV: leihyuhng * **put to use** FV: sáiyuhng; yingyuhng * **use up** RV: yuhngsaai * **what's the use?** PH: yáuh mātyéh yuhng a?

used * **be used to** FV: gwaanjó * **not used to** FV: m̀gwaan

useful SV: ❶ yáuhyuhng (ge) ❷ (helpful, of service) bōngdāksáu

useless SV: móuhyuhng

usher N: (a person) jìudoihyùhn (M: go) FV: jìudoih; yìhngjip; daai

usual SV: ❶ (ordinary) pìhngsèuhng ge ❷ pìhngsìh ge * **as usual** A: jiusèuhng

usually MA: pìhngsèuhng; pìhngsìh

usurp FV: ❶ bajim (someone's property) ❷ chàamdyuht (someone's power) ❸ saan waih (a throne)

usury VO: fong gòuleihtaai

utensil N: yuhnggeuih * **kitchen utensils** N: sābōu ngāang chāang (M: dī) * **household utensils** N; gàtìhng yuhnggeuih

uterus N: jígùng (M: go)

utilitarian SV: gùngleih ge; gùngleih jyúyih ge * **utilitarianism** N: gùngleih jyúyih

utility N: sahtyuhng; haauhyuhng * **public utility** N: gùngyuhng sihyihp

utilize FV: leihyuhng

utmost A: gihkjì SV: jeui yúhn N: gihkhaahn (M: go) * **the utmost ends of the earth** IE: tìnngàaih hóigok * **do one's utmost** PH: jeuhnlihk yìhwàih

utopia N: wūtokbòng; léihséunggwok

utter(ly) FV: ❶ góng (a sound or sounds) ❷ yùhnchyùhn; jyuhtdeui

utterance N: faatyàm; góngfaat

V

vacancy N: ❶ (position) hùngkyut (M: go) ❷ (blank) hùngbaahk (M: pin) ❸ (unoccupied space) hùnggàan SV: (lack of work) chìnghàahn

vacant SV: ❶ (empty) hùng(ge) ❷ (leisured) hùnghàahn ge ❸ (of the mind) hùnghèui (ge)

vacate FV: ❶ (give up living in) chìnchēut ❷ (leave unoccupied) hùngchēut

vacation N: ❶ (holiday) gakèih (M: go) ❷ (vacating) teuichēut FV: douhga; yàuga * **summer vacation** N: syúga * **spring vacation** N: chēunga

vaccinate VO: dáyuhfòhngjàm; jungdáu

vaccination N: jungdáu

vaccine N: dauhmìuh

vacillate SV: yàuhyìh; chàuhchyùh

vacuum N: jànhùng * **vacuum bottle** N: nyúhnséuiwú (M: go) * **vacuum brake** N: jànhùngjaahp (M: douh) * **vacuum cleaner** N: (jànhùng) kàpchàhngèi (M: go) * **vacuum pump** N: jànhùngbàm (M: go) * **vacuum tube** N: jànhùnggún; dihnjígún (M: jì)

vagabond N: làuhlohngjé (M: go) SV: làuhlohngge; yàuhdohng ge

vagina N: yàmdouh

vagrant SV: yàuhdohngge; piupokge N: làuhlohngjé; yàuhmàahn

vague SV: ❶ mchìngchó; hàhmwùh (speech) ❷ mòuhwùh (impression)

vain SV: ❶ (without result) tòuhlòuh ge * **in vain** A: baahkbaahk

vainglory N: hèuiwìhng; jihfuh

vale N: gūk; sàangūk (M: go)

valediction N: goubihtchìh (M: pìn)

valet N: ❶ (manservant) nàahmgùngyàhn (M: go) ❷ (employee in a hotel who dry-cleans or presses clothes) sáitong nàahm gùng (M: go)

valiant SV: yúhnggám N: yúhnggám ge yàhn (M: go)

valid SV: ❶ (effective) yáuhhaauh ge ❷ (well based) yáuhgàngeui ge; jingkok ge

validate FV: ❶ (make valid) sái sànghaauh ❷ (prove) jingsaht ❸ (permit) pàijéun

valise N: ❶ (small leatherbag)

léuihhàhngdói (M: go) ❷ (soldier's kit bag) builòhng (M: go)

valley N: sàangūk (M: go)

valour SV: yìngyúhng; yúhngmáahng

valuable SV: yáuhgajihk(ge); gwaijuhng(ge) N: gwaijuhngbán (M: gihn) * **valuable to . . .** PH: deui . . . yáuhgajihk

valuation N: pìhngga; gúga

value N: gajihk

valuer N: pìhnggayàhn (M: go)

valve N: ❶ (inlet or outlet) wuhtfáan (M: faai) wuhtsāk (M: go) wuhtmùhn (M: douh) ❷ (in the heart or blood vessel) fáanmók (M: faai) ❸ (in radio) jànhùnggún (M: jì)

vamp N: (upper front part of a shoe) hàaihmín (M: faai) PH: (improvise a musical accompaniment to a song or dance) jīkjihkbuhnjau VO: (repair a shoe) wuhn hàaihmín

vampire N: ❶ (spirit or ghost) kàphyutgwái; kàphyutgèungsì (M: jek) ❷ (person who preys on others) daaihyíhlūng (M: go)

van N: ❶ (vehicle) wēngjái (M: ga) ❷ (railway carriage for goods) fochèsēung (M: go) ❸ (caravan) pùhngchè (M: ga) ❹ (of an army or fleet in battle) sìnfūng (M: go)

Vancouver N/PW: Wāngōwá / wàh

vandalism N: wáiwaaih gùngmaht ge hàhngwàih (M: júng)

vane N: (wind) fùngheungbīu (M: go)

vanguard N: ❶ sìnfùng (M: go) ❷ (military) sìntàuhbouhdéui (M: deuih)

vanilla N: wàhnnēilá; hèungchóu

vanish FV: sìusāt

vanity N: ❶ (conciet) jihfuh; hèuiwìhng ❷ (worthlessness) hùnghèui * **vanity bag, vanity box, vanity case** N: sòjòngdóijái (M: go)

vanquish FV: ❶ hāakfuhk; jingfuhk ❷ yīkjai (emotion)

vantage N: singleih; yàusai * **vantage ground** N: yáuhleihdeihwaih

vaporize FV: jingfaat

vapour N: ❶ (steam) jìnghei ❷ (mist) mouh ❸ (unsubstantial thing) waahnséung * **water vapour** N: séuijìnghei * **vapour bath** N: jìnghei yuhk

variable SV: yihbinge; hóbinge N: binleuhng

variance N: bātwòh; kèihgin * **at variance with** PH: tùhng . . . bātwòh

variat N: yihtáijih

variation N: ❶ binfa; góibin ❷ (music) binjaukūk (M: sáu)

varicoloured SV: jaahpsīk ge; ńghngàahn luhksīk ge

varied SV: m̀tùhng ge; goksīkgokyeuhng ge

variety N: ❶ (not being the same at all times) binfa ❷ (number of different things) júngleuih

variform SV: yìhng yìhng sīk sīk ge

various SV: m̀tùhng ge; goksīkgokyeuhng ge

varnish N: chātyáu

vary FV: góibin; binwuhn

vascular SV: hyutgún ge; mahkgún ge * **vascular tissue** N: mahkgúnjóujīk

vase N: ❶ jēun (M: go) ❷ (for holding flowers) fājēun (M: go)

vaseline N: fàahnsihlàhm

vassal N: sàhn; nòuhdaih (M: go) * **vassal state** N: suhkgwok (M: go)

vast SV: ❶ (immense) geuihdaaih ge ❷ (extensive) gwóngfut(ge); sàmyúhn (ge) * **vast sums of money** N: geuihngáak ge gàmchìhn (M: bāt)

vat N: daaihtúng; daaihgōng (M: go) PH: jèung . . . yahptúng/yahpgōng

Vatican N/PW: Fàahndaigōng

vaudeville N: jaahpgeih

vault N: ❶ (arched roof) yùhngúng ngūkdéng (M: go) ❷ (cellar) deihlòuh (M: go) ❸ (under a church for burials) mouhyuht (M: go) ❹ (of the bank) bóuhímfu (M: go) N: ❺ (sport) chìhgòntiu * **vaulting-horse** N: muhkmáh (M: jek) FV: tiugwo

vaunt FV: chèuingàuh SV: kwàjèung; ngàhchaat

veal N: ngàuhjáiyuhk

vector N: chyùhnyíhm mùihgaai (M: júng)

veer VO: góibin fòngheung

vega N: jīknéuisìng (M: nāp)

vegetable N: sòchoi; choi SV: jihkmahtge; sòchoige

vegetarian N: sihkjàaige- yàhn; sousihkjé (M: go) * **vegetarian food** N: jàaichoi

vehemence N: yihtsàm

vehicle N: ❶ chè (M: ga) chèléung (M: léung) ❷ (of expression) mùihgaaimaht (M: júng)

veil N: mihnsā (M: faai) VO: jēmihnsā FV: jēbai

vein N: ❶ (blood-vessel) jihngmahk; hyutgún (M: tiùh) ❷ (in leaves, marbles) màhnléih ❸ (mood) chìhngséuih

velocity N: ❶ (speed) chūkdouh ❷ (rate of motion) chūkdouh; chūkléut

velvet N: tìnngòhyúng; siyúng * **an iron hand in a velvet glove** IE: siuléuih- chòhngdōu

velvety SV: chíhtìnngòhyúng ge; yàuhyúhn (ge)

vend FV: ❶ (sell) fáahn- maaih; giumaaih ❷ faatbíu (opinion) * **vending machine** N: jihduhng maaihmahtgèi (M: go)

veneration N: jyùnging; gingyi * **be filled with veneration for** Patt: deui ~ chùngmúhn gingyi

venereal SV: singgàau ge; yànsinggàauyáhnhéi ge * **venereal diseases** N:

singbehng (M: júng)

venetian blind N: baak- yihpchèung (M: tòhng)

vengeance VO: bousàuh FV: boufuhk * **take venge- ance on an enemy** PH: heung dihkyàhn bousàuh

vengeful SV: bousàuh sàm- chit ge

venial SV: ❶ (excusable) hóyíh yùhnleuhng ge ❷ (not serious) hìngmèih ge

venison N: luhkyuhk; yèh- méi

venom N: ❶ (poisonous fluid) duhkyihk ❷ (hate, spite) ngokyi; yunhahn

vent N: ❶ (inlet or outlet) tùngfùngháu (M: go) ❷ (means of escape) chēutháu; lauhduhng (M: go) FV: (outlet for one's feel- ings) faatsit; toulouh

ventilate FV: ❶ (cause air to move) sái hùnghei làuhtùng ❷ (make a question widely known) gùnghòi; syùnbou

ventilation N: tùngfùng

venture N: mouhhím FV: ❶ (take the risk) mouhhím ❷ (dare) gám; dáamgám * **nothing venture, nothing gained** IE: bātyahpfúyuht, yìn- dāk fújí

venue N: ❶ (rendezvous) jaahphahpdeihdím (M: go) ❷ (meeting-place) wúichèuhng (M: go)

Venus N: ❶ (star) Gàmsìng ❷ (Goddess) Wàihnaahpsì néuihsàhn

veracity N: sìhngsaht SV: hókaau; jànsaht

veranda(h) N: kèhláu (M: go)

verb N: duhngchìh (M: go)

verbal SV: (spoken) háutàuh (ge) * a verbal translation FV: jihkyihk * verbal account N: háutàuh gáaisīk (M: go) * verbal-warning N: háutàuh gínggou (M: go)

verbatim SV: juhkjihge; yùhnchyùhn jiu jihmín ge

verbiage N: dòyùh ge syutwah/geuijí

verbose SV: leuihjeuih; chamhei

verdant SV: ❶ (fresh and green) chìngcheui (ge)

verdict N: ❶ (decision reached by a jury) chòihkyut ❷ (decision, opinion) kyutdihng; pundyun

verdure N: cheuiluhk (sīk)

verge N: ❶ (edge) bīnyùhn ❷ (border) gaaihaahn FV: ❶ (close to) jipgahn ❷ (incline) kìngheung * on the verge of FV: jipgahn

verify FV: jingsaht; hahtdeui

veritable SV: jànjing ge PH: mìhngfùhkèihsaht ge

verity N: jànléih

vermil(l)ion N/SV: jyùhùhngsīk FV: yíhmsìhng jyùhùhngsīk

verminous SV: yáuhsāt ge; wùjòu ge

vernacular N: fòngyìhn; tóuwá SV: búndeih (ge)

versatile SV: dòchòihdò-ngaih (ge); dòfòngmihn ge * a versatile genius N: dòfòng-mihn ge tìnchòih (M: go) * a versatile mind N: dòchòih dòngaih ge yàhn (M: go)

verse N: sì (M: sáu); wáhn-màhn (M: pìn) M: jit

versed FV: jìngtùng; suhk-lihn * be versed in . . . FV: jìngtùng . . .

version N: ❶ (translation) fàanyihk; yihkbún ❷ (account of an event) góngfaat ❸ (edition) báanbún

versus FV: deui

vertebra N: jekjèuigwàt (M: jit)

vertebrate N: jekjèui-duhngmaht SV: yáuh jek-jèuigwàt ge

vertex N: díngdím; jeuigòu-dím

vertical SV: sèuihjihk (ge) * vertical line N: sèuihjihksin (M: tiùh) * out of the vertical SV: m̀sèuihjihk (ge)

very A: ❶ hóu ❷ (extreme) fèisèuhng SV: (exact, precise) ngāamngāam; jìnghaih

vesper(s) N: ❶ (church service) máahntóu ❷ (star) gàmsìng

vessel N: ❶ (hollow receptacle) yùhnghei (M: go) ❷ (ship) syùhn (M: jek) ❸ (blood vessel) hyutgún

vest N: ❶ (undergarment) dáisāam (M: gihn) ❷ (waistcoat) buisàm (M: gihn) FV: ❶ (supply) kàpyúh ❷ (vest in) gwàisuhk * vested interest N: kyùhnleih

vest N: ❶ (undergarment) dáisāam (M: gihn) ❷ (waistcoat) buisāam (M: gihn) FV: ❶ (supply) kàpyúh ❷ (vest in) gwàisuhk * **vested interest** N: kyùhnleih

vestibule N: jáulóng (M: tiuh)

vestige N: ❶ (trace) hàhnjīk; wàihjīk (M: go) ❷ (organ) teuifa heigùn (M: go)

vestment N: ❶ (garment worn by a priest in church) jaipòuh; faatyì (M: gihn) ❷ (ceremonial robe) láihfuhk (M: gihn)

vet N: sauyì (M: go)

veteran N: ❶ (person who has much experience) lóuhsáu (M: go) ❷ (soldier) lóuhbìng ❸ (ex-service man) teuinghgwànyàhn (M: go) SV: jìsàm (ge); lóuhjìgaak (ge)

veterinary N: sauyì (M: go) SV: saubehng ge

veto N: fáukyutkyùhn FV: fáukyut; gamjí

vex FV: gìknàu

vexation N: fàahnnóuh; kwanyíu

via FV: gìnggwo

viable SV: nàhngsàngchyùhn ge

viaduct N: ❶ (bridge) gahùngkìuh (M: tiuh) ❷ (road) gahùng douhlouh (M: tiuh)

vial N: yeuhkséuijēun (M: go)

vibrate FV: jànduhng; báaiduhng

vibration N: janduhng;

báaiduhng (M: chi)

vicar N: ❶ (church of England) gaaukèuimuhksì ❷ (church of Rome) doihbíu; doihléih * **vicarage** N: gaaukèuimuhksì ge jyuhjáak

vice N: ❶ (evil conduct) jeuihngok (M: júng) ❷ (bad habit) waaihjaahpgwaan (M: go) ❸ (apparatus) lóuhfúkím (M: go) FV: kìhmjyuh SV: m̀douhdāk; chèhngok (ge) BF: (deputy) fu * **vice admiral** N: hóigwàn jùngjeung (M: go) * **vice-chairman** N; fujyújihk; fuwuihjéung (M: go) * **vice-chancellor** N; daaihhohk fuhaauhjéung (M: go) * **vice-president** N: fujúngtúng (M: go) * **vice-premier** N; fujúngléih (M: go)

viceroy N: júngdūk (M: go)

vice versa PH: fáangwolàihgóng

vicinity PW: fuhgahn

vicious SV: ❶ (of vice) chèhngok (ge) ❷ (spiteful) ngokduhk (ge) ❸ (having faults) yáuh chongh (ge)

vicious circle N: ngoksingchèuhnwàahn

victim N: ❶ (person) sauhhoihhyàhn (M: go) ❷ (creature) hèisàngbán (M: gihn)

victor N: singleihjé; jinsingjé (M: go)

victory N: singleih; sìhnggùng

video FV: luhkyíng * **video game** N: dihnjí yàuhhei (M: júng) * **video tape** N: luhkyíngdáai (M: hahp) * **video tape recorder** N: luhkyínggèi (M:

bouh) * **video phone** N: dihnsih dihnwá (M: go)

vie FV: jàang

Vietnamese N: Yuhtnàahmyàhn (M: go) BF: Yuhtnàahm

view N: ❶ (scenery) fùnggíng ❷ (opinion) yigin; gingáai ❸ (intention) yitòuh; muhkdīk ❹ (power of seeing) sihlihk FV: ❶ (look at) tái ❷ (examine) gùnchaat; gímyihm ❸ (consider) háauleuih * **point of view** N: lahpchèuhng; gùndím

vigilance SV: gínggok; gíngsíng FV: sáuyé

vigilant SV: gíngsíng ge; gínggok ge

vigorous SV: jìnglihkchùngpui ge; yáuh jìnglihk ge

vigo(u)r N: jìnglihk; wuhtlihk; paaklihk

vile SV: ❶ (shamful and disgusting) bèipéi; hóchí ❷ (bad) ngoklyut (ge) ❸ (valueless) móuhgajihk ge

village N: hèungchyùn; chyùn (M: tìuh)

villager N: chyùnmàhn; hèungmàhn (M: go)

villain N: ❶ (in drama) waaihyàhn; fáanpaaigoksīk (M: go) ❷ (playful use) waaihdáan (M: go)

vim N: jìnglihk; wuhtlihk * **full of vim and vigour** Adj. PH: jìnglihk chùngpui (ge)

vindicate FV: jingsaht; bihnmìhng

vine N: ❶ (grape) pòuhtòuhsyuh (M: pò) ❷ (climbing plant) lāantàhng jihkmaht (M: pò) tàhng (M: tìuh) * **vine yard** N: pòuhtòuhyùhn (M: go)

vinegar N: chou

vintage N: ❶ (wine) pòuhtòuhjáu ❷ (grape harvesting) pòuhtòuh sàuwohkleuhng BF: (a period in the past) gúdín * **vintage car** N: lóuhpâaih mìhngchè (M: go)

vintner N: pòuhtòuh jáusèung (M: go)

viola N: jùngtàihkàhm (M: go)

violate FV: ❶ (break a treaty law) wàihfáan ❷ (act without proper respect) châmfaahn; mouhfaahn ❸ (rape) kèuhnggàan

violence N: bouhlihk; bouhhahng (M: júng) * **do violence to . . .** PH: heung . . . hàhnghùng

violent SV: ❶ (using great force) bouhlike ge; kwòhngbouh ge ❷ (severe) hehkliht (ge)

violet N: jílòhlàahn

violin N: síutàihkàhm (M: go)

violinist N: síutàihkàhmgā/ sáu (M: go)

violoncello N: daaihtàihkàhm (M: go)

V.I.P. N: gwaibān (M: wái)

viper N: ❶ (poisonous snake) duhksèh (M: tìuh) ❷ (spiteful person) yàmhímgwái (M: go)

virgin N: chyúhnéuih (M: go)

virile SV: ❶ (manly) nàahmsing ge ❷ (strong) jìnglihkchùngpui ge

virility N: nàahmjí heikoi

virology N: behngduhkhohk

virtual A: sahtjaiseuhng

virtue N: ❶ (goodness, excellence) méihdāk; dākhahng; yàudīm ❷ (chastity) jingchòu ❸ (efficacy) haauhlihk; haauhnàhng

virtuosity N: deui ngaihseuhtbán ge ngoihou; deui ngaihseuhtbán ge gaamséunglihk

virtuoso N: ngaihseuhtbán gaamséunggā (M: go)

virtuous SV: sihnlèuhng ge

virulence N: duhksing; kehkduhk (M: júng)

virus N: behngduhk (M: júng)

visa N/FV: chìmjing (M: go)

visage N: mihnmaauh

vis-a-vis Adv. PH: mihn deui mihn

viscera N: noihjohng

viscid N: nìmsing SV: ❶ (sticky) chìlahplahp ❷ (semi-fluid) bunlàuhtái (ge)

viscount N: jíjeuk (M: go)

viscountess N: jíjeuk fùyàhn (M: go)

visibility N: nàhnggindouh; hógindouh

visible SV: táidākdóu

vision N: ❶ (power of seeing) sihlihk; ngáahngwòng ❷ (imagination) waahnjeuhng; séungjeuhng

visionary SV: ❶ waahn-séung ge ❷ (impractical) m̀sahtjai ge

visit FV: ❶ chàamgùn (organization, place) ❷ taam (a friend) ❸ baaifóng (a person formally) ❹ (inspect) sihchaat N: fóngmahn (M: chi) ✳ **visiting-card** N: kāatpín; mìhngpín (M: jèung) ✳ **visiting hours (in hospital)** N: taambehng sìhgaan

vistor N: ❶ (guest) yàhnhaak (M: go) ❷ (formal vistor) lòihbàn (M: wái) ❸ (stay at a place) yàuhhaak (M: go) ✳ **vistor's book** N: lòihbàn chìmméngbóu (M: bún)

vista N: ❶ (view) yúhnging (M: fūk, mohk) ❷ jèuiyīk ✳ **vista-vision** N: sàmging dihnyíng (M: bouh)

visual SV: táige; sihgokge

visual aids N: sihgok gaaugeuih (M: júng)

visualize FV: yìhngjeuhng-fa; geuihtáifa

vital SV: hóugányiu ge

vitality N: sàngmihnglihk; wuht-lihk

vitalize VO: jàngtìm wuhtlihk

vitals N: juhngyiu heigùn; yiuhoih (M: go)

vitamin N: wàihtàmihng (M: júng) ✳ **vitamin tablets** N: wàihtàmihngyún (M: nāp)

vitascope N: dihnyíngfongyínggèi (M: bouh, go)

vitreous SV: bòlèi ge; táumihng ge

vitriol N: làuhsyùnyìhm SV: hāakbohk

vituperate FV: jaumah; yuhkmah

viva (voce) SV: háutàuh ge * **viva examination** N: háusíh

vivacious SV: ❶ (lively) wuhtput (ge) ❷ (high-spirited) hòisàm ge

vivid SV: ❶ (bright, clear) sìnmìhng ❷ (active, lively) wuhtput (ge); yáuh sàanghei ge ❸ (distinct and clear) sàangduhng ge

vixen N: (bad-tempered woman) putfúh (M: go)

viz EV: jíkhaih

vocabulary N: ❶ (range of words) chìhwuih; chìhleuih ❷ (word) sàangjih (M: go)

vocal SV: sìngyàm ge * **vocal cord** N: sìngdáai * **vocal music** N: sìngngohk

vocalist N: sìngngohkgà; gòcheunggà (M: go)

vocation N: ❶ (of religious) sàhnjiuh ❷ (a call, a career) sihyihp ❸ (trades, occupation) jīkyihp

vociferate FV: daaihsènggóng; daaihsèngngaai

vociferous SV: hóuchòuh ge; cháaunaauh ge

vodka N: fuhkdahkgàjáu

vogue N: chìuhlàuh SV: sìhmòu; làuhhàhng * **all the vogue** PH: douchyu sauh fùngyìhng ge * **in vogue** SV: sìhmòu ge

voice N: ❶ (in speaking) sìngyàm (M: go) ❷ (of a person) sèng (M: bá) ❸ (sound) sèng (M: dì) ❹ (opinion) yigin (M: go) ❺ (right to express oneself) faatyìhnkyùhn ❻ (in phonetics) juhkyàm (M: go) FV: faatbíu; bíudaaht * **with one voice** IE: yìhháutùhngsìng * **voice-over** N: pòhngbaahk

void SV: ❶ (invalid, null) mòuhhaauh ❷ (empty) hùng ge ❸ (without) kyutfaht N: taaihùng

volatile SV: ❶ (of a liquid) yìhfàifaat ge ❷ (of a person) hòilóhng ge

volatility N: (of a liquid) fàifaatsing

volcano N: fósàan (M: joh, go)

volition N: yiji; yijilìhk

volleyball N: pàaihkàuh (M: go)

volt M: (unit of electrical force) fuhkdahk

voltage N: dihnngaat

voltmeter N: dihnngaatbíu (M: go)

volubility N: hóugeháuchòih SV: yáuhháuchòih; làuhleih

voluble SV: gihntàahm

volume M: ❶ (a book) bún ❷ (one book in a set of books) bún; gyún N: ❶ (amount of space) táijīk ❷ (of sound) sèng; yàmleuhng * **a volume of** N: daaihleuhng * **speak volumes for** PH: chùngfahn bíumìhng . . .

voluntary SV: jihyuhn ge;

jihduhng ge; jiyuhn ge; yihmouh ge * **voluntary army** N: jiyuhngwān * **voluntary work** N: yihmouh gùngjok

volunteer N: ❶ jiyuhnjé (M: go) ❷ (soldier) yihyúhngbìng; jiyuhnbìng (M: go) A: jihyuhn * **volunteer corps** N: yihyúhnggwān

voluptuous SV: sīkchìhng ge BF: sīkchìhng

vomit FV: ngáu N: ngáutoumaht; ngáuchēutlàih ge yéh

voracious SV: ❶ (hungry) tāamsihk (ge) ❷ (greedy) tāamlàahm (ge)

vortex N: ❶ (wind) syùhnfūng (M: jahn) ❷ (whirlpool) syùhnwō (M: go)

votable SV: yáuhsyúngéuikyùhn ge

votary N: ngoihoujé; jìchìhjé (M: go)

vote FV: ❶ (for someone for an office) syún ❷ (by balloting) tàuhpiu; bíukyut ❸ (authorize) tùnggwo N: ❶ (right) tàupiukyùhn; bíukyutkyùhn ❷ syúnpiu (M: jèung) * **put sth. to the vote** FV: fuhjyù bíukyut * **take a vote** FV: bíukyut * **vote down** FV: fáukyut * **vote through** FV: bíukyut tùnggwo * **-voter** N: syúnmàhn (M: go)

vouch FV: bóujing; dāambóu

voucher N: (receipt) sàugeui (M: jèung)

vow VO: (take an oath, make a promise) saihyuhn FV: faatsaih N: saihyeuk; saihyihn (M: go)

vowel N: móuhyām (M: go)

voyage FV/N: hòhnhàhng (M: chi) N: léuihhàhng (M: chi)

voyager N: hòhnhàhng jé (M: go)

vulcanize FV: ngahngfa; lóuhfa

vulgar SV: ❶ (ill mannered) chòulóuh (ge) ❷ (low) hahlàuh (ge) ❸ (in common use) tùngjuhk (ge)

vulnerable SV: yihsauhsèung ge; yihsauhgùnggīk ge

vulture N: ❶ (bird) tùkyìng (M: jek) ❷ (greedy person) tāamsàmgwái (M: go)

W

wad(ding) N: gaapléih (M: júng)

waddle V. PH: yìuhyìuhbáaibáaigám hàahng

wade FV: gaangséui

wafer N: wāifabéng (M: faai)

waffle N: ❶ (utterance) mòuhliuhwá ❷ (food) daahngyún (M: tiuh) FV: lōsòu

waft FV: piufàuh; chèuisung N: fàuhduhng

wag FV: báai N: fùihàaih ge yàhn (M: go) * **wag the tail** VO: báaiméih

wage(s) N: ❶ (payment for

work) yàhngùng ❷ (reward) bouchàuh FV: jeunhàhng; chùhngsih ✳ wage earner N: lòuhduhng gùngjok jé ✳ wage scale N: gùngjì dángkāp bíu (M: go)

wager N: dóujyu FV: dádóu

waggon N: (for carrying goods) fochè (M: ga)

wail FV: haam N: hūkyāp; bēisèung

waist N: ❶ (part of the body) yìu ❷ (part of a garment) yìuwàih ✳ waist line N: yìuwàih ✳ waist band N: yìudáai (M: tìuh) ✳ waist coat N: buisàm (M: gihn)

wait FV: dáng ✳ wait on FV: jiudoih; jiufù ✳ wait till; wait until FV: dángdou ✳ wait out Patt: dángdou . . . gitchūk ✳ waiting-list N: hauhbóu mìhngdāan (M: jèung) ✳ waiting room N: ❶ (doctor's) hauhchánsāt (M: go) ❷ (airport's) hauhgēisāt (M: go)

waiter N: fógei; kéihtóng; kéihtói (M: go)

waitoress N: néuihjiudoih (M: go) néuihsihying (M: go)

waive FV: fonghei

wake FV: ❶ (stop sleeping) séng ❷ (by calling) giuséng ❸ (by pushing) ngúngséng ❹ (by disturbing) chòuhséng ✳ wake up PH: héisàn la! ✳ wake up FV: giuséng sb ✳ wake to FV: faatgok

walk FV: hàahng N: bouhhàhng; saanbouh (M: chi) ✳ take a walk FV: hàahngháh; saanháhbouh ✳ walk of life N: hòhngyihp; jīkyihp (M: júng) ✳ walking stick N: gwáai-

jéung (M: jì)

walkie-talkie N: mòuhsindihn tùngwahgèi (M: bouh, ga)

walking N: bouhhàhng SV: wúihhàahng ge ✳ walking stick N: sihdīk (M: jì)

walkout N: bahgùng

wall N: ❶ chèuhng (M: buhng) ❷ (makes an enclosure) wàihchèuhng (M: douh) VO: wàih yātbuhng chèuhng ✳ see through a brick wall SV: yáuh ngáahngwòng ✳ wall painting N: bīkwá (M: fūk) ✳ wall paper N: chèuhngjí

wallet N: (for banknotes) ngàhnbāau (M: go) hòhbāau (M: go)

walnut N: hahptòuh (M: go)

walrus N: hóijeuhng (M: jek)

waltz N: wàhyíhjìmóuh (M: jek)

wan SV: ❶ (of a person) chōngbaahk ❷ (of light) ngamdaahm ❸ (of the sky) yàmngam

wand N: ❶ gwan (M: jì) ❷ (used by magician) mōseuhtpáahng (M: jì) ❸ (used by conductor) jífàipáahng (M: jì)

wander FV: làuhlohng; yàuhdohng SV: dohngsātlóuh ✳ wanderer N: làuhlohngjé

wane FV: ❶ (become less or weaker) gáamsíu; binyeuhk ❷ (of the moon) yuhtkyut ✳ on the wane PH: yahtjihm sèuimèih

want FV: yiu; sèuiyiu AV: séung; yiu N: ❶ (lack) kyutfaht ❷ (need) sèuiyiu ✳ in want SV: kùhng

wanting SV: kyuhtsíu ge; bātjūk ge

wanton SV: ❶ (playful) wàahnpèih ❷ (capricious) fáanfūk mòuhsèuhng ge ❸ (wilful) yahmsing ge ❹ (licentious) fongdohng ge N: (unchaste woman) dohngfúh (M: go)

war N: jinjàng; daujàng FV: dájeung; daujàng; jokjin ✻ **war cry** FV: naahphaam ✻ **war head** N: dáantàuh (M: go) ✻ **world war** N: saigaai daaihjin (M: chi) ✻ **war plane** N: jingèi (M: ga) ✻ **warship** N: jinlaahm (M: jek) ✻ **war time** N/TW: jinsìh ✻ **war zone** N/PW: jinkèui (M: go) ✻ **war loard** N: gwànfaht (M: go)

warble FV: (bird) giu N: níuhmìhng

ward N: ❶ (in hospital) behngfóng; daaihfóng (M: go, gàan) ❷ (in prison) gàamfòhng; gàamchòhng (M: go) FV: ❶ (prevent, push off) dóngjyuh ❷ (guard, protect) gàamwuh

warden N: ❶ (of a school) sèhgàam (M: go) ❷ (of a prison) dínyuhkjéung (M: go)

wardrobe N: yìgwaih; sàamgwaih (M: go)

ware N: (goods) fomaht BF: hei ✻ **silver ware** N: ngàhnhei (M: gihn) ✻ **china ware** n: chìhhei (M: gihn) FV: làuhsàm; jyuyi ✻ **ware house** N: fochōng (M: go)

warfare N: jinjāng; daujàng BF: jin ✻ **chemical warfare** N: fahohkjin

warlike SV: houjin ge

warlord N: gwànfaht (M: go)

warm SV: ❶ nyúhn ❷ (hot) yiht ❸ (enthusiastic) yihtsàm; yihtsìhng ❹ (affectionate) yihtchìhng FV: yiht ✻ **warm up** FV: ❶ yiht ❷ (before exercise) yihtsàn ✻ **warm hearted** SV: yihtchìhng ge; yihtsàm ge

warming-pan N: nyúhnlòuh (M: go)

warmth N: yihtchìhng; wānnyúhn

warn FV: gínggou

warning N: gínggou (M: go, chi)

warp FV: ❶ jíngnyūn ❷ wāaikūk (fact)

warrent N: ❶ (for arrest) kèuibouh lihng (M: jèung) ❷ (to attend court) chyùhnpiu (M: jèung) ❸ (a fair cause) léihyàuh (M: go) FV: (guarantee) bóujing

warrior N: jinsìh; yúhngsih (M: go)

wart N: júngláu (M: go)

wary SV: síusàm; gánsahn

wash FV: ❶ sái ❷ (carry, sweep) chùng ✻ **washable** SV: sáidāk ge ✻ **wash basin** N: mihnpún (M: go) ✻ **washboard** N: sáisāambáan (M: faai) ✻ **wash clothes** VO: sáisàam ✻ **washing machine** N: sáiyìgèi (M: go, ga) ✻ **wash room** N: chisó; sáisáugàan (M: go)

washed-out SV: teuisīkge

washer N: ❶ (for dishes) sáiwúngèi (M: ga) ❷ (for clothes) sáiyìgèi (M: ga)

wasp N: wòhngfūng (M: jek)

wastage N: sìuhouleuhng;

faimaht

waste FV: sàai; lohngfai N: laahpsaap; faimaht SV: fòngfaige * **waste basket** N: jihjílõ (M: go) * **waste paper** N: jihjí (M: jèung) * **waste pipe** N: pàaihséuigún

wastebin N: laahpsaaptúng (M: go)

watch N: ❶ (time piece) bīu; sáubīu (M: go) ❷ (a turn to stand guard) gínggaai; jihkbāan FV: ❶ (keep looking at) táijyuh ❷ (mind, care for) hòn (jyuh) ❸ (look out for) hàujyuh * **watch out!** PH: síusàm! * **watch chain** N: bīulín (M: tìuh) * **watch maker** N: jūngbīulòu (M: go) * **watch man** N: hōngàangge (M: go) * **watch word** N: háulihng (M: go) * **watch dog** N: gínghyún (M: jek)

water N: séui FV: làhm * **water buffalo** N: séuingàuh (M: jek) * **water chestnut** N: máhtái (M: go) * **water closet** N: séuichi (M: go) * **water color** N: séuichói * **water fall** N: buhkbou (M: go) * **water front** N: hóipèih * **water level** N: ❶ (a leveling instrument) séuipìhng ❷ (water table) séuipìhng sin ❸ (height of the surface of still water) séuiwái * **water lily** N: hòhfā; lìhnfā (M: déu) * **water melon** N: sàigwà (M: go) * **water polo** N: séuikàuh * **water power** N: séuilihk * **water proof** SV: fòhngséuige * **water tower** N: séuitaap (M: go) * **water works** N: jihlòihséui chitbeih

watery SV: ❶ (of colour) táahm ❷ (of liquid) hèi ❸ (of food) móuhmeih; séuiwòngwòng (ge)

watt M: wōk; ngáhdahk

wave N: ❶ (in water) lohng; bòlohng ❷ (in a storm) fùnglohng FV: ❶ (with the hand) báai(sáu); yaahp(sáu) ❷ (as of a flag) jìujín; piuyèuhng * **wave motion** N: bōduhng * **electrical waves** N: dihnbō * **heat waves** N: yihtlohng * **light waves** N: gwōngbō * **long waves** N: chèuhngbō * **short waves** N: dyúnbō * **sound waves** N: yāmbō; sìnglohng

wavelike SV: chíh bōlohng ge

waver FV: ❶ (move unsteadily) yìuhduhng ❷ (to give way) duhngngyìuh SV: (hesitate) yàuhyìhbātkyut

wax N: laahp VO: dálaahp FV: (of the moon) binyùhn * **ear-wax** N: yíhsí * **wax paper** N: laahpjí (M: jèung)

waxen SV: laahpjouh ge

way N: ❶ (path, route) louh (M: tìuh) ❷ (method) fòngfaat; faatjí (M: go) ❸ (direction) fòngheung ❹ (custom) jaahpgwaan ❺ (manner of behaving) jokfùng; taaidouh ❻ (distance) louhchìhng * **all the way** PH: yātlouhseuhng... * **anyway** PH: mòuhleuhnyùhhòh * **by the way** A: seuhnbín * **by way of** CV: yàuh * **go out of one's way to** SV/A: jeuhnlihk; gihklihk * **give way** FV: yeuhngbouh * **have a way with** Patt: deui... hóuyáuhbaahnfaatge * **in a way** Patt: hái máuhyātfòngmihn * **pay one's way** PH: jihgéi béichìn * **put in another way** EV: wuhnyìhnjí

wayside N/PW: louhbīn

wayward SV: yahmsing

we PN: ngóhdeih

weak SV: ❶ (lacking strength) hèuiyeuhk ❷ (of the senses) sèuiyeuhk ❸ (of mixed liquids, diluted) táahm ❹ (not good) m̀haih géi hóu; chādī ❺ (not solid, frail) m̀gaulihk * **weakness** N: yeuhkdím; dyúnchu (M: go)

weaken FV: seukyeuhk

weakling N: yeuhkjé (M: go)

wealth N: chòihfu; chìhnchòih

wealthy SV: yáuhchín

wean VO: (to cause a child to stop suckling) gaaináaih

weapon N: móuhhei (M: gihn) * **atomic weapon** N: yùhnjí móuhhei * **nuclear weapon** N: hahtjí móuhhei

weaponry N: móuhhei

wear FV: ❶ jeuk (clothes, socks, trousers, shoes . . .) ❷ daai (hat, spectacles, earrings, rings) ❸ laahm (scarf, suspenders) * **wear away** RV: mòhsyún * **wear down** ① mòhwaaih ② (weaken) hāakfuhk * **wear off** (pass away) gwo * **wear on** PH: maahnmáan siusaih * **wear out** PH: (exhausted) gànpèihlihkjeuhn

weary SV: ❶ (tired) guih ❷ (causing tiredness) lihngyàhn yimgyuhn ge * **wearisome** SV: lihng yàhn fàahnmuhn ge

weather N: tìnhei FV: ❶ (come through successfully) douhgwo ❷ (discolour) lihng .

. . teuisìk * **weather chart** N: heijeuhngtòuh; tìnheitòuh (M: jèung) * **weather cock** N: fùngbìu * **in all weather** PH: fùngyúh mòuhjó * **weather proof** SV: fòhngsèui ge * **weather forecast** N; tìnhei bougou * **weather station** N: heijeuhngtòih (M: go) * **weather beaten** SV: bâauging fùngsèung

weave FV: ❶ (work at a loom) jìk; fóngjìk ❷ (compose) pìnpàaih ❸ (twist and turn) yùwùih chìhnjeun * **weaver** N: jìkbougùngyàhn (M: go)

weave FV: yìuh

web N: ❶ (any woven fabric) móhng (M: go) ❷ (of a spider) jìjyùmóhng (M: go) kàhmlòuh sì mōng (M: go) ❸ (of ducks, geese) jéung

wed VO: gitfàn FV: ❶ (to take a wife) chéui; chóu ❷ (to take a husband) ga ❸ (unite) githahp ❹ (devoted to) gìnchìh

wedding N: fànláih

wedge N: muhkseui (M: faai) FV: (fix tightly) sip, sāk

Wednesday N: sìngkèihsàam; láihbaaisàam

weed N: yéhchóu; jaahpchóu FV: ❶ chèuih (weed) ❷ (get rid of) chìngchèuih; tòuhtaai * **weeder** N: chèuihchóugèi (M: go) * **weedy** SV: ① (full of weeds) dòjaahpchóu ge ② (thin and tall) sauseuk ge

week N: láihbaai; sìngkèih (M: go) * **week in, week out** PH: yāt go láihbaai yauh yātgo láihbaai gám * **week day** N: jàuyaht * **week end** N: jàumuht (M: go) * **weekly** PH: múih sìngkèih yātchi N: jàuhón

(M: bún) ✴ **week ender** N: jàumuht douhga ge yàhn (M: go)

weep FV: haam; hūk ✴ **weep for joy** PH: héigihkyìhyāp ✴ **weeping** SV: (of trees) sèuihjì ge

weigh FV: ❶ (measure) ching; bohng ❷ (compare the importance) háauleuih SV: chúhng (NuM) ✴ **weigh down** FV: jeuihdài SV: lìhng yàhn pèihlòuh ge ✴ **weigh in with** VO: tàihchēut yíhleuhn ✴ **weigh anchor (begin a voyage)** FV: hòisàn; hòisyùhn

weight N: chúhngleuhng ✴ **gain weight** RV: chúhngjó; fèihjó ✴ **lose weight** RV: hèngjó; saujó ✴ **carry weight** SV: yáuhfahnleuhng; juhngyiu ✴ **have weight with** Patt: deui . . . juhngyiu ✴ **weight watcher** N: gáamfèih ge yàhn (M: go)

weird SV: ❶ (strange) gwaai ❷ (unnatural) bāthósìyíh

welcome FV: (act of welcoming) fùnyìhng PH: ❶ (permitted) m̀sáihaakhei; fùnyìhng ❷ (absolved of the need to express thanks) m̀sáihaakhei

weld FV: hohn N: hohnháu (M: go)

welfare N: fūkleih; hahngfūk ✴ **social welfare** N: séhwúi fūkleih

well N: ❶ (for water) jéng (M: go) ❷ (for oil) yàuhjéng (M: go) FV: làuhchēut; panchēut SV: ❶ (in good health) gihnhòng ❷ (in a desired way) hóu; tóhdong PH: (as an introductory expression of a sentence) gámàh ✴ **as well as** Patt: yihk . . . yihk; yauh .

. . yauh ✴ **might as well** MA: bātyùh ✴ **well off** SV: yáuhchín(ge) ✴ **well informed** SV: ginmàhn gwóngbok ge ✴ **well known** SV: chēutméng (ge) ✴ **well worth** SV: dái ✴ **well versed in** SV: jìngtùng ✴ **well read** SV: bokhohk (ge)

Welsh N: ❶ (people) Wāiyíhsìyàhn (M: go) ❷ (language) Wāiyíhsìwá SV: Wāiyíhsìyàhn ge

wen N: (cyst) láu (M: go)

west N: sài ✴ **(to the) west of** Patt: hái . . . ge sàibihn

western SV: sàibihn; sàifòng ge ✴ **westerner** N: sàifòngyàhn; sàiyàhn (M: go) ✴ **westernize** SV: sàifa

westward SV: heungsài (ge)

wet SV: sāp FV: jíngsāp N: ❶ (rain) yúh ❷ (moisture) sāphei; séuifahn

whale N: kìhngyùh (M: tìuh) VO: bouhkìhng ✴ **whaler** N: (ship) bouhkìhngsyùhn (M: jek)

wharf N: máhtàuh (M: go) ✴ **wharfage** N: máhtàuhfai

what N: mātyéh; mèyéh ✴ **no matter what** PH: mòuhleuhn dímyéung ✴ **what for?** MA: dímgáai? ✴ **what if . . .?** Patt: yùhgwó . . . jauh dím nē? ✴ **what about . . . ?** MA: dím a? ✴ **what kind of** SV: dímyéung ge

whatever PH: mòuhleuhn mātyéh

wheat N: síumahk

wheel N: chèlūk (M: go) FV: jyun; lūk ✴ **wheel barrow** N: sáutèuichè (M: ga) ✴ **wheel-**

man N: tòhsáu (M: go) ∗
wheel chair N: lèuhnyí (M:
jèung)

when TW: ❶ (at what time)
géisí; géisìh ❷ (at the time that)
gójahnsí; ... ge sìhhauh

whenever, whensoever
TW: ❶ (when) géisìh; géisí ❷
(at any time) mòuhleuhn géisìh;
chèuihsíh A: múihfùhng

where N: (at or in what place)
bīnsyu; bīndouh VO: (to what
place) heui bīnsyu Patt: (from
what place) hái bīnsyu làih

whereabouts PH: (in what
place) hái bīnsyu N: hahlohk

whereas Patt: yànwaih ...
ge yùhngu

whereby A: pàhng mātyéh

wherefore MA: ❶ (for which
reason) yànchí ❷ (why) dímgáai

wherein PH: ❶ (in what) hái
bīnsyu ❷ (in what respect) hái
bīn fòngmihn

wherever PH: (whatever
place) mòuhleuhnbīnsyu Patt:
bīnsyu ... bīnsyu; bīndouh ..
. bīndouh

whet FV: mòh ∗ **whet stone**
N: mòhdōusehk (M: gauh)

whether Patt: ❶ (no matter
if) mòuhleuhn ... m̀ ❷ (if)
haihm̀haih

which SP: bīn M

whiff Nu-M: yātdaahm; yātbuhng FV: chèui; pan

while N: ❶ (period of time)
sìhgaan ❷ (a time, a little while)
yātjahngāan SV: (a long while)
hóu noih TW: (during the time

that) ... gójahnsí; ... ge
sìhhauh SV: (temporarily)
jaahmsìh Patt: (and yet, but
though) sèuiyìhn ... .;
daahnhaih ... ∗ **once in a
while** MA: yáuhsìh; gaanjūng
∗ **worth one's while** SV:
jihkdāk

whim N: gwaainihmtàuh (M:
go)

whimper FV/N: hūkyāp

whimsical SV: gúgwaai (ge)

whimsy N: ❶ (fanciful idea)
gwaainihmtàuh (M: go) ❷ (odd
humour) gwaaipèihhei

whip FV: ❶ (beat, strike) bīn
❷ (beat with a beater or a fork)
faak N: bīn (M: tiuh) ∗ **whip
hand** N: yàusai ∗ **whip round**
N: mouhgyùn

whirl FV: ❶ (move quickly
round and round) tàhmtámjyun
❷ (of the brain) wàhn ∗ **whirl
pool** N: syùhnwò (M: go) ∗
whirl wind N: syùhnfùng (M:
jahn)

whirligig N: ❶ (top) tòhló
(M: go) ❷ (rovolving motion)
syùhnjyún wahnduhng

whisk FV: ❶ hehnghēng sou
❷ (whip) faak (eggs) N: ❶ (for
clothes) sàamcháat (M: go) ❷
(for flapping flies) wūyìngpáak
(M: go) ❸ (for whipping eggs)
faakdáangèi (M: go) ∗
whisker N: sòu; wùhsòu

whiskey N: wàisihgéi (M:
jēun, jì)

whisper FV: saisaisèng gám
góng N: sìyúh

whistle FV: chèuiháusaau N:
❶ saaují (M: go) ❷ (used by the
policeman) ngàhngāi (M: go) ∗

pay too dear for one's whistle IE: dāk bāt sèuhngsāt

white SV: baahk; baahksīk * **white collar** N: baahklèhng gāaikāp * **egg white** N: dáanbaahk/báak * **White House** N/PW: Baahkgùng

whiten FV: piubaahk

white wash N: fùiseúi VO: yàuh fùiséui

whither VO: heui bīnsyu

Whitsunday N: ❶ (protestant) singlìhng gonglàhmjit ❷ (Catholic) singsàhn gonglàhmjit

Whitsuntide N: ❶ (protestant) singlìhng gonglàhmjit jàu ❷ (Catholic) singsàhn gonglàhmjit jàu

whittle FV: seuk N: tòuhdōu (M: bá)

whizz PH: chahp yātsèng FV: (slang) tàusit

who N: bīngo

whoever N: ❶ yahmhòhyàhn ❷ mòuhleuhn bīngo

whole SV: yùhnjíng ge SP: sèhng — M N: chyùhnbouh; jíngtái * **whole world** N: chyùhn saigaai * **as a whole** PH: jauh chyùhntái yìh leuhn * **with one's whole heart** IE: chyùhnsàm chyùhnyi * **whole hogger** N: gihkdyùnpaai

wholesale FV/N: pàifaat * **wholesaler** N: pàifaatsèung (M: go)

wholesome SV: gihnhòngge; yáuhyīk ge

wholly A: yùhnchyùhn; tùngtùng; jyuhtdeui

whom N: bīngo

whoop N: ❶ (loud cry) daaihgiusèng ❷ (of coughing) hàauchyúnsèng FV: giu * **whooping cough** N: gāikāt; baakyahtkāt

whop FV: ❶ (beat) dá ❷ (defeat) dábaaih * **whopping** SV: fèisèuhngdaaih ge

whore N: geihnéuih; lóuhgéui (M: go) FV: maaihyàhm * **whore master** N: piuhhaak (M: go)

whose SV: bīngo ge

why MA: dímgáai; waihmātyéh; jouhmātyéh

wick N: ❶ (of lamp) dāngsàm (M: tìuh) ❷ (of candle) laahpjūksàm (M: tìuh)

wicked SV: ❶ (malevolent) hāksàm (ge) ❷ (immoral) chèhngok(ge)

wicket N: ❶ jākmùhn (M: douh) ❷ (for selling tickets) sauhpiuchyu

wide SV: fut * **wide apart** SV: gaak dāk hóu yúhn * **wide awake** SV: chìngsíng ge; gèigíng ge * **wide screen** SV: futngàhnmohk ge * **wide spread** SV: póupin ge

widen FV: jíngfut

widow N: gwáfúh (M: go) * **remain a widow** VO: sáugwá

widower N: gwàanfù (M: go)

width N: futdouh

wield FV: sáiyuhng

wife N: lóuhpòh; taaitáai; fùyán (potite form) (M: go)

wig N: gá (tàuh) faat (M: go) FV: naauh

wigwag VO: dá seunhouh

wild SV: ❶ (of animals) yéhsing ge ❷ (of plants) yéhsàang ge ✳ **wild animal** N: yéhsau (M: jek) ✳ **wild country** N: fòngyéh; fòngsàanyéhléhng ✳ **wild flowers** N: yéhfā (M: déui) ✳ **run wild** SV: fongdohng

wilderners N: kwongyéh; fòngyéh

wildfire N: yéhfó; gwáifó

wile N: gwáigai (M: go) FV: ngāak

wilful SV: yahmsing ge

will A: (indicating future time) jauhlàih; wúih AV: ❶ (indicating probability) hónàhng ❷ (indicating capacity or ability) hóyíh; nàhnggau ❸ (desire) séung N: ❶ (mental power) yiji ❷ (determination) kyutsàm; jiyuhn ❸ (statement in writing saying how sb. wishes his property to be distributed after his death) wàihjūk (M: jèung) ✳ **against one's will** PH: bātdākyíh ✳ **at will** A: chèuihyi ✳ **have one's will** PH: yùhyuhn yíhsèuhng

willing SV: háng ✳ **willingly** PH: sàmgàmchìhngyuhn

will-o'-the-wisp N: ❶ gwáifó ❷ (something or somebody that one pursues unsuccessfully because it or he is difficult to group or reach) nàahnyíh jūkmó ge sihmaht

willow N: láuhsyuh; yèuhngláuh (M: po)

willy-nilly SV: yàuhyihbātkyut

wilt SV: ❶ (of plants) dìujeh ❷ (of person) tèuihsong

wily SV: gwáimáh (ge); gáauwaaht (ge)

wimple N: tàuhgàn (M: tiuh)

win FV: ❶ yèhng ❷ (attain) dākdóu ❸ (persuade) seuifuhk N: singleih; sàuyik ✳ **win hands down** PH: hìng yìh yih géui ✳ **win over** Patt: jèung . . . jàngchéuigwolàih ✳ **win through** PH: gìnglihk gàannàahn; jùngyù sìhnggùng

wince SV: teuisūk; waisūk

wind N: ❶ fùng ❷ (breath) fùkàp ❸ (scent) heimeih ✳ **against the wind** SV: ngaahkfùng; yihkfùng ✳ **with the wind** SV: seuhnfùng ✳ **get wind of** PH: tèngdóudòsíu . . . ge sīusīk ✳ **get winded** FV: heichyún ✳ **wind bag** N: hùngtàahmjé (M: go) ✳ **wind break** N: fòhngfùnglàhm (M: go) ✳ **wind jammer** N: fàahnsyùhn (M: jek) ✳ **wind mill** N: fùngchè (M: go) ✳ **wind storm** N: bouhfùng (M: chèuhng) ✳ **wind swept** SV: dòngfùng (ge) ✳ **wind tight** SV: m̀tùngfùng (ge) ✳ **wind screen wiper (of motor vehicles)** N: séuibuht

wind FV: (blow) chèui

wind FV: ❶ (of a spring) séuhnglín ❷ (wrap or twine around) jaat, chìhn ✳ **wind off** FV: gáaihòi ✳ **wind up** FV: gitchūk N: gitguhk

winding SV: lyūnkūkge; lyūnlyūnkūkkūkge

window N: chēung; chēungmún (M: douh) ✳ **window blind** N: chēunglím (M: fūk) ✳ **window pane** N: chēung bōlēi

(M: faai)

windward SV: heungfùng-ge

windy SV: daaihfùng; dòfùng

wine N: jáu (M: júng) * **wine bibber** N: jáugwái (M: go) * **wine bibber** N: jáugwái (M: go) * **wine glass** N: jáubūi (M: jek)

wing N: ❶ (of a bird or plane) yihk (M: jek) ❷ (part of a building) jākyihk FV: ❶ (fly) fēi; fèihàhng ❷ (speed up) gàchūk; gàfaai * **wingmanship** N: fèihàhng geihseuht

wink FV: ❶ (close and open one's eyes) jáamngáahn ❷ (of a star) sím sím háh N: ❶ (act of winking) ngáahnsīk ❷ (very short time) yātsīkgāan

winner N: singleihjé; dākjéungjé (M: go)

winning SV: ❶ singleih ge ❷ (persuasive) màihyàhn ge * **winnings** N: yèhngfàanlàih ge chín

winnow FV: sài

winsome SV: ❶ (attractive) màihyàhn ge ❷ (pleasing) hóngoi ge

winter N: dūngtīn; láahngtīn FV: gwodūng * **winter sports** N: dūnggwai wahnduhng (M: júng) * **winter season** N: dùnggwai * **winter solstice** N: dùngji * **winter vacation** N: hòhnga

wintry SV: hòhnláahng (ge)

wipe FV: maat RV: ❶ (make a thing dry) maatgòn ❷ (rub away or off) maatlāt * **wipe out** PH: chitdái sìumiht *

wipe up RV: chaatjehng

wire N: ❶ (electric) dihnsin (M: tìuh) ❷ (iron or zinc) titsín (M: tìuh) ❸ (copper) tùhngsín (M: tìuh) ❹ (steel) gongsín (M: tìuh) VO: ❶ (put electric wires in) ngòndihnsin ❷ (send a message by telegraph) dádihnbou * **wire dancer** N: hàahng gongsín ge yàhn (M: go) * **wireless** N: mòuhsindihn SV: mòuhsindihn ge

wisdom N: jiwai; chòihji * **wisdomtooth** N: jiwaingàh (M: jek)

wise SV: chùngmìhng * **be (get) wise to** FV: mìhngbaahk * **in any wise** PH: mòuhleuhn yùhhòh * **wise acre** N: jihjokchùngmìhng ge yàhn (M: go) * **wise crack** N: chiupèihwá (M: geui)

wish FV: ❶ (want, want to) hèimohng ❷ (in giving an order) chéng ❸ (expressing hope to a person) jūk N: yuhnmohng; hèimohng (M: go) * **wish for** FV: hèimohng * **wish on** FV: kèuhngbīk * **wishful** SV: hotmohng ge

wishy-washy SV: ❶ (of soup) hèi ❷ (of tea) táahm ❸ (of talk) hùngduhng ge

wisp M: jaat FV: jaat

wit N: ❶ (intelligence) gèiji; jiwai ❷ (person) chòihjí (M: go) SV: gèigíng

witch N: néuihmòuh; mòuhpòh (M: go) FV: màihwaahk * **witch craft** N: mòuhseuht * **witchery** N: mòfaat; mòuhseuht * **witch hunting** PH: jingjih bīkhoih

with CV: (accompanying, going together) tùhng; tùhngmàaih

FV: ❶ (having) yáuh ❷ (using as an instrument) yuhng ❸ (including) lìhn MA: ❶ (because of) yànwaih ❷ (despite) sèuiyìhn ✳ **together with** Patt: tùhng . . . háiyātchàih ✳ **with each other** A: béichí jìgāan ✳ **be pleased with** SV: fùnhéi ✳ **with the whole heart** VO: jeuhnsàm

withdraw FV: ❶ (take back) sàufàan ❷ (from business) tìhng (yihp) ❸ (from a race) teuichēut ❹ (troops) chitteui ❺ (a motion) chitwùih; chéuisiu SV: (introverted) noihheung

wither FV: ❶ (of flower) jeh; chàahn ❷ (of plant) fù; séi

withhold FV: ❶ (keep back) yīkjai ❷ (refuse to give) kaulàuh

within PW: (inside) yahpbihn; léuihbihn Patt: (not beyond) hái . . . jìnoih; hái . . . yíhnoih

without FV: (not having) móuh PW: (outside) ngoihbihn; chēutbihn ✳ **without doubt** PH: hòuhmòuhyìhmahn ✳ **without delay** A: màhseuhng ✳ **without ceasing** A: m̀tìhng; bāttìhng ✳ **without a break** A: yāthei; yātlìhn

withstand FV: ❶ (resist) dáikong ❷ (oppose) fáankong ❸ (stand against) dóngjyuh

witness FV: ❶ (see) chànngáahn táigin ❷ (give evidence) jokjing ❸ (give evidence of) jingmìhng N: ❶ (a person) jingyàhn; ginjingyàhn; muhkgīkjingyàhn (M: go) ❷ (evidence) jinggeui; jingmìhng ✳ **call to witness** Patt: chéng . . . jokjing ✳ **witness box/witness stand** N: jingyàhnjihk

witticism N: miuhyúh

witty SV: ❶ (clever) gèiji ge ❷ (full of humour) fùihàaih (ge)

wizard N: ❶ (magician) nàahmmòuh; seuhtsih (M: go) ❷ (person with amazing abilities) kèihchòih (M: go)

wobble PH: ❶ (move unsteadily) yìuhbáai bātdihng ❷ (uncertain in making decisions) yàuhyìhbātkyut

woe N: ❶ bèingòi; fúnóuh ❷ (pl.) jòinaahn

woebegone SV: fúháufúmihn

wolf N: ❶ (animal) lòhng; chàaihlòhng (M: jek) ❷ (person) tàamsàmgwái (M: go) IE: lòhngtàn fúyin ✳ **wolf hound** N: lòhnggáu (M: jek)

woman N: néuihyán (M: go) BF: néuih — SV: néuihyányìhngge

womb N: jígùng (M: go)

womanfolk N: fúhnéuih; néuihsing

wonder N: ❶ (strange; wonderful things) kèihjìk; kèihgùn (M: go) ❷ (feeling) gìngkèih FV: ❶ (feel surprise) gokdākchēutkèih ❷ (feel curiosity) séungjìdou ✳ **no wonder** PH: m̀gwaaidāk ✳ **wonder why** MA: m̀jìdímgáai; m̀mìhngbaahk ✳ **wonderland** N: sìngíng; kèihgíng ✳ **wonderful** SV: ① (surprising) gìngyàhn ge ② (good) jànhaihhóu ge

won't P: m̀

woo VO: kàuhfàn; kàuhngoi FV: jèuikàuh ✳ **wooer** N: kàuhngoijé (M: go)

wood N: muhk (M: gauh) ✳
fire wood N: chàaih ✳ **woods**
N: sàmlàhm; syuhlàhm (M: go)
✳ **out of the woods** SV:
tyuthím ✳ **wood carving** N:
muhkhāak ✳ **wood cut** N:
muhkhāakwá (M: fūk) ✳ **wood
pulp** N: muhk (jí) jèung

wooden SV: ❶ (made of
wood) muhk ge; muhkjouh ge
❷ (stiff, clumsy) deuhn (ge) ✳
wooden headed SV: bahn ge;
chéun ge

woodland N: sàmlàhm (M:
go)

woodman N: jáamchàaih-
lóu (M: go)

woodpecker N: deuk-
muhkníuh (M: jek)

woodwork N: ❶ (things
made of wood) muhkjaibán (M:
gihn) ❷ (art of making things of
wood) muhkgùng sáungaih (M:
júng)

woody SV: ❶ (wooded)
dòsyuhmuhk ge ❷ (of or like
wood) muhkjāt ge

woof N: ❶ (weft) wáihsin (M:
tìuh) ❷ (bark) saisèng ge
faihsèng ✳ **woofer** N:
dàiyàmlabā (M: go)

wool N: ❶ yèuhngmòuh;
yúng ❷ (material similar in appearance or texture to wool) chíh
yèuhngmòuh ge yéh ❸ (thick
curly hair) háuh ge lyūn tàuhfaat ✳ **all wool and a yard
wide** IE: fojàngasaht ge ✳
dyed in the ~ SV: chitdái ge
✳ **go for wool and come
home shorn** IE: tàugàim̀dóu
siht jàmáih ✳ **pull the wool
over one's eyes** VO: ngáak
yàtgoyàhn ✳ **wool gathering**
IE: sàm bāt joih yìhn

woollden SV: yèuhngmòuh
ge N: mòuhjīkbán; yúng

wool(l)y SV: ❶ (made of
wool) yèuhngmòuh ge ❷ (of the
mind, ideas) mòuhwùhge;
m̀chìngchó ge N: pl. lāangsāam
(M: gihn)

word N: ❶ jih; chìh (M: go) ❷
(meaning message or speech)
syutwah, wá (M: geui) ❸ (news,
information) sìusīk; yàmseun ❹
(promise) nokyìhn; bóujing ❺
(command, order) mihnglihng
FV: chouchìh ✳ **at a word** A:
jīkhāak; máhseuhng ✳ **by
word of mouth** N: háutàuh
tùngjì ✳ **in a word** A: júngjì ✳
in other word A: wuhnyìhnjì
✳ **keep one's word** VO:
sáunokyìhn ✳ **word book** N:
chìhwuih; jihdín (M: bún) ✳
word perfect SV: buihsuhk ✳
word picture N: sàangduhng
ge mìuhseuht ✳ **word play** N:
sèunggwàanyúh ✳ **wording** N:
chouchìh

wordy SV: chamhei (ge),
lōsō(ge)

work N: ❶ (general work) sih;
gùngjok (M: gihn) ❷ (of art)
ngaihseuhtbán (M: gihn) ❸
(book) jyujok (M: bouh) ❹ (pl.)
gùngchóng (M: gàan) FV: ❶
jouhsih; jouhgùng ❷ (on a book)
sé ❸ (on something) sàuléih ❹
(something over) joijouh ❺
(machine cow, horse) sáiyuhng
✳ **all in the day's work** AV:
jingsèuhnggám ✳ **at work** FV:
jouhgányéh ✳ **make short
work of sth.** SV: seunchŭk
yúhnsìhng ✳ **out of work** RV:
(engine) waaihjó SV: (worker)
sātyihp ✳ **work bag** N: jām-
sinbāau (M: go) ✳ **work box**
N: gùnggeuihsèung (M: go) ✳
work house N: gámfayún (M:
gàan) ✳ **workshop** N: ①
gùngchèuhng (M: go) ② saht-

yihmbāan (M: go)

workaholic N: gùngjok-kwòhng (ge yàhn) (M: go)

worker N: gùngyàhn (M: go) * **social worker** N: séhwúi gùngjokjé (M: go)

workman N: gùngyàhn; gùngjok yàhnyùhn (M: go) * **workmanlike** SV: yáuh geihháau ge * **workmanship** N: sáugùng; gùngngaihbán

world N: ❶ (the earth) saigaai ❷ (the globe) deihkàuh ❸ (the universe) yúhjauhmaahnmaht ❹ (human affairs) saisih BF: —gaai * **for all the world** PH: mòuhleuhnyùhhòh * **in the world** PH: saigaaiseuhng * **make a noise in the world** IE: yèuhngmìhngtìnhah * **out of the world** SV: fèifàahn ge; yàusau ge * **world without end** A: wíhngyúhn gám * **world power** N: saigaai kèuhnggwok * **world wide** SV: chyùhnsaigaai ge * **business world** N: sèunggaai * **the scholastic world** N: hohkseuhtgaai

worldly SV: ❶ (material) mahtjātge ❷ (temporal) saijuhkge ❸ (interested in material things) síhkwúi * **worldly wise** SV: saigu ge

worm N: ❶ chùhng (M: tìuh) ❷ (insignificant person) síuyàhnmát (M: go) FV: hóumaahn gám hàahng

worn SV: ❶ gauh ge; laahn ge ❷ (tired) guih * **worn out** SV: ① yuhnglaahnjó ge ② (tired) hóu guih

worrisome SV: màhfàahn ge

worry FV: dàamsàm; gwa-

jyuh SV: (sàm) fàahn; sàmgàp N: yâuleuih; fàahnnóuh; guleuih * **worry oneself** IE: jihchàhm fàahnnóuh

worse SV: juhngsèui; juhngbaih N: gangwaaih ge sih * **go from bad to worse** IE: múih fong yuh hah * **none the worse** SV: yìyìhn; yìhngyìhn * **get worse, worse and worse** Patt: yuht làih yuht chà * **worse off** SV: chìhngfong bātgāai

worship N: láihbaai; sùhngbaai FV: baai * **worshipful** SV: hóging(ge)

worst SV: ❶ (in quality) jeuiyáih ❷ (in degree) jeuibaih FV: dábaaih; gīkbaaih * **give sb. the worst of it** VO: dábaaih yāt go yàhn * **make the worst** Patt: deui . . . jok jeui waaih ge dásyun

worth FV: ❶ (of a commodity) jihk ❷ (possessing) yúngyaúh N: (value) gajihk * **for all one is worth** VO: jeuhnlihk * **for what it is worth** PH: bātleuhnjàngá * **worthless** SV: móuhgajihk ge * **worthwhile** AV: jihkdāk

worthy SV: ❶ (having merit) yáuhgajihkge ❷ (deserving respect) yáuhyiyih ge N: gihtchēutyàhnsih (M: go)

would MA: (to express a condition) yùhgwó FV: (to express willingness) yuhnyi A: (to show something that went on regularly for some time) sìhsìh CV: (to make a request) m̀gòi AV: (wish) séung

wound N: sèung; chongsèung FV: sèunghoih VO: sauhsèung

wraith N: yàulìhng; gwái

wrangle FV: jàang; jàng-leuhn

wrap FV: bàau N: (pl.) ngoihtou (M: gihn) * **be wraped up in** PH: jyùnsàm yù . . .

wrapper N: ❶ (of a book) bàausyújí (M: jèung) ❷ (dressing-gown) sàhnlāu (M: gihn)

wrath SV/N: fáhnnouh

wreak FV: ❶ (give expression to) faatsit ❷ (revenge) bousàuh

wreath N: (placed on a coffin, grave, statue) fāhyún (M: go)

wreathe FV: ❶ jouh (wreath) ❷ (cover) jēkoi ❸ (wind) chìhnyíu

wreck FV: powaih; wáimiht VO: sātsih N: ❶ (ship) laahnsyùhn (M: jek) ❷ automobile) laahnchè (M: ga) * **wreckage** N: chàahnhàaih

wrecker N: ❶ (person employed to recover a wrecked ship) dálàauh yuhhím ge syùhn ge yàhn (M: go) ❷ (house breaker) chaak gauhngūk ge yàhn (M: go)

wrench N: (a tool) sìhbáná (M: go) FV: ❶ (twist) náu ❷ (in-jure by twisting) náusèung ❸ (distort facts) wāaikūk

wrest FV: ❶ (take sth. violent-ly away) chéung ❷ (twist or pervert facts, meaning of sth.) wāaikūk

wrestle FV/N: sèutgok (M: chèuhng)

wretch N: ❶ (unforturate and miserable person) hólìhn ge yàhn (M: go) ❷ (contemptible, mean person) bèipéi ge yàhn (M:

go) ❸ (rogue) waaihdáan (M: go)

wright N: gùngyàhn; gùng-jeuhng (M: go)

wring FV: náu RV: náugòn

wrinkle N: jaumàhn (M: tìuh) FV: jíngchàauh * **wrinkle up one's forehead** VO: jauhéi mèihtàuh * **be full of wrinkle** IE: jūk ji dò màuh

wrist N: sáuwún; sáungaau * **wrist band** N: jauhháu (M: go)

write FV: sé VO: séjih * **write down** FV: ① (put down) sédài; sèilohk ② (describe as, miuhsé ③ (reduce the nominal, value) bíndài * **write off** FV (cancel) chéuisìu; jyusìu * **write out** FV: tàhngsé; tàhng-chìng * **write up** FV (describe) chèuhngsai mìuhsé

writer N: (author) jokgā; jok-jé (M: go)

writing N: jokbán; jyujok (M: pīn; bún)

written SV: syùmín ge * **written examination** N: bāt-síh * **written language** N: màhnjih

wrong SV: ❶ (unjust, im-proper) cho, m̀ngāam ❷ (out of order) waaihjó; yáuhmahntàih RVE: FV cho N: chongh (M: go) FV: yùnwóng * **be in the wrong** SV: cho, chojó * **be wronged** VO: sauhjó yùnwāt * **in the wrong box** SV: chyúgíng bātleih * **go wrong with (mechanically)** SV: waaihjó * **wrong doer** N: jouhwaaihsih ge yàhn (M: go) * **wrong doing** N: waaihsih; jeuihhahng * **wrong headed** SV: wàahngu; gujáp

wurst N: hèungchéung (M: tìuh)

X

xerox FV: yíngyan; fūkyan

x-rated SV: yáuh haahnjaising ge (movie)

x-ray N: ēksìh gwōng VO: jiu ēksìhgwōng

xylophone N: muhkkàhm (M: go)

Y

yacht N: yàuhtéhng (M: jek) * **yacht club** N: yàuhtéhng kèuilohkbouh (M: go)

yak N: nèihngàuh móuhngàuh (M: jek)

yam N: fàansyú (M: go)

Yangtze River N/PW: Chèuhnggòng; Yèuhngjígòng (M: tìuh)

Yankee N: ❶ (in the American Civil War) bākfònglóu (M: go) ❷ (colloq. in Europe) Méihgwoklóu (M: go)

yap N: (of dogs) kwòhngfaihsèng FV: kwoñngfai

yard N: ❶ (measure of length) máh ❷ (courtyard) tìhngyún (M: go) ❸ (empty land) hùngdeih (M: daat) ❹ (lawn) chóudéi (M: daat) ❺ (enclosure for a special purpose) chèuhngdeih (M: go) * **lumber yard** N: muhkchóng (M: gàan) * **railroad yard** N: fóchè tìhngchèchèuhng (M: go) * **yardstick** N: máhchek (M: bá)

yarn N: ❶ (thread) sā (M: tìuh) ❷ (story) gusih (M: go) VO: gónggusih * **cotton yarn** N: mìhnsā (M: tìuh)

yawl N: saifàahnsyùhn (M: jek)

yawn VO: dá haamlòuh SV: lìhthòi N: haamlòuh (M: go)

year N: nìhn * **all the year round** PH: yātnìhndoutàuh * **from year to year** PH: yātnìhn yauh yātnìhn * **year in year out** SV: bātdyuhn * **year book** N: nìhngaam; nìhnhón (M: bún) * **school year** N: hohknìhn (M: go)

yearn FV: sìnihm; héungwóhng; hotmohng; wàaihnihm

yeast N: ❶ (for fermentation) haàumóuh(fán) ❷ (for making bread) faatfán

yell FV: ngaai; daaihsènggámngaai N: giusèng; naahphaamsèng

yellow SV: ❶ wòhng; wòhngsīk (ge) ❷ (cowardly) nohyeuhk ge N: wòhngsīk FV: binwòhng * **yellow pages** N: wòhngyihp fànleuih gwónggou * **Yellow River** N/PW: Wòhnghòh (M: tùh)

yelp FV: faih N: faihsèng

yen N: yahtyùhn

yes SV: haih; ngāam *
yesman N: yingsìngchùhng

yesterday TW: kàhmyaht; chàhmyaht; jokyaht

yet Patt: ❶ (up to now) douyìhnjoih wàih jí . . . juhng . . . ❷ (nevertheless) sèuiyihn . . . daahnhàih . . . ❸ (still) . . . juhng . . . ❹ (before all is over) . . . chìhjóu . . .

yield FV: ❶ (give way) yeuhng; yeuhngbouh ❷ (give up) fonghei ❸ (produce) sàngchàan ❹ (surrender) tàuhhòhng N: cháanleuhng; sàusìhng

Y.M.C.A. N: Chìngnìhnwúi

yoga N: yùhgā

yoke N: ❶ (a wooden frame) ngaahk ❷ (for oxen) ngàuhngaahk FV: (unite) githahp

yolk N: dáanwóng; daahnwóng (M: go)

yonder SV: yúhnchyu ge

you PN: ❶ (one person) néih ❷ (several persons) néihdeih ❸ (polite form) gokwái

young SV: ❶ hauhsàang; nìhnhèng ❷ (having little experience) móuh gìngyihm (ge) * **young people** N: nìhnhèngyàhn

youngster N: hauhsàangjái (M: go)

yourself N: néihjihgéi

youth N: ❶ (a young person) chìngnìhnyàhn; nìhnhèngyàhn (M: go) ❷ (time of being young) siunìhnsìhdoih; chìngchèunkèih * **youthful** SV: nìhnhèng; hauhsàang

yuan N/M: yùhn

Yugoslav N/PW: Nàahm sīlàaifù

Y.W.C.A. N: Néuihchìng nìhnwúi

Z

zany N: waahtkàiyínyùhn (M go) síucháu (M: go)

zeal N: yihtsàm; yihtsìhng

zebra N: bàanmáh (M: jek)

zenith N: ❶ (part of the sky directly overhead) tìndéng ❷ (highest point) díngdím

zero Nu: lihng N: (point of a scale) lihngdouh * **above zero** PH: lihngdouh yíhseuhng * **below zero** PH: lihngdouh yíhhah

zest N: ❶ (great interest) hingcheui ❷ (stimulating quality) chigīksing

zigzag SV: lyūnlyūnkūkkūk ge

zinc N: sàn

zinnia N: baakyahtchóu (M: pò)

Zionism N: Yàuhtaaifuhk gwok jyúyih

zip N: làailín (M: tìuh) VO: làaihòi/màaih làailín * **zipper, zip fasterner** N: làailín (M: tìuh)

zodiac N: sìngjoh (M: go)